ROUTLEDGE INTERNATIONAL HANDBOOK OF SOCIAL NEUROENDOCRINOLOGY

The *Routledge International Handbook of Social Neuroendocrinology* is an authoritative reference work providing a balanced overview of current scholarship spanning the full breadth of the rapidly developing field of social neuroendocrinology. Considering the relationships between hormones, the brain, and social behavior, this collection brings together groundbreaking research in the field for the first time.

Featuring 39 chapters written by leading researchers, the handbook offers impressive breadth of coverage. It begins with an overview of the history of social neuroendocrinology before discussing its methodological foundations and challenges. Other topics covered include state-of-the-art research on dominance and aggression; social affiliation; reproduction and pair bonding (e.g. sexual behavior, sexual orientation, romantic relationships); pregnancy and parenting; stress and emotion; cognition and decision making; social development; and mental and physical health. The handbook adopts a lifespan approach to the study of social neuroendocrinology throughout, covering the roles that hormones play during gestation, childhood, adolescence, and adulthood. It also illustrates the evolutionary forces that have shaped hormone-behavior associations across species, including research on humans, non-human primates, birds, and rodents.

The handbook will serve as an authoritative reference work for researchers, students, and others intrigued by this topic, while also inspiring new lines of research on interactions among hormones, the brain, and behavior in social contexts.

Oliver C. Schultheiss is Professor of Psychology at Friedrich-Alexander University, Erlangen, Germany. His research focuses on the implicit motivational needs for power, achievement, affiliation, and sex, and their interactions with the endocrine system.

Pranjal H. Mehta is Associate Professor in Experimental Psychology at University College London, UK. His research examines interactions between hormones, the social environment, and human behavior with an emphasis on status hierarchies, stress, and decision making.

ROUTLEDGE INTERNATIONAL HANDBOOK OF SOCIAL NEUROENDOCRINOLOGY

Edited by Oliver C. Schultheiss
and Pranjal H. Mehta

LONDON AND NEW YORK

First published 2019
by Routledge
2 Park Square, Milton Park, Abingdon, Oxon OX14 4RN

and by Routledge
52 Vanderbilt Avenue, New York, NY 10017

Routledge is an imprint of the Taylor & Francis Group, an informa business

British Library Cataloguing-in-Publication Data
A catalogue record for this book is available from the British Library

Library of Congress Cataloging-in-Publication Data
Names: Schultheiss, Oliver C., 1967- editor. | Mehta, Pranjal H., 1977- editor.
Title: Routledge international handbook of social neuroendocrinology / edited by Oliver C. Schultheiss and Pranjal H. Mehta.
Other titles: International handbook of social neuroendocrinology | Handbook of social neuroendocrinology
Description: Abingdon, Oxon ; New York, NY : Routledge, 2019. | Includes bibliographical references.
Identifiers: LCCN 2018020205 | ISBN 9781138711440 (hbk ; alk. paper) | ISBN 9781315200439 (ebk)
Subjects: LCSH: Human behavior—Endocrine aspects. | Psychoneuroendocrinology.
Classification: LCC QP356.4 .R68 2019 | DDC 612.8—dc23
LC record available at https://lccn.loc.gov/2018020205

ISBN: 978-1-138-71144-0 (hbk)
ISBN: 978-1-315-20043-9 (ebk)

Typeset in Bembo
by Apex CoVantage, LLC

To my family, Maria, Julian, Leo, Ben, and Jonathan
—O.C.S.

To my parents, Tarika Mehta and Hriday Mehta
—P.H.M

CONTENTS

Contents

Contents

Contents

CONTRIBUTORS

Eyal Abraham *Interdisciplinary Center Herzliya, Israel*

Jennifer A. Bartz *McGill University, Canada*

Kathryn G. Beauchamp *University of Oregon, USA*

Clancy Blair *New York University, USA*

Kira Bleck *Friedrich-Alexander University, Germany*

Stephen H. Braren *New York University, USA*

D. Michael Burt *Durham University, UK*

Brandon D. Butler *University of Texas at Arlington, USA*

Justin M. Carré *Nipissing University, Canada*

C. Sue Carter *Indiana University, USA*

Kathleen V. Casto *New College of Florida, USA*

Kristi Chin *University of Michigan, USA*

Sean P. Coyne *Notre Dame of Maryland University, USA*

Khytam Dawood *Pennsylvania State University, USA*

Birgit Derntl *University of Tübingen, Germany*

Esther K. Diekhof *Universität Hamburg, Germany*

Contributors

Andrew Richard Dismukes *Iowa State University, USA*

Gelena Dlugash *Friedrich-Alexander University, Germany*

Anna Dreber *Stockholm School of Economics, Sweden*

Robin S. Edelstein *University of Michigan, USA*

David A. Edwards *Emory University, USA*

Dorien Enter *Radboud University Nijmegen, The Netherlands*

Ruth Feldman *Interdisciplinary Center Herzliya, Israel*

Eric D. Finegood *New York University, USA*

Philip A. Fisher *University of Oregon, USA*

Jessica Flannery *University of Oregon, USA*

Zoey Forrester-Fronstin *University of Tennessee, USA*

Cheryl A. Frye *University at Albany–SUNY, USA*

Matthew J. Fuxjager *Wake Forest University, USA*

Steven W. Gangestad *University of New Mexico, USA*

Lee T. Gettler *University of Notre Dame, USA*

Malin Gingnell *University of Tübingen, Germany*

Nicholas M. Grebe *Duke University, USA*

Jennifer Hahn-Holbrook *University of California, Merced, USA*

Elizabeth A. D. Hammock *Florida State University, USA*

Elizabeth Hampson *University of Western Ontario, Canada*

Markus Hausmann *Durham University, UK*

Markus Heinrichs *Albert-Ludwigs-University of Freiburg, Germany*

Travis E. Hodges *Brock University, Canada*

Colin Holbrook *University of California, Merced, USA*

Sarah K. C. Holtfrerich *Universität Hamburg, Germany*

Sarah Horn *University of Oregon, USA*

Jonas Hornung *University of Tübingen, Germany*

Moniek H. M. Hutschemaekers *Radboud University Nijmegen, The Netherlands*

Kevin T. Janson *Friedrich-Alexander University, Germany*

Emily Jeanneault *Nipissing University, Canada*

Magnus Johannesson *Stockholm School of Economics, Sweden*

Robert A. Josephs *University of Texas at Austin, USA*

Saurabh S. Kokane *University of Texas at Arlington, USA*

Martin G. Köllner *Friedrich-Alexander University, Germany*

Sonia A. Krol *McGill University, Canada*

Brigitte M. Kudielka *University of Regensburg, Germany*

Patty X. Kuo *University of Notre Dame, USA*

Amy Lehrner *James J. Peters VA Medical Center and Icahn School of Medicine at Mount Sinai, USA*

Catherine A. Marler *University of Wisconsin, USA*

Nicole Marley *Nipissing University, Canada*

Allan Mazur *Syracuse University, USA*

Pranjal H. Mehta *University College London, UK*

Cheryl M. McCormick *Brock University, Canada*

Shannin Nicole Moody *Iowa State University, USA*

Jonas P. Nitschke *McGill University, Canada*

Leehe Peled-Avron *University of Haifa, Israel*

Allison M. Perkeybile *Indiana University, USA*

Linda I. Perrotti *University of Texas at Arlington, USA*

Rosemarie E. Perry *New York University, USA*

Jenny Mai Phan *Iowa State University, USA*

David A. Puts *Pennsylvania State University, USA*

Luise Reimers *Universität Hamburg, Germany*

Nathaniel S. Rieger *University of Wisconsin, USA*

Karin Roelofs *Radboud University Nijmegen, The Netherlands*

Nicolas Rohleder *Friedrich-Alexander University, Germany*

James R. Roney *University of California, Santa Barbara, USA*

Leslie E. Roos *University of Oregon, USA*

Kevin A. Rosenfield *Pennsylvania State University, USA*

Amar Sarkar *University of Cambridge, UK*

Bastian Schiller *Albert-Ludwigs-University of Freiburg, Germany*

Oliver C. Schultheiss *Friedrich-Alexander University, Germany*

Kalynn M. Schulz *University of Tennessee, USA*

Simone G. Shamay-Tsoory *University of Haifa, Israel*

Elizabeth Anne Shirtcliff *Iowa State University, USA*

Andrea Tountas *Iowa State University, USA*

Brian C. Trainor *University of California, Davis, USA*

Douglas W. Wacker *University of Washington Bothell, USA*

Alicia A. Walf *Rensselaer Polytechnic Institute, USA*

Oliver T. Wolf *Ruhr University Bochum, Germany*

Rachel Yehuda *James J. Peters VA Medical Center and Icahn School of Medicine at Mount Sinai, USA*

Ellen Zakreski *McGill University, Canada and Iowa State University, USA*

Sandra Zänkert *University of Regensburg, Germany*

Xin Zhao *University of Wisconsin, USA*

Contributors

Jenny Mai Phan, Iowa State University, USA

David A. Puts, Pennsylvania State University, USA

Luisa Künstler, University of Siegen, Germany

Nathaniel S. Pieper, University of Washington, USA

Katherine Reagan, Brunel University, London, UK

Nicholas Pound, Brunel University, London, UK

James R. Roney, University of California, Santa Barbara, USA

Leslie L. Knapp, University of Utah, USA

Kevin A. Rosenfield, Pennsylvania State University, USA

Amir Sarkar, University of Cumbria, UK

Bastian Schiller, Albert-Ludwigs-University of Freiburg, Germany

Oliver C. Schultheiss, Friedrich-Alexander University, Germany

Benjamin M. Schultz, University of Tennessee, USA

Simone G. Shamay-Tsoory, University of Haifa, Israel

Elizabeth Anne Shirtcliff, Iowa State University, USA

Jamie Toussaint, Iowa State University, USA

Brian C. Trainor, University of California, Davis, USA

Dennis L. Wacker, Washington State University, USA

Allen A. Wolf, German Primate Center, Germany

Oliver T. Wolf, Ruhr University, Germany

Rachel Zamzow, University of Missouri, USA

Ellen Zakreski, University of California, Berkeley, USA

Sandra Zanker, University of Siegen, Germany

Xin Zhao, University of Hawaii, USA

INTRODUCTION

Oliver C. Schultheiss and Pranjal H. Mehta

In a sense, the study of hormones has always been linked to the study of social behavior. There is a consensus that modern behavioral endocrinology started with Arnold Berthold's experiments on male chickens, in which he castrated them at a young age and then reimplanted the excised testes in some, noting the effects this had on bodily development and behavior (Soma, 2006). Not only was the presence of testes required for developing secondary sex characteristics such as a comb and wattles, but it also led to male chickens' aggression toward other males – providing a first inkling that hormones can be related to *behavior*. Other researchers later identified the invisible messenger between cells (hence the term *endocrine*) emitted by the testes and called it testosterone. Yet others eventually documented that the behavioral effects exerted by hormones were mediated by neurons within and outside the central nervous system, suggesting a *neuro-endocrine* interaction. So from the get-go of the study of the relationship between hormones and behavior, we have a tightly coupled triad: hormones, neurons, behavior.

Yet it would be wrong to identify the study of hormonal functions and hormonal involvement in behavior narrowly with *social* contexts and behaviors. For instance, hormones can influence food and water intake as well as the regulation of energy due to purely physiological reasons. In insects, hormones are associated with molting and metamorphosis. None of these endocrine functions is directly related to social context and behavior, although there may of course be remote social aspects upstream or downstream of these endocrine functions. And many endocrine effects play out in cells other than neurons, although this does not preclude them from being functionally integrated with neuronal and behavioral changes.

So for the sake of providing this handbook with a working definition, we suggest that social neuroendocrinology is the study of the links between hormones, neurons, and behaviors occurring in, influencing, and being influenced by a social context (see Figure 0.1). In many cases, the causal flow between these elements can go both ways: Hormones influence the brain by binding to receptors; the brain influences hormones by regulating their levels. Hormones influence behavior, mediated by their effects on the behavior-generating functions of the brain and its regulation of supporting physiological changes in the body. Behavior operates on the world, and its effects there feed back to the brain, thereby influencing hormones. Of course, the external world can also impact hormones independently of the organism's own behavior, such as when information about potentially rewarding or threatening events reaches the brain via the senses.

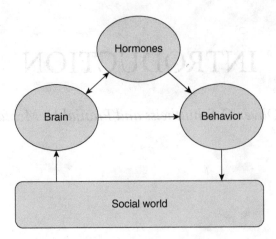

Figure 0.1 The main elements of social neuroendocrinology and their relationships with each other. Arrows represent the flow of causal effects. See text for further discussion.

What sets social neuroendocrinology apart from the more general science of behavioral endocrinology is that social neuroendocrinology studies the relationships that hormones, brain, and behavior have with the *social* world: how hormonal and behavioral changes are occasioned by certain social contexts (e.g., competition, puberty, parenthood); how they are elicited or shaped by specific social stimuli (e.g., social threat, winning or losing against someone else, encountering a sexually attractive other); and how hormonal changes in turn affect covert and overt behavior toward such social stimuli and settings (e.g., by changing cognition, learning, emotion, and motivation).

At the same time, social neuroendocrinology shares three key aspects with behavioral endo-crinology. Both disciplines have strong roots in biopsychology and its use of animal models for the experimental study of causal mechanisms in the interactions between hormones, brain, and behavior that would be difficult or impossible to conduct in humans. Both disciplines also sometimes use this cross-species approach for comparative purposes; that is, to figure out how hormones and behavior are linked in different ways in different species and how this can help to understand the broader role of a certain hormone for certain adaptive behaviors under vary-ing circumstances. And both disciplines are interested in how evolutionary forces have shaped continuity and change in hormone-brain-behavior relationships.

We think that this handbook represents a wonderful illustration of the complexity and rich-ness of social neuroendocrinological research sketched out in the previous paragraphs. The chapters contained in this handbook represent all elements of our definition of social neuroen-docrinology in many different ways, ranging from research related to dominance and aggression (Section 2), social affiliation (Section 3), mating and reproduction (Section 4), cognition and emotion in their social aspects (Section 5), to research related to social development (Section 6) and mental and physical health (Section 7). Within and across chapters and sections, the contrib-utors to this handbook review research stemming from the study of birds, rodents, non-human primates, and humans, providing readers with a rich tapestry of hormone-brain-behavior inter-actions in widely diverging social-species arenas. At the same time, this handbook also fea-tures, in Section 1, a critical review of the current state of the field, focusing on challenges of measurement and reproducibility that currently engage social neuroendocrinology, neighboring disciplines, and science in general. Many chapters revisit these challenges in their specific topical contexts.

We hope that the handbook will be useful to researchers in the field who want to get a broad view of the field as it is presently constituted, but also useful for newcomers to the field, including graduate and post-graduate students, and for interested readers from neighboring disciplines. Because its creation represents a fundamentally collaborative effort between many different individuals, we would like to thank the following people: first of all, our excellent authors, all experts in their respective fields of research, who rose to our call to contribute state-of-the-art chapters to this handbook; Ceri McLardy at Routledge who initially suggested the idea of editing a handbook of social neuroendocrinology to us, and her and Sophie Crowe for their competent handling of the book project at all stages; our mentors, colleagues, collaborators, and students who got us, kept us, and still keep us excited and engaged in research on hormones and behavior in their social context; and to our families and friends who were consistently patient with us when we dove long and deep into writing and editing this handbook. While we may have been the catalysts for making this book happen, it ultimately could not have happened without the work, dedication, and support of all these individuals. We are in your debt.

Reference

Soma, K.K. (2006). Testosterone and aggression: Berthold, birds and beyond. *Journal of Neuroendocrinology*, *18*(7), 543–551. doi:10.1111/j.1365-2826.2006.01440.x

SECTION 1

Historical and methodological issues

1

HISTORY OF SOCIAL NEUROENDOCRINOLOGY IN HUMANS

*Allan Mazur**

Introduction

Endocrinology developed during the 20th century with demonstrations, usually in animal models, that many so-called endocrine glands (e.g., pituitary, thyroid, testes, ovaries, pancreas, pineal, hypothalamus, adrenals) produce particular molecules ("hormones") that enter the bloodstream, which transports them to specialized receptors elsewhere in the body to affect physiology and behavior. Hormonal communication was distinguished from electrical signals that were recognized much earlier to travel instantly through the peripheral nervous system and brain, as in the 19th-century image of animating the Frankenstein monster with electricity.

By the early 20th century, endocrinology was producing spectacular advances in medical treatment. Hypothyroidism, in which metabolism slows down so the body lacks energy, and when severe causes death, could be treated with heterogeneous extract from animal thyroids. By the 1930s an active hormone, thyroxine, had been isolated from the extract and its structure identified. Forty years ago, when my cancerous thyroid glands were removed, a daily pill of desiccated cow thyroid adequately replaced their function. Now I use synthetic thyroid hormone with more precise dosage.

In the 1920s, after a malfunctioning pancreas had been implicated in childhood (type 1) diabetes, insulin was discovered to be the crucially missing hormone. Soon available for treatment, injections of insulin extended the short life expectancy of diabetic children to normal longevity (Bliss, 1982). By World War II, hormones including corticosterone were known to come from animal adrenals, some of them useful for reducing inflammation in humans.

Not all such interventions were successful. Early claims of restoring masculine vitality by eating bull testicles probably reflect either placebo effects or fiction (Cheney, 2006). Certainly there was some basis for this hopeful belief. Castration of animals and humans has been practiced since antiquity, with the knowledge that removing the testicles before puberty prevents the appearance of secondary male characteristics. In animals this produces more tractable oxen and geldings, and plumper capons. In eunuchs, the face remains beardless, bodies are fleshy rather than muscular, and libido is muted. Male sopranos and contraltos, emasculated to maintain the prepubescent voice range, were prominent in the opera and church music of 17th- and 18th-century Europe (Cheney, 2006). If removing testicles was emasculating, then ingesting testicular extract should masculinize, or so the logic went.

Our modern understanding began in the 1930s with the isolation and identification of testosterone and other androgens. Mashing tons of bull testicles over a 7-year period, Fred Koch and his coworkers fractionated ounces of material sufficiently pure to make the combs of capons grow bright red (McGee, 1927). Adolf Butenandt distilled 25,000 liters of policemen's urine to obtain 15 mg of androsterone, a weak androgen (De Kruif, 1945). Identification and synthesis of other androgens including testosterone followed quickly, enabling experiments to replace or enhance testosterone in animal subjects and human patients. An example is the classic study of hen pecking orders by Allee, Collias, and Lutherman (1939) who injected testosterone propionate into low-ranking hens. These females became aggressive, and each rose in her status hierarchy, some to the top position. Their comb size increased (a male characteristic), egg laying was suppressed, some began crowing (rare in hens), and a few began courting other hens.

These early investigations and interventions were made despite the inability of researchers to measure hormone levels in the blood. Over the past half century, progress in measurement has been spectacular, spurred by the development of radioimmunoassay in 1960 by Rosalyn Yalow and Solomon Berson. (Yalow earned a Nobel Prize in 1977. Berson was dead by then, making him ineligible.) Many hormones and other chemicals, in tiny amounts, are now assayed quickly, cheaply, and usually accurately. My first hormone study in the 1970s required blood to be drawn from subjects. By the 1980s, assays could be made from saliva (Wang, Plymate, Nieschlag, & Paulsen, 1981; Riad-Fahmy, Read, Walker, & Griffiths, 1982; Kirschbaum and Hellhammer, 1989), a technique popularized for human behavioral studies by psychologists James Dabbs Jr. (2000) and Douglas Granger (Granger, Shirtcliff, Booth, Kivlighan, & Schwartz, 2004). Today saliva assays are performed using enzyme-linked immunosorbent assay (ELISA), polymerase chain reaction, and high-resolution mass spectrometry. The choice involves tradeoffs between cost and accuracy (Wheeler, 2013).

Leaving hormones for a moment, we need to speak of the nervous system – headed, of course, by the brain with nerves running down the spinal cord and throughout the body. The autonomic nervous system, that part of the nervous system controlling functions not consciously directed (thus automatically or autonomously directed) has two networks that work in opposition. One, the *sympathetic* nervous system, prepares the body for vigorous actions such as are associated with "fight or flight," or stress. The other network, the *parasympathetic* nervous system, calms the body after the emergency alert ends.

If the brain senses a threat, the sympathetic nervous system dilates blood vessels in the large muscles while constricting those at the periphery of the body, thus directing oxygen-laden blood where it is most needed during emergencies; it increases heart rate and opens up the bronchial tubes of the lungs. It quickly stimulates the adrenal glands (located atop the kidneys) to release the hormones adrenalin (also called epinephrine) and norepinephrine – also secreted elsewhere in the brain and body – into the bloodstream, reinforcing the actions of the sympathetic nerves. The parasympathetic network has the opposite effects: relaxing the peripheral blood vessels so blood resumes normal flow to the extremities, and decreasing heart rate; in all, relaxing the body after the threat has passed.

The term *neuroendocrinology* was coined in the 1920s to emphasize the constant interplay between the electrical nervous system and the chemical hormones. By the 1950s it was recognized that communication between them is mediated by two small organs near the base of the brain: the hypothalamus (part of the brain) and the nearby pituitary, a pea-shaped endocrine gland. The hypothalamus and pituitary are tightly connected by nerves and ducts through which signals flow.

The hypothalamus connects the brain with the rest of the body in two ways: through the nervous system and via hormonal "releasing factors" sent to the pituitary, which in turn pumps other hormones into the bloodstream to affect distant endocrine glands, a slower and longer-lasting process than nerve transmission.

Feedbacks are essential to the neuroendocrine system. Consider, for example, high cortisol, which is functional for emergency responses to stressors but unhealthy if sustained during resting and nonthreatening periods. When high cortisol in the blood is detected by the pituitary and the hypothalamus, they respectively curtail their production of adrenocorticotropic hormone (ACTH) and corticotrophin-releasing factor (CRF), thus ceasing the adrenals' production of cortisol so it can decrease to resting level.

The neuroendocrine system is enormously complex, but limiting our focus to *social* neuroendocrinology in humans greatly simplifies matters because most socially relevant research has focused on three specific axes: the hypothalamic-pituitary-adrenal axis, the hypothalamic-pituitary-gonadal axis, and neuropeptides. Risking oversimplification, I refer to each of these by their hormone of primary interest and a more or less corresponding behavior: cortisol and stress, testosterone and dominance, and oxytocin and bonding. Cortisol and testosterone are steroid hormones, made from cholesterol; oxytocin is a peptide hormone made from amino acids. Other areas of inquiry are not covered in this chapter.

Cortisol and stress

The hypothalamic-pituitary-adrenal (HPA) axis may be activated when a stressful stimulus (perhaps an attacker) is perceived. The brain causes CRF to be released by the hypothalamus, which triggers release of ACTH from the pituitary, which in turn triggers the release of glucocorticoids (in humans, mainly cortisol) from the adrenal cortex. Cortisol is often called the "stress hormone" because it energizes the body to withstand or defend against a stressor, increasing the amount of glucose in the blood, providing energy for a sustained effort.

Walter Cannon (1932) described the stress reaction as an automatic "fight or flight" response to a perceived threat. Subjectively, this response is experienced as discomfort, whether as anxiety, fear, anger, annoyance, or depression. Physiologically, it activates the HPA axis and the sympathetic nervous system. The adrenal medulla (core of an adrenal gland) instantly secretes epinephrine (popularly known as adrenaline) and norepinephrine. ACTH released from the pituitary acts more slowly, flowing through the bloodstream to the adrenal cortex (surface of an adrenal gland), which releases cortisol, further mobilizing the body's resources.

I often visit Yosemite National Park, the mecca for rock climbers because of its steep granite walls, especially the sheer face of El Capitan rising 900 meters – three times the height of the Empire State Building – and iconic Half Dome at 620 meters. Most big-wall climbers take days to summit, sleeping in hammocks tethered to the granite, but experts can scale these faces in hours. A few "free soloists" climb with no aids other than a chalk bag to improve finger grip, and without safety ropes. Climbers are highly competitive, challenging each other in daring attainments, well-illustrated in the movie *Valley Uprising* (2014; www.youtube.com/watch?v=o86TpaSBcWw).

I do not understand how they can do it. I feel stressed watching them, a vicarious response documented on election night among voters who backed the loser (Stanton, Labar, Saini, Kuhn, & Beehner, 2010). Perhaps these individuals lack the normal fear response that keeps most of us from holding by our fingertips to a vertical rock face. Or perhaps they started climbing while young, tackling ever more difficult faces, did them repeatedly and became habituated, muting their stress. We do not know. There has been no neuroendocrine research at Yosemite because elite climbers are hard to recruit as reliable subjects.

Less spectacular than Yosemite but more convenient for study is the Trier Social Stress Test (TSST), a mock job interview that induces social-evaluative stress in laboratory subjects. Introduced in 1993 at the University of Trier by Clemens Kirschbaum, the test is now well established as an experimental paradigm (Kirschbaum, Pirke, & Hellhammer, 1993; Mahoney, Brunyé, Taylor, & Kanarek, 2014; Frisch, Häusser, & Mojzisch, 2015). It takes about 15 minutes and is divided into three periods. Subjects are first asked to imagine they are being evaluated for a dream job and to prepare a speech explaining why they are the best candidate; then they give the speech in front of an impassive selection committee; and finally, still in front of the committee, they are given a 5-minute task in mental arithmetic, all of it videoed.

Sometimes the TSST is compared to a lower-stress control condition in which subjects talk and do mental arithmetic but with no selection committee or video camera present, thus without the social evaluation component. In a majority of subjects, the Trier, but not the control condition, activates the HPA axis and sympathetic nervous system, elevating cortisol and adrenalin, quickening the pulse, and moving blood from the periphery of the body to large muscles, a shift easily measured by decreasing thumb blood volume (TBV). This basic design is modified as needed by the experimenter.

Commonly in social neuroendocrinology, the relationship of hormones to behavior is reciprocal. Hormone levels, affected by a situation, influence behavior while behavior affects hormone levels. The TSST is convenient for examining causality in both directions. Stress response can be made an independent variable by comparing subjects taking the Trier with subjects taking the lower-stress control version. Thus, for example, cortisol elevated by the Trier has been associated with subsequent prosocial behavior. Or, cortisol level can be the dependent variable in studies comparing the stress response in different types of subjects, or in subjects who have been manipulated in different ways, showing, for example, that those given empathetic social support during their Trier test have less stress than subjects without social support (see Frisch et al., 2015 for a review of Trier studies).

Considerable research with the TSST and other methods inquires how stress is related to rank in a face-to-face status hierarchy. Primate studies have long shown that the leaders of stable hierarchies have lower cortisol than subordinates, consistent with our stereotype of leaders as "cool" and unperturbed by "bending the rules," while those of low rank nervously "toe the line." Group leaders may manipulate subordinates through signals that elevate or relieve stress (Mazur, 1985). Limited evidence shows that real-world leaders, for example military officers and government officials, have lower basal cortisol than non-leaders (Sherman et al., 2012). Low autonomic arousal, indicated by as simple a measure as low pulse rate, is associated with children and adults who are prone to violate social norms, engaging in antisocial and criminal behaviors (Raine, 2002).

There are, however, conditions when leaders show relatively high adrenocortical activity, as when they take the lead in facing a predator or a hostile group of outsiders. Leaders may be unusually stressed from within their own group during periods of instability when facing challengers who were previously subordinate, or when competing with a presumptuous subordinate for a valuable prize (de Waal, 1982; Mazur, 1985; Harms, Crede, Tynan, Leon, & Jeung, 2016). Knight and Mehta (2017) gave the Trier test to subjects after manipulating both their status rank and the stability of their group's hierarchy. They found in stable hierarchies that high status muted cortisol response but that in unstable hierarchies, high status was associated with high cortisol.

The stress response, originally conceptualized as occurring in extreme situations, is more recently studied in mundane social interaction where stresses are low, and participants are barely if at all aware of them. Cortisol may be unperturbed by these low stress levels, so more sensitive measures of sympathetic nervous activity are required, including changes in pulse rate and TBV, and elevation of the salivary enzyme alpha amylase (Rohleder, Nater, Wolf, Ehlert, & Kirsch-baum, 2004).

Alan Booth pioneered the study of subtle stresses that occur during casual conversation, continuously recording pulse rate and TBV in real time. One could later watch a video of the conversation accompanied by subjects' fluctuating stress levels, making visible a previously unseen dimension of the interaction. The most striking finding was that conversation per se is more stressful than periods of non-talking, and the sympathetic nervous system is highly reactive as talking proceeds (Brinkerhoff & Booth, 1984).

Extending this method, Figure 1.1 shows a compressed waveform measured from one student in conversation with a professor. It begins (at the left) near the end of a distracting video, used to acclimate the subject to the setting, and continues through 25 minutes of talk. First the professor speaks, then the student, in alternating turns. The labels above the waveform, "Listening" and "Speaking," refer to the student-subject. TBV is indicated by the (vertical) width of the waveform. The student's waveform is wider (i.e., more relaxed) while he watches the distracting video than during the following conversation. More importantly, there is variation within the conversation. The student is more relaxed while listening to the professor than when talking to him, possibly explaining why students fall asleep during lecture. That aside, the main point is that it is more stressful to speak than to listen, at least when conversing with someone of higher rank (Mazur, 2015). During additional conversations in my lab between people initially different in status, stress response of the high-status person is muted compared to stress of the low-status person.

It has long been known that in conversations among strangers who initially are not obviously different in status, an informal ranking nonetheless emerges, often quickly (Fisek and Ofshe, 1970). Is that differentiation related to the subtle stresses occurring during their early interaction? This was queried in casual 10-minute conversations among three previously unacquainted young men. These conversations were not sufficiently competitive or stressful to elevate cortisol, however stress differences among the men could be detected with more sensitive indicators of sympathetic-nervous activity (pulse, TBV) and by salivary alpha amylase. These show that high status goes to those with lowest stress (Mazur, Welker, & Peng, 2015).

Testosterone and dominance

The hypothalamic-pituitary-gonadal (HPG) axis starts with gonadotropin-releasing hormone released by the hypothalamus, which triggers release of luteinizing hormone (LH) and follicle-stimulating hormone (FSH) by the pituitary, which in turn triggers the release of gonadal steroids. These are primarily testosterone from the male testes, and estrogen from the ovaries. In females, monthly changes of LH and FSH releases regulate the menstrual cycle. Testosterone is also produced in female ovaries but in far smaller amounts. Testosterone is often studied for its possible association with dominance behavior in face-to-face hierarchies.

Research after World War II established that the mammalian fetus of both XX and XY individuals begins with undifferentiated sexual parts. A gene on the Y chromosome causes the asexual gonads to develop as testes; lacking this gene the gonads become ovaries. So far as we know, the sex chromosomes have little more to do with sex differentiation, which hereafter is driven by hormones produced in the now sex-specific gonads. The testes produce testosterone during gestation, and production peaks again a month or two after birth, then declines by 6 months of age to the low range seen in later childhood. Testosterone and other testicular secretions cause the external genitalia to form into penis and scrotum rather than clitoris and labia, and internal

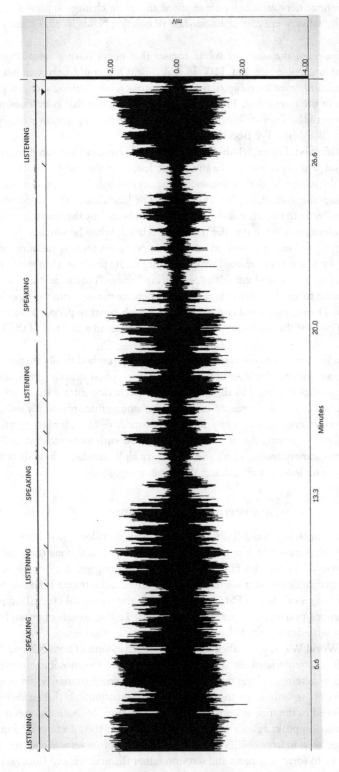

Figure 1.1 Thumb pulse of a student in conversation with Professor Mazur. Narrowing of the waveform indicates a decrease in thumb blood volume, widening an increase, coinciding with student's speaking and listening turns, respectively.

ducts take the male form. The central nervous system is masculinized in rats and probably in humans too. The general rule, somewhat simplified, is that early exposure to greater amounts of testosterone produces more male characteristics and fewer female characteristics, while less exposure to testosterone produces the reverse. Certain transgender individuals have the chromosomes of one sex, but due to abnormalities of early testosterone exposure – whether in production of the hormone or insensitivity of testosterone receptors or steroid drug treatments – do not develop the expected secondary sexual characteristics (Lee Houk, Ahmed, Hughes, & The International Consensus Conference on Intersex Organized by the Lawson Wilkins Pediatric Endocrine Society and the European Society for Paediatric Endocrinology, 2006).

The testes greatly increase production of testosterone at puberty, elevating boys' prepubescent serum levels 10 or more times, promoting growth of the penis, deeper voice, muscles, beard and body hair, sex interest, and possibly combativeness. Attempts to assess the specific contribution of sharply rising testosterone to changing behavior in adolescent boys are indecisive because of the difficulty of untangling physiology from other important changes during these years: entering high school, taking a job, prolonged absence from parents, more dependence on peer approval. Any of these may affect behavior independently of hormonal effects. Partly for this reason, most recent and ongoing research on the social neuroendocrinology of testosterone has focused on adults, when the physical features of each sex have been established (but for examples of modern research on children and adolescents, see Klipker, Wrzus, Rauers, Boker, & Riediger, 2017; Shirtcliff et al., 2015; van Bokhoven et al., 2006).

By the mid-1970s there was sufficient accumulation of testosterone studies of humans and nonhuman primates, usually mature males, to venture a generalization that elevation in that hormone facilitates "dominance" activity, while a decrease inhibits it. Conversely, an increase in the individual's dominance activity will increase production of testosterone which, in turn, will facilitate further dominance activity. A decrease in dominance activity will cause a drop in testosterone which, in turn, will inhibit further dominance activity (Rose, Bernstein, & Gordon et al., 1975; Mazur, 1976). At that time, the term *dominance* was used simply because the primate literature refers to status hierarchies in face-to-face groups as "dominance hierarchies." Perhaps that was unfortunate, leading some later authors to infer that it refers to hostile aggression by the powerful on the weak, whereas to primatologists it simply means attempting to enhance or maintain one's rank in the group's status hierarchy, irrelevantly whether by brutal or gentle means. (Dominance activity among apes and humans is usually gentle.)

At the time, only medical professionals could administer hormones (vs. placebo) to human subjects, so studies were necessarily in the other direction: the effect of dominance behavior on testosterone level. There was and still is no standard experimental paradigm for testosterone comparable to the Trier test for cortisol. Usually physically intensive athletic contests were used, comparing hormone changes in winners vs. losers. Testosterone should rise in winners and decrease in losers, contingent on their corresponding elevation or depression in mood (e.g., Mazur and Lamb, 1980; Mazur et al. 1989).

Brian Gladue introduced a non-physical competition, randomly assigning young men to "winning" and "losing" a rigged laboratory contest of reaction time. Wins and losses were further manipulated into "Decisive" vs. "Close" outcomes. Assays from repeated saliva samples, shown in Figure 2 of Gladue, Boechler, & McCaul (1989), vividly support the win-loss effect. Moods after the contest were consistent, with losers more depressed than winners. Whether the outcome was decisive or close made little difference.

Increasing interest in testosterone was reflected in two similar models associating the hormone with dominant behavior. One, dubbed the "biosocial model," was my own, formulated for primates (1985, 2005); the other, by Wingfield, Hegner, Dufty, & Ball (1990), was for birds.

In the biosocial model, every individual has certain observable signs or signals that suggest his or her social status is (or ought to be) high or low. High or rising testosterone is presumed to support the expression of high-status signs, while low or declining T shifts signaling toward deferent signs. Dominant signaling can induce stress in the interaction; deferent signaling reduces stress.

As the number of research reports from different investigators increased, continually updated reviews of the literature affirmed the relationship between testosterone and dominance, at least in men, but also noted failures to replicate (Mazur and Booth, 1998; Archer, 1991, 2006; Carré, McCormick, & Hariri, 2011; Carré and Olmstead, 2015; Geniole, Bird, Ruddick, & Carré, 2016). One recent example, essentially a replication of Gladue's study, had young men play a rigged Tetris computer game, then assigned each one randomly into outcomes: clear win, narrow win, clear loss, or narrow loss. Saliva was collected once pre-game and once 20 minutes afterward. The results were utterly different and inconsistent with those reported by Gladue. There was no main win-loss effect on testosterone; clear winners had a slight but insignificant increase in testosterone, while it dropped or barely changed in all other categories; clear vs. narrow outcome did matter, with narrow winners having a far greater drop in testosterone than other conditions (Wu, Eisenegger, Zilioli, Watson, & Clark, 2017).

Some discrepancies in the literature can be discounted because subjects were not motivated to win or showed no mood change corresponding to their outcome, perhaps because little was at stake or they were not personally concerned about the outcome. Subjects scoring high on "implicit power motivation," presumably those who most cared about winning, were especially likely to show a win-loss effect (Schultheiss, Campbell, & McClelland, 1999; Schultheiss et al., 2005; Vongas and Hajj, 2017). But as new studies seemed continually to report testosterone effects only after controlling on various mediating variables, or no effect at all, the win-loss effect could hardly be regarded as robust (Casto and Edwards, 2016). Oliveira and Oliveira (2014) suggested that discrepancies from the win-loss prediction may be due to cognitive variables such as perceived threat/challenge, and whether or not a victory or defeat is perceived by the subject as deserved. The most recent meta-analysis of these studies, by Geniole et al. (2016), gives new life to the old hypothesis. Overall, winners of a competition demonstrate a larger increase in testosterone relative to losers, especially in studies outside the lab (e.g., in sports venues). Lab studies show a relatively weak effect. Clearly, the last chapter of this story is not yet written.

Apart from sports and laboratory studies, by the 1990s another line of research led by Alan Booth and James Dabbs focused on secondary analysis of large datasets collected for other purposes but containing testosterone as one variable. Among the most important were studies funded by the US Congress to evaluate possible health effects from exposure to Agent Orange during the Vietnam War. The Army's Vietnam Experience Study (VES) is a cross-section of 4,462 male veterans given extensive medical examinations and interviews. The Air Force Health Study (AFHS) has a longitudinal design, following about a thousand male veterans through six cycles of interviews and medical examinations, spanning 20 years. These large samples have statistical power so conspicuously lacking in typical studies of testosterone and behavior.

The most important finding from the Army's VES is the reliable association between high testosterone and self-reports of diverse antisocial behaviors, including childhood truancy, trouble as an adult on the job and with the law, marital disruption, drug and alcohol abuse, violent behavior, and military AWOL – mostly indicators of rebelliousness and assertive norm breaking (Dabbs and Morris, 1990; Booth and Osgood, 1993). Another important finding is the relationship between testosterone and marriage. Booth and Dabbs (1993) reported that men with high testosterone are less likely to marry than are men with low testosterone. The longitudinal AFHS shows this to be a long-term dynamic relationship: Male testosterone declines after marriage. If a marriage fails, male testosterone rises around the time of divorce (Mazur and Michalek, 1998; Danish replication by Holmboe et al., 2017).

Despite experimenters' inability to administer exogenous testosterone until recently, earlier study designs buttressed a causal effect, showing that natural rises in testosterone, from earlier contests, predicted increased willingness to participate in a future contest (Mehta and Josephs, 2006; Carré and McCormick, 2008; Carré, Campbell, Lozoya, Goetz, & Welker, 2013).

Burnham (2007) introduced the ultimatum game (UG) into testosterone research. Here a "proposer" makes an offer to a "responder" about how to divide a fixed sum of money. If the responder accepts that offer, the split is made; if the responder refuses the offer, neither gets any money. Typically, proposers offer nearly equal splits which responders accept. Occasionally proposers offer unfair splits, which responders tend to reject. ("Rational choice" predicts that responders will accept any offer in preference to zero dollars.) In Burnham's version, male undergraduates played both roles, at different times paired randomly, and the proposer was constrained to offer either $25 or $5 out of $40. Among responders offered only $5, those who rejected had significantly higher testosterone than those accepting the unfair offer.

In the new century it became permissible for researchers to dose subjects with testosterone vs. placebo, using gels applied to the skin, injections, or nasal sprays. (This followed sharply rising popularity of prescribed testosterone, without overt ill effects, to treat symptoms of "low T," a dubious syndrome invented for advertising purposes.) This promised an era of experimentally tested causal hypotheses, but to date results have been disappointingly inconsistent. One of the first of the new experiments showed that administering testosterone to young men decreases the generosity of offers in the UG (Zak et al., 2009). This was followed by a report of seemingly opposite results, that testosterone dosing (of young females) *increases* the fairness of offers, a prosocial behavior (Eisenegger, Naef, Snozzi, Heinrichs, & Fehr, 2010). Adding to the confusion, Kopsida, Berrebi, Petrovic, and Ingvar (2016, both sexes) and Cueva et al. (2017, males) did *not* find significant effects of administered testosterone on rejecting unfair offers, contradicting Burnham's (2007) original report of an association. A later study of a Japanese rugby team found that among high-status players, high testosterone was associated with less acceptance of unfair offers, consistent with Burnham's original finding, but among low-status players, high testosterone was associated with acquiescence to unfair offers from high-status players (Inoue et al., 2017). Thus, in this context of rigid hierarchy, high testosterone enhanced whatever action was consistent with one's pre-existing status rank.

If testosterone's role in adult males is essentially to enhance status, does this occur through *prosocial* (e.g., generosity or acquiescence, as among Japanese rugby players) as well as *antisocial* (e.g., response to provocation) actions? To address this, Dreher et al. (2016) modified the UG so that, having accepted or rejected an offer, the responder has an opportunity to punish or reward the proposer at a proportionate cost to himself. Men treated with testosterone (vs. placebo) were more likely to punish proposers who made unfair offers, indicating that the hormone indeed enhances antisocial response to provocation. Testosterone-treated men who received large offers were more likely to reward the proposer. Thus, testosterone enhanced dominant behavior, whether prosocial or antisocial, as was appropriate for the situation. These results, so felicitous for the biosocial model, have not yet been replicated.

Testosterone and cortisol were from the outset both included in many studies. They are known to interact physiologically (Handa and Weiser, 2013), but only recently has attention shifted to their social behavioral connection. According to the seminal "dual hormone hypothesis" of Mehta and Josephs (2010), testosterone is associated with dominance or leadership especially (or only) when cortisol is low (also see Terburg, Morgan, & van Honk, 2009; Prasad et al., 2017). Empirical tests give mixed but usually positive results (Mehta and Prasad, 2015. Moreover, the hypothesis is intuitively appealing, suggesting that the people most likely to act assertively, to break norms or otherwise scale stressful barriers, are those least bothered by the stressor, thus low in cortisol or in trait anxiety (Hamilton, Carre, Mehta, Olmstead, & Whitaker, 2015).

Does testosterone affect women the same way it affects men? From the outset, studies have focused mostly on young men if only because it is easier to reliably measure testosterone at the higher levels found in males. Also, there are differences in the relevant organs, and in the very different roles of testosterone in male versus female development, from the embryo through maturation. Some researchers now include subjects of both sexes in the same analysis to increase statistical power, scaling the sex difference in testosterone by normalizing levels, then testing gender × testosterone interactions. I think this is a poor analytical tactic and the sexes should be analyzed separately. Overall, the evidence of testosterone effects in women is suggestive but weaker than evidence for men (van Anders and Watson, 2006; Edwards and Castro, 2013; Geniole et al., 2016). There are some suggestive findings that estradiol may be associated with dominance in women (Schultheiss, Dargel, & Rohde, 2003; Stanton and Schultheiss, 2007; Stanton and Edelstein, 2009; Oxford, Tiedtke, Ossmann, Özbe, & Schultheiss, 2017).

Oxytocin and bonding

Oxytocin was discovered in 1906 but its molecular structure not worked out until 1952. It is a peptide hormone and neurotransmitter, synthesized in the hypothalamus and released by the pituitary, reaching both the brain and the bloodstream (*Ross et al., 2009*). Oxytocin is important around childbirth, released in response to stretching of the cervix and uterus during labor and with stimulation of the nipples during breastfeeding, helping the mother lactate and bond with her baby.

Injecting oxytocin into a female rat's brain increases maternal behavior toward orphan cubs and maternal aggression. The hormone affects partner preference, pair bonding, and social recognition (Pedersen and Prange, 1979; Campbell, 2008; Carter, 1998; Bielsky and Young, 2004; Lim and Young, 2006; Williams, Insel, Harbaugh, & Carter, 1994). These animal effects, broadly interpreted as prosocial, suggest that oxytocin might promote sociability in humans as well. There has been a flurry of research in the past 15 years, partly in the hope that oxytocin, or the related peptide vasopressin, may offer therapy for mental disorders such as autism.

In an influential article in *Nature*, Kosfeld and colleagues proposed trust as one prosocial behavior that might be increased in young men receiving oxytocin (vs. placebo) via nasal spray. The experimenters adopted a two-player "trust game" from behavioral economics. One player, called "the investor," begins with a stake of money. He can keep it or endow any part to an anonymous "trustee." Whatever money the trustee receives is immediately tripled by an experimenter. Now the trustee has the choice of keeping all the money received, or of returning some to the investor. Both players can profit if the investor gives money to the trustee *and* the trustee returns a greater amount than was endowed. Thus, each player has a prosocial and an antisocial option: The investor decides whether or not to trust the trustee; and if the trustee receives money, he decides on any payment back to the investor. The result of the experiment was that oxytocin increased investors' endowments, but it did not increase trustees' generosity in back-payments (Kosfeld, Heinrichs, Zak, Fischbacher, & Fehr, 2005).

Zak, Kurzban, and Matzner (2005) soon fortified the oxytocin-trust hypothesis. Again running the trust game but without manipulating oxytocin, they reported that higher endogenous oxytocin (in blood) was associated with more generous endowments by investors and more generous back-payments by trustees. In another study, Zak, Stanton, & Ahmadi (2007) showed that administering oxytocin (vs. placebo) increased generosity as measured by donating money to a stranger.

Criticisms have been raised of this and subsequent oxytocin research in humans, including the lack of certitude that oxytocin administered by nasal spray actually reaches the brain in time to affect measured behaviors (Churchland and Winkielman, 2012; McCullough, Churchland, & Mendez, 2013; but see Daughters et al., 2015). Focusing specifically on six studies since 2005 that used variants of the trust game, Nave, Camerer, and McCullough (2015) concluded that the claimed association of intranasal oxytocin with higher trust has not replicated well (also see Walum, Waldman, & Young, 2016; and Hurlemann and Marsh, 2017).

De Dreu and his colleagues proposed a different means whereby oxytocin is prosocial or parochially altruistic, such as by increasing ethnocentrism, i.e., promoting in-group cohesion against threatening out-groups. The tendency among primates to form defensive alliances, pitting in groups against out-groups, is well known. Furthermore, this tendency increases during periods of stressful conflict, leading to the (untested) hypothesis that cortisol is the operative hormone (Mazur, 2005). Now the focus was on oxytocin.

De Dreu's group ran a series of computer-guided tasks to gage both ethnocentric in-group favoritism as well as out-group degradation, comparing young men treated with oxytocin vs. placebo. Their results showed that oxytocin motivates in-group favoritism and, to a lesser extent, out-group derogation, concluding: "These findings call into question the view of oxytocin as an indiscriminate 'love drug' or 'cuddle chemical' and suggest that oxytocin has a role in the emergence of intergroup conflict and violence" (De Dreu et al., 2010; also see De Dreu et al., 2010). De Dreu's colleagues continue to report supportive results (Daughters, Manstead, Ten Velden, & De Dreu, 2017).

Given the recent surge of oxytocin research, much of it equivocal, it is too early for firm conclusions about how it affects diverse prosocial behaviors. Some researchers are skeptical, others show enormous enthusiasm:

> Studies across multiple attachments throughout life . . . . demonstrate that the extended oxytocin system provides the neurohormonal substrate for parental, romantic, and filial attachment in humans; that the three prototypes of affiliation are expressed in similar constellations of social behavior; and that oxytocin is stable over time within individuals, is mutually influencing among partners, and that mechanisms of cross-generation and inter-couple transmission relate to coordinated social behavior.
>
> (Feldman, 2012: 380)

Perhaps, perhaps not.

Building a stronger foundation

Social neuroendocrinology and its attendant literature have grown rapidly but erratically. New articles each month seem at odds with earlier articles or go off in a new direction altogether. There is little accumulation of reliable findings. Seemingly contradictory results occur so often that reviews depend on counting the number of reports supporting a hypothesis versus the number that do not.

This happens because researchers are under pressure to squeeze out positive (and novel) findings, so they look at their data this way and that way, testing one interaction after another, until something pops out that is significant, a process called "p-hacking" (Simmons, Nelson, &

Simonsohn, 2011). As a result, we see publication of "findings" that probably are not replicable. Occasionally these come to light, as for the now infamous claim that "power posing" increases testosterone and decreases cortisol (Carney, Cuddy, & Yap, 2010), disseminated in a TED talk with over 40 million views and almost certainly not true (Ranehill et al., 2015; www.ted.com/talks/amy_cuddy_your_body_language_shapes_who_you_are). More often, false positives are allowed to stand, littering the journals, because the pedestrian work of replication is not vita-building, and editors have a bias against publishing null results (see also Schultheiss & Mehta, this volume).

A strong foundation for neuroendocrinology requires confidence in core findings. Is it *really* true that among young men in serious competition, testosterone of winners rises relative to testosterone of losers? Does increased testosterone *really* elicit status-enhancing behavior in men and improve their rank in a face-to-face hierarchy? Do such effects occur in women?

These questions are barely closer to solid answers than they were a quarter century ago. It is time for a collaboration among independent laboratories, doing parallel replications of primary hypotheses on large samples at each site. They must agree beforehand (and register publicly) what hypotheses are to be tested, predicted results, uniform procedures, assay methods, analyses to be employed, and a common format for reports so results can be easily compared.

High priority must be given to resolving doubts about the accuracy of assays for salivary testosterone (Welker et al., 2016) and oxytocin (McCullough et al., 2013). This can be done by supplying multiple laboratories with duplicate samples drawn from large pools of saliva, some pools spiked so hormone concentrations are known. Each lab would blindly assay the same samples, so different methods can be compared and either validated, improved, or rejected.

Do not mix apples and oranges. Human and nonhuman primates typically participate in face-to-face status hierarchies, their homologous evolutionary roots the basis for applying animal models to people. Personal dominance hierarchies have little in common with the large-scale socioeconomic stratification (SES) of agrarian and industrial societies, where people in one stratum – most not knowing one another – regard themselves (and are regarded by others) as superior (or inferior) to other large strata of people. SES does not occur among nonhuman primates and has been present in human society for only about 10,000 years. The physiological and behavioral mechanisms whereby individuals achieve or maintain rank in a face-to-face hierarchy are different from attainment of SES by birth, or in modern societies also by education and wealth accumulation. SES and dominance hierarchies have no common phylogenetic basis, yet they are sometimes conflated in social neuroendocrinology, a confounding to be avoided.

The early approach of studies reported here was to establish gross relationships between hormones and behaviors, with little attention to the *mechanisms* whereby these variables are related, which remain elusive. Take testosterone as an example. If it does increase social dominance, what specifically is the mechanism by which this occurs? Here are five candidates, all experimentally testable by comparing testosterone supplementation (or suppression) with placebo.

1. Signaling status

Status signs have been much discussed in humans, including erect vs. stooped postures, eye contact vs. eye aversion, dominant vs. deferent speech, or physical approach vs. retreat. Heightened testosterone may increase dominant signing; low testosterone would increase deferent signs. Results so far show that young women who received testosterone (vs. placebo) prolonged their staring into the eyes of threatening faces (Terburg, Aarts, & van Honk, 2012). Testosterone administered to young men increased their approach to angry faces during social confrontations (Wagels, Radke, Goerlich, Habel, & Votinov, 2017).

2. Reducing fear

Animal studies show a fear-reducing effect of testosterone (e.g., Aikey, Nyby, Anmuth, & James, 2002). Young women administered testosterone (vs. placebo) had reduced vigilant emotional response to fearful faces, interpreted by van Honk, Peper, and Schutter (2005) as direct evidence for fear-reducing properties of the hormone in humans (also see Hermans, Putman, Baas, Koppeschaar, & van Honk, 2006). Chichinadze, Lazarashvili, Chichinadze, and Gachechiladze (2012) propose that anxiety-reducing and pleasure-enhancing properties of testosterone underlay its relationship to dominance and the effects of winning or losing. Anecdotally, one researcher who self-administered testosterone told me that it had a calming effect. At least one study suggests that exogenous testosterone increased stress in subjects waiting to take the Trier test (Knight et al., 2017). Personally, I have never felt calmer (or more stressed) during extensive self-testing with testosterone, but if calm occurs that would confer an advantage in exchanging stress signals during a dominance contest, and it would support risk taking. Heightened cortisol might increase insecurity and susceptibility to stressors, a disadvantage during a dominance contest and a barrier to risk taking. (Do Yosemite climbers have high testosterone and low cortisol?) A simple but potentially valuable exploration would be to randomly assign subjects to hormone vs. placebo treatments, afterward asking if they feel any differently, and if so, how?

3. Vigilance to threat

One often acts dominantly when challenged by a competitor, or by the representative of a repressive institution (e.g., a police officer or high school teacher). Possibly testosterone increases vigilance or sensitivity to insult, metaphorically installing a hair trigger. This could occur by altering the activation of, or coupling between, specific brain regions, particularly the amygdala and orbitofrontal cortex, which have testosterone receptors and are responsive to fearful and angry faces (Mehta and Beer, 2010; van Wingen, Mattern, Verkes, Buitelaar, & Fernández, 2010; Eisenegger, Haushofer, & Fehr, 2011).

4. Stress resilience

During dominance contests, individuals are assumed to compete for status, each trying to "out-stress" the other. I have already noted the advantage of reduced fear, but apart from that, one would have an edge if able to stand one's ground, still feeling the fear but successfully coping with it. ("Take it like a man.") Animal studies show that testosterone downregulates stress responses in the HPA and sympathetic nervous system (Eisenegger et al., 2011).

5. Priming motivation or potency

Possibly testosterone intensifies status-relevant motivations like desire for success, rewards, thrill of victory, or need for power (Schultheiss et al., 1999; Welker, Gruber, & Mehta, 2015). Testosterone may enhance one's personal sense of stature or of potency. In a recent experiment, exogenous testosterone or a placebo was administered to men and self-perceptions of physical dominance subsequently assessed by having participants select what they believed to be their true face from an array of images digitally manipulated in masculinity. Testosterone-treated men picked a more masculine version of their own face than did those on placebo – an effect that was particularly pronounced among men with relatively low baseline testosterone. We have barely begun research on this potential mechanism.

What have we learned?

At least for me, looking back at the history of social neuroendocrinology shows that we have developed tantalizing leads and lively inquiries but not yet a stable set of findings suitable for inclusion in an undergraduate textbook. This is an exciting work in progress, energized in the past few decades by rapid increase in bright young researchers from diverse fields, applying new techniques and producing a profuse literature, though a literature rife with inconsistent findings and perhaps false positives. It is time for a pause, a refinement of methods, and a consolidation of valid results.

Note

* I appreciate the advice of R. Josephs, P. Mehta, and O. Schultheiss.

References

Aikey, J.L., Nyby, J.G., Anmuth, D.M., & James, P.J. (2002). Testosterone rapidly reduces anxiety in male house mice (*Mus musculus*). *Hormones and Behavior, 42*(4), 448–460. https://doi.org/10.1006/hbeh.2002.1838

Allee, W., Collias, N., & Lutherman, C. (1939). Modification of the social order in flocks of hens by the injection of testosterone propionate. *Physiology & Behavior, 44,* 735–740.

Archer, J. (1991). The influence of testosterone on human aggression. *British Journal of Psychology, 82*(Pt 1), 1–28. https://doi.org/10.1111/j.2044-8295.1991.tb02379.x

Archer, J. (2006). Testosterone and human aggression: An evaluation of the challenge hypothesis. *Neuroscience and Biobehavioral Reviews, 30*(3), 319–345. https://doi.org/10.1016/j.neubiorev.2004.12.007

Bielsky, I.F., & Young, L.J. (2004). Oxytocin, vasopressin, and social recognition in mammals. *Peptides, 25*(9), 1565–1574. https://doi.org/10.1016/j.peptides.2004.05.019

Bliss, M. (1982). *The discovery of insulin.* Chicago, IL: University of Chicago Press.

Booth, A., & Dabbs, J., Jr. (1993). Testosterone and men's marriages. *Social Forces, 72*(2), 463–477. https://doi.org/10.1093/sf/72.2.463

Booth, A., & Osgood, D. (1993). The influence of testosterone on deviance in adulthood. *Criminology, 31*(1), 93–117. https://doi.org/10.1111/j.1745-9125.1993.tb01123.x

Booth, A., Shelley, G., Mazur, A., Tharp, G., & Kittok, R. (1989). Testosterone, and winning and losing in human competition. *Hormones and Behavior, 23*(4), 556–571. https://doi.org/10.1016/0018-506X(89)90042-1

Brinkerhoff, D., & Booth, A. (1984). Gender, dominance and stress. *Journal of Social and Biological Structures, 7*(2), 159–177. https://doi.org/10.1016/S0140-1750(84)80007-X

Burnham, T. (2007). High-testosterone men reject low ultimatum game offers. *Proceedings of the Royal Society B: Biological Sciences, 274,* 2327–2330.

Campbell, A. (2008). Attachment, aggression and affiliation: The role of oxytocin in female social behavior. *Biological Psychology, 77*(1), 1–10. https://doi.org/10.1016/j.biopsycho.2007.09.001

Cannon, W. (1932). *Wisdom of the body.* New York, NY: W.W. Norton & Company.

Carney, D.R., Cuddy, A.J., & Yap, A.J. (2010). Power posing: Brief nonverbal displays affect neuroendocrine levels and risk tolerance. *Psychological Science, 21*(10), 1363–1368. https://doi.org/10.1177/0956797610383437

Carré, J.M., Campbell, J.A., Lozoya, E., Goetz, S.M., & Welker, K.M. (2013). Changes in testosterone mediate the effect of winning on subsequent aggressive behaviour. *Psychoneuroendocrinology, 38*(10), 2034–2041. https://doi.org/10.1016/j.psyneuen.2013.03.008

Carré, J.M., & McCormick, C.M. (2008). Aggressive behavior and change in salivary testosterone concentrations predict willingness to engage in a competitive task. *Hormones and Behavior, 54*(3), 403–409. https://doi.org/10.1016/j.yhbeh.2008.04.008

Carré, J.M., McCormick, C.M., & Hariri, A.R. (2011). The social neuroendocrinology of human aggression. *Psychoneuroendocrinology, 36*(7), 935–944. https://doi.org/10.1016/j.psyneuen.2011.02.001

Carré, J., & Olmstead, N. (2015). Social neuroendocrinology of human aggression: Examining the role of competition-induced testosterone dynamics. *Neuroscience Forefront Review, 286,* 171–186. https://doi.org/10.1016/j.neuroscience.2014.11.029

Carter, C.S. (1998). Neuroendocrine perspectives on social attachment and love. *Psychoneuroendocrinology*, *23*(8), 779–818. https://doi.org/10.1016/S0306-4530(98)00055-9

Casto, K.V., & Edwards, D.A. (2016). Testosterone, cortisol, and human competition. *Hormones and Behavior*, *82*, 21–37. https://doi.org/10.1016/j.yhbeh.2016.04.004

Cheney, V. (2006). *A brief history of castration* (2nd ed.). Bloomington, IN: Authorhouse.

Chichinadze, K., Lazarashvili, A., Chichinadze, N., & Gachechiladze, L. (2012). Testosterone dynamics during encounter: Role of emotional factors. *Journal of Comparative Physiology: A, Neuroethology, Sensory, Neural, and Behavioral Physiology*, *198*(7), 485–494. https://doi.org/10.1007/s00359-012-0726-1

Churchland, P.S., & Winkielman, P. (2012). Modulating social behavior with oxytocin: How does it work? What does it mean? *Hormones and Behavior*, *61*(3), 392–399. https://doi.org/10.1016/j.yhbeh.2011.12.003

Cueva, C., Roberts, R.E., Spencer, T.J., Rani, N., Tempest, M., Tobler, P.N., . . . Rustichini, A. (2017). Testosterone administration does not affect men's rejections of low ultimatum game offers or aggressive mood. *Hormones and Behavior*, *87*, 1–7. https://doi.org/10.1016/j.yhbeh.2016.09.012

Dabbs, J., Jr. (2000). *Heroes, rogues and lovers: Testosterone and behavior*. New York, NY: McGraw-Hill.

Dabbs, J., Jr., & Morris, R. (1990). Testosterone, social class, and antisocial behavior in a sample of 4,462 men. *Psychological Science*, *1*(3), 209–211. https://doi.org/10.1111/j.1467-9280.1990.tb00200.x

Daughters, K., Manstead, A.S., Hubble, K., Rees, A., Thapar, A., & van Goozen, S.H. (2015). Salivary oxytocin concentrations in males following intranasal administration of oxytocin: A double-blind, crossover study. *PLoS One*, *10*(12), e0145104. https://doi.org/10.1371/journal.pone.0145104

Daughters, K., Manstead, A., Ten Velden, F., & De Dreu, C. (2017). Oxytocin modulates third-party sanctioning of selfish and generous behavior within and between groups. *Psychoneuroendocrinology*, *77*, 18–24. https://doi.org/10.1016/j.psyneuen.2016.11.039

De Dreu, C.K., Greer, L.L., Handgraaf, M.J., Shalvi, S., van Kleef, G.A., Baas, M., . . . Feith, S.W. (2010). The neuropeptide oxytocin regulates parochial altruism in intergroup conflict among humans. *Science*, *328*(5984), 1408–1411. https://doi.org/10.1126/science.1189047

De Kruif, P. (1945). *The male hormone*. New York, NY: Harcourt Brace.

De Waal, F. (1982). *Chimpanzee politics*. New York, NY: Harper & Row.

Dreher, J., Dunne, S., Pazderska, A., Frodl, T., Nolan, J., & O'Doherty, J. (2016). Testosterone causes both prosocial and antisocial status-enhancing behaviors in human males. *Proceedings of the National Academy of Sciences*, *113*, 11633–11638. https://doi.org/10.1073/pnas.1608085113

Edwards, D.A., & Casto, K.V. (2013). Women's intercollegiate athletic competition: Cortisol, testosterone, and the dual-hormone hypothesis as it relates to status among teammates. *Hormones and Behavior*, *64*(1), 153–160. https://doi.org/10.1016/j.yhbeh.2013.03.003

Eisenegger, C., Haushofer, J., & Fehr, E. (2011). The role of testosterone in social interaction. *Trends in Cognitive Sciences*, *15*(6), 263–271. https://doi.org/10.1016/j.tics.2011.04.008

Eisenegger, C., Naef, M., Snozzi, R., Heinrichs, M., & Fehr, E. (2010). Prejudice and truth about the effect of testosterone on human bargaining behaviour. *Nature*, *463*(7279), 356–359. https://doi.org/10.1038/nature08711

Feldman, R. (2012). Oxytocin and social affiliation in humans. *Hormones and Behavior*, *61*(3), 380–391. https://doi.org/10.1016/j.yhbeh.2012.01.008

Fisek, M., & Ofshe, R. (1970). The process of status evolution. *Sociometry*, *33*(3), 327–346. https://doi.org/10.2307/2786161

Frisch, J.U., Häusser, J.A., & Mojzisch, A. (2015). The "Trier Social Stress Test" as a paradigm to study how people respond to threat in social interactions. *Frontiers in Psychology*, *6*, 14. https://doi.org/10.3389/fpsyg.2015.00014

Geniole, S., Bird, B., Ruddick, E., & Carré, J. (2016). Effects of competition outcome on testosterone concentrations in humans: An updated meta-analysis. *Hormones and Behavior*. https://doi.org/10.1016/j.yhbeh.2016,10.002

Giles, G.E., Mahoney, C.R., Brunyé, T.T., Taylor, H.A., & Kanarek, R.B. (2014). Stress effects on mood, HPA axis, and autonomic response: Comparison of three psychosocial stress paradigms. *PLoS One*, *9*(12), e113618. https://doi.org/10.1371/journal.pone.0113618

Gladue, B., Boechler, M., & McCaul, K. (1989). Hormonal response to competition in human males. *Aggressive Behavior*, *15*, 409–422.

Granger, D., Shirtcliff, E., Booth, A., Kivlighan, K., & Schwartz, E. (2004). The "trouble" with salivary testosterone. *Psychoneuroendocrinology*, *29*, 1229–1240.

Hamilton, L., Carre, J., Mehta, P., Olmstead, N., & Whitaker, J. (2015). Social neuroendocrinology of status: A review and future directions. *Adaptive Human Behavior and Physiology, 1*(2), 202–230. https://doi.org/10.1007/s40750-015-0025-5

Handa, R., & Weiser, M. (2013). Gonadal steroid hormones and the hypothalamo-pituitary-adrenal axis. *Frontiers in Neuroendocrinology.* https://doi.org/10.1016/j.yfrne.2013.11.001

Harms, P., Crede, M., Tynan, M., Leon, M., & Jeung, W. (2016). Leadership and stress: A meta-analytic review. *The Leadership Quarterly, 28,* 179–184. https://doi.org/10.1016/j.leaqua.2016.10.006

Hermans, E.J., Putman, P., Baas, J.M., Koppeschaar, H.P., & van Honk, J. (2006). A single administration of testosterone reduces fear-potentiated startle in humans. *Biological Psychiatry, 59*(9), 872–874. https://doi.org/10.1016/j.biopsych.2005.11.015

Holmboe, S.A., Priskorn, L., Jørgensen, N., Skakkebaek, N.E., Linneberg, A., Juul, A., & Andersson, A.M. (2017). Influence of marital status on testosterone levels – A ten year follow-up of 1113 men. *Psychoneuroendocrinology, 80,* 155–161. https://doi.org/10.1016/j.psyneuen.2017.03.010

Hurlemann, R., & Marsh, N. (2017). Deciphering the modulatory role of oxytocin in human altruism. *Reviews in the Neurosciences, 28*(4), 335–342. https://doi.org/10.1515/revneuro-2016-0061

Inoue, Y., Takahashi, T., Burriss, R.P., Arai, S., Hasegawa, T., Yamagishi, T., & Kiyonari, T. (2017). Testosterone promotes either dominance or submissiveness in the ultimatum game depending on players' social rank. *Scientific Reports, 7*(1), 5335. https://doi.org/10.1038/s41598-017-05603-7

Kirschbaum, C., & Hellhammer, D.H. (1989). Salivary cortisol in psychobiological research: An overview. *Neuropsychobiology, 22*(3), 150–169. https://doi.org/10.1159/000118611

Kirschbaum, C., Pirke, K.M., & Hellhammer, D.H. (1993). The "Trier Social Stress Test" – a tool for investigating psychobiological stress responses in a laboratory setting. *Neuropsychobiology, 28*(1–2), 76–81. https://doi.org/10.1159/000119004

Klipker, K., Wrzus, C., Rauers, A., Boker, S.M., & Riediger, M. (2017). Within-person changes in salivary testosterone and physical characteristics of puberty predict boys' daily affect. *Hormones and Behavior, 95,* 22–32. https://doi.org/10.1016/j.yhbeh.2017.07.012

Knight, E.L., Christian, C.B., Morales, P.J., Harbaugh, W.T., Mayr, U., & Mehta, P.H. (2017). Exogenous testosterone enhances cortisol and affective responses to social-evaluative stress in dominant men. *Psychoneuroendocrinology, 85,* 151–157. https://doi.org/10.1016/j.psyneuen.2017.08.014

Knight, E.L., & Mehta, P. (2017). Hierarchy stability moderates the effect of status on stress and performance in humans. *Proceedings of the National Academy of Science, 114,* 78–83. https://doi.org/10.1973/pnas.1609811114

Kopsida, E., Berrebi, J., Petrovic, P., & Ingvar, M. (2016). Testosterone administration related differences in brain activation during the ultimatum game. *Frontiers in Neuroscience, 10,* 66. https://doi.org/10.3389/fnins.2016.00066

Kosfeld, M., Heinrichs, M., Zak, P.J., Fischbacher, U., & Fehr, E. (2005). Oxytocin increases trust in humans. *Nature, 435*(7042), 673–676. https://doi.org/10.1038/nature03701

Lee, P.A., Houk, C.P., Ahmed, S.F., Hughes, I.A., & The International Consensus Conference on Intersex Organized by the Lawson Wilkins Pediatric Endocrine Society and the European Society for Paediatric Endocrinology. (2006). Consensus statement on management of intersex disorders. *Pediatrics, 118*(2), e488–e500. https://doi.org/10.1542/peds.2006-0738

Lim, M.M., & Young, L.J. (2006). Neuropeptidergic regulation of affiliative behavior and social bonding in animals. *Hormones and Behavior, 50*(4), 506–517. https://doi.org/10.1016/j.yhbeh.2006.06.028

Mazur, A. (1985). A biosocial model of status in face-to-face primate groups. *Social Forces, 64*(2), 377–402. https://doi.org/10.1093/sf/64.2.377

Mazur, A. (2005). *Biosociology of dominance and deference.* New York, NY: Rowman & Littlefield.

Mazur, A. (1976). Effects of testosterone on status in primate groups. *Folia Primatologica, 26,* 214–216.

Mazur, A. (2015). Biosociology of dominance and deference. In J. Turner, R. Machalek, & A. Maryanski (Eds.), *Handbook of evolutionary analysis in the social sciences* (pp. 474–492). Oxford: Paradigm.

Mazur, A., & Booth, A. (1998). Testosterone and dominance in men. *Behavioral and Brain Sciences, 21*(3), 353–363. https://doi.org/10.1017/S0140525X98001228

Mazur, A., & Lamb, T.A. (1980). Testosterone, status, and mood in human males. *Hormones and Behavior, 14*(3), 236–246. https://doi.org/10.1016/0018-506X(80)90032-X

Mazur, A., & Michalek, J. (1998). Marriage, divorce, and male testosterone. *Social Forces, 77*(1), 315–330. https://doi.org/10.1093/sf/77.1.315

Mazur, A., Welker, K.M., & Peng, B. (2015). Does the biosocial model explain the emergence of status differences in conversations among unacquainted men? *PLoS One, 10*(11), e0142941. https://doi.org/10.1371/journal.pone.0142941

McCullough, M.E., Churchland, P.S., & Mendez, A.J. (2013). Problems with measuring peripheral oxytocin: Can the data on oxytocin and human behavior be trusted? *Neuroscience and Biobehavioral Reviews, 37*(8), 1485–1492. https://doi.org/10.1016/j.neubiorev.2013.04.018

McKee, L. (1927). The effect of the injection of a lipoid fraction of bull testicle in capons. *Proceedings of the Institute of Medicine, 6,* 242.

Mehta, P.H., & Beer, J. (2010). Neural mechanisms of the testosterone-aggression relation: The role of orbitofrontal cortex. *Journal of Cognitive Neuroscience, 22*(10), 2357–2368. https://doi.org/10.1162/jocn.2009.21389

Mehta, P.H., & Josephs, R.A. (2006). Testosterone change after losing predicts the decision to compete again. *Hormones and Behavior, 50*(5), 684–692. https://doi.org/10.1016/j.yhbeh.2006.07.001

Mehta, P.H., & Josephs, R.A. (2010). Testosterone and cortisol jointly regulate dominance: Evidence for a dual-hormone hypothesis. *Hormones and Behavior, 58*(5), 898–906. https://doi.org/10.1016/j.yhbeh.2010.08.020

Mehta, P.H., & Prasad, S. (2015). The dual-hormone hypothesis: A brief review and future research agenda. *Current Opinion in Behavioral Sciences, 3,* 163–168. https://doi.org/10.1016/j.cobeha.2015.04.008

Nave, G., Camerer, C., & McCullough, M. (2015). Does oxytocin increase trust in humans? A critical review of research. *Perspectives on Psychological Science, 20,* 772–789. https://doi.org/10.1177/1745691615600138

Oliveira, G., & Oliveira, R. (2014). Androgen responsiveness to competition in humans: The role of cognitive variables. *Neuroscience and Neuroeconomics, 3,* 19–32. https://doi.org/10.2147/NAN.S55721

Oxford, J.K., Tiedtke, J.M., Ossmann, A., Özbe, D., & Schultheiss, O.C. (2017). Endocrine and aggressive responses to competition are moderated by contest outcome, gender, individual versus team competition, and implicit motives. *PLoS One, 12*(7), e0181610. https://doi.org/10.1371/journal.pone.0181610

Pedersen, C., & Prange, A. (1979). Induction of maternal behavior in virgin rats after intracerebroventricular administration of oxytocin. *Proceedings of the National Academy of Sciences of the United States of America, 12,* 6661–6665.

Prasad, S., Narayanan, J., Lim, V.K.G., Koh, G.C.H., Koh, D.S.Q., & Mehta, P.H. (2017). Preliminary evidence that acute stress moderates basal testosterone's association with retaliatory behavior. *Hormones and Behavior, 92,* 128–140. https://doi.org/10.1016/j.yhbeh.2016.10.020

Raine, A. (2002). Biosocial studies of antisocial and violent behavior in children and adults: A review. *Journal of Abnormal Child Psychology, 30*(4), 311–326. https://doi.org/10.1023/A:1015754122318

Ranehill, E., Dreber, A., Johannesson, M., Leiberg, S., Sul, S., & Weber, R.A. (2015). Assessing the robustness of power posing: No effect on hormones and risk tolerance in a large sample of men and women. *Psychological Science, 26*(5), 653–656. https://doi.org/10.1177/0956797614553946

Riad-Fahmy, D., Read, G.F., Walker, R.F., & Griffiths, K. (1982). Steroids in saliva for assessing endocrine function. *Endocrine Reviews, 3*(4), 367–395. https://doi.org/10.1210/edrv-3-4-367

Rohleder, N., Nater, U.M., Wolf, J.M., Ehlert, U., & Kirschbaum, C. (2004). Psychosocial stress-induced activation of salivary alpha-amylase: An indicator of sympathetic activity? *Annals of the New York Academy of Sciences, 1032*(1), 258–263. https://doi.org/10.1196/annals.1314.033

Rose, R., Bernstein, I., & Gordon, T. (1975). Consequences of social conflict on plasma testosterone levels in rhesus monkeys. *Psychosomatic Medicine, 37,* 50–61.

Ross, H.E., Cole, C.D., Smith, Y., Neumann, I.D., Landgraf, R., Murphy, A.Z., & Young, L.J. (2009). Characterization of the oxytocin system regulating affiliative behavior in female prairie voles. *Neuroscience, 162*(4), 892–903. https://doi.org/10.1016/j.neuroscience.2009.05.055

Schultheiss, O.C., Campbell, K.L., & McClelland, D.C. (1999). Implicit power motivation moderates men's testosterone responses to imagined and real dominance success. *Hormones and Behavior, 36*(3), 234–241. https://doi.org/10.1006/hbeh.1999.1542

Schultheiss, O.C., Dargel, A., & Rohde, W. (2003). Implicit motives and gonadal steroid hormones: Effects of menstrual cycle phase, oral contraceptive use, and relationship status. *Hormones and Behavior, 43*(2), 293–301. https://doi.org/10.1016/S0018-506X(03)00003-5

Schultheiss, O.C., Wirth, M.M., Torges, C.M., Pang, J.S., Villacorta, M.A., & Welsh, K.M. (2005). Effects of implicit power motivation on men's and women's implicit learning and testosterone changes after social victory or defeat. *Journal of Personality and Social Psychology, 88*(1), 174–188. https://doi.org/10.1037/0022-3514.88.1.174

Sherman, G.D., Lee, J.J., Cuddy, A.J., Renshon, J., Oveis, C., Gross, J.J., & Lerner, J.S. (2012). Leadership is associated with lower levels of stress. *Proceedings of the National Academy of Sciences of the United States of America, 109*(44), 17903–17907. https://doi.org/10.1073/pnas.1207042109

Shirtcliff, E.A., Dismukes, A.R., Marceau, K., Ruttle, P.L., Simmons, J.G., & Han, G. (2015). A dual-axis approach to understanding neuroendocrine development. *Developmental Psychobiology, 57*(6), 643–653. https://doi.org/10.1002/dev.21337

Simmons, J.P., Nelson, L.D., & Simonsohn, U. (2011). False-positive psychology: Undisclosed flexibility in data collection and analysis allows presenting anything as significant. *Psychological Science, 22*(11), 1359–1366. https://doi.org/10.1177/0956797611417632

Stanton, S.J., & Edelstein, R.S. (2009). The physiology of women's power motive: Implicit power motivation is positively associated with estradiol levels in women. *Journal of Research in Personality, 43*(6), 1109–1113. https://doi.org/10.1016/j.jrp.2009.08.002

Stanton, S.J., Labar, K.S., Saini, E.K., Kuhn, C.M., & Beehner, J.C. (2010). Stressful politics: Voters' cortisol responses to the outcome of the 2008 United States presidential election. *Psychoneuroendocrinology, 35*(5), 768–774. https://doi.org/10.1016/j.psyneuen.2009.10.018

Stanton, S.J., & Schultheiss, O.C. (2007). Basal and dynamic relationships between implicit power motivation and estradiol in women. *Hormones and Behavior, 52*(5), 571–580. https://doi.org/10.1016/j.yhbeh.2007.07.002

Terburg, D., Aarts, H., & van Honk, J. (2012). Testosterone affects gaze aversion from angry faces outside of conscious awareness. *Psychological Science, 23*(5), 459–463. https://doi.org/10.1177/0956797611433336

Terburg, D., Morgan, B., & van Honk, J. (2009). The testosterone-cortisol ratio: A hormonal marker for proneness to social aggression. *International Journal of Law and Psychiatry, 32*(4), 216–223. https://doi.org/10.1016/j.ijlp.2009.04.008

van Anders, S.M., & Watson, N.V. (2006). Social neuroendocrinology: Effects of social contexts and behaviors on sex steroids in humans. *Human Nature (Hawthorne, N.Y.), 17*(2), 212–237. https://doi.org/10.1007/s12110-006-1018-7

van Bokhoven, I., van Goozen, S.H., van Engeland, H., Schaal, B., Arseneault, L., Séguin, J.R., ... Tremblay, R.E. (2006). Salivary testosterone and aggression, delinquency, and social dominance in a population-based longitudinal study of adolescent males. *Hormones and Behavior, 50*(1), 118–125. https://doi.org/10.1016/j.yhbeh.2006.02.002

van Honk, J., Peper, J.S., & Schutter, D.J. (2005). Testosterone reduces unconscious fear but not consciously experienced anxiety: Implications for the disorders of fear and anxiety. *Biological Psychiatry, 58*(3), 218–225. https://doi.org/10.1016/j.biopsych.2005.04.003

van Wingen, G., Mattern, C., Verkes, R.J., Buitelaar, J., & Fernández, G. (2010). Testosterone reduces amygdala-orbitofrontal cortex coupling. *Psychoneuroendocrinology, 35*(1), 105–113. https://doi.org/10.1016/j.psyneuen.2009.09.007

Vongas, J.G., & Al Hajj, R. (2017). The effects of competition and implicit power motive on men's testosterone, emotion recognition, and aggression. *Hormones and Behavior, 92*, 57–71. https://doi.org/10.1016/j.yhbeh.2017.04.005

Wagels, L., Radke, S., Goerlich, K.S., Habel, U., & Votinov, M. (2017). Exogenous testosterone decreases men's personal distance in a social threat context. *Hormones and Behavior, 90*, 75–83. https://doi.org/10.1016/j.yhbeh.2017.03.001

Walum, H., Waldman, I.D., & Young, L.J. (2016). Statistical and methodological considerations for the interpretation of intranasal oxytocin studies. *Biological Psychiatry, 79*(3), 251–257. https://doi.org/10.1016/j.biopsych.2015.06.016

Wang, C., Plymate, S., Nieschlag, E., & Paulsen, C.A. (1981). Salivary testosterone in men: Further evidence of a direct correlation with free serum testosterone. *The Journal of Clinical Endocrinology and Metabolism, 53*(5), 1021–1024. https://doi.org/10.1210/jcem-53-5-1021

Welker, K.M., Gruber, J., & Mehta, P.H. (2015). A positive affective neuroendocrinology approach to reward and behavioral dysregulation. *Frontiers in Psychiatry, 6*, 93. https://doi.org/10.3389/fpsyt.2015.00093

Welker, K.M., Lassetter, B., Brandes, C.M., Prasad, S., Koop, D.R., & Mehta, P.H. (2016). A comparison of salivary testosterone measurement using immunoassays and tandem mass spectrometry. *Psychoneuroendocrinology, 71*, 180–188. https://doi.org/10.1016/j.psyneuen.2016.05.022

Wheeler, M.J. (2013, August). A short history of hormone measurement. *Hormone Assays in Biological Fluids, 1065*, 1–6.

Williams, J.R., Insel, T.R., Harbaugh, C.R., & Carter, C.S. (1994). Oxytocin administered centrally facilitates formation of a partner preference in female prairie voles (*Microtus ochrogaster*). *Journal of Neuroendocrinology, 6*(3), 247–250. https://doi.org/10.1111/j.1365-2826.1994.tb00579.x

Wingfield, J., Hegner, J., Dufty, A., Jr., & Ball, G. (1990). The "challenge hypothesis": Theoretical implications for patterns of testosterone secretion, mating systems and breeding strategies. *American Naturalist, 136*(6), 829–846. https://doi.org/10.1086/285134

Wu, Y., Eisenegger, C., Zilioli, S., Watson, N.V., & Clark, L. (2017). Comparison of clear and narrow outcomes on testosterone levels in social competition. *Hormones and Behavior, 92*, 51–56. https://doi.org/10.1016/j.yhbeh.2016.05.016

Zak, P.J., Kurzban, R., Ahmadi, S., Swerdloff, R.S., Park, J., Efremidze, L., ... Matzner, W. (2009). Testosterone administration decreases generosity in the ultimatum game. *PLoS One, 4*(12), e8330. https://doi.org/10.1371/journal.pone.0008330

Zak, P.J., Kurzban, R., & Matzner, W.T. (2005). Oxytocin is associated with human trustworthiness. *Hormones and Behavior, 48*(5), 522–527. https://doi.org/10.1016/j.yhbeh.2005.07.009

Zak, P.J., Stanton, A.A., & Ahmadi, S. (2007). Oxytocin increases generosity in humans. *PLoS One, 2*(11), e1128. https://doi.org/10.1371/journal.pone.0001128

2

HORMONE MEASUREMENT IN SOCIAL NEUROENDOCRINOLOGY

A comparison of immunoassay and mass spectroscopy methods

Oliver C. Schultheiss, Gelena Dlugash, and Pranjal H. Mehta

A primer on hormones

As a field, social neuroendocrinology almost always involves the measurement of hormones in some manner, be it as a predictor or correlate of physiology, affect, cognition, and behavior, or be it as an outcome of experimental manipulations. This applies regardless of whether the research is conducted on non-human animals or humans. Hormones differ regarding the ease and validity with which they can be measured due to their chemical structure, the properties that result from it, and their concentrations. Three large groups of hormones can be distinguished: (1) hormones that are derived from single amino acids, such as adrenaline, noradrenaline, dopamine, or the thyroid hormones; (2) hormones that are peptides and proteins, such as oxytocin or growth hormone; and (3) steroid hormones, derived from cholesterol, such as cortisol, progesterone, or testosterone (Ojeda & Kovacs, 2012).

While the first two groups comprise hormones that due to either their large molecular structure or their polarity cannot permeate the barrier of cell membranes, steroids, the third group, can do that. This means that steroid hormones, but not amines or peptides and proteins, can travel to and affect the brain (e.g., Bäckström, Carstensen, & Södergard, 1976), even though steroid hormones are released by glands in the periphery of the body (outside the central nervous system). To some extent, this eliminates the issue of whether central levels of steroids correspond to peripheral levels, which is a thorny problem in research on non-steroid hormones (e.g., Leng & Ludwig, 2016; McCullough, Churchland, & Mendez, 2013). Another crucial difference between these three groups of hormones is that amines, peptides, and proteins are broken down by enzymes and are therefore difficult to measure unambiguously (e.g., McCullough et al., 2013). In contrast, steroids represent rather robust hormones that need to be cleared from the bloodstream by the liver. This structural stability increases their attractiveness for researchers. But it also comes at the cost of a very small size that can pose its own set of challenges for measurement, as we will show below. Finally, because steroids can be found in comparable concentrations in virtually all body compartments and do not degrade quickly, they provide researchers with many substrates from which to assay these hormones. As a consequence, steroids are not only routinely measured in blood, but can also be assessed from urine (Campbell, 1994), feces (Palme, 2005), hair (Stalder & Kirschbaum, 2012), and saliva (Gröschl, 2008; Schultheiss & Stanton, 2009), with the latter showing good convergence with measurements in blood (e.g., Keevil, MacDonald, Macdowall, Lee, & Wu, 2014). For these reasons, they represent a highly attractive target for social neuroendocrinologists, particularly when researchers want to avoid the use of invasive sample collection methods such as venipuncture. For research with human participants, salivary steroid assessment has become the method of choice in many laboratories.

While salivary steroid assessment provides a rather accessible window into endocrine processes and their relationship to brain functions and behavior, considerable care and forethought need to go into all steps of the measurement process. For instance, measurement results can be biased by the devices used for stimulating saliva flow for easier sample collection (e.g., Gröschl & Rauh, 2006; Schultheiss, 2013), by improper storage (e.g., Gröschl, Wagner, Rauh, & Dörr, 2001; Whembolua, Granger, Singer, Kivlighan, & Marguin, 2006), and by the pre-processing of the samples themselves (e.g., Durdiakova, Fabryova, Koborova, Ostatnikova, & Celec, 2013). Schultheiss and Stanton (2009) and Schultheiss, Schiepe, and Rawolle (2012) provide detailed discussions and recommendations regarding these issues.

However, despite social neuroendocrinologists' awareness of these issues, the field as a whole has not paid as much attention as it should to another, more consequential problem associated with salivary steroid assessment. For quite some time, clinical endocrinologists, who are by profession particularly concerned about valid, reliable measurement from which medical diagnoses can be derived, have voiced concerns about the validity of immunoassay methods for the assessment of steroids, particularly in the low ranges that are typical of salivary steroids (e.g., Herold & Fitzgerald, 2003; Matsumoto & Bremner, 2004; Stanczyk et al., 2003; Taieb, Benattar, Birr, & Lindenbaum, 2002). By and large, these concerns have not received attention within the field of human social neuroendocrinology – many researchers continue to use steroid immunoassays, encouraged by the proliferation of specialized commercially available assay kits for salivary hormones and perhaps trusting that a technique that had worked well for other parts of endocrinology for so long could not be the wrong approach for their own area of research. Social neuroendocrinologists were largely unaware that they increasingly fell out of step with the developments in clinical endocrinology, which by 2013 even led to a de facto ban by the *Journal of Clinical Endocrinology & Metabolism* on papers based on immunoassays and the stipulation that mass spectrometry should be used instead (Handelsman & Wartofsky, 2013; but see Wierman et al., 2014). To explain how this situation arose and what practical consequences it may have for the measurement and interpretation of salivary steroids, we will first provide some background on immunoassay and mass spectrometry approaches to hormone assessment and then compare the results that these methods give for various steroids, with an emphasis on testosterone for illustrative purposes. We will also discuss the convergence between steroid measurements made with both methods and draw some conclusions about the future of steroid hormone assessment in social neuroendocrinology.

Immunoassays

Immunoassays are based on organisms' immune responses to exogenous molecules and compounds entering the body. The body's immune system analyzes the exogenous matter (also called antigen) and manufactures antibodies that fit the specific molecular surface of the antigen well enough to selectively attach to it and incapacitate it or mark it as a target for other components of the immune system. Antibodies can be raised in and harvested from animals (usually rabbits), resulting in *polyclonal* antibodies – that is, antibodies that are produced by different bone marrow cells and therefore represent a mix of heterogeneous antibodies, targeting different surface sites of the antigen. In contrast, *monoclonal* antibodies are raised in specific hybrid cell lines that can produce an unlimited and highly uniform supply of a homogenous antibody, targeting a specific antigen site (Kane & Banks, 2000).

Antibodies can be raised against specific target analytes, such as testosterone or oxytocin, that one would like to measure. This is the basic idea behind the immunoassay approach. However, most mammals do not show a strong immune system response against lipids or very small molecules (steroids are both) or substances that their own body produces in exactly the same way, too. This is why for immunization purposes the targeted analyte is usually conjugated to a protein to increase its immunogenicity, that is, its capacity to elicit an immune system response leading to the production of antibodies (Kane & Banks, 2000). For small molecules like steroid hormones, this means that some of the few binding sites that they have are occupied by the conjugated protein and are therefore not available for detection by the immune system. Because steroid hormones and their various metabolites differ only in very minute details, conjugation to a binding site that differentiates between steroid variants can therefore be one reason for an antibody's lack of specificity. And because antibodies are tailored to recognize the compound of target and conjugated protein, they may also have a binding affinity to just the protein that was used and other proteins with similar partial binding properties. This is important to keep in mind when considering the validity limits of immunoassays in endocrinology (see also Gosling, 2000, pp. 14, 15).

Having an antibody that specifically binds to a certain substance is per se insufficient for measuring the substance. Instead of one thing that is invisible and unweighable (the targeted substance), now we have two such things – the target and the antibody. Yalow and Berson (1960) solved this problem in the following way: They used a fixed amount of antibody and added a fixed amount of antigen, with a label attached that could be measured, plus a sample with an unknown amount of the unlabeled antigen. This resulted in a competition of the labeled antigen and the unlabeled antigen for antibody binding. The greater the relative amount of unlabeled antigen, the less of a signal the labeled antigen could emit after the competition was stopped. Conversely, the smaller the relative amount of unlabeled antigen, the greater the signal emitted by the labeled antigen. The meaning of variations in the signal that different amounts of labeled antigen emit, reflecting different gradations of competitive displacement by unlabeled antigen, can be derived by including samples with known concentrations of unlabeled antigen – the so-called standards or calibrators of an assay.

The majority of immunoassays used in social neuroendocrinology these days are based on this competitive binding principle, originally introduced by Yalow and Berson (1960). Yalow and Berson used a radioisotope as label and a gamma counter to measure its signal, thus creating the *radio*immunoassay (RIA) technique that is still in use today. Later, researchers developed *enzymatic* immunoassays (EIA) that replaced the radioactive label with one whose color (or sometimes luminescence) indicated the degree of antigen present in the assay. Here, the measurement is done through photometers detecting light at a wavelength corresponding to the enzyme's color. The deeper the coloration, the stronger the labeled signal and hence the less unlabeled antigen is present. So whether it is an RIA or an EIA, immunoassays do not measure the naturally occurring hormone itself, but its effect on the concentration of the labeled hormone of a fixed quantity that it competes with.

The quality and performance characteristics of an immunoassay can be gaged from several indicators. Its *validity* is usually assessed from its ability to measure the concentration of samples with known concentrations as accurately as possible (*recovery*). For instance, if a sample with known concentrations (e.g., by creating the sample through first weighing and then dissolving the analyte in a liquid matrix) of 1 and 5 ng/mL of cortisol gives readings of 1.05 and 4.85 ng/mL by cortisol immunoassay, then recovery is 105% for the former and 97% for the latter sample and thus very good. Recovery thus represents an instance of a causal link between values given by the measure and systematic variations of the measured target, a key concept in validity theory (Borsboom, Mellenbergh, & van Heerden, 2004).

An immunoassay's validity can also be gaged from its *specificity* for the targeted analyte; that is, how well it can discriminate the target from other analytes with a similar structure. For this purpose, samples are created that not only contain known amounts of the target analyte (e.g., cortisol), but also of analytes that the antibody might bind to, too, because they are structurally similar to the target analyte (e.g., other steroids). While recovery should be close to 100% for the target analyte, it should be close to 0% for all other analytes. Determining specificity usually requires a lot of work and biochemical know-how and intuition about which substances might cross-react with the antigen. Assay users rarely do their own specificity checks and instead rely on relevant information by the manufacturer. However, it is often unclear whether manufacturer-supplied information encompasses all substances that could conceivably bind to the antibody. This means that although the list may give the assay a clean bill of specificity (e.g., no cross-reactivity with other steroids), this may not be the whole story, as other substances also contained in a given sample type (e.g., saliva) may substantially cross-react with the antibody. Thus, for highly complex biological fluids like serum or saliva, lists of substances for which cross-reactivity has been determined can hardly ever be exhaustive. And one should also keep in mind that the information supplied by the manufacturer (a) may try to present a flawless picture of the assay and (b) may be based on antibodies or assay procedures at one stage on assay manufacturing and may have changed with subsequent alterations to assay ingredients and manufacturing. In the terms of psychological validity theory, specificity can be viewed as an instance of discriminant validity (e.g., Campbell & Fiske, 1959).

A third aspect of an assay's validity is its *sensitivity*, indicating the minimal concentration it can discern from a zero-concentration measurement. Most frequently, sensitivity is operationalized via the limit of detection (LOD), defined as the mean signal for a zero-concentration measurement, plus 3 times its standard deviation (SD), or the limit of quantification (LOQ), derived in the same way, but with 10 times the SD. Thus, if a cortisol assay has a SD of 0.002 ng/mL for a zero-concentration standard sample, its LOD would be 3×0.002 ng/mL $= 0.006$ ng/mL and its LOQ would be 10×0.002 ng/mL $= 0.020$ ng/mL. Note that this determination of sensitivity can be criticized for many of the same reasons that null-hypothesis testing has been criticized more generally (e.g., Nickerson, 2000). It does not positively establish a lower limit for the measurement of a non-zero-concentration sample. And its results depend on measurement error, whose magnitude is in turn influenced by the number of zero-concentration measurements that were done (10 measurements will give a lower SD and hence lower LOD and LOQ than 5 measurements).

An assay's reliability is gaged via its precision, assessed by measuring the same sample twice or more. The SD of these repeated measurements is then divided by their mean and multiplied by 100, yielding the coefficient of variation (CV) in percent. For instance, if the same saliva sample gives values of 1.03 ng/mL and 0.97 ng/mL in two successive measurements, the SD is 0.042 ng/mL and the mean is 1.00 ng/mL; hence $(0.042/1.00) \times 100 = 4.2\%$. To determine the CV of all samples measured in one and the same assay, all CVs are averaged to arrive at the *intra-assay CV*. However, an assay's precision may also vary across repeated performances of this assay, such as when one assay is run today and another next week. Will independently conducted assays give the same values for the same samples? To determine the *inter-assay CV*, the same samples are included in two or more assays that constitute an integrated measurement series (e.g., for salivary cortisol of all participants in a large panel study), and results are converted to a CV according to the same formula as the intra-assay CV. Note that intra- and inter-assay CVs again depend on measurement error and thus on the total number of measurements. Including more measurements will yield lower CVs.

Note that some of these measures of validity and reliability also apply to mass spectrometry (MS). For instance, research using MS for the assessment of hormones frequently reports the limit of detection (or quantification), recovery, and intra- and inter-assay CV (e.g., Gao, Stalder, & Kirschbaum, 2015). We will return to some of these issues in our next section, which describes the principles of the MS approach.

Mass spectrometry

(Ultra-)high pressure liquid chromatography (HPLC or simply LC), coupled with mass spectrometry (MS), has become the "gold standard" of hormone assessment. Depending on the measurement goals, components of the LC–MS system can be adjusted to better accommodate a particular analyte or matrix. In the following, we will focus only on the most important and common components of various LC–MS systems as they are applied to hormone assessment (see Gouveia et al., 2013; McDonald, Matthew, & Auchus, 2011).

The MS component is based on two physical properties of molecules: mass and charge. In the mass analyzer, the core of MS, ions are accelerated in a vacuum through an electromagnetic field toward the detector. This field can only be passed by charged molecules with a specific mass-to-charge ratio, which can be set by the user. Compounds with a different ratio get thrown off on their way through the mass analyzer and therefore do not reach the detector. MS thus measures a target analyte directly and with high specificity.

Accurately measuring a given analyte in a given substance (often called "matrix") via MS is challenging for several reasons. First, complex matrices, like serum, saliva, or urine, contain various salts and different nonvolatile compounds (e.g., Chiu et al., 2010; Selby, 1999). In an MS system, these can interfere with measurement by suppressing ionization. As a second challenge, analytes with an identical mass-to-charge ratio (= isobars), like testosterone and epitestosterone or 17-α-estradiol and 17-β-estradiol, cannot be differentiated by MS itself. A third challenge is posed by the sheer number and variety of compounds present in saliva or serum. These would let the vacuum collapse upon entering the mass analyzer.

To resolve these issues, MS is coupled to a chromatography system (either liquid chromatography, LC, for nonvolatile compounds, or gas chromatography, GC, for volatile compounds, as when fluids are vaporized by heating), which (a) purifies and (b) separates analytes by their chemical and physical properties and lets them enter MS separately. This results in an enormous improvement of measurement sensitivity and specificity. Thus, the coupling of LC (GC) and MS is the reason why this measurement approach can detect analytes with unrivaled specificity.

Generally, a LC–MS or GC–MS system can be divided into four main components: chromatography, ion source, mass analyzer, and detector (Figure 2.1).

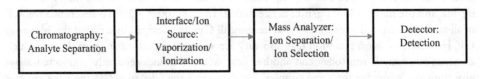

Figure 2.1 Individual components of mass spectrometry and their functions

The first part of the system is chromatography. GC features excellent resolution and separation of over 65 compounds in one single run and is therefore frequently used in steroid metabolomics of urine samples. However, because GC is only applicable to volatile and nonpolar compounds, neither of which steroids and their metabolites belong to, a time- and labor-consuming derivatization step must be executed first. *Derivatization* refers to a chemical reaction in which unwanted nonvolatile and polar properties of analytes are modified by conjunction of special derivates to the analyte, making it nonpolar and volatile. Additionally, derivatization can also enhance MS performance, resulting in lower limits of detection. Therefore, derivatization can also be used in LC assays, but only as an option.

Mostly, LC has become the chromatography method of choice. It is easy to conduct and does not generally require derivatization. It offers both a high throughput of samples and the detection of up to a dozen steroids in one run. Therefore, it is often used for analyzing steroids in blood and saliva samples. By developing efficient interfaces for transferring analytes that have been separated by LC to the vacuumed gas phase of MS, LC can now easily be coupled to MS.

The ion source is the second essential part of this system, as only ionized and gaseous components can enter the vacuumed mass analyzer. The most common ion sources are electric spray ionization (ESI), atmospheric pressure chemical ionization (APCI), and atmospheric pressure photoionization (APPI). All of these techniques can be run in a positive or negative ion mode for detecting positively or negatively charged ions. Also, they all are suitable for measuring various steroids simultaneously.

Both ESI and APCI in positive mode are often used for measuring steroid profiles (Gao et al., 2015; Gaudl et al., 2016). However, because of its gentle ionization, ESI is the most frequently used ion source. It provides high measurement sensitivity with less analyte fragmentation, but is also vulnerable to whatever matrix effects remain after LC, which, as we have pointed out above, can cause ionization and suppress evaporation. Nevertheless, ESI is particularly suitable for assessing testosterone, because it comes with a very low LOD and can therefore detect testosterone even in populations that have low circulating levels of this hormone (e.g., women and children).

In contrast to ESI, APCI is less impaired by ion suppression caused by matrix effects, but generates more analyte fragmentation and can be therefore less sensitive. APPI is a newer ion source, which was designed for a soft ionization of nonpolar compounds and steroids in particular. Using this technique combined with a negative ion mode has resulted in a huge improvement of sensitivity in estradiol detection, a hormone that is notoriously difficult to assess due to its low levels.

Nowadays, modern mass spectrometers contain several ion sources, such as a combination of ESI and APCI, and use these sources simultaneously in one single run in positive as well as in negative ion modes. Thus the mass spectrometer can be aligned to any type of analyte in any type of sample.

After ionization, analytes enter the vacuum of a mass analyzer. The most commonly used type of mass analyzer in steroid endocrinology is the triple quadrupole mass analyzer (Triple Quad or MS/MS), which is well suited for the quantification of small molecules. It consists of three quadrupoles, each of which consists of two pairs of electrically charged metal rods that select or fragment ions (Figure 2.2).

More specifically, the first quadrupole filters the analyte by its mass-to-charge ratio. Analytes that correspond to this ratio are the only ions that can travel on a stable path through the electromagnetic field toward the second quadrupole, the so-called collision cell. Here, the previously selected ion (precursor ion), which frequently does not suffice for identifying the analyte, gets fragmented in a gas. This results in characteristic, more identifiable fragments, which then travel

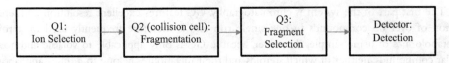

Figure 2.2 Triple quadrupole mass spectrometer (tandem mass spectrometer; Q: quadrupole)

to the third quadrupole, where they undergo further mass-to-charge ratio selection. Finally, the ions hit a detector, usually an electron multiplier.

One special feature of all mass spectrometers is the option of stable isotope analysis by using an internal standard (IS). Typically, the IS is the same type of molecule as the target analyte. Crucially, though, the IS is labeled with a stable isotope like deuterium or C^{13}. It therefore has the same chemical properties as the analyte, except for its molecular mass. Thus, both compounds can be detected and quantified by MS separately. The IS is added to all samples and calibrators before sample preparation and therefore before entering the LC–MS procedure. During sample preparation, ionization, and quantification, the IS undergoes the same losses as the target analyte and is therefore an internal control *for every single sample*. Usually, MS quantification is computed by analyte-to-IS ratio.

Comparison of mass spectrometry with immunoassays

The key difference between MS and immunoassays lies in analyte detection. While MS exploits stable physical properties of molecules for measurement, immunoassays are based on more fickle biochemical reactions, which can be affected by any little fluctuation in external factors like enzyme purity or activity, temperature, ionic strength, pH, and so on (see Selby, 1999). These factors have a big impact on assay validity; and more so for enzymatic immunoassays than for radioimmunoassays, which use a physical characteristic of molecules (i.e., radiation) for detection.

Another major problem of all immunoassay techniques is a lack of specificity due to cross-reactions between antibody and matrix compounds that are structurally similar to the targeted analyte. These interfering bindings cause immunoassays to overestimate analytes, sometimes up to a factor of three. Welker et al. (2016) showed this effect for testosterone in saliva, comparing immunoassay performance to LC–MS. They observed that the overestimation was higher when testosterone was lower (e.g., in the female range). Bae et al. (2016) reported similar results for salivary cortisol. Relative to LC–MS, immunoassay overestimated cortisol in saliva. The authors attributed this effect to the different standardization of immunoassays relative to MS and pointed out that this issue can be resolved by standardizing immunoassays against MS. While this is certainly true, they also reported the more problematic observation that at low cortisol concentrations (< 1.8 ng/mL), there was substantial cross-reactivity with cortisone (up to 254% recovery). The authors also observed interference by the protein α-amylase. The latter effect is particularly troubling, because α-amylase is proportionally the most important protein in saliva and it appears to affect the measurement of cortisol at levels that are in the typical salivary range. Most importantly, these findings provide direct evidence that a protein can bias a steroid immunoassay, and particularly at levels that are typical of salivary steroids. RIAs of gonadal steroids also suffer from cross-reactivity to other substances and can yield higher estimates in comparison to MS (e.g., Hsing et al., 2007). However, it is important to keep in mind that there can be substantial differences between immunoassays in the extent to which they are susceptible to overestimation and cross-reactivity. A lot hinges on proper standardization and antibody design (Baker, 2015).

Testosterone assessment

To illustrate the issues involved in measuring a steroid in different matrices (blood, saliva) and with different methods (LC-MS, RIA, EIA), we have compiled data from studies that looked at testosterone in combined samples of women and men (see Table 2.1). This ensures that whatever processing steps and methods were used, they were held constant within a study and thus across sample gender. Although the data listed in Table 2.1 by no means represent a comprehensive overview of all published studies, some consistent observations can be made. First, the gender difference that is typical of testosterone (Stanton, 2011) is always highest for LC-MS, followed by RIA, and then EIA. For serum, this difference is particularly dramatic, as LC-MS indicates an up to 22-fold difference, whereas for RIA and EIA the difference is only about 8- to 9-fold. For saliva, the difference is smaller, with LC-MS and RIA providing similar estimates of a 5- to 6-fold difference. This suggests that perhaps due to gender differences in protein binding of testosterone, the gender differences in testosterone in saliva, which contains only the free, unbound fraction of this hormone, is considerably less pronounced than in serum. But here, too, EIAs underestimate the difference as only about 2-fold. Second, for serum, which contains both protein-bound and unbound (or free) testosterone, male concentrations are very comparable across studies and methods. However, female testosterone is overestimated by a factor of two by all immunoassays relative to LC-MS. For salivary EIAs we specifically looked at the Salimetrics testosterone assay, which is frequently used in research with human partici-pants, and, for RIAs, the equally popular Coat-a-Count RIA by Siemens (previously manu-factured by Diagnostic Products Corporation) and the Diagnostic Systems Laboratories RIA. There are two notable observations here. One is that RIA and LC-MS yield measurements of similar magnitude, which may reflect the good measurement convergence between RIA with MS methods (for the Coat-a-Count RIA, see Groenestege et al., 2012; Taieb et al., 2003; Wang, Catlin, Demers, Starcevic, & Swerdloff, 2004). The second is the pronounced tendency of the Salimetrics assay to overestimate salivary testosterone and produce rather variable measurements across studies, despite testing similar populations. For women in particular, the average across-study testosterone level was more than 5-fold of what would be expected based on the average LC-MS results. For men, the same comparison yielded a less extreme but still 2-fold higher average than LC-MS. The peculiarity of salivary testosterone values as assayed with EIA appears not to be specific to the Salimetrics assay, however. Welker et al. (2016), who assayed the same samples also with other EIAs in addition to the one by Salimetrics, obtained average concen-trations of 82 pg/mL for women and 222 pg/mL for men for a testosterone EIA by IBL, and concentrations of 45 pg/mL and 107 pg/mL, respectively, for a testosterone EIA by DRG (see table S3 in Welker et al., 2016). Thus, both the reduced gender difference and the inflated con-centrations appear to be a more general feature of testosterone EIAs. This conclusion is further underscored by the fact that these values come from the very same samples for which Welker et al. (2016) reported considerably lower testosterone concentrations for LC-MS, and with a much larger gender difference (see Table 2.1).

So what can be concluded from the illustrative findings displayed in Table 2.1? If LC-MS with its ability to isolate and directly detect analytes is taken as a reference standard, then immunoas-says yield similar concentration estimates for testosterone as long as there is a large signal-to-noise ratio, with "signal" denoting the targeted analyte (i.e., testosterone) and "noise" denoting anything that can cross-react with the antibodies. For serum samples taken from men, there seems to be little difference overall between LC-MS and immunoassay measurements. But even with serum samples obtained in women, the first deviations between immunoassay and LC-MS become apparent, presumably due to immunoassays' susceptibility to matrix effects

Table 2.1 Illustrative findings for testosterone in saliva and serum, as assessed with liquid chromatography-mass spectrometry (LC-MS), enzyme-linked immunosorbent assays (ELISA) or enzymatic immunoassays (EIA), and radioimmunoassays (RIA)

LC-MS				ELISA/EIA				RIA			
Study	N (♀/♂)	♀	♂	Study	N (♀/♂)	♀	♂	Study	N (♀/♂)	♀	♂
Saliva											
Welker et al. (2016)	56/42	11.6	63.6	Welker et al. (2016)	57/42	63.6	146.0	Stanton (2011)	262/296	13.3	77.5
Keevil et al. (2014)	86/104	4.6	63.7	Zilioli, Caldbick, and Watson (2014)	79/85	63.4	121.8	Oxford, Tiedtke, Ossmann, Özbe, and Schultheiss (2017)	53/152	14.6	79.0
Turpeinen, Hämäläinen, Haanpää, and Dunkel (2012)	47/36	5.5	49.3	Mehta, Jones, and Josephs (2008)	91/93	38.9	119.4	Mehta and Josephs (2010)	50/50	21.7	99.9
Clifton et al. (2016)	2123/1599	10.7	64.4	Burkitt, Widman, and Saucier (2007)	39/36	96.8	183.5	Schultheiss et al. (2005)	86/125	18.0	125.0
Weighted mean	2312/1781	10.4	64.0	Weighted mean	266/256	60.0	133.6	Weighted mean	451/543	15.3	87.4
♂/♀ ratio		6.16		♂/♀ ratio		2.23		♂/♀ ratio		5.72	
Serum (total testosterone)											
Keevil et al. (2014)	91/94	231	5192	Taieb et al. (2003)	55/50	1470	6311	Taieb et al. (2003)	51/50	807	5965
Büttler et al. (2015)	23/22	228	5228	Torjesen and Sandnes (2003)	2057/1447	605	4813	Torjesen and Sandnes (2003)	2180/1505	490	4006
Wang et al. (2014)	75/75	230	5209	Häkkinen, Pakarinen, Kraemer, Newton, and Alen (2000)	11/11	490	4842	Khosla et al. (2002)	152/173	400	5370
Büttler et al. (2016)	31/29	190	3135	Evrin, Nilsson, Öberg, and Malmberg (2005)	197/189	288	4611	Söderberg et al. (2001)	45/85	317	5504
Weighted mean	220/220	225	4930	Weighted mean	2320/1697	598	4834	Weighted mean	2428/1813	487	4260
♂/♀ ratio		21.95		♂/♀ ratio		8.08		♂/♀ ratio		8.73	

Note. For Häkkinen et al. (2000), data are reported for middle-aged participants only. For Khosla et al. (2002), data are reported for premenopausal individuals and individuals up to an age of 50 years.

(e.g., protein content) and steroid cross-reactivity. These susceptibility issues are amplified at the concentrations typically observed in salivary testosterone, particularly for the female range of concentrations and particularly for EIAs. However, although not quite as dramatic, the high concentrations for male saliva samples measured with EIA are also troubling. So can testosterone immunoassays be even trusted, particularly when used with saliva samples?

Another way to look at this issue is through the prism of convergent validity. Although absolute salivary testosterone levels may differ by assay type, there still might be good convergence between LC-MS and immunoassay. While such evidence would not persuade a clinician, who needs accurate absolute measurements for diagnosis, linear shifts in value ranges are less of a concern for researchers who are less interested in absolute levels and more in measurement specificity ("Is it really testosterone I am measuring?") and covariance ("Can I use measured concentrations to explore correlations with other variables or with treatments?"). Welker et al. (2016) have addressed this question by examining the convergence between LC-MS and EIA measurements of salivary testosterone in men and women. When correlating LC-MS measurements with EIA measurements across both genders, there is some evidence of convergence, with correlations ranging from .47 (IBL) to .57 (DRG). However, these coefficients are not very meaningful, because they are mainly driven by the substantial gender difference in testosterone, which is detected more or less well by all assays (see Table 2.1). When Welker et al. (2016) looked at the more relevant within-gender correlations, results were disappointing. For men, correlations between all three EIAs and LC-MS did not exceed .17. For women, correlations ranged between −.17 (IBL) and .22 (DRG). These findings suggest that the EIAs tested by Welker et al. (2016) are not suitable to assess valid individual differences in salivary testosterone, particularly when looking at each gender separately. They thus reinforce the doubts already raised by the elevated measurement levels of salivary T as obtained via EIA and the curiously low gender difference associated with them.

What about RIA assessments of testosterone? Unfortunately, there are no published data yet on the degree of convergence between LC-MS and RIA measurements of salivary testosterone. Perhaps a study by Groenestege et al. (2012) can serve as an interim estimate. These researchers looked at the convergence between LC-MS and direct immunoassays specifically for serum samples with low testosterone concentrations (i.e., < 1,153 pg/mL). Convergence coefficients varied considerably across assays, from .59 to .92. Notably, the latter, highest value was reached by the Coat-A-Count RIA for testosterone that has also been frequently used for assessing testosterone in saliva. It is unclear, however, whether similarly high convergence coefficients would be found for samples in the actual, much lower salivary range of testosterone (i.e., from 1 to 250 pg/mL) and particularly whether substantial convergence could be reached in within-gender analyses. To some extent, such speculations are moot by now, because the Coat-a-Count RIA, like the DSL testosterone RIA, is no longer manufactured, reflecting an overall tendency of researchers to move away from RIAs and the radioactive waste they generate. Still, the illustrative data presented in Table 2.1 seem to suggest that some of the problems that testosterone EIAs are grappling with are absent or at least greatly attenuated in RIAs, presumably because the label conjugated to the target hormone is a complex, biochemically active enzyme in the former case and a simple and biochemically inert radioisotope in the latter. The mean values and gender differences RIAs produce appear to be very comparable to data generated by LC-MS.

Other steroids

In the previous paragraphs, we focused on the illustrative case of salivary testosterone assessment. We would also like to briefly comment on how immunoassay assessment of other key steroids compares to MS assessment. Cortisol is the steroid with very high salivary levels (an order of magnitude higher than testosterone) and should therefore be easier to assess by immunoassay than most other salivary steroids. While this is generally true, we have already pointed out that immunoassays tend to overestimate cortisol, reflecting cross-reactivity and protein interference effects (Baid, Sinaii, Wade, Rubino, & Nieman, 2007; Bae et al., 2016; Miller, Plessow, Rauh, Groschl, & Kirschbaum, 2013). Baid et al. (2007) report a convergence of .72 (Spearman) between RIA and LC-MS assessment of salivary cortisol; Miller et al. (2013) report convergence coefficients ranging from .90 to .97 for various EIAs with LC-MS. Welker et al. (2016) report a correlation coefficient of .80 between EIA and LC-MS cortisol.

Compared to salivary cortisol, the assessment of salivary progesterone and particularly of salivary estradiol represents much greater challenges due to the extremely low concentrations of these hormones. Even LC-MS faces a challenge when trying to detect salivary estradiol, for which measurements are typically in the low single-digit pg/mL range. For instance, Gao et al. (2015) report a limit of quantification of 1 pg/mL for salivary estradiol and of 5 pg/mL for salivary progesterone. Both boundaries are thus relatively close to the typical mean values of these hormones in the saliva of men and normally cycling women. However, LC-MS appears to be suitable for assaying salivary estradiol, as judged by its high convergence with serum estradiol (r = .82; Fiers, Dielen, Somers, Kaufman, & Gerris, 2017). Although so far no direct comparisons of immunoassay and MS assessment of salivary estradiol and progesterone appear to have been published, there are studies that compared various immunoassays with LC-MS for serum samples. Ray, Kushnir, Yost, Rockwood, and Wayne Meikle (2015) report that although an EIA of progesterone showed good convergence with LC-MS (r = .92), the former method overestimated progesterone concentrations by a factor of 2.3 relative to the latter method. Similarly, Ketha, Girtman, and Singh (2015) report that all of 14 tested EIAs overestimate estradiol, some up to 3-fold. RIAs, on the other hand, again appear to give values more similar to LC-MS methods (Rosner, Hankinson, Sluss, Vesper, & Wierman, 2013). In a concentration range of up to 330 pg/mL, Gaudl et al. (2016) observed excellent convergence between EIA and LC-MS (r = .96). However, Huhtaniemi et al. (2012) found that at the low serum estradiol concentrations (< 11 pg/mL) – that is, in the range of salivary estradiol concentrations – immunoassay and LC-MS show unacceptably low convergence (r = .32). It is safe to expect that whatever problems of overestimation or method convergence exist for serum measurements will be exacerbated for assessment of estradiol and progesterone in saliva, with its much lower steroid concentrations relative to serum.

Implications

From the detailed discussion of salivary testosterone assessment and our cursory overview of the challenges associated with the assessment of other steroids that are of interest to social neuroendocrinologists, the following picture emerges. Immunoassay approaches to measuring steroids have come under increasing fire due to their lack of sensitivity and tendency to overestimate true concentrations (e.g., Harold & Fitzgerald, 2003; Matsumoto & Bremner, 2004; Taieb et al., 2002). To the extent that overestimation is due only to a misalignment of standardization between immunoassay and LC-MS, the issue would be one of scaling only. But it appears that it is also one of validity, because antibody cross-reactivity, non-specificity, and susceptibility to the general biochemical milieu in the assay have been shown to contribute to measurement variance. Although there are some indications that these problems may be more severe in EIAs than in RIAs, there is no a priori reason why some RIAs should not also be prone to cross-reactivity and non-specificity effects. As we pointed out at the beginning, for the measurement of steroids in serum, this state of affairs has already led to a de facto ban on immunoassay methods in at least one clinical endocrinology journal (Handelsman & Wartofsky, 2013). Others have taken a more measured approach, arguing that it is unrealistic to expect all laboratories to give up immuno-assays and adopt LC-MS, as this would be tantamount to abandoning many assay techniques that work reasonably well and require a sizable investment in terms of equipment and training (Taylor, Keevil, & Huhtaniemi, 2015). Besides, a badly done LC-MS measurement can yield less valid results than a carefully validated and executed immunoassay with suitable quality controls; thus, LC-MS is not a sure-fire guarantee of better results. In the long run, however, LC-MS will become the norm not only in clinical endocrinology, but also in social neuroendocrinology, simply because scientific progress and the advancement of theory crucially depend on the most valid, accurate, and sensitive measurement available. In this regard, the sun is rising for LC-MS, while it is gradually setting for immunoassays.

In closing, we offer some more pragmatically oriented arguments that may aid researchers interested in measuring steroids. The benefits of immunoassays are clear: their performance is easy and they are relatively cheap. Researchers new to hormone assessment can readily learn how do run immunoassays, without advanced analytical knowledge. But every hormone must be assayed individually, which is time- and labor-consuming. Moreover, assays of several steroids also require larger sample volumes (50–400 µl per hormone). In comparison to immunoassays, LC-MS is an effective, high throughput method that requires only small sample volumes of 100 µl for measuring several steroids simultaneously (e.g., testosterone, estradiol, progesterone, and cortisol). Despite all performance advantages of LC-MS, this technique is very complex and requires well-advanced chemical and analytical knowledge. In comparison to immunoassays, newcomers to this technique have to be trained intensively. Due to its universal application, LC-MS/MS methods are now being developed that can be used for steroid analysis in saliva and serum as well as urine or hair. Further, several LC-MS/MS methods for quantification of estra-diol in serum with a limit of quantification < 0.5 pg/mL have already been developed (Ketha et al., 2015; Fiers et al., 2017). Modern immunoassays are generally not capable of reaching "down" this far while also retaining good precision.

In summary, immunoassays show satisfying performance in quantifying steroids in larger concentrations, such as in serum. But when it comes to measurement of hormones at lower concentrations, like testosterone in women or gonadal steroids in saliva more generally, immu-noassays' validity appears to be limited and findings should be evaluated with a healthy dose of skepticism. In the long run – that is, in the next 5 to 10 years – we anticipate that LC-MS meth-ods will become easier to use and, through methodological advances, even more sensitive so that they can provide precise and valid measurements of steroids even in the single-picogram range. By that time, they will have become the new standard for accurate hormone measurement in social neuroendocrinology.

References

Bäckström, T., Carstensen, H., & Södergard, R. (1976). Concentration of estradiol, testosterone and pro-gesterone in cerebrospinal fluid compared to plasma unbound and total concentrations. *Journal of Steroid Biochemistry*, 7(6), 469–472. https://doi.org/10.1016/0022-4731(76)90114-X

Bae, Y.J., Gaudl, A., Jaeger, S., Stadelmann, S., Hiemisch, A., Kiess, W., . . . Kratzsch, J. (2016). Immunoas-say or LC-MS/MS for the measurement of salivary cortisol in children? *Clinical Chemistry Laboratory Medicine (CCLM)*, 54(5), 811–822. doi:10.1515/cclm-2015-0412

Baid, S.K., Sinaii, N., Wade, M., Rubino, D., & Nieman, L.K. (2007). Radioimmunoassay and tandem mass spectrometry measurement of bedtime salivary cortisol levels: A comparison of assays to establish hypercor-tisolism. *The Journal of Clinical Endocrinology and Metabolism*, 92(8), 3102–3107. doi:10.1210/jc.2006-2861

Baker, M. (2015). Reproducibility crisis: Blame it on the antibodies. *Nature, 521*(7552), 274–276. doi: 10.1038/521274a

Borsboom, D., Mellenbergh, G.J., & van Heerden, J. (2004). The concept of validity. *Psychological Review, 111*(4), 1061–1071. doi:2004-19012-010 [pii] 10.1037/0033-295X.111.4.1061

Burkitt, J., Widman, D., & Saucier, D.M. (2007). Evidence for the influence of testosterone in the performance of spatial navigation in a virtual water maze in women but not in men. *Hormones and Behavior, 51*(5), 649–654. doi:10.1016/j.yhbeh.2007.03.007

Büttler, R.M., Martens, F., Ackermans, M.T., Davison, A.S., van Herwaarden, A.E., Kortz, L., . . . Heijboer, A.C. (2016). Comparison of eight routine unpublished LC-MS/MS methods for the simultaneous measurement of testosterone and androstenedione in serum. *Clinical Chimica Acta, 454*, 112–118. doi:10.1016/j.cca.2016.01.002

Büttler, R.M., Martens, F., Fanelli, F., Pham, H.T., Kushnir, M.M., Janssen, M.J., . . . Heijboer, A.C. (2015). Comparison of 7 published LC-MS/MS methods for the simultaneous measurement of testosterone, androstenedione, and dehydroepiandrosterone in Serum. *Clinical Chemistry, 61*(12), 1475–1483. doi:10.1373/clinchem.2015.242859

Campbell, D.T., & Fiske, D.W. (1959). Convergent and discriminant validation by the multitrait-multimethod matrix. *Psychological Bulletin, 56*, 81–105.

Campbell, K.L. (1994). Blood, urine, saliva and dip-sticks: Experiences in Africa, New Guinea, and Boston. *Annals of the New York Academy of Sciences, 709*, 312–330.

Chiu, M.L., Lawi, W., Snyder, S.T., Wong, P.K., Liao, J.C., & Gau, V. (2010). Matrix effects – a challenge toward automation of molecular analysis. *JALA: Journal of the Association for Laboratory Automation, 15*(3), 233–242. doi:10.1016/j.jala.2010.02.001

Clifton, S., Macdowall, W., Copas, A.J., Tanton, C., Keevil, B.G., Lee, D.M., . . . Wu, F.C.W. (2016). Salivary testosterone levels and health status in men and women in the British general population: Findings from the Third National Survey of Sexual Attitudes and Lifestyles (Natsal-3). *The Journal of Clinical Endocrinology and Metabolism, 101*(11), 3939–3951. doi:10.1210/jc.2016-1669

Durdiakova, J., Fabryova, H., Koborova, I., Ostatnikova, D., & Celec, P. (2013). The effects of saliva collection, handling and storage on salivary testosterone measurement. *Steroids, 78*(14), 1325–1331. doi:10.1016/j.steroids.2013.09.002

Evrin, P.E., Nilsson, S.E., Öberg, T., & Malmberg, B. (2005). Serum C-reactive protein in elderly men and women: Association with mortality, morbidity and various biochemical values. *Scandinavian Journal of Clinical and Laboratory Investigation, 65*(1), 23–31. doi:10.1080/00365510510013505

Fiers, T., Dielen, C., Somers, S., Kaufman, J.M., & Gerris, J. (2017). Salivary estradiol as a surrogate marker for serum estradiol in assisted reproduction treatment. *Clinical Biochemistry, 50*(3), 145–149. doi:10.1016/j.clinbiochem.2016.09.016

Gao, W., Stalder, T., & Kirschbaum, C. (2015). Quantitative analysis of estradiol and six other steroid hormones in human saliva using a high throughput liquid chromatography-tandem mass spectrometry assay. *Talanta, 143*, 353–358. doi:10.1016/j.talanta.2015.05.004

Gaudl, A., Kratzsch, J., Bae, Y.J., Kiess, W., Thiery, J., & Ceglarek, U. (2016). Liquid chromatography quadrupole linear ion trap mass spectrometry for quantitative steroid hormone analysis in plasma, urine, saliva and hair. *Journal of Chromatography A, 1464*, 64–71. doi:10.1016/j.chroma.2016.07.087

Gosling, J.P. (2000). Analysis by specific binding. In J.P. Gosling (Ed.), *Immunoassays: A practical approach* (pp. 1–17). Oxford: Oxford University Press.

Gouveia, M.J., Brindley, P.J., Santos, L.L., Correia da Costa, J.M., Gomes, P., & Vale, N. (2013). Mass spectrometry techniques in the survey of steroid metabolites as potential disease biomarkers: A review. *Metabolism, 62*(9), 1206–1217. https://doi.org/10.1016/j.metabol.2013.04.003

Groenestege, W.M.T., Bui, H.N., ten Kate, J., Menheere, P.P., Oosterhuis, W.P., Vader, H.L., . . . Janssen, M.J. (2012). Accuracy of first and second generation testosterone assays and improvement through sample extraction. *Clinical Chemistry, 58*(7), 1154–1156. doi:10.1373/clinchem.2011.181735

Gröschl, M. (2008). Current status of salivary hormone analysis. *Clinical Chemistry, 54*(11), 1759–1769. doi:clinchem.2008.108910 [pii] 10.1373/clinchem.2008.108910

Gröschl, M., & Rauh, M. (2006). Influence of commercial collection devices for saliva on the reliability of salivary steroids analysis. *Steroids, 71*(13–14), 1097–1100. doi:S0039-128X(06)00195-4 [pii] 10.1016/j.steroids.2006.09.007

Gröschl, M., Wagner, R., Rauh, M., & Dorr, H.G. (2001). Stability of salivary steroids: The influences of storage, food and dental care. *Steroids, 66*(10), 737–741. doi:S0039-128X(01)00111-8 [pii]

Häkkinen, K., Pakarinen, A., Kraemer, W.J., Newton, R.U., & Alen, M. (2000). Basal concentrations and acute responses of serum hormones and strength development during heavy resistance training in middle-aged and elderly men and women. *Journals of Gerontology Series: A Biological Sciences and Medical Sciences*, *55*(2), B95–B105.

Handelsman, D.J., & Wartofsky, L. (2013). Requirement for mass spectrometry sex steroid assays in the journal of clinical endocrinology and metabolism. *The Journal of Clinical Endocrinology and Metabolism*, *98*(10), 3971–3973. doi:10.1210/jc.2013-3375

Herold, D.A., & Fitzgerald, R.L. (2003). Immunoassays for testosterone in women: Better than a guess? *Clinical Chemistry*, *49*(8), 1250–1251.

Hsing, A.W., Stanczyk, F.Z., Belanger, A., Schroeder, P., Chang, L., Falk, R.T., & Fears, T.R. (2007). Reproducibility of serum sex steroid assays in men by RIA and mass spectrometry. *Cancer Epidemiol Biomarkers Prevention*, *16*(5), 1004–1008. doi:10.1158/1055-9965.EPI-06-0792

Huhtaniemi, I.T., Tajar, A., Lee, D.M., O'Neill, T.W., Finn, J.D., Bartfai, G., . . . Group, E. (2012). Comparison of serum testosterone and estradiol measurements in 3174 European men using platform immunoassay and mass spectrometry; relevance for the diagnostics in aging men. *European Journal of Endocrinology*, *166*(6), 983–991. doi:10.1530/EJE-11-1051

Kane, M.M., & Banks, J.N. (2000). Raising antibodies. In J.P. Gosling (Ed.), *Immunoassays: A practical approach* (pp. 19–58). Oxford: Oxford University Press.

Keevil, B.G., MacDonald, P., Macdowall, W., Lee, D.M., Wu, F.C., & Team, N. (2014). Salivary testosterone measurement by liquid chromatography tandem mass spectrometry in adult males and females. *Annals of Clinical Biochemistry*, *51*(Pt 3), 368–378. doi:10.1177/0004563213506412

Ketha, H., Girtman, A., & Singh, R.J. (2015). Estradiol assays – the path ahead. *Steroids*, *99*(Pt A), 39–44. doi:10.1016/j.steroids.2014.08.009

Khosla, S., Arrighi, H.M., Melton, I. L.J., Atkinson, E.J., O'Fallon, W.M., Dunstan, C., & Riggs, B.L. (2002). Correlates of osteoprotegerin levels in women and men. *Osteoporosis International*, *13*(5), 394–399. doi:10.1007/s001980200045

Leng, G., & Ludwig, M. (2016). Intranasal oxytocin: Myths and delusions. *Biological Psychiatry*, *79*(3), 243–250. https://doi.org/10.1016/j.biopsych.2015.05.003

Matsumoto, A.M., & Bremner, W.J. (2004). Serum testosterone assays – accuracy matters. *The Journal of Clinical Endocrinology and Metabolism*, *89*(2), 520–524. doi:10.1210/jc.2003-032175

McCullough, M.E., Churchland, P.S., & Mendez, A.J. (2013). Problems with measuring peripheral oxytocin: Can the data on oxytocin and human behavior be trusted? *Neuroscience & Biobehavioral Reviews*, *37*(8), 1485–1492. https://doi.org/10.1016/j.neubiorev.2013.04.018

McDonald, J.G., Matthew, S., & Auchus, R.J. (2011). Steroid profiling by gas chromatography–mass spectrometry and high performance liquid chromatography–mass spectrometry for adrenal diseases. *Hormones and Cancer*, *2*(6), 324–332. doi:10.1007/s12672-011-0099-x

Mehta, P.H., Jones, A.C., & Josephs, R.A. (2008). The social endocrinology of dominance: Basal testosterone predicts cortisol changes and behavior following victory and defeat. *Journal of Personality and Social Psychology*, *94*(6), 1078–1093. doi:2008-06135-011 [pii] 10.1037/0022-3514.94.6.1078

Mehta, P.H., & Josephs, R.A. (2010). Testosterone and cortisol jointly regulate dominance: Evidence for a dual-hormone hypothesis. *Hormones and Behavior*, *58*, 898–906. doi:S0018-506X(10)00241-2 [pii] 10.1016/j.yhbeh.2010.08.020

Miller, R., Plessow, F., Rauh, M., Groschl, M., & Kirschbaum, C. (2013). Comparison of salivary cortisol as measured by different immunoassays and tandem mass spectrometry. *Psychoneuroendocrinology*, *38*(1), 50–57. doi:10.1016/j.psyneuen.2012.04.019

Nickerson, R.S. (2000). Null hypothesis significance testing: A review of an old and continuing controversy. *Psychological Methods*, *5*(2), 241–301.

Ojeda, S.R., & Kovacs, W.J. (2012). Organization of the endocrine system. In W.J. Kovacs & S.R. Ojeda (Eds.), *Textbook of endocrine physiology* (6th ed., pp. 3–20). New York, NY: Oxford University Press.

Oxford, J.K., Tiedtke, J.M., Ossmann, A., Özbe, D., & Schultheiss, O.C. (2017). Endocrine and aggressive responses to competition are moderated by contest outcome, gender, individual versus team competition, and implicit motives. *PLoS One*, *12*(7), e0181610. doi:10.1371/journal.pone.0181610

Palme, R. (2005). Measuring fecal steroids: Guidelines for practical application. *Annals of the New York Academy of Sciences*, *1046*(1), 75–80. doi:10.1196/annals.1343.007

Ray, J.A., Kushnir, M.M., Yost, R.A., Rockwood, A.L., & Wayne Meikle, A. (2015). Performance enhancement in the measurement of 5 endogenous steroids by LC-MS/MS combined with differential ion mobility spectrometry. *Clinica Chimica Acta*, *438*, 330–336. doi:10.1016/j.cca.2014.07.036

Rosner, W., Hankinson, S.E., Sluss, P.M., Vesper, H.W., & Wierman, M.E. (2013). Challenges to the measurement of estradiol: An endocrine society position statement. *The Journal of Clinical Endocrinology and Metabolism*, *98*(4), 1376–1387. doi:10.1210/jc.2012-3780

Schultheiss, O.C. (2013). Effects of sugarless chewing gum as a stimulant on progesterone, cortisol, and testosterone concentrations assessed in saliva. *International Journal of Psychophysiology*, *87*, 111–114. doi:10.1016/j.ijpsycho.2012.11.012

Schultheiss, O.C., Schiepe, A., & Rawolle, M. (2012). Hormone assays. In H. Cooper, P.M. Camic, D.L. Long, A.T. Panter, D. Rindskopf & K.J. Sher (Eds.), *Handbook of research methods in psychology* (Vol. 1: Foundations, planning, measures, and psychometrics, pp. 489–500). Washington, DC: American Psychological Association.

Schultheiss, O.C., & Stanton, S.J. (2009). Assessment of salivary hormones. In E. Harmon-Jones & J.S. Beer (Eds.), *Methods in social neuroscience* (pp. 17–44). New York, NY: Guilford Press.

Schultheiss, O.C., Wirth, M.M., Torges, C.M., Pang, J.S., Villacorta, M.A., & Welsh, K.M. (2005). Effects of implicit power motivation on men's and women's implicit learning and testosterone changes after social victory or defeat. *Journal of Personality and Social Psychology*, *88*(1), 174–188.

Selby, C. (1999). Interference in immunoassay. *Annals of Clinical Biochemistry*, *36*(6), 704–721. doi:10.1177/000456329903600603

Söderberg, S., Olsson, T., Eliasson, M., Johnson, O., Brismar, K., Carlström, K., & Ahren, B. (2001). A strong association between biologically active testosterone and leptin in non-obese men and women is lost with increasing (central) adiposity. *International Journal of Obesity*, *25*(1), 98.

Stalder, T., & Kirschbaum, C. (2012). Analysis of cortisol in hair – state of the art and future directions. *Brain, Behavior, and Immunity*, *26*(7), 1019–1029. https://doi.org/10.1016/j.bbi.2012.02.002

Stanczyk, F.Z., Cho, M.M., Endres, D.B., Morrison, J.L., Patel, S., & Paulson, R.J. (2003). Limitations of direct estradiol and testosterone immunoassay kits. *Steroids*, *68*(14), 1173–1178.

Stanton, S.J. (2011). The essential implications of gender in human behavioral endocrinology studies. *Frontiers in Behavioral Neuroscience*, *5*, 9. doi:10.3389/fnbeh.2011.00009

Taieb, J., Benattar, C., Birr, A.S., & Lindenbaum, A. (2002). Limitations of steroid determination by direct immunoassay. *Clinical Chemistry*, *48*(3), 583–585.

Taieb, J., Mathian, B., Millot, F., Patricot, M.C., Mathieu, E., Queyrel, N., . . . Boudou, P. (2003). Testosterone measured by 10 immunoassays and by isotope-dilution gas chromatography-mass spectrometry in sera from 116 men, women, and children. *Clinical Chemistry*, *49*(8), 1381–1395.

Taylor, A.E., Keevil, B., & Huhtaniemi, I.T. (2015). Mass spectrometry and immunoassay: How to measure steroid hormones today and tomorrow. *European Journal of Endocrinology*, *173*(2), D1–D12. doi:10.1530/EJE-15-0338

Torjesen, P.A., & Sandnes, L. (2004). Serum testosterone in women as measured by an automated immunoassay and a RIA. *Clinical Chemistry*, *50*(3), 678; author reply 678–679. doi:10.1373/clinchem.2003.027565

Turpeinen, U., Hämäläinen, E., Haanpää, M., & Dunkel, L. (2012). Determination of salivary testosterone and androstendione by liquid chromatography–tandem mass spectrometry. *Clinica Chimica Acta*, *413*(5), 594–599. https://doi.org/10.1016/j.cca.2011.11.029

Wang, C., Catlin, D.H., Demers, L.M., Starcevic, B., & Swerdloff, R.S. (2004). Measurement of total serum testosterone in adult men: Comparison of current laboratory methods versus liquid chromatography-tandem mass spectrometry. *The Journal of Clinical Endocrinology and Metabolism*, *89*(2), 534–543.

Welker, K.M., Lassetter, B., Brandes, C.M., Prasad, S., Koop, D.R., & Mehta, P.H. (2016). A comparison of salivary testosterone measurement using immunoassays and tandem mass spectrometry. *Psychoneuroendocrinology*, *71*, 180–188. http://dx.doi.org/10.1016/j.psyneuen.2016.05.022

Whembolua, G.L., Granger, D.A., Singer, S., Kivlighan, K.T., & Marguin, J.A. (2006). Bacteria in the oral mucosa and its effects on the measurement of cortisol, dehydroepiandrosterone, and testosterone in saliva. *Hormones and Behavior*, *49*(4), 478–483. doi:S0018-506X(05)00236-9 [pii] 10.1016/j.yhbeh.2005.10.005

Wierman, M.E., Auchus, R.J., Haisenleder, D.J., Hall, J.E., Handelsman, D., Hankinson, S., . . . Stanczyk, F.Z. (2014). Editorial: The new instructions to authors for the reporting of steroid hormone measurements. *The Journal of Clinical Endocrinology and Metabolism*, *99*(12), 4375. doi:10.1210/jc.2014-3424

Yalow, R.S., & Berson, S.A. (1960). Immunoassay of endogenous plasma insulin in man. *Journal of Clinical Investigation*, *39*, 1157–1175.

Zilioli, S., Caldbick, E., & Watson, N.V. (2014). Testosterone reactivity to facial display of emotions in men and women. *Hormones and Behavior*, *65*(5), 461–468. doi:10.1016/j.yhbeh.2014.04.006

3

REPRODUCIBILITY IN SOCIAL NEUROENDOCRINOLOGY

Past, present, and future

Oliver C. Schultheiss and Pranjal H. Mehta

Many scientific disciplines are currently embroiled in what could rightfully be called a revolution. It is a revolution spurred by a crisis in scientists' trust in the reproducibility of published research, that is, whether the finding obtained in a study can be obtained again is subsequent, closely matched or even exact replications of this study. This revolution aims at changing the way we do and report science towards increased transparency and rigor. In this chapter we discuss (i) the origins of this revolution; (ii) examples from social neuroendocrinology relevant to the revolution; and (iii) practical recommendations to strengthen future research in social neuroendocrinology.

A primer on reliability, validity, and power

To better understand why reproducibility has become such an issue in the empirical sciences, we think it is useful to briefly sketch out what happens when we test hypotheses, because that will put the reader in a better position to appreciate what can go wrong in the process. The main players in issues of reproducibility are reliability, validity, and statistical power.

Imagine you are a researcher who wants to test the extent to which cortisol is associated with creativity. To examine the association, besides a good measure of creativity (we will not go into that), you need a reliable measure of cortisol. Reliability refers to the precision of a measurement. If you run a sample through a cortisol assay and repeat that process again and again for this sample, will the same value show up again and again? The answer is, of course: never exactly, but hopefully sufficiently close. Thus, measured values of 1.22 ng/mL, 1.18 ng/mL, and 1.24 ng/mL of the same sample would constitute reasonably reliable measurements, because although the values differ, they are close together in terms of absolute levels, converging on an average of 1.22 ng/mL. This would be a reliable assay. In contrast, the same average could be achieved through the following series of measurements: 0.93 ng/mL, 1.39 ng/mL, and 1.42 ng/mL. The latter measurement process is less precise, causing a lot more variance around the estimated average. This would be an unreliable assay. Because cortisol measured with an unreliable (= imprecise) assay is less likely to be correlated with a measure of creativity than cortisol measured with a reliable (= precise) assay, you will opt for the latter method. If you run several studies, you will also be more likely to reproduce a specific association with the reliable assay than with the unreliable one, all else being equal.

41

But although measure reliability is a necessary precondition for reproducible science, it is not a sufficient one. The second key element for reproducibility is validity. that is, whether a measure actually measures what it purports to measure. For instance, just because an assay kit claims that it measures cortisol does not mean that that is the case. Perhaps the assay picks up something completely different. Perhaps it measures cortisol, but also other steroids, and therefore is not a specific measure of cortisol. Or perhaps it is an exact measure of cortisol in one medium (e.g., serum), but not in another (e.g., saliva). This is a recurring topic in social neuroendocrinology (e.g., Carter et al., 2007; Horvat-Gordon, Granger, Schwartz, Nelson, & Kivlighan, 2005; Valstad et al., 2017) and an issue that we cover at length with regard to steroid measurements in a separate chapter (see Schultheiss, Dlugash, & Mehta, this volume). Clearly, as a researcher you can only test your hypothesis regarding the link between cortisol and creativity if your measures are valid. Reproducibility can be hampered if more valid measures are used in some studies and less valid ones in others, even if they are equally reliable. Thus, consistency in the use of highly valid measures is key. (Note that this also has another implication: you could get a specific result and be able to replicate it consistently with an invalid measure, but not with a valid measure. This example shows that high reproducibility is not necessarily the same as high validity!)

The third key element for reproducible science is statistical power. According to Cohen (1992), statistical power denotes the probability (in percent) of obtaining a statistically significant effect, given a certain sample size (N), statistical threshold criterion (e.g., typically $p < .05$), and population effect size (e.g., expressed as r, d, or odds ratio). Returning to our illustrative example, if you had reason to expect the association between cortisol and creativity to be $r = .40$ in the general population (e.g., based on meta-analytic estimates of associations between cortisol and other psychological variables) and you were to employ the standard two-tailed alpha level of .05 in your research, then you would have an 80% chance of obtaining a significant result if you tested $N = 47$ participants. Or, in other words, if you ran 10 studies with 47 participants each, assuming the true effect size in the population is $r = .40$, the association between cortisol and creativity could be expected to pass the .05 significance threshold in 8 of the 10 studies. The sample effect sizes picked up in those 10 studies are expected to scatter around the population effect size, with some coming out higher and some lower. Some of the latter will not exceed the .05 threshold.

Of course, if you want to make sure that you get an effect of a certain expected size with greater likelihood, then – all else being equal – you could increase N so that your power will be 99%. Now, you would need to test 106 participants to ensure that you would see the effect emerge as significant in 99 out of 100 studies. If you actually ran those 100 studies, the observed per-sample effect sizes would show much less scatter around the population effect size than effect sizes obtained in the previous set of studies with an N of 47. The reason is because the increase in sample size decreases the width of the confidence interval and thus makes the effect size estimate more precise.

Now let us revisit the population effect size we based our power calculations on. An $r = .40$, equivalent to a d of .87 or an odds ratio of 4.87, is actually a rather rare population effect size in the behavioral sciences if one uses meta-analytic findings as an approximation (and, as we will discuss below, there are good reasons to think that even those may represent overestimations). Richard, Bond, and Stokes-Zoota (2003) conducted a mega-analysis (that is, a meta-analysis of meta-analyses; see Hattie, 2008) based on a century of research in social psychology and found an average effect size of $r = .21$, equivalent to a d of .43 and an odds ratio of 2.18. If we take this as the basis of the population effect size for the hypothesized association between cortisol and creativity and want to make sure that we find a significant effect ($p < .05$) with a power of 80%, we would need to test 176 individuals. And if we want to avoid not seeing the finding in 1 out of 5 studies, but only in 1 out of 10, equivalent to a power of 90%, we would need to test 235 individuals. Samples of this size are the exception rather than the rule in social neuroendocrinology and other domains of psychology. And typically, published effect sizes are much bigger than $r = .21$, too. While this may sound like good news at first blush, small samples combined with large sample effect sizes actually hint at a problem in our field. We will later discuss why.

For now, we conclude that the likelihood of obtaining or replicating a statistically significant effect present in the overall population is a function of the reliability and validity of the measurements involved, the size of the effect, the significance threshold chosen, and the size of one's sample.

Some milestones and focal issues of the replication crisis

A key catalyst for the replication crisis and the revolution it triggered was a paper published by John Ioannidis (2005) whose title claimed that "most published research findings are false." Ioannidis argued that *low statistical power* and *bias in the way research is conducted and published* are critical factors that can lead to the publication of false-positive findings (that is, reporting a sizeable effect or a relationship in a study when in fact it is only minuscule or in a different direction altogether in the overall population).

There are several drawbacks to studies with low statistical power. Low power, by definition, indicates that there is a low chance of discovering an effect in a study that is genuinely true in the population. That is, a low-powered study is likely to produce a false negative result, or commit a Type II error (see Figure 3.1). But even when a low-powered study is "lucky" enough

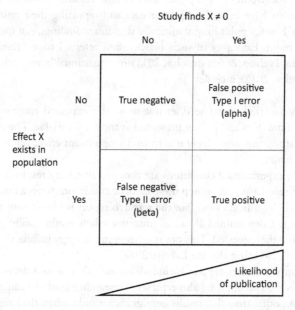

Figure 3.1 Probabilistic relationship between true effect and effect observed in a given study. Findings from a study may correctly indicate the absence (true negative) or presence (true positive) of an effect exceeding a certain size in a randomly drawn sample. But they may also falsely indicate the absence of an effect if one is present in the population (false negative) or the presence of an effect if one is absent in the population (false positive). Historically, journals in the behavioral sciences have preferred to publish positive (= significant) findings.

to discover a true effect (typically determined by a statistical significance test), the effect size observed in the low-powered study is likely to be much larger than the true effect size in the population, a phenomenon referred to as the *winner's curse* (Ioannidis, 2008). Somewhat paradoxically, in studies with low statistical power, unreliable measurement can often contribute to such inflated effect size estimates, whereas in studies with high statistical power unreliable measures almost always attenuate observed effect sizes (Loken & Gelman, 2017). And finally, even if the best measures are employed, statistically significant effects can even be obtained for an actual population effect size of 0 due to sampling fluctuations – that is, 5% of all samples drawn from such a population will yield a significant result based on standard statistical thresholding ($p < .05$; Type I error) and thus represent false positives.

This would not be a problem in a world in which all findings, significant or not, from studies with high statistical power as well as from studies with low statistical power were eventually published: after a couple of years one could take stock of all studies, meta-analyze them, and come up with a pretty clear-cut verdict whether the overall population effect reliably differs from zero and, if so, how much and in which direction. Unfortunately, in the real world of academia, there is publication bias – many journal editors and reviewers tend to favor the publication of statistically significant results. Thus, the right half of the box depicted in Figure 3.1, containing both true and false positives, is overrepresented in the literature, a phenomenon that has been termed *excess significance* (Button, Ioannidis, Mokrysz, Nosek, Flint, Robinson, & Munafo, 2013). In contrast, findings falling into the left half of the box shown in Figure 3.1, containing both true and false negatives, are less likely to get published. This could be termed, in analogy to excess significance, *rare non-significance*.

The preference of journals for positive findings leads to the second factor which according to Ioannidis (2005) contributes to the publication of false findings: *researcher bias*. This refers to the flexibility scientists have in analyzing their data and reporting their results, which, in the context of journals' bias for publishing statistically significant findings, can increase the chances of a false-positive result. Examples of such biases, often referred to as "researcher degrees of freedom" (Simmons, Nelson, & Simonsohn, 2011) or "questionable research practices" (John, Loewenstein, & Prelec, 2012), include:

- The originally targeted outcome does not show the expected relationship, but another, peripheral measure does and is then presented as the focal variable. The more measures are included in a study, the more likely it is to find a significant effect for at least one of them due to mere chance.
- Cases or entire experimental conditions are dropped that keep results from becoming statistically significant (that is, dropping these cases or conditions turns a non-significant result into a statistically significant one), but the research report is silent about this fact.
- Sample size is not determined ahead of time but when results finally get significant and data collection is then stopped. This optional stopping strategy inflates the Type I error rate (Simmons et al., 2011; but also see Lakens, 2014).
- Stringent control variables are not included, because they would decrease effect size and significance levels. The opposite also represents researcher bias: including covariates for no apparent reason other than that results get significant only when they are included.
- The original hypothesis does not pan out, but another, unexpected finding emerges from the research and is then presented in the manuscript as the a priori hypothesis (this is called *hypothesizing after results are known*, or HARKing [Kerr, 1998], and used to be the officially recommended approach for writing papers in psychology; see Bem, 2003; Sternberg, 2003).

- A less valid or less rigorous measure is preferred over a more valid or rigorous one, simply because the former is more likely to support one's hypothesis than the latter.
- Researchers typically scrutinize all methods and data-processing steps particularly carefully when a study fails to support their hypothesis, hunting for methodological glitches that could explain this negative outcome. But they do not go to the same lengths for studies that support their hypothesis.

And bias can occur in innumerable other ways, and even in the most well-intentioned and principled researchers. After all, science is a human endeavor and thus susceptible to the many ways in which we protect, defend, and uphold our most cherished concepts and hypotheses.

Meta-analyses based on such a body of literature are bound to overestimate true effect sizes and may even indicate a reliable effect size across studies when the relationship in question is nil in the population (Bakker, van Dijk, & Wicherts, 2012). Bakker et al. ran simulations showing that even for a population effect size of zero, underpowered studies that also exploit questionable research practices can lead to meta-analytical effect sizes estimates (d) of up to .48. Such estimates cover a large spectrum of the average effect sizes in actually published meta-analyses! (e.g., Richard et al., 2003).

Ioannidis's (2005) paper was largely aimed at biomedical and epidemiological research, and his key arguments had been made before (e.g., Cohen, 1962; Greenwald, 1975; Meehl, 1967; Smith, 1970). But his paper had an immense impact not only on the fields it focused on, but across many other scientific disciplines, too. One reason for this effect may have been its provocative title. The other reason may have to do with the diminishing returns on investment in biomedicine at the time. For instance, two independent investigations that examined the reproducibility of published landmark studies in oncology and drug development found that results for only 11% (Begley & Ellis, 2012; 53 studies) to 25% (Prinz, Schlange, & Asadullah, 2011; 67 studies) of them could be reproduced. One group of researchers even put a price tag on the squandering of resources on non-reproducible published findings in biomedical research: US$ 28 billion per year in the United States alone (Freedman, Cockburn, & Simcoe, 2015). Thus, although funding agencies spent more and more money on understanding and curing illnesses such as cancer, scientific progress had slowed down noticeably, thus failing to deliver to patients the effective treatments they urgently need (Harris, 2017).

But the impact of Ioannidis's paper was not limited to the biomedical sciences. Vul, Harris, Winkielman, and Pashler (2009) applied Ioannidis's argument to functional magnetic resonance imaging (fMRI) studies of emotion, personality, and social cognition, arguing that much of that research is severely underpowered and capitalizes on chance by presenting those among up to 100,000 data points representing the brain that show significant ($p < .01$) or highly significant ($p < .001$) activation (see also Button et al., 2013). Even if there is no actual systematic brain activation effect, this would still result in 1,000 or 100 significant voxels, respectively. Bennett, Miller, and Wolford (2009) provided a humorous illustration of this issue by reporting that a dead salmon completing a social-perspective-taking task in an fMRI scanner showed significant brain activation – an artifact of improper statistical thresholding.

The discussion of problematic practices in analyzing and reporting data spilled over into mainstream psychology after the publication of a paper claiming to provide evidence for precognitive abilities in humans (Bem, 2011) and the criticism it drew regarding its data-analytical strategy (Wagenmakers, Wetzels, Borsboom, & van der Maas, 2011). The discussion further intensified when the Open Science Collaboration (2015) – which included one of us (PHM) – tried to replicate findings from 100 studies published in three leading psychology journals in the year 2008, using designs with high statistical power and adhering as much as possible to the original, published study protocols. Only 39% of the studies were deemed to represent successful replications, and the effect sizes of the replication studies were almost always substantially lower than those reported in the original publication (see Camerer et al., 2016, for related observations in the field of economics). Thus, whether it is biomedical or behavioral research, Ioannidis's (2005) prediction about the low reproducibility of published research turns out to be a valid diagnosis of the state of several scientific disciplines.

The way we were: a personal look back

In the following sections of this chapter, we will present some case studies highlighting challenges with reproducibility in social neuroendocrinology. Our objective is not pointing fingers at others but presenting evidence, acknowledged by the originators of the research, for problematic research strategies in our own field. As researchers who have been, and still are, passionate about our own pet theories and hypotheses and who have been socialized into academia under the "old rules" that contributed to the replication crisis, we do not claim to have been immune to the problems of conducting and reporting research outlined previously.

As a case in point, the first author of this chapter (OCS) recognizes many of the processes that lead to published false positives in his own first published social neuroendocrinology paper (Schultheiss, Campbell, & McClelland, 1999). The study was conducted in 1997 to test a simple idea: Winning or losing a dominance contest leads to increases or decreases in testosterone in men with a high, but not in those with a low, implicit need for power (nPower). Thus, it was designed to test an interaction between an experimentally varied factor (winning versus losing) and a quantitatively assessed motivational disposition. Assuming a medium-sized (Cohen, 1992) correlation of .30 between nPower and testosterone change among winners and a similarly sized negative correlation of −.30 in losers (already a generous estimate, given the typical personality/social-psychology effect size of r = .21; Richard et al., 2003), this would have required at least 44 participants per experimental condition and thus a total of 88 participants to detect the expected effect with 80% probability at $p < .05$. But the first author only had resources to test 42 participants in total. Even if the estimated effect size had been true, this cut his effective power down to a 46% chance of observing the predicted effect, making it an underpowered study from the get-go. Then, after all data were collected, the picture stories had been coded for nPower, and the last saliva sample run through the gamma counter, the pre-planned regression analyses testing the hypothesized effect revealed – nothing! There was no sign of a significant interaction between contest outcome and nPower in the data.

When OCS had recovered from this blow, he began to scrutinize all data file processing syntax for signs of data misalignment or any evidence for data miscoding. When that could be ruled out, he remembered that in past research on power motivation, researchers had often distinguished between subtypes of power motivation that could be assessed with more differentiated coding systems than the one he had used. So he took advantage of the flexibility inherent in this approach and recoded the stories using a number of different variants of nPower coding systems. This eventually turned up the desired evidence: a highly significant three-way interaction between contest outcome, an egocentric variant of power motivation termed personalized power (p Power), and a more social variant termed socialized power (s Power). The effect was due to a positive association between p Power and testosterone changes in winners in the absence of s Power that did not occur in s Power-present winners or in losers in general. Overall, the regression model accounted for 46% of the variance, corresponding to R = .68. Individual correlation coefficients in follow-up decompositions of the interaction reached levels of almost .90, but were based on *ns* as low as 5. This is the set of findings that was eventually published.

No mention was made in the published paper that other coding systems had also been used for assessing power motivation, but without success. The published paper is thus a textbook case of the undisclosed flexibility that researchers have when analyzing and reporting their findings, the spectacular effect sizes that can be associated with underpowered samples, and the tendency of reviewers and journal editors to accept papers with such spectacular results for publication.

So were the findings ever replicated? The answer is: it depends. The first replication attempt (Schultheiss & Rohde, 2002) was unsuccessful. These authors tried the p/s Power coding approach, failed, but did not report this fact in their paper. Instead they switched to an analytic approach that combined an overall measure of nPower with a word-count index of inhibition to predict testosterone responses to a dominance contest outcome (Schultheiss et al., 1999, had tried this, too, but without success and without mentioning it in the paper). Again, the study was underpowered ($N = 66$), particularly with regard to the complex three-way interaction of contest outcome, nPower, and the inhibition index. The flexibility in OCS's switch of analytical strategy from Schultheiss et al. (1999) to Schultheiss and Rohde (2002) is only barely defensible on the grounds that previous research unrelated to hormones has documented functional similarities between p Power and uninhibited nPower and s Power and inhibited nPower (e.g., McClelland, Davis, Kalin, & Wanner, 1972), and the fact that he was generally right in the sense that high levels of power motivation did predict testosterone increases in winners and/or decreases in losers, once a moderating factor was taken into account.

The nPower × contest outcome interaction originally expected by the first author emerged in later studies with better statistical power, and not just for testosterone (Schultheiss et al., 2005; Oxford, Tiedtke, Ossmann, Özbe, & Schultheiss, 2017), but also for cortisol (Wirth, Welsh, & Schultheiss, 2006) and, in women, for estradiol (Oxford et al., 2017; Stanton & Schultheiss, 2007). Nevertheless, these studies also feature an inconsistent result, namely the reversed nPower × contest outcome effect on testosterone for men observed by Oxford et al. (2017; cf. Schultheiss et al., 2005). It remains to be resolved whether these paradoxical results may have been due to differences in the contest paradigms employed. OCS also had conducted one additional study with 56 male US students, but failed to find a significant nPower × contest outcome effect on post-contest testosterone changes. A reanalysis of the data for the purposes of this chapter suggests that the predicted effect of a positive correlation between nPower and testosterone changes among winners and a negative correlation among losers was present immediately after the contest, but did not reach accepted significance levels for the interaction, $p = .18$. The results were therefore not published (file drawer $N = 1$), although these participants were included as part of Wirth et al.'s (2006, Study 2) report on nPower × contest outcome effects on cortisol changes.

Vongas and al Hajj (2017) provide a final twist to this story. These researchers used the same experimental paradigm originally introduced by Schultheiss et al. (1999), but reframed it such that the contest outcome would be an indicator of future leadership ability and also took other steps to make it methodologically more sophisticated. Vongas and al Hajj (2017) measured p Power with a slightly different coding system than Schultheiss et al. (1999), by using all nPower coding categories of the Winter (1994) coding manual except the prosocial one that focuses on unsolicited help and advice (personal communication by John Vongas). Across two studies with statistical power approaching 80% ($N = 84$ and 72), they reported significant contest outcome × p Power interaction effects on testosterone changes. They thus provided a partial replication – *sans* the contribution of an s Power measure – of the Schultheiss et al. (1999) findings and also of the findings reported by Schultheiss et al. (2005).

What is the bottom line of this personal account of one researcher's career in social neuroendocrinology? It shows that a passion for a hypothesis, coupled with a journal system that rewards underpowered research yielding over-the-top effect sizes, is likely to produce published findings that, through no ill will or deliberate intention to deceive on the part of the author, the editor, and the reviewers, are difficult to replicate, unless some undisclosed flexibility is used, and that therefore should be viewed with caution. At least there was a trajectory from under-powered (Schultheiss et al., 1999) to less underpowered (Schultheiss & Rohde, 2002) and finally adequately powered studies (e.g., Oxford et al., 2017; $N = 326$) and towards the inclusion of data sets and data analysis scripts with the publication for the sake of transparency (Oxford et al., 2017). Still, there is a degree of variability and inconsistency in the line of work that started with Schultheiss et al. (1999) that remains to be resolved in direct replication studies, conducted as preregistered studies or registered reports (see below).

Power posing

While the aforementioned example illustrates that the field of behavioral endocrinology prob-ably has never been immune to the pitfalls of false-positive research, this study and many similar others from various laboratories did not lead to public critiques or systematic discussions of their merits and weaknesses, although this would have been justified. By contrast, Carney, Cuddy, and Yap's (2010) study did lead to public critiques and discussions. These researchers tested the idea that a brief enactment of body postures signaling high social power, compared to postures signaling low power, would lead to corresponding changes in physiology, feeling, and behavior. Testing 42 participants randomly allocated to either the high-power or the low-power condi-tion, Carney et al. found that participants in the former condition showed an increase in sali-vary testosterone, a decrease in salivary cortisol, a strong sense of subjective power, and a strong propensity towards risky decision-making. In contrast, participants in the low-power condition showed a decrease in testosterone, an increase in cortisol, felt less powerful, and also made less risky decisions after the intervention. In the abstract, the authors drew the following conclusion from these findings: "That a person can, by assuming two simple 1-min poses, embody power and instantly become more powerful has real-world, actionable implications" (Carney et al., 2010, p. 1363).

Responding to mounting criticism that power-posing effects could not be replicated in other laboratories (e.g., Simmons & Simonsohn, 2017; Davis et al., 2017; Garrison, Tang, & Schmeichel, 2016; Ranehill et al., 2015), Carney, Cuddy, and Yap (2015) argued that effects of power posing can and have been replicated in many studies (see Cuddy, Schultz, & Fosse, 2018, as well as Gronau et al., 2017, for recent updates on the effects of power posing on feelings of power). But we note that from a social neuroendocrinology perspective, it is remarkable that none of the studies Carney et al. (2015) cite in support of their hypothesis ever focused on the hormonal effects originally reported in Carney et al. (2010). These effects had already come under scrutiny by Stanton (2011), who argued that treating gender as a covariate in the analyses reported by Carney et al. (2010) did not do justice to the differences in overall levels and the specific mechanisms of testosterone release in men and women. With the benefit of hindsight, we would add that the sample collection and hormone assay methods used by Carney et al. (2010) now appear to have had doubtful validity, too (Schultheiss, 2013; Schultheiss, Dlugash, & Mehta, this volume; Welker et al., 2016) – a caveat that also applies to many other studies, including some of those from our own laboratories.

So were there any attempts at replicating Carney et al.'s (2010) endocrine effects, and what did they find? We could identify four studies that had specifically aimed to replicate these effects (Davis et al., 2017; Ranehill et al., 2015; Ronay, Tybur, van Huijstee, & Morssinkhof, 2017; Smith & Apicella, 2017) and provide an overview of them in Table 3.1, next to Carney et al.'s (2010) original results. A careful analysis of these studies and comparison with the original

Table 3.1 Overview of main methodological features and endocrine outcomes for power-pose studies, with effect sizes based on direct comparisons between high-power and low-power poses

Study	N	Power pose	Additional factors	Effect on testosterone	Effect on cortisol	Also relevant
Original study						
Carney et al. (2010)	42 (26♀,16♂)	2 × 60 s, either high or low	–	$d = 0.66$, $p < .05$	$d = -0.89$, $p < .02$	–
Replication studies						
Ranehill et al. (2015)	200 (98♀, 102♂)	2 × 180 s, either high or low	–	$d = -0.20$, ns	$d = -0.16$, ns	–
Ronay et al. (2017)	108 (64♀, 44♂)	direct replication	–	$d = -0.12$, ns	$d = -0.03$, ns	
Smith and Apicella (2017)	258 (♂ only), 160 after exclusion of neutral-posing controls	direct replication, plus neutral-posing control	winning/losing in one-on-one tug-of-war (before power posing)	$d = -0.08$, ns	$d = 0.09$, ns	For testosterone, win/lose × power pose interaction: testosterone rise in high-power-pose winners and low-power-pose losers
Davis et al. (2017)	73 (52♀, 21♂), 53 (36♀, 17♂) after exclusion of no-posing controls	direct replication, plus no-posing control		$d = -0.31$, ns	$d = 0.25$, ns	Participants had diagnosis of social anxiety disorder
Totals and weighted averages	521 (198♀, 323♂)			$\mathbf{d = -0.16}$	$\mathbf{d = -0.02}$	

power-posing study reveals the following. First, three of the four replication studies – with Davis et al. (2017) being the exception – feature substantially larger samples than the original study, determined by statistical power analyses and often increasing sample sizes beyond the results of these analyses. Second, all four attempted to replicate the original power-posing manipulation closely (i.e., taking on the two consecutive postures in each condition described in the original paper for at least 1 min), but there were some differences as well. Davis et al. (2017) manipulated power posing in participants with a diagnosis of social anxiety disorder before they entered a free-speech task. Ranehill et al. (2015) used longer times for the poses than the original study. Two studies aimed at minimizing experimenter effects by having a computer provide the instructions (Ranehill et al., 2015; Smith & Apicella, 2017). Smith and Apicella (2017) added another between-subject control condition with a neutral power pose and an additional factor, namely, whether participants had previously won or lost in a game of tug-of-war against another participant. Notably Ronay et al.'s (2017) study was a registered report that was accepted in principle before data collection even started (more on registered reports below). Third, the studies by Davis et al. (2017), Ranehill et al. (2015), and Ronay et al. (2017) suffer from the same problem of treating gender as a covariate already criticized by Stanton (2011), and all four studies, like the original study, base their conclusions on hormone assays whose validity for the accurate assessment of testosterone has recently come under scrutiny (see Schultheiss et al., this volume; Welker et al., 2016). However, because all four studies are comparable with regard to these last issues, these general criticisms cannot explain any between-study differences in the results reported.

Table 3.1 shows that none of the replication studies was able to replicate either the testosterone increase or the cortisol decrease associated with high-power postures, relative to low-power postures, reported by the original study. In fact, the pooled effect size as well as the individual effects reported by each replication study suggest that the effect of power posing on testosterone may be in the opposite direction of the effect reported in the original study (i.e., a sign, or Type S, error according to Gelman & Carlin, 2014). In terms of absolute magnitude the pooled effect sizes of all replication studies are in the small range (Cohen, 1992), whereas the effect sizes originally reported by Carney et al. (2010) are medium- to large-sized (a magnitude, or Type M, error according to Gelman & Carlin, 2014). With regard to the effects of power posing on endocrine variables, Carney et al.'s (2010) original study is thus a good example of journals favoring the publication of studies with seemingly large, positive effects that are difficult to replicate.

There is also evidence for low statistical power and undisclosed flexibility contributing to Carney et al.'s (2010) results. The low statistical power of the original study is evident from the sample size, which unrealistically presupposes a large effect ($d = .78$) for simple between-group comparisons at $p < .05$ and a power of 80%. Some of the flexibility that went into data processing is disclosed in the original publication – one outlier was omitted from the analyses for testosterone and two were omitted from the analyses for cortisol. Crede and Phillips (2017) reanalyzed the Carney et al. (2010) data and demonstrated that not only the removal of outliers played a role in obtaining the results for testosterone and cortisol eventually reported in the original publication, but also other data-analytic decisions not discussed in Carney et al. (2010; and to be fair: usually not addressed in *any* published studies). These included the use of an ANCOVA approach that treated baseline hormone measures as a covariate instead of an analysis of hormone change scores (see van Breukelen, 2006), the question of adding the baseline of the "other" hormone (e.g., cortisol) whenever an analysis was directed at a target hormone (e.g., testosterone), and the decision to use gender as a covariate instead of analyzing the data for each gender separately. Crede and Phillips (2017) identify in each of their tables for testosterone and cortisol 54 possible ways to analyze the data resulting from the permutation of decisions related to outlier omission, covariate selection, and the consideration of gender. And for each hormone, only 1 out of 54 combinations of data-analytic decision yielded the desired $p < .05$ effect. These were the effects that were eventually published.

Carney et al. (2010) have to be given credit that they made their data set available to others for reanalyses, one of which led to the Crede and Phillips (2017) publication. Dana Carney, the lead author, eventually agreed with the critics of the original study, stating that in light of the many failed replication studies and the strong reservations other researchers voiced about the original study, she does "not believe that 'power pose' effects are real" (Carney, undated). In the same statement, Carney also conceded that the sample was too small, that gender should have been treated differently than as a covariate in the analyses of testosterone, and that the sample had been filled up until effects on the original focal measure – risk taking – became significant at $p < .05$ in one type of analysis, which was eventually reported, but not in another, equally valid analytic design. She now characterizes these decisions as instances of p-hacking (i.e., ensuring that an effect just barely makes the .05 significance level; Simmons et al., 2011) and using researcher degrees of freedom (Carney, undated). In essence, she confirms Crede and Phillips's (2017) conclusion that key findings of the Carney et al. (2010) study must be attributed not to an actual effect present in the overall population, but to exploiting undisclosed flexibility in data collection, processing, and analysis (note that this may be a premature conclusion with regard to feelings of power induced by power posing; see Cuddy et al., 2018; Gronau et al., 2017).

In our experience, it is a rare case that a researcher who was once passionate about a study and its findings not only responds to criticism by making her or his data available to others, but eventually acknowledges that he or she may have gotten it wrong. We suspect that in their heart of hearts, all scientists know that some of the studies they have published over the years are less likely than others to actually represent a true effect that can be replicated. But very few would admit this openly and thus help pave the way to the self-correction that should be part and parcel of the scientific endeavor, but in reality hard to come by. Following the discussions about many other findings that have come under scrutiny in recent years (the Carney et al., 2010 study is hardly the only one), our impression is that defensiveness is the modal response of most researchers who have published findings that are then critiqued by others. Ultimately, this is a problematic response for scientists, even though it may be viewed as a very human response, because it leads to costly and unproductive debates instead of helping to clear the path toward better and more conclusive studies that can correct the scientific record. Carney, in our view, has done the painful, but right thing. Kudos.

A peek inside one laboratory's file drawer

A third illustrative example of the danger of false-positive science in social neuroendocrinology comes from the laboratory of Olivier Luminet (Lane, Luminet, Nave, & Mikolajczak, 2016). Luminet and his collaborators have conducted a series of eight studies in which oxytocin or placebo was administered via an intranasal spray to participants and the effect of this treatment on social behavior was examined. In terms of experimental design, hormone administration, and sample size, this research is similar to a large number of recent studies from various laboratories examining the effects of oxytocin administration on affiliative behavior, social cognition, and trust (e.g. De Dreu et al., 2010; Hurlemann et al., 2010; Kosfeld, Heinrichs, Zak, Fischbacher, & Fehr, 2005). And initially, Luminet's group was successful, too, with studies suggesting that oxytocin increases trust (Mikolajczak, Pinon, Lane, de Timary, & Luminet, 2010 [note that Lane et al., 2016, p. 11, later stated that if analyzed properly, the effect reported in this paper was not reliable]; Mikolajczak, Gross, Lane, Corneille, de Timary, & Luminet, 2010) and a willingness to share emotions with others (Lane et al., 2013), with one additional paper suggesting that oxytocin effects on social behavior may depend on alexithymia, a self-report measure of individual differences in accessing one's emotions (Luminet, Grynberg, Ruzette, & Mikolajczak, 2011).

However, the Luminet laboratory also conducted several studies that failed to document hypothesized effects of oxytocin on dependent measures. One was a failed replication of the oxytocin effect on trust. This paper, although initially rejected by one journal (see Lane et al., 2016), was eventually published by another journal, and its findings are therefore on record (Lane et al., 2015). Three other papers, documenting null effects of oxytocin administration on social conformity, social mimicry, and compassion, were submitted to journals, but repeatedly rejected and remain unpublished (see Lane et al., 2016), illustrating how the previously discussed "rare non-significance" in the published literature comes about. Lane et al. (2016, p. 2) drew the following conclusion from this state of affairs:

> After realising that our publication portfolio has become less and less representative of our actual findings, and because the nonpublication of our null results might contribute to generating a publication bias in [intranasal oxytocin administration] research, we decided to retrieve these studies out of our drawer, hoping that other laboratories will do the same.

Lane et al. (2016) conducted a meta-analysis of all eight studies conducted in the Luminet laboratory, comprising a total of 453 research participants, 25 research paradigms, and 13 dependent variables. It should be noted that in six of these studies, 60 participants or more were tested, thus providing these studies the statistical power to reliably (> 80%) detect mean-difference effects sizes of $d = 0.65$, which corresponds to a medium to large effect size (Cohen, 1992). It is our impression that such sample sizes are already rather high compared to many other hormone administration studies and thus provide a somewhat better basis for testing targeted hypotheses.

The results of the in-lab meta-analysis yielded sobering results. An overall analysis of all emotion, cognitive, and behavioral dependent variables revealed an average effect size of $d = .003$, which was not significantly different from a null effect. This finding was not moderated by the type of dependent measure used or the specific theory of oxytocin's effect tested.

Lane et al. (2016) state that the difficulty in replicating effects of oxytocin on theoretically relevant outcomes has turned them from believers into skeptics. Addressing the question how the large literature on oxytocin effects in humans could have accumulated in the first place, given this difficulty to replicate basic effects, they offer two explanations. One is that the publication record in its totality represents false positives, resulting from selective publication of the few studies out of many conducted that happened to cross the threshold of statistical significance. The implication is that in the overall population, the effect of intranasally administered oxytocin on social cognition and behavior of the type tested in published studies is close to zero and that the hypothesis of oxytocin effects on social cognition and behavior is plain wrong.

The other explanation Lane et al. (2016) offer is that effects of intranasal oxytocin in studies of human participants is due to methodological and statistical artifacts. These may include pre-existing differences between treatment and placebo groups, particularly in small-N studies, single-blind studies in which the experimenter knows about a participant's treatment-group assignment, although the participant is not informed (see Rosenthal & Rosnow, 1969), unsubstantiated assumptions about the dosage and timeline of intranasal delivery of oxytocin and its effects on the brain (e.g., Leng & Ludwig, 2016; Walum, Waldman, & Young, 2016), and unrealistically high targeted effect sizes, given the sample sizes tested.

Lane et al. (2016) do not rule out the possibility that effects of oxytocin on social cognition and behavior are moderated by situational or dispositional factors, leading to a strong effect under one set of boundary conditions and a null effect under another. This would be consistent with the difficulty of replicating any direct main effects of oxytocin administration. But, as the authors emphasize repeatedly in their paper, the most problematic aspect of intranasal oxytocin research is the lack of published *direct* replications, be it of the main effect of hormone administration or any interaction effects with other variables.

They draw the following conclusion from their own data and their knowledge of the field of oxytocin research:

> We believe that a systematic shift in the [intranasal oxytocin administration] publication process is essential for revealing the true state of the world. Pre-registration of ex-ante hypotheses, replication attempts of the findings before their submission, and the submission of null results and failed replications for publication, especially when the studies are well-powered to detect the original findings, should be encouraged. Review processes should insist on fully reporting all of the candidate moderators that were measured and tested and encourage publication of well-conducted studies, regardless of their results.
>
> (Lane et al., 2016, p. 13)

We fully agree with Lane et al.'s (2016) conclusions, which are also echoed by Walum et al. (2016), and applaud them for the scientific integrity they demonstrate by laying open their lab's research record.

Gathering around the campfire of highly reproducible research

Our previous examples document that social endocrinology is not immune to the factors that gave rise to the replication crisis sweeping psychology and other sciences. This should not be surprising, given that our field has been subject to the same incentives, pressures, academic socialization practices, and publication biases as other fields. It seems that the constant hunt for sexy and sensational new findings may lure our field into the dark wilderness of irreproducible research. What is a better alternative?

It is our impression that the behavioral sciences have made the greatest progress and achieved the most profound insights when they have focused on well-documented, highly reproducible findings. Pavlovian conditioning, that is, the learned association between unconditioned rewards and punishers and the stimuli that reliably predict them, is a classic example. Because Pavlovian conditioning is a very robust phenomenon resulting from a well-defined general testing paradigm, this type of learning has become a prime vehicle for research on such different topics as animal cognition, emotional processing, or molecular changes involved in learning (e.g., LeDoux, 1996, 2002). It became the backbone of research in biopsychology and neuroscience, helping to make both Nobel Prize–winning discoveries (e.g., Eric Kandel's research on synaptic changes in the *Aplysia californica*) and to further the progress of our understanding of brain functions in general. Indeed, it could be argued that biopsychology and neuroscience in their present form are inconceivable without the firm fundament of Pavlovian conditioning and its close cousin, instrumental conditioning. Over time the limits of Pavlovian learning processes also became apparent (Seligman, 1970), and some specific findings resulting from Pavlovian conditioning paradigms have turned out to be hard to replicate (e.g., Maes et al., 2016). But the phenomenon itself was so robust and pervasive that its limits were not apparent for a long time and actually required clever experimental setups to document them (Garcia & Koelling, 1966).

Other examples of strong testing paradigms producing valuable phenomena for entire scientific disciplines include the Stroop test for the cognitive sciences (MacLeod, 1991), binocular rivalry in consciousness studies (Dehaene, 2014), the ultimatum game for the study of decision-making (Güth, Schmittberger, & Schwarze, 1982), and the strange situation test (Ainsworth & Bell, 1970) and the marshmallow test in developmental psychology (Mischel, Shoda, & Rodriguez, 1989). Does social neuroendocrinology have similarly robust testing paradigms that can be used as a secure platform from which substantial questions can be addressed?

Without a doubt, our field features such robust campfires of replicable phenomena around which researchers can gather and use them to shine a light on new questions. They appear to come in two varieties: testing paradigms that are either strong for a priori, conceptual reasons or that result from a serendipitous observation with a well-replicated empirical track record. An excellent example of a strong conceptual testing paradigm in social neuroendocrinology work with animal models is gonadectomizing individuals and then reinstating hormones through external administration. This allows to bring hormone concentrations under experimental control and study their causal effects on, for instance, sexual preference, mating behavior, parenting, or aggression. This approach is typically combined with robust testing paradigms imported from other subdisciplines (e.g., learning psychology, ethology, neuroscience; see, for instance, Nelson, 2011).

Because gonadectomy, combined with hormonal reinstatement, is not a research approach feasible with human participants, options are more limited in human social neuroendocrinology. Naturally occurring variations in hormone levels, such as circadian rhythms, during the menstrual cycle, or in the transition from fertility to menopause, can serve as alternatives, again for well-established a priori reasons. But they do not allow the same strong causal inferences that can be drawn from purely experimental animal models. Moreover, for studies trying to exploit menstrual cycle effects, there is the difficulty of determining cycle phase (Blake, Dixson, O'Dean, & Denson, 2016). And this line of research is not immune to the dangers of false-positive science, as reflected by the discussions surrounding menstrual cycle "effects" on political preferences (Durante, Rae, & Griskevicius, 2013; Gelman & Carlin, 2014), mate preferences (Gildersleeve, Haselton, & Fales, 2014; Harris, Pashler, & Mickes, 2014), or clothing style (Blake, Dixson, O'Dean, & Denson, 2017; Eisenbruch, Simmons, & Roney, 2015). Still, as several chapters in this volume document, if used prudently, the natural-variation approach can yield systematic insights into neuroendocrinological phenomena such as interhemispheric coupling (Hausmann & Burt, this volume), memory and decision-making (Hampson, this volume), or emotional and motivational processes (Gingnell, Hornung, & Derntl, this volume; Diekhof, Reimers, & Holtfrerich, this volume).

One strong testing paradigm available not only to researchers working with animals, but also to those working with humans, is the administration of exogenous hormones, sometimes combined with the temporary pharmacological suppression of endogenous hormones. Although the validity of such methods is still an issue of debate in the case of peptides like oxytocin (see above; Leng & Ludwig, 2016), this method is viable for steroid hormones, whose free, unbound fraction readily passes the blood-brain barrier. Thus, the mechanism by which steroid administration affects the brain are well understood, and there is evidence of its efficacy using physiological indicators. For instance, testosterone can be administered orally and its effects on genital function have been documented (e.g., Corona et al., 2017; Tuiten et al., 2000). Moreover, testosterone administration can be combined with the administration of a gonadotropin-releasing-hormone antagonist, which results in a downregulation of the hypothalamic-pituitary-gonadal axis (Goetz et al., 2014). This treatment transiently reduces gonadal (endogenous) testosterone release to hypogonadal levels, making the experimental paradigm akin to animal studies using gonadectomy with subsequent exogenous hormone reinstatement.

Other well-documented hormone-manipulation interventions include the downregulation of the hypothalamic-pituitary-adrenal axis through dexamethasone suppression (also termed "chemical adrenalectomy"; Lupien & McEwen, 1997, p. 21) or, conversely, the simulation of a strong stress response through the administration of hydrocortisone (e.g., Schwabe, Tegenthoff, Hoffken, & Wolf, 2010). Of course, both approaches can be combined to mimic animal studies in which the hormone-producing gland is removed and hormone levels are then restored through exogenous hormone administration (Lupien & McEwen, 1997). Overall (steroid) hormone administration studies, particularly when coupled with transient glandular suppression, provide excellent testing paradigms with well-described underlying mechanisms of hormone function and proven effects on relevant outcome measures. Note, however, that this does not necessarily imply that all targeted outcomes will be affected in a hypothesized manner or that this research is immune to low statistical power, undisclosed flexibility, or publication bias. Our argument is that when these obstacles to greater scientific rigor are removed, the hormone administration/suppression approach represents a well-described, mechanistic tool for elucidating causal mechanisms of hormones in social neuroendocrinology.

Sometimes strong testing paradigms are also the result of a serendipitous observation, backed up by highly consistent empirical replications, like in the case of the Trier Social Stress Test (TSST, Kirschbaum, Pirke, & Hellhammer, 1993). In the TSST, the experimenter asks research participants to first prepare (anticipation period, 10 min) and then actually give an impromptu job application presentation in front of an unresponsive panel of two confederates of the experimenter (5 min). Subsequently, participants also perform a math task in front of the panel by counting down from 1,022 in steps of 13. If they make a mistake, a panel member asks them to start over again from 1,022 (5 min). Saliva or blood samples taken before (baseline, anticipation), during (speech, math task), and after the TSST show a robust and strong cortisol increase starting during the anticipation period, peaking about 40 min after TSST onset and returning to baseline levels about 90 min after TSST onset (Goodman, Janson, & Wolf, 2017; Kirschbaum et al., 1993). (The TSST also elicits strong responses for other hormonal and psychophysiological parameters such as prolactin, growth hormone, heart rate, or blood pressure.)

In general, salivary cortisol levels rise two- to threefold in the majority of participants (Kudielka, Hellhammer, & Kirschbaum, 2007), thus making the stress-axis effect elicited by the TSST a large-sized one. This suggests that the social-evaluative stress that characterizes the testing situation in the TSST is a near universal elicitor of strong endocrine responses in humans. Goodman et al.'s (2017) meta-analysis of the effect of the TSST on cortisol responses yields a large effect size of $d = 0.925$, based on the within-subject comparison between the pre-TSST baseline and post-TSST saliva samples (see also Dickerson & Kemeny, 2004). This suggests that in studies assessing TSST-induced cortisol changes within subjects, a sample size of nine participants would be sufficient to detect the stress-induced cortisol effect with a probability of 80% at $p < .05$. For a 90% probability, a total sample size of 12 would be sufficient. The size of the TSST effect is all the more remarkable as it goes in a direction opposite to the circadian cortisol drop during waking hours usually observed over assessments covering similar time spans as the TSST procedure. Adding a non-stressful control group therefore will typically yield similar or even higher effect sizes when comparing cortisol concentrations in samples collected after the end of the TSST and control procedures (e.g., Wiemers, Schultheiss, & Wolf, 2015). Thus, the TSST represents a robust paradigm for stimulating a strong, highly replicable endocrine stress response by psychological means.

Due to its robustness, the TSST is now a frequently used method for exploring stress responses and their relationship with other factors, such as gender differences, age, mental health, social support, or immunological changes (see Kudielka, Hellhammer, & Wüst, 2009; Kudielka & Zänkert, this volume; Rohleder, this volume). We think it is notable that so far the TSST represents the only testing paradigm in which a standardized psychological situation produces such a robust hormonal response. Similarly strong psychological-stimulation paradigms for other hormones, such as testosterone, estradiol, and progesterone, but also peptides like oxytocin or vasopressin, are sorely missing so far, and their development remains an important task for future research in social neuroendocrinology.

Conclusion and recommendations

So far in this chapter, we have chronicled the replication crisis in science, with a particular focus on the behavioral sciences and the core reasons for why the crisis came about. We have pointed out that a combination of factors on the side of journals (valuing novel, significant, strong-effect findings over replications or null results, even if based on methodologically rigorous studies) and researchers (underpowered studies, combined with undisclosed flexibility in analyzing and reporting results) has fueled this crisis by producing findings that cannot be replicated. We have shown by example that social neuroendocrinology is not immune to findings that have been difficult to replicate, but also pointed out that there are clear-cut cases of solid, replicable research built on conceptually or empirically strong testing paradigms. All is not lost, so to speak. But what can researchers in our field do to improve the quality of future studies and insure that false-positive findings are minimized?

We propose that the royal road to a better science of social neuroendocrinology is based on Chambers's (2017) model of registered studies. This approach requires authors, in a first stage, to undergo peer review of a proposed study, justifying its importance and necessity, listing and justifying the hypotheses, and detailing its methods. Requests by editors and reviewers for changes regarding the theory or the methods can be addressed in subsequent revision(s), until in-principle acceptance is given. Only then can the study author start collecting data. In a second review stage, the originally involved editor and reviewers then evaluate the final paper (now including results and discussion sections), verifying that the study has been conducted as approved and that results are presented and discussed in line with the originally proposed hypotheses. The paper can also include additional, post-hoc exploratory analyses clearly labeled as such. At this second stage, editors and reviewers can also request revisions. The final revised paper is then published. The most important aspect of registered reports is, however, that in-principle acceptance is not based on the results of a study (whether they are significant, have large effect sizes, etc.), *but on the merit of the question it tries to answer and the rigor of the methods it employs.* Registered reports thus represent a complete departure from the de facto model of scientific review and publishing, which was always overfocused on outcomes. To the extent that this model, which we deem to be the best one presently available, is gradually adopted by journals and researchers in our field, one important goal will be to monitor whether it generates unintended side effects. After all, the traditional model of publishing, which gave rise to the present reproducibility crisis, was not implemented to generate false positives. Yet it did. Incentives and their boundary conditions can sometimes generate truly weird side effects, as Skinner's (1948) famous case of superstitious behavior in pigeons illustrates.

Realistically, however, it may take a while until the journals that social neuroendocrinologists typically publish their work in will adopt the full-blown registered-study approach championed by Chambers (2017). And even if they do, at least initially this is unlikely to be a requirement for all submitted studies but rather an optional feature. In the meantime, what else can be done to enhance the quality of science in our field? We suggest the following measures might be helpful.

Preregister studies

Even if the journals you usually submit your work to do not feature full preregistration in the sense of peer review of the proposed study and its rationale and methods, you can preregister your research plan, your hypotheses, and your planned analyses in a time-stamped manner on sites such as http://aspredicted.org or http://osf.io. However, it is crucial that you be as specific as possible with regard to the hypotheses, targeted sample size and its power-analysis justification, independent and dependent variables (in the case of experimental paradigms) or measured variables (in the case of correlational research designs), analyses, and dealing with outliers and exclusions (see http://datacolada.org/64). This way, you can ensure that when the research is done and you are about to submit your work to a journal of your choice, editors and reviewers can evaluate the merits of your actual findings vis-à-vis your original research plan.

Run power analyses

Before you run a study, do a power analysis based on earlier research in your own laboratory or published studies with a similar focus, but keeping in mind that these may be biased towards larger effects than what would be realistic (see our discussion above about journal publishing biases). If there are no published or unpublished effect sizes to go by, assume a mean effect size of $r = .21$ (which corresponds to about $d = .43$) as typically found in published social-psychology studies (Richard et al., 2003). If your laboratory is unable to test samples of the sizes suggested by your power analyses, consider engaging in a multi-site collaboration with other labs (for an example, see Knight et al., submitted). Report your a priori power analysis in your method section, including whatever reasons made you deviate from it.

Practice open science

Make your data set, including raw data, and analysis scripts available in commonly accessible formats such as text files (.txt) or generic delimited file formats (e.g.,. csv) so that others can reanalyze your data or test their own hypotheses on your data. If you publish open access (OA), which we would recommend, you can submit these files as a supplement with your manuscript. If you submit your work to a subscription-only, paywalled journal, make sure your data and analysis scripts are publicly available through, for instance, the open science framework (http://osf.io). Be sure to reference these files through a permanent link in your published manuscript. Also, if your research materials and paradigms were programmed on and presented via a computer, make those scripts available, too, so that others can replicate your work or make use of whatever ingenuous idea for testing and assessment you may have developed in your own work.

Use the best available methods

With best available methods we refer to the best-validated research designs and measures (see our discussion of strong paradigms above and Schultheiss et al., this volume). Methods and measures of questionable validity can be a means to the end of hidden flexibility, "enabling" findings that would not emerge, or emerge differently, if more valid methods and measures had been used.

Run and value replication studies

If you think that your own or someone else's work in a particular area is so interesting or important that a lot could hinge upon whether the findings can be replicated or not, do a preregistered, properly powered, and methodologically rigorous replication study. If the original study was pretty rigorous to start with, do an exact replication. If it left methodological wriggle room (see our previous point), improve upon it and aim at making the replication as rigorous as possible. Regardless of the study's results, try to get the replication published and do not be deterred if some journals state that they are not interested in replication studies. Submit and submit again, and you will eventually find a journal with a sufficiently enlightened editorship. If it is not a replication of your own work but someone else's, confer with the authors of the original study before running the replication study. This can help ensure that you know everything there is to know about the original study and its methods and hence your ability to do a direct replication.

Of course, this also applies in reverse: if someone tries to replicate your own studies and contacts you with a request for more information, your very first response should be to thank those researchers for deeming your work important enough to warrant the effort, regardless of the outcome, and provide whatever information and materials are requested.

Carefully conducted, methodologically rigorous replication studies may or may not replicate the original finding. Such outcomes should not be misconstrued as verdicts of the scientific integrity of the authors of the original finding or the replicating team. Even when the best methods are used, samples are adequately powered, and all data and materials have been shared openly, neither false positives nor false negatives can ever be conclusively ruled out due to the fundamentally probabilistic nature of statistical prediction in the behavioral sciences. And sometimes a critical moderator may have eluded all contributing author teams so far. Inconsistent results should therefore be the starting point for further, ideally collaborative, replication work and aim at resolving the issue through more studies. They should not be a cause for doubting others' skills and integrity as scientists. Indeed, we think the latter way of thinking is due to our currently prevailing academic publishing practices that place a premium on the outcome of research. We believe that shifting to registered reports will also alter the standards by which scientists will be judged in the future, with a focus then on the kind of questions that are asked and the methods that are employed.

Change the standards of evaluation

The recommendations we make here are neither entirely new nor unique. Others have presented similar arguments and recommendations before us, and often more comprehensively and thoughtfully than we could do in the brevity of this chapter (see, for instance, Chambers, 2017; Ioannidis, Fanelli, Dunne, & Goodman, 2015; Munafo et al., 2017; Simmons et al., 2011). But they require, as a consequence, a sea change in how we evaluate science and scientists in the future. We need to stop valuing the churning out of many publications built on spectacular but ultimately non-replicable findings from studies with low statistical power or other methodological drawbacks. Instead, we need to start valuing carefully crafted research that is methodologically rigorous, sufficiently powered, up-front about its goals and methods via preregistration, and transparent with regard to the data collected and analyses performed. We also need to value research programs that focus a substantial part of their effort on internal and external replications and that thus contribute to building a more solid foundation of empirical knowledge. The "new" approach to doing science we espouse here will be more labor-intensive and perhaps yield publications at a slower pace. But it comes with the great advantage that those fewer publications will eventually advance science more than publications generated under the "old" approach. This should and will have important consequences for socializing undergraduate students, graduate students, and postdocs into academia, for the standards of good science we communicate to them, and of course for hiring and tenure decisions. Under the "old" standards, committees would screen candidates for number of publications, citation frequency, and acquired external funding. With the new approach we endorse here, committees should still look for productivity and relevance, but focus more on the following indicators for their evaluations:

- Are there published registered reports on the candidate's portfolio? These would signal that other scientists deemed the research important enough to endorse its execution, regardless of the outcome.
- Does the candidate employ rigorous methods, as reflected in preregistration, explicitly reported a priori power analyses, full disclosure of all experimental conditions, methods, exclusions, and data-analytic decisions?
- Does the candidate make her or his data sets, analysis scripts, and method materials freely available by submitting them as supplements to the publication or depositing them on internet repositories dedicated to open science practices, to the extent allowed by law?

The more a candidate's portfolio provides affirmative answers to these questions – less so by the time someone is hired for a tenure-track position, more so when the person is up for tenure – the more likely the candidate's research program is built on a solid foundation and will therefore make lasting contributions. We need to change the academic culture in this direction, in science in general and in social neuroendocrinology in particular.

References

Ainsworth, M.D.S., & Bell, S.M. (1970). Attachment, exploration, and separation: Illustrated by the behavior of one-year-olds in a strange situation. *Child Development, 41*(1), 49–67. doi:10.2307/1127388

Bakker, M., van Dijk, A., & Wicherts, J.M. (2012). The rules of the game called psychological science. *Perspectives on Psychological Science, 7*(6), 543–554. doi:10.1177/1745691612459060

Begley, C.G., & Ellis, L.M. (2012). Drug development: Raise standards for preclinical cancer research. *Nature, 483*(7391), 531–533. doi:10.1038/483531a

Bem, D.J. (2003). Writing the empirical journal article. In J.M. Darley, M.P. Zanna, & H.L. Roediger (Eds.), *The compleat academic: A career guide.* Washington, DC: American Psychological Association.

Bem, D.J. (2011). Feeling the future: Experimental evidence for anomalous retroactive influences on cognition and affect. *Journal of Personality and Social Psychology, 100*(3), 407–425. doi:10.1037/a0021524

Bennett, C.M., Miller, M., & Wolford, G. (2009). Neural correlates of interspecies perspective taking in the post-mortem Atlantic Salmon: An argument for multiple comparisons correction. *Neuroimage, 47*(Suppl. 1), S125.

Blake, K.R., Dixson, B.J.W., O'Dean, S.M., & Denson, T.F. (2016). Standardized protocols for characterizing women's fertility: A data-driven approach. *Hormones and Behavior, 81*(Suppl. C), 74–83. https://doi.org/10.1016/j.yhbeh.2016.03.004

Blake, K.R., Dixson, B.J.W., O'Dean, S.M., & Denson, T.F. (2017). No compelling positive association between ovarian hormones and wearing red clothing when using multinomial analyses. *Hormones and Behavior, 90*(Suppl. C), 129–135. https://doi.org/10.1016/j.yhbeh.2017.03.005

Button, K.S., Ioannidis, J.P., Mokrysz, C., Nosek, B.A., Flint, J., Robinson, E.S., & Munafo, M.R. (2013). Power failure: Why small sample size undermines the reliability of neuroscience. *Nature Reviews: Neuroscience, 14*(5), 365–376. doi:10.1038/nrn3475

Camerer, C.F., Dreber, A., Forsell, E., Ho, T-H., Huber, J., Johannesson, M., . . . Wu, H. (2016). Evaluating replicability of laboratory experiments in economics. *Science, 351*(6280), 1433–1436. doi:10.1126/science.aaf0918

Carney, D.R. (undated). *My position on "power poses."* Retrieved from http://faculty.haas.berkeley.edu/dana_carney/pdf_Dana%20Carney%20CV%201-23-17.pdf

Carney, D.R., Cuddy, A.J.C., & Yap, A.J. (2010). Power posing: Brief nonverbal displays affect neuroendocrine levels and risk tolerance. *Psychological Science, 21*(10), 1363–1368. doi:10.1177/0956797610383437

Carney, D.R., Cuddy, A.J.C., & Yap, A.J. (2015). Review and summary of research on the embodied effects of expansive (vs. contractive) nonverbal displays. *Psychological Science, 26*(5), 657–663. doi:10.1177/0956797614566855

Carter, C.S., Pournajafi-Nazarloo, H., Kramer, K.M., Ziegler, T.E., White-Traut, R., Bello, D., & Schwertz, D. (2007). Oxytocin: Behavioral associations and potential as a salivary biomarker. *Annals of the New York Academy of Sciences, 1098*, 312–322. doi:1098/1/312 [pii] 10.1196/annals.1384.006

Chambers, C. (2017). *The 7 deadly sins of psychology: A manifesto for reforming the culture of scientific practice.* Princeton, NJ: Princeton University Press.

Cohen, J. (1962). The statistical power of abnormal-social psychological research: A review. *Journal of Abnormal Social Psychology, 65*, 145–153.

Cohen, J. (1992). A power primer. *Psychological Bulletin, 112*, 155–159.

Corona, G., Rastrelli, G., Morgentaler, A., Sforza, A., Mannucci, E., & Maggi, M. (2017). Meta-analysis of results of testosterone therapy on sexual function based on international index of erectile function scores. *European Urology, 72*, 1000–1011. https://doi.org/10.1016/j.eururo.2017.03.032

Crede, M., & Phillips, L.A. (2017). Revisiting the power pose effect: How robust are the results reported by Carney, Cuddy, and Yap (2010) to data analytic decisions? *Social Psychological and Personality Science, 8*(5), 493–499. doi:10.1177/1948550617714584

Cuddy, A.J.C., Schultz, S.J., & Fosse, N.E. (2018). P-curving a more comprehensive body of research on postural feedback reveals clear evidential value for power-posing effects: Reply to Simmons and Simonsohn (2017). *Psychological Science, 29*(4), 656–666. doi:10.1177/0956797617746749

Davis, M.L., Papini, S., Rosenfield, D., Roelofs, K., Kolb, S., Powers, M.B., & Smits, J.A.J. (2017). A randomized controlled study of power posing before public speaking exposure for social anxiety disorder: No evidence for augmentative effects. *Journal of Anxiety Disorders, 52*(Suppl. C), 1–7. https://doi.org/10.1016/j.janxdis.2017.09.004

De Dreu, C.K.W., Greer, L.L., Handgraaf, M.J.J., Shalvi, S., van Kleef, G.A., Baas, M., . . . Feith, S.W.W. (2010). The neuropeptide oxytocin regulates parochial altruism in intergroup conflict among humans. *Science, 328*(5984), 1408–1411. doi:10.1126/science.1189047

Dehaene, S. (2014). *Consciousness and the brain: Discovering how the brain codes our thoughts.* New York, NY: Penguin Books.

Dickerson, S.S., & Kemeny, M.E. (2004). Acute stressors and cortisol responses: A theoretical integration and synthesis of laboratory research. *Psychological Bulletin, 130*(3), 355–391.

Durante, K.M., Rae, A., & Griskevicius, V. (2013). The fluctuating female vote: Politics, religion, and the ovulatory cycle. *Psychological Science, 24*(6), 1007–1016. doi:10.1177/0956797612466416

Eisenbruch, A.B., Simmons, Z.L., & Roney, J.R. (2015). Lady in red: Hormonal predictors of women's clothing choices. *Psychological Science, 26*(8), 1332–1338. doi:10.1177/0956797615586403

Freedman, L.P., Cockburn, I.M., & Simcoe, T.S. (2015). The economics of reproducibility in preclinical research. *PLoS Biology, 13*(6), e1002165. doi:10.1371/journal.pbio.1002165

Garcia, J., & Koelling, R.A. (1966). Relation of cue to consequence in avoidance learning. *Psychonomic Science, 4*(1), 123–124. doi:10.3758/bf03342209

Garrison, K.E., Tang, D., & Schmeichel, B.J. (2016). Embodying power: A preregistered replication and extension of the power pose effect. *Social Psychological and Personality Science, 7*(7), 623–630. doi:10.1177/1948550616652209

Gelman, A., & Carlin, J. (2014). Beyond power calculations: Assessing type S (Sign) and type M (Magnitude) errors. *Perspectives on Psychological Science, 9*(6), 641–651. doi:10.1177/1745691614551642

Gildersleeve, K., Haselton, M.G., & Fales, M.R. (2014). Do women's mate preferences change across the ovulatory cycle? A meta-analytic review. *Psychological Bulletin, 140*(5), 1205–1259. doi:10.1037/a0035438

Goetz, S.M.M., Tang, L., Thomason, M.E., Diamond, M.P., Hariri, A.R., & Carré, J.M. (2014). Testosterone rapidly increases neural reactivity to threat in healthy men: A novel two-step pharmacological challenge paradigm. *Biological Psychiatry, 76*(4), 324–331. https://doi.org/10.1016/j.biopsych.2014.01.016

Goodman, W.K., Janson, J., & Wolf, J.M. (2017). Meta-analytical assessment of the effects of protocol variations on cortisol responses to the Trier Social Stress Test. *Psychoneuroendocrinology, 80*(Suppl. C), 26–35. https://doi.org/10.1016/j.psyneuen.2017.02.030

Greenwald, A.G. (1975). Consequences of prejudice against the null hypothesis. *Psychological Bulletin, 82*(1), 1–20.

Gronau, Q.F., van Erp, S., Heck, D.W., Cesario, J., Jonas, K.J., & Wagenmakers, E-J. (2017). A Bayesian model-averaged meta-analysis of the power pose effect with informed and default priors: The case of felt power. *Comprehensive Results in Social Psychology, 2*(1), 123–138. doi:10.1080/23743603.2017.1326760

Güth, W., Schmittberger, R., & Schwarze, B. (1982). An experimental analysis of ultimatum bargaining. *Journal of Economic Behavior & Organization, 3*(4), 367–388. https://doi.org/10.1016/0167-2681(82)90011-7

Harris, C.R. (2017). *Rigor mortis: How sloppy science creates worthless cures, crushes hope, and wastes billions.* New York, NY: Basic Books.

Harris, C.R., Pashler, H., & Mickes, L. (2014). Elastic analysis procedures: An incurable (but preventable) problem in the fertility effect literature. Comment on Gildersleeve, Haselton, and Fales (2014). *Psychological Bulletin, 140*(5), 1260–1264. doi:10.1037/a0036478

Hattie, J. (2008). *Visible learning: A synthesis of over 800 meta-analyses relating to achievement.* New York, NY: Routledge.

Horvat-Gordon, M., Granger, D.A., Schwartz, E.B., Nelson, V.J., & Kivlighan, K.T. (2005). Oxytocin is not a valid biomarker when measured in saliva by immunoassay. *Physiology and Behavior, 84*(3), 445–448.

Hurlemann, R., Patin, A., Onur, O.A., Cohen, M.X., Baumgartner, T., Metzler, S., . . . Kendrick, K.M. (2010). Oxytocin enhances amygdala-dependent, socially reinforced learning and emotional empathy in humans. *The Journal of Neuroscience, 30*(14), 4999–5007. doi:10.1523/jneurosci.5538-09.2010

Ioannidis, J.P.A. (2005). Why most published research findings are false. *PLoS Medicine, 2*(8), e124. doi:04-PLME-E-0321R2 [pii] 10.1371/journal.pmed.0020124

Ioannidis, J.P.A. (2008). Why most discovered true associations are inflated. *Epidemiology, 19*(5), 640–648. doi:10.1097/EDE.0b013e31818131e7

Ioannidis, J.P.A., Fanelli, D., Dunne, D.D., & Goodman, S.N. (2015). Meta-research: Evaluation and improvement of research methods and practices. *PLOS Biology, 13*(10), e1002264. doi:10.1371/journal.pbio.1002264

John, L.K., Loewenstein, G., & Prelec, D. (2012). Measuring the prevalence of questionable research practices with incentives for truth telling. *Psychological Science, 23*(5), 524–532. doi:10.1177/0956797611430953

Kerr, N.L. (1998). HARKing: Hypothesizing after the results are known. *Personality and Social Psychology Review, 2*(3), 196–217. doi:10.1207/s15327957pspr0203_4

Kirschbaum, C., Pirke, K.M., & Hellhammer, D.H. (1993). The "Trier Social Stress Test" – a tool for investigating psychobiological stress responses in a laboratory setting. *Neuropsychobiology, 28*(1–2), 76–81.

Knight, E.L., Kutlikova, H.H., Morales, P.J., Christian, C.B., Harbaugh, W.T., Mayr, U., . . . Carré, J.M. (submitted for publication). *No robust effect of exogenous testosterone on cognitive reflection in three experiments.*

Kosfeld, M., Heinrichs, M., Zak, P.J., Fischbacher, U., & Fehr, E. (2005). Oxytocin increases trust in humans. *Nature, 435*(7042), 673–676.

Kudielka, B.M., Hellhammer, D.H., & Kirschbaum, C. (2007). Ten years of research with the Trier Social Stress Test–Revisited. In E. Harmon-Jones & P. Winkielman (Eds.), *Social neuroscience: Integrating biological and psychological explanations of social behavior* (pp. 56–83). New York, NY: Guilford Press.

Kudielka, B.M., Hellhammer, D.H., & Wüst, S. (2009). Why do we respond so differently? Reviewing determinants of human salivary cortisol responses to challenge. *Psychoneuroendocrinology, 34*(1), 2–18. doi:S0306-4530(08)00264-3 [pii] 10.1016/j.psyneuen.2008.10.004

Lakens, D. (2014). Performing high-powered studies efficiently with sequential analyses. *European Journal of Social Psychology, 44*(7), 701–710. doi:10.1002/ejsp.2023

Lane, A., Luminet, O., Nave, G., & Mikolajczak, M. (2016). Is there a publication bias in behavioural intranasal oxytocin research on humans? Opening the file drawer of one laboratory. *Journal of Neuroendocrinology, 28*(4), n/a–n/a. doi:10.1111/jne.12384

Lane, A., Luminet, O., Rimé, B., Gross, J.J., de Timary, P., & Mikolajczak, M. (2013). Oxytocin increases willingness to socially share one's emotions. *International Journal of Psychology, 48*(4), 676–681. doi:10.1080/00207594.2012.677540

Lane, A., Mikolajczak, M., Treinen, E., Samson, D., Corneille, O., de Timary, P., & Luminet, O. (2015). Failed replication of oxytocin effects on trust: The envelope task case. *PLoS One, 10*(9), e0137000. doi:10.1371/journal.pone.0137000

LeDoux, J.E. (1996). *The emotional brain.* New York, NY: Simon and Schuster.

LeDoux, J.E. (2002). *The synaptic self.* New York, NY: Viking.

Leng, G., & Ludwig, M. (2016). Intranasal oxytocin: Myths and delusions. *Biological Psychiatry, 79*(3), 243–250. https://doi.org/10.1016/j.biopsych.2015.05.003

Loken, E., & Gelman, A. (2017). Measurement error and the replication crisis. *Science, 355*(6325), 584–585. doi:10.1126/science.aal3618

Luminet, O., Grynberg, D., Ruzette, N., & Mikolajczak, M. (2011). Personality-dependent effects of oxytocin: Greater social benefits for high alexithymia scorers. *Biological Psychology, 87*(3), 401–406. https://doi.org/10.1016/j.biopsycho.2011.05.005

Lupien, S.J., & McEwen, B.S. (1997). The acute effects of corticosteroids on cognition: Integration of animal and human model studies. *Brain Research Reviews, 24*(1), 1–27. https://doi.org/10.1016/S0165-0173(97)00004-0

MacLeod, C.M. (1991). Half a century of research on the Stroop effect: An integrative review. *Psychological Bulletin, 109*, 163–203.

Maes, E., Boddez, Y., Alfei, J.M., Krypotos, A-M., D'Hooge, R., De Houwer, J., & Beckers, T. (2016). The elusive nature of the blocking effect: 15 failures to replicate. *Journal of Experimental Psychology: General, 145*(9), e49–e71. doi:10.1037/xge0000200

McClelland, D.C., Davis, W.N., Kalin, R., & Wanner, E. (1972). *The drinking man.* New York, NY: Free Press.

Meehl, P.E. (1967). Theory-testing in psychology and physics: A methodological paradox. *Philosophy of Science*, 103–115.

Mikolajczak, M., Gross, J.J., Lane, A., Corneille, O., de Timary, P., & Luminet, O. (2010). Oxytocin makes people trusting, not gullible. *Psychological Science, 21*(8), 1072–1074. doi:10.1177/0956797610377343

Mikolajczak, M., Pinon, N., Lane, A., de Timary, P., & Luminet, O. (2010). Oxytocin not only increases trust when money is at stake, but also when confidential information is in the balance. *Biological Psychology, 85*(1), 182–184. https://doi.org/10.1016/j.biopsycho.2010.05.010

Mischel, W., Shoda, Y., & Rodriguez, M.L. (1989). Delay of gratification in children. *Science, 244*, 933–938.

Munafo, M.R., Nosek, B.A., Bishop, D.V.M., Button, K.S., Chambers, C.D., Percie du Sert, N., . . . Ioannidis, J.P.A. (2017). A manifesto for reproducible science. *Nature Human Behaviour, 1*, 0021. doi:10.1038/s41562-016-0021

Nelson, R.J. (2011). *An introduction to behavioral endocrinology* (4th ed.). Sunderland, MA: Sinauer Associates Inc.

Open Science, C. (2015). Estimating the reproducibility of psychological science. *Science, 349*(6251), aac4716. doi:10.1126/science.aac4716

Oxford, J.K., Tiedtke, J.M., Ossmann, A., Özbe, D., & Schultheiss, O.C. (2017). Endocrine and aggressive responses to competition are moderated by contest outcome, gender, individual versus team competition, and implicit motives. *PLoS One, 12*(7), e0181610. doi:10.1371/journal.pone.0181610

Prinz, F., Schlange, T., & Asadullah, K. (2011). Believe it or not: How much can we rely on published data on potential drug targets? *Nature Reviews Drug Discovery, 10*(9), 712. doi:10.1038/nrd3439-c1

Ranehill, E., Dreber, A., Johannesson, M., Leiberg, S., Sul, S., & Weber, R.A. (2015). Assessing the robustness of power posing: No effect on hormones and risk tolerance in a large sample of men and women. *Psychological Science, 26*(5), 653–656. doi:10.1177/0956797614553946

Richard, F.D., Bond, C.F.J., & Stokes-Zoota, J.J. (2003). One hundred years of social psychology quantitatively described. *Review of General Psychology, 74*(4), 331–363. doi:10.1037/1089-2680.7.4.331

Ronay, R., Tybur, J.M., van Huijstee, D., & Morssinkhof, M. (2017). Embodied power, testosterone, and overconfidence as a causal pathway to risk-taking. *Comprehensive Results in Social Psychology, 2*(1), 28–43. doi:10.1080/23743603.2016.1248081

Rosenthal, R., & Rosnow, R. L. (Eds.). (1969). *Artifact in behavioral research.* New York, NY: Academic Press.

Schultheiss, O.C. (2013). Effects of sugarless chewing gum as a stimulant on progesterone, cortisol, and testosterone concentrations assessed in saliva. *International Journal of Psychophysiology, 87*, 111–114. doi:10.1016/j.ijpsycho.2012.11.012

Schultheiss, O.C., Campbell, K.L., & McClelland, D.C. (1999). Implicit power motivation moderates men's testosterone responses to imagined and real dominance success. *Hormones and Behavior, 36*(3), 234–241.

Schultheiss, O.C., & Rohde, W. (2002). Implicit power motivation predicts men's testosterone changes and implicit learning in a contest situation. *Hormones and Behavior, 41*, 195–202.

Schultheiss, O.C., Wirth, M.M., Torges, C.M., Pang, J.S., Villacorta, M.A., & Welsh, K.M. (2005). Effects of implicit power motivation on men's and women's implicit learning and testosterone changes after social victory or defeat. *Journal of Personality and Social Psychology, 88*(1), 174–188.

Schwabe, L., Tegenthoff, M., Hoffken, O., & Wolf, O.T. (2010). Concurrent glucocorticoid and noradrenergic activity shifts instrumental behavior from goal-directed to habitual control. *Journal of Neuroscience, 30*(24), 8190–8196. doi:10.1523/JNEUROSCI.0734-10.2010

Seligman, M.E.P. (1970). On the generality of the laws of learning. *Psychological Review, 77*, 406–428.

Simmons, J.P., Nelson, L.D., & Simonsohn, U. (2011). False-positive psychology: Undisclosed flexibility in data collection and analysis allows presenting anything as significant. *Psychological Science, 22*(11), 1359–1366. doi:0956797611417632 [pii] 10.1177/0956797611417632

Simmons, J.P., & Simonsohn, U. (2017). Power posing: P-curving the evidence. *Psychological Science, 28*(5), 687–693. doi:10.1177/0956797616658563

Skinner, B.F. (1948). "Superstition" in the pigeon. *Journal of Experimental Psychology, 38*, 168–172.

Smith, K.M., & Apicella, C.L. (2017). Winners, losers, and posers: The effect of power poses on testosterone and risk-taking following competition. *Hormones and Behavior, 92*(Suppl. C), 172–181. https://doi.org/10.1016/j.yhbeh.2016.11.003

Smith, N.C. (1970). Replication studies: A neglected aspect of psychological research. *American Psychologist, 25*(10), 970–975. doi:10.1037/h0029774

Stanton, S.J. (2011). The essential implications of gender in human behavioral endocrinology studies. *Frontiers in Behavioral Neuroscience, 5*, 9. doi:10.3389/fnbeh.2011.00009

Stanton, S.J., & Schultheiss, O.C. (2007). Basal and dynamic relationships between implicit power motivation and estradiol in women. *Hormones and Behavior, 52*(5), 571–580. doi:S0018-506X(07)00163-8 [pii] 10.1016/j.yhbeh.2007.07.002

Sternberg, R.J. (2003). *The psychologist's companion: A guide to scientific writing for students and researchers* (4th ed.). Cambridge: Cambridge University Press.

Tuiten, A., van Honk, J., Koppeschaar, H., Bernaards, C., Thijssen, J., & Verbaten, R. (2000). Time course of effects of testosterone administration on sexual arousal in women. *Archives of General Psychiatry, 57*(2), 149–153; discussion 155–146.

Van Breukelen, G. J. (2006). ANCOVA versus change from baseline: More power in randomized studies, more bias in nonrandomized studies [corrected]. *Journal of Clinical Epidemiology, 59*(9), 920–925.

Valstad, M., Alvares, G.A., Egknud, M., Matziorinis, A.M., Andreassen, O.A., Westlye, L.T., & Quintana, D.S. (2017). The correlation between central and peripheral oxytocin concentrations: A systematic review and meta-analysis. *Neuroscience & Biobehavioral Reviews, 78*(Suppl. C), 117–124. https://doi.org/10.1016/j.neubiorev.2017.04.017

Vongas, J.G., & Al Hajj, R. (2017). The effects of competition and implicit power motive on men's testosterone, emotion recognition, and aggression. *Hormones and Behavior, 92*, 57–71. doi:10.1016/j.yhbeh.2017.04.005

Vul, E., Harris, C., Winkielman, P., & Pashler, H. (2009). Puzzlingly high correlations in fMRI studies of emotion, personality, and social cognition. *Perspectives on Psychological Science, 4*, 274–290.

Wagenmakers, E.J., Wetzels, R., Borsboom, D., & van der Maas, H.L.J. (2011). Why psychologists must change the way they analyze their data: The case of psi: Comment on Bem (2011). *Journal of Personality and Social Psychology, 100*(3), 426–432. doi:10.1037/a0022790

Walum, H., Waldman, I.D., & Young, L.J. (2016). Statistical and methodological considerations for the interpretation of intranasal oxytocin studies. *Biological Psychiatry, 79*(3), 251–257. https://doi.org/10.1016/j.biopsych.2015.06.016

Welker, K.M., Lassetter, B., Brandes, C.M., Prasad, S., Koop, D.R., & Mehta, P.H. (2016). A comparison of salivary testosterone measurement using immunoassays and tandem mass spectrometry. *Psychoneuroendocrinology, 71*, 180–188. https:// doi.org/10.1016/j.psyneuen.2016.05.022

Wiemers, U.S., Schultheiss, O.C., & Wolf, O.T. (2015). Public speaking in front of an unreceptive audience increases implicit power motivation and its endocrine arousal signature. *Hormones and Behavior, 71*, 69–74. doi:10.1016/j.yhbeh.2015.04.007

Winter, D.G. (1994). *Manual for scoring motive imagery in running text* (4th ed.). Ann Arbor: Department of Psychology, University of Michigan, Unpublished manuscript.

Wirth, M.M., Welsh, K.M., & Schultheiss, O.C. (2006). Salivary cortisol changes in humans after winning or losing a dominance contest depend on implicit power motivation. *Hormones and Behavior, 49*(3), 346–352.

SECTION 2

Dominance and aggression

4

LEVERAGING SEASONALITY IN MALE SONGBIRDS TO BETTER UNDERSTAND THE NEUROENDOCRINE REGULATION OF VERTEBRATE AGGRESSION

Douglas W. Wacker

For any stimulus there is some probability that an animal will respond aggressively, whether with warnings, threats, attacks, or some combination thereof (Wingfield, Moore, Goymann, Wacker, & Sperry, 2006). This response can be viewed as the result of a decision based on two interdependent, non-mutually exclusive factors: (1) an animal's immediate context, including its current social and environmental setting, and (2) its physiological, morphological, and behavioral state (Greenberg, Howerton, & Trainor, 2014; Jacobs & Wingfield, 2000; Wingfield et al., 2006). An animal's state is dependent upon its evolutionary history, development (including epigenetic modifications), previous experiences, and current seasonal life history stage (Bester-Meredith & Marler, 2001; Crews, 2003; Cushing & Kramer, 2005; Jacobs & Wingfield, 2000; Provençal et al., 2013; Wingfield et al., 2006). Social behaviors, including aggression, are modulated by intersecting, steroid-sensitive neural circuits in vertebrates, including the social behavior network and mesolimbic reward system, together forming the social decision-making network (Goodson, 2005; S.W. Newman, 1999; O'Connell & Hofmann, 2012) (Table 4.1). Investigations into how predictable seasonal changes in these networks affect an animal's propensity to show aggressive behavior are necessary complements to experimental manipulations where specific signaling constituents are altered in isolation from other neural mechanisms that work in concert to alter behavior under normal conditions. Owing to the conservation of the social decision-making network across vertebrates, insights gained by studying seasonal state changes in songbirds have and will continue to illuminate the mechanisms of aggression in all vertebrates, including humans (Goodson, 2005; Maney & Goodson, 2011; Miczek, Fish, Joseph, & De Almeida, 2002; O'Connell & Hofmann, 2012).

History and value of avian models of aggression

There are numerous reviews that define types of animal aggression, often based on their function (e.g., Moyer, 1968; Nelson & Trainor, 2007; Wingfield et al., 2006). Here, I primarily discuss

Table 4.1 Brain regions discussed in this chapter, with an emphasis on nodes of the social decision-making network (SDN)

Abbreviation	Full name
AH	anterior hypothalamus
BSTl	bed nucleus of the stria terminalis, lateral division
BSTm	bed nucleus of the stria terminalis, medial division
cmTEL	central medial telencephalon (includes BST, LS, pvMSt)
periaqueductal grey	PAG, dorsal PAG is avian ICO, *see Goodson and Kingsbury (2013)*
LS	lateral septum
MeA	medial amygdala (TnA in birds)
NAcc	nucleus accumbens
POM or mPOA	medial preoptic area
POA	preoptic area
pvMSt	periventricular nucleus of medial striatum
PVN	paraventricular nucleus of the hypothalamus
TnA	nucleus taeniae of the amygdala (akin to mammalian MeA)
VMH	ventromedial nucleus of the hypothalamus
vmTEL	ventromedial telencephalon (includes TnA)
VTA	ventral tegmental area

male *territorial aggression*, where animals initiate behaviors in defense of territorial resources. Songbirds are especially amenable to studies of naturally occurring territorial aggression, as they are typically diurnal and express aggressive behaviors that are readily quantifiable in the field (Nice, 1964; Sperry, Wacker, & Wingfield, 2010; Wingfield & Hahn, 1994). The territorial song sparrow (*Melospiza melodia*) is an exemplar of songbird aggression. Male song sparrows use postures, movements, and vocalizations (points, feather puffs, wing waves, gapes, bill wipes, calls, songs) as well as attack behaviors (aggressive flights, strikes, fights) during conflicts (Nice, 1964; Wacker, Schlinger, & Wingfield, 2008; Wingfield & Hahn, 1994). Songbird aggression can be induced experimentally in the field via simulated territorial intrusion (STI), where a caged male decoy and speaker playing conspecific song are placed within a known territory and the latency to aggression, number of aggressive flights, number of songs, closest approach, and proximity to the decoy are assessed (Wingfield & Hahn, 1994) (Figure 4.1A). Some behaviors, such as feather puffing and wing waving, while observable, are not easily quantified in the field. These behaviors can be assessed with a laboratory-based simulated territorial intrusion (labSTI), where Nice's behavioral descriptions are retooled into a composite aggression score (Sperry et al., 2010; Wacker et al., 2016; Wacker et al., 2008) (Figure 4.1B). Other studies have used simplified metrics to gauge aggressiveness in the laboratory, including counting the number of contacts with a barrier separating cages of two rivals during an aggression test (Heimovics, Ferris, & Soma, 2015). Here, I will refer to all lab-based aggression tests involving a live decoy and conspecific song playback as labSTIs.

Some behaviors listed in Figure 4.1 may be considered *warning* behaviors that signal an animal's fighting ability (Wingfield et al., 2006). If one subscribes to a definition of aggression that necessarily involves physical altercation, then these behaviors may not always be aggressive, as they can serve to reduce the probability of attack. For example, Nowicki, Searcy, and Hughes (1998) removed male song sparrows from adjoining territories, and then played recorded conspecific song on one of the vacated locations; subsequent invasions occurred earlier or only on

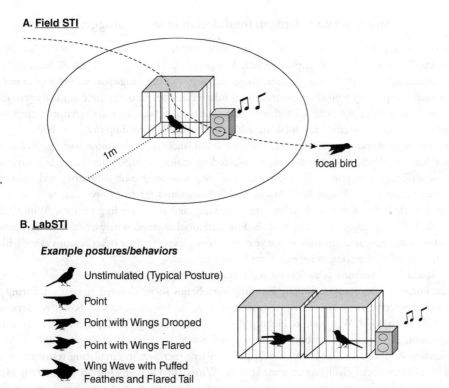

A. **Field STI**

1m

focal bird

B. **LabSTI**

Example postures/behaviors

Unstimulated (Typical Posture)

Point

Point with Wings Drooped

Point with Wings Flared

Wing Wave with Puffed
Feathers and Flared Tail

Figure 4.1 (A) In a field simulated territorial intrusion (STI), flights towards, closest approach to, and time
spent within 1m and 5m from a live caged male decoy and speaker playing conspecific song
are quantified for a male song sparrow on its territory. (B) In a labSTI, postures and behaviors
observable but difficult to quantify in the field are assessed for a male within its home cage
when challenged by a rival male in a neighboring cage and conspecific song playback. The
number of songs sung by the focal male is recorded in both behavioral tests. Based on Nice
(1964); Sperry et al. (2010); Wacker et al. (2008); Wingfield & Hahn (1994).

territories without playback, suggesting that song can reduce the probability of territorial intrusion. Such warning behavior is not restricted to birds. In perhaps the most well-known mammalian example, male red deer (*Cervus elaphus*) engage in roaring and parallel walking contests,
which only sometimes lead to actual fighting (Clutton-Brock & Albon, 1979). Other behaviors
may serve as a *threat*, which indicates not only the individual's status but also his intention to
attack (Nice, 1964). Song sometimes serves this purpose. Male song sparrows sing different
song types (sometimes matching a rival), change their song rate, perform variants of songs, and
use low amplitude soft song in territorial conflicts (Akçay, Tom, Campbell, & Beecher, 2013;
Searcy, Anderson, & Nowicki, 2006; Templeton, Akçay, Campbell, & Beecher, 2012). In male
song sparrows stimulated with song playback and then allowed to interact with a conspecific
taxidermy mount near the playback speaker, only the number of soft songs was related to subsequent attack on the mount (Searcy et al., 2006). Other research shows that song type matching
can also predict future attack in this species (Akçay et al., 2013). The extent to which the neural
and endocrine modulation of warning, threat, and attack overlap has not been fully elucidated.
Still, the many behaviors observed during agonistic interactions between rival male song sparrows allow for a richer understanding of the expression of territorial aggression.

Androgen and estrogen modulation of seasonal aggression

Territorial aggression varies across seasons/photoperiods in many vertebrates (Cavigelli & Pereira, 2000; Garrett & Campbell, 1980; Wingfield & Hahn, 1994; Wise & Jaeger, 2016). Seasonal aggression in the Pacific Northwest subspecies of the song sparrow (*Melospiza melodia morphna*) is especially well characterized. This subspecies goes through three annually repeating, seasonal life history stages associated with differential expression of male territorial aggression and circulating testosterone levels (Wingfield & Hahn, 1994). Breeding males are highly aggressive and have elevated circulating testosterone levels, molting males show low aggression and have low circulating testosterone, and non-breeding males are highly aggressive but have very low circulating testosterone. This subspecies of song sparrow is non-migratory and holds territories year-round (Wingfield & Hahn, 1994). Sometimes territories remain static across an annual cycle, other times they differ across breeding and non-breeding periods (Wingfield & Monk, 1992). So although some non-breeding territorial aggression may be related to maintaining breeding territories for later in the year, it is clearly expressed for other reasons as well, likely in defense of food resources necessary for winter survival.

Gonadal testosterone is associated with heightened male aggression in multiple vertebrate taxa. For example, many seasonally breeding vertebrates show elevated aggression during the breeding season when circulating testosterone is at its height (Gordon, Rose, & Bernstein, 1976; Lincoln, 1971; Wingfield & Hahn, 1994), castration during development can reduce male aggression in adulthood in some animals (Berthold & Quiring, 1944; Jewell, 1997; Lincoln, Guinness, & Short, 1972; Moore, 1987), and transient increases in circulating testosterone can be induced by social challenge in some species (Wingfield, Hegner, Dufty, & Ball, 1990). However, gonadal androgens are not always necessary for the activation of male aggression, as adult castration does not always reduce it (Caldwell, Glickman, & Smith, 1984; Trainor & Marler, 2001; Wingfield, 1994). Also, juvenile song sparrows, whose testes have yet to mature, respond aggressively to challenge, and adult males in the non-breeding season display robust aggression with regressed gonads and very low levels (≤ 0.01 ng/ml) of circulating testosterone (Wingfield, 1994; Wingfield & Hahn, 1994).

Wingfield, Lynn, and Soma (2001) proposed non-mutually exclusive hypotheses for circulating testosterone-independent aggression in non-breeding male song sparrows, including a "circulating precursor hypothesis" and "testosterone hypersensitivity hypothesis." Both hypotheses have been validated. The circulating precursor hypothesis predicts that a peripherally produced androgen/estrogen precursor travels to the brain where region-specific conversion to more bioactive steroids facilitates aggression, but not breeding behavior. DHEA is a testosterone/estrogen precursor produced in multiple locations, including the testes, adrenals, liver, and brain (A.E. Newman & Soma, 2011; Soma & Wingfield, 2001). Circulating DHEA levels are elevated in song sparrow life history stages associated with high aggression (breeding and non-breeding) as compared to those associated with low aggression (molt) (Soma & Wingfield, 2001). This association of DHEA and aggression is also observed in other avian species. DHEA levels in the cloacal fluid correlate with non-breeding territorial aggression in Anna's hummingbird (*Calypte anna*), and plasma DHEA levels are correlated with non-breeding aggression in response to STI in spotted antbirds (*Hylophylax naevioides*) (González-Gómez et al., 2014; Hau, Stoddard, & Soma, 2004). DHEA may also facilitate non-breeding aggression in red squirrels (*Tamiasciurus hudsonicus*) (Boonstra et al., 2008) and American alligators (*Alligator mississippiensis*) (Hamlin, Lowers, & Guillette, 2011), but more work needs to be done. Considering their phylogenetic relationship to birds, continued work on crocodilians would be valuable, but is restricted due to logistic and existential constraints. That DHEA levels are positively correlated with non-breeding aggression in multiple species suggests that this hormone may be involved in the facilitation of such behavior.

Consistent with Wingfield et al.'s circulating precursor hypothesis, evidence suggests that DHEA increases song sparrow aggression, at least in part, via conversion to 17β-estradiol (Heimovics, Trainor, & Soma, 2015; Soma, Tramontin, & Wingfield, 2000). This conversion can happen quickly, allowing birds to respond to threats immediately. For example, a 30-minute field-based STI increases aggression and the activity of 3β-hydroxysteroid dehydrogenase/Δ5–4 isomerase (3β-HSD), the enzyme that catalyzes transformation of DHEA to androstenedione, in the central medial and caudal telencephalon of non-breeding male song sparrows (Pradhan et al., 2010). Then, the activity of the enzyme aromatase, which catalyzes the transformation of androgens to estrogens, can be rapidly activated, facilitating aggression (Balthazart, Baillien, & Ball, 2001; Heimovics, Trainor et al., 2015). Interestingly, rapid, estrogen-mediated increases in aggression occur in non-breeding, but not breeding song sparrows, suggesting a seasonal difference in the physiological regulation of aggression in this species (Heimovics, Ferris et al., 2015). Such seasonal life history stage-specific effects of estrogen on aggression are not specific to birds. For example, cyclodextrin-conjugated estradiol (cE2) rapidly increases male aggression in castrated, testosterone-treated California mice (*Peromyscus californicus*), but only in animals held on short days (breeding stage), and not long days (non-breeding stage) (Trainor, Finy, & Nelson, 2008). DHEA is an important circulating androgen/estrogen precursor involved in the modulation of territorial aggression, and its effects can vary with the seasonal life history stage of an animal.

DHEA can also enhance sensitivity to androgens and estrogens by up-regulating the expression of their receptors. Resulting hypersensitivity to neurosteroids in regions of the social decision-making network may then facilitate the expression of non-breeding aggression in the absence of high circulating testosterone levels (Wacker et al., 2016; Wingfield et al., 2001). Consistent with Wingfield et al.'s testosterone hypersensitivity hypothesis, chronic (14-day) administration of DHEA concomitantly increases brain region-specific neural androgen receptor expression and aggression in non-breeding male song sparrows. DHEA-induced increases in androgen receptor mRNA in the pvMSt and aromatase mRNA in the POA and are consistent with seasonal differences in expression associated with naturally elevated DHEA levels (Wacker et al., 2016; Wacker, Wingfield, Davis, & Meddle, 2010). This suggests that circulating DHEA, transported to the brain at elevated levels during breeding and non-breeding life history stages, is converted to bioactive androgens and estrogen, which can then act directly on androgen and estrogen response elements to upregulate androgen receptor and aromatase mRNA expression in areas of the social decision-making network. Transcriptional autoregulation of androgen receptor expression by testosterone and regulation of aromatase expression by estrogen is well established in vertebrates (Fraley, Steiner, Lent, & Brenowitz, 2010; Fusani, Van't Hof, Hutchison, & Gahr, 2000; Lu, McKenna, Cologer-Clifford, Nau, & Simon, 1998; Tan et al., 1988). When circulating DHEA is lower during the molt, it would not be predicted to induce the same transcriptional changes, thereby leading to reduced androgen binding and estrogen availability and lower aggression during this life history stage.

As an animal's physiological, morphological, and behavioral state is dependent upon its current life history stage, it is not surprising that the effects of systemically administered, steroid signaling and synthesis inhibitors on aggression can vary seasonally. In male song sparrows, the androgen receptor antagonist, flutamide, is effective at reducing breeding, but not non-breeding aggression in a labSTI (Sperry et al., 2010). Interestingly, flutamide only decreases one measure of aggression in a field STI (aggressive flights), and only during the early breeding period. Flutamide also increases the latency to aggression in breeding, but not non-breeding male European robins (*Erithacus rubecula*) (Schwabl & Kriner, 1991). Evidence suggests that changes in seasonal aggression are also related to estrogen availability. Fadrozole, an inhibitor of estrogen synthesis, significantly decreases non-breeding, but not breeding song sparrow aggression in response to a field-based STI (Soma, Sullivan et al., 2000). It is possible that the administered dose of fadrozole was incapable of reducing high levels of estrogen synthesis facilitated by high circulating androgen levels in the breeding males. Alternatively, it may be that breeding aggression is under different neural control than non-breeding aggression, resulting in fadrozole being less effective. The latter hypothesis is consistent with the observation that aromatase mRNA expression differs in breeding vs. non-breeding song sparrows in some areas of the social decision-making network (Wacker et al., 2010). Fadrozole's effects on aggression also vary seasonally in other taxa. Fadrozole reduces short-day (breeding stage) but increases long-day (non-breeding) aggression in castrated male beach mice (*Peromyscus polionotus*) given exogenous testosterone (Trainor, Lin, Finy, Rowland, & Nelson, 2007). Conversely, fadrozole increases aggression in short-day (breeding stage), castrated, male California mice, but only in animals housed with Carefresh paper bedding, not those housed with corncob bedding, which may interfere with estrogen signaling (Landeros et al., 2012). Interestingly, fadrozole *increases* aggression in non-breeding male song sparrows in a labSTI (Wacker et al., 2008). This apparent discrepancy in fadrozole's effects on song sparrow aggression in the field vs. lab may be related to the type of behaviors measured in each study (Sperry et al., 2010; Wacker et al., 2008). Postures and behaviors quantified in the labSTI (e.g., points, wing waving) may represent warning behavior, while behaviors assessed in the field (e.g., flights towards a decoy and closest approach) may be more indicative of threat or attack. Again, these facets of aggression may be under different neural and endocrine control. These studies suggest that the careful examination of seasonal, population, taxonomic, and environmental differences are necessary to expand our understanding of the mechanisms underlying aggressive behavior.

Neuroendocrine modulation of seasonal aggression

The social decision-making network is a well-conserved set of interconnected brain regions that mediates changes in social behavior across vertebrate taxa (Table 4.1) (Crews, 2003; Goodson, 2005; Goodson & Kingsbury, 2013; Nelson & Trainor, 2007; S.W. Newman, 1999; O'Connell & Hofmann, 2012). These brain regions are either sensitive to or connected to regions sensitive to androgens and estrogens (Chakraborty & Burmeister, 2010; Forlano, Marchaterre, Deitcher, & Bass, 2010; Rosen, O'bryant, Matthews, Zacharewski, & Wade, 2002; Simerly, Chang, Muramatsu, & Swanson, 1990; Wacker et al., 2010). Seasonal/photoperiodic changes in the expression and activity of steroidogenic enzymes and sex steroid receptors in the social decision-making network are common (Aggarwal, Goswami, Khandelwal, & Sehgal, 2014; Santillo, Falvo, Di Fiore, & Baccari, 2017; Soma, Schlinger, Wingfield, & Saldanha, 2003; Trainor, Rowland, & Nelson, 2007; Wacker et al., 2010; Zhang et al., 2016). In male song sparrows, aromatase and androgen receptor mRNA expression are upregulated during breeding in multiple locations within the social decision-making network (Wacker et al., 2010). Within the VMH, a brain region implicated in the regulation of male aggression in rodents, aromatase expression is highest during breeding and non-breeding when aggression is also high (Falkner, Grosenick, Davidson, Deisseroth, & Lin, 2016; Wacker et al., 2010). Interestingly, no seasonal differences in the expression of estrogen receptor α or β were detected in any brain region examined in song sparrows (Wacker et al., 2010). This observation, coupled with the seasonal dependence of rapid estrogen-mediated increases in aggression leaves open the possibility that fast-acting membrane- (e.g., mER) and/or endoplasmic reticulum-associated (e.g., GPER/GPR30) estrogen receptors are more potent modulators of non-breeding vs breeding aggression (Heimovics, Ferris et al., 2015; Heimovics, Trainor et al., 2015; Qiu, Rønnekleiv, & Kelly, 2008; Revankar, Cimino, Sklar, Arterburn, & Prossnitz, 2005; Wacker et al., 2010). GPER was recently characterized in the zebra finch (*Taeniopygia guttata*) (Acharya & Veney, 2012), but mER, as of this writing, has not been identified in birds. Seasonal comparisons of GPER and mER, as well as proteins mediating ERα and β's potential associations with the cell membrane and metabotropic glutamate receptors (Mermelstein, 2009; Seredynski, Balthazart, Ball, & Cornil, 2015), are sorely needed to assess their role in the seasonal modulation of aggression.

Regions of the social decision-making network are populated by neuropeptide systems known to mediate changes in vertebrate social behaviors, including aggression (Kelly & Vitousek, 2017; Kingsbury & Wilson, 2016). For example, vasotocin (homolog of mammalian vasopressin) and vasoactive intestinal polypeptide (VIP), and their receptors have been described in regions of the social decision-making network in a multitude of vertebrate species, and signaling by these neuropeptides has been implicated in the regulation of aggression (Bester-Meredith & Marler, 2001; Dai, Swaab, & Buijs, 1997; Goodson, 1998a, 1998b; Goodson, Kelly, Kingsbury, & Thompson, 2012; Goodson, Wilson, & Schrock, 2012; Wilson, Goodson, & Kingsbury, 2016). These neuropeptide systems are sensitive to androgens and estrogens, so these steroids may induce changes to aggression, at least in part, via their modulation (Aste, Viglietti-Panzica, Balthazart, & Panzica, 1997; Grozhik et al., 2014; Scordalakes & Rissman, 2004; Wacker et al., 2008). There is evidence for such regulation. For example, exogenous testosterone increases vasopressin 1a receptor (v1ar) expression in AH, BSTm, POM, PVN, and VMH, and increases singing, and calling behavior in non-breeding, male white-throated sparrows (*Zonotrichia albicollis*) (Grozhik et al., 2014). Inhibition of estrogen synthesis by fadrozole increases non-breeding male song sparrow aggression in the labSTI, while decreasing VIP-ir in rostral regions of LS (Wacker et al., 2008). Similar to androgen and estrogen signaling systems, neuropeptide signaling machinery within the social decision-making network can vary seasonally, and the nature of such changes differs across avian species, likely relating to specific life history strategies (Goodson, Wilson et al., 2012; Wilson et al., 2016). In male song sparrows in the Midwestern United States that show non-breeding territoriality (*Melospiza melodia melodia*), VIP-ir is reduced during non-breeding versus breeding in the AH, BSTm, NAcc, POM, PVN, VTA, and subdivisions of the LS (Goodson, Wilson et al., 2012). Field sparrows (*Spizella pusilla*), which flock during non-breeding, do not show as robust non-breeding decreases in VIP-ir in PVN or BSTm, and no decrease in AH. VIP binding also varies by season in Emberizid sparrows, with breeding vs. non-breeding differences detected across multiple species in AH, BSTm, MeA, POM, and PVN, but not VMH (Wilson et al., 2016).

Molt has received less attention in seasonal comparisons of avian neuropeptide systems, at least as it relates to reduced aggression. Vasotocin-ir is lower in molting (low circulating testosterone) versus breeding (high testosterone) male canaries (*Serinus canaria*), but the function of this difference has not been explored in detail (Voorhuis, De Kloet, & De Wied, 1991). There is a well-established relationship between increased neural VIP and the photorefractory period, which is associated with molt in multiple species of seasonally breeding birds (Deviche, Saldanha, & Silver, 2000; Saldanha, Deviche, & Silver, 1994; Sharp, 2005). In male song sparrows, administration of fadrozole decreases VIP-ir in the ventral forebrain island/lateral septum organ of LS, an effect that is reversed in birds co-administered DHEA (Wacker et al., 2008). Levels of DHEA are lower in this species during the molt, when aggression in also low (Soma & Wingfield, 2001). How neuropeptide signaling systems change across life history stages, and how this variation may relate to androgen/estrogen-dependent aggression, especially reductions during molt, requires continued study.

Leveraging seasonality to better understand the neuroendocrine regulation of aggression

The seasonal modulation of territorial aggression involves a myriad of rapid activational and longer-term neural changes, which may include changes in the expression of sex steroid synthesis/signaling molecules (Wacker et al., 2010) and neuropeptide signaling machinery (Goodson, Wilson et al., 2012; Wilson et al., 2016), activity of steroidogenic enzymes and production of brain-region specific neurosteroids (Balthazart et al., 2001; Charlier, Cornil, Ball, & Balthazart, 2010; Heimovics, Prior, Ma, & Soma, 2016; Pradhan et al., 2010), availability of cofactors involved in steroid synthesis and receptor binding (Charlier et al., 2010; Pradhan et al., 2010), trafficking towards and activation of "genomic" estrogen receptors at the cell surface (Dominguez & Micevych, 2010; Heimovics, Trainor et al., 2015), and the expression and activation of fast-acting androgen and estrogen receptors (Heimovics, Trainor et al., 2015). It is not fully understood how all of these effects combine to facilitate appropriate seasonal life history stage changes in male territorial aggression in the Pacific Northwest song sparrow. However, a fairly extensive seasonal profile of steroid signaling and aggression has been established for this species (Table 4.2). Once such a seasonal profile is available for an animal, one can use this information to deliberately target relevant endocrine and/or neural signals, brain areas/connections, etc. for experimental manipulation. One can then determine not only how such manipulations affect territorial aggression, but also how they alter the overall state of relevant signaling systems across the social decision-making network.

I have reviewed work outlining the role of androgens and estrogens, as well as the neuropeptides, vasotocin, and vasoactive intestinal polypeptide in the modulation of male territorial aggression, with an emphasis on seasonally breeding songbirds. Other hormonal and neural

Table 4.2 Seasonal differences in male territorial aggression and its endocrine/neuroendocrine modulation in the Pacific Northwest subspecies of the song sparrow (*Melospiza melodia morphna*). Seasonal differences can be leveraged to deliberately target endocrine and neuroendocrine signaling systems in subsequent experimental manipulations (Heimovics, Ferris et al., 2015; Heimovics, Prior et al., 2016; Pradhan et al., 2010; Soma, Schlinger, Wingfield, & Saldanha, 2003; Soma, Sullivan, et al., 2000; Soma, Tramontin, et al., 2000; Soma & Wingfield, 2001; Sperry, Wacker, & Wingfield, 2010; Wacker, Schlinger, & Wingfield, 2008; Wacker, Wingfield, Davis, & Meddle, 2010; Wingfield, 1994; Wingfield & Hahn, 1994).

	Breeding	Prebasic Molt	Non-breeding
Territorial Aggression			
during STI	high	low	high
after STI (persistence)	yes	no	no
Sex Steroids			
hormone levels			
testosterone (circulating)	high	low	low
17β-estradiol (circulating)	low	low	low
DHEA (circulating)	high	low	high
hormone manipulations			
flutamide (18 days)	decreases*	unassessed	no effect
fadrozole (1 day)	no effect	unassessed	decreases**
fadrozole (~10 days)	no effect	unassessed	decreases***
17β-estradiol (in food)	no effect	unassessed	rapidly increases

		Breeding	Prebasic Molt	Non-breeding
Neural – sex steroid receptors				
androgen receptor mRNA				
	POA	>	=	=
	pvMSt	>	=	=
ERα mRNA		no difference in any region examined		
ERβ mRNA		no difference in any region examined		
mER		*unassessed*		
GPER		*unassessed*		
Neural – steroidogenic enzymes				
aromatase mRNA				
	POA	>	=	=
	mPOA/BSTM	>	=	=
	VMH	=	<	=
aromatase activity				
	vmTEL (contains MeA)	=	<	=
	diencephalon	>	=	=
3β-HSD activity				
	cmTEL (contains BST, LS, pvMSt)	<	=	=
	vmTEL (contains MeA)	<	intermediate	>
Neural – neurosteroids				
Testosterone				
	AH	higher	*unassessed*	lower
	POA	higher	*unassessed*	lower
	MeA (TnA)	higher	*unassessed*	lower
17β-estradiol				
	AH	higher	*unassessed*	lower
	POA	higher	*unassessed*	lower
	MeA (TnA)	higher	*unassessed*	lower
DHEA		no difference in any region examined		
Neural – challenge-induced changes****				
Testosterone		no changes in any region examined		
17β-estradiol		no changes in any region examined		
DHEA				
	AH	decreases	*unassessed*	decreases
	MeA (TnA)	decreases	*unassessed*	no effect
	medial striatum (contains pvMSt)	decreases	*unassessed*	decreases
3β-HSD activity				
	cmTEL (contains BST, LS, pvMSt)	*unassessed*	*unassessed*	increases

* Flutamide reduces aggression in birds held on long days in the lab and aggressive flights during early breeding in the field.
** Fadrozole (1 day) decreases non-breeding aggression during, but not after a field STI.
*** Fadrozole (10 days) decreases non-breeding aggression during and after a field STI, but *increases* aggression in a labSTI.
**** In dominant males in a male-male dyad compared to subordinate and control birds (AH and MeA) or subordinate birds only (medial striatum) for testosterone, 17β-estradiol, and DHEA.

signals (glucocorticoids, oxytocin/mesotocin, serotonin, etc.) have and should also be considered in studies of vertebrate social behavior and its seasonal regulation. Much of this chapter has outlined work on free-living and wild animals. It is important to note that sample sizes in such studies tend to be smaller than those on laboratory-reared rodent models. Also, comparing animals across species and life history stages will yield more variation than is typically seen in research on genetically inbred stocks. While this variation is exactly what makes the comparative approach both interesting and valuable, it is critical that statistical power be carefully considered, especially in studies showing no differences in the variables examined. Publication of such "negative" findings and deliberate replication of studies should be encouraged to gain a more comprehensive understanding of complex social behavior. I advocate an approach where studies of seasonal state change are used to guide subsequent experimental manipulations to more fully understand the mechanisms of territorial aggression in free-living animals. Extending this approach to other social behaviors and to other taxonomic groups will allow for a more complete understanding of the multifaceted neuroendocrine modulation of sociality in vertebrates.

Literature cited

Acharya, K.D., & Veney, S.L. (2012). Characterization of the G-protein-coupled membrane-bound estrogen receptor GPR30 in the zebra finch brain reveals a sex difference in gene and protein expression. *Developmental Neurobiology, 72*(11), 1433–1446.

Aggarwal, N., Goswami, S.V., Khandelwal, P., & Sehgal, N. (2014). Aromatase activity in brain and ovary: Seasonal variations correlated with circannual gonadal cycle in the catfish, *Heteropneustes fossilis. Indian Journal of Experimental Biology, 52*, 527–537.

Akçay, Ç. l., Tom, M.E., Campbell, S.E., & Beecher, M.D. (2013). Song type matching is an honest early threat signal in a hierarchical animal communication system. *Proceedings of the Royal Society of London B: Biological Sciences, 280*(1756). doi:10.1098/rspb.2012.2517.

Aste, N., Viglietti-Panzica, C., Balthazart, J., & Panzica, G. (1997). Testosterone modulation of peptidergic pathways in the septo-preoptic region of male Japanese quail. *Poultry and Avian Biology Reviews, 8*(2), 77–94.

Balthazart, J., Baillien, M., & Ball, G.F. (2001). Phosphorylation processes mediate rapid changes of brain aromatase activity. *The Journal of Steroid Biochemistry and Molecular Biology, 79*(1), 261–277.

Berthold, A.A., & Quiring, D. (1944). The transplantation of testes. *Bulletin of the History of Medicine, 16*, 399–401.

Bester-Meredith, J.K., & Marler, C.A. (2001). Vasopressin and aggression in cross-fostered California mice (*Peromyscus californicus*) and white-footed mice (*Peromyscus leucopus*). *Hormones and Behavior, 40*(1), 51–64.

Boonstra, R., Lane, J.E., Boutin, S., Bradley, A., Desantis, L., Newman, A.E., & Soma, K.K. (2008). Plasma DHEA levels in wild, territorial red squirrels: Seasonal variation and effect of ACTH. *General and Comparative Endocrinology, 158*(1), 61–67.

Caldwell, G.S., Glickman, S.E., & Smith, E.R. (1984). Seasonal aggression independent of seasonal testosterone in wood rats. *Proceedings of the National Academy of Sciences, 81*(16), 5255–5257.

Cavigelli, S.A., & Pereira, M.E. (2000). Mating season aggression and fecal testosterone levels in male ringtailed lemurs (*Lemur catta*). *Hormones and Behavior, 37*(3), 246–255.

Chakraborty, M., & Burmeister, S.S. (2010). Sexually dimorphic androgen and estrogen receptor mRNA expression in the brain of túngara frogs. *Hormones and Behavior, 58*(4), 619–627.

Charlier, T.D., Cornil, C.A., Ball, G.F., & Balthazart, J. (2010). Diversity of mechanisms involved in aromatase regulation and estrogen action in the brain. *Biochimica et Biophysica Acta (BBA)-General Subjects, 1800*(10), 1094–1105.

Clutton-Brock, T.H., & Albon, S.D. (1979). The roaring of red deer and the evolution of honest advertisement. *Behaviour, 69*(3), 145–170.

Crews, D. (2003). The development of phenotypic plasticity: Where biology and psychology meet. *Developmental Psychobiology, 43*(1), 1–10.

Cushing, B.S., & Kramer, K.M. (2005). Mechanisms underlying epigenetic effects of early social experience: The role of neuropeptides and steroids. *NeuroScience & Biobehavioral Reviews, 29*(7), 1089–1105.

Dai, J., Swaab, D.F., & Buijs, R.M. (1997). Distribution of Vasopressin and Vasoactive Intestinal Polypeptide (VIP) fibers in the human hypothalamus with special emphasis on suprachiasmatic nucleus efferent projections. *Journal of Comparative Neurology, 383*, 397–414.

Deviche, P., Saldanha, C.J., & Silver, R. (2000). Changes in brain gonadotropin-releasing hormone-and vasoactive intestinal polypeptide-like immunoreactivity accompanying reestablishment of photosensitivity in male dark-eyed juncos (*Junco hyemalis*). *General and Comparative Endocrinology, 117*(1), 8–19.

Dominguez, R., & Micevych, P. (2010). Estradiol rapidly regulates membrane estrogen receptor α levels in hypothalamic neurons. *Journal of Neuroscience, 30*(38), 12589–12596.

Falkner, A.L., Grosenick, L., Davidson, T.J., Deisseroth, K., & Lin, D. (2016). Hypothalamic control of male aggression-seeking behavior. *Nature Neuroscience, 19*(4), 596–604. doi:10.1038/nn.4264

Forlano, P.M., Marchaterre, M., Deitcher, D.L., & Bass, A.H. (2010). Distribution of androgen receptor mRNA expression in vocal, auditory, and neuroendocrine circuits in a teleost fish. *Journal of Comparative Neurology, 518*(4), 493–512.

Fraley, G.S., Steiner, R.A., Lent, K.L., & Brenowitz, E.A. (2010). Seasonal changes in androgen receptor mRNA in the brain of the white-crowned sparrow. *General and Comparative Endocrinology, 166*(1), 66–71.

Fusani, L., Van't Hof, T., Hutchison, J.B., & Gahr, M. (2000). Seasonal expression of androgen receptors, estrogen receptors, and aromatase in the canary brain in relation to circulating androgens and estrogens. *Developmental Neurobiology, 43*(3), 254–268.

Garrett, J.W., & Campbell, C.S. (1980). Changes in social behavior of the male golden hamster accompanying photoperiodic changes in reproduction. *Hormones and Behavior, 14*(4), 303–318.

González-Gómez, P.L., Blakeslee, W.S., Razeto-Barry, P., Borthwell, R.M., Hiebert, S.M., & Wingfield, J.C. (2014). Aggression, body condition, and seasonal changes in sex-steroids in four hummingbird species. *Journal of Ornithology, 155*(4), 1017–1025.

Goodson, J.L. (1998a). Territorial aggression and dawn song are modulated by septal vasotocin and vasoactive intestinal polypeptide in male field sparrows (*Spizella pusilla*). *Hormones and Behavior, 34*(1), 67–77.

Goodson, J.L. (1998b). Vasotocin and vasoactive intestinal polypeptide modulate aggression in a territorial songbird, the violet-eared waxbill (Estrildidae: *Uraeginthus granatina*). *General and Comparative Endocrinology, 111*(2), 233–244. doi:10.1006/gcen.1998.7112

Goodson, J.L. (2005). The vertebrate social behavior network: Evolutionary themes and variations. *Hormone and Behavior, 48*(1), 11–22. doi:10.1016/j.yhbeh.2005.02.003

Goodson, J.L., Kelly, A.M., Kingsbury, M.A., & Thompson, R.R. (2012). An aggression-specific cell type in the anterior hypothalamus of finches. *Proceedings of the National Academy of Sciences, 109*(34), 13847–13852.

Goodson, J.L., & Kingsbury, M.A. (2013). What's in a name? Considerations of homologies and nomenclature for vertebrate social behavior networks. *Hormones and Behavior, 64*(1), 103–112.

Goodson, J.L., Wilson, L.C., & Schrock, S.E. (2012). To flock or fight: Neurochemical signatures of divergent life histories in sparrows. *Proceedings of the National Academy of Sciences, 109*(Suppl. 1), 10685–10692.

Gordon, T.P., Rose, R.M., & Bernstein, I.S. (1976). Seasonal rhythm in plasma testosterone levels in the rhesus monkey (*Macaca mulatta*): A three year study. *Hormones and Behavior, 7*(2), 229–243.

Greenberg, G.D., Howerton, C.L., & Trainor, B.C. (2014). Fighting in the home cage: Agonistic encounters and effects on neurobiological markers within the social decision-making network of house mice (*Mus musculus*). *Neuroscience Letters, 566*, 151–155.

Grozhik, A.V., Horoszko, C.P., Horton, B.M., Hu, Y., Voisin, D.A., & Maney, D.L. (2014). Hormonal regulation of vasotocin receptor mRNA in a seasonally breeding songbird. *Hormones and Behavior, 65*(3), 254–263.

Hamlin, H.J., Lowers, R.H., & Guillette, L.J., Jr. (2011). Seasonal androgen cycles in adult male American alligators (*Alligator mississippiensis*) from a barrier island population. *Biology of Reproduction, 85*(6), 1108–1113.

Hau, M., Stoddard, S.T., & Soma, K.K. (2004). Territorial aggression and hormones during the non-breeding season in a tropical bird. *Hormones and Behavior, 45*(1), 40–49.

Heimovics, S.A., Ferris, J.K., & Soma, K.K. (2015). Non-invasive administration of 17β-estradiol rapidly increases aggressive behavior in non-breeding, but not breeding, male song sparrows. *Hormones and Behavior, 69*, 31–38.

Heimovics, S.A., Prior, N.H., Ma, C., & Soma, K.K. (2016). Rapid effects of an aggressive interaction on dehydroepiandrosterone, testosterone and oestradiol levels in the male song sparrow brain: A seasonal comparison. *Journal of Neuroendocrinology, 28*(2). doi:10.1111/jne.12345

Heimovics, S.A., Trainor, B.C., & Soma, K.K. (2015). Rapid effects of Estradiol on aggression in birds and mice: The fast and the furious. *Integrative and Comparative Biology, 55*(2), 281–293. doi:10.1093/icb/icv048

Jacobs, J.D., & Wingfield, J.C. (2000). Endocrine control of life-cycle stages: A constraint on response to the environment? *The Condor, 102*(1), 35–51.

Jewell, P. (1997). Survival and behaviour of castrated Soay sheep (*Ovis aries*) in a feral island population on Hirta, St. Kilda, Scotland. *Journal of Zoology, 243*(3), 623–636.

Kelly, A.M., & Vitousek, M.N. (2017). Dynamic modulation of sociality and aggression: An examination of plasticity within endocrine and neuroendocrine systems. *Philosophical Transactions of the Royal Society B, 372*(1727). doi:10.1098/rstb.2016.0243

Kingsbury, M.A., & Wilson, L.C. (2016). The role of VIP in social behavior: Neural hotspots for the modulation of affiliation, aggression, and parental care. *Integrative and Comparative Biology, 56*(6), 1238–1249.

Landeros, R.V., Morisseau, C., Yoo, H.J., Fu, S.H., Hammock, B.D., & Trainor, B.C. (2012). Corncob bedding alters the effects of estrogens on aggressive behavior and reduces estrogen receptor-α expression in the brain. *Endocrinology, 153*(2), 949–953.

Lincoln, G. (1971). The seasonal reproductive changes in the red deer stag (*Cervus elaphus*). *Journal of Zoology, 163*(1), 105–123.

Lincoln, G., Guinness, F., & Short, R. (1972). The way in which testosterone controls the social and sexual behavior of the red deer stag (*Cervus elaphus*). *Hormones and Behavior, 3*(4), 375–396.

Lu, S-F., McKenna, S.E., Cologer-Clifford, A., Nau, E.A., & Simon, N.G. (1998). Androgen receptor in mouse brain: Sex differences and similarities in autoregulation. *Endocrinology, 139*(4), 1594–1601.

Maney, D.L., & Goodson, J.L. (2011). Neurogenomic mechanisms of aggression in songbirds. *Advances in Genetics, 75*, 83–119.

Mermelstein, P. (2009). Membrane-localised Oestrogen receptor α and β influence neuronal activity through activation of metabotropic Glutamate receptors. *Journal of Neuroendocrinology, 21*(4), 257–262.

Miczek, K.A., Fish, E.W., Joseph, F., & De Almeida, R.M. (2002). Social and neural determinants of aggressive behavior: Pharmacotherapeutic targets at serotonin, dopamine and γ-aminobutyric acid systems. *Psychopharmacology, 163*(3–4), 434–458.

Moore, M.C. (1987). Castration affects territorial and sexual behaviour of free-living male lizards, *Sceloporus jarrovi*. *Animal Behaviour, 35*(4), 1193–1199.

Moyer, K.E. (1968). Kinds of aggression and their physiological basis. *Communications in Behavioral Biology, 2*(2), 65–87.

Nelson, R.J., & Trainor, B.C. (2007). Neural mechanisms of aggression. *Nature Reviews Neuroscience, 8*(7), 536.

Newman, A.E., & Soma, K.K. (2011). Aggressive interactions differentially modulate local and systemic levels of corticosterone and DHEA in a wild songbird. *Hormones and Behavior, 60*(4), 389–396.

Newman, S.W. (1999). The medial extended amygdala in male reproductive behavior: A node in the mammalian social behavior network. *Annals of the New York Academy of Sciences, 877*, 242–257.

Nice, M.M. (1964). *Studies in the life history of the song sparrow*. New York, NY: Dover.

Nowicki, S., Searcy, W.A., & Hughes, M. (1998). The territory defense function of song in song sparrows: A test with the speaker occupation design. *Behaviour, 135*(5), 615–628.

O'Connell, L.A., & Hofmann, H.A. (2012). Evolution of a vertebrate social decision-making network. *Science, 336*(6085), 1154–1157.

Pradhan, D.S., Newman, A.E., Wacker, D.W., Wingfield, J.C., Schlinger, B.A., & Soma, K.K. (2010). Aggressive interactions rapidly increase androgen synthesis in the brain during the non-breeding season. *Hormones and Behavior, 57*(4), 381–389.

Provençal, N., Suderman, M.J., Caramaschi, D., Wang, D., Hallett, M., Vitaro, F., . . . Szyf, M. (2013). Differential DNA methylation regions in cytokine and transcription factor genomic loci associate with childhood physical aggression. *PLoS One, 8*(8), e71691. doi:10.1371/journal.pone.0071691

Qiu, J., Rønnekleiv, O.K., & Kelly, M.J. (2008). Modulation of hypothalamic neuronal activity through a novel G-protein-coupled estrogen membrane receptor. *Steroids, 73*(9), 985–991.

Revankar, C.M., Cimino, D.F., Sklar, L.A., Arterburn, J.B., & Prossnitz, E.R. (2005). A transmembrane intracellular estrogen receptor mediates rapid cell signaling. *Science, 307*(5715), 1625–1630.

Rosen, G., O'Bryant, E., Matthews, J., Zacharewski, T., & Wade, J. (2002). Distribution of androgen receptor mRNA expression and immunoreactivity in the brain of the green anole lizard. *Journal of Neuroendocrinology, 14*(1), 19–28.

Saldanha, C.J., Deviche, P.J., & Silver, R. (1994). Increased VIP and decreased GnRH expression in photorefractory dark-eyed juncos (*Junco hyemalis*). *General and Comparative Endocrinology, 93*(1), 128–136.

Santillo, A., Falvo, S., Di Fiore, M.M., & Baccari, G.C. (2017). Seasonal changes and sexual dimorphism in gene expression of StAR protein, steroidogenic enzymes and sex hormone receptors in the frog brain. *General and Comparative Endocrinology, 246*, 226–232.

Schwabl, H., & Kriner, E. (1991). Territorial aggression and song of male European robins (*Erithacus rubecula*) in autumn and spring: Effects of antiandrogen treatment. *Hormones and Behavior, 25*(2), 180–194.

Scordalakes, E., & Rissman, E.F. (2004). Aggression and arginine vasopressin immunoreactivity regulation by androgen receptor and estrogen receptor α. *Genes, Brain and Behavior, 3*(1), 20–26.

Searcy, W.A., Anderson, R.C., & Nowicki, S. (2006). Bird song as a signal of aggressive intent. *Behavioral Ecology and Sociobiology, 60*(2), 234–241.

Seredynski, A.L., Balthazart, J., Ball, G.F., & Cornil, C.A. (2015). Estrogen receptor β activation rapidly modulates male sexual motivation through the transactivation of metabotropic glutamate receptor 1a. *Journal of Neuroscience, 35*(38), 13110–13123.

Sharp, P.J. (2005). Photoperiodic regulation of seasonal breeding in birds. *Annals of the New York Academy of Sciences, 1040*(1), 189–199.

Simerly, R.B., Chang, C., Muramatsu, M., & Swanson, L.W. (1990). Distribution of androgen and estrogen receptor mRNA-containing cells in the rat brain: An in situ hybridization study. *Journal of Comparative Neurology, 294*(1), 76–95. doi:10.1002/cne.902940107

Soma, K.K., Schlinger, B.A., Wingfield, J.C., & Saldanha, C.J. (2003). Brain aromatase, 5α-reductase, and 5β-reductase change seasonally in wild male song sparrows: Relationship to aggressive and sexual behavior. *Developmental Neurobiology, 56*(3), 209–221.

Soma, K.K., Sullivan, K.A., Tramontin, A.D., Saldanha, C.J., Schlinger, B.A., & Wingfield, J.C. (2000). Acute and chronic effects of an aromatase inhibitor on territorial aggression in breeding and nonbreeding male song sparrows. *Journal of Comparative Physiology A: Neuroethology, Sensory, Neural, and Behavioral Physiology, 186*(7), 759–769.

Soma, K.K., Tramontin, A.D., & Wingfield, J.C. (2000). Oestrogen regulates male aggression in the non-breeding season. *Proceedings of the Royal Society of London B: Biological Sciences, 267*(1448), 1089–1096.

Soma, K.K., & Wingfield, J.C. (2001). Dehydroepiandrosterone in songbird plasma: Seasonal regulation and relationship to territorial aggression. *General and Comparative Endocrinology, 123*(2), 144–155.

Sperry, T.S., Wacker, D.W., & Wingfield, J.C. (2010). The role of androgen receptors in regulating territorial aggression in male song sparrows. *Hormone and Behavior, 57*(1), 86–95. doi:10.1016/j.yhbeh.2009.09.015

Tan, J.-A., Joseph, D.R., Quarmby, V.E., Lubahn, D.B., Sar, M., French, F.S., & Wilson, E.M. (1988). The rat androgen receptor: Primary structure, autoregulation of its messenger ribonucleic acid, and immunocytochemical localization of the receptor protein. *Molecular Endocrinology, 2*(12), 1276–1285.

Templeton, C.N., Akçay, Ç., Campbell, S.E., & Beecher, M.D. (2012). Soft song is a reliable signal of aggressive intent in song sparrows. *Behavioral Ecology and Sociobiology, 66*(11), 1503–1509.

Trainor, B.C., Finy, M.S., & Nelson, R.J. (2008). Rapid effects of estradiol on male aggression depend on photoperiod in reproductively non-responsive mice. *Hormones and Behavior, 53*(1), 192–199.

Trainor, B.C., Lin, S., Finy, M.S., Rowland, M.R., & Nelson, R.J. (2007). Photoperiod reverses the effects of estrogens on male aggression via genomic and nongenomic pathways. *Proceedings of the National Academy of Sciences, 104*(23), 9840–9845.

Trainor, B.C., & Marler, C.A. (2001). Testosterone, paternal behavior, and aggression in the monogamous California mouse (*Peromyscus californicus*). *Hormones and Behavior, 40*(1), 32–42.

Trainor, B.C., Rowland, M.R., & Nelson, R.J. (2007). Photoperiod affects estrogen receptor α, estrogen receptor β and aggressive behavior. *European Journal of Neuroscience, 26*(1), 207–218.

Voorhuis, T., De Kloet, E., & De Wied, D. (1991). Ontogenetic and seasonal changes in immunoreactive vasotocin in the canary brain. *Developmental Brain Research, 61*(1), 23–31.

Wacker, D.W., Khalaj, S., Jones, L.J., Champion, T.L., Davis, J.E., Meddle, S.L., & Wingfield, J.C. (2016). Dehydroepiandrosterone (DHEA) heightens aggression and increases androgen receptor and aromatase mRNA expression in the brain of a male songbird. *Journal of Neuroendocrinology, 28*(12). doi:10.1111/jne.12443

Wacker, D.W., Schlinger, B.A., & Wingfield, J.C. (2008). Combined effects of DHEA and fadrozole on aggression and neural VIP immunoreactivity in the non-breeding male song sparrow. *Hormones and Behavior, 53*(1), 287–294.

Wacker, D.W., Wingfield, J.C., Davis, J.E., & Meddle, S.L. (2010). Seasonal changes in aromatase and androgen receptor, but not estrogen receptor mRNA expression in the brain of the free-living male song sparrow, Melospiza melodia morphna. *Journal of Comparative Neurology, 518*(18), 3819–3835.

Wilson, L.C., Goodson, J.L., & Kingsbury, M.A. (2016). Seasonal variation in group size is related to seasonal variation in neuropeptide receptor density. *Brain, Behavior and Evolution, 88*(2), 111–126.

Wingfield, J.C. (1994). Regulation of territorial behavior in the sedentary song sparrow, Melospiza melodia morphna. *Hormones and Behavior, 28*(1), 1–15.

Wingfield, J.C., & Hahn, T.P. (1994). Testosterone and territorial behaviour in sedentary and migratory sparrows. *Animal Behaviour, 47*(1), 77–89.

Wingfield, J.C., Hegner, R.E., Dufty, A.M., Jr., & Ball, G.F. (1990). The "challenge hypothesis": Theoretical implications for patterns of testosterone secretion, mating systems, and breeding strategies. *The American Naturalist, 136*(6), 829–846.

Wingfield, J.C., Lynn, S.E., & Soma, K.K. (2001). Avoiding the "costs" of testosterone: Ecological bases of hormone-behavior interactions. *Brain, Behavior and Evolution, 57*(5), 239–251.

Wingfield, J.C., & Monk, D. (1992). Control and context of year-round territorial aggression in the non-migratory song sparrow Zonotrichia melodia morphna. *Ornis Scandinavica*, 298–303.

Wingfield, J.C., Moore, I.T., Goymann, W., Wacker, D.W., & Sperry, T. (2006). Contexts and ethology of vertebrate aggression: Implications for the evolution of hormone-behavior interactions. In R.J. Nelson (Ed.), *Biology of aggression* (pp. 179–210). New York, NY: Oxford University Press.

Wise, S.E., & Jaeger, R.G. (2016). Seasonal and geographic variation in territorial conflicts by male red-backed salamanders. *Behaviour, 153*(2), 187–207.

Zhang, F., Wang, J., Jiao, Y., Zhang, L., Zhang, H., Sheng, X., . . . Weng, Q. (2016). Seasonal changes of androgen receptor, estrogen receptors and aromatase expression in the medial preoptic area of the wild male ground squirrels (*Citellus dauricus Brandt*). *European Journal of Histochemistry, 60*(2), 116–122.

5

BEHAVIORAL AND NEUROENDOCRINE PLASTICITY IN THE FORM OF WINNER AND LOSER EFFECTS

Nathaniel S. Rieger, Matthew J. Fuxjager, Brian C. Trainor,
Xin Zhao, and Catherine A. Marler

Introduction

The social lives of animals are complex. Individuals living in large populations must not only navigate a variety of affiliative relationships but also a wide range of adversarial ones (Oliveira, 2009). Furthermore, one's social landscape is always in flux, changing in response to time of year, population density, and other stochastic environmental perturbations. Accordingly, behavioral and physiological/neural mechanisms that support social agility and flexibility should evolve to allow individuals to fine-tune their behavior. One way that research has focused on this framework is by studying two related phenomena that epitomize behavioral and physiological plasticity: the winner effect and the loser effect.

The winner effect is defined as an ability to win fights following the acquisition of prior social victories, whereas the loser effect is defined as an increased propensity to lose fights following prior social defeat. Both behavioral processes are psychological in nature, and thus each potentially can occur independently of intrinsic fighting ability (Hsu & Wolf, 1999). Indeed, in an important synthesis of the winner and loser effect literature, Hsu, Early and Wolf (2006) point out that individuals form a winner effect because they have a greater willingness to engage in a fight rather than by necessarily changing intrinsic ability to become faster or stronger. The same is thought to occur for the loser effect: individuals become more likely to lose because they perceive themselves as losers, as opposed to somehow becoming intrinsically slower or weaker.

Winner and loser effects are found in a wide variety of taxa, including mammals (Huhman et al., 2003; Oyegbile and Marler, 2005), reptiles (Schuett, 1997), birds (Apfelbeck, Stegherr, & Goymann, 2011; Drummond & Canales, 1998; Popp, 1988), fish (Bakker, Feuthdebruijn, & Sevenster, 1989; Bakker & Sevenster, 1983; Beacham, 1988; Beaugrand, Goulet, & Payette, 1991; Chase, Tovey, Spangler-Martin, & Manfredonia, 2002), and invertebrates (Bergman et al., 2003; Hoefler, 2002; Whitehouse, 1997). Some work even suggests that humans form winner and loser effects (Yee, Bailenson, & Duchenaut, 2009), while other studies have considered how these effects can ripple out and have broader effects on social behavior (Coates, Gurnell, & Sarnyai, 2010). Additionally, meta-analyses of these two phenomena point out that they need not occur together – some species might show a loser effect, but not a winner effect (Hsu et al., 2006;

Mesterton-Gibbons, 1999). This suggests that while these processes are conceptually related, they are not necessarily opposite sides of the same coin. Such insight likely has implications for the physiological and neurobiological mechanisms that underlie both effects (see below). Regardless of these considerations, the taxonomic breadth in which we see evidence of robust winner and loser effects implies that these phenomena are not isolated traits that co-evolve with select aspects of social biology but instead occur in a diverse array of species that employ numerous social traits. In this way, we suspect that the winner and loser effect are relatively important behavioral mechanisms that likely help individuals contend with their environment.

However, little is actually known about the functional significance of the winner and loser effects. Few studies measure such phenomenon in free-living animals, where their direct or indirect impact on reproductive success can be measured (Rutte, Taborsky, & Brinkhof, 2006). This shortcoming means that the adaptive value of either the winner or loser effect is unclear; nonetheless, the prevailing thought is that these two events help individuals make appropriate decisions about when to engage in aggressive interactions and when to avoid them. Some of the studies highlighted below support this point of view, showing that the winner effect develops only when individuals accrue victories while defending their own territories (as reflected by the residency effect in the laboratory) (Fuxjager & Marler, 2010; Fuxjager, Mast, Becker, & Marler, 2009). In other words, the familiarity or contextual saliency of the immediate social environment might serve as a "switch" to potentiate changes in one's psychological state that occur after winning a fight, and that can lead to future aggression, agonistic persistence, and territorial vigilance. Such effects are likely adaptive because they help individuals acquire resources and reproductive opportunities. Other studies echo this finding by showing that the winner effect forms in species where the breeding environment is characterized by frequent agonism, such that only winners acquire mates (Oliveira, Silva, & Canario, 2009).

Winner and loser effects can provide other functionally important evolutionary benefits, in addition to territorial ability. For example, studies in the green swordtail fish, *Xiphophorus helleri*, show that randomly selected individuals given social victories are more likely to become the dominant individual within a linear social hierarchy (Dugatkin & Druen, 2004). The opposite is true for randomly chosen individuals who are given losing experiences, in that these individuals are more likely to emerge as low-ranking individuals. This work therefore suggests that winner and loser effects play an important role in the emergence of hierarchies that, in turn, maintain social stability within a population.

Another notable study with respect to the evolutionary significance of the loser effect is documented in crickets (Hofmann & Stevenson, 2000). When males fight, they perform a stereotyped sequence of escalating events, which end with wrestling. Either opponent can retreat at any phase of this escalation, and the one who does (the loser) displays a strong tendency to avoid further conflicts. However, this loser effect completely disappears once the loser begins to fly. Even more intriguing is that this effect does not occur when the cricket is tumbled around in a tube – it must fly to remove the loser effect. This can be traced back to the effects of a thoracic central pattern generator that controls flying in this species; once it is activated, it appears to reset the brain for aggression. These data therefore suggest that the loser effect of a cricket is purely place and time dependent, in that the phenomenon is easily erased once a losing individual relocates and has to re-establish residency. In nature, this effect likely helps individuals avoid costs associated with contests in which loss is inevitable, but still provides flexibility to allow crickets to "turn on" aggression when those costs are not severe.

With these considerations about the nature of winner and loser effects in mind, we can begin to ask how each is manifested at the physiological and neurobiological level. Indeed, for each to unfold and develop, changes in the brain must somehow underlie one's ability to "reconsider" the costs associated with aggression. Below we review these mechanisms.

Winner and loser effects in California mice

The monogamous and territorial California mouse (*Peromyscus californicus*) is developing into a unique model by which to understand winner and loser effects (Oyegbile & Marler, 2005; Fuxjager et al., 2009; Fuxjager & Marler, 2010). Both males and females strongly defend exclusive territories (Ribble, 1992), and both exhibit high levels of aggression towards the same and opposite sexes (Davis & Marler, 2003; Oyegbile & Marler, 2005; Fuxjager, Zhao, Rieger, & Marler, 2017; Rieger & Marler, 2018). Upon pair bonding, males and females share and defend a territory (Ribble, 1992), and whether an individual is in the home territory (resident) or a novel territory plays a particularly important role in physical aggression and the formation of the winner effect. Importantly, changes due to winning occur at both the behavioral and neural levels and are dependent on the interaction of residency, experience and hormones. The less researched loser effect in California mice has been studied through the lens of social defeat that acts as a stressor following repeated defeat experiences. As in the winner effect, socially defeated California mice show distinct changes at the behavioral and neural levels, with changes based on hormones and experience. The effect of residency may also play a role in social defeat with residency and status acting to create resilience against losing (Morrison et al., 2014; Morrison, Curry, & Cooper, 2012), but this has yet to be studied in California mice. California mice therefore have an integration of behavioral, neural, and hormonal processes that help to form and maintain the winner and loser effects, making them an important species through which to parse out the effects of each of these inputs.

Importantly, the differences discussed above relating to behavioral changes in both the winner and loser effect are mirrored by hormonal and neural changes that occur as a result of winning or losing fights. Internal changes occur during a fight that can rapidly influence current behavior and/or buttress future behavior, and hormonal changes are one category of mechanism through which this can occur. These hormonal changes may be important both for a permissive role in adopting a behavioral change relevant to a current social interaction, as well as modifying or stimulating neural mechanisms for maintaining long-term changes. Thus far, however, winner and loser effects do not appear to be controlled by the same behavioral and neuroendocrine mechanisms, and this is explored in detail below. Furthermore, aspects of the reward system may play a vital role in the formation and maintenance of these phenomena.

Winner effect

Behavioral mechanisms of the winner effect

The experience of winning fights is central to the formation of the winner effect (Hsu et al., 2006). The more fights an individual male California mouse wins, the more likely that individual is to win subsequent encounters against same sex conspecifics. While aggression has been studied in female California mice, the winner effect has yet to be studied. Specifically, laboratory studies have shown that winning three training fights leads to a robust winner effect being expressed in a subsequent fourth test fight (Fuxjager & Marler, 2010; Oyegbile & Marler, 2005). Subsequent aggressive encounters following a fight are marked by quicker attack latencies and greater overall aggression shown towards intruders (Trainor, Bird & Marler, 2004). Winners are also more likely to seek out aggression in the future, indicating an increased motivation to fight (Fuxjager & Marler, 2009; Fuxjager, Forbes-Lorman, et al., 2010; Hsu et al., 2006). This leads males to become more efficient at winning during fights as denoted by the winner index, a measure of the number of attack behaviors and submission behaviors completed by an individual during a fight.

The full formation of the winner effect also requires residency, a so-called home field advantage. In order to form the full winner effect, mice need both winning experience and for those experiences to happen in their home cage (Fuxjager et al., 2009). Individuals who gained their winning experiences in a novel cage showed no differences in fighting ability from inexperienced resident mice. This indicates that winning alone is not sufficient for the full formation of the winner effect. We therefore speculate that individuals are assessing their physical environment and perhaps weighing the costs and benefits associated with defending a site in a particular environment, such as an established territory that is both familiar and contains necessary resources. Studies of the closely related but polygamous and non-territorial white-footed mouse (*Peromyscus leucopus*) show that resource abundance can also affect contest outcome, with individuals who hold greater resources such as food winning more often (Fuxjager, Montgomery, Becker, & Marler, 2010) However, resource abundance shows no interaction with residency. As such, it is likely that the effect of resource abundance and the effect of experience on winning is controlled, at least in part, by different neural mechanisms. This indicates that the interaction of residency specifically with experience leads to the full formation of the winner effect and not other environmental factors (Fuxjager, Forbes-Lorman, et al., 2010; Fuxjager, Montgomery, et al., 2010; Fuxjager, Oyegbile, & Marler, 2011). This strongly ties the winner effect with residency and territoriality and indicates that the winner effect may act as a way to reinforce aggression to help maintain territories in the face of challenges.

The above described winner effect research has not incorporated the role of vocalizations and how these could be involved in the formation and maintenance of the winner effect, including the ability to communicate willingness to escalate in an aggression encounter. While we have not specifically studied the accrued effects of multiple encounters on vocalizations, we have examined vocalizations within single aggressive social interactions. California mice produce ultrasonic vocalizations (USV) in a variety of social contexts. One vocalization that shows sexual dimorphism and functions during aggression during laboratory territorial defense is the sustained vocalization (SV: previously referred to as syllable vocalizations; Kalcounis-Rueppell, Metheny, & Vonhoff, 2006; Rieger & Marler, 2018). SVs are long, low-bandwidth calls at a frequency of ~22 kHz; these vocalizations can vary in terms of total number of calls (previously referred to as syllables; Kalcounis-Rueppell, Pultorak, & Marler, 2018), duration, and calls per bout (previously referred to as syllables per phrase). Total SV calls produced by residents prior to the onset of physical aggression increased in males compared to females and predicted resident defensive behavior (Rieger & Marler, 2018). Resident SV calls therefore may act as a signal to intruders, possibly of motivation to fight that in turn alters intruder behavior. Moreover, during the transition from pre-fight to fighting, SVs are shortened. The degree of shortening of SVs predicts total offensive aggression by residents, thus corresponding with an escalation in physical aggression. Finally, along with shortening duration of calls, the number of calls per bout also decreases from pre-fight to fighting. We therefore see that the production of vocalizations prior to an aggressive encounter is increased in residents, and likely plays a role in territoriality (Rieger & Marler, 2018). An important future direction would be to study vocal signals in the context of the winner effect. For example, shortened SV duration could be used by prior winners to enhance the signals they send to intruders to convey motivation to fight or fighting quality.

We have alluded to residency as being critical for the development of the winner effect. A fundamental component of residency is that it is a preferred location such as a territory that needs to be defended. We hypothesize that the formation of conditioned place preferences (CPPs) may contribute to both the development of residency and increased aggression in that location. The conditioned place preference paradigm is classically used to examine the rewarding or addicting properties of a drug as a mechanism for conditioning an individual to a specific location (Tzschentke, 2007). Several lines of evidence suggest that attacking or experiencing victory can be rewarding and facilitate the association between the rewarding properties with the environmental cues (Fish, DeBold, & Miczek, 2005; Fish, Joseph, & Miczek, 2002). For example, in a T-shaped maze, focal male mice can learn to discriminate between the side that contains a submissive male from another strain versus the control side (Tellegen & Horn, 1972; Tellegen, Horn, & Legrand, 1969) and can run faster to the side conditioned with the submissive male for the opportunity to defeat the submissive mouse (Legrand, 1970). Martínez, Guillén-Salazar, Salvador, and Simón (1995) further found that mice can acquire a CPP for the initially less-preferred compartment wherein they defeated the submissive mouse. A similar effect was also observed in green anole lizards (*Anolis carolinensis*) that prefer an environment in which they exhibited aggressive behavior toward the reflection of themselves in a mirror (versus the nonreflective back of the mirror; Farrell & Wilczynski, 2006). From an evolutionary perspective, the development of the CPP may reflect an animal's natural capacity of associating aggressive and/or winning experience with a particular location. We speculate that the formation of CPPs could naturally contribute to the establishment or the consolidation of the residency effect (Fuxjager & Marler, 2009).

Neural and hormonal mechanisms of the winner effect

Testosterone

Winning encounters produces a significant change in androgens in individuals across species and taxa (Elekonich & Wingfield, 2000; Hau, Wikelski, Soma, & Wingfield, 2000; Jasnow, Huhman, Bartness, & Demas, 2000; Sperry, Wacker, & Wingfield, 2010; Trainor & Marler, 2001; Wingfield, Hegner, Dufty, & Ball, 1990). Most notably, individual male California mice that win fights in their home cage display increased testosterone levels 45 minutes following their winning experience, referred to as a testosterone-pulse (Oyegbile & Marler, 2005; Marler, Oyegbile, Plavicki, & Trainor, 2005). If an individual does not win, or wins in an unfamiliar environment, these testosterone-pulses do not occur (Fuxjager & Marler, 2010), illustrating that experience, environment, and hormonal mechanisms are required for the full formation of a winner effect. Moreover, testosterone-pulses are required to see an increase in aggressive behaviors in later fights following winning experiences. Castrated males that received testosterone implants to maintain baseline levels of testosterone but received post-victory saline showed no changes in future aggressive behavior. In addition, animals that received aromatase inhibitors, which prevent the conversion of testosterone to estrogen, still display increased aggression in later fights, suggesting that this experience dependent system is also androgen dependent (Trainor et al., 2004).

Interestingly, in the non-territorial and polygamous white-footed mouse, winning experiences do not alter testosterone. This species difference in post-victory hormone changes accounts for the formation of the winner effect in California mice but not white-footed mice (Oyegbile & Marler, 2006, Fuxjager & Marler, 2010). However, exogenous post-victory testosterone-pulses in white-footed mice induces a winner effect, thereby eliminating species differences in winner effect formation (Fuxjager, Oyegbile, & Marler, 2011). This provides evidence that pulsatile

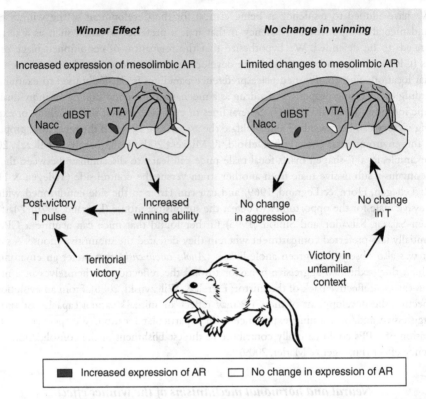

Figure 5.1 Inputs required for the winner effect in California mice. The winner effect in California mice requires multiple inputs in order to be fully realized. First, victory in an aggressive encounter must occur in a home territory. This leads to a pulse of testosterone that, in turn, increases expression of mesolimbic androgen receptors in the nucleus accumbens, dorsolateral bed nucleus of the stria terminalus, and ventral tegmental area. These changes taken together lead to increased likelihood of winning future fights. If victories occur in a novel territory, a testosterone-pulse does not occur and mesolimbic androgen receptors remain mostly unchanged.

testosterone cements the winning experience and creates the neural and psychological changes necessary for the winner effect to take hold. As such, one key to the formation of the winner effect may be the release or response to post-victory testosterone.

Testosterone-pulses following winning experiences lead to changes in androgen receptor patterns across the brain. In the bed nucleus of the stria terminalis (BNST) androgen receptors are increased following victories either in the home cage or a novel cage (Fuxjager, Forbes-Lorman, et al., 2010). This indicates that the BNST is related to aggression and winning in general but not necessarily to territoriality. Androgen receptors in the nucleus accumbens (NAc) and the ventral tegmental area (VTA) increase following wins that occur in the home territory only (Fuxjager, Forbes-Lorman, et al., 2010), indicating that these brain areas are likely vital to forming the winner effect in the context of residency. Changes in progesterone receptors following aggression in male California mice were not seen, suggesting that progesterone receptors do not play a role in the formation of the winner effect in males. We speculate that, because the NAc and VTA are tied to functions in reward and reinforcement, increased androgen receptors in these two areas may act to increase the intrinsic reward of fighting, thus increasing the motivation to fight in the future following winning experiences.

We also speculate that on a behavioral level, victory-induced testosterone-pulses contribute to residency via CPPs. On a hormonal level, testosterone has rewarding effects and can produce CPPs to the environment where the testosterone-pulses are experienced. Early studies have reported that hormone replacement therapy for hypogonadal men has been associated with enhancement of mood (Davidson, Camargo & Smith, 1979; Stuenkel, Dudley, & Yen, 1991), and rises in plasma testosterone are positively correlated with self-reports of elation in male athletes (Booth, Shelley, Mazur, Tharp, & Kittok, 1989) as well as following a decisive victory in humans (Mehta, Snyder, Knight, & Lassetter, 2015). Animal studies further provide empirical evidence revealing the rewarding effects of T. For instance, anabolic androgenic steroids can be voluntarily consumed through oral (Wood, 2002), intravenous (Wood, Johnson, Chu, Shad, & Self, 2004), and intracerebroventricular (ICV) self-administration (DiMeo & Wood, 2004; DiMeo & Wood, 2006; Triemstra et al., 2008; Wood et al., 2004) in hamsters (*Mesocricetus auratus*). In addition, the CPP can be produced via subcutaneous (Alexander, Packard, & Hines, 1994) (De Beun, Jansen, Slangen, & van de Poll, 1992), intra-nucleus accumbens (Packard, Cornell, & Alexander, 1997), and intra-medial preoptic area injections of testosterone (King, Packard, & Alexander, 1999).

In male California mice, testosterone-induced CPP is dependent on the environment and pair-bonding experience (Zhao & Marler, 2014a; Zhao & Marler, 2016). Specifically, sexually naïve male California mice can only form testosterone-induced CPP to an unfamiliar environment, not the home environment. From the perspective of ecology, before forming pair bonds most sexually naive males are usually motivated to disperse up to 80 meters and establish ownership of a territory (Ribble, 1992). Therefore, the testosterone-induced CPPs observed in sexually naïve males may reinforce the allocation of time towards exploration of a less familiar environment (Hawley et al., 2013) and/or help to initiate territoriality. In contrast to the sexually naïve mice, pair-bonded males can only form testosterone-induced CPP to home, but not an unfamiliar environment (Zhao & Marler, 2016). For monogamous species, the pair bond is a marker for an important life history stage and affects several social behaviors (Gobrogge, Liu, Jia, & Wang, 2007; Insel, Preston, & Winslow, 1995; Pultorak, Fuxjager, Kalcounnis-Rueppell, & Marler, 2015; Becker, Petruno, & Marler, 2012). The testosterone-induced CPP to the home may reflect its natural function in maintaining or strengthening residency.

This also stands in line with the need to form the winner effect in paired males (Fuxjager, Forbes-Lorman, et al., 2010; Fuxjager & Marler, 2010; Fuxjager et al., 2009). Pair-bonded males have already established their own territories, where the interactions with the partner and familiarity with the environment may increase the salience of the territory. Through the location preferences, testosterone may further promote site-specific aggressive motivation that, along with the winning experience, results in increased expression of the winner effects. We speculate that the winner effect will further contribute to behaviors such as territorial defense and possibly mate-guarding behavior, which could eventually increase the individual fitness when expressed under appropriate conditions. In comparison, the absence of cues associated with residency and the female mate may make the unfamiliar environment less salient and inhibit male responses to the rewarding properties of testosterone and the formation of the winner effects.

Progesterone

Progesterone levels change following aggression that contributes to winning experiences. In females a progesterone challenge exists, wherein levels of progesterone exhibit a transient decrease after interacting with an intruder. Progesterone generally decreases aggression, and by decreasing the progesterone/testosterone ratio in females, aggression may be increased in future encounters (Davis & Marler, 2003). In males, progesterone also decreases following aggressive encounters (Davis & Marler, unpublished data) and likely also acts to help increase aggression. Despite this work on how progesterone contributes to aggression (an important component of winning experience) its role in winning is yet to be elucidated.

Vasopressin

Vasopressin, which acts as a central neuropeptide and has a role in aggression across species, has been shown to play a role in aggression and territoriality (Albers, 2012; Caldwell & Albers, 2004; Ferris, Albers, Wesolowski, Goldman, & Luman, 1984; Ferris, Meenan, Axelson, & Albers, 1986). Administration of a vasopressin antagonist lengthened attack latencies in fights that occurred in the home cage of California mice but not in neutral cages or in white-footed mouse fights (Bester-Meredith, Martin, & Marler, 2005). Along with this, California mice cross-fostered with white-footed mice show decreased levels of aggression compared to those raised by California mice. These cross-fostered California mice also show less vasopressin immunoreactive staining in the BNST, the supraoptic nucleus (SON), and the medial amygdala (MeA). Vasopressin has also been shown to play an important role in aggression in other species including Syrian hamsters. Administration of vasopressin to the anterior hypothalamus increases offensive aggression (Ferris et al., 1984). Following repeated victories, dominant hamsters show greater vasopressin V1aR receptor binding in the ventromedial hypothalamus than their defeated counterparts. These changes indicate that vasopressin plays an important role in the expression of aggression and may also play an important role in the formation of the winner effect which is yet to be fully understood. Future research should focus on the role of both vasopressin and oxytocin on aggression and the winner effect.

Dopamine

The winner effect is also driven by reward pathways, as is demonstrated through the role of dopamine in the formation of the winner effect. Dopamine activity has been implicated in a wide array of social behaviors, including dominance and aggression (Miczek, Fish, de Bold, & Almeida, 2002; Miller & Beninger, 1991; Winberg & Nilsson, 1992). The upregulation of gene expression of various dopamine-related proteins in the VTA has been demonstrated in male mice that won 20 encounters in succession (Bondar, Boyarskikh, Kovalenko, Filipenko, & Kudryavtseva, 2009). In male Syrian hamsters (*Mesocricetus auratus*), winning all 14 consecutive agonistic encounters results in increased TH-immunoreactivity (precursor of dopamine) in the lateral septum, BNST and the NAc shell, all brain areas associated with reward-like functions. Pharmacological antagonism of dopamine receptors in loci of the social brain network diminishes the seeking of the opportunity to fight as well as the intensity of aggressive behaviors (Couppis & Kennedy, 2008; Schwartzer & Melloni Jr, 2010). Within California mice specifically, dopamine is essential for the formation of the winner effect. The peripheral administration of D1- and D2-like receptor antagonists following a victory prevents the formation of the winner effect (Becker & Marler, 2015). Moreover, DA receptor antagonists reduce the amount of aggression that occurs during a fight with a competitive opponent (Becker & Marler, 2015). Taken together, these results indicate that dopamine activity following the experience of winning is vital to the formation of the winner effect.

As discussed above, the testosterone-induced CPP may contribute to the establishment or maintenance of the residency. It has been demonstrated that the testosterone-induced CPP can be blocked by peripheral or intra-accumbens injection of dopamine receptor antagonist, a-flupenthixol, suggesting the rewarding effects of testosterone are mediated through the dopamine system (Packard, Schroeder, & Alexander, 1998) and both dopamine D1 and D2 receptor subtypes are involved in the acquisition of testosterone-induced CPPs (Schroeder & Packard, 2000). All of these results suggest that the actions of dopamine contribute to the mechanisms underlying an animal's motivation to engage aggressively and win after previous winning behaviors.

Loser effect/social defeat

BEHAVIORAL MECHANISMS

Whereas winner effects facilitate aggression and promote engagement in future contests, loser effects are usually associated with behavioral strategies that reduce the possibility of aggressive conflict. Although the effects of losing per se have not been studied in California mice in the same level of detail that winning has (e.g., effects on the probability of winning an aggressive contest), research examining the effects of social defeat on behavior can provide insights into the behavioral and neurobiological changes that occur with adverse social experiences. Furthermore, since both male and female California mice exhibit aggressive behavior, the effects of social defeat has been studied in both males and females. Just as individual winning experiences produce unique neuroendocrine profiles in males (Marler et al., 2005; Zhao & Marler, 2014b) and females (Davis & Marler, 2003; Duque-Wilckens & Trainor, 2017), the experience of losing social encounters can also produce distinct behavioral and neuroendocrine responses in males and females (Steinman & Trainor, 2017; Trainor et al., 2011).

Male California mice exposed to three short bouts of defeat with aggressive, sexually experienced males develop an intriguing behavioral phenotype. First, defeated males confronted with an intruder in the home cage show increased fear behaviors such as freezing and decreased social approach behavior such as anogenital and social sniffing (Steinman et al., 2015, Trainor et al., 2011). These behavioral responses correspond well with other studies in hamsters (Jasnow, Davis, & Huhman, 2004) and mice (Kudryavtseva, Bakshtanovskaya, & Koryankina, 1991) that observe increases in submissive behavior after losing social interactions. Curiously, defeat does not reduce aggression in male California mice, although this might be dependent on testing conditions, including cage size (Steinman et al., 2015). The cage size for these studies is relatively small and may not provide sufficient opportunities for the resident to avoid an intruder. However, it seems likely that different neuroendocrine mechanisms drive aggression in males that have experienced defeat stress versus males that have not (Watt, Burke, Renner, & Forster, 2009). Aggression in males who have experienced defeat stress is not accompanied by anogenital sniffing, which provides important olfactory stimulation to offensive aggression circuits, and as such, assessment of the intruder is less likely to have occurred.

Whereas defeated males avoid social cues in the home cage, in a novel environment stressed males exhibit levels of social approach that are no different from unstressed males. While this degree of social approach following defeat stress is sometimes referred to as an "unsusceptible" (Krishnan et al., 2007) or "resilient" (Elliott, Ezra-Nevo, Regev, Neufeld-Cohen, & Chen, 2010) phenotype, these terms are probably not accurate descriptors for male California mice because their behavioral profiles differ based on residency status (Steinman et al., 2015, Fuxjager et al., 2011). Currently, it is unclear why social approach is not reduced by social defeat in a novel environment. One possibility mentioned earlier is that novel environments can remove the loser effect (Hsu et al., 2006). Intriguingly, forgetting or the extinction of a memory is an active neurobiological process that relies in part on the frontal cortex (Milad & Quirk, 2002). The ability to maintain social approach in novel environments could be a critical strategy for forgetting losing experiences and setting up a new territory. In a field setting, it is likely that young male California mice will be more likely to lose in social encounters with older, more experienced males. Similar to the winner effect (discussed above), exhibiting stronger submissive responses in familiar environments may be an effective strategy for avoiding territorial animals while social approach is likely an essential step towards establishing a new territory.

While defeated males have high levels of social approach in novel environments, defeated female California mice exhibit reduced social approach (Greenberg et al., 2014; Trainor et al., 2013) that is typically observed in social defeat models in other species. This response is typically interpreted as a loss of social reward because it frequently coincides with other changes in reward sensitivity such as reduced preferences for sucrose (Krishnan et al., 2007). Intriguingly, while females who have experienced defeat stress do not approach unfamiliar females, they remain vigilant as characterized by orientation towards a cage containing an unfamiliar female but not an empty cage, a behavior that is not seen in males. Whether this also occurs in a familiar environment in males or females is yet to be tested.

For vocalizations, it is unknown whether calls specific to losing exist, but we have identified sex differences in ultrasonic vocalizations associated with defensive aggression, a set of behaviors we would expect to be associated with losing. Barks, short high amplitude bursts of 18–22 kHz that begin and end in the audible range, are a hallmark of aggressive behavior and produced more by females than males. These bark calls correlate highly with defensive aggression and occur almost exclusively following the onset of physical aggression (Rieger & Marler, 2018) and may function in a manner similar to rat 22 kHz calls to prevent future aggression by residents by displaying the negative affect of the caller (Riede, 2013). We predict that with repeated losing experiences, California mouse barks become a more prevalent call type by which individuals look to mitigate the amount of aggression shown against them by residents. Such barks may provide an intriguing new area of research by which to understand aggressive behaviors, particularly from the perspective of the formation of loser effects.

Hormonal and neural mechanisms of the loser effect

Testosterone

While testosterone is vital to the formation of the winner effect, to this point there is little evidence that the loser effect and social defeat in California mice are driven by androgens or androgen receptors (Trainor et al., 2013). For example, while social defeat produces social withdrawal in females but not males, gonadectomy has no effect on social withdrawal following defeat stress (Trainor et al., 2013), indicating that circulating gonadal hormones do not play a major role in social withdrawal.

Progesterone

To this point the role of progesterone in the loser effect is unknown. Across the estrous cycle in female rats, proestrous females show an increase in hippocampal progesterone (Frye & Walf, 2004; Frye, Petralia, & Rhodes, 2000). Moreover, this increase in progesterone is correlated with anxiolytic behavior, including greater exploration during open field tests (Frye and Walf, 2004; Frye et al., 2000). The administration of progesterone to ovariectomized rats is also shown to reduce anxiety across a variety of behavioral tasks. As such, progesterone may play a role in reducing stress following social defeat, though this has yet to be tested.

Arginine vasopressin

Social defeat reduces the number of vasopressin positive cells in the PVN, SON and posterior BNST (Steinman et al., 2015). Decreases in immunoreactivity in the PVN coincide with decreased vasopressin mRNA as measured with real-time PCR. Decreases in vasopressin gene expression and immunoreactivity may be mediated by glucocorticoids, as glucocorticoids can reduce vasopressin transcription and immunoreactivity in the PVN (Davis et al., 1986). Male California mice that lost aggressive encounters have elevated corticosterone levels both in the active (dark) and inactive (light) phases (Trainor et al., 2011), a change not seen following winning experiences (Marler et al., 2005). While strong effects of losing were observed on vasopressin immunoreactivity, no effects of losing were observed on vasopressin V1a receptor (V1aR) binding across several nuclei known to modulate aggression such as the bed nucleus of the stria terminalis (BNST) and lateral septum (Duque-Wilckens et al., 2016). However, V1aR has important effects on aggression and social behavior. Infusion of vasopressin V1aR antagonists into the lateral ventricle reduces aggression in a familiar environment (Bester-Meredith et al., 2005). Thus, a decrease in vasopressin synthesis is consistent with the loss of normal patterns of aggressive behavior observed in stressed males. However, the specific sites of V1aR regulation on aggression have not yet been identified in California mice. However, in hamsters (Albers et al., 2006) and prairie voles (Gobrogge et al., 2007) activation of V1aR in the anterior hypothalamus increases male aggression in a resident intruder test. Interestingly, V1aR antagonist infused in to the medioventral BNST decreases social approach behavior in male California mice (Duque-Wilckens et al., 2016). Consistent with this, selective deletion of V1aR has also been found to reduce social interaction behavior in mice (Egashira et al., 2007). Thus, while losing does not appear to affect the expression of V1aR, decreases in vasopressin likely lead to decreased V1aR activity that could contribute to loser effects in males by decreasing both social approach (via the BNST) and aggressive behavior (possibly via the anterior hypothalamus). In female California mice, social defeat may work through oxytocin instead of vasopressin; social defeat had no effects on vasopressin immunoreactivity (ref) but can increase oxytocin immunoreactivity as well as the reactivity of oxytocin neurons in social contexts (Steinman et al., 2016).

Dopamine

Social defeat induces long-lasting increases in the activity of dopamine neurons within the VTA that project to the NAc (Trainor, 2011). This pathway is an essential component of neural circuits controlling motivation and is known to be dysregulated in psychiatric disorders such as depression (Russo & Nestler, 2013). As such, the effects of social stress on the VTA-NAc circuit have been heavily studied. While the impact of these neuroadaptations on winner and loser effects have not been directly tested, several lines of evidence indicate that hyperactivity in VTA dopamine neurons may profoundly affect how experience modulates aggressive behavior. Multiple studies in male rats (Anstrom, Miczek & Budygin, 2009) and mice (Krishnan et al., 2007; Razzoli, Andreoli, Michielin, Quarta, & Sokal, 2011) show that social defeat induces burst firing in VTA dopamine neurons. In vivo recordings show that burst firing of VTA dopamine neurons occurs in response to salient cues (Brischoux, Chakraborty, Brierly, & Ungless, 2009; Schultz, Dayan, & Montague, 1997). Although the exact function of this burst firing is still debated (Berridge, 2012; Schultz, 2016; Wise, 2006), it seems clear that disruption of this process (e.g. burst firing in the absence of salient cues) would interfere with normal motivational processes. Indeed, when optogenetic stimulation was used to normalize the activity of VTA neurons projecting to the NAc, normal social approach behavior was restored in male mice exposed to defeat stress (Chaudhury et al., 2013).

Beyond firing rate within the VTA-NAc pathway, the total dopamine context in the brain is also vital to social defeat and the loser effect. Analyses of total dopamine content illustrate that male California mice exposed to social defeat had higher levels of dopamine in the NAc than control males (Campi, Greenberg, Kapoor, Ziegler, & Trainor, 2014). Higher levels of dopamine could be driven by increased dopamine synthesis and release or simply a decrease in dopamine release. Counter intuitively, higher levels of the dopamine metabolites DOPAC and homovanilic acid (HVA) in defeated males suggest that defeat increases dopamine release. Curiously, infusion of dopamine D1 receptor agonist into the NAc that decreased social motivation in females had no effect in males (Campi et al., 2014). However, the effects of D1 receptor manipulations within the NAc have not been studied in a resident intruder test and this may reveal a context dependent role of dopamine related to territoriality. As discussed previously, both D1 and D2 receptors have important effects on the winner effect. Considering that both the NAc and VTA become more sensitive to androgens with winning experience, it seems likely that defeat-induced changes in dopamine signaling within the NAc would have important effects on this process. Female California mice exposed to social defeat also exhibit increased dopamine, DOPAC, and HVA levels within the NAc. Furthermore, D1 agonists infused in to the NAc are sufficient to reduce social motivation while D1 antagonist infusion can restore social motivation in defeated females. Again, further study is needed to determine whether changes in dopaminergic signaling would affect winning or losing in female California mice.

Conclusion

In the winner effect, both intrinsic and environmental factors interact to produce long-term behavioral and neural differences. The confluence of winning fights, residency, and increased post-encounter testosterone lead to an increased ability to win future fights. Moreover, these changes may apply more broadly than just altering the probability of winning or losing future encounters. These changes, especially relating to testosterone and residency, likely play a major role in territoriality as well as reward systems. As such, our understanding of the winner effect may lead to a broader understanding of the underlying processes of environmental stimuli and reward and how these are linked with the predictability of the environment. The responses of individuals to winning and losing experiences is intriguing because it allows us to understand the plasticity of behavioral interactions that allow individuals to adjust their behavior to adapt to both their current and future social interactions.

As knowledge about the loser effect accumulates, we can examine the similarities and differences through which these pathways change behavior and illuminate mechanisms underlying sex differences in behavior. The location of past and current experiences plays such an important role in the formation of the winner effect that it is likely to influence responses to social defeat and the loser effect as described earlier. A critical question is whether the winner effect can provide a buffer or counteract past exposure to losing or defeat stress and, if so, what the genetic and molecular underpinnings are for these interactions between complex behaviors that express such plasticity. More specifically, it would be extremely valuable to understand why male California mice exhibit such resilience in the face of social defeat. As research continues in understanding the neural mechanisms of the winner and loser effects, the hippocampus may prove to be an important additional brain area to target because of the importance of spatial location and memory for such long-lasting effects.

It is also important to note that the major results relating to the winner effect and social defeat presented in this chapter have been successfully replicated in multiple experiments using different approaches. In general, throughout these studies, sufficient sample sizes for animal studies were used (no less than $n = 10$ per group). These sample sizes are typically used for laboratory animal studies because the environments of the animals are controlled from birth, greatly reducing variability and helping to increase statistical power leading us to be highly confident in these results.

A behavioral component that has been lacking in many of these studies that would better mimic natural conditions is to provide animals routes through which they can escape or retreat from aversive stimuli. We expect highly social species to integrate information around them, assess their internal states, and to make decisions about how to make the most of social situations that they cannot escape. However, although research is lacking in this area, we would also expect individuals to employ decisions to escape those social situations when possible. Overall, while extensive behavioral plasticity has been found in the development of winner and loser effects, the plasticity is likely to be much greater as we expand the choices that individuals can make to exert more control over their environment.

References

Albers, H.E. (2012). The regulation of social recognition, social communication and aggression: Vasopressin in the social behavior neural network. *Hormones and Behavior, 61*(3), 283–292. http://doi.org/10.1016/j.yhbeh.2011.10.007

Albers, H.E., Dean, A., Karom, M.C., Smith, D., & Huhman, K.L. (2006). Role of V1a vasopressin receptors in the control of aggression in Syrian hamsters. *Brain Research, 1073–1074,* 425–430.

Alexander, G.M., Packard, M.G., & Hines, M. (1994). Testosterone has rewarding affective properties in male rats: Implications for the biological basis of sexual motivation. *Behavioral Neuroscience, 108*(2), 424–428. doi:10.1037/0735-7044.108.2.424

Anstrom, K.K., Miczek, K.A., & Budygin, E.A. (2009). Increased phasic dopamine signaling in the mesolimbic pathway during social defeat in rats. *Neuroscience, 161,* 3–12.

Apfelbeck, B., Stegherr, J., & Goymann, W. (2011). Simulating winning in the wild: The behavioral and hormonal response of black redstarts to a single and repeated territorial challenges of high and low intensity. *Hormones and Behavior, 60,* 565–571.

Bakker, T.C.M., Feuthdebruijn, E., & Sevenster, P. (1989). Asymmetrical effects of prior winning and losing on dominance in sticklebacks (*Gasterosteus aculeatus*). *Ethology, 82*(3), 224–229.

Bakker, T.C.M., & Sevenster, P. (1983). Determinants of dominance in male sticklebacks (*Gasterosteus aculeatus L*). *Behaviour, 86,* 55–71.

Beacham, J.L. (1988). The relative importance of body size and aggressive experience as determinants of dominance in pumpkinseed sunfish, *Lepomis gibbosus*. *Animal Behavior, 36,* 621–623.

Beaugrand, J., Goulet, C., & Payette, D. (1991). Outcome of dyadic conflict in male green swordtail fish, *Xiphophorus helleri*: Effects of body size and prior dominance. *Animal Behavior, 41,* 417–424.

Becker, E.A., & Marler, C.A. (2015). Postcontest blockade of dopamine receptors inhibits development of the winner effect in the California mouse (*Peromyscus californicus*). *Behavioral Neuroscience, 129*(2), 205.

Becker, E.A., Petruno, S., & Marler, C.A. (2012). A comparison of scent marking between a monogamous and promiscuous species of peromyscus: Pair bonded males do not advertise to novel females. *PLoS One, 7*(2), e32002. http://doi.org/10.1371/journal.pone.0032002

Bergman, D.A., Kozlowski, C.P., McIntyre, J.C., Huber, R., Daws, A.G., & Moore, P.A. (2003). Temporal dynamics and communication of winner effects in the crayfish, *Orconectes rusticus*. *Behaviour, 140,* 805–825.

Berridge, K.C. (2012). From prediction error to incentive salience: Mesolimbic computation of reward motivation. *European Journal of Neuroscience, 35,* 1124–1143.

Bester-Meredith, J.K., Martin, P.A., & Marler, C.A. (2005). Manipulations of vasopressin alter aggression differently across testing conditions in monogamous and nonmonogamous Peromyscus mice. *Aggressive Behavior, 31*(2), 189–199.

Bondar, N.P., Boyarskikh, U.A., Kovalenko, I.L., Filipenko, M.L., & Kudryavtseva, N.N. (2009). Molecular implications of repeated aggression: Th, Dat1, Snca and Bdnf gene expression in the VTA of victorious male mice. *PLoS One*, *4*(1), e4190. http://doi.org/10.1371/journal.pone.0004190

Booth, A., Shelley, G., Mazur, A., Tharp, G., & Kittok, R. (1989). Testosterone, and winning and losing in human competition. *Hormones and Behavior*, *23*(4), 556–571. http://doi.org/10.1016/0018-506X(89)90042-1

Brischoux, F., Chakraborty, S., Brierley, D.I., & Ungless, M.A. (2009). Phasic excitation of dopamine neurons in ventral VTA by noxious stimuli. *Proceedings of National Academy of Sciences of United States of America*, *106*(12), 4894–4899. doi:10.1073/pnas.0811507106

Caldwell, H.K., & Albers, H.E. (2004). Effect of photoperiod on vasopressin-induced aggression in Syrian hamsters. *Hormones and Behavior*, *46*(4), 444–449. http://doi.org/10.1016/j.yhbeh.2004.04.006

Campi, K.L., Greenberg, G.D., Kapoor, A., Ziegler, T.E., & Trainor, B.C. (2014). Sex differences in effects of dopamine D1 receptors on social withdrawal. *Neuropharmacology*, *77*, 208–216.

Chase, I.D., Tovey, C., Spangler-Martin, D., & Manfredonia, M. (2002). Individual differences versus social dynamics in the formation of animal dominance hierarchies. *Proceedings of the National Academy of Sciences of the United States of America*, *99*(8), 5744–5749.

Chaudhury, D., Walsh, J.J., Friedman, A.K., Juarez, B., Ku, S.M., Koo, J.W., . . . Han, M.H. (2013). Rapid regulation of depression-related behaviours by control of midbrain dopamine neurons. *Nature*, *493*, 532–536.

Coates, J.M., Gurnell, M., & Sarnyai, Z. (2010). From molecule to market: Steroid hormones ad financial risk-taking. *Philosophical Transactions of Royal Society London Series B: Biological Sciences*, *365*, 331–343.

Couppis, M. H., & Kennedy, C. H. (2008). The rewarding effect of aggression is reduced by nucleus accumbens dopamine receptor antagonism in mice. *Psychopharmacology*, *197*(3), 449–456. http://doi.org/10.1007/s00213-007-1054-y

Davidson, J.M., Camargo, C.A., & Smith, E.R. (1979). Effects of androgen on sexual behavior in hypogonadal men. *The Journal of Clinical Endocrinology and Metabolism*, *48*(6), 955–958. http://doi.org/10.1210/jcem-48-6-955

Davis, E.S., & Marler, C.A. (2003). The progesterone challenge: Steroid hormone changes following a simulated territorial intrusion in female *Peromyscus californicus*. *Hormones and Behavior*, *44*, 189–198.

Davis, L.G., Arentzen, R., Reid, J.M., Manning, R.W., Wolfson, B., Lawrence, K.L., & Baldino, F.J. (1986). Glucocorticoid sensitivity of vasopressin mRNA levels in the paraventricular nucleus of the rat. *Proceedings of the National Academy of Sciences of the United States of America*, *83*, 1145–1149.

De Beun, R., Jansen, E., Slangen, J.L., & van de Poll, N.E. (1992). Testosterone as appetitive and discriminative stimulus in rats: Sex-and dose-dependent effects. *Physiology & Behavior*, *52*(4), 629–634.

DiMeo, A.N., & Wood, R.I. (2004). Circulating androgens enhance sensitivity to testosterone self-administration in male hamsters. *Pharmacology Biochemistry and Behavior*, *79*(2), 383–389.

DiMeo, A.N., & Wood, R.I. (2006). Self-administration of estrogen and dihydrotestosterone in male hamsters. *Hormones and Behavior*, *49*(4), 519–526.

Drummond, H., & Canales, C.A. (1998). Dominance between booby nestlings involves winner and loser effects. *Animal Behavior*, *55*, 1669–1676.

Dugatkin, L.A., & Druen, M. (2004). The social implications of winner and loser effects. *Proceedings of the Royal Society B*, *271*, S488–S489.

Duque-Wilckens, N., Steinman, M.Q., Laredo, S.A., Hao, R., Perkeybile, A.M., Bales, K.L., & Trainor, B.C. (2016). Anxiolytic effects of vasopressin V1a receptor in the medioventral bed nucleus of the stria terminalis: Sex specific effects in social and nonsocial contexts. *Neuropharmacology*, *110*, 59–68.

Duque-Wilckens, N., & Trainor, B. C. (2017). Behavioral neuroendocrinology of female aggression. *Oxford Encyclopedia of Neuroscience* (Vol. 1). http://doi.org/10.1093/acrefore/9780190264086.013.11

Egashira, N., Tanoue, A., Matsuda, T., Koushi, E., Harada, S., Takano, Y., . . . Fujiwara, M. (2007). Impaired social interaction and reduced anxiety-related behavior in vasopressin V1a receptor knockout mice. *Behavioral Brain Research*, *178*, 123–127.

Elekonich, M.M., & Wingfield, J.C. (2000). Seasonality and hormonal control of territorial aggression in female song sparrows (Passeriformes: Emberizidae: *Melospiza melodia*). *Ethology*, *106*(6), 493–510. http://doi.org/10.1046/j.1439-0310.2000.00555.x

Elliott, E., Ezra-Nevo, G., Regev, L., Neufeld-Cohen, A., & Chen, A. (2010). Resilience to social stress coincides with functional DNA methylation of the Crf gene in adult mice. *Nature Neuroscience*, *13*(11), 1351–1353.

Farrell, W.J., & Wilczynski, W. (2006). Aggressive experience alters place preference in green anole lizards, *Anolis carolinensis*. *Animal Behavior*, *71*(5), 1155–1164.

Ferris, C.F., Albers, H.E., Wesolowski, S.M., Goldman, B.D., & Luman, S.E. (1984). Vasopressin injected into the hypothalamus triggers a stereotypic behavior in golden hamsters. *Science, 224*(4648), 521–523. http://doi.org/10.1126/science.6538700

Ferris, C.F., Meenan, D.M., Axelson, J.F., & Albers, H.E. (1986). A vasopressin antagonist can reverse dominant/subordinate behavior in hamsters. *Physiology & Behavior, 38*(1), 135–138. http://doi.org/10.1016/0031-9384(86)90143-5

Fish, E.W., DeBold, J.F., & Miczek, K.A. (2005). Escalated aggression as a reward: Corticosterone and GABAA receptor positive modulators in mice. *Psychopharmacology, 182*(1), 116–127.

Fish, E.W., Joseph, F., & Miczek, K.A. (2002). Aggressive behavior as a reinforcer in mice: Activation by allopregnanolone. *Psychopharmacology, 163*(3–4), 459–466.

Frye, C.A., Petralia, S., & Rhodes, M. (2000). Estrous cycle and sex differences in performance on anxiety tasks coincide with increases in hippocampal progesterone and 3α, 5α-THP. *Pharmacology Biochemistry and Behavior, 67*(3), 587–596. http://doi.org/10.1016/S0091-3057(00)00392-0

Frye, C.A., & Walf, A.A. (2004). Estrogen and/or progesterone administered systemically or to the Amygdala can have anxiety-, fear-, and pain-reducing effects in ovariectomized rats. *Behavioral Neuroscience, 118*(2), 306–313. http://doi.org/10.1037/0735-7044.118.2.306

Fuxjager, M.J., Forbes-Lorman, R.M., Coss, D.J., Auger, C.J., Auger, A.P., & Marler, C.A. (2010). Winning territorial disputes selectively enhances androgen sensitivity in neural pathways related to motivation and social aggression. *Proceedings of the National Academy of Sciences of the United States of America, 107*(27), 12393–12398. doi:10.1073/pnas.1001394107

Fuxjager, M.J., Mast, G., Becker, E.A., & Marler, C.A. (2009). The "home advantage" is necessary for a full winner effect and changes in post-encounter testosterone. *Hormones and Behavior, 56,* 214–219.

Fuxjager, M. J., & Marler, C. A. (2009). How and why the winner effect forms: Influences of contest environment and species differences. *Behavioral Ecology, 21*(1), 37–45. http://doi.org/10.1093/beheco/arp148

Fuxjager, M.J., & Marler, C.A. (2010). How and why the winner effect forms: Influences of contest environment and species differences. *Behavioral Ecology, 21*(1), 37–45. doi:10.1093/beheco/arp148

Fuxjager, M.J., Montgomery, J.L., Becker, E.A., & Marler, C.A. (2010). Deciding to win: Interactive effects of residency, resources and "boldness" on contest outcome in white-footed mice. *Animal Behaviour, 80*(5), 921–927. http://doi.org/10.1016/j.anbehav.2010.08.018

Fuxjager, M.J., Oyegbile, T.O., & Marler, C.A. (2011). *Independent and additive contributions of postvictory testosterone and social experience to the development of the winner effect.* http://dx.doi.org/10.1210/en.2011-1099

Fuxjager, M.J., Zhao, X., Rieger, N.S., & Marler, C.A. (2017). Why animals fight: Uncovering the function and mechanisms of territorial aggression. In *American psychological association handbook of comparative psychology* (pp. 853–875). Washington, DC: American Psychological Association.

Gobrogge, K.L., Liu, Y., Jia, X., & Wang, Z. (2007). Anterior hypothalamic neural activation and neurochemical associations with aggression in pair-bonded male prairie voles. *Journal of Comparative Neurology, 502*(6), 1109–1122.

Greenberg, G.D., Laman-Maharg, A., Campi, K.L., Voigt, H., Orr, V.N., Schaal, L., & Trainor, B.C. (2014). Sex differences in stress-induced social withdrawal: Role of brain derived neurotrophic factor in the bed nucleus of the stria terminalis. *Frontiers in Behavioral Neuroscience, 7,* 223.

Hau, M., Wikelski, M., Soma, K.K., & Wingfield, J.C. (2000). Testosterone and year-round territorial aggression in a Tropical Bird. *General and Comparative Endocrinology, 117*(1), 20–33. http://doi.org/10.1006/gcen.1999.7390

Hawley, W.R., Grissom, E.M., Martin, R.C., Halmos, M.B., Bart, C.L., & Dohanich, G.P. (2013). Testosterone modulates spatial recognition memory in male rats. *Hormones and Behavior, 63*(4), 559–565. doi:10.1016/j.yhbeh.2013.02.007

Hoefler, C.D. (2002). Is contest experience a trump card? The interaction of residency status, experience, and body size on fighting success in *Misumenoides formosipes* (Araneae: Thomisidae). *Journal of Insect Behavior, 15*(6), 779–790.

Hofmann, H.A., & Stevenson, P.A. (2000). Flight restores fight in crickets. *Nature, 403,* 613.

Hsu, Y.Y., Earley, R.L., & Wolf, L.L. (2006). Modulation of aggressive behaviour by fighting experience: Mechanisms and contest outcomes. *Biological Reviews, 81*(1), 33–74.

Hsu, Y.Y., & Wolf, L.L. (1999). The winner and loser effect: Integrating multiple experiences. *Animal Behaviour, 57,* 903–910.

Huhman, K.L., Solomon, M.B., Janicki, M., Harmon, A.C., Lin, S.M., Israel, J.E., & Jasnow, A.M. (2003). Conditioned defeat in male and female Syrian hamsters. *Hormones and Behaviour, 44*(3), 293–299.

Insel, T.R., Preston, S., & Winslow, J.T. (1995). Mating in the monogamous male: Behavioral consequences. *Physiology & Behaviour, 57*(4), 615–627. doi:10.1016/0031-9384(94)00362-9

Jasnow, A.M., Davis, M., & Huhman, K.L. (2004). Involvement of central amygdalar and bed nucleus of the stria terminalis corticotropin-releasing factor in behavioral responses to social defeat. *Behavioural Neuroscience, 118*(5), 1051–1061.

Jasnow, A.M., Huhman, K.L., Bartness, T.J., & Demas, G.E. (2000). Short-day increases in aggression are inversely related to circulating testosterone concentrations in male Siberian Hamsters (*Phodopus sungorus*). *Hormones and Behavior, 38*(2), 102–110. http://doi.org/10.1006/hbeh.2000.1604

Kalcounis-Rueppell, M.C., Metheny, J.D., & Vonhof, M.J. (2006). Production of ultrasonic vocalizations by Peromyscus mice in the wild. *Frontiers in Zoology, 3*(1), 3. http://doi.org/10.1186/1742-9994-3-3

Kalcounis-Rueppell, M. C., Pultorak, J. D., & Marler, C. A. (2018). Ultrasonic Vocalizations of Mice in the Genus Peromyscus. *Handbook of Behavioral Neuroscience, 25*, 227–235. Academic Press: Amsterdam. http://doi.org/10.1016/B978-0-12-809600-0.00022-6

King, B.E., Packard, M.G., & Alexander, G.M. (1999). Affective properties of intra-medial preoptic area injections of testosterone in male rats. *Neuroscience Letters, 269*(3), 149–152.

Krishnan, V., Han, M-H., Graham, D.L., Berton, O., Renthal, W., Russo, S.J., . . . Nestler, E.J. (2007). Molecular adaptations underlying susceptibility and resistance to social defeat in brain reward regions. *Cell, 131*, 391–404.

Kudryavtseva, N.N., Bakshtanovskaya, I.V., & Koryankina, L.A. (1991). Social model of depression in mice of C57Bl/6J strain. *Pharmacology Biochemistry and Behavior, 38*(2), 315–320.

Legrand, R. (1970). Successful aggression as the reinforcer for runway behavior of mice. *Psychonomic Science, 20*(5), 303–305.

Marler, C.A., Oyegbile, T., Plavicki, J., & Trainor, B.C. (2005). Response to Wingfield commentary on "A continuing saga: The role of testosterone in aggression." *Hormones and Behaviour, 48*, 256–258.

Martínez, M., Guillén-Salazar, F., Salvador, A., & Simón, V.M. (1995). Successful intermale aggression and conditioned place preference in mice. *Physiology & Behaviour, 58*(2), 323–328. doi:10.1016/0031-9384(95)00061-M.

Mehta, P.H., Snyder, N.A., Knight, E.L., & Lassetter, B. (2015). Close versus decisive victory moderates the effect of testosterone change on competitive decisions and task enjoyment. *Adaptive Human Behavior and Physiology, 1*(3), 291–311. http://doi.org/10.1007/s40750-014-0014-0

Mesterton-Gibbons, M. (1999). On the evolution of pure winner and loser effects: A game-theoretic model. *Bulletin of Mathematical Biology, 61*(6), 1151–1186.

Miczek, K.A., Fish, E.W., de Bold, J.F., & de Almeida, R.M. (2002). Social and neural determinants of aggressive behavior: Pharmacotherapeutic targets at serotonin, dopamine and ?-aminobutyric acid systems. *Psychopharmacology, 163*(3–4), 434–458. http://doi.org/10.1007/s00213-002-1139-6

Milad, M.R., & Quirk, G.J. (2002). Neurons in medial prefrontal cortex signal memory for fear extinction. *Nature, 420*(6911), 70–74. http://doi.org/10.1038/nature01138

Miller, R., & Beninger, R.J. (1991). On the interpretation of asymmetries of posture and locomotion produced with dopamine agonists in animals with unilateral depletion of striatal dopamine. *Progress in Neurobiology, 36*(3), 229–256. http://doi.org/10.1016/0301-0082(91)90032-V

Morrison, K., Bader, L., Clinard, C., Gerhard, D., Gross, S., & Cooper, M. (2014). Maintenance of dominance status is necessary for resistance to social defeat stress in Syrian hamsters. *Behavioural Brain Research, 270*, 277–286. http://doi.org/10.1016/J.BBR.2014.05.041

Morrison, K., Curry, D., & Cooper, M. (2012). Social status alters defeat-induced neural activation in Syrian hamsters. *Neuroscience, 210*, 168–178. http://doi.org/10.1016/J.NEUROSCIENCE.2012.03.002

Oliveira, R.F. (2009). Social behavior in context: Hormonal modulation of behavioral plasticity and social competence. *Integrative and Comparative Biology, 49*(4), 423–440. doi:10.1093/icb/icp055

Oliveira, R.F., Silva, A., & Canario, A.V.M. (2009). Why do winners keep winning? Androgen mediation of the winner effect but not loser effect. *Proceedings of Royal Society B, 276*, 2249–2256.

Oyegbile, T.O., & Marler, C.A. (2005). Winning fights elevates testosterone levels in California mice and enhances future ability to win fights. *Hormones and Behaviour, 48*(3), 259–267.

Oyegbile, T.O., & Marler, C.A. (2006). Weak winner effect in a less aggressive mammal: Correlations with corticosterone but not testosterone. *Physiology & Behavior, 89*(2), 171–179. http://doi.org/10.1016/j.physbeh.2006.05.044

Packard, M.G., Cornell, A.H., & Alexander, G.M. (1997). Rewarding affective properties of intra-nucleus accumbens injections of testosterone. *Behavioral Neurosciences, 111*(1), 219–224. doi:10.1037/0735-7044.111.1.219

Packard, M.G., Schroeder, J.P., & Alexander, G.M. (1998). Expression of testosterone conditioned place preference is blocked by peripheral or intra-accumbens injection of α-flupenthixol. *Hormones and Behavior, 34*(1), 39–47. doi:10.1006/hbeh.1998.1461

Popp, J.W. (1988). Effects of experience on agonistic behavior among American goldfinches. *Behavioural Processes, 16*, 11–19.

Pultorak, J.D., Fuxjager, M.J., Kalcounis-Rueppell, M.C., & Marler, C.A. (2015). Male fidelity expressed through rapid testosterone suppression of ultrasonic vocalizations to novel females in the monogamous California mouse. *Hormones and Behaviour, 70*, 47–56.

Razzoli, M., Andreoli, M., Michielin, F., Quarta, D., & Sokal, D.M. (2011). Increased phasic activity of VTA dopamine neurons in mice 3 weeks after repeated social defeat. *Behavioural Brain Research, 218*(1), 253–257.

Ribble, D.O. (1992). Dispersal in a monogamous rodent, *Peromyscus californicus*. *Ecology, 73*(3), 859–866. doi:10.2307/1940163

Riede, T. (2013). Stereotypic laryngeal and respiratory motor patterns generate different call types in rat ultrasound vocalization. *Journal of Experimental Zoology: Part A, Ecological Genetics and Physiology, 319*(4), 213–224. http://doi.org/10.1002/jez.1785

Rieger, N.S., & Marler, C.A. (2018). The function of ultrasonic vocalizations during territorial defence by pair-bonded male and female California mice. *Animal Behaviour, 135*. http://doi.org/10.1016/j.anbehav.2017.11.008

Russo, S.J., & Nestler, E.J. (2013). The brain reward circuitry in mood disorders. *National Reviews Neuroscience, 14*, 609–625.

Rutte, C., Taborsky, M., & Brinkhof, M.W.G. (2006). What sets the odds of winning and losing? *Trends in Ecology & Evolution, 21*(1), 16–21.

Schroeder, J.P., & Packard, M.G. (2000). Role of dopamine receptor subtypes in the acquisition of a testosterone conditioned place preference in rats. *Neuroscience Letters, 282*(1), 17–20.

Schuett, G.W. (1997). Body size and agonistic experience affect dominance and mating success in male copperheads. *Animal Behaviour, 54*, 213–224.

Schultz, W. (2016). Dopamine reward prediction error coding. *Dialogues in Clinical Neuroscience, 18*, 23–32.

Schultz, W., Dayan, P., & Montague, P.R. (1997). A neural substrate of prediction and reward. *Science, 275*, 1593–1599.

Schwartzer, J.J., & Melloni, R.H., Jr. (2010). Dopamine activity in the lateral anterior hypothalamus modulates AAS-induced aggression through D2 but not D5 receptors. *Behavioural Neuroscience, 124*(5), 645.

Sperry, T.S., Wacker, D.W., & Wingfield, J.C. (2010). The role of androgen receptors in regulating territorial aggression in male song sparrows. *Hormones and Behavior, 57*(1), 86–95. http://doi.org/10.1016/j.yhbeh.2009.09.015

Steinman, M.Q., Duque-Wilckens, N., Greenberg, G.D., Hao, R., Campi, K.L., Laredo, S.A., . . . Trainor, B.C. (2016). Sex-specific effects of stress on oxytocin neurons correspond with responses to intranasal oxytocin. *Biological Psychiatry, 80*, 406–414.

Steinman, M.Q., Laredo, S.A., Lopez, E.M., Manning, C.E., Hao, R.C., Doig, I.E., . . . Trainor, B.C. (2015). Hypothalamic vasopressin systems are more sensitive to social defeat in males versus females. *Psychoneuroendocrinology, 51*, 122–134.

Steinman, M.Q., & Trainor, B.C. (2017). Sex differences in the effects of social defeat on brain and behavior in the California mouse: Insights from a monogamous rodent. *Seminars in Cell and Developmental Biology, 61*, 92–98.

Stuenkel, C.A., Dudley, R.E., & Yen, S.S.C. (1991). Sublingual administration of testosterone-hydroxypropyl-β-cyclodextrin inclusion complex sEpisodic androgen release in hypogonadal men★. *The Journal of Clinical Endocrinology and Metabolism, 72*(5), 1054–1059. http://doi.org/10.1210/jcem-72-5-1054

Tellegen, A., & Horn, J.M. (1972). Primary aggressive motivation in three inbred strains of mice. *Journal of Comparative and Physiological Psychology, 78*(2), 297.

Tellegen, A., Horn, J.M., & Legrand, R.G. (1969). Opportunity for aggression as a reinforcer in mice. *Psychonomic Science, 14*(3), 104–105.

Trainor, B.C. (2011). Stress responses and the mesolimbic dopamine system: Social contexts and sex differences. *Hormones and Behavior, 60*(5), 457–469.

Trainor, B.C., Bird, I.M., & Marler, C.A. (2004). Opposing hormonal mechanisms of aggression revealed through short-lived testosterone manipulations and multiple winning experiences. *Hormones and Behavior, 45*(2), 115–121. http://doi.org/10.1016/j.yhbeh.2003.09.006

Trainor, B.C., & Marler, C.A. (2001). Testosterone, paternal behavior, and aggression in the monogamous California mouse (*Peromyscus californicus*). *Hormones and Behavior, 40*(1), 32–42. http://doi.org/10.1006/hbeh.2001.1652

Trainor, B.C., Pride, M.C., Villalon Landeros, R., Knoblauch, N.W., Takahashi, E.Y., Silva, A.L., & Crean, K.K. (2011). Sex differences in social interaction behavior following social defeat stress in the monogamous California mouse (*Peromyscus californicus*). *PLoS One, 6*(2), e17405.

Trainor, B.C., Takahashi, E.Y., Campi, K.L., Florez, S.A., Greenberg, G.D., Laman-Maharg, A., ... Steinman, M.Q. (2013). Sex differences in stress-induced social withdrawal: Independence from adult gonadal hormones and inhibition of female phenotype by corncob bedding. *Hormones and Behaviour, 63*, 543–550.

Triemstra, J.L., Sato, S.M., & Wood, R.I. (2008). Testosterone and nucleus accumbens dopamine in the male Syrian hamster. *Psychoneuroendocrinology, 33*(3), 386–394.

Tzschentke, T.M. (2007). Measuring reward with the Conditioned Place Preference (CPP) paradigm: Update of the last decade. *Addiction Biology, 12*(3–4), 227–462. doi:10.1111/j.1369-1600.2007.00070.x

Watt, M.J., Burke, A.R., Renner, K.J., & Forster, G.L. (2009). Adolescent male rats exposed to social defeat exhibit altered anxiety behavior and limbic monoamines as adults. *Behavioral Neuroscience, 123*(3), 564–576. http://doi.org/10.1037/a0015752

Whitehouse, M.A. (1997). Experience influences male-male contests in the spider *Argyrodes antipodiana* (Theridiidae: Araneae). *Animal Behaviour, 53*, 913–923.

Winberg, S., & Nilsson, G.E. (1992). Induction of social dominance by L-dopa treatment in Arctic charr. *NeuroReport, 3*(3), 243–246. http://doi.org/10.1097/00001756-199203000-00006

Wise, R.A. (2006). Role of brain dopamine in food reward and reinforcement. *Philosophical Transactions of Royal Society of London Series B: Biological Sciences, 361*, 1149–1158.

Wingfield, J.C., Hegner, R.E., Dufty, A.M., & Ball, G.F. (1990). The 'challenge hypothesis': Theoretical implications for patterns of testosterone secretion, mating systems, and breeding strategies. *American Naturalist, 136*(6), 829–846.

Wood, R.I. (2002). Oral testosterone self-administration in male hamsters: Dose-response, voluntary exercise, and individual differences. *Hormones and Behaviour, 41*(3), 247–258. doi:10.1159/000054645

Wood, R.I., Johnson, L.R., Chu, L., Schad, C., & Self, D.W. (2004). Testosterone reinforcement: Intravenous and intracerebroventricular self-administration in male rats and hamsters. *Psychopharmacology, 171*(3), 298–305. doi:10.1007/s00213-003-1587-7

Yee, N., Bailenson, J.N., & Ducheneaut, N. (2009). The proteus effect: Implications of transformed digital self-representation on online and offline behavior. *Communication Research, 36*(2), 285–312. doi:10.1177/0093650208330254

Zhao, X., & Marler, C.A. (2014a). Pair bonding prevents reinforcing effects of testosterone in male California mice in an unfamiliar environment. *Proceedings of Royal Society B, 281*(1788), 20140985. doi:10.1098/rspb.2014.0985

Zhao, X. & Marler, C. A. (2014b). A timeline of testosterone response of male California mice to females over 24 hours. Unpublished raw data.

Zhao, X., & Marler, C.A. (2016). Social and physical environments as a source of individual variation in the rewarding effects of testosterone in male California mice (*Peromyscus californicus*). *Hormones and Behaviour, 85*, 30–35.

6

THE ENDOCRINOLOGY OF DOMINANCE RELATIONS IN NON-HUMAN PRIMATES

Sean P. Coyne

This chapter will explore the role hormones play in influencing dominance status in non-human primates (hereinafter referred to as primates). It starts with the definition of dominance and its importance in primate socioecology. The chapter then explores specific hormones and their role in dominance, beginning with traditionally "male hormones" (i.e., androgens). While it is clear that androgens play a role in dominance status for both males and females, this chapters makes the considerations separately. Next, the chapter explores the role of estrogens and dominance for females only. Finally, the chapter concludes with the relationship between both stress hormones (i.e., glucocorticoids) as well as neurohormones and neurotransmitters with dominance. Overall, the chapter first summarizes what is known in each of these areas and then emphasizes the areas of the literature where there are still gaps in our knowledge.

What is dominance?

Dominance hierarchies are helpful heuristics to help animals navigate social interactions

Almost all primates live in social groups, with frequent, repeated interactions between familiar individuals. Dominance relationships between these individuals are convenient ways for animals to make decisions about access to limited resources (e.g., food or mates) while minimizing the potential costs of escalated aggression. With knowledge of prior agonistic encounters, individuals can reasonably assess the likelihood of future success or defeat, and signal dominance or submission without needing to engage in physical aggression (Bernstein, 2011). Dominance status results from (and is measured by) the outcomes of repeated interactions among individuals, and is therefore a dyadic, not individual, property. Individual attributes, such as size and strength, can nevertheless contribute to the attainment of dominance, and the outcomes of dominance interactions produce important effects on individual biology, including hormones.

Hormones serve important functions in regulating dynamic processes, chiefly by signaling somatic states and environmental stimuli and coordinating appropriate physiological and behavioral responses. Hormones play a particularly important role in regulating life history strategies (Ketterson & Nolan, 1992; Finch & Rose, 1995). Life history theory is the conceptual tool long used by biologists to understand and explain the differential allocation of energetic resources by organisms as they move through various stages in the life cycle, and simply states that because organisms have a limited set of resources available, they must optimize the "spending" of these resources on different activities such as growth, reproduction, and somatic maintenance (Stearns, 1992). Thus, it is no surprise that hormones are implicated in many facets of dominance. They can prepare the body to produce the "winning" signals of dominance (e.g. colorful faces of mandrills, Setchell & Wickings, 2005; colorful genitals of vervets, Gerald, 2001), as well as the necessary behaviors to coincide with the physical signals (e.g. pant-hoot calls in chimpanzees, Fedurek et al., 2016). Dominant males will often have priority of access to fertile females, thus hormones coordinate the behaviors and necessary physiology of reproductive effort. The reason hormones are so successful as a signaling system is that the same hormone can coordinate multiple physiological and behavioral systems across the central and peripheral nervous systems simultaneously, and as such have great economy (Nelson and Kriegsfeld, 2017).

Dominance and physiology are related in complex relationships that can vary depending on species and context

It is an important consideration for researchers that dominance rank is an outcome of a complex history of behaviors, thus correlations of dominance rank with hormonal attributes are just that, correlations. This leaves important questions about how physiology is impacted by different processes contributing to and reinforcing dominance status, and what the direction of cause and effect exists between status and hormone production. For example, while androgens are understood to regulate the expression of some sexually selected morphological signals (which can indicate an individual's status), a landmark study of barn swallows showed that experimental manipulation of a male's plumage coloration, a sexual signal in this species, led to higher androgen production (Safran, Adelman, McGraw, & Hau, 2008). By contrast, some studies of primates suggest that testosterone correlates better with future dominance rank than with current rank, suggesting a role in facilitating the behaviors that contribute to rank acquisition rather than any feature of rank itself (Beehner, Bergman, Cheney, Seyfarth, & Whitten, 2006).

Androgens and male dominance relationships

Male social status in primates is linked to their ability to defeat other males in intrasexual aggressive competition for mates and resources

The highest-ranking males in a group thus tend to be prime-aged individuals in peak condition (Alberts, Watts, & Altmann, 2003; Setchell, Wickings, & Knapp, 2006; Bissonnette et al., 2015; Borries, Perlman, & Koenig, 2015; Marty, Hodges, Agil, & Engelhardt, 2015). In some species or populations, however, the highest-ranking males are not the most formidably aggressive males but those who have resided in the group the longest. This is the case with the rhesus macaques on Cayo Santiago, where rank is typically related to group tenure length (Bercovitch, 1997; Berard, 1999), although even here exceptions have been observed (Georgiev et al., 2016), raising questions as to whether this type of dominance acquisition is typical of the species as a whole or only of the provisioned, high-density population of Cayo Santiago. Even in species where aggression plays a central role in obtaining and maintaining high rank, other factors can also have a role. Social skills related to the ability of primate males to recruit alliance partners for agonistic support, for example, can augment a male's standing in the hierarchy (Schülke, Bhagavatula, Vigilant, & Ostner, 2010; Gilby et al., 2013; Neumann, 2013). With these caveats in mind, it is still clear that attaining and maintaining high dominance rank in male primates overall is influenced to a large extent by their ability to dominate others in dyadic encounters either through direct aggression or by signaling their ability to do so (e.g., somatic development, behavioral displays, special ornaments). All these pathways to dominance, in turn, are often testosterone-dependent in their expression.

Androgens and aggression are often tightly linked

Individual primates with higher levels of androgens tend to be more aggressive – whether the behavior is measured in a semi-experimental setting as their response to handling by humans (Zohdy, Bisanzio, Tecot, Wright, & Jernvall, 2017) or in naturalistic conditions when interacting with conspecifics (Muller & Wrangham, 2004). As a result, species in which social status is maintained via aggression, positive correlations between male rank and testosterone frequently emerge (Muller, 2017; Prall & Muehlenbein, 2017). Such correlations are not universally present, or even expected, however. The "Challenge Hypothesis" predicts that male androgen levels are linked closer to aggressive mating competition than to reproductive physiology per se (Wingfield, Hegner, Dufty, & Ball, 1990). While originally proposed to explain differences in male hormonal profiles among birds of different species, this hypothesis has successfully been applied to explain endocrine variation among male primates (Muller & Wrangham, 2004; Muller, 2017). Several conditions have been identified as predictors of a positive correlation between testosterone and male dominance rank: high-ranking males will have higher testosterone levels than lower-ranking males when high rank predicts mating success, is maintained by aggression, and/or when the dominance hierarchy in the group is unstable (Muller, 2017). Empirical data from a range of species support this and suggest that in species or periods when high levels of testosterone are not essential for rank maintenance or for gaining access to fertile females, high-ranking males do not differ in their androgen profiles from low-ranking males, reducing the expected detrimental correlates of elevated testosterone production (e.g., increased energy expenditure, greater vulnerability to infection) they might otherwise experience (reviewed in Muller, 2017).

Androgens can signal male dominance

Secondary sexual characteristics can be costly for males to produce or maintain, and are assumed to be honest signals indicative of male health and "quality" (Zahavi, 1975). Initially, researchers thought the exaggerated development of secondary sexual characteristics in males to be indicators of individual ability to handle parasites (e.g., Hamilton & Zuk, 1982), but Folstad and Karter (1992) expanded the handicap principle to explain differences in hormone function. Specifically, they noted that testosterone is a "double-edged sword" which promotes stronger secondary sexual traits while compromising immunocompetence. For example, one well-known male primate signal is the red facial coloration of mandrills. The redness of male mandrill faces is controlled by androgen levels and increases during periods of rank instability or in the presence of sexually receptive females. The degree of redness represents an honest signal of androgen status, competitive ability, and the willingness to engage in aggressive encounters (Setchell, Smith, Wickings, & Knapp, 2008). Interestingly, rhesus macaques also display variation in red facial color, which is attractive to females, but is not related to dominance rank (Dubuc, Allen, Maestripieri, & Higham, 2014). Therefore, the signal, while commonly related to androgen levels, is not universally related to dominance rank across the cercopithecine primates, and warrants independent examination of each species in which it occurs. For example, the redness of bare chest patches correlates clearly with status in male geladas, but it is not yet known how androgens influence this trait, and if so, how this relates to the complementary reception in females (Bergman, Ho, & Beehner, 2009). And while blue scrotal coloration serves as a signal of status in vervet monkeys (Gerald, 2001), it appears that darker scrotal color is linked to higher serotonin rather than androgen levels (Gerald & McGuire, 2007).

Most work in primates focuses on visual cues, because primates are a highly visual species. However, some recent work has shifted focus toward auditory cues of sexually selected traits. For example, both gibbons (Barelli, Mundry, Heistermann, & Hammerschmidt, 2013) and rhesus macaques (Higham, Pfefferle, Heistermann, M., Maestripieri, D., & Stevens, 2013) have been shown to have aspects of their vocalization structure relate significantly to androgen levels, where gibbons with higher androgen levels have higher pitch and longer calls, while rhesus macaques had a higher frequency calls with higher androgen levels. Further, chimpanzee vocalizations are influenced by testosterone levels such that higher testosterone levels are significantly related to higher frequency of the call and greater rates of calling (Fedurek et al., 2016). Work by Puts et al. (2016) looked at comparing the fundamental frequency of male vocalizations across multiple species of primates, including humans. Results indicate that a higher degree of mating competition (e.g., monogamy vs. polygyny) leads to a greater dimorphism between males and females in vocal pitch. Further, their work on the human sample showed that lower frequency vocalizations had specific hormone profiles of high testosterone and low cortisol. Not only did vocal frequency relate significantly to androgen levels previously described, but it was also related to dominance and attractiveness, where males who perceived themselves as dominant lowered their vocal pitch, and those with lower pitch were rated as more attractive. Therefore, it is likely that similar relationships occur widely in primates with androgen levels influencing the fundamental frequency of certain types of vocalizations, which are similarly correlated with dominance status. Therefore, there are a variety of signals produced by primates, which are costly to maintain or produce, and indicate an honest signal of that male's quality.

Androgens and female dominance relationships

Androgens play an important role in female dominance outcomes

Androgen levels in females are substantially lower than those of males, and were initially largely ignored as a factor that influenced female social relationships. However, work in species in which females dominate males shows that the relationship between androgens and behavior may operate similarly when the socioecological demands are the same.

Activation effects in sex-reversed species reflect similar relationships between androgens and dominance seen in males

Some of the earliest work investigating the role of androgens and female dominance occurred in lemurs, in which traditional sex roles are reversed and adult females outrank adult males (Jolly, 1966). Phylogenetic work has demonstrated that female social dominance in lemurs is the ancestral trait. Specifically, among ancestral lemuriform female primates, individuals show a more masculinized hormone profile, and increased social dominance over males. However, among more recently evolved clades, there is a relaxing in both masculinized female hormone profiles, and female social dominance (Petty and Drea, 2015). For example, in ring-tailed lemurs, females display a 2-fold increase in rates of both aggression and androgen concentrations in the mating season (von Engelhard, Kappeler, & Heistermann, 2000). Further, androgen increases were shown to be independent of ovarian hormone production, and therefore tied at least in part to competition over dominance, and not exclusively to sexual functioning. However, there was no significant relationship between competitive success and androgen levels at the individual level, likely because of the low sample size ($N = 12$), and the authors suggest the importance of also considering prenatal brain priming effects for female domination over males. Bonobos are another species in which females can dominate males, though not all females necessarily outrank all males. Interestingly, however, studies in captivity have shown that there is no relationship between female rank and androgen levels (Sannen, van Elsacker, Heistermann, & Eens, 2004). Whether the same holds under naturalistic condition is presently unknown.

Androgen exposure in fetal development affects lifetime dominance status in females

One putative biomarker of prenatal exposure to androgens is the ratio of the 2nd and 4th digits (2D:4D ratio) with lower ratios indicating higher levels of androgen exposure (reviewed in Manning, Kilduff, Cook, Crewther, & Fink, 2014). The benefit of using 2D:4D ratios is that one can study adult behavior without needing to have sampled individuals in utero. For example, research in rhesus macaques has shown that low 2D:4D ratios are significantly associated with higher-ranking females while high ratios were associated with low-ranking females (Nelson, Hoffman, Gerald, & Shultz, 2010). Additionally, work with female chacma baboons has shown that low 2D:4D ratios are associated with higher rank, low submission rates, and high rates of aggression (Howlett, Setchell, Hill, & Barton, 2015). Beyond the use of 2D:4D ratios, there have also been studies using captive rhesus macaques in which experimenters exposed prenatal female individuals to androgens via injections. These studies have revealed that prenatal androgen exposure has many far-reaching effects on a variety of behaviors. Interestingly, the type and degree of behavioral modification depends on the level of androgens individuals were exposed to as well as when the exposure occurred in development. For example, early androgen exposure in females resulted in male-like levels of aggressive rough and tumble play, but late androgen exposure had no effect on the rates of rough and tumble play. Alternatively, late gestational androgen exposure affects vocalizations and interest in infants, but early gestational exposure does not affect these behaviors (reviewed in Wallen, 2005). Though the focus of this research is typically on how the androgen exposure affects sex-typical sexual behavior (i.e., the ability to initiate and engage in appropriate receptive copulatory behaviors), it is clear that depending on the timing and amount of androgen exposure, many different female behaviors may be altered. Further, given that some of these behaviors are aggressive in nature (e.g., rough and tumble play) it may also be the case that prenatal androgen exposure affects female behavior in dominance interactions. Overall, these studies suggest that prenatal androgen exposure is potentially an important organizing mechanism for the lifetime maintenance of dominance relationships.

Estrogens and female dominance relationships

Dominance and reproductive success is tightly linked in female primates

In many species, female reproductive success is tied to dominance rank (e.g., chimpanzees, Pusey, Williams, & Goodall, 1997; long-tailed macaques, van Noordwijk & van Schaik, 1999). However, a large part of this differential reproductive success is likely due to differences in access to nutritional resources and may have little to do directly with dominance status limiting the ability to secure mating partners (as is the case for males). There have been a few studies in captive populations investigating the role of estrogens with mating-related aggression in primates (e.g., Zumpe & Michael, 1989), although to date there has been no work in wild populations.

Dominant callitrichine females suppress subordinates' reproduction

A notable exception to direct dominant interference on reproductive ability is the callitrichine primates of South and Central America. The callitrichine primates (i.e., marmosets and tamarins) are small, arboreal primates that tend to live in small territorial family groups. Callitrichines almost always produce twins, requiring a large amount of paternal care for offspring survival. Often older offspring will remain with their parents and provide alloparental care for their younger siblings. The family groups almost always consist of only a single breeding female, with either a single or pair of breeding males, as well as several male and female offspring (Digby, Ferrari, & Saltzman, 2011). Therefore, all but the dominant individuals in the group are being suppressed in their own reproductive effort. Reproductive suppression can be the result of an active effort by the dominant female over her daughters, or a choice by the daughters to forgo mating opportunity in less than ideal circumstances (Beehner & Lu, 2013).

Reproductive suppression is achieved by interrupting subordinate females' ovulatory cycles

An earlier theory of reproductive suppression posited that dominant females use harassment in order to increase the stress levels of subordinate females. The heightened chronic stress could in turn interrupt regular functioning of the hypothalamic-pituitary-gonadal axis, preventing proper ovulation or conception. While theoretically sound, there does not seem to be much evidence supporting this mechanism (e.g., Abbott, Saltzman, Schultz-Darken, & Smith, 1997; Sapolsky, 2005). More recently, investigators have looked at the role of chemosignals of dominant females. The callitrichines have specialized scent glands in the anogenital regions, which communicate signals about the species, gender, and even individual identity of the secretor (Ziegler, 2013). Research with cotton-top tamarins and common marmosets has shown that exposure to chemosignals is effective in suppressing subordinate females' ovulatory cycles. However, the chemosignals alone are not sufficient for maintaining the suppression, as females were able to resume normal ovulatory function a few weeks after exposure to dominant female chemosignals (Beehner & Lu, 2013). Therefore, while chemosignals are clearly a part of the picture, there are likely other factors influencing reproductive suppression, such as social cues. Regardless of the mechanism(s) dominant females use in their suppression of subordinate females' reproductive functions, the reproductive failure of subordinates is well understood, the key mechanism of which is interruption of ovulation. In common marmosets, ovulation failure occurs rather rapidly, due to a drop in chorionic gonadotropin within 1–4 days of exposure to the dominant female. However, the process can be reversed rapidly as well, and removal of exposure to the dominant female signals results in a rapid increase of chorionic gonadotropin within a few days, and normal ovulatory cycles recurring within 3–4 weeks (Saltzman, Digby, & Abbott, 2009).

Dominance and glucocorticoids

Glucocorticoids mediate the physiological stress response

Glucocorticoids are steroid hormones produced in the adrenal gland in response to a variety of stressors. In the short term, they prepare the body for the flight-or-fight response by mobilizing energy reserves and coordinating rapid, adaptive behavioral responses. However, chronically elevated levels can have detrimental effects such as a shift toward physiological dysregulation, neural reorganization, accelerated aging, and death (McEwen, 2007).

The relationship between dominance rank and stress depends on the socioecology of the species

During investigations of which dominance ranks are subject to greater stress, the findings have been conflicting, suggesting interspecific and contextual differences may be important factors. For example, one could argue that high-ranked individuals are more stressed, perhaps over resisting frequent challenges (e.g., savannah baboons, Gesquiere et al., 2011). However, another claim could be that low-ranked individuals are more stressed due their lack of access to resources. Ultimately, as Sapolsky (2005) rightly states, "rank means different things in different species" (p. 648). Some species (e.g., rhesus macaques, chimpanzees) have highly despotic, top-down hierarchies in which access to resources is extremely skewed in favor of the dominant individual. In these despotic species, low-ranked individuals should have much greater stress levels (due to their inability to successfully access resources) compared to more egalitarian species (e.g., bonobos, barbary macaques) with more equitable access to resources. Further, some species display lifelong inherited rank (e.g., Japanese macaque females) for which there is never any fluctuation. Therefore, no psychosocial stressors are associated with maintaining rank. Other species (e.g., baboons, mandrills) have highly unstable hierarchies, where individuals may constantly have to challenge and fight to attain and maintain high dominance rank, and therefore high-ranked individuals would be expected to have higher stress levels compared to individuals who have lower rank (Sapolsky, 2005).

Social factors are a major source of stress for non-human primates

There are many ways in which dominance behaviors may be related to psychosocial stressors, and therefore to glucocorticoids. For example, the Social Stress Hypothesis predicts that there should be greater variation in stress levels during periods of social instability as individuals are establishing and maintaining their dominance rank (Higham, Heistermann, & Maestripieri, 2013). For example, in male chacma baboons, changes in the dominance hierarchy were the major source of variation in increased glucocorticoid levels (Bergman, Beehner, Cheney, Seyfarth, & Whitten, 2005). Over a 14-month study period, there were three periods of dominance instability: an immigrant male takeover as alpha male, a resident male ascent to alpha male, and the rise of a natal male to higher dominance rank. During these periods, there was a significant rise of glucocorticoid levels across all males. Further, there was a significant interaction between rank and stability, such that high-ranked males had higher glucocorticoid levels during the unstable periods, whereas low-ranked males had higher glucocorticoid levels during stable periods. In a similar study on male rhesus macaques, Higham, Heistermann, et al. (2013) demonstrated that the only period during which glucocorticoid levels were significantly related to dominance rank was during a period of social instability, when high-ranked males who were being targeted by coalitions of lower ranked males had the highest glucocorticoid levels. Recent work in yellow baboons has demonstrated that rank *attainment* was associated with a significant increase in glucocorticoid levels compared to glucocorticoid levels before adult rank was attained (Akinyi et al., 2017). The authors believe that upon rank attainment the psychosocial demands on the animal, such as agonistic encounters and mating pressures, are much greater than before.

Despite the fact that female rhesus macaques typically inherit rank directly from their mother, these positions may be altered by stress physiology as well. The serotonin transporter (*SERT*) gene has been implicated for its role in dealing with psychosocial stressors, with the short (*s*) allele making individuals more susceptible to stressors, and the long (*l*) allele buffering against stressors. In a study in which female rhesus macaques were taken from their large social groups in placed into groups of five unfamiliar females, Jarrell et al. (2008) investigated how the *SERT* gene influenced subsequent dominance formation among the unfamiliar females. They found that individuals with the buffering *l* allele were more likely to overcome the psychosocial stressor of an unfamiliar social group and maintain a dominant social status than individuals with the sensitizing *s* allele.

Dominance rank can counteract negative effects of psychosocial stressors

Dominance rank can be also thought of as a buffer to, rather than a cause of, stress. Individuals of different rank wield different amounts of social capital, that is, access to social partners. This social capital can be a particularly helpful influence in relieving psychosocial stressors through positive social interactions (e.g., grooming). For example, in a study of rhesus macaque females, dominance rank interacted with measures of social connectedness to predict glucocorticoid levels. Specifically, high-ranking females with focused social networks had the lowest glucocorticoid levels, suggesting that social capital controlled by dominance rank is an important mechanism for coping with stressors (Brent, Semple, Dubuc, Heistermann, & MacLarnon, 2011). Interestingly, Barbary macaques of both sexes show a more diverse pattern of glucocorticoid amelioration compared to rhesus macaques, which is dependent on dominance rank. Among high-ranking Barbary macaques, the pattern is the same as in rhesus macaques, such that individuals with more concentrated grooming networks show the lowest glucocorticoid levels. However, among low-ranked individuals, those with more widely spread grooming networks show the lowest glucocorticoid levels (Sonnweber et al., 2015). The authors argue that the more egalitarian hierarchy of Barbary macaques allows for more diverse strategies in response to dealing with stressors.

Dominance and neurohormones

Neurohormones influence social behaviors, which in turn can influence dominance

Neurohormones and neurotransmitters such as dopamine, oxytocin, and vasopressin that derive from the central nervous system (CNS) play an important role regulating physiology and social behaviors. While these physiological measures have not directly been studied in relationship with dominance, the behaviors they regulate could influence dominance behaviors. However, obtaining non-invasive measures of CNS metabolites has proved extremely difficult for field primatology (Higham, 2016). Therefore, most work that has been done typically comes from either studies with captive animals using traditionally invasive measures, or indirect assessments of neurohormone function, such as differences in genetic polymorphisms influencing the efficiency of binding and transportation of the neurohormones to their receptors.

Dopamine influences risk-taking and boldness, important factors for achieving dominance

Dopamine is traditionally thought of a neurotransmitter involved in the reward pathway of the limbic system (Ikemoto, 2010). Additionally, recent work with various dopamine receptors has revealed that the dopaminergic system also influences risk-taking, boldness, and impulsivity behaviors as well. For example, work with juvenile rhesus macaques (Coyne et al., 2015) and vervets (Fairbanks, Way, Breidenthal, Bailey, & Jorgensen, 2012) has shown that individuals with a variant copy of the dopamine receptor D4 (*DRD4*) gene (i.e., a gene that conveys less binding affinity; 7R allele in macaques, 5R allele in vervets) are prone to more impulsive and risky behavior. These individuals were shown to be less fearful of a strange intruder to the home cage (Fairbanks et al., 2012) and to spend more time socially exploring outside maternal protection (Coyne et al., 2015). Further, Fairbanks et al. (2004) have demonstrated that impulsivity and boldness in adolescence predicts dominance attainment in adult male vervet monkeys. Similarly, work with dopamine receptor D2 (*DRD2*) in Japanese macaques has demonstrated that *DRD2* genotype does not directly influence dominance attainment. However, *DRD2* genotype does directly affect affiliative behaviors such as proximity maintenance, grooming, and playing, which in turn influenced dominance attainment (Yamaguchi, Lee, Kato, Jas, & Goto, 2017). Therefore, while dopamine levels do not directly influence dominance, this neurotransmitter plays an important role regulating social behaviors that may lead individuals to successful attempts at attaining dominance.

Oxytocin and vasopressin control social bonding, important for coalition formation

Oxytocin and vasopressin have long been implicated as important hormones that regulate the social bonding between parents and offspring as well as between mating partners (Donaldson & Young, 2008). However, more recently oxytocin has been implicated in regulating not only mating-related bonding but also stable, peaceful associations between individuals (Romero, Onishi, & Hasegawa, 2016). For example, there are interesting associations between "friendships" and oxytocin and vasopressin levels in juvenile rhesus macaques. Further, there was a sex difference such that number of friendships in females predicted oxytocin levels, while number of friendships in males predicted vasopressin levels (Weinstein et al., 2014). Similarly, Samuni et al. (2016) have recently demonstrated that chimpanzees have elevated oxytocin levels immediately prior to and during intergroup conflicts, suggesting that oxytocin plays an important role for in-group social bonding for better cohesion during these conflicts. While social cohesion is not directly related to bonding, coalition formation is a common strategy among males of many species in dominance acquisition (discussed in Bissonnette, Franz, Schülke, & Ostner, 2014). Therefore, oxytocin and vasopressin may be influencing success at dominance acquisition indirectly in those species which require successful coalitions by promoting greater social cohesion and cooperation among coalition partners.

Serotonin influences reactions to stress and anxiety, as well as life history traits that help determine dominance rank

In the central nervous system, serotonin is one of the key influences on mood, social behaviors, and stress reactivity, with high levels of serotonin leading to elevated mood and social behavior, and decreased levels or low availability of serotonin often leading to depression (Shively, Mirkes, Lu, Henderson, & Bethea, 2003). More recently, Howell et al. (2007) conducted a longitudinal study on the effects of early life serotonin levels and adult life history outcomes in male rhesus macaques. The authors evaluated serotonin levels in cerebrospinal fluid (CSF) during the juvenile through adult periods and measured aggression, age at emigration, dominance rank, and mortality in adulthood. Results indicate that CSF serotonin levels are consistent between the two sampling points, and that low early life serotonin levels delay emigration, and are associated with high levels of violence and a proneness for premature death. However, the males with low early life serotonin that survived were able to achieve high dominance rank. Similarly, Fairbanks et al. (2004) measured CSF serotonin levels of adolescent male vervet monkeys while these were still in their natal groups, then again 2 years later upon becoming adults and being introduced into a new group. Similar to rhesus macaques, vervets with low serotonin levels in adolescence were more likely to achieve a stable alpha male position in adulthood. Overall, serotonin levels seem to have a consistent relationship with dominance status, at least in male primates, where lower levels of serotonin early in life seem to predict higher, stable hierarchy positions later in life.

Conclusion

Both male and female primate dominance relations are affected by sex steroids. Empirical data, however, is still limited for females, especially in terms of the effects of androgens. The mode of rank acquisition and the fitness benefits of high rank seem to be key predictors of rank-related differences in testosterone levels among males. In both males and females, the costs of high or low rank are reflected in elevated glucocorticoid production, but whether it is the high- or the low-ranking individuals who experience greater chronic elevations varies depending on the type social stressors associated with their respective position in the hierarchy and the amount of social support available from other group members. Even though most field studies of primates have focused on the relationship between dominance and steroid hormones due to the feasibility of measuring these in feces and urine, recent work has also shown the central role of several neurohormones and neurotransmitters in mediating dominance interactions. The variety of mating and social systems observed among the non-human primates offer rich grounds for studies into the endocrinology of dominance. Despite the methodological limitations that come with observing long-lived animals in the field, long-term studies of known individual primates can provide a unique perspective not only on the physiology of dominance in mammals more broadly, but also, due to their close phylogenetic relationship to us, an important comparative point for studies of human evolutionary biology.

Acknowledgments

I would like to thank Oliver Schultheiss and Pranjal Mehta for the invitation to contribute to this volume, Melissa Emery Thompson for insightful discussion and helpful feedback, and Alex Georgiev for helpful edits and feedback on an earlier draft. Any errors and omissions are my own.

References

Abbott, D.H., Saltzman, W., Schultz-Darken, N.J., & Smith, T.E. (1997). Specific neuroendocrine mechanisms not involving generalized stress mediate social regulation of female reproduction in cooperatively breeding marmoset monkeys. *Annals of the New York Academy of Sciences, 807*(1), 219–238. https://doi.org/10.1111/j.1749-6632.1997.tb51923.x

Akinyi, M.Y., Gesquiere, L.R., Franz, M., Onyango, P.O., Altmann, J., & Alberts, S.C. (2017). Hormonal correlates of natal dispersal and rank attainment in wild male baboons. *Hormones and Behavior, 94*, 153–161. https://doi.org/10.1016/j.yhbeh.2017.07.005

Alberts, S.C., Watts, H.E., & Altmann, J. (2003). Queuing and queue-jumping: Long-term patterns of reproductive skew in male savannah baboons, Papio cynocephalus. *Animal Behaviour, 65*(4), 821–840. https://doi.org/10.1006/anbe.2003.2106

Barelli, C., Mundry, R., Heistermann, M., & Hammerschmidt, K. (2013). Cues to androgens and quality in male gibbon songs. *PLoS One, 8*(12), e82748. https://doi.org/10.1371/journal.pone.0082748

Beehner, J.C., Bergman, T.J., Cheney, D.L., Seyfarth, R.M., & Whitten, P.L. (2006). Testosterone predicts future dominance rank and mating activity among male chacma baboons. *Behavioral Ecology and Sociobiology, 59*(4), 469–479. https://doi.org/10.1007/s00265-005-0071-2

Beehner, J.C., & Lu, A. (2013). Reproductive suppression in female primates: A review. *Evolutionary Anthropology: Issues, News, and Reviews, 22*(5), 226–238. https://doi.org/10.1002/evan.21369

Berard, J. (1999). A four-year study of the association between male dominance rank, residency status, and reproductive activity in rhesus macaques (*Macaca mulatta*). *Primates, 40*, 159–175. https://doi.org/10.1007/bf02557708

Bercovitch, F.B. (1997). Reproductive strategies of rhesus macaques. *Primates, 38*, 247–263. https://doi.org/10.1007/bf02381613

Bergman, T.J., Beehner, J.C., Cheney, D.L., Seyfarth, R.M., & Whitten, P.L. (2005). Correlates of stress in free-ranging male chacma baboons, *Papio hamadryas ursinus*. *Animal Behaviour, 70*(3), 703–713. https://doi.org/10.1016/j.anbehav.2004.12.017

Bergman, T. J., Ho, L., & Beehner, J. C. (2009). Chest color and social status in male geladas (*Theropithecus gelada*). *International Journal of Primatology, 30*(6), 791–806. https://doi.org/10.1007/s10764-009-9374-x

Bernstein, I.S. (2011). Social mechanisms in the control of primate aggression. In C.J. Campbell, A. Fuentes, K.C. MacKinnon, S.K. Bearder, & R.M. Stumpf (Eds.), *Primates in perspective* (2nd ed.). Oxford: Oxford University Press.

Bissonnette, A., Franz, M., Schülke, O., & Ostner, J. (2014). Socioecology, but not cognition, predicts male coalitions across primates. *Behavioral Ecology, 25*(4), 794–801. https://doi.org/10.1093/beheco/aru054

Bissonnette, A., Perry, S., Barrett, L., Mitani, J.C., Flinn, M., Gavrilets, S., & de Waal, F.B.M. (2015). Coalitions in theory and reality: A review of pertinent variables and processes. *Behaviour, 152*, 1–56. https://doi.org/10.1163/1568539x-00003241

Borries, C., Perlman, R.F., & Koenig, A. (2015). Characteristics of alpha males in Nepal gray langurs. *American Journal of Primatology, 79*(7), e22437. https://doi.org/10.1002/ajp.22437

Brent, L.J.N., Semple, S., Dubuc, C., Heistermann, M., & MacLarnon, A. (2011). Social capital and physiological stress levels in free-ranging adult female rhesus macaques. *Physiology & Behavior, 102*(1), 76–83. https://doi.org/10.1016/j.physbeh.2010.09.022

Coyne, S.P., Lindell, S.G., Clemente, J., Barr, C.S., Parker, K.J., & Maestripieri, D. (2015). Dopamine D4 receptor genotype variation in free-ranging rhesus macaques and its association with juvenile behavior. *Behavioural Brain Research, 292*, 50–55. https://doi.org/10.1016/j.bbr.2015.06.014

Digby, L.J., Ferrari, S.F., & Saltzman, W. (2011). Callitrichines the role of competition in cooperatively breeding species. In C.J. Campbell, A. Fuentes, K.C. MacKinnon, S.K. Bearder, & R.M. Stumpf (Eds.), *Primates in perspective* (2nd ed.). Oxford: Oxford University Press.

Donaldson, Z.R., & Young, L.J. (2008). Oxytocin, vasopressin, and the neurogenetics of sociality. *Science, 322*(5903), 900–904. https://doi.org/10.1126/science.1158668

Dubuc, C., Allen, W.L., Maestripieri, D., & Higham, J.P. (2014). Is male rhesus macaque red color ornamentation attractive to females? *Behavioral Ecology and Sociobiology, 68*(7), 1215–1224. https://doi.org/10.1007/s00265-014-1732-9

Fairbanks, L.A., Jorgensen, M.J., Huff, A., Blau, K., Hung, Y.Y., & Mann, J.J. (2004). Adolescent impulsivity predicts adult dominance attainment in male vervet monkeys. *American Journal of Primatology, 64*(1), 1–17. https://doi.org/10.1002/ajp.20057

Fairbanks, L.A., Way, B.M., Breidenthal, S.E., Bailey, J.N., & Jorgensen, M.J. (2012). Maternal and offspring dopamine D4 receptor genotypes interact to influence juvenile impulsivity in vervet monkeys. *Psychological Science, 23*(10), 1099–1104. https://doi.org/10.1177/0956797612444905

Fedurek, P., Slocombe, K.E., Enigk, D.K., Thompson, M.E., Wrangham, R.W., & Muller, M.N. (2016). The relationship between testosterone and long-distance calling in wild male chimpanzees. *Behavioral Ecology and Sociobiology, 70*(5), 659–672. https://doi.org/10.1007/s00265-016-2087-1

Finch, C.E., & Rose, M.R. (1995). Hormones and the physiological architecture of life history evolution. *The Quarterly Review of Biology, 70*(1), 1–52. https://doi.org/10.1086/418864

Folstad, I., & Karter, A.J. (1992). Parasites, bright males, and the immunocompetence handicap. *The American Naturalist, 139*(3), 603–622. https://doi.org/10.1086/285346

Georgiev, A.V., Maestripieri, D., Christie, D., Maldonado, E., Emery Thompson, M., Rosenfield, K.A., & Ruiz-Lambides, A.V. (2016). Breaking the succession rule: The costs and benefits of an alpha-status take-over by an immigrant rhesus macaque on Cayo Santiago. *Behaviour, 153*(3), 325–351. https://doi.org/10.1163/1568539x-00003344

Gerald, M.S. (2001). Primate colour predicts social status and aggressive outcome. *Animal Behaviour, 61*(3), 559–566. https://doi.org/10.1006/anbe.2000.1648

Gerald, M. S., & McGuire, M. T. (2007). Secondary sexual coloration and CSF 5-HIAA are correlated in vervet monkeys (*Cercopithecus aethiops sabaeus*). *Journal of Medical Primatology, 36*(6), 348–354. https://doi.org/10.1111/j.1600-0684.2007.00227.x

Gesquiere, L.R., Learn, N.H., Simao, M.C.M., Onyango, P.O., Alberts, S.C., & Altmann, J. (2011). Life at the top: Rank and stress in wild male baboons. *Science, 333*(6040), 357–360. https://doi.org/10.1126/science.1207120

Gilby, I.C., Brent, L.J.N., Wroblewski, E.E., Rudicell, R.S., Goodall, J., & Pusey, A.E. (2013). Fitness benefits of coalitionary aggression in male chimpanzees. *Behavioral Ecology and Sociobiology, 67*, 373–381. https://doi.org/10.1007/s00265-012-1457-6

Hamilton, W.D., & Zuk, M. (1982). Heritable true fitness and bright birds: A role for parasites? *Science, 218*(4570), 384–387. https://doi.org/10.1126/science.7123238

Higham, J. P. (2016). Field endocrinology of nonhuman primates: Past, present, and future. *Hormones and Behavior, 84*, 145–155. https://doi.org/10.1016/j.yhbeh.2016.07.001

Higham, J.P., Heistermann, M., & Maestripieri, D. (2013). The endocrinology of male rhesus macaque social and reproductive status: A test of the challenge and social stress hypotheses. *Behavioral Ecology and Sociobiology, 67*(1), 19–30. https://doi.org/10.1007/s00265-012-1420-6

Higham, J.P., Pfefferle, D., Heistermann, M., Maestripieri, D., & Stevens, M. (2013). Signaling in multiple modalities in male rhesus macaques: Sex skin coloration and barks in relation to androgen levels, social status, and mating behavior. *Behavioral Ecology and Sociobiology, 67*(9), 1457–1469. https://doi.org/10.1007/s00265-013-1521-x

Howell, S., Westergaard, G., Hoos, B., Chavanne, T.J., Shoaf, S.E., Cleveland, A., . . . Dee Higley, J. (2007). Serotonergic influences on life-history outcomes in free-ranging male rhesus macaques. *American Journal of Primatology, 69*(8), 851–865. https://doi.org/10.1002/ajp.20369

Howlett, C., Setchell, J.M., Hill, R.A., & Barton, R.A. (2015). The 2D:4D digit ratio and social behaviour in wild female chacma baboons (*Papio ursinus*) in relation to dominance, aggression, interest in infants, affiliation and heritability. *Behavioral Ecology and Sociobiology, 69*(1), 61–74. https://doi.org/10.1007/s00265-014-1817-5

Ikemoto, S. (2010). Brain reward circuitry beyond the mesolimbic dopamine system: A neurobiological theory. *Neuroscience & Biobehavioral Reviews, 35*(2), 129–150. https://doi.org/10.1016/j.neubiorev.2010.02.001

Jarrell, H., Hoffman, J. B., Kaplan, J. R., Berga, S., Kinkead, B., & Wilson, M. E. (2008). Polymorphisms in the serotonin reuptake transporter gene modify the consequences of social status on metabolic health in female rhesus monkeys. *Physiology & Behavior, 93*(4–5), 807–819. https://doi.org/10.1016/j.physbeh.2007.11.042

Jolly, A. (1966). *Lemur behavior.* Chicago, IL: University of Chicago Press.

Ketterson, E.D., & Nolan, V. (1992). Hormones and life histories: An integrative approach. *The American Naturalist, 140*(Suppl. 1), S33–S62. https://doi.org/10.1086/285396

Manning, J., Kilduff, L., Cook, C., Crewther, B., & Fink, B. (2014). Digit ratio (2D:4D): A biomarker for prenatal sex steroids and adult sex steroids in challenge situations. *Frontiers in Endocrinology, 5.* https://doi.org/10.3389/fendo.2014.00009

Marty, P.R., Hodges, K., Agil, M., & Engelhardt, A. (2015). Alpha male replacements and delayed dispersal in crested macaques (*Macaca nigra*). *American Journal of Primatology, 79*(7), e22448. https://doi.org/10.1002/ajp.22448

McEwen, B.S. (2007). Physiology and neurobiology of stress and adaptation: Central role of the brain. *Physiological Reviews, 87*(3), 873–904. https://doi.org/10.1152/physrev.00041.2006

Muller, M.N. (2017). Testosterone and reproductive effort in male primates. *Hormones and Behavior, 91*, 36–51. https://doi.org/10.1016/j.yhbeh.2016.09.001

Muller, M.N., & Wrangham, R.W. (2004). Dominance, aggression and testosterone in wild chimpanzees: A test of the "challenge hypothesis". *Animal Behaviour, 67*(1), 113–123. https://doi.org/10.1016/j.anbehav.2003.03.013

Nelson, E., Hoffman, C.L., Gerald, M.S., & Shultz, S. (2010). Digit ratio (2D:4D) and dominance rank in female rhesus macaques (*Macaca mulatta*). *Behavioral Ecology and Sociobiology, 64*(6), 1001–1009. https://doi.org/10.1007/978-1-4614-1046-1_6

Nelson, R., & Kriegsfeld, L.J. (2017). *An introduction to behavioral endocrinology* (5th ed.). Sunderland, MA: Sinauer Associates Inc.

Neumann, C. (2013). *Achievement and maintenance of dominance in male crested macaques (Macaca nigra)*. PhD thesis, Leipzig University, Leipzig.

Petty, J.M., & Drea, C.M. (2015). Female rule in lemurs is ancestral and hormonally mediated. *Scientific Reports, 5*, srep09631. https://doi.org/10.1038/srep09631

Prall, S.P., & Muehlenbein, M.P. (2017). Hormonal correlates of dominance. In A. Fuentes (Ed.), *The international encyclopedia of primatology*. Hoboken, NJ: John Wiley & Sons, Inc.

Pusey, A., Williams, J., & Goodall, J. (1997). The influence of dominance rank on the reproductive success of female chimpanzees. *Science, 277*(5327), 828–831. https://doi.org/10.1126/science.277.5327.828

Puts, D.A., Hill, A.K., Bailey, D.H., Walker, R.S., Rendall, D., Wheatley, J.R., . . . Jablonski, N.G. (2016). Sexual selection on male vocal fundamental frequency in humans and other anthropoids. *Proceedings of the Royal Society of London B: Biological Sciences, 283*(1829), 20152830. https://doi.org/10.1098/rspb.2015.2830

Romero, T., Onishi, K., & Hasegawa, T. (2016). The role of oxytocin on peaceful associations and sociality in mammals. *Behaviour, 153*(9–11), 1053–1071. https://doi.org/10.1163/1568539x-00003358

Safran, R.J., Adelman, J.S., McGraw, K.J., & Hau, M. (2008). Sexual signal exaggeration affects physiological state in male barn swallows. *Current Biology, 18*, R461–R462. https://doi.org/10.1016/j.cub.2008.03.031

Saltzman, W., Digby, L.J., & Abbott, D.H. (2009). Reproductive skew in female common marmosets: What can proximate mechanisms tell us about ultimate causes? *Proceedings of the Royal Society of London B: Biological Sciences, 276*(1656), 389–399. https://doi.org/10.1098/rspb.2008.1374

Samuni, L., Preis, A., Mundry, R., Deschner, T., Crockford, C., & Wittig, R.M. (2016). Oxytocin reactivity during intergroup conflict in wild chimpanzees. *Proceedings of the National Academy of Sciences*, 201–2. https://doi.org/10.1073/pnas.1–2114

Sannen, A., van Elsacker, L., Heistermann, M., & Eens, M. (2004). Urinary testosterone-metabolite levels and dominance rank in male and female bonobos *(Pan paniscus)*. *Primates, 45*(2), 89–96. https://doi.org/10.1007/s10329-003-0066-4

Sapolsky, R.M. (2005). The influence of social hierarchy on primate health. *Science, 308*(5722), 648–652. https://doi.org/10.1126/science.1106477

Schülke, O., Bhagavatula, J., Vigilant, L., & Ostner, J. (2010). Social bonds enhance reproductive success in male macaques. *Current Biology, 20*, 2207–2210. https://doi.org/10.1016/j.cub.2010.10.058

Setchell, J.M., Smith, T., Wickings, E.J., & Knapp, L.A. (2008). Social correlates of testosterone and ornamentation in male mandrills. *Hormones and Behavior, 54*(3), 365–372. https://doi.org/10.1002/ajpa.20478

Setchell, J.M., & Wickings, E.J. (2005). Dominance, status signals and coloration in male mandrills *(Mandrillus sphinx)*. *Ethology, 111*(1), 25–50. https://doi.org/10.1111/j.1439-0310.2004.01054.x

Setchell, J.M., Wickings, E.J., & Knapp, L.A. (2006). Life history in male mandrills *(Mandrillus sphinx)*: Physical development, dominance rank, and group association. *American Journal of Physical Anthropology, 131*(4), 498–510. https://doi.org/10.1002/ajpa.20478

Shively, C.A., Mirkes, S.J., Lu, N.Z., Henderson, J.A., & Bethea, C.L. (2003). Soy and social stress affect serotonin neurotransmission in primates. *The Pharmacogenomics Journal, 3*(2), 114. https://doi.org/10.1038/sj.tpj.6500166

Sonnweber, R.S., Ravignani, A., Stobbe, N., Schiestl, G., Wallner, B., & Fitch, W. (2015). Rank-dependent grooming patterns and cortisol alleviation in Barbary macaques. *American Journal of Primatology, 77*(6), 688–700. https://doi.org/10.1002/ajp.22391

Stearns, S.C. (1992). *The evolution of life histories* (Vol. 249). Oxford: Oxford University Press.

van Noordwijk, M.A., & van Schaik, C.P. (1999). The effects of dominance rank and group size on female lifetime reproductive success in wild long-tailed macaques, *Macaca fascicularis*. *Primates, 40*(1), 105–130. https://doi.org/10.1007/bf02557705

von Engelhard, N., Kappeler, P.M., & Heistermann, M. (2000). Androgen levels and female social dominance in *Lemur catta*. *Proceedings of the Royal Society of London B: Biological Sciences, 267*(1452), 1533–1539. https://doi.org/10.1098/rspb.2000.1175

Wallen, K. (2005). Hormonal influences on sexually differentiated behavior in nonhuman primates. *Frontiers in Neuroendocrinology, 26*(1), 7–26. https://doi.org/10.1016/j.yfrne.2005.02.001

Weinstein, T.A., Bales, K.L., Maninger, N., Hostetler, C.M., & Capitanio, J.P. (2014). Early involvement in friendships predicts later plasma concentrations of oxytocin and vasopressin in juvenile rhesus macaques (*Macaca mulatta*). *Frontiers in Behavioral Neuroscience, 8,* 295–295. https://doi.org/10.3389/fnbeh.2014.00295

Wingfield, J.C., Hegner, R.E., Dufty, A.M., Jr., & Ball, G.F. (1990). The "challenge hypothesis": Theoretical implications for patterns of testosterone secretion, mating systems, and breeding strategies. *The American Naturalist, 136*(6), 829–846. https://doi.org/10.1086/285134

Yamaguchi, Y., Lee, Y. A., Kato, A., Jas, E., & Goto, Y. (2017). The roles of dopamine D2 receptor in the social hierarchy of rodents and primates. *Scientific Reports, 7,* 43348. https://doi.org/10.1038/srep43348

Zahavi, A. (1975). Mate selection – a selection for a handicap. *Journal of Theoretical Biology, 53*(1), 205–214. https://doi.org/10.1016/0022-5193(75)90111-3

Ziegler, T.E. (2013). Social effects via olfactory sensory stimuli on reproductive function and dysfunction in cooperative breeding marmosets and tamarins. *American Journal of Primatology, 75*(3), 202–211. https://doi.org/10.1002/ajp.22061

Zohdy, S., Bisanzio, D., Tecot, S., Wright, P.C., & Jernvall, J. (2017). Aggression and hormones are associated with heterogeneity in parasitism and parasite dynamics in the brown mouse lemur. *Animal Behaviour, 132,* 109–119. https://doi.org/10.1016/j.anbehav.2017.08.002

Zumpe, D., & Michael, R. P. (1989). Female dominance rank and behavior during artificial menstrual cycles in social groups of rhesus monkeys (*Macaca mulatta*). *American Journal of Primatology, 17*(4), 287–304. https://doi.org/10.1002/ajp.1350170404

7

THE DUAL-HORMONE APPROACH TO DOMINANCE AND STATUS-SEEKING

Amar Sarkar, Pranjal H. Mehta, and Robert A. Josephs

Testosterone is a steroid hormone secreted as the end product of the hypothalamic-pituitary-gonadal (HPG) axis, and is widely theorised to trigger dominance and status-seeking tendencies that support or enhance reproductive behaviour (Mazur & Booth, 1998). At the biological level, testosterone guides important aspects of male sexual development, including the growth of the testes and penis, spermatogenesis, and the appearance of secondary sexual characteristics. At the psychological level, testosterone is predicted to enhance dominance-oriented behaviours, both in the research community and in popular culture. A central theory that has guided the field of social endocrinology – and the social endocrinology of dominance in particular – has been the challenge hypothesis, proposed by Wingfield, Hegner, Dufty, and Ball (1990), which explicitly linked endogenous testosterone concentrations to dominance behaviour in birds. This testosterone-dominance link has now been explored in a range of animals, and has also been proposed for humans (Mazur & Booth, 1998). The idea of a strong testosterone-dominance association is now so entrenched that testosterone is colloquially referred to as the "power hormone", and is believed to trigger dominance, aggression, competitiveness and risk-seeking.

Certainly, there is an intuitive elegance to a single hormone exerting such widespread and profound behavioural effects. There are several approaches to understanding whether elevations in testosterone are a cause or consequence of dominance. For instance, elevated testosterone may follow the attainment of social dominance. Alternatively, social dominance may follow high or rising levels of testosterone. A bidirectional relationship has also been proposed (Mazur, 1985), such that high testosterone levels may facilitate social dominance, which further elevates testosterone levels.

While there are notable positive associations between testosterone and social dominance, especially under situations when status is challenged (Archer, 2006; Beehner, Bergman, Cheney, Seyfarth, & Whitten, 2006; Giammanco, Tabacchi, Giammanco, Di Majo, & La Guardia, 2005; Gould & Ziegler, 2007), there is also a range of results that renders such a straightforward interpretation untenable (Carré & McCormick, 2008; Mehta & Josephs, 2010; Josephs, Sellers, Newman, & Mehta, 2006; van Bokhoven et al., 2006). Similar to the weak results for testosterone and dominance, a meta-analysis also did not find more than a mild association between testosterone and aggression (Archer, Graham-Kevan, & Davies, 2005).

In particular, a great deal of research has approached the effect of testosterone on behaviour by – perhaps reasonably – analysing only testosterone. Studying only testosterone is theoretically and analytically expedient, as well as more resource friendly. However, from a physiological standpoint it is more likely that the HPG-axis does not always function in isolation. Rather, testosterone may often exert its effects in concert with – or opposition to – other hormones to jointly regulate cognition and behaviour. Not considering other theoretically relevant hormones may account for several of the weak testosterone-behaviour links that have been noted. To this extent, a recent programme of research (Mehta & Josephs, 2010; Mehta & Prasad, 2015) has adopted a novel perspective on the psychological and social effects of testosterone, based on the principle that hormones do not act in isolation. This dual-hormone hypothesis predicts that the psychophysiological effects of testosterone are moderated by a second hormone – cortisol, an end product of the hypothalamic-pituitary-adrenal (HPA) axis. Like testosterone, cortisol is a steroid hormone. It belongs to the family of glucocorticoids, and its primary physiological function is to metabolise sugar. Cortisol concentrations rise during experiences of physical or psychological stress (Dickerson & Kemeney, 2004) and this hormone exerts several other psychological effects. In the short term, cortisol induces some forms of cognitive impairment, such as weakening retrieval of information from long-term memory (Dominique, Roozendaal, Nitsch, McGaugh, & Hock, 2000), though it may also enable effective adaptation to uncertainty (Cueva et al., 2015; Plessow, Schade, Kirschbaum, & Fischer, 2017). Over longer periods, however, cortisol exposure can become maladaptive, leading to reductions in approach-oriented behaviour such as risk-taking or increases in social avoidance (Kandasmy et al., 2014; Roelofs et al., 2009). On the other hand, low levels of cortisol have been linked to lower levels of stress and a general increase in approach-related behaviour and status attainment (Roelofs et al., 2009; Sherman et al., 2012).

Importantly, the HPA-axis and the HPG-axis are known to co-regulate one another in the brain, with downstream effects on the secretion of cortisol and testosterone (Viau, 2002). Furthermore, cortisol can inhibit testosterone function (Viau, 2002), and may thus be a suitable candidate hormone for a disruptor of the testosterone-behaviour link. Within the framework of the dual-hormone hypothesis, then, the effects of testosterone are predicted to depend on concentrations of cortisol. For instance, two individuals who have similarly high levels of testosterone may have very different cortisol levels. According to the dual-hormone hypothesis, high cortisol levels should weaken the capacity of testosterone to influence status-seeking behaviours. Thus, the stereotypical effect of testosterone on dominance and status-seeking should be most likely to occur under low levels of cortisol. Studies that only consider testosterone produce analyses that collapse data across all cortisol levels, essentially diluting high testosterone concentrations in too wide a distribution of cortisol concentrations. This potentially accounts for the noisy, weak, or null testosterone-dominance associations that have repeatedly been observed.

The dual-hormone hypothesis has a particular statistical translation – an interaction term representing the product of testosterone and cortisol concentrations. According to this hypothesis, there should be a significant relationship between testosterone and the response variable in the direction of interest (e.g., a positive relationship between testosterone and dominant behaviour), but only under the condition that cortisol concentrations are low. If cortisol concentrations are high, the testosterone-behaviour association is expected to be attenuated. An analysis of the interaction yields a substantial theoretical payoff in that it enables the generation of predictions that are both richer and more precise in terms of which outcomes will occur under which combinations of endocrine conditions.

The dual-hormone hypothesis has been successfully applied to findings in several psychological domains closely related to dominance and social status. In the remainder of this chapter, we offer a brief overview of the evidence that has accrued in support of this hypothesis. We also discuss cases in which there is an interaction between testosterone and cortisol in predicting behaviour, but the pattern of the interaction deviates from the original predictions of the dual-hormone hypothesis (particularly for studies that examine aggressive and antisocial behaviour). We conclude with a discussion of future directions that will help refine and build this emerging literature.

Evidence in support of the dual-hormone hypothesis

Basal hormone profiles

Dominance

An early investigation of behaviour specifically in the context of the dual-hormone hypothesis was aimed at understanding dominance (study 1, Mehta & Josephs, 2010). In this experiment, participants ($n = 100$) were split into same-sex dyads and were randomly assigned to the role of a leader or a follower (participants later switched roles, such that followers were then observed as leaders). Leaders would give instructions for the followers to complete a standardised psychometric assessment of spatial reasoning. These interactions were filmed, and seven hypothesis-blind judges were later shown the footage and asked to rate the leader on various aspects of perceived dominance (e.g., the perceived dominance scale included terms such as "dominant", "assertive", "confident", and "leader-like"). Aggregation and analysis of the ratings revealed the first evidence of what appeared to be a dual-hormone effect on perceived dominance (see Figure 7.1): Individuals who had higher baseline testosterone were also judged to be more dominant, but this effect was conditional – it was apparent only in individuals with low cortisol. This association between testosterone and perceived dominance was not observed in individuals with high cortisol. Furthermore, the pattern was consistent across males and females.

An important feature of this experiment is the response variable: observer ratings of participant behaviour. The results suggest that the dual-hormone profile is *visible*, or expressed in an individual's behaviour in forms that can be detected by others. This is noteworthy

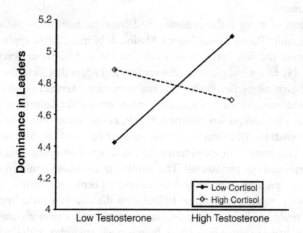

Figure 7.1 Dominance in leaders (average of observers' ratings on a 7-point scale) as a function of testosterone and cortisol levels. Hormone levels were measured at the beginning of the experiment. Low = 1 standard deviation below mean; high = 1 standard deviation above mean. The intercept and slopes from the multiple regression model were used to plot dominance scores one standard deviation above and below the means for testosterone and cortisol. *Figure and legend used from Mehta and Josephs (2010), with permission.*

because testosterone and cortisol also exert cognitive and behavioural effects that individuals themselves may not be aware of. For instance, in research that administered testosterone to females, participants were unable to introspect on its effects on their behaviour in self-reports, even though their behaviour changed (Eisenegger, Naef, Snozzi, Heinrichs, & Fehr, 2010; van Honk, Peper, & Schutter, 2005). Because the psychological effects of testosterone need not be observable, either to the individual or to others, it is particularly impressive that the dual-hormone profile was discernible by unacquainted strangers at the behavioural level.

Social status

Ultimately, many testosterone-driven behaviours can be interpreted as means to attain higher social status. For example, there is growing evidence that dominant behaviour is positively related to status attainment (Anderson & Kilduff, 2009; Cheng, Tracy, Foulsham, Kingstone, & Henrich, 2013). Furthermore, status outside of the laboratory builds on a multiplicity of sustained social relationships, quite in contrast to many laboratory-based tests of dominance which involve only dyadic communications, often between strangers. To that extent, some studies have begun investigating the joint role of testosterone and cortisol in regulating social status beyond the laboratory, accounting for both real-world significance and the fact that an individual who is dominant often exerts that dominance over several other individuals.

An examination of sportswomen in competitive collegiate teams revealed that perceived social status varied with basal concentrations of cortisol and testosterone (Edwards & Casto, 2013). In particular, participants ($n = 74$) were asked to rate other members of their specific teams in terms of perceptions of leadership capability. Consistent with the dual-hormone hypothesis, testosterone levels were positively associated with leadership ratings, but only when endogenous cortisol was low. Therefore, these hormones may regulate perceived leadership within social groups and competitive teams. This study extends the results described in Mehta and Josephs (2010) by showing the effect of the testosterone × cortisol interaction on social status among individuals who are actually in the same group rather than just strangers in a brief experimental encounter.

Another indicator of status is the centrality and connectedness of an individual in a social network. A recent study (Ponzi, Zilioli, Mehta, Maslov, & Watson, 2016) applied social network analysis to understand the link between network position and hormone levels in a sample of male athletes ($n = 44$). In a social network, the vertices and edges that form the network acquire particular psychological properties. Each individual represents a vertex in space, and the connections to or from other vertices (other individuals) represent social relationships. Importantly, the connections between vertices possess direction (that is, a connection from A to B is not the same as a connection from B to A). Features of these connections, such as their number and direction, are therefore interpretable in social terms. The number of outgoing connections from one vertex to others represents gregariousness. The number of incoming connections to one vertex from other vertices represents popularity. The number of times one vertex comes in between two other vertices represents betweenness. In line with the dual-hormone hypothesis, popularity was positively related to basal testosterone concentrations, but only if cortisol was low. Also consistent with the dual-hormone hypothesis, betweenness (an index of the individual's centrality in the network) was predicted by high basal testosterone and low basal cortisol. Furthermore, the dual-hormone effect for gregariousness was in the same direction as for popularity and betweenness but was not statistically significant (perhaps due to low statistical power). Therefore, the dual-hormone hypothesis is also able to predict – at least to some extent – social status at the level of human social networks.

Further extending the ecological validity of the testosterone × cortisol interaction on social status is an examination of male leaders who hold genuine leadership roles in major organisations. The participants were enrolled in the executive education programme offered at Harvard University (Sherman, Lerner, Josephs, Renshon, & Gross, 2016). Specifically, participants were senior-level individuals (n = 78), holding positions in the government, defence, law enforcement, and the military. The response variable in this case was a crude but effective marker of rank: the self-reported number of subordinates. Consistent with the dual-hormone hypothesis, testosterone was positively related to number of subordinates, but only if cortisol was low. Furthermore, the participants described by Sherman et al. (2016) are an important example of research participants who are *not* mostly full-time undergraduate or graduate students. These participants were fully employed and significantly older than participants in all of the other studies described here. This difference in age, employment, and general status addresses potential concerns over the dual-hormone hypothesis being restricted to only younger individuals in university settings.

Overall, it is important to note that the dual-hormone hypothesis has predicted dominance and social status across both sexes, younger and older individuals and, perhaps most importantly, across various operationalisations of dominance and social status, including observer reports of instruction-giving behaviour (Mehta & Josephs, 2010), leadership ratings provided by team members (Edwards & Casto, 2013), the number and nature of connections in graphs representing social networks (Ponzi et al., 2016), and in the self-reported number of subordinates (Sherman et al., 2016). Future work should aim to extend the repertoire of response variables that measure leadership and dominance in connection to testosterone and cortisol levels.

Risk-taking

Individuals take risks to gain rewards in the context of significant uncertainty. If unsuccessful, they may be worse off than before. One example of risky behaviour is financial risk-taking, which has been particularly tractable in laboratory investigation, because participants make financial decisions instead of entering into dangerous situations that may characterise other types of risk-taking. In the context of financial risk, pharmacologically elevated cortisol over several days suppresses financial risk appetite (Kandasamy et al., 2014). On the other hand, endogenous testosterone has been positively correlated with risk-taking behaviour (Apicella et al., 2008; Coates & Herbert, 2008), though this relationship is not strictly positive and null results have also been noted (Zethraeus et al., 2009, Boksem et al., 2013; Buskens, Raub, van Miltenburg, Montoya, & van Honk, 2016).

Two recent studies (Mehta, Welker, Zilioli, & Carré, 2015) have analysed risk-taking in the context of the dual-hormone hypothesis. In the first of these, male and female participants (n = 115) provided self-reports of their own risk-taking tendencies. Participants also nominated informants, who were then requested to rate the participant on their risk-taking tendencies. Consistent with the predictions of the dual-hormone hypothesis, higher testosterone levels predicted greater self- and informant evaluations of risk-taking, but only in individuals with lower cortisol. This relationship between testosterone and risk-taking was not observed in individuals with higher cortisol levels, and there were no differences in the pattern of the dual-hormone interaction between males and females.

In one sense, these results are even more striking than the finding that observers are able to perceive dominance behaviours in participant footage (Mehta & Josephs, 2010), because it suggests that an individual's impressions about his or her friends and colleagues may track their basal hormone levels over time. Because the informants were reporting on risk tendencies from memory, rather than by observing the participants in a risk-taking situation, their memories and judgements of the participants appear to encode the participant's basal hormone profiles as well.

The second study in this sequence examined risk-taking at the behavioural level, using performance on the Balloon Analogue Risk Task (BART; Lejuez et al., 2002). This task has a relatively high degree of construct validity, and predicts risk-taking in real-world situations (Hunt, Hopko, Bare, Lejuez, & Robinson, 2005; Lejuez et al., 2002). Participants are required to inflate digital balloons over a number of trials. Each pump yields a small number of points, and further inflates the balloon. These points are exchanged for cash at the end of the task. The balloon is programmed to burst after a random number of pumps (and the participant is aware of this random bursting). If the balloon bursts, all points earned by inflating that balloon are lost, and the next balloon is presented. The participant may choose to cash in all points on an unburst balloon and move to the next balloon. Every time the participant decides to pump the balloon further is an instance of a risky decision, because the participant does not know whether the next pump will cause the balloon to burst. It is, of course, in the participant's interest to maximise the number of points. In this study (Mehta, Welker, Zilioli, & Carré, 2015), male participants ($n = 165$) first provided a hormone sample and then completed the BART. As with the self- and informant evaluations of risk-taking, associations between hormones and BART risk-taking were also consistent with the dual-hormone hypothesis – that is, testosterone was positively associated with risk-taking (measured as the number of pumps on unburst balloons) when basal cortisol was low. This association between testosterone and risk-taking was not observed in participants who had higher cortisol levels.

A recent pre-registered study (Ronay, Oostrom, & Pollet, 2018) that used hair hormone levels provides further evidence of the dual-hormone hypothesis in relation to risk. The researchers found that, in male participants ($n = 53$ males, with a total of $n = 162$), hair testosterone was positively associated with risk-taking behaviour, but only when hair cortisol levels were low. Hair provides an index of long-term, cumulative hormone levels (Dettenborn, Tietze, Kirschbaum, & Stalder, 2012), and is freer of momentary fluctuations that characterise hormone quantifications from blood or saliva samples. Hair can be used to provide estimates of both cortisol and testosterone, though it is used only infrequently in hormone-behaviour research.

Competitive bidding

In an auction, if an individual offers more money than the estimated value of the object, the individual is said to be overbidding, as it is unlikely one values the object as much as one is willing to pay for it (if the individual truly did value the object as much as they are offering, then it cannot be considered overbidding). A relatively recent study has shown that overbidding in auctions is consistent with the dual-hormone hypothesis (van den Bos, Golka, Effelsberg, & McClure, 2013). Analysis of saliva samples provided by male participants ($n = 26$) involved in a small laboratory-based auction study revealed a positive association between testosterone and overbidding when cortisol was low. The association was not observed in participants with higher endogenous cortisol. Although there is no rational economic value to overbidding, it does signal an individual's competitiveness, and perhaps a desire to win at any cost – that is, winning itself is the goal, not the object one is bidding for. Overbidding in an auction (where others are aware of the individual's bids) could also be a channel to increase visibility, again, perhaps, acting as a signal of willingness to compete. To this extent, overbidding affects the social environment and draws attention toward the bidder.

Empathy

Empathy has been classically understood as the capacity to transpose oneself into the experiences and emotions of another individual. One large study combining both males and females ($n = 469$) found that variation in empathy as self-reported on a well-validated psychometric questionnaire (the Interpersonal Reactivity Index; Davis, 1983) was consistent with predictions of the dual-hormone hypothesis (Zilioli, Caldbick, & Watson, 2014). That is, higher basal testosterone concentrations predicted lower empathy, but only under conditions of low cortisol. This association was not apparent when cortisol was high. Indeed, the opposite tendency was observed when cortisol was high: higher testosterone appeared to predict greater empathy. This positive association between testosterone and empathy is consistent with a recent investigation of 84 males (Vongas & Al Hajj, 2017), where contest-induced increases in testosterone concentrations predicted better emotion recognition in a procedural task; however, that study did not include cortisol measures.

Importantly, although these patterns in Zilioli et al. (2014) emerged in the combined sample of males and females, when the sexes were analysed separately, the dual-hormone interaction was statistically significant only in males. This difference is consistent with some recent work that also reported a significant dual-hormone interaction only in males when males and females were analysed separately (Ronay et al., 2018). But it is a departure from several previous comparisons between males and females, where there were no sex differences (e.g., Mehta & Josephs, 2010; Mehta, Welker, Zilioli, & Carré, 2015). Whether this apparent sex difference is a true psychological difference or an artefact of the inevitable loss of statistical power that follows splitting a sample remains to be verified. Because there were over twice as many males ($n = 323$) as females ($n = 146$), it may explain why the effect was observed in the former but not the latter. However, even for the smaller group of female participants the sample was fairly large – larger than almost any other study discussed in this chapter (testosterone measurement in females is especially error-prone, providing a potential explanation for null results, Welker et al., 2016).

It should be noted that these findings characterise *self-reported* empathy. The dual-hormone effect did not extend to performance on another widely used measure of cognitive empathy, the Reading the Mind in the Eyes Test (RMET), which captures the capacity to accurately infer simple and complex emotional states expressed in the eye region of another individual, with no other portion of the face shown (Baron-Cohen, Wheelwright, Hill, Raste, & Plumb, 2001). There are also other manifestations of empathy that are behavioural (e.g., prosocial behaviour) and emotional (e.g., the extent to which viewing the emotional experiences of others causes physiological arousal in the observer). It will be important to examine how these behavioural and physiological aspects of empathy fit within the framework of the dual-hormone hypothesis (see also Sollberger, Bernauer, & Ehlert, 2016 for an interesting application of the dual-hormone hypothesis to pro-environmental behaviour, which may be driven in part by prosocial motivation, in a sample of 147 male participants).

Aggression and punishment

The link between testosterone and aggression is one of the more stereotypical associations that this hormone shares with a psychological variable. In fact, earlier research on aggression anticipated the dual-hormone effect before it was formally theorised. Aggression, especially amongst younger individuals, may also be a behavioural pathway to higher social status (Cillessen & Mayeux, 2004; Vaillancourt & Hymel, 2006). A relatively early study (Dabbs, Jurkovic, & Frady,

1991) has linked adolescent aggression and violence to endocrine profiles consistent with the dual-hormone hypothesis. In particular, delinquent adolescent males ($n = 113$) who had higher basal testosterone and low basal cortisol were also found to have been more violent, received stricter treatment from their parole boards, and also were more likely to break institutional rules. The positive correlation between testosterone and behaviour was detected among low-cortisol individuals but not among high-cortisol individuals. A more recent study also found converging evidence in this direction (Popma et al., 2007). Adolescent males ($n = 103$) on a delinquency diversion programme provided self-reports on their aggressive tendencies. The psychometric test used to measure these tendencies was the Buss-Durkee Hostility Inventory (Buss & Durkee, 1957), which captures both overt aggression (the open expressions of anger and aggression) and covert aggression (unwillingness to freely express anger and aggression). While the researchers did not find significant associations for covert aggression, the relationship between self-reported overt aggression and hormone levels was in line with the dual-hormone hypothesis. In particular, higher scores for overt aggression were positively associated with higher levels of basal testosterone when basal cortisol was low. This testosterone-behaviour association was not observed for individuals with higher levels of cortisol.

An intriguing recent study (Grotzinger et al., 2018) examined the relationships between adolescent aggression, testosterone and cortisol using hormone estimates from hair ($n = 460$). Consistent with the dual-hormone hypothesis, hair testosterone was a significant predictor of aggression at low levels of hair cortisol.

Antisocial behaviour is not, of course, restricted to aggression and violence. Indeed, there are many kinds of aggression, and many of these are not related to delinquency or delinquent-like tendencies. More recent research has examined antisocial behaviour in economic games, in which participants can opt to punish other players (in the context of economic games, punishment often entails making decisions that will reduce another player's monetary payoffs). Not all forms of punishment are antisocial. If individuals choose to punish others who are free-riding on resources in a public goods game, then that is an instance of prosocial punishment. On the other hand, individuals may sometimes choose to punish individuals who invest more than they are expected to in a common resource pool (or indeed, more than the participant). If the participant punishes such individuals, it is an instance of antisocial punishment. In a recent study (Pfattheicher, Landhäußer, & Keller, 2014) of healthy male participants ($n = 72$), testosterone was positively related to antisocial punishment among those with lower basal cortisol, but this link was not observed among individuals with high basal cortisol.

Overall, then, it appears that the dual-hormone hypothesis can predict aggressive behaviour at both the self-report and behavioural levels, and in both clinical and healthy samples.

Group performance

A recent area of enquiry is the joint influence of testosterone and cortisol on group-level decisions and performance. This is an important subfield of research both because many financial decisions and risks are executed by groups rather than individuals, and also because the consequences of such decisions extend to multiple individuals. To this extent, a recent study (Akinola, Page-Gould, Mehta, & Lu, 2016) has described a novel endocrine construct – the group-level hormone profile, obtained by aggregating individual hormone concentrations (in this case, testosterone and cortisol) using multi-level modelling (Croon & van Veldhoven, 2007). Male and female participants ($n = 370$) worked in small groups of three to six individuals to complete a complex logistics and supply chain management problem in which they were required to optimise financial performance. Importantly, there was no "correct" strategy that had to be discovered and implemented. Rather more consistent with decision-making in the real world, there were multiple approaches that could yield successful outcomes, and groups could vary multiple parameters in arriving at an optimal strategy. Consistent with the dual-hormone hypothesis, group testosterone was positively related to group performance only for those groups low in cortisol but not for those groups high in cortisol. This effect remained even when controlling for the effects of personality and hormonal variation at the group level.

Alongside providing evidence for the dual-hormone hypothesis, these results offer two key advances to the study of hormones in decision-making. First, they highlight the validity of using a hypothetical, collective-level endocrine construct to describe group decision-making. The second advance lies in the task's impressive ecological validity, being a much closer approximation of real-world decisions than many laboratory measures of decision-making.

Hormone change profiles

Aside from the effects of basal hormone profiles discussed earlier, a smaller body of research suggests that acute *changes* in hormone levels may also reliably predict behavioural outcomes. Hormone concentrations change predictably over the course of the day. However, they also change dynamically during social interactions. These intra-situational variations in hormone levels are also of significant theoretical interest in generating an understanding of how the endocrine system regulates behaviour. Two studies have found behavioural effects of changes in cortisol and testosterone concentrations that were consistent with the dual-hormone hypothesis in the context of competitive bargaining (Mehta, Mor, Yap, & Prasad, 2015).

In the first study, male and female MBA students ($n = 70$) were assigned to act out a negotiating task in pairs, with the roles of buyer and seller determined at random. Negotiations are interactions that pit at least two (often competing) motives against one another. One motive is to secure a strong financial outcome for oneself or the group one is representing (a monetary motive). A second motive is a social one. Negotiators who experience conflict between financial and social motives often end up with lower financial earnings. For example, an entrepreneur seeking to sell her business may be concerned that proposing too high a price to potential buyers could reduce social rapport and undermine her social reputation. As a result, she may offer a lower price and thus negotiate a worse financial deal for herself. The results of this study of seller-buyer negotiations were broadly consistent with the dual-hormone hypothesis. Individuals who experienced an increase in testosterone alongside a decrease in cortisol secured economically stronger bargains (a financially adaptive hormonal profile), while financial outcomes for individuals experiencing an increase in testosterone alongside an increase in cortisol were significantly weaker (a financially costly hormonal profile). Furthermore, individuals who perceived the monetary and social motives of interactions to be in conflict also showed the financially costly hormonal profile (a testosterone increase combined with a cortisol increase), while those who did not perceive monetary and social motives to be in conflict showed the financially profitable hormonal profile (a testosterone increase combined with a cortisol decrease). Importantly, the effect was specific to individuals assigned to act as the sellers in the bargain. This moderation by social role (buyer or seller) was not originally hypothesised, but was noted to be consistent with previous findings that the seller is typically the individual who has greater influence over the outcome of the negotiations (Amanatullah, Morris, & Curhan, 2008).

In the second study, the authors further examined the idea that hormones act as a proxy for social and financial concerns in the context of an ultimatum game in which male and female participants ($n = 115$) were involved. In the ultimatum game, a participant must decide whether to accept or reject a portion of money offered by another individual. The individual making the offer (the proposer) receives a fixed sum (e.g., $10) and can allocate this money between himself or herself and the other player in any ratio they please. The receiver is aware of the total sum in play, and can accept or reject the offer. If the receiver rejects the offer, both players lose all of the money. The most egalitarian allocation is a 50:50 split of this endowment. However, it is in the receiver's economic best interest to accept *any* sum offered greater than zero monetary units, as any sum renders the receiver better off than they were previously. However, a behavioural hallmark of interactions in ultimatum games is that receivers will frequently reject offers that they perceive to be unfair – that is, being offered much smaller than a 50:50 split of the initial endowment can trigger rejection of these offers, a punishment-like behaviour that is detrimental to both parties. A post-test saliva sample was obtained after the ultimatum game was completed. Consistent with high testosterone and low cortisol predicting a financially adaptive response, participants who showed an increase in testosterone and a decrease in cortisol were more likely to accept typically "unfair" offers, thus acting in their economic best interest. On the other hand, if both cortisol and testosterone increased, participants were more likely to reject the offer, thus compromising their economic interests likely in the service of social motives (e.g., the motive to punish the other player in the face of perceived social provocation).

Furthermore, both studies found that the dual-hormone interaction statistically mediated the associations between psychological traits and bargaining behaviour. For example, in the ultimatum game study, higher scores on a personality measure of trait aggression were related to increased rejection of unfair offers, and this trait aggression-behaviour association was mediated by the dual-hormone interaction. Specifically, high trait aggression predicted increased testosterone and cortisol levels, which in turn predicted rejection of unfair offers. However, low trait aggression predicted increased testosterone and decreased cortisol levels, which in turn predicted acceptance of unfair offers.

Variation in the pattern of the dual-hormone interaction

A few investigations have also observed important variations in the effects of dual-hormone interactions in regulating antisocial behaviour, such that it is the individuals with high basal testosterone and *high*, rather than low, basal cortisol who show such tendencies.

For example, research on trait psychopathy in a large sample of males and females ($n = 237$) found a positive relationship between testosterone and self-reported psychopathy in males who also had high levels of cortisol. The association was not observed in males with lower levels of cortisol, and was also not observed in females ($n = 123$). In another study of reactive aggression in females, participants ($n = 53$) were insulted by an accomplice in a pre-recorded video (Denson, Mehta, et al., 2013). Participants believed that this accomplice was another participant, and that the interaction was live. In particular, the participant first made a brief speech about her life goals. The insult comprised derogatory remarks about the quality of the speech and the participant's level of achievement and her life goals. Following this, participants were given an opportunity to retaliate by subjecting the insulter to bursts of white noise during what was presented as a competitive reaction time task against the participant who had insulted them. Testosterone was positively associated with the extent of retaliation in participants with high cortisol, but not those with moderate or low cortisol. These findings are also conceptually similar to the results of the second study in Mehta, Mor et al. (2015) described earlier, wherein participants who showed increased testosterone and increased cortisol levels also showed a greater tendency to reject unfair offers in an ultimatum game, which may be interpreted as a form of reactive aggression.

Aside from psychopathy and reactive aggression, recent work has also examined joint hormonal regulation of unethical behaviour. In particular, Lee, Gino, Jin, Rice, & Josephs (2015) investigated cheating tendencies in two studies. In the first study, with male and female participants ($n = 82$), cheating was measured by the extent to which participants overstated the number of correctly solved logic puzzles (solving a greater number of puzzles led to a higher monetary gain for participants). Individuals with higher baseline testosterone were more likely to engage in cheating behaviour only if their cortisol levels were high. The second study in this sequence, also conducted on male and female participants ($n = 117$), found an especially striking result. In addition to replicating the original testosterone × cortisol interaction on cheating found in the first study, hormone assays on post-test saliva samples revealed that the participants who had cheated showed *lower* levels of cortisol and negative affect. Furthermore, there was evidence of a dose-response relationship – the greater the extent of cheating, the greater the decrease in post-test cortisol concentrations relative to pre-test cortisol concentrations. This finding led the authors to propose a cheating-as-stress-reduction hypothesis, which suggests that intrinsically high levels of endogenous cortisol (accompanied by a generally aversive psychophysiological state) may predispose individuals to act unethically as a way to reduce stress levels that are otherwise too high.

Together, these studies suggest that high testosterone and high cortisol may also predict antisocial tendencies. However, it is unclear when these tendencies will follow from this particular combination (high testosterone, high cortisol) and when they will follow the standard predictions of the dual-hormone hypothesis (high testosterone, low cortisol), as has been the case in previous work that has examined aggressive or antisocial behaviour (Dabbs et al., 1991; Pfattheicher et al., 2014; Popma et al., 2007). We suspect that in populations and situations where aggression and violence may be harmful for status, high testosterone and low cortisol should be associated with lower levels of aggression and violence (e.g., among groups of women in which gender socialisation would suggest that aggression would have a negative effect on status). Establishing the boundary conditions for the effects of each of these hormone profiles will be an important step in understanding dual endocrine contributions to behaviour.

Moderators of the testosterone × cortisol interaction

Personality

Some studies are revealing that personality traits may also interact with hormone profiles to regulate behaviour. For instance, a recent study provides suggestive evidence that dual-hormone effects may be particularly pronounced in individuals with a high level of trait dominance (Pfattheicher, 2017). Male participants ($n = 153$) had the opportunity to make monetary gains by depriving money from another individual (selecting this option was considered to be a dominant behaviour – alternatively, participants could also choose not to take money from the other individual, which was the non-dominant option). In support of the dual-hormone hypothesis, there was a statistically significant testosterone × cortisol interaction; testosterone was positively related to dominant behaviour only among individuals with low cortisol. This study also found that testosterone and cortisol further interacted with self-reported trait dominance to predict dominant behaviour (this three-way interaction was marginally significant). Specifically, the dual-hormone interaction effect was driven by individuals high in trait dominance, and was not statistically significant in individuals low in trait dominance. While the author acknowledges that the evidence is merely suggestive and potentially underpowered, the finding does open important avenues for interactions between hormones and self-reported personality traits in explaining dominant behaviours (for some related research on exogenous testosterone × self-reported trait dominance interactions predicting competitive and aggressive behaviour, see Mehta et al., 2015; Carré et al., 2017).

Other research has focussed on problematic adolescent behaviour. One study (Tackett et al., 2014) that examined externalising behaviour in male and female adolescents ($n = 104$) found that high testosterone predicted higher rates of antisocial tendencies when cortisol was low, but only in individuals with higher levels of traits associated with personality disorders – disagreeableness and emotional instability. Furthermore, this moderation by disagreeableness and emotional instability was recapitulated in another mixed-sex adolescent sample ($n = 104$) using a different hormone, estradiol, which, like testosterone, is released by the HPG-axis (Tackett et al., 2015). This finding also extends the dual-hormone hypothesis to include HPG-hormones beyond testosterone, an important step for research in this area. The existence of personality × cortisol × testosterone (or estradiol) interactions on antisocial behaviour may have clinical relevance in terms of diagnosis, treatment, or rehabilitation.

Social context: Endocrine contributions to behaviour are also dependent on social context. For instance, the dual-hormone effect on the decision to compete again *after* a competition depends on whether one had won or lost the first competition (study 2; Mehta & Josephs, 2010). Male participants ($n = 57$) were randomly assigned to win or lose in a competitive scenario (a supposed intelligence test based on speed), and were then asked whether they wished to participate in the competition again. Basal testosterone predicted an increased likelihood of choosing to compete again only when basal cortisol was low *and* when an individual had lost, suggesting that this endocrine profile may predispose individuals to attempt to reclaim status when it is lost or compromised, as when losing a competition. Another study using female participants ($n = 120$) found a very similar effect (Henry, Sattizahn, Norman, Beilock, & Maestripieri, 2017). Participants performed a computerised competitive task in pairs, with individuals randomly allocated to win or lose the task, which entailed visual motor responses. Testosterone was positively correlated with task performance in participants with low, but not high levels of cortisol. Most importantly, this interaction was further influenced by the status of having won or lost the competition. In particular, the testosterone × cortisol interaction on competition performance was observed in the participants assigned to lose. As with Mehta and Josephs (2010), these results suggest that the status undermining effects of losing competitions may interact with baseline hormone profiles to predict performance.

Another important social context is inclusion or exclusion from a group. Social exclusion is easily induced in laboratory settings using the Cyberball task, in which a participant can be excluded from digital social interactions that others are having (Williams & Jarvis, 2006). One study on male participants ($n = 74$) found a marginally significant interaction between testosterone, cortisol, and social context in predicting a laboratory measure of aggression. Among participants in the inclusion condition, there was a positive association between basal testosterone and a laboratory measure of aggression only when basal cortisol was low (Geniole, Carré, & McCormick, 2011). But among participants who were excluded, the opposite dual-hormone interaction pattern emerged: the pattern suggested that testosterone was positively related to aggressive behaviour only among high-cortisol individuals. While this was a tentative association, it does add inductive support to the notion that social context can exert an effect on dual-hormone contributions to behaviour, and may help clarify the contexts in which different dual-hormone interaction effects occur.

Future directions

Adaptive value of dual-hormone profiles: An important unresolved question is the general adaptiveness of behaviours that appear to arise from high testosterone and low cortisol concentrations. An important example in this regard is risk-taking. A certain level of risk-seeking enables an individual to seize opportunities and rewards that may be fleeting and may therefore be quickly lost. This combination of hormones may also enable individuals to engage more effectively with high-uncertainty situations in order to gain rewards. However, risk-taking can also result in significant costs at both individual and societal levels. Excessive risk-taking is likely to compromise the health and safety of an individual and those around him or her (e.g., driving at very high speeds, unprotected sexual intercourse, drug use). Depending on the social influence of the risk-taker, excessive risk may also have enormous and wide-ranging consequences, such as destabilising markets and declaring wars. Another example is antisocial behaviour such as aggression. It may be in certain populations and contexts (e.g., male adolescents in a delinquency programme), aggressive actions such as physical violence may be more adaptive for status attainment whereas in other populations (e.g., university students, work organisations) such aggressive actions would likely impair status attainment. A better understanding of the adaptive nature of aggression may potentially help explain some of the inconsistent results. Understanding the biological bases of behaviours such as risk-taking and aggression, and the conditions in which these endocrine profiles may be adaptive or maladaptive is therefore an important goal for continued research.

Investigations of neural mechanisms: The neural processes underlying dual-hormone effects remain poorly understood. Mechanistic elucidations will enhance our knowledge of how these effects are occurring. For instance, glucocorticoids downregulate the androgen receptors to which testosterone binds (Burnstein, Maiorino, Dai, & Cameron, 1995; Chen, Wang, Yu, Liu, & Pearce, 1997). Thus, even when testosterone levels are high, if cortisol is causing androgen receptor downregulation, testosterone molecules may be unable to bind to the relevant receptors, diminishing further psychophysiological effects.

Network- and region-level neural processes are also likely to be associated with these dual-hormone effects. One possibility derives from the brain's fundamental capacity to detect and react to reward signals. At the endocrine level, increased testosterone and decreased cortisol have independently been associated with enhanced reward-processing and reward-processing (Hermans et al., 2010; Mehta, Welker, Zilioli, & Carré, 2015; Montoya, Bos, Terburg, Rosenberger, & van Honk, 2014; van Honk et al., 2004). For example, testosterone increases activity in mesolimbic reward centres, including the nucleus accumbens within the ventral striatum and the ventral tegmental area (Hermans et al., 2010; Op de Macks et al., 2011). On the other hand, some studies have shown that cortisol concentrations are positively correlated with widespread reductions in activity in reward-related networks, such as the striatum and basolateral amygdala (Montoya et al., 2014). Of course, it would also be incorrect to characterise the effects of cortisol to be generally "anti-rewarding", as there is some evidence that cortisol may stimulate dopamine release in the nucleus accumbens (Oswald et al., 2005; Pruessner, Champagne, Meaney, & Dagher, 2004). However, overall, cortisol does appear to be implicated in the brain's reward circuitry.

Reward processing is theorised to underlie some of the behaviours discussed in this chapter (e.g., risk-taking, social status). Although there are separate neural studies of testosterone and reward processing and cortisol and reward processing, there is no direct test of the dual-hormone hypothesis in relation to neural reward systems. According to the dual-hormone hypothesis, testosterone would have a positive association with reward processing (e.g., ventral striatum activity) only under low, but not high, cortisol concentrations. This reward processing may in turn mediate the effects of these hormones on behaviours such as risk-taking.

Although there is no direct evidence for the dual-hormone interaction predicting neural reward processing, there is some new indirect evidence with respect to a psychological marker of reward processing. Specifically, a recent study of male and female undergraduate participants

($n = 98$) found a particularly interesting effect: In an economic game, basal testosterone concentrations were positively correlated with self-reported enjoyment and satisfaction with the game in participants with low, but not high, cortisol concentrations (Mehta, DesJardins, van Vugt, & Josephs, 2017). This study provides initial evidence for the idea that motivation for reward, as expressed by factors such as task-enjoyment and related neural systems linked to reward, may underpin the influence of the testosterone × cortisol interaction on behaviour.

In addition to reward, another mechanism likely at play is threat, which the brain is also extremely sensitive to. Both cortisol and testosterone enhance the neural processing of threat and negative affect (Denson, Ronay, et al., 2013; Goetz et al., 2014; Hermans, Ramsey, & van Honk, 2008; Mehta & Beer, 2010). However, whereas cortisol triggers neurophysiological systems that may be more oriented toward social avoidance, testosterone triggers approach-oriented behaviours, likely to engage with the threat rather than avoid it. Covariation in endogenous cortisol and testosterone will lead to differential modulation of the relevant brain networks, which would likely manifest in different behavioural repertoires. For example, in a small study of healthy males ($n = 19$), participants with higher concentrations of testosterone and lower concentrations of cortisol showed greater activation in brain regions associated with cognitive control (the dorsolateral prefrontal cortex) in an anger-control task (Denson, Ronay, et al., 2013). In comparison, participants with high concentrations of both testosterone and cortisol did not show this pattern of activation, suggesting that prefrontal activity may mediate the effect of hormone interactions on psychological processes.

Psychopharmacological experiments to understand causality: Pharmacological approaches have the benefit of enhancing our understanding of causation. All of the effects discussed in this chapter arise from endogenous variation in steroid concentrations. That is to say, the causal theory underlying the dual-hormone hypothesis is that cortisol inhibits the action of testosterone. However, the testosterone × cortisol interaction is not truly able to offer evidence for this causal statement, as the reverse is also possible. Although it may also be the case that testosterone inhibits the action of cortisol, existing research does provide some clues that support our interpretation of the testosterone × cortisol interaction – that it is cortisol inhibiting the effects of testosterone.

By experimentally varying the concentrations of cortisol and testosterone, pharmacological manipulations will be able to generate important insights about the effects of different combinations of these hormones on behaviour. Of the four relevant pharmacological manipulations of testosterone and cortisol, three are readily and easily implemented with no health concerns. These are (1) increasing cortisol concentrations with drugs such as hydrocortisone, (2) suppressing cortisol activity with drugs such as dexamethasone and (3) increasing testosterone concentrations with drugs such as nasal sprays, topical gels and creams, or via ingestion. Researchers frequently use these approaches, especially for increasing cortisol and testosterone. The fourth possibility, pharmacologically suppressing testosterone activity, may pose some ethical and logistical issues. Antiandrogen drugs such as inhibitors of gonadotropic releasing hormone (which stimulates testosterone release), are also used for chemical castration. Though an important recent investigation has administered testosterone antagonists (cetrorelix acetate) to healthy volunteers (Goetz et al., 2014), we anticipate that there may be significant hurdles in conducting such studies, both in terms of obtaining the relevant research ethics approval, and also in recruiting male participants for such an experiment. This is not to say that experiments aiming to reduce testosterone concentrations are impossible, only that they are not nearly as expedient as those increasing testosterone, or increasing and decreasing cortisol. Fortunately, the combinations of the greatest interest (at present) are high levels of testosterone with low levels of cortisol, or high levels of both testosterone and cortisol. These can be mimicked pharmacologically by administering a testosterone enhancer alongside hydrocortisone (to increase cortisol levels) or dexamethasone (to suppress cortisol levels).

Experimental manipulations of stress to understand causality: A recent pilot study (Prasad et al., 2017) offers some evidence of a potential non-pharmacological route to understanding causality. The researchers manipulated participant stress by either engaging them in a social stress task (increasing cortisol) or in a relaxation task (decreasing cortisol). Participants ($n = 39$) were randomly assigned to either the stress or relaxation conditions. Consistent with the dual-hormone hypothesis, testosterone interacted with this acute stress manipulation to predict subsequent behaviour (retaliations in an ultimatum game). Basal testosterone was positively related to retaliatory behaviour (greater rate of rejecting offers) only in the low stress (low cortisol) condition, but this association was not seen in the high stress (high cortisol) condition. Although this is only a pilot study that requires replication and extension, it does open up avenues for new work using acute stress and relaxation tasks as cortisol manipulators. These types of study designs will be especially useful in providing non-pharmacological experimental tests of the dual-hormone hypothesis.

Other statistical models analysing two hormones: This chapter has reviewed evidence for the interaction between testosterone and cortisol concentrations as a predictor of behaviour, but other approaches also attempt to incorporate both testosterone and cortisol in describing human social behaviour. It will be important to carry out studies that test and compare different approaches directly to one another. For example, one line of research examines the coupling between testosterone and cortisol, which is captured in the magnitude of the positive correlation between the two hormones (Shirtcliff et al., 2015; Dismukes et al., 2015; Johnson et al., 2014). The notion of coupling follows on the observation that in several cases, cortisol and testosterone may share a strong positive association with one another, whereas in other cases the two hormones may show weaker or no coupling. This coupling has been used to describe antisocial aggression in adolescence. Hormone coupling is the topic of Chapter 33 (Zakreski et al., this volume), and is therefore not discussed further here.

Sex differences: The dual-hormone hypothesis appears to hold for both sexes, at least as far as several of the studies described here are concerned (Mehta & Josephs, 2010; Mehta, Mor, Yap, & Prasad, 2015; Mehta, Welker, Zilioli, & Carré, 2015, study 2; Tackett et al., 2014, 2015; Grotzinger et al., 2018). However, there are also a few differences. For instance, there are cases where an effect was noted in males but not females (Welker et al., 2014; Zilioli et al., 2014; Ronay et al., 2018). In other cases, all the participants were of only one sex, which would complicate drawing inferences for the other sex (e.g., Edward & Casto, 2013; study 2, Mehta, Welker, Zilioli, & Carré, 2015). Because studies with male-only samples outnumber those with mixed-sex or female-only samples, it is presently unclear how the dual-hormone hypothesis explains the hormone-dominance relationship in several status-seeking behaviours in females, including antisocial punishment (Pfattheicher et al., 2014), overbidding (van den Bos et al., 2013), or number of subordinates (Sherman et al., 2016), all of which were studied only in males.

At a more general level, the dual-hormone hypothesis on interactions between cortisol and testosterone is a specification of broader interactions between the HPA-axis and the HPG-axes. As the results describing estradiol × cortisol interactions suggest, the HPG-axis secretes hormones other than testosterone that may contribute to dominance and status-seeking behaviour (Tackett et al., 2015). Because only one study reports this effect, and because the result is restricted to externalising behaviours such as aggression, it is important to expand the scope of studies to include other types of dominance-oriented behaviour. To this extent, stereotypically "female" sex hormones such as estradiol and progesterone should be more widely incorporated into future research on dual-hormone contributions to social behaviour in both males and females.

Potential bias introduced by measurement techniques: A little-considered but an important issue is the technique of quantifying hormones. Typically, participants provide saliva samples from which hormone concentrations are quantified using one of several analytical approaches. Most researchers use immunoassays to measure steroid hormone concentrations, but growing evidence indicates that this technique is susceptible to measurement error (Welker et al., 2016). A devil's advocate argument against the dual-hormone hypothesis is that the testosterone × cortisol interaction does not reflect a true physiological interplay that drives behaviour, but merely indicates varying levels of glucocorticoid (or other steroid) interference of the testosterone assay, a concern that extends across immunoassay methods. Therefore, it is particularly important to consider the results from quantifications that are not reliant on immunoassays. A much more precise technique for estimating testosterone in both hair and saliva is liquid chromatography tandem mass spectrometry (Welker et al., 2016). The two hair-based studies described in this chapter that support the dual-hormone hypothesis have used this technique (Grotzinger et al., 2018; Ronay et al., 2018). Because the testosterone × cortisol interaction was detectable with liquid chromatography tandem mass spectrometry, these findings provide preliminary evidence that it is not merely an artefact arising from the use of immunoassays.

Statistical power and replication: While the testosterone × cortisol interaction has been observed in different contexts and with different response variables (hence the motivation for this chapter), it is important to acknowledge the low statistical power characterising many of the dual-hormone findings, as well as failures to replicate the key effect. As with other subdisciplines in experimental psychology, social endocrinology research is often characterised by low statistical power to detect small to medium sized effects. There are several components to statistical power, but the most commonly cited cause of low power is sample size. Although some of the studies described here have a large number of participants (e.g., 400), others have very few (under 20). Furthermore, there have also been notable failures to detect the testosterone × cortisol interaction in a few studies with large samples. For instance, in a study of competitive behaviour, aggression, and motivation ($n = 326$), Oxford, Tiedtke, Ossmann, Özbe, and Schultheiss (2017) found that aggression was associated with low cortisol levels but not with high testosterone (i.e., a main effect of cortisol, rather than a testosterone × cortisol interaction). Another study (Mazur & Booth, 2014) examined the link between testosterone, cortisol and antisocial deviance in a large data set from American army veterans ($n = 4,462$). While testosterone was, in general, positively correlated with antisocial behaviour, the relation was not moderated by cortisol.

We recommend that if researchers have data of sufficient quality for both cortisol and testosterone and a theoretically relevant psychological variable, they should perform exploratory tests for the dual-hormone hypothesis, even if it is not the hypothesis of central significance to the research. For any psychological study that analyses both testosterone and cortisol, it becomes trivially straightforward to conduct an additional analysis to test the dual-hormone hypothesis. The publication of these analyses, though exploratory, will provide at least an impression of how readily the effect replicates. In particular, if the dual-hormone hypothesis is biologically plausible, then evidence for it should appear in studies that are testing other research questions as well.

Overall, this line of research would also certainly benefit from several large, direct replications of key findings (e.g., Mehta & Josephs, 2010). These efforts should be sufficiently powered to detect even small effects, and should perhaps be pre-registered so as to guard against false discovery or undisclosed exploitation of researchers degrees of freedom during data analysis. At present, we are aware of one pre-registered study of the dual-hormone hypothesis (Ronay et al., 2018). Further efforts in these directions would add significantly to the empirical foundation of the dual-hormone hypothesis, providing researchers with more accurate estimates of the underlying effect sizes.

Conclusion

Hormones have long been known to influence human social behaviour, and the dual-hormone hypothesis provides a framework with which to both design and interpret research on these influences. It should be noted that the dual-hormone hypothesis is very much in its infancy. While the accumulation of support across a range of response variables relating to dominance and status-seeking is certainly encouraging, large knowledge gaps remain. We have described some of these gaps in the present chapter. Researchers should prioritise these important unknowns so as to shed light on how the interactions between endocrine systems influence dominance and human social behaviour.

References

Akinola, M., Page-Gould, E., Mehta, P.H., & Lu, J.G. (2016). Collective hormonal profiles predict group performance. *Proceedings of the National Academy of Sciences, 35*, 9774–9779.

Amanatullah, E.T., Morris, M.W., & Curhan, J.R. (2008). Negotiators who give too much: Unmitigated communion, relational anxieties, and economic costs in distributive and integrative bargaining. *Journal of Personality and Social Psychology, 95*, 723–738.

Anderson, C., & Kilduff, G.J. (2009). Why do dominant personalities attain influence in face-to-face groups? The competence-signaling effects of trait dominance. *Journal of Personality and Social Psychology, 96*, 491–503.

Apicella, C.L., Dreber, A., Campbell, B., Gray, P.B., Hoffman, M., & Little, A.C. (2008). Testosterone and financial risk preferences. *Evolution and Human Behavior, 29*, 384–390.

Archer, J. (2006). Testosterone and human aggression: An evaluation of the challenge hypothesis. *Neuroscience & Biobehavioral Reviews, 30*(3), 319–345.

Archer, J., Graham-Kevan, N., & Davies, M. (2005). Testosterone and aggression: A reanalysis of book, Starzyk, and Quinsey's (2001) study. *Aggression and Violent Behavior, 10*, 241–261.

Baron-Cohen, S., Wheelwright, S., Hill, J., Raste, Y., & Plumb, I. (2001). The "Reading the Mind in the Eyes" test revised version: A study with normal adults, and adults with Asperger syndrome or high-functioning autism. *The Journal of Child Psychology and Psychiatry and Allied Disciplines, 42*, 241–251.

Beehner, J. C., Bergman, T. J., Cheney, D. L., Seyfarth, R. M., & Whitten, P. L. (2006). Testosterone predicts future dominance rank and mating activity among male chacma baboons. *Behavioral Ecology and Sociobiology, 59*, 469–479.

Boksem, M.A., Mehta, P.H., van den Bergh, B., van Son, V., Trautmann, S.T., Roelofs, K., . . . Sanfey, A.G. (2013). Testosterone inhibits trust but promotes reciprocity. *Psychological Science, 24*, 2306–2314.

Burnstein, K.L., Maiorino, C.A., Dai, J.L., & Cameron, D.J. (1995). Androgen and glucocorticoid regulation of androgen receptor cDNA expression. *Molecular and Cellular Endocrinology, 115*, 177–186.

Buskens, V., Raub, W., van Miltenburg, N., Montoya, E.R., & van Honk, J. (2016). Testosterone administration moderates effect of social environment on trust in women depending on second-to-fourth digit ratio. *Scientific Reports, 6*, 27655.

Buss, A.H., & Durkee, A. (1957). An inventory for assessing different kinds of hostility. *Journal of Consulting Psychology, 21*, 343–349.

Carré, J.M., Geniole, S.N., Ortiz, T.L., Bird, B.M., Videto, A., & Bonin, P.L. (2017). Exogenous testosterone rapidly increases aggressive behavior in dominant and impulsive men. *Biological Psychiatry, 82*, 249–256.

Carré, J. M., & McCormick, C. M. (2008). Aggressive behavior and change in salivary testosterone concentrations predict willingness to engage in a competitive task. *Hormones and Behavior, 54*, 403–409.

Chen, S.Y., Wang, J., Yu, G.Q., Liu, W., & Pearce, D. (1997). Androgen and glucocorticoid receptor heterodimer formation: A possible mechanism for mutual inhibition of transcriptional activity. *Journal of Biological Chemistry, 272*, 14087–14092.

Cheng, J.T., Tracy, J.L., Foulsham, T., Kingstone, A., & Henrich, J. (2013). Two ways to the top: Evidence that dominance and prestige are distinct yet viable avenues to social rank and influence. *Journal of Personality and Social Psychology, 104*, 103–125.

Cillessen, A.H., & Mayeux, L. (2004). From censure to reinforcement: Developmental changes in the association between aggression and social status. *Child Development, 75*, 147–163.

Coates, J.M., & Herbert, J. (2008). Endogenous steroids and financial risk taking on a London trading floor. *Proceedings of the National Academy of Sciences, 105,* 6167–6172.

Croon, M.A., & van Veldhoven, M.J. (2007). Predicting group-level outcome variables from variables measured at the individual level: A latent variable multilevel model *Psychological Methods, 12,* 45–57.

Cueva, C., Roberts, R.E., Spencer, T., Rani, N., Tempest, M., Tobler, P.N., . . . Rustichini, A. (2015). Cortisol and testosterone increase financial risk taking and may destabilize markets. *Scientific Reports, 5.*

Dabbs, J.M., Jurkovic, G.J., & Frady, R.L. (1991). Salivary testosterone and cortisol among late adolescent male offenders. *Journal of Abnormal Child Psychology, 19,* 469–478.

Davis, M.H. (1983). Measuring individual differences in empathy: Evidence for a multidimensional approach. *Journal of Personality and Social Psychology, 44,* 113–126.

Dettenborn, L., Tietze, A., Kirschbaum, C., & Stalder, T. (2012). The assessment of cortisol in human hair: Associations with sociodemographic variables and potential confounders. *Stress, 15,* 578–588.

Denson, T.F., Mehta, P.H., & Tan, D.H. (2013). Endogenous testosterone and cortisol jointly influence reactive aggression in women. *Psychoneuroendocrinology, 38,* 416–424.

Denson, T.F., Ronay, R., von Hippel, W., & Schira, M.M. (2013). Endogenous testosterone and cortisol modulate neural responses during induced anger control. *Social Neuroscience, 8,* 165–177.

Dickerson, S. S., & Kemeny, M. E. (2004). Acute stressors and cortisol responses: A theoretical integration and synthesis of laboratory research. *Psychological Bulletin, 130,* 355–391. Dismukes, A.R., Johnson, M.M., Vitacco, M.J., Iturri, F., & Shirtcliff, E.A. (2015). Coupling of the HPA and HPG axes in the context of early life adversity in incarcerated male adolescents. *Developmental Psychobiology, 57,* 705–718.

Dominique, J. F., Roozendaal, B., Nitsch, R. M., McGaugh, J. L., & Hock, C. (2000). Acute cortisone administration impairs retrieval of long-term declarative memory in humans. *Nature Neuroscience, 3,* 313–314.

Edwards, D.A., & Casto, K.V. (2013). Women's intercollegiate athletic competition: Cortisol, testosterone, and the dual-hormone hypothesis as it relates to status among teammates. *Hormones and Behavior, 64,* 153–160.

Eisenegger, C., Naef, M., Snozzi, R., Heinrichs, M., & Fehr, E. (2010). Prejudice and truth about the effect of testosterone on human bargaining behaviour. *Nature, 463,* 356–359.

Geniole, S. N., Carré, J. M., & McCormick, C. M. (2011). State, not trait, neuroendocrine function predicts costly reactive aggression in men after social exclusion and inclusion. *Biological Psychology, 87,* 137–145.

Giammanco, M., Tabacchi, G., Giammanco, S., Di Majo, D., & La Guardia, M. (2005). Testosterone and aggressiveness. *Medical Science Monitor, 11,* RA136–RA145.

Goetz, S. M., Tang, L., Thomason, M. E., Diamond, M. P., Hariri, A. R., & Carré, J. M. (2014). Testosterone rapidly increases neural reactivity to threat in healthy men: A novel two-step pharmacological challenge paradigm. *Biological Psychiatry, 76,* 324–331.

Gould, L., & Ziegler, T. E. (2007). Variation in fecal testosterone levels, inter-male aggression, dominance rank and age during mating and post-mating periods in wild adult male ring-tailed lemurs (*Lemur catta*). *American Journal of Primatology, 69,* 1325–1339.

Grotzinger, A.D., Mann, F.D., Patterson, M.W., Tackett, J.L., Tucker-Drob, E.M., & Harden, K.P. (2018). Hair and salivary testosterone, hair cortisol, and externalizing behaviors in adolescents. *Psychological Science,* 0956797617742981.

Henry, A., Sattizahn, J.R., Norman, G.J., Beilock, S.L., & Maestripieri, D. (2017). Performance during competition and competition outcome in relation to testosterone and cortisol among women. *Hormones and Behavior, 92,* 82–92.

Hermans, E. J., Bos, P. A., Ossewaarde, L., Ramsey, N. F., Fernández, G., & van Honk, J. (2010). Effects of exogenous testosterone on the ventral striatal BOLD response during reward anticipation in healthy women. *Neuroimage, 52,* 277–283.

Hermans, E. J., Ramsey, N. F., & van Honk, J. (2008). Exogenous testosterone enhances responsiveness to social threat in the neural circuitry of social aggression in humans. *Biological Psychiatry, 63,* 263–270.

Hunt, M. K., Hopko, D. R., Bare, R., Lejuez, C. W., & Robinson, E. V. (2005). Construct validity of the balloon analog risk task (BART) associations with psychopathy and impulsivity. *Assessment, 12,* 416–428.

Johnson, M.M., Dismukes, A.R., Vitacco, M.J., Breiman, C., Fleury, D., & Shirtcliff, E.A. (2014). Psychopathy's influence on the coupling between hypothalamic-pituitary-adrenal and -gonadal axes among incarcerated adolescents. *Developmental Psychobiology, 56,* 448–458.

Josephs, R. A., Sellers, J. G., Newman, M. L., & Mehta, P. H. (2006). The mismatch effect: When testosterone and status are at odds. *Journal of Personality and Social Psychology, 90,* 999–1013.

Kandasamy, N., Hardy, B., Page, L., Schaffner, M., Graggaber, J., Powlson, A.S., . . . Coates, J. (2014). Cortisol shifts financial risk preferences. *Proceedings of the National Academy of Sciences, 111*, 3608–3613.

Lee, J.J., Gino, F., Jin, E.S., Rice, L.K., & Josephs, R.A. (2015). Hormones and ethics: Understanding the biological basis of unethical conduct. *Journal of Experimental Psychology: General, 144*, 891–897.

Lejuez, C.W., Read, J.P., Kahler, C.W., Richards, J.B., Ramsey, S.E., Stuart, G.L., . . . Brown, R.A. (2002). Evaluation of a behavioral measure of risk taking: The Balloon Analogue Risk Task (BART). *Journal of Experimental Psychology: Applied, 8*, 75–84.

Mazur, A., & Booth, A. (1998). Testosterone and dominance in men. *Behavioral and Brain Sciences, 21*, 353–363.

Mazur, A., & Booth, A. (2014). Testosterone is related to deviance in male army veterans, but relationships are not moderated by cortisol. *Biological Psychology, 96*, 72–76.

Mehta, P. H., & Beer, J. (2010). Neural mechanisms of the testosterone–aggression relation: The role of orbitofrontal cortex. *Journal of Cognitive Neuroscience, 22*, 2357–2368.

Mehta, P.H., DesJardins, N.M.L., van Vugt, M., & Josephs, R.A. (2017). Hormonal underpinnings of status conflict: Testosterone and cortisol are related to decisions and satisfaction in the hawk-dove game. *Hormones and Behavior, 92*, 141–154

Mehta, P.H., & Josephs, R.A. (2010). Testosterone and cortisol jointly regulate dominance: Evidence for a dual-hormone hypothesis. *Hormones and Behavior, 58*, 898–906.

Mehta, P.H., Mor, S., Yap, A.J., & Prasad, S. (2015a). Dual-hormone changes are related to bargaining performance. *Psychological Science, 26*, 866–876.

Mehta, P.H., & Prasad, S. (2015). The dual-hormone hypothesis: A brief review and future research agenda. *Current Opinion in Behavioral Sciences, 3*, 163–168.

Mehta, P.H., van Son, V., Welker, K.M., Prasad, S., Sanfey, A.G., Smidts, A., & Roelofs, K. (2015). Exogenous testosterone in women enhances and inhibits competitive decision-making depending on victory-defeat experience and trait dominance. *Psychoneuroendocrinology, 60*, 224–236.

Mehta, P.H., Welker, K.M., Zilioli, S., & Carré, J.M. (2015b). Testosterone and cortisol jointly modulate risk-taking. *Psychoneuroendocrinology, 56*, 88–99.

Montoya, E. R., Bos, P. A., Terburg, D., Rosenberger, L. A., & van Honk, J. (2014). Cortisol administration induces global down-regulation of the brain's reward circuitry. *Psychoneuroendocrinology, 47*, 31–42.

Op de Macks, Z. A., Moor, B. G., Overgaauw, S., Güroğlu, B., Dahl, R. E., & Crone, E. A. (2011). Testosterone levels correspond with increased ventral striatum activation in response to monetary rewards in adolescents. *Developmental Cognitive Neuroscience, 1*, 506–516.

Oswald, L. M., Wong, D. F., McCaul, M., Zhou, Y., Kuwabara, H., Choi, L., . . . & Wand, G. S. (2005). Relationships among ventral striatal dopamine release, cortisol secretion, and subjective responses to amphetamine. *Neuropsychopharmacology, 30*, 821–832.

Oxford, J. K., Tiedtke, J. M., Ossmann, A., Özbe, D., & Schultheiss, O. C. (2017). Endocrine and aggressive responses to competition are moderated by contest outcome, gender, individual versus team competition, and implicit motives. *PLoS One, 12*, e0181610.

Pfattheicher, S. (2017). Illuminating the dual-hormone hypothesis: About chronic dominance and the interaction of cortisol and testosterone. *Aggressive Behavior, 43*, 85–92.

Pfattheicher, S., Landhäußer, A., & Keller, J. (2014). Individual differences in antisocial punishment in public goods situations: The interplay of cortisol with testosterone and dominance. *Journal of Behavioral Decision Making, 27*, 340–348.

Ponzi, D., Zilioli, S., Mehta, P. H., Maslov, A., & Watson, N. V. (2016). Social network centrality and hormones: The interaction of testosterone and cortisol. *Psychoneuroendocrinology, 68*, 6–13.

Popma, A., Vermeiren, R., Geluk, C.A., Rinne, T., van den Brink, W., Knol, D.L., . . . Doreleijers, T.A. (2007). Cortisol moderates the relationship between testosterone and aggression in delinquent male adolescents. *Biological Psychiatry, 61*, 405–411.

Plessow, F., Schade, S., Kirschbaum, C., & Fischer, R. (2017). Successful voluntary recruitment of cognitive control under acute stress. *Cognition, 168*, 182–190.

Prasad, S., Narayanan, J., Lim, V.K., Koh, G.C., Koh, D.S., & Mehta, P.H. (2017). Preliminary evidence that acute stress moderates basal testosterone's association with retaliatory behavior. *Hormones and Behavior, 92*, 128–140.

Pruessner, J. C., Champagne, F., Meaney, M. J., & Dagher, A. (2004). Dopamine release in response to a psychological stress in humans and its relationship to early life maternal care: A positron emission tomography study using [11C] raclopride. *Journal of Neuroscience, 24*, 2825–2831.

Roelofs, K., van Peer, J., Berretty, E., de Jong, P., Spinhoven, P., & Elzinga, B. M. (2009). Hypothalamus–pituitary–adrenal axis hyperresponsiveness is associated with increased social avoidance behavior in social phobia. *Biological Psychiatry, 65,* 336–343.

Ronay, R., Oostrom, J.K., & Pollet, T. (2018). No evidence for a relationship between hair testosterone concentrations and 2D: 4D ratio or risk taking. *Frontiers in Behavioral Neuroscience, 12,* 30.

Sherman, G.D., Lee, J.J., Cuddy, A.J., Renshon, J., Oveis, C., Gross, J.J., & Lerner, J.S. (2012). Leadership is associated with lower levels of stress. *Proceedings of the National Academy of Sciences, 109,* 17903–17907.

Sherman, G. D., Lerner, J. S., Josephs, R. A., Renshon, J., & Gross, J. J. (2016). The interaction of testosterone and cortisol is associated with attained status in male executives. *Journal of Personality and Social Psychology, 110,* 921–929.

Shirtcliff, E.A., Dismukes, A.R., Marceau, K., Ruttle, P.L., Simmons, J.G., & Han, G. (2015). A dual-axis approach to understanding neuroendocrine development. *Developmental Psychobiology, 57,* 643–653.

Sollberger, S., Bernauer, T., & Ehlert, U. (2016). Salivary testosterone and cortisol are jointly related to pro-environmental behavior in men. *Social Neuroscience, 11,* 553–566.

Tackett, J.L., Herzhoff, K., Harden, K.P., Page-Gould, E., & Josephs, R.A. (2014). Personality× hormone interactions in adolescent externalizing psychopathology. *Personality Disorders: Theory, Research, and Treatment, 5,* 235–246.

Tackett, J.L., Reardon, K.W., Herzhoff, K., Page-Gould, E., Harden, K.P., & Josephs, R.A. (2015). Estradiol and cortisol interactions in youth externalizing psychopathology. *Psychoneuroendocrinology, 55,* 146–153.

Vaillancourt, T., & Hymel, S. (2006). Aggression and social status: The moderating roles of sex and peer-valued characteristics. *Aggressive Behavior, 32,* 396–408.

van Bokhoven, I., van Goozen, S. H., van Engeland, H., Schaal, B., Arseneault, L., Séguin, J. R., . . . & Tremblay, R. E. (2006). Salivary testosterone and aggression, delinquency, and social dominance in a population-based longitudinal study of adolescent males. *Hormones and Behavior, 50,* 118–125.

van den Bos, W., Golka, P.J., Effelsberg, D., & McClure, S.M. (2013). Pyrrhic victories: The need for social status drives costly competitive behavior. *Frontiers in Neuroscience, 7.*

van Honk, J., Peper, J.S., & Schutter, D.J. (2005). Testosterone reduces unconscious fear but not consciously experienced anxiety: Implications for the disorders of fear and anxiety. *Biological Psychiatry, 58,* 218–225.

van Honk, J., Schutter, D.J., Hermans, E.J., Putman, P., Tuiten, A., & Koppeschaar, H. (2004). Testosterone shifts the balance between sensitivity for punishment and reward in healthy young women. *Psychoneuroendocrinology, 29,* 937–943.

Viau, V. (2002). Functional cross-talk between the hypothalamic-pituitary-gonadal and- adrenal axes. *Journal of Neuroendocrinology, 14,* 506–513.

Vongas, J.G., & Al Hajj, R. (2017). The effects of competition and implicit power motive on men's testosterone, emotion recognition, and aggression. *Hormones and Behavior, 92,* 57–71.

Welker, K.M., Lassetter, B., Brandes, C.M., Prasad, S., Koop, D.R., & Mehta, P.H. (2016). A comparison of salivary testosterone measurement using immunoassays and tandem mass spectrometry. *Psychoneuroendocrinology, 71,* 180–188.

Welker, K.M., Lozoya, E., Campbell, J.A., Neumann, C.S., & Carré, J.M. (2014). Testosterone, cortisol, and psychopathic traits in men and women. *Physiology & Behavior, 129,* 230–236.

Welker, K.M., Prasad, S., Srivastava, S., & Mehta, P.H. (2017). Basal cortisol's relation to testosterone changes may not be driven by social challenges. *Psychoneuroendocrinology, 85,* 1–5.

Williams, K.D., & Jarvis, B. (2006). Cyberball: A program for use in research on interpersonal ostracism and acceptance. *Behavior Research Methods, 38,* 174–180.

Wingfield, J.C., Hegner, R.E., Dufty, A.M., Jr., & Ball, G.F. (1990). The "challenge hypothesis": Theoretical implications for patterns of testosterone secretion, mating systems, and breeding strategies. *The American Naturalist, 136,* 829–846.

Zethraeus, N., Kocoska-Maras, L., Ellingsen, T., Von Schoultz, B.O., Hirschberg, A.L., & Johannesson, M. (2009). A randomized trial of the effect of estrogen and testosterone on economic behavior. *Proceedings of the National Academy of Sciences, 106,* 6535–6538.

Zilioli, S., Caldbick, E., & Watson, N. V. (2014). Testosterone reactivity to facial display of emotions in men and women. *Hormones and Behavior, 65,* 461–468.

8

SOCIAL NEUROENDOCRINOLOGY OF HUMAN AGGRESSION

Progress and future directions

Justin M. Carré, Emily Jeanneault, and Nicole Marley

Basic introduction

A large body of evidence indicates that testosterone modulates various physiological, morphological and behavioural processes that play a critical to survival and reproduction (Ketterson & Nolan, 1992). In addition, a wealth of evidence indicates that changes in one's social environment can bring about changes in testosterone concentrations over both the short term (e.g., competitive interactions) and long term (e.g., acquiring a long-term mate, becoming a father). In this chapter, we provide a basic overview of research examining the role of competition-induced changes in testosterone in modulating human aggression. We also provide a brief summary of recent pharmacological challenge experiments demonstrating that a single dose of testosterone can rapidly modulate physiological, perceptual and behavioural processes of relevance to human aggression. In this chapter, we take a comparative approach drawing on both the human and non-human literature to provide a sense of the commonalities in the basic neuroendocrine mechanisms underlying complex social behaviour.

Testosterone and aggression

Research in animal models indicates that testosterone plays an important role in modulating aggressive behaviour (Nelson & Trainor, 2007). However, despite the popular belief that testosterone may also promote human aggression, meta-analytic estimates suggest that the association between testosterone and human aggression is small ($r = .08$, see Archer et al., 2005). There are several potential explanations for the weak relationship between testosterone and human aggression. For example, in contrast to work in animal models that obtain direct objective assessments of aggression (e.g., resident-intruder paradigm), most human studies rely upon self-report measures that may not accurately capture how an individual would behave in a specific circumstance. Also, self-report measures of aggression typically assess general behavioural tendencies across different contexts (i.e., trait level aggression) – and work in animal models indicates that relationships between testosterone and aggression depend highly upon social context (e.g., Wingfield et al., 1990). Finally, many studies examining links between baseline testosterone and human aggression have relied upon assessment of testosterone at a single point in time. Although testosterone concentrations are relatively stable across time (Liening et al., 2010), we know from a vast amount of research that testosterone levels do fluctuate throughout the day (Dabbs, 1990), season (Stanton et al., 2011), and in response to competitive interactions (Geniole et al., 2017). The latter findings have led researchers to speculate that perhaps acute changes in testosterone concentrations within the context of competition/social provocation may be more relevant to our understanding of the neuroendocrinology of aggressive behaviour (McGlothlin et al., 2007).

Context dependent changes in T and aggressive behaviour

A wealth of research in both non-human animal models and in humans indicates that testosterone concentrations are highly responsive to competitive interactions (Wingfield et al., 1990; Oliveira, 2009; Mazur & Booth, 1998). Moreover, a recent meta-analysis indicates that the outcome of competitive interactions modulates the pattern of T reactivity, such that winners demonstrate relatively higher testosterone concentrations post-competition relative to losers ($D = .20$; Geniole et al., 2017). Notably, this effect is most robust ($D = .43$) in studies conducted in the 'field' (e.g., with sport athletes) and is much weaker in studies conducted in the laboratory ($D = .08$).

Theoretical models suggest that acute changes in testosterone concentrations within the context of competitive interactions may function to fine-tune ongoing and/or subsequent competitive and aggressive behaviour (Leshner, 1975; Mazur, 1985; Wingfield et al., 1990; Archer, 2006; Oliveira, 2009). During the past decade, researchers have examined the role of competition-induced changes in testosterone in modulating human competitive/aggressive behaviour. In a first study, Mehta and Josephs (2006) found that a rise in testosterone during a competitive interaction predicted men's ($n = 57$) willingness to approach a subsequent competitive interaction. Similarly, Carré and McCormick (2008) examined men's ($n = 38$) willingness to approach a competitive interaction after assessing testosterone responses to an aggressive interaction. Here, they had participants play the Point Subtraction Aggression Paradigm (PSAP). In this task, participants are led to believe that they are playing a computer game with another same-sex participant (in reality, this is a fictitious opponent). Participants are instructed that they must hit a button 100 times to earn a point. They are told that their payment at the conclusion of the study would be based on the number of points they earned during the task. During the PSAP, points are stolen from participants, and this is attributed to their putative game partner. Participants are instructed that they can respond by ignoring the provocation (i.e., continue to earn points), by stealing points back, or by protecting their points from subtraction. In this task, stealing points back is a costly behaviour because participants do not get to keep the stolen points and engaging in such behaviour detracts from points earned during the game. Stealing points in this game serves the function of retaliating against one's opponent, and is considered a form of reactive aggression. Results indicated that a rise in testosterone during the PSAP was positively correlated with aggressive behaviour (stealing points back) and also predicted men's willingness to approach a subsequent competitive interaction with the same game partner (Carré & McCormick, 2008). In another study, Geniole and colleagues (2013) had male ($n = 104$) participants perform the PSAP and were then asked to decide the honorarium to be received by their game partner (participants could give as much or as little of a 5-dollar honorarium to their game partner; giving lower amounts can be considered a form of financial aggression). Results indicated that participants demonstrating a rise in testosterone during the PSAP gave lower financial allocations to their game partner (Geniole et al., 2013). Collectively, these studies suggest that changes in testosterone during competition and/or social provocation (elicited by the PSAP) predict subsequent competitive and aggressive behaviour.

In other studies, participants first engaged in a rigged competitive interaction (resulting in a clear winner and loser) and then performed the PSAP (Carré et al., 2009; Carré et al., 2013). Results indicated that a rise in testosterone during the competitive interaction was positively correlated with subsequent aggressive behaviour in men ($n = 39$ and $n = 114$, respectively), but not women ($n = 60$ and $n = 123$, respectively). Despite these findings, recent work has failed to replicate this effect. Vongas and Al Hajj (2017) found that an increase in testosterone during a competitive interaction was positively correlated with subsequent aggression (assessed using the PSAP), but this effect was not statistically significant ($n = 72$). Differences in basic methodology may in part explain the weaker effects observed by Vongas and Al Hajj (2017). Specifically, in contrast to previous work using the PSAP (e.g., Carré et al., 2009; 2013), the study by Vongas and Al Hajj (2017) did not award participants money for the points earned on the task. Without the financial consequences associated with stealing, provocations may not have been as salient, and retaliatory stealing may have been qualitatively different from the standard version of the PSAP. Also, another study that included both men ($n = 165$) and women ($n = 161$) found no relationship between testosterone responses to competition and subsequent aggressive behaviour assessed using the Taylor Aggression Paradigm (Oxford et al., 2017). Thus, more research will be needed to determine the robustness of the effect of competition-induced testosterone responses on aggressive behaviour.

Pharmacological challenge research

The correlational nature of the studies reviewed thus far limits our ability to make strong causal claims concerning the role of testosterone in modulating human aggression. One solution to this problem is to use a pharmacological challenge approach. During the past few decades, single dose pharmacological challenge research has been conducted primarily in healthy young women and has found that testosterone can indeed modulate social, cognitive, physiological and behavioural processes of relevance to human aggression (see Bos et al., 2012 for review). For instance, testosterone increases cardiac responses ($n = 16$) and amygdala reactivity ($n = 12$) to angry facial expressions (van Honk et al., 2001; Hermans et al., 2008) and induces attentional biases ($n = 12$) toward such facial cues of threat (Terburg et al., 2012). More recently, single dose testosterone administration paradigms have been developed to study the role of testosterone in modulating similar processes in young men. Results indicate that testosterone increases threat-related amygdala function ($n = 16$) (Goetz et al., 2014), increases perception of one's own physical dominance ($n = 30$) (Welling et al., 2016), enhances preferences for facial femininity in a potential short-term vs. long-term mate ($n = 93$) (Bird et al., 2016), increases anger in responses to a frustrating task ($n = 90$) (Panagiotidis et al., 2017), increases men's approach toward aggressive individuals ($n = 82$) (Wagels et al., 2017), increases risk-taking ($n = 75$) (Cueva et al., 2015), decreases cognitive reflection ($n = 243$), (Nave, Camerer, & McCullough, 2017), and increases punishment of an uncooperative game partner and increases reward toward a cooperative game partner ($n = 40$) (Dreher et al., 2016).

Notably, correlational work suggests that individual differences in personality traits (e.g., trait dominance, trait self-construal) may moderate the effects of testosterone on dominance-related outcome variables (e.g., Carré et al., 2009; Slatcher et al., 2011; Welker et al., 2017). For instance, one study found that a rise in testosterone among male winners ($n = 20$) of a competitive interaction predicted enhanced aggressive behaviour, but only for men scoring high in trait dominance (Carré et al., 2009). Going beyond correlational studies, a number of testosterone manipulation studies have found that trait dominance moderates the effect of testosterone on physiological and behavioural processes. For instance, Carré and colleagues (2017) reported that a single application of testosterone rapidly increased aggressive behaviour, but only for men ($n = 121$) scoring relatively high on trait dominance. Similarly, Mehta and colleagues (2015) reported that testosterone increased competitive motivation, but only among women ($n = 54$) scoring high in trait dominance. Finally, another experiment reported that testosterone administration lead to an increase in men's physiological stress response (cortisol) to a psycho-social stressor, but only for men scoring high in trait dominance ($n = 50$) (Knight et al., 2017). Collectively, these experiments highlight the importance of examining personality traits when attempting to detail the neuroendocrine mechanisms underlying complex human behaviour.

Animal models of testosterone and aggression

Animal models are particularly useful for testing causal mechanisms shaping complex social behaviour. In a series of experiments, researchers have found that acutely elevating testosterone after an aggressive interaction played a key role in modulating subsequent aggressive behaviour in male California mice (Fuxjager et al., 2011: Gleason, Fuxjager, Oyegbile, & Marler, 2009; Trainor, Bird, & Marler, 2004; see the other chapters in Section 2). Similarly, Oliveira and colleagues (2009) examined the role of testosterone in mediating the 'winner' and 'loser' effects in male tilapia ($n = 32$). In control fish, winners of an aggressive interaction are more likely to win a subsequent aggressive interaction (88% win second fight), whereas losers are more likely to lose subsequent interactions (87% lose second fight). Winners treated with an anti-androgen drug, which prevented the normal increase in testosterone in response to competitive interactions, were less likely to win a subsequent aggressive interaction (relative to control males). In contrast, losers treated with an androgen (11-ketotestosterone – primary testosterone metabolite in fish) were not more likely to win a subsequent aggressive interaction. These findings indicate that the 'winner effect' (but not the 'loser effect') depends critically on acute fluctuations in testosterone. In other work with male cichlid fish ($n = 105$), unresolved social conflicts increased the probability of winning future competitive interactions – an effect that was in part due to heightened testosterone levels after the unresolved conflict (Dijkstra, Schaafsma, Hofmann, & Groothuis, 2012). Collectively, these experiments provide compelling support for the role of competition-induced testosterone dynamics in mediating ongoing and/or future social behaviour. Moreover, the animal studies reviewed here are highly consistent with research in humans suggesting that competition-induced changes in testosterone may serve to modulate aggressive behaviour.

Relationship between cortisol and aggressive behaviour

Cortisol is another steroid hormone that has been linked to variability in aggressive behaviour. Research in humans suggests complex associations between cortisol and aggression. For instance, in one study of adolescent boys and girls, it was found that serum cortisol concentrations were negatively correlated with various self-report indices of aggression – an effect that was found in boys ($n = 118$) but not girls ($n = 127$) (Poustka et al., 2010). Similarly, in a relatively small sample of pre-adolescent boys ($n = 38$), McBurnett et al. found that those individuals nominated by their peers as high in aggression had significantly lower levels of salivary cortisol concentrations. In contrast, another study of young adolescent boys ($n = 194$) found that individuals with conduct disorder (characterized by elevated aggressive behaviour) had significantly higher salivary cortisol concentrations relative to those without the disorder (van Bokhoven et al., 2005). In a study using the Taylor Aggression Paradigm (TAP), Oxford and colleagues (2017) reported that baseline cortisol levels were negatively correlated with aggression in men ($n = 165$), but positively related to aggression in women ($n = 161$). Surprisingly, few studies have investigated the extent to which experimentally manipulating stress (either through pharmacological challenge or stress paradigm) influences subsequent aggressive responding. In one study, adult men and women were exposed to a physical stressor (air blast) and subsequently assessed for aggressive behaviour using the TAP. The authors reported that stress exposure increased aggression among men ($n = 56$), but decreased aggression among women ($n = 66$) (Verona and Kilmer, 2007). In another study using a similar stress manipulation, Verona and Curtin (2006) reported that men ($n = 58$) exposed to the stressor demonstrated an increase in aggression across blocks of the TAP, whereas men in the control condition demonstrated no change in aggression across blocks. In contrast, women ($n = 59$) exposed to the stressor experienced no change in aggression across blocks, whereas women in the control condition demonstrated an increase in aggression across blocks (Verona & Curtin, 2006). Another study found that stress exposure did not affect aggression among men ($n = 24$), but decreased aggression among women ($n = 25$) (Verona et al., 2007). Similarly, using rejections of unfair offers in the Ultimatum Game as an index of retaliatory aggression, Prasad et al. (2017) reported that a social stressor decreased aggression in women ($n = 19$), but increased aggression among men ($n = 20$). Böhnke et al. (2010) conducted the only pharmacological challenge study to investigate the role of cortisol in modulating human aggression. Results indicated that a single dose of cortisol increased aggressive behaviour assessed using the TAP, but only for women ($n = 96$, 50% women). Clearly, more research examining the role of acute and chronic stress on aggressive behaviour will be needed to draw more definitive conclusions concerning the role of cortisol in modulating human aggression. Finally, there is some evidence that testosterone and cortisol interact to predict various forms of dominance-related behaviours, including aggression (see Chapter 7 by Sarkar, Mehta & Josephs).

Similar to the human work, research in rodents indicates a complex relationship between corticosterone (cortisol analogue in rodents) and aggression. Some earlier studies reported that removal of the adrenal glands (and thus, the main source of corticosterone), leads to excessive forms of aggressive behaviour in rodents ($n = 7$–14/group, $n = 5$/group), characterized by fewer threat displays and more attacks to vulnerable areas of the body (Haller et al., 2004, 2001). Conversely, other research indicates that chronic physical stressors in rodent models ($n = 42$, $n = 4$–13/group) promote increased aggressive behaviour (Wood et al., 2003; van der Kooij et al., 2014). Collectively, this body of work suggests the possibility of a U-shaped relationship between stress hormones and aggression whereby both low and high corticosterone concentrations promote the expression of abnormal aggression (Walker et al., in press).

Relationship between oxytocin and aggressive behaviour

The neuropeptide oxytocin is another hormone that has been linked to aggressive behaviour. In one study, Lee and colleagues (2009) found that variability in oxytocin concentrations (measured from cerebrospinal fluid) were negatively correlated with a dimensional measure of life history of aggression ($n = 58$). Pharmacological challenge studies using intranasal oxytocin administration have reported mixed findings. In one experiment using a modified version of the PSAP, Ne'eman and colleagues (2016) reported that a single dose of oxytocin increased aggressive behaviour in men ($n = 28$) and women ($n = 20$). In another study, it was found that oxytocin increased participants' (men and women, $n = 93$) propensity toward intimate partner aggression, especially among those scoring high in trait aggression (DeWall et al., 2014). In contrast, in a relatively small within-subject cross-over design in healthy men ($n = 17$), there was no effect of intranasal oxytocin on aggressive behaviour assessed using the PSAP (Alcorn III et al., 2015). Also, in a study of young women ($n = 45$), Campbell and Hausmann (2013) found no effect of intranasal oxytocin on aggressive behaviour assessed using the PSAP. However, they found that individual differences in trait anxiety moderated the effect of oxytocin on aggression, such that oxytocin decreased aggressive behaviour, but only in women scoring high in state anxiety (Campbell & Hausmann, 2013). Further complicating the relationship between oxytocin and aggression is the finding that links between oxytocin and aggression/antisocial behaviour depend on social context. Specifically, De Dreu and colleagues (2011) have reported administration of oxytocin ($n = 70$) increases cooperative behaviour toward one's in-group, and to a lesser degree, promotes defensive aggression toward the out-group (see Simnone Shamay-Tsoory et al., for further discussion on the role of OT in modulating human behaviour).

Research with male rats ($n = 10$–17/group) indicates that administration of oxytocin leads to a reduction in aggressive behaviour, an effect that is abolished by the co-administration of an oxytocin receptor antagonist (Calcagnoli, de Boer, Althaus, den Boer, & Koolhaas, 2013). Similar anti-aggressive effects of oxytocin have been observed in male mice ($n = 6$–8/group) after intranasal administration of oxytocin (Calcagnoli, Kreutzmann, de Boer, Althaus, & Koolhaas, 2015). In addition, female hamsters ($n = 5$–12/group) show a dose-dependent reduction in aggression when administered oxytocin, an effect that can be reversed with an oxytocin receptor antagonist (Harmon, Huhman, Moore, & Albers, 2002). Despite such anti-aggressive effects, oxytocin may have aggression-potentiating effects during childbirth and lactation. Female rats selectively bred for high anxiety-related behaviour (HAB) are significantly more aggressive during a maternal defence relative to rats selectively bred for low anxiety-related behaviour (LAB). Notably, oxytocin concentrations within the periventricular nucleus of the hypothalamus (PVN) and central amygdala (CeA) were increased in HAB dams relative to LAB dams. Moreover, a positive correlation between oxytocin release within the PVN and CeA and maternal aggression was found. Finally, oxytocin receptor antagonist infused directly in the PVN or CeA lead to a reduction in maternal aggression in HAB dams, whereas infusion of oxytocin into the PVN increased maternal aggression among LAB dams. Increases in oxytocin were also observed in the central amygdala (CeA), with more significant changes within the HAB population (Bosch, Kromer, Brunton, & Neumann, 2004). Follow-up studies revealed oxytocin antagonist in HAB rats CeA decreased innate offensive behaviour (Bosch, Meddle, Beiderbeck, Douglas, & Neumann, 2005).

Relationship between vasopressin and aggressive behaviour

A closely related neuropeptide, vasopressin has also been examined with respect to its association with aggressive behaviour. In one study with a relatively small sample of male and female participants ($n = 26$) meeting criteria for personality disorder, individual differences in cerebrospinal vasopressin were positively correlated with life history of general aggression (Coccaro, Kavoussi, Hauger, Cooper, & Ferris, 1998). In golden hamsters, administration of vasopressin into either the anterior ($n = 4$–11) (Ferris et al., 1997) or ventrolateral hypothalamus ($n = 61$) (Delville et al., 1994) increases aggressive behaviour. Furthermore, Ferris and colleagues (2006) found that administration of a selective vasopressin receptor blocker significantly reduced male hamsters' aggressive behaviour during a resident-intruder paradigm.

Future directions

Neural mechanisms through which testosterone modulates human aggression: More research will be needed to elucidate the neural mechanisms through which testosterone modulates human aggression. Research in animal models indicates that several inter-connected cortical and subcortical structures within the so-called social behaviour network (Newman, 1999) are directly related to the expression of aggression (Nelson & Trainor, 2007). One model suggests a neural circuitry comprising the medial amygdala, medial hypothalamus and periaqueductal grey (PAG) positively modulates aggressive behaviour (Siegel et al., 2007; Blair, 2010). Specifically, this model suggest that the medial amygdala provides excitatory input to glutamatergic neurons located within the medial hypothalamus, which exert excitatory drive on PAG neurons, ultimately mediating aggressive behaviour (Siegel et al., 2007). Also, given the extensive projections from the orbitofrontal cortex (OFC) to the hypothalamus and amygdala, it has been proposed that the propensity to engage in aggression may emerge from impaired regulatory control of the OFC over limbic structures (see Nelson & Trainor, 2007 for review). Importantly, androgen and estrogen receptors are widely distributed throughout the neural circuitry underlying reactive aggression (Newman, 1999; Wood & Newman, 1999; Fernandez-Guasti et al., 2000; Roselli et al., 2001; Donahue et al., 2000; Murphy et al., 1999), suggesting that testosterone and/or its metabolites (e.g., estradiol) may directly modulate this circuitry by interacting with steroid hormone receptors in these regions. Notably, functional neuroimaging studies have found that individual differences in baseline testosterone concentrations are positively correlated with amygdala reactivity to facial expressions of anger and fear in men ($n = 21$, Derntl et al., 2009; $n = 41$, Manuck et al., 2010) and negatively correlated with OFC responses to social provocation in men and women ($n = 34$, Mehta and Beer, 2010). Also, exogenous administration of testosterone enhanced amygdala and hypothalamic reactivity to angry and fearful faces ($n = 12$, Hermans et al., 2008; $n = 44$, van Wingen et al., 2009; $n = 12$, Bos, van Honk, Ramsey, Stein, & Hermans, 2013) and decreased amygdala-OFC coupling during processing of angry and fearful facial expressions ($n = 25$, van Wingen et al., 2010). These findings suggest that testosterone may bias aggressive behaviour by enhancing threat-related amygdala function and/or decreasing PFC-amygdala functional coupling during the processing of social threat (e.g., angry facial expressions, social provocation).

Testosterone may also regulate aggressive behaviour through modulating the reward value of aggression. There is evidence from human studies indicating that aggression is rewarding, and that people regulate the degree/severity of aggression based on the extent to which they both self-report the behaviour to be rewarding (e.g., Ramírez et al., 2005, $n = 50$) and show activation in reward-related brain regions (e.g., nucleus accumbens) during the decision to aggress ($n = 69$, Chester & DeWall, 2016). Because testosterone increases sensitivity to reward ($n = 12$, van Honk et al., 2004) and activity in the same brain regions (e.g., ventral striatum, which includes the nucleus accumbens, Hermans et al., 2010, $n = 12$), it may upregulate subjective feelings of reward associated with retaliatory aggression. To the extent that testosterone does regulate aggression by modulating reward-related neural function, the dopaminergic system is most likely involved. In rodent models, the administration of testosterone can enhance dopaminergic activity in reward regions of the brain within 30 minutes (e.g., de Souza Silva et al., 2009, $n = 6$–7/group), and testosterone's rewarding effects are abolished when dopamine receptor antagonists are administered to the nucleus accumbens ($n = 5$–8/group, Packard et al., 1998). Additionally, post-victory surges in testosterone are also associated with greater AR expression in the nucleus accumbens and ventral tegmental area which, in turn, is associated with more aggressive behaviour during the bouts ($n = 5$–8/group, Fuxjager et al., 2010). The rewarding effects of aggression can be indexed more directly by having rodents exert effort (e.g., nose-pokes) to gain access to conspecific rivals; dopamine receptor antagonists, when administered to the nucleus accumbens, reduce this effort and, once access to the conspecific is eventually gained, reduce aggression during the bout (Couppis & Kennedy, 2008). Therefore, another mechanism through which testosterone might modulate aggression is by upregulating the pleasure derived from – or anticipated in response to – aggression, with these effects mediated by the rapid regulation of dopamine (for additional review, see Losecaat et al., 2016).

Pharmacogenetics: Testosterone's effects on cell function, and ultimately psychological and behavioural processes, are in part mediated by testosterone's binding to the androgen receptor (AR). When activated by androgens such as testosterone and dihydrotestosterone, ARs translocate to the cell nucleus where they ultimately have transcriptional control of androgen-dependent genes. Notably, the transcriptional potential of target genes by the AR is influenced by a relative expansion of a polyglutamine stretch in the N-terminal domain of the AR, which itself is encoded by a trinucleotide (CAG) repeat polymorphism of the AR gene. In vitro work indicates that the transcriptional efficiency of the AR is inversely related to the length of CAG repeats within the AR gene (i.e., fewer repeats confers a more 'efficient' AR; Chamberlain et al., 1994; Choong et al., 1996). Furthermore, in vivo work suggests that variation in the AR CAG repeat moderates the effect of testosterone replacement therapy on prostate volume growth. Specifically, testosterone increases prostate volume ($n = 131$), but only among those individuals with relatively short CAG repeats within the AR (Zitzmann, Depenbusch, Gromoll, & Nieschlag, 2003). Other research indicates that testosterone positively predicts amygdala reactivity to threat-related cues, but only among men ($n = 41$) with fewer CAG repeats within the AR gene (Manuck et al., 2010). Also, in a relatively large sample of adolescent boys ($n = 300$), Vermeersch, T'sjoen, Kaufman, and Vincke (2008) found that testosterone was positively related to aggressive and non-aggressive risk-taking, but only for those boys with relatively shorter CAG repeats within the AR gene. In light of this work, it will be critical to examine the role of the AR CAG repeat in moderating effects of exogenous testosterone on psychological, physiological and behavioural processes.

Sex differences/similarities: An important question for future research is whether testosterone's effects on aggressive behaviour are sex-dependent (Josephs et al., 2011). Previous work indicates that testosterone responses to competitive interactions positively predict subsequent aggression in men, but not women (Carré et al., 2009; 2013). Although one may conclude from this work that testosterone does not map onto aggression in women, difficulty in accurately measuring testosterone concentrations in women may contribute to additional measurement error which could obscure hormone-behaviour relationships (e.g., Welker et al., 2016). Also, it should be noted that research examining the association between baseline levels of testosterone and aggression has reported similar relationships in men ($r = .08$) and women ($r = .13$; see Archer et al., 2005 for meta-analysis). Finally, despite using different drug administration protocols, neuroimaging work indicates that exogenous testosterone administration has similar effects on threat-related neural function in women ($n = 12$, $n = 27$) (Hermans et al., 2008; van Wingen et al., 2009) and men ($n = 16$) (Goetz et al., 2014). Thus, more work will be needed to determine the extent to which effects of testosterone on various outcome measures of relevance to aggression are similar and/or different in men and women.

Moderators of the T-aggression relationship: As reviewed in this chapter, there are now several correlational and experimental studies demonstrating that associations between testosterone and dominant/aggressive behaviour depend on variability in personality traits such as dominance, impulsivity and self-construal (Carré et al., 2009; Slatcher et al., 2011; Mehta et al., 2015; Knight et al., 2017; Carré et al., 2017; Welker et al., 2017). One criticism of this moderator approach is that it is possible to measure dozens of moderator variables, which inevitably increases type I error rate and poses a serious problem for the replicability of social neuroendocrinology research (see Nave et al.'s, 2015 critique of the oxytocin literature). One way to mitigate this problem is to specify a priori the key moderator variables that are to be examined and to provide a sound theoretical and empirical rationale for examining the specific moderators (this could be done through pre-registration of study hypotheses). However, even with strong a priori predictions, another problem with examining several moderator variables is the issue of multiple comparisons, which ultimately inflates type I error rate if one does not apply stringent corrections (e.g., Bonferroni). However, stringent correction for type I error rate would ultimately increase one's chances of committing a type II error and would necessitate obtaining very large sample sizes in order to overcome this potential problem. One approach which has been used in various fields (e.g., developmental psychology, medicine, genetics) is to create a cumulative risk factor score which combines multiple individual difference variables to create a single moderator variable (e.g., Evans et al., 2013). For example, participants scoring in the top quartile for a particular moderator variable would receive a score of '1' (i.e., presence of risk), whereas all other participants would receive a score of '0' (i.e., absence of risk). Each moderator variable would be coded in this way, and the sum of these coded variables would be used as a single 'risk score' to use in moderator analyses. The main advantage of the cumulative risk approach is that it is parsimonious, insensitive to risk collinearity (i.e., insensitive to the degrees of covariation among risk factors), and provides enhanced statistical power (using multiple moderators variables with numerous interactions terms would make for incomprehensible interactions and unstable effects to due covariation among main effects; Evan et al., 2013).

Replicability of social neuroendocrine research: The intranasal oxytocin literature exploded in the early 2000s with the publication of a paper demonstrating that a single dose of oxytocin increased men's trust behaviour in an economic task (Kosfeld et al., 2005). This initial finding led to dozens of studies examining the role of oxytocin in modulating various psychological, physiological and behavioural processes (see Bartz et al., 2011 for review). Despite early excitement about the effects of intranasal oxytocin on human social behaviour (especially in terms of therapeutic potential for psychopathologies characterized by social deficits), several recent replication attempts have failed (Lane et al., 2016; Nave et al., 2015; Walum et al., 2016). Single testosterone administration research in healthy young men is in its infancy, and thus, it will be critical to replicate some of the early promising findings to examine the extent to which the effects are robust. In such replication attempts, it will be important to have well-powered studies, which will most likely require multi-laboratory collaborations to increase statistical power to detect relatively small-to-medium effects (especially when examining drug × personality, drug × gene, and drug × personality × gene interactions). In addition, pre-registration of study hypotheses will enable researchers to differentiate between confirmatory vs. exploratory analyses (van't Veer & Giner-Sorolla, 2016). Replication efforts will also need to pay close attention to potential sex differences in the effects of testosterone, the testosterone dose administered, route of administration (e.g., intra-muscular injection, transdermal gel, intranasal gel), and timing of behavioural assessment after drug application – all factors that may ultimately influence the effects of testosterone on the parameters assessed.

Summary

The research reviewed in this chapter suggests that acute fluctuations in testosterone during competition and/or social provocation may serve to modulate ongoing and/or future aggressive behaviour. Notably, correlational work and recent pharmacological challenge studies suggest that individual differences in personality traits (e.g., trait dominance, self-control, and self-construal) modulate the effect of testosterone on human aggression. Future well-powered studies using multi-method approaches (e.g., pharmacological challenge, fMRI, genetics) will be critical to furthering our understanding of the neurobiological mechanisms through which testosterone may bias aggressive behaviour.

References

Alcorn, J.L., III, Green, C.E., Schmitz, J., & Lane, S.D. (2015). Effects of oxytocin on aggressive responding in healthy adult males. *Behavioral Pharmacology, 26*, 798–804.

Archer, J. (2006). Testosterone and human aggression: An evaluation of the challenge hypothesis. *Neuroscience and Biobehavioral Reviews, 30*, 319–345.

Archer, J., Graham-Kevan, N., & Davies, M. (2005). Testosterone and aggression: A reanalysis of Book, Starzyk, and Quinsey's (2001) study. *Aggression and Violent Behavior, 10*, 241–261.

Bartz, J.A., Zaki, J., Bolger, N., & Ochsner, K.N. (2011). Social effects of oxytocin in humans: Context and person matter. *Trends in Cognitive Science, 15*, 301–309.

Bird, B.M., Welling, L.L., Ortiz, T.L., Moreau, B.J., Hansen, S., Emond, M., . . . Carré, J.M. (2016). Effects of exogenous testosterone and mating context on men's preferences for female facial femininity. *Hormones and Behavior, 85*, 76–85.

Blair, R.J.R. (2010). Neuroimaging of psychopathy and antisocial behavior: A targeted review. *Current Psychiatry Reports, 12*, 76–82.

Böhnke, R., Bertsch, K., Kruk, M.R., Richter, S., & Naumann, E. (2010). Exogenous cortisol enhances aggressive behavior in females, but not in males. *Psychoneuroendocrinology, 35*(7), 1034–1044.

Bokhoven, I.V., Goozen, S.H., Engeland, H.V., Schaal, B., Arseneault, L., Séguin, J.R., & Tremblay, R.E. (2004). Salivary cortisol and aggression in a population-based longitudinal study of adolescent males. *Journal of Neural Transmission, 112*(8), 1083–1096.

Bos, P.A., Panksepp, J., Bluthé, R.M., & van Honk, J. (2012). Acute effects of steroid hormones and neuropeptides on human social-emotional behavior: A review of single administration studies. *Frontiers in Neuroendocrinology, 33*, 17–35.

Bos, P.A., van Honk, J., Ramsey, N. F., Stein, D. J., & Hermans, E. J. (2013). Testosterone administration in women increases amygdala responses to fearful and happy faces. *Psychoneuroendocrinology, 38*, 808–817.

Bosch, O.J., Kromer, S.A., Brunton, P.J., & Neumann, I.D. (2004). Release of oxytocin in the hypothalamic paraventricular nucleus, but not Central Amygdala or lateral septum in lactating residents and virgin intruders during maternal defence. *Neuroscience, 124*, 439–448.

Bosch, O.J., Meddle, S.L., Beiderbeck, D.I., Douglas, A.J., & Neumann, I.D. (2005). Brain oxytocin correlates with maternal aggression: Link to anxiety. *The Journal of Neuroscience, 25*(29), 6807–6815.

Calcagnoli, F., de Boer, S.F., Althaus, M., den Boer, J.A., & Koolhaas, J.M. (2013). Antiaggressive activity of central oxytocin in male rats. *Psychopharmacology, 229*, 639–651.

Calcagnoli, F., Kreutzmann, J.C., de Boer, S.F., Althaus, M., & Koolhaas, J.M. (2015). Acute and repeated intranasal oxytocin administration exerts anti-aggressive and pro-affiliative effects in male rats. *Psychoneuroendocrinology, 51*, 112–121.

Campbell, A., & Hausmann, M. (2013). Effects of oxytocin on women's aggression depend on state anxiety. *Aggressive Behavior, 39*, 316–322.

Carré, J.M., Campbell, J.A., Lozoya, E., Goetz, S.M., & Welker, K.M. (2013). Changes in testosterone mediate the effect of winning on subsequent aggressive behavior. *Psychoneuroendocrinology, 38*, 2043–2041.

Carré, J.M., Geniole, S.N., Ortiz, T.L., Bird, B.M., Videto, A., & Bonin, P.L. (2017). Exogenous testosterone rapidly increases aggressive behavior in dominant and impulsive men. *Biological Psychiatry, 82*, 249–256.

Carré, J.M., & McCormick, C.M. (2008). Aggressive behaviour and change in salivary testosterone concentrations predict willingness to engage in a competitive task. *Hormones and Behavior, 54*, 403–409.

Carré, J.M., Putnam, S.K., & McCormick, C.M. (2009). Testosterone responses to competition predict future aggressive behaviour at a cost to reward in men. *Psychoneuroendocrinology, 343*, 561–570.

Chamberlain, N.L., Driver, E.D., & Miesfeld, R.L. (1994). The length and location of CAG trinucleotide repeats in the androgen receptor N-terminal domain affect transactivation function. *Nucleic Acids Research, 22*, 3181–3186.

Chester, D.S., & DeWall, C.N. (2016). The pleasure of revenge: Retaliatory aggression arises from a neural imbalance toward reward. *Social Cognitive and Affective Neuroscience, 11*, 1173–1182.

Choong, C.S., Kemppainen, J.A., Zhou, Z.X., & Wilson, E.M. (1996). Reduced androgen receptor gene expression with first exon CAG repeat expansion. *Molecular Endocrinology, 10*, 1527–1535.

Coccaro, E. F., Kavoussi, R. J., Hauger, R. L., Cooper, T. B., & Ferris, C. F. (1998). Cerebrospinal fluid vasopressin levels: Correlates with aggression and serotonin function in personality-disordered subjects. *Archives of General Psychiatry, 55*, 708–714.

Couppis, M.H., & Kennedy, C.H. (2008). The rewarding effect of aggression is reduced by nucleus accumbens dopamine receptor antagonism in mice. *Psychopharmacology (Berl), 197,* 449–456.

Cueva, C., Roberts, R.E., Spencer, T., Rani, N., Tempest, M., Tobler, P.N., . . . Rustichini, A. (2015). Cortisol and testosterone increase financial risk taking and may destabilize markets. *Scientific Reports, 5,* 11206.

Dabbs, J.M. (1990). Salivary testosterone measurements: Reliability across hours, days, and weeks. *Physiology and Behavior, 48,* 83–86.

De Dreu, C.K., Greer, L.L., van Kleef, G.A., Shalvi, S., & Handgraaf, M.J. (2011). Oxytocin promotes human ethnocentrism. *PNAS, 108,* 1262–1266.

Delville, Y., Mansour, K.M., & Ferris, C.F. (1994). Testosterone facilitates aggression by modulating vasopressin receptors in the hypothalamus. *Physiology and Behavior, 60,* 25–29.

Derntl, B., Windischberger, C., Robinson, S., Kryspin-Exner, I., Gur, R.C., Moser, E., & Habel, U. (2009). Amygdala activity to fear and anger in healthy young males is associated with testosterone. *Psychoneuroendocrinology, 34,* 687–693.

de Souza Silva, M.A., Mattern, C., Topic, B., Buddenberg, T.E., & Huston, J.P. (2009). Dopaminergic and serotonergic activity in neostriatum and nucleus accumbens enhanced by intranasal administration of testosterone. *European Neuropsychopharmacology, 19,* 53–63.

DeWall, C.N., Gillath, O., Pressman, S.D., Black, L.L., Bartz, J.A., Moskovitz, J., & Stetler, D.A. (2014). When the love hormone leads to violence: Oxytocin increases intimate partner violence inclinations among high trait aggressive people. *Social Psychological and Personality Science, 5,* 691–697.

Dijkstra, P.D., Schaafsma, S.M., Hofmann, H.A., & Groothuis, T.G. (2012). 'Winner effect' without winning: Unresolved social conflicts increase the probability of winning a subsequent contest in a cichlid fish. *Physiology Behavior, 105,* 489–492.

Donahue, J.E., Stopa, E.G., Chorsky, R.L., King, J.C., Schipper, H.M., Tobet, S.A., . . . Reichlin, S. (2000). Cells containing immunoreactive estrogen receptor-α in the human basal forebrain. *Brain Research, 856,* 142–151.

Dreher, J.C., Dunne, S., Pazderska, A., Frodl, T., Nolan, J.J., & O'Doherty, J.P. (2016). Testosterone causes both prosocial and antisocial status-enhancing behaviors in human males. *Proceedings of the National Academy of Sciences of the United States of America, 113,* 11633–11638.

Evans, G.W., Li, D., & Whipple, S.S. (2013). Cumulative risk and child development. *Psychological Bulletin, 139,* 1342–1396.

Fernández-Guasti, A., Kruijver, F.P., Fodor, M., & Swaab, D.F. (2000). Sex differences in the distribution of androgen receptors in the human hypothalamus. *Journal of Comparative Neurology, 425,* 422–435.

Ferris, C.F., Lu, S.F., Messenger, T., Guillon, C.D., Heindel, N., Miller, M., Koppel, G., Robert Bruns, F., & Simon, N.G. (2006). Orally active vasopressin V1a receptor antagonist SRX251, selectively blocks aggressive behavior. *Pharmacology Biochemistry and Behavior, 83,* 169–174.

Ferris, C.F., Melloni, R.H., Koppel, G., Perry, K.W., Fuller, R.W., & Delville, Y. (1997). Vasopressin/serotonin interaction sin the anterior hypothalamus control aggressive behavior in golden hamsters. *Journal of Neuroscience, 17,* 4331–4340.

Fuxjager, M.J., Oyegbile, T.O., & Marler, C.A. (2011). Independent and additive contributions of postvictory testosterone and social experience to the development of the winner effect. *Endocrinology, 152,* 4322–3429.

Fuxjager, M.J., Forbes-Lorman, R.M., Coss, D.J., Auger, C.J., Auger, A.P., & Marler, C.A. (2010). Winning territorial disputes selectively enhances androgen sensitivity in neural pathways related to motivation and social aggression. *Proceedings of the National Academy of Sciences of the United States of America, 107,* 12393–12398.

Geniole, S.N., Bird, B.M., Ruddick, E.L., & Carré, J.M. (2017). Effects of competition outcome on testosterone concentrations in humans: An updated meta-analysis. *Hormones and Behavior, 92,* 37–50.

Geniole, S.N., Busseri, M.A., & McCormick, C.M. (2013). Testosterone dynamics and psychopathic personality traits independently predict antagonistic behavior towards the perceived loser of a competitive interaction. *Hormones and Behavior, 64,* 790–798.

Gleason, E.D., Fuxjager, M.J., Oyegbile, T.O., & Marler, C.A. (2009). Testosterone release and social context: When it occurs and why. *Frontiers in Neuroendocrinology, 30,* 460–469.

Goetz, S.M.M., Tang, L., Thomason, M.E., Diamond, M.P., Hariri, A.R., & Carré, J.M. (2014). Testosterone rapidly increases neural reactivity to threat in healthy men: A novel two-step pharmacological challenge paradigm. *Biological Psychiatry, 76,* 324–331.

Haller, J., Halasz, J., Mikics, E., & Kruk, M.R. (2004). Chronic glucocorticoid deficiency-induced abnormal aggression, autonomic hypoarousal, and social deficit in rats. *Journal of Neuroendocrinology, 16*, 550–557.

Haller, J., Schraaf, J.V., & Kruk, M.R. (2001). Deviant forms of aggression in glucocorticoid hyporeactive rats: A model for 'Pathological' aggression? *Journal of Neuroendocrinology, 13*, 102–107.

Harmon, A.C., Huhman, K.L., Moore, T.O., & Albers, H.E. (2002). Oxytocin inhibits aggression in female Syrian hamsters. *Journal of Neuroendocrinology, 14*, 963–969.

Hermans, E.J., Ramsey, N.F., & van Honk, J. (2008). Exogenous testosterone enhances responsiveness to social threat in the neural circuitry of social aggression in humans. *Biological Psychiatry, 63*, 263–270.

Hermans, E.J., Bos, P.A., Ossewaarde, L., Ramsey, N., Fernandez, G., & van Honk, J. (2010). Effects of exogenous testosterone on the ventral striatal BOLD response during reward anticipation in healthy women. *Neuroimage, 52*, 277–283.

Josephs, R.A., Mehta, P.H., & Carré, J.M. (2011). Gender and social environment modulate the effects of testosterone on social behavior: Comment on Eisenegger et al. *Trends in Cognitive Sciences, 15*, 509–510.

Ketterson, E.D., & Nolan, V., Jr. (1992). Hormones and life histories: An integrative approach. *American Naturalist, 140*, S33–S62.

Knight, E.L., Christian, C.B., Morales, P.J., Harbaugh, W.T., Mayr, U., & Mehta, P.H. (2017). Exogenous testosterone enhances cortisol and affective responses to social-evaluative stress in dominant men. *Psychoneuroendocrinology, 85*, 151–157.

Kosfeld, M., Heinrichs, M., Zak, P.J., Fischbacher, U., & Fehr, E. (2005). Oxytocin increases trust in humans. *Nature, 435*, 673–676.

Lane, A., Luminet, O., Nave, G., & Mikolajczak, M. (2016). Is there a publication bias in behavioural intranasal oxytocin research on humans? Opening the file drawer of one laboratory. *Journal of Neuroendocrinology, 28*(4).

Lee, R., Ferris, C., van de Kar, L.D., & Coccaro, E.F. (2009). Cerebrospinal fluid oxytocin, life history of aggression, and personality disorder. *Psychoneuroendocrinology, 34*, 1567–1573.

Leshner, A. I. (1975). A model of hormones and agnostic behavior. *Physiologyy and Behavior, 15*, 225–235.

Liening, S.H., Stanton, S.J., Saini, E.K., & Schultheiss, O.C. (2010). Salivary testosterone, cortisol, and progesterone: Two-week stability, interhormone correlations, and effects of time of day, menstrual cycle, and oral contraceptive use on steroid hormone levels. *Physiology and Behavior, 99*, 8–16.

Losecaat Vermeer, A.B., Riečanský, I., & Eisenegger, C. (2016). Competition, testosterone, and adult neurobehavioral plasticity. *Progress in Brain Research, 229*, 213–238.

Manuck, S.B., Marsland, A.L., Flory, J.D., Gorka, A., Ferrell, R.E., & Hariri, A.R. (2010). Salivary testosterone and a trinucleotide (CAG) length polymorphism in the androgen receptor gene predict amygdala reactivity in men. *Psychoneuroendocrinology, 35*, 94–104.

Mazur, A. (1985). A biosocial model of status in face-to-face primate groups. *Social Forces, 64*, 377–402.

Mazur, A., & Booth, A. (1998). Testosterone and dominance in men. *Behavioral Brain Science, 21*, 353–363.

McBurnett, K., Lahey, B.B., Rathouz, P.J., & Loeber, R. (2000). Low salivary cortisol and persistent aggression in boys referred for disruptive behavior. *Archives of General Psychiatry, 57*, 38–43.

McGlothlin, J.W., Jawor, J.M., & Ketterson, E.D. (2007). Natural variation in a testosterone-mediated trade-off between mating effort and parent effort. *American Naturalist, 170*, 864–875.

Mehta, P.H., & Beer, J. (2010). Neural mechanisms of the testosterone-aggression relation: The role of the orbito-frontal cortex. *Journal of Cognitive Neuroscience, 22*, 2357–2368.

Mehta, P.H., & Josephs, R.A. (2006). Testosterone change after losing predicts the decision to compete again. *Hormones and Behavior, 50*, 684–692.

Mehta, P.H., van Son, V., Welker, K.M., Prasad, S., Sanfey, A.G., Smidts, A., & Roelofs, K. (2015). Exogenous testosterone in women enhances and inhibits competitive decision-making depending on victory-defeat experience and trait dominance. *Psychoneuroendocrinology, 60*, 224–236.

Murphy, A.Z., Shupnik, M.A., & Hoffman, G.E. (1999). Androgen and estrogen (α) receptor distribution in the periaqueductal gray of the male rat. *Hormones and Behavior, 36*, 98–108.

Nave, G., Camerer, C., & McCullough, M. (2015). Does oxytocin increase trust in humans? Critical review of research. *Perspectives on Psychological Science, 10*, 772–789.

Nave, G., Nadler, A., Zava, D., & Camerer, C. (2017). Single dose testosterone impairs cognitive reflection in men. *Psychological Science, 28*, 1398–1407.

Ne'eman, R., Perach-Barzilay, N., Fischer-Shofty, M., Atias, A., & Shamay-Tsoory, S.G. (2016). Intranasal administration of oxytocin increases human aggressive behavior. *Hormones and Behavior, 80*, 125–131.

Nelson, R.J., & Trainor, B.C. (2007). Neural mechanisms of aggression. *Nature Reviews Neuroscience, 8*, 536–546.

Newman, S. (1999). The medial extended amygdala in male reproductive behavior: A node in the mammalian social behavior network. *Annals of the New York Academy of Sciences, 877,* 242–257.

Oliveira, R.F. (2009). Social behavior in context: Hormonal modulation of behavioural plasticity and social competence. *Integrative and Comparative Biology, 49,* 423–440.

Oliveira, R.F., Silva, A., & Canario, A.V. (2009). Why do winners keep winning? Androgen mediation of winner but not loser effects in cichlid fish. *Proceedings of the Royal Society of London: Biological Sciences, 276,* 2249–2256.

Oxford, J.K., Tiedtke, J.M., Ossmann, A., Ozbe, D., & Schultheiss, O.C. (2017). Endocrine and aggressive responses to competition are moderated by contest outcome, gender, individual versus team competition, and implicit motives. *PLoS One, 12,* e0181610.

Packard, M.G., Schroeder, J.P., & Alexander, G.M. (1998). Expression of testosterone conditioned place preference is blocked by peripheral or intra-accumbens injection of α-flupenthixol. *Hormones and Behavior, 34,* 39–47.

Panagiotidis, D., Clemens, B., Habel, U., Schneider, F., Schneider, I., Wagels, L., & Votinov, M. (2017). Exogenous testosterone in a non-social provocation paradigm potentiates anger but not behavioural aggression. *European Neuropsychopharmacology, 27,* 1172–1184.

Poustka, L., Maras, A., Hohm, E., Fellinger, J., Holtmann, M., Banaschewski, T., & Laucht, M. (2010). Negative association between plasma cortisol levels and aggression in a high-risk community sample of adolescents. *Journal of Neural Transmission, 117,* 621–627.

Prasad, S., Narayanan, J., Lim, V. K. G., Koh, G. C. H., Koh, D. S. Q., & Mehta, P. H. (2017). Preliminary evidence that acute stress moderates basal testosterone's association with retaliatory behavior. *Hormones and Behavior, 92,* 128–140.

Ramírez, J.M., Bonniot-Cabanac, M.C., & Cabanac, M. (2005). Can aggression provide pleasure? *European Psychologist, 10,* 136–145.

Roselli, C.E., Klosterman, S., & Resko, J.A. (2001). Anatomic relationships between aromatase and androgen receptor mRNA expression in the hypothalamus and amygdala of adult male cynomolgus monkeys. *Journal of Comparative Neurology, 439,* 208–223.

Siegel, A., Bhatt, S., Bhatt, R., & Zalcman, S.S. (2007). The neurobiological basis for development of pharmacological treatments of aggressive disorders. *Current Neuropsychopharmacology, 5,* 135–147.

Slatcher, R.B., Mehta, P.H., & Josephs, R.A. (2011). Testosterone and self-reported dominance interact to influence human mating behaviour. *Social Psychological and Personality Science, 2,* 531–539.

Stanton, S.J., Mullette-Fillman, O.A., & Huettel, S.A. (2011). Seasonal variation of salivary testosterone in men, normal cycling women, and women using hormonal contraceptives. *Physiology and Behavior, 104,* 804–808.

Terburg, D., Aarts, H., & van Honk, J. (2012). Testosterone affects gaze aversion from angry faces outside of conscious awareness. *Psychological Science, 23,* 459–463.

Trainor, B.C., Bird, I.M., & Marler, C.A. (2004). Opposing hormonal mechanisms of aggression revealed through short-lived testosterone manipulations and multiple winning experiences. *Hormones and Behavior, 45,* 115–121.

van Bokhoven, I., van Goozen, S. H. M., van Engleand, H., Schaal, B., Arseneault, L., Séguin, J. R., . . . Tremblay, R. E. (2005). Salivary cortisol and aggression in a population-based longitudinal study of adolescent males. *Journal of Neural Transmission, 112,* 1083–1096.

van der Kooij, M.A., Fantin, M., Kraev, I., Korshunova, I., Grosse, J., Zanoletti, O., . . . Sandi, C. (2014). Impaired hippocampal neuroligin-2 function by chronic stress or synthetic peptide treatment is linked to social deficits and increased aggression. *Neuropsychopharmacology, 39,* 1148–1158.

van Honk, J., Schutter, D.J.L.G., Hermans, E.J., Putnam, P., Tuiten, A., & Koppeschaar, H. (2004). Testosterone shifts the balance between sensitivity for punishment and reward in healthy young women. *Psychoneuroendocrinology, 29,* 937–943.

van Honk, J., Tuiten, A., Hermans, E., Putnam, P., Koppeschaar, H., Thijssen, J., Verbaten, R., van Doornen, L. (2001). A single administration of testosterone induces cardiac accelerative responses to angry faces in healthy young women. *Behavioral Neuroscience, 115,* 238–242.

van't Veer, A.E., & Giner-Sorolla, R. (2016). Pre-registration in social psychology – a discussion and suggested template. *Journal of Experimental Social Psychology, 67,* 2–12.

van Wingen, G.A., Mattern, C., Verkes, R.J., Buitelaar, J., & Fernández, G. (2010). Testosterone reduces amygdala–orbitofrontal cortex coupling. *Psychoneuroendocrinology, 35,* 105–113.

van Wingen, G.A., Zylick, S.A., Pieters, S., Mattern, C., Verkes, R.J., Buitelaar, J.K., & Fernandez, G. (2009). Testosterone increases amygdala reactivity in middle-aged women to a young adulthood level. *Neuropsychopharmacology, 34,* 539–547.

Vermeersch, H., T'sjoen, G., Kaufman, J.M., & Vincke, J. (2008). The role of testosterone in aggressive and non-aggressive risk-taking in adolescent boys. *Hormones and Behavior, 53*, 463–471.

Verona, E., & Curtin, J.J. (2006). Gender differences in the negative affective priming of aggressive behavior. *Emotion, 6*, 115–124.

Verona, E., & Kilmer, A. (2007). Stress exposure and affective modulation of aggressive behavior in men and women. *Journal of Abnormal Psychology, 116*, 410–421.

Verona, E., Reed, II.A., Curtin, J.J., & Pole, M. (2007). Gender differences in emotional and overt/covert aggressive responses to stress. *Aggressive Behavior, 33*, 261–271.

Vongas, J.G., & Al Hajj, R. (2017). The effects of competition and implicit power motive on men's testosterone, emotion recognition, and aggression. *Hormones and Behavior, 92*, 57–71.

Walker, S.E., Papilloud, A., Huzard, D., & Sandi, C. (in press). The link between aberrant hypothalamic-pituitary-adrenal axis activity during development and the emergence of aggression–animal studies. *Neuroscience & Biobehavioral Reviews.*

Walum, H., Waldman, I.D., & Young, L.J. (2016). Statistical and methodological considerations for the interpretation of intranasal oxytocin studies. *Biological Psychiatry, 79*, 251–257.

Wagels, L., Radke, S., Goerlich, K.S., Habel, U., & Votinov, M. (2017). Exogenous testosterone decreases men's personal distance in a social threat context. *Hormones and Behavior, 90*, 75–83.

Welker, K.M., Lassetter, B., Brandes, C.M., Prasad, S., Koop, D.R., & Mehta, P.H. (2016). A comparison of salivary testosterone measurement using immunoassays and tandem mass spectrometry. *Psychoneuroendocrinology, 71*, 180–188.

Welker, K.M., Norman, R.E., Goetz, S., Moreau, B.J.P., Kitayama, S., & Carré, J.M. (2017). Preliminary evidence that testosterone's association with aggression depends on self-construal. *Hormones and Behavior, 92*, 117–127.

Welling, L.L., Moreau, B.J., Bird, B.M., Hansen, S., & Carré, J.M. (2016). Exogenous testosterone increases men's perceptions of their own physical dominance. *Psychoneuroendocrinology, 64*, 136–142.

Wingfield, J.C., Hegner, R.E., Dufty, A.M., Jr., & Ball, G.F. (1990). The 'Challenge Hypothesis': Theoretical implications for patterns of testosterone secretion, mating systems, and breeding strategies. *American Naturalist, 136*, 829–846.

Wood, G.E., Young, L.T., Reagan, L.P., & McEwen, B.S. (2003). Acute and chronic restraint stress alter the incidence of social conflict in male rats. *Hormones and Behavior, 43*, 205–213.

Wood, R., & Newman, S.W. (1999). Androgen receptor immunoreactivity in the male and female Syrian hamster brain. *Journal of Neurobiology, 39*, 359–370.

Zitzmann, M., Depenbusch, M., Gromoll, J., & Nieschlag, E. (2003). Prostate volume and growth in testosterone-substituted hypogonadal men are dependent on the CAG repeat polymorphism of the androgen receptor gene: A longitudinal pharmacogenetics study. *Journal of Clinical Endocrinology and Metabolism, 88*, 2049–2054.

SECTION 3

Social affiliation

9

SOCIAL ENDOCRINOLOGY IN EVOLUTIONARY PERSPECTIVE

Function and phylogeny

Nicholas M. Grebe and Steven W. Gangestad

Introduction

Humans are a highly social, interdependent species. Infant well-being depends on caregivers – parents and, in many cases, others – for extended periods (Kaplan, Hill, Lancaster & Hurtado, 2000; Hrdy, 2009). Women and men form lasting pair-bonds in virtually all human societies (e.g., Fletcher et al., 2015). Highly interdependent friendships too give meaning to people's lives (e.g., Tooby & Cosmides, 1996).

Hormonal systems play critical roles in the development, regulation, and maintenance of human social relationships. In the past 15 years, scholarly interest in "social hormones" such as oxytocin has exploded. A Web of Science search using the keywords "oxytocin" and "behavior or psychology or cognition or emotion or social" yields 91 papers published in 1997. From 1998 to 2004, little changed: the mean number of published articles per year was 91. But then the number more than doubled by 2008 (190) and re-doubled by 2013 (411). In 2017, it exceeds 600 – more than a six-fold increase over two decades. Citation rates have risen even more dramatically over that time span: by more than 16 times.

The research to date emphasizes the ways in which hormones affect social dispositions and shape interactions with others. A growing literature attempts to understand these effects in terms of systematic theory about what, fundamentally, social hormones do psychologically – the psychological mechanisms through which they exert their effects. Secondarily, the literature addresses circumstances under which social hormones are secreted into the bloodstream.

In this chapter, we offer a perspective we think deserves more attention: an explicitly evolutionary framework. Endocrine systems evolved. Their major components – titers of hormones, distributions of receptors, cellular effects of ligand-receptor units, and processes that affect hormonal secretion and bioavailability – were shaped by selection. They also often have deep evolutionary roots, having first appeared in ancestors very distant to us. The value of evolutionary theorizing in endocrinology, in our view, lies *in the context of theory development and discovery of psychological process*. In absence of explicit evolutionary theory, it is unlikely that anyone would think to ask certain questions about the way hormonal systems operate, a point illustrated in this chapter. We begin with a broad evolutionary framework for understanding hormonal mechanisms. We then illustrate this framework by discussing oxytocin, which plays a prominent role in regulating social interactions.

Evolutionary endocrinology: foundational ideas

An evolutionary perspective as a starting point

Hormones are chemical signals that communicate "messages" to multiple internal sites simultaneously. Endocrine systems share a number of features: titers of hormone circulate through the bloodstream; bioactive levels are affected by processes of secretion, binding by proteins, and clearance; each process is affected by internal and external "cues" that lead to increased or decreased concentrations, perceived by internal monitors or sensory responses to environmental features; circulating hormones are then "picked up" by receptors at multiple sites (e.g., brain structures, other organs); hormone-receptor units affect cellular activity in ways sensitive to cell types (e.g., through RNA transcription). Whereas some cellular activities are upregulated, others are downregulated. These cellular effects translate into observable phenotypic changes in the way the organism reacts to its internal or external environment (e.g., Nelson, 2011).

These features offer insight into the general nature of the selection processes that shaped endocrine systems. They produce responses to the conditions that regulate their circulating levels. To have evolved, these contingent responses are (or were, in the ancestral conditions in which they evolved) adaptive (i.e., fitness-enhancing). Naturally, to understand the specific "adaptive logic" of a particular endocrine system – how and in what ways it produces adaptive contingent responses – one must understand it *as* a system, a *functionally integrated* set of features.

Life history theory

Recent evolutionary endocrinological theory appeals to life history theory as a foundation for understanding endocrine systems (e.g., Ellison, 2017). Organisms harvest energy from the environment and allocate that energy to fitness-enhancing activities. Energy allocated to particular activities cannot be allocated to others. Organisms must, therefore, inevitably decide how to use energy. Given an ecological niche, certain systematic ways of allocating energy promote the organism's fitness better than others; natural selection sifts through the myriad possible allocation "strategies" to favor those that maximize fitness. Other limited resources of an organism – e.g., micronutrient building blocks, time, and neural or other tissue-specific resources – may also be subject to allocation decisions. Life history theory is a branch of theoretical biology that seeks to understand how selection shapes organisms' allocation decisions (e.g., Charnov, 1993; Del Giudice et al., 2015).

As an organism's best use of limited resources depends on life circumstances, selection should favor strategies that allocate resources differently depending on circumstances. For instance, the value of growth depends on whether an organism is above or below optimal body size (e.g., Charnov, 1993); when an organism is infected with pathogens or comes face-to-face with a predator, its optimal allocations very likely differ from those when it is germ-free or safely away from threats; presented with a mating opportunity, an organism might fuel activities not worthwhile absent that opportunity. Because energy and other resources are limited, any decision to allocate additional energy *toward* certain activities inevitably requires, simultaneously, decisions to draw energy *away from* alternative current or future activities. For example, an infected individual reduces muscular activity to, in part, afford greater allocation of energy to immunological activity (Lochmiller & Deerenberg, 2000).

Endocrine hormones within a life history framework

Given the many tissues a hormone may simultaneously affect, changes in cellular activity instigate diverse and numerous phenotypic changes, an idea captured by the concept of *hormonal pleiotropy* (e.g., Flatt, Tu, & Tatar, 2005). In turn, this feature inspires a straightforward claim about endocrine systems' evolved function: *Endocrine systems constitute major avenues through which selection has shaped organisms to coordinate simultaneous shift of energetic and other limited resources from one set of activities to another, contingent on life circumstances* (e.g., Finch & Rose, 1995; Ketterson & Nolan, 1999). While life history theory seeks to understand the adaptive logic of allocation attunements – *why* they make the allocation decisions they do – an understanding of *how* organisms coordinate adaptive attunements requires an appreciation of endocrine systems. Selection shapes (a) the mechanisms that dictate the circumstances triggering secretion of a hormone, (b) the distribution of receptors that receive endocrine signals, and (c) how tissues respond to receipt of signals. Through these actions, endocrine hormones function as key mediators of life history strategies and allocation trade-off decisions.

Two additional concepts flesh out the idea of hormonal pleiotropy. The first is *phenotypic integration* (e.g., Ketterson, Atwell, & McGlothlin, 2009). The multiple phenotypic changes that result from hormone-induced cascades tend to be functionally integrated; they "work together" to benefit organisms. (For example, during mating season in dark-eyed juncos, testosterone increases male attractiveness as well as range size, both of which enhance male mating success; Ketterson & Nolan, 1999.) The second is *allocation trade-offs*. To "pay for" increases in allocation of effort toward certain ends, decrements in allocation to other efforts occur. Some phenotypic changes work with others by "paying" for these changes. (For example, in dark-eyed juncos, male testosterone leads to decrements in parental effort, not because there is inherent value in doing so, but rather because other efforts – notably, efforts to find and attract mates – are prioritized; Ketterson & Nolan, 1999.)

Neuromodulation as part of an adaptive complex of modulatory responses

Hormones affect neural tissue too, and thereby affect how neural resources are utilized: the stimuli that an organism attends to, the appraisal of those stimuli, potentiation of particular "likes" and "wants," and so on. Neural impacts too should be functionally integrated with the total suite of hormonal effects.

Some hormones are projected directly into brain regions. Oxytocin, for instance, is synthesized in multiple nuclei of the hypothalamus, from where it can be projected into the central nervous system and/or stored in the posterior pituitary gland for release into the periphery. Scholars debate the extent to which central and peripheral activity of oxytocin is coordinated (McCullough, Churchland, & Mendez, 2013; Valstad et al., 2017). Release is synchronized in at least certain situations (Neumann & Landgraf, 2012). Indeed, single hypothalamic neurons project to both pituitary and central sites, at least in some species (Saito et al., 2004). From a functional standpoint, this makes sense: neuromodulatory effects likely would have evolved to coordinate with peripheral effects. The vast majority of the studies we review associating oxytocin with behavior or context assess peripheral concentrations, and as such, they (at least implicitly) assume that peripheral levels reflect activity in the central nervous system. The generalizability of this assumption remains unknown (see, e.g., Ludwig & Leng, 2006, on central release dependent upon neuronal activity).

The reverse engineering of endocrine responses

One may ask whether scholars fundamentally interested in understanding a hormone's psychological effects should also be interested in its non-psychological impacts. We think yes, for the reason implied above: Broadly speaking, the function of an endocrine hormone is to modulate allocation of energy and resources in a coordinated fashion in response to circumstances under which the hormone is released. Non-psychological effects of hormones critically inform an understanding of a hormone's specific way of doing so. They constrain the range of possible solutions to the reverse engineering question of how selection shaped an endocrine system to modulate allocation strategies.

Conditional responsivity and internal regulatory variables

Allocation decisions should be a function of circumstances, which must be perceived, interpreted, and evaluated. "Internal regulatory variables" (Tooby et al., 2008; Del Giudice et al., 2015) are gages that represent information regarding environmental predictability, exogenous mortality risk, and the state of social relationships (among other things) as neutrally instantiated parameters. Hormone production and release can be thought of as a function of these appraisals, leading to coordinated behavioral and physiological actions that function to reallocate limited resources. An individual's learned experiences and developmental background will influence these appraisals, providing yet another example of the context-dependent nature of hormone release in mediating life history strategies.

An example: cortisol as a response to perceived threat

Consider a simple example: cortisol release in response to a threat. An event is perceived, appraised, and judged to be a threat. Projections from brain regions lead to release of ACTH from the pituitary gland into the bloodstream, which stimulates release of cortisol from the adrenal medulla. Within seconds, circulating cortisol causes increases in blood glucose levels, energy available to muscles and neural systems. It promotes insulin resistance in the liver, dampening the rate at which glucose is stored as fat. At the same time, it suppresses other activities, such as inflammatory immune responses. Cortisol release, then – in response to particular circumstances (including but not limited to threat per se) – not only renders stored energy available for potential use but also modulates how energy is to be utilized, increasing its availability for some activities, and diminishing its availability for others. For similar functional analyses of the actions of testosterone, estrogen, and several other hormones, see Ellison (2017).

Phylogeny and adaptation

A life history examination of a hormonal system in a single extant species (such as humans) can, in theory, yield a coherent functional account of the system – how its effects, under the circumstances in which the system is activated, work together to produce benefits. At the same time, phylogenetic considerations – when the system made its debut in evolutionary history and how it evolved over time – can offer valuable constraints on functional interpretation. A hormonal system that exists today likely did not initially appear with precisely the same suite of coordinated effects or activating circumstances. Hormonal systems are shaped over time along lineages in ways sensitive to new demands on species in the lineage.

A key concept is *co-option*: A feature (in this context, a hormonal system) gains a new benefit that did not exist in previous species in a lineage. To do so, the outcomes that were shaped by an old benefit must serve the new benefit sufficiently well. That is, there must exist a fortuitous match between old outcomes and new benefit (see Gould & Vrba, 1982, on "exaptation"). Secondary adaptation occurs when the new function leads to modification of features in ways that serve the new function better. If the feature or system continues to serve the old function, modification should not compromise that function severely.

Co-option may be sequential, occurring at one point, leading to modification, setting the stage for further co-option, secondary adaptation, and so on. Co-option and secondary modification are also lineage-specific, meaning that a co-opted feature present in descendant species may be absent in species descended from common ancestors in which the co-option did not occur, a point that, as we discuss below, is pertinent to oxytocin.

Oxytocin

Oxytocin is perhaps the most well-known social hormone in humans. Some popular science articles deem oxytocin *the* "love," "bonding," or "trust" hormone (e.g., Stix, 2014). Over two decades of studies strongly suggest that oxytocin is a key biological component behind interdependent, psychologically "close" relationships (see, e.g., Van IJzendoorn & Bakermans-Kranenburg, 2012; Carter, 2014). That said, the literature on oxytocin yields few simple answers about what, exactly, oxytocin *does*, psychologically (though we now know it is not simply a "love," "bonding," or "trust" hormone; e.g., Bethlehem, 2014). An explicitly evolutionary perspective along the lines we propose above may offer fruitful ways toward further understanding. We illustrate the potential value of an evolutionary approach, then, with the oxytocin system.

The evolution of the oxytocin system

Oxytocin-like peptides had functions in ancestors common to both vertebrates and some invertebrates (e.g., mollusks, arthropods, annelids); their evolutionary debut was 600+ million years ago (Gruber, 2014). In ancestral invertebrate species, tocin molecules likely played a role in coordinating specialized smooth muscle contractions, often involved in reproductive processes. In an early vertebrate, genes encoding a common tocin molecule duplicated and gave rise to oxytocin homologs and vasopressin homologs, which then evolved to acquire distinct functions (e.g., Hoyle, 1999). Both vasopressin and oxytocin per se made their evolutionary debut in placental mammals ~250 million years ago. Following Kelly and Goodson (2014), we refer to all oxytocin homologs as "oxytocin" and all vasopressin homologs as "vasopressin."

Oxytocin's regulation of social behavior: its evolutionary debut

Within vertebrates, oxytocin (and vasopressin) homologs have long played social regulatory roles. Oxytocin is implicated in the social behavior of teleost fish, though its precise roles vary across species. In Mozambique tilapia, dominant males have higher levels of oxytocin in the hindbrain (Almeida et al., 2012). In a related species, daffodil cichlids, by contrast, central infusions of oxytocin leads to more submissive behavior toward high ranking males (Reddon et al., 2012). (For additional examples, see Godwin & Thompson, 2012.) Oxytocin may affect the social behavior of birds too, though, once again, in ways varying across species. In zebra finches, oxytocin affects flocking behavior, nest-building, male-female side-by-side perching (e.g., Goodson et al., 2009; Klatt & Goodson, 2013). Though evidence is scant, oxytocin also affects maternal behavior in some species (e.g., Thai hens: Chokchaloemwong et al., 2013).

Goodson (2013) argued that attempts to understand the function of oxytocin across species in terms of a single model system are doomed to fail. Though oxytocin systems across species often share broad features (e.g., they affect social behavior, broadly defined), the precise effects they have, and through which brain structures, vary across taxa – even closely related species. The reason is that, given differences in ecology and contingencies of history, oxytocin systems across species possess lineage-specific co-options. The extent to which diversification can be systematized (e.g., organized around specific ecological factors) remains unknown.

Oxytocin's involvement in maternal behavior in mammals

Physiologists realized a century ago that extracts from the pituitary gland (containing oxytocin) induce uterine contractions in pregnant humans and non-human mammals (e.g., Bell, 1909). In fact, oxytocin and/or vasopressin homologs are involved in egg-laying even in reptiles (see Knobloch & Grinevich, 2014). During mammalian lactation, oxytocin activates the milk let-down reflex, itself involving control of smooth muscle contraction (e.g., Wakerley & Lincoln, 1973).

Oxytocin is a key mediator of bonding of human mother to offspring as well as, perhaps, attachment of offspring to mothers, forged during parturition (Carter, 2014), lactation (Crowley & Armstrong, 1992), emotionally "warm" touch (Feldman et al., 2010), and responses to infant's cries (Riem et al., 2011). One possible evolutionary scenario is that, given its role in birthing and lactation, oxytocin was co-opted to possess specific neuromodulatory effects that support mothering in an early mammal (e.g., Carter, 2014; Crespi, 2016; Feldman et al., 2016). Then again, as oxytocin supports mothering in some avian species, and even promotes elaborate nesting behavior in lineages as distant as turtles (Carr et al., 2008), perhaps a more plausible scenario is that oxytocin's physiological role in reproduction set the stage for its neuromodulatory influence of maternal behavior in the common ancestor of the broad taxon Amniota (mammals, archosaurs [crocodiles, avian and non-avian dinosaurs], and reptiles; Knobloch & Grinevich, 2014) – i.e., it may have a deeper evolutionary origin, predating the evolution of mammals. Once oxytocin also came to play a critical physiological role in lactation in mammals, its regulation of maternal behavior may have evolved to become much more elaborate.

The maternal brain in rats

Classic work establishes the neurobiology of maternal behavior in rats, which speaks to how oxytocin affects this behavior (for a review, see, e.g., Numan, 2017). Nulliparous female rats actively avoid pups. New mothers, by contrast, engage in well-established maternal behaviors with pups (e.g., pup retrieval, licking, nursing), even when, after one hour of exposure post-birth, their own pups are experimentally removed, and replaced by another mother's pups a week later. Multiple hormones present at birth alter maternal brain structures that account for these effects, including estradiol, progesterone, and prolactin. Oxytocin also plays a critical role. Sophisticated experimental studies establish the neurobiological alterations involved (e.g., in conjunction with mesolimbic dopaminergic activity, oxytocin inhibits activity in the nucleus accumbens, which potentiates activity in ventral pallidum, which promotes maternal behavior; for a review, see Numan & Young, 2016).

In this framework, oxytocin affects maternal behavior through neurobiological networks that fundamentally regulate motivation. At the same time, oxytocin modulation of subcortical systems does not preclude the possibility that some key systems affected, downstream, by oxytocin neuromodulation fundamentally pertain to attentional, cognitive, or emotional processes. Such processes may carry especially important effects in species that have well-developed cortical systems (e.g., humans; see Wirth, 2015).

Oxytocin in humans

The mother-infant bond a "biological prototype" for human sociality?

Scholars have convincingly argued that, in some species (including humans), oxytocin likely plays a role in regulating responses to partners in interdependent social relationships aside from the mother-infant one (e.g., Carter, 2014; Crespi, 2016; Numan & Young, 2016). This was perhaps accomplished via additional co-options of oxytocin's role in organizing and directing maternal behavior. Carter (2014) argues that oxytocin's effects on social behavior stems from the "biological prototype" for mammalian sociality: the mother-infant bond (see also Numan & Young, 2016). One such co-option involves behavior in pair-bonds. Like the mother-infant bond, sexual pair-bonds exist within the context of reproduction and involve a coordination of social behaviors between members of a dyad. In sexual pair-bonds, partners develop selective preferences for each other, cooperate with each other to raise offspring, and in general, form a bond that reflects psychological "closeness" (Young & Wang, 2004).

Seminal studies in this domain focused on prairie voles – specifically, a comparison of closely related vole species with contrasting mating systems (e.g., Insel & Shapiro, 1992). Interestingly, oxytocin affects pair-bonding in prairie voles through networks that are overlapping if not identical to those affecting mothering (see Numan & Young, 2016), bolstering the argument that oxytocin's critical role in mothering set the stage for co-option of networks for pair-bonding in mammalian species in which pair-bonding evolved. At the same time, once again, oxytocin is implicated in courtship and mating behavior in a variety of vertebrates (e.g., Godwin & Thompson, 2012; Knobloch & Grinevich, 2014) and pair-bonding in some birds (e.g., Kelly & Goodson, 2014). Whether oxytocin's involvement in mammalian pair-bonding, then, evolved from a mother-infant "biological prototype" specific to mammals or through modifications of pre-existing adaptations supporting mating in vertebrates remains a fundamental and crucial question, not yet answered.

Oxytocin and human pair-bonds

Inspired by studies on prairie voles, psychologists have examined the role of OT in the establishment and maintenance of human pair-bonds. Schneiderman et al. (2012) found that 120 "new lovers" had elevated oxytocin compared to 43 singles. Moreover, initial oxytocin negatively predicted relationship dissolution 6 months later. Success of emotional support relationship interventions is related to oxytocin levels (Holt-Lunstad et al., 2008), as may be overall relationship satisfaction (Holt-Lunstad, Birmingham, & Light, 2015; but see Smith et al., 2013). Oxytocin administration leads to more engaged, constructive communication about relationship conflicts (Ditzen et al., 2009) and more intense orgasms and greater contentment after intercourse with a partner (Behnia et al., 2014). (We note that literature reporting effects of oxytocin administration is currently difficult to interpret due to low power coupled with publication bias, as well as ambiguity concerning whether effects are byproducts of exceedingly high peripheral levels rather than core effects of increased central levels; Walum et al., 2016; Lane et al., 2016; Leng & Ludwig, 2016.) Studies in other pair-bonding primates provide comparative evidence consistent with these findings. In male common marmosets, oxytocin levels rise after reunion with a mating partner (Seltzer & Ziegler, 2007), and black-tufted marmoset pairs engaged in increased rates of huddling and partner-seeking behavior after oxytocin administration (Smith et al., 2010).

In contrast, multiple studies have found *positive* associations between oxytocin and distress and anxiety regarding one's relationship (e.g., Taylor, 2006; Taylor et al., 2010; see also Tabak et al., 2011). Taylor (2006) proposes that distress or anxiety within relationships leads to oxytocin release, which in turn increases "appetite" for social affiliation outside of the distressful bond (Taylor, 2006).

We propose a hypothesis designed in part to reconcile these conflicting findings (Grebe et al., 2017). Under this model, "Identify and Invest," key triggers of oxytocin release are cues of challenges or threats to actual or potential valued relationships. oxytocin, in turn, then functions to re-orient psychological resources toward these relationships. Within romantic relationships, relationship threats may be signaled by a discrepancy in investment between partners. Thus, we examined associations between induced oxytocin responses (where oxytocin was assayed before and after a thought-listing task concerning the relationship in saliva) and reports of relationship involvement from both members of a romantic couple. In two studies (total sample size of 278), we found positive associations between self-reports of relationship involvement and oxytocin (Grebe et al., 2017). Yet we also found *negative* associations between an individual's oxytocin and their *partner's* reports of investment (with self-investment controlled). We propose, then, that oxytocin is naturally secreted peripherally under circumstances in which a valued relationship is threatened or vulnerable, at least in the context of romantic relationships. This model may generalize to other classes of social relationships. The mother-infant relationship, for instance, demands attention and motivational resources, due to the infant's near-complete dependence on the mother. So too do new or impending romances, before a strong bond is established between partners. Both contexts are characterized by high circulating levels of oxytocin (Carter, 2014; Schneiderman et al., 2012). (We note once again that the extent to which increased peripheral levels is coordinated with increased projection centrally remains unknown.)

A role in other social relationships?

Oxytocin has been claimed to play roles in yet other interdependent social relationships, including relationships with kin, friends, and in-group members (e.g., Crespi, 2016). As noted above, in other taxa, oxytocin homologs serve broader social functions pertaining to social aggregation (e.g., Goodson et al., 2009), dominance hierarchies (e.g., Almeida et al., 2012), and mate competition (e.g., Godwin & Thompson, 2012). Oxytocin may play such roles in some mammals too (Anacker & Beery, 2013).

A key question is whether the mother-infant relationship is the prototype from which co-options of oxytocin to other social relationships occurred, as some have argued (e.g., Carter, 2014), or oxytocin has independently evolved to play roles in multiple relationships. If the former is true, (a) oxytocin's role in the mother-infant relationship must have had psychological effects that, even without marked modification, functioned to adaptively regulate social behavior in the novel context sufficiently well; and (b) oxytocin's role in the novel context could not have led to modified social functions of oxytocin that would compromise its role in the mother-infant relationship. oxytocin's co-option for pair-bond relationships likely satisfied both (a) and (b). But oxytocin's co-option to other relationships may not have, meaning that oxytocin's involvement in other relationships would have been highly constrained. As also noted above, however, this question has not been answered; oxytocin may yet play a role in multiple relationships.

Oxytocin administration studies

In this light, it is interesting to note that the vast majority of oxytocin administration studies on humans have examined how oxytocin affects social interactions between people who had never met prior to the experimental study. Effects in these studies, by themselves, do not demonstrate that oxytocin naturally regulates behavior in such interactions. Oxytocin may be exogenously administered, and have effects, in contexts in which oxytocin is never naturally implicated. To establish that *endogenous* oxytocin is *naturally* involved in these effects, however, one must conduct studies of hormonal responses observed in natural circumstances.

Relatively few studies, however, have examined how peripheral levels of oxytocin vary with natural circumstances outside of the context of parenting. Most of those concern romantic relationships (see above). Few concern oxytocin secretion during interactions between strangers, and it is too early to tell whether clear, systematic patterns emerge (see, e.g., Christensen et al., 2014).

The oxytocin system in a life history framework

Physiological functions of oxytocin and reverse engineering an adapted response system

A powerful explanatory framework for the bonding functions of oxytocin integrates effects *and* causes of oxytocin production. As we emphasize above, however, hormones have pleiotropic effects, which are very often functionally integrated, and many of which are non-psychological in nature. Oxytocin is no exception. To understand the functional "logic" of oxytocin – how it mediates prioritization of resource utilization – one must offer a functional account of these non-psychological manifestations too. They importantly constrain appropriate interpretation. Yet the psychological literature on oxytocin has paid very little attention to the non-psychological manifestations of oxytocin.

Oxytocin's physiological effects are numerous and highly disparate in nature – falling in metabolic, immunological, and cardiac domains, among others. Table 9.1 summarizes seven generally well-established effects, along with some non-social psychological effects (see also Gimpl & Fahrenholz, 2001).

A provisional functional theory of oxytocin's pleiotropic effects

Recently, we have sought to understand oxytocin's pleiotropic effects in humans, both psychological and non-psychological, and the circumstances in which oxytocin is secreted peripherally

Table 9.1 Physiological and non-social psychologrical effects of oxytocin

1. *Mobilizes energy stores and increases energy expenditure.* Increases lipolysis and basal metabolic rate (e.g., Deblon et al., 2011; Chaves et al., 2013).
2. *Decreases energy intake.* Suppresses feeding behavior (e.g., Blevins & Baskin, 2015; Lawson et al., 2015).
3. *Has immunomodulatory effects.* Is immunosuppressive (reduces metabolically expensive pathogen resistance and sickness behavior) but may upregulate tolerance and repair functions (e.g., Wang et al., 2015; Detillion et al., 2004; Shattuck & Muehlenbein, 2015).
4. *Affects cardiac function.* Increases parasympathetic control; fosters cardiac responsiveness to and performance in recognizing negatively emotionally valenced stimuli (e.g., Norman et al., 2011; Gamer & Büchel, 2012; Striepens et al., 2012).
5. *Increases insulin sensitivity and secretion.* Increases rate of insulin secretion and sensitivity, which leads to greater uptake of glucose in the muscles and heart (e.g., Klement et al., 2017; Lee et al., 2008).
6. *Affects cortisol release.* Decouples HPA axis responses from withdrawal motivation (e.g., Yee et al., 2016; Numan, 2017).
7. *Is analgesic.* Increases pain thresholds (e.g., Tracy et al., 2015; Eliava et al., 2016).

as functionally integrated responses. That is, we have aimed to reverse-engineer the oxytocin system: Given its effects and the circumstances under which these effects are exerted, *what benefits has the human oxytocin system been designed to offer, under what circumstances, and through what processes?* The theory we have developed is provisional. More important than its details is the need to further develop and test this theory and alternatives, inspired by the evolutionary framework we laid out.

Specifically, we argue that oxytocin has evolved to become activated in the context of an important relationship (e.g., with an infant or pair-bond partner) that demands attention, either because the relationship partner is vulnerable (e.g., in the case of an infant) or the relationship itself is vulnerable (e.g., in the case of a threatened relationship). In these contexts, we propose, the oxytocin system is responsive to particular kinds of threats or potential threats, and is designed to monitor those threats and respond to them, when perceived. That is, the oxytocin system is itself *a threat-sensitive system*, much like the cortisol system is a threat-sensitive system. At the same time, the oxytocin system operates in ways very distinct from the cortisol system. Indeed, we stress that the oxytocin system is not a "stress" system. It is better understood as a system that modifies motivation and readiness for specific motivated action, and affects physiological and other psychological features in a way that prepares for readiness to act. These actions, we provisionally propose, serve to protect valued relationships (e.g., with a dependent infant, a valued romantic relationship).

Physiological effects of oxytocin are key components that inform this conceptualization. Oxytocin mobilizes energy for a reason – readiness to use it. It furthermore allocates energy away from certain potentially expensive expenditures, such as inflammatory immune responses. It affects vigilance to particular kinds of threats. It suppresses potentially competing interests, such as interest in food. It dampens other psychological states that might interfere with efforts to deal with potentiated threat, such as avoidance motivation and the experience of pain (which itself motivates withdrawal behavior).

The psychological consequences of oxytocin under naturally occurring conditions may be multiple, and they hinge on the precise context in which oxytocin release occurs. Fundamentally, oxytocin likely affects motivational states (e.g., in the context of a lactating female, pertinent to mothering), in light of neurobiological networks through which oxytocin has effects (e.g., Numan, 2017). At the same time, it likely also has downstream effects on vigilance and attention: sensitivity to potential threats as well as evidence that threats are not present. And, as has been proposed, it may affect perceptions of self (e.g., it may promote integration of relationships with others into a sense of self). Importantly, however, we argue that these psychological outcomes are likely defined by the context in which an oxytocin response occurs. It makes little adaptive sense for a mother to be attentive to social stimuli if doing so leads her to neglect her infant. Rather, she should be sensitive to her infant's emotional states as well as to social stimuli pertinent to her infant's well-being. Hence, oxytocin should not render social stimuli more salient *in general*; rather, social stimuli pertinent to the relationship context in which the oxytocin system responds should be salient. The relationship context in which the oxytocin system is upregulated important affects whether responses are prosocial or antisocial. A system adaptively designed to regulate maternal aggression should promote aggression toward agents who threaten an infant or a mother's ability to care for the infant. In the context of a vulnerable pair-bond relationship, oxytocin should facilitate prosocial and aggressive responses that serve to protect that relationship.

The blossoming of the field of human social endocrinology is, to us, a truly exciting development. Our aim in this chapter has been to present a particular meta-theoretical perspective for the study of hormones and social behavior, with the hope that it inspires future research rooted in evolutionary considerations. To provide an example of this perspective's potential usefulness, we outline a provisional evolutionary interpretation of the functions of the oxytocin system. As emphasized above, our attempt to reverse-engineer this system is provisional. Given that too little is known about the circumstances that affect activation of the oxytocin system, we fully expect that our conceptualization will need to be tweaked, overhauled, or, potentially, jettisoned, as new facts become known. At the same time, we emphasize our larger points: (a) a complete functional understanding of the oxytocin system demands such a reverse engineering, regardless of whether our conceptualization is mistaken or not; and (b) the conceptualization we offer can usefully guide development of alternatives. We believe these same points can and should be brought to bear on the many endocrine systems affecting social behavior.

References

Almeida, O., Gozdowska, M., Kulczykowska, E., & Olveira, O.F. (2012). Brain levels of arginine-vasotocin and isotocin in dominant and subordinate males of a cichlid fish. *Hormones and Behavior, 61*, 212–217.

Anacker, M.J., & Beery, A.K. (2013). Life in groups: The roles of oxytocin in mammalian sociality. *Frontiers in Behavioral Neuroscience, 7*, 185.

Behnia, B., Heinrichs, M., Bergmann, W., Jung, S., Germann, J., Schedlowski, M., . . . Kruger, T.H. (2014). Differential effects of intranasal oxytocin on sexual experiences and partner interactions in couples. *Hormones and Behavior, 65*(3), 308–318.

Bell, W.B. (1909). The pituitary body and the therapeutic value of the infundibular extract in shock, uterine atony, and intestinal paresis. *British Medical Journal, 2*(2553), 1609.

Bethlehem, R.A., Baron-Cohen, S., van Honk, J., Auyeung, B., & Bos, P.A. (2014). The oxytocin paradox. *Frontiers in Behavioral Neuroscience, 8*, 48.

Blevins, J.E., & Baskin, D.G. (2015). Translational and therapeutic potential of oxytocin as an anti-obesity strategy: Insights from rodents, nonhuman primates and humans. *Physiology & Behavior, 152*, 438–449.

Carr, J.L., Messinger, M.A., & Patton, G.M. (2008). Nesting behavior in three-toed box turtles (*Terrapene carolina triunguis*) following oxytocin-induced oviposition. *Chelonian Conservation Biology, 7*, 124–128.

Carter, C.S. (2014). Oxytocin pathways and the evolution of human behavior. *Annual Review of Psychology, 65*, 17–39.

Charnov, E.L. (1993). *Life history invariants: Some explorations of symmetry in evolutionary ecology* (Vol. 6). Oxford: Oxford University Press.

Chaves, V.E., Tilelli, C.Q., Brito, N.A., & Brito, M.N. (2013). Role of oxytocin in energy metabolism. *Peptides, 45*, 9–14.

Chokchaloemwong, D., Prakobsaeng, N., Sartsoongnoen, N., Kosonsiriluk, S., El Halawani, M., & Chaiseha, Y. (2013). Mesotocin and maternal care of chicks in native Thai hens (*Gallus domesticus*). *Hormones and Behavior, 64*(1), 53–69.

Christensen, J.C., Shiyanov, P.A., Estepp, J.R., & Schlager, J.J. (2014). Lack of association between human plasma oxytocin and interpersonal trust in a prisoner's dilemma paradigm. *PLoS One, 9*(12), e116172.

Crespi, B.J. (2016). Oxytocin, testosterone, and human social cognition. *Biological Reviews, 91*(2), 390–408.

Crowley, W.R., & Armstrong, W.E. (1992). Neurochemical regulation of oxytocin secretion in lactation. *Endocrine Reviews, 13*(1), 33–65.

Deblon, N., Veyrat-Durebex, C., Bourgoin, L., Caillon, A., Bussier Peteut, A.L., Petrosino, S., . . . Rohner-Jeanrenaud, F. (2011). Mechanisms of the anti-obesity effects of oxytocin in diet-induced obese rats. *PLoS One, 6*(9), e25565.

Del Giudice, M., Gangestad, S.W., & Kaplan, H.S. (2015). Life history theory and evolutionary psychology. In D.M. Buss (Ed.), *The handbook of evolutionary psychology*. Hoboken, NJ: John Wiley & Sons, Inc.

Detillion, C.E., Craft, T.K., Glasper, E.R., Prendergast, B.J., & DeVries, A.C. (2004). Social facilitation of wound healing. *Psychoneuroendocrinology, 29*(8), 1004–1011.

Ditzen, B., Schaer, M., Gabriel, B., Bodenmann, G., Ehlert, U., & Heinrichs, M. (2009). Intranasal oxytocin increases positive communication and reduces cortisol levels during couple conflict. *Biological Psychiatry, 65*(9), 728–731.

Eliava, M., Melchior, M., Knobloch-Bollmann, H.S., Wahis, J., de Silva Gouveia, M., Tang, Y., . . . Grinevich, V. (2016). A new population of parvocellular oxytocin neurons controlling magnocellular neuron activity and inflammatory pain processing. *Neuron, 89*, 1291–1304.

Ellison, P.T. (2017). Endocrinology, energetics, and human life history: A synthetic model. *Hormones and Behavior, 91,* 97–106.

Feldman, R., Gordon, I., Schneiderman, I., Weisman, O., & Zagoory-Sharon, O. (2010). Natural variations in maternal and paternal care are associated with systematic changes in oxytocin following parent-infant contact. *Psychoneuroendocrinology, 35*(8), 1133–1141.

Feldman, R., Monakhov, M., Pratt, M., & Ebstein, R.P. (2016). Oxytocin pathway genes: Evolutionary ancient system impacting on human affiliation, sociality, and psychopathology. *Biological Psychiatry, 79*(3), 174–184.

Finch, C.E., & Rose, M.R. (1995). Hormones and the physiological architecture of life history evolution. *Quarterly Review of Biology,* 1–52.

Flatt, T., Tu, M.P., & Tatar, M. (2005). Hormonal pleiotropy and the juvenile hormone regulation of Drosophila development and life history. *Bioessays, 27*(10), 999–1010.

Fletcher, G.J., Simpson, J.A., Campbell, L., & Overall, N.C. (2015). Pair-bonding, romantic love, and evolution: The curious case of homo sapiens. *Perspectives on Psychological Science, 10*(1), 20–36.

Gamer, M., & Büchel, C. (2012). Oxytocin specifically enhances valence-dependent parasympathetic responses. *Psychoneuroendocrinology, 37*(1), 87–93.

Gimpl, G., & Fahrenholz, F. (2001). The oxytocin receptor system: Structure, function, and regulation. *Physiological Reviews, 81*(2), 629–683.

Godwin, J., & Thompson, R. (2012). Nonapeptides and social behavior in fishes. *Hormones and Behavior, 61*(3), 230–238.

Goodson, J.L. (2013). Deconstructing sociality, social evolution and relevant nonapeptide functions. *Psychoneuroendocrinology, 38*(4), 465–478.

Goodson, J.L., Schrock, S.E., Klatt, J.D., Kabelik, D., & Kingsbury, M.A. (2009). Mesotocin and nonapeptide receptors promote estrildid flocking behavior. *Science, 325*(5942), 862–866.

Gould, S.J., & Vrba, E.S. (1982). Exaptation – a missing term in the science of form. *Paleobiology, 8*(1), 4–15.

Grebe, N.M., Kristoffersen, A.A., Grøntvedt, T.V., Thompson, M.E., Kennair, L.E.O., & Gangestad, S.W. (2017). Oxytocin and vulnerable romantic relationships. *Hormones and Behavior, 90,* 64–74.

Gruber, C.W. (2014). Physiology of invertebrate oxytocin and vasopressin neuropeptides. *Experimental Physiology, 99*(1), 55–61.

Holt-Lunstad, J., Birmingham, W.A., & Light, K.C. (2008). Influence of a "warm touch" support enhancement intervention among married couples on ambulatory blood pressure, oxytocin, alpha amylase, and cortisol. *Psychosomatic Medicine, 70*(9), 976–985.

Holt-Lunstad, J., Birmingham, W.C., & Light, K.C. (2015). Relationship quality and oxytocin influence of stable and modifiable aspects of relationships. *Journal of Social and Personal Relationships, 32*(4), 472–490.

Hoyle, C.H. (1999). Neuropeptide families and their receptors: Evolutionary perspectives. *Brain Research, 848*(1), 1–25.

Hrdy, S.B. (2009). *Mothers and others: The evolutionary origins of mutual understanding.* Cambridge, MA: Harvard University Press.

Insel, T.R., & Shapiro, L.E. (1992). Oxytocin receptor distribution reflects social organization in monogamous and polygamous voles. *Proceedings of the National Academy of Sciences, 89*(13), 5981–5985.

Kaplan, H., Hill, K., Lancaster, J., & Hurtado, A.M. (2000). A theory of human life history evolution: Diet, intelligence, and longevity. *Evolutionary Anthropology, 9*(4), 156–185.

Kelly, A.M., & Goodson, J.L. (2014). Social functions of individual vasopressin–oxytocin cell groups in vertebrates: What do we really know? *Frontiers in Neuroendocrinology, 35*(4), 512–529.

Ketterson, E.D., Atwell, J.W., & McGlothlin, J.W. (2009). Phenotypic integration and independence: Hormones, performance, and response to environmental change. *Integrative and Comparative Biology, 49*(4), 365–379.

Ketterson, E.D., & Nolan, V., Jr. (1999). Adaptation, exaptation, and constraint: A hormonal perspective. *The American Naturalist, 154*(Suppl. 1), S4–S25.

Klatt, J.D., & Goodson, J.L. (2013). Sex-specific activity and function of hypothalamic nonapeptide neurons during nest-building in zebra finches. *Hormones and Behavior, 64*(5), 818–824.

Klement, J., Ott, V., Rapp, K., Brede, S., Piccinini, F., Cobelli, C., . . . Hallschmid, M. (2017). Oxytocin improves β-cell responsivity and glucose tolerance in healthy men. *Diabetes, 66*(2), 264–271.

Knobloch, H.S., & Grinevich, V. (2014). Evolution of oxytocin pathways in the brain of vertebrates. *Frontiers in Behavioral Neuroscience, 8.*

Lane, A., Luminet, O., Nave, G., & Mikolajczak, M. (2016). Is there a publication bias in behavioural intranasal oxytocin research on humans? Opening the file drawer of one laboratory. *Journal of Neuroendocrinology, 28,* n/a–n/a.

Lawson, E.A., Marengi, D.A., DeSanti, R.L., Holmes, T.M., Schoenfeld, D.A., & Tolley, C.J. (2015). Oxytocin reduces caloric intake in men. *Obesity, 23*(5), 950–956.

Lee, E.S., Uhm, K.O., Lee, Y.M., Kwon, J., Park, S.H., & Soo, K.H. (2008). Oxytocin stimulates glucose uptake in skeletal muscle cells through the calcium-CaMKK-AMPK pathway. *Regulatory Peptides, 151*(1), 71–74.

Leng, G., & Ludwig, M. (2016). Intranasal oxytocin: Myths and delusions. *Biological Psychiatry, 79*, 243–250.

Lochmiller, R.L., & Deerenberg, C. (2000). Trade-offs in evolutionary immunology: Just what is the cost of immunity? *Oikos, 88*(1), 87–98.

Ludwig, M., & Leng, G. (2006). Dendritic peptide release and peptide-dependent behaviours. *Nature Reviews Neuroscience, 7*, 126–136.

McCullough, M.E., Churchland, P.S., & Mendez, A.J. (2013). Problems with measuring peripheral oxytocin: Can the data on oxytocin and human behavior be trusted? *Neuroscience & Biobehavioral Reviews, 37*, 1485–1492.

Nelson, R.J. (2011). *An introduction to behavioral endocrinology* (4th ed.). Sunderland, MA: Sinauer Associates Inc.

Neumann, I.D., & Landgraf, R. (2012). Balance of brain oxytocin and vasopressin: Implications for anxiety, depression, and social behaviors. *Trends in Neurosciences, 35*(11), 649–659.

Norman, G.J., Cacioppo, J.T., Morris, J.S., Karelina, K., Malarkey, W.B., DeVries, A.C., & Berntson, G.G. (2011). Selective influences of oxytocin on the evaluative processing of social stimuli. *Journal of Psychopharmacology, 25*(10), 1313–1319.

Numan, M. (2017). Parental behavior. In *Reference module in neuroscience and biobehavioral psychology*. Amsterdam: Elsevier.

Numan, M., & Young, L.J. (2016). Neural mechanisms of mother-infant bonding and pair bonding: Similarities, differences, and broader implications. *Hormones and Behavior, 77*, 98–112.

Reddon, A.R., O'Connor, C.M., Marsh-Rollo, S.E., & Balshine, S. (2012). Effects of isotocin on social responses in a cooperatively breeding fish. *Animal Behaviour, 84*(4), 753–760.

Riem, M.M., Bakermans-Kranenburg, M.J., Pieper, S., Tops, M., Boksem, M.A., Vermeiren, R.R., . . . Rombouts, S.A. (2011). Oxytocin modulates amygdala, insula, and inferior frontal gyrus responses to infant crying: A randomized controlled trial. *Biological Psychiatry, 70*(3), 291–297.

Saito, D., Komatsuda, M., & Urano, A. (2004). Functional organization of preoptic vasotocin and isotocin neurons in the brain of rainbow trout: Central and neurohypophysial projections of single neurons. *Neuroscience, 124*, 973–984.

Schneiderman, I., Zagoory-Sharon, O., Leckman, J.F., & Feldman, R. (2012). Oxytocin during the initial stages of romantic attachment: Relations to couples' interactive reciprocity. *Psychoneuroendocrinology, 37*(8), 1277–1285.

Seltzer, L.J., & Ziegler, T.E. (2007). Non-invasive measurement of small peptides in the common marmoset (*Callithrix jacchus*): A radiolabeled clearance study and endogenous excretion under varying social conditions. *Hormones and Behavior, 51*(3), 436–442.

Shattuck, E.C., & Muehlenbein, M.P. (2015). Human sickness behavior: Ultimate and proximate explanations. *American Journal of Physical Anthropology, 157*(1), 1–18.

Smith, A.S., Ågmo, A., Birnie, A.K., & French, J.A. (2010). Manipulation of the oxytocin system alters social behavior and attraction in pair-bonding primates, *Callithrix penicillata*. *Hormones and Behavior, 57*(2), 255–262.

Smith, T.W., Uchino, B.N., MacKenzie, J., Hicks, A.M., Campo, R.A., Reblin, M., . . . Light, K.C. (2013). Effects of couple interactions and relationship quality on plasma oxytocin and cardiovascular reactivity: Empirical findings and methodological considerations. *International Journal of Psychophysiology, 88*(3), 271–281.

Stix, G. (2014, September 8). *Fact or fiction? Oxytocin is the "Love Hormone."* Retrieved from www.scientificamerican.com/article/fact-or-fiction-oxytocin-is-the-love-hormone/

Striepens, N., Scheele, D., Kendrick, K.M., Becker, B., Schäfer, L., Schwalba, K., . . . Hurlemann, R. (2012). Oxytocin facilitates protective responses to aversive social stimuli in males. *Proceedings of the National Academy of Sciences, 109*(44), 18144–18149.

Tabak, B.A., McCullough, M.E., Szeto, A., Mendez, A.J., & McCabe, P.M. (2011). Oxytocin indexes relational distress following interpersonal harms in women. *Psychoneuroendocrinology, 36*(1), 115–122.

Taylor, S.E. (2006). Tend and befriend biobehavioral bases of affiliation under stress. *Current Directions in Psychological Science, 15*(6), 273–277.

Taylor, S.E., Saphire-Bernstein, S., & Seeman, T.E. (2010). Are plasma oxytocin in women and plasma vasopressin in men biomarkers of distressed pair-bond relationships? *Psychological Science, 21*(1), 3–7.

Tooby, J., & Cosmides, L. (1996, January). Friendship and the banker's paradox: Other pathways to the evolution of adaptations for altruism. In *Proceedings of the British academy* (Vol. 88, pp. 119–144). Oxford: Oxford University Press.

Tooby, J., Cosmides, L., Sell, A., Lieberman, D., & Sznycer, D. (2008). 15 internal regulatory variables and the design of human motivation: A computational and evolutionary approach. In *Handbook of approach and avoidance motivation* (Vol. 251). Mahwah, NJ: Erlbaum.

Tracy, L.M., Georgiou-Karistianis, N., Gibson, S.J., & Giummarra, M.J. (2015). Oxytocin and the modulation of pain experience: Implications for chronic pain management. *Neuroscience & Biobehavioral Reviews*, *55*, 53–67.

Valstad, M., Alvares, G.A., Egknud, M., Matziorinis, A.M., Andreassen, O.A., Westlye, L.T., & Quintana, D.S. (2017). The correlation between central and peripheral oxytocin concentrations: A systematic review and meta-analysis. *Neuroscience & Biobehavioral Reviews*, *78*, 117–124.

Van IJzendoorn, M.H., & Bakermans-Kranenburg, M.J. (2012). A sniff of trust: Meta-analysis of the effects of intranasal oxytocin administration on face recognition, trust to in-group, and trust to out-group. *Psychoneuroendocrinology*, *37*(3), 438–443.

Wakerley, J.B., & Lincoln, D.W. (1973). The milk-ejection reflex of the rat: A 20-to 40-fold acceleration in the firing of paraventricular neurones during oxytocin release. *Journal of Endocrinology*, *57*(3), 477–493.

Walum, H., Waldman, I.D., & Young, L.J. (2016). Statistical and methodological considerations for the interpretation of intranasal oxytocin studies. *Biological Psychiatry*, *79*, 251–257.

Wang, P., Yang, H.P., Tian, S., Wang, L., Wang, S.C., Zhang, F., & Wang, Y.F. (2015). Oxytocin-secreting system: A major part of the neuroendocrine center regulating immunologic activity. *Journal of Neuroimmunology*, *289*, 152–161.

Wirth, M.M. (2015). Hormones, stress, and cognition: The effects of glucocorticoids and oxytocin on memory. *Adaptive Human Behavior and Physiology*, *1*(2), 177–201.

Yee, J.R., Kenkel, W.M., Friling, J.L., Dohdia, J.S., Onishi, K.G., Tovar, S., … Carter, C.S. (2016). Oxytocin promotes functional coupling between paraventricular nucleus and both sympathetic and parasympathetic cardioregulatory nuclei. *Hormones and Behavior*, *80*, 82–91.

Young, L.J., & Wang, Z. (2004). The neurobiology of pair bonding. *Nature Neuroscience*, *7*(10), 1048–1054.

10

ORGANIZATIONAL AND ACTIVATIONAL EFFECTS OF PROGESTERONE ON SOCIAL BEHAVIOR IN FEMALE MAMMALS

Alicia A. Walf and Cheryl A. Frye

Introduction

Social behavior involves interactions between individuals, typically of the same species. Individuals begin engaging in social behaviors at birth; these interactions can be complex and are related to an ever-changing context, including changes in hormones. Social behaviors of mammals, which will be the focus herein, can take many forms, to some extent, based upon their social context, which varies. Even if we focus on social behaviors of rodents, we can see many general forms that take place. For example, naked mole rats live in a huge breeding colony, numbering in the hundreds, with a single queen who is the only female in the entire group who mates (much like social insects such as ants and bees). Adult female hamsters are solitary creatures; the social interactions relating to male hamsters can take two forms: (1) mating as long as the appropriate hormonal context exists (e.g., high progesterone) or (2) aggression towards this male if these conditions are not right. Rats and mice are considered social animals, living in small colonies. Generally, adult males and females spend time together only for reproduction, and the majority of the lives of rats and mice is spent living with sisters before becoming a dam, and then with their offspring thereafter.

Many hormones influence, regulate, and mediate social behaviors, including but not limited to social interactions between same-sex conspecifics; behaviors revolving around a limited resource as is often seen with aggression; providing care for offspring; courtship behaviors that bring conspecifics together; and the reproductive behaviors that can follow. In this chapter, we are going to review the role of progesterone for social behavior of rodents, with a focus on reproductive or reproductively relevant behaviors.

First, a brief introduction to progesterone. The word progesterone refers to this hormone's progestational, or pregnancy-maintaining, effects. Progesterone is part of the class of steroid (cholesterol-based) hormones referred to as C_{21} hormones (or the endogenous progestogens). Another related term is progestins; progestins refer to synthetic versions of the progestogens. Progesterone is made via conversion of pregnenolone. Like pregnenolone, progesterone is also a prohormone, or a substance that can act as a hormone itself or can be converted into another

163

hormone that has different endocrine properties. Progesterone is a prohormone for many other steroids, including the androgens and estrogens, which also co-vary in the natural hormonal states that will be discussed in this chapter (e.g., estrous cycle, mating, pregnancy, post-partum). Although the androgens and estrogens have robust effects for social behaviors, we will focus here solely on progesterone and its pregnane metabolites, such as allopregnanolone (a.k.a. 5α-pregnan-3α-ol-20-one, or 3α,5α-tetrahydroprogesterone, or 3α,5α-THP).

Second, it is important to consider when and where progestogens (the endogenous forms of progesterone and its metabolites, such as allopregnanolone) are released from. Production and secretion of progesterone occurs cyclically among female mammals following release of gonadotropin-releasing hormone from the hypothalamus, which stimulates release of luteinizing hormone and follicle-stimulating hormone from the anterior pituitary gland. Particularly high levels of progesterone are released from the corpora lutea[1] (more so than the ovarian follicles themselves) over this ovarian cycle. The corpora lutea are the sites of rupture of ova from the follicle, which produces progesterone; this progesterone production is timed to maintain an early pregnancy while the placenta is formed. Indeed, the placenta is another major source of progesterone, and progesterone secretion from the placenta is important for maintaining the pregnancy until parturition. A third peripheral source of progestogens are the adrenal glands particularly during times of stress and aging. Notably, progesterone can also be produced in the brain itself. Although named for their progestational, or pregnancy-maintaining, effects, progestogens are found in vertebrates wherever steroidogenesis occurs, including the brain. The effects of endogenous progestogens for varied social behaviors over the female rodents' lifespan will be discussed in this chapter.

Third, in addition to having several sources, progestogens have multiple cellular mechanisms. For example, like other steroids, progesterone has actions following binding to its nuclear receptor, referred to as the progestin receptor (PR). Additionally, our laboratory and others have investigated other nuclear and membrane receptor targets of progesterone for social behavior, including pregnane xenobiotic receptor (PXR), neurotransmitter receptors, and membrane PRs. Studies investigating these mechanisms of progesterone using social responding as a behavioral endpoint will be discussed herein.

Fourth, progesterone is involved in many social behaviors of rodents. For example, progesterone is important in maintaining pregnancy and also in the initiation and cessation of mating behavior as well as parental behaviors following parturition. These are behaviors linked directly to reproductively relevant social behaviors of rodents; these can be referred to as the activational effects of progestogens. Activational effects of hormones are those actions of hormones that occur at hormone targets (e.g., specific brain regions) that were organized during early development; these are generally noted post-puberty. Conversely, organizational effects of hormones are referred to as those that occur early in life, even before puberty when there is a cyclical secretion of hormones, such as progesterone. In this chapter, we will also discuss situations where there may be overlap in the role of progesterone for social behaviors as well as those involved in stress responding and affect. Some of these effects can also occur early in brain development, thereby they would be considered organizational effects of progestogens. Examples of both activational and organizational effects of progestogens for social behavior will be discussed in this chapter, with a focus on reproduction.

Lastly, the role of social behaviors to alter progestogen levels will be addressed. What may be particularly interesting regarding the progesterone-social behavior interactions are the observations that different social behaviors, such as mating as one example, can produce rapid changes in release of progestogens. Our laboratory's focus has been on the rapid release of progestogens in the brain following social behaviors. These responses, their relationship to stress, and their broader relevance will be discussed.

Progesterone's organizational effects relevant for social behavior

As outlined above, progesterone is secreted over ovulatory cycles, mainly from the corpora lutea. With a successful pregnancy, progesterone continues to be secreted from the corpora lutea until the placenta is formed and then becomes the primary source of progesterone during the remainder of pregnancy. In rodents that will be discussed in this chapter, progesterone secretion with successful pregnancy requires a progestational reflex triggered by copulation in most rodents. Pregnancy is associated with increasing levels of progesterone throughout, with peaks during pregnancy much higher than the female ever experiences during ovulatory cycles. Pregnancy and the post-partum period are a time for clear differences in brain and behavior; a discussion of which is beyond the scope of this review, but will be discussed later in this work (Feldman, 2018; Hahn-Holbrook, 2018) and in other recent reviews (Altemus, 2017; Brunton, 2016; Brunton & Russell, 2010; Douglas, 2010; Hirst, Kelleher, Walker, & Palliser, 2014; Craig H. Kinsley & Lambert, 2008; Craig Howard Kinsley et al., 2008; Macbeth & Luine, 2010; J.L. Pawluski & Galea, 2007; Jodi L. Pawluski, Lambert, & Kinsley, 2016; Jodi L. Pawluski, Lonstein, & Fleming, 2017).

There is an understanding that this increase in progesterone, and then a decrease around parturition, is important for the length of pregnancy in the mother, but can also have consequences for the offspring (i.e., organizational effects of progesterone). Organizational effects of any hormones, including progestogens, are those that occur during critical periods of offspring development and lead to changes in brain structure and/or function; these critical periods in early development occur prenatally and/or perinatally in both males and females. Well-known organizational effects of hormones for brain structure and function, are the sexually dimorphic areas of the hypothalamus and/or the hypothalamic-pituitary-gonadal/adrenal (HPG/HPA) axes, respectively. Some of progestogens' organizational effects are supported by findings reported during parturition and other challenging events early in development before puberty. For instance, in different mammal models, including rats, guinea pigs, and sheep, challenges such as inter-uterine growth restriction, placental insufficiency, and hypoxia can be exacerbated with decreased levels of allopregnanolone in the dam, which can translate to lower levels of allopregnanolone in the offspring and poorer pregnancy outcomes (Brunton, 2016; Hirst et al., 2014; Hirst, Palliser, Yates, Yawno, & Walker, 2008; Pluchino, Russo, & Genazzani, 2016; Westcott, Hirst, Ciurej, Walker, & Wlodek, 2008; Yawno, Yan, Walker, & Hirst, 2007). The extent to which there is protection of the fetus from mother's progestogens (like what is observed with α-fetoprotein and estradiol, or 11β-HSD and cortisol/corticosterone) likely involves steroidogenic enzymes, but this remains to be fully elucidated. Other challenges, both before and after parturition, additionally support organizational effects of progesterone; these will be described in detail later in this chapter. Another example, particularly relevant to this chapter, is the BTBR T + tf/J (a.k.a. BTBR)[2] mouse model of autism spectrum disorders. This strain of mice develops atypically, with a lack of a corpus callosum as well as impairments in social interaction, vocalization in social settings, and HPA/HPG function (as evidenced by differences in corticosterone and allopregnanolone) (Babineau, Yang, Berman, & Crawley, 2013; Frye & Llaneza, 2010; McFarlane et al., 2008; Scattoni, Ricceri, & Crawley, 2011). Puberty is another critical period for the organizational effects of progestogens (e.g., Juraska & Willing, 2017; Piekarski, Boivin, & Wilbrecht, 2017; Schulz, 2018; Smith, 2013); albeit, this transitional period and the organizational effects of any steroids is less well-characterized than pre- and peri-natal effects, which will be discussed in greater detail in this chapter (and please see Schulz, 2018). The idea that progesterone can serve to maintain the quiescence of the dam and fetus and protect the brain during parturition and other challenging events in early development and transitional periods needs further investigation.

Progesterone has activational effects to mediate social behavior in animals

Much is known about the activational effects of steroid hormones. Some of the behaviors that have been the focus in the field of behavioral endocrinology relating to the activational effects of hormones are social behaviors. Importantly, progestogens have actions for complex social interactions, including affiliation and aggression, of rodents.

Parental behavior is an example of an affiliative behavior that progesterone modifies. Parental behaviors are a suite of species-specific responses towards offspring to provide the level of care that is needed to survive. In the case of many rodents, including rats and mice, parental care is provided by the mother. Maternal behaviors in these species include nursing, grooming, maintaining a nest, and protection of the young. Engaging in these behaviors, particularly for the primiparous rodent, demonstrates a tremendous shift in social behavior. Instead of avoiding the pups (as is the typical response among nulliparous females), parous females approach and engage in specific social behaviors with the offspring (Dulac, O'Connell, & Wu, 2014; Rilling, 2013; Rilling & Young, 2014). Several hormones, including progesterone as well as estradiol, oxytocin, and prolactin, change during pregnancy and coincident with birth and the establishment of maternal behaviors in rodents (Rilling & Young, 2014). In addition to the role of progesterone and other hormones associated with maternal behavior for establishing this response, these hormones have actions for modifying this social behavior. These are activational effects of hormones, acting on regions such as the medial preoptic area of the hypothalamus, that were organized by hormones during development (Rilling & Young, 2014). Notably, the neurocircuitry of this social behavior involves activation in the medial preoptic area, a dampening of activation of the amygdala to the novel stimuli of pups, and activation of the reward pathway, including the ventral tegmental area (VTA) (Numan & Woodside, 2010; Olazábal et al., 2013; Rilling, 2013; Rilling & Young, 2014). Of additional importance, engagement in this social behavior can alter the later social responding of the offspring. For example, variation in maternal behaviors, such as licking and grooming, alter offspring's later responses. Offspring that receive the greatest amount of licking and grooming by their biological or adoptive dams show this same pattern of social behavior when they become dams; those that receive low levels of licking and grooming show low levels when they are dams (Champagne et al., 2008; Weaver, Meaney, & Szyf, 2006). There are also alterations in offsprings' stress responding and other behaviors, including anxiety as well as adult reproductive behavior of females, based upon these variations in maternal behaviors (Cameron et al., 2008; Weaver et al., 2006). These studies show the long-term consequences of maternal social behavior; the direct role and mechanisms of progesterone for these effects remain to be elucidated.

Although female rats and mice typically show less aggressive behavior than do males, progesterone may mediate some of these antagonistic encounters. Of note, progesterone can increase aggression in nulliparous (virgin) mice, and aggressive behavior peaks coincidentally with circulating progesterone levels (Mann et al., 1984). An example relevant for the well-known progestational effects of progesterone is maternal aggression, which is defined by antagonistic behaviors of a pregnant or post-partum dam to protect her young. Maternal aggression is rarely observed in the absence of offspring and is correlated with increased progesterone (Barkley, Geschwind, & Bradford, 1979). Surgical pregnancy termination reduces, and progesterone-replacement restores, maternal aggression in mice and rats (de Sousa et al., 2010; Mann, Konen, & Svare, 1984; Svare, 1979; Svare, Miele, & Kinsley, 1986). These are just a few examples of how progesterone can alter maternal aggression among female rats and mice.

Another quintessential activational effect of hormones are those relating to reproduction. This has been well-studied in mammals, in particular in rodents. Pertinent here, reproductive behaviors are a type of social behavior; details of how we use reproductive behavior to characterize the effects and mechanisms of progestogens for social behaviors will be discussed in the following sections.

Rodent reproduction as a model to look at progesterone's effects and mechanisms

To understand the effects and mechanisms for complex social behaviors of mammals, it has been useful to employ rodent reproduction as a model. This model is useful for many reasons. It has been employed since the inception of behavioral endocrinology, with the earliest studies reported by Frank Beach (Beach, 1976), and has been validated across many laboratories in the following several decades. Female rodents' mating behavior includes several specific patterns: attractivity, proceptivity, receptivity. Attractivity, as defined by Frank Beach, "refers to the female's stimulus value in evoking sexual responses by the male" (Beach, 1976); an example can be changes in female's scent (pheromones). Proceptivity is considered courtship behaviors, or those behaviors that the female engages in towards the male initiating mating behavior. Examples of proceptive behaviors in female rodents are "ear wiggling" (where the rodents move their heads rapidly producing what looks like rapid movements of their ears) as well as motor/approach behavior (e.g., "hopping/darting"). Another way that attractivity and perceptivity are now categorized is that these are appetitive behaviors to initiate and/or maintain a reproductive interaction. On the other hand, receptivity is a consummatory behavior, or all those responses of the female that are necessary and sufficient for mating. These behaviors are associated with both estradiol and progestogens, which generally co-vary over reproductive cycles of female mammals. Details about the role of progestogens for receptivity will be discussed later in this section.[3]

Behaviors that rodents engage in relating to reproduction are sexually dimorphic and have been well-characterized (Harlan, Shivers, & Pfaff, 1984). These behaviors are observed in rodents' natural environment as well as laboratory settings. There are some important differences to consider between laboratory and field work on reproductive behavior of rodents that should be noted. Using rats as the example, in the natural environment, female rats in behavioral estrous will show higher appetitive behaviors (attractivity and proceptivity) and consummatory behaviors towards many male partners; the environment will be traversed in between intromissions from males and often takes longer than what occurs most typically in the laboratory. In the laboratory, a typical set-up for testing reproductive behavior of female rodents is to put a behavioral estrous female in a much smaller environment than they would traverse naturally (e.g., a 10-gallon aquarium) with a single sexually experienced male. In this situation, the female still shows attractivity and proceptivity before receptivity, but the mating sequence is shorter because the male will intromit several times with short intervals between until ejaculation. This "standard mating" paradigm is different than the natural mating situation in that it involves fewer social interactions than what occurs outside the laboratory. A semi-naturalistic testing environment that our laboratory typically uses is called "paced mating." Paced mating assessments occur in a larger arena, with a barrier in the center that has a small hole that only a female can fit through;

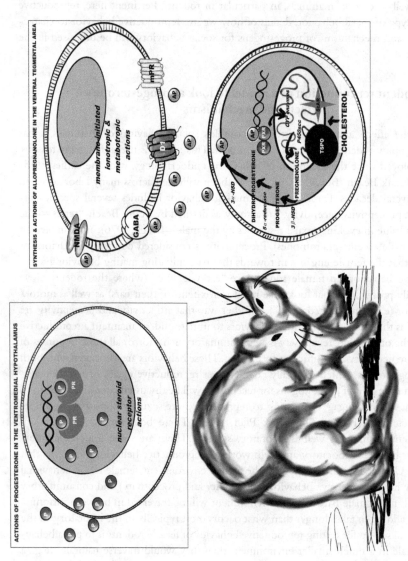

Figure 10.1 The many targets for progestogen production and action for reproductive behavior of female rodents. On the top right, actions of progesterone (P) via nuclear progestin receptors (PRs), which dimerize, bind to response elements, ultimately leading to a change in the proteins transcribed and the cell's behavior, are depicted. For reproductive behavior of female rodents, P's actions at estradiol-induced PRs in the ventromedial hypothalamus are necessary. On the left, the synthesis of allopregnanolone (AP) from cholesterol via mitochondria actions of TSPO, StAR, p450scc and CYP enzymes to produce pregnenolone and the other progestogens, including AP, is depicted. Above this on the left, the membrane-initiated actions of AP via NMDA, GABA$_A$, Type 1-like dopamine (D1), and membrane progestin (mPR) receptors in the midbrain ventral tegmental area are depicted. These actions are necessary for female rodent reproductive behavior (bottom).

male rodents, being larger than females, cannot fit through this. By using this hole, females can (and do) leave the side of the chamber that the male is on after intromissions. The timing of paced mating is similar to the timing of the natural mating sequence.

As described above, reproductive behavior of female rodents is not a single behavioral response. For simplicity, in this chapter, we will focus on the effects of progestogens for reproductive behavior (i.e., receptivity) using lordosis as our main outcome measure. Lordosis is a measure of receptivity. Lordosis is the characteristic mating posture that female rodents assume, with the back becoming arched downward, when mounted by a male (Figure 10.1 bottom, right). The lordosis response occurs with inhibition of motor behavior, which is a robust difference from the increased motor behavior females show during behavioral estrous (i.e., the word estrous coming from "possessed by the gadfly" or defined as a frenzy). Lordosis can be assessed by comparing the frequency of it occurring following a mount by a male during the testing session ("lordosis quotient," or the percentage of time lordosis is observed when a male mounts a female), as well as the extent to which the back is arched downward ("lordosis rating," scored 0–3, with a score of 3 being the maximal extent of arching; Hardy and Debold, 1971). Furthermore, in our laboratory, rodents are tested in a battery that includes social behaviors with same and opposite sex conspecifics, affective measures, and measures of motor behavior. An important note is that the results that we will be describing are those in which there was a congruent pattern on both measures of lordosis (i.e., lordosis quotient and lordosis rating) as well as other ethologically relevant social responses (i.e., coincident reduction in aggression/rejection behaviors towards males and increased proceptivity) as well as affective, motor, and cognitive responses. Affective and cognitive responses will be described later in this chapter.

There are other reasons that reproduction has been used as a research model. There is an understanding of the hormonal control of lordosis of rodents (which will be described more below). With this understanding, investigating the receptor and molecular targets of these hormones can be manipulated pharmacogenetically with robust differences in lordosis observed. This is not the case with other complex social behaviors, or many behaviors in general (cognition, emotion, etc.). Additionally, brain regions involved in reproduction generally, and lordosis specifically, have been well-studied. For example, with lordosis, there are actions of steroids in the ventromedial hypothalamus (VMH) as well as extra-hypothalamic regions, such as the midbrain ventral tegmental area (VTA) (Frye, 2001a). Lastly, reproduction is a model that can be used in several rodent species. We and others have utilized a cross-species approach using rodent reproduction; this has demonstrated the general role of hormones, including progestogens, among many rodents and differences between rodents, such as those observed in rats, mice, and hamsters, suggest differences in neural targets and mechanisms. Thus, reproduction is a good model to further understand progestogens' role in social behaviors.

Species similarities and differences reveal the role of progestogens for reproduction

Reproduction, including the receptivity measure, lordosis, occurs when there is an appropriate context, whether this be the neuroendocrine state (e.g., not during pregnancy), health of the animal (e.g., not with illness or stress), or environmental/social context (e.g., not without a male to mate with) (Frye & Rhodes, 2013; Frye, 2011; Frye et al., 2011; Uphouse et al., 2005). A typical way to assess whether a hormone is involved in a behavior is to assess co-variation in the hormone of interest and the behavior (correlational approach); remove the gland that produces the hormone and determine whether the behavior is reduced (extirpation), and administer the hormone back and determine whether the behavior is restored (replacement). In rodent models of reproduction, several studies assessing natural increases in progestogens over the estrous cycle, and after ovariectomy and progestogen-replacement support the notion that progestogens are involved in reproduction of females. For example, this approach has been used to determine the role of progesterone for lordosis of rats, mice, and hamsters; specifically, lordosis occurs coincident with high progesterone levels over the estrous cycle (Blaustein, 2010; Frye, 2001a). There are some species differences with ovariectomy and hormone replacement. Ovariectomy reduces the lordosis response of adult female hamsters, mice, and rats. Further, lordosis is only observed in ovariectomized hamsters when both estradiol and progesterone is administered within physiological ranges that mimic the estrous cycle (Frye, 2011). On the other hand, ovariectomized rats and mice will show lordosis with physiological estradiol dosing alone, but this response is strengthened with subsequent administration of progesterone (Frye, 2011). Species differences also support the neural circuitry for these effects. Specifically, there are differences in lordosis following direct administration of progesterone to the VMH and/or VTA of ovariectomized, estradiol-primed hamsters, rats, and mice. While hamsters require progesterone to be administered to both the VMH and VTA for lordosis, rats have a robust response to progesterone to the VTA and/or VMH and mice have a more moderate response (Frye, 2011). Together, these studies support the role of hypothalamic structures as targets of progestogens, but also revealed novel targets, such as the VTA. Thus, progestogens in the midbrain VTA reward system is essential for lordosis of hamsters, and can mediate the tone of lordosis following actions in the hypothalamus of estradiol-primed ovariectomized rats and mice.

Mechanisms of progestogens for reproduction

With the establishment of the role of progesterone for reproduction, the brain mechanisms for these effects can be determined. There are several receptor mechanisms for progesterone in different brain regions. Progesterone acts in the VMH through its cognate nuclear PRs, which are induced by estradiol, for initiation of lordosis (Blaustein, 2003). Progesterone binding to PRs leads to dimerization of the receptor, its binding to DNA in the nucleus, transcription and formation of messenger RNA that is translated to produce specific proteins and, thus, alter the behavior of the cell (Blaustein, 2003). Pharmacogenetically blocking PRs in the VMH attenuates lordosis initiation, and activation of PRs in VMH produces the opposite effect (Frye & Vongher, 1999; Glaser, Etgen, & Barfield, 1985; Mani et al., 1994, 1996; Ogawa, Olazábal, Parhar, & Pfaff, 1994; Olster & Blaustein, 1989). Thus, progesterone in the VMH is involved in the initiation of lordosis among female rodents; Figure 10.1 (top, right) depicts these actions of progestogens.

An important point as it relates to reproduction is that progesterone does not only have actions through PRs in the VMH for these effects. The tone (duration and intensity) of lordosis is altered by progesterone acting in the midbrain VTA (Frye, 2001a, 2001b), but the VTA has few estradiol-induced intracellular PRs (Blaustein, Tetel, Ricciardi, Delville, & Turcotte, 1994; Caldwell et al., 1995; MacLusky & McEwen, 1980; Warembourg, 1978). Yet, administration of progesterone intravenously or directly to the VTA of rodents increases firing of VTA neurons within a minute and lordosis a couple of minutes later (DeBold & Frye, 1994; Frye, Bayon, & Vongher, 2000; Pleim, Baumann, & Barfield, 1991). As well, administering progesterone that is bound to a macromolecule and thus cannot pass the cell membrane has similarly rapid effect on lordosis of rodents (Frye & Gardiner, 1996; Frye, Mermelstein, & DeBold, 1992). These data suggested that there must be a membrane target within the VTA for progesterone. Thus, progesterone can have more rapid effects than occur with nuclear PRs through acting at membrane bound PRs.

Membrane PRs (mPRs) are a target of progestogens for reproduction of rodents. For the most part, mPRs, members of the progestin and adipoQ receptor (paqr) superfamily, have been characterized based upon their expression and regulation in fish and amphibians (Thomas, 2012). However, our laboratory investigated the expression patterns as well as functional role of mPRs using lordosis as a bioassay in both rats and mice (Frye, Walf, Kohtz, & Zhu, 2013; Frye, Walf, Kohtz, & Zhu, 2014). The expression of mPRs, specifically mPRα (paqr7) and mPRβ (paqr8) was determined in the body and brain of proestrous rats. Expression of both of these receptors were higher in the brain (cortex, hypothalamus, hippocampus, midbrain) than body (spleen, heart, lung, kidney, liver, intestines), especially for mPRβ. Expression was particularly high for both mPRα (paqr7) and mPRβ (paqr8) in the midbrain (Frye, Walf, Kohtz, & Zhu, 2013, 2014). This is similar to what others have noted about mPRα and mPRβ expression increasing among proestrous compared to diestrous rats (with lower progesterone levels) in the hypothalamus (Liu & Arbogast, 2009). There are also functional effects of mPR manipulation for lordosis. Estradiol-primed ovariectomized rats and mice were administered progesterone and infused with antisense oligodeoxynucleotides (AS-ODNs) targeted against mPRα and/or mPRβ intracerebroventricularly or to the VTA (Frye, Walf, Kohtz, & Zhu, 2013, 2014). This technique of AS-ODNs is similar to other pharmacological techniques, but instead of antagonizes the target with a drug, it uses a base pair sequence complementary to the gene of interest to temporarily inhibit that gene's expression. Among both rats and mice, administration of AS-ODNs for mPRα, mPRβ, or co-administration of mPRα and mPRβ to the lateral ventricle or to the VTA, compared to vehicle, similarly attenuated lordosis (Frye, Walf, Kohtz, & Zhu, 2013, 2014). Thus, mPRs are novel targets in the brain, including the VTA, for progesterone's effects on reproduction.

In addition to these membrane effects through mPRs, there are effects of progesterone, which may be via actions of its neuroactive metabolite, allopregnanolone, for lordosis through other membrane targets. Studies assessing the traditional target of progesterone for lordosis, the VMH, have shown that progesterone may have actions not only involving nuclear PRs, but also membrane targets, such as neurotransmitter receptors (e.g., gamma-aminobutyric acid, GABA; glutamate) as well as second messengers and signal transduction pathways (Balasubramanian et al., 2008a, 2008b, Georgescu & Pfaus, 2006a, 2006b; Gonzalez et al., 2014; Hoffman et al., 2002). Figure 10.1 (top, left) depicts these membrane targets of progestogens.

In our laboratory, studies have focused on neurotransmitter and downstream molecular targets for progestogen-facilitated lordosis among rodents. This has been based upon rapid actions of progestogens in the VTA to facilitate lordosis, as well as PR expression in this region. There are few nuclear PRs in this region, but among rats there are some expressed perinatally; however, in adulthood, these regress and the few remaining in the region are not estrogen-induced (Frye, 2011; Quadros, Goldstein, De Vries, & Wagner, 2002; Warembourg, 1978). The VTA is traditionally considered for its role in dopamine reward pathways. Our studies assessing a motivated social behavior, such as reproduction, have thus focused on determining whether dopamine as well as GABA and glutamate, with inhibitory and excitatory actions, respectively, on the circuitry in this region are targets of progestogens for lordosis. Indeed, manipulating dopamine, GABA and/or glutamate receptors in the VTA, as well as their downstream signal transduction pathways, alter lordosis of female rodents with high endogenous or exogenous progesterone levels (Frye & Walf, 2008d; Frye, 2011). Conversely, altering $GABA_B$ and/or glutamate-type N-methyl-D-aspartate (NMDA) receptors can be inhibitory for lordosis (Frye & Walf, 2008d; Frye, 2011; Frye & Paris, 2011a). Additionally, these studies demonstrate that progesterone's actions through these targets may be subsequent to its metabolism to allopregnanolone, or production of allopregnanolone locally in the VTA (Frye, 2011; Frye et al., 2011; Frye, Paris, &

Rhodes, 2008). In addition to these neurotransmitter targets, there is high expression of the steroidogenic enzymes necessary for production of allopregnanolone (Cheng and Karavolas, 1975; Frye, 2001b; Frye et al., 2006; Frye, 2011; Li et al., 1997). Allopregnanolone has well-known actions to bind directly to GABA receptors, and may modulate actions of glutamate and dopamine receptors, in the VTA to increase lordosis (Frye et al., 2006; Frye & Paris, 2011a; Frye & Walf, 2008d; Frye et al., 2014b). Thus, progesterone and allopregnanolone have permissive and direct, respectively, actions at many membrane targets in the midbrain VTA, such as GABA, dopamine, glutamate, and mPRs and their associated second messengers, for social behaviors.

Rapid changes in progestogen milieu with reproductive experience

As described above, rapid changes in reproduction of female rodents is one of the best-studied animal models for elucidating novel actions of progestogens in the brain. An additional point of interest is that mating itself can alter social/reproductive responses and progestogen levels. Indeed, the nature of the mating experience, such as using a paced mating paradigm that allows female rats to control the timing of their contacts with males can have both short-term and long-term consequences. Paced mating, the ethologically typical manner of female mating behavior in which the female controls the timing and frequency of copulation, compared to a standard mating paradigm where females cannot control the timing of mating contacts with the male, rapidly increases allopregnanolone production in the midbrain as well as the hypothalamus (as well as other targets which will be discussed further in a following section) (Frye, Paris, & Rhodes, 2007, 2008; Frye & Rhodes, 2006). This is observed in naturally receptive rats in proestrus as well as rats that have had other major sources of progestogens removed (the ovaries and adrenal glands) but are primed with low dosages of estradiol which permit mating of rats, suggesting that higher allopregnanolone levels are from midbrain production of this steroid (Frye, 2011; Frye et al., 2011, 2014b, 2014c). There can be individual differences in the response of females when they are paced mated. Although the majority of females spontaneously pace their contacts with males in the laboratory setting even during their first encounter (as is what normally would occur in the wild), some females do not; in those that do not pace their mating, allopregnanolone levels are not increased in the midbrain (Frye et al., 2007). As well, reproductive experience can alter how females respond to subsequent mating experiences. For example, females with previous standard mating experience do not time their contacts with males in a subsequent paced mating test as do females that have prior experience with paced mating (Meerts, Schairer, Farry-Thorn, Johnson, & Strnad, 2014). This is important because paced mating can have long-term consequences to increase circulating progesterone levels and fertility and fecundity of dams (Frye & Erskine, 1990). Moreover, differences in receptivity, fertility, and fecundity in middle-aged rats that are transitioning to reproductive senescence are associated with reduced capacity to produce allopregnanolone in the midbrain (Walf, Paris, Llaneza, & Frye, 2011). Finally, altering the capacity for production of allopregnanolone with administration of a 5α-reductase inhibitor, finasteride, during the last week of pregnancy of rats has negative effects on birth outcomes, including reduced gestational length and fecundity (Paris, Brunton, Russell, Walf, & Frye, 2011). A similar pattern of effects was observed with other stressors during gestation as well as in offspring (Frye & Paris, 2011b; Paris, Brunton, Russell, & Frye, 2011; Paris, Brunton, Russell, Walf & Frye, 2011). For instance, in these offspring, negative consequences include early onset of puberty, morphological differences in hippocampus, and behavioral deficits in the open field and object recognition task; these studies will be addressed further in later sections. Together, these studies show that it is not only progestogens' effects for reproduction, but that the social experience with mating can alter progestogens with both short- and long-term consequences.

Pregnane xenobiotic receptors are a cellular target for progestogen formation (as a response to, and to stimulate) social behaviors

A question then is: what are the important targets of mating-induced progestogen production? Years of investigations into these potential targets have revealed several proteins and enzymes that are required for both the metabolism of progesterone to allopregnanolone as well as de novo production of allopregnanolone from brain cholesterol stores. These include highly coordinated actions of 18kDA translocator protein (TSPO), steroidogenic acute regulatory (StAR) protein, cytochrome P450-dependent C27 side chain cleavage enzymes (P450scc), 3β-hydroxysteroid dehydrogenase, 5α-reductase and 3α-hydroxysteroid dehydrogenase in neurons and glia in several brain regions (Batarseh & Papadopoulos, 2010; Baulieu, 1991; King et al., 2004; Mellon, 1994; Mellon & Deschepper, 1993; Paul & Purdy, 1992). These factors required for the production of allopregnanolone from metabolism of circulating progesterone, or brain-derived allopregnanolone are expressed in the spinal cord, cerebellum, hindbrain (e.g., pons, medulla), midbrain (e.g., VTA), and forebrain (e.g., corticolimbic regions, including the hippocampus and hypothalamus) (Cheng and Karavolas, 1975; Frye, Koonce, Walf & Rusconi, 2013; Frye, 2009, 2001b, 2001a, 2011; Furukawa et al., 1998; Li et al., 1997). When these targets are blocked by pharmacological antagonists administered to the midbrain VTA of rats, there is attenuation of lordosis (Frye, Koonce, Walf, & Rusconi, 2013; Frye, 2011, 2009) There is a newly investigated modulator in this allopregnanolone pathway – the pregnane xenobiotic receptor (PXR).

Our laboratory has been characterizing the role of PXR in the midbrain VTA as a target for allopregnanolone's actions and production. As its name implies, PXR is part of the immune system and a target of xenobiotics in body tissues, such as the liver. It also is considered a promiscuous receptor that positively modulates, or induces, many molecules, including allopregnanolone, as well as enzymes that metabolize cholesterol (Bauer et al., 2006; Forman & Dussault, 2002; Francis, Fayard, Picard, & Auwerx, 2003; Harmsen, Meijerman, Beijnen, & Schellens, 2007; Kliewer, Goodwin, & Willson, 2002; Ma, Idle, & Gonzalez, 2008; Ott, Fricker, & Bauer, 2009; Xu, 2005; Zhang, Xie, & Krasowski, 2008). There is a long list of molecules that PXR positively modulates (including several steroids, and allopregnanolone), but there are much fewer molecules that are negatively modulated or reduced by PXR. Details about how PXR is both a receptor target of allopregnanolone and involved in its production are described in the paragraphs below.

PXR is expressed in the blood-brain barrier as well as brain in many species that have been assessed (e.g., in pigs, rodents, rabbits, and humans) (Bauer et al., 2006; Frye, 2011; Lamba, 2004; Marini et al., 2007; Mellon, Gong, & Schonemann, 2008). In using microarray analysis to compare rats who were paced mated or not, the PXR gene (along with many other genes associated with metabolism/biosynthesis of progestogens and neurotransmitter targets of progestogens) was found to be expressed in the midbrain (Frye & Walf, 2008d). Subsequent investigations verified the midbrain expression of PXR with RT-PCR and western blotting (Frye et al., 2011). Moreover, expression of PXR is higher in midbrain of proestrous rats compared to diestrous rats or male rats (Frye, Paris, Walf & Rusconi, 2011; Frye, Koonce, & Walf, 2013a; Frye, Koonce, Walf & Rusconi, 2013), suggesting a relationship with progestogens and its potential role as a homeostatic regulator.

Studies manipulating PXR expression demonstrate that PXR is a target in the midbrain for allopregnanolone production as well as action. Effects of lifelong knock down of PXR, using PXR knockout rats and mice, for lordosis in proestrous rodents and ovariectomized rodents administered progesterone or allopregnanolone were investigated. Findings showed that PXR knockout rats and mice in proestrus had lower lordosis than wildtypes; this same pattern was observed with progesterone administration to ovariectomized PXR knockout rats and mice (Frye et al., 2013a). In addition to these changes in lordosis behavior, PXR knockout rats, for instance, had decreased prosocial behavior (sniffing, grooming, following with contact) with a female conspecific as well as increased anxiety-like behavior (Frye et al., 2013a). A recent study has corroborated these findings about PXR as a neural target using PXR knockout mice. In this study, PXR knockout mice and their wildtype counterparts were compared for recognition memory and anxiety-like behaviors as well as EEG responses (Boussadia et al., 2017). PXR knockout mice had increased anxiety-like responses and poorer recognition memory that occurred in concert with changes in EEG responses (i.e., lower theta frequency during sleep and abnormal delta waves) (Boussadia et al., 2017). Together, these studies support the notion that PXR is a neural target for diverse behavioral responses, including social behavior, of rodents. Later in this chapter, the significance of changes in social behavior occurring with changes in other cognitive/behavioral processes will be discussed.

A concern with using knockout animals is that there has been knockout of a gene that may regulate many targets throughout development and therefore alter the adult responses. As well, there can be possible compensatory mechanisms. Importantly, we have observed with PXR AS-ODN infusions to the midbrain VTA, which reduce PXR gene expression, corroborate the findings in animals with lifelong knockout of this gene. For example, infusions of PXR AS-ODNs to the midbrain reduce both lordosis responses and allopregnanolone levels in the midbrain of proestrous or ovariectomized and progesterone-primed rats (Frye, Koonce, & Walf, 2014abc; Frye, 2011; Frye et al., 2011; Frye & Rhodes, 2013). Furthermore, studies using sequential inhibition of both TSPO (the rate-limiting factor for synthesis of steroids from cholesterol) and PXR suggest that PXR may be upstream of TSPO for its role in allopregnanolone production in the brain – that is, PXR must be activated before TSPO, and many downstream protein and enzymes required for steroidogenesis of allopregnanolone, are activated. Additionally, blocking PXR with AS-ODNs to the midbrain attenuates the effects of manipulating major downstream targets of allopregnanolone (i.e., those receptors in the VTA that allopregnanolone binds), such as GABA receptors, for lordosis (Frye et al., 2014a). Together, these data suggest that PXR is an interesting target because it may be involved in the production of allopregnanolone via activating CYP enzymes in the steroidogenic pathway (see Figure 10.1) as well as a potential brain mechanism for allopregnanolone to bind to in the midbrain VTA for reproduction. Furthermore, PXR may be a brain target for other behaviors relevant for reproduction and social behaviors in general.

Why is there a liver (factor) in the brain? Steroids, like allopregnanolone, are labile. Allopregnanolone is working fast through steroidogenic pathways, passing through the mitochondrial membranes, and being rapidly produced in the brain (via the proteins and enzymes described above, including cholesterol metabolism via TSPO, StAR, 5α-reductase, 3α-HSD). It can be adaptive to have a mechanism like this for rapid responding to social and other challenges; much of this involves altering sympathetic and parasympathetic balance, which is usually considered when we discuss the stress response. A situation may arise that it is necessary to have a rapid response to stress (sympathetic), and then you have to be able to turn it off (parasympathetic). PXR could be a rapid regulator of this (via steroidogenic enzymes and direct binding of allopregnanolone). As such, the idea is that social challenges, such as the mating situations that have been described so far in this chapter, may also involve these rapid modulations for adaptive responses. We have focused so far in this chapter on how progestogens' actions for lordosis may involve novel receptor targets that can have such fast actions, such as PXR, mPRs, and neurotransmitter receptors; next, the focus will be on other behaviors relevant for these social interactions.

Changes in the social behavior of rodents with progesterone are coincident with changes to reduce anxiety, enhance approach, and decrease depression

Another point of interest in these studies are the extent to which manipulations of allopregnanolone, through PXR or other means, alters other behaviors of female rodents over the estrous cycle. For example, paced mating can reduce anxiety-like responding of female rodents (Frye, 2001a; Nyuyki, Waldherr, Baeuml, & Neumann, 2011) as well as condition a place preference (Frye, Bayon, Pursnani, & Purdy, 1998; Paredes & Alonso, 1997). Although we have focused in the last sections on using lordosis as a model to investigate the mechanisms and brain targets of progestogens relevant for social behaviors of mammals, there are other behaviors to consider.

In considering the content of female rodents' life experiences, there are changes in other behaviors in concert with changes in progestogens such as those that occur prior to, with, and after the reproductive experience (Carter, Lederhendler, & Kirkpatrick, 1999). Prior to reproduction, a proestrous female rodent in the wild has increased locomotion and leaves its natal group that resides in a burrow to traverse a complex and dangerous environment with potential for meeting mating partners, other females, as well as predators; in this case, females would have to overcome an avoidance pattern of responding to an approach pattern as well as suppress anxiety/fear responding (Frye and Rhodes, 2013). Following reproduction, females retreat to their burrows and then there are changes in behaviors associated with maternal care and aggression (as described above). Moreover, there are changes in other cognitive responses, such as navigating this complex environment for food, while avoiding dangers, and returning to their nest. We and others have assessed the role that progestogens have for these affective responses as well as cognitive behavior in the laboratory.

Progestogens can reduce anxiety and fear behavior of rodents, through acting in corticolimbic structures. In support, female rodents have lower anxiety responses in novel environments used in the laboratory to assess anxiety-like responding of rodents, such as the open field or elevated plus maze, when they are in proestrus compared to diestrus (Frye, Petralia, & Rhodes, 2000; Frye et al., 2008). This reduced anxiety-like behavior correlates with both increased levels of progesterone and allopregnanolone in limbic structures, such as the hippocampus (Frye, Petralia, & Rhodes, 2000). Similarly, there is reduced anxiety-like responding during pregnancy of rats, that is, a time of high progesterone levels (Macbeth & Luine, 2010). As well, progesterone or allopregnanolone administration systemically or to discrete brain regions reduces anxiety in the open field and elevated plus maze tasks or fear towards predator stimuli (Akwa, Purdy, Koob, & Britton, 1999; Engin & Treit, 2007; Frye & Walf, 2004a; Mòdol, Darbra, & Pallarès, 2011; Walf & Frye, 2003). Another important point here is that there can be concomitant changes in other indices of affect in animals, such as depression-like responding, with fluctuations in progestogens. Much like with anxiety-like behavior, reduced depression-like behavior (assessed with duration spent immobile in the forced swim task) is observed in proestrous compared to diestrous rats (Frye & Walf, 2002). As well, pregnant female rats spend less time immobile than do post-partum rats (Frye & Walf, 2004b). These effects may be task, dosing and/or site specific (e.g., Contreras & Gutiérrez-García, 2017; Członkowska, Sienkiewicz-Jarosz,

Siemiatkowski, Bidziński, & Płaźnik, 1999; Engin & Treit, 2007; Fernández-Guasti & Picazo, 1999; Laconi, Casteller, Gargiulo, Bregonzio, & Cabrera, 2001; Toufexis, Davis, Hammond, & Davis, 2004). For example, dosing effects are supported by comparing across studies using different dosages, but by also noting differences across natural cycles of females and between males and females (which are all associated with differing progestogen milieu and responsivity to allopregnanolone administration). Here, we will mainly focus the review on the role of natural fluctuations or dosing to female rodents that are within a physiological range.

Allopregnanolone has received particular interest in its role to reduce anxiety-like behaviors of rodents. Allopregnanolone, much like typical anxiolytic drugs, binds to GABA receptors with functional effects on anxiety, fear, and stress responding (reviewed in (Gunn et al., 2015). In a line of rats that were selectively bred to show high or low stress/anxiety responding as neonates (based upon the number of ultrasonic vocalizations with separation from their mothers), those in the high responding group had greater anxiety as adults as well as lower allopregnanolone levels (Zimmerberg, Brunelli, Fluty, & Frye, 2005). Blocking the conversion of progesterone to allopregnanolone with pharmacological antagonists of requisite enzymes, or with genetic knockout of these enzymes, increases anxiety-like responding of adult female rodents with high endogenous progestogen levels (de Brito Faturi, Teixeira-Silva, & Leite, 2006; Frye & Walf, 2002; Frye, Walf, Rhodes, & Harney, 2004; Koonce & Frye, 2013; Koonce, Walf, & Frye, 2012). Likewise, inhibiting neurosteroidogenesis of allopregnanolone with antagonists of metabolism or biosynthesis, such as 5α-reductase, TSPO or PXR, administered to mesocorticolimbic structures increases anxiety-like responding of adult female rodents (Frye et al., 2014; Frye, Koonce et al., 2014a, 2014b; Frye et al., 2011; Qiu et al., 2015; Rhodes & Frye, 2001). The requisite enzymes for neurosteroidogenesis of allopregnanolone are highly expressed in the subcortical limbic system as well as frontal cortex (i.e., not just in the midbrain VTA as already described above; Cheng and Karavolas, 1975; Frye, 2001a, 2001b; Furukawa et al., 1998; Li et al., 1997). Moreover, paced mating induced increases in allopregnanolone are associated with lower anxiety and paced mating increases allopregnanolone throughout the mesocorticolimbic circuit (Frye & Rhodes, 2006). So in addition to the great capacity for the midbrain to respond to allopregnanolone as well as produce it locally, as described above, the mesocorticolimbic structures are additional major targets with a role in affect.

Progestogens also alter cognitive performance of rodents. An intriguing example of this that is clearly linked to social behaviors is the role of parity/motherhood for cognitive performance. Motherhood has been associated with better spatial learning in several laboratories (Kinsley et al., 1999; Pawluski & Galea, 2007). Similarly, recognition memory is enhanced with motherhood and parity (Macbeth & Luine, 2010; Paris & Frye, 2008; Walf, Koonce, & Frye, 2015). There are also estrous cycle differences in several memory tasks, including those assessing recognition and place memory among rats (Frye, 1995; Frye, Duffy, & Walf, 2007; Paris & Frye, 2008; Walf et al., 2015; Walf, Rhodes, & Frye, 2006). Administration of progesterone post-training to rats and mice improves recognition and place memory (Frye, Duffy et al., 2007; Frye, Koonce, & Walf, 2010; Frye, Llaneza, & Walf, 2009; Frye & Walf, 2008c; Tuscher, Fortress, Kim, & Frick, 2015; Walf et al., 2006). These effects of progesterone administration for cognition are not observed among mice that cannot metabolize progesterone to allopregnanolone, such as 5α-reductase knockout mice, aged mice, and/or transgenic mice with Alzheimer's disease–like pathology (Frye, Koonce, & Walf, 2013b; Frye et al., 2010; Frye and Walf, 2008b, 2008c; Walf et al., 2015). Indeed, with aging, there can be both positive and negative effects of progestogen-administration to rodents (Koebele & Bimonte-Nelson, 2017; Walf et al., 2015). This may be due to many factors, including parity and capacity to produce allopregnanolone. In support, differences in cognitive performance were reported among middle-aged retired breeders who were maintaining or had declining reproductive function (based upon estrous cycle regularity, fertility, and fecundity) (Paris, Walf, & Frye 2011). Rats with declining reproductive function had poorer performance, compared to those with maintenance of reproductive function, in several tasks: water maze, inhibitory avoidance, object recognition and Y-maze. Moreover, behavioral differences in these tasks were associated with frontal cortex and hippocampus levels of progesterone and allopregnanolone (which depended upon the task) (Paris, Walf, & Frye, 2011). Taken together, progesterone and allopregnanolone can have effects across the lifespan, including during the estrous cycle, pregnancy, post-partum period and aging, of female rodents. Parity may have a beneficial effect on the brain in part through progestogen exposure and reorganizing/facilitating effects associated with new stimuli. Notably, elephants have among the longest gestational periods of mammals and 5α-reduced progestogens, such as allopregnanolone, are their principal circulating progestogens (Hodges, Heistermann, Beard, & van Aarde, 1997). It may be that "elephants never forget" (as the saying goes) because of these reorganizing effects of progestogens; albeit, this is purely our speculation given that the behavioral endocrinology of elephant cognition is yet unknown (but see a recent interesting report on cognitive behavior of elephants; Dale & Plotnik, 2017).

Progestogens' and stress effects

Speaking of elephants, an "elephant in the room" (or chapter) is the role of stress for the effects of progestogens relevant for social behavior. Indeed, some of the earliest studies demonstrating the dynamic release of allopregnanolone were those involving stressor exposure to rats. In adults, increases in allopregnanolone in response to acute cold-water swim, shock, ether, and/or carbon dioxide exposure have been demonstrated in intact, gonadectomized, and/or adrenalectomized animals (Paul & Purdy, 1992). We can consider the behaviors surrounding mating (i.e., leaving the safety of one's natal nest to traverse a dangerous environment with both predators and strangers) as well as the close interaction of mating as related to social challenges; with such acute stressors, there is an increase in allopregnanolone. However, with greater or more prolonged stressors, there can be suppression of reproduction (as well as allopregnanolone). As an example, female rats have lordosis suppression following restraint stress; this could be ameliorated with pretreatment with allopregnanolone (Miryala et al., 2011). As described above, mating, especially when it is paced mating, can quickly lead to an increased secretion of allopregnanolone, much like these aforementioned acute psychological or physical stressors (Frye & Bayon, 1999; Frye, Paris et al., 2007; Frye & Rhodes, 2006). This stress-induced allopregnanolone release may promote a return to homeostasis after an acute challenge; it occurs across different species, involves modulation by the primary inhibitory neurotransmitter of the brain (GABA), is associated with reduced anxiety-like responding and can dampen HPA responding (Biggio, Pisu, Biggio, & Serra, 2014; Frye, 2001b; Mensah-Nyagan et al., 2001; Patchev & Almeida, 1996; Paul & Purdy, 1992; Toufexis et al., 2004). Furthermore, withdrawal from progesterone and allopregnanolone is associated with changes in stress responding and anxiety-like behaviors (Devall et al., 2015; Lovick, 2012; Smith et al., 1998). Another consideration, though, is that social isolation is a robust chronic stressor associated with other dysfunctions in allopregnanolone. For example, social isolation in adult male mice reduces allopregnanolone and expression of 5α-reductase in addition to increasing anxiety behavior as well as aggression (Bortolato et al., 2011; Nin, Martinez, Pibiri, Nelson, & Pinna, 2011). That there can be opposite effects of allopregnanolone depending upon the nature of the stressor suggest that it is a homeostatic regulator of endocrine stress responses in adults.

There are regulating effects of allopregnanolone on stress during development, which can then alter later behavioral and stress responses in the adult. Prenatal stress, in which pregnant rats are subjected to differences stressors, can have many negative consequences during the pregnancy related to transmission of HPA reactivity to offspring in utero, pregnancy outcomes, and even much later (Weinstock, 2001). Some of these later consequences germane to this chapter are those involving long-term changes in progestogens, HPA axis regulation and behaviors. For example, a variety of different stressors among rats, including infections, restraint stress, cold or swim stress exposure of mothers (referred to as prenatal stress), produce negative effects on brain structure (e.g., hippocampus volume, dendrite branching in the corticolimbic structures) as well as function (e.g., capacity to produce allopregnanolone, HPA function) of their offspring (Frye & Paris, 2011b; Kehoe, Mallinson, McCormick, & Frye, 2000; Kellogg & Frye, 1999; Paris, Brunton, Russell, & Frye, 2011; Paris, Brunton, Russell, Walf, & Frye, 2011). Indeed, prenatally stressed rats have reduced lordosis responses during proestrus when they are tested as adults (Frye & Orecki, 2002). Neonatal maternal separation also has long-term consequences for allopregnanolone and HPA function (McCormick, Kehoe, Mallinson, Cecchi, & Frye, 2002). Some, but not all effects of early maternal separation can be ameliorated with neonatal administration of allopregnanolone. Adult exploratory behavior is reduced by neonatal maternal separation and this is reversed in rats administered allopregnanolone during the neonatal period (Llidó, Mòdol, Darbra, & Pallarès, 2013). But this allopregnanolone treatment did not reverse effects of neonatal separation on prepulse inhibition (Llidó et al., 2013). Social isolation in prepubertal juveniles also produces endocrine dysregulation. For example, effects of social isolation in prepubertal rats produces HPA dysregulation, as evidenced by lower basal levels of both corticosterone from adrenals and allopregnanolone in the brain (Pisu et al., 2017). Pregnant rats that were socially isolated as juveniles have a more precipitous reduction in allopregnanolone levels post-parturition as well as reduced nursing behavior than do those that were not isolated as juveniles (Pisu et al., 2017).[4] Maternal separation effects to increase anxiety-like responding in the elevated plus maze were mitigated with dosing with allopregnanolone during the separation (Zimmerberg & Kajunski, 2004). These data suggest that early life challenges and alterations in progestogens produce differences in the social behaviors of rodents throughout the lifespan.

Social buffers can mitigate some acute and chronic effects of stress

Another way to conceptualize the effects of progestogens and stress for social behavior are that the effects of social interactions can buffer stress effects. A well-known example of this is described by the Taylor "tend and befriend" model (in opposition to Cannon's "fight or flight" model) of stress responding (Cannon & Cannon, 1967; Cannon, 1915, 1929; Taylor et al., 2000). It has been argued that there is a sex difference with females being more likely to engage the "tend and befriend" approach and males the "fight or flight" response when faced with a challenge. A study assessing 18-month-old boys and girls supported this notion – girl infants were more likely to approach their mothers when the mother's behavior was stress-inducing than boys were (David & Lyons-Ruth, 2005). A general focus on the mechanisms underlying some of these effects has been the role of oxytocin (the reader is referred to the chapters in this volume as well as other recent reviews (Carter, 2014; Johnson & Young, 2017; Marlin & Froemke, 2017). The role of progestogens for these effects on social buffering among humans needs further investigation, but there is some support in the literature. For example, experimentally aroused or naturally varying affiliation motivation (implicitly measured) in humans is positively associated with progesterone in women (and sometimes also in men) (Schultheiss, Dargel, & Rohde, 2003; Schultheiss, Wirth, & Stanton, 2004; Wirth & Schultheiss, 2006). Recently, this laboratory has observed progesterone increases are positively associated with affiliation motivation in women teams who competed against other women teams, but not in women competing individually against other women (Oxford, Tiedtke, Ossmann, Özbe, & Schultheiss, 2017). This latter effect may indicate a stress-buffering role of progesterone, triggered by social support, in challenging competitive situations. As another example, this role is supported by the literature including the findings that women engaging in a social task with other women have increased levels of progesterone in saliva than those that completed a neutral task together (Brown et al., 2009). High progesterone levels predicted the propensity for women to help another woman in a task 1 week later (Brown et al., 2009). Moreover, female rats had a lower latency to free another female rat placed in a restrainer in a laboratory experiment (described as "empathy") and were more apt to show this behavior than eating chocolate when given the choice (Ben-Ami Bartal, Decety, & Mason, 2011). Thus, social interactions can buffer acute stress effects, there may be sex differences in these effects, and the direct effects of progestogens here are of continued interest.

Our group has been investigating these effects of social buffers for more chronic stressors in people (as well as rodents). In one example, the effects of a random environmental noise stressor were assessed in building occupants of a newly constructed laboratory. This noise stressor (fire alarms, 120 db, generally lasting several minutes) had been occurring frequently (estimates are about once per month) at random times (when newly installed HVAC system detected air pressure changes), or as scheduled, for years. The people exposed to these fire alarms verbalized that it was "stressful" to be interrupted, often when performing laboratory work; a pilot investigation of the anxiety and cortisol levels corroborated this (Paris et al., 2010). We also noticed that in some baseline measures of anxiety, such as the elevated plus maze, behavioral patterns were shifting in laboratory animals that were raised in the colonies in this building (Walf & Frye, 2009). A cross-species approach then was utilized to more systematically investigate the role of these environmental stressors by comparing stress responding in rats, mice, and humans. In all, the environmental stressor produced changes in physiological (heart rate, blood pressure), endocrine (glucocorticoids, salivary α-amylase, glucose), and/or behavioral (depression, anxiety) measures of stress, compared to a control condition; the controls were laboratory animals or people who were not exposed to the noise (unpublished results). Given the evidence of stress, an important question then became how to reduce the effects of this chronic and unpredictable stressor. To this end, over 3 weeks, rats, mice, and humans were subject to similar interventions, such as enrichment with novel objects/toys/games, social interactions (daily half hour time spent in a large cage with toys and many conspecifics in the case of rodents; going to lunch with others in the study in the case of the humans), and/or classical music. A striking result was that the intervention that worked best to reduce the many indices of stress responding that were collected were those that involved social interaction: exploring in the large, more populous cage for the rats and lunch with others in the humans (unpublished results and Figure 10.2 for summary of data in people). As has been demonstrated by our group in related studies, females were most affected by the noise stress, but this could be ameliorated with these enriching and social interventions.

More recently, our group has been investigating sex/gender differences in individuals who have suffered a traumatic brain injury. Indeed, a recent article in *ESPN* magazine outlines how, despite women athletes being more prone to brain injury, and having more symptoms, compared to male athletes (Keating, 2017), these findings to date on this have not been given the attention that is deserved. An important point that may not be satisfactorily considered is other factors in these athletes (as well as other studies on sex/gender/hormone role on traumatic brain injury). Take for example, recent analyses that our group has been completing assessing differences between adult men and women who have suffered a traumatic brain injury. In this currently ongoing study, sex/gender differences are noted, with women generally having greater symptoms following a traumatic brain injury than men. Moreover, individual variability

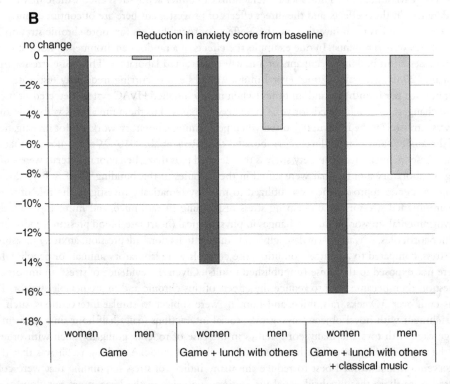

A

Daily Intervention	Baseline	Week 1	Week 2	Week 3
Play Tetris on iPod (30 min)	No	Yes	No	No
Play any iPod game (30 min)	No	No	Yes	Yes
Lunch out of work setting	No	No	Yes	Yes
Listen to Mozart (240 minutes)	No	No	No	Yes

B

Figure 10.2 Gender/sex differences in anxiety scores of people that were routinely exposed to fire alarms in the workplace following 3 weeks of interventions. Scores are depicted as a percent change from baseline (no intervention) in each group. These pilot data ($n = 6$ men, $n = 8$ women) suggest that women were more responsive than men to the stress reduction interventions, in particular those that involved a social component (i.e., going to lunch with colleagues).

in symptomology in both women and men seems to be related to social/life factors, with differences between women and men. Women with greater parity, if afflicted with traumatic brain injury, have a reduced risk for symptoms or disability. In men similarly afflicted, the number of career changes in men seems to be protective. With both parity and career changes, there are a number of coincident changes occurring. One factor that may be linking these life changes are differences in social environments and the efforts of individuals to adapt (and thrive) in them. It may be that progesterone changes, clearly occurring with parity in addition to other neuroendocrine changes, may underlie some of these protective effects of social support/environment that we have observed. The role of progestogens alone, and in concert with oxytocin, in social behaviors and bonding in humans has been recently reviewed and lends support to our interpretation of these protective effects of social environment in the face of traumatic brain injury (Gangestad & Grebe, 2017). That the social environment, including parenting, can play a large role in brain and body health has been described (Brown & Brown, 2015; Ho, Konrath, Brown, & Swain, 2014; Reblin & Uchino, 2008). Readers are also referred to a recent hypothesis paper describing how allopregnanolone may ease loneliness (Cacioppo & Cacioppo, 2015) and another recent review describing effects of pregnane neurosteroids for stress and emotion in people (Wirth, 2011). Additional studies on the role of sex/gender differences, and effects of progestogens for these effects, are warranted.

Conclusion

In summary, progestogens can have activational and organizational effects to alter broad aspects of social behavior of mammals. One focus in this chapter was using a model of rodent social behavior – reproduction. The studies described above support the idea that we can begin to understand the mechanisms and brain targets of progestogens by using behaviors (lordosis, and other social and affective behaviors), substantiating subsequent studies on these mechanisms in other brain regions, other complex behaviors, and in other species including humans. Another focus in this chapter has been on effects of progestogens in females. It should be noted that although males do not experience the same dramatic variations in progestogens as do females, males have the receptor targets of progestogens and enzymes necessary for their production that were described herein, but the role and mechanisms of progestogens in males is much less understood. Males may respond to progesterone via actions at PRs for reproductive responding (Andersen & Tufik, 2006); yet, effects of progestogens to adult male rats reduces both social interaction and social recognition (the opposite pattern as to what is observed in females administered progesterone) (Bychowski & Auger, 2012; Frye & Llaneza, 2011). Indeed, the role of progestogens among males remains to be elucidated. Lastly, social isolation is a stressor, and enriched social interactions can have effects to buffer against stress effects in individuals during early development and adulthood. Of particular interest for additional future studies is that there are organizational brain changes that appear to occur with pregnancy and rearing of offspring, all of which may have consequences for later encounters with physical and psychological stressors (including social challenges).

Acknowledgments

The authors thank the many colleagues who have provided support and help.

Notes

1 For the majority of this chapter, the role of progestogens for the social behavior of rodents will be considered. As rodents have litters of several offspring, the plural form of corpora luteum (corpora lutea) and ovum (ova) are most appropriate. In other mammals, such as humans, the singular form of these nouns would be more appropriate. For consistency, unless specifically referring to effects only observed in humans, the plural forms of these nouns will be used in this chapter.
2 This strain of mice was originally developed by Columbia University (New York, NY, USA), but is now commercially available from Jackson Laboratory (Bar Harbor, ME, USA).
3 In this chapter, we are specifically focusing on the role of progestogens, and will leave out additional details about estradiol if they are not crucial to the point being made about progestogens. It cannot be

ignored that estradiol varies before and with progesterone during reproductive cycles, pregnancy, and post-parturition among female mammals. Estradiol has actions to increase progestogens and effects on its own, or in concert with progestogens, for social and many other behaviors. Although these effects are important to consider, it is beyond the scope of this chapter to address them.

4 Although a thorough discussion is beyond the scope of this chapter, an important point related to these findings in rodent models is the role of early life social stressors among girls and how this may be a risk factor for developing post-partum depression in adulthood. A lack of social support is a well-known risk factor for post-partum depression (along with variables such as history of depression or other affective disorder (bipolar depression, premenstrual dysphoric disorder), family history of depression, stress, pregnancy/birth complications). Much less is known, as of now, about the long-term effects of social isolation during childhood as a risk factor for post-partum depression. However, recent studies have shown a relationship between childhood abuse/maltreatment and increased risk for post-partum depression (e.g., Alvarez-Segura et al., 2014; Sexton, Hamilton, McGinnis, Rosenblum, & Muzik, 2015) as well as reducing mother-infant interactions (Morelen, Menke, Rosenblum, Beeghly, & Muzik, 2016). Additionally, recent studies in women have shown that there may be an association with late pregnancy and/or early post-partum allopregnanolone levels and symptoms of depression (Schiller, Meltzer-Brody, & Rubinow, 2015; Schiller, Schmidt, & Rubinow, 2014). Moreover, changes in levels of allopregnanolone (and other reproductive hormones) may be predictive only among women who are most susceptible to such changes (Schiller et al., 2015, 2014). This is a clinically important, but poorly understood, topic.

References

Akwa, Y., Purdy, R.H., Koob, G.F., & Britton, K.T. (1999). The amygdala mediates the anxiolytic-like effect of the neurosteroid allopregnanolone in rat. *Behavioural Brain Research, 106*(1–2), 119–125.

Altemus, M. (2017). Neuroendocrine networks and functionality. *The Psychiatric Clinics of North America, 40*(2), 189–200. https://doi.org/10.1016/j.psc.2017.01.008

Alvarez-Segura, M., Garcia-Esteve, L., Torres, A., Plaza, A., Imaz, M.L., Hermida-Barros, L., . . . Burtchen, N. (2014). Are women with a history of abuse more vulnerable to perinatal depressive symptoms? A systematic review. *Archives of Women's Mental Health, 17*(5), 343–357. https://doi.org/10.1007/s00737-014-0440-9

Andersen, M.L., & Tufik, S. (2006). Does male sexual behavior require progesterone? *Brain Research Reviews, 51*(1), 136–143. https://doi.org/10.1016/j.brainresrev.2005.10.005

Babineau, B.A., Yang, M., Berman, R.F., & Crawley, J.N. (2013). Low home cage social behaviors in BTBR T+tf/J mice during juvenile development. *Physiology & Behavior, 114–115*, 49–54. https://doi.org/10.1016/j.physbeh.2013.03.006

Balasubramanian, B., Portillo, W., Reyna, A., Chen, J.Z., Moore, A.N., Dash, P.K., & Mani, S.K. (2008a). Nonclassical mechanisms of progesterone action in the brain: I. Protein kinase C activation in the hypothalamus of female rats. *Endocrinology, 149*(11), 5509–5517. https://doi.org/10.1210/en.2008-0712

Balasubramanian, B., Portillo, W., Reyna, A., Chen, J.Z., Moore, A.N., Dash, P.K., & Mani, S.K. (2008b). Nonclassical mechanisms of progesterone action in the brain: II. Role of calmodulin-dependent protein kinase II in progesterone-mediated signaling in the hypothalamus of female rats. *Endocrinology, 149*(11), 5518–5526. https://doi.org/10.1210/en.2008-0713

Barkley, M.S., Geschwind, I.I., & Bradford, G.E. (1979). The gestational pattern of estradiol, testosterone and progesterone secretion in selected strains of mice. *Biology of Reproduction, 20*(4), 733–738.

Batarseh, A., & Papadopoulos, V. (2010). Regulation of Translocator Protein 18kDa (TSPO) expression in health and disease states☆. *Molecular and Cellular Endocrinology, 327*(1–2), 1–12. https://doi.org/10.1016/j.mce.2010.06.013

Bauer, B., Yang, X., Hartz, A.M.S., Olson, E.R., Zhao, R., Kalvass, J.C., . . . Miller, D.S. (2006). In vivo activation of human pregnane X receptor tightens the blood-brain barrier to methadone through P-glycoprotein up-regulation. *Molecular Pharmacology, 70*(4), 1212–1219. https://doi.org/10.1124/mol.106.023796

Baulieu, É.-É. (1991). Neurosteroids: A new function in the brain. *Biology of the Cell, 71*(1–2), 3–10. https://doi.org/10.1016/0248-4900(91)90045-O

Beach, F.A. (1976). Sexual attractivity, proceptivity, and receptivity in female mammals. *Hormones and Behavior, 7*(1), 105–138. https://doi.org/10.1016/0018-506X(76)90008-8

Ben-Ami Bartal, I., Decety, J., & Mason, P. (2011). Empathy and pro-social behavior in rats. *Science (New York, N.Y.)*, *334*(6061), 1427–1430. https://doi.org/10.1126/science.1210789

Biggio, G., Pisu, M.G., Biggio, F., & Serra, M. (2014). Allopregnanolone modulation of HPA axis function in the adult rat. *Psychopharmacology*, *231*(17), 3437–3444. https://doi.org/10.1007/s00213-014-3521-6

Blaustein, J.D. (2003). Progestin receptors: Neuronal integrators of hormonal and environmental stimulation. *Annals of the New York Academy of Sciences*, *1007*, 238–250.

Blaustein, J.D. (2010). Hormones and female sexual behavior. In *Encyclopedia of behavioral neuroscience* (pp. 49–56). Elsevier. https://doi.org/10.1016/B978-0-08-045396-5.00199-8

Blaustein, J.D., Tetel, M.J., Ricciardi, K.H., Delville, Y., & Turcotte, J.C. (1994). Hypothalamic ovarian steroid hormone-sensitive neurons involved in female sexual behavior. *Psychoneuroendocrinology*, *19*(5–7), 505–516.

Bortolato, M., Devoto, P., Roncada, P., Frau, R., Flore, G., Saba, P., . . . Barbaccia, M.L. (2011). Isolation rearing-induced reduction of brain 5α-reductase expression: Relevance to dopaminergic impairments. *Neuropharmacology*, *60*(7–8), 1301–1308. https://doi.org/10.1016/j.neuropharm.2011.01.013

Boussadia, B., Lakhal, L., Payrastre, L., Ghosh, C., Pascussi, J-M., Gangarossa, G., & Marchi, N. (2017). Pregnane X receptor deletion modifies recognition memory and electroencephalographic activity. *Neuroscience*. https://doi.org/10.1016/j.neuroscience.2017.07.038

Brown, S.L., & Brown, R.M. (2015). Connecting prosocial behavior to improved physical health: Contributions from the neurobiology of parenting. *Neuroscience & Biobehavioral Reviews*, *55*, 1–17. https://doi.org/10.1016/j.neubiorev.2015.04.004

Brown, S.L., Fredrickson, B.L., Wirth, M.M., Poulin, M.J., Meier, E.A., Heaphy, E.D., . . . Schultheiss, O.C. (2009). Social closeness increases salivary progesterone in humans. *Hormones and Behavior*, *56*(1), 108–111. https://doi.org/10.1016/j.yhbeh.2009.03.022

Brunton, P.J. (2016). Neuroactive steroids and stress axis regulation: Pregnancy and beyond. *The Journal of Steroid Biochemistry and Molecular Biology*, *160*, 160–168. https://doi.org/10.1016/j.jsbmb.2015.08.003

Brunton, P.J., & Russell, J.A. (2010). Endocrine induced changes in brain function during pregnancy. *Brain Research*, *1364*, 198–215. https://doi.org/10.1016/j.brainres.2010.09.062

Bychowski, M.E., & Auger, C.J. (2012). Progesterone impairs social recognition in male rats. *Hormones and Behavior*, *61*(4), 598–604. https://doi.org/10.1016/j.yhbeh.2012.02.009

Cacioppo, S., & Cacioppo, J.T. (2015). Why may allopregnanolone help alleviate loneliness? *Medical Hypotheses*, *85*(6), 947–952. https://doi.org/10.1016/j.mehy.2015.09.004

Caldwell, J.D., Walker, C.H., Faggin, B.M., Carr, R.B., Pedersen, C.A., & Mason, G.A. (1995). Characterization of progesterone-3-[125I-BSA] binding sites in the medial preoptic area and anterior hypothalamus. *Brain Research*, *693*(1–2), 225–232.

Cameron, N.M., Shahrokh, D., Del Corpo, A., Dhir, S.K., Szyf, M., Champagne, F.A., & Meaney, M.J. (2008). Epigenetic programming of phenotypic variations in reproductive strategies in the rat through maternal care. *Journal of Neuroendocrinology*, *20*(6), 795–801. https://doi.org/10.1111/j.1365-2826.2008.01725.x

Cannon, W.B. (1915). *Bodily changes in pain, hunger, fear and rage : An account of recent researches into the function of emotional excitement* (1st ed.). New York, NY: Appleton-Century-Crofts.

Cannon, W.B. (1929). *Bodily changes in pain, hunger, fear and rage : An account of recent researches into the function of emotional excitement* (2nd ed.). New York, NY: Appleton-Century-Crofts.

Cannon, W.B., & Cannon, C.J. (1967). *The wisdom of the body: How the human body reacts to disturbance and danger and maintains the stability essential to life* (Rev. and enl. ed. Renewed). New York, NY: W.W. Norton & Company.

Carter, C.S. (2014). Oxytocin pathways and the evolution of human behavior. *Annual Review of Psychology*, *65*, 17–39. https://doi.org/10.1146/annurev-psych-010213-115110

Carter, C.S., Lederhendler, I.I., & Kirkpatrick, B. (Eds.). (1999). *The integrative neurobiology of affiliation*. Cambridge, MA: MIT Press.

Champagne, D.L., Bagot, R.C., van Hasselt, F., Ramakers, G., Meaney, M.J., de Kloet, E.R., . . . Krugers, H. (2008). Maternal care and hippocampal plasticity: Evidence for experience-dependent structural plasticity, altered synaptic functioning, and differential responsiveness to glucocorticoids and stress. *The Journal of Neuroscience: The Official Journal of the Society for Neuroscience*, *28*(23), 6037–6045. https://doi.org/10.1523/JNEUROSCI.0526-08.2008

Cheng, Y.J., & Karavolas, H.J. (1975). Subcellular distribution and properties of progesterone (delta4-steroid) 5alpha-reductase in rat medial basal hypothalamus. *The Journal of Biological Chemistry*, *250*(20), 7997–8003.

Contreras, C.M., & Gutiérrez-García, A.G. (2017). Progesterone modifies the responsivity of the amygdala-mPFC connection in male but not female wistar rats. *Neuroscience Letters, 649*, 1–6. https://doi.org/10.1016/j.neulet.2017.04.002

Członkowska, A.I., Sienkiewicz-Jarosz, H., Siemiatkowski, M., Bidziński, A., & Płaźnik, A. (1999). The effects of neurosteroids on rat behavior and 3H-muscimol binding in the brain. *Pharmacology, Biochemistry, and Behavior, 63*(4), 639–646.

Dale, R., & Plotnik, J.M. (2017). Elephants know when their bodies are obstacles to success in a novel transfer task. *Scientific Reports, 7*, 46309. https://doi.org/10.1038/srep46309

David, D.H., & Lyons-Ruth, K. (2005). Differential attachment responses of male and female infants to frightening maternal behavior: Tend or befriend versus fight or flight? *Infant Mental Health Journal, 26*(1), 1–18. https://doi.org/10.1002/imhj.20033

de Brito Faturi, C., Teixeira-Silva, F., & Leite, J.R. (2006). The anxiolytic effect of pregnancy in rats is reversed by finasteride. *Pharmacology, Biochemistry, and Behavior, 85*(3), 569–574. https://doi.org/10.1016/j.pbb.2006.10.011

de Sousa, F.L., Lazzari, V., de Azevedo, M.S., de Almeida, S., Sanvitto, G.L., Lucion, A.B., & Giovenardi, M. (2010). Progesterone and maternal aggressive behavior in rats. *Behavioural Brain Research, 212*(1), 84–89. https://doi.org/10.1016/j.bbr.2010.03.050

DeBold, J.F., & Frye, C.A. (1994). Genomic and non-genomic actions of progesterone in the control of female hamster sexual behavior. *Hormones and Behavior, 28*(4), 445–453. https://doi.org/10.1006/hbeh.1994.1042

Devall, A.J., Santos, J.M., Fry, J.P., Honour, J.W., Brandão, M.L., & Lovick, T.A. (2015). Elevation of brain allopregnanolone rather than 5-HT release by short term, low dose fluoxetine treatment prevents the estrous cycle-linked increase in stress sensitivity in female rats. *European Neuropsychopharmacology: The Journal of the European College of Neuropsychopharmacology, 25*(1), 113–123. https://doi.org/10.1016/j.euroneuro.2014.11.017

Douglas, A.J. (2010). Baby on board: Do responses to stress in the maternal brain mediate adverse pregnancy outcome? *Frontiers in Neuroendocrinology, 31*(3), 359–376. https://doi.org/10.1016/j.yfrne.2010.05.002

Dulac, C., O'Connell, L.A., & Wu, Z. (2014). Neural control of maternal and paternal behaviors. *Science (New York, N.Y.), 345*(6198), 765–770. https://doi.org/10.1126/science.1253291

Engin, E., & Treit, D. (2007). The anxiolytic-like effects of allopregnanolone vary as a function of intracerebral microinfusion site: The amygdala, medial prefrontal cortex, or hippocampus. *Behavioural Pharmacology, 18*(5–6), 461–470. https://doi.org/10.1097/FBP.0b013e3282d28f6f

Feldman, R. (2018). The neurobiology of human parenting. Schultheiss, O. C., & Mehta, P. H. (Eds.). (in press). In *Routledge international handbook of social neuroendocrinology*. Abingdon, UK: Routledge.

Fernández-Guasti, A., & Picazo, O. (1999). Sexual differentiation modifies the allopregnanolone anxiolytic actions in rats. *Psychoneuroendocrinology, 24*(3), 251–267.

Forman, B.M., & Dussault, I. (2002). The nuclear receptor PXR: A master regulator of "Homeland" defense. *Critical Reviews in Eukaryotic Gene Expression, 12*(1), 12. https://doi.org/10.1615/CritRev EukaryotGeneExpr.v12.i1.30

Francis, G.A., Fayard, E., Picard, F., & Auwerx, J. (2003). Nuclear receptors and the control of metabolism. *Annual Review of Physiology, 65*(1), 261–311. https://doi.org/10.1146/annurev.physiol.65.092101.142528

Frye, C.A. (1995). Estrus-associated decrements in a water maze task are limited to acquisition. *Physiology & Behavior, 57*(1), 5–14.

Frye, C.A. (2001a). The role of neurosteroids and non-genomic effects of progestins and androgens in mediating sexual receptivity of rodents. *Brain Research Reviews, 37*(1–3), 201–222.

Frye, C.A. (2001b). The role of neurosteroids and nongenomic effects of progestins in the ventral tegmental area in mediating sexual receptivity of rodents. *Hormones and Behavior, 40*(2), 226–233. https://doi.org/10.1006/hbeh.2001.1674

Frye, C.A. (2009). Neurosteroids' effects and mechanisms for social, cognitive, emotional, and physical functions. *Psychoneuroendocrinology, 34*(Suppl. 1), S143–S161. https://doi.org/10.1016/j.psyneuen.2009.07.005

Frye, C.A. (2011). Novel substrates for, and sources of, progestogens for reproduction. *Journal of Neuroendocrinology, 23*(11), 961–973. https://doi.org/10.1111/j.1365-2826.2011.02180.x

Frye, C.A., & Bayon, L.E. (1999). Mating stimuli influence endogenous variations in the neurosteroids 3alpha, 5alpha-THP and 3alpha-diol. *Journal of Neuroendocrinology, 11*(11), 839–847.

Frye, C.A., Bayon, L.E., Pursnani, N.K., & Purdy, R.H. (1998). The neurosteroids, progesterone and 3alpha, 5alpha-THP, enhance sexual motivation, receptivity, and proceptivity in female rats. *Brain Research, 808*(1), 72–83.

Frye, C.A., Bayon, L.E., & Vongher, J.M. (2000). Intravenous progesterone elicits a more rapid induction of lordosis in rats than does SKF38393. *Psychobiology*, 28, 99–109.

Frye, C.A., Duffy, C.K., & Walf, A.A. (2007). Estrogens and progestins enhance spatial learning of intact and ovariectomized rats in the object placement task. *Neurobiology of Learning and Memory*, 88(2), 208–216. https://doi.org/10.1016/j.nlm.2007.04.003

Frye, C.A., & Erskine, M.S. (1990). Influence of time of mating and paced copulation on induction of pseudopregnancy in cyclic female rats. *Journal of Reproduction and Fertility*, 90(2), 375–385.

Frye, C.A., & Gardiner, S.G. (1996). Progestins can have a membrane-mediated action in rat midbrain for facilitation of sexual receptivity. *Hormones and Behavior*, 30(4), 682–691. https://doi.org/10.1006/hbeh.1996.0069

Frye, C.A., Koonce, C.J., & Walf, A.A. (2010). Mnemonic effects of progesterone to mice require formation of 3alpha, 5alpha-THP. *Neuroreport*, 21(8), 590–595. https://doi.org/10.1097/WNR.0b013e32833a7e14

Frye, C.A., Koonce, C.J., & Walf, A.A. (2013a). Pregnane xenobiotic receptors and membrane progestin receptors: Role in neurosteroid-mediated motivated behaviours. *Journal of Neuroendocrinology*, 25(11), 1002–1011. https://doi.org/10.1111/jne.12105

Frye, C.A., Koonce, C.J., & Walf, A.A. (2013b). Progesterone, compared to medroxyprogesterone acetate, to C57BL/6, but not 5α-reductase mutant, mice enhances object recognition and placement memory and is associated with higher BDNF levels in the hippocampus and cortex. *Neuroscience Letters*, 551, 53–57. https://doi.org/10.1016/j.neulet.2013.07.002

Frye, C.A., Koonce, C.J., & Walf, A.A. (2014a). Involvement of pregnane xenobiotic receptor in mating-induced allopregnanolone formation in the midbrain and hippocampus and brain-derived neurotrophic factor in the hippocampus among female rats. *Psychopharmacology*, 231(17), 3375–3390. https://doi.org/10.1007/s00213-014-3569-3

Frye, C.A., Koonce, C.J., & Walf, A.A. (2014b). Novel receptor targets for production and action of allopregnanolone in the central nervous system: A focus on pregnane xenobiotic receptor. *Frontiers in Cellular Neuroscience*, 8. https://doi.org/10.3389/fncel.2014.00106

Frye, C.A., Koonce, C.J., & Walf, A.A. (2014c). The pregnane xenobiotic receptor, a prominent liver factor, has actions in the midbrain for neurosteroid synthesis and behavioral/neural plasticity of female rats. *Frontiers in Systems Neuroscience*, 8. https://doi.org/10.3389/fnsys.2014.00060

Frye, C.A., Koonce, C.J., Walf, A.A., & Rusconi, J.C. (2013). Motivated behaviors and levels of 3α, 5α-THP in the midbrain are attenuated by knocking down expression of pregnane xenobiotic receptor in the midbrain ventral tegmental area of proestrous rats. *The Journal of Sexual Medicine*, 10(7), 1692–1706. https://doi.org/10.1111/jsm.12173

Frye, C.A., & Llaneza, D.C. (2010). Corticosteroid and neurosteroid dysregulation in an animal model of autism, BTBR mice. *Physiology & Behavior*, 100(3), 264–267. https://doi.org/10.1016/j.physbeh.2010.03.005

Frye, C.A., & Llaneza, D.C. (2011). The role of 3α-hydroxy-5α-pregnan-20-one in mediating the development and/or expression of schizophrenia spectrum disorders: Findings in rodent models and clinical populations. In M. Ritsner (Ed.), *Brain protection in schizophrenia, mood and cognitive disorders* (Vol. 1). Berlin: Springer.

Frye, C.A., Llaneza, D.C., & Walf, A.A. (2009). Progesterone can enhance consolidation and/or performance in spatial, object and working memory tasks in Long-Evans rats. *Animal Behaviour*, 78(2), 279–286.

Frye, C.A., Mermelstein, P.G., & DeBold, J.F. (1992). Evidence for a non-genomic action of progestins on sexual receptivity in hamster ventral tegmental area but not hypothalamus. *Brain Research*, 578(1–2), 87–93.

Frye, C.A., & Orecki, Z.A. (2002). Prenatal stress produces deficits in socio-sexual behavior of cycling, but not hormone-primed, Long-Evans rats. *Pharmacology, Biochemistry, and Behavior*, 73(1), 53–60.

Frye, C.A., & Paris, J.J. (2011a). Effects of neurosteroid actions at N-methyl-D-aspartate and GABAA receptors in the midbrain ventral tegmental area for anxiety-like and mating behavior of female rats. *Psychopharmacology*, 213(1), 93–103. https://doi.org/10.1007/s00213-010-2016-3

Frye, C.A., & Paris, J.J. (2011b). Gestational exposure to variable stressors produces decrements in cognitive and neural development of juvenile male and female rats. *Current Topics in Medicinal Chemistry*, 11(13), 1706–1713. https://doi.org/10.2174/156802611796117649

Frye, C.A., Paris, J.J., & Rhodes, M.E. (2007). Engaging in paced mating, but neither exploratory, anti-anxiety, nor social behavior, increases 5alpha-reduced progestin concentrations in midbrain, hippocampus, striatum, and cortex. *Reproduction (Cambridge, England)*, 133(3), 663–674. https://doi.org/10.1530/rep.1.01208

Frye, C.A., Paris, J.J., & Rhodes, M.E. (2008). Exploratory, anti-anxiety, social, and sexual behaviors of rats in behavioral estrus is attenuated with inhibition of 3α, 5α-THP formation in the midbrain ventral tegmental area. *Behavioural Brain Research, 193*(2), 269–276. https://doi.org/10.1016/j.bbr.2008.06.005

Frye, C.A., Paris, J.J., Walf, A.A., & Rusconi, J.C. (2011). Effects and mechanisms of 3α, 5α,-THP on emotion, motivation, and reward functions involving pregnane xenobiotic receptor. *Frontiers in Neuroscience, 5*, 136. https://doi.org/10.3389/fnins.2011.00136

Frye, C.A., Petralia, S.M., & Rhodes, M.E. (2000). Estrous cycle and sex differences in performance on anxiety tasks coincide with increases in hippocampal progesterone and 3α, 5α -THP. *Pharmacology, Biochemistry, and Behavior, 67*(3), 587–596.

Frye, C.A., & Rhodes, M.E. (2006). Progestin concentrations are increased following paced mating in midbrain, hippocampus, diencephalon, and cortex of rats in behavioral estrus, but only in midbrain of diestrous rats. *Neuroendocrinology, 83*(5–6), 336–347. https://doi.org/10.1159/000096051

Frye, C.A., & Rhodes, M.E. (2013). The role and mechanisms of steroid hormones in approach-avoidance behavior. In A. J. Elliot (Ed.), *Handbook of approach and avoidance motivation* (pp. 109–126). New York, NY: Psychology Press.

Frye, C.A., Rhodes, M.E., Petralia, S.M., Walf, A.A., Sumida, K., & Edinger, K.L. (2006). 3alpha-hydroxy-5alpha-pregnan-20-one in the midbrain ventral tegmental area mediates social, sexual, and affective behaviors. *Neuroscience, 138*(3), 1007–1014. https://doi.org/10.1016/j.neuroscience.2005.06.015

Frye, C.A., & Vongher, J.M. (1999). Progestins' rapid facilitation of lordosis when applied to the ventral tegmentum corresponds to efficacy at enhancing GABA(A)receptor activity. *Journal of Neuroendocrinology, 11*(11), 829–837.

Frye, C.A., & Walf, A.A. (2002). Changes in progesterone metabolites in the hippocampus can modulate open field and forced swim test behavior of proestrous rats. *Hormones and Behavior, 41*(3), 306–315. https://doi.org/10.1006/hbeh.2002.1763

Frye, C.A., & Walf, A.A. (2004a). Estrogen and/or progesterone administered systemically or to the amygdala can have anxiety-, fear-, and pain-reducing effects in ovariectomized rats. *Behavioral Neuroscience, 118*(2), 306–313. https://doi.org/10.1037/0735-7044.118.2.306

Frye, C.A., & Walf, A.A. (2004b). Hippocampal 3alpha, 5alpha-THP may alter depressive behavior of pregnant and lactating rats. *Pharmacology, Biochemistry, and Behavior, 78*(3), 531–540. https://doi.org/10.1016/j.pbb.2004.03.024

Frye, C.A., & Walf, A.A. (2008a). Effects of progesterone administration and APPswe+PSEN1Δe9 mutation for cognitive performance of mid-aged mice. *Neurobiology of Learning and Memory, 89*(1), 17–26. https://doi.org/10.1016/j.nlm.2007.09.008

Frye, C.A., & Walf, A.A. (2008b). Progesterone enhances performance of aged mice in cortical or hippocampal tasks. *Neuroscience Letters, 437*(2), 116–120. https://doi.org/10.1016/j.neulet.2008.04.004

Frye, C.A., & Walf, A.A. (2008c). Progesterone to ovariectomized mice enhances cognitive performance in the spontaneous alternation, object recognition, but not placement, water maze, and contextual and cued conditioned fear tasks. *Neurobiology of Learning and Memory, 90*(1), 171–177. https://doi.org/10.1016/j.nlm.2008.03.005

Frye, C. A., & Walf, A.A. (2008d). Membrane actions of progestins at dopamine type 1-like and GABAA receptors involve downstream signal transduction pathways. *Steroids, 73*(9–10), 906–913. https://doi.org/10.1016/j.steroids.2008.01.020

Frye, C.A., Walf, A.A., Kohtz, A.S., & Zhu, Y. (2013). Membrane progestin receptors in the midbrain ventral tegmental area are required for progesterone-facilitated lordosis of rats. *Hormones and Behavior, 64*(3), 539–545. https://doi.org/10.1016/j.yhbeh.2013.05.012

Frye, C.A., Walf, A.A., Kohtz, A.S., & Zhu, Y. (2014). Progesterone-facilitated lordosis of estradiol-primed mice is attenuated by knocking down expression of membrane progestin receptors in the midbrain. *Steroids, 81*, 17–25. https://doi.org/10.1016/j.steroids.2013.11.009

Frye, C.A., Walf, A.A., Rhodes, M.E., & Harney, J.P. (2004). Progesterone enhances motor, anxiolytic, analgesic, and antidepressive behavior of wild-type mice, but not those deficient in type 1 5 alpha-reductase. *Brain Research, 1004*(1–2), 116–124. https://doi.org/10.1016/j.brainres.2004.01.020

Furukawa, A., Miyatake, A., Ohnishi, T., & Ichikawa, Y. (1998). Steroidogenic acute regulatory protein (StAR) transcripts constitutively expressed in the adult rat central nervous system: Colocalization of StAR, cytochrome P-450SCC (CYP XIA1), and 3beta-hydroxysteroid dehydrogenase in the rat brain. *Journal of Neurochemistry, 71*(6), 2231–2238.

Gangestad, S.W., & Grebe, N.M. (2017). Hormonal systems, human social bonding, and affiliation. *Hormones and Behavior, 91*, 122–135. https://doi.org/10.1016/j.yhbeh.2016.08.005

Georgescu, M., & Pfaus, J.G. (2006a). Role of glutamate receptors in the ventromedial hypothalamus in the regulation of female rat sexual behaviors I. Behavioral effects of glutamate and its selective receptor agonists AMPA, NMDA and kainate. *Pharmacology, Biochemistry, and Behavior, 83*(2), 322–332. https://doi.org/10.1016/j.pbb.2006.02.016

Georgescu, M., & Pfaus, J.G. (2006b). Role of glutamate receptors in the ventromedial hypothalamus in the regulation of female rat sexual behaviors. II. Behavioral effects of selective glutamate receptor antagonists AP-5, CNQX, and DNQX. *Pharmacology, Biochemistry, and Behavior, 83*(2), 333–341. https://doi.org/10.1016/j.pbb.2006.02.019

Glaser, J.H., Etgen, A.M., & Barfield, R.J. (1985). Intrahypothalamic effects of progestin agonists on estrous behavior and progestin receptor binding. *Physiology & Behavior, 34*(6), 871–877.

Gonzalez, C.L.R., Mills, K.J., Genee, I., Li, F., Piquette, N., Rosen, N., & Gibb, R. (2014). Getting the right grasp on executive function. *Frontiers in Psychology, 5*. https://doi.org/10.3389/fpsyg.2014.00285

Gunn, B.G., Cunningham, L., Mitchell, S.G., Swinny, J.D., Lambert, J.J., & Belelli, D. (2015). GABAA receptor-acting neurosteroids: A role in the development and regulation of the stress response. *Frontiers in Neuroendocrinology, 36*, 28–48. https://doi.org/10.1016/j.yfrne.2014.06.001

Hahn-Holbrook, J. (2018). Breastfeeding, pregnancy, and hormones. In Schultheiss, O. C., & Mehta, P. H. (Eds.). (in press). *Routledge international handbook of social neuroendocrinology*. Abingdon, UK: Routledge.

Hardy, D.F., & Debold, J.F. (1971). Effects of mounts without intromission upon the behavior of female rats during the onset of estrogen-induced heat. *Physiology & Behavior, 7*(4), 643–645.

Harlan, R.E., Shivers, B.D., & Pfaff, D.W. (1984). Lordosis as a sexually dimorphic neural function. *Progress in Brain Research, 61*, 239–255. https://doi.org/10.1016/S0079-6123(08)64439-8

Harmsen, S., Meijerman, I., Beijnen, J.H., & Schellens, J.H.M. (2007). The role of nuclear receptors in pharmacokinetic drug-drug interactions in oncology. *Cancer Treatment Reviews, 33*(4), 369–380. https://doi.org/10.1016/j.ctrv.2007.02.003

Hirst, J.J., Kelleher, M.A., Walker, D.W., & Palliser, H.K. (2014). Neuroactive steroids in pregnancy: Key regulatory and protective roles in the foetal brain. *The Journal of Steroid Biochemistry and Molecular Biology, 139*, 144–153. https://doi.org/10.1016/j.jsbmb.2013.04.002

Hirst, J.J., Palliser, H.K., Yates, D.M., Yawno, T., & Walker, D.W. (2008). Neurosteroids in the fetus and neonate: Potential protective role in compromised pregnancies. *Neurochemistry International, 52*(4), 602–610. https://doi.org/10.1016/j.neuint.2007.07.018

Ho, S.S., Konrath, S., Brown, S., & Swain, J.E. (2014). Empathy and stress related neural responses in maternal decision making. *Frontiers in Neuroscience, 8*. https://doi.org/10.3389/fnins.2014.00152

Hodges, J.K., Heistermann, M., Beard, A., & van Aarde, R.J. (1997). Concentrations of progesterone and the 5 alpha-reduced progestins, 5 alpha-pregnane-3,20-dione and 3 alpha-hydroxy-5 alpha-pregnan-20-one, in luteal tissue and circulating blood and their relationship to luteal function in the African elephant, Loxodonta africana. *Biology of Reproduction, 56*(3), 640–646.

Hoffman, C.S., Westin, T.M., Miner, H.M., Johnson, P.L., Summers, C.H., & Renner, K.J. (2002). GABAergic drugs alter hypothalamic serotonin release and lordosis in estrogen-primed rats. *Brain Research, 946*(1), 96–103.

Johnson, Z.V., & Young, L.J. (2017). Oxytocin and vasopressin neural networks: Implications for social behavioral diversity and translational neuroscience. *Neuroscience and Biobehavioral Reviews, 76*(Pt A), 87–98. https://doi.org/10.1016/j.neubiorev.2017.01.034

Juraska, J.M., & Willing, J. (2017). Pubertal onset as a critical transition for neural development and cognition. *Brain Research, 1654*(Pt B), 87–94. https://doi.org/10.1016/j.brainres.2016.04.012

Keating, P. (2017, July 17). The concussion gap. *ESPN Magazine*.

Kehoe, P., Mallinson, K., McCormick, C.M., & Frye, C.A. (2000). Central allopregnanolone is increased in rat pups in response to repeated, short episodes of neonatal isolation. *Developmental Brain Research, 124*(1), 133–136. https://doi.org/10.1016/S0165-3806(00)00106-1

Kellogg, C.K., & Frye, C.A. (1999). Endogenous levels of 5 alpha-reduced progestins and androgens in fetal vs. adult rat brains. *Developmental Brain Research, 115*(1), 17–24. https://doi.org/10.1016/S0165-3806(99)00041-3

King, S.R., Ginsberg, S.D., Ishii, T., Smith, R.G., Parker, K.L., & Lamb, D.J. (2004). The steroidogenic acute regulatory protein is expressed in steroidogenic cells of the day-old brain. *Endocrinology, 145*(10), 4775–4780. https://doi.org/10.1210/en.2003-1740

Kinsley, C.H., Bardi, M., Karelina, K., Rima, B., Christon, L., Friedenberg, J., & Griffin, G. (2008). Motherhood induces and maintains behavioral and neural plasticity across the lifespan in the rat. *Archives of Sexual Behavior, 37*(1), 43–56. https://doi.org/10.1007/s10508-007-9277-x

Kinsley, C.H., & Lambert, K.G. (2008). Reproduction-induced neuroplasticity: Natural behavioural and neuronal alterations associated with the production and care of offspring. *Journal of Neuroendocrinology*, *20*(4), 515–525. https://doi.org/10.1111/j.1365-2826.2008.01667.x

Kinsley, C.H., Madonia, L., Gifford, G.W., Tureski, K., Griffin, G.R., Lowry, C., . . . Lambert, K.G. (1999). Motherhood improves learning and memory. *Nature*, *402*(6758), 137–138. https://doi.org/10.1038/45957

Kliewer, S.A., Goodwin, B., & Willson, T.M. (2002). The nuclear pregnane X receptor: A key regulator of xenobiotic metabolism. *Endocrine Reviews*, *23*(5), 687–702. https://doi.org/10.1210/er.2001-0038

Koebele, S.V., & Bimonte-Nelson, H.A. (2017). The endocrine-brain-aging triad where many paths meet: Female reproductive hormone changes at midlife and their influence on circuits important for learning and memory. *Experimental Gerontology*, *94*, 14–23. https://doi.org/10.1016/j.exger.2016.12.011

Koonce, C.J., & Frye, C.A. (2013). Progesterone facilitates exploration, affective and social behaviors among wildtype, but not 5α-reductase Type 1 mutant, mice. *Behavioural Brain Research*, *253*, 232–239. https://doi.org/10.1016/j.bbr.2013.07.025

Koonce, C.J., Walf, A.A., & Frye, C.A. (2012). Type 1 5α-reductase may be required for estrous cycle changes in affective behaviors of female mice. *Behavioural Brain Research*, *226*(2), 376–380. https://doi.org/10.1016/j.bbr.2011.09.028

Laconi, M.R., Casteller, G., Gargiulo, P.A., Bregonzio, C., & Cabrera, R.J. (2001). The anxiolytic effect of allopregnanolone is associated with gonadal hormonal status in female rats. *European Journal of Pharmacology*, *417*(1–2), 111–116.

Lamba, V. (2004). PXR (NR1I2): Splice variants in human tissues, including brain, and identification of neurosteroids and nicotine as PXR activators. *Toxicology and Applied Pharmacology*, *199*(3), 251–265. https://doi.org/10.1016/j.taap.2003.12.027

Li, X., Bertics, P.J., & Karavolas, H.J. (1997). Regional distribution of cytosolic and particulate 5alpha-dihydroprogesterone 3alpha-hydroxysteroid oxidoreductases in female rat brain. *The Journal of Steroid Biochemistry and Molecular Biology*, *60*(5–6), 311–318.

Liu, B., & Arbogast, L.A. (2009). Gene expression profiles of intracellular and membrane progesterone receptor isoforms in the mediobasal hypothalamus during pro-oestrus. *Journal of Neuroendocrinology*, *21*(12), 993–1000. https://doi.org/10.1111/j.1365-2826.2009.01920.x

Llidó, A., Mòdol, L., Darbra, S., & Pallarès, M. (2013). Interaction between neonatal allopregnanolone administration and early maternal separation: Effects on adolescent and adult behaviors in male rat. *Hormones and Behavior*, *63*(4), 577–585. https://doi.org/10.1016/j.yhbeh.2013.02.002

Lovick, T.A. (2012). Estrous cycle and stress: Influence of progesterone on the female brain. *Brazilian Journal of Medical and Biological Research = Revista Brasileira De Pesquisas Medicas E Biologicas*, *45*(4), 314–320.

Ma, X., Idle, J.R., & Gonzalez, F.J. (2008). The pregnane X receptor: From bench to bedside. *Expert Opinion on Drug Metabolism & Toxicology*, *4*(7), 895–908. https://doi.org/10.1517/17425255.4.7.895

Macbeth, A.H., & Luine, V.N. (2010). Changes in anxiety and cognition due to reproductive experience: A review of data from rodent and human mothers. *Neuroscience and Biobehavioral Reviews*, *34*(3), 452–467. https://doi.org/10.1016/j.neubiorev.2009.08.011

MacLusky, N.J., & McEwen, B.S. (1980). Progestin receptors in rat brain: Distribution and properties of cytoplasmic progestin-binding sites. *Endocrinology*, *106*(1), 192–202. https://doi.org/10.1210/endo-106-1-192

Mani, S.K., Allen, J.M., Lydon, J.P., Mulac-Jericevic, B., Blaustein, J.D., DeMayo, F.J., . . . O'Malley, B.W. (1996). Dopamine requires the unoccupied progesterone receptor to induce sexual behavior in mice. *Molecular Endocrinology (Baltimore, MD)*, *10*(12), 1728–1737. https://doi.org/10.1210/mend.10.12.8961281

Mani, S.K., Blaustein, J.D., Allen, J.M., Law, S.W., O'Malley, B.W., & Clark, J.H. (1994). Inhibition of rat sexual behavior by antisense oligonucleotides to the progesterone receptor. *Endocrinology*, *135*(4), 1409–1414. https://doi.org/10.1210/endo.135.4.7925102

Mann, M.A., Konen, C., & Svare, B. (1984). The role of progesterone in pregnancy-induced aggression in mice. *Hormones and Behavior*, *18*(2), 140–160. https://doi.org/10.1016/0018-506X(84)90039-4

Marini, S., Nannelli, A., Sodini, D., Dragoni, S., Valoti, M., Longo, V., & Gervasi, P.G. (2007). Expression, microsomal and mitochondrial activities of cytochrome P450 enzymes in brain regions from control and phenobarbital-treated rabbits. *Life Sciences*, *80*(10), 910–917. https://doi.org/10.1016/j.lfs.2006.11.022

Marlin, B.J., & Froemke, R.C. (2017). Oxytocin modulation of neural circuits for social behavior. *Developmental Neurobiology*, *77*(2), 169–189. https://doi.org/10.1002/dneu.22452

McCormick, C.M., Kehoe, P., Mallinson, K., Cecchi, L., & Frye, C.A. (2002). Neonatal isolation alters stress hormone and mesolimbic dopamine release in juvenile rats. *Pharmacology Biochemistry and Behavior*, *73*(1), 77–85. https://doi.org/10.1016/S0091-3057(02)00758-X

McFarlane, H.G., Kusek, G.K., Yang, M., Phoenix, J.L., Bolivar, V.J., & Crawley, J.N. (2008). Autism-like behavioral phenotypes in BTBR T+tf/J mice. *Genes, Brain, and Behavior*, *7*(2), 152–163. https://doi.org/10.1111/j.1601-183X.2007.00330.x

Meerts, S.H., Schairer, R.S., Farry-Thorn, M.E., Johnson, E.G., & Strnad, H.K. (2014). Previous sexual experience alters the display of paced mating behavior in female rats. *Hormones and Behavior*, *65*(5), 497–504. https://doi.org/10.1016/j.yhbeh.2013.12.015

Mellon, S.H. (1994). Neurosteroids: Biochemistry, modes of action, and clinical relevance. *Journal of Clinical Endocrinology and Metabolism*, *78*(5), 1003–1008. https://doi.org/10.1210/jc.78.5.1003

Mellon, S.H., & Deschepper, C.F. (1993). Neurosteroid biosynthesis: Genes for adrenal steroidogenic enzymes are expressed in the brain. *Brain Research*, *629*(2), 283–292. https://doi.org/10.1016/0006-8993(93)91332-M

Mellon, S.H., Gong, W., & Schonemann, M.D. (2008). Endogenous and synthetic neurosteroids in treatment of Niemann-Pick type C disease. *Brain Research Reviews*, *57*(2), 410–420. https://doi.org/10.1016/j.brainresrev.2007.05.012

Mensah-Nyagan, A.G., Do-Régo, J.L., Beaujean, D., Luu-The, V., Pelletier, G., & Vaudry, H. (2001). Regulation of neurosteroid biosynthesis in the frog diencephalon by GABA and endozepines. *Hormones and Behavior*, *40*(2), 218–225. https://doi.org/10.1006/hbeh.2001.1689

Miryala, C.S.J., Hassell, J., Adams, S., Hiegel, C., Uzor, N., & Uphouse, L. (2011). Mechanisms responsible for progesterone's protection against lordosis-inhibiting effects of restraint II. Role of progesterone metabolites. *Hormones and Behavior*, *60*(2), 226–232. https://doi.org/10.1016/j.yhbeh.2011.05.005

Mòdol, L., Darbra, S., & Pallarès, M. (2011). Neurosteroids infusion into the CA1 hippocampal region on exploration, anxiety-like behaviour and aversive learning. *Behavioural Brain Research*, *222*(1), 223–229. https://doi.org/10.1016/j.bbr.2011.03.058

Morelen, D., Menke, R., Rosenblum, K. L., Beeghly, M., & Muzik, M. (2016). Understanding bidirectional mother-infant affective displays across contexts: Effects of maternal maltreatment history and postpartum depression and PTSD symptoms. *Psychopathology*, *49*, 305–314.

Nin, M.S., Martinez, L.A., Pibiri, F., Nelson, M., & Pinna, G. (2011). Neurosteroids reduce social isolation-induced behavioral deficits: A proposed link with neurosteroid-mediated upregulation of BDNF expression. *Frontiers in Endocrinology*, *2*, 73. https://doi.org/10.3389/fendo.2011.00073

Numan, M., & Woodside, B. (2010). Maternity: Neural mechanisms, motivational processes, and physiological adaptations. *Behavioral Neuroscience*, *124*(6), 715–741. https://doi.org/10.1037/a0021548

Nyuyki, K.D., Waldherr, M., Baeuml, S., & Neumann, I.D. (2011). Yes, I am ready now: Differential effects of paced versus unpaced mating on anxiety and central oxytocin release in female rats. *PLoS One*, *6*(8), e23599. https://doi.org/10.1371/journal.pone.0023599

Ogawa, S., Olazábal, U.E., Parhar, I.S., & Pfaff, D.W. (1994). Effects of intrahypothalamic administration of antisense DNA for progesterone receptor mRNA on reproductive behavior and progesterone receptor immunoreactivity in female rat. *The Journal of Neuroscience: The Official Journal of the Society for Neuroscience*, *14*(3 Pt 2), 1766–1774.

Olazábal, D.E., Pereira, M., Agrati, D., Ferreira, A., Fleming, A.S., González-Mariscal, G., . . . Uriarte, N. (2013). Flexibility and adaptation of the neural substrate that supports maternal behavior in mammals. *Neuroscience and Biobehavioral Reviews*, *37*(8), 1875–1892. https://doi.org/10.1016/j.neubiorev.2013.04.004

Olster, D.H., & Blaustein, J.D. (1989). Development of progesterone-facilitated lordosis in female guinea pigs: Relationship to neural estrogen and progestin receptors. *Brain Research*, *484*(1–2), 168–176.

Ott, M., Fricker, G., & Bauer, B. (2009). Pregnane X Receptor (PXR) regulates P-glycoprotein at the blood-brain barrier: Functional similarities between pig and human PXR. *Journal of Pharmacology and Experimental Therapeutics*, *329*(1), 141–149. https://doi.org/10.1124/jpet.108.149690

Oxford, J.K., Tiedtke, J.M., Ossmann, A., Özbe, D., & Schultheiss, O.C. (2017). Endocrine and aggressive responses to competition are moderated by contest outcome, gender, individual versus team competition, and implicit motives. *PLoS One*, *12*(7), e0181610. https://doi.org/10.1371/journal.pone.0181610

Paredes, R.G., & Alonso, A. (1997). Sexual behavior regulated (paced) by the female induces conditioned place preference. *Behavioral Neuroscience*, *111*(1), 123–128.

Paris, J.J., Brunton, P.J., Russell, J.A., & Frye, C.A. (2011). Immune stress in late pregnant rats decreases length of gestation and fecundity, and alters later cognitive and affective behaviour of surviving pre-adolescent offspring. *Stress*, *14*(6), 652–664. https://doi.org/10.3109/10253890.2011.628719

Paris, J.J., Brunton, P.J., Russell, J.A., Walf, A.A., & Frye, C.A. (2011). Inhibition of 5α-reductase activity in late pregnancy decreases gestational length and fecundity and impairs object memory and central progestogen Milieu of Juvenile rat offspring: 5α-reductase and gestational outcome. *Journal of Neuroendocrinology*, *23*(11), 1079–1090. https://doi.org/10.1111/j.1365-2826.2011.02219.x

Paris, J.J., Franco, C., Sodano, R., Freidenberg, B., Gordis, E., Anderson, D.A., . . . Frye, C.A. (2010). Sex differences in salivary cortisol in response to acute stressors among healthy participants, in recreational or pathological gamblers, and in those with posttraumatic stress disorder. *Hormones and Behavior*, *57*(1), 35–45. https://doi.org/10.1016/j.yhbeh.2009.06.003

Paris, J.J., & Frye, C.A. (2008). Estrous cycle, pregnancy, and parity enhance performance of rats in object recognition or object placement tasks. *Reproduction*, *136*(1), 105–115. https://doi.org/10.1530/REP-07-0512

Paris, J.J., Walf, A.A., & Frye, C.A. (2011). II. Cognitive performance of middle-aged female rats is influenced by capacity to metabolize progesterone in the prefrontal cortex and hippocampus. *Brain Research*, *1379*, 149–163. https://doi.org/10.1016/j.brainres.2010.10.099

Patchev, V.K., & Almeida, O.F. (1996). Gonadal steroids exert facilitating and "buffering" effects on glucocorticoid-mediated transcriptional regulation of corticotropin-releasing hormone and corticosteroid receptor genes in rat brain. *The Journal of Neuroscience: The Official Journal of the Society for Neuroscience*, *16*(21), 7077–7084.

Paul, S.M., & Purdy, R.H. (1992). Neuroactive steroids. *FASEB Journal: Official Publication of the Federation of American Societies for Experimental Biology*, *6*(6), 2311–2322.

Pawluski, J.L., & Galea, L. A.M. (2007). Reproductive experience alters hippocampal neurogenesis during the postpartum period in the dam. *Neuroscience*, *149*(1), 53–67. https://doi.org/10.1016/j.neuroscience.2007.07.031

Pawluski, J.L., Lambert, K.G., & Kinsley, C.H. (2016). Neuroplasticity in the maternal hippocampus: Relation to cognition and effects of repeated stress. *Hormones and Behavior*, *77*, 86–97. https://doi.org/10.1016/j.yhbeh.2015.06.004

Pawluski, J.L., Lonstein, J.S., & Fleming, A.S. (2017). The neurobiology of postpartum anxiety and depression. *Trends in Neurosciences*, *40*(2), 106–120. https://doi.org/10.1016/j.tins.2016.11.009

Piekarski, D.J., Boivin, J.R., & Wilbrecht, L. (2017). Ovarian hormones organize the maturation of inhibitory neurotransmission in the frontal cortex at puberty onset in female mice. *Current Biology: CB*, *27*(12), 1735–1745.e3. https://doi.org/10.1016/j.cub.2017.05.027

Pisu, M.G., Boero, G., Biggio, F., Garau, A., Corda, D., Congiu, M., . . . Serra, M. (2017). Juvenile social isolation affects maternal care in rats: Involvement of allopregnanolone. *Psychopharmacology*. https://doi.org/10.1007/s00213-017-4661-2

Pleim, E.T., Baumann, J., & Barfield, R.J. (1991). A contributory role for midbrain progesterone in the facilitation of female sexual behavior in rats. *Hormones and Behavior*, *25*(1), 19–28.

Pluchino, N., Russo, M., & Genazzani, A.R. (2016). The fetal brain: Role of progesterone and allopregnanolone. *Hormone Molecular Biology and Clinical Investigation*, *27*(1), 29–34X. https://doi.org/10.1515/hmbci-2016-0020

Qiu, Z.-K., Li, M-S., He, J-L., Liu, X., Zhang, G-H., Lai, S., . . . Chen, J-S. (2015). Translocator protein mediates the anxiolytic and antidepressant effects of midazolam. *Pharmacology, Biochemistry, and Behavior*, *139*(Pt A), 77–83. https://doi.org/10.1016/j.pbb.2015.10.005

Quadros, P.S., Goldstein, A.Y.N., De Vries, G.J., & Wagner, C.K. (2002). Regulation of sex differences in progesterone receptor expression in the medial preoptic nucleus of postnatal rats. *Journal of Neuroendocrinology*, *14*(10), 761–767.

Reblin, M., & Uchino, B.N. (2008). Social and emotional support and its implication for health. *Current Opinion in Psychiatry*, *21*(2), 201–205. https://doi.org/10.1097/YCO.0b013e3282f3ad89

Rhodes, M.E., & Frye, C.A. (2001). Inhibiting progesterone metabolism in the hippocampus of rats in behavioral estrus decreases anxiolytic behaviors and enhances exploratory and antinociceptive behaviors. *Cognitive, Affective & Behavioral Neuroscience*, *1*(3), 287–296.

Rilling, J.K. (2013). The neural and hormonal bases of human parental care. *Neuropsychologia*, *51*(4), 731–747. https://doi.org/10.1016/j.neuropsychologia.2012.12.017

Rilling, J.K., & Young, L.J. (2014). The biology of mammalian parenting and its effect on offspring social development. *Science (New York, N.Y.)*, *345*(6198), 771–776. https://doi.org/10.1126/science.1252723

Scattoni, M.L., Ricceri, L., & Crawley, J.N. (2011). Unusual repertoire of vocalizations in adult BTBR T+tf/J mice during three types of social encounters. *Genes, Brain, and Behavior, 10*(1), 44–56. https://doi.org/10.1111/j.1601-183X.2010.00623.x

Schiller, C.E., Meltzer-Brody, S., & Rubinow, D.R. (2015). The role of reproductive hormones in postpartum depression. *CNS Spectrums, 20*(1), 48–59. https://doi.org/10.1017/S1092852914000480

Schiller, C.E., Schmidt, P.J., & Rubinow, D.R. (2014). Allopregnanolone as a mediator of affective switching in reproductive mood disorders. *Psychopharmacology, 231*(17), 3557–3567. https://doi.org/10.1007/s00213-014-3599-x

Schultheiss, O.C., Dargel, A., & Rohde, W. (2003). Implicit motives and gonadal steroid hormones: Effects of menstrual cycle phase, oral contraceptive use, and relationship status. *Hormones and Behavior, 43*(2), 293–301.

Schultheiss, O.C., Wirth, M.M., & Stanton, S.J. (2004). Effects of affiliation and power motivation arousal on salivary progesterone and testosterone. *Hormones and Behavior, 46*(5), 592–599. https://doi.org/10.1016/j.yhbeh.2004.07.005

Schulz, K. (2018). The role of steroid hormones in development of brain & behavior: Insights from an animal model. In Schultheiss, O. C., & Mehta, P. H. (Eds.). (in press). *Routledge international handbook of social neuroendocrinology.* Abingdon, UK: Routledge.

Sexton, M.B., Hamilton, L., McGinnis, E.W., Rosenblum, K.L., & Muzik, M. (2015). The roles of resilience and childhood trauma history: Main and moderating effects on postpartum maternal mental health and functioning. *Journal of Affective Disorders, 174*, 562–568. https://doi.org/10.1016/j.jad.2014.12.036

Smith, S.S. (2013). The influence of stress at puberty on mood and learning: Role of the $\alpha 4\beta\delta$ GABAA receptor. *Neuroscience, 249*, 192–213. https://doi.org/10.1016/j.neuroscience.2012.09.065

Smith, S.S., Gong, Q.H., Li, X., Moran, M.H., Bitran, D., Frye, C.A., & Hsu, F.C. (1998). Withdrawal from 3alpha-OH-5alpha-pregnan-20-one using a pseudopregnancy model alters the kinetics of hippocampal GABAA-gated current and increases the GABAA receptor alpha4 subunit in association with increased anxiety. *The Journal of Neuroscience: The Official Journal of the Society for Neuroscience, 18*(14), 5275–5284.

Svare, B. (1979). Steroidal influences on pup-killing behavior in mice. *Hormones and Behavior, 13*(2), 153–164.

Svare, B., Miele, J., & Kinsley, C. (1986). Mice: Progesterone stimulates aggression in pregnancy-terminated females. *Hormones and Behavior, 20*(2), 194–200.

Taylor, S.E., Klein, L.C., Lewis, B.P., Gruenewald, T.L., Gurung, R.A., & Updegraff, J.A. (2000). Biobehavioral responses to stress in females: Tend-and-befriend, not fight-or-flight. *Psychological Review, 107*(3), 411–429.

Thomas, P. (2012). Rapid steroid hormone actions initiated at the cell surface and the receptors that mediate them with an emphasis on recent progress in fish models. *General and Comparative Endocrinology, 175*(3), 367–383. https://doi.org/10.1016/j.ygcen.2011.11.032

Toufexis, D.J., Davis, C., Hammond, A., & Davis, M. (2004). Progesterone attenuates corticotropin-releasing factor-enhanced but not fear-potentiated startle via the activity of its neuroactive metabolite, allopregnanolone. *The Journal of Neuroscience: The Official Journal of the Society for Neuroscience, 24*(45), 10280–10287. https://doi.org/10.1523/JNEUROSCI.1386-04.2004

Tuscher, J.J., Fortress, A.M., Kim, J., & Frick, K.M. (2015). Regulation of object recognition and object placement by ovarian sex steroid hormones. *Behavioural Brain Research, 285*, 140–157. https://doi.org/10.1016/j.bbr.2014.08.001

Uphouse, L., Selvamani, A., Lincoln, C., Morales, L., & Comeaux, D. (2005). Mild restraint reduces the time hormonally primed rats spend with sexually active males. *Behavioural Brain Research, 157*(2), 343–350. https://doi.org/10.1016/j.bbr.2004.08.001

Walf, A.A., & Frye, C.A. (2003). Anti-nociception following exposure to trimethylthiazoline, peripheral or intra-amygdala estrogen and/or progesterone. *Behavioural Brain Research, 144*(1–2), 77–85.

Walf, A.A., & Frye, C.A. (2009). Using the elevated plus maze as a bioassay to assess the effects of naturally occurring and exogenously administered compounds to influence anxiety-related behaviors of mice. In *Mood and anxiety related phenotypes in mice* (pp. 225–246). Totowa, NJ: Humana Press. https://doi.org/10.1007/978-1-60761-303-9_12

Walf, A.A., Koonce, C.J., & Frye, C.A. (2015). Progestogens' effects and mechanisms for object recognition memory across the lifespan. *Behavioural Brain Research, 294*, 50–61. https://doi.org/10.1016/j.bbr.2015.07.057

Walf, A.A., Paris, J.J., Llaneza, D.C., & Frye, C.A. (2011). I. Levels of 5α-reduced progesterone metabolite in the midbrain account for variability in reproductive behavior of middle-aged female rats. *Brain Research, 1379*, 137–148. https://doi.org/10.1016/j.brainres.2010.11.004

Walf, A.A., Rhodes, M.E., & Frye, C.A. (2006). Ovarian steroids enhance object recognition in naturally cycling and ovariectomized, hormone-primed rats. *Neurobiology of Learning and Memory, 86*(1), 35–46. https://doi.org/10.1016/j.nlm.2006.01.004

Warembourg, M. (1978). Radioautographic study of the rat brain, uterus and vagina after [3H]R-5020 injection. *Molecular and Cellular Endocrinology, 12*(1), 67–79.

Weaver, I.C.G., Meaney, M.J., & Szyf, M. (2006). Maternal care effects on the hippocampal transcriptome and anxiety-mediated behaviors in the offspring that are reversible in adulthood. *Proceedings of the National Academy of Sciences of the United States of America, 103*(9), 3480–3485. https://doi.org/10.1073/pnas.0507526103

Weinstock, M. (2001). Effects of maternal stress on development and behaviour in rat offspring. *Stress (Amsterdam, Netherlands), 4*(3), 157–167.

Westcott, K.T., Hirst, J.J., Ciurej, I., Walker, D.W., & Wlodek, M.E. (2008). Brain allopregnanolone in the fetal and postnatal rat in response to uteroplacental insufficiency. *Neuroendocrinology, 88*(4), 287–292. https://doi.org/10.1159/000139771

Wirth, M.M. (2011). Beyond the HPA axis: Progesterone-derived neuroactive steroids in human stress and emotion. *Frontiers in Endocrinology, 2.* https://doi.org/10.3389/fendo.2011.00019

Wirth, M.M., & Schultheiss, O.C. (2006). Effects of affiliation arousal (hope of closeness) and affiliation stress (fear of rejection) on progesterone and cortisol. *Hormones and Behavior, 50*(5), 786–795. https://doi.org/10.1016/j.yhbeh.2006.08.003

Xu, D-X. (2005). Perinatal lipopolysaccharide exposure downregulates pregnane X receptor and Cyp3a11 expression in fetal mouse liver. *Toxicological Sciences, 87*(1), 38–45. https://doi.org/10.1093/toxsci/kfi239

Yawno, T., Yan, E.B., Walker, D.W., & Hirst, J.J. (2007). Inhibition of neurosteroid synthesis increases asphyxia-induced brain injury in the late gestation fetal sheep. *Neuroscience, 146*(4), 1726–1733. https://doi.org/10.1016/j.neuroscience.2007.03.023

Zhang, B., Xie, W., & Krasowski, M.D. (2008). PXR: A xenobiotic receptor of diverse function implicated in pharmacogenetics. *Pharmacogenomics, 9*(11), 1695–1709. https://doi.org/10.2217/14622416.9.11.1695

Zimmerberg, B., Brunelli, S.A., Fluty, A.J., & Frye, C.A. (2005). Differences in affective behaviors and hippocampal allopregnanolone levels in adult rats of lines selectively bred for infantile vocalizations. *Behavioural Brain Research, 159*(2), 301–311. https://doi.org/10.1016/j.bbr.2004.11.009

Zimmerberg, B., & Kajunski, E.W. (2004). Sexually dimorphic effects of postnatal allopregnanolone on the development of anxiety behavior after early deprivation. *Pharmacology, Biochemistry, and Behavior, 78*(3), 465–471. https://doi.org/10.1016/j.pbb.2004.03.021

11

THE NEUROENDOCRINOLOGICAL BASIS OF HUMAN AFFILIATION

How oxytocin coordinates affiliation-related cognition and behavior via changing underlying brain activity

Bastian Schiller and Markus Heinrichs

Chapter overview

Humans live in complex social environments in which they survive and thrive by connecting with others via strong, often selective and lasting affiliative bonds (Baumeister & Leary, 1995; Eisenberger & Cole, 2012; House, Landis, & Umberson, 1988). To both create and maintain these social bonds, evolution has provided us with intricately engineered internal, neuroendocrinological communication systems that orchestrate a set of brain systems to coordinate affiliation-related cognition, motivation, and behavior (Donaldson & Young, 2008; Heinrichs, von Dawans, & Domes, 2009; McCall & Singer, 2012; Meyer-Lindenberg, Domes, Kirsch, & Heinrichs, 2011). The aim of this chapter is to provide an overview of the rich and growing field of research demonstrating the key role of the neuropeptide oxytocin in human affiliation. After briefly summarizing animal research on the neuroendocrinology of affiliation, we will focus on experimental studies in humans using placebo-controlled intranasal administration to manipulate the availability of oxytocin in the central nervous system, allowing causal inferences to be drawn about the impact of this neuropeptide on social affiliation (Born et al., 2002; Quintana, Alvares, Hickie, & Guastella, 2015; Quintana et al., 2015). We will further focus on studies investigating healthy participants and refer the reader to the many excellent reviews summarizing translational approaches to administering oxytocin for clinical purposes (Ma, Shamay-Tsoory, Han, & Zink, 2016; Meyer-Lindenberg et al., 2011; Yamasue & Domes, 2017). Finally, as other chapters in this handbook focus on the neuroendocrinology of pair bonding, reproduction, and parenting, and oxytocin from an individual difference and moderator perspective, this chapter will allot extra space to the research on the behavioral and neural mechanisms underlying affiliations among non-kin members (e.g., friends, group members), a social phenomenon of pivotal importance for survival and prosperity in human societies.

Animal research

Decades of animal research have shown that the neuropeptide oxytocin critically impacts affiliation-related processes (for comprehensive reviews, please see Carter, Grippo, Pournajafi-Nazarloo, Ruscio, & Porges, 2008; Donaldson & Young, 2008; Insel, 2010; McCall & Singer, 2012; van Anders, Goldey, & Kuo, 2011). In non-human mammals, oxytocin receptors are found in the various brain regions associated with the central nervous control of affiliation-relevant social cognition and behavior including parental care, pair bonding, and social memory (Heinrichs et al., 2009; Landgraf & Neumann, 2004). Evidence for oxytocin's causal role in affiliation-related behavior comes from studies that experimentally raised or lowered central oxytocin signaling either pharmacologically (via centrally infusing oxytocin or its antagonist) or genetically (via blocking oxytocin receptor activation). For example, increasing oxytocin signaling stimulated maternal behavior in virgin female rats and, conversely, decreasing oxytocin signaling reduced such behavior (Fahrbach, Morrell, & Pfaff, 1985; Pedersen, Ascher, Monroe, & Prange, 1982); increasing oxytocin signaling in monogamous prairie voles facilitated partner-preference formation and, conversely, decreasing oxytocin signaling blocked such behavior (Lim & Young, 2006; Carter, DeVries, & Getz, 1995); and genetically blocking oxytocin signaling in mice hampered social memory as evident in reduced recognition of previously encountered conspecifics (Young & Wang, 2004). In sum, research on animal neuroendocrinology has shown that oxytocin facilitates affiliative behavior in animals. It thereby provides both the roots and inspirations for research on the neuroendocrinological basis of affiliation in humans.

Human research

In humans, causal inferences about the impact of neuropeptides on social affiliation have been drawn from studies using placebo-controlled intranasal administration to modulate oxytocin availability in the central nervous system of healthy participants (for the original demonstration of the utility of the intranasal route of peptide administration, see Born et al., 2002; for evidence of heightened oxytocin levels in cerebrospinal fluid following intranasal oxytocin administration, see Striepens et al., 2013; for evidence that the effects of intranasal administration of oxytocin occur via direct intranasal delivery pathways rather than across the blood brain barrier via systematically circulating oxytocin or via stimulation of peripheral oxytocin receptors, see Quintana, Alvares et al., 2015; Quintana et al., 2015). Below, we will review the findings from these studies, demonstrating that oxytocin is a key modulator of many socio-cognitive processes and social behaviors contributing to human affiliation.

Behavioral studies

The heterogeneity of the behavioral paradigms used to study oxytocin's effects on human social cognition and behavior necessitates interpreting their findings cautiously with regard to specific changes in the socio-cognitive processes that seem to be relevant when affiliating with others. Findings from studies performed so far, however, are consistent with the general view that oxytocin reduces avoidance behavior and increases approach behavior by lowering social stress and social anxiety, by improving the decoding, encoding, and retrieving of socio-emotional cues, and by increasing the willingness to take social risks. A few studies have also provided direct evidence for oxytocin's involvement in affiliation-related behaviors by showing that intranasal oxytocin administration modulates attachment security, human parenting, sexual intercourse, and inter-group interactions (for reviews, please see De Dreu & Kret, 2016;

Heinrichs et al., 2009; Ma et al., 2016; McCall & Singer, 2012; Meyer-Lindenberg et al., 2011; Rilling & Young, 2014).

First, several studies have shown that oxytocin *lowers social stress and social anxiety*. In this regard, a seminal study suggested oxytocin as a potential biological mechanism underlying the stress-reducing effects of social support. Male participants who received both social support by their best friend and intranasal oxytocin administration exhibited the lowest cortisol responses and subjectively reported levels of anxiety during the exposure to psychosocial stress, whereas those who received no social support and placebo exhibited the highest cortisol response (Heinrichs, Baumgartner, Kirschbaum, & Ehlert, 2003). Another trial demonstrated that oxytocin might also lower stress in interaction between couples: compared to placebo, oxytocin administration both increased positive communication behavior during a couple's conflict in male and female participants and decreased stress-related cortisol reactivity (Ditzen et al., 2008). In sum, these findings suggest that oxytocin contributes to affiliative behavior among friends and romantic partners by facilitating the effects of social support by close friends and by buffering stress responses in conflict-laden interactions between couples.

Second, a group of studies has shown that oxytocin *improves the decoding, encoding, and retrieving of socio-emotional cues*. With regard to the decoding of socio-emotional cues, oxytocin improved the ability to infer the mental state of another individual from the eyes (Domes, Heinrichs, Michel, Berger, & Herpertz, 2007; task "Reading the Mind in the Eyes" from Baron-Cohen et al., 2001) and to correctly identify emotional states felt by others (operationalized by time-series correlations between a participant's ratings of a target's affect as displayed in videos and the target's own ratings of his or her affect, see Bartz et al., 2010). Two meta-analyses concluded that oxytocin enhances emotion recognition of faces overall (Shahrestani, Kemp, & Guastella, 2013; van IJzendoorn & Bakermans-Kranenburg, 2012), with apparently stronger effects for the recognition of happy and fearful faces (Shahrestani et al., 2013). With regard to the encoding and retrieving of socio-emotional cues, oxytocin, administered post-learning, improved the immediate and delayed recognition of face identities (Savaskan, Ehrhardt, Schulz, Walter, & Schächinger, 2008), and when administered pre-learning, specifically improved the recognition of faces but not that of nonsocial stimuli (Rimmele, Hediger, Heinrichs, & Klaver, 2009). These beneficial effects of oxytocin on the processing of socio-emotional cues may be due to specifically lengthened gazing time on the eye region (Guastella, Mitchell, & Dadds, 2008) and, more generally, due to the increased allocation of attention to social stimuli (Shamay-Tsoory & Abu-Akel, 2016). Whatever the exact mechanisms may be, by improving the processing of socio-emotional cues and thereby also the understanding of another's intentions and emotions, oxytocin opens doors for smoothing the social interactions that provide the basis for lasting social affiliations.

A third line of studies has demonstrated that oxytocin *increases the willingness to take social risks with regard to trusting behavior*. In a seminal pioneer study, oxytocin administration increased trusting behavior toward an anonymous interaction partner in a social decision-making paradigm involving real financial consequences, but not in a nonsocial control condition (Kosfeld, Heinrichs, Zak, Fischbacher, & Fehr, 2005). Several subsequent studies confirmed that oxytocin increases trust in social interactions (Mikolajczak, Gross et al., 2010; Mikolajczak, Pinon, Lane, de Timary, & Luminet, 2010; Theodoridou, Rowe, Penton-Voak, & Rogers, 2009), whereas other studies suggested that oxytocin's effects on trust depend on the social relationship with the interaction partner (Van IJzendoorn & Bakermans-Kranenburg, 2012). In light of some inconsistent findings regarding the effects of oxytocin on trust in studies that used highly controlled but relatively artificial designs (Nave, Camerer, & McCullough, 2015), future research might benefit from studying these effects in more natural social settings, such as in interactions including face stimuli of interaction partners or in actual face-to-face interactions. As trusting each other is a prerequisite of healthy relationships among friends, couples, and family members, such research holds the potential to provide important clues regarding oxytocin's key role in social affiliations.

Fourth, two studies reported that oxytocin is directly involved in the *experience of attachment quality*. A single dose of oxytocin administered intranasally increased the subjective experience of attachment security in male participants with an insecure attachment pattern (Buchheim et al., 2009). A recent study expanded this result by showing that two weeks of daily intranasal oxytocin treatment lowered attachment avoidance and improved the attachment quality experienced with friends, especially in participants with a general tendency for unsecure attachments (Bernaerts et al., 2017). As secure attachments are associated with lower stress reactivity and a better ability to interact socially (Ditzen et al., 2008), these findings again reveal the importance of oxytocin in social affiliation.

A fifth line of studies delivered evidence of oxytocin's key role in *human parenting behavior*. While intranasal administration oxytocin studies are rarely performed in mothers due to concerns about administering oxytocin to lactating mothers, administering oxytocin intranasally in fathers increased their stimulatory and exploratory play and their social engagement, and reduced their hostility during father-child interactions (Naber, van IJzendoorn, Deschamps, van Engeland, & Bakermans-Kranenburg, 2010; Weisman, Zagoory-Sharon, & Feldman, 2012). Thus, by potentially changing some of the socio-cognitive processes discussed above, higher central nervous system oxytocin levels seem to be associated with more sensitive fathering behavior.

Sixth, there is some, albeit inconclusive, evidence regarding the role of oxytocin in *human sexual behavior*. Intranasal oxytocin administration increased the experienced intensity of orgasm during sexual intercourse and subsequent contentment (Behnia et al., 2014), but it had no effect on self-reported appetitive, consummatory, and refractory sexual behavior during masturbation (Burri, Heinrichs, Schedlowski, & Kruger, 2008). There is thus initial evidence that oxytocin modulates human sexual behavior, a key ingredient of romantic relationships, but we obviously need more research here.

Seventh, and last, there are now several investigations pointing to oxytocin's modulatory role in *interactions among members of distinct social groups*. With regard to social cognition, oxytocin administration increased positive attitudes toward members of natural in-groups (De Dreu, Greer, van Kleef, Shalvi, & Handgraaf, 2011) and the conformity with judgments made by other in-group members, even if these were erroneous (Stallen, De Dreu, Shalvi, Smidts, & Sanfey, 2012). With regard to social behavior, oxytocin's effects have been mainly studied in interactions between members of experimentally created social groups ("minimal groups") and under conditions in which the participants could mutually affect their resources ("second party"). In these studies, oxytocin administration increased prosocial behavior toward minimal in-group members, whereas it had no effects on behavior toward minimal out-group members (for a review, see De Dreu & Kret, 2016). Members of minimal groups have never interacted before, and their group membership gains significance only during the experimental procedure. Thus, the above research indicates that oxytocin facilitates group-interested behavior among members of groups while they are forming and whose members' self-interests are interdependent. Future studies should investigate more deeply whether such findings also apply to behavior exhibited by third parties, whose resources are not affected by the behavior of other interactions partners and whose behavior is thus free of strategic considerations such as reciprocity or reputation (Fehr & Fischbacher, 2004; Schiller, Baumgartner, & Knoch, 2014). Initial evidence suggests that oxytocin's effects on inter-group behavior might differ between second- and third-party behavior (Daughters, Manstead, Ten Velden, & De Dreu, 2017). Even more important, oxytocin's effects on inter-group behavior should be studied in interactions between members of natural social groups, ensuring an ecologically authentic social setting. The first such research (Marsh et al., 2017) showed that oxytocin increases donation behavior toward disadvantaged refugees, an out-group with low status and lacking any common history of conflict with the participants, which presumably elicited empathic reactions in most participants that were reinforced by oxytocin. It is tempting to speculate whether this finding might also apply to behavior toward members of rival, natural out-groups with at least equal status and a history of previous intense and conflicting interactions (e.g., supporters of opposing political parties or sport teams; Baumgartner, Schiller, Rieskamp, Gianotti, & Knoch, 2014; Schiller et al., 2016). In sum, many studies suggest a modulatory role of oxytocin in inter-group interactions, however, its specific effects on behavior toward in- and out-group members, particularly in interactions among members of natural social groups, must still be illuminated.

Brain studies

Oxytocin's effects on social affiliation rely on its action as a neuromodulator and neurotransmitter in the brain (Heinrichs et al., 2009; Meyer-Lindenberg et al., 2011). Oxytocin is synthesized in magnocellular neurons in the paraventricular and supraoptic nuclei of the hypothalamus (Meyer-Lindenberg et al., 2011). From there, it is projected via axon transmission and dendritic release, resulting in both local action and diffusion through the brain to several brain regions rich in oxytocin receptors, such as the amygdala, hippocampus, striatum, suprachiasmatic nucleus, globus pallidus, insula, bed nucleus of the stria terminalis, and brainstem, thereby modulating neurotransmission in these areas (Gimpl & Fahrenholz, 2001; Meyer-Lindenberg et al., 2011; Paloyelis et al., 2016). Neuroscientific methods enable us to reveal neural activity in brain areas that potentially mediate oxytocin's effects on social affiliation. In the following, we will summarize findings from metabolic neuroimaging studies that in the spatial domain revealed important insights about oxytocin-induced changes in neural activity during social affiliation, as well as findings from electrophysiological studies which in the temporal domain have generated important insights about when oxytocin changes specific neurophysiological processes underlying social affiliation.

Oxytocin and metabolic neuroimaging studies

Metabolic neuroimaging studies have identified changes after intranasal oxytocin administration during the processing of social stimuli in various (sub)cortical regions, most prominently in the amygdala, striatum, insula, and prefrontal and temporal cortices (for reviews, please see Kanat, Heinrichs, & Domes, 2014; Ma, Shamay-Tsoory, Han, & Zink, 2016; Meyer-Lindenberg et al., 2011). For example, an initial fMRI study showed that oxytocin decreased amygdala reactivity to negative social cues and functional coupling of the amygdala with brainstem regions (Kirsch et al., 2005). Subsequent studies confirmed these findings by showing that oxytocin reduces amygdala activity in response to negative emotional expressions (fearful and angry faces: Domes et al., 2007; eyes of fearful faces: Kanat, Heinrichs, Mader, van Elst, & Domes, 2015; eyes of angry faces: Kanat, Heinrichs, Schwarzwald, & Domes, 2015), in response to social trust betrayal (Baumgartner, Heinrichs, Vonlanthen, Fischbacher, & Fehr, 2008), or in response to unreciprocated cooperation (Rilling et al., 2012). Other investigations have suggested a more complex scenario, with some showing that oxytocin enhances amygdala activity in response to fearful faces in women (Domes et al., 2010) and that, in men, oxytocin enhances amygdala activity in response to fearful faces in the basal nucleus and in response to happy faces in the corticomedial and lateral nucleus, but reduces amygdala activity in response to fearful faces in the corticomedial and lateral nucleus (Gamer, Zurowski, & Büchel, 2010). In sum, many studies have demonstrated that oxytocin reduces neural reactivity to negative social stimuli in regions in the "neural alarm system" (e.g., amygdala, but also anterior cingulate cortex and anterior insula; Ma et al., 2016). These anxiolytic effects of oxytocin may reduce social avoidance, thereby benefiting the creation and maintenance of social affiliations.

Another group of studies has shown that oxytocin increases neural reactivity to social stimuli in reward-related regions (e.g., ventral tegmental area, caudate), suggesting that it augments social motivation (Ma et al., 2016). For example, oxytocin administration increased reward-related activity in response to friendly faces presented as reward feedback stimuli in the social incentive delay task (Groppe et al., 2013), in response to reciprocated cooperation (Rilling et al., 2012), or in response to faces of the own partner (Scheele et al., 2013). Again, oxytocin's effects seem to be modulated by gender, with less clear evidence of increased reward-related activity after oxytocin administration in women (Domes et al., 2010). Overall, the oxytocin-induced increase in reward-related activity may represent possible biological mechanisms for oxytocin's role in attributing reward value to social stimuli, which in turn facilitates the initiation of social interactions and strengthens affiliations with others.

Still another set of studies showed that oxytocin boosts both neural reactivity to socially salient cues in general and connectivity within the saliency network (the salience network mainly includes dorsal anterior cingulate and anterior insula cortices and is thought to select specific stimuli for in-depth processing by focusing the "spotlight of attention", for details, see Uddin, 2017). For example, there is evidence that oxytocin increases activity in the ventral tegmental area to both friendly faces presented as reward feedback stimuli and to angry faces presented as punishment feedback stimuli in the social incentive delay task cues (Groppe et al., 2013), and that it increases functional connectivity between the amygdala and salience network (Hu et al., 2015). In sum, making social stimuli more salient (Shamay-Tsoory & Abu-Akel, 2016) might represent another mechanism through which oxytocin ensures that socially significant others are put in the neural-processing spotlight, which in turn provides the basis for affiliating with them.

Taken together, metabolic neuroimaging studies have demonstrated that oxytocin reduces activity in areas associated with the processing of negative emotions, and that it increases activity in areas associated with the processing of rewarding social stimuli and activity in areas associated with the allocation of attentional resources during social processing. These studies thus suggest three potential mechanisms through which oxytocin might indirectly facilitate the creation and maintenance of social affiliations with significant others. Future studies could address more directly the neural processes underlying oxytocin's effects on affiliating with friends and group members. For example, it would be very interesting to know whether the more prosocial behavior toward members of minimal in-groups after oxytocin administration is mediated by increased activity in areas involved in social cognition and mentalizing (e.g., dorsomedial prefrontal cortex, temporal parietal junction; Gallagher & Frith, 2003; van Overwalle, 2009), given that differential activation in those areas seems to contribute to the differential behavior toward in- and out-group members (Baumgartner, Gotte, Gugler, & Fehr, 2012).

Electrical neuroimaging studies

Electrical neuroimaging studies can complement findings from metabolic neuroimaging studies by generating knowledge on oxytocin's effects on the exact time course of neural activity and the specific neurophysiological processes occurring during social affiliation. Unfortunately, very few working groups have applied electrophysiology in combination with intranasal oxytocin administration so far. Inspired by early pioneering research (Fehm-Wolfsdorf, Bachholz, Born,

Voigt, & Fehm, 1988; Pietrowsky, Braun, Fehm, Pauschinger, & Born, 1991), recent event-related potential (ERP) studies have resumed investigating oxytocin's effects on electrophysiological processing. In general, these studies have provided evidence that oxytocin modulates both early (< 300ms after stimulus presentation; Huffmeijer et al., 2013; Liu, Sheng, Woodcock, & Han, 2013; Ruissen & de Bruijn, 2015; Sheng, Liu, Zhou, Zhou, & Han, 2013) and late-occurring neurophysiological processes (> 300ms; Herzmann, Bird, Freeman, & Curran, 2013; Huffmeijer et al., 2013; Waller et al., 2015; Wu, van Dijk, & Zhou, 2013).

More specifically, three studies revealed that oxytocin intensifies the processing of social stimuli in general, as indicated by increased vertex positive potentials (positive-going modulations at fronto-central electrode sites occurring between 140 and 180ms after stimulus onset and associated with the configural processing of faces; Joyce, & Rossion, 2005) and late positive potentials (positive-going modulations at centro-parietal electrode sites beginning 300–400ms after feedback onset and associated with the allocation of attention toward emotionally and motivationally significant stimuli; Hajcak, Dunning, & Foti, 2009) in response to happy and disgust faces that were presented as feedback stimuli in a flanker task (Huffmeijer et al., 2013). Furthermore, it was shown that oxytocin increases suppression of mu and beta band activity associated with social resonance processing in response to a point-light display of continuous biological motion of a human figure's walk (Perry et al., 2010), and the N2s (negative-going modulations at fronto-central electrode sites occurring around 250ms after stimulus onset and associated with response conflict; Yeung, Botvinick, & Cohen, 2004) in the social Simon task (the same stimulus represents a Go trial for one participant, but a NoGo trial for the other participant, i.e., response conflict arises from the different task rules for the two actors who jointly execute the Simon task; Ruissen & de Bruijn, 2015).

Another group of studies showed that oxytocin increases social motivation toward others, as indicated by more similar negative potentials 300–400ms after the presentation of own-child versus other-child faces (Waller et al., 2015), by more similar late positive potentials 300–1000ms after the presentation of evaluative descriptions of other-owned versus self-owned objects (Wu et al., 2013), and by more similar P2 (positive-going modulation at fronto-central electrode sites 220–280ms after stimulus presentation) and late positive potentials in response to other-judgments versus self-judgments (Liu et al., 2013).

With regard to affiliation among group members, another study showed that oxytocin increased the racial in-group bias in neurophysiological responses (indicated by larger differences in fronto-central positive potentials 120–180ms after presentation of painful vs. neutral facial expressions of racial in-group members; Sheng et al., 2013). Future studies might also illuminate how oxytocin changes neurophysiological processes underlying behavior toward members of natural social in- and out-group members in inter-group conflict.

In sum, the few initial EEG studies we can rely on provided rather inconclusive evidence on oxytocin's effects on specific socio-cognitive processes underlying social affiliation. More electrophysiological research investigating the temporal dynamics of activating distributed neural networks using spatio-temporal EEG analyses is needed. Such spatio-temporal EEG analyses utilize all spatial (reference-independent electrical field distributions across all electrodes) and temporal (data from all time points of task processing in millisecond steps) information available from multichannel EEG (for reviews, please see Michel, Koenig, Brandeis, Gianotti, & Wackermann, 2009; Murray, Brunet, & Michel, 2008). For example, by segmenting ERPs into time periods of stable neural network configurations, one can identify and time the entire sequence of functional microstates; that is, neurophysiological processes involved in a given socio-cognitive behavior (for a recent example see Schiller et al., 2016). Such an analysis generates information about the intensity, duration, and type of neurophysiological processes, holding the potential to generate highly valuable knowledge on oxytocin's effects on the temporal dynamics of socio-cognitive processes underlying human affiliation.

Summary and outlook

Relying on over a decade of oxytocin research, we now possess solid evidence that oxytocin promotes affiliation in humans by reducing stress and anxiety, by increasing the saliency of social cues, by modulating socio-cognitive functions (e.g., social memory, emotion recognition) and by facilitating trusting behavior. Such evidence could be further bolstered by demonstrating that oxytocin administration increases specific affective responses associated with affiliation motivation (McClelland, 1987), for example genuine smiling in response to affiliative stimuli (which could be measured by electromyography of facial muscle activity that is indicative of subtle smiling; Dufner, Arslan, Hagemeyer, Schonbrodt, & Denissen, 2015). Given the plethora of intranasal application studies supporting oxytocin's role in affiliation-related processes, we still possess little knowledge about the effects of oxytocin on specific socio-cognitive processes. Neuroimaging methods enable us to empirically investigate the neural correlates involved in the underlying socio-cognitive processes, thereby providing clues to the mechanisms underlying oxytocin's effect. In the spatial domain, metabolic neuroimaging studies have generated important insights regarding oxytocin-induced changes in neural activity during social interactions. In contrast, in the temporal domain, we still do not really understand how oxytocin administration affects the dynamics of socio-cognitive neural processes. Spatio-temporal analysis of electrophysiological brain activity holds the potential to illuminate how and when oxytocin changes the temporal dynamics of social cognition and behavior underlying social affiliation, a little explored research field thus far with great potential to reveal the still not well understood neurophysiological mechanisms of oxytocin's effects in humans. Ultimately, research applying multiple methodologies combining electrical and metabolic neuroimaging with intranasal oxytocin administration using large sample sizes will integrate our knowledge about hormonal effects on neural processing in the spatial and temporal domain and further deepen our understanding of the neurobiological mechanisms of human social affiliation.

References

Baron-Cohen, S., Wheelwright, S., Hill, J., Raste, Y., & Plumb, I. (2001). The "Reading the Mind in the Eyes" test revised version: A study with normal adults, and adults with Asperger syndrome or high-functioning autism. *Journal of Child Psychology and Psychiatry, 42*(2), 241–251.

Bartz, J.A., Zaki, J., Bolger, N., Hollander, E., Ludwig, N.N., Kolevzon, A., & Ochsner, K.N. (2010). Oxytocin selectively improves empathic accuracy. *Psychological Science, 21*(10), 1426–1428.

Baumeister, R.F., & Leary, M.R. (1995). The need to belong – desire for interpersonal attachments as a fundamental human motivation. *Psychological Bulletin, 117*(3), 497–529.

Baumgartner, T., Gotte, L., Gugler, R., & Fehr, E. (2012). The mentalizing network orchestrates the impact of parochial altruism on social norm enforcement. *Human Brain Mapping, 33*(6), 1452–1469.

Baumgartner, T., Heinrichs, M., Vonlanthen, A., Fischbacher, U., & Fehr, E. (2008). Oxytocin shapes the neural circuitry of trust and trust adaptation in humans. *Neuron, 58*(4), 639–650.

Baumgartner, T., Schiller, B., Rieskamp, J., Gianotti, L.R., & Knoch, D. (2014). Diminishing parochialism in intergroup conflict by disrupting the right temporo-parietal junction. *Social Cognitive and Affective Neuroscience, 9*(5), 653–660.

Behnia, B., Heinrichs, M., Bergmann, W., Jung, S., Germann, J., Schedlowski, M., . . . Kruger, T.H.C. (2014). Differential effects of intranasal oxytocin on sexual experiences and partner interactions in couples. *Hormones and Behavior, 65*(3), 308–318.

Bernaerts, S., Prinsen, J., Berra, E., Bosmans, G., Steyaert, J., & Alaerts, K. (2017). Long-term oxytocin administration enhances the experience of attachment. *Psychoneuroendocrinology, 78*(Suppl. C), 1–9.

Born, J., Lange, T., Kern, W., McGregor, G.P., Bickel, U., & Fehm, H.L. (2002). Sniffing neuropeptides: A transnasal approach to the human brain. *Nature Neuroscience, 5*(6), 514–516.

Buchheim, A., Heinrichs, M., George, C., Pokorny, D., Koops, E., Henningsen, P., . . . Gündel, H. (2009). Oxytocin enhances the experience of attachment security. *Psychoneuroendocrinology, 34*(9), 1417–1422.

Burri, A., Heinrichs, M., Schedlowski, M., & Kruger, T.H.C. (2008). The acute effects of intranasal oxytocin administration on endocrine and sexual function in males. *Psychoneuroendocrinology, 33*(5), 591–600.

Carter, C.S., Devries, C.A., & Getz, L.L. (1995). Physiological substrates of mammalian monogamy: The prairie vole model. *Neuroscience & Biobehavioral Reviews, 19*(2), 303–314.

Carter, C.S., Grippo, A.J., Pournajafi-Nazarloo, H., Ruscio, M.G., & Porges, S.W. (2008). Oxytocin, vasopressin and sociality. *Progress in Brain Research, 170,* 331–336.

Daughters, K., Manstead, A.S.R., Ten Velden, F.S., & De Dreu, C.K.W. (2017). Oxytocin modulates third-party sanctioning of selfish and generous behavior within and between groups. *Psychoneuroendocrinology, 77,* 18–24.

De Dreu, C.K.W., Greer, L.L., van Kleef, G.A., Shalvi, S., & Handgraaf, M.J.J. (2011). Oxytocin promotes human ethnocentrism. *Proceedings of the National Academy of Sciences of the United States of America, 108*(4), 1262–1266.

De Dreu, C.K.W., & Kret, M.E. (2016). Oxytocin conditions intergroup relations through upregulated in-group empathy, cooperation, conformity, and defense. *Biological Psychiatry, 79*(3), 165–173.

Ditzen, B., Schmidt, S., Strauss, B., Nater, U.M., Ehlert, U., & Heinrichs, M. (2008). Adult attachment and social support interact to reduce psychological but not cortisol responses to stress. *Journal of Psychosomatic Research, 64*(5), 479–486.

Domes, G., Heinrichs, M., Glascher, J., Buchel, C., Braus, D.F., & Herpertz, S.C. (2007). Oxytocin attenuates amygdala responses to emotional faces regardless of valence. *Biological Psychiatry, 62*(10), 1187–1190.

Domes, G., Heinrichs, M., Michel, A., Berger, C., & Herpertz, S.C. (2007). Oxytocin improves "mind-reading" in humans. *Biological Psychiatry, 61*(6), 731–733.

Domes, G., Lischke, A., Berger, C., Grossmann, A., Hauenstein, K., Heinrichs, M., & Herpertz, S.C. (2010). Effects of intranasal oxytocin on emotional face processing in women. *Psychoneuroendocrinology, 35*(1), 83–93.

Donaldson, Z.R., & Young, L.J. (2008). Oxytocin, vasopressin, and the neurogenetics of sociality. *Science, 322*(5903), 900–904.

Dufner, M., Arslan, R.C., Hagemeyer, B., Schonbrodt, F.D., & Denissen, J.J. (2015). Affective contingencies in the affiliative domain: Physiological assessment, associations with the affiliation motive, and prediction of behavior. *Journal of Personality and Social Psychology, 109*(4), 662–676.

Eisenberger, N.I., & Cole, S.W. (2012). Social neuroscience and health: Neurophysiological mechanisms linking social ties with physical health. *Nature Neuroscience, 15*(5), 669–674.

Fahrbach, S.E., Morrell, J.I., & Pfaff, D.W. (1985). Possible role for endogenous oxytocin in estrogen-facilitated maternal behavior in rats. *Neuroendocrinology, 40*(6), 526–532.

Fehm-Wolfsdorf, G., Bachholz, G., Born, J., Voigt, K., & Fehm, H.L. (1988). Vasopressin but not oxytocin enhances cortical arousal: An integrative hypothesis on behavioral effects of neurohypophyseal hormones. *Psychopharmacology (Berl), 94*(4), 496–500.

Fehr, E., & Fischbacher, U. (2004). Third-party punishment and social norms. *Evolution and Human Behavior, 25*(2), 63–87.

Gallagher, H.L., & Frith, C.D. (2003). Functional imaging of "theory of mind". *Trends in Cognitive Sciences, 7*(2), 77–83.

Gamer, M., Zurowski, B., & Büchel, C. (2010). Different amygdala subregions mediate valence-related and attentional effects of oxytocin in humans. *Proceedings of the National Academy of Sciences of the United States of America, 107*(20), 9400–9405.

Gimpl, G., & Fahrenholz, F. (2001). The oxytocin receptor system: Structure, function, and regulation. *Physiological Reviews, 81*(2), 629–683.

Groppe, S.E., Gossen, A., Rademacher, L., Hahn, A., Westphal, L., Gründer, G., & Spreckelmeyer, K.N. (2013). Oxytocin influences processing of socially relevant cues in the ventral tegmental area of the human brain. *Biological Psychiatry, 74*(3), 172–179.

Guastella, A.J., Mitchell, P.B., & Dadds, M.R. (2008). Oxytocin increases gaze to the eye region of human faces. *Biological Psychiatry, 63*(1), 3–5.

Hajcak, G., Dunning, J.P., & Foti, D. (2009). Motivated and controlled attention to emotion: Time-course of the late positive potential. *Clinical Neurophysiology, 120*(3), 505–510.

Heinrichs, M., Baumgartner, T., Kirschbaum, C., & Ehlert, U. (2003). Social support and oxytocin interact to suppress cortisol and subjective responses to psychosocial stress. *Biological Psychiatry, 54*(12), 1389–1398.

Heinrichs, M., von Dawans, B., & Domes, G. (2009). Oxytocin, vasopressin, and human social behavior. *Frontiers in Neuroendocrinology, 30*(4), 548–557.

Herzmann, G., Bird, C.W., Freeman, M., & Curran, T. (2013). Effects of oxytocin on behavioral and ERP measures of recognition memory for own-race and other-race faces in women and men. *Psychoneuroendocrinology, 38*(10), 2140–2151.

House, J., Landis, K., & Umberson, D. (1988). Social relationships and health. *Science, 241*(4865), 540.

Hu, J., Qi, S., Becker, B., Luo, L., Gao, S., Gong, Q., . . . Kendrick, K.M. (2015). Oxytocin selectively facilitates learning with social feedback and increases activity and functional connectivity in emotional memory and reward processing regions. *Human Brain Mapping, 36*(6), 2132–2146.

Huffmeijer, R., Alink, L.R.A., Tops, M., Grewen, K.M., Light, K.C., Bakermans-Kranenburg, M.J., & van IJzendoorn, M.H. (2013). The impact of oxytocin administration and maternal love withdrawal on Event-Related Potential (ERP) responses to emotional faces with performance feedback. *Hormones and Behavior, 63*(3), 399–410.

Insel, T.R. (2010). The challenge of translation in social neuroscience: A review of oxytocin, vasopressin, and affiliative behavior. *Neuron, 65*(6), 768–779.

Joyce, C., & Rossion, B. (2005). The face-sensitive N170 and VPP components manifest the same brain processes: The effect of reference electrode site. *Clinical Neurophysiology, 116*(11), 2613–2631.

Kanat, M., Heinrichs, M., & Domes, G. (2014). Oxytocin and the social brain: Neural mechanisms and perspectives in human research. *Brain Research, 1580*, 160–171.

Kanat, M., Heinrichs, M., Mader, I., van Elst, L.T., & Domes, G. (2015). Oxytocin modulates amygdala reactivity to masked fearful eyes. *Neuropsychopharmacology, 40*(11), 2632–2638.

Kanat, M., Heinrichs, M., Schwarzwald, R., & Domes, G. (2015). Oxytocin attenuates neural reactivity to masked threat cues from the eyes. *Neuropsychopharmacology, 40*(2), 287–295.

Kirsch, P., Esslinger, C., Chen, Q., Mier, D., Lis, S., Siddhanti, S., . . . Meyer-Lindenberg, A. (2005). Oxytocin modulates neural circuitry for social cognition and fear in humans. *Journal of Neuroscience, 25*(49), 11489–11493.

Kosfeld, M., Heinrichs, M., Zak, P.J., Fischbacher, U., & Fehr, E. (2005). Oxytocin increases trust in humans. *Nature, 435*(7042), 673–676.

Landgraf, R., & Neumann, I.D. (2004). Vasopressin and oxytocin release within the brain: A dynamic concept of multiple and variable modes of neuropeptide communication. *Frontiers in Neuroendocrinology, 25*, 150–176.

Lim, M.M., & Young, L.J. (2006). Neuropeptidergic regulation of affiliative behavior and social bonding in animals. *Hormones and Behavior, 50*(4), 506–517.

Liu, Y., Sheng, F., Woodcock, K.A., & Han, S. (2013). Oxytocin effects on neural correlates of self-referential processing. *Biological Psychology, 94*(2), 380–387.

Ma, Y., Shamay-Tsoory, S., Han, S., & Zink, C.F. (2016). Oxytocin and social adaptation: Insights from neuroimaging studies of healthy and clinical populations. *Trends in Cognitive Sciences, 20*(2), 133–145.

Marsh, N., Scheele, D., Feinstein, J.S., Gerhardt, H., Strang, S., Maier, W., & Hurlemann, R. (2017). Oxytocin-enforced norm compliance reduces xenophobic outgroup rejection. *Proceedings of the National Academy of Sciences of the United States of America, 114*(35), 9314–9319.

McCall, C., & Singer, T. (2012). The animal and human neuroendocrinology of social cognition, motivation and behavior. *Nature Neuroscience, 15*(5), 681–688.

McClelland, D.C. (1987). *Human motivation*. New York, NY: Cambridge University Press.

Meyer-Lindenberg, A., Domes, G., Kirsch, P., & Heinrichs, M. (2011). Oxytocin and vasopressin in the human brain: Social neuropeptides for translational medicine. *Nature Reviews Neuroscience, 12*(9), 524–538.

Michel, C.M., Koenig, T., Brandeis, D., Gianotti, L.R., & Wackermann, J. (2009). *Electrical neuroimaging*. London: Cambridge University Press.

Mikolajczak, M., Gross, J.J., Lane, A., Corneille, O., de Timary, P., & Luminet, O. (2010). Oxytocin makes people trusting, not gullible. *Psychological Science, 21*(8), 1072–1074.

Mikolajczak, M., Pinon, N., Lane, A., de Timary, P., & Luminet, O. (2010). Oxytocin not only increases trust when money is at stake, but also when confidential information is in the balance. *Biological Psychology, 85*(1), 182–184.

Murray, M.M., Brunet, D., & Michel, C.M. (2008). Topographic ERP analyses: A step-by-step tutorial review. *Brain Topography, 20*(4), 249–264.

Naber, F., van IJzendoorn, M.H., Deschamps, P., van Engeland, H., & Bakermans-Kranenburg, M.J. (2010). Intranasal oxytocin increases fathers' observed responsiveness during play with their children: A double-blind within-subject experiment. *Psychoneuroendocrinology, 35*(10), 1583–1586.

Nave, G., Camerer, C., & McCullough, M. (2015). Does oxytocin increase trust in humans? A critical review of research. *Perspectives on Psychological Science, 10*(6), 772–789.

Paloyelis, Y., Doyle, O.M., Zelaya, F.O., Maltezos, S., Williams, S.C., Fotopoulou, A., & Howard, M.A. (2016). A spatiotemporal profile of in vivo cerebral blood flow changes following intranasal oxytocin in humans. *Biological Psychiatry, 79*(8), 693–705.

Pedersen, C.A., Ascher, J.A., Monroe, Y.L., & Prange, A.J., Jr. (1982). Oxytocin induces maternal behavior in virgin female rats. *Science, 216*(4546), 648–650.

Perry, A., Bentin, S., Shalev, I., Israel, S., Uzefovsky, F., Bar-On, D., & Ebstein, R.P. (2010). Intranasal oxytocin modulates EEG mu/alpha and beta rhythms during perception of biological motion. *Psychoneuroendocrinology, 35*(10), 1446–1453.

Pietrowsky, R., Braun, D., Fehm, H.L., Pauschinger, P., & Born, J. (1991). Vasopressin and oxytocin do not influence early sensory processing but affect mood and activation in man. *Peptides, 12*(6), 1385–1391.

Quintana, D.S., Alvares, G.A., Hickie, I.B., & Guastella, A.J. (2015). Do delivery routes of intranasally administered oxytocin account for observed effects on social cognition and behavior? A two-level model. *Neuroscience & Biobehavioral Reviews, 49*(Suppl. C), 182–192.

Quintana, D.S., Westlye, L.T., Rustan, Ø.G., Tesli, N., Poppy, C.L., Smevik, H., . . . Andreassen, A. (2015). Low-dose oxytocin delivered intranasally with breath powered device affects social-cognitive behavior: A randomized four-way crossover trial with nasal cavity dimension assessment. *Translational Psychiatry, 5*(e602).

Rilling, J.K., DeMarco, A.C., Hackett, P.D., Thompson, R., Ditzen, B., Patel, R., & Pagnoni, G. (2012). Effects of intranasal oxytocin and vasopressin on cooperative behavior and associated brain activity in men. *Psychoneuroendocrinology, 37*(4), 447–461.

Rilling, J.K., & Young, L.J. (2014). The biology of mammalian parenting and its effect on offspring social development. *Science, 345*(6198), 771–776.

Rimmele, U., Hediger, K., Heinrichs, M., & Klaver, P. (2009). Oxytocin makes a face in memory familiar. *The Journal of Neuroscience, 29*(1), 38–42.

Ruissen, M.I., & de Bruijn, E.R.A. (2015). Is it me or is it you? Behavioral and electrophysiological effects of oxytocin administration on self-other integration during joint task performance. *Cortex, 70*, 146–154.

Savaskan, E., Ehrhardt, R., Schulz, A., Walter, M., & Schächinger, H. (2008). Post-learning intranasal oxytocin modulates human memory for facial identity. *Psychoneuroendocrinology, 33*(3), 368–374.

Scheele, D., Wille, A., Kendrick, K.M., Stoffel-Wagner, B., Becker, B., Gunturkun, O., . . . Hurlemann, R. (2013). Oxytocin enhances brain reward system responses in men viewing the face of their female partner. *Proceedings of the National Academy of Sciences of the United States of America, 110*(50), 20308–20313.

Schiller, B., Baumgartner, T., & Knoch, D. (2014). Intergroup bias in third-party punishment stems from both ingroup favoritism and outgroup discrimination. *Evolution and Human Behavior, 35*(3), 169–175.

Schiller, B., Gianotti, L.R.R., Baumgartner, T., Nash, K., Koenig, T., & Knoch, D. (2016). Clocking the social mind by identifying mental processes in the IAT with electrical neuroimaging. *Proceedings of the National Academy of Sciences of the United States of America, 113*(10), 2786–2791.

Shamay-Tsoory, S.G., & Abu-Akel, A. (2016). The social salience hypothesis of oxytocin. *Biological Psychiatry, 79*(3), 194–202.

Shahrestani, S., Kemp, A.H., & Guastella, A.J. (2013). The impact of a single administration of intranasal oxytocin on the recognition of basic emotions in humans: A meta-analysis. *Neuropsychopharmacology, 38*(10), 1929–1936.

Sheng, F., Liu, Y., Zhou, B., Zhou, W., & Han, S.H. (2013). Oxytocin modulates the racial bias in neural responses to others' suffering. *Biological Psychology, 92*(2), 380–386.

Stallen, M., De Dreu, C.K., Shalvi, S., Smidts, A., & Sanfey, A.G. (2012). The herding hormone: Oxytocin stimulates in-group conformity. *Psychological Science, 23*(11), 1288–1292.

Striepens, N., Kendrick, K.M., Hanking, V., Landgraf, R., Wüllner, U., Maier, W., & Hurlemann, R. (2013). Elevated cerebrospinal fluid and blood concentrations of oxytocin following its intranasal administration in humans. *Scientific Reports, 3*, 3440.

Theodoridou, A., Rowe, A.C., Penton-Voak, I.S., & Rogers, P.J. (2009). Oxytocin and social perception: Oxytocin increases perceived facial trustworthiness and attractiveness. *Hormones and Behavior, 56*(1), 128–132.

Uddin, L.Q. (2017). *Salience network of the human brain*. New York, NY: Elsevier.

van Anders, S.M., Goldey, K.L., & Kuo, P.X. (2011). The steroid/peptide theory of social bonds: Integrating testosterone and peptide responses for classifying social behavioral contexts. *Psychoneuroendocrinology, 36*(9), 1265–1275.

Van IJzendoorn, M.H., & Bakermans-Kranenburg, M.J. (2012). A sniff of trust: Meta-analysis of the effects of intranasal oxytocin administration on face recognition, trust to in-group, and trust to out-group. *Psychoneuroendocrinology, 37*(3), 438–443.

Van Overwalle, F. (2009). Social cognition and the brain: A meta-analysis. *Human Brain Mapping, 30*(3), 829–858.

Waller, C., Wittfoth, M., Fritzsche, K., Timm, L., Wittfoth-Schardt, D., Rottler, E., . . . Gündel, H. (2015). Attachment representation modulates oxytocin effects on the processing of own-child faces in fathers. *Psychoneuroendocrinology, 62*, 27–35.

Weisman, O., Zagoory-Sharon, O., & Feldman, R. (2012). Oxytocin administration to parent enhances infant physiological and behavioral readiness for social engagement. *Development, Autism, and Aggression, 72*(12), 982–989.

Wu, Y., van Dijk, E., & Zhou, X. (2013). Evaluating self- vs. other-owned objects: The modulatory role of oxytocin. *Biological Psychology, 92*(2), 179–184.

Yamasue, H., & Domes, G. (2017). *Oxytocin and autism spectrum disorders*. Berlin: Springer.

Yeung, N., Botvinick, M.M., & Cohen, J.D. (2004). The neural basis of error detection: Conflict monitoring and the error-related negativity. *Psychological Review, 111*(4), 931–959.

Young, L.J., & Wang, Z. (2004). The neurobiology of pair bonding. *Nature Neuroscience, 7*(10), 1048–1054.

12

OXYTOCIN AND HUMAN SOCIALITY

An interactionist perspective on the "hormone of love"

Jonas P. Nitschke, Sonia A. Krol, and Jennifer A. Bartz

Introduction

Humans need social bonds to maintain physical and emotional well-being (e.g., Baumeister & Leary, 1995). It is, thus, crucial to understand the factors that facilitate developing and sustaining healthy social connections. In this regard, oxytocin has been identified as an important neuro-chemical substrate of attachment and affiliation. A nine-amino-acid peptide that asserts its effects peripherally as a hormone, oxytocin has been implicated in various physiological processes including childbirth, lactation, and thermoregulation (Lee, Macbeth, Pagani, & Young, 2009). Oxytocin, however, also acts centrally as a neuromodulator, influencing social cognition and behavior related to attachment/bonding, social memory, care-taking, and parenting (for reviews: Bielsky & Young, 2004; Carter, 1998; Feldman, Weller, Zagoory-Sharon, & Levine, 2007; Insel, 2010). To date, most work on oxytocin and sociality has been in non-human animals, largely because methodological constraints have made it difficult to empirically investigate the role of oxytocin in human sociality. However, research in humans has increased exponentially in the past 15 years with the emergence of intranasal administration technology to facilitate delivery of peptides to the central nervous system (Born et al., 2002). Studies using this technology to manipulate the availability of oxytocin in humans indicate some notable similarities with the animal literature. Indeed, oxytocin was quickly dubbed the "love hormone" for its capacity to promote a range of affiliative processes including trust (Baumgartner, Heinrichs, Vonlanthen, Fischbacher, & Fehr, 2008; Kosfeld, Heinrichs, Zak, Fischbacher, & Fehr, 2005; also see Schiller and Hausmann, this volume), eye contact (Guastella, Howard, Dadds, Mitchell, & Carson, 2009; Guastella, Mitchell, & Dadds, 2008), inferring others' mental states (Domes et al., 2007), and more general social information processing (Kirsch et al., 2005; Rimmele, Hediger, Heinrichs, & Klaver, 2009; Savaskan, Ehrhardt, Schulz, Walter, & Schächinger, 2008). As research in this area began to accumulate, however, inconsistencies in oxytocin's capacity to unilaterally enhance social cognition and behavior became apparent. Some subsequent studies showed null effects, and some indicated socially *detrimental* effects – for example, increasing levels of *mistrust* (Bartz, Zaki, Ochsner, et al., 2010; Declerck, Boone, & Kiyonari, 2010; Mikolajczak et al., 2010; also see Peled-Avron & Shamay-Tsoory, this volume), envy and gloating (Shamay-Tsoory et al., 2009), negative emotions (Hirosawa et al., 2012; MacDonald et al., 2013), and negative social percep-tions (Bartz et al., 2010; Gao et al., 2016).

One interpretation of these inconsistencies is that there is no meaningful effect of oxytocin on human sociality. For example, Nave and colleagues (2015) conducted a meta-analysis of research on oxytocin and trust and argued that there is not enough reliable evidence to conclude that oxytocin increases trust in humans. Notwithstanding this important work, the wealth of findings seem hard to explain if intranasal oxytocin is having *no* effect. Of course, it is possible that findings in this area are "false positives," resulting from the small samples that often characterize intranasal administration studies due to their expense and logistical difficulties (see Button et al., 2013; Lane, Luminet, Nave, & Mikolajczak, 2016), and/or "researcher degrees of freedom" (Simmons, Nelson, & Simonsohn, 2011). It is also possible that journal preferences for publishing significant effects paint a rosier picture than is warranted (Ioannidis, 2012). At this point it is difficult to rule out these possibilities; however, we propose an alternative perspective that the effect of intranasal oxytocin on human sociality is real, but more nuanced than the simplistic love hormone view suggests.

Careful inspection of the data indicates that oxytocin's social effects often depend on contextual and/or person factors (Bartz, Zaki, Bolger, & Ochsner, 2011). As Bartz, Zaki, et al. (2011; also see Bartz, 2016) proposed, oxytocin's various social effects can be understood by considering an *interactionist's perspective* that recognizes how features of the situation combine with characteristics of the person to produce differential effects on cognition and behavior. About 50 years ago the field of personality psychology faced a somewhat analogous situation to the one facing human oxytocin researchers today. Based on the observation of surprisingly low correlations between traits and behaviors and/or traits measured on multiple occasions, many questioned whether it was meaningful, scientifically, to measure and investigate the effects of "personality" (e.g., Ross & Nisbett, 2011). One influential response to this crisis was put forward by Walter Mischel and colleagues (Mischel, 1973; Shoda, Mischel, & Wright, 1994), who emphasized the role of individual-specific cognitive and affective processes that mediate the situation to behavior relationship; according to this theory, situational inputs are filtered by the idiosyncratic ways people encode and construe (social) situations, their expectancies and beliefs, their unique affective and self-regulatory styles, competencies, and goals and values. It is the variability in these "cognitive and affective mediating units" that explains why one person responds to a social overture with a smile and prosocial talk, whereas another responds with aggression, expecting, perhaps based on personal history, that others cannot be trusted (Shoda et al., 1994). We propose that this *interactionist* view may also account for oxytocin's nuanced effects, and, in particular, oxytocin's person-dependent effects: if experience is filtered through person-specific cognitive and affective mediating units, then oxytocin should have differential effects on social cognition and behavior depending on these individual differences. Of note, our perspective not only offers an explanation for the aforementioned inconsistencies in the literature, but it also clarifies the noted failures to replicate and reported smaller effects – specifically, if the effects of oxytocin depend on the context in which it is administered and/or the person to whom it is given.

In the following sections, we review evidence of oxytocin's nuanced social effects. Although both context- and person-dependent effects have been reported (Bartz, Zaki, et al., 2011), here we focus on the latter. As we argue, oxytocin's person-dependent effects are somewhat systematic in that oxytocin appears to largely facilitate sociality in individuals who are less motivated to engage socially, and/or those who lack the skills to do so. Conversely, oxytocin appears to have either negligible or even (socially) detrimental effects in individuals who are anxious about, and preoccupied with, social closeness and sensitive to rejection. We focus our review on studies in healthy individuals but reference data from clinical populations that, arguably, reflect "extremes" in the personality dimension under consideration – in particular, autism spectrum disorder (ASD) and borderline personality disorder (BPD).

As we review this literature, it is important to keep in mind that the mechanism(s) by which oxytocin modulates human sociality is/are not well-understood. However, as argued elsewhere (Bartz, 2016; Bartz, Zaki, et al., 2011), understanding oxytocin's context- and person-dependency may in fact shed light on the underlying mechanism(s) at play. To date, several hypotheses have been put forward. A thorough discussion of this topic is beyond the scope of this chapter, but in Table 12.1 we present an overview of three hypothesized mechanisms: Affiliative Motivation, Social Salience, and Anxiety Reduction (interested readers are referred to Bartz, Zaki, et al., 2011 for a more detailed discussion of this topic). We refer to these mechanistic hypotheses as appropriate in our review.

Personality moderators of intranasal oxytocin: the good, the bad, and the null

Beneficial social effects

In one of the first studies to demonstrate person-moderated effects, Bartz, Zaki, Bolger, et al. (2010) found that oxytocin selectively improved empathic accuracy in participants who scored higher (vs. lower) on the Autism Quotient (AQ; Baron-Cohen, Wheelwright, Skinner, Martin, & Clubley, 2001), a 50-item self-report questionnaire assessing traits associated with autism (i.e., deficits in social and communication skills, imagination, attention to details, and intolerance of change). Participants ($N = 27$, within-subject) randomly received intranasal oxytocin or placebo on separate occasions, approximately 3 weeks apart; after both oxytocin/placebo (drug administration order was counterbalanced), participants completed a naturalistic empathic accuracy task in which they watched videos of targets discussing emotional autobiographical events and provided continuous ratings of how they thought the target was feeling. These ratings were compared to the target's ratings of how they were actually feeling, as an index of empathic accuracy. Consistent with prior work using other measures of mental state attribution accuracy like the Reading the Mind in the Eyes Test (RMET; Baron-Cohen, Wheelwright, Hill, Raste, & Plumb, 2001), AQ was negatively associated with empathic accuracy in the placebo condition – that is, the more a person endorsed traits of autism, the poorer their empathic accuracy performance. Critically, however, oxytocin selectively improved empathic accuracy for high AQ participants, such that following oxytocin administration, their performance was indistinguishable from their low AQ counterparts.

This effect has now been conceptually replicated in several investigations (and has been directly replicated by our group in a pre-registered study, also within-subject; Bartz, Nitschke, Krol, & Tellier, under review). Specifically, Radke and de Bruijn (2015) found that individual differences in emotional empathy, as assessed by the empathic concern subscale of the Interpersonal Reactivity Index (Davis, 1980), moderated the effects of oxytocin on the RMET. Again, oxytocin administration selectively benefitted those with lower baseline empathic concern ($N = 24$; within-subject). Similarly, Feeser et al. (2015) found that individual differences in trait empathy, measured with the Empathy Quotient (which is negatively correlated with the AQ; Baron-Cohen & Wheelwright, 2004) moderated the effects of oxytocin on the RMET, with oxytocin selectively facilitating performance in low, but not high, empathy participants ($N = 71$; between-subjects). In another studying focusing on the RMET, Luminet et al. (2011) found that individual differences in alexithymia (i.e., an inability to describe one's own emotional experience; Sifneos, 1973; Cook, Brewer, Shah, & Bird, 2013) moderated the effects of oxytocin, with oxytocin selectively improving RMET performance for those individuals high in alexithymia ($N = 60$; between-subjects). Finally, Leknes et al. (2013) found that individual differences in

Table 12.1 Three hypothesized mechanisms for oxytocin's social effects in humans

	Affiliative motivation	Social salience	Anxiety reduction
Hypothesis	Oxytocin increases social motivation and/or a "communal" other-orientation associated with the motivation to attend to and/or care for others (e.g., Bartz, 2016; Gordon, Martin, Feldman, & Leckman, 2011; Ross & Young, 2009)	Oxytocin increases the (perceptual) salience of, and attention to, social cues in the environment (e.g., Bartz, Zaki, et al., 2011; Shamay-Tsoory et al., 2009; Shamay-Tsoory & Abu-Akel, 2016)	Oxytocin reduces anxiety, especially social anxiety (e.g., Bartz & Hollander, 2006; Heinrichs & Domes, 2008; Neumann & Landgraf, 2012)
Evidence	• Oxytocin plays a critical role in mother-infant and adult-adult pair-bonding in non-human animals (e.g., Bielsky & Young, 2004; Carter, 1998; Carter, Devries, & Getz, 1995) • Oxytocin is critically involved in the onset of maternal behaviors (e.g., Bosch & Neumann, 2012; Pedersen et al., 1992) and alloparental care (e.g., Olazábal & Young, 2006) • Oxytocin increases trust (e.g., Kosfeld et al., 2005), a communal orientation (Bartz et al., 2015), and various other prosocial behaviors in humans (e.g., see Bartz, Zaki, et al., 2011 for review)	• Oxytocin promotes selective recognition of offspring in sheep by augmenting neuronal sensitivity to social stimuli (e.g., Keverne & Kendrick, 1992) • Oxytocin increases the salience of acoustic social stimuli and, as a result, promotes maternal behavior in mice (Marlin, Mitre, D'amour, Chao, & Froemke, 2015) • Oxytocin augments emotional salience of social memories (e.g., Bartz, Zaki, Ochsner, et al., 2010; Guzmán et al., 2013, 2014)	• Oxytocin attenuates HPA axis and stress reactivity (e.g., Heinrichs, Baumgartner, Kirschbaum, & Ehlert, 2003; Neumann & Landgraf, 2012; Quirin, Kuhl, & Düsing, 2011) • Oxytocin attenuates amygdala activity in men (e.g., Kirsch et al., 2005)
Explanatory value	• Explains the selectively beneficial (social) effects of oxytocin displayed by those who are preoccupied with closeness and rejection sensitive (e.g., anxiously attached individuals or those with BPD), since heightening the desire to affiliate may bring to mind people's negative expectancies, memories of failures to achieve affiliative goals, and/or maladaptive strategies to pursue affiliation goals. An increase in goal states does not mean that people will be equipped with the skills to pursue that goal (e.g., Bartz, 2016) • Explains "anti-social" effects displayed by those who are less socially proficient/more socially aloof, if the underlying reason for those social impairments is social amotivation (cf. Chevallier, Kohls, Troiani, Brodkin, & Schultz, 2012)	• Explains why context can critically shape the social effects of oxytocin: Increasing attention to social cues should augment prosociality when interacting with familiar, close or reliable others but diminish prosociality under situations of competition, uncertainty, or when interacting with out-group members (Bartz, Zaki, et al., 2011) • Explains the selectively beneficial (social) effects of oxytocin displayed by individuals with ASD, augmenting the salience of social cues should be beneficial to those who are less attuned to such cues at baseline like, e.g., individuals on the autism spectrum • Explains "anti-social" effects displayed by those who are preoccupied with closeness and rejection sensitive (e.g., anxiously attached individuals or those with BPD), since increasing attention to social cues would likely amplify pre-existing negative expectancies	• Explains the selectively beneficial (social) effects of oxytocin displayed by individuals with ASD, and those who are less socially proficient/more socially aloof, if the underlying reason for those social impairments is anxiety in social situations (cf. Bellini, 2006) • Unclear why oxytocin would produce "anti-social" effects in some individuals; however, easing anxiety may increase their confidence (e.g., Panksepp & Biven, 2012) or reduce their inhibitions and, consequently, prompt them engage in behaviors that they feel they must stifle to ingratiate themselves with others (e.g., non-cooperation)

Note: The above listed theories can work independently or in conjunction with each other to explain the effects of oxytocin.

emotional sensitivity (in this study, emotional sensitivity was not assessed via self-report, but was operationalized as better task performance in the placebo condition) moderated the effects of oxytocin on emotion recognition ($N = 40$; within-subject). That is, individuals scoring lower on a task measuring emotional sensitivity in the placebo condition benefited more from oxytocin administration than individuals high in emotion sensitivity. Additionally, they found that oxytocin increased stimulus-driven pupil dilation – suggesting increased attentional resources devoted to the task – but again, only for those low in emotional sensitivity.

Other studies indicate similar person-dependent effects on more general affiliative cognitions and behaviors. For example, Arueti et al. (2013) investigated the effects of oxytocin on cooperation using a computerized drawing task, which was either performed individually or, in the cooperation condition, as a team ($N = 42$; within-subject). Following placebo, participants working individually performed better than those working as a team. However, following oxytocin, team performance levels were comparable (and high) to those working individually. Notably, oxytocin's enhancing effects in the team-work condition were only observed in highly competitive individuals, as measured by the Social Value Orientation scale (Messick & McClintock, 1968; van Lange & Liebrand, 1991), suggesting that oxytocin is especially likely to facilitate cooperation and teamwork in those who do not show this tendency at baseline. A similar finding was reported by De Dreu (2012) but rather than focusing on competitiveness, De Dreu focused on differences in attachment avoidance, which is associated with a fear of and/ or discomfort with emotional closeness and intimacy, and extreme self-reliance. Participants received intranasal oxytocin or placebo and then played the classic "prisoner's dilemma" game with another player ($N = 77$; between-subjects). As expected, attachment avoidance was negatively associated with trust and cooperation in the placebo group. However, oxytocin selectively increased trust and cooperation for avoidant individuals, who, following oxytocin, were indistinguishable from more secure individuals (similar to Bartz, Zaki, Ochsner et al., 2010, in this study oxytocin had no effect on trust and cooperation for secure individuals, who scored relatively high on these variables in general).

More recently, Bartz and colleagues (2015) also observed selectively beneficial effects of oxytocin for avoidant individuals ($N = 40$; within-subject). This study assessed whether intranasal oxytocin augments a "communal" other-orientation, associated with care and concern for others, as it appears to do in non-human animals. Overall, there was a trend-level increase in communion for the average participant. However, as predicted, results showed that attachment moderated the effect of oxytocin such that avoidant individuals, who are low in communion at baseline, showed the most robust increase in communion – describing themselves as significantly more "warm," "caring," "gentle," "understanding," "cooperative," etc., following oxytocin (vs. placebo). These findings suggest that oxytocin may facilitate trust and cooperation in avoidant individuals by making them more motivated to attend to others and less concerned with self-reliance. Finally, across two relatively large-scale studies (Study 1: $N = 121$; Study 2: $N = 112$), Human and colleagues (2016) found that extraversion (which is also negatively correlated with attachment avoidance, Shaver & Brennan, 1992) moderated the effects of oxytocin on prosocial behavior. Specifically, oxytocin (vs. placebo) led to greater perceived social connection and prosocial tendencies (Study 1) and more positive responses to help and greater trust (Study 2), in individual low in extraversion. Again, as with Bartz, Simeon, et al. (2011) and De Dreu (2012), oxytocin was not particularly beneficial for individuals high in extraversion who were already fairly social.

Taken together, these studies suggest that those who, at baseline, are less socially proficient and/or more aloof and introverted are especially likely to benefit, socially, from oxytocin administration. By contrast, those who are more socially competent and/or more socially inclined (less avoidant, more extraverted) show no, or only negligible, effects following oxytocin. Regarding the latter group, it is unclear whether intranasal oxytocin has no effect, or whether task ceiling/floor effects preclude the detection of oxytocin's effects on sociality. As noted, many of the individual differences described in the previous section (e.g., AQ, alexithymia, avoidance, extraversion) have been found to be correlated. At this point we do not know the specific latent factor, or factors, that moderate oxytocin's social effect, but this will be an important direction for future work (e.g., Krol, Nitschke, Sunahara & Bartz, in prep). Not only will such knowledge help researchers identify the people for whom oxytocin would be expected to have positive social effects, this information can also shed light on underlying mechanisms (e.g., Bartz, 2016; Bartz, Zaki, et al., 2011). Take, for example, the aforementioned cluster involving AQ, attachment avoidance, and introversion; research indicates that people characterized by low extraversion and/or high neuroticism are particularly responsive to signals of punishment (Gray, 1981; Gray, 1987). That these individuals also selectively respond to oxytocin in a prosocial manner lends credence to the notion that oxytocin may promote sociality by attenuating anxiety and/or punishment aversion. Of course, these findings are also consistent with the Social Salience and/ or Affiliative Motivation hypotheses (see Table 12.1).

Although this review is not specifically concerned with clinical populations, we conclude this section reviewing work on oxytocin and autism spectrum disorders (ASD). ASD is a heterogeneous disorder, but a core symptom domain is impairments in understanding social cues and adequately responding to them (Volkmar & Klin, 2005). Indeed, people diagnosed with ASD tend to score high on many of the personality moderators reported above (e.g., AQ, alexithymia); thus, ASD can be seen as an "extreme exemplar" of these individual differences. In fact, some of the first human studies that manipulated the availability of oxytocin were conducted in individuals on the autism spectrum. Inspired by work showing altered peripheral oxytocin levels in children with autism (Modahl et al., 1998), Hollander and colleagues (Hollander et al., 2007) administered oxytocin to 15 adults diagnosed with autism or Asperger's disorder (within-subject) and found that oxytocin significantly reduced repetitive behaviors (Hollander et al., 2003) and improved retention of social cognition – specifically, the ability to identify emotional content in auditory cues.

Since this pioneering work, others have found that oxytocin benefits individuals with ASD by facilitating emotion recognition in both speech and visual cues (Anagnostou et al., 2012; Guastella et al., 2010). Others have shown that oxytocin augments attention to social stimuli more generally in ASD (Andari et al., 2010; Xu et al., 2015). For example, Andari et al. (2010) administered oxytocin/placebo and had study ASD participants ($N = 13$; within-subject) play a modified version of "cyberball" (Williams & Jarvis, 2006), in which participants played a simulated ball toss game with three fictitious players who varied in their levels of cooperation (as indexed by the likelihood that each would reciprocate ball tosses to the participant; i.e., cooperative, neutral, or non-cooperative). In the placebo condition, individuals with ASD tossed the ball equally to all players and, in this way, seemed unaware of the player's level of cooperation. However, following oxytocin, ASD participants showed an increase in interactive behaviors towards the most cooperative partner, versus the less cooperative players, suggesting that oxytocin administration normalized the processing of social cues in these individuals. Importantly, this behavior change was accompanied by increased self-reported trust towards the fictitious cooperative player. In addition, following oxytocin administration, ASD participants spend more time gazing at socially relevant facial regions (e.g., eyes) in an accompanying facial recognition task. In a subsequent fMRI study ($N = 20$; between-subjects) that used a modified cyberball task, Andari et al. (2016) report that oxytocin selectively increased brain activity in visual areas in response to faces (vs. non-social stimuli) in patients with ASD. Again, these changes in brain activity were accompanied by behavioral and cognitive changes, including increased feelings of trust towards partners in the cyberball paradigm. Piqued by these and related findings, Bakermans-Kranenburg and van IJzendoorn (2013) conducted a meta-analysis and concluded that individuals with ASD may reap the strongest benefits from oxytocin in terms of behavioral and cognitive outcomes, compared to other psychopathologies. That said, some studies examining the effects of oxytocin in ASD report mixed or null effects (Anagnostou et al., 2012; Dadds et al., 2014; Guastella et al., 2015). However, some of these studies were treatment trials and the mixed/null effects could be related to sample sizes, dose, duration, the dependent variable, and/or age (two of these studies focused on youth samples).

Null and detrimental social effects

In contrast to the aforementioned selectively beneficial effects, other studies show null or even socially detrimental effects of oxytocin administration (see Bartz, Zaki, et al., 2011). Such detrimental effects are less common, but nonetheless appear to be systematic in that they often involve those who are highly motivated to connect with others but anxious about, and preoccupied with, closeness and/or rejection. In other words, using the vocabulary of the "big five," those high in extraversion, and high in neuroticism (who, according to Gray, 1981, are both reward- and punishment-sensitive).

In one such study, Bartz, Zaki, Ochsner, et al. (2010) investigated the effects of oxytocin on recollections of maternal care and closeness in childhood. This work was motivated by work in non-human animals showing that oxytocin plays a critical role in social memory and, more generally, the notion that oxytocin is involved in attachment bond formation. To investigate whether oxytocin plays a role in human attachment representations, the authors administered oxytocin/placebo ($N = 31$; within-subject) and measured memories of maternal care and closeness, two key features of the attachment bond. Maternal care was measured with the widely used Parental Bonding Instrument (Parker, Tupling, & Brown, 1979) a retrospective self-report measure of parenting styles; items included "frequently smiled at me" and "could make me feel better when I was upset." Maternal closeness was measured with the Inclusion of Other in Self Scale (Aron, Aron, & Smollan, 1992). Results showed no main effect of oxytocin on maternal recollections; rather the effect was moderated by individual differences in attachment anxiety. Specifically, less anxiously attached/more secure participants remembered their mother as more caring, and felt closer to their mother, when they received oxytocin compared to when those same participants received placebo; conversely, more anxiously attached participants remembered their mothers as *less* caring, and reported feeling *less* close to their mother, when they received oxytocin (vs. placebo). These results suggest that oxytocin may augment the salience of these social-emotional experiences, be they positive or negative. Interestingly, subsequent work in mice corroborates the idea (Guzmán et al., 2013, 2014); as Guzmán and colleagues note, oxytocin likely heightens the emotional salience of the social context to "improve cognitive tuning of emotional processes." Indeed, such effects are arguably adaptive since a child in danger would not do well to misremember mom as consistently caring and reliable when, in fact, she is not (Bartz, 2016).

Other work also suggests moderation by attachment/interpersonal insecurity. Rockliff et al. (2011) showed that attachment security moderated the effect of oxytocin on compassion-focused imagery. Following drug/placebo administration, participants ($N = 41$; between-subjects) imagined themselves as recipients of compassion and positive feelings; compared to placebo, oxytocin increased the ease with which securely attached participants were able to conjure up these positive images, but oxytocin had no effect for more insecurely attached participants, who, notably, reported more negative experiences during the task following oxytocin. In the aforementioned study by Bartz et al. (2015) looking at the effects of oxytocin on communion, *agency* was also measured – that is, feeling "independent," "self-confident," etc. Here, there was no main effect of oxytocin on agency. However, anxiously attached individuals showed a selective *decrease* in agency following oxytocin. This finding resonates well with the idea that oxytocin heightens anxious individuals' sense of vulnerability (Bartz, 2016), as does entering into uncertain interpersonal contexts more generally (Bartz & Lydon, 2006, 2008). Indeed, consistent with this, DeWall et al. (2014) found that oxytocin administration led individuals with high (vs. low) levels of trait aggression to endorse greater intimate partner violence (IPV) inclinations ($N = 93$; between-subjects). Finally, other work suggests that interpersonally vulnerable individuals may be less likely to benefit from the anxiolytic effects of oxytocin. Meinlschmidt and Heim (2007) found oxytocin administration attenuated cortisol in controls but not in men who had experienced early parental separation, and Norman et al. (2010) found that oxytocin increases autonomic cardiac control (i.e., heart-rate variability) in control subjects but not in those who were more lonely.

In addition to attachment anxiety and loneliness, other work suggests that the experience of early life stress/adversity (ELA) moderates the effects of oxytocin administration. In general (i.e., in the absence of oxytocin administration), individuals with ELA show increased sensitivity towards emotional stimuli, especially negative stimuli (Dannlowski et al., 2013; Fonzo et al., 2016; Tottenham et al., 2011), and, like Rockliff et al. (2011), studies show that those with ELA do not benefit from oxytocin in the way others do. In a study investigating the effects of oxytocin on helping behavior (operationalized as cooperation towards an excluded player), Riem, van IJzendoorn, et al. (2013) found that while oxytocin administration led to increased cooperation in low ELA individuals, it had no effect on cooperation for those with high ELA ($N = 54$; between-subjects). Similarly, van IJzendoorn et al. (2011) report that oxytocin increased willingness to donate money to a charity but, again, only for individuals low in ELA ($N = 57$; within-subject). Finally, Bakermans-Kranenburg et al. (2012) report that ELA also moderates the effects of oxytocin on sensitive caregiving, operationalized as excessive handgrip force in response to an infant crying, which is thought to indicate hostility and harsh parenting ($N = 44$; between-subjects). Whereas oxytocin decreased handgrip force for low ELA women, it had no effect on handgrip force for women with high ELA (who demonstrated the same high levels of force under placebo and oxytocin).

Finally, in a study looking at neural mechanisms, Riem, Bakermans-Kranenburg, Huffmeijer, & van IJzendoorn (2013) found that oxytocin increased functional connectivity for brain areas associated with emotion and cognition in low ELA individuals, notably between the posterior cingulate cortex (PCC) and the brainstem ($N = 42$; between-subjects). The PCC has been found to play an important role in default networks associated with social cognition, in particular mind-reading abilities (e.g., Wolf, Dziobek, & Heekeren, 2010). Compared to the placebo condition, oxytocin administration increased resting state connectivity for individuals with little or no ELA experiences (also see Bos, Panksepp, Bluthé, & van Honk, 2012; Riem, Bakermans-Kranenburg, Voorthuis, & van IJzendoorn, 2014), whereas oxytocin again had no effect on functional connectivity for those with higher levels of ELA. Of note, work in non-human animals indicates that early caregiving experiences can affect the development of the endogenous oxytocin system. For example, in on such study, Winslow et al. (Winslow, Noble, Lyons, Sterk, & Insel, 2003) showed that compared to mother-reared monkeys, nursery-reared monkeys had lower cerebrospinal-fluid (CSF) oxytocin levels and, critically, were unable to benefit from provision of social support in an anxiety inducing context. These and other related findings implicating early life experiences suggest that in addition to differences in expectancies and construal, the differential effects of oxytocin in these individuals may be rooted in differences in the endogenous oxytocin system.

As in the section outlining selective beneficial effects of oxytocin, we end this section discussing findings from work in a clinical population that could be characterized as an "extreme exemplar" of interpersonal anxiety: Borderline Personality Disorder (BPD). BPD is associated with a range of symptoms including impulsivity, emotion dysregulation, a lack of sense of self, and, of particular relevance, interpersonal dysfunction (Stanley & Siever, 2010), which is characterized by, on one hand, needy reassurance seeking, and, on the other, impulsive and retaliative behaviors in response to perceived injustice and social rejection, as well as a diminished capacity to trust and respond appropriately to others (King-Casas et al., 2008). Given work on oxytocin and trust (e.g., Kosfeld et al., 2005), at first blush, oxytocin might seem like an ideal treatment candidate for BPD; however, the aforementioned studies showing socially detrimental effects of oxytocin in anxiously attached individuals suggest otherwise.

In one of the first studies to investigate the effects of intranasal oxytocin in BPD, Bartz, Simeon, et al. (2011) administered oxytocin or placebo to healthy adults and adults with BPD; participants then played the "assurance game" (a variant of the prisoner's dilemma that incentivizes trust and cooperation) with another player (a research confederate). Rather than increasing interpersonal trust, oxytocin significantly decreased interpersonal trust and the likelihood of cooperation in BPD participants. Oxytocin's effects on cooperation are noteworthy because participants were instructed to indicate how likely it would be that they would cooperate *if they knew for sure their partner would choose the cooperative strategy*. As noted the assurance game incentivizes cooperation: participants make the most money when both players cooperate; conversely, choosing to defect, punishes the partner (who makes $0), but is also costly to the participant. Nonetheless, BPD participants, following oxytocin, chose to punish their partner – a finding possibly reminiscent of the impulsive aggression individuals with BPD can display when they feel interpersonally vulnerable (and also in line with the aforementioned study by DeWall et al., 2014). Of note, consistent with the data in non-clinical populations, this effect held whether groups were categorized by diagnosis (BPD vs. healthy), or whether we collapsed across groups and looked at the effects of attachment anxiety. Although the sample in this study was relatively small ($N = 27$; between-subjects), this finding was replicated by Ebert et al. (2013) who showed that oxytocin decreased trust and prosocial actions (i.e., money transfer) in the trust game in BPD ($N = 26$).

Other work has focused specifically on oxytocin's effects attenuating psychosocial stress and hypersensitivity to social threat in BPD. Specifically, Simeon et al. (2011) administered oxytocin or placebo to healthy adults and adults with BPD ($N = 27$; within-subject); participants then underwent the Trier Psychosocial Stress Test (Kirschbaum, Pirke, & Hellhammer, 1993). Results showed that oxytocin attenuated stress reactivity (both mood dysphoria and cortisol) in BPD participants. Although these findings suggest possible positive effects of oxytocin for BPD participants, it is interesting to note that while BPD-oxytocin participants had the lowest cortisol levels, BPD-placebo had lower cortisol levels than did the healthy controls under placebo or under oxytocin. In another study, Bertsch et al. (2013) administered intranasal oxytocin or placebo to healthy adults and women with BPD ($N = 79$, between-subjects); they then presented participants with a series of emotionally expressive faces and measured gaze fixation and brain activity with fMRI. In the placebo condition, BPD participants (vs. controls) showed an elevated initial fixation on angry faces, which was accompanied by enhanced activity in the right amygdala; however, oxytocin administration reversed this effect in the BPD participants, attenuating activity in the right amygdala and fixations. Interestingly, the opposite pattern was observed for the healthy control women in this study, with oxytocin heightening activity in the right amygdala in response to angry (minus happy) faces, a finding consistent with Domes et al. (Domes et al., 2010). Based on these findings, the authors conclude that oxytocin may decrease BPD "hypersensitivity to social threat" and, in this way, may be helpful in reducing anger and aggressive behavior in this population, and explanation that is consistent with the anxiety reduction hypothesis of oxytocin.

Regarding possible mechanisms, the findings by Simeon et al. (2011) and Bertsch et al. (2013) are consistent with the anxiety reduction hypothesis of oxytocin. Conversely, Bartz, Simeon, et al.'s (2011) and Ebert et al.'s (2013) findings, as well as the findings in anxiously attached individuals more generally, are more consistent with the social salience and affiliative motivation hypotheses: If oxytocin increases the salience of social cues and/or the desire to affiliate, then it should amplify attention to those cues and the expectancies associated with those cues – be they positive or negative; such amplification could then have downstream consequences on expectations and behavior. Here it is noteworthy that studies showing contextual moderation in healthy adults are in line with this interpretation. In particular, although oxytocin increases trust and cooperation when people are interacting with familiar others, research indicates that oxytocin can *decrease* trust when people are interacting with strangers, for example (Declerck et al., 2010; Declerck, Boone, & Kiyonari, 2014) and out-group members, at least under conditions of fear (De Dreu et al., 2010). One possibility is that while oxytocin might reduce attention to threating faces in more neutral contexts and/or with task-based measures, such effects may not extend to highly charged social contexts that involve a great deal of uncertainly (like the assurance or trust games). Others have argued that oxytocin may strengthen self-confidence (Panksepp & Biven, 2012), perhaps giving those with BPD the courage to engage in more anti-social behaviors. Although plausible, this does not explain why oxytocin increases mistrust in BPD; moreover, the aforementioned work showing a selective decrease in agency – i.e., feelings of self-confidence (Bartz et al., 2015) in anxiously attached individuals, and work showing that interpersonally vulnerable individuals do not show the typical anxiolytic response from oxytocin (Meinlschmidt & Heim, 2007; Norman et al., 2010) speak against this argument. Future work is needed to both better understand the factors that influence trust and cooperation in BPD as well as the effects of oxytocin in this population.

Beyond personality: the oxytocin receptor gene

In addition to personality, other factors including context, gender and/or sex, as well as variability in the endogenous oxytocin system can moderate the effects of intranasal oxytocin. Given space constraints, we focus on one such factor: variation in the oxytocin receptor gene (*OXTR*; Gimpl & Fahrenholz, 2001; Inoue et al., 2010; Tost et al., 2010). To date, most studies examining the *OXTR* focus on two single nucleotide polymorphisms (SNPs): rs53576 and rs2254298 (see Kumsta & Heinrichs, 2013). Although the exact functional significance of these polymorphisms is not known, it is thought that these genetic variations may influence the number of oxytocin receptors and/or their sensitivity to oxytocin (Chen, Heinrichs, & Johnson, 2017). A comprehensive review of this literature is beyond the scope of this chapter; below we provide an overview specifically focusing on studies that suggests these polymorphisms may track with the personality moderating factors described above.

A number of studies have linked *OXTR* polymorphisms with empathy/empathic abilities. In one of the first such studies, Rodrigues, Saslow, Garcia, John, and Keltner (2009), sample size 192, showed that individuals homozygous for the G allele (i.e., GG) of rs53576, compared to those with at least one copy of the A allele (i.e., AA, AG), exhibited higher dispositional empathy and performed better on the RMET. Similarly, Smith and colleagues (Smith, Porges, Norman, Connelly, & Decety, 2014) had participants ($N = 51$) view people experiencing physical pain; individuals with rs53576 GG showed stronger levels of sympathetic arousal and greater empathic concern, compared to A allele carriers. In another study investigating how people respond when a close other is threatened ($N = 162$), Buffone and Poulin (2014) found that participants with the rs53576 GG allele were more likely to display aggression (measured by a rating scale) on the other person's behalf, compared to those who did not carry the GG allele. Of note, these findings are consistent with recent animal research linking oxytocin with maternal aggression (Bosch, Meddle, Beiderbeck, Douglas, & Neumann, 2005; Pedersen, Caldwell, Peterson, Walker, & Mason, 1992; Rickenbacher, Perry, Sullivan, & Moita, 2017), and the "Tend and Defend" model of oxytocin (De Dreu et al., 2010).

In addition to empathy, *OXTR* polymorphisms have also been associated with differences in emotion regulation. For example, in the aforementioned study by Rodriguez et al. (2009), individuals with an A allele on rs53576 (compared to those homozygous for the G allele), showed a higher psychological (i.e., subjective feelings) and physiological (i.e., heart rate) stress response in anticipation of a stress task. Other research has looked at *OXTR* and the capacity to receive social support in anticipation of a psychosocial stressor. Specifically, in a study of 173 participants, Chen et al. (2011) used the aforementioned TSST to manipulate psychosocial stress; participants were randomly assigned to a social support condition (i.e., they brought a close friend to the testing session), or control condition (they came alone). Only participants carrying at least one copy of the G allele (i.e., GG, AG) on rs53576 showed a reduction in physiological stress (i.e., cortisol) after receiving social support; homozygous A allele carriers did not. Kanthak, Chen, Kumsta, Hill, Thayer, and Heinrichs (2016) conceptually replicated this effect in a sample of 203 participants. They found that only GG genotype carriers of rs53576 (10 GG allele carriers in total; 5 in the experimental group) showed increased heart-rate variability – an indicator of stress regulation via the recruitment of the autonomic nervous system (Gerteis & Schwerdtfeger, 2016; Kok & Fredrickson, 2010) – after receiving social support in anticipation of a psychosocial stressor.

In sum, these findings suggest that, compared to those carrying at least one A allele, individuals homozygous for the G allele of rs53576 appear to possess higher levels of social-emotional sensitivity and a greater capacity to benefit from the provision of social support. As with the nasal administration research, however, caution is warranted when interpreting these data as it does not appear to be a simple good-bad story. Bradley et al. (2011) conducted a large-scale genetics study involving 1,632 participants, 308 of which completed measures of adult attachment. The found that GG genotype carriers actually had a *greater* risk for emotion dysregulation and were more likely to be characterized by disorganized attachment in adulthood if they had experienced significant childhood abuse. Similarly, McQuaid et al. (2013, 2014) showed that GG (vs. AA) genotype carriers had higher levels of depressive symptomatology if they had experienced early life maltreatment ($N = 288$). The data suggest that while GG allele carriers' increased social sensitivity can be beneficial in positive social environments, their increased social sensitivity can be *detrimental* in more negative social environments; conversely, the decreased social sensitivity of A allele carriers may make them more resilient to the effects of severe childhood adversity. This interpretation is consistent with the more general "sensitivity hypothesis" (Belsky, Bakermans-Kranenburg, & van IJzendoorn, 2007; Boyce & Ellis, 2005). Of course, as with the intranasal oxytocin work, these differential effects could also be due to false positives and/or false negatives.

In sum, although more work is needed, studies show that *OXTR* polymorphisms track with key individual difference moderators of exogenous oxytocin's effects; this raises the intriguing possibility that (at least some of) intranasal oxytocin's person-dependent effects may be related to variations in the sequences on oxytocin genes.

4. Concluding comments

In conclusion, research in non-human animals, and recent work in humans, suggests that oxytocin is a key factor in attachment and affiliative behavior. We argued, however, that the "love hormone" view of oxytocin is overly simplistic and that the effects of oxytocin, while real, are nuanced and, specifically, critically depend on person factors. It is well-established that the same situation can yield very different behavioral responses because of individual differences. We argue that such a person X situation *interactionist* perspective can also explain peoples' differential response to oxytocin. In particular, individual differences in the way people construe and encode information, their expectancies and beliefs, their unique affective and self-regulatory styles, competencies, goals, and values will critically shape their response to intranasal oxytocin. Critically though, we further argue that the person-dependent effects of oxytocin are systematic in that oxytocin appears to facilitate social cognition and behavior in individuals who are less motivated to engage socially, or who lack the skills to do so, but that oxytocin can have detrimental (social) effects for those who are excessively preoccupied with closeness and the possibility of rejection – in particular, those characterized by attachment anxiety, early life adversity and Borderline Personality Disorder. Although beyond the scope of this review, as argued here and elsewhere (Bartz, 2016; Bartz, Zaki,et al., 2011), these individual difference effects may, in fact, shed light on the underlying mechanism(s) by which oxytocin modulates human sociality; in particular, adjudicating between the social salience, affiliative motivation, and anxiety reduction hypotheses (see Table 12.1). It is our hope that future research will begin to tackle this question of mechanism as this knowledge will be critical for making predictions about when and for whom oxytocin augmentation might be expected to have socially beneficial effects and when it might be expected to have null or detrimental social effects.

References

Anagnostou, E., Soorya, L., Chaplin, W., Bartz, J.A., Halpern, D., Wasserman, S., . . . Hollander, E. (2012). Intranasal oxytocin versus placebo in the treatment of adults with autism spectrum disorders: A randomized controlled trial. *Molecular Autism, 3*(1), 16.

Andari, E., Duhamel, J-R., Zalla, T., Herbrecht, E., Leboyer, M., & Sirigu, A. (2010). Promoting social behavior with oxytocin in high-functioning autism spectrum disorders. *Proceedings of the National Academy of Sciences, 107*(9), 4389–4394. https://doi.org/10.1073/pnas.0910249107

Andari, E., Richard, N., Leboyer, M., & Sirigu, A. (2016). Adaptive coding of the value of social cues with oxytocin, an fMRI study in autism spectrum disorder. *Cortex, 76,* 79–88. https://doi.org/10.1016/j.cortex.2015.12.010

Aron, A., Aron, E.N., & Smollan, D. (1992). Inclusion of other in the self scale and the structure of interpersonal closeness. *Journal of Personality and Social Psychology, 63*(4), 596.

Arueti, M., Perach-Barzilay, N., Tsoory, M.M., Berger, B., Getter, N., & Shamay-Tsoory, S.G. (2013). When two become one: The role of oxytocin in interpersonal coordination and cooperation. *Journal of Cognitive Neuroscience, 25*(9), 1418–1427. https://doi.org/10.1162/jocn_a_00400

Bakermans-Kranenburg, M.J., van IJzendoorn, M.H., Riem, M.M., Tops, M., & Alink, L.R. (2012). Oxytocin decreases handgrip force in reaction to infant crying in females without harsh parenting experiences. *Social Cognitive and Affective Neuroscience, 7*(8), 951–957. https://doi.org/10.1093/scan/nsr067

Bakermans-Kranenburg, M.J., & van IJzendoorn, M.H.V. (2013). Sniffing around oxytocin: Review and meta-analyses of trials in healthy and clinical groups with implications for pharmacotherapy. *Translational Psychiatry, 3*(5), e258. https://doi.org/10.1038/tp.2013.34

Baron-Cohen, S., & Wheelwright, S. (2004). The empathy quotient: An investigation of adults with Asperger syndrome or high functioning autism, and normal sex differences. *Journal of Autism and Developmental Disorders, 34*(2), 163–175. https://doi.org/10.1023/B:JADD.0000022607.19833.00

Baron-Cohen, S., Wheelwright, S., Hill, J., Raste, Y., & Plumb, I. (2001). The "Reading the Mind in the Eyes" test revised version: A study with normal adults, and adults with Asperger syndrome or high-functioning autism. *Journal of Child Psychology and Psychiatry, 42*(2), 241–251. https://doi.org/10.1111/1469-7610.00715

Baron-Cohen, S., Wheelwright, S., Skinner, R., Martin, J., & Clubley, E. (2001). The Autism-Spectrum Quotient (AQ): Evidence from Asperger syndrome/high-functioning autism, males and females, scientists and mathematicians. *Journal of Autism and Developmental Disorders, 31*(1), 5–17. https://doi.org/10.1023/A:1005653411471

Bartz, J.A. (2016). Oxytocin and the pharmacological dissection of affiliation. *Current Directions in Psychological Science, 25*(2), 104–110. https://doi.org/10.1177/0963721415626678

Bartz, J.A., & Hollander, E. (2006). The neuroscience of affiliation: Forging links between basic and clinical research on neuropeptides and social behavior. *Hormones and Behavior, 50*(4), 518–528. https://doi.org/10.1016/j.yhbeh.2006.06.018

Bartz, J.A., & Lydon, J.E. (2006). Navigating the interdependence dilemma: Attachment goals and the use of communal norms with potential close others. *Journal of Personality and Social Psychology, 91*(1), 77.

Bartz, J.A., & Lydon, J.E. (2008). Relationship-specific attachment, risk regulation, and communal norm adherence in close relationships. *Journal of Experimental Social Psychology, 44*(3), 655–663. https://doi.org/10.1016/j.jesp.2007.04.003

Bartz, J.A., Lydon, J.E., Kolevzon, A., Zaki, J., Hollander, E., Ludwig, N., & Bolger, N. (2015). Differential effects of oxytocin on agency and communion for anxiously and avoidantly attached individuals. *Psychological Science*, 0956797615580279. https://doi.org/10.1177/0956797615580279

Bartz, J.A., Zaki, J., Ochsner, K.N., Bolger, N., Kolevzon, A., Ludwig, N., & Lydon, J.E. (2010). Effects of oxytocin on recollections of maternal care and closeness. *Proceedings of the National Academy of Sciences, 107*(50), 21371–21375. https://doi.org/10.1073/pnas.1012669107Bartz, J.A., Zaki, J., Bolger, N., Hollander, E., Ludwig, N.N., Kolevzon, A., & Ochsner, K.N. (2010). Oxytocin selectively improves empathic accuracy. *Psychological Science, 21*(10), 1426–1428. https://doi.org/10.1177/0956797610383439Bartz, J.A., Zaki, J., Bolger, N., & Ochsner, K.N. (2011). Social effects of oxytocin in humans: Context and person matter. *Trends in Cognitive Sciences.* https://doi.org/10.1016/j.tics.2011.05.002

Bartz, J.A., Simeon, D., Hamilton, H., Kim, S., Crystal, S., Braun, A., . . . Hollander, E. (2011). Oxytocin can hinder trust and cooperation in borderline personality disorder. *Social Cognitive and Affective Neuroscience, 6*(5), 556–563. https://doi.org/10.1093/scan/nsq085

Baumeister, R.F., & Leary, M.R. (1995). The need to belong: Desire for interpersonal attachments as a fundamental human motivation. *Psychological Bulletin, 173*(3).

Baumgartner, T., Heinrichs, M., Vonlanthen, A., Fischbacher, U., & Fehr, E. (2008). Oxytocin shapes the neural circuitry of trust and trust adaptation in humans. *Neuron, 58*(4), 639–650. https://doi.org/10.1016/j.neuron.2008.04.009

Bellini, S. (2006). The development of social anxiety in adolescents with autism spectrum disorders. *Focus on Autism and Other Developmental Disabilities, 21*(3), 138–145. https://doi.org/10.1177/10883576060210030201

Belsky, J., Bakermans-Kranenburg, M.J., & van IJzendoorn, M.H. (2007). For better and for worse: Differential susceptibility to environmental influences. *Current Directions in Psychological Science, 16*(6), 300–304. https://doi.org/10.1111/j.1467-8721.2007.00525.x

Bertsch, K., Gamer, M., Schmidt, B., Schmidinger, I., Walther, S., Kästel, T., . . . Herpertz, S. C. (2013). Oxytocin and reduction of social threat hypersensitivity in women with borderline personality disorder. *American Journal of Psychiatry, 170*(10), 1169–1177. https://doi.org/10.1176/appi.ajp.2013.13020263

Bielsky, I.F., & Young, L.J. (2004). Oxytocin, vasopressin, and social recognition in mammals. *Peptides, 25*(9), 1565–1574. https://doi.org/10.1016/j.peptides.2004.05.019

Born, J., Lange, T., Kern, W., McGregor, G.P., Bickel, U., & Fehm, H.L. (2002). Sniffing neuropeptides: A transnasal approach to the human brain. *Nature Neuroscience, 5*(6), 514–516. https://doi.org/10.1038/nn849

Bos, P.A., Panksepp, J., Bluthé, R-M., & van Honk, J. (2012). Acute effects of steroid hormones and neuropeptides on human social-emotional behavior: A review of single administration studies. *Frontiers in Neuroendocrinology, 33*(1), 17–35. https://doi.org/10.1016/j.yfrne.2011.01.002

Bosch, O.J., Meddle, S.L., Beiderbeck, D.I., Douglas, A.J., & Neumann, I.D. (2005). Brain oxytocin correlates with maternal aggression: Link to anxiety. *Journal of Neuroscience, 25*(29), 6807–6815. https://doi.org/10.1523/JNEUROSCI.1342-05.2005

Bosch, O.J., & Neumann, I.D. (2012). Both oxytocin and vasopressin are mediators of maternal care and aggression in rodents: From central release to sites of action. *Hormones and Behavior, 61*(3), 293–303. https://doi.org/10.1016/j.yhbeh.2011.11.002

Boyce, W.T., & Ellis, B.J. (2005). Biological sensitivity to context: I. An evolutionary-developmental theory of the origins and functions of stress reactivity. *Development and Psychopathology, 17*(02). https://doi.org/10.1017/S0954579405050145

Bradley, B., Westen, D., Mercer, K.B., Binder, E.B., Jovanovic, T., Crain, D., . . . Heim, C. (2011). Association between childhood maltreatment and adult emotional dysregulation in a low-income, urban, African American sample: Moderation by oxytocin receptor gene. *Development and Psychopathology, 23*(2), 439–452. https://doi.org/10.1017/S0954579411000162

Buffone, A.E.K., & Poulin, M.J. (2014). Empathy, target distress, and neurohormone genes interact to predict aggression for others – even without provocation. *Personality and Social Psychology Bulletin, 40*(11), 1406–1422. https://doi.org/10.1177/0146167214549320

Button, K.S., Ioannidis, J.P.A., Mokrysz, C., Nosek, B.A., Flint, J., Robinson, E.S.J., & Munafò, M.R. (2013). Power failure: Why small sample size undermines the reliability of neuroscience. *Nature Reviews Neuroscience, 14*(5), 365–376. https://doi.org/10.1038/nrn3475

Carter, C.S. (1998). Neuroendocrine perspectives on social attachment and love. *Psychoneuroendocrinology, 23*(8), 779–818. https://doi.org/10.1016/S0306-4530(98)00055-9

Carter, C.S., Devries, A.C., & Getz, L.L. (1995). Physiological substrates of mammalian monogamy: The prairie vole model. *Neuroscience & Biobehavioral Reviews, 19*(2), 303–314. https://doi.org/10.1016/0149-7634(94)00070-H

Chen, F.S., Heinrichs, M., & Johnson, S.C. (2017). Oxytocin and the emergence of individual differences in the social regulation of stress. *Social and Personality Psychology Compass, 11*(8), n/a–n/a. https://doi.org/10.1111/spc3.12332

Chen, F.S., Kumsta, R., von Dawans, B., Monakhov, M., Ebstein, R.P., & Heinrichs, M. (2011). Common Oxytocin Receptor gene (OXTR) polymorphism and social support interact to reduce stress in humans. *Proceedings of the National Academy of Sciences, 108*(50), 19937–19942. https://doi.org/10.1073/pnas.1113079108

Chevallier, C., Kohls, G., Troiani, V., Brodkin, E.S., & Schultz, R.T. (2012). The social motivation theory of autism. *Trends in Cognitive Sciences, 16*(4), 231–239. https://doi.org/10.1016/j.tics.2012.02.007

Cook, R., Brewer, R., Shah, P., & Bird, G. (2013). Alexithymia, not autism, predicts poor recognition of emotional facial expressions. *Psychological Science, 24*(5), 723–732.

Dadds, M.R., MacDonald, E., Cauchi, A., Williams, K., Levy, F., & Brennan, J. (2014). Nasal oxytocin for social deficits in childhood autism: A randomized controlled trial. *Journal of Autism and Developmental Disorders, 44*(3), 521–531. https://doi.org/10.1007/s10803-013-1899-3

Dannlowski, U., Kugel, H., Huber, F., Stuhrmann, A., Redlich, R., Grotegerd, D., . . . Suslow, T. (2013). Childhood maltreatment is associated with an automatic negative emotion processing bias in the amygdala: Amygdalar emotion processing bias. *Human Brain Mapping, 34*(11), 2899–2909. https://doi.org/10.1002/hbm.22112

Davis, M.H. (1980). A multidimensional approach to individual differences in empathy. *JSAS Catalog of Selected Documents in Psychology, 10*(85).

De Dreu, C.K.W. (2012). Oxytocin modulates the link between adult attachment and cooperation through reduced betrayal aversion. *Psychoneuroendocrinology, 37*(7), 871–880. https://doi.org/10.1016/j.psyneuen.2011.10.003

De Dreu, C.K.W., Greer, L.L., Handgraaf, M.J.J., Shalvi, S., Kleef, G.A.V., Baas, M., . . . Feith, S.W.W. (2010). The neuropeptide oxytocin regulates parochial altruism in intergroup conflict among humans. *Science, 328*(5984), 1408–1411. https://doi.org/10.1126/science.1189047

Declerck, C.H., Boone, C., & Kiyonari, T. (2010). Oxytocin and cooperation under conditions of uncertainty: The modulating role of incentives and social information. *Hormones and Behavior, 57*(3), 368–374. https://doi.org/10.1016/j.yhbeh.2010.01.006

Declerck, C.H., Boone, C., & Kiyonari, T. (2014). The effect of oxytocin on cooperation in a prisoner's dilemma depends on the social context and a person's social value orientation. *Social Cognitive and Affective Neuroscience, 9*(6), 802–809. https://doi.org/10.1093/scan/nst040

DeWall, C.N., Gillath, O., Pressman, S.D., Black, L.L., Bartz, J.A., Moskovitz, J., & Stetler, D.A. (2014). When the love hormone leads to violence: Oxytocin increases intimate partner violence inclinations among high trait aggressive people. *Social Psychological and Personality Science*, 5(6), 691–697. https://doi.org/10.1177/1948550613516876

Domes, G., Heinrichs, M., Gläscher, J., Büchel, C., Braus, D.F., & Herpertz, S.C. (2007). Oxytocin attenuates amygdala responses to emotional faces regardless of valence. *Biological Psychiatry*, 62(10), 1187–1190. https://doi.org/10.1016/j.biopsych.2007.03.025

Domes, G., Lischke, A., Berger, C., Grossmann, A., Hauenstein, K., Heinrichs, M., & Herpertz, S.C. (2010). Effects of intranasal oxytocin on emotional face processing in women. *Psychoneuroendocrinology*, 35(1), 83–93. https://doi.org/10.1016/j.psyneuen.2009.06.016

Ebert, A., Kolb, M., Heller, J., Edel, M-A., Roser, P., & Brüne, M. (2013). Modulation of interpersonal trust in borderline personality disorder by intranasal oxytocin and childhood trauma. *Social Neuroscience*, 8(4), 305–313. https://doi.org/10.1080/17470919.2013.807301

Feeser, M., Fan, Y., Weigand, A., Hahn, A., Gärtner, M., Böker, H., . . . Bajbouj, M. (2015). Oxytocin improves mentalizing – pronounced effects for individuals with attenuated ability to empathize. *Psychoneuroendocrinology*, 53, 223–232.

Feldman, R., Weller, A., Zagoory-Sharon, O., & Levine, A. (2007). Evidence for a neuroendocrinological foundation of human affiliation. *Psychological Science*, 18.

Fonzo, G.A., Ramsawh, H.J., Flagan, T.M., Simmons, A.N., Sullivan, S.G., Allard, C.B., . . . Stein, M.B. (2016). Early life stress and the anxious brain: Evidence for a neural mechanism linking childhood emotional maltreatment to anxiety in adulthood. *Psychological Medicine*, 46(5), 1037–1054. https://doi.org/10.1017/S0033291715002603

Gao, S., Becker, B., Luo, L., Geng, Y., Zhao, W., Yin, Y., . . . Kendrick, K.M. (2016). Oxytocin, the peptide that bonds the sexes also divides them. *Proceedings of the National Academy of Sciences*, 113(27), 7650–7654. https://doi.org/10.1073/pnas.1602620113

Gerteis, A.K.S., & Schwerdtfeger, A.R. (2016). When rumination counts: Perceived social support and heart rate variability in daily life. *Psychophysiology*, 53(7), 1034–1043. https://doi.org/10.1111/psyp.12652

Gimpl, G., & Fahrenholz, F. (2001). The oxytocin receptor system: Structure, function, and regulation. *Physiological Reviews*, 81(2), 629–683.

Gordon, I., Martin, C., Feldman, R., & Leckman, J.F. (2011). Oxytocin and social motivation. *Developmental Cognitive Neuroscience*, 1(4), 471–493. https://doi.org/10.1016/j.dcn.2011.07.007

Gray, J.A. (1981). A critique of Eysenck's theory of personality. In *A model for personality* (pp. 246–276). Berlin, Heidelberg: Springer. https://doi.org/10.1007/978-3-642-67783-0_8

Gray, J.A. (1987). *The psychology of fear and stress*. Cambridge: Cambridge University Press.

Guastella, A.J., Einfeld, S.L., Gray, K.M., Rinehart, N.J., Tonge, B.J., Lambert, T.J., & Hickie, I.B. (2010). Intranasal oxytocin improves emotion recognition for youth with autism spectrum disorders. *Biological Psychiatry*, 67(7), 692–694. https://doi.org/10.1016/j.biopsych.2009.09.020

Guastella, A.J., Gray, K.M., Rinehart, N.J., Alvares, G.A., Tonge, B.J., Hickie, I.B., . . . Einfeld, S.L. (2015). The effects of a course of intranasal oxytocin on social behaviors in youth diagnosed with autism spectrum disorders: A randomized controlled trial. *Journal of Child Psychology and Psychiatry*, 56(4), 444–452. https://doi.org/10.1111/jcpp.12305

Guastella, A.J., Howard, A.L., Dadds, M.R., Mitchell, P., & Carson, D.S. (2009). A randomized controlled trial of intranasal oxytocin as an adjunct to exposure therapy for social anxiety disorder. *Psychoneuroendocrinology*, 34(6), 917–923. https://doi.org/10.1016/j.psyneuen.2009.01.005

Guastella, A.J., Mitchell, P.B., & Dadds, M.R. (2008). Oxytocin increases gaze to the eye region of human faces. *Biological Psychiatry*, 63(1), 3–5. https://doi.org/10.1016/j.biopsych.2007.06.026

Guzmán, Y.F., Tronson, N.C., Jovasevic, V., Sato, K., Guedea, A.L., Mizukami, H., . . . Radulovic, J. (2013). Fear-enhancing effects of septal oxytocin receptors. *Nature Neuroscience*, 16(9), 1185–1187. https://doi.org/10.1038/nn.3465

Guzmán, Y.F., Tronson, N.C., Sato, K., Mesic, I., Guedea, A.L., Nishimori, K., & Radulovic, J. (2014). Role of oxytocin receptors in modulation of fear by social memory. *Psychopharmacology*, 231(10), 2097–2105. https://doi.org/10.1007/s00213-013-3356-6

Heinrichs, M., Baumgartner, T., Kirschbaum, C., & Ehlert, U. (2003). Social support and oxytocin interact to suppress cortisol and subjective responses to psychosocial stress. *Biological Psychiatry*, 54(12), 1389–1398. https://doi.org/10.1016/S0006-3223(03)00465-7

Heinrichs, M., & Domes, G. (2008). Neuropeptides and social behaviour: Effects of oxytocin and vasopressin in humans. In *Progress in brain research* (Vol. 170, pp. 337–350). Elsevier.

Hirosawa, T., Kikuchi, M., Higashida, H., Okumura, E., Ueno, S., Shitamichi, K., . . . Minabe, Y. (2012). Oxytocin attenuates feelings of hostility depending on emotional context and individuals' characteristics. *Scientific Reports*, *2*, 384. https://doi.org/10.1038/srep00384

Hollander, E., Bartz, J.A., Chaplin, W., Phillips, A., Sumner, J., Soorya, L., . . . Wasserman, S. (2007). Oxytocin increases retention of social cognition in autism. *Biological Psychiatry*, *61*(4), 498–503. https://doi.org/10.1016/j.biopsych.2006.05.030

Hollander, E., Novotny, S., Hanratty, M., Yaffe, R., DeCaria, C.M., Aronowitz, B.R., & Mosovich, S. (2003). Oxytocin infusion reduces repetitive behaviors in adults with autistic and Asperger's disorders. *Neuropsychopharmacology; New York*, *28*(1), 193–198. http://dx.doi.org/10.1038/sj.npp.1300021

Human, L.J., Thorson, K.R., & Mendes, W.B. (2016). Interactive effects between extraversion and oxytocin administration: Implications for positive social processes. *Social Psychological and Personality Science*, *7*(7), 735–744. https://doi.org/10.1177/1948550616644964

Inoue, H., Yamasue, H., Tochigi, M., Abe, O., Liu, X., Kawamura, Y., . . . Kasai, K. (2010). Association between the oxytocin receptor gene and amygdalar volume in healthy adults. *Biological Psychiatry*, *68*(11), 1066–1072. https://doi.org/10.1016/j.biopsych.2010.07.019

Insel, T.R. (2010). The challenge of translation in social neuroscience: A review of oxytocin, vasopressin, and affiliative behavior. *Neuron*, *65*(6), 768–779. https://doi.org/10.1016/j.neuron.2010.03.005

Ioannidis, J.P.A. (2012). Why science is not necessarily self-correcting. *Perspectives on Psychological Science*, *7*(6), 645–654. https://doi.org/10.1177/1745691612464056

Kanthak, M.K., Chen, F.S., Kumsta, R., Hill, L.K., Thayer, J.F., & Heinrichs, M. (2016). Oxytocin receptor gene polymorphism modulates the effects of social support on heart rate variability. *Biological Psychology*, *117*, 43–49. https://doi.org/10.1016/j.biopsycho.2016.02.007

Keverne, E.B., & Kendrick, K.M. (1992). Oxytocin facilitation of maternal behavior in sheep. *Annals of the New York Academy of Sciences*, *652*(1), 83–101.

King-Casas, B., Sharp, C., Lomax-Bream, L., Lohrenz, T., Fonagy, P., & Montague, P.R. (2008). The rupture and repair of cooperation in borderline personality disorder. *Science*, *321*(5890), 806–810. https://doi.org/10.1126/science.1156902

Kirsch, P., Esslinger, C., Chen, Q., Mier, D., Lis, S., Siddhanti, S., . . . Meyer-Lindenberg, A. (2005). Oxytocin modulates neural circuitry for social cognition and fear in humans. *Journal of Neuroscience*, *25*(49), 11489–11493. https://doi.org/10.1523/JNEUROSCI.3984-05.2005

Kirschbaum, C., Pirke, K-M., & Hellhammer, D.H. (1993). The Trier Social Stress Test – a tool for investigating psychobiological stress responses in a laboratory setting. *Neuropsychobiology*, *28*, 76–81.

Kok, B.E., & Fredrickson, B.L. (2010). Upward spirals of the heart: Autonomic flexibility, as indexed by vagal tone, reciprocally and prospectively predicts positive emotions and social connectedness. *Biological Psychology*, *85*(3), 432–436. https://doi.org/10.1016/j.biopsycho.2010.09.005

Kosfeld, M., Heinrichs, M., Zak, P.J., Fischbacher, U., & Fehr, E. (2005). Oxytocin increases trust in humans. *Nature*, *435*(7042), 673–676. https://doi.org/10.1038/nature03701

Kumsta, R., & Heinrichs, M. (2013). Oxytocin, stress and social behavior: Neurogenetics of the human oxytocin system. *Current Opinion in Neurobiology*, *23*(1), 11–16. https://doi.org/10.1016/j.conb.2012.09.004

Lane, A., Luminet, O., Nave, G., & Mikolajczak, M. (2016). Is there a publication bias in behavioural intranasal oxytocin research on humans? Opening the file drawer of one laboratory. *Journal of Neuroendocrinology*, *28*(4). https://doi.org/10.1111/jne.12384

Lee, H-J., Macbeth, A.H., Pagani, J., & Young, W.S. (2009). Oxytocin: The great facilitator of life. *Progress in Neurobiology*, *88*(2), 127–151. https://doi.org/10.1016/j.pneurobio.2009.04.001

Leknes, S., Wessberg, J., Ellingsen, D-M., Chelnokova, O., Olausson, H., & Laeng, B. (2013). Oxytocin enhances pupil dilation and sensitivity to "hidden" emotional expressions. *Social Cognitive and Affective Neuroscience*, *8*(7), 741–749. https://doi.org/10.1093/scan/nss062

Luminet, O., Grynberg, D., Ruzette, N., & Mikolajczak, M. (2011). Personality-dependent effects of oxytocin: Greater social benefits for high alexithymia scorers. *Biological Psychology*, *87*(3), 401–406. https://doi.org/10.1016/j.biopsycho.2011.05.005

MacDonald, K., MacDonald, T.M., Brüne, M., Lamb, K., Wilson, M.P., Golshan, S., & Feifel, D. (2013). Oxytocin and psychotherapy: A pilot study of its physiological, behavioral and subjective effects in males with depression. *Psychoneuroendocrinology*, *38*(12), 2831–2843. https://doi.org/10.1016/j.psyneuen.2013.05.014

Marlin, B.J., Mitre, M., D'Amour, J.A., Chao, M.V., & Froemke, R.C. (2015). Oxytocin enables maternal behaviour by balancing cortical inhibition. *Nature, 520*(7548), 499–504. https://doi.org/10.1038/nature14402

McQuaid, R.J., McInnis, O.A., Abizaid, A., & Anisman, H. (2014). Making room for oxytocin in understanding depression. *Neuroscience & Biobehavioral Reviews, 45*, 305–322. https://doi.org/10.1016/j.neubiorev.2014.07.005

McQuaid, R.J., McInnis, O.A., Stead, J.D., Matheson, K., & Anisman, H. (2013). A paradoxical association of an oxytocin receptor gene polymorphism: Early-life adversity and vulnerability to depression. *Frontiers in Neuroscience, 7.* https://doi.org/10.3389/fnins.2013.00128

Meinlschmidt, G., & Heim, C. (2007). Sensitivity to intranasal oxytocin in adult men with early parental separation. *Biological Psychiatry, 61*(9), 1109–1111. https://doi.org/10.1016/j.biopsych.2006.09.007

Messick, D.M., & McClintock, C.G. (1968). Motivational bases of choice in experimental games. *Journal of Experimental Social Psychology, 4*(1), 1–25. https://doi.org/10.1016/0022-1031(68)90046-2

Mikolajczak, M., Gross, J.J., Lane, A., Corneille, O., de Timary, P., & Luminet, O. (2010). Oxytocin makes people trusting, not gullible. *Psychological Science, 21*(8), 1072–1074. https://doi.org/10.1177/0956797610377343

Mischel, W. (1973). Toward a cognitive social learning reconceptualization of personality. *Psychological Review, 80*(4).

Modahl, C., Green, L.A., Fein, D., Morris, M., Waterhouse, L., Feinstein, C., & Levin, H. (1998). Plasma oxytocin levels in autistic children. *Biological Psychiatry, 43*(4), 270–277. https://doi.org/10.1016/S0006-3223(97)00439-3

Nave, G., Camerer, C., & McCullough, M. (2015). Does oxytocin increase trust in humans? A critical review of research. *Perspectives on Psychological Science, 10*(6), 772–789. https://doi.org/10.1177/1745691615600138

Neumann, I.D., & Landgraf, R. (2012). Balance of brain oxytocin and vasopressin: Implications for anxiety, depression, and social behaviors. *Trends in Neurosciences, 35*(11), 649–659. https://doi.org/10.1016/j.tins.2012.08.004

Norman, G.J., Karelina, K., Morris, J.S., Zhang, N., Cochran, M., & Courtney DeVries, A. (2010). Social interaction prevents the development of depressive-like behavior post nerve injury in mice: A potential role for oxytocin. *Psychosomatic Medicine, 72*(6), 519–526. https://doi.org/10.1097/PSY.0b013e3181de8678

Olazábal, D.E., & Young, L.J. (2006). Oxytocin receptors in the nucleus accumbens facilitate "spontaneous" maternal behavior in adult female prairie voles. *Neuroscience, 141*(2), 559–568. https://doi.org/10.1016/j.neuroscience.2006.04.017

Panksepp, J., & Biven, L. (2012). *The archaeology of mind: Neuroevolutionary origins of human emotions.* New York, NY: W.W. Norton & Company.

Parker, G., Tupling, H., & Brown, L.B. (1979). A parental bonding instrument. *British Journal of Medical Psychology, 52*(1), 1–10. https://doi.org/10.1111/j.2044-8341.1979.tb02487.x

Pedersen, C.A., Caldwell, J.D., Peterson, G., Walker, C.H., & Mason, G.A. (1992). Oxytocin activation of maternal behavior in the Rata. *Annals of the New York Academy of Sciences, 652*(1), 58–69. https://doi.org/10.1111/j.1749-6632.1992.tb34346.x

Quirin, M., Kuhl, J., & Düsing, R. (2011). Oxytocin buffers cortisol responses to stress in individuals with impaired emotion regulation abilities. *Psychoneuroendocrinology, 36*(6), 898–904. https://doi.org/10.1016/j.psyneuen.2010.12.005

Radke, S., & de Bruijn, E.R.A. (2015). Does oxytocin affect mind-reading? A replication study. *Psychoneuroendocrinology, 60*, 75–81. https://doi.org/10.1016/j.psyneuen.2015.06.006

Rickenbacher, E., Perry, R.E., Sullivan, R.M., & Moita, M.A. (2017). Freezing suppression by oxytocin in central amygdala allows alternate defensive behaviours and mother-pup interactions. *ELife, 6.*

Riem, M.M.E., van IJzendoorn, M.H., Tops, M., Boksem, M.A.S., Rombouts, S.A.R.B., & Bakermans-Kranenburg, M.J. (2013). Oxytocin effects on complex brain networks are moderated by experiences of maternal love withdrawal. *European Neuropsychopharmacology, 23*(10), 1288–1295. https://doi.org/10.1016/j.euroneuro.2013.01.011

Riem, M.M.E., Bakermans-Kranenburg, M.J., Huffmeijer, R., & van IJzendoorn, M.H. (2013). Does intranasal oxytocin promote prosocial behavior to an excluded fellow player? A randomized-controlled trial with Cyberball. *Psychoneuroendocrinology, 38*(8), 1418–1425. https://doi.org/10.1016/j.psyneuen.2012.12.023

Riem, M.M.E., Bakermans-Kranenburg, M.J., Voorthuis, A., & van IJzendoorn, M.H. (2014). Oxytocin effects on mind-reading are moderated by experiences of maternal love withdrawal: An fMRI study.

Progress in Neuro-Psychopharmacology and Biological Psychiatry, 51, 105–112. https://doi.org/10.1016/j.pnpbp.2014.01.014

Rimmele, U., Hediger, K., Heinrichs, M., & Klaver, P. (2009). Oxytocin makes a face in memory familiar. *Journal of Neuroscience, 29*(1), 38–42. https://doi.org/10.1523/JNEUROSCI.4260-08.2009

Rockliff, H., Karl, A., McEwan, K., Gilbert, J., Matos, M., & Gilbert, P. (2011). Effects of intranasal oxytocin on "compassion focused imagery". *Emotion, 11*(6), 1388–1396. https://doi.org/10.1037/a0023861

Rodrigues, S.M., Saslow, L.R., Garcia, N., John, O.P., & Keltner, D. (2009). Oxytocin receptor genetic variation relates to empathy and stress reactivity in humans. *Proceedings of the National Academy of Sciences, 106*(50), 21437–21441. https://doi.org/10.1073/pnas.0909579106

Ross, H.E., & Young, L.J. (2009). Oxytocin and the neural mechanisms regulating social cognition and affiliative behavior. *Frontiers in Neuroendocrinology, 30*(4), 534–547. https://doi.org/10.1016/j.yfrne.2009.05.004

Ross, L., & Nisbett, R.E. (2011). *The person and the situation: Perspectives of social psychology.* London: Pinter & Martin Publishers.

Savaskan, E., Ehrhardt, R., Schulz, A., Walter, M., & Schächinger, H. (2008). Post-learning intranasal oxytocin modulates human memory for facial identity. *Psychoneuroendocrinology, 33*(3), 368–374. https://doi.org/10.1016/j.psyneuen.2007.12.004

Shamay-Tsoory, S.G., & Abu-Akel, A. (2016). The social salience hypothesis of oxytocin. *Biological Psychiatry, 79*(3), 194–202. https://doi.org/10.1016/j.biopsych.2015.07.020

Shamay-Tsoory, S.G., Fischer, M., Dvash, J., Harari, H., Perach-Bloom, N., & Levkovitz, Y. (2009). Intranasal administration of oxytocin increases envy and schadenfreude (Gloating). *Biological Psychiatry, 66*(9), 864–870. https://doi.org/10.1016/j.biopsych.2009.06.009

Shaver, P.R., & Brennan, K.A. (1992). Attachment styles and the "Big Five" personality traits: Their connections with each other and with romantic relationship outcomes. *Personality and Social Psychology Bulletin, 18*(5), 536–545. https://doi.org/10.1177/0146167292185003

Shoda, Y., Mischel, W., & Wright, J.C. (1994). Intraindividual stability in the organization and patterning of behavior: Incorporating psychological situations into the idiographic analysis of personality. *Journal of Personality and Social Psychology, 67*(4), 674.

Sifneos, P.E. (1973). The prevalence of "alexithymic" characteristics in psychosomatic patients. *Psychotherapy and Psychosomatics, 22*(2–6), 255–262. https://doi.org/10.1159/000286529

Simeon, D., Bartz, J.A., Hamilton, H., Crystal, S., Braun, A., Ketay, S., & Hollander, E. (2011). Oxytocin administration attenuates stress reactivity in borderline personality disorder: A pilot study. *Psychoneuroendocrinology, 36*(9), 1418–1421. https://doi.org/10.1016/j.psyneuen.2011.03.013

Simmons, J.P., Nelson, L.D., & Simonsohn, U. (2011). False-positive psychology undisclosed flexibility in data collection and analysis allows presenting anything as significant. *Psychological Science,* 0956797611417632. https://doi.org/10.1177/0956797611417632

Smith, K.E., Porges, E.C., Norman, G.J., Connelly, J.J., & Decety, J. (2014). Oxytocin receptor gene variation predicts empathic concern and autonomic arousal while perceiving harm to others. *Social Neuroscience, 9*(1), 1–9. https://doi.org/10.1080/17470919.2013.863223

Stanley, B., & Siever, L.J. (2010). The interpersonal dimension of borderline personality disorder: Toward a neuropeptide model. *American Journal of Psychiatry, 167*(1), 24–39. https://doi.org/10.1176/appi.ajp.2009.09050744

Tost, H., Kolachana, B., Hakimi, S., Lemaitre, H., Verchinski, B.A., Mattay, V.S., . . . Meyer-Lindenberg, A. (2010). A common allele in the Oxytocin Receptor gene (OXTR) impacts prosocial temperament and human hypothalamic-limbic structure and function. *Proceedings of the National Academy of Sciences, 107*(31), 13936–13941. https://doi.org/10.1073/pnas.1003296107

Tottenham, N., Hare, T. A., Millner, A., Gilhooly, T., Zevin, J. D., & Casey, B. J. (2011). Elevated amygdala response to faces following early deprivation. *Developmental Science, 14*(2), 190–204. https://doi.org/10.1111/j.1467-7687.2010.00971.x

van IJzendoorn, M.H., Huffmeijer, R., Alink, L.R.A., Bakermans-Kranenburg, M.J., & Tops, M. (2011). The impact of oxytocin administration on charitable donating is moderated by experiences of parental love-withdrawal. *Frontiers in Psychology, 2.* https://doi.org/10.3389/fpsyg.2011.00258

Van Lange, P.A.M., & Liebrand, W.B.G. (1991). Social value orientation and intelligence: A test of the goal prescribes rationality principle. *European Journal of Social Psychology, 21*(4), 273–292. https://doi.org/10.1002/ejsp.2420210402

Volkmar, F.R., & Klin, A. (2005). Issues in the classification of autism and related conditions. In F.R. Volkmar, R. Paul, A. Klin, & D. Cohen (Eds.), *Handbook of autism and pervasive developmental disorders* (pp. 5–41). Hoboken, NJ: John Wiley & Sons, Inc. https://doi.org/10.1002/9780470939345.ch1

Williams, K.D., & Jarvis, B. (2006). Cyberball: A program for use in research on interpersonal ostracism and acceptance. *Behavior Research Methods, 38*(1), 174–180. https://doi.org/10.3758/BF03192765

Winslow, J.T., Noble, P.L., Lyons, C.K., Sterk, S.M., & Insel, T.R. (2003). Rearing effects on cerebrospinal fluid oxytocin concentration and social buffering in rhesus monkeys. *Neuropsychopharmacology, 28*(5), 910–918. https://doi.org/10.1038/sj.npp.1300128

Wolf, I., Dziobek, I., & Heekeren, H.R. (2010). Neural correlates of social cognition in naturalistic settings: A model-free analysis approach. *NeuroImage, 49*(1), 894–904. https://doi.org/10.1016/j.neuroimage.2009.08.060

Xu, L., Ma, X., Zhao, W., Luo, L., Yao, S., & Kendrick, K.M. (2015). Oxytocin enhances attentional bias for neutral and positive expression faces in individuals with higher autistic traits. *Psychoneuroendocrinology, 62*, 352–358. https://doi.org/10.1016/j.psyneuen.2015.09.002

13

AFFILIATIVE OR AGGRESSIVE? THE ROLE OF OXYTOCIN IN ANTISOCIAL BEHAVIOUR THROUGH THE LENS OF THE SOCIAL SALIENCE HYPOTHESIS

Leehe Peled-Avron and Simone G. Shamay-Tsoory

Oxytocin regulates prosocial and antisocial behaviours: the social salience hypothesis

Antisocial behaviours are actions that do not take the welfare of others and/or of society into consideration or that may cause harm to others or society (Berger, 2003). Furthermore, antisocial behaviours also include acts deemed contrary to prevailing norms of social conduct (Calkins & Keane, 2009). Research has shown that the nonapeptide oxytocin is one of the neurochemical compounds participating in the formation and modulation of both pro- and antisocial behaviours.

Oxytocin is a nine-amino-acid peptide hormone known mainly for its role in enhancing uterine contractions during childbirth and in mediating milk secretion from mammary glands during lactation (for a comprehensive review see Lee, Macbeth, Pagani, & Young, 2009). It is synthesized in the magnocellular neurons of the paraventricular and supraoptic nuclei of the hypothalamus (Gimpl & Fahrenholz, 2001). These nuclei project into the posterior pituitary and release the peptide via axonal transport into the bloodstream, via which it is then transported to multiple peripheral tissues (Gainer, Yamashita, Fields, House, & Rusnak, 2002). Carried by the cerebrospinal fluid (CSF), oxytocin works globally in the brain as a neuro-hormone, exerting its influence on all cells that express the oxytocin receptor (Ludwig & Leng, 2006). As recently discovered, oxytocin also exerts its influence on cells that express arginine-vasopressin receptors (Song & Albers, 2017).

Animal studies have demonstrated that oxytocin plays a major role in social behaviour and affiliation (Donaldson & Young, 2008; Winslow & Insel, 2002; Young & Wang, 2004). These studies inspired a surge of interest in how oxytocin affects prosocial behaviours in humans. Kosfeld, Heinrichs, Zak, Fischbacher, and Fehr (2005) were among the first to find that oxytocin increases trust in cooperative settings ($N = 58$ in experiment 1 out of 2). Later studies partially replicated this finding, showing that individuals ($N = 49$) treated with oxytocin did not decrease their trust even after they were betrayed several times, while those treated with placebo decreased their trust in response to their counterparts' betrayal (Baumgartner, Heinrichs, Vonlanthen, Fischbacher, & Fehr, 2008). Individuals ($N = 68$) treated with oxytocin were found to donate more money in a money-gifting generosity game (Zak, Stanton, & Ahmadi, 2007). Oxytocin has also been implicated in various social cognition skills. Intranasal oxytocin administration improved the ability to infer the emotions and mental states of others (Domes, Heinrichs, Michel, Berger, & Herpertz, 2007 ($N = 30$)) and to recognize emotions in other people's facial expressions (Lischke et al., 2012 ($N = 14$); Marsh, Henry, Pine, & Blair, 2010 ($N = 50$)). Oxytocin also improved eye contact in social situations and gaze towards the eye region (Andari et al., 2010 ($N = 13$); Domes et al., 2013 ($N = 14$); Guastella, Mitchell, & Dadds, 2008 ($N = 52$)).

Many of the earlier findings support the prosocial hypothesis of oxytocin, namely that oxytocin primarily enhances affiliative and prosocial behaviour (Kosfeld et al., 2005; Zak et al., 2007). Nevertheless, other conflicting results imply that oxytocin's effects are far more complex in humans. A growing body of evidence demonstrates that oxytocin can increase antisocial behaviours, including violence and aggression (DeWall et al., 2014 ($N = 93$); Ne'eman, Perach-Barzilay, Fischer-Shofty, Atias, & Shamay-Tsoory, 2016 ($N = 45$)). Moreover, high levels of plasma oxytocin have been linked to interpersonal difficulties and relational distress (Tabak, McCullough, Szeto, Mendez, & McCabe, 2011 ($N = 39$); Taylor et al., 2006 ($N = 85$)). It is important to note that measurements of plasma oxytocin in many studies are highly questionable and several studies have erroneously suggested that plasma levels of oxytocin reflect central oxytocin release (Leng & Ludwig, 2016). Hence, their implications for central oxytocin activity are debatable.

In an attempt to resolve the incongruence pertaining to the role of oxytocin in social behaviour, researchers have recently proposed a theory that focuses on the role of oxytocin in increasing social salience (Bartz, Zaki, Bolger, & Ochsner, 2011; Shamay-Tsoory et al., 2009; Shamay-Tsoory & Abu-Akel, 2016). According to this hypothesis, oxytocin elevates the salience of social cues so that its effects depend both on the external context in which it is administered (e.g., competitive vs. cooperative) and on individual baseline characteristics (Figure 13.1). For example, oxytocin was shown to increase feelings of trust, empathy and love for ingroup members but not for outgroup members (De Dreu et al., 2010 ($N = 49$). Oxytocin was even found to instigate defensive forms of aggression towards outgroup members (De Dreu et al., 2010; 2012) as well as towards intimate partners (DeWall et al., 2014, N = 93). This finding signifies that whether oxytocin encourages aggressive propensities toward the other depends on the type of external context (group membership of the individual to whom the oxytocin was administered and the target explored in the task). Interestingly, oxytocin has been shown to enhance anthropomorphism in inanimate objects (Peled-Avron, Perry, & Shamay-Tsoory, 2016; Scheele et al., 2015), further strengthening the notion that it enhances the salience of social cues even in nonhuman objects to make them appear human. Nonetheless, oxytocin's effects are also modulated by internal contextual cues such as individual traits. For instance, intranasal oxytocin improved empathic accuracy among individuals who were less socially capable but not among those who already demonstrated high social capabilities (Bartz et al., 2010 ($N = 27$); Feeser et al., 2015 ($N = 71$)). Oxytocin's effects can also vary between men and women. For example, oxytocin facilitates accurate perception of kinship in women but competition in men (Fischer-Shofty, Levkovitz, & Shamay-Tsoory, 2013 ($N = 62$)). According to the biosocial origin theory (Wood & Eagly, 2002), biological hormonal factors combined with cultural and social factors influence behavioural sex differences. Women act according to prosocial behavioural tendencies while men act according to a more agentic, masterful, competitive manner in order to improve their social statues. Oxytocin might be a key neuro-hormone facilitating these sex

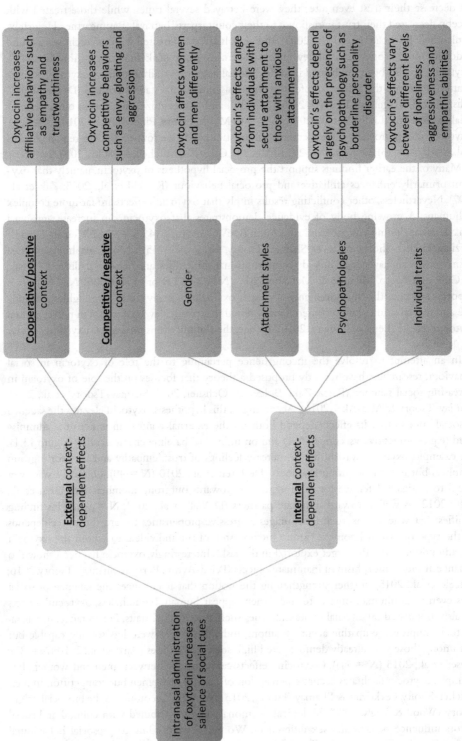

Figure 13.1 Intranasal oxytocin regulates the salience of social cues and its effects depend both on the external context in which it is administered (e.g., competitive vs. cooperative) and on internal individual baseline characteristics, such as personality traits, degree of psychopathology, gender and attachment style

dependent behaviours. This view is in consonance with the social salience hypothesis since oxytocin increased the salience of social cues in a sex dependent manner – it increased women's prosocial, kinship tendencies whereas it increased men's competitive tendencies.

In this chapter we discuss the social salience hypothesis, with special emphasis on the anti-social effects of oxytocin on social cognition. Focusing on the antisocial effects of oxytocin can offer an opposing critical view to the prevailing hypothesis regarding oxytocin's prosocial effects (Striepens, Kendrick, Maier, & Hurlemann, 2011; Yamasue et al., 2012; Insel, 2010).

The effect of oxytocin on antisocial behaviours

Envy and gloating

A study examining the effect of oxytocin on envy and schadenfreude (Shamay-Tsoory et al., 2009 ($N = 56$)) was one of the firsts to challenge the prevailing prosocial literature on oxytocin. The incongruence generated by this study led to the need to reframe the traditional view of how the peptide regulates social behaviour to include other less positive social effects. The study employed the paradigm of a game of chance involving monetary gains. The game was designed to provoke competitive emotions such as envy and gloating in a controlled laboratory setting. The authors speculated that if the oxytocinergic system is indeed generally involved in the modulation of social emotions, the administration of oxytocin would increase ratings of envy and gloating following unequal monetary gains. The results demonstrated that participants who lost more money than their counterparts exhibited greater levels of envy following oxytocin administration than following placebo. Conversely, participants who won more money than their counterparts gloated more following oxytocin administration than following placebo. These results served as the seminal evidence in suggesting that oxytocin may have effects that contradict the widely acknowledged prosocial hypothesis. The authors concluded that these findings indicate that the oxytocinergic system may modulate the salience of social agents depending on context. As a result, oxytocin administration may provoke an extensive range of emotions and behaviours related to social behaviour that may be either positive or negative in nature. Following this finding, the social salience hypothesis was later extended by Bartz et al. (2011), who suggested that oxytocin's effects are modulated by the individual to whom the hormone is administered and the context in which it is given. The hypothesis was further addressed by Olff et al. (2013), who similarly suggested that interindividual variables and contextual factors increase oxytocin's sensitivity to social cues. Finally, the theory was recently reformulated by Shamay-Tsoory and Abu-Akel (2016) to include the interaction between the oxytocinergic system and the dopaminergic system.

Aggression

Aggression is usually described as a behaviour aimed at harming another individual (Baron, 1977). It plays an evolutionary role in survival during searches for food or mates (Berger and Kathleen, 2007). Oxytocin has been linked to aggression, mainly in animal studies. In a study of female golden hamsters, oxytocin facilitated maternal aggression towards an outside intruder (Ferris et al., 1992). Likewise, the infusion of oxytocin antagonist into the central nucleus of the amygdala of rat dams resulted in increased aggression towards intruders (Lubin, Elliot, Black, & Johns, 2003 ($N = 70$)). Mutant mice that underwent targeted disruption of the gene encoding for oxytocin demonstrated a decrease in aggressive behaviour towards an intruder (DeVries, Young

III, & Nelson, 1997). Moreover, neonatal female prairie voles that were infused with oxytocin exhibited intra-sexual aggression after exposure to a male (Bales & Carter, 2003 (N = 43)).

In humans, breastfeeding mothers were found to inflict more severe punishment on unduly aggressive confederates than formula-feeding mothers or women who had never been pregnant (Hahn-Holbrook, Holt-Lunstad, Holbrook, Coyne, & Lawson, 2011 (N = 40)). A possible interpretation of this finding relates to the increased secretion of oxytocin among breastfeeding mothers, which may have increased the salience of their opponents' behaviours and caused the said aggression.

A study that examined the direct influence of intranasal oxytocin administration on aggression in humans (Ne'eman et al., 2016 (N = 45)) employed the social orientation paradigm in the form of a competitive monetary game played against a fictitious (computerized) partner. The game included repeated provocation of aggressive responses by the partner and measured three types of responses in the context of provocation: an aggressive response, an individualistic response and a collaborative response. Participants completed the task following administration of oxytocin or placebo. The results showed that following provocation, oxytocin increased aggressive responses compared with placebo. There were no differences between the number of responses following oxytocin or placebo in either individualistic or collaborative responses. These findings suggest that the effects of oxytocin are likely to vary depending on environmental social cues. Hence, according to the social salience hypothesis, if oxytocin elevates the salience of social cues in a hostile/confrontational environment, an individual will appraise the other as more dangerous and threatening and thereby adopt aggressive behaviour.

Another study examined the relation between oxytocin and intimate partner violence (DeWall et al., 2014 (N = 93)). In this study, participants varying in physical aggression tendencies were provoked. Following either oxytocin or placebo administration, they then rated the probability that they would engage in aggressive behaviours such as throwing an object that might inflict pain or slapping their partner. The results showed that oxytocin increased inclinations toward intimate partner violence, but only among individuals who were prone to physical aggression. This result is also in line with the social salience hypothesis, as oxytocin exerted a differential effect depending on individual traits. For people prone to aggressive behaviour, oxytocin elevates the salience of this trait and mediates a more aggressive antisocial response rather than a more cooperative or prosocial response.

Intergroup conflict

Interesting results pertaining to individuals' preferences and predispositions towards either their ingroup or outgroup counterparts further corroborate the social salience hypothesis. The first study to examine the effect of oxytocin on intergroup relations demonstrated that oxytocin regulates parochial altruism. In three experiments, male participants made decisions that had monetary consequences for their ingroup member, their outgroup member and themselves. The results showed that oxytocin promoted ingroup trust and cooperation as well as defensive, but not offensive, outgroup aggression (De Dreu et al., 2010 (N = 49)). Similarly, another study found oxytocin involvement in ethnocentrism. The hormone was found to promote ingroup cooperation, trust and coordination and stimulate outgroup violence, prejudice and xenophobia. Oxytocin was found to raise ingroup favouritism on the one hand and outgroup derogation on the other, though to a lesser extent (De Dreu, Greer, van Kleef, Shalvi, & Handgraaf, 2011 (5 experiments: N = 63, 70, 66, 71, and 77, respectively)). Furthermore, oxytocin was found to strengthen ingroup conformity (Stallen, De Dreu, Shalvi, Smidts, & Sanfey, 2012 (N = 74)). Participants who were administered oxytocin conformed to ratings of unfamiliar visual stimuli made by their ingroup members rather than those made by outgroup members. This important finding suggests that oxytocin influences subjective preferences according to group attribution (Stallen et al., 2012 ($N = 74$)). A pharmaco-electroencephalography study found that oxytocin increased empathic neural responses to ingroup members, but not to outgroup members. Specifically, larger P2 amplitudes were elicited in response to facial expressions of pain compared to neutral expressions among racial ingroup members but not racial outgroup members (Sheng, Liu, Zhou, Zhou, & Han, 2013 ($N = 16$)). Cohen et al. (2017 ($N = 19$)) recently demonstrated that oxytocin administration significantly increased the amount of interpersonal space participants preferred to maintain between themselves and strangers but did not decrease the interpersonal space they maintained with friends. In consonance with the social salience hypothesis, when an unfamiliar and possibly threatening context is present, such as an approaching stranger, oxytocin may increase the salience of this social cue and therefore increase the interpersonal distance maintained from this individual, resulting in an increase in the antisocial behaviour of keeping one's distance from other individuals. Yet contrary to the social salience hypothesis, oxytocin did not decrease the personal distance kept from a friend. In this particular case, a plausible explanation is that individuals already maintain close personal distances between themselves and their friends and that there is a certain ceiling effect below which this distance cannot decrease any further, even under the influence of oxytocin.

In contrast to the findings discussed thus far, oxytocin was found to increase empathy for pain towards outgroup members but not towards ingroup members in the context of the Israeli-Palestinian conflict (Shamay-Tsoory et al., 2013 ($N = 55$)). Yet in line with the social salience hypothesis, a plausible explanation for this contrasting finding might be that in particular contexts in which an outgroup member is linked with a conspicuous conflictual outgroup, such as an Israeli-Palestinian (outgroup) to an Israeli-Jew (ingroup), the outgroup member becomes more prominent and salient to ingroup members. As a result, this outgroup member would attract the attention and consequently the emotions of the ingroup members, even if these emotions are prosocial, as in the case of empathy for pain.

Considering the various group-dependent effects of oxytocin, it appears that the hormone is rather susceptible to external contextual factors. Depending on the context, e.g., on whether actions are required towards ingroup or outgroup members, oxytocin is liable to exert positive/prosocial as well as negative/antisocial effects.

The neural underpinnings of the effects of oxytocin

Several pharmaco-imaging studies using functional magnetic resonance imaging and intranasal oxytocin administration have tapped into the neural underpinnings of oxytocin's behavioural effects. A study that examined the effects of oxytocin on the neural processing of socially salient cues found that oxytocin increased activity in the ventral tegmental area (VTA) for angry faces as well as for friendly faces (Groppe et al., 2013 ($N = 28$)). This finding suggests that oxytocin attaches salience to social cues irrespective of their valence, such that prosocial signals portrayed in friendly faces are as salient as antisocial, aggressive signals portrayed in angry faces. Further, another study found that during social judgements, oxytocin increased activity in reward-related areas such as the nucleus accumbens, the striatum and the orbitofrontal cortex and in social-related areas including the posterior superior temporal sulcus and premotor cortex, yet decreased activity in those areas during non-social judgements (Gordon et al., 2013 ($N = 17$)). Consistent with this, Rilling et al. (2012 ($N = 91$)) demonstrated that oxytocin increased functional connectivity between the amygdala and the salience network: insula and caudate. This increased connectivity has been linked to improved social learning (Hu et al., 2015 ($N = 106$)).

Oxytocin has multiple binding sites, including the autonomic and limbic areas (Loup, Tribollet, Dubois-Dauphin, & Dreifuss, 1991; Loup, Tribollet, Dubois-Dauphin, Pizzolato, & Dreifuss, 1989). One study demonstrated that among men who were shown photos of their female partners, oxytocin administration resulted in heightened responses in the nucleus accumbens and VTA, as opposed to among those who were shown photos of unfamiliar women (Scheele et al., 2013 ($N = 20$)). Another study found that oxytocin increased activation within the caudate nucleus and the amygdala in response to reciprocated cooperation (Rilling et al., 2012 ($N = 91$)). Evidence for the role of oxytocin in the processing of rewarding events and the assignment of salience suggests that oxytocin plays a key role in these functions (Sanna, Argiolas, & Melis, 2012). With regards to antisocial neural effects, oxytocin, vasopressin release and receptor activation in the central amygdala and the bed nucleus of the stria terminalis were found to play an important role in maternal aggression (for review see Bosch & Neuman, 2012). Future studies should examine the neural underpinnings of the effect of oxytocin on antisocial behaviours in humans.

Implications for psychopathology

It is crucial to bear in mind that given the antisocial effects outlined in this chapter, the therapeutic potential of oxytocin should be considered with caution. For example, administering oxytocin to individuals in a hostile, dangerous environment might result in exacerbation of threat signals. In turn, this might lead to elevated levels of anxiety that might be problematic for individuals with anxiety disorders or borderline personality disorders (Bartz et al., 2011). Moreover, treating individuals with oxytocin in uncontrolled situations that may include negative social interactions has the potential to stimulate defensive or aggressive reactions. Since complete social control outside the clinic or hospital ward is impossible to achieve, chronic daily administration of oxytocin should be handled with caution.

Oxytocin shows much promise as an adjunct therapeutic agent for individuals with autism spectrum disorders and schizophrenia (Cochran, Fallon, Hill, & Frazier, 2013). Nevertheless, individuals with autism exhibit deficits in attending to socially salient stimuli (Bird, Catmur, Silani, Frith, & Frith, 2006), while schizophrenic patients have difficulties suppressing socially salient information (Hahn et al., 2010). Therefore, it is imperative to decipher how each psychopathology processes socially salient stimuli in order to properly characterize the therapeutic potential of oxytocin for each specific pathology.

Limitations in human oxytocin research

Despite the wide array of effects of intranasal oxytocin on human behaviour, there are several limitations in this field of research that need to be addressed.

The issue of low statistical power is of particular significance. Walum, Waldman, and Young (2016) examined the averaged statistical power of intranasal oxytocin studies both in healthy and in clinical populations and discovered that these studies are often underpowered, thus putting the validity of the findings into question. It is interesting to note that most of the studies in this field report at least one positive finding, suggesting that almost all investigated hypotheses within intranasal oxytocin studies are true. A plausible explanation for this is the publication bias problem (Rosenthal, Archer, Hall, DiMatteo, & Rogers, 1979; Schooler, 2011) characterized by withholding the many unpublished negative or unsatisfying results in this field. One laboratory tried to address this problem by reporting their null and unpublished results regarding the effects of intranasal oxytocin on human behaviour (Lane, Luminet, Nave, & Mikolajczak, 2016). The authors found a significant main effect of oxytocin in only one out of 25 tasks they examined and a significant interaction with oxytocin treatment in only 5 of the 25 tasks. They proposed that the majority of significant findings in this field may stem either from type I error, in which the accepted P-value allows a false positive rate of 5%, or from statistical artefacts. Such statistical artefacts may include the following: a small sample using between-subject design that is internally invalid; single blind studies in which the researcher influences the results; and insufficient knowledge of intranasal oxytocin pharmacokinetics. Moreover, research practices such as multiple analyses on the same data and insufficient correction for multiple comparisons may be improperly used, often leading to inflation of statistical effects. Studies in this field often use post-hoc analyses and unexplained exclusion of outliers, which again undermine the reliability of the findings. For these reasons, published results in this field may represent false positives instead of true findings. One such example pertains to the connection between oxytocin and trust. A recent and intriguing suggestion is that the basic connection between oxytocin and trust is not particularly robust (Nave, Camerer, & McCullough, 2015). Specifically, attempts to replicate this finding demonstrated small effect sizes that are not reliably different from zero.

Possible ways of addressing these limitations include the following: conducting large-scale meta-analyses that can aid in interpreting the validity of the current findings; performing a priori power calculations; publishing negative and null results; adjusting the alpha level to the number of tests performed; disclosing methods by making all data available to others within the field; cooperating in order to increase power and replicate findings; and using more efficient routes of oxytocin administration, such as stimulating endogenous oxytocin release through melanocortin receptor agonists that have shown promising social effects (Modi et al., 2015).

Conclusion, inconsistencies and future directions

It is evident that oxytocin is deeply involved in the entire spectrum of social behaviour. Its effects, nonetheless, are complex and highly differential, depending on the person treated with oxytocin and the context and situation in which it is administered. As emphasized throughout the chapter, although oxytocin can exert prosocial effects, it can also exert antisocial effects, such as increasing envy, social distance and even aggression, depending on the external context of the social situation and the internal context of the person to whom the oxytocin is administered. Still, some theories posit that oxytocin does not increase the salience of social cues per se, but rather facilitates the salience of emotionally evocative and personally salient cues in the environment (Kemp & Guastella, 2010, 2011; Harari-Dahan & Bernstein, 2014). Specifically, according to these theories, the known social effects of oxytocin may not be limited to social behaviours but may extend to a wide range of adaptive and maladaptive behaviours modulated by approach and avoidance processes. For example, oxytocin's effect on envy and gloating can be interpreted as a general effect on approach behaviour since jealousy, an emotion similar to envy, promotes approach behaviour (Lazarus, 1991) and is associated with the left fronto-cortical regions known to be associated with approach behaviours (Carver & Harmon-Jones, 2009). The general approach-avoidance hypothesis (Harari-Dahan & Bernstein, 2014) suggests that oxytocin's activations in the mesocorticolimbic circuitry are linked to general approach and reward motivation (Berridge, 2007; Berridge et al., 2009; Treadway & Zald, 2011) rather than specifically linked to increased social salience (Ma, Shamay-Tsoory, Han, & Zink, 2016). We believe that the social salience hypothesis can be congruent with the approach-avoidance hypotheses, since increasing the salience of social cues can result either in an approach-motivated behaviour such as trust and generosity or in an avoidance-motivated behaviour such as aggression that is instigated to protect the individual from harm. Future studies would benefit from examining the effects of oxytocin while manipulating two different social contexts, for example by administering oxytocin in both competitive and cooperative social contexts in the same experiment in order to compare the effect sizes of both influences on the same sample. Future studies would also benefit from examining the antisocial effects of oxytocin in psychopathology to determine the degree to which oxytocin might induce hostile and harmful inclinations in patients. It is also crucial to examine oxytocin's influence during real-life interactions between humans, with special emphasis on aggressive and envious interactions. Finally, the neurological underpinnings of the oxytocinergic system should be examined during antisocial interactions in order to decipher its antisocial neural bases in addition to the prosocial neural bases already known in the field.

References

Andari, E., Duhamel, J-R., Zalla, T., Herbrecht, E., Leboyer, M., & Sirigu, A. (2010). Promoting social behavior with oxytocin in high-functioning autism spectrum disorders. *Proceedings of the National Academy of Sciences, 107*(9), 4389–4394.

Bales, K.L., & Carter, C.S. (2003). Sex differences and developmental effects of oxytocin on aggression and social behavior in prairie voles (*Microtus ochrogaster*). *Hormones and Behavior, 44*(3), 178–184.

Baron, R. A. (1977). The prevention and control of human aggression. In *Human aggression* (pp. 225–274). Boston, MA: Springer.

Bartz, J., Simeon, D., Hamilton, H., Kim, S., Crystal, S., Braun, A., . . . Hollander, E. (2010). Oxytocin can hinder trust and cooperation in borderline personality disorder. *Social Cognitive and Affective Neuroscience, 6*(5), 556–563.

Bartz, J.A., Zaki, J., Bolger, N., & Ochsner, K.N. (2011). Social effects of oxytocin in humans: Context and person matter. *Trends in Cognitive Sciences, 15*(7), 301–309.

Baumgartner, T., Heinrichs, M., Vonlanthen, A., Fischbacher, U., & Fehr, E. (2008). Oxytocin shapes the neural circuitry of trust and trust adaptation in humans. *Neuron, 58*(4), 639–650.

Berger, K. S., & Kathleen, B. (2007). The developing person through the life span (7th ed.). New York, NY: Worth Publishers.

Berridge, K.C. (2007). The debate over dopamine's role in reward: The case for incentive salience. *Psychopharmacology (Berl), 191*(3), 391–431.

Berridge, K.C., Robinson, T.E., & Aldridge, J.W. (2009). Dissecting components of reward: "liking," "wanting," and learning. *Current Opinion in Pharmacology, 9*(1), 65–73.

Bird, G., Catmur, C., Silani, G., Frith, C., & Frith, U. (2006). Attention does not modulate neural responses to social stimuli in autism spectrum disorders. *Neuroimage, 31*(4), 1614–1624.

Bosch, O.J., & Neumann, I.D. (2012). Both oxytocin and vasopressin are mediators of maternal care and aggression in rodents: From central release to sites of action. *Hormones and Behavior, 61*(3), 293–303.

Carver, C.S., & Harmon-Jones, E. (2009). Anger is an approach-related affect: Evidence and implications. *Psychological Bulletin, 135*(2), 183.

Cochran, D., Fallon, D., Hill, M., & Frazier, J.A. (2013). The role of oxytocin in psychiatric disorders: A review of biological and therapeutic research findings. *Harvard Review of Psychiatry, 21*(5), 219.

Cohen, D., Perry, A., Gilam, G., Mayseless, N., Gonen, T., Hendler, T., & Shamay-Tsoory, S.G. (2017). The role of oxytocin in modulating interpersonal space: A pharmacological fMRI study. *Psychoneuroendocrinology, 76*, 77–83.

Calkins, S. D., & Keane, S. P. (2009). Developmental origins of early antisocial behavior. *Development and Psychopathology, 21*(4), 1095–1109.

De Dreu, C.K., Greer, L.L., Handgraaf, M.J., Shalvi, S., van Kleef, G.A., Baas, M., & Feith, S.W. (2010). The neuropeptide oxytocin regulates parochial altruism in intergroup conflict among humans. *Science, 328*(5984), 1408–1411.

De Dreu, C.K., Greer, L.L., van Kleef, G.A., Shalvi, S., & Handgraaf, M.J. (2011). Oxytocin promotes human ethnocentrism. *Proceedings of the National Academy of Sciences, 108*(4), 1262–1266.

De Dreu, C.K., Shalvi, S., Greer, L.L., van Kleef, G.A., & Handgraaf, M.J. (2012). Oxytocin motivates non-cooperation in intergroup conflict to protect vulnerable in-group members. *PLoS One, 7*(11), e46751.

DeVries, A.C., Young, III. W.S., & Nelson, R.J. (1997). Reduced aggressive behaviour in mice with targeted disruption of the oxytocin gene. *Journal of Neuroendocrinology, 9*(5), 363–368.

DeWall, C.N., Gillath, O., Pressman, S.D., Black, L.L., Bartz, J.A., Moskovitz, J., & Stetler, D.A. (2014). When the love hormone leads to violence oxytocin increases intimate partner violence inclinations among high trait aggressive people. *Social Psychological and Personality Science*, 1948550613516876.

Domes, G., Heinrichs, M., Kumbier, E., Grossmann, A., Hauenstein, K., & Herpertz, S.C. (2013). Effects of intranasal oxytocin on the neural basis of face processing in autism spectrum disorder. *Biological Psychiatry*, *74*, 164–171.

Domes, G., Heinrichs, M., Michel, A., Berger, C., & Herpertz, S.C. (2007). Oxytocin improves "mind-reading" in humans. *Biological Psychiatry*, *61*, 731–733.

Donaldson, Z.R., & Young, L.J. (2008). Oxytocin, vasopressin, and the neurogenetics of sociality. *Science*, *322*(5903), 900–904.

Feeser, M., Fan, Y., Weigand, A., Hahn, A., Gärtner, M., Böker, H., Bajbouj, M. (2015). Oxytocin improves mentalizing – pronounced effects for individuals with attenuated ability to empathize. *Psychoneuroendocrinology*, *53*, 223–232.

Ferris, C., Foote, K., Meltser, H., Plenby, M., Smith, K., & Insel, T. (1992). Oxytocin in the amygdala facilitates maternal aggression. *Annals of the New York Academy of Sciences*, *652*(1), 456–457.

Fischer-Shofty, M., Levkovitz, Y., & Shamay-Tsoory, S.G. (2013). Oxytocin facilitates accurate perception of competition in men and kinship in women. *Social Cognitive and Affective Neuroscience*, *8*(3), 313–317.

Gainer, H., Yamashita, M., Fields, R.L., House, S.B., & Rusnak, M. (2002). The magnocellular neuronal phenotype: Cell-specific gene expression in the hypothalamo-neurohypophysial system. *Progress in Brain Research*, *139*, 1–14.

Gimpl, G., & Fahrenholz, F. (2001). The oxytocin receptor system: Structure, function, and regulation. *Physiological Reviews*, *81*(2), 629–683.

Gordon, I., Vander Wyk, B.C., Bennett, R.H., Cordeaux, C., Lucas, M.V., Eilbott, J.A., & Pelphrey, K.A. (2013). Oxytocin enhances brain function in children with autism. *Proceedings of the National Academy of Sciences*, *110*(52), 20953–20958.

Groppe, S.E., Gossen, A., Rademacher, L., Hahn, A., Westphal, L., Gründer, G., & Spreckelmeyer, K.N. (2013). Oxytocin influences processing of socially relevant cues in the ventral tegmental area of the human brain. *Biological Psychiatry*, *74*(3), 172–179.

Guastella, A.J., Mitchell, P.B., & Dadds, M.R. (2008). Oxytocin increases gaze to the eye region of human faces. *Biological Psychiatry*, *63*(1), 3–5.

Hahn, B., Robinson, B.M., Kaiser, S.T., Harvey, A.N., Beck, V.M., Leonard, C.J., & Gold, J.M. (2010). Failure of schizophrenia patients to overcome salient distractors during working memory encoding. *Biological Psychiatry*, *68*(7), 603–609.

Hahn-Holbrook, J., Holt-Lunstad, J., Holbrook, C., Coyne, S.M., & Lawson, E.T. (2011). Maternal defense: Breast feeding increases aggression by reducing stress. *Psychological Science*, *22*(10), 1288–1295.

Harari-Dahan, O., & Bernstein, A. (2014). A general approach-avoidance hypothesis of oxytocin: Accounting for social and non-social effects of oxytocin. *Neuroscience & Biobehavioral Reviews*, *47*, 506–519.

Hu, J., Qi, S., Becker, B., Luo, L., Gao, S., Gong, Q., & Kendrick, K.M. (2015). Oxytocin selectively facilitates learning with social feedback and increases activity and functional connectivity in emotional memory and reward processing regions. *Human Brain Mapping*, *36*(6), 2132–2146.

Insel, T.R. (2010). The challenge of translation in social neuroscience: A review of oxytocin, vasopressin, and affiliative behavior. *Neuron*, *65*(6), 768–779.

Kemp, A.H., & Guastella, A.J. (2010). Oxytocin: Prosocial behavior, social salience, or approach-related behavior? *Biological Psychiatry*, *67*(6), e33–e34.

Kemp, A.H., & Guastella, A.J. (2011). The role of oxytocin in human affect: A novel hypothesis. *Current Directions in Psychological Science*, *20*(4), 222–231.

Kosfeld, M., Heinrichs, M., Zak, P.J., Fischbacher, U., & Fehr, E. (2005). Oxytocin increases trust in humans. *Nature*, *435*(7042), 673–676.

Lane, A., Luminet, O., Nave, G., & Mikolajczak, M. (2016). Is there a publication bias in behavioural intranasal oxytocin research on humans? Opening the file drawer of one laboratory. *Journal of Neuroendocrinology*, *28*(4).

Lazarus, R.S. (1991). *Emotion and adaptation*. Oxford: Oxford University Press.

Lee, H.J., Macbeth, A.H., Pagani, J.H., & Young, W.S. (2009). Oxytocin: The great facilitator of life. *Progress in Neurobiology*, *88*(2), 127–151.

Leng, G., & Ludwig, M. (2016). Intranasal oxytocin: Myths and delusions. *Biological Psychiatry*, *79*(3), 243–250.

Lischke, A., Berger, C., Prehn, K., Heinrichs, M., Herpertz, S.C., & Domes, G. (2012). Intranasal oxytocin enhances emotion recognition from dynamic facial expressions and leaves eye-gaze unaffected. *Psychoneuroendocrinology, 37*(4), 475–481.

Loup, F., Tribollet, E., Dubois-Dauphin, M., & Dreifuss, J.J. (1991). Localization of high-affinity binding sites for oxytocin and vasopressin in the human brain: An autoradiographic study. *Brain Research, 555*(2), 220–232.

Loup, F., Tribollet, E., Dubois-Dauphin, M., Pizzolato, G., & Dreifuss, J.J. (1989). Localization of oxytocin binding sites in the human brainstem and upper spinal cord: An autoradiographic study. *Brain Research, 500*(1), 223–230.

Lubin, D.A., Elliot, J.C., Black, M.C., & Johns, J.M. (2003). An oxytocin antagonist infused into the central nucleus of the amygdala increases maternal aggressive behavior. *Behavioral Neuroscience, 117*(2), 195.

Ludwig, M., & Leng, G. (2006). Dendritic peptide release and peptide-dependent behaviours. *Nature reviews. Neuroscience, 7*(2), 126–136. doi:10.1038/nrn1845

Ma, Y., Shamay-Tsoory, S., Han, S., & Zink, C.F. (2016). Oxytocin and social adaptation: Insights from neuroimaging studies of healthy and clinical populations. *Trends in Cognitive Sciences, 20*(2), 133–145.

Marsh, A.A., Henry, H.Y., Pine, D.S., & Blair, R. (2010). Oxytocin improves specific recognition of positive facial expressions. *Psychopharmacology (Berl), 209*(3), 225–232.

Modi, M.E., Inoue, K., Barrett, C.E., Kittelberger, K.A., Smith, D.G., Landgraf, R., & Young, L.J. (2015). Melanocortin receptor agonists facilitate oxytocin-dependent partner preference formation in the prairie vole. *Neuropsychopharmacology, 40*(8), 1856–1865.

Nave, G., Camerer, C., & McCullough, M. (2015). Does oxytocin increase trust in humans? A critical review of research. *Perspectives on Psychological Science, 10*(6), 772–789.

Ne'eman, R., Perach-Barzilay, N., Fischer-Shofty, M., Atias, A., & Shamay-Tsoory, S.G. (2016). Intranasal administration of oxytocin increases human aggressive behavior. *Hormones and Behavior, 80*, 125–131.

Olff, M., Frijling, J. L., Kubzansky, L. D., Bradley, B., Ellenbogen, M. A., Cardoso, C., & van Zuiden, M. (2013). The role of oxytocin in social bonding, stress regulation and mental health: an update on the moderating effects of context and interindividual differences. *Psychoneuroendocrinology, 38*(9), 1883–1894.

Peled-Avron, L., Perry, A., & Shamay-Tsoory, S.G. (2016). The effect of oxytocin on the anthropomorphism of touch. *Psychoneuroendocrinology, 66*, 159–165. doi:10.1016/j.psyneuen.2016.01.015

Rilling, J.K., DeMarco, A.C., Hackett, P.D., Thompson, R., Ditzen, B., Patel, R., & Pagnoni, G. (2012). Effects of intranasal oxytocin and vasopressin on cooperative behavior and associated brain activity in men. *Psychoneuroendocrinology, 37*(4), 447–461. doi:10.1016/j.psyneuen.2011.07.013

Rosenthal, R., Archer, D., Hall, J. A., DiMatteo, M. R., & Rogers, P. L. (1979). Measuring sensitivity to nonverbal communication: The PONS test. In *Nonverbal behavior* (pp. 67–98). Baltimore, MD: The Johns Hopkins University Press.

Sanna, F., Argiolas, A., & Melis, M.R. (2012). Oxytocin-induced yawning: Sites of action in the brain and interaction with mesolimbic/mesocortical and incertohypothalamic dopaminergic neurons in male rats. *Hormones and Behavior, 62*(4), 505–514.

Scheele, D., Schwering, C., Elison, J.T., Spunt, R., Maier, W., & Hurlemann, R. (2015). A human tendency to anthropomorphize is enhanced by oxytocin. *European Neuropsychopharmacology, 25*(10), 1817–1823. doi:10.1016/j.euroneuro.2015.05.009

Scheele, D., Wille, A., Kendrick, K.M., Stoffel-Wagner, B., Becker, B., Güntürkün, O., & Hurlemann, R. (2013). Oxytocin enhances brain reward system responses in men viewing the face of their female partner. *Proceedings of the National Academy of Sciences, 110*(50), 20308–20313.

Schooler, J. (2011). Unpublished results hide the decline effect: Some effects diminish when tests are repeated. Jonathan Schooler says being open about findings that don't make the scientific record could reveal why. *Nature, 470*(7335), 437–438.

Shamay-Tsoory, S.G., & Abu-Akel, A. (2016). The social salience hypothesis of oxytocin. *Biological Psychiatry, 79*(3), 194–202. doi:10.1016/j.biopsych.2015.07.020

Shamay-Tsoory, S.G., Abu-Akel, A., Palgi, S., Sulieman, R., Fischer-Shofty, M., Levkovitz, Y., & Decety, J. (2013). Giving peace a chance: Oxytocin increases empathy to pain in the context of the Israeli-Palestinian conflict. *Psychoneuroendocrinology, 38*(12), 3139–3144.

Shamay-Tsoory, S.G., Fischer, M., Dvash, J., Harari, H., Perach-Bloom, N., & Levkovitz, Y. (2009). Intranasal administration of oxytocin increases envy and schadenfreude (gloating). *Biological Psychiatry, 66*, 864–870.

Sheng, F., Liu, Y., Zhou, B., Zhou, W., & Han, S. (2013). Oxytocin modulates the racial bias in neural responses to others' suffering. *Biological Psychology, 92*(2), 380–386.

Song, Z., & Albers, H.E. (2017). Cross-talk among oxytocin and arginine-vasopressin receptors: Relevance for basic and clinical studies of the brain and periphery. *Frontiers in Neuroendocrinology.* In press.

Stallen, M., De Dreu, C.K., Shalvi, S., Smidts, A., & Sanfey, A.G. (2012). The herding hormone oxytocin stimulates in-group conformity. *Psychological Science,* 0956797612446026.

Striepens, N., Kendrick, K.M., Maier, W., & Hurlemann, R. (2011). Prosocial effects of oxytocin and clinical evidence for its therapeutic potential. *Frontiers in Neuroendocrinology, 32*(4), 426–450.

Tabak, B.A., McCullough, M.E., Szeto, A., Mendez, A.J., & McCabe, P.M. (2011). Oxytocin indexes relational distress following interpersonal harms in women. *Psychoneuroendocrinology, 36*(1), 115–122.

Taylor, S.E., Gonzaga, G.C., Klein, L.C., Hu, P., Greendale, G.A., & Seeman, T.E. (2006). Relation of oxytocin to psychological stress responses and hypothalamic-pituitary-adrenocortical axis activity in older women. *Psychosomatic Medicine, 68*(2), 238–245.

Treadway, M. T., & Zald, D. H. (2011). Reconsidering anhedonia in depression: Lessons from translational neuroscience. *Neuroscience & Biobehavioral Reviews, 35*(3), 537–555.

Walum, H., Waldman, I.D., & Young, L.J. (2016). Statistical and methodological considerations for the interpretation of intranasal oxytocin studies. *Biological Psychiatry, 79*(3), 251–257.

Winslow, J., & Insel, T. (2002). The social deficits of the oxytocin knockout mouse. *Neuropeptides, 36*(2), 221–229.

Wood, W., & Eagly, A.H. (2002). A cross-cultural analysis of the behavior of women and men: Implications for the origins of sex differences. *Psychological Bulletin, 128*(5), 699.

Yamasue, H., Yee, J.R., Hurlemann, R., Rilling, J.K., Chen, F.S., Meyer-Lindenberg, A., & Tost, H. (2012). Integrative approaches utilizing oxytocin to enhance prosocial behavior: From animal and human social behavior to autistic social dysfunction. *Journal of Neuroscience, 32*(41), 14109–14117a.

Young, L.J., & Wang, Z. (2004). The neurobiology of pair bonding. *Nature Neuroscience, 7*(10), 1048.

Zak, P.J., Stanton, A.A., & Ahmadi, S. (2007). Oxytocin increases generosity in humans. *PLoS One, 2*(11), e1128.

SECTION 4

Pair bonding, reproduction, and parenting

14

FUNCTIONAL ROLES OF GONADAL HORMONES IN HUMAN PAIR BONDING AND SEXUALITY

James R. Roney

In most mammalian species, sexual behavior is mostly or entirely confined to days on which it is possible for females to conceive (for reviews, see Adkins-Regan, 2005; Beach, 1976; Carter, 1992; Roney, 2015). In species in which there are clearly diagnostic cues of female fecundity, furthermore, even males refrain from sexual behavior when such cues are absent. For example, male hamsters rendered anosmic (and thus unable to detect olfactory cues of fecundity) fail to mount females who are sexually receptive (e.g., Devor & Murphy, 1973). Likewise, male dogs refrain from mounting females in heat that have been treated with an antibiotic that alters their vaginal flora and thereby removes olfactory cues of estrus (Dzieciol et al., 2013). Thus, in many species, cues from females indicate potentially conceptive days (i.e., female fecundity), and both male and female sexual motivation is largely restricted to exactly these days.

In functional terms, this coupling of sexuality to fecundity should often maximize the net fitness benefits of sexual behavior.[1] Sexual behavior entails fitness costs – ranging from risks of infection, injury, and predation to opportunity costs associated with other behaviors – and thus sex must have countervailing fitness benefits to explain selection for motivational systems that encourage its pursuit. Conception is the most obvious of such benefits. In those species in which males provide no investment in females or their offspring beyond the contribution of their genes, the possibility of conception may be the only fitness benefit that outweighs the costs of sex. Thus, in such species, both males and females appear designed to restrict copulation to fecund time periods.

In proximate terms, the endocrine signals that index fluctuations in mammalian fecundity also appear to explain changes in female sexual receptivity (willingness to accept copulation attempts by males), proceptivity (the active soliciting of sexual contact), and attractiveness (the extent to which males are motivated to pursue copulation with a female), as argued in a number of early reviews (e.g., Beach, 1949, 1976; Young, 1961). In mammalian estrous or menstrual cycles, developing follicles containing fertilizable gametes produce steep rises in estradiol just before ovulation, such that increasing estradiol is a reliable index of impending fecundity. Consistent with a signal that links sexual behavior to fecundity, then, both correlational and experimental studies confirm positive effects of estradiol on female sexual motivation across essentially all nonhuman mammalian species that have been directly investigated (for reviews, see Blaustein, 2008; Carter, 1992; Roney, 2015, 2016; Thornhill & Gangestad, 2008). In species in which a corpus luteum forms spontaneously during non-fecund cycle regions, the elevated progesterone that it produces tends to have strongly inhibitory associations with both female sexual motivation and attractiveness (reviewed in Beach, 1976; Roney, 2015). Thus, in many nonhuman mammals, opposing effects of estradiol and progesterone on female sexual motivation and attractiveness generate behavioral patterns in which copulation is largely restricted to time periods when conception is possible.

It is against the background of this general mammalian pattern that we can view the endocrine correlates of human sexuality. Humans engage in sexual behaviors across all phases of the menstrual cycle and also during anovulatory cycles and other non-fecund states such as pregnancy. What explains this change, and what are the phylogenetic precursors of it among nonhuman primates? Finally, how has the endocrine regulation of human sexuality changed relative to other mammalian species, and how can research on endocrinology help inform our understanding of the evolved functions of human sexual and relationship psychology? The remainder of the chapter will address possible answers to these questions.

Human pair bonding and sexuality

Most theories of the evolution of human pair bonding postulate that concealment of cues of ovulatory timing is necessary for the emergence of male long-term investment in mates and offspring (Alexander & Noonan, 1979; Lovejoy, 2009; Strassmann, 1981; Symons, 1979). The general reasoning here is that clear cues of ovulatory timing would select for males who compete to inseminate females during those times, but who then move on to inseminate other females as they become fecund. Furthermore, even if some males were inclined to form long-term bonds and invest in offspring, they might not have been able to prevent more dominant males from inseminating their mates if fecund time periods were accurately perceivable. Strassmann (1981) persuasively pushed this logic further to argue that females who suppressed cues of ovulatory timing could have specifically attracted less physically dominant males whose best reproductive strategy was to guard, copulate with and invest in the offspring of women who were unattractive to dominant males specifically because of their suppressed cues of fecundity. But given the potentially large benefits of male paternal investment for offspring fitness (see Kaplan, Hill, Lancaster, & Hurtado, 2000), women who concealed ovulation and men who invested in them may have outcompeted competitors across generations until both concealed ovulation and male provisioning became the dominant human phenotypes.

Sexual behavior can act as a cue of ovulatory timing if female sexual receptivity is confined to fecund cycle days. Both mathematical modeling (e.g., Rodriguez-Girones & Enquist, 2001) and verbal arguments (Alexander & Noonan, 1979; Strassmann, 1981) have therefore postulated that sexual receptivity must be extended beyond fecund days in order to conceal ovulatory timing and promote male non-genetic investments in females and their offspring. This in turn requires alteration of the general mammalian pattern whereby opposing effects of estradiol and progesterone largely confine female sexual motivation and attractiveness to only fecund cycle days. Before turning to how this alteration may have occurred in humans, it may be worthwhile to briefly review phylogenetic precursors to non-fecund (or "extended") sexuality among nonhuman primates.

Hormones and sexuality in nonhuman primates

A number of nonhuman primates exhibit extended sexuality in which copulations take place on days when conception probability is zero or very low (for a review, see Thornhill & Gangestad,

2008). In chimpanzees (*Pan troglodytes*), for instance, females have sexual swellings for more days than their likely fecundity, and will often copulate with multiple adult males in a social group while in a swollen state (Deschner, Heistermann, Hodges, & Boesch, 2004; Heistermann, Mole, Vervaecke, van Elsacker, & Hodges, 1996). Swelling size appears to be a probabilistic but imperfect predictor of fecundity (Nunn, 1999), unlike the more clearly diagnostic cues of fecundity that appear to be present in many other mammals. Theorists have argued that nonconceptive sexuality can evolve when females obtain non-genetic ("direct") benefits from males as a result of such behavior (e.g., Rodriguez-Girones & Enquist, 2001). In species like chimpanzees, one such benefit may be paternity confusion, as males who have copulated with a female in a swollen state may be less likely to mistreat her offspring if there is a positive probability that they could be the father (for a review of this and other possible benefits of extended sexuality in female primates, see Thornhill & Gangestad, 2008).

Although extended sexuality does occur in multiple nonhuman primate species, its occurrence is usually temporally proximate to fecund cycle days, and the hormonal correlates of female sexual motivation and attractiveness are still very similar to those seen in other mammals. Sexual swellings in chimps appear to be promoted by estradiol but inhibited by progesterone (Deschner et al., 2004; Emery & Whitten, 2003), and copulations likewise occur when females are swollen but tend to cease entirely after the luteal phase rise in progesterone triggers sex skin detumescence (Deschner et al., 2004). This pattern of positive effects of estradiol but negative effects of progesterone on the probability of primate sexual behavior is a widespread pattern found across many genera, with sexual behavior often absent entirely during most of the nonfecund luteal phase (for reviews, see Dixson, 1998; Emery Thompson, 2009; for an apparent exception to this pattern in a specific macaque species, see Furtbauer, Heistermann, Schulke, & Ostner, 2011). Thus, extended sexuality in nonhuman primates often involves a broadening of sexual behavior into days adjacent to the small number of fecund cycle days, but does not usually entail the expansion of sexuality across the entire menstrual cycle.

Hormones and sexuality in women

Humans do engage in sexual behavior across the entire menstrual cycle and during completely anovulatory time periods, and thus exhibit an expansion of extended sexuality relative to the majority of nonhuman primates. This raises questions regarding how endocrine regulation of sexuality may have changed in humans relative to both other primates and mammalian species that more tightly restrict copulations to fecund cycle days. The following sections introduce different theoretical positions regarding this issue, as well as an evaluation of the evidence for each position. This general section will focus on women's sexuality, with a subsequent section briefly addressing the endocrine regulation of men's sexual psychology and behavior.

Release from hormonal control

One possible means to extend sexuality is to de-couple its regulation from the fluctuations in estradiol and progesterone that have clear facilitating and inhibiting effects, respectively, on sexual motivation in other mammals. Symons (1979) endorsed this position in his discussion of the role of sexuality in human pair bonding: "Human females deviate from this [nonhuman] pattern in that the preovulatory rise in estrogen is accompanied neither by increased desire and responsiveness to sexual stimulation nor increased attractiveness to males" (p. 105). Symons came to this conclusion – as well as others, such as sexual desire being unaffected by menopause or ovariectomy in humans – despite the fact that very little research at that time had systematically investigated the hormonal predictors of women's sexual motivation. What have we learned about this topic in the ensuing three to four decades?

We have learned, in short, that ovarian hormones do in fact have effects on women's sexual desire and behavior. Multiple studies and reviews have converged on the conclusion that natural or surgical menopause is associated, on average, with declines in women's sexual motivation (e.g., Alexander et al., 2004; Dennerstein, Lehert, & Burger, 2005; Dennerstein, Wood, & Burrows, 1977; Freeman et al., 2007; Gracia, Freeman, Sammel, Lin, & Mogul, 2007). Longitudinal studies show that it is declining estradiol (and not declining androgens) that best predicts drops in sexual function across the menopausal transition (Dennerstein et al., 2005; Dennerstein, Randolph, Taffe, Dudley, & Burger, 2002; Freeman et al., 2007; McCoy, 1990). Causal effects of hormones are supported by clinical trials showing that menopausal declines in sexual desire can be at least partially reversed via administration of estrogens (Dennerstein, Burrows, Wood, & Hyman, 1980; Nathorst-Boos, Wiklund, Mattsson, Sandin, & von Schoultz, 1993; Sherwin, 1991), testosterone combined with estrogen (Braunstein et al., 2005; Floter, Nathorst-Boos, Carlstrom, & von Schoultz, 2002; Sherwin, Gelfand, & Brender, 1985), or testosterone alone (Davis et al., 2008; for a general review, see Alexander et al., 2004). Although androgens like testosterone have shown efficacy in hormone replacement trials, Cappelletti and Wallen (2016) argued that only supra-physiological doses of testosterone have produced such effects, whereas estradiol treatments at doses typical of natural, preovulatory concentrations can improve sexual desire. (Testosterone may also increase desire by increasing the bioavailability of estrogens; see Wallen, 2001.) Finally, Schmidt et al. (2009) showed that chemical suppression of ovarian hormone production in healthy premenopausal women led to clear declines in sexual functioning, including drops in desire-related outcomes such as rates of sexual fantasy.

Many other studies have provided evidence for increased sexual desire or behavior on fecund, preovulatory cycle days relative to other phases of the menstrual cycle (for reviews, see Roney, 2015; Wallen, 2001). Such effects are especially reliable in studies that have confirmed ovulatory timing via luteinizing hormone (LH) tests or frequent hormone sampling (e.g., Bullivant et al., 2004; Dennerstein et al., 1994; Diamond & Wallen, 2011; Hedricks, Schramm, & Udry, 1994; Wilcox et al., 2004). Although these cycle phase shifts are consistent with ovarian hormone regulation of sexual motivation given the prototypical hormone shifts across the menstrual cycle, early studies had nonetheless reported null effects for tests of whether within-cycle fluctuations in hormones were associated with day-to-day changes in measures of sexual motivation (Dennerstein et al., 1994; Morris, Udry, Khan-Dawood, & Dawood, 1987; Persky, Charney, Lief, et al., 1978; Persky, Lief, Strauss, Miller, & O'Brien, 1978; van Goozen, Wiegant, Endert, Helmond, & van de Poll, 1997). These studies were limited, however, by small sample sizes, relatively infrequent hormone sampling, and underpowered statistical techniques for the analysis of non-independent data.

In light of the lack of direct evidence for hormonal predictors of cycle phase shifts in women's desire, my lab undertook a large study to address some of the limitations in this literature (Roney & Simmons, 2013). Young women collected daily saliva samples across 1–2 menstrual cycles, while also completing online self-reports of their sexual desire on corresponding days. We assayed the saliva samples for estradiol, progesterone, and testosterone on every day in a nine-day window in the middle of the cycle, and on alternating days outside of this window. Employing mixed regression models to correctly account for repeated measurements nested within women, we found that estradiol concentrations measured two days before the response day positively predicted self-reports of sexual desire. Progesterone concentrations were even stronger negative predictors of desire, whether measured the same day as the response day, or one or two days earlier. Figure 14.1 provides a visual depiction of the association of desire

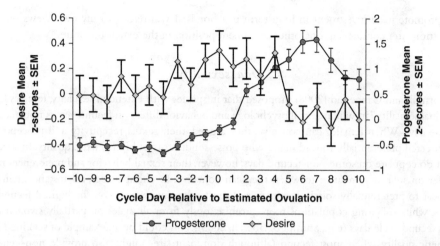

Figure 14.1   Mean desire for sex and mean progesterone concentrations aligned against estimated day of cycle (day 0 represents the estimated day of ovulation) in a sample of young women with confirmed ovulatory cycles (*n* = 53 cycles). Values are standardized within-cycles such that zero points on the y-axes represent the mean values within a given cycle.

Reprinted from "Hormonal Predictors of Sexual Desire in Natural Menstrual Cycles," by J.R. Roney and Z.L. Simmons, *Hormones and Behavior*, *63*, 636–645. Copyright 2013 by Elsevier. Reprinted with permission.

with current day progesterone. Because estradiol peaks one to two days before ovulation, while progesterone peaks after ovulation in the non-fecund luteal phase, opposing effects of these hormones could explain the ovulatory peak in sexual desire that has been demonstrated in the prior literature and that was also replicated in this study.

The findings of the Roney and Simmons (2013) study directly contradicted Symons's (1979) claim that women do not experience increased desire associated with the preovulatory estrogen surge. They also provided perhaps the first direct evidence that progesterone has inhibitory effects on women's desire. Although many nonhuman primates do exhibit some extended sexuality, progesterone at mid-luteal concentrations is usually associated with a complete absence of sexual behavior under natural living conditions (reviewed in Dixson, 1998), and the clear drop in desire associated with the luteal progesterone peak in our study (see Figure 14.1) suggests that a weakened form of inhibitory effects of progesterone may be conserved in humans. Recently, Jones et al. (in press) in a study with over 300 women measured at least five times in weekly sessions, found that within-women shifts in progesterone were significantly negatively correlated with changes in measures of sexual desire, while shifts in estradiol had positive but weaker and less consistent associations with desire.[2] Their findings appear to represent an independent replication of the basic pattern of results reported in Roney and Simmons (2013).

A strong version of the release from hormonal control position thus appears to be false. Not only do ovarian hormones affect women's sexual motivation, but evidence suggests that the same pattern of facilitating effects of estradiol combined with inhibitory effects of progesterone characterizes humans in common with most mammalian species. Nonetheless, distinct from most other mammals, sexual behavior is expressed at all cycle phases – as reported in all studies that have examined this, including Roney and Simmons (2013) – and the assumption of essentially continuous capacity for sexual receptivity that undergirds theories of human pair bonding is surely correct. What then explains the conservation of these hormone effects in humans – even if in a weakened form – given that continuous receptivity may have been selected specifically to promote male investment in long-term pair bonds? I will return to my own views on this question after considering one other prominent position in the extant literature.

Dual sexuality

Thornhill and Gangestad (2008) proposed that in species with extended sexuality, females have a "dual sexuality" in which sexual psychology and behavior differs on fecund versus non-fecund cycle days. When females can conceive, they argued, their sexual receptivity and proceptivity is directed preferentially toward males who possess indicators of high genetic quality. In species that do copulate on some non-fecund days, however, their sexual behavior and preferences may differ on such days relative to when they can conceive. In chimpanzees, for instance, females appear to preferentially solicit dominant and resist subordinate males on the highest fecundity days, while soliciting copulations more promiscuously from all males on partially swollen but less fecund cycle days (e.g., Stumpf & Boesch, 2005). This could be an example of seeking high genetic quality when most fecund (although dominant sires might also provide non-genetic benefits in chimpanzees) but then shifting standards for sexual partners during extended sexuality as a means of confusing paternity.

Application of the dual sexuality idea to humans suggests that women may be especially sexually interested in men with putative markers of genetic quality on days before ovulation when conception is possible, but then have potentially distinct sexual desires related to pair-bond maintenance at other times (Grebe, Emery Thompson, & Gangestad, 2016; Thornhill & Gangestad, 2008). Thus, the evidence reviewed above regarding women's higher sexual motivation near ovulation when estradiol is high and progesterone is low could be qualified by shifts in the targets of desire: peri-ovulatory desire may preferentially target sexually attractive men, whereas desire at other times may be more targeted toward men who are high-investing pair-bond partners. This idea of human dual sexuality has been tested with respect to both women's mate preferences and their target-specific sexual desires.

With respect to mate preferences, a fairly large number of studies have reported that women express stronger preferences for putative indicators of men's genetic quality – including, for example, facial or body masculinity, symmetry, low voice pitch, and behavioral displays of dominance – when women are tested near ovulation than when they are surveyed at other points of the menstrual cycle (for reviews, see Gangestad & Thornhill, 2008; Roney, 2009; Thornhill & Gangestad, 2008). Most such studies have estimated ovulatory timing using counting methods for which evidence suggests reliability is low (see Gangestad et al., 2016), however, and the diversity of counting algorithms that have been employed has raised issues regarding possible researcher degrees of freedom in the identification of fecund cycle days (e.g., Wood, Kressel, Joshi, & Louie, 2014). Two large-scale meta-analyses came to conflicting conclusions regarding whether mate preference cycle phase shifts are in fact robust (Gildersleeve, Haselton, & Fales, 2014; Wood et al., 2014). Since their publication, additional studies with large sample sizes have reported null findings for cycle phase shifts (e.g., Zietsch, Lee, Sherlock, & Jern, 2015) and hormonal predictors (Jones et al., 2017) of women's preferences for masculinity in men's faces, as well as null effects for cycle phase shifts in preferences for more masculine bodies (Junger, Kordsmeyer, & Penke, 2017). Thus, one of the main empirical lines of support for the dual sexuality position – that women are more attracted to men with cues of good genes on fecund vs. non-fecund cycle days – stands in some doubt, and further research appears necessary to resolve this question.

More directly related to the themes of this chapter is the question of whether the hormonal predictors of women's sexual desire exhibit target-specificity in ways that are consistent with the dual sexuality position. Grebe et al. (2016) argued that progesterone may *positively* predict women's sexual desire for their own long-term, romantic partners, which would be a reversal of the inhibitory effects of progesterone documented in most primates and thus perhaps represent an evolved specialization for promoting pair bonds via sexual behavior during the non-fecund luteal phase. In a sample of 33 naturally cycling, partnered women, they showed that changes in salivary progesterone assessed one week apart positively predicted changes in women's sexual attraction to their own partners, whereas changes in estradiol negatively predicted such attraction. For attraction to men other than their partners ("extra-pair" men), non-significant trends were in the opposite direction. One limitation of this study, however, is that absolute progesterone concentrations suggested that the majority of saliva samples (48 out of 61) came from the luteal phase, which, if true, would mean that the study was unable to clearly test whether progesterone values characteristic of the luteal phase up-regulate in-pair desire relative to the lower progesterone concentrations that characterize the follicular phase before ovulation. Nonetheless, the findings of Grebe et al. (2016) were highly intriguing for their suggestion of a possible reversal of endocrine effects on sexual motivation when the target of desire was a long-term romantic partner.

To test the robustness of this reversal, Roney and Simmons (2016) analyzed data from the Roney and Simmons (2013) study that pertained specifically to women in relationships. These women were asked to report daily their sexual attraction toward and fantasy about both their own partners and other, extra-pair men. Although only 15 women in this study were in relationships, many were sampled repeatedly across two cycles, and, in all, 24 cycles of data were available from partnered women with over 300 data-points for each measured hormone and over 700 survey responses for the measures of in-pair and extra-pair attraction. The findings were unambiguous: contrary to Grebe et al. (2016), within-cycle fluctuations in progesterone negatively predicted day-to-day changes in women's desire for both their own partners and for other men. Furthermore, desire for both categories of men was significantly higher during the fertile window (i.e., the cycle days when conception is possible; see Wilcox, Weinberg, & Baird, 1998) relative to other days in the same cycles. Although the small number of partnered women in this study raises issues regarding the generalizability of its findings, a recent study with hundreds of partnered women and pre-registered methods for estimating cycle phase likewise found peri-ovulatory peaks in women's desire for both their own partners and for extra-pair men (Arslan, Schilling, Gerlach, & Penke, 2017). Taken together, the findings from this larger study and that of Roney and Simmons (2016) argue against the idea that women's desire for their own partners is facilitated by the elevated progesterone concentrations that characterize the non-fecund luteal phase.

In summary, evidence is converging on the conclusion that sexual desire in general is enhanced during fecund phases of women's menstrual cycles, whether measured as general desire, desire targeted to pair-bond partners, or desire directed toward other men. Whether preferences for specific traits in men shift across the cycle is a question that appears to be in need of additional research, with a particular need for highly powered studies that can simultaneously pinpoint ovulatory timing and assess the hormonal predictors of potential preference shifts. With respect to sexual desire, though, the studies that have sampled hormones repeatedly and broadly across cycle regions have converged in reproducing in humans the general mammalian pattern of positive effects of estradiol and negative effects of progesterone on measures of female sexual motivation (Jones et al., in press; Roney & Simmons, 2013, 2016). What functional considerations may explain the conservation of this pattern in humans?

Motivational priorities theory

Estrus is typically defined as the period of time during which females are sexually receptive and are capable of conceiving. In proposing their dual sexuality position, Thornhill and Gangestad (2008) described the function of estrus as follows: "We also propose that estrus shares a basic function across all vertebrates: to obtain sires of superior genetic quality" (p. 189). In most mammals, males provide no direct parental care and females obtain no benefits from mates other than genes, and thus female sire choice during estrus is expected to focus on male genetic quality. Nonetheless, in an important sense, I disagree that the function of having a restricted time period during which females are sexually receptive is sire choice for good genes. Instead, a much more basic function is to couple the expression of sexual behavior to the time periods when its fitness benefits are the highest relative to its fitness costs. In other words, the main function of estrus is to shift motivational priorities toward sexual behavior when conception provides a fitness benefit that can outweigh the fitness costs of sex.

Consider an analogy with temporal cycles of hunger and satiety. The main function of hunger is logically to motivate a search for food when internal energy availability has decreased. The function of satiety is to shift motivational priorities to problems other than feeding when energy availability is sufficient (persistence in feeding and foraging during such times could present large opportunity costs with respect to the neglect of other adaptive problems). To argue that the function of estrus is sire choice for good genes seems analogous to arguing that the function of hunger is the choice of nutritious foods. Food choice is expected to be focused on cues of nutritive value (at least in ancestral environments), of course, and specific food preferences may even undergo slight shifts when hungry versus sated, but clearly the more basic function of hunger is to shift motivational priorities toward eating when energy stores are dropping or low. The question of specific food preferences is potentially orthogonal and certainly secondary to this more basic function of adaptive adjustments in motivational priorities.

Sexual behavior should have had fitness costs as well benefits in ancestral humans, as in other species. Such costs could include risk of infection or injury, diversion of attention from monitoring the environment for threats or opportunities, and loss of time and energy that could be invested in other behaviors. Conception would have been an important countervailing fitness benefit, although in a pair-bonding species with extended sexuality there should have been other benefits related to pair-bond establishment and maintenance. If the relationship-related benefits were not strongly coupled to temporal fluctuations in fecundity, however, then other things equal, the benefit-to-cost ratio of sexual behavior should have been higher for women on average on days when conception was possible than when it was not. My proposal is that positive effects of estradiol and negative effects of progesterone on sexual motivation were conserved in humans due to the selection pressures associated with these fecundity-related changes in the average fitness costs and benefits of sexual behavior. In the next section, I will propose that relationship-related variables also affect women's sexual motivation, but that these influences are largely independent of the hormone effects. Together, these hormonal and non-hormonal influences may explain how fecundity-related shifts in sexual motivation can co-exist with the continuous potential for sexual receptivity that may have been necessary to conceal ovulatory timing and thus promote the evolution of human pair bonding.

I will use "motivational priorities theory" as a label for the position that one function of many hormonal signals is to regulate temporal changes in behavioral priorities. If motivational priorities theory explains hormonal influences on women's sexual motivation, then one might expect that ovarian hormones will have effects on competing motivational priorities that are opposite in sign to their effects on sexual desire. Consistent with motivational priorities theory, in many nonhuman mammalian species, feeding and foraging drop during time periods when females can conceive, but then return to baseline outside of fecund time periods when sexual receptivity has declined (for reviews, see Fessler, 2003; Schneider, Wise, Benton, Brozek, & Keen-Rhinehart, 2013). Ovarian hormones regulate these shifts via opposite effects on feeding and sexual motivation. In nonhuman primates, in particular, estradiol administration decreases females' food intake, progesterone reverses the inhibitory effects of estradiol, and the combined effects of the two hormones in natural cycles lead to a pronounced nadir in eating just before ovulation when females are fecund (e.g., Bielert & Busse, 1983; Czaja & Goy, 1975; Kemnitz, Gibber, Lindsay, & Eisele, 1989). Ovarian hormone effects on feeding are a nearly perfect mirror image of their effects on sexuality, suggesting special design to shift between these priorities depending on females' fecundity.

A number of studies have likewise provided evidence for drops in women's food intake just before ovulation (for reviews, see Buffenstein, Poppitt, McDevitt, & Prentice, 1995; Fessler, 2003). Early studies did not have data regarding hormonal predictors of women's food intake, however, and did not directly test for possible tradeoffs between eating and sexual motivation. In the Roney and Simmons (2013, 2016) study described earlier that collected daily saliva samples, women in the second menstrual cycle of data collection were also surveyed daily regarding their overall levels of food intake. Hormonal predictors of food intake were remarkably similar to those seen in nonhuman primates: fluctuations in estradiol negatively predicted within-cycle shifts in food intake, progesterone fluctuations positively predicted them, and the two hormones together statistically mediated a significant drop in food intake during the fertile window (Roney & Simmons, 2017). Furthermore, since this study was unique in having measures of food intake and sexual motivation from the same women on the same days, it was able to test endocrine correlates of tradeoffs between these motivational priorities. In fact, fluctuations in estradiol and progesterone were oppositely associated with shifts in a variable computed as the difference between standardized daily measures of food intake and sexual desire, and the cycle phase peak in sexual desire was temporally aligned with the nadir in food intake (see figure 4 in Roney & Simmons, 2017). Thus, endocrine regulation of women's sexual motivation may be part of a broader system that is designed to shift multiple motivational priorities based on circumstances that predicted changes in their relative fitness benefits, on average, during human evolution.

To be clear, I do not think that the reciprocal hormonal regulation of sexual and feeding motivation necessarily or primarily results from temporal or energetic constraints that preclude performing both behaviors on the same cycle days. Rather, sexual motivation may drop outside of fecund cycle days, on average, in order to avoid the fitness costs of sex while focusing instead on alternative adaptive problems, such as foraging. However, during the fertile windows of fecund cycles, a relative shift in motivation to sexuality should have reduced the probability of missing important conceptive opportunities. Since one means of increasing the motivation for one goal is to reduce the motivation for competing ones (Fessler, 2003), the drop in feeding motivation on fecund cycle days may function to further enhance the motivation for sexual behavior when conception is possible.

Motivational priorities theory can also be extended to explain changes in sexual motivation at time-scales broader than individual menstrual cycles. The drops in sexual motivation that occur on average with menopause (reviewed above) and during intensive lactation (e.g., Avery, Duckett, & Frantzich, 2000; Forster, Abraham, Taylor, & Llewellyn-Jones, 1994; Rupp et al., 2013) are consistent with the calibration of desire to the benefit-to-cost ratio of sexual behavior, since these are time periods when conception is absent as a possible fitness benefit. During events such as lactation, furthermore, attention should be adaptively allocated to more pressing adaptive problems related to infant care, and a reduction in sexual motivation may facilitate this process by reducing the salience of competing motivational priorities.

Motivational priorities theory may provide a general explanation for the phylogenetic conservation of the endocrine regulators of female sexual motivation. As reviewed above, hormone signals associated with elevated fecundity increase measures of sexual motivation across most mammalian species, and evidence is converging that these same effects are found in humans. The dual sexuality position – via its postulation of the function of estrus being choice of males with high genetic quality – may have obscured a more basic and general function of estrus as a means of adaptively shifting motivational priorities based on the relative fitness benefits of alternative behaviors under different circumstances. Motivational priorities theory can efficiently explain both within-cycle and life-stage shifts in women's sexuality associated with corresponding changes in hormone concentrations, and can also account for additional effects of ovarian hormones on variables such as food intake. Although I believe that the weight of current evidence supports motivational priorities theory as the best available explanation for hormonal influences on women's sexuality, non-hormonal variables in all likelihood also play extremely important roles, as argued in the next section.

Synthesis: dual regulation of women's sexuality

My proposal here is that women's sexuality is also strongly influenced by variables related to mate choice, relationship initiation, and relationship maintenance, and that these variables operate largely independently of hormonal influences. If this postulation of independence is correct, then there may be a type of "dual regulation" of sexual motivation, with hormonal and non-hormonal influences having additive effects. If the non-hormonal influences are potent enough, furthermore, they may produce sexual receptivity and proceptivity that are sufficiently distributed across time periods that ovulatory timing is not clearly revealed by changes in sexual behaviors. In fact, the non-hormonal influences may exhibit design specifically for the promotion and maintenance of pair bonds, and thus in effect add relationship-related factors to the more phylogenetically conserved cost-benefit calculus that is implemented by endocrine influences on sexual motivation.

Exposure to attractive potential mates may be one variable that increases sexual desire. Such desire could be part of the subjective phenomenology of mate choice and may also signal interest to potential partners as a courtship tactic. Because desirable long-term mates could be met at any time of the menstrual cycle, however, or during anovulatory time periods, opportunities for relationship initiation and pair-bond establishment could have been missed if sexual desire was exclusively coupled to endocrine signals of fecundity. This may have selected for a capacity to respond to desirable partners with heightened sexual motivation regardless of the current baseline concentrations of ovarian hormones.

Perhaps consistent with this, in the Roney and Simmons (2013) study, there was a strong positive effect of weekend timing on women's self-reports of sexual desire. Because social events are concentrated on weekends in the undergraduate women who comprised this sample, this heightened desire may have occurred in response to social interactions with potential mates. Interestingly, the weekend timing effect was statistically independent of the significant hormonal influences on desire in this same sample: weekend timing did not interact with any hormone variable, and regression coefficients for the weekend and hormone variables were not affected by whether they were included in the same regression models or were entered into separate models.

Another line of evidence for relationship-related variables as calibrators of women's sexual motivation concerns effects of relationship length on measures of sexual desire. A number of studies have reported that women's sexual desire and initiation is highest early in relationships and tends to decline with increasing relationship length (e.g., Dennerstein et al., 2005; Murray and Milhausen, 2012; Pillsworth, Haselton, & Buss, 2004). Because frequent sexual activity must be mostly nonconceptive given the minority of cycle days on which conception is possible, heightened sexual motivation early in relationships is unlikely to be explained by fecundity-related shifts in ovarian hormones, and may instead represent a behavioral strategy that signals commitment to a partner and helps to establish a pair bond (see Roney, 2015). In a longitudinal study of women going through the menopausal transition, Dennerstein et al. (2005) reported that entry into a new relationship was a stronger predictor of women's sexual desire and responsiveness than was their estradiol concentration, although estradiol was also a significant positive predictor of sexual functioning in the same structural equation model. Thus, even among women whose estradiol concentrations were undergoing relatively steep decline across the course of a longitudinal study, entry into a new relationship – as well as feelings for a current partner – were strong positive predictors of sexual motivation, with effects that were statistically significant after controlling for simultaneous hormonal influences on desire. These patterns are consistent with relationship-related variables acting to modulate women's sexual motivation regardless of whether baseline hormone concentrations are high or low.

Dual regulation of sexual motivation could be achieved by way of hormonal and non-hormonal influences acting as additive inputs to the neural structures that produce desire. Hormones do not generally trigger behaviors directly, but instead modulate their likelihoods of occurrence in response to stimuli via effects such as alteration of the firing thresholds of neurons (Becker, Breedlove, & Crews, 1992). In female rats, for instance, the lordosis response occurs in response to tactile stimulation from males, but only if hypothalamic neurons are in a responsive state as determined by estrogen priming (Pfaff & Schwartz-Giblin, 1988). In this case, as in many rodents, the hormone effects are strong enough that mating does not take place at all unless ovarian hormone concentrations exceed a critical threshold. In most primates, however, these influences have been weakened such that mating can take place even when females have been ovariectomized (as has been observed in captivity), but ovarian hormones still have strong effects on the motivation for sexual behavior (for reviews, see Dixson, 1998; Wallen, 1990). In humans, evidence suggests that particular networks of neural structures that involve a number of transmitter systems are involved in the regulation of women's sexual motivation (for a review, see Pfaus, 2009). These are neural structures known to express ovarian hormone receptors, but a dampening of the priming effects of hormones combined with an increase in the potency of social stimuli in activating these networks may be sufficient to explain the capacity of relationship-related variables to induce sexual desire even in states of low ovarian hormone concentrations. Phylogenetically, this dual regulation of sexuality may have required only incremental changes in the functions relating hormone concentrations and social stimuli to levels of sexual motivation, rather than the evolution of entirely new regulatory mechanisms. These changes could have promoted pair bonding via their production of the continuous capacity for sexual receptivity, while also maintaining the fitness advantages of using hormone fluctuations to shift motivational priorities based on their relative fitness benefits in different circumstances.

Hormones and sexuality in men

Although the focus of this chapter is on the endocrinology of women's sexuality, the arguments herein carry implications for how men's sexual behavior may be designed to respond to women's sexuality. A brief examination of men's sexuality can thus help test the theoretical arguments that were presented in the above sections.

If women's continuous capacity for sexual receptivity and desire does help to obscure cues of ovulatory timing well enough that male partners cannot reliably diagnose fecund time periods, then men's sexual interest in their partners should be relatively invariant across cycle days. Most studies that have examined this have in fact found that male rates of sexual initiation are flat across regions of the menstrual cycle (Adams, Gold, & Burt, 1978; Caruso et al., 2014; van Goozen et al., 1997; cf. Harvey, 1987), even though these same studies demonstrated increases in measures of women's sexual motivation just before ovulation. Strom, Ingberg, Druvefors, Theodorsson, and Theodorsson (2012) likewise reported that men's testosterone concentrations did not fluctuate, on average, across days of their partners' cycles. Finally, unlike women, data suggests that men's sexual desire for their partners does not decline with increasing relationship length (Murray & Milhausen, 2012). Women's desire may decline to avoid the fitness costs of sex, other things equal, after a pair bond has been established, while still capturing conceptive opportunities via increases in desire during the fertile windows of fecund cycles. But if over evolutionary time men have been unable to detect when such fertile windows occurred, their ancestral fitness-maximizing strategy may have been relatively constant sexual interest regardless of relationship length (or cycle phase) in order to ensure that unpredictable insemination opportunities were captured whenever they arose.

Relatively constant sexual interest may help explain why men's sexual desire does not appear to closely track variability in gonadal hormones within the normal range. Chemical suppression of gonadotropin-releasing hormone (GnRH) that results in hypogonadal testosterone concentrations does produce significant declines in men's sexual desire, fantasy, and intercourse frequency (Bagatell, Heiman, Rivier, & Bremner, 1994). However, in this same study, testosterone replacement doses at only half the average normal concentrations fully restored all sexual measures to their pre-treatment baselines (for some evidence of more continuous effects of replacement doses, see Finkelstein et al., 2013). Likewise, administration of high doses of exogenous testosterone to eugonadal men did not produce significant changes in sexual desire or behavior (Bagatell, Heiman, Matsumoto, Rivier, & Bremner, 1994). Such findings suggest that men's sexual motivation may require only minimum threshold concentrations of gonadal hormones rather than closely tracking endocrine fluctuations across the normal range.

Rather than regulating sexual motivation, fluctuations in men's gonadal hormones may be more closely linked to somatic and behavioral investments in mate competition versus alternative motivational priorities. Androgens appear to promote muscle development, intrasexual competitiveness and status-seeking, and direct pursuit of potential mates, while potentially drawing energy away from competing survival-related investments in fat storage and some forms of immune function (for reviews, see Bribiescas, 2001; Ellison, 2001; Roney, 2016). In species in which males invest paternally in offspring, furthermore, testosterone tends to drop during offspring care (for reviews, see Muller, 2017; Wingfield, Hegner, Dufty, & Ball, 1990) and experimental elevations of testosterone after the birth of offspring can reduce paternal effort in favor of mate pursuit (e.g., Hegner & Wingfield, 1987). Humans appear to exhibit this same endocrine signature of male investment in pair bonds and offspring, as multiple studies have converged in showing declines in men's testosterone after entry into committed romantic relationships, with further declines associated with fatherhood (for reviews, see Gettler, 2014; Gray & Campbell, 2009; Roney & Gettler, 2015). Roney and Gettler (2015) used such findings to propose a simple model – the testosterone-relationship cycle – in which elevated testosterone promotes the successful attainment of long-term relationship entry, which in turn causes reductions in testosterone production in order to focus motivational priorities on pair bond and offspring investment instead of on the pursuit of new mating opportunities.

In summary, men's sexual psychology and its endocrine correlates exhibit patterns that suggest design for pair bonding and a functional responsiveness to women's reproductive strategies. Instead of sexual motivation being strongly coupled to clearly diagnostic cues of female fecundity – as in most mammalian males – men's sexual interest appears to be relatively constant with respect to women's cycle phase, consistent with the idea that women's ovulatory timing is effectively concealed. Hormones like testosterone, rather than modulating temporal shifts in sexual motivation, appear to modulate efforts at mate pursuit. These endocrine effects may be adaptive responses to pair bonding plus concealed ovulation, since they produce shifts in motivational priorities from courtship effort to paternal investment based on current circumstances, but also allow relatively constant sexual interest in long-term partners despite the drops in testosterone that are associated with relationship entry and fatherhood.

Conclusion

Evidence is accumulating that women's sexual motivation is higher during fecund time periods, and that positive and negative effects of estradiol and progesterone, respectively, cause temporal shifts in desire. Motivational priorities theory provides an efficient explanation for why these hormone effects may have been conserved from a wide range of nonhuman species. In particular, sexual motivation decreases during non-fecund time periods in order to avoid the fitness costs of sex, other things equal, when conception is not possible, but then increases during elevated fecundity in order to capture conceptive opportunities. Competing motivational priorities – such as feeding and foraging – exhibit an inverse pattern, decreasing in salience during fecund time periods. Whether elements of a "dual sexuality" are overlain onto phylogenetically conserved shifts in motivational priorities is a question with mixed findings that requires additional research. Despite the conservation of endocrine influences on women's desire, social and relationship variables also have strong effects that may be independent of and additive to the hormone effects. The mechanisms that respond to social variables should exhibit special design for relationship initiation and pair-bond maintenance, though future research is necessary to better test functional hypotheses regarding the non-hormonal branch of the proposed dual regulation of women's sexual psychology. Finally, men's hormone production and sexual psychology appear to exhibit design for long-term mating and paternal investment, as evidenced by the well-replicated finding that testosterone drops with relationship entry and fatherhood. That pattern may also demonstrate an endocrine-mediated shift in motivational priorities – between mate pursuit and paternal investment – based on temporal shifts in the net fitness benefits of alternative behaviors.

Notes

1 Fitness is used as in evolutionary biology and refers to the effects of traits or behaviors on gene replication. A fitness benefit thus refers to the effect of a behavior that promotes the gene replication of the organism that exhibited the behavior, whereas a fitness cost is an effect that reduces the rate of gene replication. Natural selection designs behavior-regulating mechanisms that promoted higher fitness (i.e., greater gene replication) relative to alternative designs in the environments in which the mechanisms evolved, but there is no necessary assumption that organisms consciously represent biological fitness as a motivational goal.

2 Although such findings on their face suggest that effects of estradiol may be weaker than effects of progesterone in predicting women's desire, caution is warranted in drawing this conclusion. Estradiol peaks are more restricted in time to specific preovulatory days, whereas progesterone peaks extend across a larger number of luteal phase days. Weekly measurements may therefore fail to sample estradiol peaks more often than they miss peaks in progesterone.

References

Adams, D.B., Gold, A.R., & Burt, A.D. (1978). Rise in female-initiated sexual activity at ovulation and its suppression by oral contraceptives. *New England Journal of Medicine, 299*, 1145–1150.

Adkins-Regan, E. (2005). *Hormones and animal social behavior*. Princeton, NJ: Princeton University Press.

Alexander, J.L., Kotz, K., Dennerstein, L., Kutner, S.J., Wallen, K., & Notelovitz, M. (2004). The effects of postmenopausal hormone therapies on female sexual functioning: A review of double-blind, randomized controlled trials. *Menopause, 11*, 749–765.

Alexander, R.D., & Noonan, K.M. (1979). Concealment of ovulation, paternal care, and human social evolution. In N.A. Chagnon & W.G. Irons (Eds.), *Evolutionary biology and human social behavior: An anthropological perspective* (pp. 436–453). Scituate, MA: North Duxbury.

Arslan, R., Schilling, K., Gerlach, T.M., & Penke, L. (2017, June). *Ovulatory shifts in women's extra-pair and in-pair sexual desire in two large pre-registered studies*. Paper presented at the 29th annual conference of the Human Behavior and Evolution Society, Boise, ID.

Avery, M.D., Duckett, L., Frantzich, C.R. (2000). The experience of sexuality during breast-feeding among primiparous women. *Journal of Midwifery and Women's Health, 45*, 227–237.

Bagatell, C.J., Heiman, J.R., Matsumoto, A.M., Rivier, J.E., & Bremner, W.J. (1994). Metabolic and behavioral effects of high-dose, exogenous testosterone in healthy men. *Journal of Clinical Endocrinology & Metabolism, 79*, 561–567.

Bagatell, C.J., Heiman, J.R., Rivier, J.F., & Bremner, W.J. (1994). Effects of endogenous testosterone and estradiol on sexual behavior in normal young men. *Journal of Clinical Endocrinology & Metabolism, 78*, 711–716.

Beach, F.A. (1949). *Hormones and behavior*. New York, NY: Paul B. Hoeber.

Beach, F.A. (1976). Sexual attractivity, proceptivity, and receptivity in female mammals. *Hormones and Behavior, 7*, 105–138.

Becker, J.B., Breedlove, S.M., & Crews, D. (1992). *Behavioral endocrinology*. Cambridge, MA: MIT Press.

Bielert, C., & Busse, C. (1983). Influences of ovarian hormones on the food intake and feeding of captive and wild chacma baboons (*Papio ursinus*). *Physiology & Behavior, 30*, 103–111.

Blaustein, J.D. (2008). Neuroendocrine regulation of feminine sexual behavior: Lessons from rodent models and thoughts about humans. *Annual Review of Psychology, 59*, 93–118.

Braunstein, G.D., Sundwall, D.A., Katz, M., Shifren, J.L., Buster, J.E., Simon, J.A., . . . Watts, N.B. (2005). Safety and efficacy of a testosterone patch for the treatment of hypoactive sexual desire disorder in surgically menopausal women. *Archives of Internal Medicine, 165*, 1582–1589.

Bribiescas, R.G. (2001). Reproductive ecology and life history of the human male. *Yearbook of Physical Anthropology, 44*, 148–176.

Buffenstein, R., Poppitt, S.D., McDevitt, R.M., & Prentice, A.M. (1995). Food intake and the menstrual cycle: A retrospective analysis, with implications for appetite research. *Physiology & Behavior, 58*, 1067–1077.

Bullivant, S.B., Sellergren, S.A., Stern, K., Spencer, N.A., Jacob, S., Mennella, J.A., & McClintock, M.K. (2004). Women's sexual desire during the menstrual cycle: Identification of the sexual phase by noninvasive measurement of luteinizing hormone. *Journal of Sex Research, 41*, 82–93.

Cappelletti, M., & Wallen, K. (2016). Increasing women's sexual desire: The comparative effectiveness of estrogens and androgens. *Hormones and Behavior, 78*, 178–193.

Carter, C.S. (1992). Neuroendocrinology of sexual behavior in the female. In J.B. Becker, S.M. Breedlove, & D. Crews (Eds.), *Behavioral endocrinology* (pp. 71–95). Cambridge, MA: MIT Press.

Caruso, S., Agnello, C., Malandrino, C., Lo Presti, L., Cicero, C., & Cianci, S. (2014). Do hormones influence women's sex? Sexual activity over the menstrual cycle. *Journal of Sexual Medicine, 11*, 211–221.

Czaja, J.A., & Goy, R.W. (1975). Ovarian hormones and food intake in female guinea pigs and rhesus monkeys. *Hormones and Behavior, 6*, 329–349.

Davis, S.R., Moreau, M., Kroll, R., Bouchard, C., Panay, N., Gass, M., . . . Studd, J. (2008). Testosterone for low libido in postmenopausal women not taking estrogen. *New England Journal of Medicine, 359*, 2005–2017.

Dennerstein, L., Burrows, G.D., Wood, C., & Hyman, G. (1980). Hormones and sexuality: Effect of estrogen and progesterone. *Obstetrics & Gynecology, 56*, 316–322.

Dennerstein, L., Gotts, G., Brown, J.B., Morse, C.A., Farley, T.M.M., & Pinol, A. (1994). The relationship between the menstrual cycle and female sexual interest in women with PMS complaints and volunteers. *Psychoneuroendocrinology, 19*, 293–304.

Dennerstein, L., Lehert, P., & Burger, H. (2005). The relative effects of hormones and relationship factors on sexual function of women through the natural menopausal transition. *Fertility and Sterility, 84*, 174–180.

Dennerstein, L., Randolph, J., Taffe, J., Dudley, E., & Burger, H. (2002). Hormones, mood, sexuality, and the menopausal transition. *Fertility and Sterility*, 77, S42–S48.

Dennerstein, L., Wood, C., & Burrows, G.D. (1977). Sexual response following hysterectomy and oophorectomy. *Obstetrics & Gynecology, 49*, 92–96.

Deschner, T., Heistermann, M., Hodges, K., & Boesch, C. (2004). Female sexual swelling size, timing of ovulation, and male behavior in wild West African chimpanzees. *Hormones and Behavior, 46*, 204–215.

Devor, M., & Murphy, M.R. (1973). The effect of peripheral olfactory blockade on the social behavior of the male golden hamster. *Behavioral Biology, 9*, 31–42.

Diamond, L.M., & Wallen, K. (2011). Sexual minority women's sexual motivation around the time of ovulation. *Archives of Sexual Behavior, 40*, 237–246.

Dixson, A.F. (1998). *Primate sexuality: Comparative studies of the prosimians, monkeys, apes, and humans*. Oxford: Oxford University Press.

Dzieciol, M., Nizański, W., Stańczyk, E., Kozdrowski, R., Najder-Kozdrowska, L., & Twardoń, J. (2013). The influence of antibiotic treatment of bitches in oestrus on their attractiveness to males during mating. *Polish Journal of Veterinary Science, 16*, 509–516.

Ellison, P.T. (2001). *On fertile ground*. Cambridge, MA: Harvard University Press.

Emery, M.A., & Whitten, P.L. (2003). Size of sexual swellings reflects ovarian function in chimpanzees (*Pan troglodytes*). *Behavioral Ecology and Sociobiology, 54*, 340–351.

Emery Thompson, M. (2009). The endocrinology of intersexual relationships in the apes. In P.T. Ellison & P.B. Gray (Eds.), *The endocrinology of social relationships* (pp. 196–222). Cambridge, MA: Harvard University Press.

Fessler, D.M.T. (2003). No time to eat: An adaptationist account of periovulatory behavioral changes. *Quarterly Review of Biology, 78*, 3–21.

Finkelstein, J. S., Lee, H., Burnett-Bowie, S-A.M., Carl Pallais, J., Yu, E.W., Borges, L.F., . . . Leder, B. Z. (2013). Gonadal steroids and body composition, strength, and sexual function in men. *New England Journal of Medicine, 369*, 1011–1022.

Floter, A., Nathorst-Boos, J., Carlstrom, K., & von Schoultz, B. (2002). Addition of testosterone to estrogen replacement therapy in oophorectomized women: Effects on sexuality and well-being. *Climacteric, 5*, 357–365.

Freeman, E.W., Sammel, M.D., Lin, H., Gracia, C.R., Pien, G.W., Nelson, D.B., & Sheng, L. (2007). Symptoms associated with menopausal transition and reproductive hormones in midlife women. *Obstetrics & Gynecology, 110*, 230–240.

Forster, C., Abraham, S., Taylor, A., & Llewellyn-Jones, D. (1994). Psychological and sexual changes after the cessation of breast-feeding. *Obstetrics & Gynecology, 84*, 872–873.

Furtbauer, I., Heistermann, M., Schulke, O., & Ostner, J. (2011). Concealed fertility and extended sexuality in a nonhuman primate (*Macaca assamensis*). *PLoS One, 6*, e23015.

Gangestad, S.W., Haselton, M.G., Welling, L.L.M., Gildersleeve, K., Pillsworth, E.G., Burriss, R.P., . . . Puts, D.A. (2016). How valid are assessments of conception probability in ovulatory cycle research? Evaluations, recommendations, and theoretical implications. *Evolution and Human Behavior, 37*, 85–96.

Gangestad, S.W., & Thornhill, R. (2008). Human oestrus. *Proceedings of the Royal Society of London B, 275*, 991–1000.

Gettler, L.T. (2014). Applying socioendocrinology to evolutionary models: Fatherhood and physiology. *Evolutionary Anthropology, 23*, 146–160.

Gildersleeve, K., Haselton, M.G., & Fales, M.R. (2014). Do women's mate preferences change across the ovulatory cycle? A meta-analytic review. *Psychological Bulletin, 140*, 1205–1259.

Gracia, C.R., Freeman, E.W., Sammel, M.D., Lin, H., & Mogul, M. (2007). Hormones and sexuality during the transition to menopause. *Obstetrics & Gynecology, 109*, 831–840.

Gray, P.B., & Campbell, B.C. (2009). Human male testosterone, pair-bonding and fatherhood. In P.T. Ellison & P.B. Gray (Eds.), *The endocrinology of social relationships* (pp. 270–293). Cambridge, MA: Harvard University Press.

Grebe, N.M., Emery Thompson, M.E., & Gangestad, S.W. (2016). Hormonal predictors of women's extrapair vs. in-pair sexual attraction: Implications for extended sexuality. *Hormones and Behavior, 78*, 211–219.

Harvey, S.M. (1987). Female sexual behavior: Fluctuations during the menstrual cycle. *Journal of Psychosomatic Research, 31*, 101–110.

Hedricks, C.A., Schramm, W., & Udry, J.R. (1994). Effects of creatinine correction to urinary LH levels on the timing of the LH peak and distribution of coitus within the human menstrual cycle. *Annals of the New York Academy of Sciences, 709*, 204–206.

Hegner, R.E., & Wingfield, J.C. (1987). Effects of experimental manipulation of testosterone levels on parental investment and breeding success in male house sparrows. *Auk, 104*, 462–469.

Heistermann, M., Mole, U., Vervaecke, H., van Elsacker, L., & Hodges, J.K. (1996). Application of urinary and fecal steroid measurements for monitoring ovarian function and pregnancy in the bonobo (*Pan paniscus*) and evaluation of perineal swelling patterns in relation to endocrine events. *Biology of Reproduction, 55*, 844–853.

Jones, B., Hahn, A., Fisher, C., Wang, H., Kandrik, M., & DeBruine, L. (in press). General sexual desire, but not desire for uncommitted sexual relationships, tracks changes in women's hormonal status. *Psychoneuroendocrinology*.

Jones, B., Hahn, A., Fisher, C., Wang, H., Kandrik, M., Han, C., . . . DeBruine, L. (2017, June). *Women's preferences for facial masculinity are not related to their hormonal status.* Paper presented at the 29th annual conference of the Human Behavior and Evolution Society, Boise, ID.

Jünger, J., Kordsmeyer, T., & Penke, L. (2017, June). *Menstrual cycle shifts in female mate preferences for male body masculinity: An estrus effect instead of good genes sexual selection?* Paper presented at the 29th annual conference of the Human Behavior and Evolution Society, Boise, ID.

Kaplan, H., Hill, K., Lancaster, J., & Hurtado, A.M. (2000). A theory of human life history evolution: Diet, intelligence, and longevity. *Evolutionary Anthropology, 9*, 156–185.

Kemnitz, J.W., Gibber, J.R., Lindsay, K.A., & Eisele, S.G. (1989). Effects of ovarian hormones on eating behaviors, body weight, and glucoregulation in rhesus monkeys. *Hormones and Behavior, 23*, 235–250.

Lovejoy, C.O. (2009). Re-examining human origins in light of *Ardipithecus ramidus*. *Science, 326*, 74e1–74e8.

McCoy, N.L. (1990). Estrogen levels in relation to self-reported symptoms and sexuality in perimenopausal women. *Annals of the New York Academy of Sciences, 592*, 450–452.

Morris, N.M., Udry, R.J., Khan-Dawood, F., & Dawood, M.Y. (1987). Marital sex frequency and midcycle female testosterone. *Archives of Sexual Behavior, 16*, 27–37.

Muller, M.N. (2017). Testosterone and reproductive effort in male primates. *Hormones and Behavior, 91*, 36–51.

Murray, S.H., & Milhausen, R.R. (2012). Sexual desire and relationship duration in young men and women. *Journal of Sex and Marital Therapy, 38*, 28–40.

Nathorst-Boos, J., Wiklund, I., Mattsson, L.A., Sandin, K., & von Schoultz, B. (1993). Is sexual life influenced by transdermal estrogen therapy? A double blind placebo controlled study in postmenopausal women. *Acta Obstetrics Gynecology Scandinavica, 72*, 656–660.

Nunn, C.L. (1999). The evolution of exaggerated sexual swellings in primates and the graded-signals hypothesis. *Animal Behaviour, 58*, 229–246.

Persky, H., Charney, N., Lief, H.I., O'Brien, C.P., Miller, W.R., & Strauss, D. (1978). The relationships of plasma estradiol level to sexual behavior in young women. *Psychosomatic Medicine, 40*, 523–535.

Persky, H., Lief, H.I., Strauss, D., Miller, W.R., & O'Brien, C.P. (1978). Plasma testosterone level and sexual behavior of couples. *Archives of Sexual Behavior, 7*, 157–173.

Pfaff, D., & Schwartz-Giblin, S. (1988). Cellular mechanisms of female reproductive behaviors. In E. Knobil, J. Neill, L. Ewing, G. Greenwald, C. Markett, & D. Pfaff (Eds.), *The physiology of reproduction* (pp. 1487–1568). New York, NY: Raven Press.

Pfaus, J.G. (2009). Pathways of sexual desire. *Journal of Sexual Medicine, 6*, 1506–1533.

Pillsworth, E.G., Haselton, M.G., & Buss, D.M. (2004). Ovulatory shifts in female sexual desire. *Journal of Sex Research, 41*, 55–65.

Rodriguez-Girones, M.A., & Enquist, M. (2001). The evolution of female sexuality. *Animal Behaviour, 61*, 695–704.

Roney, J.R. (2009). The role of sex hormones in the initiation of human mating relationships. In P.T. Ellison & P.B. Gray (Eds.), *The endocrinology of social relationships* (pp. 246–269). Cambridge, MA: Harvard University Press.

Roney, J.R. (2015). An evolutionary functional analysis of the hormonal predictors of women's sexual motivation. In T.K. Shackelford & R.D. Hansen (Eds.), *The evolution of sexuality* (pp. 99–121). Cham, Switzerland: Springer.

Roney, J.R. (2016). Theoretical frameworks for human behavioral endocrinology. *Hormones and Behavior, 84*, 97–110.

Roney, J.R., & Gettler, L.T. (2015). The role of testosterone in human romantic relationships. *Current Opinion in Psychology, 1*, 81–86.

Roney, J.R., & Simmons, Z.L. (2013). Hormonal predictors of sexual motivation in natural menstrual cycles. *Hormones and Behavior, 63*, 636–645.

Roney, J.R., & Simmons, Z.L. (2016). Within-cycle fluctuations in progesterone negatively predict changes in both in-pair and extra-pair desire among partnered women. *Hormones and Behavior, 81*, 45–52.

Roney, J.R., & Simmons, Z.L. (2017). Ovarian hormone fluctuations predict within-cycle shifts in women's food intake. *Hormones and Behavior, 90*, 8–14.

Rupp, H.A., James, T.W., Ketterson, E.D., Sengelaub, D.R., Ditzen, B., & Heiman, J.R. (2013). Lower sexual interest in postpartum women: Relationship to amygdala activation and intranasal oxytocin. *Hormones and Behavior, 63*, 114–121.

Schmidt, P.J., Steinberg, E.M., Negro, P.P., Haq, N., Gibson, C., & Rubinow, D.R. (2009). Pharmacologically induced hypogonadism and sexual function in healthy young women and men. *Neuropsychopharmacology, 34*, 565–576.

Schneider, J.E., Wise, J.D., Benton, N.A., Brozek, J.M., & Keen-Rhinehart, E. (2013). When do we eat? Ingestive behavior, survival, and reproductive success. *Hormones and Behavior, 64*, 702–728.

Sherwin, B.B. (1991). The impact of different doses of estrogen and progestin on mood and sexual behavior in postmenopausal women. *Journal of Clinical Endocrinology & Metabolism, 72*, 336–343.

Sherwin, B.B., Gelfand, M.M., & Brender, W. (1985). Androgen enhances sexual motivation in females: A prospective, crossover study of sex steroid administration in the surgical menopause. *Psychosomatic Medicine, 47*, 339–351.

Strassmann, B.I. (1981). Sexual selection, paternal care, and concealed ovulation in humans. *Ethology and Sociobiology, 2*, 31–40.

Strom, J.O., Ingberg, E., Druvefors, E., Theodorsson, A., & Theodorsson, E. (2012). The female menstrual cycle does not influence testosterone concentrations in male partners. *Journal of Negative Results in Biomedicine, 11*, 1–7.

Stumpf, R.M., & Boesch, C. (2005). Does promiscuous mating preclude female choice? Female sexual strategies in chimpanzees (*Pan troglodytes verus*) of the Tai national park, Cote d'Ivoire. *Behavioral Ecology and Sociobiology, 57*, 511–524.

Symons, D. (1979). *The evolution of human sexuality*. Oxford: Oxford University Press.

Thornhill, R., & Gangestad, S.W. (2008). *The evolutionary biology of human female sexuality*. Oxford: Oxford University Press.

Van Goozen, S.H.M., Wiegant, V.M., Endert, E., Helmond, F.A., & van de Poll, N.E. (1997). Psychoneuroendocrinological assessment of the menstrual cycle: The relationship between hormones, sexuality, and mood. *Archives of Sexual Behavior, 26*, 359–382.

Wallen, K. (1990). Desire and ability: Hormones and the regulation of female sexual behavior. *Hormones and Behavior, 14*, 233–241.

Wallen, K. (2001). Sex and context: Hormones and primate sexual motivation. *Hormones and Behavior, 40*, 339–357.

Wilcox, A.J., Baird, D.D., Dunson, D.B., McConnaughey, D.R., Kesner, J.S., & Weinberg, C.R. (2004). On the frequency of intercourse around ovulation: Evidence for biological influences. *Human Reproduction, 19*, 1539–1543.

Wilcox, A.J., Weinberg, C.R., & Baird, D.D. (1998). Post-ovulatory ageing of the human oocyte and embryo failure. *Human Reproduction, 13*, 394–397.

Wingfield, J.C., Hegner, R.E., Dufty, A.M., & Ball, G.F. (1990). The "challenge hypothesis": Theoretical implications for patterns of testosterone secretion, mating systems, and breeding strategies. *American Naturalist, 136*, 829–846.

Wood, W., Kressel, L., Joshi, P.D., & Louie, B. (2014). Meta-analysis of menstrual cycle effects on women's mate preferences. *Emotion Review, 6*, 229–249.

Young, W.C. (1961). The hormones and mating behavior. In W.C. Young (Ed.), *Sex and internal secretions* (pp. 1173–1239). Baltimore, MD: Williams & Wilkins.

Zietsch, B.P., Lee, A. G., Sherlock, J.M., & Jern, P. (2015). Variation in women's preferences regarding male facial masculinity is better explained by genetic differences than by previously identified context-dependent effects. *Psychological Science, 26*, 1440–1448.

15

ORGANIZATIONAL EFFECTS OF HORMONES ON SEXUAL ORIENTATION

Kevin A. Rosenfield, Khytam Dawood, and David A. Puts

Introduction

Sexual orientation refers to relative sexual attraction to men (androphilia), women (gynephilia), or both (Bailey et al., 2016) and is one of the most sexually dimorphic human psychological traits. In most Western surveys, more than 95% of genetic (XY) males report exclusive or near-exclusive gynephilia, and a similar proportion of women report exclusive or near-exclusive androphilia (Bailey et al., 2016), resulting in a sex difference of approximately six standard deviations (Hines, 2011). However, despite this large sex difference, non-trivial proportions of both sexes report not only non-heterosexual orientations, but also non-heterosexual behavior (e.g., Grulich et al., 2014; Wienke & Whaley, 2015) and identity (e.g., Pakula & Shoveller, 2013). How and why variations in sexual orientation arise is a matter of fascination and debate within and outside of the scientific community. What are the genetic, environmental, and neurophysiological factors responsible for variation in sexual orientation? Researchers in the social and life sciences have made significant progress toward answering these questions (Hill, Dawood, & Puts, 2013), and much evidence suggests that activities of the neuroendocrine system during prenatal or early postnatal development exert an influence on sexual orientation later in life.

In this chapter, we review this evidence. After exploring how sexual orientation is measured, we turn our attention to studies relating variation in sexual orientation to sex hormone signaling, by which we mean both production of and sensitivity to sex hormones. We consider cases of gender reassignment during infancy or early childhood, followed by evidence regarding specific classes of hormones: androgens and estrogens. We review data from studies examining hormone levels during fetal development, medical conditions associated with atypical hormone levels or sensitivity, normal variation in hormone sensitivity, manipulations of hormone levels via pharmaceutical treatment or castration, as well as endogenous hormone levels in adulthood. We also examine indirect evidence – hormone biomarkers, such as finger length ratios. Finally, we consider possible targets of hormonal signaling: how sexual orientation is represented in the brain. Throughout, we incorporate relevant data from animal models. Whenever possible, we have indicated the sample sizes and effect sizes associated with the studies cited in the text. While some of these are reported in the text itself, for ease of comparison we have presented the vast majority of these figures in several tables, along with information on the study variables, predicted associations, and statistical significance.

Measuring sexual orientation

Whereas some researchers simply ask study participants whether they consider themselves heterosexual, homosexual, or bisexual (Sell, 2007), perhaps the most widely used instruments for measuring sexual orientation are the Kinsey Scale (Kinsey, Pomeroy, & Martin, 1948) and Klein Sexual Orientation Grid (Klein, Sepekoff, & Wolf, 1985). The Kinsey Scale measures sexual orientation along four dimensions: attraction, fantasy, behavior, and identity using 7-point scales ranging from exclusive heterosexual orientation to exclusive homosexual orientation. The Klein Grid evaluates sexual orientation along dimensions of attraction, behavior, fantasy, social and emotional preferences, self-identification, and heterosexual/homosexual lifestyle, also using 7-point scales. Within each dimension, subjects are asked to report their past, present, and ideal behavior/preferences. Responses to the 21 questions of this instrument loaded onto a single factor in a factor analysis, suggesting considerable redundancy (Weinrich et al., 1993). However, it is important to note that the various dimensions sometimes measured under the rubric of sexual orientation are not perfectly correlated. For example, one may identify as heterosexual and engage only in heterosexual sex, yet be attracted to and sexually fantasize only about members of one's own sex. In such cases, most researchers would say that one has a homosexual orientation. This is because sexual behavior and identity can be constrained by local culture, and because sexual attraction motivates behavior and identity, not vice versa (Bailey et al., 2016). In both sexes, self-report measures of sexual orientation generally correlate well with more objective measures, such as reaction time (Wright, 1994), viewing time (Israel & Strassberg, 2009), genital arousal (Chivers, Rieger, Latty, & Bailey, 2005), and pupil dilation (Rieger & Savin-Williams, 2012; Rieger et al., 2015; Watts, Holmes, Savin-Williams, & Rieger, 2017) in response to male vs. female stimuli, although these relationships are often stronger in men than in women. This may be related to increased plasticity of sexual orientation in women compared to men (Bailey, 2009), but there remains disagreement as to whether this difference in plasticity results in part from sex differences in gender socialization (Baumeister, 2000; Shibley-Hyde & Durik, 2000).

Gender reassignment

Among vertebrates, sex differences in the brain and behavior emerge when androgens divert development onto a masculine trajectory (Morris, Jordan, & Breedlove, 2004). This cascade of events commences with the differentiation of the gonads, which is triggered by the expression of sex-determining region Y (*Sry*) gene as early as gestation day 10 in mammals (Wilhelm, Palmer, & Koopman, 2007). It is thus logical to hypothesize that the human sex difference in gynephilic vs. androphilic orientation also arises from males' higher androgen levels. However, the different social environments of males and females, namely, their upbringing as boys and girls respectively, may also contribute to sex differences in sexual attraction. If one could design the ideal experiment for disentangling the role of intrinsic physiological sex differences from gender socialization it would likely resemble the following: From infancy, expose a randomly selected cohort of children of one genetic sex (male: XY, female: XX), who were exposed to sex-typical hormonal regimes prenatally, to a social environment typical of the opposite sex (i.e., raise XY individuals as girls and XX as boys), including by changing the child's appearance so that others would perceive the child as the opposite sex. Later, ascertain sexual orientation (Bailey et al., 2016). The larger the role of gender socialization, the more typical the child should be of the reassigned gender.

Such manipulations are obviously unethical, but several cases of gender reassignment at birth have nevertheless occurred for various reasons. Gender was reassigned in several hormonally typical males whose penises were accidentally destroyed during circumcision, or were malformed due to cloacal exstrophy, in which the abdomen and penis develop abnormally. The medical community once recommended reassigning these males as female, both surgically (via castration, penectomy, and vaginoplasty) and socially (e.g., encouraging female-typical play, playmates, and dress behavior). While castration necessarily leads to male-atypical hormone levels subsequently, the organizational effects of prenatal hormones on the developing brain will remain. Data on adult sexual orientation are available for seven such natal males whose gender was reassigned as described above between birth and 17 months (Bailey et al., 2016). In all cases, adult sexual attraction was gynephilic (Figure 15.1), an extremely improbable outcome (less than 2 in 100 trillion) if prenatal development were irrelevant (Bailey et al., 2016). Thus, postnatal gender socialization appears generally insufficient to produce androphilia in individuals with male-typical early androgen exposure. We now turn our attention to evidence concerning such androgenic influences on sexual orientation.

Androgens

Androgen signaling in genetic females

Findings from studies measuring fetal hormones are mixed. However, studies of genetic or endocrine disorders that lead to atypical production of or sensitivity to gonadal hormones (disorders of sexual development) indicate that androgens promote gynephilia in genetic females (summarized in Table 15.1).

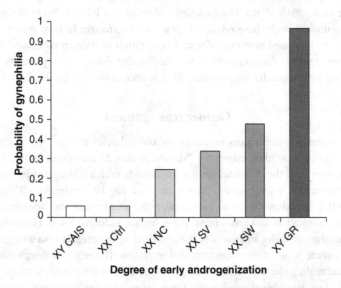

Figure 15.1   Proportion of individuals experiencing gynephilia as a function of early androgen signaling in individuals raised as females. Gynephilia is defined here as Kinsey 2–6 (regular attractions to and fantasies about women). Degree of androgenization refers to both exposure and sensitivity to androgens. XY = genetic male, XX = genetic female. Categories are rank-ordered: CAIS = complete androgen insensitivity syndrome (sexual orientation does not differ from female controls; Hines, Ahmed, & Hughes, 2003), Ctrl = women recruited without regard to diagnosis or sexual orientation (Gangestad, Bailey, & Martin, 2000), NC = non-classical CAH, SV = simple virilizing CAH, SW = salt-wasting CAH (Meyer-Bahlburg, Dolezal, Baker, & New, 2008 for all CAH), GR = gender-reassigned natal males (Bailey et al., 2016). In general this indicates that increased androgen signaling is related to increasing incidence of gynephilia.

Fetal hormone levels

The relationship between fetal hormones and sexual orientation itself has not been systematically studied. However, several groups have tested the hypothesis that children's gender-typical play behavior, a correlate of adult sexual orientation (Cohen, 2002; Rieger, Linsenmeier, & Bailey, 2008), is associated with fetal hormone levels. While one study found a relationship between male-typical behavior and testosterone sampled from amniotic fluid in genetic females (Auyeung et al., 2009), two others did not (Knickmeyer et al., 2005; van De Beek, Van Goozen, Buitelaar, & Cohen-Kettenis, 2009). van De Beek et al. (2009) also observed no relationship between amniotic progesterone or estrogen and girls' female-typical play behavior, or between any of the three steroids. In addition, maternal blood testosterone assayed once between weeks 5 and 36 of pregnancy predicted male-typical play behavior in preschool girls (Hines, Golombok, Rust, Johnston, & Golding, 2002). These studies indirectly hint at a relationship between maternal hormone levels and sexual orientation, but they did not measure sexual orientation directly and only sampled testosterone during small developmental windows. Experimental manipulation of fetal hormones would be conclusive but unethical in humans. However, several disorders of sexual development are associated with altered androgen signaling and hence can serve as "natural experiments" – or quasi-experiments, as "treatments" are not randomly assigned.

Congenital adrenal hyperplasia

Congenital adrenal hyperplasia (CAH) is an autosomal recessive disorder of sexual development characterized by underproduction of one of the five enzymes responsible for glucocorticoid synthesis in the adrenal cortex. Unable to synthesize glucocorticoids, the adrenal cortex converts a portion of the unusually abundant glucocorticoid precursors to androgens, leading to excess androgen (hyperandrogenism) (Merke & Bornstein, 2005; Speiser & White, 2011). During early development, this hyperandrogenism may masculinize brain structures underlying sexually differentiated cognitive and behavioral traits. Despite postnatal hormone replacement therapy, females with CAH sometimes present with more male-typical toy choice, play behavior, vocational preferences, maternal behavior (Meyer-Bahlburg, 2001), and cognition (Puts, McDaniel, Jordan, & Breedlove, 2008).

Published evidence overwhelmingly suggests that CAH also leads to an increased chance of non-heterosexuality in women (Hines, 2011). Ten studies with age-matched (or in one case, unaffected sister-matched) control groups have reported that women with CAH are more likely to identify as non-heterosexual, have a history of engaging in homosexual relationships, or report attraction to members of the same sex (Dittmann, Kappes, & Kappes, 1992; Frisén et al., 2009; Gastaud et al., 2007; Hines, Brook, & Conway, 2004; Johannsen, Ripa, Mortensen, & Main, 2006; May, Boyle, & Grant, 1996; Meyer-Bahlburg et al., 2008; Money, Schwartz, & Lewis, 1984; Zucker, Bradley, Oliver, Blake, & Fleming, 1996). Four of these studies found that CAH severity (assessed by hormonal assay, specific mutation of the 21-hydroxlase gene, or degree of genital virilization at birth) positively predicted the likelihood of non-heterosexuality (Figure 15.1). Additionally, two studies reported a high incidence of homosexual behavior or fantasies, but did not use a control group for comparison (Ehrhardt, Evers, & Money, 1968; Khorashad et al., 2017). Three studies failed to replicate a relationship between CAH and female non-heterosexuality Kuhnle & Bullinger, 1997: no data provided; Lev-Ran, 1974: 0 of 18 patients reporting non-heterosexual behavior or attraction, with no control group; Slijper et al., 1992: 0 of 18 patients reporting non-heterosexual behavior or attraction, with no control group. Several authors have questioned the methodologies employed in these unsupportive studies (e.g., Hines, 2011), but their criticisms,

Table 15.1 Summary of results for studies linking androgen levels and receptors to sexual orientation in genetic females (see section "Androgen signaling in genetic females")

Reference	Predictor variable	Dependent variable	Predicted association	Significant?	N	T	C	ES	Stat	Method
Auyeung et al., 2009	Testosterone in amniotic fluid	Male-typical play behavior	Positive	Yes	100	n/a	n/a	0.42	r	From paper
Knickmeyer et al., 2005	Testosterone in amniotic fluid	Male-typical play behavior	Positive	No	21	n/a	n/a	−0.19	r	From paper
Van De Beek et al., 2009	Testosterone in amniotic fluid	Male-typical toy preference	Positive	No	63	n/a	n/a	0.00	r	From paper
Van De Beek et al., 2009	Estradiol in amniotic fluid	Male-typical toy preference	Positive	No	63	n/a	n/a	−0.04	r	From paper
Van De Beek et al., 2009	Progesterone in amniotic fluid	Male-typical toy preference	Positive	No	63	n/a	n/a	0.07	r	From paper
Van De Beek et al., 2009	Testosterone in amniotic fluid	Female-typical toy preference	Positive	No	63	n/a	n/a	0.03	r	From paper
Van De Beek et al., 2009	Estradiol in amniotic fluid	Female-typical toy preference	Positive	No	63	n/a	n/a	0.14	r	From paper
Van De Beek et al., 2009	Progesterone in amniotic fluid	Female-typical toy preference	Positive	No	63	n/a	n/a	0.00	r	From paper
Van De Beek et al., 2009	Testosterone in maternal blood	Male-typical toy preference	Positive	No	58	n/a	n/a	−0.01	r	From paper
Van De Beek et al., 2009	Estradiol in maternal blood	Male-typical toy preference	Positive	No	58	n/a	n/a	0.06	r	From paper
Van De Beek et al., 2009	Progesterone in maternal blood	Male-typical toy preference	Positive	No	58	n/a	n/a	0.22	r	From paper
Van De Beek et al., 2009	Testosterone in maternal blood	Female-typical toy preference	Positive	No	58	n/a	n/a	0.09	r	From paper
Van De Beek et al., 2009	Estradiol in maternal blood	Female-typical toy preference	Positive	No	58	n/a	n/a	−0.05	r	From paper
Van De Beek et al., 2009	Progesterone in maternal blood	Female-typical toy preference	Positive	No	58	n/a	n/a	−0.05	r	From paper
Hines et al., 2004	CAH vs. non-CAH unrelated	Gynephilia	Higher in CAH	Yes	31	16	15	0.82	d	From paper
Johannsen et al., 2006	CAH vs. non-CAH unrelated	Gynephilia	Higher in CAH	Yes	110	40	70	0.24	V	Calculated
Meyer-Bahlburg et al., 2008	CAH vs. non-CAH unrelated	Gynephilia	Higher in CAH	Yes	167	143	24	0.60	d	Calculated
Money et al., 1984	CAH vs. CAIS (XX) or MRKS (XX)	Gynephilia	Higher in CAH	Yes	57	30	27	1.03	d	Calculated
Zucker et al., 1996	CAH vs. non-CAH unrelated	Gynephilia	Higher in CAH	Yes	45	30	15	0.47	d	From paper
Dittmann et al., 1992	CAH vs. non-CAH sisters	Gynephilia	Higher in CAH	Yes	48	34	14	1.03	d	Calculated
Frisén et al., 2009	CAH vs. non-CAH unrelated	Gynephilia	Higher in CAH	Yes	124	62	62	0.59	d	Calculated
Gastaud et al., 2007	CAH vs. non-CAH unrelated	Gynephilia	Higher in CAH	Yes	104	35	69	0.45	d	Calculated
Khorashad et al., 2017	CAH with no control group	Gynephilia	High in CAH	45% gynephilic	18	18	0	n/a	n/a	n/a
Ehrhardt et al., 1968	CAH with no control group	Gynephilia	High in CAH	48% gynephilic	23	23	0	n/a	n/a	n/a
May et al., 1996	CAH vs. non-CAH w/ diabetes	Gynephilia	Higher in CAH	Yes	36	17	19	0.43	V	Calculated
Agrawal et al., 2004	Homosexual vs. heterosexual	Incidence of PCO	Higher in homosexual	Yes	618	254	364	1.07	d	Calculated
Agrawal et al., 2004	Homosexual vs. heterosexual	Incidence of PCOS	Higher in homosexual	Yes	618	254	364	0.58	d	Calculated
Smith et al., 2011	Homosexual vs. heterosexual	Incidence of PCO	Higher in homosexual	No	211	114	97	0.16	d	Calculated

Study	Measure	Comparison	Direction	Significant	N	T	C	ES	Stat	Method
Smith et al., 2011	Incidence of PCOS	Homosexual vs. heterosexual	Higher in homosexual	No	211	114	97	0.16	d	Calculated
Loraine, Ismail, Adamopoulos, & Dove, 1970	Testosterone in urine	Homosexual vs. heterosexual	Higher in homosexual	Yes	18	4	14	n/a	n/a	n/a
Griffiths et al., 1974	Testosterone in urine	Homosexual vs. heterosexual	Higher in homosexual	n/a	42	42	0	n/a	n/a	n/a
Downey, Ehrhardt, Schiffman, Dyrenfurth, Becker, 1987	Testosterone in plasma	Homosexual vs. heterosexual	Higher in homosexual	No	14	7	7	0	d	Calculated
Dancey, 1990	Testosterone in urine	Homosexual vs. heterosexual	Higher in homosexual	No	20	10	10	−0.39	d	Calculated
Singh, Vidaurri, Zambarano, & Dabbs Jr., 1999	Testosterone in saliva	Butch rating	Positive	Yes	33	33	0	0.59	r	From paper
Pearcey, Docherty, & Dabbs, 1996	Within-couple salivary T difference	Within-couple butch rating difference	Negative	No	26	n/a	n/a	−0.35	r	From paper
Pearcey et al., 1996	Within-couple salivary T difference	Within-couple butch rating difference	Above omitting outlier	Yes	25	n/a	n/a	−0.54	r	From paper
Pearcey et al., 1996	Testosterone in saliva	Butch rating	Higher in butch	No	54	n/a	n/a	−0.03	r	From paper

Note: N: Total sample size, T: Treatment group sample size, C: Control group sample size, ES: Effect size, Stat: Effect size statistic used, Method: Method used to obtain effect size.

such as "inadequate assessments of sexual orientation" (Meyer-Bahlburg, 2001), could also be applied to many studies supporting the relationship. Overall, 11 of 14 published studies (summarized above) report increased (or in the case of Ehrhardt et al., 1968 and Khorashad et al., 2017, substantially higher than the general population) incidence of non-heterosexuality in female CAH patients. Given these results (see also Table 15.1), the relationship between CAH and sexual orientation in women is ripe for meta-analysis, so that more general conclusions can be drawn. To reduce the chance of publication bias, such an analysis should include any unpublished results that can be obtained, as these would be more likely to be unsupportive of the hypothesized relationship.

Polycystic ovary syndrome

Polycystic ovary syndrome (PCOS) is the most common endocrine disorder in women (Barry et al., 2010). Symptoms appear around menarche or slightly before and may include polycystic ovaries, hyperandrogenism, and irregular or infrequent menstrual cycling (Silfen et al., 2003). Genetic and prenatal environmental causes of PCOS have been suggested (Abbott, Barnett, Bruns, & Dumesic, 2005; Barry et al., 2010; Bronstein et al., 2011; Goodarzi, Guo, Yildiz, Stanczyk, & Azziz, 2007), and some evidence implicates elevated early androgens. For example, female rhesus macaques (*Macaca mulatta*) and sheep (*Ovis aries*) exposed to exogenous androgen during fetal development present with PCOS-like symptoms, including hypersecretion of luteinizing hormone, oligomenorrhoea (infrequent menstrual cycles), irregular follicular development, and insulin resistance (Franks, 2002). In addition, androgen levels in umbilical vein blood were elevated in daughters of women with PCOS (Barry et al., 2010), who themselves are more likely to have PCOS, given its high heritability (approximately 70%; Vink, Sadrzadeh, Lambalk, & Boomsma, 2006). If women with PCOS were exposed to excess androgen during early development, and if prenatal androgens contribute to later gynephilia, then the incidence of non-heterosexuality might be elevated in PCOS women. In fact, a far higher prevalence of both PCO (polycystic ovaries with or without other PCOS symptoms; Cohen's $d = 1.07$) and PCOS (Cohen's $d = 0.58$) was observed in 254 self-identifying lesbians than in 364 non-lesbians attending a fertility clinic (Agrawal et al., 2004). In a smaller sample of 114 lesbian and 97 heterosexual women, only 13 of whom were diagnosed with PCOS, non-significant trends were observed toward increased PCOS (Cohen's $d = 0.16$), polycystic ovaries (Cohen's $d = 0.16$), hirsutism, testosterone, and androstenedione in lesbians compared to heterosexual women (Smith et al., 2011). Additional studies are needed before any firm conclusions regarding the relationship between PCOS and sexual orientation can be drawn, although given their general consistency, meta-analysis of the studies already conducted may yield significant results.

Studies of PCOS thus suggest that hyperandrogenism and/or exposure to elevated prenatal androgens from hyperandrogenic mothers increases the probability of gynephilia. The late emergence of observable symptoms in PCOS helps rule out differential rearing as an explanation for elevated homosexuality in women with PCOS. However, mothers of women with PCOS may exhibit different rearing practices regardless of daughters' condition, so it would be useful to compare sexual orientation in sisters with and without PCOS, but to our knowledge, no sibling study relating PCOS and sexual orientation has yet been undertaken.

Adult hormone levels

Some evidence indicates that homosexual women exhibit higher androgen levels than heterosexual women in adulthood (Griffiths et al., 1974; Loraine et al., 1970); one of these studies reported no statistical results, while the other compared testosterone levels of only four lesbians to a "normal" population range in four separate statistical tests. In addition, several studies have found no differences (Dancey, 1990; Downey et al., 1987). However, homosexual women self-identifying as "butch" had higher salivary testosterone that those identifying as "femme" in two samples (Pearcey et al., 1996; Singh et al., 1999). Very little has been published on the effects of testosterone treatment on sexual orientation in women; however, a case report of an androphilic female-to-male transsexual indicates that testosterone treatment did not produce gynephilic interests (Blanchard, 1990).

Androgen signaling in genetic males

Studies of reduced androgen signaling or production suggest that androgens promote gynephilia in genetic males (summarized in Table 15.2).

Fetal hormone levels

Four studies have investigated the relationship between prenatal hormone levels and childhood male-typical play behavior, reaching contradictory conclusions. Auyeung et al. (2009) found that testosterone levels in amniotic fluid were positively associated with male-typical play behavior in genetic males, while Knickmeyer et al. (2005) and van De Beek et al. (2009) found no such relationship. In addition, maternal blood testosterone assayed once between weeks 5 and 36 of pregnancy did not predict male-typical play behavior in preschool boys (Hines et al., 2002). The methods employed in these studies differ substantially, which may account for the difference in findings. More studies utilizing these and other methodologies are needed before any firm conclusions can be drawn.

Adult hormone levels

In contrast to evidence that prenatal or early postnatal androgens promote androphilia in genetic males, research on adult hormones and sexual orientation has produced mixed but generally null results (Meyer-Bahlburg, 1977). An early study found that plasma testosterone levels were significantly lower in exclusively homosexual (Kinsey 6; $N = 8$), and almost exclusively homosexual (Kinsey 5; $N = 7$) men than heterosexual men (Kolodny, Masters, Hendryx, & Toro, 1971). Meyer-Bahlburg (1977) notes that a disproportionate number of homosexual subjects were drug users, suggesting that sexual orientation could have been confounded by drug use. However, all 13 of these men reported marijuana use and virtually no experience with other drugs. Analogous numbers are not reported for the heterosexual controls. Loraine et al. (1970) reported lower average testosterone levels in three homosexual men compared to 14 heterosexual controls, but the small sample size impedes generalization of these results. Two other studies found relationships between adult testosterone and sexual orientation in men, but were criticized on the basis of methodological problems such as small samples and inappropriate controls (reviewed by Meyer-Bahlburg, 1977), and six studies found no relationship between adult hormones and sexual orientation (see Table 15.2 in Meyer-Bahlburg, 1977).

In addition, testosterone treatment in adulthood did not produce gynephilic interests in homosexual men (Barahal, 1940), and removal of testicular androgen via castration appears not to produce androphilic interests. Of 36 men who reported being mostly or exclusively attracted to women prior to voluntary castration without hormone replacement, none reported a change to being mostly or exclusively attracted to men after castration, and three reported

Table 15.2 Summary of results for studies linking androgen levels and receptors to sexual orientation in genetic males (see section "Androgen signaling in genetic males")

Reference	Predictor variable	Dependent variable	Predicted association	Significant?	N	T	C	ES	Stat	Method
Van De Beek et al., 2009	Testosterone in amniotic fluid	Male-typical toy preference	Positive	No	63	n/a	n/a	0.11	r	From paper
Van De Beek et al., 2009	Estradiol in amniotic fluid	Male-typical toy preference	Positive	No	63	n/a	n/a	−0.05	r	From paper
Van De Beek et al., 2009	Progesterone in amniotic fluid	Male-typical toy preference	Positive	Yes	63	n/a	n/a	0.30	r	From paper
Van De Beek et al., 2009	Testosterone in amniotic fluid	Female-typical toy preference	Positive	No	63	n/a	n/a	0.01	r	From paper
Van De Beek et al., 2009	Estradiol in amniotic fluid	Female-typical toy preference	Positive	No	63	n/a	n/a	0.04	r	From paper
Van De Beek et al., 2009	Progesterone in amniotic fluid	Female-typical toy preference	Positive	No	63	n/a	n/a	−0.19	r	From paper
Auyeung et al., 2009	Testosterone in amniotic fluid	Male-typical play behavior	Positive	Yes	112	n/a	n/a	0.20	r	From paper
Knickmeyer et al., 2005	Testosterone in amniotic fluid	Male-typical play behavior	Positive	No	31	n/a	n/a	0.00	r	From paper
Van De Beek et al., 2009	Testosterone in maternal blood	Male-typical toy preference	Positive	No	57	n/a	n/a	0.09	r	From paper
Van De Beek et al., 2009	Estradiol in maternal blood	Male-typical toy preference	Positive	No	57	n/a	n/a	−0.13	r	From paper
Van De Beek et al., 2009	Progesterone in maternal blood	Male-typical toy preference	Positive	No	57	n/a	n/a	0.12	r	From paper
Van De Beek et al., 2009	Testosterone in maternal blood	Female-typical toy preference	Positive	No	57	n/a	n/a	−0.17	r	From paper
Van De Beek et al., 2009	Estradiol in maternal blood	Female-typical toy preference	Positive	No	57	n/a	n/a	0.05	r	From paper
Van De Beek et al., 2009	Progesterone in maternal blood	Female-typical toy preference	Positive	No	57	n/a	n/a	−0.07	r	From paper
Kolodny et al., 1971	Kinsey rating	Testosterone in plasma	Lower in Kinsey 5 and 6	Yes	65	15	50	−2.26	d	Calculated
Loraine et al., 1970	Homosexual vs. heterosexual	Testosterone in urine	Higher in heterosexual	Yes	17	3	14	n/a	n/a	n/a
Hines et al., 2003	CAIS vs non-CAIS women	Gynephilia	Higher in CAIS	No	44	22	22	−0.10	d	Calculated

Note: N: Total sample size, T: Treatment group sample size, C: Control group sample size, ES: Effect size, Stat: Effect size statistic used, Method: Method used to obtain effect size.

equal attraction to men and women after castration (E. Wibowo, T. Johnson, and R. Wassersug, personal communications; September 3–5, 2017; data from Handy, Jackowich, Wibowo, Johnson, & Wassersug, 2016). These results are consistent with no overall activational effect of androgens on sexual orientation, but a depressed libido leading to more equal (reduced) attraction to women and men following castration (Handy et al., 2016; Wassersug, Westle, & Dowsett, 2017).

Androgen sensitivity

Complete androgen insensitivity syndrome (CAIS) is a genetic disorder in which XY individuals (i.e., genetic males) have a nonfunctional androgen receptor. Individuals with CAIS are born with undescended testes and produce normal-to-high male levels of circulating androgen, but their androgen insensitivity results in a female appearance. Likewise, individuals with CAIS have a female gender identity and are female-typical psychologically: No significant differences were found between XX female controls and XY women with CAIS in aspects of gender identity, gender role, childhood play behavior, or sexual orientation (Hines et al., 2003). Other studies have found extremely low levels of non-heterosexuality in women with CAIS (Money et al., 1984; Wisniewsky et al., 2000; Figure 15.1).

Like CAIS, partial androgen insensitivity syndrome stems from mutations in the androgen receptor gene. However, there is wide variation in the extent of androgen insensitivity across patients with partial androgen insensitivity syndrome (PAIS) and some (Quigley, 2002; Oakes, Eyvazzadeh, Quint, & Smith, 2008), but not all (Bouvattier, Mignot, Lefèvre, Morel, & Bougnères, 2006), evidence indicates increased androphilia in XY individuals with partial androgen insensitivity syndrome compared to genetic males with fully functional androgen receptor genes, perhaps reflecting the variability in insensitivity (Oakes et al., 2008).

Studies relating sexual orientation to either normal variation in androgen receptor gene sequence (Macke et al., 1993; $N = 410$) or androgen receptor immunoreactivity (a measure of androgen receptor density) in the brain (Kruijver, Fernández-Guasti, Fodor, Kraan, & Swaab, 2001; $N = 33$) have produced null findings. Why typical variation in androgen receptor function is not reliably associated with sexual orientation has yet to be resolved. Perhaps such variation has modest effects on function or is compensated by feedback on circulating androgen levels or androgen receptor transcriptional activity or distribution.

α-reductase deficiency

The enzyme 5α-reductase-2 converts testosterone into the more potent androgen dihydrotestosterone. A number of genetic mutations lead to 5α-reductase-2 deficiency, resulting in a significant shortage of dihydrotestosterone in males (Imperato-McGinley & Zhu, 2002). At birth, XY males born with 5α-reductase-2 deficiency present with ambiguous external genitalia and reduced prostate volume, but remaining internal structures are consistent with genetic sex. Until puberty, affected individuals have often been raised as girls and identified as girls. However, at the onset of puberty, genital masculinization occurs, along with male-typical increases in muscle mass and decreases in vocal pitch. The majority of affected individuals have identified as men after this transition (Imperato-McGinley & Zhu, 2002) and are gynephilic in adulthood (Garcia-Falgueras & Swaab, 2009). Thus, in general, sexual orientation is more consistent with early testosterone exposure than gender of rearing in this population. Although effects of pubertal or adult androgens on the brain, as well on appearance and hence social interactions, cannot be ruled out, cases of gender reassignment at birth (Section 3) suggest that these influences are minimal.

Estrogens

Despite their common characterization as "female" hormones, estrogens exert masculinizing effects in some mammals, including rats and mice (McEwen, Lieberburg, Chaptal, & Krey, 1977; Wu et al., 2009). In these species, most brain masculinization is accomplished through the conversion via the enzyme aromatase of androgens to estrogens and subsequent binding of estrogen to estrogen receptors (Naftolin, Ryan, Davies, Petro, & Kuhn, 1975). It has been hypothesized that estrogens also play a part in masculinizing the human brain, but little evidence supports this hypothesis (Motta-Mena & Puts, 2017; Puts & Motta-Mena, 2017; Zuloaga, Puts, Jordan, & Breedlove, 2008).

Diethylstilbestrol

Diethylstilbestrol (DES) is a synthetic estrogen that was administered to pregnant women during the mid-twentieth century with the intended effect of reducing the risk of abnormal pregnancy and miscarriage, but with many unintended negative consequences (Titus-Ernstoff et al., 2003). For women exposed to DES in utero, these include increased incidence of breast cancer, structural abnormalities of the reproductive tract, infertility, and abnormal pregnancies (Schrager & Potter, 2004).

A sample of women exposed prenatally to DES scored higher on several dimensions of same-sex orientation (including behavior and attraction variables) than both an unrelated control group and their unexposed sisters (Ehrhardt et al., 1985; $N = 60$), and a follow-up study (Meyer-Bahlburg et al., 1995; $N = 217$) replicated some associations but not others. However, these results were not replicated in subsequent larger studies (Newbold, 1993). In by far the largest study of this type ($N > 5,500$), women exposed to DES were significantly *less likely* than controls to report homosexual behavior (Titus-Ernstoff et al., 2003).

Other evidence that sexual orientation is not estrogen-mediated

Additional data cast further doubt on the role of estrogens in masculinizing the human brain (see Puts & Motta-Mena, 2017 for a more complete review). First, dihydrotestosterone has similar effects to testosterone on female sexually differentiated behavior in rhesus macaques (Wallen, 2005). Because dihydrotestosterone cannot be aromatized into estrogen, this means that estrogen-to-estrogen-receptor binding must not be essential to brain and behavior masculinization in a close human relative. Second, eight case studies reviewed in Cooke, Nanjappa, Ko, Prins, and Hess (2017) found no differences in self-reported sexual orientation between men with and without functioning aromatase genes, and an additional case study reported male-typical gender identity and sexual orientation in a man lacking a functional estrogen receptor (Smith et al., 1994). Although larger samples are clearly desirable, these results provide evidence that men can have masculine behavior despite the inability to aromatize testosterone to estrogen. This indicates that estrogen-to-estrogen-receptor binding is not essential for masculinizing the human brain in general and sexual orientation in particular.

Hormone biomarkers

Researchers have also used several morphological or behavioral traits as putative biomarkers of prenatal sex hormone exposure (e.g., Rahman & Wilson, 2003). In general, these data indicate increased masculinization in gynephilic females, but mixed results in males (summarized in Table 15.3).

Table 15.3 Summary of results for studies linking hormonal biomarkers to sexual orientation (see section "Harmone biomarkers")

Reference	Predictor variable	Dependent variable	Sex	Predicted association	Significant?	N	T	C	ES	Stat	Method
McFadden & Pasanen, 1998	Sexual orientation	Otoacoustic emissions	F	Stronger in heterosexual	Yes	94	37	57	0.37	d	From paper
McFadden & Champlin, 2000	Sexual orientation	Auditory evoked potentials	F	Different in two samples	Yes (5 of 19)	105	57	49	0.37–0.62	d	From paper
McFadden & Champlin, 2000	Sexual orientation	Auditory evoked potentials	F	Different in two samples	No (14 of 19)	105	57	49	0.01–0.30	d	From paper
Martin & Nguyen, 2004	Andro- vs. gynophilia	Bone growth/body size	Both	Androphilia = female-typical	Yes (7 of 10)	412	228	184	0.20–0.38	d	From paper
McFadden & Champlin, 2000	Sexual orientation	Auditory evoked potentials	M	Different in two samples	Yes (5 of 19)	103	53	50	0.38–0.47	d	From paper
McFadden & Champlin, 2000	Sexual orientation	Auditory evoked potentials	M	Different in two samples	No (14 of 19)	103	53	50	0.03–0.26	d	From paper
Bogaert & Hershberger, 1999	Sexual orientation	Penile length (flaccid)	M	Different in two samples	Yes	4230	813	3417	0.65	d	Calculated
Bogaert & Hershberger, 1999	Sexual orientation	Penile length (erect)	M	Different in two samples	Yes	4230	813	3417	1.28	d	Calculated
Valentova & Havlíček, 2013	Sexual orientation	Ratings of SO from vocal recordings	M (F raters)	Ratings match actual orientation	Yes	20	n/a	n/a	0.92	d	From paper
Valentova & Havlíček, 2013	Sexual orientation	Ratings of SO from vocal recordings	M (M raters)	Ratings match actual orientation	Yes	19	n/a	n/a	0.61	d	From paper
Valentova & Havlíček, 2013	Sexual orientation	Ratings of SO from facial images	M (F raters)	Ratings match actual orientation	Yes	20	n/a	n/a	0.32	d	From paper
Valentova & Havlíček, 2013	Sexual orientation	Ratings of SO from facial images	M (M raters)	Ratings match actual orientation	Yes	19	n/a	n/a	0.58	d	From paper
Valentova, Kleisner, & Havlíček, 2014	Sexual orientation	Ratings of SO from facial images	M (F raters)	Ratings match actual orientation	No	20	n/a	n/a	0.31	d	Calculated
Valentova et al., 2014	Sexual orientation	Ratings of SO from facial images	M (M raters)	Ratings match actual orientation	No	20	n/a	n/a	-0.10	d	Calculated

(Continued)

Table 15.3 (Continued)

Reference	Predictor variable	Dependent variable	Sex	Predicted association	Significant?	N	T	C	ES	Stat	Method
Valentova et al., 2014	Ratings of masculinity	Ratings of SO from facial images	M	Positive – feminine & gynephilia	Yes	66	n/a	n/a	0.46	*r*	Calculated
Hall & Kimura, 1994	Sexual orientation	Asymmetry of dermal ridge direction	M	Higher in homosexuals	Yes	248	66	182	0.37	*d*	Calculated
Forastieri et al., 2017	Sexual orientation	Asymmetry of dermal ridge direction	M	Higher in homosexuals	No	136	60	76	n/a	n/a	n/a
Mustanski et al., 2002	Sexual orientation	Asymmetry of dermal ridge direction	M	Higher in homosexuals	No	333	169	164	−0.28	*d*	Calculated

Note: N: Total sample size, T: Treatment group sample size, C: Control group sample size, ES: Effect size, Stat: Effect size statistic used, Method: Method used to obtain effect size.

Biomarkers in women

The ratio of the lengths of the 2nd digit (index finger) to the 4th digit (ring finger; 2D:4D) is a widely used biomarker. Males have lower ratios than do females from the end of the first trimester through adulthood (Galis, Ten Broek, Dongen, & Wijnaendts, 2010; Malas, Dogan, Evcil, & Desdicioglu, 2006). A more masculine 2D:4D has been associated with testosterone relative to estradiol in amniotic fluid (Lutchmaya, Baron-Cohen, Raggatt, Knickmeyer, & Manning, 2004; Ventura, Gomes, Pita, Neto, & Taylor, 2013), as well as CAH (Brown, Hines, Fane, & Breedlove, 2002; Ciumas, Hirschberg, & Savic, 2009; Okten, Kalyoncu, & Yaris, 2002: but see Buck, Williams, Hughes, & Acerini, 2003), and XY androgen insensitive individuals have a feminine 2D:4D (Berenbaum, Bryk, Nowak, Quigley, & Moffat, 2009). Thus, 2D:4D is utilized as a proxy for prenatal androgen signaling, and meta-analysis of 18 studies indicated that non-heterosexual women indeed have more masculine 2D:4D than do heterosexual women (Grimbos, Dawood, Burriss, Zucker, & Puts, 2010; total $N = 2,707$).

Because left-handedness is more common in males, it may also reflect prenatal androgen. In a meta-analysis of 20 studies comprising over 20,000 participants, homosexual women were 91% more likely than heterosexual women to be left-handed (Lalumiere, Blanchard, & Zucker, 2000). It is possible that this difference reflects greater developmental instability in homosexual individuals rather than hormonal influences (Mustanski, Bailey, & Kaspar, 2002; see Conclusion), but Martin, Puts, and Breedlove (2008) found little evidence of increased developmental instability in homosexual individuals.

Also used as a biomarker for early androgen signaling are the extremely subtle sounds produced by the inner ear in response to short click sounds known as click-evoked otoacoustic emissions (henceforth: otoacoustic emissions). Otoacoustic emissions are stronger in women than in men (McFadden & Pasanen, 1998), and stronger in women without male co-twins than in those with male co-twins, whose androgen may have masculinized their sisters in utero (McFadden, Loehlin, & Pasanen, 1996). In one study, non-heterosexual women had masculinized otoacoustic emissions compared to heterosexual women (McFadden & Pasanen, 1998).

Like otoacoustic emissions, auditory evoked potentials can be elicited by click stimuli, and some of their features are sexually dimorphic. Auditory evoked potentials are measured via electrodes attached to subjects' heads and ears, resulting in a series of peaks and waves that are thought to represent neuronal firing in response to acoustic stimuli. Some of these features have been found to be masculinized in homosexual women (McFadden & Champlin, 2000).

Finally, Martin and Nguyen (2004) found that long bone growth in the arms, hands, and legs, another sexually dimorphic putative biomarker for early steroid exposure, was more masculine (greater) in homosexual women compared to heterosexual women and homosexual men.

Biomarkers in men

Some putative biomarkers of early androgen signaling have been reported to be more masculine in homosexual men compared to heterosexual men. For example, meta-analysis of 20 studies (total $N = 20,990$) homosexual men were 34% more likely than heterosexual men to be left-handed (Lalumiere et al., 2000). In addition, features of auditory evoked potentials that differed by sexual orientation were more masculine in homosexual men (McFadden & Champlin, 2000), homosexual men have been reported to have hypermasculinized penis size (Bogaert & Hershberger, 1999), and homosexual men's faces were rated as more masculine than heterosexual men's faces (Valentova & Havlíček, 2013; Valentova et al., 2014).

Other biomarkers show mixed or no associations with men's sexual orientation. For instance, sexual orientation was unrelated to both 2D:4D in a meta-analysis of 18 studies (Grimbos et al., 2010; total N = 3,121) and otoacoustic emissions (McFadden & Pasanen, 1998; N = 108, d = 0.07). Moreover, although the shapes of several facial features differed between homosexual and heterosexual men, about half of these features were more masculine, and half more feminine, in homosexual men (Valentova et al., 2014). Fingertip dermal ridge count is also sexually dimorphic: Women are likelier than men to have more ridges on the left than right hand. Hall and Kimura (1994) found that dermal ridge asymmetry was more feminine in homosexual men, but Forastieri et al. (2017) and Mustanski et al. (2002) failed to replicate this, and neither sexual orientation nor genetic sex was related to dermal ridge asymmetry in male-to-female transsexuals (Slabbekoorn, van Goozen, Sanders, Gooren, & Cohen-Kettenis, 2000).

Finally, Martin and Nguyen (2004) found that homosexual men were more feminine in long bone growth of the arms, hands, and legs.

Neurobiology of sexual orientation

Research into the neurobiology underlying sexual orientation has benefited from both non-human animal models and comparisons of sexually dimorphic brain regions in people of different sexual orientations (Rahman, 2005). In many cases, the finding that certain brain regions are sexually dimorphic has led researchers to posit that prenatal hormones play a part in determining their size or neuronal density, which would account for sex – and potentially sexual orientation – differences in these characteristics (summarized in Table 15.4).

SDN-POA/INAH-3

The sexually dimorphic nucleus of the preoptic area (SDN-POA) is a cluster of cells in the hypothalamic medial preoptic area of rats. It is larger in males than in females, and this difference is abolished by neonatal castration and restored by administration of exogenous androgen (Arnold & Gorski, 1984). Lesions to the SDN-POA of male rats reduced male-typical sexual behavior, including mounting, intromission, and ejaculation (De Jonge et al., 1989). In sheep, Roselli, Larkin, Resko, Stellflug, and Stormshak (2004) demonstrated that rams displaying sexual partner preference for other rams had feminized (smaller) sexually dimorphic nuclei than female-oriented rams. The closest homologue in humans to the SDN-POA of rats and the sexually dimorphic nucleus of sheep may be the third interstitial nucleus of the anterior hypothalamus (INAH-3; e.g., Allen, Hines, Shryne, & Gorski, 1989). In support of a connection between INAH-3 size and sexual orientation in humans, LeVay (1991) found that it is on average twice as voluminous in heterosexual men as it is in heterosexual women and homosexual men. Another study failed to reproduce the significant relationship between sexual orientation and INAH-3 volume in men (Byne et al., 2001). However, the large effect size calculated from Byne et al.'s (2001) data (d = 1.22; see Table 15.4) suggests that a larger sample may have produced a result supportive of the hypothesized relationship.

Suprachiasmatic nucleus

The suprachiasmatic nucleus is a cell group located in the hypothalamus. It is primarily responsible for maintenance of circadian rhythms (Marieb & Hoehn, 2010) but may also be related to reproduction (Södersten, Hansen, & Srebro, 1981). Swaab and Hofman (1990) found that the suprachiasmatic nucleus was on average 1.7 times as large and contained 2.1 times as many

Table 15.4 Summary of results for studies linking neurobiology to sexual orientation (see section "Neurobiology of sexual orientation")

Reference	Predictor variable	Dependent variable	Sex	Predicted association	Significant?	N	T	C	ES	Stat	Method
Byne et al., 2001	Genetic sex	INAH-3 volume	Both	Higher in males	Yes	65	31	34	2.62	d	Calculated
Byne et al., 2001	Sexual orientation	INAH-3 volume	Male	Higher in heterosexuals	No	45	31	14	1.22	d	Calculated
LeVay, 1991	Genetic sex	INAH-3 volume	Both	Higher in males	Yes	22	16	6	3.2	d	Calculated
LeVay, 1991	Sexual orientation	INAH-3 volume	Male	Higher in heterosexuals	Yes	35	19	16	5.63	d	Calculated
Swaab & Hofman, 1990	Sexual orientation	Suprachiasmatic nucleus volume	Male	Higher in heterosexuals	Yes	28	10	18	4.72	d (non-par)	Calculated
Swaab & Hofman, 1990	Sexual orientation	Suprachiasmatic nucleus # of neurons	Male	Higher in heterosexuals	Yes	28	10	18	5.76	d (non-par)	Calculated
Allen & Gorski, 1991	Genetic sex	Area of midsagittal plane of anterior commissure	Both	Higher in males	Yes	60	30	30	n/a	n/a	n/a
Allen & Gorski, 1991	Sexual orientation	Area of midsagittal plane of anterior commissure	Male	Higher in heterosexuals	No	60	30	30	n/a	n/a	n/a
Lasco et al., 2002	Genetic sex	Area of midsagittal plane of anterior commissure	Both	Higher in males	No	101	58	43	1.02	d	Calculated
Lasco et al., 2002	Sexual orientation	Area of midsagittal plane of anterior commissure	Male	Higher in heterosexuals	No	78	20	58	-0.42	d	Calculated
Ponseti et al., 2007	Genetic sex	Grey matter volume	Both	Higher in males	Yes	49	24	25	1.99	d	Calculated
Ponseti et al., 2007	Sexual orientation	Grey matter volume	Male	Higher in heterosexuals	No	30	16	24	0.19	d	Calculated
Ponseti et al., 2007	Sexual orientation	Grey matter volume	Female	Higher in heterosexuals	No	40	15	25	0	d	Calculated
Ponseti et al., 2007	Sexual orientation	Perirhinal cortex volume	Male	Higher in homosexuals	No	30	16	24	n/a	n/a	n/a
Ponseti et al., 2007	Sexual orientation	Perirhinal cortex volume	Female	Higher in homosexuals	Yes	40	15	25	n/a	n/a	n/a
Abé et al., 2014	Sexual orientation	Cortical thickness	Male	Higher in heterosexuals	Yes for 6 of 8 regions	40	19	21	n/a	n/a	n/a
Abé, Johansson, Allzén, & Savic, 2014	Sexual orientation	Cortical thickness	Male	Higher in heterosexuals	No for 2 of 8 regions	40	19	21	n/a	n/a	n/a

Note: N: Total sample size, T: Treatment group sample size, C: Control group sample size, ES: Effect size, Stat: Effect size statistic used, Method: Method used to obtain effect size.

neurons in homosexual compared to heterosexual men. The authors to posited that the differences found between heterosexual and homosexual men were hormonally mediated. To test this, the same research group treated male rats with an aromatase-inhibitor. Rats treated pre- and postnatally possessed on average 59% more vasopressin-expressing neurons in the suprachiasmatic nucleus than untreated controls and expressed bisexual social and sexual partner preference. Groups that were untreated or treated only prenatally developed sexual and social partner preference toward females (Swaab, Slob, Houtsmuller, Brand, & Zhou, 1995).

Anterior commissure

The anterior commissure is one of several white matter brain regions connecting the hemispheres of the cerebral cortex (Marieb & Hoehn, 2010). It is not implicated in the regulation of sexual behavior, but the size of its midsagittal area was found to be larger in women than men, and also larger in homosexual men than in both heterosexual men and heterosexual women (Allen & Gorski, 1991). Allen and Gorski speculated that (1) size differences in this structure may be related to differences between homosexual and heterosexual men in cerebral lateralization, given that homosexual men are more likely than heterosexual men to be left-handed, and (2) anterior commissure size is mediated by levels of steroid hormones such as testosterone. While the latter hypothesis has not been tested, Lasco, Jordan, Edgar, Petito, and Byne (2002) failed to replicate the relationship between anterior commissure size and sexual orientation in men; this association has yet to be investigated in female subjects. Finally, there is some evidence that two thyroid hormones, thyroxin and triiodothyronine, play a part in determining the size of the anterior commissure in rats (Ferraz, Escobar, & De Escobar, 1994). These hormones have not been studied in the context of sexual orientation, but if their levels differ in homosexual and heterosexual populations, then this may help to explain the sexual orientation–based difference in size.

Perirhinal cortex

Using structural magnetic resonance imaging (sMRI) and voxel-based morphometry, Ponseti et al. (2007) investigated sex and sexual orientation differences in gray matter concentrations in the brains of living people. While they found sex differences in global gray matter concentrations, heterosexual men and women did not differ from their homosexual counterparts on this global measure. However, heterosexual women showed higher gray matter concentrations than homosexual women in several regions, including the perirhinal cortex (this was not the case for heterosexual vs. homosexual men). The perirhinal cortex is a cell group located in the medial temporal lobe and is associated with olfactory and spatial processing, as well as memory encoding. Although the authors note that spatial processing may differ according to sexual orientation, there is no direct evidence of a functional link between the perirhinal cortex and sexual orientation. With regard to a hormonal mechanism, neither hormone levels, nor the expression of hormone receptors has been studied in the context of perirhinal cortex dimorphism. However, the sex difference in its size suggests that the development of this region may be influenced by steroid hormones, as has been found in several of the other brain regions discussed in this section.

Cortical thickness

Finally, it has been shown that cortical thickness is sexually dimorphic and that this difference may be related to androgen exposure (Bramen et al., 2012). The relationships are complex;

cortical thickness in pubescent boys and girls was inversely related to androgen levels (Bramen et al., 2012), and the cortices of men were thicker than women's in some regions and thinner in others (Lv et al., 2010). Abé et al. (2014) hypothesized a difference in cortical thickness between heterosexual and homosexual men. Using sMRI, they found that heterosexual men had larger thalamus volumes and thicker cortices in several areas than both homosexual men and heterosexual women. Whether cortical thickness has any causal connection to sexual orientation has yet to be determined, but relationships between cortical thickness and androgens suggest that prenatal hormonal environment may play a role.

Conclusion

Although research into the endocrinology of human sexual orientation is almost entirely correlational, and much work has yet to be done, some tentative inferences are possible. First, androgen signaling at or below female-typical levels leads to androphilia. Both typical genetic females and genetic males with no androgen signaling due to complete androgen insensitivity syndrome are highly likely to be androphilic.

Second, individuals whose androgen signaling exceeds female-typical levels are more likely than typical females to be gynephilic. Whether they are raised as boys or girls, natal males with male-typical prenatal androgen signaling are nearly always gynephilic. Genetic males exposed to androgen signaling that is intermediate between typical males and females due to partial androgen insensitivity syndrome or 5α-reductase-2 deficiency are intermediate in their probability of gynephilic orientation. Likewise, genetic females exposed to intermediate androgen signaling are intermediate in their probability of gynephilic orientation, as indicated by studies of congenital adrenal hyperplasia, polycystic ovary syndrome, 2D:4D, handedness, otoacoustic emissions, auditory evoked potentials, and long bone growth.

Third, androgens act on the neural substrates underlying sexual orientation primarily by binding directly to androgen receptor rather than being aromatized into estrogen and binding to estrogen receptor. Prenatal exposure to a synthetic estrogen has little or no effect on women's sexual orientation, and genetic males with nonfunctional aromatase and estrogen receptor genes apparently have male-typical sexual orientation. By contrast, studies of partial and complete androgen insensitivity syndrome indicate that androgen receptor function is critical to sexual orientation.

Fourth, the influence of androgens on sexual orientation is organizational rather than activational. Adult hormone concentrations are weakly correlated, if at all, with sexual orientation within men. Moreover, testosterone treatment does not produce gynephilia in androphilic men, and removal of androgen signaling due to castration does not produce androphilia in gynephilic men. Although homosexual women, especially those identifying as "butch" lesbians, may have higher testosterone levels than heterosexual women, this may be explained by the higher incidence of polycystic ovary syndrome in lesbians. The scanty available evidence indicates that testosterone treatment does not produce gynephilia in androphilic women.

Fifth, most variation in sexual orientation among genetic males is not due to chronic, systemic differences in androgen signaling. Disorders of sexual development such as complete androgen insensitivity syndrome, partial androgen insensitivity syndrome, and 5α-reductase-2 deficiency demonstrate that decreases in androgen signaling increase the probability of androphilia in genetic males, but little evidence links such global alterations in androgenization to sexual orientation in males without disorders of sexual development. Indeed, handedness, auditory evoked potentials, penile size, and facial appearance have been found to be more masculine in homosexual compared to heterosexual men, contrary to the prediction that lower overall androgenization produces androphilia in homosexual men. Other biomarkers such as 2D:4D, click-evoked otoacoustic emissions, objective facial measures, and fingertip dermal ridge asymmetry have shown mixed or no associations with men's sexual orientation, or have been found to be more feminine in the case of long bone growth.

Perhaps acute decreases in androgen signaling during a developmental window when sexual orientation is organized lead to compensatory increases in androgen during other developmental windows, hypermasculizating some biomarkers (McFadden, 2017). Or perhaps elevated androgens when some biomarkers develop leads to compensatory decreases in androgenization when sexual orientation differentiates. Perhaps the mixed associations reflect varied androgen signaling across anatomical regions of the brain and body, with lower androgenization in brain regions associated with sexual orientation as well as the epiphyses of the long bones in homosexual men, and higher androgenization in regions associated with handedness and auditory evoked potentials, for example. More research is needed to discriminate between these possibilities.

Finally, more work is needed to clarify the neural substrates of sexual orientation. For example, although the perirhinal cortex has been found to be masculinized in lesbians, this region is not directly related to sexual attraction, and no research has compared the third interstitial nucleus of the anterior hypothalamus or nearby nuclei in homosexual women to heterosexual women or men. Some brain regions and attributes such as interstitial nucleus of the anterior hypothalamus, suprachiasmatic nucleus, and anterior commissure size, and cortical thickness have been found to vary with sexual orientation in men, but the identification of causal relationships to sexual orientation require further investigation, as does how development in these regions may be influenced by sex hormones.

Overall, however, a wide variety of evidence compellingly indicates that androgens acting during the pre-and perinatal periods of human development influence sexual orientation in adulthood.

References

Abbott, D.H., Barnett, D.K., Bruns, C.M., & Dumesic, D.A. (2005). Androgen excess fetal programming of female reproduction: A developmental aetiology for polycystic ovary syndrome? *Human Reproduction Update, 11*(4), 357–374. https://doi.org/10.1093/humupd/dmi013

Abé, C., Johansson, E., Allzén, E., & Savic, I. (2014). Sexual orientation related differences in cortical thickness in male individuals. *PLoS One, 9*(12), 1–14. https://doi.org/10.1371/journal.pone.0114721

Agrawal, R., Sharma, S., Bekir, J., Conway, G., Bailey, J., Balen, A.H., & Prelevic, G. (2004). Prevalence of polycystic ovaries and polycystic ovary syndrome in lesbian women compared with heterosexual women. *Fertility and Sterility, 82*(5), 1352–1357. https://doi.org/10.1016/j.fertnstert.2004.04.041

Allen, L.S., & Gorski, R.A. (1991). Sexual dimorphism of the anterior commissure and massa intermedia of the human brain. *The Journal of Comparative Neurology, 312*(1), 97–104. https://doi.org/10.1002/cne.903120108

Allen, L.S., Hines, M., Shryne, E., & Gorski, A. (1989). Two sexually dimorphic cell groups in the human brain. *The Journal of Neuroscience, 9*(2), 497–506.

Arnold, A.P., & Gorski, R.A. (1984). Induction of structural sex differences in the central nervous system. *Annual Review of Neuroscience, 7*, 413–442.

Auyeung, B., Baron-Cohen, S., Ashwin, E., Knickmeyer, R., Hackett, G., & Hines, M. (2009). Fetal testosterone predicts sexually differentiated childhood behavior in girls and in boys. *Psychological Science, 20*(2), 144–148. https://doi.org/10.1111/j.1467-9280.2009.02279.x.Fetal

Bailey, J.M. (2009). What is sexual orientation and do women have one? In D.A. Hope (Ed.), *Contemporary perspectives on gay, lesbian, and bisexual identities* (Vol. 54). New York, NY: Springer. https://doi.org/10.1007/978-0-387-09556-1

Bailey, J.M., Vasey, P.L., Diamond, L.M., Breedlove, S.M., Vilain, E., & Epprecht, M. (2016). Sexual orientation, controversy, and science. *Psychological Science in the Public Interest, 17*(2), 45–101. https://doi.org/10.1177/1529100616637616

Barahal, H.S. (1940). Testosterone in psychotic male homosexuals. *Psychiatric Quarterly, 14*(2), 319–330. https://doi.org/10.1007/BF01573190

Barry, J.A., Kay, A.R., Navaratnarajah, R., Iqbal, S., Bamfo, J.E.A.K., David, A.L., . . . Hardiman, P.J. (2010). Umbilical vein testosterone in female infants born to mothers with polycystic ovary syndrome is elevated to male levels. *Journal of Obstetrics and Gynaecology, 30*(5), 444–446. https://doi.org/10.3109/01443615.2010.485254

Baumeister, R.F. (2000). Gender differences in erotic plasticity: The female sex drive as socially flexible and responsive. *Psychological Bulletin, 126*(3), 347–374. https://doi.org/10.1037/0033-2909.126.3.347

Berenbaum, S.A., Bryk, K.K., Nowak, N., Quigley, C.A., & Moffat, S. (2009, November). Fingers as a marker of prenatal androgen exposure. *Endocrinology, 150*, 5119–5124. https://doi.org/10.1210/en.2009-0774

Blanchard, R. (1990). Gender identity disorders in adult women. In R. Blanchard & B.W. Steiner (Eds.), *Clinical management of gender identity disorders in children and adults* (pp. 79–91). Washington, DC: American Psychiatric Association.

Bogaert, A.F., & Hershberger, S. (1999). The relation between sexual orientation and penile size. *Archives of Sexual Behavior, 28*(3).

Bouvattier, C., Mignot, B., Lefèvre, H., Morel, Y., & Bougnères, P. (2006). Impaired sexual activity in male adults with partial androgen insensitivity. *The Journal of Clinical Endocrinology & Metabolism, 91*(9), 3310–3315.

Bramen, J.E., Hranilovich, J.A., Dahl, R.E., Chen, J., Rosso, C., Forbes, E.E., . . . Sowell, E.R. (2012). Sex matters during adolescence : Testosterone-related cortical thickness maturation differs between boys and girls. *PLoS One, 7*(3), 1–9. https://doi.org/10.1371/journal.pone.0033850

Bronstein, J., Tawdekar, S., Liu, Y., Pawelczak, M., David, R., & Shah, B. (2011). Age of onset of polycystic ovarian syndrome in girls may be earlier than previously thought. *Journal of Pediatric and Adolescent Gynecology, 24*(1), 15–20. https://doi.org/10.1016/j.jpag.2010.06.003

Brown, W.M., Hines, M., Fane, B.A., & Breedlove, S.M. (2002). Masculinized finger length patterns in human hyperplasia. *Hormones and Behavior, 386*, 380–386. https://doi.org/10.1006/hbeh.2002.1830

Buck, J.J., Williams, R.M., Hughes, I.A., & Acerini, C.L. (2003). In-utero androgen exposure and 2nd to 4th digit length ratio comparisons between healthy controls and females with classical congenital adrenal hyperplasia. *Human Reproduction, 18*(5), 2–5. https://doi.org/10.1093/humrep/deg198

Byne, W., Tobet, S., Mattiace, L.A., Lasco, M.S., Kemether, E., Edgar, M.A., . . . Jones, L.B. (2001). The interstitial nuclei of the human anterior hypothalamus: An investigation of variation with sex, sexual orientation, and HIV Status. *Hormones and Behavior, 40*(2), 86–92. https://doi.org/10.1006/hbeh.2001.1680

Chivers, M.L., Rieger, G., Latty, E., & Bailey, J.M. (2005). A sex in the specificity of sexual arousal. *Psychological Science, 15*(11), 736–744. https://doi.org/10.1111/j.0956-7976.2004.00750.x

Ciumas, C., Hirschberg, A.L., & Savic, I. (2009, May). High fetal testosterone and sexually dimorphic cerebral networks in females. *Cerebral Cortex*, 1167–1174. https://doi.org/10.1093/cercor/bhn160

Cohen, K.M. (2002). Relationships among childhood sex-atypical behavior, spatial ability, handedness, and sexual orientation in men, *31*(1), 129–143.

Cooke, P.S., Nanjappa, X.M.K., Ko, C., Prins, G.S., & Hess, R.A. (2017). Estrogens in male physiology. *Physiological Reviews*, 995–1043. https://doi.org/10.1152/physrev.00018.2016

Dancey, C. (1990). Sexual orientation in women: An investigation of hormonal and personality variables. *Biological Psychology, 30*(3), 251–264. https://doi.org/10.1016/0301-0511(90)90142-J

De Jonge, F.H., Louwerse, A.L., Ooms, M.P., Evers, P., Endert, E., & van De Poll, N.E. (1989). Lesions of the SDN-POA inhibit sexual behavior of male wistar rats. *Brain Research Bulletin, 23*(6), 483–492. https://doi.org/10.1016/0361-9230(89)90194-9

Dittmann, R.W., Kappes, M.E., & Kappes, M.H. (1992). Sexual behavior in adolescent and adult females with congenital adrenal hyperplasia. *Psychoneuroendocrinology, 17*(2–3), 153–170. https://doi.org/10.1016/0306-4530(92)90054-B

Downey, J., Ehrhardt, A. A., Schiffman, M., Dyrenfurth, I., & Becker, J. (1987). Sex hormones in lesbian and heterosexual women. *Hormones and Behavior, 21*(3), 347–357. https://doi.org/10.1016/0018-506X(87)90019-5

Ehrhardt, A.A., Evers, K., & Money, J. (1968). Influence of androgen and some aspects of sexually dimorphic behavior in women with the late-treated adrenogenital syndrome. *The Johns Hopkins Medical Journal, 123*(3).

Ehrhardt, A.A., Meyer-Bahlburg, H.F.L., Rosen, L.R., Feldman, J.F., Veridiano, N.P., Zimmerman, I., & McEwen, B.S. (1985). Sexual orientation after prenatal exposure to exogenous estrogen. *Archives of Sexual Behavior, 14*(1), 57–77. https://doi.org/10.1007/BF01541353

Ferraz, A.G., Escobar, F., & De Escobar, G.M. (1994). The development of the anterior commissure in normal and hypothyroid rats. *Developmental Brain Research, 81,* 293–308.

Forastieri, V., Andrade, C.P., Souza, A.L.V., Silva, S., El-hani, C.N., Maria, L., . . . Flores, R.Z. (2017). Evidence against a relationship between dermatoglyphic asymmetry and male sexual orientation, 74(6), 861–870.

Franks, S. (2002). Adult polycystic ovary syndrome begins in childhood. *Best Practice and Research: Clinical Endocrinology and Metabolism, 16*(2), 263–272. https://doi.org/10.1053/beem.2002.0203

Frisén, L., Nordenström, A., Falhammar, H., Filipsson, H., Holmdahl, G., Janson, P.O., . . . Nordenskjöld, A. (2009). Gender role behavior, sexuality, and psychosocial adaptation in women with congenital adrenal hyperplasia due to CYP21A2 deficiency. *Journal of Clinical Endocrinology and Metabolism, 94*(9), 3432–3439. https://doi.org/10.1210/jc.2009-0636

Galis, F., Ten Broek, C.M.A., Dongen, S. Van, & Wijnaendts, L.C.D. (2010). Sexual dimorphism in the prenatal digit ratio (2D:4D). *Archives of Sexual Behavior, 39,* 57–62. https://doi.org/10.1007/s10508-009-9485-7

Gangestad, S.W., Bailey, M., & Martin, N.G. (2000). Taxometric analyses of sexual orientation and gender identity. *Journal of Personality and Social Psychology, 78*(6).

Garcia-Falgueras, A., & Swaab, D.F. (2009). Sexual hormones and the brain: An essential alliance for sexual identity and sexual orientation. *Pediatric Neuroendocrinology, 17,* 22–35. https://doi.org/10.1159/000262525

Gastaud, F., Bouvattier, C., Duranteau, L., Brauner, R., Thibaud, E., Kutten, F., & Bougneres, P. (2007). Impaired sexual and reproductive outcomes in women with classical forms of congenital adrenal hyperplasia. *The Journal of Clinical Endocrinology & Metabolism, 92*(4), 1391–1396.

Goodarzi, M.O., Guo, X., Yildiz, B.O., Stanczyk, F.Z., & Azziz, R. (2007). Correlation of adrenocorticotropin steroid levels between women with polycystic ovary syndrome and their sisters. *American Journal of Obstetrics and Gynecology, 196*(4), 1–6. https://doi.org/10.1016/j.ajog.2006.12.009

Griffiths, P.D., Merry, J., Browning, M.C.K., Eisinger, A.J., Huntsman, R.G., Lord, E.J.A., . . . Whitehouse, R.H. (1974). Homosexual women: An endocrine and psychological study. *Journal of Endocrinology, 63,* 549–556.

Grimbos, T., Dawood, K., Burriss, R., Zucker, K.J., & Puts, D.A. (2010). Sexual orientation and the second to fourth finger length ratio: A meta-analysis in men and women. *Behavioral Neuroscience, 124*(2), 278–287. https://doi.org/10.1037/a0018764

Grulich, A.E., De Visser, R.O., Badcock, P.B., Smith, A.M.A., Heywood, W., Richters, J., . . . Simpson, J.M. (2014). Homosexual experience and recent homosexual encounters: The second Australian study of health and relationships. *Sexual Health, 11*(5), 439–450. https://doi.org/10.1071/SH14122

Hall, J.A.Y., & Kimura, D. (1994). Dermatoglyphic asymmetry and sexual orientation in men. *Behavioral Neuroscience, 108*(6), 1203–1206.

Handy, A.B., Jackowich, R.A., Wibowo, E., Johnson, T.W., & Wassersug, R.J. (2016). Gender preference in the sexual attractions, fantasies, and relationships of voluntarily castrated men. *Sexual Medicine, 4*(1), e51–e59. https://doi.org/10.1016/j.esxm.2015.11.001

Hill, A., Dawood, K., & Puts, D.A. (2013). Biological foundations of sexual orientation. In C.J. Patterson & A.R. D'Augelli (Eds.), *Handbook of psychology and sexual orientation* (pp. 55–68). Oxford: Oxford University Press.

Hines, M. (2011). Prenatal endocrine influences on sexual orientation and on sexually differentiated childhood behavior. *Frontiers in Neuroendocrinology, 32*(2), 170–182. https://doi.org/10.1016/j.yfrne.2011.02.006

Hines, M., Ahmed, S.F., & Hughes, I.A. (2003). Psychological outcomes and gender-related development in complete androgen insensitivity syndrome. *Archives of Sexual Behavior, 32*(2), 93–101. https://doi.org/10.1023/A:1022492106974

Hines, M., Brook, C., & Conway, G.S. (2004). Androgen and psychosexual development: Core gender identity, sexual orientation and recalled childhood gender role behavior in women and men with Congenital Adrenal Hyperplasia (CAH). *Journal of Sex Research, 41*(1), 75–81. https://doi.org/10.1080/00224490409552215

Hines, M., Golombok, S., Rust, J., Johnston, K.J., & Golding, J. (2002). Testosterone during pregnancy and gender role behavior of preschool children: A longitudinal, population study. *Child Development, 73*(6), 1678–1687.

Imperato-McGinley, J., & Zhu, Y.S. (2002). Androgens and male physiology the syndrome of 5α-reductase-2 deficiency. *Molecular and Cellular Endocrinology, 198*(1–2), 51–59. https://doi.org/10.1016/S0303-7207 (02)00368-4

Israel, E., & Strassberg, D.S. (2009). Viewing time as an objective measure of sexual interest in heterosexual men and women. *Archives of Sexual Behavior, 38*(4), 551–558. https://doi.org/10.1007/s10508-007-9246-4

Johannsen, T.H., Ripa, C.P.L., Mortensen, E.L., & Main, K.M. (2006). Quality of life in 70 women with disorders of sex development. *European Journal of Endocrinology, 155*(6), 877–885. https://doi.org/10.1530/eje.1.02294

Khorashad, B.S., Roshan, G.M., Reid, A.G., Aghili, Z., Hiradfar, M., Afkhamizadeh, M., . . . Reza, M. (2017). Sexual orientation and medical history among Iranian people with complete androgen insensitivity syndrome and congenital adrenal hyperplasia. *Journal of Psychosomatic Research, 92*, 55–62. https://doi.org/10.1016/j.jpsychores.2016.12.002

Kinsey, A.C., Pomeroy, W.R., & Martin, C.E. (1948). *Sexual behavior in the human male*. Philadelphia, PA: Saunders. Retrieved from www.ncbi.nlm.nih.gov/pmc/articles/PMC1447861/

Klein, F., Sepekoff, B., & Wolf, T.J. (1985). Sexual orientation: A multi-variable dynamic process. *Journal of Homosexuality, 11*(1–2), 35–49. https://doi.org/10.1300/J082v11n01_04

Knickmeyer, R.C., Wheelwright, S., Taylor, K., Raggatt, P., Hackett, G., & Baron-Cohen, S. (2005). Gender-typed play and amniotic testosterone. *Developmental Psychology, 41*(3), 517–528. https://doi.org/10.1037/0012-1649.41.3.517

Kolodny, R.C., Masters, W.H., Hendryx, J., & Toro, G. (1971). Plasma testosterone and semen analysis in male homosexuals. *The New England Journal of Medicine, 319*(26). https://doi.org/10.1056/nejm198811243192103

Kruijver, F.P.M., Fernández-Guasti, A., Fodor, M., Kraan, E.M., & Swaab, D.F. (2001). Sex differences in androgen receptors of the human mamillary bodies are related to endocrine status rather than to sexual orientation or transsexuality. *Journal of Clinical Endocrinology and Metabolism, 86*(2), 818–827. https://doi.org/10.1210/jc.86.2.818

Kuhnle, U., & Bullinger, M. (1997). Outcome of congenital adrenal hyperplasia. *Pediatric Surgery International, 12*, 511–515. https://doi.org/10.1016/S0022-3468(98)90265-2

Lalumiere, M.L., Blanchard, R., & Zucker, K.J. (2000). Sexual orientation and handedness in men and women : A meta-analysis, *126*(4), 575–592.

Lasco, M.S., Jordan, T.J., Edgar, M.A., Petito, C.K., & Byne, W. (2002). A lack of dimorphism of sex or sexual orientation in the human anterior commissure. *Brain Research, 936*, 95–98.

Lev-Ran, A. (1974). Sexuality and educational levels of women with the late-treated adrenogenital syndrome. *Archives of Sexual Behavior, 3*(1), 27–32. https://doi.org/10.1007/BF01541040

LeVay, S. (1991). A difference in hypothalamic structure between heterosexual and homosexual men. *Science, 253*(5023), 1034–1037. https://doi.org/10.1126/science.1887219

Loraine, J.A., Ismail, A.A.A., Adamopoulos, D.A., & Dove, G.A. (1970). Endocrine function in male and female homosexuals. *British Medical Journal, 4*, 406–408.

Lutchmaya, S., Baron-Cohen, S., Raggatt, P., Knickmeyer, R., & Manning, J.T. (2004). 2nd to 4th digit ratios, fetal testosterone and estradiol. *Early Human Development, 77*(1–2), 23–28. https://doi.org/10.1016/j.earlhumdev.2003.12.002

Lv, B., Li, J., He, H., Li, M., Zhao, M., Ai, L., . . . Wang, Z. (2010). NeuroImage gender consistency and difference in healthy adults revealed by cortical thickness. *NeuroImage, 53*(2), 373–382. https://doi.org/10.1016/j.neuroimage.2010.05.020

Macke, J.P., Hu, N., Hu, S., Bailey, M., King, V.L., Brown, T., . . . Nathans, J. (1993). Sequence variation in the androgen receptor gene is not common determinant of male sexual orientation. *American Journal of Human Genetics, 53*, 844–852.

Malas, M.A., Dogan, S., Evcil, E.H., & Desdicioglu, K. (2006). Fetal development of the hand, digits and digit ratio (2D:4D). *Early Human Development, 82*, 468–475. https://doi.org/10.1016/j.earlhumdev.2005.12.002

Marieb, E.N., & Hoehn, K. (2010). *Human anatomy & physiology*. San Francisco: Benjamin Cummings.

Martin, J.T., & Nguyen, D.H. (2004). Anthropometric analysis of homosexuals and heterosexuals: Implications for early hormone exposure. *Hormones and Behavior, 45*, 31–39. https://doi.org/10.1016/j.yhbeh.2003.07.003

Martin, J.T., Puts, D.A., & Breedlove, S.M. (2008). Hand asymmetry in heterosexual and homosexual men and women : Relationship to 2D : 4D digit ratios and other sexually dimorphic anatomical traits. *Archives of Sexual Behavior, 37*, 119–132. https://doi.org/10.1007/s10508-007-9279-8

May, B., Boyle, M., & Grant, D. (1996). A comparative study of sexual experiences: Women with diabetes and women with congenital adrenal hyperplasia due to 21-hydroxylase deficiency. *Journal of Health Psychology, 1*(4), 479–492.

McEwen, B.S., Lieberburg, I., Chaptal, C., & Krey, L.C. (1977). Aromatization: Important for sexual differentiation of the neonatal rat brain. *Hormones and Behavior, 9*(3), 249–263. https://doi.org/https://doi.org/10.1016/0018-506X(77)90060-5

McFadden, D. (2017). On possible hormonal mechanisms affecting sexual orientation. *Archives of Sexual Behavior, 46*(6), 1609–1614. https://doi.org/10.1007/s10508-017-0995-4

McFadden, D., & Champlin, C.A. (2000). Comparison of auditory evoked potentials in heterosexual, homosexual, and bisexual males and females. *Journal of the Association for Research in Otolaryngology, 1*, 89–99. https://doi.org/10.1007/s101620010008

McFadden, D., Loehlin, J.C., & Pasanen, E.G. (1996). Additional findings on heritability and prenatal masculinization of cochlear mechanisms: Click-evoked otoacoustic emissions, *97*(1991).

McFadden, D., & Pasanen, E.G. (1998, March). Comparison of the auditory systems of heterosexuals and homosexuals: Click-evoked otoacoustic emissions. *Proceedings of the National Academy of Sciences, 95*, 2709–2713.

Merke, D.P., & Bornstein, S.R. (2005). Congenital adrenal hyperplasia. *Lancet, 365*, 2125–2136. https://doi.org/10.1016/B978-0-12-374430-2.00015-8

Meyer-Bahlburg, H.F.L. (1977). Sex hormones and male homosexuality in comparative perspective. *Archives of Sexual Behavior, 6*(4), 297–325. https://doi.org/10.1007/BF01541203

Meyer-Bahlburg, H.F.L. (2001). Gender and sexuality in classic congenital adrenal hyperplasia. *Endocrinology and Metabolism Clinics of North America, 30*(1), 155–171. https://doi.org/10.1016/S0889-8529(08)70024-0

Meyer-Bahlburg, H.F.L., Dolezal, C., Baker, S.W., & New, M.I. (2008). Sexual orientation in women with classical or non-classical congenital adrenal hyperplasia as a function of degree of prenatal androgen excess. *Archives of Sexual Behavior, 37*(1), 85–99. https://doi.org/10.1007/s10508-007-9265-1

Meyer-Bahlburg, H.F.L., Ehrhardt, A.A., Rosen, L.R., Gruen, R.S., Veridiano, N.P., Vann, F.H., & Neuwalder, H.F. (1995). Prenatal estrogens and the development of homosexual orientation. *Developmental Psychology, 31*(1), 12–21. https://doi.org/10.1037/0012-1649.31.1.12

Money, J., Schwartz, M., & Lewis, V.G. (1984). Adult erotosexual status and fetal hormonal masculinization and demasculinization: 46,XX congenital virilizing adrenal hyperplasia and 46,XY androgen-insensitivity syndrome compared. *Psychoneuroendocrinology, 9*(4), 405–414. https://doi.org/10.1016/0306-4530(84)90048-9

Morris, J.A., Jordan, C.L., & Breedlove, S.M. (2004). Sexual differentiation of the vertebrate nervous system. *Nature Neuroscience, 7*(10), 1034–1039. https://doi.org/10.1038/nn1325

Motta-Mena, N. V, & Puts, D.A. (2017). Endocrinology of human female sexuality, mating, and reproductive behavior. *Hormones and Behavior, 91*, 19–35. https://doi.org/10.1016/j.yhbeh.2016.11.012

Mustanski, B.S., Bailey, J.M., & Kaspar, S. (2002). Dermatoglyphics, handedness, sex, and sexual orientation. *Archives of Sexual Behavior, 31*(1), 113–122. https://doi.org/10.1023/A

Naftolin, F., Ryan, K., Davies, I., Petro, Z., & Kuhn, M. (1975). The formation and metabolism of estrogens in brain tissues. *Advances in the Biosciences, 15*, 105–121.

Newbold, R.R. (1993). Gender-related behavior in women exposed prenatally to diethylstilbestrol. *Environmental Health Perspectives, 101*(3), 208–213.

Oakes, M.B., Eyvazzadeh, A.D., Quint, E., & Smith, Y.R. (2008). Mini-reviews complete androgen insensitivity syndrome – a review. *Journal of Pediatric and Adolescent Gynecology, 21*(6), 305–310. https://doi.org/10.1016/j.jpag.2007.09.006

Okten, A., Kalyoncu, M., & Yaris, N. (2002). The ratio of second- and fourth-digit lengths and congenital adrenal hyperplasia due to 21-hydroxylase deficiency. *Early Human Development, 70*, 47–54.

Pakula, B., & Shoveller, J.A. (2013). Sexual orientation and self-reported mood disorder diagnosis among Canadian adults. *BMC Public Health, 13*(1), 209. https://doi.org/10.1186/1471-2458-13-209

Pearcey, S.M., Docherty, K.J., & Dabbs, J.M. (1996). Testosterone and sex role identification in lesbian couples. *Physiology & Behavior, 60*(3), 1033–1035. https://doi.org/10.1016/0031-9384(96)00132-1

Ponseti, J., Siebner, H.R., Klöppel, S., Wolff, S., Granert, O., Jansen, O., . . . Bosinski, H.A. (2007). Homosexual women have less grey matter in perirhinal cortex than heterosexual women. *PLoS One, 2*(8), 1–5. https://doi.org/10.1371/journal.pone.0000762

Puts, D.A., McDaniel, M.A., Jordan, C.L., & Breedlove, S.M. (2008). Spatial ability and prenatal androgens: Meta-analyses of CAH and digit ratio (2D:4D) studies. *Archives of Sexual Behavior, 37*(1), 100–111. https://doi.org/10.1007/s10508-007-9271-3.Spatial

Puts, D., & Motta-Mena, N.V. (2017). Is human brain masculinization estrogen receptor-mediated? Reply to Luoto and Rantala. *Hormones and Behavior, 97*, 3–4.

Quigley, C.A. (2002). Editorial: The postnatal gonadotropin and sex steroid surge-insights from the androgen insensitivity syndrome. *The Journal of Clinical Endocrinology & Metabolism, 87*(1), 24–28. https://doi.org/10.1210/jc.87.1.24

Rahman, Q. (2005). The neurodevelopment of human sexual orientation. *Neuroscience and Biobehavioral Reviews, 29*(7), 1057–1066. https://doi.org/10.1016/j.neubiorev.2005.03.002

Rahman, Q., & Wilson, G.D. (2003). Sexual orientation and the 2nd to 4th finger length ratio: Evidence for organising effects of sex hormones or developmental instability? *Psychoneuroendocrinology, 28*(3), 288–303. https://doi.org/10.1016/S0306-4530(02)00022-7

Rieger, G., Cash, B.M., Merrill, S.M., Jones-Rounds, J., Muralidharan, S., & Savin-Williams, R.C. (2015). Sexual arousal: The correspondence of eyes and genitals. *Biological Psychology, 104*, 56–64. https://doi.org/10.1016/j.biopsycho.2014.11.009

Rieger, G., Linsenmeier, J.A.W., & Bailey, J.M. (2008). Sexual orientation and childhood gender nonconformity : Evidence from home videos, *44*(1), 46–58. https://doi.org/10.1037/0012-1649.44.1.46

Rieger, G., & Savin-Williams, R.C. (2012). The eyes have it: Sex and sexual orientation differences in pupil dilation patterns. *PLoS One, 7*(8). https://doi.org/10.1371/journal.pone.0040256

Roselli, C.E., Larkin, K., Resko, J.A., Stellflug, J.N., & Stormshak, F. (2004). The volume of a sexually dimorphic nucleus in the ovine medial preoptic area/anterior hypothalamus varies with sexual partner preference. *Endocrinology, 145*(2), 478–483. https://doi.org/10.1210/en.2003-1098

Schrager, S., & Potter, B.E. (2004). Diethylstilbestrol exposure. *American Family Physician, 69*(10), 2395–2400. Retrieved from http://europepmc.org/abstract/MED/15168959

Sell, R.L. (2007). Defining and measuring sexual orientation for research. *The Health of Sexual Minorities: Public Health Perspectives on Lesbian, Gay, Bisexual and Transgender Populations*, (1941), 355–374. https://doi.org/10.1007/978-0-387-31334-4_14

Shibley-Hyde, J., & Durik, A.M. (2000). Gender differences in erotic plasticity – evolutionary or sociocultural forces? Comment on Baumeister (2000). *Psychological Bulletin, 126*(3), 375–379. https://doi.org/10.1037/0033-2909.126.3.375

Silfen, M.E., Denburg, M.R., Manibo, A.M., Lobo, R.A., Jaffe, R., Ferin, M., . . . Oberfield, S.E. (2003). Early endocrine, metabolic, and sonographic characteristics of Polycystic Ovary Syndrome (PCOS): Comparison between nonobese and obese adolescents. *Journal of Clinical Endocrinology and Metabolism, 88*(10), 4682–4688. https://doi.org/10.1210/jc.2003-030617

Singh, D., Vidaurri, M., Zambarano, R.J., & Dabbs, J.M., Jr. (1999). Lesbian erotic role identification: Behavioral, morphological, and hormonal correlates. *Journal of Personality and Social Psychology, 76*(6), 1035–1049.

Slabbekoorn, D., van Goozen, S.H.M., Sanders, G., Gooren, L.J.G., & Cohen-Kettenis, P.T. (2000). The dermatoglyphic characteristics of transsexuals: Is there evidence for an organizing effect of sex hormones. *Psychoneuroendocrinology, 25*, 365–375.

Slijper, F.M.E., van der Kamp, H.J., Brandenburg, H., Keizer-Schrama, S.D.M., Drop, S.L.S., & Molenaar, J.C. (1992). Evaluation of psychosexual development of young women with congenital adrenal hyperplasia: A pilot study. *Journal of Sex Education and Therapy, 18*(3), 200–207.

Smith, E.P., Boyd, J., Frank, G.R., Takahashi, H., Cohen, R.M., Specker, B., . . . Korach, K.S. (1994). Estrogen resistance caused by a mutation in the estrogen-receptor gene in a man. *The New England Journal of Medicine, 331*(16), 11056–11061. https://doi.org/10.1056/nejm198811243192103

Smith, H.A., Markovic, N., Matthews, A.K., Danielson, M.E., Kalro, B.N., Youk, A.O., & Talbott, E.O. (2011). A comparison of polycystic ovary syndrome and related factors between lesbian and heterosexual women. *Women's Health Issues, 21*(3), 191–198. https://doi.org/10.1016/j.whi.2010.11.001

Södersten, P., Hansen, S., & Srebro, B. (1981). Suprachiasmatic lesions disrupt the daily rhythmicity in the sexual behaviour of normal male rats and of male rats treated neonatally with antioestrogen. *The Journal of Endocrinology, 88*(1), 125–130. https://doi.org/10.1677/joe.0.0880125

Speiser, P.W., & White, P.C. (2011). Congenital adrenal hyperplasia. *The New England Journal of Medicine*, *349*(8), 776–788. https://doi.org/10.1542/pir.30-7-e49

Swaab, D.F., & Hofman, M.A. (1990). An enlarged suprachiasmatic nucleus in homosexual men. *Brain Research*, *537*(1–2), 141–148. https://doi.org/10.1016/0006-8993(90)90350-K

Swaab, D.F., Slob, A.K., Houtsmuller, E.J., Brand, T., & Zhou, J.N. (1995). Increased number of vasopressin neurons in the Suprachiasmatic Nucleus (SCN) of "bisexual" adult male rats following perinatal treatment with the aromatase blocker ATD. *Developmental Brain Research*, *85*(2), 273–279. https://doi.org/10.1016/0165-3806(94)00218-O

Titus-Ernstoff, L., Perez, K., Hatch, E.E., Troisi, R., Palmer, J.R., Hartge, P., . . . Hoover, R. (2003). Psychosexual characteristics of men and women exposed prenatally to diethylstilbestrol. *Epidemiology*, *14*, 155–160. https://doi.org/10.1097/01.EDE.0000039059.38824.B2

Valentova, J.V., & Havlíček, J. (2013). Perceived sexual orientation based on vocal and facial stimuli is linked to self-rated sexual orientation in Czech men. *PLoS One*, *8*(12). https://doi.org/10.1371/journal.pone.0082417

Valentova, J.V., Kleisner, K., & Havlíček, J. (2014). Shape differences between the faces of homosexual and heterosexual men. *Archives of Sexual Behavior*, *43*, 353–361. https://doi.org/10.1007/s10508-013-0194-x

Van De Beek, C., van Goozen, S.H.M., Buitelaar, J.K., & Cohen-Kettenis, P.T. (2009). Prenatal sex hormones (maternal and amniotic fluid) and gender-related play behavior in 13-month-old infants. *Archives of Sexual Behavior*, *38*(1), 6–15. https://doi.org/10.1007/s10508-007-9291-z

Ventura, T., Gomes, M.C., Pita, A., Neto, M.T., & Taylor, A. (2013). Digit ratio (2D:4D) in newborns: Influences of prenatal testosterone and maternal environment. *Early Human Development*, *89*(2), 107–112. https://doi.org/10.1016/j.earlhumdev.2012.08.009

Vink, J.M., Sadrzadeh, S., Lambalk, C.B., & Boomsma, D.I. (2006). Heritability of polycystic ovary syndrome in a Dutch twin-family study. *The Journal of Clinical Endocrinology & Metabolism*, *91*(6), 2100–2104. https://doi.org/10.1210/jc.2005-1494

Wallen, K. (2005). Hormonal influences on sexually differentiated behavior in nonhuman primates. *Frontiers in Neuroendocrinology*, *26*, 7–26. https://doi.org/10.1016/j.yfrne.2005.02.001

Wassersug, R.J., Westle, A., & Dowsett, G.W. (2017). Men's sexual and relational adaptations to erectile dysfunction after prostate cancer treatment. *International Journal of Sexual Health*, *29*(1), 69–79. https://doi.org/10.1080/19317611.2016.1204403

Watts, T.M., Holmes, L., Savin-Williams, R.C., & Rieger, G. (2017). Pupil dilation to explicit and non-explicit sexual stimuli. *Archives of Sexual Behavior*, *46*(1), 155–165. https://doi.org/10.1007/s10508-016-0801-8

Weinrich, J.D., Snyder, P.J., Pillard, R.C., Grant, I., Jacobson, D.L., Robinson, S.R., & McCutchan, J.A. (1993). A factor analysis of the Klein sexual orientation grid in two disparate samples. *Archives of Sexual Behavior*, *22*(2), 157–168. https://doi.org/10.1007/BF01542364

Wienke, C., & Whaley, R.B. (2015). Same-gender sexual partnering: A re-analysis of trend data. *Journal of Sex Research*, *52*(2), 162–173. https://doi.org/10.1080/00224499.2013.819066

Wilhelm, D., Palmer, S., & Koopman, P. (2007). Sex determination and gonadal development in mammals. *Physiological Reviews*, *87*(1), 1–28. https://doi.org/10.1152/physrev.00009.2006

Wisniewsky, A.B., Migeon, C.J., Meyer-Bahlburg, H.F.L., Gearhart, J.P., Berkovitz, G.D., & Money, J. (2000). Complete androgen insensitivity syndrome: Long-term medical, surgical, and psychosexual outcome. *Journal of Clinical Endocrinology and Metabolism*, *85*(8), 2664–2669. https://doi.org/10.1210/jcem.85.8.6742

Wright, L.W. (1994). Assessment of sexual preference using a choice reaction time task. *Journal of Psychopathology and Behavioral Assessment*, *20*(3), 230–231. https://doi.org/10.1007/BF02229209

Wu, M.V., Manoli, D.S., Fraser, E.J., Coats, J.K., Tollkuhn, J., Honda, S.I., . . . Shah, N.M. (2009). Estrogen masculinizes neural pathways and sex-specific behaviors. *Cell*, *139*(1), 61–72. https://doi.org/10.1016/j.cell.2009.07.036

Zucker, K., Bradley, S.J., Oliver, G., Blake, J., & Fleming, S. (1996). Psychosexual development of women with congenital adrenal hyperplasia. *Hormones and Behavior*, *30*(4), 300–318. https://doi.org/10.1006/hbeh.1996.0038

Zuloaga, D.G., Puts, D.A., Jordan, C.L., & Breedlove, S.M. (2008). The role of androgen receptors in the masculinization of brain and behavior: What we've learned from the testicular feminization mutation. *Hormones and Behavior*, *53*(5), 613–626. https://doi.org/10.1016/j.yhbeh.2008.01.013.The

16

HORMONES AND CLOSE RELATIONSHIP PROCESSES

Neuroendocrine bases of partnering and parenting

Robin S. Edelstein and Kristi Chin

Introduction

In this chapter, we review research on the social neuroendocrinology of close relationship processes, with special attention to human romantic relationships and the context of parenthood. We focus primarily on steroid hormones – including testosterone, cortisol, estradiol, and progesterone – that have important implications for the development and maintenance of pair- and parent-child bonds (see Feldman, 2012; Johnson & Young, 2015, for recent reviews on peptide hormones such as oxytocin and vasopressin). Although these hormones have been studied fairly extensively in humans and other animals, relatively less is known about their role in romantic relationships. Further, most hormones tend to be studied and conceptualized in isolation from one another (but see Schneiderman, Kanat-Maymon, Zagoory-Sharon, & Feldman, 2014; van Anders, Goldey, & Kuo, 2011; Wardecker, Smith, Edelstein, & Loving, 2015, for some notable exceptions). Thus, we aim to synthesize current knowledge about the implications of these different hormones, with the goal of better understanding their unique and shared contributions to human romantic relationships.

Further, and perhaps surprisingly, although both partnering and parenting are inherently *dyadic* processes that unfold *over time*, the vast majority of research on neuroendocrine processes in close relationships has been conducted with individuals (as opposed to couples or parent-child dyads) and at one point in time (rather than longitudinally). This work also tends to be somewhat sex-stereotyped, in that (for instance) stereotypically "male" hormones such as testosterone are much more likely to be assessed in research on men versus women, whereas stereotypically "female" hormones such as estradiol are much more likely to be assessed in research on women versus men. Additionally, relatively few studies assess individual differences in associations between hormones and relationship processes or outcomes. Thus, in this review, we highlight understudied topics such as (a) how hormone levels may change over time as a function of relationship experiences such as parenting, (b) how one individual's hormones may be associated with his or her partner's relationship functioning, and (c) how these processes may differ across people, including the extent to which hormone-relationship links may differ by sex or gender.

We also acknowledge that psychologists and neuroscientists alike have become increasingly concerned with issues of replicability and reproducibility, particularly in the last 5–10 years (e.g., Barch & Yarkoni, 2013; Simmons, Nelson, & Simonsohn, 2011), and that "best practices" for data collection and reporting have changed fairly significantly as a result (Shrout & Rodgers, 2018). Thus, particularly in retrospect, at least some of the studies we discuss may have been limited in statistical power due to relatively small sample sizes and/or limited in generalizability due to flexibility in data-analytic decisions. We therefore report sample sizes and effect sizes for key studies when relevant (and when they could be estimated) and consider statistical power and data-analytic flexibility as possible explanations for seemingly inconsistent patterns of findings.

Overview of steroid hormones

Testosterone, cortisol, estradiol, and progesterone have been studied fairly extensively in humans and other animals; they fluctuate in response to relationship experiences and have important downstream implications for close relationship processes (e.g., Loving & Slatcher, 2013; Wardecker et al., 2015; Wynne-Edwards & Reburn, 2000). As described in more detail in the following sections, these hormones have been linked with interpersonal processes across the lifespan in both humans and other animals, including changes that may occur as a function of partnering and parenting and individual differences in orientations toward close relationships. In most cases, we review studies in which hormone data were obtained from salivary measures and note exceptions as relevant. Salivary hormone measures have been widely used in research with humans, in part because they are generally less intrusive and less expensive to collect compared to other bodily substances, such as blood (Schultheiss & Stanton, 2009). However, as noted elsewhere in this handbook, immunoassays of salivary hormones may be more prone to measurement error than other techniques, particularly at lower concentrations, as is often the case for women's testosterone (Miller, Plessow, Rauh, Gröschl, & Kirschbaum, 2013; Welker et al., 2016). Thus there are reasons to expect that other techniques, such as mass spectrometry, may ultimately become a preferred assessment tool over immunoassays.

Briefly, *testosterone* has been associated with both dominance and parental care (Mazur & Michalek, 1998; van Anders et al., 2011; Wingfield, Hegner, Dufty, & Ball, 1990). In both men and women, higher levels of testosterone appear to support the initiation and establishment of sexual relationships (e.g., Edelstein, Chopik, & Kean, 2011; McIntyre et al., 2006); lower levels of testosterone appear to support more nurturant behaviors such as caregiving and the longer-term maintenance of close relationships (e.g., Edelstein et al., 2017; Gettler, McDade, Feranil et al., 2011). *Cortisol* is a stress hormone that is particularly responsive to social stressors and challenges (Dickerson & Kemeny, 2004). Although short-term increases in cortisol are thought to be adaptive for coping with acute stressors, long-term or chronic cortisol reactivity can be problematic for health and relationship functioning (e.g., Adam et al., 2017; Loving & Slatcher, 2013). *Estradiol* is generally thought to support caregiving and bonding in humans and other mammals (Mileva-Seitz & Fleming, 2011), and has been associated with individual differences in desire for and responses to emotional closeness (e.g., Edelstein et al., 2010). However, there is some evidence that parental behavior might benefit from declines and/or lower levels of estradiol that occur during the transition to parenthood (e.g., Edelstein et al., 2017; Glynn et al., 2016). Finally, *progesterone* has been associated with social closeness, maternal behavior, and affiliation in humans and other mammals (e.g., Brown et al., 2009). However, like cortisol, progesterone also increases in response to stress, and is thought to down-regulate physiological stress responses (Wirth, 2011).

Although all four hormones have clear implications for close relationship processes, research in this area has focused most extensively on testosterone (more so in men than women) and cortisol; thus, our review is necessarily weighted more heavily toward these hormones. However, we argue that a more complete understanding of the social neuroendocrinology of close relationship processes necessitates understanding the contributions of multiple hormones, and that future research should more fully explicate the roles of estradiol and progesterone in both men and women.

Hormones in the context of partnering

Differences in hormones as function of relationship status

At perhaps the most basic level of analysis, hormones appear to vary systematically as a function of people's partnered status: People in committed romantic relationships tend to have lower baseline levels of testosterone compared to single people, a difference that is thought to reflect a focus on relationship maintenance versus initiation (see Roney & Gettler, 2015; Wardecker et al., 2015, for review). For instance, in a study of 4,462 United States Army veterans, men who were married had significantly lower serum testosterone levels than those who were divorced, $d = -.45$, and those who had never been married, $d = -.26$ (Mazur, 2014). Fewer studies include women, but those that do generally find similar patterns (e.g., Edelstein et al., 2011; van Anders & Goldey, 2010; van Anders & Watson, 2006), with effect sizes ranging from $d = -.09$ (Edelstein et al., 2011, in a sample of 134 undergraduate students) to $d = -.22$ (van Anders & Watson, 2006, in a sample of 72 heterosexual women). Although these findings allude to smaller effect sizes for women compared to men, in most studies, data are typically presented only for men or for women, or are analyzed separately if both men and women are included. Thus, there are relatively few formal statistical tests of gender differences (e.g., interactions between gender and the construct of interest), making it difficult to draw firm conclusions about such differences (Nieuwenhuis et al., 2011). Additionally, measurement error tends to be higher for assays of women's versus men's salivary testosterone (e.g., Welker et al., 2016), which could contribute to differences in effect sizes across studies.

Although most research has focused on North American (male) participants, differences in testosterone as a function of relationship status have also been observed cross-culturally, including among men in Senegal, Japan, and China, and women in Norway and the Philippines (e.g., Alvergne et al., 2009; Barrett et al., 2013; Gray et al., 2006; Kuzawa et al., 2010; Sakaguchi et al., 2006). Sample sizes tend to be somewhat smaller in cross-cultural studies (e.g., 67 Pilipino women in Kuzawa et al., 2010, $d = -.68$; 81 Senegalese men in Alvergne et al., 2009, $d = -1.84$), but these findings suggest that the mechanisms that drive differences or changes in testosterone as a function of relationship status may be somewhat universal. However, as we describe later, these mechanisms have been understudied, leaving major gaps in our understanding of the processes that might support relationship-status differences or changes in testosterone, let along with other hormones.

Individual differences research points to a similar conclusion: Partnered men who are less invested in or committed to their relationships tend to have testosterone levels that are more similar to single men (e.g., Edelstein et al., 2011; McIntyre et al., 2006). Men and women who engage in simultaneous emotional and/or sexual relationships with multiple partners also typically have higher levels of testosterone than those who are involved with only one partner (e.g., Alvergne et al., 2009; van Anders et al., 2007), again suggesting that commitment to a single partner may be a key determinant of differences in testosterone levels. Further, partnered women appear to have testosterone levels more similar to single women to the extent that they report higher levels of uncommitted sexual activity, extraversion, and sensation-seeking (Costa et al., 2015; Edelstein et al., 2011), traits that could promote interest in alternative romantic or sexual partners (Penke & Asendorpf, 2008).

Much less is known about how other hormones might differ according to partnered status. However, like testosterone, cortisol appears to be lower among people who are partnered compared to those who are single (e.g., $d = -.38$ in a sample of 152 adults, Maestripieri et al., 2013; $d = -.16$ in a comparison between 484 single men and 146 men who were married and/or fathers, Gettler, McDade, & Kuzawa, 2011). These differences may even be apparent in the early stages of romantic relationships: In one study, 79 people who had become partnered in the last 3 months were compared to 34 demographically matched single people (Weisman et al., 2015). Those who had recently become partnered showed lower overall cortisol production, $d = -.44$, and smaller cortisol awakening responses, $d = -.53$ (suggesting potentially attenuated stress responses; Fries et al., 2009). Moreover, in sample of 572 adults, people who were married showed lower overall cortisol output compared to never- or previously married individuals, $d = -.25$ and $-.28$, respectively, and a more rapid decline of cortisol levels throughout the day (Chin et al., 2017), again suggesting better health outcomes (Adam et al., 2017). Together, these findings suggest that changes in cortisol might be one pathway through which close social bonds can have positive effects on health (e.g., Slatcher & Selcuk, 2017).

Very few studies explicitly examine or report differences in estradiol or progesterone as a function of partnered status; however, in a study of 185 normally cycling Norwegian women, Barrett et al. (2015) found that women (ages 25–35) who were married or living as married had higher average estradiol and progesterone (both $d = .40$) levels averaged over a 1-month period compared to unmarried women. Their analyses adjusted for women's age, body mass index (BMI), history of contraceptive use, and several other demographic variables known to influence hormone levels. In our own study of 212 undergraduate students, including 108 women, we did not find evidence for differences in estradiol between single and partnered people, $d = .08$, including when analyses were conducted separately by gender (Edelstein et al., 2012). However, single men and women (65% of the sample) showed larger estradiol *responses* after watching a video clip that depicted an emotionally intimate father-daughter exchange, $d = .52$, compared to an equally positive but less emotionally intimate social interaction, $d = .12$ (Edelstein et al., 2012). These differences might reflect a stronger drive for emotional connection among single versus partnered individuals, or perhaps single participants' greater ability to identify with the protagonists in the video.

Differences across studies with respect to relationship status-hormone associations could also reflect differences between the samples in terms of age (adult women versus undergraduate students) or simply greater statistical power in the Barrett et al. (2015) study. It is also worth noting that Barrett et al. restricted their sample to normally cycling women, due to the effects of hormonal contraceptives on neuroendocrine levels, whereas the sample in Edelstein et al. (2012) included 18 women taking hormonal contraceptives. (Excluding women taking hormonal contraceptives did not change any of the reported findings.) More generally, such differences across studies could obscure findings when comparing hormone levels for single versus partnered women, and there is fairly little consistency across studies with respect to this important inclusion criterion. Issues surrounding contraception also raise an important question about sample generalizability: National surveys suggest that approximately 20%–30% of sexually active women ages 15 to 44 are using some form of hormonal contraceptive at any given time, and nearly 80% have done so at some point in their lives (Jones et al., 2012). Thus, excluding women taking hormonal contraceptives necessarily limits the extent to which conclusions can be drawn about the larger population.

Changes in hormones as a function of relationship status

Relationship status effects are generally assumed to be causal, in that experiences related to partnering are thought to lead to changes in hormones over time, most notably to declines in testosterone and cortisol. Although the mechanisms that might support such changes have not yet been well articulated, nurturant experiences that occur in the context of close relationships (e.g., close physical contact, emotional support) can have short-term effects on hormones that are consistent with the presumably long-term changes described earlier. For instance, nurturant or affectionate interactions can lead to short-term declines in testosterone (e.g., Kuo et al., 2016; see Zilioli & Bird, 2017). Physical touch and intimacy have also been associated with lower daily cortisol output and attenuated cortisol reactivity to laboratory stressors (Ditzen et al., 2008; Ditzen et al., 2007).

Most research on relationship status "effects" has thus far been cross-sectional, making it difficult to determine whether changes in partnered status in fact *lead* to changes in hormones. However, the few longitudinal studies of testosterone-partnering links provide fairly convincing support that changes in partnering generally precede changes in hormones (Das & Sawin, 2016; e.g., Gettler, McDade, Feranil et al., 2011; but see Goldey et al., in press; van Anders & Watson, 2006). For instance, in a 10-year longitudinal study of 2,100 male air force veterans (mean age of 43 at the first assessment), men's serum testosterone levels showed a pattern of increase prior to divorce and decrease following remarriage (Mazur & Michalek, 1998). Another 10-year longitudinal study of 1,113 Danish men (ages 30–60 at the initial assessment) provides further support for the idea that changes in relationship status lead to changes in testosterone (Holmboe et al., 2017): Men's serum testosterone levels declined with age, overall, but men who went from unmarried to married over the course of the study showed an accelerated decline, $d = -.55$, whereas those who went from married to unmarried showed an attenuated decline, $d = .26$. These findings held even when controlling for BMI, smoking, and physical activity, suggesting that changes in marital status may moderate normative age-related declines in testosterone over and above other lifestyle variables. Moreover, there was relatively little evidence that baseline levels of testosterone *predicted* changes in marital status in this sample; that is, findings were more consistent with the idea that changes in relationship status precede changes in testosterone, at least for men.

In a similar vein, in a 1-year longitudinal study of 78 first-year male college students, men who were single had higher testosterone compared to men in committed relationships (Dibble et al., 2017). Relationship dissolution was also associated with increases in men's testosterone; however, men who became partnered additionally showed pre-emptive testosterone declines, providing some reason to believe that causality may ultimately be bidirectional. It is worth noting, however, that the vast majority of participants in this study (more than 95% of cases across repeated measurements) did not experience changes in relationship status during the study period, so findings regarding testosterone changes as a function of relationship status in this study should be treated cautiously. Dibble et al. (2017) also examined several potential mediators of the testosterone-relationship status link – partnered sexual activity, masturbation, and relationship desires – but did not find that any of these variables could help to explain why partnered men tended to have lower testosterone overall compared to their single counterparts. These findings beg the question of potential mechanisms; future research might explore whether other kinds of relationship experiences, such as physical contact and emotional intimacy, might contribute to long-term changes in testosterone as a function of partnering. More generally, to our knowledge, all published longitudinal research on hormone changes as a function of partnering has focused on testosterone in virtually all male samples (see Goldey et al., in press; van Anders & Watson, 2006, for exceptions that include women). Of course, insofar as null findings have historically been more difficult to publish than significant effects, it is possible that at least some of the underrepresentation of women in testosterone research, or the lack of published research on other hormones, could be due to file drawer effects resulting from null effects for women and/or other hormones. Future research should examine whether and how other hormones fluctuate as a function of changes in relationship status and how these fluctuations might differ by sex or gender.

Hormones and romantic relationship outcomes: individual and dyadic associations

Regardless of their source, changes in hormones related to partnering are generally thought to be functional, in that they support the establishment and maintenance of romantic relationships (Roney & Gettler, 2015; Wardecker et al., 2015). Evidence consistent with this idea indicates that, among people involved in committed romantic relationships, lower levels of testosterone and/or cortisol are associated with indicators of better relationship functioning, such as greater relationship, commitment, satisfaction, and investment; less interest in alternative relationship partners; greater empathy; more self-disclosure and intimacy; and lower levels of partner-directed verbal and physical aggression and hostility (Denes et al., 2017; Ditzen et al., 2008; Edelstein et al., 2014; Gray et al., 2017; McIntyre et al., 2006; Schneiderman et al., 2014; Soler et al., 2000). For instance, in sample of 54 men in committed relationships, those with higher baseline testosterone levels reported higher levels of both verbal and physical partner-direction aggression, $r = .37$ and .24, respectively. Schneiderman et al. (2014) similarly reported positive associations between cortisol and hostility in both men and women in a sample of 60 couples. Taken together, these findings suggest that the changes that occur once people enter into relationships may well promote better relationship functioning in the long-term.

Much less is known about the implications of estradiol and progesterone for romantic relationship functioning; however, both hormones appear to be positively related to physical intimacy and/or feelings of closeness, especially among women (e.g., Schultheiss et al., 2003; Wardecker et al., 2015). For example, in a sample of 100 undergraduate students, endogenous estradiol levels were positively associated with individual differences in implicit (i.e., nonconscious) intimacy motivation among men and women who were more comfortable with closeness, $\beta = .39$ (Edelstein et al., 2010). As described earlier, emotionally intimate experiences may also lead to short-term increases in estradiol (Edelstein et al., 2012). Among women, estradiol and progesterone levels have additionally been associated with higher levels of sexual motivation and desire (Grammer et al., 2004; van Anders & Dunn, 2009). For instance, sexually explicit stimuli (i.e., videos depicting heterosexual encounters) may temporarily increase women's estradiol levels (van Anders et al., 2009, $d = .38$ in a sample of 31 naturally cycling women).

Further, in a study of 33 naturally cycling partnered women, women's endogenous progesterone levels were positively linked with greater partner-directed sexual desire, $\beta = .38$ (Grebe et al., 2016), whereas estradiol levels were positively associated with greater sexual attraction toward other men as opposed to partners, $\beta = .39$. Roney and Simmons (2013), however, found that within-cycle changes in progesterone were *negatively* associated with day-to-day changes in sexual desire in a sample of 43 normally cycling women (approximately one-third of whom were partnered); within-cycle changes in estradiol were largely unrelated to changes in sexual desire. As noted earlier, inconsistent findings across studies could simply reflect low statistical power; it is also possible that unique characteristics of these samples and/or differences in data-analytic approaches contributed to these differences. Future research would benefit from higher-powered replication efforts to more fully assess links between estradiol, progesterone, and sexual desire.

Further, as with research on effects of partnering per se, most studies of hormone-relationship quality links are cross-sectional; thus it is difficult to determine whether differences in hormones lead to changes in relationship quality, whether differences in relationship quality lead to changes in hormones, or (perhaps most likely) whether these changes might be bidirectional. In one notable exception, Das and Sawin (2016) examined relationship quality and endogenous testosterone in a representative sample of 1,270 older Americans (average age of 67 at the first assessment). For men, higher testosterone at the first assessment was predictive of lower relationship quality at the second assessment 5 years later, but the reverse causal pathway was not significant, suggesting that changes in testosterone may have led to differences in men's relationship quality. For women, testosterone at the first assessment was not significantly associated with relationship quality at the second assessment; however, there was a trend in support of the reverse causal pathway. These findings provide some evidence for the primacy of testosterone in predicting relationship outcomes, at least in men, and for potentially different causal pathways for men versus women. This study is notable in terms of its sample size and composition, as well as its longitudinal design; however, because data from men and women were analyzed separately, it would be premature to conclude that the pattern of findings in fact differs significantly by gender. Moreover, it is unclear whether these results might generalize to younger populations, particularly given that testosterone levels generally decline with age (e.g., Leifke et al., 2000).

Even less is known about longitudinal changes in other hormones with respect to relationship quality. Although some work has investigated changes in women's estradiol and progesterone as a function of the menstrual cycle (e.g., Grebe et al., 2016; Roney & Simmons, 2013), these studies have generally focused on women's sexual desire as opposed to relationship quality and have not explicitly addressed issues of causality between hormones and relationship outcomes. Future research should examine such links in both men and women, ideally including more than two time points to more fully document patterns of change.

We also currently know very little about *dyadic* links between hormones and relationship outcomes because the vast majority of relevant studies focus on individuals rather than couples (e.g., men and women in the Das & Sawin, 2016, study were in romantic relationships but not with other study participants). Yet extant data provide growing evidence that individual differences in hormones have implications not only for individuals, but also for their partners (Schneiderman et al., 2014). For example, men and women report higher relationship satisfaction and commitment when their *partners* have lower testosterone levels (r ranging from $-.37$ to $-.51$ in a sample of 39 couples, Edelstein et al., 2014). Couples in which both partners have relatively high levels of testosterone also tend to show higher levels of partner-directed hostility and aggression (Kaiser & Powers, 2006; Schneiderman et al., 2014).

Although not focused on romantic relationships per se, one recent study investigated changes in testosterone and cortisol as a function of an experimental manipulation designed to increase intimacy among previously unacquainted individuals (Ketay et al., 2017). In a sample of 58 undergraduate students, participants with lower baseline testosterone levels, and those who showed larger pre- to post-task declines in testosterone, reported greater desired and actual closeness toward their partner following the manipulation (a self-disclosure task) compared to a less intimate task. Participants with lower baseline cortisol, and those who showed larger pre- to post-task declines in cortisol, similarly reported greater desired and actual closeness to their partner following the intimate task, suggesting that cortisol and related stress-linked changes might impair relationship processes (friendship formation in this case). Moreover, people whose interaction *partners* had lower baseline cortisol, or showed larger cortisol declines, reported greater desires for closeness toward those individuals following the intimate task, providing some evidence for dyadic associations between cortisol and interpersonal outcomes. Taken together, these findings are consistent with the idea that lower levels of testosterone and cortisol may support or promote relationship functioning, and that positive intimate interactions may be a particularly fruitful context in which to investigate dyadic associations between hormones and interpersonal outcomes (Loving & Slatcher, 2013). The extent to which these findings might generalize to romantic relationships, and particularly whether such intimacy "interventions" might lead to changes in hormones among those in long-term relationships, is a promising direction for future research.

In addition to illuminating within-dyad associations, studies that include both partners also provide intriguing evidence that hormonal coordination or synchrony *between* partners may be important for romantic relationship functioning. For instance, couples often show between-partner correlations in cortisol, and those with stronger correlations tend to report poorer relationship quality and show evidence of less optimal relationship functioning (e.g., Saxbe & Repetti, 2010; Schneiderman et al., 2014; see Timmons et al., 2015, for a review). Insofar as cortisol production is a marker of stress, these finding suggest that couples who are "in sync" in cortisol might experience more relationship stress, be more impacted by their partner's experiences of stress, and/or have more difficulty coping with stressful experiences.

Cortisol has been most often investigated compared to other hormones in studies of coordination or synchrony (Timmons et al., 2015); however, there is limited evidence for within-couple correlations in testosterone and progesterone (Booth et al., 2005; Edelstein et al., 2014; Edelstein et al., 2015; Saxbe et al., 2017). Moreover, as we describe in the section on parenting, within-couple correlations in testosterone may predict positive relationship outcomes during the transition to parenthood (Saxbe et al., 2017).

Summary and implications

In sum, partnering appears to have important implications for baseline levels of steroid hormones, particularly testosterone and cortisol. Both men and women in committed relationships tend to have lower levels of testosterone and cortisol compared to single people, yet there may be differences depending on the specific type of partnering and gender. Lower levels of testosterone and cortisol have also been linked with more positive relationship outcomes, suggesting that changes that occur when people become partnered may be adaptive or beneficial in maintaining that relationship. Most work remains somewhat gendered, however, in that differences in testosterone have been more fully explored among men versus women. Moreover, very few studies include *both* men and women, and those that do typically analyze data separately by gender, making it difficult to formally assess gender differences. More work is also needed to tease apart issues of causality, and to better understand the mechanisms that might contribute to changes in hormones over time. Moreover, relatively little is known about how estradiol and progesterone may differ according to partnered status, how these hormones might change over time as a function of changes in partnering, and whether they are associated with relationship outcomes. Finally, there is emerging evidence to suggest that an individual's hormone levels have implications for his or her partner's relationship well-being as well as their own, and that coordination or synchrony in hormones between couples may be an important indicator of relationship functioning. The vast majority of studies on hormone-partnering links do not include both couple members, however, and further research is needed to more fully understand how hormones influence and are influenced by dyadic processes.

Hormones in the context of parenting

Differences in hormones as a function of parental status

Hormones appear to vary systematically as a function of parental status, in that men and women with children typically have lower testosterone compared to those without, even when controlling for potentially important covariates such as age and BMI (e.g., Barrett et al., 2013; Gettler & Oka, 2016; Gray et al., 2006). For instance, in a sample of 75 Swiss men, fathers had lower testosterone than men without children, $d = -.59$ (Perini et al., 2012). Kuzawa et al. (2010) similarly found, in a sample of 67 Pilipino women, that mothers had higher levels of waking testosterone compared to women without children, $d = -1.02$; mothers and non-mothers did not significantly differ in their levels of evening testosterone, $d = -.38$, but this difference was significant when only mothers with children younger than 2 years of age were included in analyses, $d = -.81$. Further evidence that children's age may be an important consideration comes from a study of 195 Norwegian women: Women with children ages three and under had lower testosterone levels compared to women without children and those with children older than 3 years, both $d = -1.58$ (Barrett et al., 2013). Studies on parenting are more likely to include women compared to those focused on partnered status exclusively, but again it is very rare for both men and women to be included in the same study. Further, the consistency of findings across cultures suggests that there could be some universal mechanisms underlying changes in hormones associated with parenthood, such as physical contact with infants, changes in the parental relationship, or changes in identity as one becomes a parent; yet as with research on partnering, there are relatively few direct investigations of such mechanisms.

It is also worth noting a recent exception to this pattern of findings: In the large sample of military veterans described earlier, married men with children living in the home had *higher* serum testosterone than married men who did not, $d = .28$ (Mazur, 2014). A similar, albeit somewhat weaker, pattern emerged when *number* of children rather than presence or absence of children was considered. The reasons for the discrepancy between these results and those of previous research are not entirely clear, but Mazur's findings are particularly notable given the statistical power of this compared to most samples. However, the ages of the children in this sample were unknown and thus not accounted for. As described above, there is some evidence that women with younger children have lower testosterone than women with older children, and most studies of fatherhood focus on those with infants or relatively young children (e.g., Gettler, McDade, Feranil et al., 2011; Perini et al., 2012). It is also possible that men involved in the military, such as those in this sample, are particularly competitive and/or dominant; perhaps in this context fathers may feel more competitive or protective of their children, in some cases leading to increases in testosterone when children are present. Of course, these possibilities remain to be tested and would present interesting avenues for future research. Moreover, as described in the following section, cross-sectional data, even in such a highly powered sample, cannot speak to *changes* in testosterone over time, as opposed to pre-existing differences between men who do and do not become fathers; it is certainly possible that men in this sample experienced declines in testosterone when they initially became fathers.

There are very few systematic assessments of cross-sectional differences in hormones other than testosterone as a function of parenthood; however, there is some evidence, from a sample of 346 naturally cycling women, that women without children may have higher baseline urinary estradiol levels than women who had given birth in the last 3 years, $d = -.53$, and those who had given birth more than 3 years earlier, $d = -.28$ (Barrett et al., 2014). Gettler, McDade, and Kuzawa (2011) also found that men who were neither married nor fathers had higher morning and evening cortisol levels compared to men who were married and/or fathers, $d = .16$ and $.20$, respectively (in a sample of 630 Pilipino men that was not stratified by fatherhood status per se).

Changes in hormones as a function of parental status

As with research on partnering, the vast majority of work on hormone-parenting links has thus far been cross-sectional. Based on these data alone, it is difficult to assess whether it is parenthood per se, rather than other changes or demographic factors associated with parenthood, that lead to between-person differences in hormones. However, several longitudinal studies have recently begun to address this gap by investigating changes in women's (and in some cases men's) hormones throughout the transition to parenthood. Findings from these studies indicate that expectant mothers show large prenatal increases in testosterone, cortisol, estradiol, and progesterone (Edelstein et al., 2015; Fleming et al., 1997; Glynn et al., 2016); these changes are thought to support fetal development, maintain the pregnancy, initiate parturition, and generally prepare women to become mothers (Makieva et al., 2014). After delivery, new mothers' hormone levels gradually decline closer to pre-pregnancy levels, with estradiol and progesterone dropping most rapidly (Fleming et al., 1997). Given that cross-sectional comparisons indicate *lower* baseline levels of testosterone and estradiol among mothers compared to women without children, these findings suggest that the short-term hormone changes observed during pregnancy may not extend into the postpartum, and may in fact reverse when women become mothers. Yet longitudinal data assessing women's hormones from the prenatal to the postpartum period are rare, so it remains somewhat unclear whether and how mothers' hormones may change long term as a function of parenting experiences.

Less is known about hormone changes among expectant fathers compared to mothers, but there is some evidence that men show declines in testosterone and estradiol and increases in cortisol during the transition to parenthood, and that these changes may begin even during the prenatal period (Berg & Wynne-Edwards, 2001; Storey et al., 2000). For instance, in our longitudinal study of 29 first-time couples, expectant fathers showed declines in testosterone and estradiol from the beginning through the end of the prenatal period, $d = -.58$ and $-.63$, respectively (versus increases among expectant mothers, with d ranging from 1.09 for cortisol to 3.05 for progesterone; Edelstein et al., 2015). Given cross-sectional findings that fathers typically have lower testosterone compared to men without children, these data suggest that the changes that begin during the prenatal period, perhaps as men prepare to become fathers, likely continue or are maintained once babies are born. As with mothers, there are relatively few longitudinal studies of changes in men's hormones that span the prenatal to postpartum period. However, in one notable exception, Gettler, McDade, Feranil et al. (2011) followed a representative sample of 624 men in the Philippines over a 4-year period as they experienced transitions in partnering and parenthood. Men who became partnered fathers during this time showed larger declines in testosterone than single men who did not have children; those who became partnered but did not have children had testosterone levels that were not significantly different from men who remained unpartnered at the follow-up assessment. These findings suggest that fatherhood specifically, rather than partnering more generally and/or the passage of time, may be an important contributor to longitudinal changes in testosterone. Moreover, testosterone declines were most pronounced among fathers who were more directly involved in infant care. This study is notable in that it is among the few to follow participants over time, thus more directly addressing issues of causality, and because the data can speak to potential mechanisms (e.g., preparing for and/or interacting with children) that might drive changes in hormones as a function of parenthood.

Hormones and parenting outcomes: individual and dyadic associations

Like hormone changes associated with partnering, those associated with parenting are thought to be functional in that they may support care of offspring and the relationship between parents (Wynne-Edwards & Reburn, 2000). For example, long-term declines in testosterone are thought to reduce aggression toward infants, focus attention away from mating effort and toward the pair-bond relationship, and/or facilitate infant-parent attachment (Zilioli & Bird, 2017).

Indeed, in a sample of 149 couples, lower paternal testosterone (assessed at 6–9 months postpartum) was associated with lower mother-reported rates of intimate aggression, $\beta = .18$, and lower maternal depressive symptoms, $\beta = -.21$ (Saxbe et al., in press). Moreover, the association between paternal testosterone and maternal depressive symptoms was mediated by maternal relationship satisfaction, such that mothers were more satisfied when their partners had lower testosterone. These findings are consistent with those indicating that people may experience better relationship quality when their partners have lower levels of testosterone (Edelstein et al., 2014); they also extend that work into the realm of intrapersonal adjustment, suggesting that one's well-being may influence or be influenced by his or her partner's hormones. Interestingly, however, in this study, fathers with lower testosterone reported *more* depressive symptoms, $\beta = -.17$, suggesting that what might be advantageous with respect to the parental relationship might confer risk for fathers themselves. Further research is needed to better understand how these processes might play out over time and the extent to which similar associations would be observed for mother's testosterone (which was not collected in this study) or for other hormones.

Lower levels of estradiol have been similarly linked with more adaptive postpartum outcomes in other longitudinal studies. For instance, Fleming et al. (1997) found that expectant mothers with lower levels of serum estradiol, and lower estradiol-to-progesterone ratios (thought to be related to the onset of maternal behavior; Mileva-Seitz & Fleming, 2011), reported stronger postpartum feelings of attachment toward their infant, *r* ranging from −.34 to −.60 ($n = 16$–20) depending on the timing and measure. In another study, women's ($n = 177$) hormones were assessed from blood samples at multiple time points throughout the prenatal period, and their behavior was observed during a free play interaction with their infants at 12 months (Glynn et al., 2016). Again, mothers with lower levels of estradiol, lower estradiol-to-progesterone ratios, and smaller increases in estradiol over time, were rated as being more sensitive during the play session.

Our longitudinal study of expectant couples provides additional evidence for links between prenatal hormones and postpartum outcomes, as well as for the dyadic implications of these links. At 3 months postpartum, fathers who had larger prenatal declines in testosterone and estradiol reported that they provided more infant care and that they were more satisfied with, committed to, and invested in their romantic relationships (Edelstein et al., 2017; Saxbe et al., 2017). Their female partners corroborated these reports, indicating that they received more postpartum support and assistance with household tasks from fathers who showed larger prenatal declines in testosterone. Similarly, despite normative prenatal increases in testosterone and estradiol, expectant mothers who showed smaller increases in these hormones were rated by their male partners as providing more postpartum parenting support.

These data are consistent with the idea that hormone changes associated with parenthood may help people become more effective caregivers and more responsive relationship partners. However, it is worth noting the different patterns of findings for estradiol in the context of parenthood versus those in the context of romantic relationships: Estradiol has generally been positively associated with romantic partnering and romantic relationship outcomes (e.g., Edelstein et al., 2010), but as just described, is often *negatively* associated with parenting-related outcomes (e.g., Glynn et al., 2016). There is currently relatively little human research on this topic, but animal research also provides evidence for both facilitative and inhibitory effects of estradiol on parental behavior (see Wardecker et al., 2015). Thus, it is possible that estradiol plays a different role in the context of romantic versus parent-child relationships. It is also possible that demographic differences across studies (e.g., in age or relationship status) or small sample sizes contribute to different patterns of findings. Given that there is relatively little human research to date, particularly high-powered studies of individuals or couples over time, more research is clearly needed to better understand the role of estradiol in human interpersonal relationships.

Additionally, as described earlier, in our longitudinal sample, we found that average levels of testosterone, progesterone, and cortisol were correlated within couples throughout the prenatal period, r ranging from .32 to .62 (Edelstein et al., 2015). Moreover, the magnitude of within-couple correlations in testosterone increased over time, and fathers who showed stronger correlations in testosterone with their female partners reported greater relationship satisfaction, commitment, and investment at 3 months postpartum (Saxbe et al., 2017). These findings were specific to testosterone, in that within-couple synchrony in other hormones did not predict fathers' postpartum outcomes in our sample. We also found some evidence in support of causality from hormone synchrony to relationship outcomes, in that prenatal relationship quality was *not* associated with subsequent within-couple correlations in testosterone (although any null effects should be interpreted cautiously given the relatively small size of our sample). Thus, within-dyad covariation in testosterone (unlike cortisol) may reflect or predict positive relationship processes, perhaps due to links between testosterone and nurturance or caregiving (van Anders et al., 2011). Nevertheless, given the dearth of work on this topic, further research is warranted to better understand the extent of within-dyad covariation of hormones, including hormones other than testosterone and cortisol, and the implications of such covariation for parenting and romantic relationship processes.

Summary and implications

In sum, parenthood appears to have important implications for hormones, and changes in hormones appear to have downstream consequences for parenting and relationship outcomes. Most research has focused on testosterone; this work indicates that parents generally have lower levels of testosterone than people without children, and that declines in testosterone may facilitate parental care. As is the case for partnering, research on hormone-parenting links tends to be somewhat gendered, in that we know much more about testosterone among fathers than mothers, and (relatively) more about estradiol and progesterone among mothers versus fathers. However, recent findings point to the importance of estradiol for both mothers and fathers, and suggest that estradiol may have different associations with behavior in the context of parent-child versus romantic relationships. Further, limited longitudinal data (mostly conducted with men) suggests that hormone changes associated with parenthood may occur over and above those attributed to partnering, and that these changes may be most evident among those who are most invested in the parental role. There is also emerging evidence that hormone changes associated with parenthood may have consequences for both the individual and his or her partner. Further research is needed to better understand these associations and, more broadly, to understand the implications of multiple hormones for parenthood and vice versa.

Conclusions and future directions

Taken together, the findings reviewed here suggest that relationship transitions are closely tied to baseline hormone levels and changes in hormones over time. Most work in this area has thus far been cross-sectional, however, which makes it difficult to tease apart the causal nature of any links between hormones and relationship processes or outcomes. The few notable exceptions provide evidence that changes in relationship status are more likely to precede changes in hormones than vice versa, and that differences in hormones may then lead to differences in relationship quality or outcomes; yet there is also some evidence for bidirectional associations between hormones and relationship processes. Future research would benefit from more comprehensive assessments of changes in hormones and relationship processes over time, in both men and women, ideally including repeated assessments of multiple hormones so that changes can be documented more precisely.

Most neuroendocrine research on partnering and parenting also tends to focus on individuals as opposed to couples, which has critically limited our understanding of dyadic effects. The few notable exceptions suggest that hormones may have implications not only for one's own adjustment and interpersonal outcomes, but also for his or her partner's. Moreover, the extent to which couples' hormones are coordinated or synchronized may be an important predictor of relationship outcomes; coordination of cortisol appears to reflect more negative relationship outcomes, whereas coordination of testosterone appears to reflect more positive outcomes. As with other areas of research, however, much less is known about dyadic effects of estradiol and progesterone, and we believe that this would be a fruitful area of research.

Future research might also focus on moderators or correlates of hormone changes and dyadic effects; for instance, who might be most likely to show hormone changes associated with partnering or parenting? Do partner effects become more or less influential over time as relationships develop? What are the predictors and long-term consequences of hormonal synchrony? Further, to our knowledge, the vast majority of research in these areas has been conducted with heterosexual couples and in two-parent households. What might such associations look like in same-sex couples or people engaged in consensually non-monogamous relationships? Expanding the scope of this work to include same-sex couples and more diverse family configurations would not only increase generalizability and inclusivity but could help to shed light on potential boundary conditions and moderators of hormone-relationship links.

Additionally, although many studies of basic partnering and parenting effects are fairly high-powered, sample sizes in many longitudinal and/or dyadic studies tend to be relatively small. There are certainly practical and financial reasons for such choices, but future research would benefit from higher-powered investigations to assess more nuanced questions about hormone changes over time and dyadic interdependence between couple members. Meta-analytic work could also be helpful in reconciling inconsistent findings across studies, particularly those that tend to be less highly powered, and to provide more precise estimates of basic effect sizes and the robustness of these effects. Such efforts have been useful for understanding links between testosterone and aggression (Book et al., 2001) and cortisol and health outcomes (Adam et al., 2017), for instance; to our knowledge, however, such efforts have not yet focused on the social neuroendocrinology of close relationship processes.

Finally, although the resources required to collect hormone data from both couple members can be fairly prohibitive, especially longitudinally and in samples large or diverse enough to make strong causal inferences, future research would benefit from study designs that assess multiple hormones as people become partnered, prepare for parenthood, and ultimately become parents. Such data could provide important new information about a wider variety of hormones, individual and gender differences in hormone-relationship links, and the implications of hormone changes for parenting and interpersonal outcomes. Longitudinal study designs could also contribute much needed data on the mechanisms that may contribute to long-term changes in hormones and links between hormones and relationship outcomes. We hope that research will continue to move in these exciting directions to advance knowledge about the social neuroendocrine bases of partnering and parenting.

References

Adam, E.K., Quinn, M.E., Tavernier, R., McQuillan, M.T., Dahlke, K.A., & Gilbert, K.E. (2017). Diurnal cortisol slopes and mental and physical health outcomes: A systematic review and meta-analysis. *Psychoneuroendocrinology, 83*, 25–41.

Alvergne, A., Faurie, C., & Raymond, M. (2009). Variation in testosterone levels and male reproductive effort: Insight from a polygynous human population. *Hormones and Behavior, 56*, 491–497.

Barch, D., & Yarkoni, T. (2013). Introduction to the special issue on reliability and replication in cognitive and affective neuroscience research. *Cognitive, Affective & Behavioral Neuroscience, 13*, 687–689.

Barrett, E.S., Parlett, L.E., Windham, G.C., & Swan, S.H. (2014). Differences in ovarian hormones in relation to parity and time since last birth. *Fertility and Sterility, 101*, 1773–1780.

Barrett, E.S., Tran, V., Thurston, S.W., Frydenberg, H., Lipson, S.F., Thune, I., & Ellison, P.T. (2015). Women who are married or living as married have higher salivary estradiol and progesterone than unmarried women. *American Journal of Human Biology, 27*, 501–507.

Barrett, E.S., Tran, V., Thurston, S.W., Jasienska, G., Furberg, A-S., Ellison, P.T., & Thune, I. (2013). Marriage and motherhood are associated with lower testosterone concentrations in women. *Hormones and Behavior, 63*, 72–79.

Berg, S.J., & Wynne-Edwards, K.E. (2001). Changes in testosterone, cortisol, and estradiol levels in men becoming fathers. *Mayo Clinic Proceedings, 76*, 582–592.

Book, A.S., Starzyk, K.B., & Quinsey, V.L. (2001). The relationship between testosterone and aggression: A meta-analysis. *Aggression and Violent Behavior, 6*, 579–599.

Booth, A., Johnson, D.R., & Granger, D.A. (2005). Testosterone, marital quality, and role overload. *Journal of Marriage and Family, 67*, 483–498.

Brown, S.L., Fredrickson, B.L., Wirth, M.M., Poulin, M.J., Meier, E., A., Heaphy, E.D., . . . Schultheiss, O.C. (2009). Social closeness increases salivary progesterone in humans. *Hormones and Behavior, 56*, 108–111.

Chin, B., Murphy, M.L., Janicki-Deverts, D., & Cohen, S. (2017). Marital status as a predictor of diurnal salivary cortisol levels and slopes in a community sample of healthy adults. *Psychoneuroendocrinology, 78*, 68–75.

Costa, R.M., Correia, M., & Oliveira, R.F. (2015). Does personality moderate the link between women's testosterone and relationship status? The role of extraversion and sensation seeking. *Personality and Individual Differences, 76*, 141–146.

Das, A., & Sawin, N. (2016). Social modulation or hormonal causation? Linkages of testosterone with sexual activity and relationship quality in a nationally representative longitudinal sample of older adults. *Archives of Sexual Behavior, 45*, 2101–2115.

Denes, A., Afifi, T.D., & Granger, D.A. (2017). Physiology and pillow talk: Relations between testosterone and communication post sex. *Journal of Social and Personal Relationships, 34*, 281–308.

Dibble, E.R., Goldey, K.L., & van Anders, S.M. (2017). Pair bonding and testosterone in men: Longitudinal evidence for trait and dynamic associations. *Adaptive Human Behavior and Physiology, 3*, 1–20.

Dickerson, S.S., & Kemeny, M.E. (2004). Acute stressors and cortisol responses: A theoretical integration and synthesis of laboratory research. *Psychological Bulletin, 130*, 355–391.

Ditzen, B., Hoppmann, C., & Klumb, P. (2008). Positive couple interactions and daily cortisol: On the stress-protecting role of intimacy. *Psychosomatic Medicine, 70*, 883–889.

Ditzen, B., Neumann, I., Bodenmann, G., von Dawans, B., Turner, R., Ehlert, U., & Heinrichs, M. (2007). Effects of different kinds of couple interaction on cortisol and heart rate responses to stress in women. *Psychoneuroendocrinology, 32*, 565–574.

Edelstein, R.S., Chopik, W.J., & Kean, E.L. (2011). Sociosexuality moderates the association between testosterone and relationship status in men and women. *Hormones and Behavior, 60*, 248–255.

Edelstein, R.S., Chopik, W.J., Saxbe, D.E., Wardecker, B.M., Moors, A.C., & LaBelle, O.P. (2017). Prospective and dyadic associations between expectant parents' prenatal hormone changes and postpartum parenting outcomes. *Developmental Psychobiology, 59,* 77–90.

Edelstein, R.S., Kean, E.L., & Chopik, W.J. (2012). Women with an avoidant attachment style show attenuated estradiol responses to emotionally intimate stimuli. *Hormones and Behavior, 61,* 167–175.

Edelstein, R.S., Stanton, S.J., Henderson, M.M., & Sanders, M.R. (2010). Endogenous estradiol levels are associated with attachment avoidance and implicit intimacy motivation. *Hormones and Behavior, 57,* 230–236.

Edelstein, R.S., van Anders, S.M., Chopik, W.J., Goldey, K.L., & Wardecker, B.M. (2014). Dyadic associations between testosterone and relationship quality in couples. *Hormones and Behavior, 65,* 401–407.

Edelstein, R.S., Wardecker, B.M., Chopik, W.J., Moors, A.C., Shipman, E.L., & Lin, N.J. (2015). Prenatal hormones in first-time expectant parents: Longitudinal changes and within-couple correlations. *American Journal of Human Biology, 27,* 317–325.

Feldman, R. (2012). Oxytocin and social affiliation in humans. *Hormones and Behavior, 61,* 380–391.

Fleming, A.S., Ruble, D., Krieger, H., & Wong, P.Y. (1997). Hormonal and experiential correlates of maternal responsiveness during pregnancy and the puerperium in human mothers. *Hormones and Behavior, 31,* 145–158.

Fries, E., Dettenborn, L., & Kirschbaum, C. (2009). The Cortisol Awakening Response (CAR): Facts and future directions. *International Journal of Psychophysiology, 72,* 67–73.

Gettler, L.T., McDade, T.W., Feranil, A.B., & Kuzawa, C.W. (2011). Longitudinal evidence that fatherhood decreases testosterone in human males. *Proceedings of the National Academy of Sciences, 108,* 16194–16199.

Gettler, L.T., McDade, T.W., & Kuzawa, C.W. (2011). Cortisol and testosterone in Filipino young adult men: Evidence for co-regulation of both hormones by fatherhood and relationship status. *American Journal of Human Biology, 5,* 609–620.

Gettler, L.T., & Oka, R.C. (2016). Are testosterone levels and depression risk linked based on partnering and parenting? Evidence from a large population-representative study of US men and women. *Social Science & Medicine, 163,* 157–167.

Glynn, L.M., Davis, E.P., Sandman, C.A., & Goldberg, W.A. (2016). Gestational hormone profiles predict human maternal behavior at 1-year postpartum. *Hormones and Behavior, 85,* 19–25.

Goldey, K.L., Conley, T.D., & van Anders, S.M. (in press). Dynamic associations between testosterone, partnering, and sexuality during the college transition in women. *Adaptive Human Behavior and Physiology.*

Grammer, K., Renninger, L., & Fischer, B. (2004). Disco clothing, female sexual motivation, and relationship status: Is she dressed to impress? *Journal of Sex Research, 41,* 66–74.

Gray, P.B., Reece, J., Coore-Desai, C., Dinall, T., Pellington, S., & Samms-Vaughan, M. (2017). Testosterone and Jamaican fathers: Exploring links to relationship dynamics and paternal care. *Human Nature,* 1–18.

Gray, P.B., Yang, C-F.J., & Pope, H.G. (2006). Fathers have lower salivary testosterone levels than unmarried men and married non-fathers in Beijing, China. *Proceedings of the Royal Society B: Biological Sciences, 273,* 333–339.

Grebe, N.M., Thompson, M.E., & Gangestad, S.W. (2016). Hormonal predictors of women's extra-pair vs. in-pair sexual attraction in natural cycles: Implications for extended sexuality. *Hormones and Behavior, 78,* 211–219.

Holmboe, S.A., Priskorn, L., Jørgensen, N., Skakkebaek, N.E., Linneberg, A., Juul, A., & Anderson, A-M. (2017). Influence of marital status on testosterone levels – a ten year follow-up of 1113 men. *Psychoneuroendocrinology, 80,* 155–161.

Johnson, Z.V., & Young, L.J. (2015). Neurobiological mechanisms of social attachment and pair bonding. *Current Opinion in Behavioral Sciences, 3,* 38–44.

Jones, J., Mosher, W., & Daniels, K. (2013). Current contraceptive use in the united states, 2006–2010, and changes in patterns of use since 1995. In *Sexual statistics: select reports from the national center for health statistics* (pp. 127–173). Nova Science Publishers, Inc.

Kaiser, H., & Powers, S. (2006). Testosterone and conflict tactics within late-adolescent couples: A dyadic predictive model. *Journal of Social and Personal Relationships, 23,* 231–248.

Ketay, S., Welker, K.M., & Slatcher, R.B. (2017). The roles of testosterone and cortisol in friendship formation. *Psychoneuroendocrinology, 76,* 88–96.

Kuo, P.X., Saini, E.K., Thomason, E., Schultheiss, O.C., Gonzalez, R., & Volling, B.L. (2016). Individual variation in fathers' testosterone reactivity to infant distress predicts parenting behaviors with their 1-year-old infants. *Developmental Psychobiology, 58,* 303–314.

Kuzawa, C.W., Gettler, L.T., Huang, Y., & McDade, T.W. (2010). Mothers have lower testosterone than non-mothers: Evidence from the Philippines. *Hormones and Behavior, 57,* 441–447.

Leifke, E., Gorenoi, V., Wichers, C., von zur Mühlen, A., von Büren, E., & Brabant, G. (2000). Age-related changes of serum sex hormones, insulin-like growth factor, and sex-hormone binding globulin levels in men: Cross-sectional data from a healthy male cohort. *Clinical Endocrinology, 53,* 689–695.

Loving, T.J., & Slatcher, R.B. (2013). Romantic relationships and health. In J.A. Simpson & L. Campbell (Eds.), *The Oxford handbook of close relationships* (pp. 617–637). Oxford: Oxford University Press.

Maestripieri, D., Klimczuk, A.C., Seneczko, M., Traficonte, D.M., & Wilson, M.C. (2013). Relationship status and relationship instability, but not dominance, predict individual differences in baseline cortisol levels. *PLoS One, 8,* e84003.

Makieva, S., Saunders, P.T., & Norman, J.E. (2014). Androgens in pregnancy: Roles in parturition. *Human Reproduction Update, 20,* 542–559.

Mazur, A. (2014). Testosterone of young husbands rises with children in the home. *Andrology, 2,* 125–129.

Mazur, A., & Michalek, J. (1998). Marriage, divorce, and male testosterone. *Social Forces, 77,* 315–330.

McIntyre, M.H., Gangestad, S.W., Gray, P.B., Chapman, J.F., Burnham, T.C., O'Rourke, M.T., & Thornhill, R. (2006). Romantic involvement often reduces men's testosterone levels – but not always: The moderating role of extrapair sexual interest. *Journal of Personality and Social Psychology, 91,* 642–651.

Mileva-Seitz, V., & Fleming, A.S. (2011). How mothers are born: A psychobiological analysis of mothering. In A. Booth, S.M. McHale, & N.S. Landale (Eds.), *Biosocial foundations of family processes* (pp. 3–34). New York, NY: Springer.

Miller, R., Plessow, F., Rauh, M., Gröschl, M., & Kirschbaum, C. (2013). Comparison of salivary cortisol as measured by different immunoassays and tandem mass spectrometry. *Psychoneuroendocrinology, 38,* 50–57.

Nieuwenhuis, S., Forstmann, B.U., & Wagenmakers, E-J. (2011). Erroneous analyses of interactions in neuroscience: A problem of significance. *Nature Neuroscience, 14,* 1105–1107.

Penke, L., & Asendorpf, J. (2008). Beyond global sociosexual orientations: A more differentiated look at sociosexuality and its effects on courtship and romantic relationships. *Journal of Personality and Social Psychology, 95,* 1113–1135.

Perini, T., Ditzen, B., Hengartner, M., & Ehlert, U. (2012). Sensation seeking in fathers: The impact on testosterone and paternal investment. *Hormones and Behavior, 61,* 191–195.

Roney, J.R., & Gettler, L.T. (2015). The role of testosterone in human romantic relationships. *Current Opinion in Psychology, 1,* 81–86.

Roney, J.R., & Simmons, Z.L. (2013). Hormonal predictors of sexual motivation in natural menstrual cycles. *Hormones and Behavior, 63,* 636–645.

Sakaguchi, K., Oki, M., Honma, S., & Hasegawa, T. (2006). Influence of relationship status and personality traits on salivary testosterone among Japanese men. *Personality and Individual Differences, 41,* 1077–1087.

Saxbe, D.E., Edelstein, R.S., Lyden, H.M., Wardecker, B.M., Chopik, W.J., & Moors, A.C. (2017). Fathers' decline in testosterone and synchrony with partner testosterone predicts greater postpartum relationship investment. *Hormones and Behavior, 90,* 39–47.

Saxbe, D.E., & Repetti, R.L. (2010). For better or worse? Coregulation of couples' cortisol levels and mood states. *Journal of Personality and Social Psychology, 98,* 92–103.

Saxbe, D.E., Schetter, C., Simon, C., Adam, E., & Shalowitz, M. (in press). High paternal testosterone may protect against postpartum depressive symptoms in fathers, but confer risk to mothers and children. *Hormones and Behavior.*

Schneiderman, I., Kanat-Maymon, Y., Zagoory-Sharon, O., & Feldman, R. (2014). Mutual influences between partners' hormones shape conflict dialog and relationship duration at the initiation of romantic love. *Social Neuroscience, 9,* 337–351.

Schultheiss, O.C., Dargel, A., & Rohde, W. (2003). Implicit motives and gonadal steroid hormones: Effects of menstrual cycle phase, oral contraceptive use, and relationship status. *Hormones and Behavior, 43,* 293–301.

Schultheiss, O.C., & Stanton, S.J. (2009). Assessment of salivary hormones. In E. Harmon-Jones & J.S. Beer (Eds.), *Methods in social neuroscience* (pp. 17–44). New York, NY: Guilford Press.

Shrout, P.E., & Rodgers, J.L. (2018). Psychology, science, and knowledge construction: Broadening perspectives from the replication crisis. *Annual Review of Psychology, 69,* 487–510.

Simmons, J.P., Nelson, L.D., & Simonsohn, U. (2011). False-positive psychology: Undisclosed flexibility in data collection and analysis allows presenting anything as significant. *Psychological Science, 22,* 1359–1366.

Slatcher, R.B., & Selcuk, E. (2017). A social psychological perspective on the links between close relationships and health. *Current Directions in Psychological Science, 26,* 16–21.

Soler, H., Vinayak, P., & Quadagno, D. (2000). Biosocial aspects of domestic violence. *Psychoneuroendocrinology, 25*, 721–739.

Storey, A.E., Walsh, C.J., Quinton, R.L., & Wynne-Edwards, K.E. (2000). Hormonal correlates of paternal responsiveness in new and expectant fathers. *Evolution and Human Behavior, 21*, 79–95.

Timmons, A.C., Margolin, G., & Saxbe, D.E. (2015). Physiological linkage in couples and its implications for individual and interpersonal functioning: A literature review. *Journal of Family Psychology, 29*, 720–731.

van Anders, S.M., & Dunn, E.J. (2009). Are gonadal steroids linked with orgasm perceptions and sexual assertiveness in women and men? *Hormones and Behavior, 56*, 206–213.

van Anders, S.M., & Goldey, K.L. (2010). Testosterone and partnering are linked via relationship status for women and "relationship orientation" for men. *Hormones and Behavior, 58*, 820–826.

van Anders, S.M., Goldey, K.L., & Kuo, P.X. (2011). The steroid/peptide theory of social bonds: Integrating testosterone and peptide responses for classifying social behavioral contexts. *Psychoneuroendocrinology, 36*, 1265–1275.

van Anders, S.M., Hamilton, L.D., & Watson, N.V. (2007). Multiple partners are associated with higher testosterone in North American men and women. *Hormones and Behavior, 51*, 454–459.

van Anders, S.M., & Watson, N.V. (2006). Relationship status and testosterone in North American heterosexual and non-heterosexual men and women: Cross-sectional and longitudinal data. *Psychoneuroendocrinology, 31*, 715–723.

Wardecker, B.M., Smith, L.K., Edelstein, R.S., & Loving, T.J. (2015). Intimate relationships then and now: How old hormonal processes are influenced by our modern psychology. *Adaptive Human Behavior and Physiology, 1*, 150–176.

Weisman, O., Schneiderman, I., Zagoory-Sharon, O., & Feldman, R. (2015). Early stage romantic love is associated with reduced daily cortisol production. *Adaptive Human Behavior and Physiology, 1*, 41–53.

Welker, K.M., Lassetter, B., Brandes, C.M., Prasad, S., Koop, D.R., & Mehta, P.H. (2016). A comparison of salivary testosterone measurement using immunoassays and tandem mass spectrometry. *Psychoneuroendocrinology, 71*, 180–188.

Wingfield, J.C., Hegner, R.E., Dufty, A.M., & Ball, G.F. (1990). The "challenge hypothesis": Theoretical implications for patterns of testosterone secretion, mating systems, and breeding strategies. *The American Naturalist, 136*, 829–846.

Wirth, M.M. (2011). Beyond the HPA axis: Progesterone-derived neuroactive steroids in human stress and emotion. *Frontiers in Endocrinology, 2*, 19.

Wynne-Edwards, K.E., & Reburn, C.J. (2000). Behavioral endocrinology of mammalian fatherhood. *Trends in Ecology and Evolution, 15*, 464–468.

Zilioli, S., & Bird, B.M. (2017). Functional significance of men's testosterone reactivity to social stimuli. *Frontiers in Neuroendocrinology, 47*, 1–18.

17

THE MANY FACES OF HUMAN CAREGIVING

Perspective on flexibility of the parental brain, hormonal systems, and parenting behaviors and their long-term implications for child development

Eyal Abraham and Ruth Feldman

While we tend to believe that parental care, typically maternal care, marks the epitome of unconditional love, an anthropological examination of human caregiving across cultures and throughout history suggests a more complex story. In fact, wide variability in human caregiving approaches have been deeply rooted in Western heritage and can be traced back to the engrossing stories of the ancient Greek mythology: from Demeter, the protective mother who stopped at nothing to save her kidnapped daughter back from the dark underworld; to Anticleia, mother of Odysseus, who died from grief and sorrow after her son's long absence; to Alcinoe, who decided to abandon her young children and sailed away with her lover yet could not stand the guilt and drowned herself in the sea; and to Medea's words "I will slay the children I have borne" in an act of revenge against her deserting husband (Geary & Flinn, 2001; Hard, 2003).

Parental care is the most critical component in supporting growth and survival of the young. Across species, parental care is provided by mothers alone, fathers alone in non-mammalian species, both parents, or parents with the help of conspecifics, with some species expressing more than one mode of care (Royle et al., 2014). In humans, childrearing patterns are diverse, influenced, and molded by a multitude of cultural and ecological factors (Hewlett, 1992; Kramer, 2010). While male parental care is extremely facultative in humans and is characterized by greater variability among and within societies and across cultures as compared to maternal care (Rilling & Mascaro, 2017), both mothering and fathering vary according to local ecological conditions, social environments, culturally derived systems of belief and behavior, and the individual's unique interpretations and coordination of caregiving responses during caregiver-infant interactions (Barrett & Fleming, 2011; Hrdy, 2011). Still, cross-cultural investigations highlight the universal cooperative nature of human childrearing (Crittenden & Marlowe, 2008; Hewlett & Winn, 2014). Since human babies, beginning at birth, are typically surrounded and carried by group members, human maternal care relies heavily on caregiving and provisioning provided by allomothers, group members other than the biological mother, including the father, family members (e.g., grandmothers and older siblings), and other women and men in the group who provide voluntary supplemental or substitute care for the helpless and demanding babies

(Hewlett & Winn, 2014; Hrdy, 2011). Over the last two decades, researchers have begun to characterize the neurobiological and neuroendocrinological mechanisms that regulate the flexibility and complexity of human parental care, the expression of cooperative behaviors, and the phenomenon of allomaternal care and explored their long-term effects on children's development. In this chapter, we address the brain basis of human caregiving and its variability across person and context, highlighting the great neural plasticity and neuroendocrine substrates associated with human caregiving.

In mammals, the postpartum marks the period of greatest plasticity in the adult brain (Cohen & Mizrahi, 2015). This plasticity is indexed by the increased functionality and connectivity of key brain areas implicated in mammalian parenting during the postpartum months and is accompanied by structural and functional changes in the parent's brain that become sensitized to infant cues and initiate the expression of species-typical caregiving behavior (Featherstone et al., 2000; Lambert et al., 2011). Such plasticity is partly triggered by the release of neuropeptides, such as oxytocin, arginine vasopressin and steroids associated with sociality and stress management, including testosterone and cortisol (Feldman, 2016a, 2017; Stolzenberg & Numan, 2011; Cohen & Mizrahi, 2015). Natural variations in early females' and males' parental behaviors, in turn, shape the infant's neurobehavioral maturation and organize the infant's lifetime capacity for social life via a process of *biobehavioral synchrony* (Feldman, 2012a, 2015a, 2017) – the coordination between the biological and social processes of parent and infant during moments of social contact. Yet, as will be further discussed, the effects of such biobehavioral processes in humans are not merely pregnancy dependent but rather rely on mechanisms of experience-dependent plasticity and are strongly influenced by environmental, social, cultural, and personal factors.

Due to the extensive literature on the topic of neurobiology of human parental care, this chapter is by no means comprehensive and addresses mainly the hormonal changes that accompany caregiving and their neural, behavioral, and mental correlates, and includes the following sections. We first begin with a brief overview of the neuroendocrinology of human parental care. Next, we describe the human parental brain as comprising several interconnected neural networks that underpin parental care as based on human imaging studies. Third, we address hormonal and behavioral correlates of the maternal brain. Fourth, we discuss the neurobiology of human allomaternal care as well as its implications to fathering, adoptive parenting, and coparenting. In the final section we describe the non-genomic cross-generational effects of human parental care; how neural and hormonal changes in the parent's brain in the postpartum translate into long-term child social competencies, provide a protective buffer, and support maturation of children's neural and hormonal systems that enable participation in social life.

The neuroendocrinology of human parental care

Nonhuman mammalian mothering is hormone dependent; hormonal changes occurring during pregnancy and labor causally determine the expression of maternal behavior. Studies in animal models have shown that experimental manipulations on the expression of key hormones markedly alter or totally eliminate the expression of maternal care (Feldman, 2012b; Lonstein, Lévy & Fleming, 2015; Pryce, 1996; Rosenblatt, 1994, 2003). Research in rodents describes the critical role of oxytocin and prolactin, which undergo substantial changes during late pregnancy (prolactin) and surge at birth (oxytocin), for the onset of maternal behavior. However, hormones associated with the stress response, particularly corticosterone (cortisol in humans), modulate maternal vigilance and active protection of offspring (Brummelte & Galea, 2010; Mann & Bridges, 2001; Pedersen & Prange, 1985). In addition, animal studies point to the involvement of vasopressin and testosterone in the emergence of fatherhood and the expression of mammalian paternal care (Carter, 2014; Wynne-Edwards, 2001). In combination with sex-related hormones (estradiol, progesterone), these hormones establish the neuroendocrine milieu that enables rodent mothers and fathers, in the 3%–5% of mammalian species who are bi-parental (Braun & Champagne, 2014; Kleiman, 1977) – two parent. The aforementioned hormones enable parents to recognize infants as rewarding stimuli, protect infants from harm, nurse, express species-typical parental behavior, and provide external regulation for the infant's immature regulatory systems, including sleep organization, thermoregulation, autonomic functions, attention, and exploration (Feldman, 2016b; Hofer, 1995; Numan & Stolzenberg, 2009). These hormones also help parents usher their young into the social niche and accommodate its distinct features. Finally, the neuroendocrinology of parenting promotes the infant's ability to manage life in harsh ecologies via mechanisms of endocrine fit and the effects of parental hormones on the infant's brain maturation and social fittedness (Feldman, Monakhov, Pratt, & Ebstein, 2016).

In contrast, human parenting is not hormone dependent. While hormonal changes during pregnancy, birth, and the postpartum period prime and accompany the expression of parenting (Apter-Levi et al., 2016; Galbally, Lewis, IJzendoorn, & Permezel, 2011; Feldman, 2016b, 2017; Gordon et al., 2010a, 2010b), humans' large associative cortex, neural plasticity, and massive limbic-cortical projections enable bottom-up, behavior-based processing so that committed parental care can trigger the hormones of parenting even without pregnancy and childbirth; for instance in primary-caregiving fathers or adoptive parents (Abraham et al., 2014; Bick & Dozier, 2013).

The social neuroendocrinology of human parental care comprises four main lines of current research. The first assesses the hormonal basis of parenting in healthy parents. The second line of research on parental hormones examines "endocrine fit" – the "match" or synchrony between parent and child hormonal levels. The third line addresses parental hormones under high-risk conditions, whether the risk stems from mother-related conditions (e.g., maternal depression, anxiety), child-related conditions (prematurity, autism spectrum disorders), or contextual adversities (poverty, abuse, war exposure). In this chapter we will focus on the fourth area of research in the neuroendocrinology of human parenting, and by no means the least abundant, which views the neurobiology of human parenting as a global area of research, and includes the brain networks, hormonal systems, and specific behaviors that activate in mothers, fathers, or other caregivers with the birth of an infant (Figure 17.1).

The flexible human parental brain

Human infants require the longest period of dependence to reach maturity of all species, rendering the caregiver's automatic response to infant cues insufficient. Thus, abilities such as emotion regulation, affect sharing, biobehavioral synchrony, self-other differentiation, mental flexibility, and perspective-taking evolved to increase parental scaffolding of infants' social adaptation (Decety, 2015; de Waal, 2015; Feldman, 2015a).

Investigations into the human parental brain typically used brain imaging techniques to test parents' brain response to auditory, visual, or multimodal infants' stimuli, such as infant pictures, movies, or sounds of infant cries, often comparing "own infant" to a standard infant or control condition. Within this body of research, most studies examined mothers, few tested fathers, and very few examined adoptive parents' and nonparents' brain response to infant cues. Using functional magnetic resonance imaging (fMRI), several brain areas in human adults were repeatedly shown to activate in response to infant cues, charting a "global caregiving" network that integrates functioning of several interconnected neural networks supporting multiple interacting processes that underpin human caregiving, while some brain areas participate in more than one system.

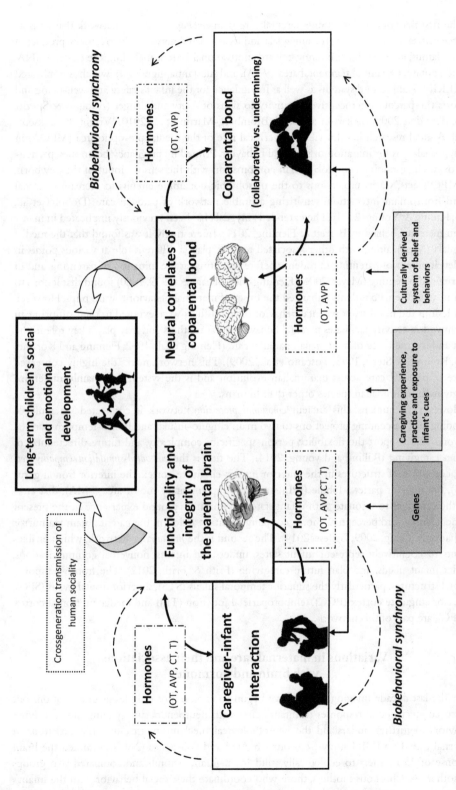

Figure 17.1. Neural and hormonal mechanisms underlying human caregiving, the coparental bond, and the cross-generational transmission of human sociality from flexibility of the parental brain in the postpartum to the development of children's social competencies and well-being modulated by the social hormones

The first network underpinning parental care is an *emotional processing* network that consists of three critical limbic circuits: the amygdala and its associated network, the oxytocin-producing hypothalamus, and the dopaminergic-reward motivational system including the striatum (NA, caudate, putamen), ventral tegmental area (VTA), and substantia nigra (SN), which is implicated in SEEKING and reward systems as well as in vigilance for the infant's safety and well-being and supports the parent's interoceptive sensitivity to signs of safety and danger (Adolphs & Spezio, 2006; Berridge, 2009; Bickart et al., 2014; Bromberg-Martin et al., 2010; Wright & Panksepp, 2012). Animal research has described the critical role of the medial pre-optic area (MPOA) in the hypothalamus for initiation of maternal behavior. Primed by pregnancy hormones, particularly oxytocin, estradiol, and prolactin, in combination with the sensory input of the newborn, the MPOA acts, via its projections to the mesolimbic dopamine circuits to increase maternal reward from infant interaction, sensitizing a limbic network of parental care (Dobolyi et al., 2014; Rilling & Young, 2014). The extended amygdala has been previously implicated in mammalian maternal behavior (Barrett & Fleming, 2011). Interestingly, it was found that the medial amygdala (MeA), along with other associated regions, plays a different role at various points in the development of parenting in rodents; before parenting, at the initiation of parenting, and in experienced parenting (Mayes, 2006). Fleming and colleagues (1979, 1980) found that lesions to MeA in virgin female rodents enhanced the onset of maternal behavior toward pups. However, MeA lesions did not disrupt parental behavior once mothers were exposed to their offspring; in fact, amygdala activity facilitates parental behavior in rat mothers and may play a key role in the onset and maintenance of mammalian parental care (Fleming et al., 1992; Fleming and Korsmit, 1996; Kolunie & Stern, 1995; Toscano et al., 2009). This network marks the highly conserved nature of parental care across mammalian evolution and is the system that mainly underpins caregiving in mammalian species other than humans.

However, in humans, this ancient *emotional processing* network is connected via multiple ascending and descending projections to two main cingulo-insular and fronto-temporo-parietal networks that support the flexibility, person-specificity, complexity, and future-directedness of human caregiving (Rilling and young, 2014). The first is the *embodied-simulation/empathy network*, consisting of structures in the anterior insular-cingulate cortex, the inferior frontal gyrus (IFG), the inferior parietal lobule (IPL), and the supplementary motor area (SMA), that enables the caregiver to resonate with infant state and emotion, ground experience in the present moment, and afford perceptual-motor coupling of infant action in the parent's brain via mirror mechanisms (Craig, 2009; Gallese, 2014). The second is the *mentalizing* network, which enables parents to cognitively represent infant states, understand infants' nonverbal communications, predict infant needs, and plan future caregiving (Frith & Frith, 2012). The fronto-temporo-parietal structures, particularly the superior temporal sulcus (STS), superior frontal gyrus (SFG), posterior cingulate cortex (PCC), temporoparietal junction (TPJ) and medial prefrontal cortex (mPFC), are part of this network.

Variations in maternal care and their associations with brain and hormones

Over the last decade imaging studies have begun to explore not only levels of activations but also to connect neural responses to infant's cues with neuroendocrine systems and caregiving behaviors to further understand the neurobiological mechanisms that underlie variations in maternal care. In a fMRI study from our lab, Atzil and colleagues (2011) examined the brain response of 23 mothers to ecologically valid "own-infant" stimuli and compared two groups of mothers: synchronous mothers, those who coordinate their social behavior with the infant's signals; and intrusive mothers, those who provide excessive parenting when the infant signals a need for rest. Findings showed that synchronous mothers exhibited greater activations in the left NAcc, whereas intrusive mothers activated the right amygdala. Functional connectivity analysis showed that among the synchronous mothers, left NAcc and right amygdala were functionally correlated with *mentalizing* and *empathy* networks, whereas among intrusive mothers, left NAcc and right amygdala were functionally correlated with premotor cortex. Finally, correlations between plasma oxytocin and NAcc and amygdala activations emerged only in the synchronous group, suggesting that parenting of synchronous mothers is more closely associated with the emotional processing circuit.

These findings highlight the link between individual variations in caregiving behaviors and altered neuroendocrine sensitivity in brain regions supporting maternal care, and are consistent with five other fMRI studies. First, a study assessing the brain reponse to own infant-cry stimuli in six mothers who delivered vaginally compared to six mothers who had an elective cesarean section delivery 2–4 weeks after delivery found greater activations in the caudate, thalamus, and hypothalamus, part of the subcortical dopaminergic circuit, and in the sensory processing and *empathy* network, including the middle temporal gyri, superior frontal gyrus and superior parietal lobe, in mothers who delivered vaginally compared to those who delivered by cesarean section (Swain et al., 2008). Another study examined associations between attachment representations, peripheral oxytocin levels, and brain activity in 30 first-time new mothers. Securely attached mothers exhibited greater activations of ventral striatum, a key node of the subcortical dopaminergic circuit, and hypothalamus, the structure where oxytocin is produced, to infant's smiling and crying faces, which were correlated with peripheral oxytocin, compared to insecure/dismissing mothers who showed greater insular activation to their infant's sad expression (Strathearn et al., 2009). Laurent and colleagues (2011) tested brain activations in 22 primiparous mothers while they were listening to their own infant, unfamiliar infant and control sounds. Salivary cortisol was collected at four time points during the Strange Situation paradigm, a commonly used stressor for caregiver-infant dyads that involves a series of separations and reunions (Ainsworth, Blehar, Waters, & Wall, 1978). The authors found that mothers with less reactive hypothalamic-pituitary-adrenal (HPA) responses during the Strange Situation showed greater activation to their own infant cry in limbic, paralimbic, and stress-regulation prefrontal circuits. Ho and colleagues (2014) investigated the link between brain activity, personal distress, and cortisol reactivity in 14 mothers in response to unfamiliar children's unpleasant feedback, and found that mothers with higher dispositional personal distress showed greater amygdala and hypothalamus activation to negative (vs. positive) feedback from the child and higher salivary cortisol levels as compared to mothers with lower levels of personal distress. Findings suggest the involvement of the limbic-hypothalamus end of HPA-axis reactivity in maternal care. Finally, a recent fMRI-PET imaging study found that synchronous maternal behavior was linked with increased dopamine responses in the NAcc and pallidum in 19 mothers to their own-infant videos, which was associated with stronger integrity within the medial amygdala network, and with lower plasma oxytocin levels (Atzil et al., 2017).

Breastfeeding also appears to play a role in the maternal brain. An fMRI study examined 17 mothers divided into two groups according to feeding method: exclusive breastfeeding and exclusive formula feeding. All mothers were scanned in the postpartum and were observed interacting with their infants at 4 months. While listening to their own infants cry, breastfeeding mothers showed greater activation in *emotional processing* and *empathy* networks, including amygdala, insula, and striatum, compared to formula-feeding mothers. For both groups of mothers, positive associations were found between activations in limbic and prefrontal areas, including the amygdala and superior frontal gyrus and observed maternal sensitivity. Results highlight the emotional salience of negative infant signals to human mothering. Authors also suggest that greater responses to infant cues in brain regions triggered by breastfeeding, which are associated with greater coordination between mothers and their infants, may be due to the effects of oxytocin release that involved in nursing (Kim et al., 2011).

Three other studies measured associations between brain activity, oxytocin levels, and maternal sensitivity and warmth. In one study authors examined levels of maternal sensitivity and intrusiveness during mother-infant free play in 22 primiparous mothers, coded by objective observers, as correlates of mothers' brain response to the cries of their own infants. Results revealed that higher levels of maternal sensitivity were associated with greater activation in the IFG and frontal pole to own infant-cry sounds, brain regions implicated in emotional and cognitive empathy. Mothers who displayed less sensitive caregiving behaviors toward their infant exhibited greater activation in the anterior insula (AI) and temporal pole, which have been implicated in pain perception. These findings suggest that intrusive mothers are more reactive to their own infant's distress signals which may lead to over-involved behavior (Musser et al., 2012). In another sample researchers compared mothers' brain activation to viewing videos of their own in infants in three affective states (neutral, happy, sad) between two groups of mothers: 15 mothers who were objectively rated as "highest sensitivity" and 15 mothers who were rated as "lowest sensitivity" during mother-infant play. Compared with "low sensitivity" mothers, "high sensitivity" mothers exhibited greater activation in the superior temporal gyrus (STG), part of the *mentalizing* network, to both own neutral and happy infants' stimuli, which was negatively correlated with plasma oxytocin levels (Elmadih et al., 2016). Moreover, Wan and colleagues (2014) found that both sensitive maternal behavior during mother-infant interaction, evaluated by objective raters, and self-reported maternal warmth were associated with greater activation in the putamen and middle frontal gyrus, part of the *emotional processing* and *mentalizing*/emotion regulation networks, respectively, in 20 mothers watching their own infants' videos. These findings suggest that greater prefrontal activations serve to regulate negative emotions and inhibit initial vigilance and stress responses while recognizing their infant's emotional state in the service of sensitive responding.

In a longitudinal study aimed to describe mechanism of plasticity in the parental brain in response to active caregiving, Kim and colleagues (2010) examined gray matter changes of 19 mothers' brains at two time points: 2–4 weeks postpartum and 3–4 months postpartum. Researchers found increased gray matter volume across these two time points in *emotional processing* network implicated in salience detection and processing reward signals (e.g., hypothalamus, SN, and amygdala). Furthermore, increased gray matter was positively correlated with maternal positive perception of her infant. Such findings provide strong evidence that the postpartum period marks a critical time for the development of sensitive parenting supported by structural brain changes, and is consistent with the animal literature reporting structural organization during postpartum as a function of postpartum experience (Featherstone et al., 2000).

Recent discoveries about the impact of hormones on neural responses to infant stimuli have been made using intranasal administration, though this approach has recently been criticized for its lack of direct replication and the poor knowledge of pharmacokinetic properties of oxytocin (Lane, Luminet, Nave, & Mikolajczak, 2016). Riem and colleagues (2011, 2013) found that oxytocin reduced amygdala activation to infant cry, while it increased activations in areas implicated in *empathy/simulation* processes in a group of 21 women who were administered oxytocin compared 21 women who were administered placebo. In the placebo group, increased activation in the amygdala was found in response to infant crying. The authors suggested that decreased amygdala activity may promote responsiveness to infant crying by preventing parents from excessive distress. Oxytocin was also found to enhance functional connectivity between the amygdala and cortical and subcortical regions involved in emotion regulation. Such findings highlight the amygdala's role in modulating negative emotional arousal and distressing the service of parenting. However, since there are inconsistencies and vagueness within literature as to whether or not own infant's cue increases or decreases amygdala activation in the parent's brain, further studies are needed to explore the role of the extended amygdala network and characterize its multiple role in the processing negative and positive infant cues.

The steroid hormone testosterone and its metabolite estradiol have been implicated in mammalian parental responsiveness (Kuo et al., 2016; Wynne-Edwards & Reburn, 2000), Bos and colleagues (2010) conducted a testosterone administration experiment in 16 women and found heightened activation in the testosterone condition compared to placebo in the thalamocingulate circuit and insula when those women listened to an infant cry. The authors suggest a potential mechanism by which testosterone acts on the thalamocingulate circuit after it metabolizes to estradiol, which is critical for the synthesis of oxytocin to upregulate parental care (Donaldson & Young, 2016).

Finally, research has begun to address the effects of adversity on a mother's brain. Overall, studies found dampened neural responses in emotion regulation circuits, greater increase in vigilance, emotional salience, and stress-related neural circuitry and impaired cortical-limbic connectivity among mothers with postpartum depression (Ho & Swain, 2017; Lenzi et al., 2016; Moses-Kolko et al., 2011), suggesting a disintegration of neural networks that normally support social behavior. Taken together, the aforementioned findings show that while each of these brain region plays an essential role in maternal response to infant's cues (for review, see Feldman, 2015a, 2017), they have distinct and specific roles in supporting a wide range of caregiving styles and behaviors human mothers express. These studies suggest that optimal human maternal care is supported by neural mechanisms related to motivation, social cognition, and emotion regulation. They also show that variations in maternal behavior and brain reactivity are related to oxytocin, cortisol, and testosterone. Findings provide evidence that human mothering is a complex and a multifaceted process underpinned by structural and functional brain sensitivity to infant cues and caregiving behavior.

Neural correlates of human allomaternal care: implications for fathering, adoptive parenting, and coparenting

Allomothering – the care of infants by adults other than the biological mother – is particularly common in primates but also observed in some birds and other mammalian species (Hrdy, 2011). It is hypothesized that as inter-birth intervals grew shorter, infant dependence longer, and female reproductive cycle increased from that of the Great Apes, hominin mothers needed a system of alloparental care in place to assure the survival and growth of the increasingly larger brains of co-dependent infants (Gettler, 2014). Since both alloparenting and father presence improved offspring's well-being and reduced rates of infant abandonment, it is argued that unless mothers were able to trust and cooperate with other group members, including male partners, to provide adequate care for their slow-maturing young, the human species could not have evolved (Hewlett, 1992).

Fathering

Our first examination of the paternal brain focused on assessment of structures that were activated in 15 fathers compared to their female partners in response to video clips showing their own infant in neutral and positive affect versus an unfamiliar infant. Atzil and colleagues (2012) found that mothers showed higher limbic activations, particularly in the amygdala, compared to fathers, and activation in the limbic-reward-motivational circuit positively correlated with maternal plasma oxytocin. Fathers, on the other hand, exhibited greater activations in socio-cognitive cortical and mentalizing areas, particularly in the mPFC, dorsolateral PFC, dorsal ACC (dACC) and IPL, which negatively correlated with plasma oxytocin, while higher activation in the amygdala was associated with higher plasma vasopressin levels. Such findings suggest oxytocin may be linked to different aspects of mothering and fathering. Vasopressin-amygdala correlation in fathers may highlight the essential role of vasopressin in the male's ability to protect and immediately respond to his offspring.

In order to tease out the effect of parent's sex from their caregiving role (primary versus secondary caregiving role) on the parental brain, in a fMRI study Abraham and colleagues (2014) recruited 89 first-time parents raising their infant within a partnered relationship: primary-caregiving heterosexual mothers, secondary-caregiving heterosexual fathers, and a unique group of primary-caregiving homosexual fathers living in a committed two-parent family and raising their infants without maternal involvement since birth. In each two-father family, one father was the biological father and the other was the adoptive father, genetically unrelated to the infant. Salivary oxytocin samples were collected from parents, parent-infant interactions were videotaped and coded for levels of parent-infant synchrony, and parental brain response were measured while parent were watching their own parent-infant interaction videos and an unfamiliar parent-infant interaction video. Since this is the first time in human history when men are able to raise children within a partnered relationship with no maternal involvement since birth, our study was the first to empirically investigate the parental brain in such a novel family setting. Several interesting findings emerged from our data. First, we found a remarkable similarity across parents (men and women, biological and adoptive parents) in the activation of a "global caregiving" network that underpins parental care across individuals. Although mothers' and fathers' brain responses to infant stimuli showed more commonalities than differences, consistent with findings in other mammals (Bales & Saltzman, 2016; Lambert et al., 2011), two important differences emerged. Primary-caregiving mothers showed greater amygdala activation, a key component of the *emotional processing* network, in response to own parent-infant interaction stimuli than secondary-caregiving fathers. Amygdala activation was positively linked to maternal salivary oxytocin and mother-infant synchrony. In comparison, secondary-caregiving fathers displayed higher STS activation than mothers. The STS, a key structure in the *mentalizing* network which plays a vital role in social cognition (Frith & Frith, 2006), was also positively associated with father's salivary oxytocin levels and father-infant synchrony. Of special interest, primary-caregiving fathers exhibited higher amygdala activation, similar to mothers, alongside greater STS activation comparable to secondary-caregiving fathers, and stronger functional connectivity between amygdala and STS was found in their brains. Amygdala-STS connectivity has been associated with better detection of social cues and was stronger in individuals with more complex social networks (Bickart et al., 2012). While significant stronger connectivity was found in primary-caregiving fathers compared to the other parent groups, in all fathers the amount of time each father spent in direct childcare was positively correlated with the degree of amygdala-STS connectivity.

Importantly, in the context of neural flexibility, we found no differences between mothers and primary-caregiving fathers in relation to *emotional processing, empathy/embodied simulation* and *mentalizing* network integrity – the strength of the average correlation within a set of brain regions defined as a networks and between networks (Abraham et al., 2016), and that exposure to own-infant stimuli increased within- and between-*empathy* and *mentalizing* network coherence in both mothers and primary-caregiving fathers (Abraham, Raz, et al., 2017).

Consistent with our findings, more fMRI studies showed that infant stimuli activated the neural "caregiving network," including the *emotional processing, empathy/simulation* and *mentalizing* networks in fathers' brains and demonstrated associations between fathers' brain activations in response to their own infant's stimuli in the subcortical motivation/reward circuitry and cortical networks, paternal caregiving behaviors and testosterone levels. For instance, Kuo and colleagues (2012) tested parental sensitivity and brain activity of 10 heterosexual fathers in response to their own infant video clips and found a negative association between paternal sensitivity and orbito-frontal cortex (OFC) activation, but a positive correlation between salivary testosterone and the caudate. The authors interpreted these findings by suggesting that testosterone increase may be associated with paternal protective behavior. Mascaro and colleagues (2013) measured paternal caregiving behavior, plasma testosterone, testes volumes, and brain activity in 70 biological heterosexual fathers and found a positive correlation between VTA activation in response to own infant photos and paternal caregiving behavior, and a negative correlation with testes volume. These findings suggest a positive feedback loop in which fathers with greater neural response in the VTA are more motivated to care of their child, which, in turn, increases paternal caregiving and enhances their brain response to the infant. Again, the inconsistencies in research highlight the need for more studies on the links between fathers' neural activity, testosterone levels, and parental behaviors. In another longitudinal fMRI study, Kim and colleagues (2014) investigated structural brain changes in 16 heterosexual biological fathers during the first 4 months postpartum. Fathers were scanned at 2–4 weeks postpartum and again at 12–16 weeks postpartum and exhibited increases in gray matter volume in brain regions involved in motivation, reward, and mentalizing, including the amygdala, straitum, hypothalamus, and PFC, but decreases in gray matter volume in the right OFC and insula, areas that activate under the context of threats and stress (Morris & Dolan, 2004). Wittfoth-Schardt and colleagues (2012) examined the effect of oxytocin on fathers' neural activity in response to infant cues. Twenty-one heterosexual fathers of kindergarten-aged children attended two fMRI sessions, one under oxytocin, the other under placebo while viewing pictures of their own child, a familiar child, and an unfamiliar child. Results indicated that oxytocin administration attenuated brain responses to pictures of own child and unfamiliar child in the subcortical dopaminergic circuit, mainly the globus pallidus (GP), and altered functional connectivity between GP and hippocampus and frontopolar cortex. The authors interpreted their findings as evidence that oxytocin reduces automatic neural responses to social stimuli as a function of their salience which is related to their reward and attachment values (own and familiar child's pictures) in human fathers. Such findings emphasize the role of oxytocin in the down-regulation of physiological responses to salient cues which eventually increases social approach tendencies. Finally, authors of a recent near-infrared spectroscopy (NIRS) study investigated the link between neural activity in the anterior PFC in 43 mothers and 41 fathers in response to their child smiling video stimuli in relation to genetic variability on the oxytocin receptor (*OXTR*) and vasopressin receptor 1A (*AVPR1A*). The authors found differential hemispheric activation of the anterior PFC observed in mothers carrying the *OXTR* rs2254298-G/G genotype compared with A carriers, but not in fathers while functional differences in anterior PFC activation between *AVPR1A* RS3-non-334 and -334 carrier fathers that was not found in mothers. These findings suggest that the A-allele of *OXTR* rs2254298 in mothers and the 334-allele of *AVPR1A* RS3 in fathers may be linked with greater risk, associated with attenuated neural response in mothers and fathers to their child's positive affect (Nishitani et al., 2017).

In sum, the abovementioned findings provide evidence of mechanism for experience-dependent neural flexibility in human fathers, and underscore both similarities in the brain response of fathers and mothers to their infant cues as well as father-specific neural pathways, via the later-developing prefrontal temporoparietal circuits, that support the development of their allomaternal role in human evolution. Overall, and consistent with animal studies (Bardi et al., 2011; Kozorovitskiy et al., 2006; Lambert et al., 2011), it appears that direct childcare experiences shape the paternal brain and increase functional connectivity both within and between networks, particularly when the father is the primary-caregiving adult.

Adoptive parenting

In our studies on the neurobiology of human paternal care, no differences emerged between biological and adoptive primary-caregiving fathers raising their infant since birth in brain activation, degree of functional connectivity within and between networks, oxytocin and vasopressin levels, and parenting behavior (Abraham et al., 2014, 2016; Abraham, Raz, et al., 2017; Abraham, Hendler, et al., 2017). Importantly, we found increased functional connectivity within and between *emotional processing, empathy*, and *mentalizing* networks in both primary-caregiving biological and adoptive fathers' brains when exposed to their interactions with their own infants' video clips compared to unfamiliar father-infant interaction video clips. Such increased coherence in both biological fathers' and adoptive fathers' brains to attachment stimuli may constitute a survival advantage for human offspring (Abraham, Raz, et al., 2017).

As for adoptive mothers, a small number of electroencephalography (EEG) studies compared neural responses to infant cues in biological and adoptive mothers. Yet findings are mixed. An EEG study found that urinary oxytocin levels in 41 foster mothers were positively associated with their behavioral expression of delight toward their infant during interaction, with quality of maternal behavior, and with greater parietal maximal P3 amplitude, which is related to the dopaminergic reward circuit (Aston-Jones & Cohen, 2005) in response to images of their foster infant (Bick & Dozier2013). These findings suggest that increased motivation, reward, and attention neural processing to infant cues were not determined by genetic relatedness. Two other ERP studies reported that both biological and adoptive mothers showed greater and similar cortical functionality associated with greater allocation of attention, during observation of their own children photos than non-mothers (Grasso et al., 2009; Hernandez-Gonzalez et al., 2016). However, Hernandez-Gonzalez and colleagues (2016) recruited 30 women, at 6 months to 2.5 years after having their first baby, divided them into two groups: 10 biological mothers and 10 adoptive mothers, and a control group of 10 non-mothers. Interestingly, these authors found that adoptive mothers showed significant higher EEG changes in the alpha, beta, and gamma bands in the cortical areas during observation of infant crying than biological mothers, which suggest that adoptive mothers were more sensitive to their infants' cry.

Coparenting

The human coparental bond is defined as a relationship of solidarity, coordinated action, and commitment to the child's well-being, and the extent to which two or more adults who actively involved in raising the child support one another's parenting efforts (McHale, 1997). While adaptive coparenting is considered a central contributor to infant survival since the dawn of humanity (Hrdy, 2011), there is a much cultural, ethnic, and individual variation within and across societies in the extent of cooperative coparenting. Such variability depends on multiple factors, such as paternity certainty, exposure to infant cues, and the amount of alloparental care provided by other females from the group (e.g., grandmothers) (Kramer, 2010). Recent developmental and social models describe the coparental bond as distinct from the marital relationship by isolating the effects of romantic relationship between partners (McHale & Irase, 2011) and highlight the importance of a mutually supportive coparenting for the development of children's mental health and social competencies (Teubert and Pinquart, 2010). In a series of studies we explored the behavioral, hormonal, and neural networks underlying coparenting, focusing on two types of coparenting described in the literature: collaborative coparenting and undermining coparenting.

In an fMRI study, Atzil et al. (2012) found online synchrony implying online correlations in the time-course of activation of a structure between mother's and father's brain to their infant's video, in the right anterior insula, the IFG, IPL, mPFC, lPFC, part of the *empathy/embodied simulation* and *mentalizing* networks. These findings show that the coupling between healthy mothers and fathers in brain networks implicated in empathy and mentalization enable parents to synchronize their efforts in order to provide optimal care and protection for their children.

In a recent fMRI longitudinal study, we followed couples across the first 6 years of family formation, including 42 couples, both opposite-sex and same-sex couples. Parents' brain responses to coparental stimuli (video clips of their partners interacting with the infants) were measured and salivary oxytocin and vasopressin were assayed when children were infants. Collaborative (e.g., supportive presence/communication, cooperation-mutual adaptation, acknowledgment, expressing empathy and positive affect) and undermining (e.g., negative affect, withdrawal-avoidance, competition, intrusiveness, and criticism) coparental behaviors were observed and coded in infancy (during a triadic two-parent-and-infant interaction) and in preschool (during a 10-minute coparental conversation discussing a topic of continuous childrearing conflict, and pleasant topic of mutual joy in their coparental relationship). In addition, coparenting and child behavior problems at 6 years were measured by using parents' self-report. Results revealed that coparental behaviors were individually stable across time and measurement methods. Across all parents, the ventral striatum (VS) and caudate, striatal nodes implicated in motivational goal-directed social behavior, activated while participants were viewing video clips of their partner interacting with their infant. Whole brain psychophysiological interactions analysis indicated that both the ventral striatum and the caudate were functionally coupled with the ventromedial PFC (vmPFC), dlPFC and left OFC, part of the *mentalizing* network, in support of the human coparental bond and this connectivity was stronger as collaborative coparental behavior increased. However, only the caudate showed distinct functional connectivity patterns positively associated with two stable coparental behavioral styles, the collaborative and the undermining. Stronger caudate-vmPFC connectivity, which has previously been linked with cooperation, flexible goal-directed behavior, consideration of multiple outcomes to guide behavior and delayed gratification (Benningfield et al., 2014; de Wit et al., 2012; Rilling et al., 2002), was positively associated with more collaborative coparenting and was positively associated with salivary oxytocin. Stronger caudate-dACC connectivity, on the other hand, which is involved in competition and conflict (Aupperle et al., 2015), was linked with an increase in undermining coparenting and was related to salivary vasopressin, a hormone implicated in mammalian social behavior, including aggression, competition, and the guarding of relationship exclusively (Neumann & Landgraf, 2012). Finally, a dyadic path model showed that parental caudate-vmPFC connectivity in infancy predicted lower child externalizing symptoms at 6 years as mediated by collaborative coparenting in preschool (Abraham, Gilam, et al., 2017). Such findings provide the first neurobiological evidence that distinct neural pathways in the parent's brain in response to the other coparent and the endocrine systems and behavioral mechanisms related to those, serve an important regulatory role in children's development and may confer evolutionary advantages for the child, the family, and the whole group.

Non-genomic cross-generational effects of parental care: from parents' brains to children's social development and mental health

During an initial sensitive period in the life of young mammals, patterns of maternal and paternal care influence offspring neural architecture and behavioral repertoire which regulate stress reactivity and sociality, creating a cross-generational pathway that is not based on genetic transmission (Curley & Champagne, 2016; Feldman, 2015b; Stolzenberg & Champagne, 2016). These environmental effects allow the next generation to display developmental flexibility and adapt to their ecological niche and its socioecological conditions. While there is now ample evidence that quality of human parental care shapes children's development and social adaptation, the molecular and neurobiological effects that may shape the offspring's developing brain by the caregiver's behavioral and neural systems have just begun to be explored. Recently, emerging research has described the associations between normative mothering (Brauer et al., 2016; Sethna et al., 2017), maternal adversity (Foland-Ross et al., 2015; Pratt et al., 2017; Quevedo et al., 2017; Wonch et al., 2016), and children's brain functionality, connectivity, and gray matter volumes.

In three longitudinal studies (Abraham et al., 2016; Abraham, Raz, et al., 2017; Abraham, Hendler, et al., 2017), we followed the same sample of 45 primary-caregiving mothers and fathers that described in the previous sections, from their children's infancy and up to 6 years to elucidate how mechanisms underpinning the parental brain responses to infant's stimuli support the development of children's social competencies over time. In two of the follow-up studies, we used Network Cohesion Indices (NCI, Raz et al., 2012) in the parental brain as predictors of children's social competencies at the preschool (3–4 years) and school entry (6–7 years) stages. NCIs probe the dynamics of coordination both within a defined network and between networks. We expected that the parent's complex social functions that are critical for offspring survival (e.g., social motivation, empathy/embodied-simulation, theory of mind) would emerge from interactions within and between distributed brain networks rather than from the activity of single regions, and such integrity indices would play a role in shaping offspring social outcomes.

Findings of these studies revealed how changes in the parental brain in the postpartum impact children's long-term outcomes. Integrity of parents' *emotional processing* network positively predicted children's expression of positive emotions and use of simple self-regulatory strategies at preschool years. This likely describes a mammalian-general mechanism that accounts for the transmission from optimal parenting to social behavior in juveniles. Integrity of the parent's *mentalizing* network positively predicted children's self-regulated socialization, which has been associated with theory-of-mind development. Integrity of the parent's *embodied simulation/empathy* network predicted children's use of more complex emotion regulation tactics, such as symbolization and attention diversion, to manage moments of heightened emotional arousal. This link from integrity of the parent's *embodied simulation/empathy* network and children's mature self-regulation was mediated by parent-infant synchrony in infancy, the first experience that sensitizes infants to the dyadic "here-and-now." Prediction of preschooler's oxytocin levels by parent's inter-connectivity between the *emotional processing* and the *embodied simulation* networks was moderated by parental oxytocin when children were infants (Abraham et al., 2016). Under condition of high parental oxytocin levels a significant positive correlation emerged between parents' *emotional processing-embodied simulation*-NCI and child's oxytocin levels, but such correlation was not found under low parent's oxytocin. In addition, higher child's oxytocin levels were associated with more frequent child use of complex regulatory strategies. We also found that a greater degree of connectivity between the *embodied-simulation/empathy* network and the *mentalizing* network in the parent's brain was longitudinally linked with lower child cortisol production in preschool. Greater between-network connectivity of the *embodied-simulation/*

empathy and the *mentalizing* networks in the parent's brain when children's were infants was longitudinally associated with children's lower internalizing problems 6 years later, as mediated by the child's regulatory behavior in preschool (Abraham, Raz, et al., 2017).

In another study from the same sample, we focused on neural pathways that underpin human interoception, the perception of one's own bodily signals, investigating how parent's interoceptive neural circuit is linked to the child's somatic problems. We found that increased activations in the parent's bilateral anterior insula (AI) in response to parent-own infant interaction video clips predicted lower child somatic problems at 6 years. Parent sensitivity levels partially mediated the links between parental AI activation and child somatic symptoms. In addition, greater parental bilateral amygdala activity predicted higher child salivary oxytocin levels at preschool years, and parental salivary oxytocin moderated the relations between preschoolers' oxytocin and later somatic symptoms. Under condition of low parental oxytocin levels significant negative correlation emerged between child's oxytocin levels during preschool years and child's somatic symptoms, but such correlation was not found under high parent's oxytocin. We also found that parental sensitivity, measured during parent-preschooler play interaction, was positively associated with preschooler's oxytocin level (Abraham, Hendler, et al., 2017). Overall, these findings provide compelling evidence of human non-genomic mechanism of the cross-generational transmission of social adaptation from parent to child. We suggest a cross-generational mechanism by which neural networks implicated in emotion regulation, simulation, mentalizing, and interoception in the parent's brain linked to hormones such as oxytocin, vasopressin, testosterone, and cortisol, which initiate caregiving behaviors. In turn, we speculate that through mechanisms of *brain-to-brain synchrony* (Feldman, 2016a; Hasson et al., 2012; Hasson & Frith, 2016) during synchronous parent-infant interactions, caregiving behaviors may tune the infant's brain, probably resulting in epigenetic alterations of hormone receptor genes expressions in the infant's key brain areas underlying mental processes that support social functions (Champagne, 2008; Liu et al., 1997; Weaver et al., 2004; Figure 17.2).

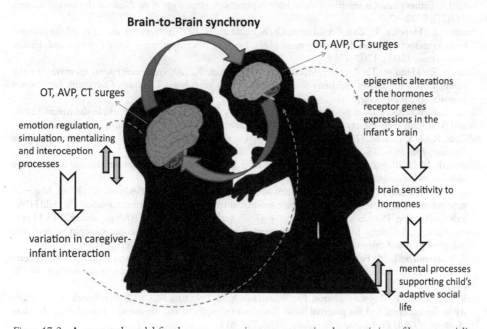

Figure 17.2   A suggested model for the non-genomic cross-generational transmission of human sociality

The neurobiology and neuroendocrinology of human caregiving; future directions and open questions

While there are remarkable variations throughout human history and across cultures in the way mothers, fathers, and other adult members participate in childcare, we assume that human caregiving may build on an ancient evolutionary alloparenting neural systems and neurohormonal coordination that support a parental role in both females and males as caregivers with the capacity to nurture the young.

Still, most of our knowledge on the neurobiology and neuroendocrinology of human caregiving is based primarily on studies in healthy mothers during postpartum raising their newborn infants within a two-parent family. Future studies may look into the neural correlates and hormonal profiles of parental care in other populations, including divorced parents, single parents, parenting in high-risk contexts (e.g., family adversity, maternal depression, poverty, marital discord), and multi-generational caregivers. Finally, how parent's and child's neural and hormonal systems "tick together" during social interactions, how such *brain-to-brain synchrony* and neuroendocrine synchronization shape child's neural, hormonal, and behavioral systems that support social adaptation at different developmental stages, and how gender differences in both parents and children modulate these neurobiological and neuroendocrinological mechanisms are exciting questions for future research to investigate. Focusing on a two-person neuroscience approach will allow new and exciting discoveries in the fields of social neuroscience and social neuroendocrinology.

References

Abraham, E., Gilam, G., Kanat-Maymon, Y., Jacob, Y., Zagoory-Sharon, O., Hendler, T., & Feldman, R. (2017). The human coparental bond implicates distinct corticostriatal pathways: Longitudinal impact on family formation and child well-being. *Neuropsychopharmacology, 42*(12), 2301.

Abraham, E., Hendler, T., Shapira-Lichter, I., Kanat-Maymon, Y., Zagoory-Sharon, O., & Feldman, R. (2014). Father's brain is sensitive to childcare experiences. *Proceedings of the National Academy of Sciences, 111*(27), 9792–9797.

Abraham, E., Hendler, T., Zagoory-Sharon, O., & Feldman, R. (2016). Network integrity of the parental brain in infancy supports the development of children's social competencies. *Social Cognitive and Affective Neuroscience, 11*(11), 1707–1718.

Abraham, E., Hendler, T., Zagoory-Sharon, O., & Feldman, R. (2017). Interoception sensitivity in the parental brain modulates children's somatic problems six years later: The role of oxytocin. *International Journal of Psychophysiology*.

Abraham, E., Raz, G., Zagoory-Sharon, O., & Feldman, R. (2017). Empathy networks in the parental brain and their long-term effects on children's stress reactivity and behavior adaptation. *Neuropsychologia*.

Adolphs, R., & Spezio, M. (2006). Role of the amygdala in processing visual social stimuli. *Progress in Brain Research, 156*, 363–378.

Ainsworth, M.D., Blehar, M.C., Waters, E., & Wall, S. (1978). *Patterns of attachment: Assessed in the strange situation and at home.* Hillsdale, NJ: Erlbaum.

Apter-Levi, Y., Pratt, M., Vakart, A., Feldman, M., Zagoory-Sharon, O., & Feldman, R. (2016). Maternal depression across the first years of life compromises child psychosocial adjustment; relations to child HPA-axis functioning. *Psychoneuroendocrinology, 64*, 47–56. https://doi.org/10.1016/j.psyneuen.2015.11.006

Aston-Jones, G., & Cohen, J.D. (2005). An integrative theory of locus coeruleus-norepinephrine function: Adaptive gain and optimal performance. *Annual Review of Neuroscience, 28*, 403–450.

Atzil, S., Hendler, T., & Feldman, R. (2011). Specifying the neurobiological basis of human attachment: Brain, hormones, and behavior in synchronous and intrusive mothers. *Neuropsychopharmacology, 36*(13), 2603–2615.

Atzil, S., Hendler, T., Zagoory-Sharon, O., Winetraub, Y., & Feldman, R. (2012). Synchrony and specificity in the maternal and the paternal brain: Relations to oxytocin and vasopressin. *Journal of the American Academy of Child & Adolescent Psychiatry, 51*(8), 798–811.

Atzil, S., Touroutoglou, A., Rudy, T., Salcedo, S., Feldman, R., Hooker, J.M., . . . Barrett, L.F. (2017). Dopamine in the medial amygdala network mediates human bonding. *Proceedings of the National Academy of Sciences, 114*(9), 2361–2366.

Aupperle, R.L., Melrose, A.J., Francisco, A., Paulus, M.P., & Stein, M.B. (2015). Neural substrates of approach-avoidance conflict decision-making. *Human Brain Mapping, 36*(2), 449–462.

Bales, K.L., & Saltzman, W. (2016). Fathering in rodents: Neurobiological substrates and consequences for offspring. *Hormones and Behavior, 77*, 249–259.

Bardi, M., Franssen, C.L., Hampton, J.E., Shea, E.A., Fanean, A.P., & Lambert, K.G. (2011). Paternal experience and stress responses in California mice (*Peromyscus californicus*). *Comparative Medicine, 61*(1), 20–30.

Barrett, J., & Fleming, A.S. (2011). Annual research review: All mothers are not created equal: Neural and psychobiological perspectives on mothering and the importance of individual differences. *Journal of Child Psychology and Psychiatry, 52*(4), 368–397.

Benningfield, M.M., Blackford, J.U., Ellsworth, M.E., Samanez-Larkin, G.R., Martin, P.R., Cowan, R.L., & Zald, D.H. (2014). Caudate responses to reward anticipation associated with delay discounting behavior in healthy youth. *Developmental Cognitive Neuroscience, 7*, 43–52.

Berridge, K.C. (2009). "Liking" and "wanting" food rewards: Brain substrates and roles in eating disorders. *Physiology & Behavior, 97*(5), 537–550.

Bick, J., & Dozier, M. (2013). The effectiveness of an attachment-based intervention in promoting foster mothers' sensitivity toward foster infants. *Infant Mental Health Journal, 34*(2), 95–103.

Bickart, K.C., Dickerson, B.C., & Barrett, L.F. (2014). The amygdala as a hub in brain networks that support social life. *Neuropsychologia, 63*, 235–248.

Bickart, K.C., Hollenbeck, M.C., Barrett, L.F., & Dickerson, B.C. (2012). Intrinsic amygdala-cortical functional connectivity predicts social network size in humans. *Journal of Neuroscience, 32*(42), 14729–14741.

Bos, P.A., Hermans, E.J., Montoya, E.R., Ramsey, N.F., & van Honk, J. (2010). Testosterone administration modulates neural responses to crying infants in young females. *Psychoneuroendocrinology, 35*(1), 114–121.

Brauer, J., Xiao, Y., Poulain, T., Friederici, A.D., & Schirmer, A. (2016). Frequency of maternal touch predicts resting activity and connectivity of the developing social brain. *Cerebral Cortex, 26*(8), 3544–3552.

Braun, K., & Champagne, F.A. (2014). Paternal influences on offspring development: Behavioural and epigenetic pathways. *Journal of Neuroendocrinology, 26*(10), 697–706.

Bromberg-Martin, E.S., Matsumoto, M., & Hikosaka, O. (2010). Dopamine in motivational control: Rewarding, aversive, and alerting. *Neuron, 68*(5), 815–834.

Brummelte, S., & Galea, L.A.M. (2010). Chronic corticosterone during pregnancy and postpartum affects maternal care, cell proliferation and depressive-like behavior in the dam. *Hormones and Behavior, 58*(5), 769–779.

Carter, C.S. (2014). Oxytocin pathways and the evolution of human behavior. *Annual Review of Psychology, 65*, 17–39.

Champagne, F.A. (2008). Epigenetic mechanisms and the transgenerational effects of maternal care. *Frontiers in Neuroendocrinology, 29*(3), 386–397.

Cohen, L., & Mizrahi, A. (2015). Plasticity during motherhood: Changes in excitatory and inhibitory layer 2/3 neurons in auditory cortex. *Journal of Neuroscience, 35*(4), 1806–1815.

Craig, A.D. (2009). How do you feel – now? The anterior insula and human awareness. *Nature Reviews Neuroscience, 10*(1).

Crittenden, A.N., & Marlowe, F.W. (2008). Allomaternal care among the Hadza of Tanzania. *Human Nature, 19*(3), 249.

Curley, J.P., & Champagne, F.A. (2016). Influence of maternal care on the developing brain: Mechanisms, temporal dynamics and sensitive periods. *Frontiers in Neuroendocrinology, 40*, 52–66.

De Waal, F.B. (2015). Prosocial primates. In *The Oxford handbook of prosocial behavior* (pp. 61–85). Oxford, New York: Oxford University Press.

De Wit, F. R., Greer, L. L., & Jehn, K. A. (2012). The paradox of intragroup conflict: A meta-analysis. *Journal of Applied Psychology, 97*(2), 360.

Decety, J. (2015). The neural pathways, development and functions of empathy. *Current Opinion in Behavioral Sciences, 3*, 1–6.

Dobolyi, A., Grattan, D.R., & Stolzenberg, D.S. (2014). Preoptic inputs and mechanisms that regulate maternal responsiveness. *Journal of Neuroendocrinology, 26*(10), 627–640.

Donaldson, Z.R., & Young, L.J. (2016). The neurobiology and genetics of affiliation and social bonding in animal models. In *Animal models of behavior genetics* (pp. 101–134). New York, NY: Springer.

Elmadih, A., Wan, M.W., Downey, D., Elliott, R., Swain, J.E., & Abel, K.M. (2016). Natural variation in maternal sensitivity is reflected in maternal brain responses to infant stimuli. *Behavioral Neuroscience, 130*(5), 500.

Featherstone, R.E., Fleming, A.S., & Ivy, G.O. (2000). Plasticity in the maternal circuit: Effects of experience and partum condition on brain astroctye number in female rats. *Behavioral Neuroscience, 114*(1), 158.

Feldman, R. (2012a). Parent-infant synchrony: A biobehavioral model of mutual influences in the formation of affiliative bonds. *Monographs of the Society for Research in Child Development, 77*(2), 42–51.

Feldman, R. (2012b). Oxytocin and social affiliation in humans. *Hormones and Behavior, 61*(3), 380–391. https://doi.org/10.1016/j.yhbeh.2012.01.008

Feldman, R. (2015a). The adaptive human parental brain: Implications for children's social development. *Trends in Neurosciences, 38*(6), 387–399.

Feldman, R. (2015b). Sensitive periods in human social development: New insights from research on oxytocin, synchrony, and high-risk parenting. *Development and Psychopathology, 27*(2), 369–395.

Feldman, R. (2016a). The neurobiology of mammalian parenting and the biosocial context of human caregiving. *Hormones and Behavior, 77*, 3–17.

Feldman, R. (2016b). Affiliation, reward, and immune biomarkers coalesce to support social synchrony during periods of bond formation in humans. *Brain, Behavior, and Immunity, 56*, 130–139.

Feldman, R. (2017). The neurobiology of human attachments. *Trends in Cognitive Sciences, 21*(2), 80–99.

Feldman, R., Monakhov, M., Pratt, M., & Ebstein, R.P. (2016). Oxytocin pathway genes: Evolutionary ancient system impacting on human affiliation, sociality, and psychopathology. *Biological Psychiatry, 79*(3), 174–184.

Fleming, A.S., Gavarth, K., & Sarker, J. (1992). Effects of transections to the vomeronasal nerves or to the main olfactory bulbs on the initiation and long-term retention of maternal behavior in primiparous rats. *Behavioral and Neural Biology, 57*(3), 177–188.

Fleming, A.S., & Korsmit, M. (1996). Plasticity in the maternal circuit: Effects of maternal experience on Fos-Lir in hypothalamic, limbic, and cortical structures in the postpartum rat. *Behavioral Neuroscience, 110*(3), 567.

Fleming, A.S., Vaccarino, F., & Luebke, C. (1980). Amygdaloid inhibition of maternal behavior in the nulliparous female rat. *Physiology & Behavior, 25*(5), 731–743.

Fleming, A., Vaccarino, F., Tambosso, L., & Chee, P. (1979). Vomeronasal and olfactory system modulation of maternal behavior in the rat. *Science, 203*(4378), 372–374.

Foland-Ross, L.C., Gilbert, B.L., Joormann, J., & Gotlib, I.H. (2015). Neural markers of familial risk for depression: An investigation of cortical thickness abnormalities in healthy adolescent daughters of mothers with recurrent depression. *Journal of Abnormal Psychology, 124*(3), 476.

Frith, C.D., & Frith, U. (2006). The neural basis of mentalizing. *Neuron, 50*(4), 531–534.

Frith, C.D., & Frith, U. (2012). Mechanisms of social cognition. *Annual Review of Psychology, 63*, 287–313.

Galbally, M., Lewis, A.J., IJzendoorn, M. van, & Permezel, M. (2011). The role of oxytocin in mother-infant relations: A systematic review of human studies. *Harvard Review of Psychiatry, 19*(1), 1–14.

Gallese, V. (2014). Bodily selves in relation: Embodied simulation as second-person perspective on intersubjectivity. *Philosophical Transactions of the Royal Society B, 369*(1644), 20130177.

Geary, D.C., & Flinn, M.V. (2001). Evolution of human parental behavior and the human family. *Parenting, 1*(1–2), 5–61.

Gettler, L.T. (2014). Applying socioendocrinology to evolutionary models: Fatherhood and physiology. *Evolutionary Anthropology: Issues, News, and Reviews, 23*(4), 146–160.

Gordon, I., Zagoory-Sharon, O., Leckman, J.F., & Feldman, R. (2010a). Oxytocin and the development of parenting in humans. *Biological Psychiatry, 68*(4), 377–382.

Gordon, I., Zagoory-Sharon, O., Leckman, J.F., & Feldman, R. (2010b). Prolactin, oxytocin, and the development of paternal behavior across the first six months of fatherhood. *Hormones and Behavior, 58*(3), 513–518.

Grasso, D.J., Moser, J.S., Dozier, M., & Simons, R. (2009). ERP correlates of attention allocation in mothers processing faces of their children. *Biological Psychology, 81*(2), 95–102.

Hard, R. (2003). *The Routledge handbook of Greek mythology: Based on HJ Rose's handbook of Greek mythology.* London: Routledge.

Hasson, U., & Frith, C.D. (2016). Mirroring and beyond: Coupled dynamics as a generalized framework for modelling social interactions. *Philosophical Transactions of the Royal Society B, 371*(1693), 20150366.

Hasson, U., Ghazanfar, A.A., Galantucci, B., Garrod, S., & Keysers, C. (2012). Brain-to-brain coupling: A mechanism for creating and sharing a social world. *Trends in Cognitive Sciences, 16*(2), 114–121.

Hernández-González, M., Hidalgo-Aguirre, R.M., Guevara, M.A., Pérez-Hernández, M., & Amezcua-Gutiérrez, C. (2016). Observing videos of a baby crying or smiling induces similar, but not identical, electroencephalographic responses in biological and adoptive mothers. *Infant Behavior and Development*, *42*, 1–10.

Hewlett, B.S. (Ed.). (1992). Father-child relations: Cultural and biosocial contexts. New York, NY: Routledge

Hewlett, B.S., & Winn, S. (2014). Allomaternal nursing in humans. *Current Anthropology*, *55*(2), 200–229.

Ho, S.S., Konrath, S., Brown, S., & Swain, J.E. (2014). Empathy and stress related neural responses in maternal decision making. *Frontiers in Neuroscience*, 8.

Ho, S.S., & Swain, J.E. (2017). Depression altered limbic response and functional connectivity related to self-oriented distress signals. *Behavioral Brain Research*, *325*, 290–296.

Hofer, M.A. (1995). Hidden regulators. *Attachment Theory: Social, Developmental and Clinical Perspectives*, 203–230.

Hrdy, S.B. (2011). *Mothers and others*. Cambridge, MA: Harvard University Press.

Kim, P., Feldman, R., Mayes, L.C., Eicher, V., Thompson, N., Leckman, J.F., & Swain, J.E. (2011). Breastfeeding, brain activation to own infant cry, and maternal sensitivity. *Journal of Child Psychology and Psychiatry*, *52*(8), 907–915.

Kim, P., Leckman, J.F., Mayes, L.C., Feldman, R., Wang, X., & Swain, J.E. (2010). The plasticity of human maternal brain: Longitudinal changes in brain anatomy during the early postpartum period. *Behavioral Neuroscience*, *124*(5), 695.

Kim, P., Rigo, P., Mayes, L.C., Feldman, R., Leckman, J.F., & Swain, J.E. (2014). Neural plasticity in fathers of human infants. *Social Neuroscience*, *9*(5), 522–535.

Kleiman, D.G. (1977). Monogamy in mammals. *The Quarterly Review of Biology*, *52*(1), 39–69.

Kolunie, J.M., & Stern, J.M. (1995). Maternal aggression in rats: Effects of olfactory bulbectomy, ZnSO 4-induced anosmia, and vomeronasal organ removal. *Hormones and Behavior*, *29*(4), 492–518.

Kozorovitskiy, Y., Hughes, M., Lee, K., & Gould, E. (2006). Fatherhood affects dendritic spines and vasopressin V1a receptors in the primate prefrontal cortex. *Nature Neuroscience*, *9*(9), 1094–1095.

Kramer, K.L. (2010). Cooperative breeding and its significance to the demographic success of humans. *Annual Review of Anthropology*, *39*, 417–436.

Kuo, P.X., Carp, J., Light, K.C., & Grewen, K.M. (2012). Neural responses to infants linked with behavioral interactions and testosterone in fathers. *Biological Psychology*, *91*(2), 302–306.

Kuo, P.X., Saini, E.K., Thomason, E., Schultheiss, O.C., Gonzalez, R., & Volling, B.L. (2016). Individual variation in fathers' testosterone reactivity to infant distress predicts parenting behaviors with their 1-year-old infants. *Developmental Psychobiology*, *58*(3), 303–314.

Lambert, K.G., Franssen, C.L., Bardi, M., Hampton, J.E., Hainley, L., Karsner, S., . . . Ferguson, T. (2011). Characteristic neurobiological patterns differentiate paternal responsiveness in two *Peromyscus* species. *Brain, Behavior and Evolution*, *77*(3), 159–175.

Lane, A., Luminet, O., Nave, G., & Mikolajczak, M. (2016). Is there a publication bias in behavioural intranasal oxytocin research on humans? Opening the file drawer of one laboratory. *Journal of Neuroendocrinology*, *28*(4).

Laurent, H.K., Stevens, A., & Ablow, J.C. (2011). Neural correlates of hypothalamic-pituitary-adrenal regulation of mothers with their infants. *Biological Psychiatry*, *70*(9), 826–832.

Lenzi, D., Trentini, C., Macaluso, E., Graziano, S., Speranza, A.M., Pantano, P., & Ammaniti, M. (2016). Mothers with depressive symptoms display differential brain activations when empathizing with infant faces. *Psychiatry Research: Neuroimaging*, *249*, 1–11.

Liu, D., Diorio, J., Tannenbaum, B., Caldji, C., Francis, D., Freedman, A., . . . Meaney, M.J. (1997). Maternal care, hippocampal glucocorticoid receptors, and hypothalamic-pituitary-adrenal responses to stress. *Science*, *277*(5332), 1659–1662.

Lonstein, J.S., Lévy, F., & Fleming, A.S. (2015). Common and divergent psychobiological mechanisms underlying maternal behaviors in non-human and human mammals. *Hormones and Behavior*, *73*, 156–185. https://doi.org/10.1016/j.yhbeh.2015.06.011

Mann, P.E., & Bridges, R.S. (2001). Lactogenic hormone regulation of maternal behavior. *Progress in Brain Research*, *133*, 251–262.

Mascaro, J.S., Hackett, P.D., & Rilling, J.K. (2013). Testicular volume is inversely correlated with nurturing-related brain activity in human fathers. *Proceedings of the National Academy of Sciences*, *110*(39), 15746–15751.

Mayes, L.C. (2006). Arousal regulation, emotional flexibility, medial amygdala function, and the impact of early experience. *Annals of the New York Academy of Sciences*, *1094*(1), 178–192.

McHale, J.P. (1997). Overt and covert coparenting processes in the family. *Family Process, 36*(2), 183–201.

McHale, J.P., & Irase, K. (2011). Coparenting in diverse family systems. In J.P. McHale & K.M. Lindahl (Eds.), *Coparenting-a conceptual and clinical examination of family systems* (pp. 15–38). Washington, DC: American Psychological Association.

Morris, J.S., & Dolan, R.J. (2004). Dissociable amygdala and orbitofrontal responses during reversal fear conditioning. *Neuroimage, 22*(1), 372–380.

Moses-Kolko, E.L., Fraser, D., Wisner, K.L., James, J.A., Saul, A.T., Fiez, J.A., & Phillips, M.L. (2011). Rapid habituation of ventral striatal response to reward receipt in postpartum depression. *Biological Psychiatry, 70*(4), 395–399.

Musser, E.D., Kaiser-Laurent, H., & Ablow, J.C. (2012). The neural correlates of maternal sensitivity: An fMRI study. *Developmental Cognitive Neuroscience, 2*(4), 428–436.

Neumann, I.D., & Landgraf, R. (2012). Balance of brain oxytocin and vasopressin: Implications for anxiety, depression, and social behaviors. *Trends in Neurosciences, 35*(11), 649–659.

Nishitani, S., Ikematsu, K., Takamura, T., Honda, S., Yoshiura, K.I., & Shinohara, K. (2017). Genetic variants in oxytocin receptor and arginine-vasopressin receptor 1A are associated with the neural correlates of maternal and paternal affection towards their child. *Hormones and Behavior, 87*, 47–56.

Numan, M., & Stolzenberg, D.S. (2009). Medial preoptic area interactions with dopamine neural systems in the control of the onset and maintenance of maternal behavior in rats. *Frontiers in Neuroendocrinology, 30*(1), 46–64.

Pedersen, C.A., & Prange, A.J. (1985). Oxytocin and mothering behavior in the rat. *Pharmacology and Therapeutics, 28*(3), 287–302.

Pratt, M., Goldstein, A., Levy, J., & Feldman, R. (2017). Maternal depression across the first years of life impacts the neural basis of empathy in preadolescence. *Journal of the American Academy of Child & Adolescent Psychiatry, 56*(1), 20–29.

Pryce, C.R. (1996). Socialization, hormones, and the regulation of maternal behavior in nonhuman simian primates. *Advances in the Study of Behavior, 25*, 423–473.

Quevedo, K., Waters, T.E., Scott, H., Roisman, G.I., Shaw, D.S., & Forbes, E.E. (2017). Brain activity and infant attachment history in young men during loss and reward processing. *Development and Psychopathology, 29*(2), 465–476.

Raz, G., Winetraub, Y., Jacob, Y., Kinreich, S., Maron-Katz, A., Shaham, G., . . . Hendler, T. (2012). Portraying emotions at their unfolding: A multilayered approach for probing dynamics of neural networks. *Neuroimage, 60*(2), 1448–1461.

Riem, M.M., Bakermans-Kranenburg, M.J., Pieper, S., Tops, M., Boksem, M.A., Vermeiren, R.R., . . . Rombouts, S.A. (2011). Oxytocin modulates amygdala, insula, and inferior frontal gyrus responses to infant crying: A randomized controlled trial. *Biological Psychiatry, 70*(3), 291–297.

Riem, M.M., van IJzendoorn, M.H., Tops, M., Boksem, M.A., Rombouts, S.A., & Bakermans-Kranenburg, M.J. (2013). Oxytocin effects on complex brain networks are moderated by experiences of maternal love withdrawal. *European Neuropsychopharmacology, 23*(10), 1288–1295.

Rilling, J.K., Gutman, D.A., Zeh, T.R., Pagnoni, G., Berns, G.S., & Kilts, C.D. (2002). A neural basis for social cooperation. *Neuron, 35*(2), 395–405.

Rilling, J.K., & Mascaro, J.S. (2017). The neurobiology of fatherhood. *Current Opinion in Psychology, 15*, 26–32.

Rilling, J.K., & Young, L.J. (2014). The biology of mammalian parenting and its effect on offspring social development. *Science, 345*(6198), 771–776.

Rosenblatt, J.S. (1994). Psychobiology of maternal behavior: Contribution to the clinical understanding of maternal behavior among humans. *Acta Paediatrica, 83*(s397), 3–8.

Rosenblatt, J.S. (2003). Outline of the evolution of behavioral and nonbehavioral patterns of parental care among the vertebrates: Critical characteristics of mammalian and avian parental behavior. *Scandinavian Journal of Psychology, 44*(3), 265–271. https://doi.org/10.1111/1467-9450.00344

Royle, N.J., Russell, A.F., & Wilson, A.J. (2014). The evolution of flexible parenting. *Science, 345*(6198), 776–781.

Sethna, V., Pote, I., Wang, S., Gudbrandsen, M., Blasi, A., McCusker, C., . . . Busuulwa, P. (2017). Mother-infant interactions and regional brain volumes in infancy: An MRI study. *Brain Structure and Function, 222*(5), 2379–2388.

Stolzenberg, D.S., & Champagne, F.A. (2016). Hormonal and non-hormonal bases of maternal behavior: The role of experience and epigenetic mechanisms. *Hormones and Behavior, 77*, 204–210.

Stolzenberg, D.S., & Numan, M. (2011). Hypothalamic interaction with the mesolimbic DA system in the control of the maternal and sexual behaviors in rats. *Neuroscience & Biobehavioral Reviews, 35*(3), 826–847.

Strathearn, L., Fonagy, P., Amico, J., & Montague, P.R. (2009). Adult attachment predicts maternal brain and oxytocin response to infant cues. *Neuropsychopharmacology, 34*(13), 2655–2666.

Swain, J.E., Tasgin, E., Mayes, L.C., Feldman, R., Todd Constable, R., & Leckman, J.F. (2008). Maternal brain response to own baby-cry is affected by cesarean section delivery. *Journal of Child Psychology and Psychiatry, 49*(10), 1042–1052.

Teubert, D., & Pinquart, M. (2010). The association between coparenting and child adjustment: A meta-analysis. *Parenting: Science and Practice, 10*(4), 286–307.

Toscano, J.E., Bauman, M.D., Mason, W.A., & Amaral, D.G. (2009). Interest in infants by female rhesus monkeys with neonatal lesions of the amygdala or hippocampus. *Neuroscience, 162*(4), 881–891.

Wan, M.W., Downey, D., Strachan, H., Elliott, R., Williams, S.R., & Abel, K.M. (2014). The neural basis of maternal bonding. *PLoS One, 9*(3), e88436.

Weaver, I.C., Cervoni, N., Champagne, F.A., D'Alessio, A.C., Sharma, S., Seckl, J.R., . . . Meaney, M.J. (2004). Epigenetic programming by maternal behavior. *Nature Neuroscience, 7*(8), 847–854.

Wittfoth-Schardt, D., Gründing, J., Wittfoth, M., Lanfermann, H., Heinrichs, M., Domes, G., . . . Waller, C. (2012). Oxytocin modulates neural reactivity to children's faces as a function of social salience. *Neuropsychopharmacology, 37*(8), 1799–1807.

Wonch, K.E., de Medeiros, C.B., Barrett, J.A., Dudin, A., Cunningham, W.A., Hall, G.B., . . . Fleming, A.S. (2016). Postpartum depression and brain response to infants: Differential amygdala response and connectivity. *Social Neuroscience, 11*(6), 600–617.

Wright, J.S., & Panksepp, J. (2012). An evolutionary framework to understand foraging, wanting, and desire: The neuropsychology of the SEEKING system. *Neuropsychoanalysis, 14*(1), 5–39.

Wynne-Edwards, K.E. (2001). Hormonal changes in mammalian fathers. *Hormones and Behavior, 40*(2), 139–145. https://doi.org/10.1006/hbeh.2001.1699

Wynne-Edwards, K.E., & Reburn, C.J. (2000). Behavioral endocrinology of mammalian fatherhood. *Trends in Ecology & Evolution, 15*(11), 464–468.

18

THE SOCIAL NEUROENDOCRINOLOGY OF PREGNANCY AND BREASTFEEDING IN MOTHERS (AND OTHERS)

Jennifer Hahn-Holbrook and Colin Holbrook

Introduction

Over deep evolutionary time, the fitness advantages of the large brains and flexible cognitive and behavioral repertoires that are the hallmarks of our altricial species compensated for the fitness costs of parental investment over an extended period of child development (Kaplan, Lancaster, & Robson, 2003), favoring the selection of traits which ultimately produced psychobiological adaptations for parental nurturance and defense (Hahn-Holbrook, Holbrook, & Haselton, 2011). The neuroendocrine changes that support human parenting appear to have been co-opted and elaborated, both over evolutionary time and during ontogeny, to support nonparental forms of social attachment and affiliation (e.g., Carter, 2014; Hazan & Shaver, 1987). Thus, while phenomena addressed in this volume such as romantic bonding, friendship, or group identification doubtless constitute complex and distinct topics of study, each plausibly derives from neuroendocrine mechanisms originally evolved to enable parental caregiving. Given the centrality of hormonal changes related to pregnancy and lactation to derived modes of social affiliation, programmatic research on the social neuroendocrinology of these topics is in surprisingly short supply. We hope that the present chapter helps to inspire the next generation of researchers to fill this gap.

As the social neuroendocrinology of labor and delivery has been recently reviewed elsewhere (Saxbe, 2017), we concentrate on pregnancy and lactation. We begin with an overview of the dramatic neuroendocrine shifts characteristic of pregnancy, including emerging evidence of effects on brain physiology, behavior, and social judgment, as well as bidirectional effects of pregnancy-related shifts on fathers and other caregivers. Following childbirth, we review models of the effects of lactation on outcomes for both mother and child, with an emphasis on affiliation, stress-attenuation, and defensive maternal aggression. We conclude by highlighting a number of translationally vital and theoretically intriguing open questions demanding further research.

Pregnancy

To begin to fathom the dramatic nature of the neuroendocrine changes accompanying pregnancy, consider the remarkable fact that expectant mothers grow an entirely new organ: the placenta. The placenta responds to hormonal signals provided by both mother and fetus, creating reciprocal feedback loops between the neuroendocrine systems of the maternal-fetal dyad and producing a variety of hormones (e.g., CRH, cortisol, estradiol, estrone) to be selectively released into the maternal bloodstream or intrauterine environment (Sandman, Davis, Buss, & Glynn, 2011). Key hormones dramatically heighten during pregnancy, with the most marked changes occurring during the third trimester, when estradiol levels increase by approximately 50-fold, progesterone levels increase by approximately 10-fold (Tulchinsky, Hobel, Yeager, & Marshall, 1972), and prolactin levels increase by approximately 7-fold (Bloch, Daly, & Rubinow, 2003). One of the most remarkable neuroendocrine changes in pregnancy arises from the placenta's ability to produce corticotropin-releasing hormone (CRH). CRH produced by the placenta (pCRH) enters the maternal bloodstream at levels ranging from 60 to 700 times higher than CRH levels observed before pregnancy (Campbell et al., 1987). In contrast to CRH release from the hypothalamus in healthy non-pregnant individuals, which ultimately triggers the release of cortisol and a negative feedback dynamic restoring CRH to baseline levels (Smith & Vale, 2006), pCRH initiates a positive feed-forward process. Specifically, placental tissue exposed to cortisol up-regulates the production of pCRH, causing pCRH levels in blood to heighten exponentially over the course of pregnancy along with increases in other HPA products such as ACTH by 3-fold and total and free cortisol by 2-fold to 5-fold (Lindsay & Nieman, 2005; McLean, Thompson, Zhang, Brinsmead, & Smith, 1994). Levels of CRH in cerebrospinal fluid are higher in pregnant compared to non-pregnant women, suggesting that peripheral increases in pCRH correlate with CRH in the pregnant brain (Zaconeta et al., 2015). (Later in this chapter, we will discuss recent research suggesting that social relationships can influence trajectories of pCRH during pregnancy.)

The dramatic shifts in gonadal and neuropeptide hormones associated with the placenta, and the concomitant effects on HPA activity, halt with the expulsion of the placenta at birth. Levels of CRH typically return to pre-pregnancy levels within days, and other gonadal and steroid hormones typically return to baseline levels within a few weeks (Bloch et al., 2003). Although the dramatic hormonal shifts associated with pregnancy are temporary, evidence derived from both rodent and human studies indicates that having experienced these changes lays the foundation for attentional, behavioral, and motivational shifts away from self-directed effort and toward the provision of parental resources and protection.

Pregnancy and the maternal brain

Natural selection appears to have shaped the pattern of endocrinological changes typical of pregnancy not only to enable gestation, but to alter the social brain in parentally adaptive ways (Glynn, 2010; Kinsley & Lambert, 2008). In rodents, nulliparous females produce lasting maternal behavior following blood transfusions from pregnant rats (Terkel & Rosenblatt, 1972), and the time-sequence of changes in both the increasing levels and relative ratios of estrogen and progesterone track the onset of maternal behaviors in rats (Bridges, 1984) and macaques (Maestripieri & Zehr, 1998). Illustrative of the causal impact of pregnancy hormones on maternal motivation in nonhuman animals, treating marmosets with estradiol and progesterone in patterns parallel to those characterizing pregnancy causes non-pregnant females to press bars more often to see an infant or to silence infant distress cries (Pryce, 1996).

Estradiol and progesterone exposure during pregnancy may induce maternal behavior indirectly by heightening sensitivity to oxytocin and prolactin. Pedersen and Prange (1979) administered oxytocin to virgin rats, finding that only those females whose estradiol levels were relatively high at the time of transfusion exhibited maternal behavior. Follow-up studies confirmed that administering estradiol prior to oxytocin administration caused full maternal behavior to emerge in virtually all animals, possibly because estradiol exposure in virgin rats significantly increases oxytocin receptor binding in the medial preoptic area (arguably the region most closely linked with maternal caregiving) and the lateral septum (a key motivational region) (Champagne, Diorio, Sharma, & Meaney, 2001). Interestingly, rats whose mothers exhibited greater licking and grooming behaviors evinced increased oxytocin receptor density in the medial preoptic area and lateral septum, whereas rodents lacking comparable experience of early maternal grooming do not show changes in oxytocin receptor density in these regions despite estradiol exposure, suggesting a biological pathway for intergenerational transmission of individual differences in maternal behavior (Champagne et al., 2001). In a similar pattern, infusions of prolactin into the medial preoptic area induce maternal behavior in virgin rats previously given estradiol and progesterone – but not in untreated females (Bridges, Numan, Ronsheim, Mann, & Lupini, 1990). In sum, classic comparative work sketches how mounting estradiol and progesterone exposure over the course of pregnancy may similarly lay the foundations for the spikes in oxytocin and prolactin exposure near parturition that help to induce maternal behavior.

The limited extant work in humans broadly accords with the rodent literature suggesting that the relative ratios of estrogen and progesterone in pregnancy help to prime the maternal brain. In a longitudinal study of 177 mothers, Glynn and colleagues (2016) assessed estradiol and progesterone at five points during pregnancy, then investigated whether hormonal trajectories predicted mothers' sensitivity towards their infants during play sessions 1 year postbirth. Mothers with lower estradiol-to-progesterone ratios at 20–34 weeks of pregnancy were more sensitive to their infants' cues (but see Sollberger & Ehlert, 2016 on the complexities of using hormone ratios). These results correspond with prior findings that mothers with lower estradiol-to-progesterone ratios in early pregnancy self-report greater infant attachment at 4 days postpartum (Fleming, Ruble, Krieger, & Wong, 1997). Glynn and colleagues also found that gonadal hormone exposures were more important predictors of maternal sensitivity in first-time mothers, a parity effect that may owe to the fact that new mothers evinced higher levels of progesterone than multiparous women, possibly to further cement long-term changes in the maternal brain.

Echoing the rodent literature, a handful of human studies indicate that higher levels of oxytocin in pregnancy engender maternal behaviors postpartum (for more details on the role of oxytocin in social behavior, see the chapter by Abraham and Feldman in this handbook). For example, higher levels of plasma oxytocin over the course of human pregnancy predict maternal vocalizations (e.g., cooing), self-reported positive emotion, infant-directed eye gaze, and infant ideation (Feldman et al., 2007). Elevated plasma oxytocin levels similarly predict more frequent affectionate maternal touch during play (Feldman et al., 2010). In a complementary finding, the magnitude of the increase in oxytocin from early to late pregnancy positively predicts the quality of maternal-infant attachment (Levine et al., 2007).

While these findings jibe with experimental studies in other mammals, the human oxytocin literature has been notably characterized by controversy. For example, some researchers have observed that blood levels of oxytocin may not reflect those in the brain (McCullough, Churchland, & Mendez, 2013), whereas others have highlighted problems with replication and low statistical power (Lane, Luminet, Nave, & Mikolajczak, 2016; Walum, Waldman, & Young, 2016). One way to circumvent these methodological issues is to compare the psychology and behavior of women who are naturally exposed to high doses of oxytocin (e.g., via natural childbirth or breastfeeding) to comparable women not exposed to high doses of oxytocin (e.g., due to C-section delivery or reliance on infant formula). With regard to natural childbirth, oxytocin levels spike to induce contractions that push the baby down the birth canal, and may also play an important role in shaping the maternal brain (see Saxbe, 2017, for a review). For example, Swain and colleagues (2011) asked six mothers who delivered vaginally and six mothers who had planned cesarean sections to listen to their own babies' cries during neuroimaging, and found that vaginal childbirth was associated with greater sensitivity to their infant's cries in areas of the brain related to sensory processing, empathy, arousal, motivation, and habit-regulation – in short, key brain correlates of maternal attention and care. However, this study was low-powered and suffered the confound that individual differences in maternal motivation prior to childbirth may covary with the decision to give birth vaginally. Further research is therefore required to ascertain whether and to what extent the mode of delivery determines changes to the maternal brain.

Ideally, research in humans would include studies investigating potential interactions between gonadal hormones and the actions of oxytocin and prolactin. Recall that, in rodents, early increases in estradiol and progesterone over pregnancy help to sensitive the brains of prospective mothers to the social and anxiolytic actions of oxytocin and prolactin, which increase during labor and lactation (Champagne, Diorio, Sharma, & Meaney, 2001). Unfortunately, no studies in humans have simultaneously assessed gonadal hormones, oxytocin, and/or prolactin during pregnancy. Even when expanding beyond studies of pregnant women to the expansive oxytocin administration literature, we found only a few studies that investigated gonadal hormones and oxytocin simultaneously (Zak, Kurzban, & Matzner, 2005; Rilling et al., 2014). The lack of attention to these potential interactions likely owes to the fact that the vast majority of oxytocin administration studies have been conducted with exclusively male participants, whose estradiol and progesterone levels are rarely considered. Also, there are likely sex differences in the effects of gonadal hormones on the actions of oxytocin (Bale & Dorsa, 1995). Hence, future research to elucidate how interactions between gonadal hormones and oxytocin and prolactin shape parenting behavior should include multiple measures of these hormones in pregnancy and post-partum in samples of mothers (and their partners – more on this below).

Beyond domain-specific effects on maternal caregiving, there is also limited evidence suggesting that pregnancy-related endocrine changes may shape more general aspects of social cognition. For example, Jones et al. (2005) hypothesized that pregnant women should have evolved an aversion towards the faces of diseased people because pathogen exposure in pregnancy would be harmful for the baby. To test this, they first manipulated the apparent health of composite faces by blending them with the real faces of individuals rated by strangers as appearing 'healthy' vs. 'unhealthy'. Although this method is limited insofar as it relies on subjective assessments of health cues, Jones and colleagues found higher preferences for facial cues that were associated with health in pregnant compared to non-pregnant women. The authors conjectured that this increased preference for healthy-looking faces in pregnancy might be mediated by heightened progesterone, citing their own studies showing similar preferences observed in women taking progesterone-based birth control or during high-progesterone phases of the menstrual cycle (Jones et al., 2005). Women also appear to favor in-group over out-group members during early pregnancy, as expectant mothers have been found to display more intense ethnocentrism during the first trimester relative to the second and third trimesters of pregnancy (Navarrete, Fessler, & Eng, 2007). These shifts in preferences away from cues of ill-health or out-group membership have been hypothesized to reflect similar functional design to (1) avoid disease, particularly during the immunosuppressed period of early pregnancy when pathogen exposure would pose a greater risk, and/or (2) to affiliate with in-group members for access to protection and resources. The spike in human chorionic gonadotropin (HCG) observed during the first trimester, while untested, is a possible hormonal mediator of this out-group avoidance pattern, given that HCG helps to coordinate immune suppression in the first trimester and also correlates with pregnancy sickness, another form of pathogen avoidance (Fessler et al., 2002). While intriguing, these interpretations should be treated with caution pending replication, including direct measures of pregnancy hormones.

Co-regulation in mothers and others

Highlighting the apparent functional aspects of the neuroendocrinology of pregnancy and lactation could create the false impression that parents who do not gestate or lactate must consequently experience less love for, or commitment to, their children. To the contrary, fathers, adoptive parents, stepparents, and other caregivers develop close bonds with children via pathways independent of those neuroendocrinologically mediated by pregnancy, natural childbirth, or breastfeeding. Likewise, hormonal changes associated with pregnancy and lactation do not occur in a vacuum, and can be influenced by social relationships. Here we summarize the handful of studies reporting on how hormonal changes in fathers can impact mothers, and how social relationships with others can influence maternal hormones during pregnancy.

New research shows that neuroendocrine changes in fathers predict paternal adjustment to parenthood and, by doing so, influence maternal adjustment as well (Edelstein et al., 2017; Saxbe et al., 2016; Storey et al., 2000). For example, a study by Edelstein and colleagues (2017) assessed estradiol and testosterone three times during pregnancy in 27 first-time expectant couples and asked about relationship satisfaction and parental engagement when the child was 3 months old. Researchers observed that expectant fathers who showed greater prenatal declines in testosterone and estradiol self-reported larger contributions to household tasks and infant care postpartum. Women whose partners showed larger testosterone declines also reported receiving more social support and more help with household tasks (Edelstein et al., 2017). Moreover, within this sample, levels of testosterone in men and women were correlated at three time points during pregnancy, revealing that fathers' whose testosterone levels were in greater synchrony with mothers' testosterone levels reported greater commitment, satisfaction, and investment in their relationship with the mother postpartum (Saxbe, Schetter, Simon, Adam, & Shalowitz, 2017). Lower testosterone was also related to better maternal postpartum adjustment in a study of 149 couples that measured testosterone at 2, 9, and 15 months postpartum. This study showed that fathers with lower average testosterone levels postpartum were more likely to report symptoms of postpartum depression, whereas mothers of these lower testosterone partners were less likely to report symptoms of postpartum depression (Saxbe et al., 2017). The negative correlation between women's depressive symptoms and their partners' testosterone seemed to be mediated by the fact that women with lower testosterone partners reported greater relationship satisfaction, which in turn predicted lower levels of depressive symptoms in mothers. Hopefully, future research will illuminate whether the co-regulatory dynamics observed between mothers and fathers hold downstream consequences for infant development or long-term family dynamics.

Just as paternal hormones appear to influence mothers, research also suggests that support provided by others can influence mothers' hormones in pregnancy and related health outcomes. A study of 210 mothers found that perceived social support during pregnancy protected women against postpartum depression by dampening maternal pCRH trajectories during pregnancy (Hahn-Holbrook et al., 2013). Specifically, women who perceived themselves as enjoying greater support from their families during pregnancy evinced slower rises in pCRH during late pregnancy, mediating fewer postpartum depressive symptoms compared to women who perceived themselves as possessing relatively poor family support. In a somewhat surprising twist, however, the perceived support of fathers did not significantly influence pCRH trajectories in this sample, although perceived paternal support did attenuate subsequent depressive symptoms.

Future work may nonetheless detect effects of perceived paternal (or non-paternal partner) support on pCRH and other maternal hormones, as the null results may owe to the notable heterogeneity in types of male partner support in this sample.

Lactation

Oxytocin and prolactin are the primary hormones involved in lactation. Oxytocin facilitates smooth muscle contraction and thereby facilitates the release of breastmilk; prolactin, as the term suggests, is the primary hormone responsible for the production of milk in breast tissue. Oxytocin is released into the bloodstream to aid in milk ejection prior to breastfeeding (McNeilly, Robinson, Houston, & Howie, 1983; White-Traut et al., 2009), and this dynamic appears driven by infant cues, as mothers separated from their infants prior to feeding do not evince a prefeeding oxytocin release (McNeilly et al., 1983). As tactile nipple stimulation occurs during feeding, oxytocin and prolactin are released in pulsating patterns directed by nerve fibers linked to the hypothalamus (Gimpl & Fahrenholz, 2001). The supply/demand dynamic intrinsic to infant suckling means that timing is key in research on the social neuroendocrinology of breastfeeding. For example, oxytocin is upregulated in response to each breastfeeding session and returns to baseline shortly thereafter. Consequently, mothers who breastfeed once daily will display similar baseline oxytocin levels to non-lactating mothers unless they are either about to nurse or have recently nursed. By contrast, mothers who breastfeed in short sessions every 15 minutes or so during waking hours, as has been reported in several small-scale horticulturalist societies (Konner & Worthman1980), and as is not unusual for mothers who feed on demand, may display highly elevated levels of oxytocin throughout the day. Thus, investigators should never regard breastfeeding status alone as a reliable proxy for oxytocin or other hormone levels.

Nursing mothers typically exhibit higher overall prolactin levels than women who are not breastfeeding, although prolactin levels, like oxytocin levels, vary in proportion to breastfeeding frequency and spacing (Battin, Marrs, Fleiss, & Mishell, 1985). Unlike oxytocin, prolactin does not show an anticipatory rise before feeding (McNeilly, Robinson, Houston, & Howie, 1983), instead direct nipple stimulation is needed to cause prolactin release, with levels in blood peaking approximately 40 minutes post-feeding (Battin, Marrs, Fleiss, & Mishell, 1985). Using an electric breast pump to express milk may cause larger increases in prolactin than direct breastfeeding (Zinaman et al., 1992). Researchers should take care to consider potential moderators such as participants' breastfeeding or breast-pumping frequency, number of breastfeeding or pumping sessions over the preceding 24 hours, time since and duration of last breastfeeding or pumping session, anticipated time of the next feeding session, and percentage of the child's diet composed of breastmilk.

In addition, studies should take the age of the child into account, as milk production transitions from primarily endocrine control to autocrine control in the first week postpartum (Hill, Chatterton, & Aldag, 1999). In the endocrine control stage in the first days after birth, breastmilk production is governed by oxytocin and prolactin released from the pituitary and suckling stimulus from the infant is a less important predictor of hormone levels (e.g., mother's breasts fill with milk after birth, whether the mother breastfeeds or not). In the autocrine control stage once breastfeeding has been established, milk supply is regulated by milk transfer from the breast in a supply-and-demand system. The implication for researchers is that, in the early days postpartum, levels of oxytocin and prolactin will be less correlated with infant sucking behavior, whereas once lactation has been established, hormone levels are more tightly governed by the timing of individual feeding bouts and total milk transfer.

Breastfeeding and the maternal-child bond

One of the chief motives for breastfeeding reported by new mothers is the desire to further bond with their infants (Arora et al., 2000). Indeed, breastfeeding is frequently assumed to foster maternal behavior in the scientific literature (Jansen et al., 2008). Folk intuition notwithstanding, surprisingly few studies have actually tested this hypothesis (Jansen et al., 2008).

The release of oxytocin and prolactin linked with lactation appears integral for evoking maternal caregiving in many nonhuman species (Kendrick, 2000). In rats, injection of oxytocin (Pedersen et al., 1992) or prolactin (Bridges et al., 1985) into the brain after pregnancy experimentally triggers maternal behaviors, whereas the injection of oxytocin- or prolactin-blocking agents shortly after giving birth prevents the onset of maternal behaviors (Bridges et al., 2001; van Leengoed et al., 1987). Heightened prolactin, characteristic of lactation, also promotes maternal responses in marmosets (Dixson & George, 1982), tamarins (Ziegler et al., 2000), and mice (Voci & Carlson, 1973). Notably, however, lactation-associated hormonal shifts appear less determinative of maternal caregiving in primates, for whom social and developmental experience are more relevant to later maternal behavior (Pedersen, 2004). For instance, among rhesus monkeys, the injection of oxytocin antagonists into the brain impairs select maternal behaviors while leaving others in place (Boccia et al., 2007). Likewise, maternal behaviors often emerge in nonhuman primates in the absence of lactation (e.g., nulliparous females often carry or groom others' infants) (Hrdy, 1999; Hrdy, 2011).

Only a handful of studies have investigated whether oxytocin or prolactin predict maternal behavior in humans. Plasma oxytocin levels assessed postpartum (and during pregnancy) correlate with maternal positive vocalizations (e.g., cooing), self-reported positive emotion, infant-directed eye gaze, and infant ideation (Feldman et al., 2007). Bewilderingly, research on the effects of prolactin on parenting motivation in humans has focused almost exclusively on . . . fathers (Rilling & Young, 2014). In the lone study of human mothers that we are aware of, prolactin levels increased more after holding a doll in pregnant and postpartum women than in women without children (Delahunty, McKay, Noseworthy, & Storey, 2007). To date, no studies have provided evidence that breastfeeding-induced increases in oxytocin or prolactin influence caregiving.

Although far from direct neuroendocrine evidence, breastfeeding and bottle-feeding mothers behave detectably differently during infant interaction. Else-Quest and colleagues (2003) reported that breastfeeders displayed more positive mother-infant interactions at 12 months than formula-feeding mothers, and Nishioka and colleagues (2011) found that mothers whose infants derived most of their nutrition from breastmilk during the first 5 months reported heightened maternal bonding relative to mothers who primarily relied on formula or did not breastfeed at all. In a complementary set of findings, Britton et al. (2006) found that those mothers who were not breastfeeding by the third month reported less sensitivity to their infants' needs than those who were breastfeeding. Mothers who were still breastfeeding at 3 months (compared to those who had weaned) were rated by independent observers as evincing greater sensitivity to their infants' cues during a 30-minute play session conducted at 6 months postpartum (Jonas et al., 2015). Intriguingly, the latter association between breastfeeding and heightened maternal sensitivity was only evident among mothers who experienced a high degree of psychological stress – mothers who reported little stress evinced relatively high maternal sensitivity regardless of breastfeeding behaviors (Jonas et al., 2015). With respect to maternal sensitivity to cues of infant distress, a large longitudinal study of 675 mother-infant dyads found that the amount of time spent breastfeeding predicted greater maternal sensitivity at 14 months (Tharner et al., 2012), and a functional neuroimaging paradigm revealed greater activation of brain regions implicated in maternal-infant bonding and empathy in response to hearing their infant cry among exclusively breastfeeding mothers compared to exclusively formula-feeding mothers at 1 month after childbirth (Kim et al., 2011).

Although the foregoing results broadly accord with the claim that breastfeeding facilitates maternal bonding and caregiving, no firm conclusions may yet be drawn given the potential self-selection factors independent of the effects of breastfeeding. Indeed, mothers who express a willingness to breastfeed while pregnant also report greater maternal sensitivity at 3 months, and this prior willingness to breastfeed correlates with the reported strength of the mother-infant bond (Britton et al., 2006). In addition, the quality of mother-infant bonding observed 2 days following parturition predicts exclusive breastfeeding at 6 months (Cernadas et al., 2003), suggesting that it is bonding that contributes to breastfeeding duration rather than the reverse. Further, it is unclear at the time of writing whether the heighted maternal sensitivity associated with breastfeeding may be somewhat accounted for by the experience of frequent, close contact between mothers and infants as opposed to the neuroendocrine effects of lactation. It is also important to stress that, regardless of whether breastfeeding may help to facilitate maternal sensitivity, the formula-feeding mothers in the studies discussed above displayed maternal sensitivity well within a normal range. Thus, additional research is required to clarify both the extent and the means by which breastfeeding may influence bonding or related outcomes such as maternal sensitivity.

Approaching maternal-infant bonding from the infant's perspective, breastfeeding could plausibly facilitate attachment for a number of reasons, including direct skin-to-skin contact between mother and child, encouragement of early maternal-child social interactions, and the calming effect of the sucking reflex. Here again, however, surprisingly few studies have investigated the putative relationship between breastfeeding and infant attachment, and those that have reveal a mixed empirical picture (Jansen et al., 2008). For example, in a study of 152 mother-infant pairs examining the association between breastfeeding and the quality of infant attachment by the first year of life, infants who had been breastfed displayed comparable secure maternal attachment to infants who had been formula-fed (Britton et al., 2006). This result may reflect the fact that infants are evolutionarily motivated to develop secure attachment relationships with non-lactating caregivers (e.g., fathers). However, breastfed infants have also been found more likely than formula-fed infants to orient their bodies towards gauze pads carrying the scent of their mothers than to gauze pads carrying the scent of unfamiliar breastfeeding women at the second week of life, consistent with the premise that breastfeeding facilitates early recognition of and attraction to maternal scent (Cernoch & Porter, 1985).

Moving from mode of consumption to the biopsychosocial effects of breastmilk itself, emerging research suggests that exposure to bioactive hormones in breastmilk may shape infant temperament. In a recent study, for example, infants exposed to higher levels of milk cortisol scored higher in negative affect in comparison to infants whose milk possessed relatively low cortisol (Grey, Davis, Sandman, & Glynn, 2013), a relationship which was not accounted for by covarying environmental factors (e.g., maternal education, age, or income) nor by negative maternal affect (e.g., depression and perceived stress). This finding converges with research showing that circulating infant cortisol levels are more closely correlated with circulating maternal cortisol in breastfed infants compared to formula-feeders (Glynn et al., 2007). Interestingly, a somewhat distinct effect of milk cortisol on infant temperament has been reported among rhesus macaques (Hinde et al., 2015), in that higher levels of milk cortisol were found to predict greater social confidence. Notably, studies suggest that early exposure to milk cortisol also shapes body composition, with higher milk cortisol exposure predicting heavier monkeys (Hinde et al., 2015) and taller humans (Hahn-Holbrook et al., 2016). While further work is needed, this overall pattern of findings suggests that lactation may be regarded as a veritable 'fourth trimester', during which breastmilk provides a direct conduit between the endocrine systems of mother and infant, shaping both physical and psychological development.

Breastfeeding attenuates maternal social stress

Maternal caregiving can be intensely challenging, particularly during the initial months following childbirth. Maternal stressors run the gamut from sexual dysfunction and sleep deprivation (Gjerdingen et al., 1993) to preoccupations with being a 'good' mother. New parents also typically experience a sustained state of heightened vigilance toward potential hazards to children largely instantiated within neurobiological stress systems (Hahn-Holbrook et al., 2011). Understandably, given the array of demands placed on new mothers, approximately 20% report depressive symptoms within the first year following childbirth (Gavin et al., 2005; Hahn-Holbrook, Cornwell-Hinrichs, & Anaya, 2017). Deleterious levels of maternal stress adversely affect child health and behavior outcomes, suggesting that selection pressures favored mechanisms to attenuate maternal stress during early childhood, and which might be expected to efficiently co-opt time-matched adaptations for lactation. Indeed, breastfeeders display lower cardiovascular stress reactions (e.g., higher cardiac parasympathetic control, lower basal systolic blood pressure) than formula-feeders or nulliparous women to the Trier Social Stress Task (Altemus et al., 2001), and similar cardiovascular benefits have been observed in breastfeeding mothers during the period of anxious anticipation prior to the Trier ordeal (Light et al., 2000). The stress-reducing effects of lactation appear to be particularly notable immediately following feeding sessions, as mothers who breastfeed just before the Trier task display blunted hormonal cortisol responses in comparison to control breastfeeding mothers who hold their infants without nursing (Heinrichs et al., 2001). A number of studies indicate that breastfeeders experience greater emotional equanimity and positive mood, as well as diminished anxiety, relative to formula-feeding mothers (Altshuler et al., 2000; Carter & Altemus, 1997). Crucially, the aforementioned differences between breastfeeders and formula-feeders persist when controlling for potential confounds such as differences in income, age, health, or employment (Mezzacappa & Katlin, 2002).

Oxytocin and prolactin appear integral to the stress-attenuation effects of breastfeeding. Oxytocin mediates lactation-related reductions in stress in rodent experiments (Neumann et al., 2000), with comparable results observed with regard to prolactin (Freeman et al., 2000). In humans, correlational studies similarly show that both higher plasma oxytocin and prolactin predict reductions in early postpartum anxiety (Nissen et al., 1998). Complementarily, mothers who release relatively greater levels of oxytocin in response to suckling display lower cortisol (Chiodera et al., 1991). In sum, the overall pattern of findings derived from both comparative and human studies suggests that lactation attenuates social stress, and that these effects are likely mediated by increases in oxytocin and prolactin, although direct evidence for the roles played by oxytocin and prolactin in buffering human maternal stress is quite thin at present.

Breastfeeding and maternal aggression

As a singularly altricial species, humans invest enormous resources in relatively few, highly vulnerable offspring who require protection over a period of years. Given the high fitness stakes, human mothers are likely to have evolved mechanisms to facilitate protection of their young against potentially dangerous conspecifics and predators, particularly during the early period of greatest infant helplessness. Fellow humans posed a serious risk to infants in the ancestral past, particularly unrelated males whose reproductive incentives conflicted with those of mothers and their children (Hrdy, 1999; Hahn-Holbrook et al., 2010). In many other mammals, lactation coincides with a period of heightened defensive aggression toward hostile conspecifics or predators characteristic of the months following birth (Lonstein & Gammie, 2002). In rats, the release of oxytocin and prolactin during lactation increases aggression toward potentially threatening conspecifics (Hansen & Ferreira, 1986), and a parallel dynamic has recently been documented in human mothers. In a behavioral paradigm, breastfeeders evinced lower systolic blood pressure (a proxy of stress) and were more aggressive (i.e., administering louder, longer aversive sound bursts) during a conflictual encounter with a confederate than were either formula-feeding mothers or women who had never given birth, suggesting that you may not want to steal a breastfeeder's parking space (Hahn-Holbrook et al., 2011).

Conclusion

The discoveries regarding the social neuroendocrinology of pregnancy and lactation accumulated to date have both challenged common assumptions and illuminated key biopsychosocial determinants of maternal and infant well-being. Remarkable though the extant literature may be, the relative dearth of human studies and over-reliance on indirect proxies rather than actual biological measures are frankly concerning given the theoretical and translational importance of these issues. Consider, for example, that only one study to date has investigated how prolactin influences maternal behavior (Delahunty et al., 2007), whereas many studies have examined the effects of prolactin on fathers (Gangestad & Grebe, 2017). Without speculating unduly into the biases underlying such an asymmetry – which is absurd on its face given the central role of prolactin in lactation and the abundance of comparative work indicating an important role in maternal anxiety-reduction and maternal motivation – it seems fair to suggest that the community of scholars may have deprioritized understanding the psychobiology of human motherhood.

On a more optimistic note, any number of enticing research opportunities are now available to the enterprising social neuroendocrinologist. To cite just one direction, the emerging indications of a rich bidirectional interplay between the endocrine systems of expectant mothers and others raises provocative possibilities with regard to effects on mothers' alloparenting kin (e.g., siblings) and friends. Similarly, with respect to breastfeeding, researchers might examine the extent to which mothers' local environments (e.g., harsh, resource-poor, and/or dangerous social settings) may be transmitted to their infants via mother's milk, with potentially lifelong personality effects (e.g., risk tolerance as an adaptive response to uncertain environments). The gold standard for future research needed to test such hypotheses will be longitudinal studies incorporating both biological and psychosocial measures. However, experimental approaches are also invaluable given the inherent limitations of correlational research. In particular, experimentally manipulating natural parental behaviors (e.g., randomly assigning mothers to breast-feed vs. hold their baby) affords social neuroendocrinologists ready alternatives to reliance on methods such as the administration of synthetic oxytocin or prolactin, which may not invoke physiologically normal or ecologically valid responses. Finally, very little research has yet been conducted on the impact of either pregnancy or breastfeeding on mothers' social interactions with romantic partners, fellow caregivers, unrelated children, or strangers, although the limited work that has been done hints at the existence of a range of functional shifts. From our vantage point here in the early 21st century, research on how mind, brain, body, and social context conspire to produce parental behavior has taken important first steps, but there's considerable growing up left to do.

References

Altemus, M., Redwine, L.S., Leong, Y.M., Frye, C.A., Porges, S.W., & Carter, C.S. (2001). Responses to laboratory psychosocial stress in postpartum women. *Psychosomatic Medicine, 63*(5), 814–821. doi:0033-3174/01/6305-0814

Altshuler, L.L., Hendrick, V., & Cohen, L.S. (2000). An update on mood and anxiety disorders during pregnancy and the postpartum period. *Primary Care Companion to the Journal of Clinical Psychiatry, 2*(6), 217–222.

Arora, S., McJunkin, C., Wehrer, J., & Kuhn, P. (2000). Major factors influencing breastfeeding rates: Mother's perception of father's attitude and milk supply. *Pediatrics, 106*(5), e67–e67. doi:10.1542/peds.106.5.e67

Bale, T.L., & Dorsa, D.M. (1995). Sex differences in and effects of estrogen on oxytocin receptor messenger ribonucleic acid expression in the ventromedial hypothalamus. *Endocrinology, 136*(1), 27–32. doi:10.1210/endo.136.1.7828541

Battin, D.A., Marrs, R.P., Fleiss, P.M., & Mishell, D.R., Jr. (1985). Effect of suckling on serum prolactin, luteinizing hormone, follicle-stimulating hormone, and estradiol during prolonged lactation. *Obstetrics & Gynecology, 65*(6), 785–788.

Bloch, M., Daly, R.C., & Rubinow, D.R. (2003). Endocrine factors in the etiology of postpartum depression. *Comprehensive Psychiatry, 44*, 234–246. doi:10.1016/S0010-440X(03)00034-8

Boccia, M.L., Goursaud, A.P., Bachevalier, J., Anderson, K.D., & Pedersen, C.A. (2007). Peripherally administered non-peptide oxytocin antagonist, L368, 899, accumulates in limbic brain areas: A new pharmacological tool for the study of social motivation in non-human primates. *Hormones and Behavior, 52*(3), 344–351. doi:10.1016/j.yhbeh.2007.05.009

Bridges, R.S. (1984). A quantitative analysis of the roles of dosage, sequence, and duration of estradiol and progesterone exposure in the regulation of maternal behavior in the rat. *Endocrinology, 114*(3), 930–940.

Bridges, R.S., DiBiase, R., Loundes, D.D., & Doherty, P.C. (1985). Prolactin stimulation of maternal behavior in female rats. *Science, 227*(4688), 782–784. doi:10.1210/endo-114-3-930

Bridges, R.S., Numan, M., Ronsheim, P.M., Mann, P.E., & Lupini, C.E. (1990). Central prolactin infusions stimulate maternal behavior in steroid-treated, nulliparous female rats. *Proceedings of the National Academy of Sciences, 87*(20), 8003–8007.

Bridges, R.S., Rigero, B.A., Byrnes, E.M., Yang, L., & Walker, A.M. (2001). Central infusions of the recombinant human prolactin receptor antagonist, S179D-PRL, delay the onset of maternal behavior in steroid-primed, nulliparous female rats. *Endocrinology, 142*(2), 730–739. doi:10.1210/endo.142.2.7931

Britton, J.R., Britton, H.L., & Gronwaldt, V. (2006). Breastfeeding, sensitivity, and attachment. *Pediatrics, 118*(5), e1436–e1443. doi:10.1542/peds.2005-2916

Campbell, E.A., Linton, E.A., Wolfe, C.D.A., Scraggs, P.R., Jones, M.T., & Lowry, P.J. (1987). Plasma corticotropin-releasing hormone during pregnancy and parturition. *Journal of Clinical Metabolism, 63*, 1054–1059. doi:10.1210/jcem-64-5-1054

Carter, C.S. (2014). Oxytocin pathways and the evolution of human behavior. *Annual Review of Psychology, 65*, 17–39. doi:10.1146/annurev-psych-010213-115110

Carter, C.S., & Altemus, M. (1997). Integrative functions of lactational hormones in social behavior and stress management. *Annals of the New York Academy of Sciences, 807*, 164–174. doi:10.1111/j.1749-6632.1997.tb51918.x

Cernadas, J.M., Noceda, G., Barrera, L., Martinez, A.M., & Garsd, A. (2003). Maternal and perinatal factors influencing the duration of exclusive breastfeeding during the first 6 months of life. *Journal of Human Lactation, 19*(2), 136–144.

Cernoch, J.M., & Porter, R.H. (1985). Recognition of maternal axillary odors by infants. *Child Development, 56*(6), 1593–1598. doi:10.1177/0890334403253292

Champagne, F., Diorio, J., Sharma, S., & Meaney, M.J. (2001). Naturally occurring variations in maternal behavior in the rat are associated with differences in estrogen-inducible central oxytocin receptors. *Proceedings of the National Academy of Sciences, 98*(22), 12736–12741. doi:10.1073/pnas.221224598

Chiodera, P., Salvarani, C., Bacchi-Modena, A., Spallanzani, R., Cigarini, C., Alboni, A., Gardini, E., & Coiro, V. (1991). Relationship between plasma profiles of oxytocin and adrenocorticotropic hormone during suckling or breast stimulation in women. *Hormone Research, 35*(3–4), 119–123. doi:10.1159/000181886

Delahunty, K.M., McKay, D.W., Noseworthy, D.E., & Storey, A.E. (2007). Prolactin responses to infant cues in men and women: Effects of parental experience and recent infant contact. *Hormones and Behavior, 51*(2), 213–220. doi:10.1016/j.yhbeh.2006.10.004

Dixson, A., & George, A. (1982). Prolactin and parental behavior in a male new world primate. *Nature, 299*, 551–553. doi:10.1038/299551a0

Edelstein, R.S., Chopik, W.J., Saxbe, D.E., Wardecker, B.M., Moors, A.C., & LaBelle, O.P. (2017). Prospective and dyadic associations between expectant parents' prenatal hormone changes and postpartum parenting outcomes. *Developmental Psychobiology, 59*(1), 77–90. doi:10.1002/dev.21469

Else-Quest, N.M., Hyde, J.S., & Clark, R. (2003). Breastfeeding, bonding, and the mother-infant relationship. *Journal of Developmental Psychology, 49*(4), 495–517. doi:10.1353/mpq.2003.0020

Feldman, R., Weller, A., Zagoory-Sharon, O., & Levine, A. (2007). Evidence for a neuroendocrinological foundation of human affiliation: Plasma oxytocin levels across pregnancy and the postpartum period predict mother-infant bonding. *Psychological Science, 18*(11), 965–970. doi:10.1111/j.1467-9280.2007.02010.x

Feldman, R., Gordon, I., Schneiderman, I., Weisman, O., & Zagoory-Sharon, O. (2010). Natural variations in maternal and paternal care are associated with systematic changes in oxytocin following parent-infant contact. *Psychoneuroendocrinology, 35*(8), 1133–1141. doi:10.1016/j.psyneuen.2010.01.013.

Fleming, A. S., Ruble, D., Krieger, H., & Wong, P. Y. (1997). Hormonal and experiential correlates of maternal responsiveness during pregnancy and the puerperium in human mothers. *Hormones and Behavior, 31*(2), 145–158.

Freeman, M.E., Kanyicska, B., Lerant, A., & Nagy, G. (2000). Prolactin: Structure, function, and regulation of secretion. *Physiological Reviews, 80*(4), 1523–1631. doi:10.1152/physrev.2000.80.4.1523

Fessler, D.T., Bayley, T., Dye, L., Brown, J., Flaxman, S., Leeners, B., . . . Tepper, B. (2002). Reproductive immunosuppression and diet: An evolutionary perspective on pregnancy sickness and meat consumption. *Current Anthropology, 43*(1), 19–61. doi:10.1086/324128

Gangestad, S.W., & Grebe, N.M. (2017). Hormonal systems, human social bonding, and affiliation. *Hormones and Behavior, 91*, 122–135. doi:10.1016/j.yhbeh.2016.08.005

Gavin, N.I., Gaynes, B.N., Lohr, K.N., Meltzer-Brody, S., Gartlehner, G., & Swinson, T. (2005). Perinatal depression: A systematic review of prevalence and incidence. *Obstetrics & Gynecology, 106*, 1071–1083. doi:10.1097/01.AOG.0000183597.31630.db

Gimpl, G., & Fahrenholz, F. (2001). The oxytocin receptor system: Structure, function, and regulation. *Physiological Reviews, 81*(2), 629–683. doi:10.1152/physrev.2001.81.2.629

Gjerdingen, D.K., Froberg, D.G., Chaloner, K.M., & McGovern, P.M. (1993). Changes in women's physical health during the first postpartum year. *Archives of Family Medicine, 2*(3), 277–283.

Glynn, L.M. (2010). Giving birth to a new brain: Hormone exposures of pregnancy influence human memory. *Psychoneuroendocrinology, 35*(8), 1148–1155. doi:10.1016/j.psyneuen.2010.01.015

Glynn, L., Davis, E.P., Dunkel Schetter, C., Chicz-Demet, A., Hobel, C.J., & Sandman, C.A. (2007). Postnatal maternal cortisol levels predict temperament in healthy breastfed infants. *Early Human Development, 83*, 675–681. doi:10.1016/j.earlhumdev.2007.01.003

Glynn, L.M., Davis, E.P., Sandman, C.A., & Goldberg, W.A. (2016). Gestational hormone profiles predict human maternal behavior at 1-year postpartum. *Hormones and Behavior, 85*, 19–25. doi:10.1016/j.yhbeh.2016.07.002

Grey, K.R., Davis, E.P., Sandman, C.A., & Glynn, L.M. (2013). Human milk cortisol is associated with infant temperament. *Psychoneuroendocrinology, 38*(7), 1178–1185. doi:10.1016/j.psyneuen.2012.11.002

Hahn-Holbrook, J., Cornwell-Hinrichs, T., & Anaya, I. (2017). Economic and health predictors of national postpartum depression prevalence: A systematic review, meta-analysis and meta-regression of 291 studies from 56 countries. *Frontiers in Psychiatry, 8*, 248. doi:10.3389/fpsyt.2017.00248

Hahn-Holbrook, J., Holbrook, C., & Bering, J. (2010). Snakes, spiders, strangers: How the evolved fear of strangers may misdirect efforts to protect children from harm. In J.M. Lampinen & K. Sexton-Radek (Eds.), *Protecting children from violence: Evidence-based interventions*. New York, NY: Psychology Press.

Hahn-Holbrook, J., Holbrook, C., & Haselton, M.G. (2011). Parental precaution: Neurobiological means and adaptive ends. *Neuroscience & Biobehavioral Reviews, 35*(4), 1052–1066. doi:10.1016/j.neubiorev.2010.09.015

Hahn-Holbrook, J., Le, T.B., Chung, A., Davis, E.P., & Glynn, L.M. (2016). Cortisol in human milk predicts child BMI. *Obesity, 24*(12), 2471–2474. doi:10.1002/oby.21682

Hahn-Holbrook, J., Dunkel Schetter, C., Arora, C., & Hobel, C.J. (2013). Placental corticotropin-releasing hormone mediates the association between prenatal social support and postpartum depression. *Clinical Psychological Science, 1*(3), 253–265. doi:10.1177/2167702612470646

Hansen, S., & Ferreira, A. (1986). Food intake, aggression, and fear behavior in the mother rat: Control by neural systems concerned with milk ejection and maternal behavior. *Behavioral Neuroscience, 100*(1), 64–70. doi:10.1037/0735-7044.100.1.64

Hazan, C., & Shaver, P. (1987). Romantic love conceptualized as an attachment process. *Journal of Personality and Social Psychology, 52*, 511–524. doi:10.1037/0022-3514.52.3.511

Heinrichs, M., Meinlschmidt, G., Neumann, I., Wagner, S., Kirschbaum, C., Ehlert, U., & Hellhammer, D.H. (2001). Effects of suckling on hypothalamic–pituitary–adrenal axis responses to psychosocial stress in postpartum lactating women. *Journal of Clinical Endocrinology & Metabolism, 86*(10), 4798–4804. doi:10.1210/jcem.86.10.7919

Hinde, K., Skibiel, A.L., Foster, A.B., Del Rosso, L., Mendoza, S.P., & Capitanio, J.P. (2015). Cortisol in mother's milk across lactation reflects maternal life history and predicts infant temperament. *Behavioral Ecology, 26*(1), 269–281. doi:10.1093/beheco/aru186

Hill, P.D., Chatterton, R.T., Jr., & Aldag, J.C. (1999). Serum prolactin in breastfeeding: State of the science. *Biological Research for Nursing, 1*(1), 65–75. doi:10.1177/109980049900100109

Hrdy, S.B. (1999). *Mother nature: A history of mothers, infants, and natural selection.* New York, NY: Pantheon Books.

Hrdy, S.B. (2011). *Mothers and others.* Cambridge, MA: Harvard University Press.

Jansen, J., de Weerth, C., & Riksen-Walraven, J.M. (2008). Breastfeeding and the mother-infant relationship – a review. *Developmental Review, 28*(4), 503–521. doi:10.1016/j.dr.2008.07.001

Jonas, W., Atkinson, L., Steiner, M., Meaney, M.J., Wazana, A., & Fleming, A.S. (2015). Breastfeeding and maternal sensitivity predict early infant temperament. *Acta Paediatrica, 104*(7), 678–686. doi:10.1111/apa.12987.

Jones, B.C., Perrett, D.I., Little, A.C., Boothroyd, L., Cornwell, R.E., Feinberg, D.R., . . . Burt, D.M. (2005). Menstrual cycle, pregnancy and oral contraceptive use alter attraction to apparent health in faces. *Proceedings of the Royal Society of London B: Biological Sciences, 272*(1561), 347–354. doi:10.1098/rspb.2004.2962

Kaplan, H., Lancaster, J., & Robson, A. (2003). Embodied capital and the evolutionary economics of the human life span. *Population and Development Review, 29*, 152–182.

Kendrick, K.M. (2000). Oxytocin, motherhood and bonding. *Experimental Physiology, 85*, 111S–124S.

Kim, P., Feldman, R., Mayes, L.C., Eicher, V., Thompson, N., Leckman, J.F., & Swain, J.E. (2011). Breast-feeding, brain activation to own infant cry, and maternal sensitivity. *Journal of Child Psychology and Psychiatry, 52*(8), 907–915. doi:10.1111/j.1469-7610.2011.02406.x

Kinsley, C.H., & Lambert, K.G. (2008). Reproduction-induced neuroplasticity: Natural behavioural and neuronal alterations associated with the production and care of offspring. *Journal of Neuroendocrinology, 20*(4), 515–525. doi:10.1111/j.1365-2826.2008.01667.x

Konner, M., & Worthman, C. (1980). Nursing frequency, gonadal function, and birth spacing among! Kung hunter-gatherers. *Science, 207*(4432), 788–791.

Lane, A., Luminet, O., Nave, G., & Mikolajczak, M. (2016). Is there a publication bias in behavioural intra-nasal oxytocin research on humans? Opening the file drawer of one laboratory. *Journal of Neuroendocrinology, 28*(4). doi:10.1111/jne.12384

Levine, A., Zagoory-Sharon, O., Feldman, R., & Weller, A. (2007). Oxytocin during pregnancy and early postpartum: Individual patterns and maternal-fetal attachment. *Peptides, 28*(6), 1162–1169. doi:10.1016/j.peptides.2007.04.016

Light, K.C., Smith, T.E., Johns, J.M., Brownley, K.A., Hofheimer, J.A., & Amico, J.A. (2000). Oxytocin responsivity in mothers of infants: A preliminary study of relationships with blood pressure during laboratory stress and normal ambulatory activity. *Health Psychology, 19*(6), 560–567. doi:10.1037/0278-6133.19.6.560

Lindsay, J.R., & Nieman, L.K. (2005). The hypothalamic-pituitary-adrenal axis in pregnancy: Challenges in disease detection and treatment. *Endocrine Reviews, 26*(6), 775–799. doi:10.1210/er.2004-0025

Lonstein, J.S., & Gammie, S.C. (2002). Sensory, hormonal, and neural control of maternal aggression in laboratory rodents. *Neuroscience and Biobehavioral Reviews, 26*(8), 869–888. doi:10.1016/S0149-7634(02)00087-8

Maestripieri, D., & Zehr, J.L. (1998). Maternal responsiveness increases during pregnancy and after estrogen treatment in macaques. *Hormones and Behavior, 34*(3), 223–230.

McCullough, M.E., Churchland, P.S., & Mendez, A.J. (2013). Problems with measuring peripheral oxytocin: Can the data on oxytocin and human behavior be trusted? *Neuroscience & Biobehavioral Reviews, 37*(8), 1485–1492. doi:10.1006/hbeh.1998.1470

McLean, M., Thompson, D., Zhang, H.P., Brinsmead, M., & Smith, R. (1994). Corticotropin-releasing hormone and beta-endorphin in labour. *European Journal of Endocrinology, 131*, 167–172. doi:10.1530/acta.0.1280339

McNeilly, A.S., Robinson, I.C., Houston, M.J., & Howie, P.W. (1983). Release of oxytocin and prolactin in response to suckling. *British Medical Journal (Clinical Research Ed.)*, *286*(6361), 257–259.

Mezzacappa, E.S., & Katlin, E.S. (2002). Breast-feeding is associated with reduced perceived stress and negative mood in mothers. *Health Psychology*, *21*(2), 187–193. doi:10.1037/0278-6133.21.2.187

Navarrete, C.D., Fessler, D.M.T., & Eng, S.J. (2007). Elevated ethnocentrism in the first trimester of pregnancy. *Evolution and Human Behavior*, *28*(1), 60–65. doi:10.1016/j.evolhumbehav.2006.06.002

Neumann, I.D., Torner, L., & Wigger, A. (2000). Brain oxytocin: Differential inhibition of neuroendocrine stress responses and anxiety-related behaviour in virgin, pregnant and lactating rats. *Neuroscience*, *95*(2), 567–575. doi:10.1016/S0306-4522(99)00433-9

Nishioka, E., Haruna, M., Ota, E., Matsuzaki, M., Murayama, R., Yoshimura, K., & Murashima, S. (2011). A prospective study of the relationship between breastfeeding and postpartum depressive symptoms appearing at 1–5 months after delivery. *Journal of Affective Disorders*, *133*(3), 553–559. doi:10.1155/2016/4765310

Nissen, E., Gustavsson, P., Widström, A.M., & Uvnäs-Moberg, K. (1998). Oxytocin, prolactin, milk production and their relationship with personality traits in women after vaginal delivery or Cesarean section. *Journal of Psychosomatic Obstetrics & Gynecology*, *19*, 49–58. doi:10.3109/01674829809044221

Pedersen, C.A., Caldwell, J.D., Peterson, G., Walker, C.H., & Mason, G.A. (1992). Oxytocin activation of maternal behavior in the rat. *Annals of the New York Academy of Sciences*, *652*(1), 58–69. doi:10.1111/j.1749-6632.1992.tb34346.x

Pedersen, C.A., & Prange, A.J. (1979). Induction of maternal behavior in virgin rats after intracerebroventricular administration of oxytocin. *Proceedings of the National Academy of Sciences*, *76*(12), 6661–6665. doi:10.1016/0031-9384(81)90002-0

Pedersen, C.A. (2004). Biological aspects of social bonding and the roots of human violence. *Annals of the New York Academy of Sciences*, *1036*(1), 106–127. doi:10.1196/annals.1330.006

Pryce, C.R. (1996). Socialization, hormones, and the regulation of maternal behavior in nonhuman simian primates. *Advances in the Study of Behavior*, *25*, 423–473. doi:10.1016/S0065-3454(08)60340-X

Rilling, J.K., DeMarco, A.C., Hackett, P.D., Chen, X., Gautam, P., Stair, S., . . . Pagnoni, G. (2014). Sex differences in the neural and behavioral response to intranasal oxytocin and vasopressin during human social interaction. *Psychoneuroendocrinology*, *39*, 237–248. doi:10.1016/j.psyneuen.2013.09.022.

Rilling, J.K., & Young, L.J. (2014). The biology of mammalian parenting and its effect on offspring social development. *Science*, *345*(6198), 771–776. doi:10.1126/science.1252723

Sandman, C.A., Davis, E.P., Buss, C., & Glynn, L.M. (2011). Prenatal programming of human neurological function. *International Journal of Peptides*, 2011, 837596. doi:10.1155/2011/837596

Saxbe, D.E. (2017). Birth of a new perspective? A call for biopsychosocial research on childbirth. *Current Directions in Psychological Science*, *26*(1), 81–86. doi:10.1177/0963721416677096

Saxbe, D.E., Edelstein, R.S., Lyden, H.A., Wardecker, B.M., Chopik, W.J., & Moors, A.C. (2016). Fathers' prenatal testosterone decline and synchrony with partner testosterone predicts greater postpartum relationship investment. *Hormones and Behavior*, *90*, 39–47. doi:10.1016/j.yhbeh.2016.07.005.

Saxbe, D.E., Schetter, C.D., Simon, C.D., Adam, E.K., & Shalowitz, M.U. (2017). High paternal testosterone may protect against postpartum depressive symptoms in fathers, but confer risk to mothers and children. *Hormones and behavior*, *95*, 103–112. doi:10.1016/j.yhbeh.2017.07.014.

Smith, S.M., & Vale, W.W. (2006). The role of the hypothalamic-pituitary-adrenal axis in neuroendocrine responses to stress. *Dialogues in Clinical Neuroscience*, *8*, 383–395.

Sollberger, S., & Ehlert, U. (2016). How to use and interpret hormone ratios. *Psychoneuroendocrinology*, *63*, 385–397. doi:10.1016/j.psyneuen.2015.09.031

Storey, A.E., Walsh, C.J., Quinton, R.L., & Wynne-Edwards, K.E. (2000). Hormonal correlates of paternal responsiveness in new and expectant fathers. *Evolution and Human Behavior*, *21*(2), 79–95. doi:10.1016/S1090-5138(99)00042-2

Swain, J.E., Kim, P., & Ho, S.S. (2011). Neuroendocrinology of parental response to baby-cry. *Journal of Neuroendocrinology*, *23*(11), 1036–1041. doi:10.1111/j.1365-2826.2011.02212.x

Terkel, J., & Rosenblatt, J.S. (1972). Humoral factors underlying maternal behavior at parturition: Cross transfusion between freely moving rats. *Journal of Comparative and Physiological Psychology*, *80*(3), 365. doi:10.1037/h0032965

Tharner, A., Luijk, M.P., Raat, H., IJzendoorn, M.H., Bakermans-Kranenburg, M.J., Moll, H.A., . . . Tiemeier, H. (2012). Breastfeeding and its relation to maternal sensitivity and infant attachment. *Journal of Developmental and Behavioral Pediatrics*, *33*(5), 396–404. doi:10.1097/DBP.0b013e318257fac3

Tulchinsky, D., Hobel, C.J., Yeager, E., & Marshall, J.R. (1972). Plasma estrone, estradiol, estriol, progesterone, and 17-hydroxyprogesterone in human pregnancy. *American Journal of Obstetrics & Gynecology, 112,* 1095–1100. doi:10.1016/0002-9378(72)90185-8

Walum, H., Waldman, I.D., & Young, L.J. (2016). Statistical and methodological considerations for the interpretation of intranasal oxytocin studies. *Biological Psychiatry, 79*(3), 251–257. doi:10.1016/0002-9378(72)90185-8

White-Traut, R., Watanabe, K., Pournajafi-Nazarloo, H., Schwertz, D., Bell, A., & Carter, S. (2009). Detection of salivary oxytocin levels in lactating women. *Developmental Psychobiology, 51*(4), 367–373. doi:10.1002/dev.20376

Van Leengoed, E., Kerker, E., & Swanson, H.H. (1987). Inhibition of post-partum maternal behaviour in the rat by injecting an oxytocin antagonist into the cerebral ventricles. *Journal of Endocrinology, 112*(2), 275–282. doi:10.1677/joe.0.1120275

Voci, V.E., & Carlson, N.R. (1973). Enhancement of maternal behavior and nest building following systemic and diencephalic administration of prolactin and progesterone in the mouse. *Journal of Comparative and Physiological Psychology, 83*(3), 388–393. doi:10.1037/h0034663

Zaconeta, A.M., Amato, A.A., Barra, G.B., Casulari da Motta, L.D., de Souza, V.C., Karnikowski, M.G.D.O., & Casulari, L.A. (2015). Cerebrospinal fluid CRH levels in late pregnancy are not associated with new-onset postpartum depressive symptoms. *The Journal of Clinical Endocrinology & Metabolism, 100*(8), 3159–3164. doi:10.1210/jc.2014-4503.

Zak, P.J., Kurzban, R., & Matzner, W.T. (2005). Oxytocin is associated with human trustworthiness. *Hormones and Behavior, 48*(5), 522–527. doi:10.1016/j.yhbeh.2005.07.009

Ziegler, T.E., Carlson, A.A., Ginther, A.J., & Snowdon, C.T. (2000). Gonadal source of testosterone metabolites in urine of male cotton-top tamarin monkeys (*Saguinus oedipus*). *General and Comparative Endocrinology, 118,* 332–343. doi:10.1006/gcen.2000.7476

Zinaman, M.J., Queenan, J.T., Labbok, M.H., Albertson, B., & Hughes, V. (1992). Acute prolactin and oxytocin responses and milk yield to infant suckling and artificial methods of expression in lactating women. *Pediatrics, 89*(3), 437–440.

19

THE NEUROENDOCRINOLOGY OF FATHERHOOD

Patty X. Kuo and Lee T. Gettler

Although fathers are still largely underrepresented in studies of child development, compared to mothers, it is now widely recognized that fathers make important contributions to the health and developmental trajectories of their children (Lamb, 2004). As part of increasing interest in understanding how variations in human fathering are related to neuroendocrine systems, a growing body of research has uncovered that testosterone, prolactin, cortisol, oxytocin, and arginine vasopressin (AVP) are broadly related to fathering and fatherhood (Gettler, 2014; Gray, McHale, & Carré, 2017; Rilling, 2013; Storey & Ziegler, 2016; Trumble, Jaeggi, & Gurven, 2015; van Anders et al., 2011). Although scholars have theorized that the associations between hormones and parenting are dependent on social context (van Anders et al., 2011), previous reviews have yet to delineate how these hormones are related to different facets of fathering, with most focusing on fatherhood status and generic quantity of paternal care measures. In this chapter, we offer a context-based framework to understand the social neuroendocrinology of fatherhood and identify strengths and weaknesses of previous research. This chapter has three major goals: (1) summarize relevant theoretical frameworks to understanding neuroendocrine systems and fathering, (2) review literature based on measured paternal outcomes, and (3) offer suggestions for future directions.

Theories relevant to hormones and parenting

In this section we summarize two sets of theories are useful for conceptualizing father-hormone research. First, we summarize life history theory, parental investment theory, and the challenge hypothesis, which have collectively been used to argue that changes in men's hormonal production varies based on men's investments in parenting effort. Second, we summarize the Steroid/Peptide Theory of Social Bonds (van Anders et al., 2011), which explains how different demands within parenting elicit differential hormonal responses to facilitate the necessary behaviors, and also builds off of life history perspectives. Finally, we note that a third theoretical framework, the bio-behavioral synchrony model (Feldman, 2012a, 2012b), has been used extensively to frame research on oxytocin and familial dynamics. For more information on this model (Feldman, 2012a, 2012b), see this volume, chapter 17.

Life history theory, parental investment theory, and the challenge hypothesis

Evolutionary perspectives, particularly parental investment theory and life history theory, have served as framing lenses for much of the research on the physiological underpinnings of fathering among humans and other animals. Life history theory focuses on the ways in which organisms must allocate energy to mutually exclusive physiological demands related to growth, reproduction, and survival. Physiological signals (such as hormones) mediate the trade-offs between various time and energy demands, and it is expected that organisms will have some adaptive capacity to flexibly adjust their individual allocation strategies in relation to their current circumstances. Environmentally sensitive, within-individual life-history shifts and accompanying variations in behavioral strategies manifest themselves through physiological pathways (e.g., hormonal axes and neurobiological systems). In terms of fathering and its underlying biology, parental investment and life history theories offer complementary predictive frameworks for the ways in which adults (particularly male mammals) face core trade-offs between mating and parenting within bi-parental species.

In that vein, a substantial amount of the existing research on the biology of fatherhood (across taxa) has focused on variability in testosterone based on the Challenge Hypothesis (Wingfield, Hegner, Dufty, & Ball, 1990). Drawing on extensive ornithological research, Wingfield and colleagues proposed that among species in which males invested time and energy in raising their young, fathers' testosterone would decline during the stages of the breeding season in which their offspring were dependent. Meanwhile, among species in which males had not evolved to invest in their young, their testosterone would remain elevated across the breeding season. Because the hypothalamic-pituitary-gonadal axis that produces testosterone is evolutionarily ancient and shared across vertebrates, the Challenge Hypothesis opened the door for scientists to make predictions regarding shifts in testosterone production based on mating and parenting effort in other species in which bi-parental care evolved.

This evolutionary-grounded approach to the study of the biology of vertebrate fathering has led to the observation that pair-bonded and/or invested vertebrate fathers commonly show similar physiological profiles, including some combination of reduced T, elevated prolactin, and heightened oxytocin and AVP (Gettler, 2014; Gray and Anderson, 2010; Storey and Ziegler, 2016; Trumble et al., 2015). Thus, this comparative perspective has served as a pillar for hypothesis testing aimed towards testing whether human fathers express psychobiological profiles similar to other invested vertebrate fathers (Gettler, 2014; Gray and Anderson, 2010; Feldman et al., 2013; Storey and Ziegler, 2016; Trumble et al., 2015; van Anders et al., 2011; van Anders, 2013). Yet, importantly, recent psychobiological heuristic frameworks (van Anders et al., 2011; van Anders, 2013) have made the observation that "parenting" represents a diffuse range of demands that might be most optimally met by varied levels of hormones (e.g., testosterone), rather than a singular profile of invested fathers having low testosterone.

Steroid/peptide theory of social bonds

The Steroid/Peptide Theory of Social Bonds argues that behavioral contexts within parenting and partnering elicit changes in steroid hormones (testosterone) and peptides (oxytocin, AVP), which in turn, facilitate bonding between partners or between parent and child. With respect to parenting, nurturant behaviors, such as comforting and cuddling should decrease testosterone, whereas "competitive" behaviors, such as protecting offspring, should increase testosterone. A central tenet of this theory is that low testosterone should not facilitate all types of parenting behaviors, but should only facilitate nurturant ones. For example, in situations where infant protection is needed, testosterone will rise to facilitate defensive behavior. The authors also argue that higher oxytocin and AVP would not only promote bonding between parents and offspring in nurturant contexts, but parents' increases in oxytocin and AVP will also facilitate defensive and protective behaviors in contexts in which such demands arise.

Review of literature by measured father outcomes

Below we review the literature on hormones by measured father outcomes to provide a contextually based understanding of the social neuroendocrinology of fatherhood. We also have included tables that summarize findings by testosterone (Table 19.1), prolactin (Table 19.2), oxytocin and AVP (Table 19.3), and cortisol (Table 19.4).

Comparisons by fathering status

Research comparing hormone levels by fathering status have typically used Life History Theory based predications and the Challenge Hypothesis, which respectively hypothesize that hormonal shifts will accompany men's transitions to invested fatherhood. Regarding T, studies across many cultural contexts have shown that partnered fathers have reduced testosterone compared to single non-fathers (Alvergne, Faurie, & Raymond, 2009; Gray, Jeffrey Yang, & Pope, 2006; Gray, Kahlenberg, Barrett, Lipson, & Ellison, 2002; Kuzawa, Gettler, Muller, McDade, & Feranil, 2009; Perini, Ditzen, Fischbacher, & Ehlert, 2012) and testosterone declines across men's transition to fatherhood (Gettler, McDade, Agustin, Feranil, & Kuzawa, 2015; Saxbe, Edelstein et al., 2017). In contrast to testosterone, human evidence for fathering status differences in baseline levels of prolactin, cortisol, oxytocin, and AVP has been limited. In a large study of Filipino men, fathers had higher levels of prolactin than non-fathers (Gettler, McDade, Feranil, & Kuzawa, 2012), but smaller studies of Jamaican and Canadian men found no overall differences in prolactin levels between fathers and non-fathers (Delahunty, McKay, Noseworthy, & Storey, 2007; Gray, Parkin, & Samms-Vaughan, 2007), which may have been underpowered to find significant differences in prolactin between fathers and non-fathers. Earlier studies found no significant differences in cortisol between expectant fathers and non-fathers (Berg & Wynne-Edwards, 2001) or between fathers and non-fathers (Fleming, Corter, Stallings, & Steiner, 2002). Two studies have found that fathers' plasma oxytocin was higher than non-fathers' oxytocin (Feldman et al., 2012; Mascaro, Hackett, & Rilling, 2014), whereas another study did not find any differences in fathers' and non-fathers' urinary oxytocin (Gray et al., 2007). Differences in findings may be attributed to differences in sample collection (urinary vs plasma) or differences in sample size. Small sample sizes may have resulted in Type II errors – for further discussion on sample sizes and neuroendocrinology, see chapter 3, this volume. Gray et al. (2007) also found no differences in urinary AVP between fathers and non-fathers, and others have not found significant differences in plasma AVP between mothers and fathers (Apter-Levi, Zagoory-Sharon, & Feldman, 2014; Atzil, Hendler, Zagoory-Sharon, Winetraub, & Feldman, 2012), or between expectant fathers and non-fathers (Cohen-Bendahan, Beijers, van Doornen, & de Weerth, 2015). Given the diversity of designs within the small literature on AVP and fatherhood, it is difficult to draw conclusions. Taken together, there is evidence that becoming a father and specifically engaging in direct care of children is associated with lowered basal testosterone. Less research has been conducted on comparing basal differences in prolactin, oxytocin, or AVP by men's parenting status. Given that null results regarding prolactin and oxytocin were found in studies with smaller sample sizes (Delahunty et al., 2007; Gray et al., 2006), but not studies with larger

Table 19.1 Testosterone (T)[a,b,c]

Study authors & year	Sample size	Biological media	Hormonal measurement (baseline, acute change, exogenous)	Key methodological or measurement details	Core findings
Dorius et al., 2011	352	saliva	baseline; morning wake samples	home interviews of US mothers and fathers; children 6–18 years old reported on closeness to mother and father	~T (baseline) in fathers not associated with child reported father-child relationship
Edelstein et al., 2017	27	saliva	baseline; longitudinal change during 6 time points prepartum	prenatal hormone sampling of first-time expectant US couples at 12, 20, 28, 36 weeks' gestation; 3 months postpartum self-report on parenting	↓T (longitudinal change), more involvement in household and infant care tasks
Endendijk et al., 2016	217	saliva	baseline; diurnal change (1st sample prior to bed, 2nd sample after waking)	two home visits with Dutch families (fathers, mothers, two children (younger = 3 years, older = 5 years); videotaped during dyadic parent-child play; scored for sensitivity and respect for autonomy	~T (levels) not associated with parenting quality; ↑T (diurnal change), more sensitivity and respect towards younger child; ~T (diurnal change) not associated with parenting with older child
Fleming et al., 2002	67	saliva	baseline; acute change (immediately after stimulus, 20 min after baseline)	cross-sectional measures from Canadian fathers of newborns and non-father control men; fathers heard recorded infant cries, smelled infant t-shirts, or heard control noises	↑T (acute change) in fathers hearing cries compared to controls; ↓T (baseline and post stimulus) related to greater sympathy and need to respond
Gettler, McDade, Feranil, et al., 2011; Gettler, McKenna, et al. 2012; Gettler et al. 2015	624 (2011) 362 (2012) 906 (2015)	saliva	baseline; diurnal (prior to bed and immediately upon waking); diurnal change (2012); long-term change	longitudinal measures from men (fathers vs. non-fathers) from the Philippines; survey measures of involvement in childcare (2011a, 2015); reported on co-sleeping with child (2012)	↓T (follow up), more childcare (2011a); ↓T (long-term change), more childcare (2015); ↓T (follow up) fathers compared to non-fathers (2011a, 2015); ↑T (baseline) predicted father status at follow up (2011a); ↓T (PM levels) in co-sleepers vs. solitary sleepers (2012)
Gettler, McDade, Agustin, et al., 2011	42	saliva	acute change	cross-sectional measures from fathers and toddlers in the Philippines; father-child play interaction at home;	~No average change in T in response to interaction (T acute change), stronger caregiving identity and partner view of father as caregiver

Study	N	Sample	Measure	Methodology	Results
Gordon et al. 2017	80	plasma (venipuncture)	baseline; long-term change	two home visits at 1 and 6 months postpartum of first-time parents free-play interactions micro-coded for vocalization, affect, proximity, and touch. interacted T and OT to predict parenting behavior	In context of high T, ↘OT related to more affectionate touch ↘T, higher synchrony, affectionate touch
Gray et al., 2002	58	saliva	baseline; diurnal (two AM and PM samples)	cross-sectional comparisons of fathers with non-fathers in US	↘T (PM levels) in married fathers compared to unmarried men ~T (diurnal change, AM levels) no differences based on father status
Gray et al., 2007	43	saliva	baseline; acute change	one hospital visit with Jamaican fathers (residential and non-residential) and single non-fathers; fathers interacted with their partners and toddlers (20 min) in a controlled setting; non-father controls read a newspaper (20 min)	↘T (baseline) in fathers compared to single men ~No average change in T between single men reading newspaper or fathers interacting with child and partner
Kuo et al., 2016	174	saliva	baseline; acute change	lab visit with US father-infant dyads; videotaped Strange Situation procedure (20 min) and father-infant teaching interaction (15 min); teaching interaction scored for positive father behaviors (e.g., sensitivity; positive regard)	↘T (acute change) from baseline to after Strange Situation ↘T (acute change) during Strange Situation predicted more positive father behaviors during teaching interaction ~T (baseline) not associated with father behaviors
Kuzawa et al., 2009	890	saliva; plasma (venipuncture)	baseline; diurnal (prior to bed and immediately upon waking)	compared fathers with non-fathers in birth cohort study in the Philippines	↘T (AM & PM) in fathers compared to non-fathers ↘T (AM & PM), involvement in childcare
Mascaro et al., 2013	70	plasma (venipuncture)	baseline	two lab sessions, first to acquire child photographs and mother-reported parenting questions. fMRI visit with fathers from US with 1–2 year old children; fMRI protocol: photos of own child vs. other child or adult; mother-reported paternal involvement in caregiving	↘T (baseline), more paternal caregiving ~T (baseline) not associated with neural activity to own infant vs. adult

(Continued)

Table 19.1 (Continued)

Study authors & year	Sample size	Biological media	Hormonal measurement (baseline, acute change, exogenous)	Key methodological or measurement details	Core findings
Mascaro et al., 2014	138	plasma (venipuncture)	baseline	one lab visit with heterosexual US fathers and non-father controls; during fMRI, subjects exposed to: happy, sad, and neutral faces from an unknown child and adult; photos of own child; sexually provocative images of women, neutral images of women, and neutral images of men; tested for brain activity differences (child vs. adult faces; sexual vs. non-sexual images) relative to hormone levels as well as based on parenting status	↖T fathers compared to non-fathers ~T age of child, number of children ~T neural activity during sexual visual task ↘T, increased activity in regions important face emotion processing during child task
Mazur, 2014	4,462	serum	baseline (morning samples)	Collected serum samples of US veteran men aged 30–48 Men participated in psychological and physical examinations	↖T, number of children living at home
Perini et al., 2012	75	saliva	baseline (AUC scores); long-term change; diurnal (waking, 5 pm, 9 pm)	longitudinal study of fathers vs. men in committed relationships in Switzerland; for fathers, saliva was collected pre and postpartum, control men provided samples 3 months apart	↘T (post-birth level) in fathers compared to controls ~T (longitudinal change) for fathers and non-fathers
Saxbe, Edelstein, et al. 2017	27	saliva	baseline; long-term change	prenatal hormone sampling of first-time expectant US couples at 12, 20, 28, 36 weeks' gestation; 3 months postpartum self-report on relationship investment	↘T across assessments ↘T, higher postpartum investment, commitment in relationship with partner
Saxbe, Schetter, et al. 2017	149	saliva	baseline; diurnal (wake, wake + 30 min, evening)	longitudinal study of parenting stress, depression, and intimate partner aggression of couples with infants in US T measure was aggregated from across diurnal sampling points at 9 months after birth of infant	↘T (baseline), more paternal depression, less parenting stress, less intimate partner aggression

Study	n[a]	Sample	Focus	Description	Findings[b]
Storey et al., 2000	34	serum (venipuncture)	baseline; acute change	compared pre and postpartum Canadian couples' hormone response to infant cues; all couples listened to infant cries, watched breastfeeding video; expectant fathers held doll, fathers held newborn	↑T (acute change) in new fathers with infants < 3 weeks old, compared to other groups (expectant fathers, fathers in with 4- to 7-week-old infants)
Storey et al., 2011	12	serum (finger stick)	baseline; acute change	two home visits with Canadian fathers of toddlers; naturalistic interaction on with–child or without–child day	~T (acute change) after interaction with toddler ↓T (acute change), more direct father-toddler interaction on "with child" day
Weisman et al., 2014	35	saliva	baseline; oxytocin-induced change in T	two lab visits with Israeli fathers with infants; fathers were administered OT or placebo, counterbalanced between visits; father-infant dyads participated in an 8-minute videotaped interaction; scored for gaze, affect, touch, vocalizations, and synchrony.	↑T (baseline), less touch, vocalization, gaze ↑T levels post-OT administration, relative to placebo

a Sample sizes listed in Tables 19.1–19.4 may differ from the published total sample sizes, which reflects our attempts to focus on the number of fathers (only) and controls in each study.

b ↑ indicates high or increased. ↓ indicates low or decreased. ~ indicates no significant relationship or difference observed or no change in the focal hormone.

c We define studies as having: "acute change" data if they focus on hormonal reactivity or short-term change (typically over 15 to 70 minutes) in response to stimuli; "diurnal" data if they focus on baseline measurements and have both morning and evening samples; "diurnal change" data if they focus on the change in hormones between the morning and evening samples; "long–term change" data if they focus on the change in hormones between time points separated by weeks, months, or years.

Table 19.2 Prolactin (PRL)

Study authors & year	Sample size	Biological media	Hormonal measurement (baseline, acute change, exogenous)	Key hormonal or psychobiological methodological or measurement details	Core findings
Delahunty et al., 2007	21	dried blood spots; serum (finger sticks)	baseline; acute change	multiple home visits with Canadian fathers from late prepartum through early postpartum, subsample repeated from birth of 1st to 2nd child; fathers heard recorded infant cries, watched breastfeeding and fathering video, held dolls (prepartum) or their infants (postpartum)	↑PRL (acute change), in response to holding second-born infants compared to first-born infants; ~PRL difference (baseline), new fathers vs. controls
Fleming et al., 2002	67	dried blood spots	baseline; acute change	see Table 19.1	↑PRL (baseline), more alert to cries; ↑PRL (acute change), in response to infant cries among experienced fathers compared to first-time fathers or control conditions.
Getler, McDade, Agustin, et al., 2011	42	dried blood spots	acute change	see Table 19.1	↘PRL (acute change), in response to father–child interaction; ↘PRL (acute change), among first-time fathers in response to father–child interaction
Getler, McDade, et al. 2012; Gettler et al., 2015	289 (2012) 304 (2015)	dried blood spots	baseline	single clinic visits with Filipino fathers and non-fathers; comparison of PRL among fathers and non-fathers, within-fathers based on fathers' self-reported total involvement in childcare	↑PRL among fathers vs. non-fathers; ~PRL difference, fathers' childcare involvement
Gordon et al., 2010b	43	plasma (venipuncture)	baseline; longitudinal change	longitudinal measures of first-time Israeli fathers at 2 mos. and 6 mos. postpartum; at 2nd visit, father-infant dyads videotaped during social and exploratory play at home; scored for parental gaze, affect, vocalizations, and touch	~PRL change, at 2 mos. and 6 mos. postpartum; ↑PRL, more coordinated exploratory play with infant

Study	N	Sample type	Measure		Findings
Gray et al., 2007	43	dried blood spots	baseline; acute change	see Table 19.1	~PRL difference (baseline), fathers vs. controls ↓PRL (acute change), in response to neutral stimuli among controls, differing from static PRL among non-residential fathers
Storey et al., 2000	34	serum (venipuncture)	baseline; acute change	see Table 19.1	↑PRL (baseline) in 37+ wks prepartum group compared to 12–16 wks prepartum group ↑PRL (baseline), more responsive to cries ↓PRL (acute change), in response to infant stimuli
Storey et al., 2011	12	serum (finger sticks)	baseline; acute change	see Table 19.1	~PRL difference (baseline), on with-child vs. without-child days ↓PRL (acute change), after fathers interacted with their toddlers

Table 19.3 Oxytocin (OT)

Study authors & year	Sample size	Biological media	Hormonal measurement (baseline, acute change, exogenous)	Key hormonal or psychobiological methodological or measurement details	Core findings
Abraham et al., 2014	69	saliva	average measure of pre & post values	two visits (home and lab) with Israeli fathers (heterosexual secondary caregivers and gay primary caregivers); OT average calculated from levels from before and after child interaction; father–child dyads videotaped during free, unstructured interactions at home; scored for fathers' gaze, affect, vocalizations, touch, father–infant synchrony during fMRI, fathers exposed to the prior recorded video of their parent–infant interaction and two control videos; tested for region of interest brain activity differences relative to hormone levels as well as based on primary vs. secondary caregiving	~OT difference, among fathers based on being primary caregivers vs. secondary or compared to mothers ↑OT, ↑ brain activity in a cortical region related to mentalizing–empathy (superior temporal sulcus [STS]) path analysis indicated this pathway: STS→ OT→ synchrony ~OT, brain activity in emotional processing pathways
Apter-Levi et al., 2014	48	plasma (venipuncture)	baseline	single lab visit with Israeli parents, videotaped interaction with 4–6 month old infant, micro-coded for gaze, affect, vocalization, and touch	~OT difference fathers and mothers ↑OT, ↑ affectionate contact, social salience
Atzil et al., 2012	15	plasma (venipuncture)	baseline	one home visit with Israeli families, videotaped for parent–infant and infant solitary play fMRI follow up, infant solitary play was used as stimuli examined neural activity within couples	↓OT, lower neural activity in cognitive brain regions
Cohen-Bendahan et al., 2015	66	urine	baseline; exogenous	measured caregiving interest in expectant fathers and control men from the Netherlands used virtual reality helmets that showed infants, infants interacting with fathers, a moving toy, and an exercising woman	~basal OT, expectant fathers and controls ~basal OT, caregiving interest

Study	N	Sample	Measure	Methods	Findings
Feldman, Gordon, Schneiderman, et al. 2010	41	saliva, plasma	acute change	lab visit with Israeli fathers and mothers; parents interacted with 4–6 month old infants (15 min); interactions micro-coded for gaze, affect, vocalizations, touch	↑OT during interaction when fathers ↑ stimulatory contact; ~OT differences between mothers and fathers
Feldman, Gordon, & Zagoory-Sharon, 2010	19	saliva, plasma	baseline; acute change	lab visit with Israeli fathers, mothers, and infants; sampled infant and parent OT; parents interacted with infants; interactions micro-coded for gaze, vocalizations, affect, touch	↑OT during interaction in parents and infants; OT change during interaction correlated between parent and infant levels; ↑OT social engagement and affect synchrony
Feldman et al., 2011	41	urine, saliva, plasma (venipuncture)	baseline	one lab visit with Israeli fathers and mothers; fathers interacted with 4–6 mos. old infants (15 min); father-infant dyads videotaped during interactions at a laboratory (infant seated); scored for fathers' and infants' gaze, affect, vocalizations, and touch	~OT difference, mothers vs. fathers ↑OT (plasma), ↑OT (saliva) ~OT (urine), OT (plasma) or OT (saliva) ↑OT (plasma, saliva), ↑ positive engagement and communication, affect synchrony ↑OT (urine), ↑ infant negative engagement, interactive stress
Feldman et al., 2012	121	plasma (venipuncture), mouthwash samples (for genetic analyses)	baseline	one lab visit with Israeli fathers and non-father controls; mouthwash samples analyzed for genetic polymorphisms related to OT function; fathers interacted with 4–6 mos. old infants; father-infant dyads videotaped during seated side-by-side interactions at a laboratory; scored for gaze, affect, vocalization, touch	↑OT (plasma, saliva), ↑ paternal attachment ↑OT, among parents vs. non-parents ↑OT, ↑ parental touch ↓OT, carriers of "risk alleles" ↑OT + low risk allele, ↑ parent-infant gaze synchrony ↑OT + low-risk allele, among parents reporting higher care from *own* parents
Feldman et al., 2013	80	saliva, plasma (venipuncture), mouthwash samples (for genetic analyses)	average measure of OT across sampling points	longitudinal measures of first-time Israeli fathers and mothers at 1 mos., 6 mos., and 3-years postpartum; blood draws at first two visits (parents only); saliva sampling (parents and child) at 3rd visit; fathers' OT values across the 3 time points were combined into "stable OT" scores; mouthwash samples analyzed for genetic polymorphisms related to OT function;	↑OT among fathers, ↑OT among mothers ↑OT among fathers, ↑OT among children ↑OT among parents, ↑ child social reciprocity with best friend ~fathers' cumulative OT genetic risk and child social reciprocity with best friend.

(Continued)

Table 19.3 (Continued)

Study authors & year	Sample size	Biological media	Hormonal measurement (baseline, acute change, exogenous)	Key hormonal or psychobiological methodological or measurement details	Core findings
Gordon et al., 2010b	37	plasma (venipuncture)	baseline; long-term change	father-child dyads videotaped during unstructured interactions at home; child videotaped during play with best friend (at age 3) infancy visit recordings scored for fathers' and infants' gaze, affect, vocalizations, and touch age 3 visit recordings (parent-child; child-best friend) scored for social reciprocity	↑OT, ↑ triadic synchrony
Gordon et al., 2017	80	plasma (venipuncture) urine	baseline; long-term change	see Table 19.1	In context of high T, ↓OT related to more affectionate touch
Gray et al., 2007	43	urine	baseline	see Table 19.1	~OT difference, by fatherhood status or fathers vs. controls
Mascaro et al., 2014	138	plasma (venipuncture)	baseline	see Table 19.1	↑OT fathers compared to non-fathers; ~OT, age or number of fathers' children; ↑OT, ↑ hippocampus activity during child task (when fathers and controls considered together); ~OT, brain activity during sexual imagery task; ~OT, brain activity in regions of interest during either imagery task
Naber et al., 2010	17	exogenous (intranasal spray)	acute change (exogenous administration)	two lab visits with Dutch fathers; double-blind, crossover within-subject study; fathers received 24 IU intranasal OT or placebo; fathers played with their toddlers (15 min) at home;	↑OT, ↑ paternal stimulation of exploration and learning; ~OT, paternal intrusiveness or sensitivity; ~OT, child involvement or responsiveness

Study	N	Source (measure)	baseline / acute change	Methods	Findings
Weisman et al., 2012	35	saliva, exogenous (intranasal spray)	acute change	father-toddler dyads videotaped during interactions; scored for fathers' structuring, sensitivity, non-hostility, and non-intrusiveness; infants' child responsiveness and involvement two lab visits with Israeli fathers; double-blind, crossover within-subject study; fathers received 24 IU intranasal OT or placebo; fathers interacted with 4–8 mo. old infants (7 min; Still-face Paradigm); scored for fathers' gaze, affect, infant-directed speech, and touch; infants' gaze, affect, and exploratory play	↑OT (saliva), among fathers at 20 min. and 40-min post-interaction in experimental vs. placebo ↑OT (saliva), among infants at 20 min. and 40-min post-interaction in experimental (fathers receive OT) vs. placebo ↑paternal social reciprocity, infant-directed positive vocalizations and encouragement in OT admin vs. placebo ↑infant object manipulation and social gaze in OT admin vs. placebo
Arginine vasopressin (AVP)					
Apter-Levi et al., 2014	119 (48 fathers)	plasma (venipuncture)	baseline	see oxytocin table	~AVP differences between mothers and fathers
Atzil et al., 2012	15	plasma (venipuncture)	baseline	see oxytocin table	↑AVP(baseline), more touch, object salience ~AVP differences between mothers and fathers ↓AVP, greater neural activity in brain areas related to social cognition in fathers only
Cohen-Bendahan et al., 2015	66	urine exogenous (intranasal spray of OT or VP)	baseline; exogenous VP	see oxytocin table	~AVP (baseline) not related to caregiving interest in expectant dads or controls ↑AVP condition, expectant fathers watched baby avatars longer than control men
Gray et al., 2007	43	urine	baseline	see Table 19.1	~AVP difference, by fatherhood status or fathers vs. controls ↓AVP among fathers with older youngest children

Table 19.4 Cortisol (CORT)

Study authors & year	Sample size	Biological media	Hormonal measurement (baseline, acute change, awakening response, exogenous)	Key hormonal or psychobiological methodological or measurement details	Core findings
Berg & Wynne-Edwards, 2001	37	saliva	longitudinal change	weekly samples collected from partner's first trimester to after birth in Canadian families compared expectant fathers with non-fathers	↓CORT in expectant dads vs. non-dads. ↑CORT in expectant fathers week prior to birth
Fleming et al., 2002	67	saliva	baseline; acute change	see Table 19.1	~CORT (baseline) in fathers vs. non-fathers
Gettler, McDade, Agustin, et al. 2011	42	saliva	acute change	see Table 19.1	↓CORT after interaction
Gettler, McDade, & Kuzawa, 2011	630	saliva	baseline; diurnal	longitudinal measures from men (fathers vs. non-fathers) from the Philippines; examined coregulation of CORT and T	↓CORT (PM levels) in pair-bonded men and fathers
Gordon et al., 2010b	37	saliva	baseline; diurnal; longitudinal change	two home visits: at 2 months and 6 months after infant's birth to Israeli families. videotaped triadic (mother–father–infant) free-play interactions at 6 months, coded for triadic synchrony	~CORT (longitudinal change) for fathers ↓CORT in fathers compared to mothers at 6 months ~CORT difference between mothers and fathers at 2 months ~CORT levels, synchrony
Gray et al., 2007	43	saliva	baseline; acute change	see Table 19.1	~CORT change across visit ~CORT differences between fathers, single men, and non-residential fathers
Storey et al., 2000	34	serum (venipuncture)	baseline; acute change	see Table 19.1	Fathers' CORT highest prior to birth ↓CORT (acute change) in response to infant stimuli
Storey et al., 2011	12	serum (finger sticks)	baseline; acute change	see Table 19.1	↓CORT (acute change) in response to toddler interaction
Weisman et al., 2013	35	saliva	baseline; OT-induced CORT change	Israeli fathers self-administered intranasal OT or placebo during two lab visits Videotaped father-infant interactions micro-coded for gaze synchrony Father and infants provided saliva samples for CORT at four time points	↑CORT in fathers in OT condition across visit ↓CORT (acute change) in response to infant interaction

sample sizes, null results may have been due to type II error, an issue in hormone research (see chapter 3, this volume).

In line with fathering status differences, some researchers have tested for hormonal differences based on parity (first-time vs. experienced fathers) or for associations with age of the youngest child. Although none of these papers specifically used the Steroid/Peptide Theory of Social Bonds (van Anders et al., 2011), contexts which facilitate greater levels of nurturance, including caring for multiple children or for infants, could theoretically generate differences in hormonal profiles of experienced fathers or fathers with younger children compared to first-time fathers or fathers of older children. Filipino fathers had larger longitudinal declines in testosterone over a 4.5-year period when their children were younger (Gettler, McDade, Agustin, Feranil, & Kuzawa, 2013; Gettler, McDade, Feranil, & Kuzawa, 2011). Another large study of American servicemen found that men residing with more children had higher testosterone levels than men with fewer or no children (Mazur, 2014), which is contrary to theoretical predictions. Mazur hypothesized that testosterone levels may have varied by fathering behaviors (protective or nurturant), which was not measured in the study. Alternatively, perhaps men with higher sexual activity, and therefore, more children, also have higher testosterone. Cortisol levels were lower and prolactin levels increased more in response to hearing infant cries in experienced fathers compared to first-time fathers (Fleming et al., 2002). Experienced fathers also reported a greater need to respond when hearing infant cries compared to first-time fathers, potentially indicating that experiences with nurturing and caring for infants is shapes hormone profiles in men (Fleming et al., 2002). Fathers with older children had lower AVP levels than fathers with younger children (Gray et al., 2007) and fathers of infants had higher prolactin levels than fathers of older children (Gettler, McDade et al., 2012). Previously, men's higher prolactin prior to the birth of an infant has been argued to facilitate bonding between father and child (Storey, Walsh, Quinton, & Wynne-Edwards, 2000). Gray et al. (2007) hypothesized that higher AVP levels among men with younger children reflected anxious arousal in response to unpredictable infant cues or physical exertion from infant care in fathers with younger children. Gettler, McDade, et al., 2012 similarly hypothesized that elevated prolactin could potentially reflect or facilitate the physically and emotionally taxing care of infants and young children.

Exposure to infant cues and interactions with children

Experimental designs that investigated hormone changes in response to visual, olfactory, or auditory infant stimuli aimed to uncover if exposure to infant cues precipitated hormone changes (e.g., decreased testosterone, increased oxytocin) that would presumably be favorable for positive, nurturing interactions with infants. The Bio-behavioral Synchrony Model (Feldman, 2012a) and the Steroid/Peptide Theory of Social Bonds (van Anders et al., 2011) both make predictions about the bidirectional influence between parent-infant interaction and/or situational context and hormone changes. In one study, fathers of newborns increased in testosterone in response to a "situational reactivity" test which included listening to 6 minutes of audio-taped infant cries and then watching a 5-minute breastfeeding video while holding their infant in a blanket (Storey et al., 2000). Storey et al. (2000) argued that new fathers' increases in testosterone to the situational reactivity test may be indicative of a "challenge" response that could motivate protection of a crying infant. Storey et al.'s interpretations are consistent with the Steroid/Peptide Theory of Social Bonds' Offspring Defense Paradox, in which high testosterone, along with high oxytocin/AVP should be linked with parental effort only within the context of infant defense. That said, it is hard to imagine what "threats" are being perceived while listening to audio-taped infant cries and watching a breastfeeding video in a home environment. Instead, these increases in testosterone to audio-taped infant cries may reflect fathers' ambivalent emotional reactions to aversive stimuli. In a different study on fathers' emotional and hormonal responses to recorded infant cries, fathers not only reported greater sympathy and alertness, but also greater annoyance, irritation, and distress than men in the non-cry conditions (Fleming et al., 2002). In tandem with these varied emotional responses, fathers also increased in testosterone (Fleming et al., 2002). It is easy to imagine that hearing infant cries from an audiotape can cause a range of emotional responses, especially when devoid of interaction with a living, breathing baby. Although these early studies were certainly foundational for the study of human paternal psychobiology, the emphasis on experimental control but lower ecological validity limits the application to real-life father-infant interactions.

Research that followed investigated changes in fathers' hormones in response to interactions with their own children, but findings across measured hormones have been mixed, which may have resulted as a function of study design or lack of statistical power. Predominating designs that used playful interactions between fathers and toddlers found decreases in fathers' cortisol, possibly reflecting an anxiolytic effect of father-child play (Gettler, McDade, Agustin, & Kuzawa, 2011; Storey, Noseworthy, Delahunty, Halfyard, & McKay, 2011), but no change in testosterone (Gettler, McDade, Agustin et al., 2011; Gray et al., 2007; Kuo et al., 2016; Storey et al., 2011). Playful interactions in smaller studies with toddlers decreased fathers' prolactin (Gettler, McDade, Agustin et al., 2011; Storey et al., 2011) or exhibited no statistically significant change (Gray et al., 2007). Collectively, these findings appeared to contradict existing theoretical notions that decreased testosterone and increased prolactin facilitate "fathering behavior," although psychobiological systems are likewise responsive to social interactions and context so these short-term reactivity patterns may also reflect that bi-directionality. Perhaps playful interactions require a different set of behavioral competencies (and therefore different biological changes) than soothing a crying infant, disciplining a misbehaving child, or engaging in other types of physical care, such as diapering an infant. Only one study has assessed hormone changes during two different types of father-infant interactions in a single laboratory visit and found that fathers' testosterone significantly decreased while they participated in the Strange Situation (a series of separations and reunions between parent and infant that frequently elicits infant distress) (Kuo et al., 2016), but there were no significant changes in testosterone during the subsequent father-infant play task. However, Kuo et al. did not counterbalance the Strange Situation and play interactions, thus it is unclear whether the Strange Situation decreases testosterone more than diurnal decline. Kuo et al.'s results contrast with Storey et al. (2000) and Fleming et al. (2002), who both found increases in testosterone in response to audio-taped infant cries in smaller samples, further highlighting the importance of context when making predictions about testosterone and fathering, consistent with the predictions of the Steroid/Peptide Theory of Social Bonds (van Anders et al., 2011). Future designs need to incorporate different types of interactions, not just play, to uncover how hormones are related to the "effort" of parenting.

Links with quantity and quality of fathering

Related to the "effort" of parenting, scholars have tried to uncover whether hormones (measured as either baseline/basal levels or acute reactivity) are associated with increased fathering quality, typically operationalized as sensitivity, affection, or synchrony. Multiple theoretical perspectives including the Challenge Hypothesis (Wingfield et al., 1990), Steroid/Peptide Theory of Social Bonds (van Anders et al., 2011), and the Bio-behavioral Synchrony Model (Feldman, 2012a) have been used to frame this area of research. Links between basal levels of testosterone and parenting quality are mixed. Multiple studies with larger sample sizes ($N = 174$–352)

have found that basal levels of testosterone are uncorrelated with fathers' parenting quality with their children (Dorius, Booth, Hibel, Granger, & Johnson, 2011; Endendijk et al., 2016; Kuo et al., 2016). In contrast, other research has found that fathers with lower basal testosterone expressed more affectionate touch and positive forms of infant-directed speech (Weisman, Zagoory-Sharon, & Feldman, 2014) and higher father-infant synchrony (Gordon, Pratt, Bergunde, Zagoory-Sharon, & Feldman, 2017), and lower levels of parenting stress (Saxbe, Schetter, Simon, Adam, & Shalowitz, 2017). These seemingly inconsistent findings may stem from differences in measures of parenting "quality" across studies. Dorius et al. (2011) used children's reports of parent-child relationship quality, whereas Kuo et al. (2016) coded fathers' sensitivity, intrusiveness, detachment, stimulation of cognitive development, and positive and negative regard. Endendijk et al. (2016) coded for sensitivity and respect for children's autonomy. In contrast to the mixed literature on basal testosterone and fathering quality, several links between baseline levels of endogenous oxytocin and fathering quality have been established. For example, higher levels of oxytocin in fathers are associated with greater synchrony in parent-infant interactions (Feldman, Gordon, & Zagoory-Sharon, 2011; Feldman et al., 2012) and triadic (mother-father-infant) interactions (Gordon, Zagoory-Sharon, Leckman, & Feldman, 2010a). Similarly, higher AVP levels were related to more touch and joint attention between parents and infants (Apter-Levi et al., 2014), and higher prolactin was related to more coordinated exploratory play between fathers and infants (Gordon, Zagoory-Sharon, Leckman, & Feldman, 2010b).

Studies that examined oxytocin reactivity found that parents' oxytocin levels increased during playful interactions with their infants (Feldman, Gordon, & Zagoory-Sharon, 2010), and when fathers engage in greater stimulatory contact (Feldman, Gordon, Schneiderman, Weisman, & Zagoory-Sharon, 2010). Elsewhere, studies have found links between changes in testosterone (either acute or diurnal; see Table 19.1) with parenting quality (Endendijk et al., 2016; Kuo et al., 2016). Fathers' declines in testosterone in response to viewing their infants in distress was predictive of fathers' sensitive parenting behaviors with infants in a subsequent playful teaching task (Kuo et al., 2016). Greater decreases in daytime testosterone were associated with more sensitivity and respect towards fathers' younger child, but not with their older child (Endendijk et al., 2016). Thus, parenting quality may not be related to trait levels of testosterone, but instead may be related to the magnitude of fathers' testosterone changes, in the short-term. It is possible that within-individual long-term changes in baseline testosterone production (e.g., across fathers' transition to parenthood) also relate to the quality of fathering, but this remains to be tested.

A different, but related literature on father involvement in childcare, has attempted to uncover links between *quantity* of childcare with hormone variation. Unlike parenting *quality*, short-term *changes* in testosterone appear to be unrelated to quantity of father involvement, at least in families with two children (Endendijk et al., 2016; Kuo et al., 2016). Several studies have found links between lower baseline or longitudinal declines in basal testosterone and fathers' increased involvement in childcare (Alvergne et al., 2009; Edelstein et al., 2017; Gettler et al., 2015; Gettler, McDade, Feranil et al., 2011; Kuzawa et al., 2009; Mascaro, Hackett, & Rilling, 2013). We note that only one large-scale study of men has examined longer-term change (over years) in men's testosterone in relation to father involvement in childcare. In that study, Filipino fathers' testosterone declined if they increased their caregiving across a 4.5-year follow-up period (Gettler et al., 2015). In a different longitudinal study of prenatal testosterone changes, expectant fathers with greater declines in testosterone were more involved in childcare tasks postpartum (Edelstein et al., 2017). Thus, there appear to be bidirectional associations between testosterone and childcare involvement. Additional studies have found that co-sleeping with children was related to lower baseline testosterone among fathers (Gettler, McKenna, McDade, Agustin, & Kuzawa,

2012; Lawson et al., 2017). Baseline prolactin was not associated with quantity of childcare (Gettler et al., 2015). One study that examined oxytocin levels in primary- and secondary-caregiving fathers did not find differences in oxytocin levels between the two types of fathers (Abraham et al., 2014).

Effects of induced hormone changes

Limitations linked to oxytocin's inability to cross the blood-brain barrier (Evans, Dal Monte, Noble, & Averbeck, 2014) resulted in increased use of exogenous, intranasal oxytocin. Studies that used experimental manipulations of oxytocin primarily have focused on whether increasing oxytocin would lead to increased fathering quality. One study found that induced oxytocin led to more stimulating parenting behaviors, but there was no difference with sensitivity or intrusiveness (Naber, van IJzendoorn, Deschamps, van Engeland, & Bakermans-Kranenburg, 2010). A different study found that induced oxytocin was predictive of greater touch and social reciprocity (Weisman, Zagoory-Sharon, & Feldman, 2012). The only study on exogenous AVP found that expectant fathers administered AVP watched baby avatars longer than control men (Cohen-Bendahan et al., 2015).

A few studies have also investigated how oxytocin administration affects other hormone levels (i.e., testosterone and cortisol) in the context of father-infant interaction and found some surprising results. For example, fathers receiving intranasal oxytocin maintained higher levels of testosterone during the father-infant interaction, whereas fathers receiving placebo decreased in testosterone (Weisman et al., 2014). Weisman et al. inferred that oxytocin administration could increase reward processing from social interactions, which in turn could facilitate fathers' caregiving behaviors. In a different study, fathers who were administered intranasal oxytocin maintained higher levels of cortisol than those receiving placebo across a still-face interaction with their infants (Weisman, Zagoory-Sharon, & Feldman, 2013). The still-face interaction can be distressing for the infant as they try to regulate their emotions without the help of their parent. oxytocin administration in fathers also appeared to affect infants' cortisol reactivity. Within high-synchrony dyads which exhibited high levels of joint social gaze between parents and infants, infants showed cortisol increases when their fathers were in the oxytocin condition. Oxytocin administration in low-synchrony dyads resulted in the opposite effect: low-synchrony infants experienced declines. Together, these studies show the importance of considering hormones within social context (i.e., playful or stressful interaction) and coregulation of multiple hormones. Despite significant effects of intranasal oxytocin on social behavior (Naber et al., 2010; Weisman et al., 2012), the mechanisms by which intranasal oxytocin affects parenting are poorly understood. More work is needed to elucidate these mechanisms and caution may be needed when drawing conclusions about oxytocin and fathering under naturalistic conditions when drawing from experimental manipulations of oxytocin.

Future directions and conclusions

The bulk of this chapter has been devoted to addressing how various behavioral contexts may lead to different associations between fathering behavior and hormones. In summary, basal testosterone appears to decline during men's transition to fatherhood, whereas evidence for changes in oxytocin, prolactin, cortisol, and AVP in response to becoming a father are less robust. Basal oxytocin is related to parenting quality, but basal testosterone is only related to quantity of childcare, at least in larger studies for this area. Playful interactions between fathers and children do not always stimulate hormone reactivity, but different paradigms, particularly those that provoke infant distress, may elicit hormone changes. Intranasal oxytocin seems to elicit higher quality parenting behaviors, but also increases testosterone and cortisol. In highlighting different patterns of associations for basal and reactivity measures with fathering outcomes, we recommend that future research needs to consider whether to assess basal hormone levels or reactivity and the bi-directionality between psychobiological systems and behavior. For example, we noted above that there are inconsistencies and seemingly opposing findings for basal prolactin and prolactin reactivity in terms of paternal engagement during play. This may reflect differences in physiological function, within the same system, between long-term exposures to hormones facilitating behavior (Gordon et al., 2010b) versus shorter-term hormonal responses to social interactions (Gettler, McDade, Agustin et al., 2011). Kuo and colleagues' (2016) approach, which focused on T, represents an intermediate between these dynamics, linking fathers' testosterone reactivity in one parenting context to their nurturing behavior in another task, minutes later. Attention to the details of how neuroendocrine axes function and interrelate with behavior over multiple time scales is critical.

Along those lines, increasing specificity in how "paternal behavior" is operationalized and understanding how different contexts may lead to different hormonal responses could resolve some of the mixed findings in this literature. Another angle to take towards resolving inconsistencies is to consider how testosterone, oxytocin, AVP, prolactin, and cortisol are possibly coregulated. Some other areas of social neuroendocrinology are considering coregulation of hormones in the determination of behavior, specifically testosterone and cortisol in social dominance (Mehta & Josephs, 2010). Only one study has examined coregulation of basal testosterone and cortisol in the context of fatherhood, there did not appear to be antagonistic associations between testosterone and cortisol, rather testosterone and cortisol tended to be co-elevated among single non-fathers or co-downregulated among partnered fathers (Gettler, McDade, & Kuzawa, 2011). A recent study on changes in endogenous hormones after the transition to parenthood found that testosterone moderated the link between oxytocin and fathering behaviors. Specifically, lower oxytocin predicted fathers' greater affectionate behaviors with their infants but only among high testosterone men (Gordon et al., 2017). Future research may need to model interactive effects between multiple hormones to uncover the complex associations between multiple hormonal systems and paternal behavior.

References

Abraham, E., Hendler, T., Shapira-Lichter, I., Kanat-Maymon, Y., Zagoory-Sharon, O., & Feldman, R. (2014). Father's brain is sensitive to childcare experiences. *Proceedings of the National Academy of Sciences*, *111*(27), 9792–9797. doi:10.1073/pnas.1402569111

Alvergne, A., Faurie, C., & Raymond, M. (2009). Variation in testosterone levels and male reproductive effort: Insight from a polygynous human population. *Hormones and Behavior*, *56*(5), 491–497. http://dx.doi.org/10.1016/j.yhbeh.2009.07.013

Apter-Levi, Y., Zagoory-Sharon, O., & Feldman, R. (2014). Oxytocin and vasopressin support distinct configurations of social synchrony. *Brain Research*, *1580*, 124–132. http://dx.doi.org/10.1016/j.brainres.2013.10.052

Atzil, S., Hendler, T., Zagoory-Sharon, O., Winetraub, Y., & Feldman, R. (2012). Synchrony and specificity in the maternal and the paternal brain: Relations to oxytocin and vasopressin. *Journal of the American Academy of Child & Adolescent Psychiatry*, *51*(8), 798–811. https://doi.org/10.1016/j.jaac.2012.06.008

Berg, S.J., & Wynne-Edwards, K.E. (2001). Changes in testosterone, cortisol, and estradiol levels in men becoming fathers. *Mayo Clinic Proceedings*, *76*(6), 582–592.

Cohen-Bendahan, C.C.C., Beijers, R., van Doornen, L.J.P., & de Weerth, C. (2015). Explicit and implicit caregiving interests in expectant fathers: Do endogenous and exogenous oxytocin and vasopressin matter? *Infant Behavior and Development*, *41*, 26–37. http://dx.doi.org/10.1016/j.infbeh.2015.06.007

Delahunty, K.M., McKay, D.W., Noseworthy, D.E., & Storey, A.E. (2007). Prolactin responses to infant cues in men and women: Effects of parental experience and recent infant contact. *Hormones and Behavior, 51*(2), 213–220. http://dx.doi.org/10.1016/j.yhbeh.2006.10.004

Dorius, C., Booth, A., Hibel, J., Granger, D.A., & Johnson, D. (2011). Parents' testosterone and children's perception of parent-child relationship quality. *Hormones and Behavior, 60*(5), 512–519. doi:10.1016/j.yhbeh.2011.07.020

Edelstein, R.S., Chopik, W.J., Saxbe, D.E., Wardecker, B.M., Moors, A.C., & LaBelle, O.P. (2017). Prospective and dyadic associations between expectant parents' prenatal hormone changes and postpartum parenting outcomes. *Developmental Psychobiology, 59*(1), 77–90. doi:10.1002/dev.21469

Endendijk, J.J., Hallers-Haalboom, E.T., Groeneveld, M.G., van Berkel, S.R., van der Pol, L.D., Bakermans-Kranenburg, M.J., & Mesman, J. (2016). Diurnal testosterone variability is differentially associated with parenting quality in mothers and fathers. *Hormones and Behavior, 80*, 68–75. http://dx.doi.org/10.1016/j.yhbeh.2016.01.016

Evans, S.L., Dal Monte, O., Noble, P., & Averbeck, B.B. (2014). Intranasal oxytocin effects on social cognition: A critique. *Brain Research, 1580*, 69–77. http://dx.doi.org/10.1016/j.brainres.2013.11.008

Feldman, R. (2012a). Bio-behavioral synchrony: A model for integrating biological and microsocial behavioral processes in the study of parenting. *Parenting, 12*(2–3), 154–164. doi:10.1080/15295192.2012.683342

Feldman, R. (2012b). Parent-infant synchrony: A biobehavioral model of mutual influences in the formation of affiliative bonds. *Monographs of the Society for Research in Child Development, 77*(2), 42–51. doi:10.1111/j.1540-5834.2011.00660.x

Feldman, R., Gordon, I., Influs, M., Gutbir, T., & Ebstein, R. P. (2013). Parental oxytocin and early caregiving jointly shape children's oxytocin response and social reciprocity. *Neuropsychopharmacology, 38*(7), 1154–1162. doi:10.1038/npp.2013.22

Feldman, R., Gordon, I., Schneiderman, I., Weisman, O., & Zagoory-Sharon, O. (2010). Natural variations in maternal and paternal care are associated with systematic changes in oxytocin following parent-infant contact. *Psychoneuroendocrinology, 35*(8), 1133–1141. https://doi.org/10.1016/j.psyneuen.2010.01.013

Feldman, R., Gordon, I., & Zagoory-Sharon, O. (2010). The cross-generation transmission of oxytocin in humans. *Hormones and Behavior, 58*(4), 669–676.

Feldman, R., Gordon, I., & Zagoory-Sharon, O. (2011). Maternal and paternal plasma, salivary, and urinary oxytocin and parent-infant synchrony: Considering stress and affiliation components of human bonding. *Developmental Science, 14*(4), 752–761. doi:10.1111/j.1467-7687.2010.01021.x

Feldman, R., Zagoory-Sharon, O., Weisman, O., Schneiderman, I., Gordon, I., Maoz, R., ... Ebstein, R.P. (2012). Sensitive parenting is associated with plasma oxytocin and polymorphisms in the OXTR and CD38 genes. *Biological Psychiatry, 72*(3), 175–181. https://doi.org/10.1016/j.biopsych.2011.12.025

Fleming, A.S., Corter, C., Stallings, J., & Steiner, M. (2002). Testosterone and prolactin are associated with emotional responses to infant cries in new fathers. *Hormones and Behavior, 42*(4), 399–413. doi:10.1006/hbeh.2002.1840

Gettler, L.T. (2014). Applying socioendocrinology to evolutionary models: Fatherhood and physiology. *Evolutionary Anthropology: Issues, News, and Reviews, 23*(4), 146–160. doi:10.1002/evan.21412

Gettler, L.T., McDade, T.W., Agustin, S.S., Feranil, A.B., & Kuzawa, C.W. (2013). Do testosterone declines during the transition to marriage and fatherhood relate to men's sexual behavior? Evidence from the Philippines. *Hormones and Behavior, 64*(5), 755–763. doi:10.1016/j.yhbeh.2013.08.019

Gettler, L.T., McDade, T.W., Agustin, S.S., Feranil, A.B., & Kuzawa, C.W. (2015). Longitudinal perspectives on fathers' residence status, time allocation, and testosterone in the Philippines. *Adaptive Human Behavior and Physiology, 1*(2), 124–149. doi:10.1007/s40750-014-0018-9

Gettler, L.T., McDade, T.W., Agustin, S.S., & Kuzawa, C.W. (2011). Short-term changes in fathers' hormones during father-child play: Impacts of paternal attitudes and experience. *Hormones and Behavior, 60*(5), 599–606. http://dx.doi.org/10.1016/j.yhbeh.2011.08.009

Gettler, L.T., McDade, T.W., Feranil, A.B., & Kuzawa, C.W. (2011). Longitudinal evidence that fatherhood decreases testosterone in human males. *Proceedings of the National Academy of Sciences of the United States of America, 108*(39), 16194–16199. doi:10.1073/pnas.1105403108

Gettler, L.T., McDade, T.W., Feranil, A.B., & Kuzawa, C.W. (2012). Prolactin, fatherhood, and reproductive behavior in human males. *American Journal of Physical Anthropology, 148*(3), 362–370. doi:10.1002/ajpa.22058

Gettler, L.T., McDade, T.W., & Kuzawa, C.W. (2011). Cortisol and testosterone in Filipino young adult men: Evidence for co-regulation of both hormones by fatherhood and relationship status. *American Journal of Human Biology, 23*(5), 609–620. doi:10.1002/ajhb.21187

Gettler, L.T., McKenna, J.J., McDade, T.W., Agustin, S.S., & Kuzawa, C.W. (2012). Does cosleeping contribute to lower testosterone levels in fathers? Evidence from the Philippines. *PLoS One, 7*(9). http://dx.doi.org/10.1371/journal.pone.0041559

Gordon, I., Pratt, M., Bergunde, K., Zagoory-Sharon, O., & Feldman, R. (2017). Testosterone, oxytocin, and the development of human parental care. *Hormones and Behavior.* doi:10.1016/j.yhbeh.2017.05.016

Gordon, I., Zagoory-Sharon, O., Leckman, J.F., & Feldman, R. (2010a). Oxytocin, cortisol, and triadic family interactions. *Physiology & Behavior, 101*(5), 679–684. http://dx.doi.org/10.1016/j.physbeh.2010.08.008

Gordon, I., Zagoory-Sharon, O., Leckman, J.F., & Feldman, R. (2010b). Prolactin, oxytocin, and the development of paternal behavior across the first six months of fatherhood. *Hormones and Behavior, 58*(3), 513–518. https://doi.org/10.1016/j.yhbeh.2010.04.007

Gray, P. B., & Anderson, K. G. (2010). *Fatherhood: Evolution and Human Paternal Behavior.* Cambridge, MA: Harvard University Press.

Gray, P.B., Jeffrey Yang, C.-F., & Pope, H.G. (2006). Fathers have lower salivary testosterone levels than unmarried men and married non-fathers in Beijing, China. *Proceedings of the Royal Society of London B: Biological Sciences, 273*(1584), 333–339.

Gray, P.B., Kahlenberg, S.M., Barrett, E.S., Lipson, S.F., & Ellison, P.T. (2002). Marriage and fatherhood are associated with lower testosterone in males. *Evolution and Human Behavior, 23*(3), 193–201. http://dx.doi.org/10.1016/S1090-5138(01)00101-5

Gray, P.B., McHale, T.S., & Carré, J.M. (2017). A review of human male field studies of hormones and behavioral reproductive effort. *Hormones and Behavior, 91*, 52–67. http://dx.doi.org/10.1016/j.yhbeh.2016.07.004

Gray, P.B., Parkin, J.C., & Samms-Vaughan, M.E. (2007). Hormonal correlates of human paternal interactions: A hospital-based investigation in urban Jamaica. *Hormones and Behavior, 52*(4), 499–507. http://dx.doi.org/10.1016/j.yhbeh.2007.07.005

Kuo, P.X., Saini, E.K., Thomason, E., Schultheiss, O.C., Gonzalez, R., & Volling, B.L. (2016). Individual variation in fathers' testosterone reactivity to infant distress predicts parenting behaviors with their 1-year-old infants. *Developmental Psychobiology, 58*(3), 303–314. doi:10.1002/dev.21370

Kuzawa, C.W., Gettler, L.T., Muller, M.N., McDade, T.W., & Feranil, A.B. (2009). Fatherhood, pair-bonding and testosterone in the Philippines. *Hormones and Behavior, 56*(4), 429–435. http://dx.doi.org/10.1016/j.yhbeh.2009.07.010

Lamb, M.E. (2004). *The role of the father in child development.* Hoboken, NJ: John Wiley & Sons, Inc.

Lawson, D.W., Nuñez-de la Mora, A., Cooper, G.D., Prentice, A.M., Moore, S.E., & Sear, R. (2017). Marital status and sleeping arrangements predict salivary testosterone levels in rural Gambian men. *Adaptive Human Behavior and Physiology, 3*(3), 221–240. doi:10.1007/s40750-017-0066-z

Mascaro, J.S., Hackett, P.D., & Rilling, J.K. (2013). Testicular volume is inversely correlated with nurturing-related brain activity in human fathers. *Proceedings of the National Academy of Sciences of the United States of America, 110*(39), 15746–15751. doi:10.1073/pnas.1305579110

Mascaro, J.S., Hackett, P.D., & Rilling, J.K. (2014). Differential neural responses to child and sexual stimuli in human fathers and non-fathers and their hormonal correlates. *Psychoneuroendocrinology, 46*, 153–163. http://dx.doi.org/10.1016/j.psyneuen.2014.04.014

Mazur, A. (2014). Testosterone of young husbands rises with children in the home. *Andrology, 2*(1), 125–129. doi:10.1111/j.2047-2927.2013.00164.x

Mehta, P.H., & Josephs, R.A. (2010). Testosterone and cortisol jointly regulate dominance: Evidence for a dual-hormone hypothesis. *Hormones and Behavior, 58*(5), 898–906. http://dx.doi.org/10.1016/j.yhbeh.2010.08.020

Naber, F., van IJzendoorn, M.H., Deschamps, P., van Engeland, H., & Bakermans-Kranenburg, M.J. (2010). Intranasal oxytocin increases fathers' observed responsiveness during play with their children: A double-blind within-subject experiment. *Psychoneuroendocrinology, 35*(10), 1583–1586. https://doi.org/10.1016/j.psyneuen.2010.04.007

Perini, T., Ditzen, B., Fischbacher, S., & Ehlert, U. (2012). Testosterone and relationship quality across the transition to fatherhood. *Biological Psychology, 90*(3), 186–191. http://dx.doi.org/10.1016/j.biopsycho.2012.03.004

Rilling, J.K. (2013). The neural and hormonal bases of human parental care. *Neuropsychologia, 51*(4), 731–747. http://dx.doi.org/10.1016/j.neuropsychologia.2012.12.017

Saxbe, D.E., Edelstein, R.S., Lyden, H.M., Wardecker, B.M., Chopik, W.J., & Moors, A.C. (2017). Fathers' decline in testosterone and synchrony with partner testosterone during pregnancy predicts greater postpartum relationship investment. *Hormones and Behavior, 90*, 39–47. http://dx.doi.org/10.1016/j.yhbeh.2016.07.005

Saxbe, D.E., Schetter, C.D., Simon, C.D., Adam, E.K., & Shalowitz, M.U. (2017). High paternal testosterone may protect against postpartum depressive symptoms in fathers, but confer risk to mothers and children. *Hormones and Behavior, 95*(Suppl. C), 103–112. https://doi.org/10.1016/j.yhbeh.2017.07.014

Storey, A.E., Noseworthy, D.E., Delahunty, K.M., Halfyard, S.J., & McKay, D.W. (2011). The effects of social context on the hormonal and behavioral responsiveness of human fathers. *Hormones and Behavior, 60*(4), 353–361. http://dx.doi.org/10.1016/j.yhbeh.2011.07.001

Storey, A.E., Walsh, C.J., Quinton, R.L., & Wynne-Edwards, K.E. (2000). Hormonal correlates of paternal responsiveness in new and expectant fathers. *Evolution and Human Behavior, 21*(2), 79–95. doi:10.1016/s1090-5138(99)00042-2

Storey, A.E., & Ziegler, T.E. (2016). Primate paternal care: Interactions between biology and social experience. *Hormones and Behavior, 77,* 260–271. http://dx.doi.org/10.1016/j.yhbeh.2015.07.024

Trumble, B.C., Jaeggi, A.V., & Gurven, M. (2015). Evolving the neuroendocrine physiology of human and primate cooperation and collective action. *Philosophical Transactions of the Royal Society of London B: Biological Sciences, 370*(1683).

van Anders, S. M. (2013). Beyond masculinity: Testosterone, gender/sex, and human social behavior in a comparative context. *Frontiers in Neuroendocrinology, 34*(3), 198–210. doi:http://dx.doi.org/10.1016/j.yfrne.2013.07.001

van Anders, S.M., Goldey, K.L., & Kuo, P.X. (2011). The steroid/peptide theory of social bonds: Integrating testosterone and peptide responses for classifying social behavioral contexts. *Psychoneuroendocrinology, 36*(9), 1265–1275. http://dx.doi.org/10.1016/j.psyneuen.2011.06.001

Weisman, O., Zagoory-Sharon, O., & Feldman, R. (2012). Oxytocin administration to parent enhances infant physiological and behavioral readiness for social engagement. *Biological Psychiatry, 72*(12), 982–989. https://doi.org/10.1016/j.biopsych.2012.06.011

Weisman, O., Zagoory-Sharon, O., & Feldman, R. (2013). Oxytocin administration alters HPA reactivity in the context of parent-infant interaction. *European Neuropsychopharmacology, 23*(12), 1724–1731. http://dx.doi.org/10.1016/j.euroneuro.2013.06.006

Weisman, O., Zagoory-Sharon, O., & Feldman, R. (2014). Oxytocin administration, salivary testosterone, and father-infant social behavior. *Progress in Neuro-Psychopharmacology and Biological Psychiatry, 49,* 47–52. http://dx.doi.org/10.1016/j.pnpbp.2013.11.006

Wingfield, J.C., Hegner, R.E., Dufty, A.M., & Ball, G.F. (1990). The "Challenge Hypothesis": Theoretical implications for patterns of testosterone secretion, mating systems, and breeding strategies. *The American Naturalist, 136*(6), 829–846.

SECTION 5

Cognition and emotion

20

SEX HORMONAL EFFECTS ON BRAIN LATERALIZATION

Markus Hausmann and D. Michael Burt

Introduction

Brain lateralization or *functional cerebral asymmetries* (FCAs) refer to the relative differences between the left and right cerebral hemisphere in some neural functions, including cognitive and emotional processing. Within the cognitive domain, it is well established that the left hemisphere predominates in different language processes and complex motor coordination, whereas the right dominates in spatial abilities, non-verbal memory and face recognition (Corballis, 2015).

In addition to these well-established FCAs, emotional and social processes also appear to be asymmetrically organized in the brain. There is convincing empirical evidence that emotions are asymmetrically processed, although the pattern of asymmetry is debated. The *right-hemisphere hypothesis* (Borod et al., 1998) states that all six basic emotions (i.e., anger, disgust, fear, happiness, sadness, surprise) are exclusively processed in the right hemisphere. In contrast, the *valence model* of emotion lateralization (e.g., Stafford & Brandaro, 2010) suggests that the right hemisphere dominates processing of negatively valenced emotions (sadness, anger, fear, and disgust), whereas positively valenced emotions (happiness and surprise) are dominantly processed by the left. This model was originally based on studies of patients with unilateral lesions, but later received support from neurologically intact participants (e.g., Silberman & Weingartner, 1986). A variation of the valence model categorizes emotions in terms of approach and avoidance rather than positive and negative valence (e.g., Harmon-Jones, 2004). The valence and approach–avoidance models overlap but also differ because motivation is not the same as valence. For instance, anger is associated with approach behavior but is negative in valence.

Behavioral approach and avoidance tendencies have been associated with both the experience and the expression of emotion (e.g., Davidson, 1992), and studies indicate that the left frontal area is associated with behaviors facilitating approach, such as fine motor behavior, language, and the expression of certain positive emotions (e.g., Fox & Davidson, 1984). In contrast, the right frontal area is associated with behaviors facilitating avoidance from novel or stressful stimuli, such as gross motor movement, autonomic reactivity, and the expression of certain negative emotions (Fox & Davidson, 1984).

One frequent approach to investigate the relationship between FCAs and both affective and social behavior is to explore the perception of emotional facial expressions using behavioral paradigms such as the visual half-field technique (Bourne, 2006) and the emotional chimeric faces test (e.g., Sackheim & Gur, 1978). Typically, in the emotional chimeric faces test, participants are presented with two mirror image faces, one which displays an emotion on the left and the other on the right (see Figure 20.1)

Although the contents of the stimuli are identical mirror images, participants tend to find the face presenting the emotional expression on the left hemiface more emotional, a finding that is generally interpreted as support for the right hemisphere hypothesis (Innes et al., 2016). In a typical visual half-field technique, an emotional and a neutral face are presented briefly (to avoid eye movement) to either side of fixation and participants decide as quickly and as accurate as possible which face displays an emotional facial expression. Response times and accuracy data revealed by the visual half-field technique sometimes support the right hemisphere hypothesis (e.g., Alves, Aznar-Casanova, & Fukusima, 2009), but at other times the related valence and approach–avoidance models (e.g., Reuter-Lorenz & Davidson, 1981). Both paradigms appear to measure somewhat different aspects of emotion lateralization and face processing, with the visual half-field technique showing greater variation in findings. This variation may be more related to specific emotion, as recent research using music to induce emotion altered FCAs for facial expressions (e.g., Hausmann, Hodgetts, & Eerola, 2016), possibly due to the music affecting the lateralized patterns of frontal brain activity. Specifically, this study found that listening to a happy music excerpt revealed a reliable increase in left language lateralization in verbal dichotic listening and reduced right lateralization in emotional lateralization and spatial attention, as measured with emotional chimeric faces and line bisection tasks, respectively. However, whether the effect of listening to music was driven by the induced emotion induction or by basic musical and acoustic features that are typical for happy music (e.g., higher tempo, etc.) requires more research.

Frontal alpha asymmetry offers another approach to understanding emotion lateralization, as Wheeler, Davidson and Tomarken's (1993) found that individuals with greater left frontal activation reported more intense feelings to positive stimuli, whereas individuals with greater right frontal activation reported more intense feelings to negative stimuli. Their findings have led to a body of research implicating asymmetry in frontal alpha activity as a potentially concurrent and prospective marker of affective processing and psychopathology. However, there are several

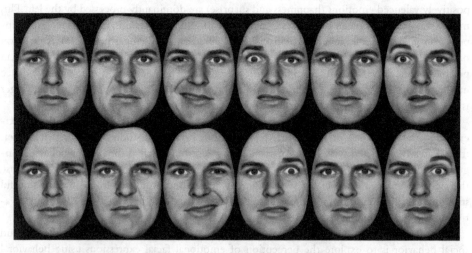

Figure 20.1   Which image looks more emotional? The upper and lower chimeric faces are mirror versions with the left of the upper face and right of the lower face being emotional.

conceptual and methodological issues with this measurement (see Reznik & Allen, 2017 for review), and it not only reflects traits but also states of affective style (Harmon-Jones & Gable, 2017; Coan & Allen, 2003).

Sex-related variation in FCAs

There is substantial variation between individuals in the magnitude and direction of FCAs, with about half of the variation in FCAs attributable to individual differences (Kim et al., 1990). Such variation has generally been ignored as random error (Hellige, 1993). However, there are many inter- *and* intra-individual factors contributing to the variation in FCAs, including longstanding factors such as age, handedness and biological sex, but also factors which vary within an individual such as hormonal and emotional states. In the section that follows, we will outline evidence that sex and sex hormones are two important factors which contribute to inter- and intra-individual variations in FCAs in the cognitive domain.

Early clinical findings suggested that unilateral lesions are more likely to result in severe cognitive deficits for men than women, for whom deficits are less hemisphere-specific (e.g., McGlone, 1977; 1978). Although the majority of studies focusing on FCAs in neurotypical participants found no significant interaction of hemisphere with sex (partly because of insufficient statistical power), several meta-analyses and large-scale studies, which included several hundreds of participants (e.g., Hirnstein, Westerhausen, Korsnes, & Hugdahl, 2013; Bless et al., 2015), revealed generally larger FCAs in men than women (Voyer, 1996, 2011), leading to the conclusion that, at the population level, larger FCAs in men than women are small but reliable. In addition to sex differences in the magnitude and direction of cognitive FCAs, there is evidence that women demonstrate greater variation in FCAs than men (Hausmann et al., 1998).

Until recently, research focused mainly on sex differences in FCAs in cognitive domains, but current research has found that several key neural correlates of emotion and decision making show sex-related variation in FCAs (Reber & Tranel, 2017), particularly in the ventromedial prefrontal cortex and the amygdala, "in which men with right-side lesions and women with left-side lesions display significant behavioral impairments, yet men with left-side lesions and women with right-side lesions display relatively unimpaired performance on emotion and decision-making tasks" (p. 270). The ventromedial prefrontal cortex is known to be significantly involved in emotion regulation, decision making, and social functioning (e.g., Damasio et al., 1994).

Patterns of activation for emotionally arousing memories reveal sex differences in FCAs, with a stronger relationship between memory of emotionally arousing stimuli and right amygdala activation in men but left amygdala activation in women (e.g., Cahill et al., 2001). In line with this, extensive social conduct deficits in men after unilateral right amygdala damage but in women after left amygdala damage were found (Tranel & Bechara, 2009). These asymmetries in the social domain appear paralleled in patterns of neural connectivity of the amygdala, with men showing higher connectivity in the right than left amygdala but the opposite pattern in women (Kilpatrick, Zald, Pardo, & Cahill, 2006).

For FCAs to develop, be maintained, and vary, interhemispheric connections appear to be vital (e.g., Chiarello & Maxfield, 1996). Despite interhemispheric connections being mainly excitatory, their long-lasting effect is inhibitory (Innocenti, 1986; Kawaguchi, 1992), with inhibition by the dominant hemisphere resulting in FCAs and, conversely, the reduction of interhemispheric inhibition resulting in increased bilateral activation (e.g., Cook, 1984; Regard, Cook, Wieser, & Landis, 1994).

Early studies aimed at linking sex differences in structural and functional interhemispheric interaction directly to the size and shape of the corpus callosum, but instead led to an ongoing debate as to whether sex differences in the macro- and microanatomy of the corpus callosum even exist and, if so, what their potential functional relevance may be (see Bishop & Wahlsten, 1997 for review). Interhemispheric transfer time (IHTT) of visually evoked potentials is faster in the right-to-left direction than left-to-right direction (e.g., Marzi, 2010), and this directional asymmetry appears less pronounced in women than men (Moes, Brown, & Minnema, 2007; Nowicka & Fersten, 2001). However, the extent to which interhemispheric inhibition related to FCAs and IHTT share the same transcallosal mechanisms is not entirely clear (Hausmann et al., 2013).

The patterns of neutral connectivity discussed above might be revealed with Diffusion Tensor Imaging (DTI), which has recently been used to investigate sex differences (see Gong et al., 2011, for a review). Studies generally find greater overall cortical connectivity in women (e.g., Gong et al., 2009) and greater *interhemispheric* connectivity in women than men (e.g., Duarte-Carvajalino et al., 2012; Ingalhalikar et al., 2014), but greater structural connectivity in men *within* hemispheres, leading Ingalhalikar et al. to speculate that male brains' structure facilitates connectivity between perception and coordinated action, whereas female brains facilitate communication between analytical and intuitive processing modes. Although the extent to which developmental trajectories of sexual dimorphisms in the human connectome (e.g., Ingalhalikar et al., 2014) and sex differences in, for example, language lateralization (Hugdahl, 1995) coincide is currently unknown, sex hormone fluctuations during adolescence are likely to play an important role (e.g., Neufang et al., 2009).

The pattern of interhemispheric connectivity may vary depending upon functions. For example, Tunc et al. (2016) found higher structural connectivity between motor, sensory (auditory and visual) and default mode subnetworks associated with executive control tasks (fronto-parietal and cingulo-opercular) in men but higher structural connectivity in women among subcortical, sensory, and attention subnetworks. Another recent structural connectivity study which investigated a large sample of 312 males and 362 females aged 9–22 years also suggested that sex differences in patterns of brain connectivity relate to male and female profiles of cognitive performance (Satterthwaite et al., 2015). Although these studies indicated clear sex differences in structural and functional connectivity, other studies did not (e.g., Nielsen et al., 2013). Variation between studies may to some extent be due to differences in DTI techniques, which are still developing and debated (Björnholm et al., 2017).

However, sex alone does not explain the large variation in FCAs between studies. Instead, sex may be "an imperfect, temporary proxy for yet-unknown factors, such as hormones or sex-linked genes, that explain variation better than sex" (Maney, 2016, p. 1). In line with this, variation in sex hormone levels, such as during the menstrual cycle, reveal that hormones account for inter- and intra-individual variation in FCAs.

Organizing effects of sex hormones effects on FCAs

Sex hormones are categorized as having either organizing effects, affecting neuronal development, or activating effects, modulating functional interactions within existing neuronal structures (Phoenix, Goy, Gerall, & Young, 1959), but these effects overlap rather than being highly distinct (Arnold & Breedlove, 1985).

The organizing effects of sex hormones have, for example, been assessed in individuals exposed to atypical (prenatal) hormonal environments, such as those with Congenital Adrenal Hyperplasia (CAH), which causes prenatal overproduction of androgens (that are normally medically corrected after birth). Although Tirosh, Rod, Cohen and Hochberg (1993) found significantly enhanced FCAs in verbal tasks, particularly in CAH women, suggesting an androgenic role in language lateralization, their finding has not been replicated (e.g., Helleday, Siwers, Ritzen, & Hugdahl, 1994; Mathews, Fane, Pasterski, Conway, Brook, & Hines, 2004). Studies of FCAs in individuals with hormonal atypicalities due to chromosomal aberrations have, for example, found that men with XXY Klinefelter syndrome, which results typically in decreased androgen levels but increased follicle-stimulating hormone and luteinizing hormone levels, have inverse or weak dominance of hand, language, and visuospatial abilities (Ganou, Grouios, Koidou, & Aleveriadou, 2010). The reduced FCAs for language have been shown to be related to decreased structural asymmetries in the superior temporal gyrus and the supramarginal gyrus (part of Wernicke's area) (Van Rijn, Aleman, Swaab, Vink, Sommer, & Kahn, 2008). Thus, although the results are mixed, possibly due to variation in androgen supplementation later in life, evidence from individuals with atypical hormonal levels points to androgens increasing FCAs.

Activating effects of sex hormones on FCAs

In comparison to the *organizing effects* of sex hormones on the brain, *activating effects* are acute and reversible (Arnold, 2009), enabling dynamic changes in FCAs, functional connectivity, and consequently behavior (Wisniewski, 1998). It is the activating effects which are in the focus of our own research and the current review.

The effects of sex hormones can be mediated by slow genomic mechanisms through nuclear receptors as well as by fast nongenomic mechanisms through membrane-associated receptors and signaling cascades (e.g., McEwen & Alves, 1999). Thus, sex hormones have many varied effects on both brain functioning and plasticity. Rather than being restricted to sexual and reproductive behavior, sex hormones have more general effects such as on higher cognitive functioning. However, the underlying hormonal mechanisms that modulate FCAs and cognitive behavior are generally unclear (Wisniewski, 1998). The well-known, relatively short-time fluctuations in estradiol and progesterone levels of the menstrual cycle have led to a focus on these hormones in women (Figure 20.2).

Moreover, it has been shown in behavioral (e.g., Bibawi et al., 1995; Hampson, 1990; Hausmann, 2005; Hausmann and Güntürkün, 2000; Hausmann et al., 2002; Mead & Hampson, 1996; McCourt, Mark, Radonovich, Willison, & Freeman, 1997; Sanders & Wenmoth, 1998) and neuroimaging studies (e.g., Weis et al., 2008; Weis et al., 2011; Thimm et al., 2014) that FCAs and the functional connectivity related to cognitive processes change across the menstrual cycle. However, results are controversial (Compton, Costello, & Diepold, 2004; see Hausmann, 2017, Hausmann and Bayer, 2010, for review) as some studies (e.g., Hausmann et al., 2002; Hausmann & Güntürkün, 2000; Mead & Hampson, 1996; Sanders & Wenmoth, 1998; Weis et al., 2008) found a reduction in FCAs related to high estradiol levels and/or progesterone levels, whereas other studies found the opposite, significant and larger FCAs related to high estradiol levels and/or progesterone levels in comparison to reduced FCAs during menstruation (e.g., Hampson, 1990; Mead & Hampson, 1996; Sanders & Wenmoth, 1998). Such conflicting results sometimes even occurred in the same study, though with different stimuli or tasks (e.g., Mead & Hampson, 1996; Sanders & Wenmoth, 1998), indicating that size and direction of the effects partly depend on the specific task and test modality (Hausmann & Bayer, 2010; Hodgetts, Weis, & Hausmann, 2015).

The search for underlying mechanisms

The mechanisms by which sex hormones modulate FCAs appear to be complex, with some inconsistencies occurring due to methodological differences between studies, such as the task

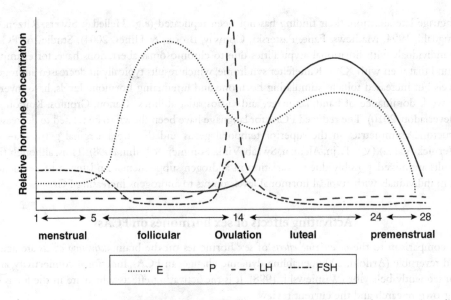

Figure 20.2 Schematic figure of the menstrual cycle, illustrating fluctuations in sex hormones (estradiol, E; progesterone, P) and gonadotropin levels (luteinizing hormone, LH; follicle-stimulating hormone, FSH) during an average 28-day menstrual cycle.

(adopted from Hausmann & Bayer, 2010; reprinted with permission from MIT Press).

and hormone assessment method used. Some studies found that hormones affect only one hemisphere, but some implicated the left (e.g., Hampson, 1990, Bibawi, Cherry, & Hellige, 1995) and others the right (e.g., Sanders & Wenmoth, 1998). An alternative mechanism was proposed by McCourt et al. (1997), who concluded that the increase of a leftward bias in a visuomotor task during the luteal phase as compared to menstrual phase might indicate that both the left and right hemisphere might have been non-specifically activated midluteally, and a slight FCA favoring the right hemisphere may have been promoted. Unfortunately, however, no attempt was made by McCourt et al. to assess directly concentrations of sex hormones, leaving it unclear whether the effect was related to progesterone and/or estradiol levels.

Findings from work with rats led Bianki and Filippova (2000) to a different approach centered on hemispheric interaction to explain cycle-related effects of sex hormones on FCAs in which increased estrogen levels during proestrus increased left hemisphere interhemispheric inhibition on the right hemisphere, whereas lower estrogen levels weakened this inhibitory action. In humans, based upon findings that FCAs were reduced for both for left and right hemisphere tasks during the midluteal phase, Hausmann and Güntürkün (2000) proposed that it was the interaction between hemispheres that was hormonally mediated rather than influence on one or both hemispheres. The authors suggested that the hormonal effect on FCAs was caused by progesterone reducing interhemispheric inhibition via suppressing the excitatory responses of neurons to glutamate (e.g., Smith et al., 1987), as well as by enhancing their inhibitory responses to GABA (Smith, 1991), resulting in hemispheric decoupling. This hypothesis of progesterone-mediated interhemispheric decoupling (Hausmann & Güntürkün, 2000) has received empirical support from studies using various techniques, including behavioral experiments (e.g., Hausmann et al., 2002; Hausmann & Güntürkün, 2000), transcranial magnetic stimulation (Hausmann et al., 2006), and fMRI (Weis et al., 2008, 2011). Weis et al (2008) also found reduced FCAs in the behavioral data when hormonal levels were high. However, the effect occurred in the follicular phase when only levels of estradiol were high. In addition, and in line with the hypothesis, the functional connectivity analysis based upon the same participants found an inhibitory influence of the dominant over the non-dominant hemisphere that varied with the menstrual cycle, but again with estradiol levels relating to the reduction in functional connectivity between hemispheres.

Estradiol, progesterone, or both?

The reduction in FCAs during high estradiol levels found by Weis et al. (2008) has also been found in other studies (e.g., Hausmann, 2005; Hausmann et al., 2006). Such findings are difficult to explain in terms of progesterone-mediated interhemispheric decoupling mainly because estradiol typically has an excitatory effect (but one which is complex and may occasionally be inhibitory, Taubøll, Sveberg, & Svalheim, 2015) whereas progesterone's effects are mainly inhibitory (Majewska et al., 1986). However, the neuromodulatory effects of estrogen and progesterone appear to interact. For example, prior estradiol administration "rendered the system refractory to neuromodulation by progesterone" (Smith, 1994, p. 66). Thus, explanations of cycle-related FCAs must at least take into account the interaction between estrogen and progesterone (Hodgetts et al., 2015).

The model of progesterone-mediated interhemispheric decoupling initially assumed that excitatory callosal fibers activated GABA-initiated inhibition in homotopic areas of the contralateral hemisphere and that high progesterone levels inhibit the interhemispheric inhibition, thereby increasing activation in the non-dominant hemisphere for a given task (Hausmann & Güntürkün, 2000). If the effect of estradiol on glutamate receptors is mainly excitatory, then we would assume both an increase in interhemispheric inhibition and larger FCAs when estradiol levels are high in the follicular phase. Although there is evidence for sex hormone–linked increased and decreased interhemispheric inhibition, it has been shown that high estradiol levels generally increase neural activity in both hemispheres (Dietrich et al., 2001; Hausmann et al., 2002), suggesting that the combination of high levels of progesterone together with high levels of estradiol results in increased activation in both the non-dominant and dominant hemispheres. In contrast to progesterone, however, GABA-ergic mechanisms seem to be unaffected by estradiol in isolation as an acute response (Taubøll et al., 2015). The combined effect of progesterone on the glutamatergic and GABA-ergic systems may be required to inhibit interhemispheric inhibition, whereas the acute excitatory effect of estradiol on the glutamatergic system increases activation in both hemispheres with a significant effect on the less active, non-dominant hemisphere. Overall, the results suggest that high estradiol levels increase activation in both cerebral hemispheres, whereas high progesterone levels rather activate the subdominant hemisphere, probably via inhibition of interhemispheric decoupling. However, there are exceptions to this; for example, Weis et al. (2008) found reduced interhemispheric inhibition, and consequently reduced FCAs when estradiol levels were elevated during the follicular phase.

The effects of estrogen on prefrontal functioning

The effects discussed so far have predominantly suggested that estrogen modulates the stimulus-driven bottom-up aspects of FCAs. However, some previous studies have also shown effects of estrogen on prefrontal function such as working memory and tasks requiring high levels of cognitive control (e.g., Colzato, Hertsig, van den Wildenberg, & Hommel, 2012; Hampson & Morley, 2013; Rosenberg & Park, 2002; but also see Colzato, Pratt, & Hommel, 2010; Gasbarri et al., 2008; Hatta & Nagaya, 2009). Thus, cycle-related effects of estradiol may affect cognition via prefrontal cortex (Keenan, Ezzat, Ginsburg, & Moore, 2001), an area with a particularly high estrogen receptor concentration in humans (Bixo, Backstrom, Winblad, & Andersson, 1995). The hypothesis that estradiol affects FCAs via its effects on cognitive control was first tested by Hjelmervik et al. (2012) using a dichotic listening task (Hugdahl, 1995) that had previously demonstrated both a larger left hemispheric bias in men than women (e.g., Hirnstein et al., 2013) and fluctuations in language lateralization across the menstrual cycle (e.g., Hampson, 1990; Sanders & Wenmoth, 1998). Specifically, Hjelmervik et al. instructed participants to pay attention and report stimuli presented to the left ear (or right ear), and cognitive control was defined as the ability to override a stimulus-driven response in the favor of an instruction-driven one (i.e., top – down process). Results revealed high estradiol levels during the follicular phase were associated with an increased left-ear advantage but only when participants were cued to shift attention to stimuli presented to the non-dominant left ear. As no menstrual cycle effect was observed when participants were not cued to shift their attention, Hjelmervik et al. (2012) concluded that the influence of estradiol was on cognitive control rather than language lateralization per se.

However, a subsequent replication attempt (Hodgetts et al., 2015) found reduced FCAs in women with high estradiol levels regardless of level of cognitive control, leading to the conclusion that estradiol reduces the stimulus-driven (bottom-up) aspect of language lateralization rather than the cognitive control component. Notably, Hjelmervik et al. (2012) used a within-subject design, repeatedly testing the same individuals, whereas Hodgetts et al.'s design was between subjects comparing individuals who were higher and lower than median levels of estradiol. Thus, different findings may be due to differences in the study design and sample size. A cycle-related modulation of the top-down aspect of FCAs was recently found in an emotional prosody task, in which participants were asked to identify the emotional tone of a target (Hodgetts, Weis & Hausmann, 2017), supporting the potential role of estradiol in the modulation of cognitive control.

Hormonal effects on FCAs related to affective and social behavior

Menstrual cycle–related effects of estradiol on cognition and FCAs are likely to involve the prefrontal cortex (Keenan et al., 2001; Hjelmervik et al., 2012, respectively). Since asymmetries in frontal activation have been linked to approach and withdrawal tendencies (Davidson, 1992), we might expect fluctuations in estradiol levels to alter approach and withdrawal tendencies which are likely to be critical for social interactions (Coan & Allen, 2003).

Although fontal alpha asymmetry as neural marker of approach and avoidance tendencies is assumed to be relatively robust over a lifetime, there is still variation due to environmental/situational factors (Harmon-Jones & Gable, 2017; Coan & Allen, 2003), such as changes in the hormonal environment as discussed previously. In line with the idea of sex hormones affecting emotion by modulating asymmetry in frontal activation, women suffering from premenstrual dysphoric disorder showed greater right (than left) frontal alpha activity during the luteal phase (Baehr et al., 2004). In healthy women, a different pattern has been found with MEG, revealing higher activation over left than right frontal electrodes during the menstrual phase, when levels of estradiol and progesterone are relatively low, compared to the periovulatory phase, when only estradiol levels are high (Hwang et al., 2008). In contrast, Solis-Ortiz et al. (1994) found no menstrual cycle-related variation in frontal alpha asymmetries, possibly due to a small sample. But they did find significantly higher interhemispheric correlation in alpha$_1$ (8–10 Hz) activity between frontal electrodes (F3 and F4) during ovulation and for occipital electrodes (O1 and O2) during the premenstrual phase, supporting the idea that hormonal fluctuations modulate interhemispheric oscillations. This is in line with the suggestion that the corpus callosum may provide a neuroanatomical correlate for frontal cortical asymmetries and that interhemispheric crosstalk plays a significant role in approach–avoidance motivation and behavior (Schutter & Harmon-Jones, 2013). Inconsistent findings may be due to the fact that previous studies did not distinguish between healthy women who are susceptible and unsusceptible to emotion-related symptoms of the menstrual cycle (Huang et al., 2015). Huang et al. hypothesized that women high in neuroticism are more susceptible and are more likely to experience cycle-related fluctuations in resting frontal alpha asymmetry. Indeed, their results revealed lower relative left prefrontal alpha during the midluteal phase (days 22–24) in high-neuroticism women than lower-neuroticism women, implying that estradiol and progesterone play a role. However, the only significant (positive) relationship for the midluteal phase in Huang et al. was reported for estradiol levels and alpha$_1$ asymmetry at prefrontal electrode positions ($r = .342$, $p < .05$). Overall, the authors concluded that resting frontal alpha asymmetry is a reliable neural marker of positive versus negative affective styles that are influenced by the state of the menstrual cycle.

Little research has been conducted on the hormonal effects on FCAs in the perception of social emotional cues such as facial expressions. This is surprising not only because such cues are important but also because similar sex differences with reduced FCAs in women have been found for facial expression perception (e.g., Bourne, 2005, 2008) as have been found in the cognitive domain (Voyer, 1996, 2011). Recently, Bourne and Vladeanu (2017) found more socially anxious women to show a reduced right-hemisphere bias in the emotional chimeric faces task that used six emotions. A similar but less pronounced pattern was also found in more socially anxious men. Using the chimeric faces task with expressions of only happiness and anger, Bourne and Gray (2009) found the second-to-fourth finger (2D:4D) ratio, which is assumed to reflect prenatal testosterone and estradiol exposure (e.g., Manning et al., 1998), to be associated with a stronger right hemisphere bias, suggesting that higher levels of prenatal testosterone exposure and low levels of estrogen exposure result in a stronger right hemisphere bias in the perception of happy and angry facial expressions. However, the 2D:4D ratio is a very indirect and highly controversial measurement of the prenatal hormonal environment, and further research is needed to understand hormonal effects on FCAs involved in social perception. We are currently starting to address this by investigating women across different cycle phases (Birch, Burt, & Hausmann, in progress).

Concluding remarks

Until now, research has mainly focused on the hormonal effects of sex and sex hormones on FCAs in the cognitive domain. While further work is needed to clarify the relationship and mechanisms in the cognitive domain, our understanding of the relationship between emotion lateralization and approach and avoidance behavior, though of key importance to social behavior, is in its infancy.

The organizing and activating effects of sex hormones modulate FCAs underlying cognitive processing. As similar FCAs have been found related to emotional and social behavior, it is likely that these will also be modulated by hormonal fluctuation. While sex hormones are certainly not the exclusive cause of variations in FCAs, including those responsible for sex differences, the lack of control for potential hormonal effects is likely to explain some of the inconsistencies in reports of FCAs in the current literature.

The mechanisms underlying the organizing and activating effects of sex hormones on FCAs are unclear. Three potential activating mechanisms on FCAs have been suggested: (i) sex hormones affect only one hemisphere (e.g., Hampson, 1990), (ii) both hemispheres are non-specifically activated hormonally, accentuating slight asymmetries, and (iii) sex hormones affect the interhemispheric crosstalk, probably via the corpus callosum (e.g., Hausmann & Güntürkün, 2000). In line with the latter hypothesis, a direct relationship between the corpus callosum and emotion has been reported, highlighting the importance of considering the direction of signal transfer between the cerebral hemispheres in studying approach- and avoidance-related motivation (Schutter & Harmon-Jones, 2013). These authors concluded that the corpus callosum provides a possible neuroanatomical correlate for frontal cortical asymmetries and that interhemispheric signal transfer plays a role in the emergence of approach-related motivation and behavior. However, for FCAs in general, all proposed mechanisms have received some empirical support, and a combination of these mechanisms is likely (Hausmann, 2017).

References

Alves, N. T., Aznar-Casanova, J. A., & Fukusima, S. S. (2009). Patterns of brain asymmetry in the perception of positive and negative facial expressions. *Laterality, 14*, 256–272.

Arnold, A. P. (2009). The organizational-activational hypothesis as the foundation for a unified theory of sexual differentiation of all mammalian tissues. *Hormones and Behavior, 55*, 570–578.

Arnold, A. P., & Breedlove, S. M. (1985). Sexual differentiation of the brain and behaviour: A re-analysis, *Hormones and Behavior, 19*, 469–498.

Baehr, E., Rosenfeld, P., Miller, L., & Baehr, R. (2004). Premenstrual dysphoric disorder and changes in frontal alpha asymmetry. *International Journal of Psychophysiology, 52*, 159–167.

Bianki, V. L., & Filippova, E. B. (2000). *Sex differences in lateralization in the animal brain*. Newark, NJ: Harwood Academic Publishers.

Bibawi, D., Cherry, B., & Hellige, J. B. (1995). Fluctuations of perceptual asymmetry across time in women and men: Effects related to the menstrual cycle. *Neuropsychologia, 33*, 131–138.

Birch, Y. K., Burth, D. M., & Hausmann, M. (2017). *Functional cerebral asymmetries of emotional face perception across the menstrual cycle*.

Bishop, K. M., & Wahlsten, D. (1997). Sex differences in the human corpus callosum: Myth or reality? *Neuroscience and Biobehavioral Review, 21*, 581–601.

Bixo, M., Backstrom, T., Winblad, B., & Andersson, A. (1995). Estradiol and testosterone in specific regions of the human female brain in different endocrine states. *Journal of Steroid, Biochemical, and Molecular Biology, 55*, 297–303.

Björnholm, L., Nikkinen, J., Kiviniemi, V., Nordström, T., Niemeläe, S., Drakesmith, M., . . . Paus, T. (2017). Structural properties of the human corpus callosum: Multimodal assessment and sex differences. *Neuroimage, 152*, 108–118.

Bless, J. J., Westerhausen, R., von Koss Torkildsen, J., Gudmundsen, M., Kompus, K., & Hugdahl, K. (2015). Laterality across languages: Results from a global dichotic listening study using a smartphone application. *Laterality, 20*, 434–452.

Borod, J. C., Cicero, B. A., Obler, L. K., Welkowitz, J., Erhan, H. M., Santschi, C., . . . Whalen, J. R. (1998). Right hemisphere emotional perception: Evidence across multiple channels. *Neuropsychology, 12*, 446–458.

Bourne, V. J. (2005). Lateralised processing of positive facial emotion: Sex differences in strength of hemispheric dominance. *Neuropsychologia, 43*, 953–956.

Bourne, V. J. (2006). The divided visual-field paradigm: Methodological considerations. *Laterality, 11*, 373–393.

Bourne, V. J. (2008). Examining the relationship between degree of handedness and degree of cerebral lateralization for processing facial emotion. *Neuropsychology, 22*, 350–356.

Bourne, V. J., & Gray, D. L. (2009). Hormone exposure and functional lateralisation: Examining the contributions of prenatal and later life hormonal exposure. *Psychoneuroendocrinology, 34*, 1214–1221.

Bourne, V. J., & Vladeanu, M. (2017). Depression or anxiety: Which is the best able to predict patterns of lateralization for the processing of emotional faces? *Cognition and Emotion, 31*, 201–208.

Cahill, L., Haier, R. J., White, N. S., Fallon, J., Kilpatrick, L., Lawrence, C., . . . Alkire, M. T. (2001). Sex-related difference in amygdala activity during emotionally influenced memory storage. *Neurobiology of Learning and Memory, 75*, 1–9.

Chiarello, C., & Maxfield, L. (1996). Varieties of interhemispheric inhibition, or how to keep a good hemisphere down. *Brain and Cognition, 30*, 81–108.

Coan, J. A., & Allen, J. J. B. (2003). The state and trait nature of frontal EEG asymmetry in emotion. In K. Hugdahl & R. J. Davidson (Eds.), *The asymmetrical brain* (2nd ed., pp. 565–615). Cambridge, MA: MIT Press.

Colzato, L. S., Hertsig, G., van den Wildenberg, W. P., & Hommel, B. (2010). Estrogen modulates inhibitory control in healthy human females: Evidence from the stop-signal paradigm. *Neuroscience, 167*, 709–715.

Colzato, L. S., Pratt, J., & Hommel, B. (2012). Estrogen modulates inhibition of return in healthy human females. *Neuropsychologia, 50*, 98–103.

Compton, R. J., Costello, C., & Diepold, J. (2004). Interhemispheric integration during the menstrual cycle: Failure to confirm progesterone-mediated interhemispheric decoupling. *Neuropsychologia, 42*, 1496–1503.

Cook, N. D. (1984). Callosal inhibition: The key to the brain code. *Behavioral Science, 29*, 98–110.

Corballis, M. C. (2015). What's left in language? Beyond the classical model. *Annals of the New York Academy of Sciences, 1359*, 14–29.

Damasio, H., Grabowski, T., Frank, R., Galaburda, A. M., & Damasio, A. R. (1994). The return of Phineas Gage: Clues about the brain from the skull of a famous patient. *Science, 264*, 1102–1105.

Davidson, R. J. (1992). Prolegmenon to the structure of emotion: Gleanings from neuropsychology. *Cognition and Emotion, 6*, 245–268.

Dietrich, T., Krings, T., Neulen, J., Willmes, K., Erberic, S., Thron, A., & Sturm, W. (2001). Effects of blood estrogen level on cortical activation patterns during cognitive activation as measures by functional MRI. *Neuroimage, 13*, 425–432.

Duarte-Carvajalino, J. M., Jahanshad, N., Lenglet, C., McMahon, K. L., de Zubicaray, G. I., Martin, N. G., . . . Sapiro, G. (2012). Hierarchical topological network analysis of anatomical human brain connectivity and differences related to sex and kinship. *Neuroimage, 59*, 3784–3804.

Fox, N. A., & Davidson, R. J. (1984). Hemispheric substrates for affect: A developmental model. In N. A. Fox & R. J. Davidson (Eds.), *The psychobiology of affective development* (pp. 353–382). Hillsdale, NJ: Erlbaum.

Ganou, M., Grouios, G., Koidou, I., & Aleveriadou, A. (2010). The concept of anomalous cerebral lateralization in Klinefelter syndrome. *Applied Neuropsychology, 17*, 144–152.

Gasbarri, A., Pompili, A., D'Onofrio, A., Cifariello, A., Tavares, M. C., & Tomaz, C. (2008). Working memory for emotional facial expressions: Role of the estrogen in young women. *Psychoneuroendocrinology, 33*, 964–972.

Gong, G., He, Y., & Evans, A. C. (2011). Brain connectivity: Gender makes a difference. *Neuroscientist, 17*, 575–591.

Gong, G., Rosa-Neto, P., Carbonell, F., Chen, Z. J., He, Y., & Evans, A. C. (2009). Age-and gender-related differences in the cortical anatomical network. *Journal of Neuroscience, 29*, 15684–15693.

Hampson, E. (1990). Estrogen-related variations in human spatial and articulatory-motor skills. *Psychoneuroendocrinology, 15*, 97–111.

Hampson, E., & Morley, E. E. (2013). Estradiol concentrations and working memory performance in women of reproductive age. *Psychoneuroendocrinology, 38*, 2897–2904.

Harmon-Jones, E. (2004). On the relationship of anterior brain activity and anger: Examining the role of attitude toward anger. *Cognition and Emotion, 18*, 337–361.

Harmon-Jones, E., & Gable, P. A. (2017). On the role of asymmetric frontal cortical activity in approach and withdrawal motivation: An updated review of the evidence. *Psychophysiology, 55*, e12879. doi:10.1111/psyp.12879

Hatta, T., & Nagaya, K. (2009). Menstrual cycle phase effects on memory and Stroop task performance. *Archives of Sexual Behavior, 38*, 821–827.

Hausmann, M. (2005). Hemispheric asymmetry in spatial attention across the menstrual cycle. *Neuropsychologia, 43*, 1559–1567.

Hausmann, M. (2017). Why sex hormones matter for neuroscience: A very short review on sex, sex hormones, and functional brain asymmetries. *Journal of Neuroscience Research, 95*, 40–49.

Hausmann, M., & Bayer, U. (2010). Sex hormonal effects on hemispheric asymmetry and interhemispheric interaction. In K. Hugdahl & R. Westerhausen (Eds.), *The two halves of the brain: Information processing in the cerebral hemispheres* (pp. 253–283). Cambridge, MA: MIT Press.

Hausmann, M., Becker, C., Gather, U., & Güntürkün, O. (2002). Functional cerebral asymmetries during the menstrual cycle: A cross sectional and longitudinal analysis. *Neuropsychologia, 40,* 808–816.

Hausmann, M., Behrendt-Körbitz, S., Kautz, H., Lamm, C., Radelt, F., & Güntürkün, O. (1998). Sex differences in oral asymmetries during word repetition. *Neuropsychologia, 36,* 1397–1402.

Hausmann, M., & Güntürkün, O. (2000). Steroid fluctuations modify functional cerebral asymmetries: The hypothesis of progesterone-mediated interhemispheric decoupling. *Neuropsychologia, 38,* 1362–1374.

Hausmann, M., Hamm, J. P., Waldie, K. E., & Kirk, I. J. (2013). Sex hormonal modulation of interhemispheric transfer time. *Neuropsychologia, 51,* 1734–1741.

Hausmann, M., Hodgetts, S., & Eerola, T. (2016). Music-induced changes in functional cerebral asymmetries. *Brain and Cognition, 104,* 58–71.

Hausmann, M., Tegenthoff, M., Sänger, J., Janssen, F., Güntürkün, O., & Schwenkreis, P. (2006). Transcallosal inhibition across the menstrual cycle: A TMS study. *Clinical Neurophysiology, 117,* 26–32.

Helleday, J., Siwers, B., Ritzen, E. M., & Hugdahl, K. (1994). Normal lateralization for handedness and ear advantage in a verbal dichotic listening task in women with Congenital Adrenal Hyperplasia (CAH). *Neuropsychologia, 32,* 875–880.

Hellige, J. B. (1993). *Hemispheric asymmetry: What's right and what's left.* Cambridge, MA: Harvard University Press.

Hirnstein, M., Westerhausen, R., Korsnes, M. S., & Hugdahl, K. (2013). Sex differences in language asymmetry are age-dependent and small: A large-scale, consonant-vowel dichotic listening study with behavioral and fMRI data. *Cortex, 49,* 1910–1921.

Hjelmervik, H., Westerhausen, R., Osnes, B., Endresen, C. B., Hugdahl, K., Hausmann, M., & Specht, K. (2012). Language lateralization and cognitive control across the menstrual cycle assessed with a dichotic-listening paradigm. *Psychoneuroendocrinology, 37,* 1866–1875.

Hodgetts, S., Weis, S., & Hausmann, M. (2015). Sex hormones affect language lateralisation but not cognitive control in normally cycling women. *Hormones and Behavior, 74,* 194–200.

Hodgetts, S., Weis, S., & Hausmann, M. (2017). Estradiol does not enhance top-down processes in dichotic listening task when tasks demands are high. *Neuropsychology, 31,* 319–327.

Huang, Y., Zhou, R., Cui, H., Wu, M., Wang, Q., Zhao, Y., & Liu, Y. (2015). Variations in resting frontal alpha asymmetry between high- and low-neuroticism females across the menstrual cycle. *Psychophysiology, 52,* 182–191.

Hugdahl, K. (1995). Dichotic listening: Probing temporal lobe functional integrity. In R. J. Davidson & K. Hugdahl (Eds.), *Brain asymmetry* (pp. 123–156). Cambridge, MA: MIT Press.

Hwang, R. J., Chen, L-F., Yeh, T-C., Tu, P-C., Tu, C-H., & Hsieh, J-C. (2008). The resting frontal alpha asymmetry across the menstrual cycle: A magnetoencephalographic study. *Hormones and Behavior, 54,* 28–33.

Ingalhalikar, M., Smith, A., Parker, D., Satterthwaite, T. D., Elliott, M. A., Ruparel, K., . . . Verma, R. (2014). Sex differences in the structural connectome of the human brain. *Proceedings of the National Academy of Science USA, 111,* 823–828.

Innes, B. R., Burt, D. M., Birch, Y., & Hausmann, M. (2016). A leftward bias however you look at it: Revisiting the emotional chimeric face task as a tool for measuring emotion lateralization. *Laterality, 21,* 643–661.

Innocenti, G. M. (1986). The general organization of callosal connections in the cerebral cortex. In E. G. Jones & A. A. Peters (Eds.), *Cerebral cortex* (pp. 291–354). New York, NY: Plenum Press.

Kawaguchi, Y. (1992). Receptor subtypes involved in callosal-induced postsynaptic potentials in rat frontal agranular cortex in vitro. *Experimental Brain Research, 88,* 33–40.

Keenan, P. A., Ezzat, W. H., Ginsburg, K., & Moore, G. J. (2001). Prefrontal cortex as the site of estrogen's effect on cognition. *Psychoneuroendocrinology, 26,* 577–590.

Kilpatrick, L. A., Zald, D. H., Pardo, J. V., & Cahill, L. F. (2006). Sex-related differences in amygdala functional connectivity during resting conditions. *Neuroimage, 30,* 452–461.

Kim, H., Levine, S. C., & Kertesz, S. (1990). Are variations among subjects in lateral asymmetry real individual differences or random error in measurement? Putting variability in its place. *Brain and Cognition, 14,* 220–242.

Majewska, M. D., Harrison, N. L., Schwartz, R. D., Barker, J. L., & Paul, S. M. (1986). Steroid hormone metabolites are barbiturate-like modulators of the GABA receptor. *Science, 232,* 1004–1007.

Maney, D. L. (2016). Perils and pitfalls of reporting sex differences. *Philosophical Transaction of the Royal Society B, 371,* 20150119.

Manning, J. T., Scutt, D., Wilson, J., & Lewis-Jones, D. I. (1998). The ratio of 2nd to 4th digit length: A predictor of sperm numbers and concentrations of testosterone, luteinizing hormone and oestrogen. *Human Reproduction, 13,* 3000–3004.

Marzi, C. A. (2010). Asymmetry of interhemispheric communication. *Wiley Interdisciplinary Review Cognitive Science, 1,* 433–438.

Mathews, G. A., Fane, B. A., Pasterski, V. L., Conway, G. S., Brook, C., & Hines, M. (2004). Androgenic influences on neural asymmetry: Handedness and language lateralization in individuals with congenital adrenal hyperplasia, *Psychoneuroendocrinology, 29,* 810–822.

McCourt, M. E., Mark, V. W., Radonovich, K. J., Willison, S. K., & Freeman, P. (1997). The effects of gender, menstrual phase and practice on the perceived location of the midsagittal plane. *Neuropsychologia, 35,* 717–724.

McEwen, B. S., & Alves, S. E. (1999). Estrogen actions in the central nervous system. *Endocrinology Review, 20,* 279–307.

McGlone, J. (1977). Sex differences in the cerebral organization of verbal functions in patients with unilateral brain lesions. *Brain, 100,* 775–793.

McGlone, J. (1978). Sex differences in functional brain asymmetry. *Cortex, 14,* 122–128.

Mead, L. A., & Hampson, E. (1996). Asymmetric effects of ovarian hormones on hemispheric activity: Evidence from dichotic and tachistoscopic tests. *Neuropsychology, 10,* 578–587.

Moes, P. E., Brown, W. S., & Minnema, M. T. (2007). Individual differences in Interhemispheric Transfer Time (IHTT) as measured by event related potentials. *Neuropsychologia, 45,* 2626–2630.

Neufang, S., Specht, K., Hausmann, M., Güntürkün, O., Herpertz-Dahlmann, B., Fink, G., & Konrad, K. (2009). Sex differences and the impact of steroid hormones on the developing human brain. *Cerebral Cortex, 19,* 464–473.

Nielsen, J. A., Zielinski, B. A., Ferguson, M. A., Lainhart, J. E., & Anderson, J. S. (2013). An evaluation of the left-brain vs. right-brain hypothesis with resting state functional connectivity magnetic resonance imaging. *PLoS One, 8,* e71275.

Nowicka, A., & Fersten, E. (2001). Sex-related differences in interhemispheric transmission time in the human brain. *Neuroreport, 12,* 4171–4175.

Phoenix, C. H., Goy, R. W., Gerall, A. A., & Young, W. C. (1959). Organizing action of prenatally administered testosterone propionate on the tissue mediating mating behavior in the female guinea pig, *Endocrinology, 65,* 369–382.

Regard, M., Cook, N. D., Wieser, H. G., & Landis, T. (1994). The dynamics of cerebral dominance during unilateral limbic seizures. *Brain, 117,* 91–104.

Reber, J., & Tranel, D. (2017). Sex differences in the functional lateralization of emotion and decision making in the human brain. *Journal of Neuroscience Research, 95,* 270–278.

Reuter-Lorenz, P., & Davidson, R. J. (1981). Differential contributions of the two cerebral hemispheres to the perception of happy and sad faces. *Neuropsychologia, 19,* 609–613.

Reznik, J. S., & Allen, J. J. B. (2017). Frontal asymmetry as a mediator and moderator of emotion: An updated review. *Psychophysiology, 55,* e12965. doi:10.1111/psyp.12965

Rosenberg, L., & Park, S. (2002). Verbal and spatial functions across the menstrual cycle in healthy young women. *Psychoneuroendocrinology, 27,* 835–841.

Sackheim, H. A., & Gur, R. (1978). Lateral asymmetry in intensity of emotional expression. *Neuropsychologia, 16,* 473–481.

Sanders, G., & Wenmoth, D. (1998). Verbal and music dichotic listening tasks reveal variations in functional cerebral asymmetry across the menstrual cycle that are phase and task dependent. *Neuropsychologia, 36,* 869–874.

Satterthwaite, T. D., Wolf, D. H., Roalf, D. R., Ruparel, K., Erus, G., Vandekar, S., ... Gur, R. C. (2015). Linked sex differences in cognition and functional connectivity in youth. *Cerebral Cortex, 25,* 2383–2394.

Schutter, D. J. L. G., & Harmon-Jones, E. (2013). The corpus callosum: A commissural road to anger and aggression. *Neuroscience & Biobehavioral Reviews, 37,* 2481–2488.

Silberman, E. K., & Weingartner, H. (1986). Hemispheric lateralisation of functions related to emotion. *Brain and Cognition, 5,* 322–353.

Solis-Ortiz, S., Ramos, J., Arce, C., Guevara, M. A., & Corsicabrera, M. (1994). EEG oscillations during menstrual-cycle. *International Journal of Neuroscience, 76,* 279–292.

Smith, S. S. (1991). Progesterone administration attenuates excitatory amino acid responses of cerebellar Purkinje cells. *Neuroscience, 42,* 309–320.

Smith, S. S. (1994). Female sex steroid hormones: From receptors to networks to performance-actions on the sensorimotor system. *Progress in Neurobiology, 44,* 55–86.

Smith, S. S., Waterhouse, B. D., & Woodward, D. J. (1987). Locally applied progesterone metabolites alter neuronal responsiveness in the cerebellum. *Brain Research Bulletin, 18,* 739–747.

Stafford, L. D., & Brandaro, N. (2010). Valence specific laterality effects in free viewing conditions: The role of expectancy and gender of image. *Brain and Cognition, 74,* 324–331.

Taubøll, E., Sveberg, L., & Svalheim, S. (2015). Interactions between hormones and epilepsy. *Seizure, 28,* 3–11.

Thimm, M., Weis, S., Hausmann, M., & Sturm, W. (2014). Menstrual cycle effects on selective attention and its underlying cortical networks. *Neuroscience, 258,* 307–317.

Tirosh, E., Rod, R., Cohen, A., & Hochberg, Z. (1993). Congenital adrenal hyperplasia and cerebral lateralizations. *Pediatric Neurology, 9,* 198–201.

Tranel, D., & Bechara, A. (2009). Sex-related functional asymmetry of the amygdala: Preliminary evidence using a case-matched lesion approach. *Neurocase, 15,* 217–234.

Tunc, B., Solmaz, B., Parker, D., Satterthwaite, T. D., Elliott, M. E., Calkins, M. E., . . . Verma, R. (2016). Establishing a link between sex-related differences in the structural connectome and behavior. *Philosophical Transaction of the Royal Society B, 371,* 20150111.

Van Rijn, S., Aleman, A., Swaab, H., Vink, M., Sommer, I., & Kahn, R. S. (2008). Effects of an extra X chromosome on language lateralization: An fMRI study with Klinefelter men (47,XXY). *Schizophrenia Research, 101,* 17–25.

Voyer, D. (1996). On the magnitude of laterality effects and sex differences in functional literalities. *Laterality, 1,* 51–83.

Voyer, D. (2011). Sex differences in dichotic listening. *Brain and Cognition, 76,* 245–255.

Weis, S., Hausmann, M., Stoffers, B., & Sturm, W. (2011). Dynamic changes in functional cerebral connectivity of spatial cognition during the menstrual cycle. *Human Brain Mapping, 32,* 1544–1556.

Weis, S., Hausmann, M., Stoffers, B., Vohn, R., Kellermann, T., & Sturm, W. (2008). Estradiol modulates functional brain organization during the menstrual cycle: An analysis of interhemispheric inhibition. *Journal of Neuroscience, 28,* 13401–13410. Wheeler, R. E., Davidson, R. J., & Tomarken, A. J. (1993). Frontal brain asymmetry and emotional reactivity – a biological substrate of affective style. *Psychophysiology, 30,* 82–89.

Wisniewski, A. B. (1998). Sexually-dimorphic pattern of cortical asymmetry, and the role of sex steroid hormones in determining cortical patterns of lateralization, *Psychoneuroendocrinology, 23,* 519–547.

21

ESTROGENS AND ANDROGENS IN THE PREFRONTAL CORTEX

Relevance for cognition and decision-making

Elizabeth Hampson

Introduction

Reproductive hormones have wide-ranging effects in the central nervous system (CNS). In the past 50 years, basic science has revealed effects at all levels, from molecular to behavioral. Once thought to be important only in the body periphery, androgens and estrogens during early brain development sculpt the architecture of the nervous system in a sex-dependent manner, and in reproductively mature adults these families of hormones intricately modulate the physiology and function of the CNS, outfitting both body and mind for reproductive function. The CNS effects of sex steroids were first discovered in other species, but they operate in the human CNS too. Importantly, hormone-driven processes include sex-typed modifications in certain cognitive functions. Although men and women do not differ in general intelligence, modest sex differences are seen in a range of more specific cognitive functions, and it is the latter where the footprint of sex steroids is most readily found. Until recently, human work focused largely on the role of estrogens in episodic memory, with post-menopausal women the most common population studied. However, the CNS effects of reproductive steroids extend well beyond the medial temporal lobe. Newer work involves regions of the prefrontal cortex (PFC) that participate in social decision-making such as the ventromedial/orbitofrontal cortex (VMPFC/OFC) and dorsolateral prefrontal cortex (DLPFC). It is these socially relevant functions that are the subject of the present chapter.

What are organizational and activational effects?

Androgens (e.g., testosterone) and estrogens (e.g., 17β-estradiol, the dominant estrogen in women of reproductive age) are potent modulators of CNS function. Briefly, their actions fall into two major classes, called *organizational* and *activational* effects (Phoenix et al., 1959). *Organizational effects* are long-term changes in the morphological and functional differentiation of the CNS caused by exposure to specific steroids during critical periods in early brain development, which occur mainly in the prenatal or early postnatal period. (Some organizational effects might also occur at puberty; Schulz & Forrester-Fronstin, this volume). *Activational effects*, on the other hand, are reversible and occur in reproductively mature adults. They are caused by androgens or estrogens currently in the bloodstream and reflect their available concentrations. Examples of activational effects include changes in the numbers of synaptic contacts or changes in neurotransmitter availability in a particular brain region. Both organizational and activational effects have repercussions for brain function, and both require the presence of specific hormone receptors in a target brain region in order for effects to be seen. Many actions of testosterone or its metabolite dihydrotestosterone are mediated by androgen receptors, while at least three forms of the estrogen receptor have been identified, two of which (ERα, ERβ) act by regulating gene transcription upon binding to estrogens, allowing for the endocrine control of a vast array of CNS-related gene products.

Organizational and activational effects were first demonstrated in guinea pigs in the context of mating behaviors (Phoenix et al., 1959), establishing that steroids are able to modify the behavioral output of the CNS. Applicability of these principles to *cognitive* functions (including memory) was slower to be recognized. However, research accelerated in the 1990s, triggered by data showing a remarkable 30% change over the female rat's five-day estrous cycle in the density of axospinous synapses (synapses that occur on dendritic spines – tiny projections found on dendrites) in the hippocampus (Woolley & McEwen, 1992), and data demonstrating that neonatal steroid exposure could produce enduring (organizational) changes in spatial memory in the rat (Williams et al., 1990). These findings reinforced parallel work on cognitive function already underway in humans and other primates. In humans, work by Resnick et al. (1986) in people exposed to excess androgens *in utero*, and our own work on variations in estradiol over the menstrual cycle (Hampson, 1990; Hampson & Kimura, 1988) provided some of the first evidence for organizational and activational effects, respectively, on cognitive functions. They also underscored the selectivity of these effects – not all aspects of cognitive function are similarly affected (or affected at all) by reproductive steroids. Around the same time, Clark and Goldman-Rakic (1989) discovered that manipulating testosterone levels in rhesus monkeys during the prenatal or early postnatal infant period influenced their ability to perform an object reversal task dependent on the orbitofrontal cortex at later ages – a first indication of the possible hormone-responsivity of the PFC. Together, these early studies supported the view that sex steroids can affect higher cortical function. Only in the past decade or so has attention turned in earnest to the PFC as a potential site of steroid action.

Hand in hand with the possibility of regulatory actions of steroids in the PFC is the idea that the PFC may be a sexually differentiated region of the primate brain. Historically, sex differences in the PFC have not been widely entertained, despite occasional reports of sex-related volumetric or biochemical differences (e.g., Schlaepfer et al., 1995). Thus, the discovery of regulatory actions of sex steroids in the PFC pushes outward the boundaries of our current understanding of this highly complex brain region. The mapping between sex differences at the functional level and hormonal effects is not a simple one, however. On the one hand, the presence of a qualitative or quantitative sex difference in overt performance is often a signal that an organizational or activational effect of sex steroids is acting (or has acted) upon underlying neural pathways. Recognizing that many of the effects of sex steroids occur at the neurochemical level, a morphological sex difference will not always be seen. On the other hand, steroid-generated effects sometimes serve to help equalize overt outcomes in the two sexes, by compensating for brain differences generated through other mechanisms (de Vries, 2004). Therefore, the presence of an observable sex difference in a specific cognitive process may signal a hormone effect, but the absence of an observable sex difference does not guarantee that hormone effects are absent (see also McCarthy & Konkle, 2005). Obsolete expectations premised on morphometric sex differences underestimate the true pervasiveness of sex steroid effects in the CNS.

The prefrontal cortex and decision-making

Over the past decade, cognitive neuroscience has devoted increasing attention to the study of decision-making and the complex cognitive and motivational processes that underlie it (see Fellows, 2013). The frontal cortex has long been acknowledged to play a key role in adaptive decision-making, providing behavioral flexibility in response to environmental context and its ever-changing demands. Indeed, early studies revealed impaired decision-making in neurological patients with acquired lesions of the PFC or conditions that involve perturbed development of the frontal cortex (Milner & Petrides, 1984). What's new in the past decade, though, is a greater recognition that 'decision-making' is not unitary. It is in fact a complex outcome that represents an emergent property of many fundamental subprocesses that must be finely orchestrated and are exquisitely tuned to current contingencies in the environment (Kennerley & Walton, 2011). Together, these processes yield the surface behavior that we observe ('adaptive decision-making'). Changes in any of the latent processes may alter the surface behavior we see expressed.

Two regions of the PFC of particular importance for social and non-social decision-making are the DLPFC, a region critical to the executive control processes of planning and working memory (the ability to temporarily hold information 'on-line' and manipulate it over short timeframes of up to a few minutes, Funahashi, 2017) and the VMPFC/OFC which, together with its connections to the amygdala and ventral striatum, is important in reward-based learning, valuation of reinforced outcomes, and their anticipated probabilities in light of recent experience (Kringelbach & Rolls, 2004). VMPFC/OFC is also thought to help regulate negative affect via the top-down inhibition of brain regions involved in processing negative emotion, particularly the amygdala (Motzkin et al., 2015). It has been proposed that the DLPFC and VMPFC/OFC represent significant nodes in two distinct but interacting functional–anatomical control networks that provide non-emotive and affective guidance, respectively, over decision-making and its expression in overt behavior (e.g., Baumgartner et al., 2011; Gläscher et al., 2012; Krawczyk, 2002). While not yet on the radar of most cognitive neuroscientists, a body of neuroendocrine evidence has emerged over the past 10–15 years to suggest that these segments of the PFC may be modulated by sex steroids.

Estrogens and the DLPFC

Our own work on estrogens and the frontal cortex began in 1997. In 2000 we were the first to show that circulating levels of estrogens may enhance the frontal executive components of working memory (Duff & Hampson, 2000). In a sample of 96 healthy post-menopausal women, we found that women receiving estrogen replacement performed significantly better than untreated women on three tests of working memory (Figure 21.1), regardless of whether or not a progestin was simultaneously being used.[1] No significant difference was observed between the two treated groups, suggesting that estrogens, not progestins, were the primary source of the effect. Our tests included standard working memory tasks (Digit Ordering, Petrides et al., 1993; Digits Backward, Wechsler, 1987; see Table 21.1 for task overview), plus a newly developed test of spatial working memory (the SPWM; Duff & Hampson, 2001) known to correlate well with established working memory tasks having a high cognitive load (see, e.g., Table 21.2 below). The effects in our study were seen robustly only on memory tasks that required the active manipulation of items within working memory, a process that recruits the DLPFC (Owen et al., 1999; Petrides et al., 1993). At the same time, no significant group differences were found on control tasks that required only the immediate passive recall of short sequences, i.e., tasks that rely on more posterior brain regions.

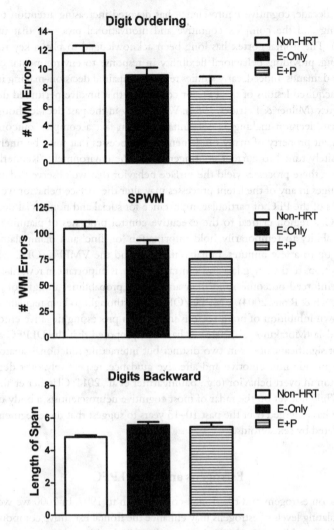

Figure 21.1 Working memory performance in post–menopausal women (*n* = 96) from Duff and Hampson (2000). Healthy women *not* using replacement estrogens (Non-HRT, *n* = 35) made significantly greater numbers of working memory errors on the Digit Ordering task (top) and SPWM task (middle) compared with women taking either estrogen alone (E-Only, *n* = 38) or estrogen plus a progestin (E + P, *n* = 23), and showed a poorer score on Digits Backward (bottom). Thus on all three tests of working memory, superior performance was observed among estrogen users. In contrast, there was no effect of estrogen use on Digits Forward (*p* = 0.563) or on the Corsi Blocks (*p* = 0.588) (data not shown). The latter tasks require only passive immediate recall, not active maintenance or manipulation of information within working memory.

Table 21.1 Glossary of cognitive tasks (with example references)

Name of task	Brief description
Delayed Response (Jacobsen, 1936)	A type of task originally used to study working memory in nonhuman primates. Each trial involves the presentation of a simple stimulus that is then removed or hidden from view. Its location (or identity) must be remembered following a short delay. Typically only a small pool of items is used (e.g., two possible locations), and the choice that is the correct one is randomized from trial to trial. On each trial, therefore, the animal must keep track of the *current* location in order to receive a food reward.
Digit Ordering (Petrides et al., 1993)	Using a set of digits provided by the experimenter, each trial involves generating aloud a re-ordered sequence of the digit set, arranged according to some pre-specified criterion. Because the original stimuli must be mentally re-arranged and temporarily held in mind, the task requires working memory. Ordering constraints might include, for example, saying the digit set aloud in ascending or descending numerical order, arranging them into a random string, or repeating them in backwards order relative to their position in the original set (as in the Digits Backward task, for example).
SPWM (Duff & Hampson, 2001)	Involves finding matching pairs of colored tokens, which are hidden beneath the identical-appearing flaps of a response board. In order to locate correct matches, the spatial locations of the hidden tokens must be temporarily held in mind until all of the pairs have been successfully discovered and matched. Thus, spatial working memory is required.
N-back task (Kirchner, 1958)	The participant is asked to monitor a series of rapidly presented auditory or visual stimuli and indicate (usually by a button press) whenever the identity (or location) of the current stimulus is the same as the stimulus that appeared 'N' stimuli back in the series (e.g., 1-back, 2-back). This working memory task is often used in functional imaging studies.
Self-Ordered Pointing (Petrides & Milner, 1982)	Each trial involves a small array of stimuli, which are shown on successive cards (or successive computer screens) in differing spatial arrangements. The participant is asked to point to one item on each card (or screen) so that by the end of the set, each item in the array has been pointed to once and only once, without skipping or repeating any of the items. Working memory is required, in that a participant must keep track of which stimuli have already been pointed to, and which remain to be pointed to, within a given trial. Array size can be varied to increase or decrease the load on working memory.
Attentional Set-Shifting (Roberts et al., 1988)	A type of cognitive task that involves switching attention to a formerly irrelevant feature of a complex stimulus after having learned previously over a set of trials to pay attention to a different feature.
Reversal Learning (Clark & Goldman-Rakic, 1989)	A type of task that involves learning over a set of trials to choose the one of two paired stimuli that is most consistently associated with receiving a reward, then, when the reward contingencies switch without warning, efficiently switching to the other member of the pair.
Delay Discounting (Reynolds & Schiffbauer, 2004)	Temporal discounting tasks typically involve establishing how long a participant is willing to wait to receive a larger delayed reward rather than an immediate but smaller reward, or how rapidly the perceived value of a reward falls off as a function of the duration of time to its receipt.
Iowa Gambling Task (Bechara et al., 1994)	A decision-making task that involves choosing from four decks of 'cards' which vary in their payoffs, penalties, and the probabilities of each, with the goal of maximizing one's winnings by the end of the task.

Multiple sources now support the idea that circulating estrogen levels do influence frontally mediated elements of the working memory system. In the first study subsequent to ours, Keenan et al. (2001) found superior performance on an auditory *N*-back task of working memory (for a brief task description see Table 21.1) in a small group of post-menopausal women taking estrogens compared with control women not on treatment. Later, using a randomized double-blind crossover design, Krug et al. (2006) confirmed an effect of 17β-estradiol using the Digit Ordering task (as in our own study) and showed that the effects generalized to a task involving memory for temporal order (another potential indication of a frontal lobe effect, Romine & Reynolds, 2004). The short latency of the effects (improvement in memory was seen after just a three-day treatment with estradiol versus placebo) is consistent with the hypothesized activational nature of the hormone action. Early tests of the estrogen hypothesis focused on post-menopausal women, but the effect on working memory has been confirmed recently using a broader range of research paradigms (see below).

Cognitive studies illustrate the functional impact of higher estrogen levels and speak to the efficiency of recruitment of the working memory network during everyday decision-making. However, functional magnetic resonance imaging (*f*MRI) has been a valuable tool to confirm a PFC locus of estrogen action. Half a dozen studies have now demonstrated increased neuronal activity at prefrontal sites during the performance of working memory tasks in women treated with estrogens compared with placebo. Smith et al. (2006), for example, in a placebo-controlled crossover trial found increased blood oxygen level-dependent (BOLD) activation under 17β-estradiol treatment in the PFC during a working memory task emphasizing active maintenance. In a monkey study, positron-emission tomography (PET) found that endogenous estradiol correlated positively with resting metabolism in the DLPFC and anterior cingulate cortex (Rilling et al., 2008). Sample sizes used in most imaging studies tend to be small, and therefore the effects of estrogens on working memory are not always significant at a behavioral level in such studies, particularly in light of the effect sizes that can realistically be expected. However, imaging has been an important tool to visualize the precise loci of significant change and, as expected, implicates sites in PFC classically associated with working memory processes.

Post-menopausal women have been the most heavily studied population to date vis-à-vis the impact of estrogens on working memory. Endogenous estradiol production is negligible after menopause, but 17β-estradiol or other forms of estrogen may be given exogenously and the outcomes studied using various research designs. Existing work includes observational studies and placebo-controlled trials. In post-menopausal women, the question of whether estrogens positively influence working memory is of clinical and not just theoretical importance. Following menopause, women commonly self-report modest reductions in memory function. Efforts to study *episodic* memory, the assumed substrate for women's self-impressions, have produced very equivocal results (Hogervorst & Bandelow, 2010). It is possible that these impressions might instead reflect a reduction in the working memory system. Interestingly, post-menopausal rhesus monkeys make higher numbers of working memory errors on the classical delayed-response task of working memory than female monkeys who are matched on chronological age but still retain a regular menstrual cycle (Roberts et al., 1997). This observation suggests generalizability to other female primates and supports an estrogen- rather than age-dependent mechanism.

Working memory has been studied extensively in monkeys using the spatial delayed-response task since the pioneering work of Jacobsen (1936) (see Table 21.1 for task description). The performance of delayed-response is impaired by lesions of DLPFC (Passingham, 1985), demonstrating a direct anatomical parallel with the human working memory system (Barbey et al., 2013). The monkey is thus considered a useful model of human working memory (whereas in rats working memory is sometimes conceptualized in a slightly different manner and may be operationalized by laboratory tasks that recruit the hippocampus). As we might predict based on the estrogen hypothesis, female monkeys display reduced accuracy on delayed-response after menopause (Roberts et al., 1997) or after ovariectomy (Tinkler & Voytko, 2005) and, consistent with estradiol as the causal agent, their performance can be restored substantially by exogenous treatments with estradiol (Kohama et al., 2016; Rapp et al., 2003).

Besides offering convergent support for the human cognitive data, nonhuman primates have afforded preliminary insights into molecular mechanisms. When our lab's work began, the existence of estrogen receptors in the adult PFC was still uncertain. But the presence of the ERα receptor in DLPFC has now been confirmed in both humans and other primate brains (Montague et al., 2008; Perlman et al., 2005; Wang et al., 2004). Montague et al. (2008) specifically targeted the DLPFC in a comparative anatomical study examining human, monkey, and rat brains. Immunohistochemistry showed abundant ERα-positive cells throughout all layers of DLPFC in the monkey and human specimens. In female monkeys, dendritic spine densities have been found to vary within DLPFC as a function of both age and estradiol levels (Hao et al., 2007), and the density of a particular type of spine, the 'thin' spine, is associated with accuracy on delayed-response in aged ovariectomized monkeys and is up-regulated by estradiol (Hara et al., 2015), making it a possible candidate mechanism to explain estradiol's effects on working memory. However, several other mechanisms also have been proposed, including regulatory effects of estradiol on serotonergic (Epperson et al., 2012), cholinergic (Dumas et al., 2012), and dopaminergic pathways (e.g., Duff & Hampson, 2000; Jacobs & D'Esposito, 2011), all of which are implicated in working memory processes (Arnsten & Robbins, 2002) and are also subject to modulation by circulating estradiol levels (e.g., Bethea et al., 2002).

It is important to realize that the effects of estrogens on working memory are not confined to *deficiency* conditions. Past work on post-menopausal women (or animal models of aging and menopause, e.g., Rapp et al., 2003) has focused on conditions characterized by extremely low estrogen availability and its remediation with estrogens given exogenously. But recent work in younger women conversely asks whether *high-estrogen* states (e.g., pregnancy, higher-estradiol stages of the menstrual cycle) that occur under natural conditions, may be associated with *superior* working memory. If, in fact, high estradiol promotes the functioning of frontal control elements of the working memory system, positive effects on working memory can be hypothesized. (Estradiol is higher at all phases of the menstrual cycle, including the lowest-estradiol phase (menses), than after menopause). Knock-down of estradiol in young women by drugs that inhibit estrogen synthesis has been shown to reduce women's performance on the N-back task of working memory (Grigorova et al., 2006). More importantly, higher-estradiol concentrations *do* seem to be associated with *improvements* in working memory performance. This has been found, for example, at high-estradiol phases of the menstrual cycle, in pregnant women evaluated during the third trimester of pregnancy, and in women actively taking oral contraceptives containing ethinyl estradiol (Hampson, in press; Hampson et al., 2015; Hampson & Morley, 2013; but see Leeners et al., 2017). One small *f*MRI study has reported a possible estradiol x genotype interaction (Jacobs & D'Esposito, 2011). These studies suggest that greater cognitive control via the dorsal frontocortical network is available during high-estrogen conditions.

To summarize, it is increasingly clear that at least some working memory processes are hormonally modulated, but the ancillary question of whether sex differences in working memory performance occur as a result of this hormonal modulation (and if so, under which conditions) has seldom been addressed. Present findings are heterogeneous, reflecting diversity in task demands and likely also uncontrolled hormonal variation. In adults of reproductive age, we discovered that men and women performed equivalently on the SPWM task of working memory if women were explicitly tested at menses (lowest-estradiol levels), but when tested at high-estradiol phases of the natural menstrual cycle then women performed superiorly (Hampson & Morley, 2013). The same pattern was observed in women using oral contraceptives when they were tested during the 'on' phase of the contraceptive cycle where ethinyl estradiol is given exogenously versus the 'off' phase where ethinyl estradiol is not given (Hampson, in press; Figure 21.2). Older work not controlling for cycle-related differences in sex steroid concentrations showed an overall female advantage in groups of unselected young adults on the SPWM, Digit Ordering, or other working memory tasks having similar cognitive demands (Duff & Hampson, 2001; Lejbak et al., 2009; Voyer et al., 2017; see also Anderson et al., 2001). (Note that under random conditions only a minority of women would be expected by chance to be tested in their lowest-estradiol state). Even older data suggest a female advantage can be seen on the delayed-response task in primates (McDowell et al., 1960).

Findings for the *N*-back task are mixed but are often an exception to this pattern and even show a male advantage in a few studies (Voyer et al., 2017; but see Speck et al., 2000) for reasons that are not well understood. Because the *N*-back is often used in the context of functional imaging, inadequate sample size combined with a potentially smaller effect size on the *N*-back

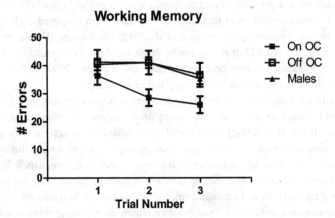

Figure 21.2 Working memory errors on the SPWM, a test of spatial working memory, in oral contraceptive users (OC users) and a group of demographically matched male controls. Three trials were given. The total number of working memory errors is shown separately for each trial. All study participants were tested on a brief set of cognitive tasks, including the SPWM, during active OC use (On OC; *n* = 40) or during the one-week interval of the contraceptive cycle when no active hormone is taken (Off OC; *n* = 20). For the male controls, *n* = 96. All the women shown here were regular users of combined OCs that consisted of ethinyl estradiol (15–35 ug/day, depending on the brand of OC being used) combined with a progestin. Participants were tested blind (without experimenter knowledge of OC use, brands used, or phase of the contraceptive cycle), and then were classified retrospectively into groups based on OC details provided by the participants at the end of the test session. ANOVA revealed that women using exogenous estradiol in the form of OCs at time of testing made significantly fewer WM errors on the SPWM than either women who were tested during the washout week of the contraceptive cycle or matched male controls. Women on OCs also showed more rapid improvement over the three trials. Among naturally cycling women (non-OC users) who participated in the same study (not shown in figure), a similar pattern was found – higher levels of estradiol, measured in saliva, were associated with superior WM performance on the SPWM (Hampson & Morley, 2013). See Hampson, in press, for further details of the data plotted here.

(Cohen's $d \approx 0.20$ versus $d \approx 0.60$–0.75 for the SPWM; see Duff & Hampson, 2001; Voyer et al., 2017) might explain some of the inconsistencies. But features of the N-back task that vary from study to study (e.g., whether the stimuli are auditory or visual; the level of cognitive load assessed), and differences in the brain regions it recruits, might also be relevant. A sex difference would be expected only if working memory demands are sufficiently high, not under low-load conditions that are insensitive to individual differences in performance (e.g., 0-back, 1-back). Theoretical models of working memory suggest that the active maintenance versus manipulative processes of working memory may recruit slightly different anatomical regions within the PFC (Owen et al., 1999), with maintenance/monitoring (of the sort required by the N-back) recruiting ventrolateral regions but less prominently recruiting the DLPFC than tasks that emphasize manipulation (Barbey et al., 2013; Hoshi et al., 2003). Given that ERα is densely expressed in the DLPFC whereas ventrolateral PFC appears to be more lightly populated, it might help to explain the discrepant N-back findings.

Table 21.2 Pearson's correlations between working memory errors on the SPWM and working memory errors on Self-Ordered Pointing (SOPT) ($n = 38$ adult females; from Hampson et al., 2015)

	SOPT 6-item	8-item	10-item	12-item	SOPT total errors
SPWM total errors	$r = .37\star$	$r = .34\star$	$r = .48\star\star$	$r = .65\star\star$	$r = .57\star\star$

Note. Correlations represent the Pearson's correlations between the total number of WM errors committed on the SPWM (summed over two trials; only two trials were administered in Hampson et al., 2015) and the total number of WM errors committed on the SOPT by the same women at each set size used, ranging from 6-item sets to the maximum 12-item sets. Also shown is the grand correlation between WM errors on the two tasks as a whole. Both tasks are thought to measure WM. Note that the size of the correlation increases with greater cognitive load on the SOPT.

$\star$ $p < .05$; $\star\star$ $p < .01$, two-tailed

In this chapter, working memory is emphasized because it is a core process important for cognitive control, sustained representation of context, planning, and goal-directed decision-making. Working memory, though, is unlikely to be the only process mediated by the PFC that is influenced by estrogens, given confirmation of estrogen receptor expression in the dorsolateral cortex and the multiple cognitive processes that rely upon the region. We investigated working memory in our studies as a representative frontocortical function, but the hypothesis that 17β-estradiol is active in adult female PFC is theoretically broader and encompasses other functions, too, that likewise depend on the DLPFC. While our own initial work was underway, PET imaging showed that estradiol treatment normalized regional activation seen in the DLPFC during the performance of an attentional set-shifting task (Berman et al., 1997), whereas ovarian suppression produced by a gonadotropin-releasing hormone analog decreased it. Effects at the cognitive/behavioral level were not found but might be observable with more refined tasks or greater statistical power. The presence of a sex difference in other frontally mediated control processes might signal their receptivity to hormonal modulation by estrogens (e.g., set-shifting, Kuptsova et al., 2015), but functions other than working memory have rarely been studied. Going forward, it will be important to begin to test the range and limits of estrogen's effects on functionality within the dorsal frontal cortex.

Androgens and the VMPFC/OFC

DLPFC is not the only region of prefrontal cortex that is subject to hormonal regulation by sex steroids. A growing body of work suggests that testosterone (and possibly other androgens) plays a role in the VMPFC/OFC. Because VMPFC/OFC participates in the representation and updating of anticipated rewards, risks, and emotional regulation (Bechara et al., 2000; Kennerley & Walton, 2011; Krawczyk, 2002; Sinha et al., 2016), testosterone too may influence decision-making processes, especially in males where it is present in the greatest abundance.

Testosterone is the primary endocrine signal that drives sexual differentiation of the male CNS. In many species, programmed release of testosterone by the testes during a defined prenatal or early postnatal period permanently masculinizes certain features of the brain via genomic actions of testosterone or its active metabolites (for a review see Breedlove & Hampson, 2002). During adulthood, testosterone may also modify specific neurochemical/anatomical parameters to promote a male phenotype. Activational effects do not always follow organizational ones, however, and may be independent. In humans, some organizational effects of testosterone are thought to occur prenatally, mediated by androgen receptors expressed in selective regions of the CNS during that time.

Regarding the VMPFC/OFC, structural imaging has revealed a regional sex difference in the volume of the VMPFC/OFC in adult male and female brains (e.g., Welborn et al., 2009). The male brain on average is larger but after correcting for whole-brain volume, further sex differences in grey and white matter organization are evident. For instance, men possess stronger fiber connections between the striatum and OFC and ventrolateral PFC than women do; conversely, women have stronger fiber connections between the striatum and DLPFC (Lei et al., 2016). A volumetric sex difference in lateral OFC is already visible in childhood, and prenatal testosterone concentrations predict local grey matter volumes among boys (Lombardo et al., 2012). Testosterone at puberty too has been found to relate predictively to grey and especially white matter volumes in male adolescents (Paus et al., 2010), including the orbital cortex, and an association with a functional polymorphism in the androgen receptor has been observed. While these findings are only correlational, they suggest the operation of an androgen-dependent mechanism (and further CNS changes at puberty when testosterone begins its climb toward adult levels).

Consistent with an organizational effect of early testosterone, monkey studies confirm that androgen receptors are in fact expressed in the primate OFC during prenatal and early postnatal life (Clark et al., 1988). Male but not female OFC also displays a right hemisphere bias in receptor density (Sholl & Kim, 1990). In human adults undergoing PET imaging, a lateralized sex difference may be seen in activation of the VMPFC/OFC (Bolla et al., 2004) during the Iowa Gambling Task (IGT; Bechara et al., 1997), a widely used measure of decision-making that recruits a network of brain regions including, importantly, VMPFC/OFC (Bechara et al., 1998; Lawrence et al., 2009). Specifically, PET showed significantly greater task-related activation in the right lateral OFC in men's than women's brains during the IGT (Bolla et al., 2004). In principle, a sex difference in adult brains could be caused by *activational* effects of hormones. But differences between men and women in the clinical symptoms of lateralized brain lesions (damage to the right VMPFC/OFC causes severe impairment in socioemotional functioning and decision-making in men, whereas it is *left* VMPFC/OFC lesions that most adversely affect women) favor a true sex difference in the local functional organization of the cortex (Reber & Tranel, 2017).

Currently the best evidence for an organizational effect of testosterone in VMPFC/OFC is behavioral. Clark and Goldman-Rakic (1989) found that female monkeys treated with testosterone prenatally or in early infancy displayed masculinized performance on an object reversal task (see Table 21.1) that relies on the OFC, when later tested at 75 days of age. (Reversal tasks require efficiently switching between two choice options as the rewards or payouts associated with each option change and alternate throughout the task). The importance of OFC for reversal learning is well established (e.g., Fellows, 2013; O'Doherty et al., 2001). Male monkeys outperform females on object reversal at this young age (Clark & Goldman-Rakic, 1989), whereas females outperform males on a different reward-based implicit learning task that depends on other brain pathways. The male advantage in object reversal is seen in human children, too (Overman et al., 1996). Only recently, Evans and Hampson (2015a) found that the sex difference can be demonstrated in *adults*, providing a sufficiently demanding reversal task is used. Extension of these observations to adults is important because it reinforces the probability that a true organizational effect is present, not simply a transient developmental delay in the maturation of the female primate OFC relative to the male, as proposed by Clark and Goldman-Rakic (1989).

VMPFC/OFC has been implicated in a number of different processes, but progress in exploring whether androgens organizationally modify other aspects of VMPFC/OFC function has been slow. This reflects the limited paradigms currently available to study organizational effects in humans (prenatal exposure to sex steroids cannot ethically be manipulated for research purposes). In principle, the second-to-fourth digit ratio (so-called 2D:4D ratio), a putative somatic biomarker of testosterone concentrations present prenatally (Manning et al., 1998), could be used to study organizational questions, and in fact, associations between individual differences in 2D:4D ratio and risk-taking propensity (for example) have been identified in a few studies (e.g., Evans & Hampson, 2014; Stenstrom et al., 2011). However, these findings are difficult to interpret because of lingering doubts about the validity of the 2D:4D ratio as a legitimate reflection of prenatal testosterone activity (for discussion see Hampson & Sankar, 2012).

Growing evidence suggests that *adult* testosterone levels exert a modulatory influence on processes governed by the VMPFC/OFC, too. Existing data are largely correlational but support the view that one or more latent processes that underlie performance on the IGT or other laboratory tasks may be androgen-dependent in an *activational* sense. One recent study reported that adult testosterone levels positively predicted the ability to flexibly adjust responding on a reversal learning task (Diekhof & Kraft, 2017). Taking the IGT as a more often-studied example, healthy adults of either sex can learn the task in a moderate number of trials, but on average men learn the deck contingencies more rapidly than women and adjust their decision-making patterns accordingly (Reavis & Overman, 2001; van den Bos et al., 2013). However, among adult men, a high endogenous testosterone level measured in serum or saliva predicts *poorer* rather than better performance on the IGT (Evans & Hampson, 2014; Reavis & Overman, 2001; Stanton et al., 2011). In women, too, higher testosterone predicts *poorer* performance (Stanton et al., 2011). The direction of the association is consistent across both sexes, but is surprising in light of the male advantage seen on the task as a whole, reinforcing the concept that on a complex task like the IGT, composed of multiple converging subprocesses, a sex difference does not always straightforwardly predict activational control by sex steroids. More than one dimension of the IGT task might be subject to hormonal regulation. Although current evidence is largely correlational, a double-blind crossover trial (van Honk et al., 2004) showed that women treated acutely with a high dose of sublingual testosterone chose more cards from disadvantageous decks, confirming that high testosterone is disadvantageous to IGT decision-making. In favor of the view that VMPFC/OFC is responsive to adult testosterone levels, androgen receptors have now been identified in the *adult* OFC (Finley & Kritzer, 1999).

Which cognitive process is subject to regulation by testosterone? The IGT has been a fruitful tool and starting point for studying decision-making, but is a complex task that evokes multiple latent processes, including decision-making under uncertainty, reinforcement-based learning, and inhibitory control (for discussion see Evans & Hampson, 2015a, 2015b). Exactly which process(es) are modulated by testosterone is not presently understood. In keeping with current conceptualizations of the VMPFC/OFC, prominent ideas regarding the source of the testosterone effect (and the male advantage on the IGT as a whole) include risk evaluation/ updating, risk-averseness, sensitivity to reward and/or punishment, or emphasis on immediate versus long-term outcomes (e.g., Evans & Hampson, 2014, 2015a, 2015b; Overman et al., 2011; Stanton et al., 2011; van den Bos et al., 2013) – processes that also apply to decisions made under many everyday conditions.

Motivational processes are likely to be involved. Functional imaging studies reveal that testosterone levels modify activity in neural circuitry important for the regulation of emotion and reward, including activity in the VMPFC/OFC, amygdala, and ventral striatum. Under resting state conditions, VMPFC-amygdala functional connectivity is enhanced in men compared with women (Engman et al., 2016). A review of functional imaging studies suggested that high endogenous testosterone concentrations are associated with greater activation in the amygdala and VMPFC/OFC in reaction to stimuli signaling threat or reward (van Wingen et al., 2011). In placebo-controlled trials, testosterone administration increased amygdala reactivity (and in some studies activation in OFC; e.g., Hermans et al., 2008) elicited under conditions of social threat or vigilance, but at very high levels such as those produced by a supraphysiological dose of testosterone, testosterone decreased amygdala connectivity with the OFC (Bos et al., 2012; van Wingen et al., 2010), indicating functional decoupling. Exogenous testosterone increases the motivation to seek rewards (van Honk et al., 2004) and heightens the BOLD response in the ventral striatum during anticipation of reward (Hermans et al., 2010). Although fewer studies have examined VMPFC/OFC, the levels of BOLD activation observed in VMPFC/OFC in anticipation of reward, in response to social threat, or during risky decision-making all show graded correlations with endogenous levels of testosterone measured in saliva or plasma (e.g., Op de Macks et al., 2016; Stanton et al., 2009; see also Mehta & Beer, 2009). In short, imaging studies suggest that adult testosterone levels do influence activity in VMPFC/OFC under certain conditions.

Our own early work on testosterone and decision-making began by studying associations between endogenous testosterone levels and entrepreneurial business ventures (White et al., 2006). We found that risk-taking was one mediator of the associations we observed. Neurons exist in the OFC that code a risk signal (O'Neill & Schultz, 2015), but whether these cells are modulated by testosterone is currently unknown. Opinions diverge on whether testosterone's influence on risk-taking is organizational or activational or both (Brañas-Garza & Rustichini, 2011; Stenstrom et al., 2011; but see Apicella et al., 2014; Goudriaan et al., 2010) and on how (or if) a willingness to incur risk is conceptually separable from VMPFC/OFC's role in the anticipatory evaluation of punishment and reward contingencies. Holding sex constant, Evans and Hampson (2014) suggested that the organizational and activational effects of testosterone might act on different latent processes relevant to decision-making on the IGT – whereas androgen exposure during early development may act to increase risk-taking, at least part of the effect of adult testosterone may be independent of risk and due to an activational influence on the weights afforded to different reinforcement outcomes (Evans & Hampson, 2014). Related though not identical concepts regarding reinforcement processing have been advanced by others to explain *sex differences* on the IGT (Overman & Pierce, 2013; van den Bos et al., 2013). Alternative hypotheses concerning the underlying processes responsible for sex- and testosterone-dependent differences in performance have received less empirical support (e.g., impulsivity).

VMPFC/OFC is not completely devoid of estrogen receptors. But if estradiol plays any role, preliminary evidence suggests its effect at high levels is to promote *decreased* not increased risk-taking (Barel et al., 2017; Op de Macks et al., 2016). Present findings with regard to estradiol must be treated with caution because few studies currently exist and small sample sizes can give rise to inaccurate findings (Button et al., 2013; Schultheiss & Mehta, this volume). However, the picture emerging so far suggests that high estradiol unopposed by progesterone[2] is associated with increased activation in subcortical regions responsive to reward, but also increased top-down control via VMPFC/OFC (e.g., Thomas et al., 2014). High estradiol seems to be associated with increased behavioral restraint and decreased reactivity to negative emotional stimuli compared with low estradiol conditions. For example, brain responses in the mesocorti-colimbic reward circuit to certain primary and secondary reinforcers vary across the menstrual cycle in women (Dreher, 2015) including responses to men's faces as sexual stimuli, which elicit a larger BOLD response in the medial OFC during the late follicular (fertile) phase of the cycle (Rupp et al., 2009). Response magnitude in the OFC was positively correlated with serum estradiol concentration, peaking at that time (also see Zeidan et al., 2011). Conversely, activation in the amygdala and OFC in response to stressful or negative stimuli is *lower* during the late follicular phase (Goldstein et al., 2005; Goldstein et al., 2010; Jacobs et al., 2015; Protopopescu et al., 2005), indicating reduced reactivity of the stress circuitry. Both men, and women tested at the beginning of the menstrual cycle when estradiol is low, had a greater BOLD signal increase in OFC and amygdala in response to negative emotional stimuli than women tested at high-estradiol levels (Goldstein et al., 2010). Despite suggestions that reward salience increases under high-estradiol conditions, the tendency for women to choose immediate rewards over larger delayed rewards is *reduced* at midcycle when estradiol is high, with the magnitude of reduction correlating directly with the circulating concentration of estradiol (Smith et al., 2014). In short, present evidence suggests that estradiol's actions differ considerably from testosterone's: high estradiol appears to promote a lower-risk, controlled mode of thinking, while high testosterone is associated with increased risk-taking and reward-seeking. Animal studies tell us that testosterone sometimes acts in the CNS via intracellular conversion to estradiol, but the data reviewed here suggest that binding to ER after conversion to estradiol is not the basis for testosterone's actions in the VMPFC/OFC.

A working model of sexual differentiation in the PFC

The frontal association cortex is often overlooked as a site of sexual differentiation or modulation by reproductive steroids because the cognitive and socioemotional functions it governs do not on the surface seem relevant to reproductive function. However, growing evidence supports the idea that sex steroids are important modulators of two partially distinct but interfacing regulatory control systems vested in the dorsal and ventral PFC (Gläscher et al., 2012) that assist in decision-making by reference to external contextual cues and internal body-related or motivational cues, respectively, and that may be differentially sensitive to estrogens and androgens.

Given that sex hormones generally act in the CNS to promote reproductive outcomes, why is endocrine control present in the PFC? This can be understood within an evolutionary framework by considering the classes of cognitive functions that are modulated, and when. Past arguments have often been based on the assumption of a sex difference, but many cognitive sex differences reported for the PFC appear to depend on reproductive states. Therefore, the proper question to ask is not why is there a sex difference, but why is there state-dependent endocrine control? What is it about high levels of estradiol or testosterone that requires sharpening of specific cognitive processes in one sex more than the other?

Among other theoretical speculations, it has been suggested that steroid-driven changes in the reactivity of the reward network might facilitate procreation by increasing sexual receptivity or desire (Caldú & Dreher, 2007). Existing theories, however, are narrowly focused and do not adequately explain the full spectrum of hormonal effects beginning to emerge. We propose, alternatively, that regulation of the PFC by sex steroids during the prime reproductive years evolved as a mechanism to promote a type of decision-making bias in each sex that best facilitates reproductive success ('fitness'). The targets of this modulation are reproductively relevant decisions such as acquiring suitable sexual partners, mates, and raising offspring that survive and thrive, but might extend to non-social decisions that recruit the same neuronal pathways. According to parental investment theory (Trivers, 1972), males can increase their chances of reproductive success by acquiring resources and pursuing mating opportunities (both require willingness to engage in risk and are motivated by anticipated rewards), while not being easily deterred when faced with short-term negative outcomes. Males must defend their acquired social status against competitors and accurately discern when it is necessary. This behavioral phenotype may be promoted by testosterone, a hormonal signal of both reproductive maturity and viability. Females, on the other hand, have greater obligatory parental investment so may benefit more than males (especially at times of increased conception risk or if reproductive effort is already underway, as signaled by a high estradiol level) from increased deliberative top-down cognitive control. Optimal gating by the dorsal and ventral control networks may optimize outcomes for both sexes.

Consistent with the idea of enhanced dorsal network function when estradiol is high, a growing body of evidence suggests that working memory, a central element of planning, is improved during high-estradiol conditions. Data for functions other than working memory are scarce, but reports of greater inhibitory control when estradiol is highest (Amin et al., 2006; Hjelmervik et al., 2012), greater delay of gratification (Diekhof, 2015; Smith et al., 2014), or facilitated attentional-switching (Colzato et al., 2012) are consistent with amplified dorsal network function and are core cognitive processes important for child-rearing. Sex differences have been reported intermittently for these same processes (e.g., Bjorklund & Kipp, 1996), but further study is required to establish if the magnitude of the sex difference is dependent upon endocrine state (i.e., upon activational effects of steroids). High testosterone during the organizational period of the CNS and high (but not excessive) testosterone at reproductive maturity may enhance ventral network function in the male brain and promote regulatory control by VMPFC/OFC over linked subcortical structures. Heightened estradiol production by the ovaries and/or placenta may serve as a biological signal to the CNS that elicits heightened dorsal network function in women.

Acknowledgments

Some of the work reported in this chapter was funded by a pilot grant from the Society for Women's Health Research through its Isis Fund Network on Sex, Gender, Drugs and the Brain, and by Discovery Grants to the author from the Natural Sciences and Engineering Research Council of Canada (NSERC). Erin Morley was supported by an NSERC Undergraduate Summer Research Award and I thank Erin for her help in collecting the oral contraceptive data.

Notes

1 Unless the uterus has been removed, progestins are prescribed to reduce the risk of endometrial carcinoma in women using estrogen replacement.
2 Progesterone conceivably plays a role in adaptive functioning, perhaps through synergistic motivational effects (but also antagonistic ones; e.g., Dreher et al., 2007). Its relevance for processes in the PFC is largely unknown.

References

Amin, Z., Epperson, C. N., Constable, R. T., & Canli, T. (2006). Effects of estrogen variation on neural correlates of emotional response inhibition. *NeuroImage, 32*, 457–464.

Anderson, V. A., Anderson, P., Northam, E., Jacobs, R., & Catroppa, C. (2001). Development of executive functions through late childhood and adolescence in an Australian sample. *Developmental Neuropsychology, 20*, 385–406.

Apicella, C. L., Dreber, A., & Mollerstrom, J. (2014). Salivary testosterone change following monetary wins and losses predicts future financial risk-taking. *Psychoneuroendocrinology, 39*, 58–64.

Arnsten, A. F. T., & Robbins, T. W. (2002). Neurochemical modulation of prefrontal cortical function in humans and animals. In D. T. Stuss & R. T. Knight (Eds.), *Principles of frontal lobe function* (pp. 51–84). New York, NY: Oxford University Press.

Barbey, A. K., Koenigs, M., & Grafman, J. (2013). Dorsolateral prefrontal contributions to human working memory. *Cortex, 49*, 1194–1205.

Barel, E., Shahrabani, S., & Tzischinsky, O. (2017). Sex hormone/cortisol ratios differentially modulate risk-taking in men and women. *Evolutionary Psychology, 15*(1), 1–10. doi:10.1177/1474704917697333

Baumgartner, T., Knoch, D., Hotz, P., Eisenegger, C., & Fehr, E. (2011). Dorsolateral and ventromedial prefrontal cortex orchestrate normative choice. *Nature Neuroscience, 14*, 1468–1474.

Bechara, A., Damasio, A. R., Damasio, H., & Anderson, S. W. (1994). Insensitivity to future consequences following damage to human prefrontal cortex. *Cognition, 50*, 7–15.

Bechara, A., Damasio, H., & Damasio, A. R. (2000). Emotion, decision making and the orbitofrontal cortex. *Cerebral Cortex, 10*, 295–307.

Bechara, A., Damasio, H., Tranel, D., & Anderson, S. W. (1998). Dissociation of working memory from decision-making within the human prefrontal cortex. *Journal of Neuroscience, 18*, 428–437.

Bechara, A., Damasio, H., Tranel, D., & Damasio, A. R. (1997). Deciding advantageously before knowing the advantageous strategy. *Science, 275*, 1293–1295.

Berman, K. F., Schmidt, P. J., Rubinow, D. R., Danaceau, M. A., van Horn, J. D., Esposito, G., . . . Weinberger, D. R. (1997). Modulation of cognition-specific cortical activity by gonadal steroids: A positron-emission tomography study in women. *Proceedings of the National Academy of Sciences, 94*, 8836–8841.

Bethea, C. L., Lu, N. Z., Gundlah, C., & Streicher, J. M. (2002). Diverse actions of ovarian steroids in the serotonin neural system. *Frontiers in Neuroendocrinology, 23*, 41–100.

Bjorklund, D. F., & Kipp, K. (1996). Parental investment theory and gender differences in the evolution of inhibition mechanisms. *Psychological Bulletin, 120*, 163–188.

Bolla, K. I., Eldreth, D. A., Matochik, J. A., & Cadet, J. L. (2004). Sex-related differences in a gambling task and its neurological correlates. *Cerebral Cortex, 14*, 1226–1232.

Bos, P. A., Hermans, E. J., Ramsey, N. F., & van Honk, J. (2012). The neural mechanisms by which testosterone acts on interpersonal trust. *NeuroImage, 61*, 730–737.

Brañas-Garza, P., & Rustichini, A. (2011). Organizing effects of testosterone and economic behavior: Not just risk taking. *PLoS One, 6*(12), e29842.

Breedlove, S. M., & Hampson, E. (2002). Sexual differentiation of the brain and behavior. In J. B. Becker, S. M. Breedlove, D. Crews, & M. M. McCarthy (Eds.), *Behavioral endocrinology* (pp. 75–114). Cambridge, MA: MIT Press.

Button, K. S., Ioannidis, J. P., Mokrysz, C., Nosek, B. A., Flint, J., Robinson, E. S., & Munafò, M. R. (2013). Power failure: Why small sample size undermines the reliability of neuroscience. *Nature Reviews Neuroscience, 14*, 365–376.

Caldú, X., & Dreher, J-C. (2007). Hormonal and genetic influences on processing reward and social information. *Annals of the New York Academy of Sciences, 1118*, 43–73.

Clark, A. S., & Goldman-Rakic, P. S. (1989). Gonadal hormones influence the emergence of cortical function in nonhuman primates. *Behavioral Neuroscience, 103*, 1287–1295.

Clark, A. S., MacLusky, N. J., & Goldman-Rakic, P. S. (1988). Androgen binding and metabolism in the cerebral cortex of the developing rhesus monkey. *Endocrinology, 123*, 932–940.

Colzato, L. S., Pratt, J., & Hommel, B. (2012). Estrogen modulated inhibition of return in healthy human females. *Neuropsychologia, 50*, 98–103.

de Vries, G. J. (2004). Sex differences in adult and developing brains: Compensation, compensation, compensation. *Endocrinology, 145*, 1063–1068.

Diekhof, E. K. (2015). Be quick about it: Endogenous estradiol level, menstrual cycle phase and trait impulsiveness predict impulsive choice in the context of reward acquisition. *Hormones and Behavior, 74*, 186–193.

Diekhof, E. K., & Kraft, S. (2017). The association between endogenous testosterone level and behavioral flexibility in young men – evidence from stimulus-outcome reversal learning. *Hormones and Behavior, 89*, 193–200.

Dreher, J-C. (2015). Neuroimaging evidences of gonadal steroid hormone influences on reward processing and social decision-making in humans. *Brain Mapping: An Encyclopedic Reference*, 3, 1011–1018.

Dreher, J-C., Schmidt, P. J., Kohn, P., Furman, D., Rubinow, D., & Berman, K. F. (2007). Menstrual cycle phase modulates reward-related neural function in women. *Proceedings of the National Academy of Sciences*, 104, 2465–2470.

Duff, S. J., & Hampson, E. (2000). A beneficial effect of estrogen on working memory in postmenopausal women taking hormone replacement therapy. *Hormones and Behavior*, 38, 262–276.

Duff, S. J., & Hampson, E. (2001). A sex difference on a novel spatial working memory task in humans. *Brain and Cognition*, 47, 470–493.

Dumas, J. A., Kutz, A. M., Naylor, M. R., Johnson, J. V., & Newhouse, P. A. (2012). Estradiol treatment altered anticholinergic-related brain activation during working memory in postmenopausal women. *NeuroImage*, 60, 1394–1403.

Engman, J., Linnman, C., van Dijk, K. R. A., & Milad, M. R. (2016). Amygdala subnuclei resting-state functional connectivity sex and estrogen differences. *Psychoneuroendocrinology*, 63, 34–42.

Epperson, C. N., Amin, Z., Ruparel, K., Gur, R., & Loughead, J. (2012). Interactive effects of estrogen and serotonin on brain activation during working memory and affective processing in menopausal women. *Psychoneuroendocrinology*, 37, 372–382.

Evans, K. L., & Hampson, E. (2014). Does risk-taking mediate the relationship between testosterone and decision-making on the Iowa gambling task? *Personality and Individual Differences*, 61, 57–62.

Evans, K. L., & Hampson, E. (2015a). Sex differences on prefrontally-dependent cognitive tasks. *Brain and Cognition*, 93, 42–53.

Evans, K. L., & Hampson, E. (2015b). Sex-dependent effects on tasks assessing reinforcement learning and interference inhibition. *Frontiers in Psychology*, 6, 1044. doi:10.3389/fpsyg.2015.01044

Fellows, L. K. (2013). Decision making: Executive functions meet motivation. In D. T. Stuss & R. T. Knight (Eds.), *Principles of frontal lobe function* (pp. 490–499). New York, NY: Oxford University Press.

Finley, S. K., & Kritzer, M. F. (1999). Immunoreactivity for intracellular androgen receptors in identified subpopulations of neurons, astrocytes and oligodendrocytes in primate prefrontal cortex. *Journal of Neurobiology*, 40, 446–457.

Funahashi, S. (2017). Working memory in the prefrontal cortex. *Brain Sciences*, 7, 49. doi:10.3390/brainsci7050049.

Gläscher, J., Adolphs, R., Damasio, H., Bechara, A., Rudrauf, D., Calamia, M., . . . Tranel, D. (2012). Lesion mapping of cognitive control and value-based decision making in the prefrontal cortex. *Proceedings of the National Academy of Sciences*, 109, 14681–14686.

Goldstein, J. M., Jerram, M., Abbs, B., Whitfield-Gabrieli, S., & Makris, N. (2010). Sex differences in stress response circuitry activation dependent on female hormonal cycle. *Journal of Neuroscience*, 30, 431–438.

Goldstein, J. M., Jerram, M., Poldrack, R., Ahern, T., Kennedy, D. N., Seidman, L. J., & Makris, N. (2005). Hormonal cycle modulates arousal circuitry in women using functional magnetic resonance imaging. *Journal of Neuroscience*, 25, 9309–9316.

Goudriaan, A. E., Lapauw, B., Ruige, J., Feyen, E., Kaufman, J-M., Brand, M., & Vingerhoets, G. (2010). The influence of high-normal testosterone levels on risk-taking in healthy males in a 1-week letrozole administration study. *Psychoneuroendocrinology*, 35, 1416–1421.

Grigorova, M., Sherwin, B. B., & Tulandi, T. (2006). Effects of treatment with leuprolide acetate depot on working memory and executive functions in young premenopausal women. *Psychoneuroendocrinology*, 31, 935–947.

Hampson, E. (1990). Estrogen-related variations in human spatial and articulatory-motor skills. *Psychoneuroendocrinology*, 15, 97–111.

Hampson, E. (in press). Sex differences in cognition: Evidence for the organizational-activational hypothesis. In L. L. M. Welling & T. K. Shackelford (Eds.), *Oxford handbook of evolutionary psychology and behavioral endocrinology*. New York, NY: Oxford University Press.

Hampson, E., & Kimura, D. (1988). Reciprocal effects of hormonal fluctuations on human motor and perceptual-spatial skills. *Behavioral Neuroscience*, 102, 456–459.

Hampson, E., & Morley, E. E. (2013). Estradiol concentrations and working memory performance in women of reproductive age. *Psychoneuroendocrinology*, 38, 2897–2904.

Hampson, E., Phillips, S. D., Duff-Canning, S. J., Evans, K. L., Merrill, M., Pinsonneault, J. K., . . . Steiner, M. (2015). Working memory in pregnant women: Relation to estrogen and antepartum depression. *Hormones and Behavior*, 74, 218–227.

Hampson, E., & Sankar, J. S. (2012). Re-examining the Manning hypothesis: Androgen receptor polymorphism and the 2D:4D digit ratio. *Evolution and Human Behavior, 33,* 557–561.

Hao, J., Rapp, P. R., Janssen, W. G. M., Lou, W., Lasley, B. L., Hof, P. R., & Morrison, J. H. (2007). Interactive effects of age and estrogen on cognition and pyramidal neurons in monkey prefrontal cortex. *Proceedings of the National Academy of Sciences, 104,* 11465–11470.

Hara, Y., Waters, E. M., McEwen, B. S., & Morrison, J. H. (2015). Estrogen effects on cognitive and synaptic health over the lifecourse. *Physiological Reviews, 95,* 785–807.

Hermans, E. J., Bos, P. A., Ossewaarde, L., Ramsey, N. F., Fernández, G., & van Honk, J. (2010). Effects of exogenous testosterone on the ventral striatal BOLD response during reward anticipation in healthy women. *NeuroImage, 52,* 277–283.

Hermans, E. J., Ramsey, N. F., & van Honk, J. (2008). Exogenous testosterone enhances responsiveness to social threat in the neural circuitry of social aggression in humans. *Biological Psychiatry, 63,* 263–270.

Hjelmervik, H., Westerhausen, R., Osnes, B., Endresen, C. B., Hugdahl, K., Hausmann, M., & Specht, K. (2012). Language lateralization and cognitive control across the menstrual cycle assessed with a dichotic-listening paradigm. *Psychoneuroendocrinology, 37,* 1866–1875.

Hogervorst, E., & Bandelow, S. (2010). Sex steroids to maintain cognitive function in women after the menopause: A meta-analysis of treatment trials. *Maturitas, 66,* 56–71.

Hoshi, Y., Tsou, B. H., Billock, V. A., Tanosaki, M., Iguchi, Y., Shimada, M., . . . Oda, I. (2003). Spatiotemporal characteristics of hemodynamic changes in the human lateral prefrontal cortex during working memory tasks. *NeuroImage, 20,* 1493–1504.

Jacobs, E. G., & D'Esposito, M. (2011). Estrogen shapes dopamine-dependent cognitive processes. Implications for women's health. *Journal of Neuroscience, 31*(14), 5286–5293.

Jacobs, E. G., Holsen, L. M., Lancaster, K., Makris, N., Whitfield-Gabrieli, S., Remington, A., . . . Goldstein, J. M. (2015). 17β-estradiol differentially regulates stress circuitry activity in healthy and depressed women. *Neuropsychopharmacology, 40,* 566–576.

Jacobsen, C. F. (1936). The functions of the frontal association areas in monkeys. *Comparative Psychology Monographs, 13,* 1–60.

Keenan, P. A., Ezzat, W. H., Ginsburg, K., & Moore, G. J. (2001). Prefrontal cortex as the site of estrogen's effect on cognition. *Psychoneuroendocrinology, 26,* 577–590.

Kennerley, S. W., & Walton, M. E. (2011). Decision making and reward in frontal cortex: Complementary evidence from neurophysiological and neuropsychological studies. *Behavioral Neuroscience, 125,* 297–317.

Kirchner, W. K. (1958). Age differences in short-term retention of rapidly changing information. *Journal of Experimental Psychology, 55,* 352–358.

Kohama, S. G., Renner, L., Landauer, N., Weiss, A. R., Urbanski, H. F., Park, B., . . . Neuringer, M. (2016). Effect of ovarian hormone therapy on cognition in the aged female rhesus macaque. *Journal of Neuroscience, 36,* 10416–10424.

Krawczyk, D. C. (2002). Contributions of the prefrontal cortex to the neural basis of human decision making. *Neuroscience and Biobehavioral Reviews, 26,* 631–664.

Kringelbach, M. L., & Rolls, E. T. (2004). The functional neuroanatomy of the human orbitofrontal cortex: Evidence from neuroimaging and neuropsychology. *Progress in Neurobiology, 73,* 341–372.

Krug, R., Born, J., & Rasch, B. (2006). A 3-day estrogen treatment improves prefrontal cortex-dependent cognitive function in postmenopausal women. *Psychoneuroendocrinology, 31,* 965–975.

Kuptsova, S. V., Ivanova, M. V., Petrushevsky, A. G., Fedina, O. N., & Zhavoronkova, L. A. (2015). Sex-related differences in task-switching: An fMRI study. *Human Physiology, 41*(6), 611–624.

Lawrence, N. S., Jollan, F., O'Daly, O., Zelaya, F., & Phillips, M. L. (2009). Distinct roles of prefrontal cortical subregions in the Iowa gambling task. *Cerebral Cortex, 19,* 1134–1143.

Leeners, B., Kruger, T. H. C., Geraedts, K., Tronci, E., Mancini, T., Ille, F., . . . Hengartner, M. P. (2017). Lack of associations between female hormone levels and visuospatial working memory, divided attention and cognitive bias across two consecutive menstrual cycles. *Frontiers in Behavioral Neuroscience, 11,* 120. doi:10.3389/fnbeh.2017.000120

Lei, X., Han, Z., Chen, C., Bai, L., Xue, G., & Dong, Q. (2016). Sex differences in fiber connection between the striatum and subcortical and cortical regions. *Frontiers in Computational Neuroscience, 10,* 100. doi:10.3389/fncom.2016.00100

Lejbak, L., Vrbancic, M., & Crossley, M. (2009). The female advantage in object location memory is robust to verbalizability and mode of presentation of test stimuli. *Brain and Cognition, 69,* 148–153.

Lombardo, M. V., Ashwin, E., Auyeung, B., Chakrabarti, B., Taylor, K., Hackett, G., . . . Baron-Cohen, S. (2012). Fetal testosterone influences sexually dimorphic gray matter in the human brain. *Journal of Neuroscience, 32*, 674–680.

Manning, J. T., Scutt, D., Wilson, J., & Lewis-Jones, D. I. (1998). The ratio of the 2nd to the 4th digit length: A predictor of sperm numbers and concentrations of testosterone, luteinizing hormone and oestrogen. *Human Reproduction, 13*, 3000–3004.

McCarthy, M. M., & Konkle, A. T. M. (2005). When is a sex difference not a sex difference? *Frontiers in Neuroendocrinology, 26*, 85–102.

McDowell, A. A., Brown, W. L., & McTee, A. C. (1960). Sex as a factor in spatial delayed-response performance by rhesus monkeys. *Journal of Comparative and Physiological Psychology, 53*, 420–432.

Mehta, P. H., & Beer, J. (2009). Neural mechanisms of the testosterone-aggression relation: The role of orbitofrontal cortex. *Journal of Cognitive Neuroscience, 22*, 2357–2368.

Milner, B., & Petrides, M. (1984). Behavioural effects of frontal-lobe lesions in man. *Trends in Neurosciences, 7*, 403–407.

Montague, D., Weickert, C. S., Tomaskovic-Crook, E., Rothmond, D. A., Kleinman, E., & Rubinow, D. R. (2008). Oestrogen receptor α localisation in the prefrontal cortex of three mammalian species. *Journal of Neuroendocrinology, 20*, 893–903.

Motzkin, J. C., Philippi, C. L., Wolf, R. C., Baskaya, M. K., & Koenigs, M. (2015). Ventromedial prefrontal cortex is critical for the regulation of amygdala activity in humans. *Biological Psychiatry, 77*, 276–284.

O'Doherty, J. O., Kringelbach, M. L., Rolls, E. T., Hornak, J., & Andrews, C. (2001). Abstract reward and punishment representations in the human orbitofrontal cortex. *Nature Neuroscience, 4*, 95–102.

O'Neill, M., & Schultz, W. (2015). Economic risk coding by single neurons in the orbitofrontal cortex. *Journal of Physiology-Paris, 109*, 70–77.

Op de Macks, Z. A., Bunge, S. A., Bell, O. N., Wilbrecht, L., Kriegsfeld, L. J., Kayser, A. S., & Dahl, R. E. (2016). Risky decision-making in adolescent girls: The role of pubertal hormones and reward circuitry. *Psychoneuroendocrinology, 74*, 77–91.

Overman, W. H., Bachevalier, J., Schuhmann, E., & Ryan, P. (1996). Cognitive gender differences in very young children parallel biologically based cognitive gender differences in monkeys. *Behavioral Neuroscience, 116*, 673–684.

Overman, W. H., Boettcher, L., Watterson, L., & Walsh, K. (2011). Effects of dilemmas and aromas on performance of the Iowa gambling task. *Behavioral Brain Research, 218*, 64–72.

Overman, W. H., & Pierce, A. (2013). Iowa gambling task with non-clinical participants: Effects of using real + virtual cards and additional trials. *Frontiers in Psychology, 4*, 935. doi:10.3389.fpsyg.2013.00935

Owen, A. M., Herrod, N. J., Menon, D. K., Clark, J. C., Downey, S. P. M. J., Carpenter, A., . . . Pickard, J. D. (1999). Redefining the functional organization of working memory processes within human lateral prefrontal cortex. *European Journal of Neuroscience, 11*, 567–574.

Passingham, R. E. (1985). Memory of monkeys (*Macaca mulatta*) with lesions in prefrontal cortex. *Behavioral Neuroscience, 99*, 3–21.

Paus, T., Nawaz-Khan, I., Leonard, G., Perron, M., Pike, G. B., Pitiot, A., . . . Pausova, Z. (2010). Sexual dimorphism in the adolescent brain: Role of testosterone and androgen receptor in global and local volumes of grey and white matter. *Hormones and Behavior, 57*, 63–75.

Perlman, W. R., Matsumoto, M., Beltaifa, S., Hyde, T. M., Saunders, R. C., Webster, M. J., . . . Weickert, C. S. (2005). Expression of estrogen receptor alpha exon-deleted mRNA variants in the human and non-human primate frontal cortex. *Neuroscience, 134*, 81–95.

Petrides, M., Alivisatos, B., Meyer, E., & Evans, A. C. (1993). Functional activation of the human frontal cortex during the performance of verbal working memory tasks. *Proceedings of the National Academy of Sciences, 90*, 878–882.

Petrides, M., & Milner, B. (1982). Deficits on subject-ordered tasks after frontal- and temporal-lobe lesions in man. *Neuropsychologia, 20*, 249–262.

Phoenix, C. H., Goy, R. W., Gerall, A. A., & Young, W. C. (1959). Organizing action of prenatally administered testosterone propionate on the tissues mediating mating behavior in the female guinea pig. *Endocrinology, 65*, 369–382.

Protopopescu, X., Pan, H., Altemus, M., Tuescher, O., Polanecsky, M., McEwen, B., . . . Stern, E. (2005). Orbitofrontal cortex activity related to emotional processing changes across the menstrual cycle. *Proceedings of the National Academy of Sciences, 102*, 16060–16065.

Rapp, P. R., Morrison, J. H., & Roberts, J. A. (2003). Cyclic estrogen replacement improves cognitive function in aged ovariectomized rhesus monkeys. *Journal of Neuroscience, 23*, 5708–5714.

Reavis, R., & Overman, W. H. (2001). Adult sex differences on a decision-making task previously shown to depend on the orbital prefrontal cortex. *Behavioral Neuroscience, 115*, 196–206.

Reber, J., & Tranel, D. (2017). Sex differences in the functional lateralization of emotion and decision-making in the human brain. *Journal of Neuroscience Research, 95*, 270–278.

Resnick, S. M., Berenbaum, S. A., Gottesman, I. I., & Bouchard, T. J. (1986). Early hormonal influences on cognitive functioning in congenital adrenal hyperplasia. *Developmental Psychology, 22*, 191–198.

Reynolds, B., & Schiffbauer, R. (2004). Measuring state changes in human delay discounting: An experiential discounting task. *Behavioural Processes, 67*, 343–356.

Rilling, J. K., Lacreuse, A., Barks, S. K., Elfenbein, H. A., Pagnoni, G., Votaw, J. R., & Herndon, J. G. (2008). Effect of menstrual cycle on resting brain metabolism in female rhesus monkeys. *NeuroReport, 19*, 537–541.

Roberts, A. C., Robbins, T. W., & Everitt, B. J. (1988). The effects of intradimensional and extradimensional shifts on visual discrimination learning in humans and non-human primates. *Quarterly Journal of Experimental Psychology, 40B*, 321–341.

Roberts, J. A., Gilardi, K. V. K., Lasley, B., & Rapp, P. R. (1997). Reproductive senescence predicts cognitive decline in aged female monkeys. *NeuroReport, 8*, 2047–2051.

Romine, C. B., & Reynolds, C. R. (2004). Sequential memory: A developmental perspective on its relation to frontal lobe functioning. *Neuropsychology Review, 14*, 43–64.

Rupp, H. A., James, T. W., Ketterson, E. D., Sengelaub, D. R., Janssen, E., & Heiman, J. R. (2009). Neural activation in the orbitofrontal cortex in response to male faces increases during the follicular phase. *Hormones and Behavior, 56*, 66–72.

Schlaepfer, T. E., Harris, G. J., Tien, A. Y., Peng, L., Lee, S., & Pearlson, G. D. (1995). Structural differences in the cerebral cortex of healthy female and male subjects: A magnetic resonance imaging study. *Psychiatry Research: Neuroimaging, 61*, 129–135.

Schulz, K., & Forrester-Fronstin, Z. (this volume). Sensitive periods of development and the organizing actions of gonadal steroid hormones on the adolescent brain. In O. C. Schultheiss & P. H. Mehta (Eds.), *International handbook of social neuroendocrinology*. London: Routledge.

Sholl, S. A., & Kim, K. L. (1990). Androgen receptors are differentially distributed between right and left cerebral hemispheres of the fetal male rhesus monkey. *Brain Research, 516*, 122–126.

Sinha, R., Lacadie, C. M., Constable, T., & Seo, D. (2016). Dynamic neural activity during stress signals resilient coping. *Proceedings of the National Academy of Sciences, 113*, 8837–8842.

Smith, C. T., Sierra, Y., Oppler, S. H., & Boettiger, C. A. (2014). Ovarian cycle effects on immediate reward selection bias in humans: A role for estradiol. *Journal of Neuroscience, 34*, 5468–5476.

Smith, Y. R., Love, T., Persad, C. C., Tkaczyk, A., Nichols, T. E., & Zubieta, J. K. (2006). Impact of combined estradiol and norethindrone therapy on visuospatial working memory assessed by functional magnetic resonance imaging. *Journal of Clinical Endocrinology & Metabolism, 91*, 4476–4481.

Speck, O., Ernst, T., Braun, J., Koch, C., Miller, E., & Chang, L. (2000). Gender differences in the functional organization of the brain for working memory. *Brain Imaging, 11*, 2581–2585.

Stanton, S. J., Liening, S. H., & Schultheiss, O. C. (2011). Testosterone is positively associated with risk-taking in the Iowa Gambling Task. *Hormones and Behavior, 59*, 252–256.

Stanton, S. J., Wirth, M. M., Waugh, C. E., & Schultheiss, O. C. (2009). Endogenous testosterone levels are associated with amygdala and ventromedial prefrontal cortex responses to anger faces in men but not women. *Biological Psychology, 81*, 118–122.

Stenstrom, E., Saad, G., Nepomuceno, M. V., & Mendenhall, Z. (2011). Testosterone and domain-specific risk: Digit ratios (2D:4D and rel2) as predictors of recreational, financial, and social risk-taking behaviors. *Personality and Individual Differences, 51*, 412–416.

Thomas, J., Météreau, E., Déchaud, H., Pugeat, M., & Dreher, J-C. (2014). Hormonal treatment increases the response of the reward system at the menopause transition: A counterbalanced randomized placebo-controlled fMRI study. *Psychoneuroendocrinology, 50*, 167–180.

Tinkler, G. P., & Voytko, M. L. (2005). Estrogen modulates cognitive and cholinergic processes in surgically menopausal monkeys. *Progress in Neuro-Psychopharmacology & Biological Psychiatry, 29*, 423–431.

Trivers, R. L. (1972). Parental investment and sexual selection. In B. Campbell (Ed.), *Sexual selection and the descent of man, 1871–1971* (pp. 136–179). Chicago, IL: Aldine.

van den Bos, R., Homberg, J., & de Visser, L. (2013). A critical review of sex differences in decision-making tasks: Focus on the Iowa Gambling Task. *Behavioural Brain Research, 238*, 95–108.

van Honk, J., Schutter, D. J. L. G., Hermans, E. J., Putman, P., Tuiten, A., & Koppeschaar, H. (2004). Testosterone shifts the balance between sensitivity for punishment and reward in healthy young women. *Psychoneuroendocrinology, 29*, 937–943.

van Wingen, G. A., Mattern, C., Verkes, R. J., Buitelaar, J., & Fernández, G. (2010). Testosterone reduces amygdala-orbitofrontal cortex coupling. *Psychoneuroendocrinology, 35*, 105–113.

van Wingen, G. A., Ossewaarde, L., Bäckström, T., Hermans, E. J., & Fernández, G. (2011). Gonadal hormone regulation of the emotion circuitry in humans. *Neuroscience, 191*, 38–45.

Voyer, D., Voyer, S. D., & Saint-Aubin, J. (2017). Sex differences in visual-spatial working memory: A meta-analysis. *Psychonomic Bulletin and Review, 24*, 307–334.

Wang, J., Cheng, C. M., Zhou, J., Smith, A., Weickert, C. S., Perlman, W. R., . . . Bondy, C. A. (2004). Estradiol alters transcription factor gene expression in primate prefrontal cortex. *Journal of Neuroscience Research, 76*, 306–314.

Wechsler, D. (1987). *Wechsler memory scale – revised*. San Antonio, TX: Psychological Corporation.

Welborn, B. L., Papademetris, X., Reis, D. L., Rajeevan, N., Bloise, S. M., & Gray, J. R. (2009). Variation in orbitofrontal cortex volume: Relation to sex, emotion regulation and affect. *Social Cognitive and Affective Neuroscience, 4*, 328–339.

White, R. E., Thornhill, S., & Hampson, E. (2006). Entrepreneurs and evolutionary biology: The relationship between testosterone and new venture creation. *Organizational Behavior and Human Decision Processes, 100*, 21–34.

Williams, C. L., Barnett, A. M., & Meck, W. H. (1990). Organizational effects of early gonadal secretions on sexual differentiation in spatial memory. *Behavioral Neuroscience, 104*, 84–97.

Woolley, C. S., & McEwen, B. S. (1992). Estradiol mediates fluctuation in hippocampal synapse density during the estrous cycle in the adult rat. *Journal of Neuroscience, 12*, 2549–2554.

Zeidan, M. A., Igoe, S. A., Linnman, C., Vitalo, A., Levine, J. B., Klibanski, A., . . . Milad, M. R. (2011). Estradiol modulates medial prefrontal cortex and amygdala activity during fear extinction in women and female rats. *Biological Psychiatry, 70*, 920–927.

22

SEX HORMONES AND ECONOMIC DECISION MAKING IN THE LAB

A review of the causal evidence

Anna Dreber and Magnus Johannesson

Introduction

While hormones have been linked to social behaviors in animals and humans in a large body of work, the potential link to economic decision making is relatively less explored, although it has received increasing attention over the last decade. Deviations in decision making from the predictions of the standard economic model of selfish rational preferences have been documented for a long time, and economic theories have to some extent taken these deviations into account (see e.g. Camerer, 2003). For example, it is often observed that people are more altruistic and care about fairness than what standard models would predict, and that people often do not maximize expected utility in the domain of risk. Some of the deviations from the standard models have been linked to cultural variables (e.g. Henrich et al., 2001), and twin research also suggests genetic components (e.g. Cesarini, Dawes, Johannesson, Lichtenstein, & Wallace, 2009). In this chapter we describe the current literature on studies attempting to causally link sex hormones to economic decision making in the lab. We focus on social preferences as measured from economic games, as well as financial risk taking and willingness to compete. While there also are studies on related topics, these are the most commonly explored preferences in the experimental economics literature. To various degrees, variation in these preferences has also been linked to important economic outcomes. For example, Henrich et al. (2001) show that in 15 small-scale societies, behavior in the social preference games is linked to economic organization and market integration. Buser, Niederle and Oosterbeek (2014) find that more competitive individuals are more likely to choose more math-oriented and more prestigious university majors, and risk preferences have been found to correlate with financial market participation (e.g. Almenberg & Dreber, 2015).

While the most famous and cited paper on a hormone and economic decision making explores the influence of oxytocin on trust behavior (Kosfeld, Heinrichs, Zak, Fischbacher & Fehr, 2005), testosterone has been the main focus in the literature attempting to link sex hormones and economic decision making.[1] Testosterone is a steroid hormone mainly produced by the testes in men. It is also present in women, but in much smaller quantities: approximately one-eighth of the male amount. Testosterone plays an important role in reproductive physiology and development and is thought to modulate several behavioral processes related to survival and reproduction, in humans and other animals, and in particular in males. There is a vast literature attempting to link testosterone to social behaviors, including aggression, dominance and mate seeking, in both men and women – see for example Sections 2 and 4 in this handbook.

Most studies attempting to link testosterone to economic decision making are correlational, involving measuring testosterone from saliva or blood.[2] This review instead focuses on pharmacological testosterone administration with double-blind placebo-controlled designs, which allows us to interpret results causally. The relation between behaviors and hormones can often be bi-directional, making correlational results hard to interpret. This review also discusses the few existing studies on administration of two other sex hormones, estrogen and progesterone, and economic decision making. These hormones play important roles for female physiology and could potentially play a role in economic decision making. There are a handful of correlational studies on this topic, mainly exploring the correlation between economic decision making and self-reported menstrual cycle phase or self-reported oral contraceptive use. Administration studies on these hormones allow us to test whether there are causal relations.

It is important to point out that administration studies are not unproblematic – the results can also be hard to interpret for these studies. For example, the results from studies giving rise to hormone levels well above the normal range can be unclear since high-dose effects could be different from effects within the normal physiological range. There could also be behavioral effects in administration studies due to other mechanisms besides the targeted hormone system, and these effects might deviate from what we would observe from endogenous hormones. These caveats are clearly relevant when interpreting the literature below.

Economic games and measures

Before discussing the specific games, there are some differences between experiments in psychology and economics that are worth mentioning. In experimental economics the norm is to not use deception, and it is almost impossible to publish experiments with deception in economic journals. Incentives are typically monetary; thus, when measuring risk preferences or willingness to compete, for example, money is at stake. Whether the no-deception rule and monetary incentives matter for the actual results is another topic (see, for example, Camerer & Hogarth, 1999 on the latter).

Social preferences within the field of economics are typically measured by the dictator game, the ultimatum game, the trust game, the prisoner's dilemma or the multiplayer continuous public goods game (see e.g. Camerer & Fehr, 2004 for more discussion of these games). In the dictator game, two participants are randomly matched, where one is randomly picked to be the dictator and one to be the recipient.[3] The dictator is typically endowed with some initial amount of money, say $10, and can choose to keep the money or give some or all to the recipient, who has received $0. In the most anonymous version of this game, the modal offer is to give 0 of the initial endowment, but there is typically also some giving, with the second most common level of giving being 50%. Giving behavior in the dictator game is often interpreted as altruism or generosity, though this interpretation has been questioned (e.g. List, 2007).[4]

In the ultimatum game, two participants are randomly matched, where one is randomly picked to be the proposer and one to be the responder. The proposer is typically endowed with some initial amount of money, unlike the responder, as in the dictator game. But in the ultimatum game, giving cannot be unconditional as in the dictator game. In the ultimatum game, the proposer makes an offer of how to split the money between the proposer and the responder. The responder can then either accept the offer, in which case the offer is implemented, or reject the offer, so that neither participant ends up with any money. The focus in this game is typically on responder behavior, where rejections of low offers are often interpreted in terms of fairness preferences or reciprocity. Proposer behavior in this game is a mix of different factors like strategic concerns, fairness and altruism: participants may give high offers because they are altruistic but also because they are strategic. Due to the difficulty of disentangling these factors, proposer behavior is typically not the focus of these studies. Responder behavior is sometimes elicited with the strategy method where responders say whether they would accept or reject several types of offers before the actual proposed offer is implemented. This method is incentive-compatible – participants are incentivized to behave according to their actual preferences – since what the responder has answered to the various offers is binding for the actual offer. Another common way of eliciting responder behavior is to ask responders for their minimum acceptable offer (MAO). All offers above this MAO are automatically accepted and all offers below are rejected.[5] In the ultimatum game, offers are typically in the interval of 40–50% and rarely above 50%. Low offers are often rejected (e.g. Güth & Kocher, 2014).

In the trust game, or the investment game, two participants are randomly matched, where one is randomly picked to be the trustor (or the investor) and one to be the trustee. The trustor is typically endowed with some initial amount of money, unlike the trustee, and can choose to send some to the trustee. Whatever is sent is multiplied, often by three, and allocated to the trustee, who then chooses whether to return something to the trustor. Whatever is returned is not multiplied. Trustor behavior is thought to capture trust as well as altruism, whereas trustee behavior is thought to capture trustworthiness (which could be due to reciprocity and altruism) (Cox, 2004). In the trust game the average amount sent by trustors is often half and the average amount returned by trustees is typically similar.

In the prisoner's dilemma, two players are randomly matched and can both choose to either cooperate or defect. The game is such that both players receive a monetary payoff that is higher when both cooperate than when both defect, but defecting against a cooperator leads to the highest payoff and cooperating with a defector leads to the lowest payoff. In the one-shot or finitely repeated version of the game, the rational choice given selfish preferences is to defect since it is payoff-maximizing. The public goods game is a multiplayer continuous version of the prisoner's dilemma, where each player in a group simultaneously decides how much of an endowment to contribute to a public good. The sum of the monetary payoffs is the highest if all players fully cooperate by contributing the whole endowment, but each player maximizes their individual payoff by contributing zero (defecting). In both games, a substantial fraction of players cooperates in the one-shot or finitely repeated game, though in the latter cooperation typically decays over time.

Financial risk taking is typically measured through having participants choose between either different incentivized gambles or between safe options and gambles. With the multiple price list approach that many studies use, participants choose between a 50–50 gamble and a safe amount that varies across choices. Risk taking can be measured as the share of risky options chosen.[6] Participants are informed about probabilities and potential outcomes in economic risk tasks (if for example probabilities are not known then the study is instead about ambiguity aversion, a literature that we do not discuss here). People are typically risk averse in the domain of gains and risk taking in the domain of losses (Kahneman & Tversky, 1979).

When measuring willingness to compete within the field of economics, participants typically first perform a task (often simple arithmetics) for a few minutes and are paid according to an individual piece-rate scheme.[7] After this first stage, they then perform the same task but are matched with random others and paid according to a competitive tournament scheme, where only the best performer is paid but the stakes are higher. During a third stage participants are then asked to choose which payment scheme they prefer when performing the task again. The self-selection into a piece-rate scheme or a tournament scheme in the third stage is the binary variable on willingness to compete (Niederle & Vesterlund, 2007). A secondary measure of competitiveness is typically the absolute change in performance in the competitive stage two compared to the non-competitive piece-rate stage one.

There is substantial variation in economic decision making between individuals with these measures, and also some evidence suggesting that context can matter (e.g. the famous framing example of Tversky & Kahneman, 1981) but also that for example framing in the dictator game does not matter (Dreber, Ellingsen, Johanneson, & Rand, 2013). Some work suggests that variables such as gender, age and whether the participant is a student or not correlate with decision making. For example, students are typically less altruistic in the dictator game than other populations (Carpenter et al., 2008). Women are typically on average more risk averse and more altruistic in the dictator game than men (e.g. Croson & Gneezy, 2009; Engel, 2011). Younger individuals are typically more risk loving than older individuals (Dohmen et al., 2011). Women are typically less willing to compete than men in math-related tasks but not necessarily in other tasks (e.g. Dreber, von Essen & Ranehill, 2014), and evidence suggests that culture matters for the gender gap in competitiveness (e.g. Gneezy, Leonard, & List, 2009; Cárdenas, Dreber, von Essen, & Ranehill, 2012). Studies also suggest a genetic component in for example dictator game giving, ultimatum game rejections, trust game behavior and risk preferences (e.g. Wallace, Cesarini, Lichtenstein, & Johannesson, 2007, Cesarini et al., 2009), and cultural variation in for example dictator game and ultimatum game behavior (e.g. Henrich et al., 2001).

When it comes to hormones and economic decision making, most studies have been correlational, and the results are typically not conclusive. The literature on financial risk taking and endogenous testosterone is a good example (see Apicella et al., 2015 for a review). While Apicella et al. (2008) find a positive correlation between testosterone and risk taking in men, Sapienza, Zingales and Mastripieri (2009) find no correlation among their full sample of men but a positive correlation in women. Stanton et al. (2011) instead find a non-linear relationship in a sample of men and women, whereas Schipper (2012) finds a positive correlation for men but not women. This illustrates the need for causal studies in order to draw more concrete conclusions.

Results: economic games and hormones

Dictator games

Zak et al. (2009) administered testosterone with 10 g of Androgel (1% testosterone gel) or placebo to 25 men in a double-blind within-subject design. At each of the two occasions of data collection 16 hours after administration, participants made four dictator decisions where another participant is the recipient. The results suggest no impact of testosterone on dictator game giving. In the analysis, the four decisions by each participant at each of the two occasions were treated as separate data points, making the sample end up being 25 participants * 4 decisions * 2 times (placebo vs testosterone) = 200 observations that were treated as independent even though they are correlated.

Zethraeus et al. (2009) administered testosterone (Testosterone undecanoate, 40 mg/day), estrogen (Estradiol 2 mg/day) or placebo to 200 postmenopausal women aged 50–65 over a period of four weeks in a double-blind between-subject design. Participants made one decision in a dictator game where the recipient is a charity. They find no effect of either hormone on dictator game giving.

Buskens, Raub, van Miltenburg, Montoya and van Honk (2016) administer testosterone (0.5mg sublingually) or placebo at one occasion to 82 women four hours before the main tasks in a double-blind between-subject study. Participants play a dictator game with an anonymous other participant. In the final sample of 81 women, they find no effect of testosterone on dictator game giving.

Ranehill et al. (2017) administer an oral contraceptive (Neovletta®, containing 150 μg levonorgestrel and 30 μg ethinylestradiol) or placebo to 340 women aged 18–35 years over a period of three months in a double-blind between-subject design. Synthetic progesterone is the main ingredient in this oral contraceptive. Participants make five dictator game decisions where in each decision the recipient is a different charity. The average donation in these five decisions is the dictator game outcome variable. In this study, the main analysis was performed as an intention to treat analysis for the 333 participants who completed data collection, but the results are similar in various robustness tests. The results suggest no impact of the oral contraceptive on dictator game giving.

Ultimatum games

One of the earliest studies on testosterone and economic decision making is Burnham (2007), who looks at ultimatum game behavior. In a correlational study of 26 men, Burnham found that men who rejected low offers in the ultimatum game had significantly higher testosterone levels than those that accepted low offers. In terms of causal studies, only a handful of results have thus far been reported.

Zak et al. (2009) study not only the dictator game but also the effect of testosterone on ultimatum game behavior in men. Instead of simply focusing on proposer and responder behavior separately, they define generosity as the difference between a participant's offer as proposer and MAO as responder. Participants make four proposer decisions and four responder decisions. As mentioned for the dictator game, although the individual's multiple decisions are clearly correlated, they are treated as independent data points in the analysis, inflating sample sizes and deflating standard errors without being corrected. In this statistically problematic analysis, Zak et al. interpret the results as suggesting that testosterone decreases generosity and increases MAOs.

Zethraeus et al. (2009) also study the ultimatum game in their sample of 200 women. Almost all participants (92%) offered a 50–50 split as proposers, and thus there is no evidence of testosterone or estrogen affecting proposer behavior. Responders answer for each possible proposal (400 Swedish krona divided between the two players in increments of 50 Swedish krona) whether they would accept or reject the proposal. A responder's acceptance threshold was defined as the midpoint of the lowest offer accepted and the previous offer. Zethraeus et al. find no effect of testosterone or estrogen on the acceptance threshold.

Eisenegger, Naef, Snozzi, Heinrichs and Fehr (2010) administer a single dose of sublingual testosterone (0.5 mg) or placebo to a total sample size of 121 women four hours before they play the ultimatum game in a double-blind between-subject design. The main focus in the paper are the 60 women who play as proposers. Participants were also asked about their beliefs of having received testosterone or placebo, with the results suggesting that participants were unaware of what they received. Each proposer played three independent ultimatum games with three different responders and could offer 0, 2, 3 or 5 out of 10 monetary units to the responder that the responder then chose to accept or reject. Eisenegger et al. find that testosterone leads to higher offers in the ultimatum game controlling for beliefs, and that those that believed they received testosterone made lower offers than those that believed they received placebo. Beliefs were, however, collected after participants played the ultimatum game, leading to a potential reverse causality problem. When beliefs are not controlled for there is no statistically significant effect of testosterone on offers in the ultimatum game. Among responders, there is no significant effect of testosterone on behavior.

Dreher et al. (2016) inject testosterone enanthate (250 mg; Androtardyl/Testoviron Depot) or placebo in a sample of 40 men 17.5–20 hours before performing a double-blind between-subject modified ultimatum game study. In this version of the ultimatum game, responders were after choosing to accept or reject the offer given the opportunity to decrease, increase or do nothing to the payoff of the proposer at a cost to themselves. This setup changes the interpretation of behavior in the ultimatum game since there is now a second stage that both the proposer and responder should consider in the ultimatum game stage. Participants in this study played a large number of rounds of this task, all as responders, with three fixed proposers (probably involving deception). Dreher et al. find no effect of testosterone on responder behavior in the ultimatum game, but that those given testosterone were more likely to punish proposers with low offers and reward proposers with high offers.

Kopsida, Berrebi, Petrovic and Ingvar (2016) administer a single dose of testosterone gel (3g containing 60 mg Tostrex) or placebo to a sample of 40 men and 28 women three hours before participants take part in a double-blind between-subject ultimatum game study in the fMRI. Participants are only responders and reacted to proposals of 45 different proposers that they could accept or reject. Fifteen offers were fair (50–50), 15 were unfair (80–20) and 15 were neutral. They find no effect of testosterone on responder behavior.[8]

Cueva et al. (2017) administer three doses of testosterone gel (10g containing Testogel™ (1% T gel)) or placebo to 41 men 48 hours, 24 hours and 0 hours prior to the experiment in a double-blind within-subject study. Participants are responders in the ultimatum game. Due to incomplete data for three participants, the final sample size is 38. Participants reacted to four different proposals that they could accept or reject. Cueva et al. find no effect of testosterone on responder behavior.

Trust games

Zethraeus et al. (2009) also include the trust game. Trustors were endowed with 150 Swedish krona that they could send to the trustee (with a multiplier of three), and trustees were asked to decide how much they would send back to the trustor for each of the three possible amounts sent (50, 100 and 150 Swedish krona). The 200 women in the study played the trust game as both trustors and trustees. Zethraeus et al. find no effect of testosterone or estrogen on trust or trustworthiness.

Boksem et al. (2013) administer testosterone (0.5mg sublingually) or placebo at one occasion to 54 women taking hormonal contraceptives in a double-blind between-subject study. Participants played once as trustors and once as trustees. Trustors were endowed with €20 that they could send to the trustee (with a multiplier of three). This experiment involves deception: trustees were always given €60 no matter what the trustors actually sent and were asked to decide how much to send back to the trustor. The final sample size for this game is 51. Unlike Zethraeus et al., Boksem et al. find that testosterone decreases trust and increases trustworthiness.

Buskens et al. (2016) also study trust game behavior. Each of the 82 female participants played six one-shot trust games with different partners and a repeated six-round game with the same partner. Participants were provided with feedback about their partner's decision after each game. Participants remained in the role as trustor or trustee throughout. Unlike Boksem et al., Buskens et al. find no effect of testosterone on trust or trustworthiness. Buskens et al. instead find different effects of testosterone depending on 2D:4D, a putative proxy of prenatal testosterone exposure, and whether the trust game is repeated or one-shot: they find that participants with low 2D:4D (potentially indicating high prenatal testosterone exposure) who were given testosterone were not more trusting in the repeated trust game than in the one-shot trust game, but the other three groups (high 2D:4D given testosterone, low and high 2D:4D in the placebo group) were more trusting in the repeated trust game compared to the one-shot trust game.

Prisoner's dilemmas/public goods games

van Honk, Montoya, Bos, van Vugt and Terburg (2012) administer testosterone (unclear how much) or placebo at two occasions to 24 women in a double-blind within-subject study. Participants played a three-player eight-round public goods game. van Honk et al. find no main effect of testosterone on cooperation, but an interaction with 2D:4D. The results suggest that participants with high 2D:4D contributed more to the public good after receiving testosterone compared to placebo, whereas there was no change in behavior for low 2D:4D participants.

Risk preferences

Zethraeus et al. (2009) also explore whether testosterone or estrogen affects risk taking in their sample of 200 women. Participants made six choices between a certain payoff and a gamble where they can win a high payoff or nothing with equal probability, with the certain payoff increasing for each choice. As all participants made monotonic choices, they use the certainty equivalent for each participant (from the midpoint of the relevant certainty equivalent interval) as their measure of risk aversion. Zethraeus et al. find no effect of either hormone on risk aversion.[9]

Boksem et al. (2013) also included measures for risk and ambiguity preferences in their sample of 54 women. Participants made 18 choices similar to Zethraeus et al., where they chose between a certain payoff and a gamble where they can win a high payoff or nothing with equal probability. Risk aversion is inferred from the share of gambles chosen. Boksem et al. find no effect of testosterone on risk aversion (or ambiguity aversion).

Buskens et al. (2016) also have participants perform a risk task consisting of seven incentivized gambles. Using a sample of 81 participants, they find no effect of testosterone administration on risk aversion.

Ranehill et al. (2017) also included a measure for financial risk taking, with 18 choices similar to what is described above. They find no effect of the oral contraceptive on risk aversion.

Willingness to compete

There is thus far only one reported study on hormone administration and the economic measure of willingness to compete.[10] Ranehill et al. (2017) have participants solve math problems as in the description of the task above, where they compete against one other participant when competing. They find no effect on the oral contraceptive on willingness to compete.

Discussion

The results from this reviewed literature on sex hormone administration and economic decision making suggests no clear pattern where a hormone causally influences economic decision making. Whereas some studies find an effect on some behavior, the results sometimes go in opposite directions, and the studies with the largest sample sizes systematically fail to find any effects (Zethraeus et al., 2009 and Ranehill et al., 2017). What is going on?

One potential explanation lies in the variation in dosages and time periods for the hormone administration. There is also some variation in subject pools, administration procedures, game setups and measures. For example, while Eisenegger et al. (2010) only include women who are not taking oral contraceptives in their testosterone administration study, Boksem et al. (2013) and Kopsida et al. (2016) only include women taking hormonal contraceptives. There are also examples where one study only explores men and one study only explores women, while the administered hormone may act differently depending on the sex of the recipient. Moreover, there is variation in dosages, the type of drug and method used to manipulate the hormone (e.g. Androgel vs Natesto), how the hormonal impact is measured (blood versus saliva) as well as variation in the time between the hormone administration and the behavioral testing between studies. There is also variation in how the economic games and measures are administrated, with some using more "cold" methods than others (e.g. using the strategy method). These factors may contribute to the variation in results.

Most estimates fail to reject the null hypothesis of an effect of sex hormones on economic behavior. The few that reported significant findings need to be interpreted cautiously due to lack of robustness in results across studies and the limited sample sizes. The lack of robustness of published significant results is not unique to the literature on hormones and economic decision making. In many literatures, the share of reproducible results has turned out to be substantial: see for example Open Science Collaboration (2015) on experiments in psychology and Camerer et al. (2016) on experiments in economics.[11] There are several reasons for why there could be a substantial fraction of false results in the literature even when scientists are not actively faking data or acting scrupulous (Ioannidis, 2005). Publication bias (Sterling, 1959) and file-drawer effects (Rosenthal, 1979) are two important reasons, as evidenced in for example Franco, Malhotra and Simonovits (2014). P-values and statistical power are also key. Low power is typically recognized as a source of an increased chance of false negative results. It has recently been documented that low power is a common phenomenon. In empirical economics, Ioannidis, Stanley and Doucouliagos (2017) find that the median power is just 18%. In neuroscience, Button et al. (2013) report a median power of 21%. And looking at dictator game experiments, Zhang and Ortmann (2013) find that the median power is 25%. Low power in combination with a statistically significant result can be very problematic (Leamer, 1983; Ioannidis, 2005; Ioannidis & Trikalinos, 2007). When power is lower than 0.5 and there is a statistically significant (p < 0.05) result, there is a high probability of a type M (Magnitude) error (a.k.a. exaggeration ratio), where the reported effect is much larger than the true effect. When power is lower than 0.1, there is also a high probability of a type S (Sign) error, where the reported effect is in the wrong direction of the true effect (Gelman & Carlin, 2014). Given the typically low sample sizes in the reviewed literature in this chapter on sex hormones and economic decision making, both of these two errors may have affected reported positive findings.[12]

Other types of research practices can also contribute to the prevalence of false positives. These are related to the various "researcher degrees of freedom" (Simmons, Nelson, & Simonsohn, 2011; Gelman & Loken, 2013). These vary according to the intentions of the researcher. Fishing implies simply correlating some number of variables with each other and only reporting significant correlations while ignoring insignificant ones. Most researchers know that this type of analysis is typically problematic, while many are unaware of the problems with the two more common practices. P-hacking (Simmons et al., 2011) refers to researchers testing a single hypothesis and actively trying to achieve statistical significance. This can be done by for example including or excluding control variables, analyzing many measure, analyzing many conditions, testing different functional forms, and at the end of the day only focusing on the results that have p < 0.05. The "garden of forking paths" (Gelman & Loken, 2013) implies a less active search, again with a single hypothesis being tested. As long as the exact analysis has not been pre-specified and when the researchers let the analysis be result contingent, there are so many potential paths to wander away on that the p-value ends up being meaningless. "Forking" is a common and natural type of data analysis which does not necessarily involve actively deceiving anyone – typically the researcher is as much deceived themselves.

For the hormone and behavior literature, it is easy to see how the various researcher degrees of freedom can be a problem. Since it is typically expensive and cumbersome to run experiments involving hormones, many outcome measures are usually studied and several control variables collected. Besides studying main effects, adding interactions with for example endogenous hormone levels or 2D:4D also contribute to more tests being performed. There are also some degrees of freedom in terms of how to define outcome variables and "outliers."

Future directions

We believe there are a number of ways to improve the way that experiments on hormones and decision making are conducted. We believe the solutions relate to sample sizes, pre-analysis plans, making datasets open, replications and lower p-value thresholds. Larger sample sizes not only decrease the false negative probability but also the problems with type M and type S errors. Larger sample sizes should also make it more difficult to p-hack, since smaller samples give more extreme results compared to larger samples. Pre-analysis plans, where the researcher states exactly what tests will be performed down to the functional form, control variables and sample, decreasing the potential for researcher degrees of freedom (fishing, p-hacking and forking) to explain statistically significant results. A common objection to pre-analysis plans is that the researcher might miss out on something unexpected. But exploratory analyses can of course still be performed – it will just be clear that this analysis is exactly exploratory and not something pre-specified.[13] Replications can thereafter be used to explore results from both pre-specified tests and exploratory tests. In order to increase sample sizes, use pre-analysis plans and perform replications, perhaps we should rely more on team science where several study sites collaborate in order to ensure high power (Klein et al., 2014; Ebersole et al., 2016; Munafo et al., 2017). To reduce the risk of false positives, we also recommend using the recently suggested 0.005 threshold for findings referred to as statistically significant (Benjamin et al., 2017).

In summary, there is little experimental evidence so far for sex hormones having consistent effects on economic behavior. However, as most existing studies are small and underpowered to detect small or medium effects, it cannot be ruled out that sex hormones affect economic behavior. We recommend large-scale studies to collect more informative and robust evidence on the effects of sex hormones on economic behavior.

Notes

1 The results from Nave, Camerer and McCullough's (2015) literature review suggest that this result most likely was a false positive since it has failed to replicate in later studies.
2 There is also a literature on 2D:4D, a putative marker of testosterone exposure in utero, and economic decision making. See Apicella, Carré and Dreber (2015) for a review on financial risk taking and 2D:4D.
3 There are also versions of the dictator game where the recipient is a charity instead of another participant.
4 For example, Benz and Meier (2008) find a positive correlation between dictator game giving and charitable giving. List (2007) finds, however, that when the strategy space of the dictator increases so the dictator can also take money from the recipient, this changes giving behavior, indicating that social norms and reference points matter and that all giving in the standard dictator game is not due to altruism.

5 Decision making under the strategy method can be interpreted as "cold" decision making, while "hot" decision making would be responding to an actual offer. Brandts and Charness (2011) compare the standard direct-response method to the strategy method and find that out of 29 comparisons, 16 find no difference, 9 find mixed evidence and 4 find differences. In particular, levels of punishment are lower with the strategy method. However, Brandts and Charness find no case of the strategy method leading to a treatment effect that is not found using the direct-response method.

6 When the gamble is kept constant while the safe amount increases for each choice, risk taking can also be inferred from when participants switch from preferring the gamble to the safe amount. However, this can be problematic when participants are inconsistent in their switching.

7 There is a large literature outside of economics defining willingness to compete differently – see for example Mehta and Josephs (2006).

8 It is likely that this experiment entailed deception as the proposer data had been collected earlier as part of another study.

9 Zethraeus et al. (2009) also had participants answer two hypothetical questions about risk attitudes and found no effect of hormones on either.

10 See for example Mehta et al. (2015) for another measure and testosterone administration.

11 See Camerer, Dreber and Johannesson (forthcoming) for more information about the replication projects, various reasons for false positive results and potential solutions.

12 For a related discussion on oxytocin, see Walum, Waldman and Young (2016).

13 See for example aspredicted.org for more information on how to preregister as well as Nosek, Ebersole, DeHaven & Mellor (forthcoming) for more discussion of the associated benefits.

References

Almenberg, J., & Dreber, A. (2015). Gender, financial literacy and stock market participation. *Economics Letters, 137*, 140–142.

Apicella, C. L., Carré, J. M., & Dreber, A. (2015). Testosterone and economic risk taking: A review. *Adaptive Human Behavior and Physiology, 1*, 358–385.

Apicella, C. L., Dreber, A., Campbell, B., Gray, P., Hoffman, M., & Little, A. C. (2008). Testosterone and financial risk preferences. *Evolution and Human Behavior, 29*, 384–390.

Benz, M., & Meier, S. (2008). Do people behave in experiments as in the field? Evidence from donations. *Experimental Economics, 11*(3), 268–281.

Benjamin, D. J., Berger, J. O., Johannesson, M., Nosek, B. A., Wagenmakers, E.–J., Berk, R., . . . Johnson, V. E. (2018). Redefine statistical significance. *Nature Human Behavior, 2*, 6–10.

Boksem, M. A. S., Mehta, P. H., van den Bergh, B., van Son, V., Trautmann, S. T., Roelofs, K., . . . Sanfey, A. G. (2013). Testosterone inhibits trust but promotes reciprocity. *Psychological Science, 24*(11), 2306–2314.

Brandts, J., & Charness, G. (2011). The strategy versus the direct-response method: A first survey of experimental comparisons. *Experimental Economics, 14*(3), 375–398.

Burnham, T. C. (2007). High-testosterone men reject low ultimatum game offers. *Proceedings of the Royal Society B, 274*, 2327–2330.

Buser, T., Niederle, M., & Oosterbeek, H. (2014). Gender, competitiveness, and career choices. *Quarterly Journal of Economics, 129*(3), 1409–1447.

Buskens, V., Raub, W., van Miltenburg, N., Montoya, E. R., & van Honk, J. (2016). Testosterone administration moderates effect of social environment on trust in women depending on second-to-fourth digit ratio. *Scientific Reports, 6*, 27655.

Button, K. S., Ioannidis, J. P. A., Mokrysz, C., Nosek, B. A., Flint, J., Robinson, E. S. J., & Munafò, M. R. (2013). Power failure: Why small sample size undermines the reliability of neuroscience. *Nature Reviews. Neuroscience, 14*(5), 365–376.

Camerer, C. F. (2003). *Behavioral game theory: Experiments in strategic interaction*. Princeton, NJ: Princeton University Press.

Camerer, C. F., Dreber, A., Forsell, E., Ho, T-H., Huber, J., Johannesson, M., . . . Wu, H. (2016). Evaluating replicability of laboratory experiments in economics. *Science, 351*, 1433–1436.

Camerer, C. F., Dreber, A., & Johannesson, M. (forthcoming). Replication and other practices for improving scientific quality in experimental economics. In A. Schram & A. Ule (Eds.), *Handbook of research methods and applications in experimental economics*.

Camerer, C. F., & Fehr, E. (2004). Measuring social norms and preferences using experimental games: A guide for social scientists. In J. Henrich, R. Boyd, S. Bowles, C. Camerer, E. Fehr, & H. Gintis (Eds.), *Foundations of human sociality*. Oxford: Oxford University Press.

Camerer, C. F., & Hogarth, R. M. (1999). The effects of financial incentives in experiments: A review and capital-labor-production framework. *Journal of Risk and Uncertainty, 19*(1–3), 7–42.

Cárdenas, J-C., Dreber, A., von Essen, E., & Ranehill, E. (2012). Gender differences in competitiveness and risk taking: Comparing children in Colombia and Sweden. *Journal of Economic Behavior and Organization, 83*(1), 11–23.

Carpenter, J., Connolly, C., & Myers, C. K. (2008). Altruistic behavior in a representative dictator experiment. *Experimental Economics, 11*(3), 282–298.

Cesarini, D., Dawes, C. T., Johannesson, M., Lichtenstein, P., & Wallace, B. (2009). Genetic variation in preferences for giving and risk taking. *Quarterly Journal of Economics, 124*(2), 809–842.

Cox, J. C. (2004). How to identify trust and reciprocity. *Games and Economic Behavior, 46*, 260–281.

Croson, R., & Gneezy, U. (2009). Gender differences in preferences. *Journal of Economic Literature, 47*(2), 448–474.

Cueva, C., Roberts, R. E., Spencer, T. J., Rani, N., Tempest, M., Tobler, P. N., . . . Rustichini, A. (2017). Testosterone administration does not affect men's rejections of low ultimatum game offers or aggressive mood. *Hormones and Behavior, 87*, 1–7.

Dohmen, T., Falk, A., Huffman, D., Sunde, U., Schupp, J., & Wagner, G. G. (2011). Individual risk attitudes: Measurement, determinants and behavioral consequences. *Journal of the European Economic Association, 9*(3), 522–550.

Dreber, A., von Essen, E., & Ranehill, E. (2014). Gender and competition in adolescence: Tasks matter. *Experimental Economics, 17*(1), 154–172.

Dreber, A., Ellingsen, T., Johannesson, M., & Rand, D. G. (2013). Do people care about social context? Framing effects in dictator games. *Experimental Economics, 16*(3), 349–371.

Dreher, J-C., Dunne, S., Pazderska, A., Frodl, T., Nolan, J. J., & Doherty, J. P. (2016). Testosterone causes both prosocial and antisocial status-enhancing behaviors in human males. *Proceedings of the National Academy of Sciences, 113*(41), 11633–11638.

Ebersole, C. R., Atherton, O. E., Belanger, A. L., Skulborstad, H. M., Allen, J. M., Banks, J. B., . . . Nosek, B. A. (2016). Many Labs 3: Evaluating participant pool quality across the academic semester via replication. *Journal of Experimental Social Psychology, 67*, 68–82.

Eisenegger, C., Naef, M., Snozzi, R., Heinrichs, M., & Fehr, E. (2010). Prejudice and truth about the effect of testosterone on human bargaining behaviour. *Nature, 463*, 356–359.

Engel, C. (2011). Dictator games: A meta study. *Experimental Economics, 14*(4), 583–610.

Franco, A., Malhotra, N., & Simonovits, G. (2014). Publication bias in the social sciences: Unlocking the file drawer. *Science, 345*(6203), 1502–1505.

Gelman, A., & Carlin, J. (2014). Beyond power calculations: Assessing type S (sign) and type M (magnitude) errors. *Perspectives in Psychological Science, 9*, 641–651.

Gelman, A., & Loken, E. (2013). *The garden of forking paths: Why multiple comparisons can be a problem, even when there is no "fishing expedition" or "p-hacking" and the research hypothesis was posited ahead of time.* Working Paper.

Gneezy, U., Leonard, K. L., & List, J. A. (2009). Gender differences in competition: Evidence from a matrilineal and a patriarchal society. *Econometrica, 77*(5), 1637–1664.

Güth, W., & Kocher, M. (2014). More than thirty years of ultimatum bargaining experiments: Motives, variations, and a survey of the recent literature. *Journal of Economic Behavior and Organization, 108*, 396–409.

Henrich, J., Boyd, R., Bowles, S., Camerer, C., Fehr, E., Gintis, H., & McElreath, R. (2001). In search of homo economicus: Behavioral experiments in 15 small-scale societies. *American Economic Review Papers and Proceedings, 91*, 73–78.

Ioannidis, J. P. A. (2005). Why most published research findings are false. *PLoS Medicine, 2*(8), e124.

Ioannidis, J. P. A., Stanley, T. D., & Doucouliagos, H. (2017). The power of bias in economics research. *Economic Journal, 127*, F236–F265.

Ioannidis, J. P. A., & Trikalinos, T. A. (2007). An exploratory test for an excess of significant findings. *Clinical Trials, 4*, 245–253.

Kahneman, D., & Tversky, A. (1979). Prospect theory: An analysis of decision under risk. *Econometrica, 47*(2), 263–291.

Klein, R. A., Ratliff, K. A., Vianello, M., Adams, R. B., Jr., Stephan, B., Bernstein, M. J., . . . Nosek, B. A. (2014). Investigating variation in replicability: A "Many Labs" replication project. *Social Psychology, 45*, 142–152.

Kopsida, E., Berrebi, J., Petrovic, P., & Ingvar, M. (2016). Testosterone administration related differences in brain activation during the ultimatum game. *Frontiers in Neuroscience, 10*, 66.

Kosfeld, M., Heinrichs, M., Zak, P. J., Fischbacher, U., & Fehr, E. (2005). Oxytocin increases trust in humans. *Nature, 435*, 673–676.

Leamer, E. E. (1983). Let's take the con out of econometrics. *American Economic Review, 73*, 31–43.

List, J. (2007). On the interpretation of giving in dictator games. *Journal of Political Economy, 115*, 482–493.

Munafò, M. R., Nosek, B. A., Bishop, D. V. M., Button, K. S., Chambers, C. D., Percie du Sert, N., . . . Ioannidis, J. P. A. (2017). A manifesto for reproducible science. *Nature Human Behavior, 1*, 0021.

Nave, G., Camerer, C. F., & McCullough, M. (2015). Does oxytocin increase trust in humans? Critical review of research. *Perspectives on Psychological Science, 10*(6), 772–789.

Niederle, M., & Vesterlund, L. (2007). Do women shy away from competition? Do men compete too much? *Quarterly Journal of Economics, 122*, 1067–1101.

Nosek, B. A., Ebersole, C. R., DeHaven, A., & Mellor, D. (forthcoming). The preregistration revolution. *Proceedings of the National Academy of Sciences.*

Open Science Collaboration. (2015). Estimating the reproducibility of psychological science. *Science, 349*(6251).

Mehta, P. H., & Josephs, R. A. (2006). Testosterone change after losing predicts the decision to compete again. *Hormones and Behavior, 50*(5), 684–692.

Mehta, P. H., van Son, V., Welker, K. M., Prasad, S., Sanfey, A. G., Smidts, A., & Roelofs, K. (2015). Exogenous testosterone in women enhances and inhibits competitive decision-making depending on victory – defeat experience and trait dominance. *Psychoneuroendocrinology, 60*, 224–236.

Ranehill, E., Zethraeus, N., Blomberg, L., von Schoultz, B., Hirschberg, A. L., Johannesson, M., & Dreber, A. (2017). Hormonal contraceptives do not impact economic preferences: Evidence from a randomized trial. *Management Science*, Articles in Advance, 1–18.

Rosenthal, R. (1979). The file drawer problem and tolerance for null results. *Psychological Bulletin, 86*(3), 638–641.

Sapienza, P., Zingales, L., & Maestripieri, D. (2009). Gender differences in financial risk aversion and career choices are affected by testosterone. *Proceedings of the National Academy of Sciences, 106*, 15268–15273.

Schipper, B. C. (2012). *Sex hormones and choice under risk.* SSRN Scholarly Paper ID 2046324. Social Science Research Network, Rochester, NY

Simmons, J. P., Nelson, L. D., & Simonsohn, U. (2011). False-positive psychology: Undisclosed flexibility in data collection and analysis allows presenting anything as significant. *Psychological Science, 22*, 1359–1366.

Stanton, S. J., Mullette-Gillman, O., McLaurin, R., Kuhn, C., LaBar, K., Platt, M., & Huettel, S. (2011). Low- and high-testosterone individuals exhibit decreased aversion to economic risk. *Psychological Science, 22*, 447–453.

Sterling, T. D. (1959). Publication decisions and their possible effects on inferences drawn from tests of significance – or vice versa. *Journal of the American Statistical Association, 54*(285), 30–34.

Tversky, A., & Kahneman, D. (1981). The framing of decisions and the psychology of choice. *Science, 211*, 453–458.

van Honk, J., Montoya, E. R., Bos, P. A., van Vugt, M., & Terburg, D. (2012). New evidence on testosterone and cooperation. *Nature, 485*, E4–E5.

Wallace, B., Cesarini, D., Lichtenstein, P., & Johannesson, M. (2007). Heritability of ultimatum game responder behavior. *Proceedings of the National Academy of Sciences, 104*(15), 15631–15615634.

Walum, H., Waldman, I. D., & Young, L. J. (2016). Statistical and methodological considerations for the interpretation of intranasal oxytocin studies. *Biological Psychiatry, 79*(3), 251–257.

Zak, P. J., Kurzban, R., Ahmadi, S., Swerdloff, R. S., Park, J., Efremidze, L., . . . Matzner, W. (2009). Testosterone administration decreases generosity in the ultimatum game. *PLoS One, 4*(12), e8330.

Zethraeus, N., Kocoska-Maras, L., Ellingsen, T., von Schoultz, B., Hirschberg, A. L., & Johannesson, M. (2009). A randomized trial of the effect of estrogen and testosterone on economic behavior. *Proceedings of the National Academy of Sciences, 106*, 6535–6538.

Zhang, L., & Ortmann, A. (2013). *Exploring the meaning of significance in experimental economics.* Discussion Paper, School of Economics, UNSW, 2013–32.

23

EMOTIONAL PROCESSING AND SEX HORMONES

Malin Gingnell, Jonas Hornung, and Birgit Derntl

Introduction and definition

The interpretation and expression of emotions are an important part of all social interactions. With this chapter we aim to give an overview of how major sex hormones, i.e. estradiol, progesterone, and testosterone, affect emotional processes ranging from emotion perception to emotional memory and empathy. We will discuss the main findings, covering behavioral outcomes as well as brain activation related to these selected emotional capacities. In general, only data on healthy adult human participants will be presented. However, as fluctuations of sex hormone levels are also associated with mental disorders, we will briefly address this aspect by highlighting findings on premenstrual dysphoria.

Defining an emotion

Definitions and models of emotion seem to be infinite. Kleinginna and Kleinginna (1981) ordered nearly 100 different definitions into 11 categories of emotion, including definitions emphasizing affective (the experience of feelings), cognitive (acts of appraisal or labeling), physiological (pointing to bodily states) and expressive behavior (pointing to observable behavioral consequences) aspects of emotion. More recently, with the rise of neuroscientific methods, it is possible to add neural definitions (attributing patterns of brain activation to specific emotions). Given this heterogeneity of definitions, we adopt a broader approach here, which sees emotion as a composite of several aspects. We particularly emphasize the following components, as they are especially important for studying the connection of sex hormones and emotions.

Physiological/endocrinological component: This refers to autonomic nervous system processes e.g. visible in changes of body temperature, heart rate or skin conductance and the associated release of hormones. A meta-analysis by Cacioppo, Berntson, Larsen, Poehlmann, and Ito (2000) suggested that mere autonomic variability may be used to separate emotions with subjective reports of anger, fear, and sadness leading to a stronger heart rate increase than disgust, anger inducing higher diastolic blood pressure than fear, and disgust increasing skin conductance more strongly than happiness.

Central nervous component: This refers to findings that experience of an emotion may evoke a brain pattern that differs between categories of emotions (see e.g. Lindquist, Wager,

Kober, Bliss-Moreau, & Barrett, 2012 for a review of emotion-specific and unspecific patterns of brain activation).

Expressive behavior: This refers to characteristic bodily or facial expressions that accompany emotions. These may in part be controlled voluntarily as part of a social encounter but may also occur as a reflexive response to emotional stimuli. However, there are small variations in the voluntary expression of emotions and the reflexive response indicating that facial expressions that mirror genuine emotions cannot be produced voluntarily (e.g. Mehu, Mortillaro, Banziger, & Scherer, 2012).

Affective component: This refers to the phenomenology or how it feels like to have an emotion. It must be noted that this aspect has been quite heavily debated in the past (Damasio, 1998; LeDoux, 1998). We still think that, although several subjective states may share commonalities both at a lower level autonomic processing and at a higher cognitive state, it is instrumental at least in human beings to view basic emotions like happiness, fear, anger, sadness, disgust, and surprise (Ekman and Cordaro, 2011) to include an affective component.

Sex hormones and the brain

Steroidal hormones such as estrogens, progesterone, and testosterone regulate physical changes associated with reproduction as well as physical responses during reproductive behavior. Although both adipose tissue and the adrenals may excrete steroid hormones, the main source for these hormones during fertile years are hormonal feedback loops via the hypothalamus to the gonads, inducing cyclic changes in levels of estrogens and progesterone across the menstrual cycle (see Figure 23.1) or a rather continuous, but with diurnal cyclicity, production of testosterone from the testicles. These changes are related to potential reproduction in various ways: e.g. across a menstrual cycle, the follicular phase is a period when the gonadal system is preparing

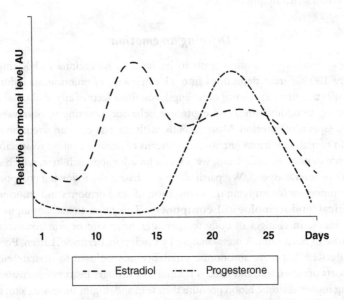

Figure 23.1 Schematic figure of variations in estradiol and progesterone from day 0 to 28 of a standardized menstrual cycle. For illustrational purpose, levels of estradiol and progesterone are given in relative arbitrary units, as the concentration of the two hormones differs substantially (progesterone is usually measured in nmol/l and estradiol in pmol/l).

for ovulation, but conception is unlikely; around ovulation the possibility for pregnancy to occur is increased; and during the luteal phase a potential pregnancy may be developing. During an actual pregnancy, multiple endocrine changes occur, predominantly orchestrated via the placenta, including a successive increase in levels of both estrogens and progesterone as pregnancy develops, followed by a dramatic drop in levels almost immediately after childbirth. The close relationship between reproductive state and steroidal hormones makes it reasonable that variation in steroid hormones could affect emotion processes important for social interaction, such as interpretation of emotional stimuli, recognition of facial expressions, or regulation of own behavior, as those can be assumed to be of varying importance based on the reproductive demands.

Steroid hormones have the potential to influence emotion processing by activating receptors in brain tissue. Steroid receptors for estradiol (ERα and ERβ) and progesterone (PRA and PRB) are highly expressed in many brain areas, especially in areas associated with emotional processing such as the hypothalamus and the limbic system (for review, see Gruber, Tschugguel, Schneeberger, & Huber, 2002; Brinton et al., 2008). In addition to these traditional receptors, animal research indicates that rapid non-genomic effects may arise after the activation of G protein-coupled estrogen receptors (GPERs), which may potentially affect behavior by increasing the release of oxytocin (Hazell et al., 2009) or the progesterone receptor membrane component 1 (PGRMC1) (Intlekofer and Petersen, 2011). Moreover, progesterone can be metabolized into neuroactive steroids such as allopregnanolone and pregnanolone, which potentiate the predominantly inhibitory $GABA_A$ receptor in a manner similar to barbiturates and benzodiazepines (Melcangi, Panzica, & Garcia-Segura, 2011). Acute administration of allopregnanolone thus has sedative, anxiolytic, and anti-convulsant properties but may also negatively influence cognitive function (Johansson, Birzniece, Lindblad, Olsson, & Backstrom, 2002; Kask, Backstrom, et al., 2008; Melcangi et al., 2011). Perhaps through the interaction of allopregnanolone and GABA, progesterone can thus have both anxiogenic (low progesterone levels) and anxiolytic effects (high progesterone levels) (Andreen et al., 2009). For testosterone, traditional androgen receptors (ARs) are distributed throughout the nervous system with high concentrations in the hypothalamus and amygdala (Cunningham, Lumia, & McGinnis, 2012). ARs can either be directly activated by testosterone or by its more potent metabolite dihydroxytestosterone (Davey and Grossmann, 2016). However, testosterone is also converted via aromatase into estradiol and thereby affects also signaling pathways for estradiol. This poses an interpretational conundrum as it is difficult to track whether observed effects are due to testosterone or dihydroxytestosterone action on ARs and/or action of testosterone converted to estradiol on ERs. As for estradiol and progesterone, there are also indications of more rapid acting, membrane-bound receptors for testosterone (Su et al., 2012) present in the prefrontal cortex (DonCarlos et al., 2006) and the hippocampus (Tabori et al., 2005).

Methods to study the effects of sex hormones

In general, we differentiate between three methods to study the effects of sex hormones on human behavior and brain activation: The first is an ***experimental approach*** with the administration of exogenous steroid hormones, ideally in a placebo-controlled, randomized and double-blind manner, together with the observation of concomitant effects. The second method is a ***correlational approach***, involving point estimates of endogenous levels of sex hormones, e.g. via saliva or blood samples. Finally, a ***quasi-experimental approach*** utilizes naturally occurring fluctuations of hormone levels, e.g. as observed during the female menstrual cycle. During the course of a menstrual cycle, a low-hormone profile of progesterone and estradiol is generally observed during the early follicular phase, followed by a first mid-cycle estradiol peak combined with low levels of progesterone around ovulation and generally increased levels of both hormones in the mid- to late-luteal phase, after which both hormones decline relatively rapidly (Sakaki and Mather, 2012) (see Figure 23.1). Before menarche and after menopause, both hormones are present in very low levels. Finally, treatment with hormonal contraception can be assumed to induce high levels of synthetic hormones during treatment (i.e. usually the first 21 cycle days starting with menses onset) and low levels of endogenous hormones (for a review see Montoya and Bos, 2017).

Emotion recognition

Implicit emotion recognition

A number of experiments have used rather low-level cognitive tasks such as gender discrimination, visual matching, or passive viewing of emotional faces and thus investigated implicit, nonverbal emotion recognition.

Estradiol/progesterone

Van Wingen et al. (2007) administered progesterone to follicular women and asked them to perform gender judgments of emotional faces. This led to bilaterally decreased amygdala and fusiform gyrus activation compared to placebo. However, this result is contradicted by several studies. First, administration of progesterone in follicular women led to increased bilateral amygdala activation in an emotional matching paradigm (van Wingen et al., 2008). Using a similar emotion matching paradigm and in line with this finding, Gingnell, Morell, Bannbers, Wikström, & Poromaa. (2012) reported stronger left amygdala reactivity during the luteal (high estradiol and progesterone) compared to the follicular phase (low progesterone). In addition, Marečková et al. (2014) also observed stronger activation of the right fusiform face area for women in mid-cycle compared to menstruation during passive viewing of angry and ambiguous faces. Given that both amygdala and fusiform gyrus are hubs in emotion and facial processing (Lindquist et al., 2012; Dricu and Frühholz, 2016), these results tend to suggest that higher levels of female sex hormones observable during mid-cycle throughout the luteal phase lead to brain activation patterns that are attributed to increased reactivity in response to facial stimuli.

Testosterone

Investigating men and women, one study showed that only in men endogenous levels of testosterone correlated negatively with bilateral amygdala reactivity during passive viewing of angry faces (Stanton, Wirth, Waugh, & Schultheiss, 2009). This is in opposition to repeated findings among women of higher emotional reactivity after testosterone administration which reliably led to increased activation in emotion processing areas like the amygdala, hypothalamus, or orbitofrontal cortex during passive viewing of emotional faces (Hermans, Ramsey, & van Honk, 2008; Bos et al., 2013) or visual matching of emotional to target faces (van Wingen et al., 2009). For testosterone in women it can thus be most consistently assumed that with rising levels emotional reactivity increases, which can be expected to also have behavioral and neuronal consequences. One report of such consequences is that testosterone increases approach behavior to threatening faces as well as increasing amygdala reactivity during approach. This has been observed in women (Radke et al., 2015) as well as men (Volman et al., 2011) and is accompanied by an increase of connectivity between frontal and temporal brain areas.

Explicit emotion recognition

According to Ekman and Davidson (1994), emotion recognition is the ability to correctly label the emotional state of a conspecific based on facial, bodily, or prosodic expressions. As the interpretation of reactions in other individuals are a core feature of social interaction, the effects of variations in steroid hormones on basic emotion recognition could be of great importance to study. Commonly, explicit emotion recognition is measured by presenting facial expressions depicting an emotion and asking participants to categorize these expressions by forced choice. While some studies also report reaction times, accuracy is most often reported, and thus we will only discuss this in the following section.

Estradiol/progesterone

In a previous study, Kamboj et al. (2015) used a dynamic morphing task during which neutral faces changed towards one of five basic emotions. Participants were given a forced choice and were instructed to respond as soon as they had recognized the emotion. Women were measured either during late follicular, early luteal or late-luteal phase. Results did not reveal any group differences with respect to recognition accuracy. However, estradiol levels were negatively correlated with recognition accuracy for disgusted faces across all groups, while progesterone was positively connected to an overall slowing of responses. Guapo et al. (2009) measured recognition for six basic emotions investigating men and women during their follicular, ovulatory, and luteal phase. The early follicular group was more accurate in recognizing angry faces compared to all other groups and sad faces compared to luteal women. For fear, ovulatory women showed significantly better performance than men. Furthermore, across women, estrogen levels were negatively correlated with recognition accuracy for angry male faces. Similarly, Derntl, Kryspin-Exner, et al. (2008) investigated follicular and luteal women with respect to six basic emotions. Follicular women had an overall better accuracy across all emotions. Furthermore, a negative correlation between progesterone levels and recognition accuracy emerged indicating higher accuracy with lower progesterone levels. In a follow-up study of the same group (Derntl, Windischberger, et al., 2008), better emotion recognition in follicular than mid-luteal women was replicated which was accompanied by stronger amygdala responses during recognition of fearful, neutral, and sad faces. Moreover, a negative correlation between amygdala activation and progesterone levels across all women emerged, which was not the case for estradiol.

Regarding the impact of estradiol and progesterone on emotion recognition performance in naturally cycling women, previous results thus most consistently point to impoverished accuracy when both estradiol and progesterone are high.

Testosterone

Van Honk and Schutter (2007) administered testosterone to follicular women in a placebo-controlled cross-over study. Participants were then presented with morphed faces of six basic emotions ranging from neutral to full-blown expressions of each emotion and asked in increments to give a forced choice categorization of the perceived emotion. Results show that accuracy for correctly labeling threatening faces was reduced after testosterone application. Furthermore, Derntl et al. (2009) investigated men by using an emotion recognition task and observed increased amygdala activation in individuals with higher endogenous testosterone levels during presentation of fearful and angry faces. However, testosterone levels were not significantly correlated with recognition accuracy. In another study, Vongas et al. (2017) investigated recognition accuracy of the six basic emotions in men and reported a positive association between testosterone levels and recognition accuracy suggesting a better recognition with higher testosterone levels.

All in all, surprisingly little is known about the direct effects of testosterone on emotion recognition or on the underlying neural activation. The available studies provide contradictory results and therefore it is not possible at the moment to make definite claims. Systematic studies are needed to address this issue and to alleviate methodological flaws of previous studies (see also Limitations and conclusions).

Emotion regulation

Successful social interaction involves experiencing emotions, but also regulation of the evoked emotion and the inhibition of behavioral responses. The concept of emotion regulation refers to a diverse set of processes influencing which emotions individuals have, when and how they experience them, and how and when they express these emotions (Gross, 1999). The process model (Gross, 2013) postulates a dynamic interplay between emotion generation and emotion regulation: At any stage of emotion generation, individuals can apply strategies to regulate their emotions, which influences emotional experience. The most frequently investigated strategies include reappraisal and suppression of emotions, which respectively refer to reframing an emotional situation and inhibiting an emotion once it has emerged (Gross, 2002; see also Morawetz et al., 2017 for meta-analysis on brain activation).

Estradiol/progesterone

In a recent EEG-study, Lusk et al. (2017) compared men and women during their follicular or mid-luteal phase regarding down-regulation of negative emotions. Participants were presented with negatively valenced or neutral pictures taken from the International Affective Pictures System (IAPS) and were instructed to perform suppression or reappraisal. During suppression, mid-luteal women had a higher N2 amplitude over fronto-central locations than men. The authors interpreted their finding as more conscious allocation of attention to emotional stimuli. At the same time, mid-luteal women also reported trendwise higher effort during suppression than follicular women and significantly higher effort than men (Lusk et al., 2017). These results give a first hint that higher levels of estradiol and progesterone as observed during the mid-luteal phase may lead to higher effort in suppressing negative emotions. Investigating naturally cycling women, Graham et al. (2017) observed that after a cognitive restructuring training including reappraisal, women high in estradiol showed reduced skin conductance in response to conditioned stimuli during fear conditioning, suggesting reduced physiological arousal. Thus, in periods when estradiol is naturally high, women especially benefit from cognitive emotion regulation. Notably, self-reports of reappraisal were not related to hormone levels and progesterone was not associated with any outcome measure. In another study, Wu et al. (2014) investigated women during the early follicular, ovulation, and mid-late luteal phase. Participants were watching a sad movie and asked to use reappraisal for emotion regulation. Results indicate that during the early follicular phase, women subjectively reported highest levels of reappraisal compared to the ovulation and mid-luteal groups. However, at the same time women in the early follicular phase also showed decreased change in skin conductance comparing reappraisal to baseline. The authors interpret these findings as higher reappraisal effort but less reappraisal success during the early follicular phase when female sex hormones are low. Taken together, in women preliminary results tend to support that higher levels of estradiol observed during ovulation improve regulation success both for reappraisal and suppression, whereas higher levels of progesterone (mid-luteal phase) are associated with higher effort during suppression. Notably, results are not unanimous as to whether behavioral or physiological regulation was successful.

Testosterone

Regarding testosterone, a study by Denson et al (2013) asked healthy men to regulate their anger feelings when reacting to personal insults. While no behavioral association existed between testosterone and anger regulation, testosterone levels were positively correlated with activation in the dorsolateral prefrontal cortex (dlPFC) and thalamus. Given the assumed role of the dlPFC in self- and emotion regulation, these results give a weak hint that higher testosterone levels in men improve emotion regulation (Denson et al., 2013). Unfortunately, further studies investigating the link between testosterone levels and emotion regulation are missing and are urgently needed.

Emotional memory

The individual memory system is often divided into memories that a subject is consciously aware of and which can be verbalized and memories that may be less conscious and rely on other systems such as motor skills. Verbally linked memories include episodic and semantic memories and are as a group called explicit or declarative. In humans such memories are often studied using verbal recall of an event or image. Implicit or non-declarative memories, on the other hand, may be expressed non-verbally, e.g. as a conditioned response to stimuli or as a learned procedural sequence of action. Here we discuss aspects of memory and learning that involve encoding and retrieval of emotional stimulus material as well as aspects of procedural memory involving affective responses during competition and conditioning.

Explicit emotional memory

Estradiol/progesterone

Ertman et al. (2011) showed better free recall but not recognition memory for negatively valenced images in luteal compared to follicular women, with a positive correlation between progesterone and both free recall and recognition memory (when identification of previously presented stimuli were based on re-presentation of old stimuli mixed with new stimuli with the subjects indicating whether they had viewed the stimuli before or not). Felmingham et al. (2012) showed that free recall of negatively valenced images was increased for women with high compared to low progesterone levels when combined with a stress induction using a cold pressor task. Spontaneous intrusive recollections after an emotional film clip have also been reported to increase during periods of increased estradiol and progesterone concentration (Ferree et al., 2011) during ovulation (Soni et al., 2013) but also to be increased in states of low as compared to high estradiol (Wegerer et al., 2014). Performing encoding and retrieval two days apart, Bayer et al. (2014) detected a trendwise advantage for recollection memory of negatively valenced pictures in follicular compared to luteal women. For positive emotions, reports of better free recall during ovulation compared to early follicular women have been shown (Pompili et al., 2016).

Regarding short-term memory, using a delayed matching-to-sample task with emotional pictures, one study found that late-follicular women made more errors compared to women in their early follicular phase (Gasbarri et al., 2008). This is in contrast to no differences between OC-users, luteal, and follicular women for short-term free recall of emotional words (Merz, 2017).

In sum, results most consistently point to a better recall of especially negative emotional stimuli with higher progesterone levels in women.

Testosterone

For men, high endogenous testosterone levels at encoding have been reported to be accompanied by increased amygdala reactivity to and better recall of neutral pictures, while no such effects were observed in women (Ackermann et al., 2012). Unfortunately, further studies investigating the link between testosterone and declarative memory are missing and thus prevent any clear conclusions about the role of testosterone in both men and women.

Implicit emotional memory/fear conditioning

To study learning and memory processes underlying naturally occurring fears, classical Pavlovian fear conditioning is frequently employed. In this context, fear acquisition involves the pairing of an initially neutral stimulus (conditioned stimulus; CS+) with an intrinsically aversive stimulus capable of eliciting a fear response (unconditioned stimulus; US). Subsequent presentation of CS+ induces a conditioned fear response that includes increased physiological arousal and enhanced activity in fear-related neural circuits. Conversely, the counteraction of fear acquisition is achieved through fear extinction, where repeated exposure of a feared stimulus (e.g. CS+) leads to a gradual attenuation of the fear response both on a physiological and neural level. The contemporary view is that extinction does not erase the fear memory, but rather induces a safety memory (i.e. CS+ is now associated with safety) (Dunsmoor, Niv, Daw, & Phelps, 2015). However, the safety memory is context-specific and labile, which is reflected by the return of the CS+ elicited fear response after change of context, passage of time, or stress provocation. Extinction recall refers to the process that occurs when an extinguished stimulus is displayed after extinction. Individuals may then react either with extinction recall, i.e. not showing a fear response, or with return of fear, i.e. showing the conditioned response de novo.

Estradiol/progesterone

Milad et al. (2010) reported that increasing estradiol levels in women during extinction learning were positively correlated with subsequent extinction recall but did not affect fear acquisition or extinction learning. States of high endogenous estradiol during ovulation have also been associated with decreased return of fear during extinction recall (Zeidan et al., 2011; Graham and Milad, 2013). This effect seems linked to endogenous release of estradiol as treatment with hormonal contraception (which increases exogenous estradiol while suppressing endogenous estradiol release) reduces extinction recall (Graham and Milad, 2013). Wegerer et al. (2014) also showed that women during the early follicular phase had significantly elevated conditioned responses during fear extinction than women during the luteal phase. Antov and Stockhorst (2014) observed better extinction recall for women during their late-follicular phase compared to early follicular women when fear acquisition had been preceded by psychosocial stress. Finally, in another study measuring 32 naturally cycling women and performing a median split on estradiol levels, women high in estradiol showed stronger activation in regions such as the insula, middle as well as rostral anterior cingulate cortices, amygdala, hippocampus, and hypothalamus during extinction recall (Hwang et al., 2015). Taken together, previous research strongly suggests a modulating role of endogenous estradiol in conditioning with an increased extinction recall during states of high estradiol. For progesterone, studies are scarce, but among those who have assessed progesterone, no significant effects have been reported (Milad et al., 2010; Zeidan et al., 2011; Antov and Stockhorst, 2014)

Testosterone

The role of testosterone is sparsely studied in conditioning but may, due to the potential conversion of testosterone into estradiol, affect extinction recall in a way similar to the one observed by estradiol in women. Preliminary support for this is given by findings from animal studies, where an inhibition of the conversion of testosterone to estradiol impaired fear extinction (Graham and Milad, 2014). Extinction learning has also been reported to be increased in men with high testosterone levels (Pace-Schott et al., 2013).

Empathy

Empathy is a complex and multidimensional construct that can be divided at least into two categories: affective and cognitive empathy (Decety and Jackson, 2004; Walter, 2012). Affective empathy is the ability to affectively experience the emotions of other persons, at the same time being aware of the self–other distinction. The cognitive component of empathy is the ability to take the perspective and cognitively understand emotions of others.

Estradiol/progesterone

Regarding the impact of female sex hormones on empathy, little is known. One previous study (Derntl et al., 2013) investigated early follicular and mid-luteal women with respect to cognitive and affective empathy. For assessing cognitive empathy, the authors presented social scenes depicting two actors. The faces of one of these actors was masked and participants were asked to infer the emotional expression of this face by forced choice. For affective empathy, short sentences describing emotional real-life situations were presented. Participants were asked to imagine how they would feel being in that situation, again selecting an emotion by forced choice. While no group differences emerged for cognitive empathy, for affective empathy mid-luteal women gave faster responses for sad and angry stimuli. Furthermore, higher progesterone levels in mid-luteal women were accompanied by higher overall affective responsiveness (Derntl et al., 2013). To our knowledge, further studies addressing the connection of female sex hormones and empathy are missing, thus making clear conclusions about the connection of female sex hormones and empathic abilities not possible at the moment.

Testosterone

Administering testosterone to women taking oral contraceptives, van Honk et al. (2011) investigated the impact of testosterone on the performance in the Reading the Mind in the Eyes Test (RMET). In this test only the eyes of human faces are presented and participants are asked to indicate the underlying emotion by forced choice. The test is believed to measure cognitive empathy. After testosterone compared to a placebo application, women had a lower accuracy in correctly identifying the emotion of the actors (van Honk et al., 2011). In the same study, the authors could also show an association between performance in the RMET, testosterone application and the 2D:4D ratio of the right hand, which is assumed to indicate fetal testosterone levels: those individuals who had high fetal testosterone and thus a lower 2D:4D-ratio also showed most pronounced empathy deficits after testosterone administration (van Honk et al., 2011). While the behavioral effect was not replicated in a recent neuroimaging study and also no direct effect of testosterone administration on task-based activation was present, changes in functional connectivity of the inferior frontal gyrus to the supplementary motor area extending to the anterior cingulate cortex (placebo > testosterone) were reported by the same group (Bos et al., 2016). Another study by Carré et al. (2015) was not able to extend above described findings to men. Here again the RMET was used and testosterone or placebo administered. Testosterone administration alone did not change recognition performance. Only when considering the 2D:4D-ratio of the left hand, a correlation emerged in the placebo condition as testosterone values were negatively correlated with RMET accuracy, again suggesting that higher prenatal testosterone has a modulatory role on the action of current testosterone. However, surprisingly, the same correlation was not significant after testosterone administration, which puts doubt on the robustness of findings.

In summary regarding testosterone-action, available evidence most consistently suggests that current levels of testosterone may not be sufficient to have an impact on cognitive empathy. It may rather be prenatal organizational effects of testosterone that alone or in connection with current testosterone levels can reduce cognitive empathy. Surprisingly little is known about the role of female sex hormones on empathic abilities, making explicit claims impossible at the moment.

Hormonal states as confounders

Apart from the fact that the variation in levels of sex steroid hormones calls for extra attention when assessing emotion-related procedures, variations in exposure may also have clinically relevant effects, which may be important to take into account.

Premenstrual symptoms

Even if the majority of women remain rather unaffected by the hormonal changes across the menstrual cycle (Sveindóttir and Bäckström, 2000), approximately 20% of women experience some sort of affective symptoms (Wittchen et al., 2002). For 3–5% of women in childbearing ages, the menstrual cycle is associated with such a pronounced cyclical affective symptomatology that they fulfill the criteria for premenstrual dysphoric disorder (PMDD, Sveindóttir and Bäckström, 2000). PMDD is characterized by a cluster of distress symptoms such as depressed mood, irritability, or increased anxiety that regularly appear during the luteal phase of the menstrual cycle. Symptom onset is usually in the early or mid-luteal phase, with a gradual worsening in the late luteal phase. In the majority of cases, symptoms continue during the first 2–3 days of menses (Hartlage et al., 2012), after which complete remission is experienced (Halbreich et al., 2003).

As far as it has been investigated, the presence of PMDD highly influences some of the described emotional capacities. For example, during the luteal phase women with PMDD show impaired recognition of emotional facial expressions with a tendency for a negativity bias, i.e. neutral faces are more often mistaken as negative expressions (Rubinow et al., 2007). Several neuroimaging studies further suggest altered neural responsivity during emotion processing across the menstrual cycle in this population. Tentative evidence for an overactive limbic reactivity during the luteal phase among women with PMDD comes from studies investigating the startle response (which is an amygdala-dependent, reflexive tendency to close the eyes in response to a sudden stimulus) with increased startle responses being observed in the luteal phase (Epperson et al., 2007) as well as differential regulation of the startle response by pre-pulse inhibition (Kask, Gulinello, et al., 2008) and during anticipation of emotional stimuli (Bannbers, Kask, Wikström, & Sundström Poromaa, 2010). Additionally, compared with their own follicular phase of the menstrual cycle and compared to healthy controls, women with PMDD show different activation of prefrontal areas during both anticipation of IAPS images inducing affective responses (Gingnell et al., 2013) and exposure to these affect-inducing images (Comasco et al., 2014). While the field is still rather juvenile, there are indications of the luteal phase being associated with an increased affective and limbic response, especially to negative social stimuli in PMDD (Gingnell et al., 2014).

In summary, this means that women with PMDD tend to respond differently to endogenous hormonal fluctuations, with a tendency to react more intense to negative stimuli during the luteal phase, apparent not only behaviorally but also on a neural level. Thus, studies aiming at disentangling the general effect of sex hormones need to take the presence of PMDD into account. Ideally, PMDD is diagnosed by administering daily ratings of mood during at least two consecutive menstrual cycles, when due care is taken to assess also presence of ovulation either through LH-assays or progesterone assessments in combination with records of menstrual bleeding.

Oral contraceptives

While the choice of available contraceptive methods has increased in recent years, OCs, first introduced in the 1960s, remain the method of choice for contraception among most women around the world. While most women report high levels of satisfaction with treatment (Skouby, 2010), a considerable percentage also reports negative side effects such as depressive symptoms, irritability, and mood swings (Ernst et al., 2002; Kelly et al., 2010) which may potentially affect assessments of emotion processing. Recently, a large register study also reported that OC-intake was associated with subsequent use of antidepressants and a first diagnosis of depression, particularly among adolescents (Skovlund et al., 2016).

Of great importance is also to take into account that the hormonal profile may differ substantially between brands, with a huge variation especially in the progesterone-analogue and its affinity to both progesterone receptors but also androgenic receptors.

OC-intake may also be used as a model to study the effects of exogenous hormones, in combination with the suppression of the endogenous hormone system through a negative feedback loop. Exploratory data in a small sample indicate impaired emotion recognition performance for sad, angry, and disgusted faces in females taking OCs vs. naturally cycling women (Hamstra et al., 2014). Additionally, affective responsiveness was significantly reduced during the pill-free week (Radke and Derntl, 2016). Moreover, Marečková et al. (2014) observed stronger reactivity in the right fusiform face area to angry and ambiguous faces in women taking combined OCs (high in synthetic hormones, i.e. ethinylestradiol and progestin, and low in endogenous hormones) compared to women in the early follicular phase (low in endogenous hormones). In the same study, also a positive correlation between activation of the fusiform face area and duration of OC-intake was observed. Furthermore, Petersen and Cahill (2015) reported significantly reduced amygdala activation in OC-taking women compared to naturally cycling women when confronted with IAPS stimuli. Taken together, only a few studies have investigated the impact of OC-intake on emotional capacities, and results are quite inconsistent. Therefore, further research is mandatory to highlight effects of OC-intake as well as to deepen our understanding of synthetic hormone action on behavioral and neuronal processes underlying emotional abilities.

Future directions

First, we want to mention important limitations of previous studies and suggest how those could be addressed in future studies. Several findings indicate changes in emotional competencies, particularly during the mid-luteal phase. Here, we face an attribution problem as levels of both estradiol and progesterone are high during this cycle phase, making it hard to disentangle whether it is the effect of both hormones or just one hormone that contributes to the observed effects. The use of placebo-controlled hormone-administration trials is a suitable way to assess this more specifically, but repeated assessments in the same individuals may also assist in clarifying the underlying effects, e.g. specific effect of one hormone vs. additive effects vs. estradiol:progesterone ratio (see also Sollberger & Ehlert, 2016). Moreover, as most findings are correlational in nature, administration studies could be a better way to study the link between hormone concentration and behavioral and neural outcome. Finally, when assessing variations in relation to the menstrual cycle, it is highly important to take into account intra-individual variability. Ideally, a longitudinal design should be applied, preferably with a randomized phase-of-entry into the study and with due caution that a suggested luteal phase assessment has been preceded by a positively detected ovulation. As previous studies have shown that OC-intake and PMDD affect emotional abilities, it is also important that future studies take this information into account and assess e.g. the presence of PMS/PMDD. Apart from longitudinal designs and the use of placebo-controlled administration of exogenous and synthetic hormones, there is also a need for studies assessing sex hormone concentrations in both sexes (e.g. little is known about estradiol in men). Another important aspect to consider is the impact of sex hormones on neuroplasticity in the brain and how that might contribute to the reported results. Barth et al. (2016) recently showed that fluctuating levels of estradiol obtained repeatedly across two menstrual cycles affects hippocampus volume, further supporting other findings on menstrual cycle related changes in morphology of the amygdala or the fusiform gyrus (Pletzer et al., 2010). In the same line, findings from Lisofsky et al. (2016) point to a reduction in amygdala volume, as well as changes in functional connectivity of the amygdala after three months of OC-intake.

Limitations and conclusions

Psychological and neuroscientific studies often yield contradictory results, a phenomenon that has been termed a "replication crisis" (e.g. Anderson and Kichkha, 2017). Also, with respect to research on emotional processing and sex hormones, inconsistencies are apparent, making it very difficult to make clear conclusions about the role of sex hormones in many of the above presented domains. In the present book chapter, most studies share small sample sizes, leading to insufficient statistical power. Furthermore, many studies are hard to compare due to the heterogeneity of paradigms and tasks used. Thus, it is difficult to tell whether results are due to specific paradigms or can be transferred to other similar approaches. Furthermore, with respect to analyses of hormone samples, large differences exist between studies with respect to whether blood or saliva samples were taken and how these samples were analyzed. Finally, the overall number of studies that related sex hormones to emotional processing is small, which might also be due to the phenomenon of not reporting non-significant results (e.g. Nissen et al., 2016). Having these limitations in mind, we propose the following conclusions:

Regarding **estradiol and progesterone** in women, several studies suggested higher emotional reactivity with higher levels of female sex hormones in brain regions like the amygdala and fusiform gyrus that are important hubs in emotion processing. Surprisingly, this increased reactivity goes hand in hand with reduced accuracy in correctly labeling emotional faces, as indicated by several studies investigating emotion recognition in naturally cycling women. For emotion regulation, previous findings indicate that high levels of estradiol are accompanied by better cognitive emotion regulation, while high levels of progesterone are associated with more effort to suppress negative feelings. The memory of an emotional event also seems to be affected by hormonal states, with high levels of progesterone at encoding increasing the recall of negative stimuli and high levels of estradiol facilitating extinction of a previously learned conditioned response, which is also reflected in stronger neural activation. Regarding empathic abilities, the lack of studies in connection with female sex hormones allows no clear conclusions. However, as no previous study assessed more than one domain in the same sample, it is only speculative to relate the different effects to each other.

Concerning the effects of **testosterone**, results are even more diverse than for estradiol and progesterone. Most consistently, in women testosterone application has been found to increase brain activation in regions including the amygdala. However, studies investigating behavioral consequences only yielded contradictory results, leading to both an increase and a decrease of emotion recognition or report null-findings. For emotion regulation, there is a lack of studies to make definite claims and only a weak hint exists that higher testosterone levels in men improve emotion regulation. The effect of testosterone on emotional memory has scarcely been investigated, making definite claims impossible. Moreover, high endogenous and/or prenatal testosterone levels have been associated with worse cognitive empathy.

Moreover, we incorporated two chapters sharing current knowledge on i) how endogenous fluctuations of sex hormones can affect clinical symptoms and ii) how intake of exogenous sex hormones can modulate emotion processing in adult women. In both areas only a limited amount of studies is available, definitely calling for more research and thus broadening our understanding of sex hormone actions on emotion and cognition.

Taken together, with this chapter we intended to highlight that research on the impact of sex hormone concentration and their fluctuations on emotional competencies has provided tentative evidence that estradiol, progesterone, and testosterone affect these abilities in women and men although, the underlying mechanisms by which these sex steroids impact our emotional responses on a behavioral and neural level are far from being understood.

References

Ackermann, S., Spalek, K., Rasch, B., Gschwind, L., Coynel, D., Fastenrath, M., . . . de Quervain, D. J. (2012). Testosterone levels in healthy men are related to amygdala reactivity and memory performance. *Psychoneuroendocrinology, 37,* 1417–1424.

Anderson, R. G., & Kichkha, A. (2017). Replication, meta-analysis, and research synthesis in economics. *American Economic Review, 107,* 56–59.

Andreen, L., Nyberg, S., Turkmen, S., van Wingen, G., Fernandez, G., & Backstrom, T. (2009). Sex steroid induced negative mood may be explained by the paradoxical effect mediated by GABAA modulators. *Psychoneuroendocrinology, 34,* 1121–1132.

Antov, M. I., & Stockhorst, U. (2014). Stress exposure prior to fear acquisition interacts with estradiol status to alter recall of fear extinction in humans. *Psychoneuroendocrinology, 49,* 106–118.

Bannbers, E., Kask, K., Wikström, J., & Sundström Poromaa, I. (2010). Lower levels of prepulse inhibition in luteal phase cycling women in comparison with postmenopausal women. *Psychoneuroendocrinology, 35,* 422–429.

Barth, C., Steele, C. J., Mueller, K., Rekkas, V. P., Arelin, K., Pampel, A., & Sacher, J. (2016). In-vivo dynamics of the human hippocampus across the menstrual cycle. *Scientific Reports, 6*, 32833.

Bayer, J., Schultz, H., Gamer, M., & Sommer, T. (2014). Menstrual-cycle dependent fluctuations in ovarian hormones affect emotional memory. *Neurobiology of Learning and Memory, 110*, 55–63.

Bos, P. A., Hofman, D., Hermans, E. J., Montoya, E. R., Baron-Cohen, S., & van Honk, J. (2016). Testosterone reduces functional connectivity during the "Reading the Mind in the Eyes" test. *Psychoneuroendocrinology, 68*, 194–201.

Bos, P. A., van Honk, J., Ramsey, N. F., Stein, D. J., & Hermans, E. J. (2013). Testosterone administration in women increases amygdala responses to fearful and happy faces. *Psychoneuroendocrinology, 38*, 808–817.

Brinton, R. D., Thompson, R. F., Foy, M. R., Baudry, M., Wang, J., Finch, C. E., . . . Nilsen, J. (2008). Progesterone receptors: Form and function in brain. *Frontiers in Neuroendocrinology, 29*, 313–339.

Cacioppo, J. T., Berntson, G. G., Larsen, J. T., Poehlmann, K. M., & Ito, T. A. (2000). The psychophysiology of emotion. *Handbook of Emotions, 2*, 173–191.

Carré, J. M., Ortiz, T. L., Labine, B., Moreau, B. J., Viding, E., Neumann, C. S., & Goldfarb, B. (2015). Digit ratio (2D:4D) and psychopathic traits moderate the effect of exogenous testosterone on socio-cognitive processes in men. *Psychoneuroendocrinology, 62*, 319–326.

Comasco, E., Hahn, A., Ganger, S., Gingnell, M., Bannbers, E., Oreland, L., . . . Sundstrom-Poromaa, I. (2014). Emotional fronto-cingulate cortex activation and brain derived neurotrophic factor polymorphism in premenstrual dysphoric disorder. *Human Brain Mapping, 35*, 4450–4458.

Cunningham, R. L., Lumia, A. R., & McGinnis, M. Y. (2012). Androgen receptors, sex behavior, and aggression. *Neuroendocrinology, 96*, 131–140.

Damasio, A. R. (1998). Emotion in the perspective of an integrated nervous system. *Brain Research Reviews, 26*, 83–86.

Davey, R. A., & Grossmann, M. (2016). Androgen receptor structure, function and biology: From bench to bedside. *The Clinical Biochemist Reviews, 37*, 3.

Decety, J., & Jackson, P. L. (2004). The functional architecture of human empathy. *Behavioral and Cognitive Neuroscience Reviews, 3*, 71–100.

Denson, T. F., Mehta, P. H., & Ho Tan, D. (2013). Endogenous testosterone and cortisol jointly influence reactive aggression in women. *Psychoneuroendocrinology, 38*, 416–424.

Derntl, B., Hack, R. L., Kryspin-Exner, I., & Habel, U. (2013). Association of menstrual cycle phase with the core components of empathy. *Hormones and Behavior, 63*, 97–104.

Derntl, B., Kryspin-Exner, I., Fernbach, E., Moser, E., & Habel, U. (2008). Emotion recognition accuracy in healthy young females is associated with cycle phase. *Hormones Behaviour, 53*, 90–95.

Derntl, B., Windischberger, C., Robinson, S., Kryspin-Exner, I., Gur, R. C., Moser, E., & Habel, U. (2009). Amygdala activity to fear and anger in healthy young males is associated with testosterone. *Psychoneuroendocrinology, 34*, 687–693.

Derntl, B., Windischberger, C., Robinson, S., Lamplmayr, E., Kryspin-Exner, I., Gur, R. C., & Habel, U. (2008). Facial emotion recognition and amygdala activation are associated with menstrual cycle phase. *Psychoneuroendocrinology, 33*, 1031–1040.

DonCarlos, L., Sarkey, S., Lorenz, B., Azcoitia, I., Garcia-Ovejero, D., Huppenbauer, C., & Garcia-Segura, L-M. (2006). Novel cellular phenotypes and subcellular sites for androgen action in the forebrain. *Neuroscience, 138*, 801–807.

Dricu, M., & Frühholz, S. (2016). Perceiving emotional expressions in others: Activation likelihood estimation meta-analyses of explicit evaluation, passive perception and incidental perception of emotions. *Neuroscience Biobehavioral Reviews, 71*, 810–828.

Dunsmoor, J. E., Niv, Y., Daw, N., & Phelps, E. A. (2015). Rethinking Extinction. *Neuron, 88*, 47–63.

Ekman, P. E., & Cordaro, D. (2011). What is meant by calling emotions basic. *Emotions Reviews, 3*, 364–370.

Ekman, P. E., & Davidson, R. J. (1994). *The nature of emotion: Fundamental questions*. Oxford: Oxford University Press.

Epperson, C. N., Pittman, B., Czarkowski, K. A., Stiklus, S., Krystal, J. H., & Grillon, C. (2007). Luteal-phase accentuation of acoustic startle response in women with premenstrual dysphoric disorder. *Neuropsychopharmacology, 32*, 2190–2198.

Ernst, U., Baumgartner, L., Bauer, U., & Janssen, G. (2002). Improvement of quality of life in women using a low-dose desogestrel-containing contraceptive: Results of an observational clinical evaluation. *The European Journal of Contraception & Reproductive Health Care, 7*, 238–243.

Ertman, N., Andreano, J. M., & Cahill, L. (2011). Progesterone at encoding predicts subsequent emotional memory. *Learning & Memory, 18*, 759–763.

Felmingham, K. L., Fong, W. C., & Bryant, R. A. (2012). The impact of progesterone on memory consolidation of threatening images in women. *Psychoneuroendocrinology, 37*, 1896–1900.

Ferree, N. K., Kamat, R., & Cahill, L. (2011). Influences of menstrual cycle position and sex hormone levels on spontaneous intrusive recollections following emotional stimuli. *Consciousness and Cognition, 20*, 1154–1162.

Gasbarri, A., Pompili, A., D'Onofrio, A., Cifariello, A., Tavares, M. C., & Tomaz, C. (2008). Working memory for emotional facial expressions: Role of the estrogen in young women. *Psychoneuroendocrinology, 33*, 964–972.

Gingnell, M., Ahlstedt, V., Bannbers, E., Wikström, J., Sundström-Poromaa, I., & Fredrikson, M. (2014). Social stimulation and corticolimbic reactivity in premenstrual dysphoric disorder: A preliminary study. *Biology of Mood & Anxiety Disorders, 4*, 3.

Gingnell, M., Bannbers, E., Wikstrom, J., Fredrikson, M., & Sundstrom-Poromaa, I. (2013). Premenstrual dysphoric disorder and prefrontal reactivity during anticipation of emotional stimuli. *European Neuropsychopharmacology, 23*, 1474–1483.

Gingnell, M., Morell, A., Bannbers, E., Wikström, J., & Poromaa, I. S. (2012). Menstrual cycle effects on amygdala reactivity to emotional stimulation in premenstrual dysphoric disorder. *Hormones and Behavior, 62*, 400–406.

Graham, B. M., Ash, C., & Den, M. L. (2017). High endogenous estradiol is associated with enhanced cognitive emotion regulation of physiological conditioned fear responses in women. *Psychoneuroendocrinology, 80*, 7–14.

Graham, B. M., & Milad, M. R. (2013). Blockade of estrogen by hormonal contraceptives impairs fear extinction in female rats and women. *Biological Psychiatry, 73*, 371–378.

Graham, B. M., & Milad, M. R. (2014). Inhibition of estradiol synthesis impairs fear extinction in male rats. *Learning & Memory, 21*, 347–350.

Gross, J. J. (1999). Emotion and emotion regulation. *Handbook of Personality: Theory and Research, 2*, 525–552.

Gross, J. J. (2002). Emotion regulation: Affective, cognitive, and social consequences. *Psychophysiology, 39*, 281–291.

Gross, J. J. (2013). Emotion regulation: Taking stock and moving forward. *Emotion, 13*, 359–365.

Gruber, C. J., Tschugguel, W., Schneeberger, C., & Huber, J. C. (2002). Production and actions of estrogens. *The New England Journal of Medicine, 346*, 340–352.

Guapo, V. G., Graeff, F. G., Zani, A. C., Labate, C. M., dos Reis, R. M., & Del-Ben, C. M. (2009). Effects of sex hormonal levels and phases of the menstrual cycle in the processing of emotional faces. *Psychoneuroendocrinology, 34*, 1087–1094.

Halbreich, U., Borenstein, J., Pearlstein, T., & Kahn, L. S. (2003). The prevalence, impairment, impact, and burden of premenstrual dysphoric disorder (PMS/PMDD). *Psychoneuroendocrinology, 28*(Suppl. 3), 1–23.

Hamstra, D. A., De Rover, M., De Rijk, R. H., & van der Does, W. (2014). Oral contraceptives may alter the detection of emotions in facial expressions. *European Neuropsychopharmacology, 24*, 1855–1859.

Hartlage, S. A., Freels, S., Gotman, N., & Yonkers, K. (2012). Criteria for premenstrual dysphoric disorder: Secondary analyses of relevant data sets. *Archives of General Psychiatry, 69*, 300–305.

Hazell, G. G., Yao, S. T., Roper, J. A., Prossnitz, E. R., O'Carroll, A. M., & Lolait, S. J. (2009). Localisation of GPR30, a novel G protein-coupled oestrogen receptor, suggests multiple functions in rodent brain and peripheral tissues. *Journal Endocrinology, 202*, 223–236.

Hermans, E. J., Ramsey, N. F., & van Honk, J. (2008). Exogenous testosterone enhances responsiveness to social threat in the neural circuitry of social aggression in humans. *Biological Psychiatry, 63*, 263–270.

Hwang, M. J., Zsido, R. G., Song, H., Pace-Schott, E. F., Miller, K. K., Lebron-Milad, K., & Milad, M. R. (2015). Contribution of estradiol levels and hormonal contraceptives to sex differences within the fear network during fear conditioning and extinction. *BMC Psychiatry, 15*, 295.

Intlekofer, K. A., & Petersen, S. L. (2011). Distribution of mRNAs encoding classical progestin receptor, progesterone membrane components 1 and 2, serpine mRNA binding protein 1, and progestin and ADIPOQ receptor family members 7 and 8 in rat forebrain. *Neuroscience, 172*, 55–65.

Johansson, I. M., Birzniece, V., Lindblad, C., Olsson, T., & Backstrom, T. (2002). Allopregnanolone inhibits learning in the Morris water maze. *Brain Research, 934*, 125–131.

Kamboj, S. K., Krol, K. M., & Curran, H. V. (2015). A specific association between facial disgust recognition and estradiol levels in naturally cycling women. *PLoS One, 10*, e0122311.

Kask, K., Backstrom, T., Nilsson, L. G., & Sundstrom-Poromaa, I. (2008). Allopregnanolone impairs episodic memory in healthy women. *Psychopharmacology (Berl.), 199*, 161–168.

Kask, K., Gulinello, M., Bäckström, T., Geyer, M. A., & Sundström-Poromaa, I. (2008). Patients with premenstrual dysphoric disorder have increased startle response across both cycle phases and lower levels of prepulse inhibition during the late luteal phase of the menstrual cycle. *Neuropsychopharmacology, 33,* 2283–2290.

Kelly, S., Davies, E., Fearns, S., McKinnon, C., Carter, R., Gerlinger, C., & Smithers, A. (2010). Effects of oral contraceptives containing ethinylestradiol with either drospirenone or levonorgestrel on various parameters associated with well-being in healthy women. *Clinical Drug Investigation, 30,* 325–336.

Kleinginna, P. R., & Kleinginna, A. M. (1981). A categorized list of emotion definitions, with suggestions for a consensual definition. *Motivation and Emotion, 5,* 345–379.

LeDoux, J. E. (1998). *The emotional brain: The mysterious underpinnings of emotional life.* New York, NY: Simon and Schuster.

Lindquist, K. A., Wager, T. D., Kober, H., Bliss-Moreau, E., & Barrett, L. F. (2012). The brain basis of emotion: A meta-analytic review. *Behavioral Brain Sciences, 35,* 121–143.

Lisofsky, N., Riediger, M., Gallinat, J., Lindenberger, U., & Kuhn, S. (2016). Hormonal contraceptive use is associated with neural and affective changes in healthy young women. *Neuroimage, 134,* 597–606.

Lusk, B. R., Carr, A. R., Ranson, V. A., & Felmingham, K. L. (2017). Women in the midluteal phase of the menstrual cycle have difficulty suppressing the processing of negative emotional stimuli: An event-related potential study. *Cognitive, Affective, & Behavioral Neuroscience,* 1–18.

Marečková, K., Perrin, J. S., Nawaz Khan, I., Lawrence, C., Dickie, E., McQuiggan, D. A., . . . Consortium, I. (2014). Hormonal contraceptives, menstrual cycle and brain response to faces. *Social Cognitive and Affective Neuroscience, 9,* 191–200.

Mehu, M., Mortillaro, M., Banziger, T., & Scherer, K. R. (2012). Reliable facial muscle activation enhances recognizability and credibility of emotional expression. *Emotion, 12,* 701–715.

Melcangi, R. C., Panzica, G., & Garcia-Segura, L. M. (2011). Neuroactive steroids: Focus on human brain. *Neuroscience, 191,* 1–5.

Merz, C. J. (2017). Contribution of stress and sex hormones to memory encoding. *Psychoneuroendocrinology, 82,* 51–58.

Milad, M. R., Zeidan, M. A., Contero, A., Pitman, R. K., Klibanski, A., Rauch, S. L., & Goldstein, J. M. (2010). The influence of gonadal hormones on conditioned fear extinction in healthy humans. *Neuroscience, 168,* 652–658.

Montoya, E. R., & Bos, P. A. (2017). How oral contraceptives impact social-emotional behavior and brain function. *Trends in Cognitive Sciences, 21,* 125–136

Morawetz, C., Bode, S., Derntl, B., & Heekeren, H. R. (2017). The effect of strategies, goals and stimulus material on the neural mechanisms of emotion regulation: A meta-analysis of fMRI studies. *Neuroscience & Biobehavioral Reviews, 72,* 111–128.

Nissen, S. B., Magidson, T., Gross, K., & Bergstrom, C. T. (2016). Publication bias and the canonization of false facts. *Elife, 5,* e21451.

Pace-Schott, E. F., Spencer, R. M., Vijayakumar, S., Ahmed, N. A., Verga, P. W., Orr, S. P., . . . Milad, M. R. (2013). Extinction of conditioned fear is better learned and recalled in the morning than in the evening. *Journal of Psychiatric Research, 47,* 1776–1784.

Petersen, N., & Cahill, L. (2015). Amygdala reactivity to negative stimuli is influenced by oral contraceptive use. *Social, Cognitive and Affective Neuroscience, 10,* 1266–1272.

Pletzer, B., Kronbichler, M., Aichhorn, M., Bergmann, J., Ladurner, G., & Kerschbaum, H. H. (2010). Menstrual cycle and hormonal contraceptive use modulate human brain structure. *Brain Research, 1348,* 55–62.

Pompili, A., Arnone, B., D'Amico, M., Federico, P., & Gasbarri, A. (2016). Evidence of estrogen modulation on memory processes for emotional content in healthy young women. *Psychoneuroendocrinology, 65,* 94–101.

Radke, S., & Derntl, B. (2016). Affective responsiveness is influenced by intake of oral contraceptives. *European Neuropsychopharmacology, 26,* 1014–1019.

Radke, S., Volman, I., Mehta, P., van Son, V., Enter, D., Sanfey, A., . . . Roelofs, K. (2015). Testosterone biases the amygdala toward social threat approach. *Science Advances, 1,* e1400074.

Rubinow, D. R., Smith, M. J., Schenkel, L. A., Schmidt, P. J., & Dancer, K. (2007). Facial emotion discrimination across the menstrual cycle in women with Premenstrual Dysphoric Disorder (PMDD) and controls. *Journal of Affective Disorders, 104,* 37–44.

Sakaki, M., & Mather, M. (2012). How reward and emotional stimuli induce different reactions across the menstrual cycle. *Social and Personality Psychology Compass, 6,* 1–17.

Skouby, S. (2010). Contraceptive use and behavior in the 21st century: A comprehensive study across five European countries. *The European Journal of Contraception & Reproductive Health Care, 15,* S42–S53.

Skovlund, C. W., Mørch, L. S., Kessing, L. V., & Lidegaard, Ø. (2016). Association of hormonal contraception with depression. *JAMA Psychiatry, 73,* 1154–1162.

Sollberger, S., & Ehlert, U. (2016). How to use and interpret hormone ratios. *Psychoneuroendocrinology, 63,* 385–397.

Soni, M., Curran, V. H., & Kamboj, S. K. (2013). Identification of a narrow post-ovulatory window of vulnerability to distressing involuntary memories in healthy women. *Neurobiology of Learning and Memory, 104,* 32–38.

Stanton, S. J., Wirth, M. M., Waugh, C. E., & Schultheiss, O. C. (2009). Endogenous testosterone levels are associated with amygdala and ventromedial prefrontal cortex responses to anger faces in men but not women. *Biological Psychology, 81,* 118–122.

Su, C., Rybalchenko, N., Schreihofer, D. A., Singh, M., Abbassi, B., & Cunningham, R. L. (2012). Cell models for the study of sex steroid hormone neurobiology. *Journal of Steroids & Hormonal Science, S2,* pii: 003

Sveindóttir, H., & Bäckström, T. (2000). Prevalence of menstrual cycle symptom cyclicity and premenstrual dysphoric disorder in a random sample of women using and not using oral contraceptives. *Acta Obstetrica Gynecologica Scandinavica, 79,* 405–413.

Tabori, N., Stewart, L., Znamensky, V., Romeo, R., Alves, S., McEwen, B., & Milner, T. (2005). Ultrastructural evidence that androgen receptors are located at extranuclear sites in the rat hippocampal formation. *Neuroscience, 130,* 151–163.

van Honk, J., & Schutter, D. J. (2007). Testosterone reduces conscious detection of signals serving social correction: Implications for antisocial behavior. *Psychological Science, 18,* 663–667.

van Honk, J., Schutter, D. J., Bos, P. A., Kruijt, A. W., Lentjes, E. G., & Baron-Cohen, S. (2011). Testosterone administration impairs cognitive empathy in women depending on second-to-fourth digit ratio. *Proceedings of the National Academy of Sciences of the United States of America, 108,* 3448–3452.

van Wingen, G., van Broekhoven, F., Verkes, R. J., Petersson, K. M., Backstrom, T., Buitelaar, J., & Fernandez, G. (2007). How progesterone impairs memory for biologically salient stimuli in healthy young women. *Journal of Neuroscience, 27,* 11416–11423.

van Wingen, G. A., van Broekhoven, F., Verkes, R. J., Petersson, K. M., Backstrom, T., Buitelaar, J. K., & Fernandez, G. (2008). Progesterone selectively increases amygdala reactivity in women. *Molecular Psychiatry, 13,* 325–333.

van Wingen, G. A., Zylicz, S. A., Pieters, S., Mattern, C., Verkes, R. J., Buitelaar, J. K., & Fernandez, G. (2009). Testosterone increases amygdala reactivity in middle-aged women to a young adulthood level. *Neuropsychopharmacology, 34,* 539–547.

Volman, I., Toni, I., Verhagen, L., & Roelofs, K. (2011). Endogenous testosterone modulates prefrontal – amygdala connectivity during social emotional behavior. *Cerebral Cortex, 21,* 2282–2290.

Vongas, J. G., & Al Hajj, R. (2017). The effects of competition and implicit power motive on men's testosterone, emotion recognition, and aggression. *Hormones and Behavior, 92,* 57–71

Walter, H. (2012). Social cognitive neuroscience of empathy: Concepts, circuits, and genes. *Emotion Review, 4,* 9–17.

Wegerer, M., Kerschbaum, H., Blechert, J., & Wilhelm, F. H. (2014). Low levels of estradiol are associated with elevated conditioned responding during fear extinction and with intrusive memories in daily life. *Neurobiology of Learning and Memory, 116,* 145–154.

Wittchen, H-U., Becker, E., Lieb, R., & Krause, P. (2002). Prevalence, incidence and stability of premenstrual dysphoric disorder in the community. *Psychological Medicine, 32,* 119–132.

Wu, M., Zhou, R., & Huang, Y. (2014). Effects of menstrual cycle and neuroticism on females' emotion regulation. *International Journal of Psychophysiology, 94,* 351–357.

Zeidan, M. A., Igoe, S. A., Linnman, C., Vitalo, A., Levine, J. B., Klibanski, A., & Milad, M. R. (2011). Estradiol modulates medial prefrontal cortex and amygdala activity during fear extinction in women and female rats. *Biological Psychiatry, 70,* 920–927.

24

HORMONAL MODULATION OF REINFORCEMENT LEARNING AND REWARD-RELATED PROCESSES – A ROLE FOR 17ß-ESTRADIOL, PROGESTERONE AND TESTOSTERONE

Esther K. Diekhof, Luise Reimers, and Sarah K. C. Holtfrerich

The steroid hormones 17ß-estradiol (estradiol in the following), progesterone and testosterone play an important role in the modulation of human behavior. Beyond a simple role in reproductive function, these hormones may also modulate human cognition in general and reward-related processing in particular (Sakaki & Mather, 2012; Wood, 2004). It has been repeatedly demonstrated that transient short-term changes in the concentration of these hormones (e.g., across the menstrual cycle) are potent intra-individual modulators of reward processing. Likewise, a trait-like hormone level that is relatively stable over several months (e.g., morning testosterone level in young men) may also be a valuable indicator of inter-individual variations in neural responses to reward. Taking into account individual variations in hormone level could help to advance the understanding of the etiology of certain psychiatric disorders related to the reward system (e.g., addiction, major depression). Evidence from neuroendocrinological research may therefore be of crucial importance for a better understanding of the mechanisms implicated in reward processing in the healthy and disordered human brain.

In women, the natural menstrual cycle offers a physiologically plausible model to track the effect of transient changes in endogenous estradiol and progesterone on reward processing. During the first half of the menstrual cycle, the follicular phase (FP), estradiol is continuously rising to its peak right before ovulation, when it shows a sudden drop. In contrast, progesterone is only slightly increasing during this phase. In the subsequent luteal phase (LP), progesterone increases to its cyclic maximum in the mid LP, while the second rise in estradiol only reaches an intermediate level (Sakaki & Mather, 2012). The menstrual cycle thus incorporates an experimental baseline of low hormone availability (early FP), a phase in which high estradiol is rather unopposed by progesterone (late FP) and a phase during which high progesterone should exert its maximum effect (mid LP).

Similar to estradiol, endogenous testosterone in women also shows a follicular rise. Yet, the effect of this rise on female reward processing has been widely neglected. The primary focus of previous research on human reward-related behavior was on male endogenous testosterone, which may represent a trait-like marker in men. If women were assessed, studies mainly tested women with hormonal contraception, who either received a single dose of testosterone versus placebo or who were free of any treatment except from hormonal contraception. Hormonal contraception suppresses follicular growth and ovulation and thus inhibits the cycle-dependent rise of estradiol and testosterone, leaving a quite stable, yet reduced endogenous testosterone level (Zimmerman, Eijkemans, Coelingh Bennink, Blankenstein, & Fauser, 2014). Pharmacological intervention with testosterone or other hormones quickly increases endogenous concentration, which is intended to enhance any associated behavioral or neural effects. But it may have several disadvantages: Firstly, it often leads to supraphysiological concentrations relative to those naturally experienced in the body, and this can lead to a reversal of the expected effects (Hu & Becker, 2008). Secondly, if pharmacological hormones are assessed in older populations, the neurofunctional architecture under research may already be compromised by the longer absence of natural hormones, which limits the generalizability of the results. Thirdly, if testosterone is administered to young women, they may not only experience supraphysiological testosterone, but part of it will be converted to estradiol through aromatization, which may again render the interpretation of the results difficult. In this chapter, we will particularly focus on evidence from young healthy populations (mainly women) and the influence of endogenous hormone levels on reward-related processing. For this purpose, different lines of behavioral and neuroimaging evidence will be reviewed.

Reinforcement learning I – menstrual cycle dependent modulation of probabilistic feedback learning

The human capacity to learn from errors or the positive outcomes of one's actions may be influenced by endogenous variations in estradiol and progesterone across the menstrual cycle (e.g., Diekhof & Ratnayake, 2016). Yet, estradiol and progesterone may not directly affect sensitivity for performance feedback, but may rather interact with other neurotransmitter systems like the mesolimbic dopamine system, which are crucial for this type of motivational learning. Converging evidence suggests that fluctuations in central dopamine may drive differences in reward learning and punishment avoidance. This is in part achieved through dopamine's differential action at two subgroups of dopamine receptors, DRD1 and DRD2, that are located at the direct and the indirect pathways of the basal ganglia, respectively. Phasic dopamine release after a rewarded action promotes learning via long-term potentiation at corticostriatal synapses of the direct, so-called Go-pathway that expresses DRD1. At the same time, avoidance learning capacity is suppressed through DRD2-dependent long-term depression of the indirect 'NoGo-pathway'. Conversely, when an action is followed by a dip in tonic dopamine, such as the one following a negative action outcome or reward omission, the NoGo-pathway is strengthened and avoidance responses are facilitated at the expense of reward learning capacity (Bromberg-Martin, Matsumoto, & Hikosaka, 2010; Maia & Frank, 2011). The effect of variations in central dopamine on the opponent processes of reward versus punishment learning has been repeatedly confirmed through pharmacological intervention (e.g., Frank, Seeberger, & O'Reilly, 2004) or neurogenetic approaches (Klein et al., 2007). Yet, similar changes in reinforcement learning capacity can also be attained by natural variations in the level of estradiol and progesterone (Diekhof & Ratnayake, 2016). Through their multiple actions in the brain, these hormones do not only affect the functional integrity of neural circuits and synapses (Gillies & McArthur, 2010) but may also be implicated in the release and turn-over of other neurotransmitters such as dopamine (Becker, 1999). In rodents, estradiol in the range of physiological concentrations has been demonstrated to have dopamine-agonistic properties (Becker, 1999). Estradiol may thereby amplify the dopaminergic response by (a.) promoting stimulated dopamine release in the striatum (Xiao & Becker, 1998), (b.) increasing striatal dopamine synthesis capacity (Pasqualini, Olivier, Guibert, Frain, & Leviel, 1995) and (c.) decreasing the affinity of inhibitory DRD2, which may in turn reduce dopamine autoregulation (Lévesque & Di Paolo, 1988). Interestingly, progesterone and its metabolites may partially oppose the effects of estradiol on dopamine transmission by promoting dopamine degradation and by attenuating dopamine release (Motzo et al., 1996). In an initial study on probabilistic feedback learning Diekhof and Ratnayake (2016) observed a relative increase in the ability to learn from the rewarding feedback of one's actions, while the capacity to avoid negative feedback was reduced during the late FP in comparison to the mid-LP. The probabilistic feedback task used by Diekhof and Ratnayake (2016) is subdivided into two parts. In the initial learning phase, subjects acquire stimulus-reward contingencies by trial-and-error from three fixed stimulus pairs of Japanese symbols, so-called pairs AB, CD and EF, with fixed reward contingencies for each option in a pair. Option A is the best one of all options and offers rewarding feedback in 80% of selections, while B is the worst option of all, with negative feedback in 80% of selections. In the subsequent transfer phase, the pairs are no longer fixed and options are combined to form new pairs. This allows one to disentangle the extent to which subjects used positive or negative feedback to guide their actions during learning. For example, if a person is good at learning from reward, she should have developed the highest preference for the most rewarded option A during learning, which should also affect selections in the new stimulus pairs (indicated by a high percentage of 'Choose A' performance). Similarly, someone that has an enhanced ability to learn from punishment should be good at avoiding the worst option B in the transfer phase, which is reflected by an increased 'Avoid B' performance. Consistent with the assumption of antagonistic effects of estradiol and progesterone on central dopamine transmission, Diekhof and Ratnayake (2016) found that when the heightened concentration of salivary estradiol of the late FP was accompanied by rather low progesterone, participants were better in learning from reward than punishment. In contrast, when progesterone rose to its maximum in the mid LP, the behavioral pattern reversed, which resulted in a significant rise in 'Avoid B' performance (see Figure 24.1A). Further, women with a higher luteal progesterone concentration were less likely to choose stimulus A in the new pairs, suggesting that a reduced Go-learning capacity was related to the increasing luteal progesterone level. In line with the behavioral findings, in the late FP the activation of the rostral cingulate zone (RCZ) in the anterior cingulate cortex (ACC) was reduced during processing of negative feedback. This was in contrast to the mid LP, when progesterone was high, during which subjects became more sensitive to punishing feedback and the response of the RCZ to negative feedback was enhanced (see Figure 24.1B). Given the theory that the RCZ may optimize action selection during avoidance learning (Ridderinkhof, Ullsperger, Crone, & Nieuwenhuis, 2004), a reduced response of the RCZ in the late FP may fit well with the dopamine-agonistic properties of estradiol, which could have strengthened Go-learning through weakening DRD2-mediated action selection and NoGo-learning (Becker, 1999). Similarly, the observed increase in activation of the RCZ following negative feedback in the mid LP, which was accompanied by an enhanced punishment learning ability (Figure 24.1A), may suggest an increased NoGo-learning ability in line with the functional opposition of the proposed Go- and NoGo-pathways (Maia & Frank, 2011).

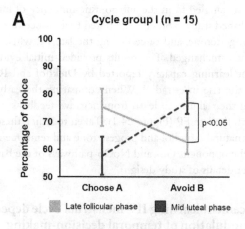

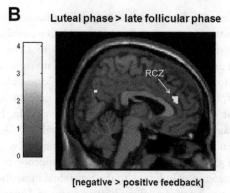

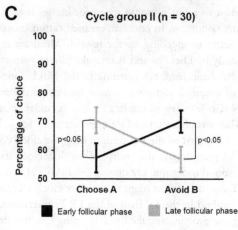

Figure 24.1 Reinforcement learning capacity changes across the menstrual cycle. (A) Reduced punishment learning (Avoid B performance) in the late FP is accompanied by a reduction of activation of the RCZ for negative feedback when compared to the middle LP (adapted from Diekhof & Ratnayake, 2016). (B) Punishment learning is reduced in the late versus early FP, while reward sensitivity (Choose A performance) is enhanced (unpublished data).

Yet, in the study of Diekhof and Ratnayake (2016), the influence of the follicular rise in estradiol could not be disentangled from the antagonistic influence of luteal progesterone. In a second, currently unpublished study, women were tested twice, once during the early FP, at the nadir of estradiol and progesterone, and once during the late FP, when estradiol level peaked but progesterone remained unchanged. The results provided initial evidence that the relative reduction in punishment learning capacity reported by Diekhof and Ratnayake (2016) may be indeed attributed to the rise in estradiol. When comparing the early and late FP, women became compromised in their ability to learn from negative feedback, while reward learning capacity increased towards the late FP (Figure 24.1). Taken together, these two studies demonstrate a relation between natural estradiol and progesterone and reinforcement learning capacity through modulation of the opponent Go- and NoGo-pathways of the basal ganglia (please also see Table 24.1 for further details of study design).

Reinforcement learning II – menstrual cycle dependent modulation of temporal decision-making

Similar to reinforcement learning, temporal decision-making has also been shown to underlie hormonal variations across the menstrual cycle. Go- and NoGo-learning processes can also be transferred to the capacity to adapt one's response time (RT) to a fast or slow response speed for reward maximization. Further, the ability to learn to speed up or to slow down for reward is affected by differences in dopamine transmission (Moustafa, Cohen, Sherman, & Frank, 2008). In the so-called clock task, subjects are presented with three different clock faces and have to figure out the optimal time to stop the clock to maximize reward. In the fast clock condition, a quick response yields maximum points (i.e., learning through the Go-pathway), whereas in the slow clock condition subjects have to postpone responding and wait longer to win a high reward (i.e., NoGo-learning). A random clock with no contingency between RT and reward controls for baseline RT preference. In line with the functional opposition of Go- and NoGo-learning preferences, Parkinson's patients off medication (state of depleted dopamine) displayed an impaired ability to adapt to a fast response speed for higher reward, but showed enhanced learning in the slow clock condition. In contrast, on medication (normalized dopamine state) the same patients were better in speeding up for reward (Moustafa et al., 2008). The sample that participated in the study by Diekhof and Ratnayake (2016) performed the clock task after they had completed probabilistic feedback learning in the MRI scanner. Consistent with the above described effects of estradiol and progesterone on central dopamine, subjects displayed an impaired ability for NoGo-learning in the late FP, that is, under conditions of high estradiol and low progesterone. This was characterized by a greater need for RT adaptation to achieve optimal performance from the first to the last trials in the slow clock condition as compared to the LP. This greater RT adaptation over the course of the slow clock trials supposedly indicates the initial tendency to respond more quickly during the FP (i.e., Go-learning bias in the presence of high estradiol). Thus, in order to adapt to the slow clock a greater learning-related RT change may have been required in the FP than in the LP. Furthermore, feedback-related brain activity measured during the probabilistic feedback learning task was predictive of RT adaptation, but only in the late FP (Figure 24.2). Activation of the inferior frontal junction (IFJ), a region implicated in cognitive control (e.g., Brass, Derrfuss, Forstmann, & von Cramon, 2005), and the RCZ correlated with better adapted RTs in the slow clock condition towards the end of the task. Thus, increased reactivity of these regions to feedback may indicate the individual ability to compensate for impaired NoGo-learning abilities in the presence of heightened follicular estradiol. Conversely, a stronger feedback-related signal in the ventromedial prefrontal

Table 24.1 Overview of studies that assessed different aspects of reward processing in relation to menstrual cycle phase

Authors	Sample size	Determination of cycle phase[1] by ...	Average cycle length in days (mean ± SD)	Test was carried out during ...				Subchapter (test domain)
				Early follicular phase on cycle day(s)[2]	Late follicular phase on cycle day(s)	Mid luteal phase on cycle day(s)	Premenstrual phase on cycle day(s)	
Diekhof and Ratnayake (2016)	15	• lutropin ovulation test • salivary estradiol and progesterone	30 ± 3	–	13 (about 4 days before ovulation)	24 (about 7 days after positive ovulation test and 5 days before next menstruation)	–	Reinforcement learning I (probabilistic feedback task)
Diekhof (2015)	28	• salivary estradiol and progesterone	–	1–3	12 (15 to 17 days before next menstruation)	–	–	Reinforcement learning II (temporal response adaptation)
Reimers et al. (2014)	14	• lutropin ovulation test • salivary estradiol and progesterone	30 ± 3	–	13 (about 4 days bevor ovulation)	24 (about 7 days after positive ovulation test and 5 days before next menstruation)	–	Reinforcement learning II (temporal response adaptation)
Smith et al. (2014)	87	• salivary estradiol in a subgroup of 34 women; of these 23 showed a rise in follicular estradiol level	28	1–2	11–12	–	–	Reinforcement learning II (delay discounting)
Alonso-Alonso et al. (2011)	9	• no additional method used	29 ± 1	3–6	10–13		–	Reward anticipation and outcome processing (food-related reward)
Frank et al. (2010)	12	• lutropin ovulation test	–	–	about 4 days before ovulation	about 4 days before next menstruation	–	Reward anticipation and outcome processing (food-related reward)
Bayer et al. (2013)	23	• salivary estradiol and progesterone	28 ± 1	0–4	–	17–23 (11 to 5 days before next menstruation)	–	Reward anticipation and outcome processing (MID)

(Continued)

Table 24.1 (Continued)

Authors	Sample size	Determination of cycle phase[1] by ...	Average cycle length in days (mean ± SD)	Test was carried out during ...				Subchapter (test domain)
				Early follicular phase on cycle day(s)[2]	Late follicular phase on cycle day(s)	Mid luteal phase on cycle day(s)	Premenstrual phase on cycle day(s)	
Bonenberger et al. (2013)	12	• lutropin ovulation test	–	3–6	–	6–10 days after positive ovulation test	–	Reward anticipation and outcome processing (MID)
Dreher et al. (2007)	11	• lutropin ovulation test • plasma estradiol and progesterone	29	4–8	–	6–10 days after positive ovulation test	–	Reward anticipation and outcome processing (gambling task)
Ossewaarde et al. (2011)	27	• lutropin ovulation test • salivary allopregnanolone	–	–	10 (8–12)	–	about 14 days after positive ovulation test and 2 days before next menstruation	Reward anticipation and outcome processing (MID)

1 Cycle phase was always determined by self-reported cycle day. Here we report all other measures used to further ascertain cycle phase.
2 The term 'cycle day' indicates the day after onset of menstruation. The data provided either indicate the average day or range of test days.

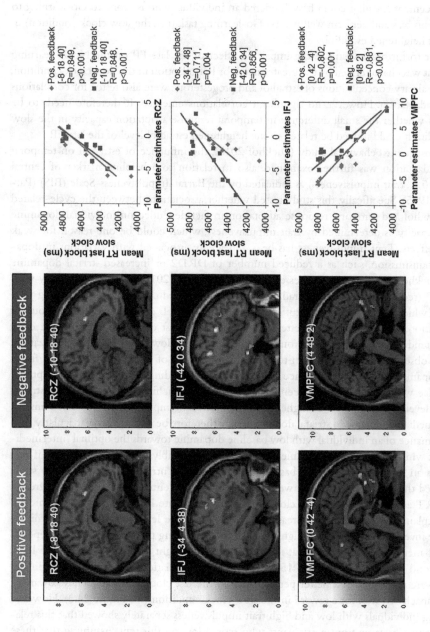

Figure 24.2 Feedback-related activation in the FP was associated with the ability to adapt to a slow response speed. Corresponding to the greater need of adaptation to a slow RT in the late FP, associations between feedback-related brain activation and performance in the slow clock condition indicated a compensatory neural mechanism. Increased activation in the RCZ and IFJ were associated with better final RT adaptation. Conversely, a stronger response of the vmPFC correlated with poorer performance in the last trial block. Adapted from Reimers et al. (2014).

cortex (vmPFC), a region involved in the representation of reward value (Grabenhorst & Rolls, 2011), the preference for immediate rewards (McClure, Laibson, Loewenstein, & Cohen, 2004) and Go-learning ability (Jocham, Klein, & Ullsperger, 2011) was related to poorer optimized performance in the slow clock condition. This suggests that increased vmPFC activation during reinforcement learning could have hindered an individual who is prone to Go-learning to overcome this bias and perform well in a NoGo-learning task (i.e., the slow clock condition) in the state of heightened estradiol.

In order to further investigate the impairing effect of the late FP on the NoGo-learning abilities that was characterized by the greater need for RT adaption in the slow clock condition, individual salivary concentrations of estradiol and progesterone were also tested for correlations with RT adaptation. However, no significant correlations emerged. It therefore needs to be ascertained whether the small difference in temporal response adaptation capacity in the slow clock condition could indeed be related to the heightened estradiol level of the late FP.

In a subsequent behavioral study (Diekhof 2015), the influence of estradiol on temporal response adaptation was further examined, also in relation to a baseline marker of central dopamine (i.e., trait impulsiveness) as indicated by the Barrat-Impulsiveness-Scale (BIS) (Patton et al., 1995). Specifically, this study tested whether associations between the cycle-related rise in estradiol and temporal response adaptation in fact depended on individual dopamine baseline capacity as determined by trait impulsiveness, which could be one reason for weak statistical effects. Trait impulsiveness has been repeatedly associated with variations in dopaminergic transmission, such as a reduced number of DRD2 or increased striatal dopamine release (Buckholtz et al., 2010; Forbes et al., 2009). Diekhof (2015) compared the early with the late FP (reduced versus high estradiol) and thus precluded the effects of increasing progesterone, which were possibly captured by Reimers, Büchel, & Diekhof (2014). Counter to expectation, women showed a better adaptation to the fast clock condition in the early FP and a tendency towards a compromised ability to slow down for reward maximization. Yet, these observations may conform to the heuristic model of an inverted U-shaped function of dopamine-related performance (Cools, 2008). According to this model, an optimal performance with respect to reinforcement learning is only achieved at intermediate striatal dopamine levels, whereas lower or higher dopamine results in impaired behavior. The transient estradiol-mediated increase in striatal dopamine may therefore be expected to particularly shift the performance of an individual with low baseline dopamine towards the optimal (intermediate) range, while the effect of the same hormone could possibly impair performance, if one already has an intermediate to high baseline dopamine concentration. In fact, the two studies that used the clock task conform well to this model: In Reimers et al. (2014), the greater need for RT adaptation in the slow clock condition in the late FP compared to the mid LP may be explained by a follicular increase of striatal dopamine level towards the right direction of the inverted U-curve. This might impair NoGo-learning performance, which depends on DRD2-mediated transmission that is more sensitive to slight increases in dopamine level. In the second study by Diekhof (2015), inter-individual variations in estradiol level in the early FP were predictive of a better performance in the fast clock and a tendency towards a reduced capacity to wait for a reward in the slow clock condition (see Figure 24.3). However, considering individuals with low and high trait impulsiveness separately showed that this relationship primarily came from participants who scored low on this trait. Assuming that these subjects may have a lower striatal dopamine baseline (e.g., Buckholtz et al., 2010), they may especially benefit from the enhancing effect of relatively higher estradiol levels during the early FP (i.e., become more impulsive choice in the form of faster RTs in the fast clock) that would shift their performance towards the point of optimality on the inverted U. Yet, when

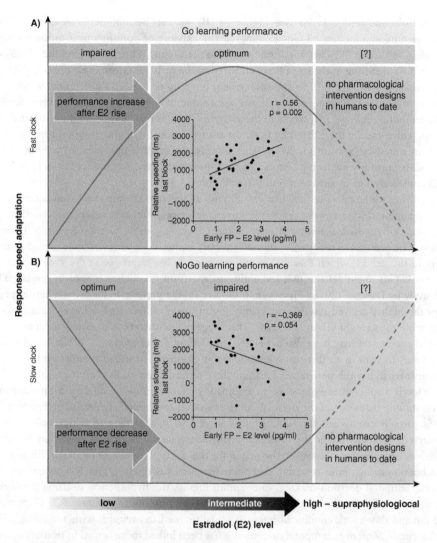

Figure 24.3 Non-linear relationship between preference during temporal response adaptation and estradiol in the early FP as a proxy of central dopamine. (A) A higher estradiol level (E2) was associated with better adjustment to fast (Go-learning). (B) A higher estradiol level (E2) predicted the impaired ability to wait for a reward (NoGo-learning). This indicates that natural variations in estradiol may influence dopamine-dependent learning performance from the low to the intermediate range of dopamine. However, to fully understand the hormone-behavior relationship, performance in the clock task should be investigated in the presence of high to supraphysiological estradiol levels (adapted from Diekhof (2015).

estradiol exceeds a certain concentration towards the late FP, this relationship may disappear or could even be reversed, as with the performance-enhancing effect of estradiol. Moreover, when progesterone reaches its maximum in the mid LP, the participant may end up even lower on the inverted U and would express a further reduced Go-learning ability. Interestingly, the latter effect was also demonstrated in a related task when comparing the late FP and mid LP (Diekhof & Ratnayake, 2016; see above). Yet, when comparing the early and late FP using the probabilistic feedback task (see Figure 24.1B), subjects became better at learning from a positive outcome (enhanced Go-learning) at the expense of punishment avoidance (NoGo-learning) in the late FP. This stands in contrast to the finding reported by Diekhof (2015) with reduced Go-learning in the late FP as compared to the early FP. Given these opposing findings, one may speculate that different reinforcement learning tasks have a differential sensitivity to hormone-induced changes in dopamine. For example, in contrast to the probabilistic feedback task, temporal response adaptation in the range of seconds may also depend on internal clock speed, which can be modulated by both variations in dopamine and estradiol level, as well as their interactions (Sandstrom, 2007). Alternatively, the small sample sizes of previous studies and other, currently neglected factors like inter-individual genetic variance could have equally well contributed to inconsistent results (see Figure 24.3).

Evidence for an effect of follicular estradiol on an inverted U-shaped relation between baseline dopamine, this time in the prefrontal cortex, and reward valuation emerged in another study that used a hypothetical temporal discounting paradigm (Smith, Sierra, Oppler, & Boettiger, 2014). The preference for smaller immediate over higher delayed rewards decreased from the early to the late FP, which means that subjects became less impulsive in the state of increased estradiol. This resembles the reduced ability to speed up for higher reward in the late FP in the study by Diekhof (2015). However, in the late FP, the preference for the smaller immediate over the higher delayed reward was mainly found in individuals with a lower frontal baseline dopamine capacity (Smith et al., 2014). This suggests that the effect of estradiol on immediate reward preferences may have also depended on baseline dopamine levels. While low dopamine levels may increase with increasing estradiol to an optimal performance range on the inverted U-curve regarding the preference for immediate reward, individuals with high baseline dopamine levels would rather experience an attenuating effect of estradiol on their frontal dopamine levels shifting them out of the optimal dopamine range for immediate reward preferences. This result partially contradicts the finding of Diekhof (2015), according to which only early follicular estradiol was predictive of better performance in the fast clock condition in subjects with low impulsiveness. However, the reason for this discrepancy might lie in the different tasks and brain systems under research. Although temporal discounting and RT adaptation both require temporal decision-making, discounting implies the hypothetical decision between an immediate and delayed reward in the range of days to months. In contrast, RT adaptation in the fast and slow clock conditions refers to actual (immediate) rewards with a maximum delay of 5 seconds. Moreover, temporal discounting has been linked to variations in frontal dopamine (Smith & Boettiger, 2012), while RT adaptation may primarily depend on striatal dopamine levels (Moustafa et al., 2008). Nonetheless, these studies on temporal decision-making provided initial evidence for an effect of cycle-dependent variations in estradiol on the inverted U-shaped function of dopamine-related processes (Diekhof, 2015; Reimers, Büchel, & Diekhof, 2014; Smith, Sierra, Oppler, & Boettiger, 2014). Yet, further studies are definitely needed, given the low statistical power of most previous studies (the number of subjects with a verified estradiol rise from early to late FP was below 30 in both Smith et al. (2014) and Diekhof (2015); see also Leeners et al., 2017 for a critical perspective on statistically underpowered results and Table 24.1 for further details on the experimental designs applied previously). Moreover, the many currently unexplored interconnections with other endocrine or genetic agents that may affect dopamine-related processing could have also contributed to inconsistent findings. Overall, the link between estradiol and dopamine in temporal decision-making still remains elusive compared to the well-established animal models for estradiol effects on dopamine-modulated behaviors (e.g., Becker, 1999).

Menstrual cycle dependent modulation of reward anticipation and receipt

Apart from its role in probabilistic feedback learning and temporal decision-making, dopamine has been implicated in the representation of the incentive salience of the reward outcome and – following successful pavlovian conditioning – of reward predictors (Schultz, 1997). Paradigms that dissociated the two phases of reward anticipation and receipt, like the monetary incentive delay task (MID; Knutson & Cooper, 2005), have identified brain regions that were consistently associated with reward prediction (ventral striatum) and/or reward outcome (both medial orbitofrontal cortex and ventral striatum) (Diekhof, Kaps, Falkai, & Gruber, 2012). Taking into account that endogenous estradiol and progesterone should antagonistically modulate striatal dopamine transmission across the menstrual cycle, one would predict a reduced response of the ventral striatum to reward predictors and its receipt during the mid LP, while an increased responsiveness should be expected during the late FP. Unfortunately, neuroimaging studies yielded rather mixed results (see Table 24.1 for details on study designs). Two studies were interested in the processing of food pictures as primary rewards during the late FP compared to the mid LP (Frank, Kim, Krzemien, & van Vugt, 2010) or the early FP (Alonso-Alonso et al., 2011). Frank et al. (2010) found increased follicular food-related activation in the ventral striatum, amygdala and hippocampus. Yet, Alonso-Alonso et al. (2011) were unable to replicate this supposedly estradiol-mediated effect when comparing the late and early FP. Instead, they identified increased activation in the inferior frontal cortex, insula and fusiform gyrus during viewing of food pictures in the late FP, but only when subjects were in the fed state. Another four studies assessed monetary reward anticipation and outcome processing using modified versions of the MID or a simple gambling task, either by comparing the (early) FP and mid LP (Bayer, Bandurski, & Sommer, 2013; Bonenberger et al., 2013; Dreher et al., 2007) or the late FP and late LP (Ossewaarde et al., 2011). Dreher et al. (2007) observed enhanced reward-related activation in several structures of the mesolimbic dopamine system, except for the ventral striatum, in the FP relative to the mid LP when subjects anticipated or received a reward after using a simple slot machine. These included the amygdala and orbitofrontal cortex during expectancy of uncertain reward, while reward delivery was accompanied by increased activation of the amygdala, mesencephalon, caudate nuclei and inferior frontal cortex. Dreher and colleagues (2007) also reported positive correlations between follicular estradiol and anticipatory activation in the amygdala and hippocampus, while the correlations found during the mid LP worked in opposite directions for estradiol and progesterone. There was a positive correlation between estradiol and activation of the amygdala and orbitofrontal cortex, and a negative correlation between estradiol and frontal regions and the ACC, while the correlation pattern was reversed for progesterone, again underscoring the opposite effects of these hormones on central dopamine function. Contrary to these findings, Ossewaarde et al. (2011) were unable to identify an enhanced follicular response of mesolimbic activation in the MID. In this version of the MID, the participants were confronted with predictors of potential reward or non-reward (i.e., cues). Following cue-offset, they were required to respond to a target stimulus as fast as possible irrespective of cue type. When the target was hit and the cue indicated a potential reward, subjects received one Euro. Ossewaarde et al. (2011) reported a significant rise in striatal activation during reward anticipation when subjects were in the very late LP (i.e., the premenstrual phase). Ossewaarde et al. (2011) proposed that this finding, which was also related to premenstrual symptom severity, might result from a hormone withdrawal-like state caused by the rather abrupt reduction in hormone level towards the end of the cycle. This could have in turn increased the sensitivity for predictors of reward, an effect often observed during drug withdrawal in substance abuse. Yet, since Ossewaarde et al. (2011) only measured the concentration of the progesterone metabolite allopregnanolone, which was significantly enhanced premenstrually as compared to the FP, this interpretation remains speculative until further replication. Adding to these inconsistent findings, Bayer et al. (2013) compared the early FP with the mid LP using a modified MID that incorporated both potential gains and losses of varying magnitudes. They found increased activation of the ACC and ventral striatum during anticipation of high losses, but in the early FP that was characterized by low estradiol and progesterone. In contrast, no phase-related change in reward processing (during neither anticipation nor outcome processing) could be observed in these brain regions. Instead, the medial orbitofrontal cortex showed a reduced responsiveness to anticipation of low as opposed to high gains in the early FP. Bonenberger et al. (2013) used a version of the MID with different reward probabilities and assessed the effect of hormonal contraception on reward anticipation by comparing hormonal contraception users during the intake phase with naturally cycling women. The latter group was tested twice in the early FP and mid LP. Bonenberger et al. (2013) found that reward-related processing remained widely unaffected by hormonal state and treatment and observed no cycle-dependent differences in brain activation. In fact, only one region at the intersection of the anterior insular and the inferior frontal cortex showed enhanced activation during reward expectation in hormonal contraception users in comparison to women during the early FP.

Taken together, previous studies on reward processing *per se* demonstrated the hormonal modulation of activation in regions of the meso- and corticolimbic dopamine system (ventral striatum, ACC, orbitofrontal cortex, amygdala), but not always in the expected direction. This may be related to study specifics like slight variations in experimental designs used (e.g., different versions of the MID or the comparison of slightly different cycle phases), limitations in sample size (see Table 24.1), or other currently undetermined noise parameters (e.g., genetic variation, circadian rhythms) that were not controlled for. Since none of these previous studies assed the association between cycle-related estradiol concentration, brain activation, and the dopaminergic baseline, we are further unable to rule out that the model of the inverted U-shape may have reconciled some of these apparent inconsistencies.

Testosterone and reward processing in general

Similar to estradiol, the androgen testosterone and its androgenic metabolites may act as intrinsic dopamine agonists and may have rewarding properties by themselves (Wood, 2004). In the rodent model, it has been demonstrated that testosterone may change the concentration of dopamine receptors, transporters and the enzymes involved in dopamine degradation through activation of a positive feedback loop via action at androgen receptors. Similar to estradiol, increased testosterone may thereby support DRD1-mediated processing at the expense of a reduced sensitivity of DRD2 (e.g., Kindlundh, Lindblom, & Nyberg, 2003), and both effects combined may shift the balance towards an increased reward processing capacity. Human evidence supports this assumption, at least in tasks using secondary reinforcers like monetary reward, positive feedback or points earned. In young women, exogenous testosterone was perceived as rewarding and promoted activation in the ventral striatum during reward anticipation in the MID (Hermans et al., 2010). In addition, testosterone may shift attention towards the rewarding properties of a stimulus and may increase reward-related risk-taking of women in the IOWA gambling task (van Honk et al., 2004). In young men, endogenous testosterone showed a positive correlation with the reward-related prediction error in the ventral striatum (Morris et al., 2015), as did testosterone levels in male and female adolescents during performance of a gambling task that included rewards and losses (Op de Macks et al., 2011). Additionally, endogenous testosterone in young men also showed a positive correlation with the ability to shift responding after a reversal of the reward-outcome association and allowed them to more flexibly adapt behavior to the new reward contingency (Diekhof & Kraft, 2017). Interestingly, this latter relationship was particularly pronounced when working memory demands were high and several reward contingencies had to be updated at the same time, suggesting a testosterone-related modulation of prefrontal capacity rather than reward prediction ability *per se*.

In sum, these studies provide preliminary evidence that endogenous testosterone may enhance reward sensitivity of the male ventral striatum. In women, exogenous testosterone may have comparable effects on reward prediction. Yet, the data are limited to a few, currently unreplicated studies, and conclusions were mostly drawn from small samples (e.g., 12 women in van Honk et al., 2004 and Hermans et al., 2010). Further, the role of endogenous testosterone has not been assessed in adult women. Therefore, future evidence is needed to enable solid inferences. In the next section, we will focus on a rather different line of studies that has demonstrated an interaction between endogenous testosterone and the peptide hormone oxytocin in the processing of the naturally rewarding properties of infant faces.

A special case for testosterone and oxytocin in the processing of the baby schema as a natural reinforcer

Attentional processing of biologically salient information, like potential threat or naturally rewarding stimuli, depends on its relevance for survival and reproduction. Apart from finding suitable mating partners, in mammals nurturing behavior is vital for reproductive success. This could explain why special reward-related information is represented by the infant's face, characterized as the 'baby schema'. Big eyes, a small mouth and nose, chubby cheeks, a round face and a large forehead form this key stimulus (Lorenz, 1943). The baby schema increases attention and promotes caretaking behavior in adults (Luo et al., 2015; Saltzman & Maestripieri, 2011). Simple viewing of infant faces elicits activation in the reward system [for review see (Kringelbach, Stark, Alexander, Bornstein, & Stein, 2016)], independent of species and, in humans, ethnicity (Golle, Probst, Mast, & Lobmaier, 2015). In that way, the baby schema may be considered a salient rewarding stimulus that acts as a natural reinforcer of nurturing behavior. Glocker et al. (2009) tested young women while viewing pictures of babies with a manipulated baby schema. Baby schema varied from low (reduced infant features) to neutral (unmanipulated infant faces) to high (exaggerated infant features). They found that activity in the ventral striatum increased with increasing baby schema. Other studies confirmed this finding and underscore the involvement of dopamine and the reward system in the processing of the baby schema (Wigton et al., 2015).

Moreover, individual sensitivity to the baby schema may also be influenced by different interacting hormones and neurotransmitters (Luo et al., 2015), and an imbalance in the relevant neuroendocrine interactions can affect nurturing behavior and parental attachment (Strathearn, 2011). The neuropeptide oxytocin has been implicated in maternal behavior (Wigton et al., 2015). It plays a major role in the induction of labor and lactation and is crucial for mother–infant bonding (Kendrick, 2000). Gregory et al. (2015) demonstrated that oxytocin administration in women increased activation of the ventral tegmental area, the origin of dopamine neurons (Oades & Halliday, 1987), in response to infant stimuli. Projections of the dopamine neurons form the mesocorticolimbic pathway that responds to motivationally relevant stimuli, whereas projections of oxytocin (originating from the paraventricular nucleus) are sent to regions of the mesocorticolimbic pathway, including the ventral tegmental area, influencing reactions to social salient stimuli (Love, 2014). Therefore, it is well conceivable that dopamine-induced motivation evokes oxytocin-induced reactions to social stimuli. Since oxytocin receptors were found in several dopamine-rich regions (for example substantia nigra, globus pallidus and preoptic area in humans), it seems probable that oxytocin and dopamine may interact and influence attachment through mesocorticolimbic pathways that are associated with processing of reward (Insel & Young, 2001). Atzil et al. (2017) investigated the role of dopamine in human mothers' bonding behavior using combined MRI–PET measurement. A stronger intrinsic connectivity of the medial amygdala network (synchronous firing of the network regions) as response to

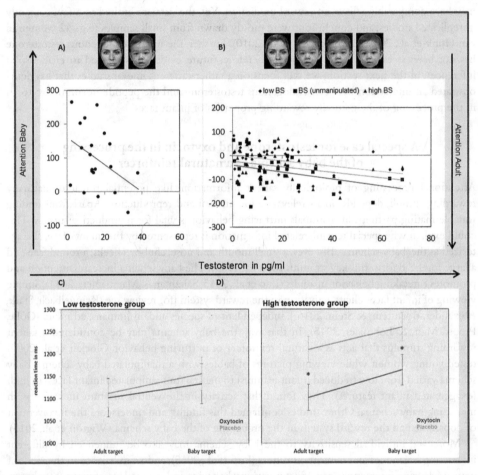

Figure 24.4 The negative effect of high testosterone on selective attention to human infants in women is compensated by oxytocin administration. Selective attention to faces representing the baby schema was calculated by subtracting the low distracting condition (baby target with adults distractors) from the high distracting condition (adult target with infant distractors). More positive values indicate increased attention to the baby schema. A negative correlation of testosterone and selective attention to infants was found both when using (A) unmanipulated stimuli and (B) a parametric variation of the baby schema. (C) and (D) display the mean reaction times to select a biologically salient target amongst distractors as a function of baseline testosterone and oxytocin versus placebo. Oxytocin thereby counteracts the negative effects of high baseline testosterone and supports rapid selection of a pop-out stimulus that could be either an adult or an infant target among distractors.

Data used from Holtfrerich et al. (2016).

the mothers' infants was positively associated with an increase of dopamine, but a decrease of plasma oxytocin. Although animal models also show involvement of the medial amygdala in maternal aggression (Haller, 2018), there is evidence that dopamine facilitates maternal behavior in rodents by acting on the medial preoptic area, which is included in the medial amygdala network (Stolzenberg et al., 2007). Yet, a trend for a positive correlation between plasma oxytocin and dopamine in the left ventral striatum could also be observed by Atzil et al. (2017). Unlike oxytocin, high endogenous testosterone in females seems to antagonize aspects of nurturing behavior that may be linked to the rewarding properties of the baby schema (e.g., the reflexive enhancement of selective attention to the baby schema). For instance, female rats treated with testosterone 4 days after birth showed reduced adult maternal behavior during interactions with their own offspring (Quadagno & Rockwell, 1972). Holtfrerich et al. (2016) found a negative correlation between the attention to infant faces and the habitual testosterone concentration of nulliparous women. Most notably, oxytocin treatment reduced this attentional deficit in women with high testosterone concentrations, but left women with low testosterone, whose attention was already directed towards the infants, unaffected (Figure 24.4). Considering this, it might be adaptive that the endogenous testosterone concentration decreases in parents of young children (Gettler, McDade, Feranil, & Kuzawa, 2011) as well as in mothers shortly after childbirth (Wynne-Edwards, 2001), which should in turn increase parental investment. Given the contrasting influence of testosterone and oxytocin on processing of the baby schema in women, both hormones can yet also promote the protection of the offspring against potential threat, especially in fathers (Rickenbacher, Perry, Sullivan, & Moita, 2017; Rilling & Young, 2014). Thus, a positive interaction of both hormones in the modulation of parental behavior is also possible. A study by Weisman and colleagues (2014) observed that lower baseline testosterone in fathers was positively correlated with paternal behavior. Yet, a greater increase in testosterone after oxytocin administration was also associated with increased paternal investment. Based on this, it was presumed that the transiently enhanced testosterone might have interacted with the male reward system to promote caretaking behavior. Consequently, fathers with a greater increase in testosterone might have received greater reward from father–infant interactions. Interestingly, behaviors like positive arousal, touch, social gaze and vocal synchrony with the infant also increased through oxytocin administration, supporting this claim. Nevertheless, it is likely that testosterone and oxytocin interactions play an important role in the intensity of social bonds in general, and nurturing behavior in particular, and that they exert paradox effects on the promotion of nurturing behavior (for more details see the Steroid/Peptide Framework of Social Bonds from van Anders, Goldey, & Kuo (2011)).

Conclusion and future directions

This review of studies from the field of reward processing and reinforcement learning demonstrated that the steroid hormones estradiol, progesterone and testosterone may significantly affect reward-related behaviors by modulating neural activation in structures of the mesolimbic dopamine system of the human brain. Collectively, previous studies formed a more or less conclusive yet quite complex picture of steroid action on human reward processing (e.g., suggesting an inverted U-shaped relationship in some cases), which might offer a good starting point for future studies to further disentangle the relation of these hormones with other systems also implicated in reward processing and reinforcement learning (e.g., the serotonin system). Through their antagonistic action on dopamine transmission, cycle-dependent variations in estradiol and progesterone may modulate reinforcement learning capacity by shifting the balance between Go- and NoGo-learning during probabilistic feedback learning or temporal response adaptation. Estradiol and progesterone may also influence the anticipation and valuation of reward receipt, yet current evidence appears to be less consistent. Research on the effects of (endogenous) testosterone in the human reward system was in line with its proposed dopamine-agonistic properties. Intervention studies with women and studies assessing endogenous testosterone in men pointed towards a relationship between increased testosterone and enhanced reward-related responses during the anticipation or receipt of secondary reinforcers like money. In contrast to that, higher endogenous testosterone levels in nulliparous women might have an attenuating effect on aspects of nurturing behavior that involve the reward system (e.g., the prioritization of attention to the baby schema). In that particular context, it has been assumed that higher endogenous testosterone may reduce the rewarding properties of the key stimulus 'baby schema' at the expense of other socially salient stimuli like adult faces that also have a high subjective relevance (e.g., as potential mating partners). Interestingly, this negative effect of testosterone on the baby schema, presumably a primary reinforcer, was counteracted by administration of the neuropeptide oxytocin, which was found to enhance activation of the ventral striatum during processing of infant faces.

What needs to be further taken into account in future research is that previous results were not always consistent. This was the case despite comparable experimental approaches (e.g., use of similar paradigms or assessment of similar cycle phases), which strongly suggests other, currently neglected physiological factors. Individual predispositions may be one such factor that may significantly interact with hormonal variations. For instance, hormone–genotype interactions have already been described in other cognitive domains (Jacobs & D'Esposito, 2011) and may certainly contribute to inter-individual differences in reward processing. Moreover, organizational effects of hormones on the developing brain could already predispose the individual to a different susceptibility for the activational hormonal effects in later life. Also, estradiol and progesterone may not only affect one isolated system such as the dopamine system but could also exert complex effects in the different intertwined emotional systems of the brain (LeDoux, 2012). Most importantly, the majority of studies published so far have only tested small samples (less than 30 persons) and very often independent replication studies with larger samples are lacking. This could have led to false-positive reporting or null-results (see Leeners et al., 2017). Future studies should therefore assess possible hormone–genotype interactions in the reward system in more detail and, most importantly, in bigger samples. This could either be done by using well-established polymorphisms implicated in dopamine transmission or by employing whole-genome approaches to identify new candidate genes.

This chapter focused on the fundamental reward-related processes in the healthy human brain. Nevertheless, research in the field of psychiatric disorders might also benefit from a closer look at the role of hormones in the etiology of disorders of the reward system as well as their impact in relation to therapeutic outcome. For example, late-onset schizophrenia and Parkinson's disease in women have been hypothesized to be partially related to the sudden drop in estradiol availability after menopause (Häfner, Hambrecht, Löffler, Munk-Jørgensen, & Riecher-Rössler, 1998; Labandeira-Garcia, Rodriguez-Perez, Valenzuela, Costa-Besada, & Guerra, 2016), while estradiol-treatment may counteract psychotic symptoms in this phase (Brzezinski, Brzezinski-Sinai, & Seeman, 2017). Further, during the FP the risk of relapse in substance dependency is enhanced, particularly for drugs that strongly affect the dopamine system (e.g., cocaine), and female substance abusers reported higher pleasure during drug intake and used higher doses in the FP compared to the LP (Terner & de Wit, 2006). In a similar vein, with the onset of puberty the activational effects of (fluctuating) estradiol may represent a developmental vulnerability for drug abuse and dependency in girls (see Kuhn et al., 2010, for review). These findings suggest an important involvement of steroid hormones in the reinstatement and maintenance of female drug addiction, which may probably contribute to sex differences in the neural mechanisms mediating addiction (Becker, Perry, & Westenbroek, 2012). Considering inter- and intra-individual hormonal variation in therapeutic approaches could therefore be another important step towards a more effective, individualized medicine.

References

Alonso-Alonso, M., Ziemke, F., Magkos, F., Barrios, F. A., Brinkoetter, M., Boyd, I., . . . Mantzoros, C. S. (2011). Brain responses to food images during the early and late follicular phase of the menstrual cycle in healthy young women: Relation to fasting and feeding. *American Journal of Clinical Nutrition, 94*(2), 377–384. https://doi.org/10.3945/ajcn.110.010736

Atzil, S., Touroutoglou, A., Rudy, T., Salcedo, S., Feldman, R., Hooker, J. M., . . . Barrett, L. F. (2017). Dopamine in the medial amygdala network mediates human bonding. *Proceedings of the National Academy of Sciences, 114*(9), 2361–2366. https://doi.org/10.1073/pnas.1612233114

Bayer, J., Bandurski, P., & Sommer, T. (2013). Differential modulation of activity related to the anticipation of monetary gains and losses across the menstrual cycle. *European Journal of Neuroscience, 38*(10), 3519–3526. https://doi.org/10.1111/ejn.12347

Becker, J. B. (1999). Gender Differences in dopaminergic function in striatum and nucleus accumbens. *Pharmacology Biochemistry and Behavior, 64*(4), 803–812. https://doi.org/10.1016/S0091-3057(99)00168-9

Becker, J. B., Perry, A. N., & Westenbroek, C. (2012). Sex differences in the neural mechanisms mediating addiction: A new synthesis and hypothesis. *Biology of Sex Differences, 3*(1), 14. https://doi.org/10.1186/2042-6410-3-14

Bonenberger, M., Groschwitz, R. C., Kumpfmueller, D., Groen, G., Plener, P. L., & Abler, B. (2013). It's all about money: Oral contraception alters neural reward processing. *Neuroreport, 24*(17), 951–955. https://doi.org/10.1097/WNR.0000000000000024

Brass, M., Derrfuss, J., Forstmann, B., & von Cramon, D. Y. (2005). The role of the inferior frontal junction area in cognitive control. *Trends in Cognitive Sciences, 9*(7), 314–316. https://doi.org/10.1016/J.TICS.2005.05.001

Bromberg-Martin, E. S., Matsumoto, M., & Hikosaka, O. (2010). Dopamine in motivational control: Rewarding, aversive, and alerting. *Neuron, 68*(5), 815–834. https://doi.org/10.1016/j.neuron.2010.11.022

Brzezinski, A., Brzezinski-Sinai, N. A., & Seeman, M. V. (2017). Treating schizophrenia during menopause. *Menopause, 24*(5), 582–588. https://doi.org/10.1097/GME.0000000000000772

Buckholtz, J. W., Treadway, M. T., Cowan, R. L., Woodward, N. D., Li, R., Ansari, M. S., . . . Zald, D. H. (2010). Dopaminergic network differences in human impulsivity. *Science, 329*(5991), 532–532. https://doi.org/10.1126/science.1185778

Cools, R. (2008). Role of dopamine in the motivational and cognitive control of behavior. *The Neuroscientist, 14*(4), 381–395. https://doi.org/10.1177/1073858408317009

Diekhof, E. K. (2015). Be quick about it: Endogenous estradiol level, menstrual cycle phase and trait impulsiveness predict impulsive choice in the context of reward acquisition. *Hormones and Behavior, 74*, 186–193. https://doi.org/10.1016/j.yhbeh.2015.06.001

Diekhof, E. K., Kaps, L., Falkai, P., & Gruber, O. (2012). The role of the human ventral striatum and the medial orbitofrontal cortex in the representation of reward magnitude – an activation likelihood estimation meta-analysis of neuroimaging studies of passive reward expectancy and outcome processing. *Neuropsychologia, 50*(7), 1252–1266. https://doi.org/10.1016/j.neuropsychologia.2012.02.007

Diekhof, E. K., & Kraft, S. (2017). The association between endogenous testosterone level and behavioral flexibility in young men – evidence from stimulus-outcome reversal learning. *Hormones and Behavior, 89*, 193–200. https://doi.org/10.1016/j.yhbeh.2017.02.006

Diekhof, E. K., & Ratnayake, M. (2016). Menstrual cycle phase modulates reward sensitivity and performance monitoring in young women: Preliminary fMRI evidence. *Neuropsychologia, 84*, 70–80. https://doi.org/10.1016/j.neuropsychologia.2015.10.016

Dreher, J-C., Schmidt, P. J., Kohn, P., Furman, D., Rubinow, D., & Berman, K. F. (2007). Menstrual cycle phase modulates reward-related neural function in women. *Proceedings of the National Academy of Sciences of the United States of America, 104*(7), 2465–2470. https://doi.org/10.1073/pnas.0605569104

Forbes, E. E., Brown, S. M., Kimak, M., Ferrell, R. E., Manuck, S. B., & Hariri, A. R. (2009). Genetic variation in components of dopamine neurotransmission impacts ventral striatal reactivity associated with impulsivity. *Molecular Psychiatry, 14*(1), 60–70. https://doi.org/10.1038/sj.mp.4002086

Frank, M. J., Seeberger, L. C., & O'Reilly, R. C. (2004). By Carrot or by Stick: Cognitive Reinforcement Learning in Parkinsonism. *Science, 306*(5703), 1940–1943. https://doi.org/10.1126/science.110 2941

Frank, T. C., Kim, G. L., Krzemien, A., & van Vugt, D. A. (2010). Effect of menstrual cycle phase on corticolimbic brain activation by visual food cues. *Brain Research, 1363*, 81–92. https://doi.org/10.1016/j. brainres.2010.09.071

Gettler, L. T., McDade, T. W., Feranil, A. B., & Kuzawa, C. W. (2011). Longitudinal evidence that fatherhood decreases testosterone in human males. *Proceedings of the National Academy of Sciences, 108*(39), 16194–16199. https://doi.org/10.1073/pnas.1105403108

Gillies, G. E., & McArthur, S. (2010). Estrogen actions in the brain and the basis for differential action in men and women: A case for sex-specific medicines. *Pharmacological Reviews, 62*(2), 155–198. https:// doi.org/10.1124/pr.109.002071

Glocker, M. L., Langleben, D. D., Ruparel, K., Loughead, J. W., Valdez, J. N., Griffin, M. D., . . . Gur, R. C. (2009). Baby schema modulates the brain reward system in nulliparous women. *Proceedings of the National Academy of Sciences, 106*(22), 9115–9119. https://doi.org/10.1073/pnas.0811620106

Golle, J., Probst, F., Mast, F. W., & Lobmaier, J. S. (2015). Preference for cute infants does not depend on their ethnicity or species: Evidence from hypothetical adoption and donation paradigms. *PLoS One, 10*(4), 1–19. https://doi.org/10.1371/journal.pone.0121554

Grabenhorst, F., & Rolls, E. T. (2011). Value, pleasure and choice in the ventral prefrontal cortex. *Trends in Cognitive Sciences, 15*(2), 56–67. https://doi.org/10.1016/j.tics.2010.12.004

Gregory, R., Cheng, H., Rupp, H. A., Sengelaub, D. R., & Heiman, J. R. (2015). Oxytocin increases VTA activation to infant and sexual stimuli in nulliparous and postpartum women. *Hormones and Behavior, 69*, 82–88. https://doi.org/10.1016/j.yhbeh.2014.12.009

Häfner, H., Hambrecht, M., Löffler, W., Munk-Jørgensen, P., & Riecher-Rössler, A. (1998). Is schizophrenia a disorder of all ages? A comparison of first episodes and early course across the life-cycle. *Psychological Medicine, 28*(2), 351–365. Retrieved from www.ncbi.nlm.nih.gov/pubmed/9572092

Haller, J. (2018). The role of central and medial amygdala in normal and abnormal aggression: A review of classical approaches. *Neuroscience and Biobehavioral Reviews, 85*, 34–43. https://doi.org/10.1016/j. neubiorev.2017.09.017

Hermans, E. J., Bos, P. A., Ossewaarde, L., Ramsey, N. F., Fernández, G., & van Honk, J. (2010). Effects of exogenous testosterone on the ventral striatal BOLD response during reward anticipation in healthy women. *NeuroImage, 52*(1), 277–283. https://doi.org/10.1016/j.neuroimage.2010.04.019

Holtfrerich, S. K. C., Schwarz, K. A., Sprenger, C., Reimers, L., & Diekhof, E. K. (2016). Endogenous testosterone and exogenous oxytocin modulate attentional processing of infant faces. *PLoS One, 11*(11), 1–19. https://doi.org/10.1371/journal.pone.0166617

Hu, M., & Becker, J. B. (2008). Acquisition of cocaine self-administration in ovariectomized female rats: Effect of estradiol dose or chronic estradiol administration. *Drug and Alcohol Dependence, 94*(1–3), 56–62. https://doi.org/10.1016/j.drugalcdep.2007.10.005

Insel, T. R., & Young, L. J. (2001). The neurobiology of attachment. *Nature Neuroscience, 2*, 129–136. Retrieved from www.nature.com/nrn/journal/v2/n2/pdf/nrn0201_129a.pdf

Jacobs, E., & D'Esposito, M. (2011). Estrogen shapes dopamine-dependent cognitive processes: Implications for women's health. *Journal of Neuroscience, 31*(14), 5286–5293. https://doi.org/10.1523/ JNEUROSCI.6394-10.2011

Jocham, G., Klein, T. A., & Ullsperger, M. (2011). Dopamine-mediated reinforcement learning signals in the striatum and ventromedial prefrontal cortex underlie value-based choices. *Journal of Neuroscience, 31*(5), 1606–1613. https://doi.org/10.1523/JNEUROSCI.3904-10.2011

Kendrick, K. M. (2000). Oxytocin, motherhood and bonding. *Experimental Physiology, 85 Spec No*, 111S–124S. Retrieved from www.ncbi.nlm.nih.gov/pubmed/10795913

Kindlundh, A. M. S., Lindblom, J., & Nyberg, F. (2003). Chronic administration with nandrolone decanoate induces alterations in the gene-transcript content of dopamine D(1)- and D(2)-receptors in the rat brain. *Brain Research, 979*(1–2), 37–42. Retrieved from www.ncbi.nlm.nih.gov/pubmed/12850568

Klein, T. A., Neumann, J., Reuter, M., Hennig, J., von Cramon, D. Y., & Ullsperger, M. (2007). Genetically determined differences in learning from errors. *Science, 318*(5856), 1642–1645. https://doi. org/10.1126/science.1145044

Knutson, B., & Cooper, J. C. (2005). Functional magnetic resonance imaging of reward prediction. *Current Opinion in Neurology, 18*(4), 411–417. Retrieved from www.ncbi.nlm.nih.gov/pubmed/160 03117

Kringelbach, M. L., Stark, E. A., Alexander, C., Bornstein, M. H., & Stein, A. (2016). Julio'16: Cuteness: Unlocking the parental brain and beyond. *Trends in Cognitive Sciences, 20*(7), 545–558.

Kuhn, C., Johnson, M., Thomae, A., Luo, B., Simon, S. A., Zhou, G., & Walker, Q. D. (2010). The emergence of gonadal hormone influences on dopaminergic function during puberty. *Hormones and Behavior, 58*(1), 122–137. https://doi.org/10.1016/j.yhbeh.2009.10.015

Labandeira-Garcia, J. L., Rodriguez-Perez, A. I., Valenzuela, R., Costa-Besada, M. A., & Guerra, M. J. (2016). Menopause and Parkinson's disease: Interaction between estrogens and brain renin-angiotensin system in dopaminergic degeneration. *Frontiers in Neuroendocrinology, 43*, 44–59. https://doi.org/10.1016/j.yfrne.2016.09.003

LeDoux, J. (2012). Rethinking the emotional brain. *Neuron, 73*(4), 653–676. https://doi.org/10.1016/J.NEURON.2012.02.004

Leeners, B., Kruger, T. H. C., Geraedts, K., Tronci, E., Mancini, T., Ille, F., . . . Hengartner, M. P. (2017). Lack of associations between female hormone levels and visuospatial working memory, divided attention and cognitive bias across two consecutive menstrual cycles. *Frontiers in Behavioral Neuroscience, 11*, 120. https://doi.org/10.3389/fnbeh.2017.00120

Lévesque, D., & Di Paolo, T. (1988). Rapid conversion of high into low striatal D2-dopamine receptor agonist binding states after an acute physiological dose of 17 beta-estradiol. *Neuroscience Letters, 88*(1), 113–118. Retrieved from www.ncbi.nlm.nih.gov/pubmed/2969467

Lorenz, K. (1943). Die angeborenen Formen möglicher Erfahrung. *Zeitschrift Für Tierpsychologie, 5*(2), 235–409. https://doi.org/10.1111/j.1439-0310.1943.tb00655.x

Love, T. M. (2014). Oxytocin, motivation and the role of dopamine. *Pharmacology Biochemistry and Behavior, 119*, 49–60. https://doi.org/10.1016/j.pbb.2013.06.011

Luo, L., Ma, X., Zheng, X., Zhao, W., Xu, L., Becker, B., & Kendrick, K. M. (2015, July). Neural systems and hormones mediating attraction to infant and child faces. *Frontiers in Psychology, 6*, 1–22. https://doi.org/10.3389/fpsyg.2015.00970

Maia, T. V., & Frank, M. J. (2011). From reinforcement learning models to psychiatric and neurological disorders. *Nature Neuroscience, 14*(2), 154–162. https://doi.org/10.1038/nn.2723

McClure, S. M., Laibson, D. I., Loewenstein, G., & Cohen, J. D. (2004). Separate neural systems value immediate and delayed monetary rewards. *Science, 306*(5695), 503–507. https://doi.org/10.1126/science.1100907

Morris, R. W., Purves-Tyson, T. D., Weickert, C. S., Rothmond, D., Lenroot, R., & Weickert, T. W. (2015). Testosterone and reward prediction-errors in healthy men and men with schizophrenia. *Schizophrenia Research, 168*(3), 649–660. https://doi.org/10.1016/j.schres.2015.06.030

Motzo, C., Porceddu, M. L., Maira, G., Flore, G., Concas, A., Dazzi, L., & Biggio, G. (1996). Inhibition of basal and stress-induced dopamine release in the cerebral cortex and nucleus accumbens of freely moving rats by the neurosteroid allopregnanolone. *Journal of Psychopharmacology, 10*(4), 266–272. https://doi.org/10.1177/026988119601000402

Moustafa, A. A., Cohen, M. X., Sherman, S. J., & Frank, M. J. (2008). A role for dopamine in temporal decision making and reward maximization in parkinsonism. *Journal of Neuroscience, 28*(47), 12294–12304. https://doi.org/10.1523/JNEUROSCI.3116-08.2008

Oades, R. D., & Halliday, G. M. (1987). Ventral tegmental (A10) system: Neurobiology. 1. Anatomy and connectivity. *Brain Research Reviews, 12*(2), 117–165. https://doi.org/10.1016/0165-0173(87)90011-7

Op de Macks, Z. A., Moor, B. G., Overgaauw, S., Güroğlu, B., Dahl, R. E., & Crone, E. A. (2011). Testosterone levels correspond with increased ventral striatum activation in response to monetary rewards in adolescents. *Developmental Cognitive Neuroscience, 1*(4), 506–516. https://doi.org/10.1016/j.dcn.2011.06.003

Ossewaarde, L., van Wingen, G. A., Kooijman, S. C., Bäckström, T., Fernández, G., & Hermans, E. J. (2011). Changes in functioning of mesolimbic incentive processing circuits during the premenstrual phase. *Social Cognitive and Affective Neuroscience, 6*(5), 612–620. https://doi.org/10.1093/scan/nsq071

Patton, J. H., Stanford, M. S., & Barratt, E. S. (1995). Factor structure of the Barratt Impulsiveness Scale. *Journal of Clinical Psychology*, 51, 768–774.

Pasqualini, C., Olivier, V., Guibert, B., Frain, O., & Leviel, V. (1995). Acute stimulatory effect of estradiol on striatal dopamine synthesis. *Journal of Neurochemistry, 65*(4), 1651–1657. Retrieved from www.ncbi.nlm.nih.gov/pubmed/7561861

Quadagno, D. M., & Rockwell, J. (1972). The effect of gonadal hormones in infancy on maternal behavior in the adult rat. *Hormones and Behavior, 3*(1), 55–62. Retrieved from www.ncbi.nlm.nih.gov/pubmed/4680507

Reimers, L., Büchel, C., & Diekhof, E. K. (2014, December). How to be patient: The ability to wait for a reward depends on menstrual cycle phase and feedback-related activity. *Frontiers in Neuroscience, 8,* 401. https://doi.org/10.3389/fnins.2014.00401

Rickenbacher, E., Perry, R. E., Sullivan, R. M., & Moita, M. A. (2017). Freezing suppression by oxytocin in central amygdala allows alternate defensive behaviours and mother-pup interactions. *eLife, 6,* 1–17. https://doi.org/10.7554/eLife.24080

Ridderinkhof, K. R., Ullsperger, M., Crone, E. A., & Nieuwenhuis, S. (2004). The role of the medial frontal cortex in cognitive control. *Science, 306*(5695), 443–447. https://doi.org/10.1126/science.1100301

Rilling, J. K., & Young, L. J. (2014). The biology of mammalian parenting and its effect on offspring social development. *Science (New York, N.Y.), 345*(6198), 771–776. https://doi.org/10.1126/science.1252723

Sakaki, M., & Mather, M. (2012). How reward and emotional stimuli induce different reactions across the menstrual cycle. *Social and Personality Psychology Compass, 6*(1), 1–17. https://doi.org/10.1111/j.1751-9004.2011.00415.x

Saltzman, W., & Maestripieri, D. (2011). The neuroendocrinology of primate maternal behavior. *Progress in Neuro-Psychopharmacology and Biological Psychiatry, 35*(5), 1192–1204. https://doi.org/10.1016/j.pnpbp.2010.09.017

Sandstrom, N. J. (2007). Estradiol modulation of the speed of an internal clock. *Behavioral Neuroscience, 121*(2), 422–432. https://doi.org/10.1037/0735-7044.121.2.422

Schultz, W. (1997). Dopamine neurons and their role in reward mechanisms. *Current Opinion in Neurobiology, 7*(2), 191–197. Retrieved from www.ncbi.nlm.nih.gov/pubmed/9142754

Smith, C. T., & Boettiger, C. A. (2012). Age modulates the effect of COMT genotype on delay discounting behavior. *Psychopharmacology, 222*(4), 609–617. https://doi.org/10.1007/s00213-012-2653-9

Smith, C. T., Sierra, Y., Oppler, S. H., & Boettiger, C. A. (2014). Ovarian cycle effects on immediate reward selection bias in humans: A role for estradiol. *The Journal of Neuroscience : The Official Journal of the Society for Neuroscience, 34*(16), 5468–5476. https://doi.org/10.1523/JNEUROSCI.0014-14.2014

Stolzenberg, D. S., McKenna, J. B., Keough, S., Hancock, R., Numan, M. J., & Numan, M. (2007). Dopamine D_1 receptor stimulation of the nucleus accumbens or the medial preoptic area promotes the onset of maternal behavior in pregnancy-terminated rats. *Behavioral Neuroscience, 121*(5), 907–919. https://doi.org/10.1037/0735-7044.121.5.907

Strathearn, L. (2011). Maternal neglect: Oxytocin, dopamine and the neurobiology of attachment. *Journal of Neuroendocrinology, 23*(11), 1054–1065. https://doi.org/10.1111/j.1365-2826.2011.02228.x

Terner, J. M., & de Wit, H. (2006). Menstrual cycle phase and responses to drugs of abuse in humans. *Drug and Alcohol Dependence, 84*(1), 1–13. https://doi.org/10.1016/j.drugalcdep.2005.12.007

Van Anders, S. M., Goldey, K. L., & Kuo, P. X. (2011). The steroid/peptide theory of social bonds: Integrating testosterone and peptide responses for classifying social behavioral contexts. *Psychoneuroendocrinology, 36*(9), 1265–1275. https://doi.org/10.1016/j.psyneuen.2011.06.001

van Honk, J., Schutter, D. J. L. G., Hermans, E. J., Putman, P., Tuiten, A., & Koppeschaar, H. (2004). Testosterone shifts the balance between sensitivity for punishment and reward in healthy young women. *Psychoneuroendocrinology, 29*(7), 937–943. https://doi.org/10.1016/j.psyneuen.2003.08.007

Weisman, O., Zagoory-Sharon, O., & Feldman, R. (2014). Progress in neuro-psychopharmacology & biological psychiatry oxytocin administration, salivary testosterone, and father – infant social behavior. *Progress in Neuropsychopharmacology & Biological Psychiatry, 49,* 47–52. https://doi.org/10.1016/j.pnpbp.2013.11.006

Wigton, R., Radua, J., Allen, P., Averbeck, B., Meyer-Lindenberg, A., McGuire, P., . . . Fusar-Poli, P. (2015). Neurophysiological effects of acute oxytocin administration: Systematic review and meta-analysis of placebo-controlled imaging studies. *Journal of Psychiatry and Neuroscience, 40*(1), 1–22. https://doi.org/10.1503/jpn.130289

Wood, R. I. (2004). Reinforcing aspects of androgens. *Physiology & Behavior, 83*(2), 279–289. https://doi.org/10.1016/j.physbeh.2004.08.012

Wynne-Edwards, K. E. (2001). Hormonal changes in mammalian fathers. *Hormones and Behavior, 40*(2), 139–145. https://doi.org/10.1006/hbeh.2001.1699

Xiao, L., & Becker, J. B. (1998). Effects of estrogen agonists on amphetamine-stimulated striatal dopamine release. *Synapse, 29*(4), 379–391. https://doi.org/10.1002/(SICI)1098-2396(199808)29:4<379::AID-SYN10>3.0.CO;2-M

Zimmerman, Y., Eijkemans, M. J. C., Coelingh Bennink, H. J. T., Blankenstein, M. A., & Fauser, B. C. J. M. (2014). The effect of combined oral contraception on testosterone levels in healthy women: A systematic review and meta-analysis. *Human Reproduction Update, 20*(1), 76–105. https://doi.org/10.1093/humupd/dmt038

25

THE IMPACT OF PSYCHOSOCIAL STRESS ON COGNITION

Oliver T. Wolf

What is stress?

Stress has obtained a rather bad reputation nowadays. This is based on the fact that chronic stress is associated with physical and mental health problems (Wolf, 2008). However, research has illustrated that the impact of stress on cognitive functions such as learning, memory and decision making are far more complex than initially assumed. Stress may enhance or impair a specific cognitive function depending on several key modulators and mediators. Both quantitative and qualitative shifts take place. These will be described and discussed in the present chapter

A common definition is that stress occurs when a person perceives a challenge to their internal or external balance (homeostasis; De Kloet et al., 2005). Thus, a discrepancy between what "should be" and "what is" induces stress (Ursin & Eriksen, 2010). A stressor can be physical (e.g. cold, hunger, pain) or psychological (e.g. work overload, mobbing, marital problems). Moreover, stressors can be acute or chronic (McEwen, 1998). For us humans, a threat to the social self (social evaluative threat), in combination with uncontrollability of the situation, is especially potent in triggering a stress response (Dickerson & Kemeny, 2004). The subjective evaluation of the stressor (primary appraisal) and of available coping resources (secondary appraisal) determines its impact on the individual (Lazarus, 1993). Something perceived as a substantial threat by one person might be perceived as an exciting challenge by another. There is substantial interindividual variability in the response to stress, an issue discussed at the end of the chapter.

The stress response evolved as an adaptive reaction aimed at maintaining physiologic integrity (homeostasis) in the face of anticipated or actual threat to physiological or psychological well-being (De Kloet et al., 2005; McEwen, 1998). The effects of stress manifest themselves on multiple levels, including behavior, subjective experience, cognitive function and physiology. The same responses which are mostly adaptive under acute stress can, however, promote disease processes in vulnerable individuals under chronic conditions (De Kloet et al., 2005; McEwen, 1998).

The neuroendocrine stress response

Stress leads to hormonal responses aimed at facilitating adaptation. The sympathetic nervous system (SNS) and the hypothalamic–pituitary–adrenal (HPA) axis are the two key players (see

Figure 25.1). SNS activity causes the rapid release of (nor)adrenaline from the adrenal medulla. This constitutes the first rapid response wave. Increased activity of the HPA axis induces the release of glucocorticoids (cortisol in humans) from the adrenal cortex. This response is slower and therefore constitutes the second response wave (De Kloet et al., 2005). Salivary cortisol concentrations start to rise approximately 10–15 minutes after stress onset and typically reach their peak at around 30 minutes after stress onset (Dickerson & Kemeny, 2004).

Glucocorticoids are lipophilic hormones and therefore can enter the brain easily. There they affect regions involved in cognitive functions (e.g. prefrontal cortex, amygdala, hippocampus, striatum). These effects are mediated by two receptors: the mineralocorticoid receptor (MR) and the glucocorticoid receptor (GR). They differ in their affinity for the hormone, with the MR having a tenfold higher affinity and their localization with the MR occurring predominantly in limbic areas and the hypothalamus. While MR activation leads to enhanced neuronal excitability, GR activation causes a delayed suppression or normalization of the neuronal

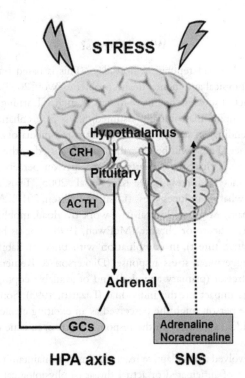

Figure 25.1 Stress activates two neuroendocrine systems: the rapidly acting sympathetic nervous system (SNS) and the slower hypothalamic–pituitary–adrenocortical (HPA) axis. Activation of the hypothalamus stimulates the SNS to secrete (nor)adrenaline from the adrenal medulla. These hormones can indirectly influence the brain via acting on the vagus nerve. The hypothalamus also releases corticotropin-releasing hormone (CRH), which stimulates the secretion of adrenocorticotropin (ACTH) from the anterior pituitary gland into the blood stream. ACTH stimulates the adrenal cortex to release glucocorticoids (GCs), which can pass the blood–brain barrier and modulate brain functions involved in cognition. GCs exert negative feedback effects on the hypothalamus and the pituitary gland, leading to reduced activity of the HPA axis.

Reprinted from Merz & Wolf, 2015 with permission from Elsevier.

network (Joels et al., 2008). In addition, GCs can exert rapid non-genomic effects which, in part, are mediated by recently described membrane-bound MRs (Joels et al., 2008) and GRs (Roozendaal et al., 2010). Thus, as illustrated in Figure 25.2, glucocorticoids have time-dependent effects comprising rapid non-genomic effects and later-occurring slower genomic effects (Wolf, 2017).

After acute stress, the HPA axis' negative feedback system leads to glucocorticoid levels returning to baseline concentrations within hours (De Kloet et al., 2005; Dickerson & Kemeny, 2004). In periods of chronic stress, persistent changes of the HPA axis can occur, leading to permanently elevated cortisol levels. However, high cortisol levels, as often observed in major depressive disorder, are not always the consequence of chronic stress (Wolf, 2008). For example, lower cortisol levels occur in several stress-associated somatoform disorders (Fries et al., 2005) as well as in post-traumatic stress disorder (Wolf, 2008; Yehuda, 2002).

Stress in the laboratory

When psychologists want to study stress experimentally, they face the dilemma as to how to induce moderate stress in the laboratory. Two paradigms have been used frequently. The Trier

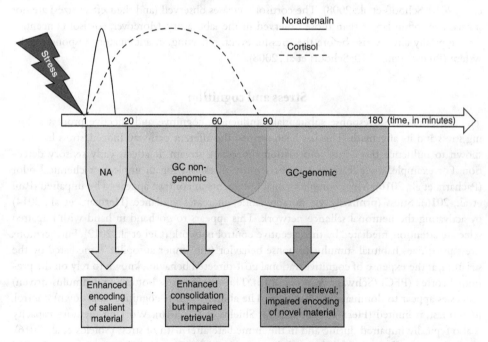

Figure 25.2 Neuroendocrine stress responses to a brief stressor (e.g. the Trier Social Stress Test) and their transcriptional and cognitive consequences. Stress influences the brain via a rapid increase in noradrenaline (NA). With a slight delay, glucocorticoids (GCs) are released. These hormones can exert rapid non-genomic and delayed genomic effects. Both effects are likely to co-occur around one hour after stress exposure. Genomic and non-genomic GC effects typically cause impaired memory retrieval. In contrast, initial encoding as well as consolidation of material perceived around the time of the stressor is enhanced. Note: The depicted temporal development is based on a rough estimate derived from the literature. For further explanations, see the associated text.

Social Stress Test (TSST; Kirschbaum et al., 1993) combines a videotaped free speech (a job interview roleplay) in front of a neutral and reserved acting committee with a mental arithmetic task (also in front of a committee). It reliably induces negative affect and activates the SNS and the HPA. The combination of social evaluative threat, motivated performance and uncontrollability makes this stressor so powerful (Dickerson & Kemeny, 2004).

The socially evaluated cold pressor task (SECPT) combines a painful stimulation (putting the hand in ice cold water) with social evaluation by an observer and a video camera (Schwabe et al., 2008). The paradigm also leads to robust SNS and HPA activations even though typically somewhat smaller in size compared to the TSST. While both stressors are typically conducted in single participant sessions, group versions of the paradigms are also effective (von Dawans et al., 2011; Minkley et al., 2014).

Stress in the field

The neuroendocrine stress response has, of course, also been studied in the field. Sport events (Rohleder et al., 2007) or exams at schools or universities (Preuss et al., 2010; Schoofs et al., 2008) have been investigated repeatedly. Especially oral exams with their strong and direct component of social evaluative threat lead to marked increases of the SNS and HPA axis (Preuss et al., 2010; Schoofs et al., 2008). The cortisol increases observed (and their effect sizes) are not surprisingly often larger than those observed in the laboratory. Moreover, cortisol concentrations typically already rise before the stressful event, reflecting an anticipatory response of the system (Preuss et al., 2010; Schoofs et al., 2008).

Stress and cognition

The hormonal stress response substantially influences cognitive and affective processes during stress and its aftermath. This has been termed the afferent pathway. Indeed, stress has been shown to influence the entire information processing stream. It affects early sensory detection. For example, stress leads to a lower sensory threshold for an unpleasant chemical odor (Pacharra et al., 2016). More complex visual judgments in contrast appear to be impaired (Paul et al., 2016). Stress (primarily via noradrenaline) increases vigilance (Hermans et al., 2014) by activating the neuronal salience network. This appears to go hand in hand with impaired selective attention, mediated by the executive control network (Oei et al., 2012). Furthermore, stress prioritizes habitual stimulus-response behavior (the "inner autopilot"), mediated by the striatum, at the expense of cognitive/rational goal-directed behavior, known to rely on the prefrontal cortex (PFC) (Schwabe & Wolf, 2013). Thus, under stress bottom-up (stimulus-driven) processes appear to dominate our behavior. The ability to exert cognitive (top-down) control, in contrast, is limited (Hermans et al., 2014; Shields et al., 2016). Working memory capacity is also typically impaired during and in the immediate aftermath of stress (Shields et al., 2016). Similarly, stress affects our abilities to make good decisions. For example, participants who had experienced a stressful laboratory situation displayed riskier and less successful behavior in a gambling task (game of dice task; Starcke et al., 2008). A recent meta-analysis concluded that stress impairs decision making, especially under those conditions where reward seeking and risk taking is disadvantageous (Starcke & Brand, 2016). The findings on decision making are in line with the stress-induced deficits in executive functions mentioned above. Impaired decision making under risk can have substantial relevance for safety behavior of employees (Starcke et al., 2016) or for traders deciding on when to buy or sell stocks (Coates & Herbert, 2008; Cueva et al., 2015).

The effects of stress on long-term memory (LTM) have received considerable attention. LTM can be subdivided into declarative or explicit and non-declarative or procedural (implicit) memory. Based on its content, declarative memory can be subdivided into episodic memory (recall of a specific event which can be located in space and time) and semantic memory (factual knowledge of the world) (Squire, 1992). The medial temporal lobe is critical for declarative memory, with the hippocampus being especially important for episodic memory (Nadel & Moscovitch, 1997).

LTM consists of at least three memory phases, namely acquisition (or encoding), consolidation (or storage) and retrieval (or recall). The literature on the impact of stress on episodic memory was initially divergent and confusing, with groups reporting both enhancing as well as impairing effects of GCs on this form of memory. However, it has become apparent that this is largely due to the fact that the different memory phases outlined above are modulated by GCs in an opposing fashion (Shields et al., 2017; Wolf, 2009).

Pre-learning stress studies have led to a somewhat inconsistent picture. The exact timing of the stressor, the emotionality of the learning material and the relation of the learning material to the stressor appear to be important modulatory factors (Wolf, 2009). A recent meta-analysis (Shields et al., 2017) revealed that pre-encoding stress typically was associated with impaired long-term memories, especially when the stressor and the memory task were separated in space and time and the learning material was not related to the stressor. Thus, a social stressor (peer conflict) experienced during a school break might impair the ability of the pupil to acquire new knowledge in the next lesson. At the same time, the memory of the peer conflict is most likely quite strong (as outlined in more depth below).

Stress boosts memory consolidation, this process representing the adaptive and beneficial side of the action of stress hormones in the central nervous system (see Figure 25.2). It has been conceptualized as the beneficial effects of "stress within the learning context" or "intrinsic stress" (Joels et al., 2006). The terminology used emphasizes the fact that the central aspects of a stressful episode are remembered better. For example, we could demonstrate that participants exposed to the TSST displayed superior long-term memory for items and faces which were part of the stress procedure in comparison to participants experiencing a well-matched control condition (Wiemers et al., 2013).

Similarly, immediate post-learning stress has repeatedly been linked to enhanced memory consolidation. For example, participants who were exposed to the cold pressor stressor directly after viewing a series of slides had better long-term memories of the slides compared to the stress free control group (Cahill et al., 2003). Supporting evidence comes from pharmacological cortisol administration studies revealing enhanced long-term memories (e.g. Buchanan & Lovallo, 2001). Often these enhancing effects of stress on consolidation are stronger for emotional material, even though they also have been observed when neutral material only was used. Neuroimaging studies have provided further evidence for a stress-induced modulation of amygdala and hippocampal activity (Wolf, 2009). These effects are mediated by the action of stress-released glucocorticoids on the hippocampal formation. Studies in rodents have shown that a stress-induced release of noradrenaline in the basolateral amygdala (BLA) appears to be a pre-requisite for the modulating effects of glucocorticoids on other brain regions (e.g. the hippocampus). Lesions of the BLA as well as administration of a beta blocker (e.g. proporanolol) abolish the enhancing effects of post-training stress (Roozendaal et al., 2009).

While an enhanced memory consolidation is adaptive and beneficial, this process appears to occur at the cost of impaired retrieval (see Figure 25.2). Using a one-day delay, scientists were able to show that stress or treatment with glucocorticoids shortly before retrieval testing impairs memory retrieval in rats in a water maze task (de Quervain et al., 1998). Again, very similar findings were observed in humans. Participants exposed to the TSST showed poorer memory retrieval of words encoded 24 hours earlier (Kuhlmann et al., 2005). Similar retrieval impairing effects were observed for social stimuli like faces and autobiographical notes (Merz et al., 2010). In line with these examples, the aforementioned meta-analysis (Shields et al., 2017) also reported a significant impairing effect of stress on memory retrieval. Roozendaal has summarized these findings as indicative of stress putting the brain into a consolidation mode, accompanied by impaired retrieval (Roozendaal et al., 2009). A reduction in retrieval might support consolidation by reducing interference (Wolf, 2017; Wolf, 2009).

Such an impairing effect of social stress on memory retrieval might explain retrieval deficits observed during school or university exams. Especially oral exams, which exert a strong social evaluative threat, lead to a pronounced activation of stress hormones (Preuss et al., 2010). Another area where the impact of stress needs to be considered more is eyewitness memories. Last but not least, these findings have obvious relevance for the development and treatment of anxiety disorders and post-traumatic stress disorder (de Quervain et al., 2017)

Initially, the impairing effects of stress on memory retrieval were thought to be restricted to episodic memories known to rely on the hippocampus. However, research conducted during the last years revealed that stress also impairs striatum-dependent stimulus-response memory retrieval or prefrontal dependent extinction memory retrieval. In addition, the effect appears to be rather long lasting (up to several hours). A summary of the effects of stress on long-term memory is provided in Figure 25.2. A recent review on this topic can be found by Wolf (2017).

Stress and social cognition

For the present chapter, the impact of acute stress on social cognition is especially relevant. As mentioned above, social evaluative threat is a potent stressor for us humans (Dickerson & Kemeny, 2004). In contrast, experiencing prosocial behavior in the form of social support is a very effective stress buffer (Ditzen & Heinrichs, 2014). Relatively little is known about how the experience of a stressful episode influences the cognitive and emotional abilities to understand and feel for another person, i.e. empathy. Early concepts of the stress response focusing on the rapid response of the sympathetic nervous system have characterized this first response as the fight or flight response (Cannon, 1932). However, somewhat later in the course of the stress response, a different bio-behavioral response pattern characterized by tending and befriending might occur, especially in women (Taylor et al., 2000). The latter concept predicts enhanced prosocial behavior and enhanced empathy in the aftermath of stress. Of note, it has been proposed that this effect occurs in men as well (Geary & Flinn, 2002).

There is agreement that empathy cannot be considered as a single process but, in contrast, as a construct consisting of at least two separable aspects, namely emotional and cognitive empathy (Blair, 2005). Cognitive empathy, often referred to as mindreading or mentalizing, refers to the capacity to consciously understand and interpret the affective state of another person. In contrast, emotional empathy describes an observer's emotional response to another person's emotional state (Singer & Lamm, 2009). Patient studies as well as human neuroimaging experiments have contributed substantially during the last decades to characterizing the neural correlates involved in these processes (Gonzalez-Liencres et al., 2013).

Our group conducted two experiments to investigate the impact of stress (exposure to the TSST) on empathy. In the first study, we used an empathy test allowing the differentiation of cognitive and emotional empathy (Multifaceted Empathy Test, MET; (Dziobek et al., 2008). Stress caused an increase in self-reported emotional empathy (Wolf et al., 2015). This effect occurred for pictures displaying people experiencing negative as well as positive emotions. In contrast, no effect on cognitive empathy (emotion recognition) was observed. The findings are highly similar to a pharmacological study reported by Wingenfeld and colleagues. The authors administered a drug which specifically stimulates the MR before participants conducted the MET. In line with the stress findings, MR stimulation also enhanced emotional but not cognitive empathy (Wingenfeld et al., 2014). In two other experiments, the impact of stress on empathy for pain was tested. Again, participants exposed to the TSST reported more emotional empathy (Gonzalez-Liencres et al., 2016; Tomova et al., 2017). Thus, while the literature is far from homogenous (e.g. Buruck et al., 2014), recent findings repeatedly observed enhanced empathy in the aftermath of acute stress.

One important question is the relevance of enhanced empathy for behavior. Will stressed participants indeed act more pro-socially? This question was initially addressed by an experiment that used economic games. In this study, male participants were exposed to the TSST for groups or a standardized control condition. Participants from the stress group performed more prosocial actions than control group participants, as evidenced by increases in trust and sharing behavior (von Dawans et al., 2012). This was taken as support for the tend-and-befriend hypothesis. A conceptual replication of these findings using the individual instead of the group version of the TSST, however, found no evidence for prosocial actions in the aftermath of stress (Steinbeis et al., 2015). More recent findings on stress and social discounting provide evidence that the prosocial effect of stress on social decision making might be restricted to close others (Margittai et al., 2015). In this study, stress boosted generosity towards close others only. Social closeness or in-group versus out-group membership appear to be important moderators to be considered in future research (see Oxford et al., 2017). They might constitute boundary conditions for the prosocial effect of stress observed in some of these laboratory studies.

Taken together, evidence is mounting that people often show enhanced prosocial behavior in the aftermath of acute stress. How these findings can be reconciled with the well-known effects of stress on aggression (Veenema, 2009; van Goozen & Fairchild, 2006) remains an empirical and conceptual challenge for the future. One possible explanation could be that during or immediately after stress, the increased SNS mediated arousal enhances aggression and antisocial behavior. In the aftermath of stress, the second response wave mediated via the HPA axis, possibly in interaction with gonadal steroids and oxytocin, might promote prosocial behavior as suggested by the tend-and-befriend hypothesis (Taylor et al., 2000; Wirth, 2011; Wolf et al., 2015). The effects of stress on social behavior are thus most likely time- and task- dependent. A review on the topic of stress and prosocial behavior can be found by (Buchanan & Preston, 2014)

Some moderators to be considered

Sex differences

Men and women differ in their psychosocial stress response and apparently also in the impact of the stress response on cognition. Studies using the TSST repeatedly observed more pronounced responses in men when compared to women (see for a recent meta-analysis Liu et al., 2017). In order to complicate things, it has to be mentioned that the menstrual cycle and especially the usage of oral contraceptives influences the (salivary) cortisol response to acute stress. Women using oral contraceptives (OCs) typically display a rather blunted cortisol increase (Kirschbaum et al., 1999), which appears to be primarily caused by an OC-induced increase in sex hormone binding globulin. These sex and sex hormone effects need to be considered when designing experiments and when trying to interpret empirical findings (Merz & Wolf, 2017).

In addition to sex differences in neuroendocrine stress responsivity, there is also evidence for sex differences in the sensitivity to stress hormones when it comes to cognition. Differential effects of stress or cortisol on a variety of cognitive processes have been reported, even though the findings are currently far from being consistent. Often the impact of stress on cognition appears to be stronger and more robust for men when compared to women. Moreover, again an impact of menstrual cycle phase and even more so of OC usage appears to exist (Merz & Wolf, 2017). For example, the impairing effect of stress on memory retrieval could not be detected in a sample of women in the luteal phase (Schoofs & Wolf, 2009). Cortisol, which impairs memory retrieval in men, did not do so in women using OCs (Kuhlmann & Wolf, 2005). Neuroimaging studies in the domain of fear conditioning repeatedly observed almost opposing effects of stress or cortisol administration on the neural correlates of emotional learning in men and women using OCs (Merz et al., 2012; Merz et al., 2013). Recent reviews on this topic can be found by Merz & Wolf (2017) and Stockhorst and Antov (2015).

Regarding the impact of stress on social cognition, little empirical data is available. In one previous study, we observed opposing associations between the stress-induced cortisol increase and cognitive empathy (Smeets et al., 2009). In men, a larger cortisol response was associated with better cognitive empathy as assessed with the movie for the assessment of social cognition (Dziobek et al., 2006). In contrast, in women the opposite pattern was observed, that is, a larger cortisol response was associated with worse cognitive empathy. Another study observed that stress enhanced self-other distinction in women, but reduced it in men (Tomova et al., 2014). How this finding might translate into empathy and prosocial behavior remains to be determined. These examples illustrate that sex appears to be a variable to be considered when trying to understand the effects of stress on social cognition. Having said this, strong and opposing effects of stress on social behavior as initially postulated by Taylor and colleagues (2000) have not been observed reliably in human experimental studies.

Taken together, conceptual (Taylor et al., 2000) as well as empirical (Merz & Wolf, 2017) evidence emphasizes the need to consider sex differences in psychoneuroendocrine stress research. The usage of small sample sizes with convenience sampling from both sexes is not advisable since it may mask stress effects, thereby hindering scientific progress in this important area. The exclusive focus on one sex (most often men in this sort of research) can be understood from a pragmatic point of view but has led to a lack of information on stress effects in women. This state of affairs cannot be accepted anymore and is increasingly being recognized by journals and funding agencies (see (Cahill, 2017)).

Genetic influences

Genes involved in the regulation of the SNS and HPA response to stress can substantially influence the effects of stress on cognition. For example, variations in a gene encoding the alpha 2 receptor influence the ability to form emotional memories (de Quervain, Kolassa, et al., 2007; Rasch et al., 2009). Moreover, it also modulates the impact of acute stress on emotional memories and their neural correlates (Li et al., 2014; Li et al., 2013). Thus, genetic alterations within the stress system can influence the susceptibility to stressful events.

Other examples are alterations in the genes encoding the MR and GR. Under stress, the MR might be responsible for switching cognitive processing towards simpler, habitual/automatic response styles (Schwabe & Wolf, 2013). The GR appears to be especially important for memory consolidation (Roozendaal et al., 2009). Variability in the function and balance of these key stress mediators is likely to be related to interindividual differences in stress responsivity and sensitivity. Studies have recently begun to characterize the impact of genetic polymorphisms in the MR and GR genes on HPA axis (re)activity and disease risk (De Kloet et al., 2016). The discovery of epigenetic modulation of these receptors by early life stress allows a new look at gene-environment interplay (Turecki & Meaney, 2016). Thus, we are at the beginning of a new area in psychoneuroendocrinology that combines experimental laboratory studies with behavioral genetics.

Interventions

Some of the effects of stress on cognition might not be desirable in a specific situation. For example, the impairing effects of stress on memory retrieval could lead to sub-optimal performance in an exam. Here, stress reduction techniques or social support might be useful strategies to buffer the stress response (Ditzen & Heinrichs, 2014). In addition, specific learning techniques might be able to reduce or prevent these stress effects (Smith et al., 2016; Wolf & Kluge, 2017). Last but not least, pharmacological interventions (e.g. the beta-blocker propranolol) can protect memory retrieval from the impairing effect of stress (de Quervain, Aerni, et al., 2007). Similar studies on the effects of stress on social cognition are currently lacking and thus represent an important area for future research.

Conclusion and outlook

In this chapter, the impact of acute stress on (social) cognition has been reviewed. Stress has been shown to influence almost all cognitive processes. A stronger stimulus-driven response type and opposing effects on memory consolidation versus memory retrieval are two fairly well established effects. With respect to social behavior, the initially somewhat surprising finding of enhanced emotional empathy and increased prosocial behavior in the aftermath of acute stress illustrates the need for new frameworks in the conceptualization of the impact of stress on social behavior. Last but not least, sex differences and genetic influences are important moderators to be considered. An enhanced understanding and a more differentiated view of the beneficial and detrimental effects of acute stress on human (social) cognition will in the long run help to foster individual and societal well-being.

Acknowledgments

The work of the author presented and discussed in this chapter has been supported by several grants from the German Research Foundation (DFG). Project B4 of the collaborative research center (SFB) 874; Project A9 of the collaborative research center (SFB) 1280, and DFG project WO 733/15–1.

References

Blair, R. J. (2005). Responding to the emotions of others: Dissociating forms of empathy through the study of typical and psychiatric populations. *Consciousness and Cognition, 14*, 698–718.
Buchanan, T. W., & Lovallo, W. R. (2001). Enhanced memory for emotional material following stress-level cortisol treatment in humans. *Psychoneuroendocrinology, 26*, 307–317.
Buchanan, T. W., & Preston, S. D. (2014). Stress leads to prosocial action in immediate need situations. *Frontiers in Behavioral Neuroscience, 8*, 5.
Buruck, G., Wendsche, J., Melzer, M., Strobel, A., & Dorfel, D. (2014). Acute psychosocial stress and emotion regulation skills modulate empathic reactions to pain in others. *Frontiers in Psychology, 5*, 517.
Cahill, L. (2017). An issue whose time has come. *Journal of Neuroscience Research, 95*, 12–13.

Cahill, L., Gorski, L., & Le, K. (2003). Enhanced human memory consolidation with post-learning stress: Interaction with the degree of arousal at encoding. *Learning & Memory, 10,* 270–274.

Cannon, W. (1932). *Wisdom of the body.* New York, NY: W. W. Norton & Company.

Coates, J. M., & Herbert, J. (2008). Endogenous steroids and financial risk taking on a London trading floor. *Proceedings of the National Academy of Sciences of the United States of America, 105,* 6167–6172.

Cueva, C., Roberts, R. E., Spencer, T., Rani, N., Tempest, M., Tobler, P. N., . . . Rustichini, A. (2015). Cortisol and testosterone increase financial risk taking and may destabilize markets. *Scientific Reports, 5,* 11206.

De Kloet, E. R., Joels, M., & Holsboer, F. (2005). Stress and the brain: From adaptation to disease. *Nature Reviews Neuroscience, 6,* 463–475.

De Kloet, E. R., Otte, C., Kumsta, R., Kok, L., Hillegers, M. H., Hasselmann, H., . . . Joëls, M. (2016). Stress and depression a crucial role of the mineralocorticoid receptor. *Journal of Neuroendocrinology, 28.* doi:10.1111/jne.12379

de Quervain, D. J., Aerni, A., & Roozendaal, B. (2007). Preventive effect of {beta}-adrenoceptor blockade on glucocorticoid-induced memory retrieval deficits. *The American Journal of Psychiatry, 164,* 967–969.

de Quervain, D. J., Kolassa, I. T., Ertl, V., Onyut, P. L., Neuner, F., Elbert, T., & Papassotiropoulos, A. (2007). A deletion variant of the alpha2b-adrenoceptor is related to emotional memory in Europeans and Africans. *Nature Neuroscience, 10,* 1137–1139.

de Quervain, D. J., Roozendaal, B., & McGaugh, J. L. (1998). Stress and glucocorticoids impair retrieval of long-term spatial memory. *Nature, 394,* 787–790.

de Quervain, D. J., Schwabe, L., & Roozendaal, B. (2017). Stress, glucocorticoids and memory: Implications for treating fear-related disorders. *Nature Reviews Neuroscience, 18,* 7–19.

Dickerson, S. S., & Kemeny, M. E. (2004). Acute stressors and cortisol responses: A theoretical integration and synthesis of laboratory research. *Psychological Bulletin, 130,* 355–391.

Ditzen, B., & Heinrichs, M. (2014). Psychobiology of social support: The social dimension of stress buffering. *Restorative Neurology and Neuroscience, 32,* 149–162.

Dziobek, I., Fleck, S., Kalbe, E., Rogers, K., Hassenstab, J., Brand, M., . . . Convit, A. (2006). Introducing MASC: A movie for the assessment of social cognition. *Journal of Autism and Developmental Disorders, 36,* 623–636.

Dziobek, I., Rogers, K., Fleck, S., Bahnemann, M., Heekeren, H. R., Wolf, O. T., & Convit, A. (2008). Dissociation of cognitive and emotional empathy in adults with asperger syndrome using the Multifaceted Empathy Test (MET). *Journal of Autism and Developmental Disorders, 38,* 464–473.

Fries, E., Hesse, J., Hellhammer, J., & Hellhammer, D. H. (2005). A new view on hypocortisolism. *Psychoneuroendocrinology, 30,* 1010–1016.

Geary, D. C., & Flinn, M. V. (2002). Sex differences in behavioral and hormonal response to social threat: Commentary on Taylor et al. (2000). *Psychological Review, 109,* 745–750.

Gonzalez-Liencres, C., Breidenstein, A., Wolf, O. T., & Brüne, M. (2016). Sex-dependent effects of stress on brain correlates to empathy for pain. *International Journal of Psychophysiology, 105,* 47–56.

Gonzalez-Liencres, C., Shamay-Tsoory, S. G., & Brüne, M. (2013). Towards a neuroscience of empathy: Ontogeny, phylogeny, brain mechanisms, context and psychopathology. *Neuroscience & Biobehavioral Reviews, 37,* 1537–1548.

Hermans, E. J., Henckens, M. J., Joels, M., & Fernandez, G. (2014). Dynamic adaptation of large-scale brain networks in response to acute stressors. *Trends in Neurosciences, 37,* 304–314.

Joels, M., Karst, H., DeRijk, R., & De Kloet, E. R. (2008). The coming out of the brain mineralocorticoid receptor. *Trends in Neurosciences, 31,* 1–7.

Joels, M., Pu, Z., Wiegert, O., Oitzl, M. S., & Krugers, H. J. (2006). Learning under stress: How does it work? *Trends in Cognitive Sciences, 10,* 152–158.

Kirschbaum, C., Kudielka, B. M., Gaab, J., Schommer, N. C., & Hellhammer, D. H. (1999). Impact of gender, menstrual cycle phase, and oral contraceptives on the activity of the hypothalamus-pituitary-adrenal axis. *Psychosomatic Medicine, 61,* 154–162.

Kirschbaum, C., Pirke, K. M., & Hellhammer, D. H. (1993). The "Trier Social Stress Test" – a tool for investigating psychobiological stress responses in a laboratory setting. *Neuropsychobiology, 28,* 76–81.

Kuhlmann, S., Piel, M., & Wolf, O. T. (2005). Impaired memory retrieval after psychosocial stress in healthy young men. *Journal of Neuroscience, 25,* 2977–2982.

Kuhlmann, S., & Wolf, O. T. (2005). Cortisol and memory retrieval in women: Influence of menstrual cycle and oral contraceptives. *Psychopharmacology, 183,* 65–71.

Lazarus, R. S. (1993). Coping theory and research: Past, present, and future. *Psychosomatic Medicine, 55*, 234–247.

Li, S., Weerda, R., Guenzel, F., Wolf, O. T., & Thiel, C. M. (2013). ADRA2B genotype modulates effects of acute psychosocial stress on emotional memory retrieval in healthy young men. *Neurobiology of Learning and Memory, 103*, 11–18.

Li, S., Weerda, R., Milde, C., Wolf, O. T., & Thiel, C. M. (2014). ADRA2B genotype differentially modulates stress-induced neural activity in the amygdala and hippocampus during emotional memory retrieval. *Psychopharmacology (Berl), 232*, 755–764.

Liu, J. J. W., Ein, N., Peck, K., Huang, V., Pruessner, J. C., & Vickers, K. (2017). Sex differences in salivary cortisol reactivity to the Trier Social Stress Test (TSST): A meta-analysis. *Psychoneuroendocrinology, 82*, 26–37.

Margittai, Z., Strombach, T., van, W. M., Joels, M., Schwabe, L., & Kalenscher, T. (2015). A friend in need: Time-dependent effects of stress on social discounting in men. *Hormones and Behavior, 73*, 75–82.

McEwen, B. S. (1998). Protective and damaging effects of stress mediators. *New England Journal of Medicine, 338*, 171–179.

Merz, C. J., Tabbert, K., Schweckendiek, J., Klucken, T., Vaitl, D., Stark, R., & Wolf, O. T. (2012). Oral contraceptive usage alters the effects of cortisol on implicit fear learning. *Hormones and Behavior, 62*, 531–538.

Merz, C. J., & Wolf, O. T. (2017). Sex differences in stress effects on emotional learning. *Journal of Neuroscience Research, 95*, 93–105.

Merz, C. J., & Wolf, O. T. (2015). Stress and emotional learning in humans: Evidence for sex differences. In R. Shansky (Ed.), *Sex differences in the central nervous system* (pp. 149–170). Oxford: Elsevier.

Merz, C. J., Wolf, O. T., & Hennig, J. (2010). Stress impairs retrieval of socially relevant information. *Behavioral Neuroscience, 124*, 288–293.

Merz, C. J., Wolf, O. T., Schweckendiek, J., Klucken, T., Vaitl, D., & Stark, R. (2013). Stress differentially affects fear conditioning in men and women. *Psychoneuroendocrinology, 38*, 2529–2541.

Minkley, N., Schroder, T. P., Wolf, O. T., & Kirchner, W. H. (2014). The Socially Evaluated Cold-Pressor Test (SECPT) for groups: Effects of repeated administration of a combined physiological and psychological stressor. *Psychoneuroendocrinology, 45*, 119–127.

Nadel, L., & Moscovitch, M. (1997). Memory consolidation, retrograde amnesia and the hippocampal complex. *Current Opinion in Neurobiology, 7*, 217–227.

Oei, N. Y., Veer, I. M., Wolf, O. T., Spinhoven, P., Rombouts, S. A., & Elzinga, B. M. (2012). Stress shifts brain activation towards ventral "affective" areas during emotional distraction. *Social Cognitive and Affective Neuroscience, 7*, 403–412.

Oxford, J. K., Tiedtke, J. M., Ossmann, A., Ozbe, D., & Schultheiss, O. C. (2017). Endocrine and aggressive responses to competition are moderated by contest outcome, gender, individual versus team competition, and implicit motives. *PLoS One, 12*, e0181610.

Pacharra, M., Schaper, M., Kleinbeck, S., Blaszkewicz, M., Wolf, O. T., & van Thriel, C. (2016). Stress lowers the detection threshold for foul-smelling 2-mercaptoethanol. *Stress, 19*, 18–27.

Paul, M., Lech, R. K., Scheil, J., Dierolf, A. M., Suchan, B., & Wolf, O. T. (2016). Acute stress influences the discrimination of complex scenes and complex faces in young healthy men. *Psychoneuroendocrinology, 66*, 125–129.

Preuss, D., Schoofs, D., Schlotz, W., & Wolf, O. T. (2010). The stressed student: Influence of written examinations and oral presentations on salivary cortisol concentrations in university students. *Stress, 13*, 221–229.

Rasch, B., Spalek, K., Buholzer, S., Luechinger, R., Boesiger, P., Papassotiropoulos, A., & de Quervain, D. J. (2009). A genetic variation of the noradrenergic system is related to differential amygdala activation during encoding of emotional memories. *Proceedings of the National Academy of Sciences of the United States of America, 106*, 19191–19196.

Rohleder, N., Beulen, S. E., Chen, E., Wolf, J. M., & Kirschbaum, C. (2007). Stress on the dance floor: The cortisol stress response to social-evaluative threat in competitive ballroom dancers. *Social Cognitive and Affective Neuroscience, 33*, 69–84.

Roozendaal, B., Hernandez, A., Cabrera, S. M., Hagewoud, R., Malvaez, M., Stefanko, D. P., . . . Wood, M. A. (2010). Membrane-associated glucocorticoid activity is necessary for modulation of long-term memory via chromatin modification. *Journal of Neuroscience, 30*, 5037–5046.

Roozendaal, B., McEwen, B. S., & Chattarji, S. (2009). Stress, memory and the amygdala. *Nature Reviews Neuroscience, 10*, 423–433.

Schoofs, D., Hartmann, R., & Wolf, O. T. (2008). Neuroendocrine stress responses to an oral academic examination: No strong influence of sex, repeated participation and personality traits. *Stress, 11*, 52–61.

Schoofs, D., & Wolf, O. T. (2009). Stress and memory retrieval in women: No strong impairing effect during the luteal phase. *Behavioral Neuroscience, 123*, 547–554.

Schwabe, L., Haddad, L., & Schachinger, H. (2008). HPA axis activation by a socially evaluated cold-pressor test. *Psychoneuroendocrinology, 33*, 890–895.

Schwabe, L., & Wolf, O. T. (2013). Stress and multiple memory systems: From "thinking" to "doing". *Trends in Cognitive Sciences, 17*, 60–68.

Shields, G. S., Sazma, M. A., McCullough, A. M., & Yonelinas, A. P. (2017). The effects of acute stress on episodic memory: A meta-analysis and integrative review. *Psychological Bulletin, 143*, 636–675.

Shields, G. S., Sazma, M. A., & Yonelinas, A. P. (2016). The effects of acute stress on core executive functions: A meta-analysis and comparison with cortisol. *Neuroscience & Biobehavioral Reviews, 68*, 651–668.

Singer, T., & Lamm, C. (2009). The social neuroscience of empathy. *Annals of the New York Academy of Sciences, 1156*, 81–96.

Smeets, T., Dziobek, I., & Wolf, O. T. (2009). Social cognition under stress: Differential effects of stress-induced cortisol elevations in healthy young men and women. *Hormones and Behavior, 55*, 507–513.

Smith, A. M., Floerke, V. A., & Thomas, A. K. (2016). Retrieval practice protects memory against acute stress. *Science, 354*, 1046–1048.

Squire, L. R. (1992). Memory and the hippocampus: A synthesis from findings with rats, monkeys, and humans. *Psychological Review, 99*, 195–231.

Starcke, K., & Brand, M. (2016). Effects of stress on decisions under uncertainty: A meta-analysis. *Psychological Bulletin, 142*, 909–933.

Starcke, K., Brand, M., & Kluge, A. (2016). Stress influences decisions to break a safety rule in a complex simulation task in females. *Biological Psychology, 118*, 35–43.

Starcke, K., Wolf, O. T., Markowitsch, H. J., & Brand, M. (2008). Anticipatory stress influences decision making under explicit risk conditions. *Behavioral Neuroscience, 122*, 1352–1360.

Steinbeis, N., Engert, V., Linz, R., & Singer, T. (2015). The effects of stress and affiliation on social decision-making: Investigating the tend-and-befriend pattern. *Psychoneuroendocrinology, 62*, 138–148.

Stockhorst, U., & Antov, M. I. (2015). Modulation of fear extinction by stress, stress hormones and estradiol: A review. *Frontiers in Behavioral Neuroscience, 9*, 359.

Taylor, S. E., Klein, L. C., Lewis, B. P., Gruenewald, T. L., Gurung, R. A., & Updegraff, J. A. (2000). Biobehavioral responses to stress in females: Tend-and-befriend, not fight-or-flight. *Psychological Review, 107*, 411–429.

Tomova, L., Majdandzic, J., Hummer, A., Windischberger, C., Heinrichs, M., & Lamm, C. (2017). Increased neural responses to empathy for pain might explain how acute stress increases prosociality. *Social Cognitive and Affective Neuroscience, 12*, 401–408.

Tomova, L., von Dawans, B., Heinrichs, M., Silani, G., & Lamm, C. (2014). Is stress affecting our ability to tune into others? Evidence for gender differences in the effects of stress on self-other distinction. *Psychoneuroendocrinology, 43*, 95–104.

Turecki, G., & Meaney, M. J. (2016). Effects of the social environment and stress on glucocorticoid receptor gene methylation: A systematic review. *Biological Psychiatry, 79*, 87–96.

Ursin, H., & Eriksen, H. R. (2010). Cognitive Activation Theory of Stress (CATS). *Neuroscience & Biobehavioral Reviews, 34*, 877–881.

Van Goozen, S. H., & Fairchild, G. (2006). Neuroendocrine and neurotransmitter correlates in children with antisocial behavior. *Hormones and Behavior, 50*, 647–654.

Veenema, A. H. (2009). Early life stress, the development of aggression and neuroendocrine and neurobiological correlates: What can we learn from animal models? *Frontiers in Neuroendocrinology, 30*, 497–518.

von Dawans, B., Fischbacher, U., Kirschbaum, C., Fehr, E., & Heinrichs, M. (2012). The social dimension of stress reactivity: Acute stress increases prosocial behavior in humans. *Psychological Science, 23*, 651–660.

von Dawans, B., Kirschbaum, C., & Heinrichs, M. (2011). The Trier Social Stress Test for Groups (TSST-G): A new research tool for controlled simultaneous social stress exposure in a group format. *Psychoneuroendocrinology, 36*, 514–522.

Wiemers, U. S., Sauvage, M. M., Schoofs, D., Hamacher-Dang, T. C., & Wolf, O. T. (2013). What we remember from a stressful episode. *Psychoneuroendocrinology, 38*, 2268–2277.

Wingenfeld, K., Kuehl, L. K., Janke, K., Hinkelmann, K., Dziobek, I., Fleischer, J., . . . Roepke, S. (2014). Enhanced emotional empathy after mineralocorticoid receptor stimulation in women with borderline personality disorder and healthy women. *Neuropsychopharmacology, 38*, 1799–1804.

Wirth, M. M. (2011). Beyond the HPA Axis: Progesterone-derived neuroactive steroids in human stress and emotion. *Frontiers Endocrinology, 2*, 19.

Wolf, O. T. (2008). The influence of stress hormones on emotional memory: Relevance for psychopathology. *Acta Psychologica, 127*, 513–531.

Wolf, O. T. (2009). Stress and memory in humans: Twelve years of progress? *Brain Research, 1293*, 142–154.

Wolf, O. T. (2017). Stress and memory retrieval: Mechanisms and consequences. *Current Opinion in Behavioral Sciences, 4*, 40–46.

Wolf, O. T., & Kluge, A. (2017). Commentary: Retrieval practice protects memory against acute stress. *Frontiers in Behavioral Neuroscience, 11*, 48.

Wolf, O. T., Schulte, J. M., Drimalla, H., Hamacher-Dang, T. C., Knoch, D., & Dziobek, I. (2015). Enhanced emotional empathy after psychosocial stress in young healthy men. *Stress, 18*, 631–637.

Yehuda, R. (2002). Post-traumatic stress disorder. *The New England Journal of Medicine, 346*, 108–114.

26

INTRA- AND INTERINDIVIDUAL DIFFERENCES IN CORTISOL STRESS RESPONSES

Sandra Zänkert and Brigitte M. Kudielka

1 Outline

This chapter focuses on psychoneuroendocrine stress regulation, highlighting intra- and interindividual differences in the human cortisol stress response and its relation to health and disease. First, we introduce basic concepts of stress and the biology of stress, especially the hypothalamic–pituitary–adrenal (HPA) axis. Then, we provide a brief overview of methodological aspects of social neuroendocrine stress research, with a focus on psychosocial stress induction paradigms in laboratory settings and magnetic resonance imaging (MRI) environments as well as recent developments in ambulatory assessment (AA). In the second part, we focus on sources of intra- and interindividual differences in salivary cortisol responses to psychosocial stress in humans.

2 Basic concepts of stress and stress biology

2.1 Basic theoretical conceptions of stress

The first to introduce the term stress to medical research was Selye, the father of modern stress research. He conceptualized stress as a non-specific response of the body to non-specific biological, chemical, physical, or social challenges that were assumed to elicit a 'general adaptation syndrome' (GAS) via the secretion of glucocorticoids (Selye, 1950). Earlier, Cannon had described the role of the sympathetic nervous system in response to an acute threat and coined the term 'fight-or-flight response' (Cannon, 1914). Soon, the conceptualization of stress as a sole physiological reaction of an organism had to be revised when Mason (1975) demonstrated that specific situational and personal characteristics are crucial elements in the stress process. He showed that factors like novelty, ambiguity, or a person's sense of control over a threatening challenge were triggering different autonomic and neuroendocrine responses. This led to the understanding that stress responses varied according to the quality of a challenge and the availability of a person's coping abilities. The transactional stress model of Lazarus and Folkman (1984) extended this notion by emphasizing the role of subjective appraisal processes as determinants of emotional and physiological responses to challenging situations. They defined stress as the experience of a mismatch between the demands put on an individual and his or her coping abilities. Finally, with their 'cognitive activation theory of stress' (CATS), Ursin and Eriksen

454

(2004) offer a more comprehensive definition of stress, which distinguishes four aspects: input or stress stimuli (stressor); the individual processing; the non-specific, general stress response; and the experience of the stress response. The stress response as an essential and necessary physiological response serves as a general alarm in a homeostatic system. That alarm elicits specific coping behaviors, which are dependent on acquired expectancies of the outcomes of stimuli and available responses.

For the understanding of how chronic stress can lead to health impairments, McEwen's 'allostatic load model' offers a theoretical framework. Allostasis is defined as a physiological principle to maintain stability through change (Sterling & Eyer, 1988). If an organism aims to maintain stability, it must vary all parameters of its internal milieu and match them appropriately to environmental demands. The coordination of allostatic responses depends on the brain's evaluation of a given challenge (McEwen, 2007) and subsequent physiological responses that are dependent on individual differences regarding personal experiences (trauma, life events), coping styles, health behaviors, and others. Overall, an allostatic response represents a complex pathway for adaptation and coping and is shut off when the challenge is over. However, the same processes that are adaptive under acute stress conditions may ultimately promote disease development when occurring chronically (McEwen, 2007). Thus, if allostatic responses are sustained over months and years, the individual reaches the state of allostatic load, a chronic hyperactivity of some physiological systems and a hypoactivity of others, leading to wear-and-tear on the body and brain. According to this model, catecholamines and the glucocorticoid cortisol are primary endocrine stress mediators promoting secondary outcomes (like metabolic, immunological, blood coagulation, and cardiovascular changes), which potentially lead to manifest disease endpoints (tertiary outcomes). In the following section, we introduce the biological basis of these endocrine stress responses.

2.2 Biological bases of the stress response

When we encounter a psychosocial stressor, two physiological pathways get activated. A first and faster pathway is represented by the sympathetic–adrenal–medullary (SAM) axis. The SAM axis initiates an endocrine reaction, releasing catecholamines from the adrenal glands (about 80% adrenaline and 20% noradrenaline). It also acts through innervation of effector organs by noradrenergic synapses leading to a rapid mobilization of energy, a down-regulation of less important organ functions, and impacts cardiovascular functioning, increasing heart rate, cardiac output, and blood pressure (for an overview see Kudielka & Kirschbaum, 2007).

The second and slower pathway is represented by the activation of the hypothalamus–pituitary–adrenal (HPA) axis. When encountering a challenge, neural stimulation of the paraventricular nucleus of the hypothalamus (PVN) leads to the release of corticotropin-releasing hormone (CRH). After secretion into the hypophyseal portal system, CRH initiates the cleavage of pro-opiomelanocortin (POMC) into adrenocorticotropin (ACTH), beta-endorphin, and other peptides and their subsequent release from the anterior pituitary gland into the blood stream. The primary target of ACTH is the adrenal cortex, where it triggers the secretion of glucocorticoids and adrenal androgens. The main glucocorticoid in humans is the steroid hormone cortisol. Cortisol has a variety of physiological effects. In order to adapt to the increased metabolic demands under acute stress, cortisol enhances circulating levels of energy substrates like glucose, free amino acids, and free fatty acids by acting on a number of enzyme systems in liver, muscles, and fat tissue. In the liver, for example, cortisol enhances gluconeogenesis. Additionally, cortisol may increase circulating free fatty acids by inhibiting lipoprotein lipase, initiating lipolysis and mobilizing free fatty acids from fat depots (McEwen, 2003). To ensure access to resources essential for coping with challenge, cortisol temporarily dampens processes involved in reproduction and cellular growth and immune system activity. Additionally, cortisol has important regulatory effects on the cardiovascular system, regulation of fluid volume, and response to hemorrhage as well as on behavior, appetite control, and affective and cognitive processes like learning and memory (McEwen, 2003). Glucocorticoids also play a key role in the termination of the stress response. A negative feedback action of cortisol on receptors in the hippocampus, hypothalamus, and pituitary gland suppresses the secretion of CRH, ACTH, and cortisol itself. Further, the secretion of cortisol follows a distinct circadian rhythm with an increase (about 50–100%) during the first hour after awakening, the so-called cortisol awakening response (CAR), and decreasing levels over the remaining day (Stalder et al., 2016). Cortisol is mostly bound to proteins, and only 5–10% of the released cortisol circulates as unbound (so-called free) cortisol that exerts its effects on target tissues. In blood, total cortisol (bound plus unbound) is typically determined in plasma or serum, whereas salivary cortisol reflects the free, biologically active fraction. Because cortisol is a lipid-soluble steroid hormone, free cortisol enters saliva by passive diffusion through the cells of the salivary glands. Besides methodological differences between cortisol as measured in blood (total cortisol) versus saliva (free cortisol), there are also some practical issues that are important to be acknowledged (for further discussion see Hellhammer, Wüst, & Kudielka, 2009). The collection of saliva samples is non-invasive, whereas the procedure of drawing a blood sample requires medically trained staff and triggers a physiological response to venepuncture, including an increase of cortisol in some participants (Weckesser et al., 2014). Interestingly, cortisol and its metabolites also accumulate in other organic material such as urine and hair, reflecting aggregated hormone levels (Stalder & Kirschbaum, 2012). This may be beneficial for research questions on the effect of chronic stress.

3 Psychosocial stress in laboratory settings and in the field

Naturally occurring acute and chronic stress responses can be studied outside the laboratory, although researchers have also devised standardized paradigms to elicit acute stress responses in controlled laboratory settings. As reported elsewhere, HPA axis responses can also be directly triggered at different functional levels via pharmacological provocation tests (see Kudielka, Hellhammer, & Wüst, 2009; Seeman & Robbins, 1994). To date, there exist a variety of laboratory stressors that aim to elicit an emotional, cardiovascular, or endocrine stress response. These laboratory stressors can be categorized into four types of stressors: (1) cognitive stressors (cognitive load; e.g., mental arithmetic tasks, academic exams), (2) social stressors (peer rejection, social evaluation; e.g., Trier Social Stress Test, Kirschbaum, Pirke, & Hellhammer, 1993), (3) emotional stressors (perception of emotional material inducing negative emotions; e.g., presentation of emotional pictures or videos), and (4) physical stressors (physical exercise, pain; e.g., Cold Pressor Test) (see Strahler, Skoluda, Kappert, & Nater, 2017). Besides this, intake of meals can activate an endocrine reaction (see Kudielka et al., 2009).

3.1 Psychosocial stress paradigms in laboratory settings

In search of a valid and reliable social stressor for laboratory environments, a meta-analysis by Dickerson and Kemeny (2004) concluded that the key psychological elements in motivated performance tasks to activate the HPA axis are a combination of social-evaluative threat and uncontrollability. The Trier Social Stress Test (TSST) (Kirschbaum, Pirke, & Hellhammer, 1993), which was found to produce the highest and most robust HPA axis activation, incorporates each of these elements, including threat to the social self. The TSST has become one of the most established psychosocial stress paradigms in modern stress research to investigate the psychological and physiological mechanisms of the stress process itself and emotional, cognitive, and behavioral consequences (Kudielka, Hellhammer, & Kirschbaum, 2007). The TSST comprises a free speech on the participant's personal qualities and a surprise mental arithmetic task in front of a two-person committee. In this paradigm, the committee is non-responsive to any attempts of social engagement and trained to withhold any non-verbal feedback. There exists a variety of modified versions of the TSST. For example, to overcome the resource-intensive protocol of the standard TSST and to be able to stress several subjects at once, von Dawans et al. (2011) developed the TSST for groups for up to six participants (TSST-G). Other versions of the original setup are the TSST for children (Buske-Kirschbaum, Jobst, Wustmans, Kirschbaum, Rauh, & Hellhammer, 1997) or elderly subjects (Kudielka et al., 1998) with respectively adapted tasks (see Allen et al., 2016; Kudielka et al., 2007). Recently, a placebo version was also established (Het, Rohleder, Schoofs, Kirschbaum, & Wolf, 2009). The PTSST is a parallelized non-stress control condition that lacks the main stress-inducing components of the TSST (i.e., no committee, no video camera), while being comparable to the original TSST in terms of the general procedure, duration, and cognitive and physical load. Alternatively, also a friendly version, the so-called f-TSST, can be used as control condition, where subjects interact with a friendly committee as opposed to the neutral and reserved behavior shown in the original TSST (Wiemers, Schoofs, & Wolf, 2013). In healthy humans, the TSST reliably induces a two-to-threefold increase in cortisol levels in approximately 70–80% of participants with a reported average effect size of d' = .93 (Dickerson & Kemeny, 2004; Frisch, Häusser, & Mojzisch, 2015; Goodman, Janson, & Wolf, 2017; Kudielka et al., 2007). Although the ecological validity of the TSST has been critically discussed, studies are still sparse (see Kudielka & Wüst, 2010). Recently, we compared salivary cortisol responses to a naturalistic stressor in the form of an oral university exam and TSST in the same subjects (Henze et al., 2017). Findings provide evidence for the view that cortisol as well as subjective stress responses to the TSST are significantly associated with acute stress responses in real life (with a correlation of r = .67 between cortisol increases during the TSST and oral examination).

Recently, Skoluda et al. (2015) investigated whether there exists a 'stimulus-response specificity', comparing the TSST with other commonly used laboratory stressors (namely, Stroop, Cold Pressor Test, ergometry) and a resting control condition. The Stroop Color–Word Interference Test is a cognitive task which requires selective attention and behavioral inhibition of a dominant reaction (subjects are instructed to name printed colors of color words). The Cold Pressor Test (CPT) requires subjects to place their non-dominant hand up to the wrist in a box filled with ice-cold water (temperature held constant at 3–4°C) for as long as possible (maximum immersion duration 3 min). In the bicycle ergometer task, subjects cycle on a stationary bike (e.g., 2 min warm up + 8 min at high level). All paradigms provoked increases in self-reported stress, reaching the highest scores in the TSST, followed by ergometry, Stroop, and CPT. The highest HPA axis response was found in the TSST, followed by ergometry, CPT, and Stroop. Other established psychosocial stress paradigms are, for example, public speech tasks like the Leiden Public Speaking Task (Westenberg et al., 2009), encompassing a speech prepared at home and given in front of a pre-recorded audience, or combined tasks like the Maastricht Acute Stress Test (MAST) (Smeets et al., 2012), recombining the mental arithmetic elements of the TSST with the physical aspects of the CPT under a condition of social evaluation. Stroud and colleagues (2000) developed the Yale Interpersonal Stressor (YIPS), an interpersonal social rejection paradigm that targets the stimulation of negative mood and activation of the HPA axis (see also below).

During the last decade, there have been several attempts to transfer the TSST into virtual reality environments (VR-TSST). This methodological development promises a reduction of cost while increasing experimental control for stress-evoking elements of the task, control for evaluator characteristics (e.g., by standardization/adjustment of sex, race, age, and physical attractiveness of the avatar), control of between-participant session replicability, and location of the task (e.g., applicable from home) (Fallon, Careaga, Sbarra, & O'Connor, 2016). So far, VR-TSSTs have been conducted simply via monitor or projection (Fallon et al., 2016), via head mounted displays (Kelly, Matheson, Martinez, Merali, & Anisman, 2007; Shiban et al., 2016), or inside a VR-Cave, which is a VR system with three rear projected walls and a floor projection (Jönsson et al., 2015; Wallergård, Jönsson, Johansson, & Karlson, 2011). The type of employed VR technology seems to be important in producing a robust stress response (Allen et al., 2016). Level of immersion did not elicit differences in HPA axis activation (Montero-López et al., 2016), whereas adding a virtual competitor more likely leads to a robust cortisol response (Shiban et al., 2016). Important issues for future research on VR paradigms will be the testing of their respective stress-eliciting potency and ecological validity.

Finally, a less resource-intensive alternative might be the socially evaluated cold pressor test (SECPT), combining the thermal pain component of the classical CPT with a social-evaluative component (Schwabe, Haddad, & Schächinger, 2008). Recent evidence shows that the SECPT indeed has the potential to provoke significant HPA axis and subjective stress responses (Schwabe et al., 2008).

3.2 Stress induction in MRI environments

Recent advances in neuroimaging techniques have enabled the investigation of regulatory networks and central nervous processing of acute stress. Several methods have been used to induce stress in the scanner but most of them fail to reliably induce a robust cortisol response (for overview see Dedovic, Aguiar, & Pruessner, 2009). However, in order to be able to study central nervous HPA axis regulation, it is essential that the applied neuroimaging stress paradigm reliably induces HPA axis responses under stress. Furthermore, significant cortisol responses are important as they validate that observed brain activation changes are a response to psychological stress and do not simply reflect the processing of the task itself, e.g., cognitive load.

Thus, Pruessner and colleagues (Dedovic et al., 2005) developed the Montreal Imaging Stress Task (MIST). It comprises a series of computerized challenging mental arithmetic tasks with an induced failure component. During a serial subtraction task, subjects are prompted for faster performance and forced to restart the task upon making a mistake. Additionally, after each run negative feedback regarding the performance is provided. The MIST has been adapted in several studies using fMRI and positron emission tomography (PET). Meanwhile, the MIST has been repeatedly employed successfully (Kogler et al., 2015).

A more recently developed paradigm for the induction of stress in MRI environments is the ScanSTRESS paradigm. Conceptually, the ScanSTRESS is closely based on the TSST and it has been shown to induce robust neuronal, heart rate, and cortisol stress responses (Dahm et al., 2017; Lederbogen et al., 2011; Streit et al., 2014). It is particularly focused on the 'Mason factors' uncontrollability and ego-involvement, implemented by pressure to perform a forced-failure component (adaptive difficulty), and social-evaluative threat induced by an observer panel that is presented to the participant via live video transmission during the scanning procedure. Like the TSST, the ScanSTRESS comprises two different tasks, namely serial subtraction and a mental rotation task (Lederbogen et al., 2011; Streit et al., 2014).

3.3 Stress in everyday settings – ambulatory assessment designs

For most research questions, laboratory stress protocols offer the advantage of standardization across sessions, but they lack the ecological validity of field studies. We now summarize some issues relevant for studying psychosocial stress in real-life settings.

Ambulatory assessment (AA) is an important research tool that allows the describing and understanding of biopsychosocial mechanisms that can (only) be observed in real-life conditions and that are not restricted to laboratory settings while minimizing retrospective biases when gathering ecologically valid data (Kudielka, Gierens, Hellhammer, Wüst, & Schlotz, 2012; Trull & Ebner-Priemer, 2013). AA can be defined as the use of field methods to assess ongoing behavior, physiology, subjective experience, and environmental aspects of humans in their unconstrained natural setting (see www.ambulatory-assessment.org). During the last decade, AA designs have been used increasingly due to the availability of computerized and digitized methods allowing the collection of self-report, observational, physiological and behavioral data. AA also allows investigation into alterations in HPA axis regulation, either under basal conditions or in response to stress, by integrating saliva samples collected by participants in research protocols. AA designs determine the time points and frequency for saliva sampling and are dependent on the particular research question. For example, event-related designs are often used to study infrequent events or cortisol responses to a specific event with high sampling frequency. The combination with time-based designs allows inclusion of baseline (pre-event) cortisol measures. Time-based designs schedule assessments of cortisol at specific time points during a given period. Furthermore, fixed-occasion and variable-occasion designs can be implemented depending on the specific research question (Kudielka et al., 2012; Schlotz, 2011). A recent review summarizes empirical examples on ambulatory psychobiological stress research (Rodrigues, Kaiseler, & Queirós, 2015).

4 Determinants of salivary cortisol responses to challenge

Salivary cortisol responses to psychosocial challenges are characterized by large variation in response magnitude both between individuals in a given context and within individuals across different contexts. Therefore, to unveil psychoneuroendocrine pathways connecting altered stress regulation with ill health, a thorough phenotyping of individual stress reactivity is of major importance. Thus, we now summarize basic knowledge on intra- and interindividual variability in cortisol stress responses. Finally, we address some general methodological issues that should be considered when conducting biopsychosocial stress research.

4.1 Sex, sex steroid-related factors, and age

Sex is an important source of variability for HPA axis stress responses (see Kajantie & Phillips, 2006; Kudielka, Buske-Kirschbaum, Hellhammer, & Kirschbaum, 2004; Kudielka & Kirschbaum, 2005; Kudielka et al., 2009; Otte et al., 2005). Men consistently show higher elevations of free cortisol levels to psychosocial challenge tasks compared to women, an effect which emerged consistently in younger as well as older adults (Kirschbaum, Wüst, & Hellhammer, 1992; Kudielka et al., 1998; Kumsta, Entringer, Hellhammer, & Wüst, 2007). For example, in response to the TSST, males are more likely to respond with increased cortisol levels than females, showing longer peak latencies and higher post-stress peaks (up to twice as high)

(Lopez-Duran, Mayer, & Abelson, 2014). Higher salivary cortisol responses to the TSST in men are also reported by a recent meta-analysis comparing 34 studies with a total sample size of 1350 individuals (640 women) (Liu et al., 2017). This sex-related variation has been attributed to differences in the internal endocrine milieu (see below). However, there has also been a discussion on the nature of the stressor. In contrast to the TSST, the cortisol response to the YIPS (see above) has been reported to be greater in females than males. This suggests that women might be more biologically reactive to interpersonal stress like social rejection challenges than men (Stroud, Papandonatos, D'Angelo, Brush, & Lloyd-Richardson, 2017; Stroud, Salovey, & Epel, 2002). However, this result fails to replicate in other studies (Linnen, Ellenbogen, Cardoso, & Joober, 2012). Regarding the endocrine milieu, the female menstrual cycle as well as intake of oral contraceptives appear to be crucial. In a study exposing a total of 81 male and female adults to the TSST, we had observed that women in the luteal phase (N = 21) show comparable salivary cortisol responses to men (N = 20) while women in the follicular phase (N = 19) and women taking oral contraceptives (N = 21) have significantly lower salivary cortisol responses (Kirschbaum, Kudielka, Gaab, Schommer, & Hellhammer, 1999). Corroborating this observation, Stephens et al. (2016) recently reported a more robust activation of the HPA axis in men compared to women in the follicular phase of the menstrual cycle. However, other studies failed to detect HPA axis response differences across the follicular, ovulatory, or luteal phase (Duchesne & Pruessner, 2013; Herbison et al., 2016). The relatively consistent finding that intake of oral contraceptives leads to reduced free salivary cortisol responses points to a moderating role of corticosteroid–binding–globulin (CBG), because oral contraceptives containing an ethinyl-estradiol component can alter endogenous CBG concentrations (Kirschbaum et al., 1996; Kumsta, Entringer, & Hellhammer, 2007). Finally, as a note of caution, it cannot be ruled out that premenstrual syndrome as well as postmenopausal status or hormone replacement therapy may alter cortisol reactivity to acute stress (for review see Kudielka et al., 2009). In sum, in women the menstrual cycle phase and use of oral contraceptives should be controlled for when investigating HPA axis reactivity. Also, any sex steroid treatment should be excluded or at least reported.

It was assumed that age might be related to a reduced resilience of the HPA axis. However, the question of whether aging comes along with a less flexible functioning of the HPA axis is still unclear. After pharmacological stimulation, the majority of studies showed elevated HPA axis responses in elderly men and women (for reviews and meta-analysis see Kudielka et al., 2009; Otte et al., 2005; Seeman & Robbins, 1994). But, a different picture emerged for studies applying psychosocial stress, with no or somewhat higher responses in older adults, primarily in men (Almela et al., 2011; Rohleder, Kudielka, Hellhammer, Wolf, & Kirschbaum, 2002; for a reanalysis of five independent studies see Kudielka, Buske-Kirschbaum, et al., 2004). From a biological point of view, there exist two explanatory approaches. On the one hand, the so-called glucocorticoid cascade hypothesis explains age-related changes in HPA axis functioning due to a decrease in the ability of hippocampal neurons to maintain sufficient negative feedback, leading to a vicious cycle of continuously increasing HPA axis responses (Sapolsky, Krey, & McEwen, 1986). On the other, as proposed by the 'corticosteroid receptor balance theory', similar endocrine responses to stress in younger and older adults could result from homeostatic control that maintains a new balance between GR and MR, even with older age, leading to a propensity for unchanged HPA axis responses (de Kloet, 1998; de Kloet et al., 1991). Empirical results are rather heterogeneous and it remains unclear if old age is characterized by a 'cascade of events' or a new 'compensatory receptor balance'. Thus, we recommend either assessing the participants' age and controlling for it when it is statistically associated with the outcome or using predefined age restrictions.

4.2 Pregnancy-related factors

Pregnancy, in general, is associated with fundamental changes in HPA axis physiology, characterized by increases in CRH, ACTH, and cortisol levels (for review see La Marca-Ghaemmaghami & Ehlert, 2015). While basal cortisol levels are increased, Entringer et al. (2010) reported decreased psychological stress reactivity to the TSST. However, it cannot be ruled out that, depending on the stressor, maternal psychological reactivity might change across gestation (La Marca-Ghaemmaghami & Ehlert, 2015). Postpartum breast-feeding in lactating women dampens the free cortisol stress response to acute psychosocial stress (for review see Heinrichs, Neumann, & Ehlert, 2002). However, at least in humans, there does not seem to be a difference in salivary cortisol reactions to psychosocial stress in lactating versus non-lactating mothers (Altemus et al., 2001).

Variation in the stress response to challenge in adulthood can also be attributed to factors originating from early life. Early life predictors like fetal growth and length of gestation as well as early life environmental adversity like prenatal substance exposure or psychosocial adversity during childhood have been shown to potentially exert a lifelong impact on HPA axis responses to stress (Hunter, Minnis, & Wilson, 2011; Kajantie & Räikkönen, 2010). Fetal programming of the HPA axis has been proposed as one key pathway for how prenatal stress, adverse birth outcomes (e.g., low birth weight), and later vulnerabilities for numerous diseases might be causally linked (Entringer, Kumsta, Hellhammer, Wadhwa, & Wüst, 2009; Seckl & Meaney, 2004; Wüst, Entringer, Federenko, Schlotz, & Hellhammer, 2005). Furthermore, individuals who experienced high degrees of adversity prior to age 16 also showed a reduced cortisol reactivity to psychosocial challenge (Lovallo, 2013).

As a practical consequence, if not centrally related to the study question, it is advisable to exclude pregnant and lactating women from study participation. In addition, it might be informative to inquire if study participants had been exposed to severe pre- or postnatal adversity.

4.3 (Epi)genetic factors

Interindividual variation in HPA axis stress regulation is under significant influence from genetic factors. For instance, twin studies documented a moderate to high heritability of the cortisol response to psychosocial stress (Federenko, Nagamine, Hellhammer, Wadhwa, & Wüst, 2004). Moreover, significant associations between cortisol regulation and sequence variation in candidate genes belonging to the HPA axis pathway in a narrow sense as well as with variation in more 'distant' genes have repeatedly been reported. For example, GR and MR gene variants have been shown to be related to ACTH and plasma as well as salivary cortisol responses to psychosocial stress (Kumsta, Entringer, Hellhammer et al., 2007; Kumsta, Entringer, Koper, et al., 2007; Wüst et al., 2004). Variation in the gene coding for FK506 binding protein (FKBP5), an important GR regulator, and variation in the CRH receptor gene (CRHR1) were associated with altered cortisol reactivity to the TSST (Bradley et al., 2008; Ising et al., 2008). Genetic variations in other neuroendocrine systems, like the serotonergic or dopaminergic system, that have been shown to be associated with psychosocial stress responses were also found (for reviews see Allen et al., 2016; Foley & Kirschbaum, 2010; Miller, Wankerl, Stalder, Kirschbaum, & Alexander, 2013). Some of these gene variants have been scrutinized in gene-environment interaction studies, like the 5-HTTLPR (serotonin-transporter-linked polymorphic region) where participants homozygous for the s-allele and a significant history of stressful life events show an elevated cortisol secretion in response to the TSST (Alexander et al., 2009). Additionally, initial findings suggest that epigenetic mechanisms might be important modulators of the neurobiological stress response. Epigenetic processes are under the control of environmental factors (including psychological factors like early life stress) and they influence gene activity and expression (for a general overview see Isles, 2015; for an overview on epigenetics and cortisol reactivity see Allen et al., 2016). For example, findings on gene–environment interactions in variation of the 5-HTTLPR have been extended through epigenetic research investigating methylation and gene expression profiles (Alexander et al., 2014; Duman & Canli, 2015).

Overall, the use of (epi)genetic approaches including quantitative genetics, candidate gene, and genome-wide approaches as well as study designs allowing the identification of gene-environment interactions offer great potential to detect stress-related disease mechanisms in humans.

4.4 Lifestyle and behavioral variables

Various lifestyle and behavioral factors, from consumption of alcohol, nicotine, coffee, or dietary energy supplements and intake of medication to physical exercise, body composition, and sleep habits, have been discussed as potential moderators of HPA axis stress responses.

Chronic alcohol consumption (including alcohol dependency), a positive family history of alcohol dependency, and acute ethanol intake have shown to potentially impact HPA axis stress reactivity (for reviews see Foley & Kirschbaum, 2010; Kudielka et al., 2009; van Hedger, Bershad, & de Wit, 2017). However, results remain somewhat heterogeneous, showing blunted or unchanged HPA axis responses to psychosocial stress. Inconsistent findings might, at least in part, be explained by different dosages and low statistical power in some studies. Thus, heavy users should not be eligible in basic research, subjects should be instructed to refrain from alcohol intake the day before study participation, and regular and recent alcohol consumption should be assessed.

Acute as well as habitual smoking can significantly modulate HPA axis stress responses. Since nicotine is a potent acute HPA axis stimulator (through induction of CRH release after binding to cholinergic receptors), acute smoking itself triggers free cortisol increases. Therefore, we recommend strictly avoiding acute smoking before and during stress testing. Furthermore, in consequence, habitual cigarette smokers show attenuated HPA axis responses to psychosocial stress (for reviews see Rohleder & Kirschbaum, 2006; van Hedger et al., 2017). Since it cannot be ruled out that acute nicotine withdrawal does not affect cortisol stress responses, we advise assessing smoking status and excluding smokers or, at least, controlling (statistically) for smoking status.

For caffeine, its pure stimulatory potency for HPA axis activation is not unequivocal (for review see van Hedger et al., 2017). However, there seems to be at least a combined stimulatory effect of acute coffee consumption and psychosocial stress exposure (Lovallo, Farag, Vincent, Thomas, & Wilson, 2006). Also, habitual caffeine consumption was associated with a greater cortisol stress reactivity to the TSST (Vargas & Lopez-Duran, 2017). Therefore, we recommend inquiring into habitual coffee consumption and instructing study participants to refrain from coffee consumption before and during laboratory testing.

Furthermore, cortisol not only affects energy metabolism but is itself also influenced by energy intake. For example, low glucose levels have been associated with a blunted free cortisol response, whereas in glucose-treated subjects stress exposure induced a large salivary cortisol response (while basal cortisol levels remained unchanged). At first glance, this appears to contradict the classical view of the proposed primary glucocorticoid function of providing the individual with energy in stress situations (for review see Rohleder & Kirschbaum, 2007). As a practical consequence, we suggest standardizing blood glucose levels when studying salivary cortisol in response to stress by providing a standardized meal or administration of a glucose-containing standard beverage about 45 minutes before stress exposition (Kudielka et al., 2009).

Stress researchers should also be aware of the fact that not only long- but also short-term medication, vaccines, or dietary supplements (irrespective of route of administration) can potentially alter salivary cortisol responses to psychosocial stress in patient groups and healthy controls. Amongst others, prominent candidates are, e.g., synthetic glucocorticoids and psychotropic drugs (see Strahler et al., 2017). A recent review details the effects of single doses of typical pharmacological agents (e.g., anxiolytics, antidepressants and sedatives, analgesics, beta blockers, etc.) on subjective as well as HPA axis stress responses (Van Hedger et al., 2017). The variety of active pharmaceutical ingredients is tremendous, and thus, the underlying chemical pathways are manifold (see Granger, Hibel, Fortunato, & Kapelewski, 2009; Holsboer & Barden, 1996; Pariante & Miller, 2001). Therefore, not surprisingly, available evidence so far is still fragmentary and very selective. Just to give two empirical examples: While some over-the-counter drugs like aspirin (acetylsalicylic acid) did not alter free cortisol stress responses to the TSST after a five-day treatment (Kudielka, Fischer, et al., 2007), a two-week vitamin C treatment (ascorbic acid) led to a faster salivary cortisol recovery (but not a smaller overall cortisol response) in healthy subjects (Brody, Preut, Schommer, & Schürmeyer, 2002). In sum, we recommend excluding chronic as well as acute medication and recent inoculation/vaccination or, at least, inquiring about on subjects' medication intake. If medication cannot be precluded, it is advisable to account for the half-life of the substance as indicated in the package insert.

Obesity, at least abdominal obesity, is associated with a greater cortisol stress response to psychosocial stress across a majority of studies (Rodriguez, Epel, White, Standen, Seckl, & Tomiyama, 2015). In slightly overweight but otherwise healthy participants, there are also reports of normal salivary cortisol responses to stress (Herbison et al., 2016; Jayasinghe, Torres, Nowson, Tilbrook, & Turner, 2014). Additionally, high levels of physical exercise as well as physical fitness have been associated with a blunted cortisol response to acute psychosocial stress, as shown in group comparisons (between-subjects designs) as well as in interventional studies (within-subject designs) (Klaperski, von Dawans, Heinrichs, & Fuchs, 2013; Rimmele et al., 2009). In consideration of such evidence, stress researchers should make a deliberate decision about their targeted study population (e.g., define obesity as exclusion criteria), instruct study participants to refrain from heavy physical exercise before study participation (even the day before), and assess and (statistically) control for physical fitness.

Evidence on the effects of sleep length on cortisol stress responses the night before testing does not support strong effects, while sleep deprivation (Vargas & Lopez-Duran, 2017) or low sleep quality (Bassett, Lupis, Gianferante, Rohleder, & Wolf, 2015; Mrug, Tyson, Turan, & Granger, 2016; Wright, Valdimarsdottir, Erblich, & Bovbjerg, 2007) might be associated with a blunted acute cortisol response the day after. Beside the assessment of sleep habits (if necessary), we strongly recommend ensuring that laboratory appointments do not interfere with the CAR (Stalder et al., 2016), daytime napping, shift work, or jet-lag (Federenko, Nagamine, et al., 2004).

4.5 Psychological factors and interventions

Psychosocial stress paradigms like the TSST rely on contextual factors to elicit HPA axis activation. Therefore, it seems natural that the social environment can exert modulating effects on endocrine responses. It has been shown that social support, at least in men, attenuated the HPA axis response to the TSST (Kirschbaum, Klauer, Filipp, & Hellhammer, 1995; Ditzen et al., 2008). This effect might be biologically moderated by the neuropeptide oxytocin (for further discussion see Hostinar, Sullivan, & Gunnar, 2014), as it enhanced the buffering effect of social support on salivary cortisol stress responsiveness in young men (Heinrichs, Baumgartner, Kirschbaum, & Ehlert, 2003). Women who received positive physical partner contact (i.e., a massage) before being exposed to a psychosocial stressor exhibited significantly lower cortisol responses compared to women who received social support or had no social interaction with their partner (Ditzen et al., 2007). Also, psychological interventions like relaxing music, brief group-based cognitive–behavioral stress management, mind–body practices like progressive muscle relaxation or Taiji practice, and some forms of meditation have been shown to dampen the endocrine stress response to TSST exposure (Gaab et al., 2003; Hammerfald et al., 2006). Such results remind us that investigators should strictly adhere to given standardized instructions in order to avoid any unintended social effects between subjects and investigators that might (un)systematically alter subjects' stress responses.

4.6 Personality

Repeatedly, it was hypothesized that salivary cortisol responses to stress are closely related to stable personality traits since the endocrine response to psychosocial stress can be viewed as a close interaction between situation and person variables within a given context (see Kudielka et al., 2009). However, it should be of note that novelty may cover the impact of personality on HPA axis regulation on the first exposure to a stress task, as indicated by studies showing that the relationship between salivary cortisol responses and personality factors only became apparent after repeated stress exposure (Pruessner et al., 1997). Personality traits that have traditionally been associated with greater psychopathology (like high neuroticism or lower extraversion) do occasionally show an effect on HPA axis regulation after onetime stress exposure (Oswald et al., 2006). Also, trait rumination has been shown to prolong the salivary cortisol response to stress in some (Shull et al., 2016; Stewart, Mazurka, Bond, Wynne-Edwards, & Harkness, 2013; Zoccola, Quas, & Yim, 2010) but not all studies (Young & Nolen-Hoeksema, 2001; Zoccola & Dickerson, 2015). In their meta-analysis, Chida and Hamer (2008) could not find any evidence for an association between negative psychological states or traits (e.g., negative affect, neuroticism, hostility, anxiety, aggression, etc.) and acute HPA axis stress responses, while they found evidence for associations between decreased HPA axis reactivity and positive psychological states or traits (e.g., happiness, positive mood, internal locus of control, self-esteem, empathy, spirituality, active coping, etc.). In sum, data aggregation over repeated stress exposures appear to enhance the chance to uncover otherwise predominantly masked relationships between self-reported personality traits and salivary cortisol stress responses. Therefore, if researchers are interested in studying associations between stable personality traits and acute cortisol stress responses, it might be advisable to apply multiple stress exposure sessions. Another promising approach to gain valuable insight in such relationships could be the use of implicit measures instead of self-reports (e.g., Schultheiss, Wiemers, & Wolf, 2014).

4.7 Chronic stress

Chronic stress, states of exhaustion, and burnout impact on acute stress responses should therefore be considered when studying HPA axis reactivity to psychosocial stress (for overviews and a meta-analysis see Chida & Hamer, 2008; Heim, Ehlert, & Hellhammer, 2000; Kudielka et al., 2006). However, conceptualizations of chronic stress (for example family caregiving, job strain, effort–reward imbalance, unemployment including financial strain, etc.) and applied assessment tools vary substantially. This might, at least in part, explain the great variability in reported results, ranging from hyper- to hyporesponsivity of the HPA axis to acute stress in chronically stressed individuals (see also below). Heim and colleagues (2000) carefully screened the then-existing literature and found evidence for hypocortisolism in individuals living under conditions of chronic stress. A thorough discussion of potential mechanistic pathways (like reduced bio-synthesis or depletion of CRH, ACTH, and cortisol, CRH hypersecretion and adaptive down-regulation of pituitary CRH receptors or changes in receptor sensitivity, increased feedback sensitivity of the HPA axis, or morphological changes) can be found there.

Studies on chronic work stress and burnout (as a potential consequence of adverse working conditions) are somewhat mixed, reporting either hyper- or hyporesponsivity (for review see Kudielka et al., 2006). However, the few studies that assessed chronic work stress according to the effort–reward imbalance model appear to be more consistent, merely pointing to HPA axis hyporeactivity (for review see Bellingrath & Kudielka, 2017). This model builds on the notion of social reciprocity, stating that the experience of a failed reciprocity between high work-related effort and low occupational rewards leads to a state of chronic stress. In accordance, more recent studies on severe burnout, clinical cases of burnout, or insufficient long-term recovery after exhaustion disorder also merely point to blunted salivary cortisol responses to psychosocial stress (Jönsson et al., 2015; De Vente, van Amsterdam, Olff, Kamphuis, & Emmelkamp, 2015; Lennartsson, Sjörs, Währborg, Ljung, & Jonsdottir, 2015).

Besides the already-mentioned marked differences in the conceptualization of chronic stress, it is reasonable to assume that chronic stress leads to HPA axis regulation changes over time. According to a time-course or two-stage model (see Bellingrath & Kudielka, 2017; Kudielka et al., 2006), an early state of chronic stress (characterized by hyperactivity of the HPA axis) could, in the long run, lead to a hyperactive state as result of a functional adaptation to excessive exposure to stress hormones. In consequence, such changes over time could then blur results pattern, and hyper- and hypocortisolemic effects in different individuals could cancel each other out in group analysis.

4.8 Psychopathology

Meanwhile, there is clear evidence for a causal role of stress in the genesis, development, and progression of numerous diseases. Simultaneously, evidence has accumulated that shows that HPA axis responses to acute stress are altered in clinical populations encompassing various somatic as well as psychiatric diseases (Chrousos, 2009; Kudielka & Wüst, 2010). Detailed summaries and meta-analysis can be found elsewhere, as for somatic illnesses (Strahler, Skoluda, Rohleder, & Nater, 2016); autoimmune disorders (Buske-Kirschbaum, Geiben, Höllig, Morschhäuser, & Hellhammer, 2002; Tsigos & Chrousos, 1994); psychiatric diseases including depression, schizophrenia, post-traumatic stress disorder, anxiety and panic disorders etc. (Bradley & Dinan, 2010; Burke, Davis, Otte, & Mohr, 2005; Ciufolini, Dazzan, Kempton, Pariante, & Mondelli, 2014; Knorr, Vinberg, Kessing, & Wetterslev, 2010; Zorn et al., 2016); or, in particular, health and disease in children (Jessop & Turner-Cobb, 2008). From a mechanistic point of view, it is not always clear whether HPA axis alterations lead to health impairments, if an illness leads to altered HPA axis alterations, or both. In any case, in non-clinical studies, subjects should carefully be screened for health impairments and respective exclusion criteria should be established defining study eligibility.

4.9 Methodological issues

Finally, some methodological issues, like habituation, time of testing (additional) collection of blood samples, anticipation effects, and the concomitant assessment of stress appraisal and inter-laboratory effects need to be briefly discussed.

A prominent feature of HPA axis responses to acute psychosocial stress is its strong habituation over repeated exposures (Pruessner et al., 1997; Schommer, Wiemers, & Wolf, 2003;

Federenko, Wüst, et al., 2004). In this regard, the HPA axis is different from the sympathetic nervous, immune, and blood coagulation system, as well as indices of hemoconcentration, which all show rather uniform activation patterns after repeated stress exposures (see Kudielka et al., 2009). In more detail, Wüst, Federenko, van Rossum, Koper, and Hellhammer (2005) reported a substantial variability of salivary cortisol response habituation patterns in healthy individuals. While 52% of the participants showed the well-known response habituation across three TSST test sessions (indicated by a response reduction across TSST exposures), 30% did not show an obvious response alteration and almost 16% of participants showed a response sensitization (indicated by a response increase across testings). The authors speculated that the specific habituation of the HPA axis to psychosocial stress is due to a reduction in context variables across sessions due to the decreasing experience of task novelty, unpredictability, and uncontrollability by subjects (Kudielka et al., 2009; Wüst, Federenko, et al., 2005). From a methodological point of view, due to such habituation effects, a within-subjects design with repeated pre- and post-interventional TSST exposure does not qualify as valid proof of stress-reducing effects of a given treatment on acute HPA axis stress regulation (e.g., psychotherapy, stress management training, etc.) since it would remain unclear whether the treatment or the familiarization with the TSST exposure had caused a potential stress response reduction. However, when planning studies with repeated exposition to the TSST, pure habituation effects might potentially be prevented, or at least be minimized, with large enough between-trial intervals and changing test settings (see Foley & Kirschbaum, 2010). Having said that, the repeated exposure to the same stressor can help to unveil associations with factors that might be otherwise overlooked at first testing, like personality traits (Pruessner et al., 1997), effects of genetic make-up (Federenko, Wüst, et al., 2004), or work-related exhaustion (Kudielka, von Känel, et al., 2006).

Due to the diurnal rhythm of cortisol secretion, and to avoid any interference with the CAR (Kudielka & Wüst, 2010; Stalder et al., 2016), acute stress sessions should ideally be scheduled in the afternoon. In a reanalysis of five independent studies comparing morning and afternoon stress sessions, we found that net salivary cortisol stress responses to the TSST can be assessed with comparable reliability in the morning or afternoon, taking into account that pre-stress cortisol levels are systematically higher during the morning compared to the afternoon (Kudielka, Schommer, Hellhammer, & Kirschbaum, 2004). Nevertheless, we could observe that higher basal cortisol levels were slightly (but significantly) related to a lower response after stress, pointing to the possibility that higher baseline levels might reduce the net stress response to some degree. In accordance, in a recent meta-analytical assessment (based on 186 TSST studies), Goodman et al. (2017) did not observe pronounced differences in effects sizes regarding cortisol responses at different times of day, but cortisol responses were slightly lower and more variable during morning sessions. Altogether, these findings suggest that performing TSST sessions during the afternoon may increase the likelihood of strong cortisol stress responses, while other time windows (if avoiding meal times) still present feasible alternatives. At least, all testings of an experimental study should be performed during the same time window.

When planning on taking (additional) blood samples to measure ACTH, total cortisol, or other biological compounds, it should be considered that venepunctures elicit a cortisol response in more than one-third of subjects. To level venepuncture-related cortisol responses on subsequent measurements, it is advised to take samples only after an extended relaxation period that follows cannula insertion (Weckesser et al., 2014).

As is already known, cortisol stress responses can be evoked, at least in men, by the sole anticipation of an upcoming psychosocial stress task (Kirschbaum, Wüst, & Hellhammer, 1992). Recently, Engert et al. (2013) found a positive correlation between anticipatory and reactive cortisol stress responses. This points to the necessity of standardized study instructions (e.g., its timing) as well as relaxation periods (e.g., its minimum length) in which subjects should not ruminate about the upcoming stress task (see also Goodman et al., 2017).

In respect to concomitant psychometric assessments, Gaab and colleagues reported that differences in anticipatory cognitive appraisal of a psychosocial challenge (in contrast to retrospective stress appraisal) explains up to 35% of the variance of the salivary cortisol stress response (Gaab, Rohleder, Nater, & Ehlert, 2005). With this, we recommend assessing not only post-stress appraisal but also anticipatory appraisal directly before stress exposure. However, a close correspondence between biological and subjective emotional stress responses is rarely reported (for a meta-analysis see Campbell & Ehlert, 2012), pointing to a lack of covariance between physiological and subjective stress markers. At first glance, this appears to be surprising because, from a theoretical point of view, psychological and biological responses represent indicators of the same construct, speaking for a strong association. Interestingly, recent work could show that psycho-endocrine responses are indeed coupled with cortisol levels. Schlotz and colleagues (2008) applied time-lagged correlations and showed that the so-far described lack of covariance might be, at least in part, explained by the different time courses of endocrine and psychological responses to stress, with subjective-psychological responses preceding HPA axis responses. That means, if we want to draw valid conclusions about psycho-endocrine covariance in response to acute stress, the different time courses of psychological and biological responses need to be accounted for.

Last but not least, it should be noted that although stress protocols like the TSST are basically highly standardized paradigms, there exists certain methodological variability between laboratories in practical implementation. For the case of the TSST, Goodman et al. (2017) recently analyzed various effects of protocol variations across laboratories and provided a list of recommendations to ensure a robust activation of the HPA axis, like frequent sampling between 30 and 45 minutes after TSST onset. Although the effectiveness of the TSST appears to be relatively robust to some methodological variation, they recommend adhering to the original protocol specifications to ensure maximized cortisol responses and to enable better comparability across studies.

5 Final remarks

Identifying sources of intra- and interindividual differences of HPA axis responses to psycho-social stress in humans is a challenging, laborious, and time-consuming task. Obviously, detailed knowledge on such differences in cortisol stress responses is essential in psychoneuroendocrine research. Here, we aimed to discuss the most prominent factors that have emerged over the last decades. Such factors need to be adequately considered when conducting studies on HPA axis reactivity. This global recommendation is certainly highly challenging since it is not possible to control for countless potential confounders in each study, especially if study samples are modest. Therefore, we aimed to give more specific recommendations as to how researchers might handle the respective variables. However, researchers should be aware of the fact that still this list is selective and new insight is accumulating continuously.

Nevertheless, we figure that the given knowledge might be helpful at different stages of a study project. During the planning stage, it might guide the researchers' decisions on exclusion criteria, eligibility and selection of study participants, factors that could be held constant across participants, information that should be provided by subjects, and issues relevant for instructions. At this stage, researchers should decide if a critical factor should be defined as an exclusion variable, held constant, used later as covariate, or even serve as experimental variation. Important aspects that direct such decisions are the central study question, the available sample size, the need for generalizability of results, and, of course, issues regarding practicability. During data analysis, the presented knowledge could help to decide for the most relevant moderating and intervening variables that should enter the statistical model, depending in number on the given study sample. Finally, such knowledge is essential when it comes to results interpretation. The discussion of sources of intra- and interindividual differences might also help to explain conflicting or contradictory data that exists in the available literature. With this, we hope to contribute to the understanding of pathways leading from individual psychobiological stress regulation to health and disease.

References

Alexander, N., Kuepper, Y., Schmitz, A., Osinsky, R., Kozyra, E., & Hennig, J. (2009). Gene-environment interactions predict cortisol responses after acute stress: Implications for the etiology of depression. *Psychoneuroendocrinology*, *34*(9), 1294–1303. doi:10.1016/j.psyneuen.2009.03.017

Alexander, N., Wankerl, M., Hennig, J., Miller, R., Zänkert, S., Steudte-Schmiedgen, S., . . . Kirschbaum, C. (2014). DNA methylation profiles within the serotonin transporter gene moderate the association of 5-HTTLPR and cortisol stress reactivity. *Translational Psychiatry*, *4*, e443. doi:10.1038/tp.2014.88

Allen, A. P., Kennedy, P. J., Dockray, S., Cryan, J. F., Dinan, T. G., & Clarke, G. (2016). The Trier Social Stress Test: Principles and practice for submission to neurobiology of stress. *Neurobiology of Stress*, *6*, 113–126. doi:10.1016/j.ynstr.2016.11.001

Almela, M., Hidalgo, V., Villada, C., van der Meij, L., Espin, L., Gomez-Amor, J., & Salvador, A. (2011). Salivary alpha-amylase response to acute psychosocial stress: The impact of age. *Biological Psychology*, *87*(3), 421–429. doi:10.1016/j.biopsycho.2011.05.008

Altemus, M., Redwine, L. S., Leong, Y. M., Frye, C. A, Porges, S. W., & Carter, C. S. (2001). Responses to laboratory psychosocial stress in postpartum women. *Psychosomatic Medicine*, *63*(5), 814–821. doi:10.1097/00006842-200109000-00015

Bassett, S. M., Lupis, S. B., Gianferante, D., Rohleder, N., & Wolf, J. M. (2015). Sleep quality but not sleep quantity effects on cortisol responses to acute psychosocial stress. *Stress*, *18*(6), 638–644. doi:10.3109/10253890.2015.1087503

Bellingrath, S., & Kudielka, B. M. (2017). Biological pathways to stress-related disease vulnerability in educators. In T. M. McIntyre, S. E. McIntyre, & D. J. Francis (Eds.), *Educator stress: An occupational health perspective*. Berlin: Springer.

Bradley, A. J., & Dinan, T. G. (2010). A systematic review of hypothalamic-pituitary-adrenal axis function in schizophrenia: Implications for mortality. *Journal of Psychopharmacology*, *24*(Suppl. 4), 91–118. doi:10.1177/1359786810385491

Bradley, R. G., Binder, E. B., Epstein, M. P., Tang, Y., Nair, H. P., Liu, W., . . . Ressler, K. J. (2008). Influence of child abuse on adult depression: Moderation by the corticotropin-releasing hormone receptor gene. *Archives of General Psychiatry*, *65*(2), 190–200. doi:10.1001/archgenpsychiatry.2007.26

Brody, S., Preut, R., Schommer, K., & Schürmeyer, T. H. (2002). A randomized controlled trial of high dose ascorbic acid for reduction of blood pressure, cortisol, and subjective responses to psychological stress. *Psychopharmacology*, *159*(3), 319–324. doi:10.1007/s00213-001-0929-6

Burke, H. M., Davis, M. C., Otte, C., & Mohr, D. C. (2005). Depression and cortisol responses to psychological stress: A meta-analysis. *Psychoneuroendocrinology*, *30*(9), 846–856. doi:10.1016/j.psyneuen.2005.02.010

Buske-Kirschbaum, A., Geiben, A., Höllig, H., Morschhäuser, E., & Hellhammer, D. (2002). Altered responsiveness of the hypothalamus-pituitary-adrenal axis and the sympathetic adrenomedullary system to stress in patients with atopic dermatitis. *The Journal of Clinical Endocrinology and Metabolism*, *87*(9), 4245–4251. doi:10.1210/jc.2001-010872

Buske-Kirschbaum, A., Jobst, S., Wustmans, A., Kirschbaum, C., Rauh, W., & Hellhammer, D. (1997). Attenuated free cortisol response to psychosocial stress in children with atopic dermatitis. *Psychosomatic Medicine*, *59*(4), 419–426.

Campbell, J., & Ehlert, U. (2012). Acute psychosocial stress: Does the emotional stress response correspond with physiological responses? *Psychoneuroendocrinology*, *37*(8), 1111–1134. doi:10.1016/j.psyneuen.2011.12.010

Cannon, W. B. (1914). The interrelations of emotions as suggested by recent physiological researches. *The American Journal of Psychology*, *25*(2), 256. doi:10.2307/1413414

Chida, Y., & Hamer, M. (2008). Chronic psychosocial factors and acute physiological responses to laboratory-induced stress in healthy populations: A quantitative review of 30 years of investigations. *Psychological Bulletin, 134*(6), 829–885. doi:10.1037/a0013342

Chrousos, G. P. (2009). Stress and disorders of the stress system. *Nature Reviews Endocrinology, 5*(7), 374–381. doi:10.1038/nrendo.2009.106

Ciufolini, S., Dazzan, P., Kempton, M. J., Pariante, C., & Mondelli, V. (2014). HPA axis response to social stress is attenuated in schizophrenia but normal in depression: Evidence from a meta-analysis of existing studies. *Neuroscience and Biobehavioral Reviews, 47*, 359–368. doi:10.1016/j.neubiorev.2014.09.004

Dahm, A-S., Schmierer, P., Veer, I. M., Streit, F., Görgen, A., Kruschwitz, J., . . . Erk, S. (2017). The burden of conscientiousness? Examining brain activation and cortisol response during social evaluative stress. *Psychoneuroendocrinology, 78*, 48–56. doi:10.1016/j.psyneuen.2017.01.019

de Kloet, E. R. (1998). Brain corticosteroid receptor balance in health and disease. *Endocrine Reviews, 19*(3), 269–301. doi:10.1210/er.19.3.269

de Kloet, E. R., Sutanto, W., Rots, N., van Haarst, A., van den Berg, D., Oitzl, M., . . . Voorhuis, D. (1991). Plasticity and function of brain corticosteroid receptors during aging. *Acta Endocrinologica*, 65–72.

de Vente, W., van Amsterdam, J. G. C., Olff, M., Kamphuis, J. H., & Emmelkamp, P. M. G. (2015). Burnout is associated with reduced parasympathetic activity and reduced HPA axis responsiveness, predominantly in males. *BioMed Research International*, 431725. doi:10.1155/2015/431725

Dedovic, K., D'Aguiar, C., & Pruessner, J. C. (2009). What stress does to your brain: A review of neuroimaging studies. *The Canadian Journal of Psychiatry, 54*(1), 6–15. doi:10.1177/070674370905400104

Dedovic, K., Renwick, R., Mahani, N. K., Engert, V., Lupien, S. J., & Pruessner, J. C. (2005). The montreal imaging stress task: Using functional imaging to investigate the effects of perceiving and processing psychosocial stress in the human brain. *Journal of Psychiatry & Neuroscience, 30*(5), 319–325. Retrieved from www.ncbi.nlm.nih.gov/pmc/articles/PMC1197276/

Dickerson, S. S., & Kemeny, M. E. (2004). Acute stressors and cortisol responses: A theoretical integration and synthesis of laboratory research. *Psychological Bulletin, 130*(3), 355–391. doi:10.1037/0033-2909.130.3.355

Ditzen, B., Neumann, I. D., Bodenmann, G., von Dawans, B., Turner, R. A., Ehlert, U., & Heinrichs, M. (2007). Effects of different kinds of couple interaction on cortisol and heart rate responses to stress in women. *Psychoneuroendocrinology, 32*(5), 565–574. doi:10.1016/j.psyneuen.2007.03.011

Ditzen, B., Schmidt, S., Strauss, B., Nater, U. M., Ehlert, U., & Heinrichs, M. (2008). Adult attachment and social support interact to reduce psychological but not cortisol responses to stress. *Journal of Psychosomatic Research, 64*(5), 479–486. doi:10.1016/j.jpsychores.2007.11.011

Duchesne, A., & Pruessner, J. C. (2013). Association between subjective and cortisol stress response depends on the menstrual cycle phase. *Psychoneuroendocrinology, 38*(12), 3155–3159. doi:10.1016/j.psyneuen.2013.08.009

Duman, E. A., & Canli, T. (2015). Influence of life stress, 5-HTTLPR genotype, and SLC6A4 methylation on gene expression and stress response in healthy Caucasian males. *Biology of Mood & Anxiety Disorders, 5*, 1–14. doi:10.1186/s13587-015-0017-x

Engert, V., Efanov, S. I., Duchesne, A., Vogel, S., Corbo, V., & Pruessner, J. C. (2013). Differentiating anticipatory from reactive cortisol responses to psychosocial stress. *Psychoneuroendocrinology, 38*(8), 1328–1337. doi:10.1016/j.psyneuen.2012.11.018

Entringer, S., Buss, C., Shirtcliff, E. A., Cammack, A. L., Yim, I. S., Chicz-DeMet, A., . . . Wadhwa, P. D. (2010). Attenuation of maternal psychophysiological stress responses and the maternal cortisol awakening response over the course of human pregnancy. *Stress, 13*(3), 258–268. doi:10.3109/10253890903349501

Entringer, S., Kumsta, R., Hellhammer, D. H., Wadhwa, P. D., & Wüst, S. (2009). Prenatal exposure to maternal psychosocial stress and HPA axis regulation in young adults. *Hormones and Behavior, 55*(2), 292–298. doi:10.1016/j.yhbeh.2008.11.006

Fallon, M. A., Careaga, J. S., Sbarra, D. A., & O'Connor, M-F. (2016). Utility of a virtual Trier Social Stress Test: Initial findings and benchmarking comparisons. *Psychosomatic Medicine, 78*(7), 835–840. doi:10.1097/PSY.0000000000000338

Federenko, I. S., Nagamine, M., Hellhammer, D. H., Wadhwa, P. D., & Wüst, S. (2004). The heritability of hypothalamus pituitary adrenal axis responses to psychosocial stress is context dependent. *The Journal of Clinical Endocrinology and Metabolism, 89*(12), 6244–6250. doi:10.1210/jc.2004-0981

Federenko, I., Wüst, S., Hellhammer, D. H., Dechoux, R., Kumsta, R., & Kirschbaum, C. (2004). Free cortisol awakening responses are influenced by awakening time. *Psychoneuroendocrinology, 29*(2), 174–184. doi:10.1016/S0306-4530(03)00021-0

Foley, P., & Kirschbaum, C. (2010). Human hypothalamus-pituitary-adrenal axis responses to acute psychosocial stress in laboratory settings. *Neuroscience and Biobehavioral Reviews, 35*(1), 91–96. doi:10.1016/j.neubiorev.2010.01.010

Frisch, J. U., Häusser, J. A., & Mojzisch, A. (2015). The Trier Social Stress Test as a paradigm to study how people respond to threat in social interactions. *Frontiers in Psychology, 6,* 1–14. doi:10.3389/fpsyg.2015.00014

Gaab, J., Blättler, N., Menzi, T., Pabst, B., Stoyer, S., & Ehlert, U. (2003). Randomized controlled evaluation of the effects of cognitive-behavioral stress management on cortisol responses to acute stress in healthy subjects. *Psychoneuroendocrinology, 28*(6), 767–779. doi:10.1016/S0306-4530(02)00069-0

Gaab, J., Rohleder, N., Nater, U. M., & Ehlert, U. (2005). Psychological determinants of the cortisol stress response: The role of anticipatory cognitive appraisal. *Psychoneuroendocrinology, 30*(6), 599–610. doi:10.1016/j.psyneuen.2005.02.001

Goodman, W. K., Janson, J., & Wolf, J. M. (2017). Meta-analytical assessment of the effects of protocol variations on cortisol responses to the Trier Social Stress Test. *Psychoneuroendocrinology, 80,* 26–35. doi:10.1016/j.psyneuen.2017.02.030

Granger, D. A., Hibel, L. C., Fortunato, C. K., & Kapelewski, C. H. (2009). Medication effects on salivary cortisol: Tactics and strategy to minimize impact in behavioral and developmental science. *Psychoneuroendocrinology, 34*(10), 1437–1448. doi:10.1016/j.psyneuen.2009.06.017

Hammerfald, K., Eberle, C., Grau, M., Kinsperger, A., Zimmermann, A., Ehlert, U., & Gaab, J. (2006). Persistent effects of cognitive-behavioral stress management on cortisol responses to acute stress in healthy subjects – a randomized controlled trial. *Psychoneuroendocrinology, 31*(3), 333–339. doi:10.1016/j.psyneuen.2005.08.007

Heim, C., Ehlert, U., & Hellhammer, D. H. (2000). The potential role of hypocortisolism in the pathophysiology of stress-related bodily disorders. *Psychoneuroendocrinology, 25*(1), 1–35. doi:10.1016/S0306-4530(99)00035-9

Heinrichs, M., Baumgartner, T., Kirschbaum, C., & Ehlert, U. (2003). Social support and oxytocin interact to suppress cortisol and subjective responses to psychosocial stress. *Biological Psychiatry, 54*(12), 1389–1398. doi:10.1016/S0006-3223(03)00465-7

Heinrichs, M., Neumann, I., & Ehlert, U. (2002). Lactation and stress: Protective effects of breast-feeding in humans. *Stress, 5*(3), 195–203. doi:10.1080/1025389021000010530

Hellhammer, D. H., Wüst, S., & Kudielka, B. M. (2009). Salivary cortisol as a biomarker in stress research. *Psychoneuroendocrinology, 34*(2), 163–171. doi:10.1016/j.psyneuen.2008.10.026

Henze, G-I., Zänkert, S., Urschler, D. F., Hiltl, T. J., Kudielka, B. M., Pruessner, J. C., & Wüst, S. (2017). Testing the ecological validity of the Trier Social Stress Test: Association with real-life exam stress. *Psychoneuroendocrinology, 75,* 52–55. doi:10.1016/j.psyneuen.2016.10.002

Herbison, C. E., Henley, D., Marsh, J., Atkinson, H., Newnham, J. P., Matthews, S. G., . . . Pennell, C. E. (2016). Characterization and novel analyses of acute stress response patterns in a population-based cohort of young adults: Influence of gender, smoking, and BMI. *Stress, 19*(2), 139–150. doi:10.3109/10253890.2016.1146672

Het, S., Rohleder, N., Schoofs, D., Kirschbaum, C., & Wolf, O. T. (2009). Neuroendocrine and psychometric evaluation of a placebo version of the "Trier Social Stress Test". *Psychoneuroendocrinology, 34*(7), 1075–1086. doi:10.1016/j.psyneuen.2009.02.008

Holsboer, F., & Barden, N. (1996). Antidepressants and hypothalamic-pituitary-adrenocortical regulation. *Endocrine Reviews, 17*(2), 187–205. doi:10.1210/edrv-17-2-187

Hostinar, C. E., Sullivan, R. M., & Gunnar, M. R. (2014). Psychobiological mechanisms underlying the social buffering of the hypothalamic – pituitary – adrenocortical axis: A review of animal models and human studies across development. *Psychological Bulletin, 140*(1), 256–282. doi:10.1037/a0032671

Hunter, A. L., Minnis, H., & Wilson, P. (2011). Altered stress responses in children exposed to early adversity: A systematic review of salivary cortisol studies. *Stress, 14*(6), 614–626. doi:10.3109/10253890.2011.577848

Incollingo Rodriguez, A. C., Epel, E. S., White, M. L., Standen, E. C., Seckl, J. R., & Tomiyama, A. J. (2015). Hypothalamic-pituitary-adrenal axis dysregulation and cortisol activity in obesity: A systematic review. *Psychoneuroendocrinology, 62,* 301–318. doi:10.1016/j.psyneuen.2015.08.014

Ising, M., Depping, A-M., Siebertz, A., Lucae, S., Unschuld, P. G., Kloiber, S., . . . Holsboer, F. (2008). Polymorphisms in the FKBP5 gene region modulate recovery from psychosocial stress in healthy controls. *The European Journal of Neuroscience, 28*(2), 389–398. doi:10.1111/j.1460-9568.2008.06332.x

Isles, A. R. (2015). Neural and behavioral epigenetics; what it is, and what is hype. *Genes, Brain and Behavior, 14*(1), 64–72. doi:10.1111/gbb.12184

Jayasinghe, S. U., Torres, S. J., Nowson, C. A., Tilbrook, A. J., & Turner, A. I. (2014). Physiological responses to psychological stress: Importance of adiposity in men aged 50–70 years. *Endocrine Connections, 3,* 110–119. doi:10.1530/EC-14-0042

Jessop, D., & Turner-Cobb, J. (2008). Measurement and meaning of salivary cortisol: A focus on health and disease in children. *Stress, 11*(1), 1–14. doi:10.1080/10253890701365527

Jönsson, P., Österberg, K., Wallergård, M., Hansen, Å. M., Garde, A. H., Johansson, G., & Karlson, B. (2015). Exhaustion-related changes in cardiovascular and cortisol reactivity to acute psychosocial stress. *Physiology & Behavior, 151,* 327–337. doi:10.1016/j.physbeh.2015.07.020

Kajantie, E., & Phillips, D. I. W. (2006). The effects of sex and hormonal status on the physiological response to acute psychosocial stress. *Psychoneuroendocrinology, 31*(2), 151–178. doi:10.1016/j.psyneuen.2005.07.002

Kajantie, E., & Räikkönen, K. (2010). Early life predictors of the physiological stress response later in life. *Neuroscience and Biobehavioral Reviews, 35*(1), 23–32. doi:10.1016/j.neubiorev.2009.11.013

Kelly, O., Matheson, K., Martinez, A., Merali, Z., & Anisman, H. (2007). Psychosocial stress evoked by a virtual audience: Relation to neuroendocrine activity. *Cyberpsychology & Behavior, 10*(5), 655–662. doi:10.1089/cpb.2007.9973

Kirschbaum, C., Klauer, T., Filipp, S. H., & Hellhammer, D. H. (1995). Sex-specific effects of social support on cortisol and subjective responses to acute psychological stress. *Psychosomatic Medicine, 57*(1), 23–31. doi:0033-3174/95/570100234$0300/0

Kirschbaum, C., Kudielka, B. M., Gaab, J., Schommer, N. C., & Hellhammer, D. H. (1999). Impact of gender, menstrual cycle phase, and oral contraceptives on the activity of the hypothalamus-pituitary-adrenal axis. *Psychosomatic Medicine, 61*(2), 154–162.

Kirschbaum, C., Pirke, K-M., & Hellhammer, D. H. (1993). The "Trier Social Stress Test" – a tool for investigating psychobiological stress responses in a laboratory setting. *Neuropsychobiology, 28*(1–2), 76–81. doi:10.1159/000119004

Kirschbaum, C., Schommer, N., Federenko, I., Gaab, J., Neumann, O., Oellers, M., . . . Hellhammer, D. H. (1996). Short-term estradiol treatment enhances pituitary-adrenal axis and sympathetic responses to psychosocial stress in healthy young men. *The Journal of Clinical Endocrinology and Metabolism, 81*(10), 3639–3643. doi:10.1210/jcem.81.10.8855815

Kirschbaum, C., Wüst, S., & Hellhammer, D. (1992). Consistent sex differences in cortisol responses to psychological stress. *Psychosomatic Medicine, 54*(6), 648–657. doi:10.1097/00006842-199211000-00004

Klaperski, S., von Dawans, B., Heinrichs, M., & Fuchs, R. (2013). Does the level of physical exercise affect physiological and psychological responses to psychosocial stress in women? *Psychology of Sport and Exercise, 14*(2), 266–274. doi:10.1016/j.psychsport.2012.11.003

Knorr, U., Vinberg, M., Kessing, L. V., & Wetterslev, J. (2010). Salivary cortisol in depressed patients versus control persons: A systematic review and meta-analysis. *Psychoneuroendocrinology, 35*(9), 1275–1286. doi:10.1016/j.psyneuen.2010.04.001

Kogler, L., Müller, V. I., Chang, A., Eickhoff, S. B., Fox, P. T., Gur, R. C., & Derntl, B. (2015). Psychosocial versus physiological stress – meta-analyses on deactivations and activations of the neural correlates of stress reactions. *NeuroImage, 119,* 235–251. doi:10.1016/j.neuroimage.2015.06.059

Kudielka, B. M., Bellingrath, S., & Hellhammer, D. H. (2006). Cortisol in burnout and vital exhaustion: An overview. *Giornale Italiano Di Medicina Del Lavoro Ed Ergonomia, 28*(1 Suppl. 1), 34–42.

Kudielka, B. M., Buske-Kirschbaum, A., Hellhammer, D., & Kirschbaum, C. (2004). HPA axis responses to laboratory psychosocial stress in healthy elderly adults, younger adults, and children: Impact of age and gender. *Psychoneuroendocrinology, 29*(1), 83–98. doi:10.1016/S0306-4530(02)00146-4

Kudielka, B. M., Fischer, J. E., Metzenthin, P., Helfricht, S., Preckel, D., & von Känel, R. (2007). No effect of 5-day treatment with acetylsalicylic acid (aspirin) or the beta-blocker propranolol (inderal) on free cortisol responses to acute psychosocial stress: A randomized double-blind, placebo-controlled study. *Neuropsychobiology, 56*(2–3), 159–166. doi:10.1159/000115783

Kudielka, B. M., Gierens, A., Hellhammer, D. H., Wüst, S., & Schlotz, W. (2012). Salivary cortisol in ambulatory assessment – some dos, some don'ts, and some open questions. *Psychosomatic Medicine, 74*(4), 418–431. doi:10.1097/PSY.0b013e31825434c7

Kudielka, B. M., Hellhammer, D. H., & Kirschbaum, C. (2007). Ten years of research with the Trier Social Stress Test – revisited. In E. Harmon-Jones & P. Winkielman (Eds.), *Social neuroscience* (pp. 56–83). New York, NY: Guilford Press.

Kudielka, B. M., Hellhammer, D. H., & Wüst, S. (2009). Why do we respond so differently? Reviewing determinants of human salivary cortisol responses to challenge. *Psychoneuroendocrinology, 34*(1), 2–18. doi:10.1016/j.psyneuen.2008.10.004

Kudielka, B. M., Hellhammer, J., Hellhammer, D. H., Wolf, O. T., Pirke, K. M., Varadi, E., . . . Kirschbaum, C. (1998). Sex differences in endocrine and psychological responses to psychosocial stress in healthy elderly subjects and the impact of a 2-week dehydroepiandrosterone treatment. *Journal of Clinical Endocrinology and Metabolism, 83*(5), 1756–1761. doi:10.1210/jc.83.5.1756

Kudielka, B. M., & Kirschbaum, C. (2005). Sex differences in HPA axis responses to stress: A review. *Biological Psychology, 69*(1), 113–132. doi:10.1016/j.biopsycho.2004.11.009

Kudielka, B. M., & Kirschbaum, C. (2007). Biological bases of the stress response. In M. Al'Absi (Ed.), *Stress and addiction: Biological and psychological mechanisms* (chapter 1, pp. 3–19). Amsterdam: Elsevier. doi:10.1016/B978-012370632-4/50004-8

Kudielka, B. M., Schommer, N. C., Hellhammer, D. H., & Kirschbaum, C. (2004). Acute HPA axis responses, heart rate, and mood changes to psychosocial stress (TSST) in humans at different times of day. *Psychoneuroendocrinology, 29*(8), 983–992. doi:10.1016/j.psyneuen.2003.08.009

Kudielka, B. M., von Känel, R., Preckel, D., Zgraggen, L., Mischler, K., & Fischer, J. E. (2006). Exhaustion is associated with reduced habituation of free cortisol responses to repeated acute psychosocial stress. *Biological Psychology, 72*(2), 147–153. doi:10.1016/j.biopsycho.2005.09.001

Kudielka, B. M., & Wüst, S. (2010). Human models in acute and chronic stress: Assessing determinants of individual hypothalamus – pituitary – adrenal axis activity and reactivity. *Stress, 13*(1), 1–14. doi:10.3109/10253890902874913

Kumsta, R., Entringer, S., Hellhammer, D. H., & Wüst, S. (2007). Cortisol and ACTH responses to psychosocial stress are modulated by corticosteroid binding globulin levels. *Psychoneuroendocrinology, 32*(8–10), 1153–1157. doi:10.1016/j.psyneuen.2007.08.007

Kumsta, R., Entringer, S., Koper, J. W., van Rossum, E. F. C., Hellhammer, D. H., & Wüst, S. (2007). Sex specific associations between common glucocorticoid receptor gene variants and hypothalamus-pituitary-adrenal axis responses to psychosocial stress. *Biological Psychiatry, 62*(8), 863–869. doi:10.1016/j.biopsych.2007.04.013

La Marca-Ghaemmaghami, P., & Ehlert, U. (2015). Stress during pregnancy. *European Psychologist, 20*(2), 102–119. doi:10.1027/1016-9040/a000195

Lazarus, R. S., & Folkman, S. (1984). *Stress, appraisal, and coping.* New York, NY: Springer Publishing Company, Inc.

Lederbogen, F., Kirsch, P., Haddad, L., Streit, F., Tost, H., Schuch, P., . . . Meyer-Lindenberg, A. (2011). City living and urban upbringing affect neural social stress processing in humans. *Nature, 474*(7352), 498–501. doi:10.1038/nature10190

Lennartsson, A. K., Sjörs, A., Währborg, P., Ljung, T., & Jonsdottir, I. H. (2015). Burnout and hypocortisolism – a matter of severity? A study on ACTH and cortisol responses to acute psychosocial stress. *Frontiers in Psychiatry, 6*, 1–8. doi:10.3389/fpsyt.2015.00008

Linnen, A-M., Ellenbogen, M. A., Cardoso, C., & Joober, R. (2012). Intranasal oxytocin and salivary cortisol concentrations during social rejection in university students. *Stress, 15*(4), 393–402. doi:10.3109/10253890.2011.631154

Liu, J. J. W., Ein, N., Peck, K., Huang, V., Pruessner, J. C., & Vickers, K. (2017). Sex differences in salivary cortisol reactivity to the Trier Social Stress Test (TSST): A meta-analysis. *Psychoneuroendocrinology, 82*, 26–37. doi:10.1016/j.psyneuen.2017.04.007

Lopez-Duran, N. L., Mayer, S. E., & Abelson, J. L. (2014). Modeling neuroendocrine stress reactivity in salivary cortisol: Adjusting for peak latency variability. *Stress, 17*(4), 285–295. doi:10.3109/10253890.2014.915517

Lovallo, W. R. (2013). Early life adversity reduces stress reactivity and enhances impulsive behavior: Implications for health behaviors. *International Journal of Psychophysiology, 90*(1), 8–16. doi:10.1016/j.ijpsycho.2012.10.006

Lovallo, W. R., Farag, N. H., Vincent, A. S., Thomas, T. L., & Wilson, M. F. (2006). Cortisol responses to mental stress, exercise, and meals following caffeine intake in men and women. *Pharmacology Biochemistry and Behavior, 83*(3), 441–447. doi:10.1016/j.pbb.2006.03.005

Mason, J. W. (1975). A historical view of the stress field. *Journal of Human Stress, 1*(1), 6–12. doi:10.1080/0097840X.1975.9940399

McEwen, B. S. (2003). Interacting mediators of allostasis and allostatic load: Towards an understanding of resilience in aging. *Metabolism, 52*(10 Suppl. 2), 10–16. doi:10.1016/S0026-0495(03)00295-6

McEwen, B. S. (2007). Physiology and neurobiology of stress and adaptation: Central role of the brain. *Physiological Reviews, 87*(3), 873–904. doi:10.1152/physrev.00041.2006

Miller, R., Wankerl, M., Stalder, T., Kirschbaum, C., & Alexander, N. (2013). The serotonin transporter gene-linked polymorphic region (5-HTTLPR) and cortisol stress reactivity: A meta-analysis. *Molecular Psychiatry, 18*(9), 1018–1024. doi:10.1038/mp.2012.124

Montero-López, E., Santos-Ruiz, A., García-Ríos, M. C., Rodríguez-Blázquez, R., Pérez-García, M., & Peralta-Ramírez, M. I. (2016). A virtual reality approach to the Trier Social Stress Test: Contrasting two distinct protocols. *Behavior Research Methods, 48*(1), 223–232. doi:10.3758/s13428-015-0565-4

Mrug, S., Tyson, A., Turan, B., & Granger, D. A. (2016). Sleep problems predict cortisol reactivity to stress in urban adolescents. *Physiology and Behavior, 155*, 95–101. doi:10.1016/j.physbeh.2015.12.003

Oswald, L. M., Zandi, P., Nestadt, G., Potash, J. B., Kalaydjian, A. E., & Wand, G. S. (2006). Relationship between cortisol responses to stress and personality. *Neuropsychopharmacology, 31*(7), 1583–1591. doi:10.1038/sj.npp.1301012

Otte, C., Hart, S., Neylan, T. C., Marmar, C. R., Yaffe, K., & Mohr, D. C. (2005). A meta-analysis of cortisol response to challenge in human aging: Importance of gender. *Psychoneuroendocrinology, 30*(1), 80–91. doi:10.1016/j.psyneuen.2004.06.002

Pariante, C. M., & Miller, A. H. (2001). Glucocorticoid receptors in major depression: Relevance to pathophysiology and treatment. *Biological Psychiatry, 49*(5), 391–404. doi:10.1016/S0006-3223(00)01088-X

Pruessner, J. C., Gaab, J., Hellhammer, D. H., Lintz, D., Schommer, N., & Kirschbaum, C. (1997). Increasing correlations between personality traits and cortisol stress responses obtained by data aggregation. *Psychoneuroendocrinology, 22*(8), 615–625. doi:10.1016/S0306-4530(97)00072-3

Rimmele, U., Seiler, R., Marti, B., Wirtz, P. H., Ehlert, U., & Heinrichs, M. (2009). The level of physical activity affects adrenal and cardiovascular reactivity to psychosocial stress. *Psychoneuroendocrinology, 34*(2), 190–198. doi:10.1016/j.psyneuen.2008.08.023

Rodrigues, S., Kaiseler, M., & Queirós, C. (2015). Psychophysiological assessment of stress under ecological settings: A systematic review. *European Psychologist, 20*(3), 204–226. doi:10.1027/1016-9040/a000222

Rohleder, N., & Kirschbaum, C. (2006). The hypothalamic-pituitary-adrenal (HPA) axis in habitual smokers. *International Journal of Psychophysiology, 59*(3), 236–243. doi:10.1016/j.ijpsycho.2005.10.012

Rohleder, N., & Kirschbaum, C. (2007). Effects of nutrition on neuro-endocrine stress responses. *Current Opinion in Clinical Nutrition and Metabolic Care, 10*(4), 504–510. doi:10.1097/MCO.0b013e3281e38808

Rohleder, N., Kudielka, B. M., Hellhammer, D. H., Wolf, J. M., & Kirschbaum, C. (2002). Age and sex steroid-related changes in glucocorticoid sensitivity of pro-inflammatory cytokine production after psychosocial stress. *Journal of Neuroimmunology, 126*(1–2), 69–77. doi:10.1016/S0165-5728(02)00062-0

Sapolsky, R. M., Krey, L. C., & McEwen, B. S. (1986). The neuroendocrinology of stress and aging: The glucocorticoid cascade hypothesis. *Endocrine Reviews, 7*(3), 284–301. doi:10.1210/edrv-7-3-284

Schlotz, W. (2011). Ambulatory psychoneuroendocrinology: Assessing salivary cortisol and other hormones in daily life. In M. R. Mehl & T. S. Conner (Eds.), *Handbook of research methods for studying daily life* (pp. 193–209). New York, NY: Guilford Press.

Schlotz, W., Kumsta, R., Layes, I., Entringer, S., Jones, A., & Wüst, S. (2008). Covariance between psychological and endocrine responses to pharmacological challenge and psychosocial stress: A question of timing. *Psychosomatic Medicine, 70*(7), 787–796. doi:10.1097/PSY.0b013e3181810658

Schommer, N. C., Hellhammer, D. H., & Kirschbaum, C. (2003). Dissociation between reactivity of the hypothalamus-pituitary-adrenal axis and the sympathetic-adrenal-medullary system to repeated psychosocial stress. *Psychosomatic Medicine, 65*(3), 450–460. doi:10.1097/01.PSY.0000035721.12441.17

Schultheiss, O. C., Wiemers, U. S., & Wolf, O. T. (2014). Implicit need for achievement predicts attenuated cortisol responses to difficult tasks. *Journal of Research in Personality, 48*, 84–92. doi:10.1016/j.jrp.2013.10.004

Schwabe, L., Haddad, L., & Schachinger, H. (2008). HPA axis activation by a socially evaluated cold-pressor test. *Psychoneuroendocrinology, 33*(6), 890–895. doi:10.1016/j.psyneuen.2008.03.001

Seckl, J. R., & Meaney, M. J. (2004). Glucocorticoid programming. *Annals of the New York Academy of Sciences, 1032*, 63–84. doi:10.1196/annals.1314.006

Seeman, T. E., & Robbins, R. J. (1994). Aging and hypothalamic-pituitary-adrenal response to challenge in humans. *Endocrine Reviews, 15*(2), 233–260. doi:10.1210/edrv-15-2-233

Selye, H. (1950). *The physiology and pathology of exposure to stress: A treatise based on the concepts of the general-adaptation-syndrome and the diseases of adaptation.* Montreal: Acta Inc. Medical Publishing.

Shiban, Y., Diemer, J., Brandl, S., Zack, R., Mühlberger, A., & Wüst, S. (2016). Trier Social Stress Test in vivo and in virtual reality: Dissociation of response domains. *International Journal of Psychophysiology, 110*, 47–55. doi:10.1016/j.ijpsycho.2016.10.008

Shull, A., Mayer, S. E., McGinnis, E., Geiss, E., Vargas, I., & Lopez-Duran, N. L. (2016). Trait and state rumination interact to prolong cortisol activation to psychosocial stress in females. *Psychoneuroendocrinology, 74*, 324–332. doi:10.1016/j.psyneuen.2016.09.004

Skoluda, N., Strahler, J., Schlotz, W., Niederberger, L., Marques, S., Fischer, S., . . . Nater, U. M. (2015). Intra-individual psychological and physiological responses to acute laboratory stressors of different intensity. *Psychoneuroendocrinology, 51*, 227–236. doi:10.1016/j.psyneuen.2014.10.002

Smeets, T., Cornelisse, S., Quaedflieg, C. W. E. M., Meyer, T., Jelicic, M., & Merckelbach, H. (2012). Introducing the Maastricht Acute Stress Test (MAST): A quick and non-invasive approach to elicit robust autonomic and glucocorticoid stress responses. *Psychoneuroendocrinology, 37*(12), 1998–2008. doi:10.1016/j.psyneuen.2012.04.012

Stalder, T., & Kirschbaum, C. (2012). Analysis of cortisol in hair – state of the art and future directions. *Brain, Behavior, and Immunity, 26*(7), 1019–1029. doi:10.1016/j.bbi.2012.02.002

Stalder, T., Kirschbaum, C., Kudielka, B. M., Adam, E. K., Pruessner, J. C., Wüst, S., . . . Clow, A. (2016). Assessment of the cortisol awakening response: Expert consensus guidelines. *Psychoneuroendocrinology, 63*, 414–432. doi:10.1016/j.psyneuen.2015.10.010

Stephens, M. A. C., Mahon, P. B., McCaul, M. E., & Wand, G. S. (2016). Hypothalamic-pituitary-adrenal axis response to acute psychosocial stress: Effects of biological sex and circulating sex hormones. *Psychoneuroendocrinology, 66*(4), 47–55. doi:10.1016/j.psyneuen.2015.12.021

Sterling, P., & Eyer, J. (1988). Allostasis: A new paradigm to explain arousal pathology. In S. Fisher & J. Reason (Eds.), *Handbook of life stress, cognition and health* (pp. 629–649). New York, NY: John Wiley & Sons, Inc.

Stewart, J. G., Mazurka, R., Bond, L., Wynne-Edwards, K. E., & Harkness, K. L. (2013). Rumination and impaired cortisol recovery following a social stressor in adolescent depression. *Journal of Abnormal Child Psychology, 41*(7), 1015–1026. doi:10.1007/s10802-013-9740-1

Strahler, J., Skoluda, N., Kappert, M. B., & Nater, U. M. (2017). Simultaneous measurement of salivary cortisol and alpha-amylase: Application and recommendations. *Neuroscience and Biobehavioral Reviews.* doi:10.1016/j.neubiorev.2017.08.015

Strahler, J., Skoluda, N., Rohleder, N., & Nater, U. M. (2016). Dysregulated stress signal sensitivity and inflammatory disinhibition as a pathophysiological mechanism of stress-related chronic fatigue. *Neuroscience and Biobehavioral Reviews, 68*, 298–318. doi:10.1016/j.neubiorev.2016.05.008

Streit, F., Haddad, L., Paul, T., Frank, J., Schäfer, A., Nikitopoulos, J., . . . Wüst, S. (2014). A functional variant in the neuropeptide S receptor 1 gene moderates the influence of urban upbringing on stress processing in the amygdala. *Stress, 17*(4), 352–361. doi:10.3109/10253890.2014.921903

Stroud, L. R., Papandonatos, G. D., D'Angelo, C. M., Brush, B., & Lloyd-Richardson, E. E. (2017). Sex differences in biological response to peer rejection and performance challenge across development: A pilot study. *Physiology and Behavior, 169*, 224–233. doi:10.1016/j.physbeh.2016.12.005

Stroud, L. R., Salovey, P., & Epel, E. S. (2002). Sex differences in stress responses: Social rejection versus achievement stress. *Biological Psychiatry, 52*(4), 318–327. doi:10.1016/S0006-3223(02)01333-1

Stroud, L. R., Tanofsky-Kraff, M., Wilfley, D. E., & Salovey, P. (2000). The Yale Interpersonal Stressor (YIPS): Affective, physiological, and behavioral responses to a novel interpersonal rejection paradigm. *Annals of Behavioral Medicine, 22*(3), 204–413. doi:10.1007/BF02895115

Trull, T. J., & Ebner-Priemer, U. (2013). Ambulatory assessment. *Annual Review of Clinical Psychology, 9*, 151–176. doi:10.1146/annurev-clinpsy-050212-185510

Tsigos, C., & Chrousos, G. P. (1994). Physiology of the hypothalamic-pituitary-adrenal axis in health and dysregulation in psychiatric and autoimmune disorders. *Endocrinology and Metabolism Clinics of North America, 23*(3), 451–466.

Ursin, H., & Eriksen, H. R. (2004). The cognitive activation theory of stress. *Psychoneuroendocrinology, 29*(5), 567–592. doi:10.1016/S0306-4530(03)00091-X

Vargas, I., & Lopez-Duran, N. (2017). Investigating the effect of acute sleep deprivation on hypothalamic-pituitary-adrenal-axis response to a psychosocial stressor. *Psychoneuroendocrinology, 79*, 1–8. doi:10.1016/j.psyneuen.2017.01.030

Van Hedger, K., Bershad, A. K., & de Wit, H. (2017). Pharmacological challenge studies with acute psychosocial stress. *Psychoneuroendocrinology, 85*, 123–133. doi:10.1016/j.psyneuen.2017.08.020

von Dawans, B., Kirschbaum, C., & Heinrichs, M. (2011). The Trier Social Stress Test for Groups (TSST-G): A new research tool for controlled simultaneous social stress exposure in a group format. *Psychoneuroendocrinology, 36*(4), 514–522. doi:10.1016/j.psyneuen.2010.08.004

Wallergård, M., Jönsson, P., Johansson, G., & Karlson, B. (2011). A virtual reality version of the Trier Social Stress Test: A pilot study. *Presence: Teleoperators and Virtual Environments, 20*(4), 325–336. doi:10.1162/PRES_a_00052

Weckesser, L. J., Plessow, F., Pilhatsch, M., Muehlhan, M., Kirschbaum, C., & Miller, R. (2014). Do venepuncture procedures induce cortisol responses? A review, study, and synthesis for stress research. *Psychoneuroendocrinology, 46*, 88–99. doi:10.1016/j.psyneuen.2014.04.012

Westenberg, P. M., Bokhorst, C. L., Miers, A. C., Sumter, S. R., Kallen, V. L., van Pelt, J., & Blöte, A. W. (2009). A prepared speech in front of a pre-recorded audience: Subjective, physiological, and neuroendocrine responses to the Leiden public speaking task. *Biological Psychology, 82*(2), 116–124. doi:10.1016/j.biopsycho.2009.06.005

Wiemers, U. S., Schoofs, D., & Wolf, O. T. (2013). A friendly version of the Trier Social Stress Test does not activate the HPA axis in healthy men and women. *Stress, 16*(2), 254–260. doi:10.3109/10253890.2012.714427

Wright, C. E., Valdimarsdottir, H. B., Erblich, J., & Bovbjerg, D. H. (2007). Poor sleep the night before an experimental stress task is associated with reduced cortisol reactivity in healthy women. *Biological Psychology, 74*(3), 319–327. doi:10.1016/j.biopsycho.2006.08.003

Wüst, S., Entringer, S., Federenko, I. S., Schlotz, W., & Hellhammer, D. H. (2005). Birth weight is associated with salivary cortisol responses to psychosocial stress in adult life. *Psychoneuroendocrinology, 30*(6), 591–598. doi:10.1016/j.psyneuen.2005.01.008

Wüst, S., Federenko, I. S., van Rossum, E. F. C., Koper, J. W., & Hellhammer, D. H. (2005). Habituation of cortisol responses to repeated psychosocial stress–further characterization and impact of genetic factors. *Psychoneuroendocrinology, 30*(2), 199–211. doi:10.1016/j.psyneuen.2004.07.002

Wüst, S., van Rossum, E. F. C., Federenko, I. S., Koper, J. W., Kumsta, R., & Hellhammer, D. H. (2004). Common polymorphisms in the glucocorticoid receptor gene are associated with adrenocortical responses to psychosocial stress. *The Journal of Clinical Endocrinology & Metabolism, 89*(2), 565–573. doi:10.1210/jc.2003-031148

Young, E. A., & Nolen-Hoeksema, S. (2001). Effect of ruminations on the saliva cortisol response to a social stressor. *Psychoneuroendocrinology, 26*(3), 319–329. doi:10.1016/S0306-4530(00)00059-7

Zoccola, P. M., & Dickerson, S. S. (2015). Extending the recovery window: Effects of trait rumination on subsequent evening cortisol following a laboratory performance stressor. *Psychoneuroendocrinology, 58*, 67–78. doi:10.1016/j.psyneuen.2015.04.014

Zoccola, P. M., Quas, J. A., & Yim, I. S. (2010). Salivary cortisol responses to a psychosocial laboratory stressor and later verbal recall of the stressor: The role of trait and state rumination. *Stress, 13*(5), 435–443. doi:10.3109/10253891003713765

Zorn, J. V., Schür, R. R., Boks, M. P., Kahn, R. S., Joëls, M., & Vinkers, C. H. (2016). Cortisol stress reactivity across psychiatric disorders: A systematic review and meta-analysis. *Psychoneuroendocrinology, 77*, 25–36. doi:10.1016/j.psyneuen.2016.11.036

SECTION 6

Developmental aspects

27

STRESS AND SOCIAL DEVELOPMENT IN ADOLESCENCE IN A RODENT MODEL

Travis E. Hodges and Cheryl M. McCormick

Introduction

Neuroscientists (Cajal, 1967) and psychologists (Beach, 1950) have long recognized the importance of a comparative approach to understanding brain and behaviour relationships. The primary contribution of investigations in non-human animals for research in humans and vice versa is the generation of testable hypotheses and principles of development (Gottlieb & Lickliter, 2004). Nevertheless, research studies with animal models are increasingly conducted predominantly in rodents. Because of the increasing interest in the "social brain" in human adolescence and how stressors may influence its development, we review here, first, the typical social behaviour of adolescent laboratory rats, how social behaviour is measured and the development of the social brain in rats. Second, we review evidence from our lab of how social stress exposures (involving our social instability stress model) in adolescence influences social development. The majority of this research was conducted in males, and results described will be for males unless otherwise noted. We have reviewed the benefits and challenges of the use of rats for translational research on the consequences of stressors in adolescence (McCormick, Green, & Simone, 2017), and a greater discussion of the parallels and differences in adolescent development between the two species can be found in that review. For a review of other models of social stress used with adolescent rats, see Burke and colleagues (Burke, McCormick, Pellis, & Lukkes, 2017).

Adolescence, social behaviour and hypothalamic–pituitary–adrenal function in rats

Defining adolescence in rats

The specific ages in rats that define the adolescent period are variable across studies and across strains of rats. Although a liberal definition starts the adolescent period in rats at weaning from the mother (typically in the lab on postnatal day (PND) 21) and ends the adolescent period on PND 59 (with sexual maturity attained at about PND 60), this definition involves a lengthy prepubertal period. In contrast, in humans, adolescence is defined as beginning at puberty (reviewed in McCormick, Green, et al., 2017). In rats, the physical markers of puberty appear in males at around PND 40–47 (as marked by separation of the prepuce from the glans penis, i.e., balanopreputial separation, and sperm in the epididymis) and in females at around PND 32–36 (as marked by vaginal opening and first ovulation) (reviewed in McCormick, Green, et al., 2017). Throughout this chapter, we will define the ages of PND 30–45 as mid-adolescence in rats and adulthood as PND 60 and beyond.

The measurement of social behaviour in rats

Across development, engaging in positive social interactions with members of the same species promotes health by enhancing resilience to stressors (social buffering) (reviewed in Hostinar, Sullivan, & Gunnar, 2014). In a laboratory setting, social interaction tests involve observing and scoring two or more rats as they perform several social behaviours (i.e., social investigation, following, grooming of peer, sniffing, social play, lying flat or standing still while maintaining physical contact with partner) with each other compared to non-social behaviours (i.e., exploring, inactivity without touching peer, self-grooming) (as in Cirulli, Terranova, & Laviola, 1996) in either a familiar or novel environment. It is also common for rats to spend more time investigating unfamiliar rats than investigating rats with which they are familiar (Cirulli et al., 1996; Hodges et al., 2017; Perkins et al., 2016). Tests that involve recording the time a rat spends in proximity to another rat but for which no active interaction is possible (e.g., the stimulus rat is behind wire mesh) have been referred to as tests of social interaction, but are perhaps better termed as tests of social approach (see Figure 27.1 for depictions of social interaction and social approach tests). Social interaction tests also are used as a measure of social anxiety in rats and other mammals; a decrease in social interaction from the norm is interpreted as more anxious (reviewed in File & Seth, 2003). Nevertheless, the reduction in social interaction may be secondary to a general increase in fear or anxiety rather than a reduction in sociality. For example, bright lighting is anxiogenic for rats, and lighting conditions can thereby increase or decrease "social anxiety" (File & Hyde, 1978). Further, social interaction is dissociable from social reward; for example, we have found that rats that have decreased social interaction in tests allowing for social contact will show no decrement in social approach when the peer is behind wire mesh (e.g., Green, Barnes, & McCormick, 2013).

The primary social behaviour in adolescent rats is social play with peers. Social play is found across many species and improves social, emotional and cognitive skills (reviewed in Pellis & Pellis, 2017; Pellis, Pellis, & Himmler, 2014). This increase in interaction with peers parallels the social restructuring in human adolescents, who increasingly value peer interactions over family interactions (reviewed in Nelson, Leibenluft, McClure, & Pine, 2005). Although there are some differences in the development of social play across strains of rats (Himmler, Stryjek, et al., 2013; Himmler, Modlinska, et al., 2014; Ku, Weir, Silverman, Berman, & Bauman, 2016; Siviy, Love, DeCicco, Giordano, & Seifert, 2003), same-sex play and social investigatory behaviours are consistently higher in adolescent rats than in adult rats (Klein, Padow, & Romeo, 2010; Perkins et al., 2016; Primus & Kellogg, 1989). Further, a short period of isolation increases social play behaviours to a greater extent in adolescent rats (PND 40–45) than it does in young adult rats (PND 67–72) (Lampe, Burman, Würbel, & Melotti, 2017).

Social play in adolescence is critical for normal adolescent behavioural development into adulthood. For example, rats housed without a cage partner (social isolation) for 13 or more days during adolescence displayed abnormal behaviour in situations of conflict (Einon & Potegal, 1991; Tulogdi et al., 2014; van den Berg et al., 1999), had impaired object memory (Einon & Morgan, 1976; Einon & Potegal, 1991), had reduced social interaction with a peer (van den Berg et al., 1999; Lukkes, Mokin, Scholl, & Forster, 2009), had increased anxiety-like

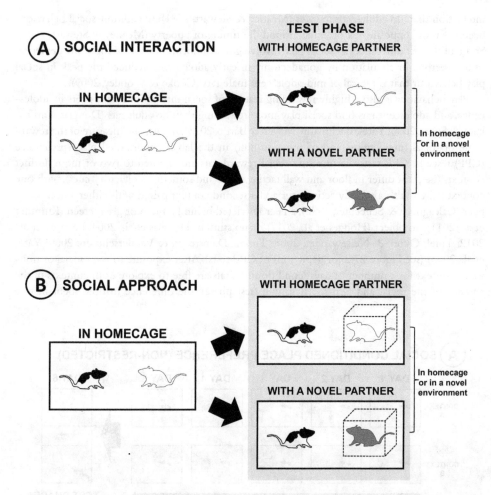

Figure 27.1 Illustrations of (A) the Social Interaction Test and the (B) Social Approach Test procedures in which (A) time spent in physical interaction is measured or (B) time spent near the barrier between the rats is measured in the test phase.

behaviour (Wright, Upton, & Marsden, 1991), exhibited awkward behaviour with a sexual partner in adulthood (van den Berg et al., 1999), showed increased conditioned fear (Lukkes et al., 2009), displayed greater aggressive behaviour with peers (Wall, Fischer, & Bland, 2012), and had impaired social recognition memory (Shahar-Gold, Gur, & Wagner, 2013). Social play behaviours (defined by chasing, wrestling, pinning, pouncing, role reversals) emerge as early as PND 17 (Bolles & Woods, 1964), peak in early to mid-adolescence (Klein et al., 2010; Panksepp, Siviy, & Normansell, 1984; Takahashi & Lore, 1983) and then change in function into precopulatory behaviours (e.g., male–male competition) in adulthood (see review by Pellis & Pellis, 2017). Moreover, the wrestling behaviours that occur during play fighting in adolescence decrease, and more aggressive behaviours (e.g., boxing) increase, into adulthood (Meaney & Stewart, 1981). In addition to the age differences in social interaction and social play, there are sex differences in the development of social behaviours in adolescent rats. Social play behaviours peak earlier in adolescent male rats than in adolescent female rats, and adolescent males engage in more social interaction than do adolescent females (Meaney & Stewart, 1981). In addition, social behaviour becomes more opposite-sex oriented around the timing of puberty (Meaney & Stewart, 1981). Some of the sex differences in social play involve gonadal hormones; for example, the depletion of testosterone in circulation by gonadectomy in early adolescence reduced the peak in social play behaviour that is typical of mid-adolescent male rats (Cooke & Woolley, 2009).

Play behaviour is also a highly rewarding feature of social interactions with peers in adolescence, and adolescent rats find social play more rewarding than do adult rats (Douglas, Varlinskaya, & Spear, 2004; Yates, Bechmann, Meyer, & Bardo, 2013). In rats, one measure of the reward value of social interactions (and of other stimuli) in the lab is conditioned place preference (CPP) tests. In CPP tests that measure social reward, rats are exposed to two or more distinct contexts (i.e., that differ in floor and wall tactile, visual and sometimes olfactory cues), with one context paired with a socially active peer and a second context paired with either a non-social peer (Calcagnetti & Schechter, 1992), a peer restricted behind a mesh or glass screen (Kummer et al., 2011), an object (Hodges et al., 2017) or no stimuli (Douglas et al., 2004; Peartree et al., 2012; Thiel, Okun, & Neisewander, 2008; Trezza, Damsteegt, & Vanderschuren, 2009; Yates et al., 2013) (see Figure 27.2 for depictions of CPP tests). After exposure to each social or non-social context for a number of days (conditioning), rats are free to explore both contexts in the absence of the social and non-social stimuli (test phase); the difference in time spent in one

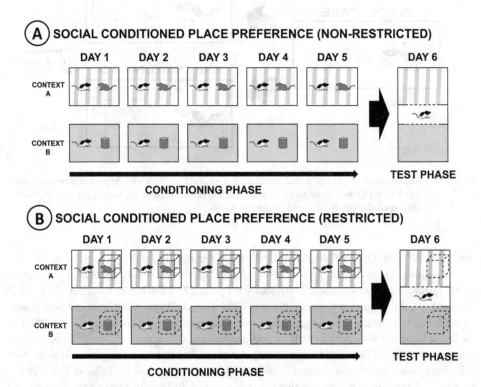

Figure 27.2 Illustrations of conditioned place preference procedures for conditioning between one context and a social stimulus and between another context and a non-social stimulus. (A) allows for unrestricted physical contact with the stimuli and (B) does not allow for direct physical context. In the test phase, the time spent in one context versus the other is the index of preference for a social or non-social stimulus.

context versus the other is indicative of the extent to which the social context was rewarding. In general, adolescent rats spend more time in a place that has become associated with social interaction than in control places.

Social cognition, which involves perceiving, recognizing and evaluating social stimuli before performing a social behaviour, also undergoes change in adolescence in rats, with social recognition being the most used measure (reviewed in McCall & Singer, 2012; van der Kooij & Sandi, 2012). Social recognition is tested with habituation/dishabituation or social discrimination paradigms (see Figure 27.3 for depictions of these paradigms). The social habituation/dishabituation paradigm involves first presenting the test rat with the same stimulus rat multiple times, and then presenting the test rat with a novel stimulus rat (reviewed in Gabor, Phan, Clipperton-Allen, Kavaliers, & Choleris, 2012). During social habituation/dishabituation, typically the test rat will show habituation (a reduction in social investigation) to the first stimulus rat after each presentation, and then a dishabituation response (a return to initial social investigation levels) to the novel stimulus rat. A more direct measure of social recognition is

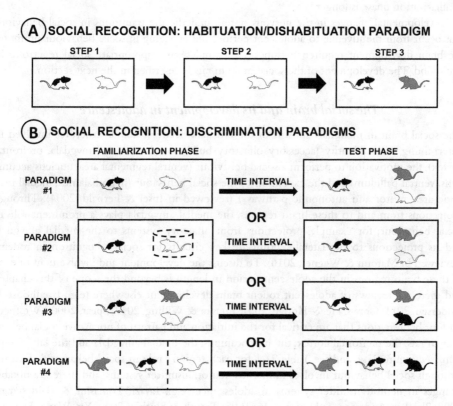

Figure 27.3 Illustrations of Social Recognition Test procedures. In (A), in Step 1, time spent investigating a novel rat is measured. In Step 2, a reduction in time spent investigating (habituation) the rat from Step 1 is expected. In Step 3, a greater time spent investigating (dishabituation) a new novel rat than spent investigating the rat in Step 2 is the index of social recognition. In (B), discrimination paradigms of social recognition involve a familiarization phase to either one or two rats with which physical contact is possible (paradigms #1 and #3) or not (paradigms #2 and #4). In the test phase, a novel rat is introduced (paradigms #1 and #2) or replaces a rat from the familiarization phase (paradigms #3 and #4), and a preference for investigating the novel vs the familiar rat is the measure of social recognition.

the social discrimination paradigm. The social discrimination paradigm of social recognition consists of presenting the test rodent with one or two stimulus rodents that are either socially restricted (kept behind either transparent plastic or wire mesh, e.g., Gur, Tendler, & Wagner, 2014; Hodges et al., 2017) or free to socially interact (e.g., Markham & Juraska, 2007; Veenema, Bredewold, & De Vries, 2012). The test phase occurs after this familiarization phase and after a time interval without the stimulus rat(s) present. The test phase involves presenting the test rat with one stimulus rodent from the familiarization phase and a novel stimulus rodent. The social discrimination paradigm relies on rats' preference for novelty, with rats typically spending more time engaging with novel versus familiar stimuli (reviewed in Gabor et al., 2012). Thus, a rat is said to have exhibited social recognition when they spend more time investigating the novel stimulus rat than the familiar stimulus rat. Social recognition performance declines with age in rats (Markham & Juraska, 2007; Perkins et al., 2016; Prediger, Batista, & Takahashi, 2005). Typically, social recognition after a four to five minute familiarization phase is absent after a two-hour interval (Dantzer, Koob, Bluthé, & Le Moal, 1988; Landgraf et al., 1995; Veenema et al., 2012). Social recognition after intervals longer than two hours can be observed when the familiarization phase is longer.

Developmental changes in the nervous system underlie the transitions in social behaviour that occur from the juvenile to adolescent period, and engaging in social behaviour promotes the brain development required to support a complete and appropriate social repertoire in adulthood. The development of the social brain in rats is described in the next section.

The social brain and its development in adolescence

The social brain in mammals consists of the crosstalk between neural structures involved in determining social identity (accessory olfactory bulb), social salience (amygdala, prefrontal cortex), the motivation to perform a social behaviour (ventral tegmental area, nucleus accumbens, ventral pallidum) and the execution of the social behaviour (hypothalamus, medial preoptic area, motor and autonomic pathways) (reviewed in Insel & Fernald, 2004). Through projections from and to these brain regions, the medial amygdala plays a prominent role in social behaviour; for example, projections from olfactory systems to the medial amygdala and its projections to the lateral septum are key circuits for social recognition in rodents (reviewed in Maroun & Wagner, 2016). To discuss the development and involvement of each of these brain regions in the adolescent period in length is beyond the scope of this chapter, and there are reviews of adolescent rodent brain development elsewhere (e.g., Brenhouse & Andersen, 2011; Crews, He, & Hodge, 2007; Juraska & Willing, 2017; Spear, 2000). We focus on four brain regions that are critical for the initiation and pattern of normative social behaviour in rats: the prefrontal cortex, the hippocampus, the medial amygdala and the lateral septum (see Figure 27.4, and see Table 27.1 for each region's role in social behaviour). Further, although social behaviour involves numerous neurotransmitter systems, and there are notable changes in neurotransmitter systems in adolescence (e.g., Tarazi, Tomasini, & Baldessarini, 1998; Teicher, Andersen, & Hostetter Jr., 1995; Trauth & Slotkin, 2000; Yu, Wang, Fritschy, Witte, & Redecker, 2006), we focus on changes in the neuropeptides oxytocin and vasopressin and their receptors from adolescence to adulthood. Although oxytocin and vasopressin are implicated in anxiety and physiological responses to stressors, they are best known for their role in the regulation of social behaviour, including aggression, maternal behaviour, sexual behaviour, social preference and social cognition (reviewed in Maroun & Wagner, 2016; Neumann & Landgraf, 2012).

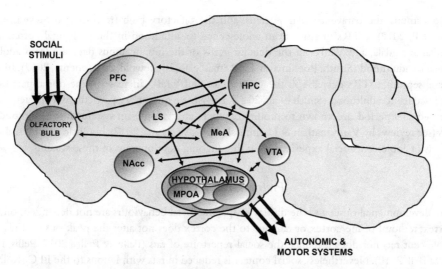

Figure 27.4   Cartoon of a sagittal view of the rat brain illustrating the main brain regions involved in social behaviour. Arrows indicate the main pathways between the regions. PFC = prefrontal cortex; LS = lateral septum; NAcc = nucleus accumbens; HPC = hippocampus; MeA = medial amygdala; MPOA = medial preoptic area; VTA = ventral tegmental area.

Table 27.1 Main role of brain regions in social behaviours

Social roles of the brain regions of interest.	
Prefrontal cortex	coordination of behaviour with a peer, maternal behaviour, sexual interest, social buffering, social interaction
Hippocampus	aggressive behaviour, behavioural sequencing, performing specific social behaviours, social recognition (CA2 subregion), submissive behaviour
Medial amygdala	aggressive behaviour, forming a social hierarchy, sexual behaviour, social interaction, social recognition
Lateral septum	affiliative behaviour, sexual behaviour, social fear behaviour, social interaction, social recognition

Oxytocin and vasopressin

Oxytocin and vasopressin are peptides synthesized primarily in the supraoptic and paraventricular nuclei of the hypothalamus. Oxytocin may be synthesized in some other hypothalamic and extra-hypothalamic sites, and vasopressin is also synthesized in the bed nucleus of the stria terminalis, the medial amygdala, the locus coeruleus, and the olfactory bulb (Veenema, 2012). Oxytocin exerts its effects in the brain primarily through binding at oxytocin receptor (OTR), whereas vasopressin exerts its effects in the brain at 1a and 1b receptor subtypes (V1aR and V1bR, respectively) (actions in the periphery also involve these, as well as additional, receptor subtypes) (Dumais & Veenema, 2016). OTR expression is evident in embryonic rats by about day 15 (Tribollet et al., 1989). Although OTRs and V1aRs are widely distributed in the central nervous system, V1bRs are limited primarily to the Cornu Ammonis 2 (CA2) region of the hippocampus, the paraventricular nucleus, and the olfactory bulb (reviewed in Stevenson & Caldwell, 2012). OTRs increase from adolescence to adulthood in the prefrontal cortex and medial amygdala, and V1aRs in the dentate gyrus of the hippocampus decrease from adolescence to adulthood (Smith, Poehlmann, Li, Ratnaseelan, Bredewold, & Veenema, 2017). In the lateral septum, OTRs decrease in the ventral part and V1aRs increase in the dorsal part from adolescence to adulthood (Smith et al., 2017). Early life experiences, particularly experiences in the neonatal period, are known to modify oxytocin and vasopressin systems into adulthood in rats (see reviews by Vaidyanathan & Hammock, 2017; Veenema, 2012), but little is known about effects of adolescent social experiences on the ongoing development of these systems.

Prefrontal cortex (PFC)

The developmental onset and the display of specific social behaviours are not dependent on the cortex; removal of the cortex or damage to the cortex does not alter the peak of social play in adolescent rats nor does it reduce the social repertoire of rats (Pellis & Pellis, 2017; Pellis, Pellis, & Bell, 2010). Nevertheless, social contact is reduced in rats with lesions to the PFC (Kolb & Nonneman, 1974), and the context-dependent coordination of behaviour with a peer requires the PFC across development (Bell, McCaffrey, Forgie, Kolb, & Pellis, 2009; Himmler, Bell, et al., 2014). Several social behaviours are modified by oxytocin in the PFC. For example, oxytocin in the medial PFC was a critical factor in the greater reduction of fear in rats when with a peer than when alone (Brill-Maoz & Maroun, 2016), OTR in the medial PFC were required for female mice to show sexual interest in males (Nakajima, Görlich, & Heintz, 2014) and OTR blockade attenuated maternal behaviour in postpartum rats (Sabihi, Durosko, Dong, & Leuner, 2014). Anxiolytic effects of oxytocin administered to the prelimbic region of the medial PFC (Sabihi et al., 2014) may lead to increased social interaction.

Changes in dendritic morphology in the PFC from adolescence to adulthood have been described in rats. For example, dendritic spines in the PFC peak at PND 31 and thereafter decrease into adulthood (Gourley, Olevska, Warren, Taylor, & Koleske, 2012; Koss, Belden, Hristov, & Juraska, 2014). Moreover, white matter increases (indicative of myelination) in the medial PFC from adolescence to adulthood (Markham, Morris, & Juraska, 2007; Willing and Juraska, 2015). There are also sex differences in the adolescent development of the medial PFC, and these involve the sex differences in sex steroids in circulation that increase in adolescence. Neurons in the adolescent female medial PFC decrease from PND 35 to PND 45 and further into adulthood, but no decrease is found in adolescent males (Markham et al., 2007; Willing and Juraska, 2015) or in ovariectomized adolescent females (Koss et al., 2014), suggesting a role of ovarian hormones in apoptosis in the medial PFC.

Depriving adolescent rats of social behaviour can alter the morphological development (Bell, Pellis, & Kolb, 2010; Himmler, Pellis, & Kolb, 2013) and function (Wall et al., 2012) of the orbitofrontal and prefrontal cortices. For example, dendritic basilar branching (dendritic branching allows for greater neural connectivity) in the orbitofrontal cortex was greater in adolescent rats housed with multiple peers than in those housed alone, and dendritic apical branching in the medial PFC was greater in adolescent rats housed singly than in adolescents that were socially housed (Bell et al., 2010). Further, rats housed with adult rats during adolescence (thus spent less time in social play) had greater basilar and apical dendritic spines, which are critical for efficient signal transmission, in the medial PFC and orbitofrontal cortex than did rats housed with other adolescents (Bell et al., 2010). Functional differences in these regions were investigated by measuring changes in expression of the immediate early gene protein products such as Fos and

Arc; increased expression these proteins is a marker of neural activation. For example, exposure to a novel peer in adolescence increased neural activation in the medial PFC of group-housed adolescent rats but not in singly housed adolescent rats (Wall et al., 2012).

Hippocampus

There is little neuronal activation in the hippocampus in rats while in social interaction (von Heimendahl, Rao, & Brecht, 2012). Nevertheless, the hippocampus is essential for the performance of several social behaviours. In turn, social behaviours influence the development of the hippocampus. Rats deprived of social interaction had a smaller hippocampal volume compared with rats housed with peers or single-housed rats briefly exposed to a conspecific each day (Kalman & Keay, 2017), and lesions to the hippocampus reduced the time rats spent in social contact with a peer (Kolb & Nonneman, 1974). The hippocampus, like the PFC, has a role in social coordination, but in rodents it has a greater involvement in the correct sequencing of behaviours during social interactions with a partner than does the PFC. For example, rats with damage to the hippocampus displayed a different set of behaviours in response to an affiliative approach by a novel peer than did control rats; specifically, behaviour became less dependent on that of the peer, and the predictability of aggressive behaviour was diminished (Maaswinkel, Gispen, & Spruijt, 1997). Damage to the hippocampus also increased the amount of aggressive behaviour displayed in social interaction (Becker, Grecksch, Bernstein, Höllt, & Bogerts, 1999; Kolb & Nonneman, 1974; Maaswinkel et al., 1997). The CA2 subfield of the hippocampus is essential for social recognition (Alexander et al., 2016; Hitti & Siegelbaum, 2014; Smith, Avram, Cymerblit-Sabba, Song, & Young, 2016). Further, activation of vasopressinergic neurons in the CA2 region during the familiarization phase (but not the retrieval phase) increased the retention of the social recognition memory from under two hours to seven days (Bluthé, Gheusi, & Dantzer, 1993; Smith et al., 2016). In addition, knocking out V1bRs in the CA2 region reduces social aggression in mice (Pagani et al., 2015; Wersinger, Ginns, O'Carroll, Lolait, & Young, 2002).

In contrast to the peak and pruning of dendritic spines in the PFC that occurs during adolescence, the spine density and length of dendrites in the hippocampus increases from weaning to adulthood in male rats (Gourley et al., 2012; Pokorný & Yamamoto, 1981). Conversely, a reduction in hippocampal dendritic spines between the pre- and post-pubertal period was found in females (Yildirim et al., 2008), consistent with other reports of sex differences in the development of the hippocampus (e.g., Roof & Havens, 1992). In addition, neurogenesis (formation of new neurons) decreases in the hippocampus from adolescence to adulthood (He & Crews, 2007).

Medial amygdala

The medial amygdala has a key role in several social behaviours (including aggressive behaviour, sexual behaviour, social interaction, social odour processing) (Knapska, Radwanska, Werka, & Kaczmarek, 2007; Newman, 1999). OTR and V1aR mRNA expression in the medial amygdala is positively associated with time spent in social interaction in mice (Murakami, Hunter, Fontaine, Ribeiro, & Pfaff, 2011). Oxytocin in the medial amygdala in males has proven to be essential for the maintenance of memory for familiar females in a social recognition paradigm (Lukas, Toth, Veenema, & Neumann, 2013). Protein synthesis and oxytocin-dependent long-term depression in the medial amygdala is necessary for the consolidation of long-term (24 hour interval) but not short-term (30 minute interval) social recognition (Gur et al., 2014).

In addition, the ability to form a lasting social hierarchy (dominant–subordinate relationship) between rats is dependent on the expression and the activation of OTR in the medial amygdala after their first social encounter (Timmer et al., 2011).

At birth, males and females have the same size of medial amygdala, and its volume becomes larger in males than in females around the beginning of the adolescent period (Hines, Allen, & Gorski, 1992; Mizukami, Nishizuka, & Arai, 1983). The medial amygdala expresses many androgen and estrogen receptors (reviewed in Newman, 1999), and gonadal hormones, the concentrations in circulation of which increase significantly in adolescence, modulate the morphology and functionality of the medial amygdala; removal of the male gonads in adolescence or adulthood reduces the volume, number of the dendritic spines and number of excitatory synapses in the medial amygdala, and results in deficits in male sexual behaviour (Cooke, Breedlove, & Jordan, 2003; Cooke & Woolley, 2009; Zancan, Dall'Oglio, Quagliotto, & Rasia Filho, 2017).

Lateral septum

The lateral septum modulates the motivation for affiliative behaviours with peers and for mating (Luo, Tahsili-Fahadan, Wise, Lupica, & Aston-Jones, 2011; Sartor & Aston-Jones, 2012). Moreover, lesions to the lateral septum increase the non-social and retreating behaviours of rats when with a peer (Kolb & Nonneman, 1974). Oxytocin and vasopressin are involved in the lateral septum's modulation of the motivation for social play in adolescent rats, and in both a sex- and context-specific manner. Oxytocin administered into the lateral septum reduced social play behaviour in adolescent females but not in adolescent males (Bredewold, Smith, Dumais, & Veenema, 2014), and administering a V1aR antagonist to the lateral septum increased social play behaviour in adolescent males and decreased social play behaviour in adolescent females, but only in the home cage and not in a novel environment (Bredewold et al., 2014; Veenema, Bredewold, & De Vries, 2013). As for the medial amygdala, oxytocin in the lateral septum may be essential for social recognition; the administration of an OTR antagonist immediately after the familiarization phase in the lateral septum abolished social recognition (Lukas et al., 2013). Moreover, the overexpression of V1aR in the lateral septum improved social recognition after intervals of 2–24 hours, whereas the reduction of V1AR in the lateral septum reduced social recognition (Bielsky, Hu, Ren, Terwilliger, & Young, 2005; Landgraf et al., 1995). In addition, the lateral septum plays a role in both social and non-social anxiety-like behaviours (Cordero, Just, Poirier, & Sandi, 2016; Liebsch, Montkowski, Holsboer, & Landgraf, 1998), and OTR in the dorsal lateral septum are involved in the acquisition and extinction of social fear behaviour (reduced social investigation after the conditioned pairing of social stimuli with a foot-shock). For example, OTR expression in the dorsal lateral septum increased during social fear conditioning and oxytocin infusion into the dorsal lateral septum during extinction abolished social fear behaviour (specifically increased social investigation, Zoicas, Slattery, & Neumann, 2014).

Neuronal density in the lateral septum increases from birth to about PND 14 and thereafter decreases until adulthood (Verney, Gaspar, Alvarez, & Berger, 1987). In the lateral septum, the density of vasopressinergic fibres becomes adult-like in males as early as PND 17, whereas the density of vasopressinergic fibres increase from adolescence to adulthood in females (De Vries, Buds, & Swaab, 1981). In addition, adolescent males have greater vasopressinergic fibres in the lateral septum than do adolescent females, and this sex difference is dependent on the presence of androgens in early life (De Vries, Best, & Sluiter, 1983; De Vries et al., 1981).

Maturation of the hypothalamic–pituitary–adrenal (HPA) in adolescence

Glucocorticoids (primarily corticosterone in rats and cortisol in humans) are released in response to stressors as the endpoint of activation of the hypothalamic–pituitary–adrenal (HPA) axis, which involves the release of corticotropin releasing hormone (CRH) from the paraventricular nucleus of the hypothalamus, and the release of adrenocorticotropic hormone (ACTH) from the anterior pituitary. The actions of glucocorticoids are mediated to a large extent through actions at their cognate intracellular receptors, the glucocorticoid receptors and mineralocorticoid receptors (GR and MR, respectively). Adolescent rats do not differ from adult rats for many features of the HPA axis: morphology of the paraventricular nucleus, expression of GR and MR mRNA and protein in the paraventricular nucleus and hippocampus, basal ACTH, basal corticosterone and concentrations of corticosteroid binding globulin (reviewed in Eiland & Romeo, 2013; Green & McCormick, 2016). Nevertheless, adolescent rats have a greater and/ or more prolonged release of corticosterone in response to several (but perhaps not all) stressors (reviewed in McCormick, Green, et al., 2017; Romeo, Patel, Pham, & So, 2016). Some features of the HPA axis continue to mature from adolescence to adulthood; prepubertal adolescent male rats had greater restraint-stress induced vasopressin heteronuclear RNA expression in the paraventricular nucleus (Viau, Bingham, Davis, Lee, & Wong, 2005); this source of vasopressin is known to increase HPA stress responses in adults, and thus increased vasopressin in young rats may be a basis for their higher stress responses than that in adults. The adrenals of prepubertal adolescent male rats had both a greater expression of adrenal melanocortin 2 receptor accessory protein mRNA (to which ACTH binds) and a greater sensitivity to ACTH (Romeo et al., 2014) than do adult male rats, which also is a likely basis for their increased release of corticosterone in response to stressors compared with adults. Further, prepubertal adolescent rats have greater expression of FKBP4 mRNA (which encodes FK506 binding protein 52 to promote the translocation of GR to the nucleus) in the hippocampus than do adult rats (Green, Nottrodt, Simone, & McCormick, 2016), although the functional significance of this increase in prepubertal rats is unknown.

In adult rats, there are clear sex differences in the regulation of the HPA axis; basal estradiol stimulates the release of corticosterone in adult females and basal testosterone inhibits the release of corticosterone in adult males (reviewed in Handa & Weiser, 2014; McCormick & Mathews, 2007). Nevertheless, gonadal hormone concentrations do not seem to be the basis of the sex differences in the prepubertal period (Romeo, Lee, & McEwen, 2004), and there is some evidence that gonadal hormones may regulate HPA function differently in post-pubertal adolescents than in adulthood (Green & McCormick, 2016). The regulation of adolescent HPA function by gonadal hormones is not well understood.

Social instability stress and social behaviour

Social instability stress in adolescence as a means of investigating the malleability of social development

Our lab first began investigating the long-lasting consequences of stress exposures experienced in adolescence in the early 2000s. At that time, there were few investigations of HPA function in response to an acute stressor in adolescence in rats and even fewer that involved repeated stress exposures (reviewed in McCormick & Mathews, 2007). Our choice of a relatively mild social stress procedure was an attempt to obtain effects that might be specific to adolescence; social stressors such as social defeat and isolation housing can result in long-lasting effects in adult rats (Buwalda, Geerdink, Vidal, & Koolhaas, 2011; Einon & Morgan, 1977; Panksepp & Beatty, 1980). Further, although often referred to as a social stressor, isolation housing does not produce the steep rise and prolonged elevation in glucocorticoids that is characteristic of other stress exposures and instead may involve dysfunction resulting from a lack of stimulation (reviewed in Green & McCormick, 2013b).

Our social stress procedure was designed to have two components, an isolation/confinement component and a social instability component, with the procedures administered daily for 16 days covering the range of mid-adolescence. Although the first two publications of our research involved postnatal days (PND) 33–48 (McCormick, Robarts, Gleason, & Kelsey, 2004; McCormick, Robarts, Kopeikina, & Kelsey, 2005), we subsequently changed the days to PND 30–45, which provides more days after the procedure in which to conduct behavioural testing while the animals are still in adolescence. The one hour isolation/confinement component was chosen because it elevates corticosterone concentrations in adolescents for the duration of the session (and there is a rapid recovery to baseline, consistent with milder stress exposures) (McCormick, Kehoe, Mallinson, Cecchi, & Frye, 2002; McCormick et al., 2001) and because of the similarity of the procedure to one of the most commonly used "psychological" stress procedures in adult rats, restraint stress (involves confinement to a tube-like container of dimensions that restrict movement). Adolescents and adults do not differ significantly in corticosterone release to one session of one hour of isolation/confinement (Hodges, Green, Simone, & McCormick, 2014). Neonatal rats show a greater release of corticosterone to repeated isolation/confinement compared with age-matched rats undergoing a first isolation/confinement (Knuth & Etgen, 2005; McCormick, Kehoe, & Kovacs, 1998), whereas in adults, there typically is a reduction in corticosterone release to repeated restraint stress relative to that in response to the first restraint session, which has been termed habituation (Grissom & Bhatnagar, 2009). Whether adolescents would show sensitization or habituation to repeated isolation/confinement was unknown.

The social instability component of our procedure involves daily changes of cage partners (pair-housed from the time of weaning) for the same 16-day period as the change of cage partners. Social instability has a long history of use as a stressor in adult rats, with early studies characterizing neuroendocrine changes that occur in groups of males in which the males are interchanged from group to group (e.g., Barnett, 1958; Taylor, Weiss, & Rupich, 1987). For example, increased sympathetic nervous system function was reported after changes in group membership among males, and HPA changes only resulted in the males when cohabitating with females (Mormede et al., 1990). The extent to which social instability would be a stressor for adolescents was not known; given the reward value of social interaction in adolescence, it was possible that new cage partners would be a positive experience. Social relationships, however, were known to be important in the recovery from stressor exposures. For example, PND 35 rats had lower corticosterone concentrations when placed in a novel environment (which typically elevates corticosterone concentrations) with a familiar peer than when with an unfamiliar peer (e.g., Gordon, 2002). Thus, our social instability stress procedure involves introducing a new cage partner after the isolation/confinement stress exposure.

We have monitored the behaviour of adolescent male rats after one hour daily isolation/confinement and upon return to a new cage partner (new cage partners also are undergoing the social instability stress procedure) and compared their behaviour to that of rats also undergoing daily isolation/confinement but always returned to their familiar cage partner (which is also undergoing daily isolation/confinement). We also have investigated the age specificity of the behavioural effects of the procedure by comparing effects with those resulting from administering the social instability stress procedure to adult rats from postnatal day 70 to 85.

The differences between adolescent rats that are isolated daily and returned to the same familiar cage partner and those isolated daily and returned to a new unfamiliar partner are minimal; although after the first few daily isolations, the males were less social when with an unfamiliar partner than with a familiar partner, this difference diminished in later blocks of days (Hodges & McCormick, 2015; McCormick, Merrick, Secen, & Helmreich, 2007). In adolescents, isolation/confinement increased affiliative behaviour, irrespective of partner familiarity, whereas in adults, the same procedures led to decreased affiliative behaviour (Hodges & McCormick, 2015). Aggressive behaviour was not observed in either age group or partner familiarity condition. When returned to an unfamiliar partner after isolation, adolescent females exhibited fewer differences in behaviour from that of control (undisturbed) females and females returning to a familiar partner than did males (McCormick et al., 2007). We have not compared the procedure administered in adolescence versus in adulthood on behaviour after isolation in females.

The influence of partner (un)familiarity in HPA responding to stressors in adolescence versus in adulthood

We investigated HPA function in male rats undergoing the social instability stress procedure in either adolescence or in adulthood. Adolescent and adult males both showed a reduction in corticosterone release in response to the sixteenth isolation (i.e., habituation) compared with age-matched controls undergoing a first isolation, irrespective of whether returned to a familiar or unfamiliar peer after previous isolations (Hodges & McCormick, 2015; McCormick et al., 2007). The role of partner familiarity was evident, however, in other measures. Adolescent rats undergoing a sixteenth isolation and that were housed with an unfamiliar partner after each previous isolation did not differ in expression of corticotrophin releasing hormone (CRH) mRNA in the central nucleus of the amygdala from rats undergoing their first isolation, and both of these groups had higher expression of CRH mRNA compared with rats undergoing their sixteenth isolation but housed with their familiar partner after each previous isolation (McCormick et al., 2007); thus, the habituation of CRH mRNA in the CEA evident in those returned repeatedly to a familiar partner was not found in those returned to an unfamiliar partner. Further, and in contrast to the habituation of corticosterone release to repeated isolation, adolescent male rats returned after isolation to their sixteenth new cage partner had higher corticosterone concentrations after one hour than did age-matched rats undergoing a first isolation and change of cage partner (Hodges & McCormick, 2015); repeated exposure to a novel peer thus potentiated corticosterone release. In contrast, adult male rats returned after isolation to their sixteenth new cage partner had lower corticosterone concentrations after one hour than did age-matched rats undergoing a first isolation and change of cage partner, suggesting that adult males habituate to the daily change in cage partners (Hodges & McCormick, 2015). Habituation is more likely to occur after repeated exposures to the same stressor (homotypic stressor) such as daily isolation/confinement than to a variety in stressors (heterotypic stressor). In sum, adolescents show potentiation of corticosterone release whereas adults show habituation of corticosterone release to repeated exposures to novel cage partners. Thus, we proposed that for adolescents, new cage partners represent a heterotypic stressor, whereas the same experience may represent a homotypic stressor for adults.

We have fewer data on neuroendocrine function during the social isolation stress procedure for females. It appears, however, that in contrast to results for males, changes of cage partners impede the habituation to repeated isolation/confinement in adolescent females (McCormick et al., 2007). Nevertheless, despite sex-specificity in the effects of the procedure on neuroendocrine function, daily isolation/confinement results in greater exposure to glucocorticoids in both sexes in adolescence when combined with social instability than when cage partners are kept in stable pairs.

Any changes in HPA function after the social instability stress (SS) procedure in adolescence are short-lived. When tested a minimum of two weeks after the SS procedure in adolescence, no differences between SS rats and control rats are found in corticosterone release in response to, and during recovery from, various stressors in either males or females (Mathews, Wilton, Styles, & McCormick, 2008; McCormick et al., 2005; McCormick, Smith, & Mathews, 2008). In contrast, in our one study of HPA function 2–3 weeks after the SS procedure administered to adult rats, SS males did not differ from non-stressed controls in corticosterone release before and after 30 min of restraint, whereas SS females showed exaggerated corticosterone release relative to control females (McCormick et al., 2005). We have not resolved why adult-stressed females show the prolonged change in HPA function that is absent in the other groups, but the results do highlight the importance of both sex and developmental stage in the consequences of social stressors. Further, that no effect of adolescent SS on HPA function was found in adulthood suggests any long-term alterations in social behaviour are not the result of a dysregulated HPA axis.

Enduring effects of SS in adolescence on social behaviour

Despite minimal differences in social behaviour between newly paired rats after isolation stress in adolescence in the colony home cages, there is much evidence that the social repertoire is modified by the adolescent SS experience from investigations conducted after the end of the SS procedure and in test arenas rather than in the home cages. When tested after the SS procedure either soon after in adolescence (Hodges et al., 2017) or weeks after in adulthood (Green et al., 2013), SS male rats spent less time initiating social interactions with an unfamiliar peer than did control rats. Nevertheless, SS rats either did not differ from control rats (Green et al., 2013) or spent more time than did control rats (Hodges et al., 2017) in proximity to an unfamiliar peer in a social approach test, which indicates that SS rats are not socially avoidant. Instead, SS rats may be socially anxious, and this anxiety may be limited to direct physical interactions with conspecifics. SS rats also exhibit more general anxiety-like behaviour in adulthood in tests that involve venturing out onto high, narrow, elevated ledges (Elevated Plus Maze Test) (McCormick et al., 2008), entering the centre of an open field (as opposed to staying close to walls), approaching novel objects (Green et al., 2013) and the latency to drink novel substances (ethanol or 1% sucrose; Marcolin, Hodges, & McCormick in preparation). One difference between social anxiety and these other measures of anxiety in SS rats is that social anxiety does not seem to require the incubation period that the other indices do; specifically, whereas social anxiety was manifested both soon after and long after the SS procedure, the other forms of anxiety were only evident in SS rats in adulthood. Thus, the social anxiety of SS rats may be somewhat independent of a more general anxiety.

Our results from conditioned place preference tests also suggest that social interactions have the same reward value for male SS rats as for control rats despite the anxiety such interactions may provoke. After repeated pairings of one context with interactions with a novel peer and another context with a non-social stimulus, SS and control rats both chose to spend more time in the context previously paired with the social stimulus than that paired with the non-social one (Hodges et al., 2017).

An alternative, but not mutually exclusive, possibility is that the reduction in social interactions occurs because SS in adolescence thwarts the development of a complete, appropriate, social repertoire. For example, behavioural sequencing (the predictability of the behaviour of one rat by the behaviour of its partner (Maaswinkel et al., 1997) involves the medial PFC and the hippocampus, neural structures that are still developing in adolescence. Thus, a disruption in behavioural sequencing may underlie the effects of SS in adolescence on social interactions.

When social interactions in a novel test arena with the cage partner are compared with social interactions with a novel peer, control and SS male rats did not differ in time spent with the familiar cage partner, and control rats spent more time in social interaction with an unfamiliar peer than did SS rats (Hodges et al., 2017). Further, the increase in time in social interaction with a novel peer relative to that with a familiar peer was significant only for control rats. A possibility that emerges from the latter finding is that SS rats may be impaired in social recognition. This possibility was tested (Hodges et al., 2017), and SS rats did not exhibit the preference for investigating a novel rat relative to a rat investigated in the familiarization phase that was exhibited by control rats. This result was found despite SS rats spending more time investigating the stimulus rats (kept behind mesh at all times) than did control rats.

Male SS rats also exhibit evidence of an altered social repertoire in adulthood when competing against their cage partner for access to sweetened condensed milk that is available daily for five minutes for five days (Cumming, Thompson, & McCormick, 2014) and when provided with the opportunity to mate with a receptive female (McCormick et al., 2013). Both SS and control rats increased aggressive behaviour from the first day to the last day when competing for sweetened condensed milk; the increase in aggression was greater for SS rats than for control rats, and SS rats were more aggressive than were control rats on the fifth day (Cumming et al., 2014). The aggression displayed is typically "face whacks", whereby one rat tries to displace the other from the feeder of sweetened condensed milk by striking its snout; thus, the increased aggression in SS rats may involve a higher motivation for the food. Male SS rats show impairments in their sexual performance with females, such as a reduction in the likelihood to ejaculate compared with the likelihood in control males (McCormick et al., 2013). A second study investigated whether females would prefer mating opportunities with control males than with SS males. This experiment revealed that social status may mitigate some of the effects of the SS procedure; when SS rats were the subordinate rat in the dyad, females showed a marked preference for the control male over the SS male (McCormick, Cameron, et al., 2017). In contrast, when SS rats were the dominant rat in the dyad, females preferred the SS male over the control male. Dominant–subordinate status of the rats in the dyad was for pairs of SS rats housed together and pairs of control rats housed together; we do not know how whether SS rats would be dominant or subordinate when housed with control males. The important finding was that SS in adolescence leads to long-lasting changes in males that were perceptible to females.

Neural mechanisms that may underlie the effects of SS in adolescence on social behaviour

Most of the investigations of neural differences between SS and control rats are preliminary and not yet published (see Table 27.2 for a summary of the findings). Regardless, the extent to which differences in the various neural measures underlie the differences in social behaviour between SS and control rats is unknown. That differences are observed in the key neural regions supporting social behaviour, however, is consistent with the possibility that the neural differences underlie the behavioural differences between SS and control males.

Hippocampus

We first investigated the hippocampus of SS rats because of our findings of reduced performance on spatial tasks in SS rats compared with control rats in males (Green & McCormick, 2013a;

Table 27.2 Summary of differences observed between SS and control rats in selected subregions of the brain contributing to social behaviour

Brain region	SS rats relative to control rats	Implication
Hippocampus	• As adolescents and as adults, increased survival of immature neurons in the dentate gyrus. • As adolescents, reduced glutamic acid decarboxylase isoform 67 (GAD67a marker for GABA neurons). • As adults, higher expression of calcium/calmodulin-dependent protein kinase II (CAMKIIα), and lower expression of the autonomously active form of CamKII.	• May underlie the reduced hippocampal-dependent memory of SS rats vs control rats.
Prefrontal cortex	• As adults, reduced CAMKIIα and PSD-95 (post-synaptic density protein 95; a scaffolding protein in synapses).	• Suggests reduced synaptic connectivity in SS rats.
Lateral septum	• As adolescents, increased CAMKIIα in the lateral septum. • As adolescents, higher oxytocin receptor binding density and reduced vasopressin receptor V1a density.	• May be implicated in reward value of social interactions.
Medial amygdala	• As adolescents, reduced number of basal dendrite terminals (reduced dendritic branches). • As adolescents, reduced expression of synaptophysin.	• Suggests reduced synaptic connectivity in SS rats.

McCormick et al., 2012; Morrissey, Mathews, & McCormick, 2011) and in females (McCormick, Nixon, Thomas, Lowie, & Dyck, 2010). As described earlier, the CA2 subregion of the hippocampus is essential for social recognition, and the hippocampus is implicated in anxiety in social interaction tests (e.g., File, Kenny, & Ouagzzal, 1998; Hollis, Wang, Dietz, Gunjan, & Kabbaj, 2010; Marco et al., 2011). In male rats, although the number of proliferating cells in the hippocampus did not differ between SS and control rats, new neurons survived longer in SS rats than in control rats (McCormick et al., 2012); the functional significance of the increased survival, however, is unknown. Signalling cascades in the hippocampus also differ between SS and control rats, with SS having a higher expression of CamKIIα (calcium/calmodulin-dependent protein kinase II; important for memory formation) and reduced expression of the autonomously active form of CamKII compared with expression in control rats tested as adults (McCormick et al., 2012). In adolescence, SS rats had reduced GAD67 (glutamic acid decarboxylase isoform 67, a marker for GABA neurons) in the pyramidal blade of the hippocampus compared with control rats (Hodges, Marcolin, & McCormick, unpublished data). Others have found that in adult rats, repeated administration of corticosterone reduced hippocampal GAD67 whereas 21 days of chronic restraint was without effect. Thus, adolescent rats may be more susceptible to GAD67 reduction by stressors than are adults (Lussier, Romay-Tallón, Caruncho, & Kalynchuk, 2013). The reductions in GAD67 and CamKIIα are consistent with the hippocampal-dependent memory impairments observed in SS rats compared with controls (Morrissey, Mathews, & McCormick, 2011; McCormick et al., 2012; Green & McCormick, 2013a; Hodges et al., 2017).

Prefrontal cortex (PFC)

In adolescence, there were few differences between SS rats and control rats in the amount of proteins involved in synaptic plasticity in various brain regions when tested at PND 46. When tested in adulthood, rats that underwent SS in adolescence had less CAMKIIα and PSD-95 (post-synaptic density protein 95; a scaffolding protein in synapses) in the PFC than did control rats (Marcolin, Hodges, & McCormick, unpublished data), which suggests reduced synaptic transmission in the PFC.

Lateral septum

When tested in adolescence, SS rats had more CAMKII in the lateral septum (Hodges et al., unpublished data). SS rats also had higher oxytocin receptor binding density in the dorsal lateral septum and nucleus accumbens than did control rats (Hodges et al., 2017). The vasopressin 1a receptor binding density of SS rats was higher in the ventral lateral septum and lower in the nucleus accumbens relative to that of control rats (Hodges et al., 2017). The infusion of an OTR antagonist into the nucleus accumbens was found to reduce social novelty-seeking of adolescent males (Smith et al., 2017) and reduce the rewarding properties of social interactions (Dolen, Darvishzadeh, Huang, & Malenka, 2013). Thus, enhanced OTR binding density (which may reflect either an increase in receptors or an increase in the affinity of the receptors for oxytocin) in the nucleus accumbens may play a role in the increased social investigatory behaviour of peers found in SS rats when the peer is confined behind mesh, but does not explain the reduced time that SS rats spend in unfettered social interactions with a novel peer.

Medial amygdala

When tested in adolescence, Golgi-staining of stellate neurons indicated that SS rats had a reduced number of basal dendrite terminals (reduced dendritic branches) in the posterodorsal medial amygdala compared with control rats (Hodges et al., unpublished data). SS rats also had reduced expression of synaptophysin (an indicator of number of synapses) in the medial amygdala than did control rats (Hodges et al., unpublished data). Combined, these results suggest reduced synaptic connectivity in the medial amygdala.

Neural activations during social interactions

We have preliminary evidence of functional differences between SS and control rats when engaging in social interactions as adolescents. SS rats had reduced neural activations (as measured by immunoreactive cell counts of the protein product of the immediate early gene c-fos) in several brain regions (paraventricular nucleus, arcuate nucleus, lateral septum, medial amygdala) compared with control rats. Further, Fos-immunoreactivity in the arcuate nucleus (which may reflect stress responding) was positively associated with time in social interaction in the SS rats, whereas Fos-immunoreactivity in the medial amygdala was associated with time in social interaction in the control rats. Thus, social interactions may be a qualitatively different experience for SS than for control rats.

Conclusion

Humans and rats undergo important shifts in social behaviour and in HPA function in adolescence (McCormick, Green, et al., 2017; McCormick, Hodges, & Simone, 2015). Research from our lab indicates that the experience of social stressors in adolescence can have immediate and enduring consequences for a broad range of social function in males; we are in early stages of investigation of social behaviour in females, for which we have noted effects on other endpoints (e.g., vulnerability to drugs of abuse, McCormick, 2010). Our findings highlight the unique plasticity of the adolescent period; the same stressor exposures in adulthood typically have little lasting effect. Although the use of rodents has proven to be of value for both translational and back-translational research (Insel et al., 2013), there is concern over the extent to which behavioural assessments in rodents reflect psychiatric disorders in human (Stanford, 2017). Thus, although the extent to which adolescent social stress in rats can be used to model human depression, social anxiety or other psychopathology is a matter of much debate, the general principles of adolescent social development that emerge from investigations in rats facilitate the generation of testable hypotheses of adolescent social development and how stressors perturb such development in humans.

References

Alexander, G. M., Farris, S., Pirone, J. R., Zheng, C., Colgin, L. L., & Dudek, S. M. (2016). Social and novel contexts modify hippocampal CA2 representations of space. *Nature Communications*, 7, 10300.

Barnett, S. A. (1958). Physiological effects of social stress in wild rats. I. The adrenal cortex. *Journal of Psychosomatic Research*, 3, 1–11.

Beach, F. A. (1950). The Snark was a Boojum. *American Psychologist*, 5, 115–124.

Becker, A., Grecksch, G., Bernstein, H. G., Höllt, V., & Bogerts, B. (1999). Social behaviour in rats lesioned with ibotenic acid in the hippocampus: Quantitative and qualitative analysis. *Psychopharmacology*, 144, 333–338.

Bell, H. C., McCaffrey, D. R., Forgie, M. L., Kolb, B., & Pellis, S. M. (2009). The role of the medial prefrontal cortex in the play fighting of rats. *Behavioral Neuroscience*, 123, 1158–1168.

Bell, H. C., Pellis, S. M., & Kolb, B. (2010). Juvenile peer play experience and the development of the orbitofrontal and medial prefrontal cortices. *Behavioural Brain Research*, 207, 7–13.

Bielsky, I. F., Hu, S. B., Ren, X., Terwilliger, E. F., & Young, L. J. (2005). The V1a vasopressin receptor is necessary and sufficient for normal social recognition: A gene replacement study. *Neuron*, 47, 503–513.

Bluthé, R. M., Gheusi, G., & Dantzer, R. (1993). Gonadal steroids influence the involvement of arginine vasopressin in social recognition in mice. *Psychoneuroendocrinology*, 18, 323–335.

Bolles, R. C., & Woods, P. J. (1964). The ontogeny of behaviour in the albino rat. *Animal Behaviour*, 12, 427–441.

Bredewold, R., Smith, C. J., Dumais, K. M., & Veenema, A. H. (2014). Sex-specific modulation of juvenile social play behavior by vasopressin and oxytocin depends on social context. *Frontiers in Behavioral Neuroscience*, 8, 1–11.

Brenhouse, H. C., & Andersen, S. L. (2011). Developmental trajectories during adolescence in males and females: A cross-species understanding of underlying brain changes. *Neuroscience and Biobehavioral Reviews*, 35, 1687–1703.

Brill-Maoz, N., & Maroun, M. (2016). Extinction of fear is facilitated by social presence: Synergism with prefrontal oxytocin. *Psychoneuroendocrinology*, 66, 75–81.

Burke, A., McCormick, C., Pellis, S., & Lukkes, J. (2017). Impact of adolescent social experiences on behavior and neural circuits. *Neuroscience and Biobehavioral Reviews*, 76, 280–300.

Buwalda, B., Geerdink, M., Vidal, J., & Koolhaas, J. M. (2011). Social behavior and social stress in adolescence: A focus on animal models. *Neuroscience and Biobehavioral Reviews*, 32, 1713–1721.

Cajal, S. R. Y. (1967). The structure and connexions of neurons. Amsterdam: Elsevier.

Calcagnetti, D. J., & Schechter, M. D. (1992). Place conditioning reveals the rewarding aspect of social-interaction in juvenile rats. *Physiology & Behavior*, 51, 667–672.

Cirulli, F., Terranova, M. L., & Laviola, G. (1996). Affiliation in periadolescent rats: Behavioral and corticosterone response to social reunion with familiar or unfamiliar partners. *Pharmacology, Biochemistry, and Behavior*, 54, 99–105.

Cooke, B. M., Breedlove, S. M., & Jordan, C. L. (2003). Both estrogen receptors and androgen receptors contribute to testosterone-induced changes in the morphology of the medial amygdala and sexual arousal in male rats. *Hormones and Behavior*, 43, 336–346.

Cooke, B. M., & Woolley, C. S. (2009). Effects of prepubertal gonadectomy on a male-typical behavior and excitatory synaptic transmission in the amygdala. *Developmental Neurobiology, 69*, 141–152.

Cordero, M. I., Just, N., Poirier, G. L., & Sandi, C. (2016). Effects of paternal and peripubertal stress on aggression, anxiety, and metabolic alterations in the lateral septum. *European Neuropsychopharmacology, 26*, 357–367.

Crews, F., He, J., & Hodge, C. (2007). Adolescent cortical development: A critical period of vulnerability for addiction. *Pharmacology, Biochemistry, and Behavior, 86*, 189–199.

Cumming, M. J., Thompson, M. A., & McCormick, C. M. (2014). Adolescent social instability stress increases aggression in a food competition task in adult male Long-Evans rats. *Developmental Psychobiology, 56*, 1575–1588.

Dantzer, R., Koob, G. F., Bluthé, R. M., & Le Moal, M. (1988). Septal vasopressin modulates social memory in male rats. *Brain Research, 457*, 143–147.

De Vries, G. J., Best, W., & Sluiter, A. A. (1983). The influence of androgens on the development of a sex difference in the vasopressinergic innervation of the rat lateral septum. *Brain Research, 284*, 377–380.

De Vries, G. J., Buds, R. M., & Swaab, D. F. (1981). Ontogeny of the vasopressinergic neurons of the suprachiasmatic nucleus and their extrahypothalamic projections in the rat brain – presence of a sex difference in the lateral septum. *Brain Research, 218*, 67–78.

Dolen, G., Darvishzadeh, A., Huang, K. W., & Malenka, R. C. (2013). Social reward requires coordinated activity of nucleus accumbens oxytocin and serotonin. *Nature, 501*, 179–184.

Douglas, L. A., Varlinskaya, E. I., & Spear, L. P. (2004). Rewarding properties of social interactions in adolescent and adult male and female rats: Impact of social versus isolate housing of subjects and partners. *Developmental Psychobiology, 45*, 153–162.

Dumais, K. M., & Veenema, A. H. (2016). Vasopressin and oxytocin receptor systems in the brain: Sex differences and sex-specific regulation of social behavior. *Frontiers in Neuroendocrinology, 40*, 1–23.

Eiland, L., & Romeo, R. D. (2013). Stress and the developing adolescent brain. *Neuroscience, 249*, 162–171.

Einon, D. F., & Morgan, M. J. (1976). Habituation of object contact in socially-reared and isolated rats (Rattus norvegicus). *Animal Behaviour, 24*, 415–420.

Einon, D. F., & Morgan, M. J. (1977). A critical period for social isolation in the rat. *Developmental Psychobiology, 10*, 123–132.

Einon, D. F., & Potegal, M. (1991). Enhanced defense in adult rats deprived of playfighting experience as juveniles. *Aggressive Behavior, 17*, 27–40.

File, S. E., & Hyde, J. R. (1978). Can social interaction be used to measure anxiety? *British Journal of Pharmacology, 62*, 19–24.

File, S. E., Kenny, P. S., & Ouagazzal, A. M. (1998). Bimodal modulation by nicotine of anxiety in the social interaction test: Role of the dorsal hippocampus. *Behavioral Neuroscience, 112*, 1423–1429.

File, S. E., & Seth, P. (2003). A review of 25 years of the social interaction test. *European Journal of Pharmacology, 463*, 35–53.

Gabor, C. S., Phan, A., Clipperton-Allen, A. E., Kavaliers, M., & Choleris, E. (2012). Interplay of oxytocin, vasopressin, and sex hormones in the regulation of social recognition. *Behavioral Neuroscience, 126*, 97–109.

Gordon, H. W. (2002). Early environmental stress and biological vulnerability to drug abuse. *Psychoneuroendocrinology, 27*, 115–126.

Gottlieb, G., & Lickliter, R. (2004). The various roles of animal models in understanding human development. *Social Development, 13*, 311–325.

Gourley, S. L., Olevska, A., Warren, M. S., Taylor, J. R., & Koleske, A. J. (2012). Arg kinase regulates prefrontal dendritic spine refinement and cocaine-induced plasticity. *Journal of Neuroscience, 32*, 2314–2323.

Green, M. R., Barnes, B., & McCormick, C. M. (2013). Social instability stress in adolescence increases anxiety and reduces social interactions in adulthood in male Long-Evans rats. *Developmental Psychobiology, 55*, 849–859.

Green, M. R., & McCormick, C. M. (2013a). Effects of social instability stress in adolescence on long-term, not short-term, spatial memory performance. *Behavioural Brain Research, 256*, 165–171.

Green, M. R., & McCormick, C. M. (2013b). Effects of stressors in adolescence on learning and memory in rodent models. *Hormones and Behavior, 64*, 364–379.

Green, M. R., & McCormick, C. M. (2016). Sex and stress steroids in adolescence: Gonadal regulation of the hypothalamic-pituitary-adrenal axis in the rat. *General and Comparative Endocrinology, 234*, 110–116.

Green, M. R., Nottrodt, R., Simone, J. J., & McCormick, C. M. (2016). Glucocorticoid receptor translocation and expression of relevant genes in hippocampus in adolescent and adult male rats. *Psychoneuroendocrinology, 73*, 32–41.

Grissom, N., & Bhatnagar, S. (2009). Habituation to repeated stress: Get used to it. *Neurobiology of Learning and Memory*, *92*, 215–224.

Gur, R., Tendler, A., & Wagner, S. (2014). Long-term social recognition memory is mediated by oxytocin-dependent synaptic plasticity in the medial amygdala. *Biological Psychiatry*, *76*, 377–386.

Handa, R. J., & Weiser, M. J. (2014). Gonadal steroid hormones and the hypothalamo–pituitary–adrenal axis. *Frontiers in Neuroendocrinology*, *35*, 197–220.

He, J., & Crews, F. T. (2007). Neurogenesis decreases during brain maturation from adolescence to adulthood. *Pharmacology, Biochemistry, and Behavior*, *86*, 327–333.

Himmler, B. T., Bell, H. C., Horwood, L., Harker, A., Kolb, B., & Pellis, S. M. (2014). The role of the medial prefrontal cortex in regulating inter-animal coordination of movements. *Behavioral Neuroscience*, *128*, 603–613.

Himmler, B. T., Pellis, S. M., & Kolb, B. (2013). Juvenile play experience primes neurons in the medial prefrontal cortex to be more responsive to later experiences. *Neuroscience Letters*, *556*, 42–45.

Himmler, B. T., Stryjek, R., Modlinska, K., Derksen, S. M., Pisula, W., & Pellis, S. M. (2013). How domestication modulates play behavior: A comparative analysis between wild rats and a laboratory strain of Rattus norvegicus. *Journal of Comparative Psychology*, *127*, 453–465.

Himmler, S. M., Modlinska, K., Stryjek, R., Himmler, B. T., Pisula, W., & Pellis, S. M. (2014). Domestication and diversification: A comparative analysis of the play fighting of the Brown Norway, Sprague-Dawley, and Wistar laboratory strains of (Rattus norvegicus). Journal of Comparative Psychology, 128(3), 318; *Journal of Comparative Psychology*, *128*, 1–10.

Hines, M., Allen, L. S., & Gorski, R. A. (1992). Sex differences in subregions of the medial nucleus of the amygdala and the bed nucleus of the stria terminalis of the rat. *Brain Research*, *579*, 321–326.

Hitti, F. L., & Siegelbaum, S. A. (2014). The hippocampal CA2 region is essential for social memory. *Nature*, *508*, 88–92.

Hodges, T. E., Baumbach, J. L., Marcolin, M. L., Bredewold, R., Veenema, A. H., & McCormick, C. M. (2017). Social instability stress in adolescent male rats reduces social interaction and social recognition performance and increases oxytocin receptor binding. *Neuroscience*, *359*, 172–182.

Hodges, T. E., Green, M. R., Simone, J. J., & McCormick, C. M. (2014). Effects of social context on endocrine function and Zif268 expression in response to an acute stressor in adolescent and adult rats. *International Journal of Developmental Neuroscience*, *35*, 25–34.

Hodges, T. E., Marcolin, M. L., & McCormick, C. M. (unpublished data). Brock University.

Hodges, T. E., & McCormick, C. M. (2015). Adolescent and adult rats habituate to repeated isolation, but only adolescents sensitize to partner unfamiliarity. *Hormones and Behavior*, *69*, 16–30.

Hollis, F., Wang, H., Dietz, D., Gunjan, A., & Kabbaj, M. (2010). The effects of repeated social defeat on long-term depressive-like behavior and short-term histone modifications in the hippocampus in male Sprague – Dawley rats. *Psychopharmacology*, *211*, 69–77.

Hostinar, C. E., Sullivan, R. M., & Gunnar, M. R. (2014). Psychobiological mechanisms underlying the social buffering of the hypothalamic – pituitary – adrenocortical axis: A review of animal models and human studies across development. *Psychological Bulletin*, *140*, 256–282.

Insel, T. R., & Fernald, R. D. (2004). How the brain processes social information: Searching for the social brain. *Annual Review of Neuroscience*, *27*, 697–622.

Insel, T. R., Voon, V., Nye, J. S., Brown, V. J., Altevogt, B. M., Bullmore, E. T., . . . Marston, H. M. (2013). Innovative solutions to novel drug development in mental health. *Neuroscience and Biobehavioral Reviews*, *37*, 2438–2444.

Juraska, J. M., & Willing, J. (2017). Pubertal onset as a critical transition for neural development and cognition. *Brain Research*, *1654*, 87–94.

Kalman, E., & Keay, K. A. (2017). Hippocampal volume, social interactions, and the expression of the normal repertoire of resident – intruder behavior. *Brain and Behavior*, e00775, 1–7.

Klein, Z. A., Padow, V. A., & Romeo, R. D. (2010). The effects of stress on play and home cage behaviors in adolescent male rats. *Developmental Psychobiology*, *52*, 62–70.

Knapska, E., Radwanska, K., Werka, T., & Kaczmarek, L. (2007). Functional internal complexity of amygdala: Focus on gene activity mapping after behavioral training and drugs of abuse. *Physiology Reviews*, *87*, 1113–1173.

Knuth, E. D., & Etgen, A. M. (2005). Corticosterone secretion induced by chronic isolation in neonatal rats is sexually dimorphic and accompanied by elevated ACTH. *Hormones and Behavior*, *47*, 65–75.

Kolb, B., & Nonneman, A. J. (1974). Frontolimbic lesions and social behavior in the rat. *Physiology & Behavior*, *13*, 637–643.

Koss, W. A., Belden, C. E., Hristov, A. D., & Juraska, J. M. (2014). Dendritic remodeling in the adolescent medial prefrontal cortex and the basolateral amygdala of male and female rats. *Synapse, 68*, 61–72.

Ku, K. M., Weir, R. K., Silverman, J. L., Berman, R. F., & Bauman, M. D. (2016). Behavioral phenotyping of juvenile Long-Evans and Sprague-Dawley rats: Implications for preclinical models of autism spectrum disorders. *PLoS One, 11*, e0158150.

Kummer, K., Klement, S., Eggart, V., Mayr, M. J., Saria, A., & Zernig, G. (2011). Conditioned place preference for social interaction in rats: Contribution of sensory components. *Frontiers in Behavioral Neuroscience, 5*, 1–5.

Lampe, J. F., Burman, O., Würbel, H., & Melotti, L. (2017). Context dependent individual differences in playfulness in male rats. *Developmental Psychobiology, 59*, 460–472.

Landgraf, R., Gerstberger, R., Montkowski, A., Probst, J. C., Wotjak, C. T., Holsboer, F., & Engelmann, M. (1995). V1 vasopressin receptor antisense oligodeoxynucleotide into septum reduces vasopressin binding, social discrimination abilities, and anxiety-related behavior in rats. *Journal of Neuroscience, 15*, 4250–4258.

Liebsch, G., Montkowski, A., Holsboer, F., & Landgraf, R. (1998). Behavioural profiles of two Wistar rat lines selectively bred for high or low anxiety-related behaviour. *Behavioural Brain Research, 94*, 301–310.

Lukas, M., Toth, I., Veenema, A. H., & Neumann, I. D. (2013). Oxytocin mediates rodent social memory within the lateral septum and the medial amygdala depending on the relevance of the social stimulus: Male juvenile versus female adult conspecifics. *Psychoneuroendocrinology, 38*, 916–926.

Lukkes, J. L., Mokin, M. V., Scholl, J. L., & Forster, G. L. (2009). Adult rats exposed to early-life social isolation exhibit increased anxiety and conditioned fear behavior, and altered hormonal stress responses. *Hormones and Behavior, 55*, 248–256.

Luo, A. H., Tahsili-Fahadan, P., Wise, R. A., Lupica, C. R., & Aston-Jones, G. S. (2011). Linking context with reward: A functional circuit from hippocampal CA3 to ventral tegmental area. *Science, 333*, 353–357.

Lussier, A. L., Romay-Tallón, R., Caruncho, H. J., & Kalynchuk, L. E. (2013). Altered GABAergic and glutamatergic activity within the rat hippocampus and amygdala in rats subjected to repeated corticosterone administration but not restraint stress. *Neuroscience, 231*, 38–48.

Maaswinkel, H., Gispen, W., & Spruijt, B. (1997). Executive function of the hippocampus in social behavior in the rat. *Behavioral Neuroscience, 111*, 777–784.

Marco, E. M., Rapino, C., Caprioli, A., Borsini, F., Maccarrone, M., & Laviola, G. (2011). Social encounter with a novel partner in adolescent rats: Activation of the central endocannabinoid system. *Behavioural Brain Research, 220*, 140–145.

Marcolin, M. L., Hodges, T. E., & McCormick, C. M. (unpublished data). Brock University.

Marcolin, M. L., Hodges, T. E., & McCormick, C. M. (in preparation). Social instability stress in adolescence increases ethanol and sucrose intake, depending on the social context.

Markham, J. A., & Juraska, J. M. (2007). Social recognition memory: Influence of age, sex, and ovarian hormonal status. *Physiology & Behavior, 92*, 881–888.

Markham, J. A., Morris, J. R., & Juraska, J. M. (2007). Neuron number decreases in the rat ventral, but not dorsal, medial prefrontal cortex between adolescence and adulthood. *Neuroscience, 144*, 961–968.

Maroun, M., & Wagner, S. (2016). Oxytocin and memory of emotional stimuli: Some dance to remember, some dance to forget. *Biological Psychiatry, 79*, 203–212.

Mathews, I. Z., Wilton, A., Styles, A., & McCormick, C. M. (2008). Heightened neuroendocrine function in males to a heterotypic stressor and increased depressive behaviour in females after adolescent social stress in rats. *Behavioural Brain Research, 190*, 33–40.

McCall, C., & Singer, T. (2012). The animal and human neuroendocrinology of social cognition, motivation and behavior. *Nature Neuroscience, 15*, 681–688.

McCormick, C. M. (2010). An animal model of social instability stress in adolescence and risk for drugs of abuse. *Physiology & Behavior, 99*, 194–203.

McCormick, C. M., Cameron, N. M., Thompson, M. A., Cumming, M. J., Hodges, T. E., & Langett, M. (2017). The sexual preference of female rats is influenced by males' adolescent social stress history and social status. *Hormones and Behavior, 89*, 30–37.

McCormick, C. M., Green, M. R., Cameron, N. M., Nixon, F., Levy, M. J., & Clark, R. A. (2013). Deficits in male sexual behavior in adulthood after social instability stress in adolescence in rats. *Hormones and Behavior, 63*, 5–12.

McCormick, C. M., Green, M. R., & Simone, J. J. (2017). Translational relevance of rodent models of hypothalamic-pituitary-adrenal function and stressors in adolescence. *Neurobiology of Stress, 6*, 31–43.

McCormick, C. M., Hodges, T. E., & Simone, J. J. (2015). Peer pressures: Social instability stress in adolescence and social deficits in adulthood in an animal model. *Developmental Cognitive Neuroscience, 11*, 2–11.

McCormick, C. M., Kehoe, P., & Kovacs, S. (1998). Corticosterone release in response to repeated, short episodes of neonatal isolation: Evidence of sensitization. *International Journal of Developmental Neuroscience, 16*, 175–185.

McCormick, C. M., Kehoe, P., Mallinson, K., Cecchi, L., & Frye, C. A. (2002). Neonatal isolation alters stress hormone and mesolimbic dopamine release in juvenile rats. *Pharmacology, Biochemistry, and Behavior, 73*, 77–85.

McCormick, C. M., & Mathews, I. Z. (2007). HPA function in adolescence: Role of sex hormones in its regulation and the enduring consequences of exposure to stressors. *Pharmacology, Biochemistry, and Behavior, 86*, 220–233.

McCormick, C. M., Merrick, A., Secen, J., & Helmreich, D. L. (2007). Social instability in adolescence alters the central and peripheral hypothalamic-pituitary-adrenal responses to a repeated homotypic stressor in male and female rats. *Journal of Neuroendocrinology, 19*, 116–126.

McCormick, C. M., Nixon, F., Thomas, C., Lowie, B., & Dyck, J. (2010). Hippocampal cell proliferation and spatial memory performance after social instability stress in adolescence in female rats. *Behavioural Brain Research, 208*, 23–29.

McCormick, C. M., Rioux, T., Fisher, R., Lang, K., MacLaury, K., & Teillon, S. M. (2001). Effects of neonatal corticosterone treatment on maze performance and HPA axis in juvenile rats. *Physiology & Behavior, 74*, 371–379.

McCormick, C. M., Robarts, D., Gleason, E., & Kelsey, J. E. (2004). Stress during adolescence enhances locomotor sensitization to nicotine in adulthood in female, but not male, rats. *Hormones and Behavior, 46*, 458–466.

McCormick, C. M., Robarts, D., Kopeikina, K., & Kelsey, J. E. (2005). Long-lasting, sex-and age-specific effects of social stress on corticosterone responses to restraint and locomotor responses to psychostimulants in rats. *Hormones and Behavior, 48*, 64–74.

McCormick, C. M., Smith, C., & Mathews, I. Z. (2008). Effects of chronic social stress in adolescence on anxiety and neuroendocrine response to mild stress in male and female rats. *Behavioural Brain Research, 187*, 228–238.

McCormick, C. M., Thomas, C. M., Sheridan, C. S., Nixon, F., Flynn, J. A., & Mathews, I. Z. (2012). Social instability stress in adolescent male rats alters hippocampal neurogenesis and produces a deficit in spatial location memory in adulthood. *Hippocampus, 22*, 1300–1312.

Meaney, M. J., & Stewart, J. (1981). A descriptive study of social development in the rat (Rattus norvegicus). *Animal Behaviour, 29*, 34–45.

Mizukami, S., Nishizuka, M., & Arai, Y. (1983). Sexual difference in nuclear volume and its ontogeny in the rat amygdala. *Experimental Neurology, 79*, 569–575.

Mormede, P., Lemaire, V., Castanon, N., Dulluc, J., Laval, M., & Le Moal, M. (1990). Multiple neuroendocrine responses to chronic social stress: Interaction between individual characteristics and situational factors. *Physiology & Behavior, 47*, 1099–1105.

Morrissey, M. D., Mathews, I. Z., & McCormick, C. M. (2011). Enduring deficits in contextual and auditory fear conditioning after adolescent, not adult, social instability stress in male rats. *Neurobiology of Learning and Memory, 95*, 46–56.

Murakami, G., Hunter, R. G., Fontaine, C., Ribeiro, A., & Pfaff, D. W. (2011). Relationships among estrogen receptor, oxytocin and vasopressin gene expression and social interaction in male mice. *European Journal of Neuroscience, 34*, 469–477.

Nakajima, M., Görlich, A., & Heintz, N. (2014). Oxytocin modulates female sociosexual behavior through a specific class of prefrontal cortical interneuron. *Cell, 159*, 295–305.

Nelson, E. E., Leibenluft, E., McClure, E. B., & Pine, D. S. (2005). The social re-orientation of adolescence: A neuroscience perspective on the process and its relation to psychopathology. *Psychological Medicine, 35*, 163–174.

Neumann, I. D., & Landgraf, R. (2012). Balance of brain oxytocin and vasopressin: Implications for anxiety, depression, and social behaviors. *Trends in Neuroscience, 35*, 649–659.

Newman, S. W. (1999). The medial extended amygdala in male reproductive behavior: A node in the mammalian social behavior network. *Annals of the New York Academy of Science, 877*, 242–257.

Pagani, J. H., Zhao, M., Cui, Z., Williams Avram, S. K., Dudek, S. M., & Young, W. S. (2015). Role of the vasopressin 1b receptor in rodent aggressive behavior and synaptic plasticity in hippocampal area CA2. *Molecular Psychiatry, 20*, 490–499.

Panksepp, J., & Beatty, W. W. (1980). Social deprivation and play in rats. *Behavioral and Neural Biology, 30*, 197–206.

Panksepp, J., Siviy, S., & Normansell, L. (1984). The psychobiology of play: Theoretical and methodological perspectives. *Neuroscience and Biobehavioral Reviews, 8*, 465–492.

Peartree, N. A., Hood, L. E., Thiel, K. J., Sanabria, F., Pentke, N. S., Chandler, K. N., & Neisewander, J. L. (2012). Limited physical contact through a mesh barrier is sufficient for social reward-conditioned place preference in adolescent male rats. *Physiology & Behavior, 105*, 749–756.

Pellis, S. M., & Pellis, V. C. (2017). What is play fighting and what is it good for? *Learning & Behavior. 45*(4), 355–366.

Pellis, S. M., Pellis, V. C., & Bell, H. C. (2010). The function of play in the development of the social brain. *American Journal of Play, 2*, 278–298.

Pellis, S. M., Pellis, V. C., & Himmler, B. T. (2014). How play makes for a more adaptable brain: A comparative and neural perspective. *American Journal of Play, 7*, 73–98.

Perkins, A. E., Doremus-Fitzwater, T. L., Spencer, R. L., Varlinskaya, E. I., Conti, M. M., Bishop, C., & Deak, T. (2016). A working model for the assessment of disruptions in social behavior among aged rats: The role of sex differences, social recognition, and sensorimotor processes. *Experimental Gerontology, 76*, 46–57.

Pokorný, J., & Yamamoto, T. (1981). Postnatal ontogenesis of hippocampal CA1 area in rats. I. Development of dendritic arborisation in pyramidal neurons. *Brain Research Bulletin, 7*, 113–120.

Prediger, R. D., Batista, L. C., & Takahashi, R. N. (2005). Caffeine reverses age-related deficits in olfactory discrimination and social recognition memory in rats: Involvement of adenosine A1 and A2A receptors. *Neurobiology of Aging, 26*, 957–964.

Primus, R. J., & Kellogg, C. K. (1989). Pubertal related changes influence the development of environment related social interaction in the male rat. *Developmental Psychobiology, 22*, 633–643.

Romeo, R. D., Lee, S. J., & McEwen, B. S. (2004). Differential stress reactivity in intact and ovariectomized prepubertal and adult female rats. *Neuroendocrinology, 80*, 387–393.

Romeo, R. D., Minhas, S., Svirsky, S. E., Hall, B. S., Savenkova, M., & Karatsoreos, I. N. (2014). Pubertal shifts in adrenal responsiveness to stress and adrenocorticotropic hormone in male rats. *Psychoneuroendocrinology, 42*, 146–152.

Romeo, R. D., Patel, R., Pham, L., & So, V. M. (2016). Adolescence and the ontogeny of the hormonal stress response in male and female rats and mice. *Neuroscience and Biobehavioral Reviews, 70*, 206–216.

Roof, R. L., & Havens, M. D. (1992). Testosterone improves maze performance and induces development of a male hippocampus in females. *Brain Research, 572*, 310–313.

Sabihi, S., Durosko, N. E., Dong, S. M., & Leuner, B. (2014). Oxytocin in the prelimbic medial prefrontal cortex reduces anxiety-like behavior in female and male rats. *Psychoneuroendocrinology, 45*, 31–42.

Sartor, G. C., & Aston-Jones, G. S. (2012). A septal-hypothalamic pathway drives orexin neurons, which is necessary for conditioned cocaine preference. *Journal of Neuroscience, 32*, 4623–4631.

Shahar-Gold, H., Gur, R., & Wagner, S. (2013). Rapid and reversible impairments of short-and long-term social recognition memory are caused by acute isolation of adult rats via distinct mechanisms. *PLoS One, 8*, e65085.

Siviy, S. M., Love, N. J., DeCicco, B. M., Giordano, S. B., & Seifert, T. L. (2003). The relative playfulness of juvenile Lewis and Fischer-344 rats. *Physiology & Behavior, 80*, 385–394.

Smith, A. S., Avram, S. K. W., Cymerblit-Sabba, A., Song, J., & Young, W. S. (2016). Targeted activation of the hippocampal CA2 area strongly enhances social memory. *Molecular Psychiatry, 21*, 1137–1144.

Smith, C. J., Poehlmann, M. L., Li, S., Ratnaseelan, A. M., Bredewold, R., & Veenema, A. H. (2017). Age and sex differences in oxytocin and vasopressin V1a receptor binding densities in the rat brain: Focus on the social decision-making network. *Brain Structure and Function, 222*, 981–1006.

Spear, L. P. (2000). The adolescent brain and age-related behavioral manifestations. *Neuroscience and Biobehavioral Reviews, 24*, 417–463.

Stanford, S. C. (2017). Confusing preclinical (predictive) drug screens with animal "models" of psychiatric disorders, or "disorder-like" behaviour, is undermining confidence in behavioural neuroscience. *Journal of Psychopharmacology, 31*, 641–643.

Stevenson, E. L., & Caldwell, H. K. (2012). The vasopressin 1b receptor and the neural regulation of social behavior. *Hormones and Behavior, 61*, 277–282.

Takahashi, L. K., & Lore, R. K. (1983). Play fighting and the development of agonistic behavior in male and female rats. *Aggressive Behavior, 9*, 217–227.

Tarazi, F. I., Tomasini, E. C., & Baldessarini, R. J. (1998). Postnatal development of dopamine and serotonin transporters in rat caudate-putamen and nucleus accumbens septi. *Neuroscience Letters, 254*, 21–24.

Taylor, G. T., Weiss, J., & Rupich, T. (1987). Male rat behavior, endocrinology and reproductive physiology in a mixed-sex, socially stressful colony. *Physiology & Behavior, 39*.

Teicher, M. H., Andersen, S. L., & Hostetter, J. C., Jr. (1995). Evidence for dopamine receptor pruning between adolescence and adulthood in striatum but not nucleus accumbens. *Developmental Brain Research, 89*, 167–172.

Thiel, K. J., Okun, A. C., & Neisewander, J. L. (2008). Social reward-conditioned place preference: A model revealing an interaction between cocaine and social context rewards in rats. *Drug and Alcohol Dependence, 96*, 202–212.

Timmer, M., Cordero, M. I., Sevelinges, Y., & Sandi, C. (2011). Evidence for a role of oxytocin receptors in the long-term establishment of dominance hierarchies. *Neuropsychopharmacology, 36*, 2349–2356.

Trauth, J. A., & Slotkin, T. A. (2000). Persistent and delayed behavioral changes after nicotine treatment in adolescent rats. *Brain Research, 880*, 167–172.

Trezza, V., Damsteegt, R., & Vanderschuren, L. J. (2009). Conditioned place preference induced by social play behavior: Parametrics, extinction, reinstatement and disruption by methylphenidate. *European Neuropsychopharmacology, 19*, 659–669.

Tribollet, E., Charpak, S., Schmidt, A., Dubois-Dauphin, M., & Dreifuss, J. J. (1989). Appearance and transient expression of oxytocin receptors in fetal, infant, and peripubertal rat brain studied by autoradiography and electrophysiology. *Journal of Neuroscience, 9*, 1764–1773.

Tulogdi, Á., Tóth, M., Barsvári, B., Biró, L., Mikics, É., & Haller, J. (2014). Effects of resocialization on post weaning social isolation induced abnormal aggression and social deficits in rats. *Developmental Psychobiology, 56*, 49–57.

Vaidyanathan, R., & Hammock, E. A. (2017). Oxytocin receptor dynamics in the brain across development and species. *Developmental Neurobiology, 77*, 143–157.

van den Berg, C. L., Hol, T., van Ree, J. M., Spruijt, B. M., Everts, H., & Koolhaas, J. M. (1999). Play is indispensable for an adequate development of coping with social challenges in the rat. *Developmental Psychobiology, 34*, 129–138.

van der Kooij, M. A., & Sandi, C. (2012). Social memories in rodents: Methods, mechanisms and modulation by stress. *Neuroscience and Biobehavioral Reviews, 36*, 1763–1772.

Veenema, A. H. (2012). Toward understanding how early-life social experiences alter oxytocin- and vasopressin-regulated social behaviors. *Hormones and Behavior, 61*, 304–312.

Veenema, A. H., Bredewold, R., & De Vries, G. J. (2012). Vasopressin regulates social recognition in juvenile and adult rats of both sexes, but in sex-and age-specific ways. *Hormones and Behavior, 61*, 50–56.

Veenema, A. H., Bredewold, R., & De Vries, G. J. (2013). Sex-specific modulation of juvenile social play by vasopressin. *Psychoneuroendocrinology, 38*, 2554–2561.

Verney, C., Gaspar, P., Alvarez, C., & Berger, B. (1987). Postnatal sequential development of dopaminergic and enkephalinergic perineuronal formations in the lateral septal nucleus of the rat correlated with local neuronal maturation. *Anatomy and Embryology, 176*, 463–475.

Viau, V., Bingham, B., Davis, J., Lee, P., & Wong, M. (2005). Gender and puberty interact on the stress-induced activation of parvocellular neurosecretory neurons and corticotropin-releasing hormone messenger ribonucleic acid expression in the rat. *Endocrinology, 146*, 137–146.

von Heimendahl, M., Rao, R. P., & Brecht, M. (2012). Weak and nondiscriminative responses to conspecifics in the rat hippocampus. *Journal of Neuroscience, 32*, 2129–2141.

Wall, V. L., Fischer, E. K., & Bland, S. T. (2012). Isolation rearing attenuates social interaction-induced expression of immediate early gene protein products in the medial prefrontal cortex of male and female rats. *Physiology & Behavior, 107*, 440–450.

Wersinger, S. R., Ginns, E. I., O'Carroll, A-M., Lolait, S. J., & Young, W. S. (2002). Vasopressin V1b receptor knockout reduces aggressive behavior in male mice. *Molecular Psychiatry, 7*, 975–984.

Willing, J., & Juraska, J. M. (2015). The timing of neuronal loss across adolescence in the medial prefrontal cortex of male and female rats. *Neuroscience, 301*, 268–275.

Wright, I. K., Upton, N., & Marsden, C. A. (1991). Resocialisation of isolation-reared rats does not alter their anxiogenic profile on the elevated X-maze model of anxiety. *Physiology & Behavior, 50*, 1129–1132.

Yates, J. R., Beckmann, J. S., Meyer, A. C., & Bardo, M. T. (2013). Concurrent choice for social interaction and amphetamine using conditioned place preference in rats: Effects of age and housing condition. *Drug and Alcohol Dependence, 129*, 240–246.

Yildirim, M., Mapp, O. M., Janssen, W. G. M., Yin, W. L., Morrison, J. H., & Gore, A. C. (2008). Postpubertal decrease in hippocampal dendritic spines of female rats. *Experimental Neurology, 210*, 339–348.

Yu, Z. Y., Wang, W., Fritschy, J. M., Witte, O. W., & Redecker, C. (2006). Changes in neocortical and hippocampal GABAA receptor subunit distribution during brain maturation and aging. *Brain Research*, *1099*, 73–81.

Zancan, M., Dall'Oglio, A., Quagliotto, E., & Rasia Filho, A. A. (2017). Castration alters the number and structure of dendritic spines in the male posterodorsal medial amygdala. *European Journal of Neuroscience*, *45*, 572–580.

Zoicas, I., Slattery, D. A., & Neumann, I. D. (2014). Brain oxytocin in social fear conditioning and its extinction: Involvement of the lateral septum. *Neuropsychopharmacology*, *39*, 3027–3035.

28

OXYTOCIN AND VASOPRESSIN SYSTEMS IN THE DEVELOPMENT OF SOCIAL BEHAVIOR

Elizabeth A. D. Hammock

Introduction

Social behavior is both the cause of and solution to most human problems. War, racism, and inequality stem from types of territorial aggression toward out-groups, while nurturing care and ensuring equitable access to resources are arguably supported by ancient affiliative mechanisms directed toward in-group members. These social behavior domains (aggression and affiliation) and the antecedent social categorization of in-group and out-group membership can be studied in fine detail in animals to uncover their causal contextual and neural bases and developmental origins. Decades of research on the oxytocin and arginine vasopressin (AVP) neuropeptides, and their cognate receptors, have begun to reveal such mechanisms. The majority of this work has been performed in adult animals, while there is much left to learn about the roles of oxytocin and AVP in the developmental emergence of species-typical social behavior.

While not an exhaustive review, this chapter will present examples from the available evidence regarding the roles of oxytocin and AVP and their receptors in social behavior. In addition, this chapter will discuss examples of research indicating their roles in development as both effectors and targets of the developmental environment during sensitive periods for attachment and socialization. Finally, this chapter describes the Developmental Uncanny Valley Hypothesis as a framework for organizing the vast literature on oxytocin and AVP in social behavior. This framework generates several falsifiable predictions regarding the roles of oxytocin and AVP in the developmental emergence of social behavior and can potentially account for contextual, individual, sex, and species differences in social behavior throughout life.

Robust causal experiments in adult animals

The earliest experiments to establish causal roles for oxytocin and AVP in the brain regulation of behavior involved direct injections of oxytocin and AVP, and their receptor antagonists, into the brains of rodents. Brain manipulations of oxytocin and AVP signaling in rodents have influenced parental care (Pedersen, Ascher, Monroe, & Prange, 1982; Pedersen & Prange, 1979), pair bonding (Carter, Williams, Witt, & Insel, 1992; Williams, Insel, Harbaugh, & Carter, 1994; Winslow, Hastings, Carter, Harbaugh, & Insel, 1993), social recognition (Engelmann & Landgraf,

1994; Ferguson, Aldag, Insel, & Young, 2001; Popik, Vetulani, & van Ree, 1992; Wacker & Ludwig, 2012), infant attachment-like behaviors (Hammock, Law, & Levitt, 2013; He et al., 2017; Nelson & Panksepp, 1998; Sigling, Wolterink-Donselaar, & Spruijt, 2009), and most recently sensory processing (Choe et al., 2015; Marlin, Mitre, D'Amour, Chao, & Froemke, 2015; Oettl et al., 2016; Wacker & Ludwig, 2012; Zheng et al., 2014). In a series of studies in the late 1970s and early 1980s, oxytocin injected into the brains of estrogen-primed female rats enhanced the transition from naïve and pup-avoidant behavior to full maternal behavior toward infant rats (Pedersen et al., 1982; Pedersen & Prange, 1979). By applying the logic that brain oxytocin enhanced maternal affiliation toward pups, in the early 1990s it was established that brain injections of oxytocin enhanced partner preference affiliative behavior in female prairie voles toward an adult male partner (Carter et al., 1992; Williams, Carter, & Insel, 1992; Williams, Catania, & Carter, 1992).

The first experiments to establish that brain manipulation of AVP affected social behavior demonstrated a role for AVP in flank-marking behavior in hamsters (Ferris, Albers, Wesolowski, Goldman, & Luman, 1984). Flank-marking is a form of chemosensory social communication in which a dominant male, previously determined by overt physical aggression, signals this status to subordinate males. A few years after oxytocin was shown to enhance female partner preference behavior, brain AVP injections were demonstrated to enhance partner preference behavior in male prairie voles (Winslow et al., 1993). Injection of AVP into the brain of mice or other non-monogamous species does not lead to partner preference behavior. A comparative approach determined that the brain distributions of these receptors are not conserved even among closely related species (Young, Wang, & Insel, 1998; Young, Winslow, Nilsen, & Insel, 1997). In particular, there seemed to emerge a pattern where species with monogamous social structures had relative enrichment of oxytocin receptor and AVP 1a receptors (AVPR1A) in ventral forebrain reward areas (nucleus accumbens and ventral pallidum), while non-monogamous species did not (Young, 1999). This led to the hypothesis that the brain location of the receptor matters for species-typical social behavior. To directly test this hypothesis, AVPR1A receptors were added to the ventral pallidum of non-monogamous male meadow voles using a viral vector (Lim et al., 2004). This gene therapy approach increased the density of AVPR1A in this ventral forebrain reward area and conferred the ability of males to form partner preferences with mated females in this non-monogamous species. Surprisingly, when the same experiment was tried with a viral vector expressing the oxytocin receptor, while it increased the probability of partner preference formation in females of the already monogamous prairie vole species, this gene therapy approach was not sufficient to promote partner preference behavior in the non-monogamous meadow vole (Ross et al., 2009). This suggests that some additional, as yet undetermined species differences in brain organization are necessary to explain the species differences in oxytocin-dependent modulation of partner preference behavior.

In summary, decades of research in rodents have demonstrated the importance of oxytocin and AVP and their receptors in social behavior (recently reviewed in Caldwell & Albers, 2016; Johnson & Young, 2017). It has taken some time to begin to figure out where oxytocin and AVP act within the brain to achieve these effects, and specifically how these neuropeptides modulate neural activity. Newer research with more precise circuit-based manipulations (e.g. Dolen, Darvishzadeh, Huang, & Malenka, 2013; Hung et al., 2017; Marlin et al., 2015; Oettl et al., 2016; Smith, Williams Avram, Cymerblit-Sabba, Song, & Young, 2016) continues to refine our understanding of the roles of oxytocin and AVP in social behavior, including data that demonstrate a role for oxytocin in processing primary sensory information to enhance detection/perception of social stimuli. These newer studies all focus on precise manipulations of system components in adult brains. Critically, to best understand the social brain, we must understand its development. Available data strongly implicate oxytocin and AVP in the development of social behavior. The rest of the chapter will be devoted to examples of this progress.

Oxytocin and vasopressin as effectors and targets of development

Compared to the quantity of research of oxytocin and AVP in adults, there is a significantly smaller body of literature on the roles of oxytocin and AVP in development. Despite the limited insight into mechanisms, all indications thus far suggest that both hormones play significant roles (Hammock, 2015; Miller & Caldwell, 2015). The species diversity in receptor distribution, which appears causal in adult animals, is also evident during early sensitive periods of behavioral development (Vaidyanathan & Hammock, 2016). In addition to species diversity, there are developmentally transient periods of heightened expression, suggesting that oxytocin and AVP could potentially have particularly robust effects during these developmental periods of higher expression. For example, in mice, AVPR1A ligand binding is evident in the hippocampus and the neocortex during pre-weaning development, with a peak around the second postnatal week (Hammock & Levitt, 2012). The oxytocin receptor shows a slightly delayed peak of expression in the cortex, particularly upper layers II–III during mouse postnatal development (Hammock & Levitt, 2013). In rats, there are also several areas where oxytocin receptor and AVPR1A demonstrate elevations in ligand binding during pre-weaning development that are well above adult levels (Smith et al., 2017).

Both oxytocin and AVP can be conceptualized as effectors and as targets of experience (reviewed in Hammock, 2015). This conceptualization has emerged from empirical research using causal research designs in rodents, suggesting a role for oxytocin and AVP in development when these neuropeptides are manipulated as the independent variable (effectors) during development or measured as the dependent variable (targets) after development. An "effector" of experience will be a gene product that transduces the environment from outside to inside the organism or is needed for such experience-dependent plasticity, while a "target" is some gene activity that the environment changes, possibly long-term. Effectors can also be characterized as plasticity genes – the genes necessary for the environment to shape the organism (Halldorsdottir & Binder, 2017). Targets can be conceptualized as genes with an epigenetic type change where the environment leaves a mark which impacts the long-term function of the target gene (Klengel & Binder, 2015).

What is the evidence that hormone functions as either effectors or targets, or as both? There is evidence that both oxytocin and AVP systems are targets of developmental experience, in other words, the developmental environment shapes the adult expression of these system components (reviewed in Veenema, 2012). Experimental models in rodents (Figure 28.1) of social deprivation and social enrichment lead to alterations in oxytocin and AVP systems (Veenema, 2012). Examples of rodent models of social deprivation include prolonged maternal separation, reduced bedding (the dam cannot make an adequate nest), single-parent rearing in biparental prairie voles, and early weaning. Models of enriched care include brief handling, communal nesting, and late weaning. The effects of modulation of the social environment on oxytocin are currently hard to interpret. It appears that some models of social deprivation lead to increased production, while others lead to decreased production of oxytocin. Further, the modulation of the environment also can affect oxytocin receptor and AVPR1A levels. Zheng et al. (Zheng et al., 2014) demonstrated that sensory deprivation (by dark rearing or whisker trimming) from birth in mice reduced the production of oxytocin mRNA and peptide in the paraventricular nucleus of the hypothalamus (PVN) measured at postnatal day 14 (P14). Presumably, more mRNA would lead to the increased production of oxytocin peptide as observed in these mice.

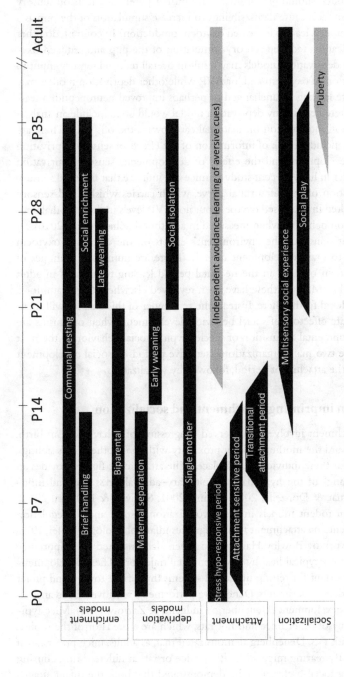

Figure 28.1 Rodent models of early life experience modulate socio-emotional behavioral traits in adulthood. Both relative enrichment and deprivation models can produce alterations in adult stress reactivity, trait anxiety, social behavior, and intergenerational transmission of mothering styles. Average ranges of important attachment and socialization processes are included for data primarily obtained from rats, but also from mice and voles. In the early neonatal period, rodents are in a stress hyporesponsive period with relatively little experience-dependent activity of the hypothalamic–pituitary–adrenal axis. The first two postnatal weeks include the attachment-sensitive period wherein stimulation by and interaction with the mother induces proximity seeking and separation-induced distress in the offspring. A transitional attachment period emerges near the end of the second postnatal week; in the absence of the mother, pups can begin to show HPA axis reactivity to stressors, leading to aversion learning. However, during this time, if the mother is present, aversive cues are blocked. Beyond this transitional attachment period, aversive stimuli elicit avoidance responses regardless of the presence of the absence of the mother. The socialization period emerges as the attachment period closes when pups can first start to assemble full multisensory representations of social stimuli (e.g. auditory and visual inputs can be co-registered in the neocortex with other sensory inputs for the first time). Social play emerges in rats by the end of the third postnatal week and lasts for 2–3 weeks, terminating near the full emergence of puberty.

Dark rearing, but not whisker deprivation, reduced AVP mRNA levels at P14. The mechanisms by which sensory input changes the developmental production of oxytocin and AVP are unknown. Given that Zheng et al. showed that sensory input can drive production of oxytocin, perhaps social deprivation models should be considered from their potential effects on sensory input. Do some deprivation models cause dams/siblings to increase stimulation of the pup as a compensation, and do those models lead to increased oxytocin production? In contrast, do other sensory deprivation models lead to reduced sensory stimulation of the pup and reduced oxytocin levels? In essence, some deprivation models may result in overall reduced sensory input to the pup and lowered production of oxytocin and/or AVP, while other deprivation models may evoke enhanced maternal care leading to unchanged or perhaps improved neuropeptide measures in the offspring. A key ingredient in any deprivation model would be to include an analysis of the effects of the deprivation intervention on maternal care toward the offspring. There are several missing puzzle pieces, including lack of information of the effects of sensory deprivation on social behavior during development and the effects of developmental sensory deprivation on oxytocin/AVP systems later in life. A recent study in mice did indicate that neonatal sensory deprivation by nerve transection of the infraorbital nerve, which carries whisker pad sensory input, on postnatal day 3 resulted in decreased oxytocin but not AVP levels in the hypothalamus and impaired social recognition behavior when measured in adulthood (Zhang et al., 2016).

As effector molecules that transduce the environment's effects on the organism, oxytocin and AVP would contribute to brain development directly. There are numerous examples of single manipulations of oxytocin or AVP in the neonatal period leading to changes in adult behavior (Simmons et al., 2017). Many of these have been reviewed elsewhere (e.g. Hammock, 2015), and will not be considered further here. Instead, the remainder of this chapter will focus on oxytocin and AVP as acute effectors of social behavior development, when organisms are in sensitive periods for developmental acquisition of species-typical social behavior. In the next section, I will briefly describe two main organizational sensitive periods of social development in mammals (Figure 28.1) – the attachment period, followed by socialization.

Mammalian imprinting/attachment and socialization

Mammalian imprinting/attachment involves a conserved progression of behaviors from birth, which includes orienting toward the mother, seeking proximity with the mother, one's siblings, or the nest, and preferences for these individuals and places. The attachment figure provides an external regulation (dampening) of the hypothalamic–pituitary–adrenal stress axis and influences its development (Gunnar & Donzella, 2002; Levine, 2001; Sullivan & Holman, 2010). Evidence for "attachment" in rodent models includes vocalization distress and dysregulation upon separation – when present, the attachment figure regulates infant physiology (Hofer, 1975, 1976; Shair, 2014). Seminal work by Bowlby, Harlow, and others demonstrated the importance of attachment to a caregiver for a typical healthy developmental trajectory. These developmentally sensitive periods are important for setting up neural systems that orient toward and prefer particular social stimuli. In rodent experiments, Denenberg performed a sensitive period analysis of key components of social development (Denenberg, Hudgens, & Zarrow, 1964). Mice typically prefer the social company of other mice and not rats, which are a predator of the mouse. However, by rearing mice with rats, Denenberg demonstrated that, as adults, mice prefer rats if they were reared with them. By rearing mice with either mice or rats at different times during development and later testing social preferences, he demonstrated that both the infant attachment period and the juvenile socialization period significantly contribute to the formation of social preferences based on social experience rather than genetic relatedness (i.e. kin selection).

Attachment period manipulations influence subsequent socialization-related behaviors (Veenema & Neumann, 2009), which is consistent with a hierarchical view of experience-dependent brain development where early experiences lay the foundation for subsequent development (Hammock & Levitt, 2006). Socialization is a developmental period in which the organism begins to build a multisensory mental template of conspecifics and learn species-appropriate social skills. Socialization occurs after the attachment period. Sometimes socialization is used as an umbrella term referring to both attachment and a later socialization period (e.g. van Leeuwen, Mulenga, & Chidester, 2014). But findings suggest they should be considered separately (Kalcher, Franz, Crailsheim, & Preuschoft, 2008), and it would therefore be helpful to have separate names for these periods. From the rodent literature, there is ample evidence to consider attachment and socialization separately. During socialization, play behavior (e.g. play fighting, rough-and-tumble play) emerges, and individuals begin to gain a multisensory neural representation of the stereotype of the in-group (Baarendse, Counotte, O'Donnell, & Vander-schuren, 2013; Baarendse, Limpens, & Vanderschuren, 2014; Meng, Li, Han, Shao, & Wang, 2010; Terranova, Laviola, & Alleva, 1993; Wei, Meaney, Duman, & Kaffman, 2011). Social play is an important aspect of socialization and social skill development across numerous species (Burghardt, 2005; Cordoni & Palagi, 2011; Hol, van den Berg, van Ree, & Spruijt, 1999; Trezza, Baarendse, & Vanderschuren, 2010). In rats, lack of access to social play decreases adult social interactions (Hol et al., 1999). The quantity of play varies across species. For example, rats are considered to have high levels of social play during the socialization period, while mice are considered to have low levels of social play. In rats, social isolation after weaning was observed to lead to changes in behavior (Hatch et al., 1965), which seem to recover with re-socialization (Meng et al., 2010). The socialization sensitive period in rats lasts up until about postnatal day 50 and is heavily dependent on play activity during this time. Mice appear to have less robust play than rats, but still show a social sensitivity during the socialization period. In a classic experiment in mice (Dyer & Southwick, 1974), males were isolated from weaning at postnatal day 21 through postnatal day 42. This leads to increased aggression and a decrease in the tendency to huddle in a social group when tested as adolescents. To more precisely identify the potential sensitive window for the socialization of mice, the experimenters co-housed these mice during three-day windows in the P21–P42 period to see if the aggression and low sociability phenotype could be rescued with some exposure. Aggression was measured with a wound index score after five days of cohousing, and co-sleeping was measured as an index of sociability during this same period. In male CFW (Carworth Farms Webster) mice, cohousing with another mouse from postnatal days 27–30 or postnatal days 30–33 were significantly less likely to show wounding aggression when tested at P42–P47. Socializing during this developmental period (P27–P30 or P30–P33) also increased the probability that adolescents were found co-sleeping in the same huddle. More recent studies have investigated different strains of mice (An et al., 2017). During the socialization period, neurogenesis seems to play an important role in the development of social behavior (Wei et al., 2011). Female mice were weaned at postnatal day 21 and co-housed until postnatal day 27, when they underwent a surgery to place a cannula to allow for 30 days of treatment to block neurogenesis. When later tested as adults, mice treated with neurogenesis blockers during the socialization period displayed almost no social exploration when tested with a novel stimulus female. These females exhibited escape behavior when the stimulus females approached. Finally, in a maternal behavior test, these mice were less likely to retrieve pups in a pup retrieval test. Treatment with the same neurogenesis-blocking procedure in adulthood did not result in these social behavior changes. Therefore, even in the absence of social experience (all animals were housed in isolation during the period of treatment), neurogenesis during the normal period of socialization is important for some level of social investigation and pup retrieval in adult mice.

The study did not include a group that was not treated and not isolated, so it is inappropriate to conclude that neurogenesis is sufficient for social behavior development. The socially isolated mice were probably still atypical compared to non-isolated mice.

Evidence for oxytocin and vasopressin systems as effectors in attachment and socialization

For oxytocin and AVP and their receptors to play a role in these developmental processes, they must be present during developmentally sensitive periods for attachment and socialization. Both oxytocin and AVP are produced by the infant brain during attachment-sensitive periods (Hammock, 2015), with AVP production appearing before oxytocin production in all species examined. In mice and rats, initial AVP synthesis (mRNA) can be detected prenatally, while oxytocin production appears perinatally. Further, oxytocin production (as measured by mRNA) appears in females before it is detectable in male neonates (Tamborski, Mintz, & Caldwell, 2016). Both males and females have production of oxytocin by postnatal day 2. In humans, both oxytocin and AVP are detectable prenatally (reviewed in [Swaab, 1995]). This species difference relative to birth is not surprising, as rats and mice at birth are in a more altricial developmental state than humans at birth (Clancy, Darlington, & Finlay, 2001; Clancy et al., 2007; Workman, Charvet, Clancy, Darlington, & Finlay, 2013). Finally, while oxytocin production in females seems to precede that for males, AVP production is more robust in males, with males producing more.

Oxytocin receptor and AVPR1A are present in the developing brain, and each has a transient time course of expression with peak expression in some (but not all) brain areas during certain phases of development (Vaidyanathan & Hammock, 2016). These transient peaks may represent species-specific developmental plasticity. For example, in the rat, there is a peak of oxytocin receptor ligand binding that is present in the cingulate cortex toward the end of the second postnatal week and the beginning of the third postnatal week (Shapiro & Insel, 1989; Snijdewint, van Leeuwen, & Boer, 1989; Tribollet, Charpak, Schmidt, Dubois-Dauphin, & Dreifuss, 1989). The mouse also has a peak of oxytocin receptor during this time, but instead of expression in the cingulate cortex, the expression is present in all primary sensory cortices and is significantly enriched in the upper cortex layers II and III as measured in somatosensory cortex (Hammock & Levitt, 2013). In this way, the rat cingulate cortex might be developmentally sensitive to oxytocin, while the mouse primary sensory cortex might be developmentally sensitive to oxytocin. AVPR1A peaks in the cortex in mouse (Hammock & Levitt, 2012) and AVP-binding sites peak in the facial nucleus of the rat (Tribollet, Goumaz, Raggenbass, & Dreifuss, 1991; Tribollet, Goumaz, Raggenbass, Dubois-Dauphin, & Dreifuss, 1991) around the end of the first postnatal week. There are numerous areas identified in the rat brain where both oxytocin receptor and AVPR1A show higher levels of receptor binding in the juvenile compared to the adult rat (Smith et al., 2017). Sex differences in the expression of these components may contribute to sex differences in behavior (Dumais & Veenema, 2016). In summary, there are developmentally transient peaks of both oxytocin receptor and AVPR1A during attachment and socialization phases of social behavior development. Future research will be required to determine if these developmentally transient peaks confer sensitive period plasticity. It is still unclear if the peak expression of either receptor translates into enhanced sensitivity to oxytocin and AVP as mechanisms of enriched plasticity during these developmental time frames. In contrast to the uncertain role for the intriguing developmentally transient receptor profiles during sensitive periods, variation in hormone levels have well-documented effects on developmental social behavior during the attachment period and the socialization period, to be discussed in detail below.

Attachment

In this section, I will discuss the evidence for oxytocin and AVP-dependent modulation of attachment-related behaviors such as separation distress as measured by separation-induced vocalizations and selective social proximity seeking behaviors.

Ultrasonic vocalizations

Upon separation from the mother, typically, developing rat pups will emit ultrasonic vocalizations (USV) in the 35–40kHz range at approximately 60–80 dB (Hofer, 1996; Hofer & Shair, 1978). This response is present within hours after birth, peaks between postnatal days 7 and 9 (Branchi, Santucci, & Alleva, 2001), and disappears by weaning (Hofer, Shair, & Brunelli, 2002). Rat pups will call at their highest rates when immediately placed in a novel environment. Familiar stimuli such as familiar bedding type will result in slightly reduced calls and soiled bedding from the home cage will reduce calls even further (Oswalt & Meier, 1975). Each additional familiar stimulus has a blunting effect on the separation-induced vocalization. As development proceeds, this separation-induced vocalization response is reduced, such that by postnatal day 18 this USV response is no longer evoked with maternal separation, at least at ambient temperatures in rats (Allin & Banks, 1971). Because of the robust behavior and its clear modulation by attachment stimuli, separation-induced ultrasonic vocalizations are widely considered to be a marker of neonatal separation distress (Hofer, 1996; Hofer et al., 2002; Panksepp, 2003; Winslow & Insel, 1991). Both oxytocin and AVP seem to modulate USV call rates, although the data do not necessarily reflect a straightforward answer about their roles (e.g. it is not clear if the peptides promote or inhibit call rates as a direct reflection of separation distress). There are two main difficulties associated with interpreting USV call rates as a measure of separation distress, and by extension attachment: 1) there are context × age dependent interactions influencing USV call rates and 2) there are often conflicting results depending on whether the neuropeptide manipulation is made to the brain or the periphery. I will describe the context × age dependent interactions first and then describe results with oxytocin and AVP manipulations in the brain and periphery.

Hofer and colleagues outline the developmental emergence of context × age interactions in the expression of USV in rats and mice (Hofer et al., 2002). Importantly, the separation-induced ultrasonic vocalization response is not just modulated by isolation. As described already, this isolation-induced USV is evident within the first day or two of postnatal development and is absent by weaning age in mice and rats. Very close to the onset of the capacity for isolation-induced USV is the ability of contact quieting – littermates or an anesthetized dam can significantly reduce the isolation-induced USV, which makes sense, given that this would mean that the infant is no longer isolated. Interestingly, by around P7 in the rat, predator-induced suppression of isolation-induced USV emerges. This means that if a neonatal rat is isolated and making a high rate of USV consistent with isolation-induced distress, if exposed to a predator odor, the rate of USV will plummet. The infant is still isolated but is actively suppressing call rates. Therefore, the separation-induced vocalization behavior which indicates infant distress, and reduced when reunited with the attachment figure, will also be reduced by a stimulus antithetical to attachment – namely a predator. This predator-induced suppression of USV is associated with sudden flinching at the odor onset, prolonged immobility, urination, and ACTH release. Therefore, by this developmental age, experimenters should be cautious in interpreting low levels of separation-induced USV as a representation of lack of distress/poor attachment, because it may also represent predator-induced behavior in the context of typical behavior. Notably, most studies of oxytocin and AVP modulated USV have been conducted around this age, without also noting the qualitative aspect of the reduction in USV; therefore, it is difficult to determine if the observed reductions in USV are due to atypical distress related to attachment (infantile aloofness) or perhaps active suppression of USV due to artificial activation of predator detection mechanisms (or conversely, if USV call rates are elevated after a manipulation, it is unclear if this is due to activation of infant distress or lack of response to predator odors). It is also possible for neonates to show a maternal potentiation of isolation-induced USV. If a rat was isolated, then briefly reunited with the dam, then isolated again, the isolation-induced USV in the second isolation would be higher than in the first isolation. This maternal potentiation effect does not emerge until P9/10 in rats, and may show a slightly different presentation in mice (Scattoni, Crawley, & Ricceri, 2009). Future studies should look carefully at the role of oxytocin and AVP in separation-induced USV across development during the attachment period under a variety of contextual conditions.

As an example of the careful attention that should be paid to these variations in isolation-induced USV across neonatal rat and mouse development, the AVP 1B receptor (AVPR1B) may play a role in the later-developing maternal potentiation of separation-induced USV, but not in baseline separation-induced USV. When tested at P3, P6, P9, and P12, AVPR1B knock-out mice and their heterozygous and wild-type littermates do not differ in separation-induced USV call rates. However, when tested at P9 in a modified test that included a brief reunion with the dam, both AVPR1B knockouts and heterozygous mice failed to show maternal potentiation of separation-induced USV, while their wild-type littermates did (Scattoni et al., 2008).

The impact of oxytocin and AVP in separation-induced USV depends on the site of delivery. Central and peripheral manipulations appear to yield contradictory results. When 6–8-day-old rat pups were given ICV injections of oxytocin, they displayed lower USV call frequency, an effect which was blocked with an oxytocin receptor antagonist (Insel & Winslow, 1991). In contrast, peripheral subcutaneous injections of oxytocin had a biphasic response: a low dose (1ug) increased USV frequency, while a 10ug dose decreased USV. An ICV injection of 0.5ug oxytocin receptor antagonist did not block the effect of a high peripheral dose of oxytocin, suggesting that the brain oxytocin receptor was not mediating this dampened response. This treatment also reduced core body temperature by approximately 2°C. Oxytocin knockout mouse pups tested on P7–P8, with no endogenous central or peripheral oxytocin signal, showed reduced separation-induced vocalizations (Winslow et al., 2000), as did oxytocin receptor knockout mice tested at P7 (Takayanagi et al., 2005). To summarize, manipulating oxytocin in the rodent neonate affects the rates of separation-induced vocalizations, but there are some serious gaps in our understanding of the mechanism. It is difficult to say if oxytocin improves or exacerbates the feeling of distress upon separation. Because of the ages tested, it is also difficult to disentangle a role for oxytocin in modulating the separation distress component or the predator-induced suppression of USV when isolated.

In a similar fashion to oxytocin, AVP effects on USV depend on the location of drug delivery. In wild-type rats tested on postnatal days 8–9, separation-induced ultrasonic vocalization is inhibited by central injections of AVP, but increased by peripheral injection of AVP (Winslow & Insel, 1993). Some of the earliest data on the acute roles of AVP in neonatal social behavior come from studies of the Brattleboro rat strain, which is sometimes referred to as an AVP knockout rat. Brattleboro rats carry a frameshift mutation in the AVP gene (Schmale, Ivell, Breindl, Darmer, & Richter, 1984), resulting in impaired AVP signaling. They have central diabetes insipidus due to the well-known role of AVP as anti-diuretic hormone: without AVP, the animals cannot retain water, and thus drink water and urinate with extraordinary frequency. As adults, these rats have well-established social behavior deficits, including deficits in social recognition behavior and atypical social interactions (Engelmann & Landgraf, 1994; Feifel et al., 2009; Lin et al., 2013). Several studies have been carried out on social behavior in early life of this AVP-deficient strain of rat, and most of these studies have focused on a role in the first two postnatal weeks (Lin et al., 2013; Nelson & Panksepp, 1998; Schank, 2009; Varga, Fodor, Klausz, & Zelena, 2015; Zelena et al., 2008), which includes the attachment period.

Brattleboro rat pups have atypical call behavior beginning by at least postnatal day 9 (Lin et al., 2013). They have reduced separation-induced call frequency, increased inter-call interval, and reduced call power when measured on postnatal days 9 and 12, but not earlier at postnatal days 2 or 5 (Lin et al., 2013). These results have been replicated in postnatal day 7–8 AVP-deficient Brattleboro male and female pups, who also showed significant reductions in the duration of calls and the frequency of calls after maternal separation compared to their AVP-producing littermates (Varga et al., 2015). Given the observation that in the AVP "knock out" rat that the change in USV is not evident until postnatal day 7, which coincides with the typical emergence of predator-induced suppression of USV, it is tempting to consider a role for AVP in the predator-dependent modulation of USV call rates. Future experiments will be needed to test this speculation. A receptor antagonist for the AVP 1B receptor (AVPR1B) given by injection in the periphery (intraperitoneal) to wild-type rats at P7–P8 (Varga et al., 2015) or P7–10 (Hodgson et al., 2007) also reduced ultrasonic vocalizations. Without AVP (as in the Brattleboro rat) or with an AVPR1B antagonist, separation-induced USV levels are low. The working hypothesis is that AVP in the anterior pituitary would bind to AVPR1B receptors and enhance the activity of the HPA axis to increase separation-induced USV. Several other studies have explored the effects of peripheral AVP receptor antagonists in rat pups. These reports all show trend level significance for AVP receptor antagonists (not always strictly selective for AVPR1B) to reduce separation-induced USV (Iijima & Chaki, 2005; Iijima et al., 2014). One study did show a statistically significant reduction in USV with peripheral injection of an AVPR antagonist in P11 male and female rat pups (Bleickardt et al., 2009). The significant results in this study might be because they pre-screened all of their study subjects to make sure that the pups were high callers to be able to observe a call-reducing effect of the AVP receptor antagonist, which appears to be a reasonable strategy.

Future studies are needed to better clarify the role of oxytocin and vasopressin in modulating this ethologically valuable behavior. For an infant, crying at the wrong time can be just as costly as not crying when the attachment figure is needed.

Proximity seeking/social orienting

Oxytocin influences early infant proximity seeking to a caregiver during the attachment period. In neonatal rodents, oxytocin given into the brain ventricles increases the preference for maternal contact (Kojima & Alberts, 2011; Nelson & Panksepp, 1996). In a recent study in monogamous mandarin voles (He et al., 2017), pups given an intraperitoneal injection of an oxytocin receptor antagonist ([d(CH$_2$)$_5$^{1}, Tyr(Me)^2, Thr^4, Orn^8, des–Gly–NH$_2$^{9}]-Vasotocin trifluoroacetate salt) 30 minutes before a test trial showed reduced attachment-like behavior in a two choice test (i.e. time spent with the familiar dam compared to a unfamiliar female matched on maternal status) as well as reduced markers of dopamine system function in reward circuitry including the ventral tegmental area and the nucleus accumbens. These studies were conducted in the third postnatal week, at a time when developmentally transient oxytocin receptor quantities in some areas of the brain are known to be at their highest levels in rodents like voles (Vaidyanathan & Hammock, 2016) and when pre-weaning animals are beginning to leave the nest for brief periods. While there is evidence for oxytocin receptor mRNA in the nucleus accumbens of the mandarin vole (Du et al., 2017), there is not yet further corroboration of the oxytocin receptor distribution profile in this species.

Not only does oxytocin seem to increase attachment-related behaviors in rodents, intranasal treatment with oxytocin increases markers of social behavior, such as social attention and orienting, in both nursery-reared and mother-reared rhesus macaques. While outside the scope of this chapter, it is important to note here that there is some controversy in the field as to the effectiveness of intranasal delivery of drug to target the brain (Leng & Ludwig, 2016; Walum, Waldman, & Young, 2016) and, perhaps more controversial, the potential current value (or lack thereof) of measurement of peripheral levels of oxytocin in either blood products or saliva as biomarkers that relate to behavioral measures (Leng & Sabatier, 2016; McCullough, Churchland, & Mendez, 2013). While the mechanisms of action are unknown, there may be value in well-designed studies which deliver oxytocin to the periphery. Such studies in animal models may help reveal important developmental contributions. Simpson et al. (2014) reported that intranasal oxytocin given to nursery-reared male and female rhesus macaque infants (n = 28) aged 7 to 14 days old while being held by the experimenter increased the frequency of infant facial gestures. Specifically, the facial gestures were measured while the experimenter made these faces and during a period where the experimenter maintained a still face. An increase in these gestures by the infant when the experimenter is also making them is considered a sign of imitation. The facial gestures included affiliative lipsmacking and tongue protrusions/retractions. There was a significant main effect of oxytocin on facial gestures (oxytocin increased facial gestures) and a main effect of condition (the infants made more facial gestures during the imitation condition than the still face condition). However, there was no interaction between oxytocin treatment and imitation condition. This means that oxytocin did not preferentially increase facial gestures under imitation, but instead just increased facial gestures produced by the infant. In this set of experiments, the researchers measured the acute behavioral response to intranasal oxytocin. They observed that intranasal oxytocin resulted in increased salivary oxytocin, measured at two hours, but by four hours, the effect was no longer significant. It is unclear if the measured oxytocin reflects endogenous release or detection of the applied oxytocin. They delivered 25IU oxytocin per infant which is on the order of 50ug. At 26ng/mL (0.026ug/mL) measured in saliva, it is possible that some of this oxytocin in saliva is what was delivered through the nose. Either way, this value of oxytocin in the saliva was positively correlated with time spent in close proximity with the caregiver. Next, they determined whether imitation skill in the first postnatal week predicted the behavioral response to intranasal oxytocin in the second week. Infants who were more likely in the first postnatal week to make face gestures in response to experimenter face gestures were also more likely after oxytocin treatment to show more lipsmacking, longer duration in close proximity with the experimenter, and longer duration of looking at the caregiver than infants with low imitation strength. These studies in infant macaques suggest an acute modulation of social gesturing in response to intranasal oxytocin, but they do not include the long-term developmental effects of chronic exposure.

The potential impact of chronic oxytocin dosing on developing social behavior was recently tested by a separate research group (Parr et al., 2016). Beginning at 2 months of age, healthy mother-reared group living male rhesus macaque infants (n = 24, data available from n = 19) were treated with placebo or oxytocin using aerosolized oxytocin in a pediatric nebulizer, while being restrained by an experimenter. By 16 weeks of age, the macaques were dosed in a dosing box without experimenter restraint. Nebulized oxytocin was given oronasally to infants at either a low frequency (once per week, with two doses of saline) or a high frequency (3x per week), compared to saline placebo (3x per week). During test procedures, the infants rested on the ventrum of the anesthetized mother, while 10-second videos of other rhesus macaques played on a nearby video screen. Videos included other rhesus monkeys with either a neutral face, open-mouth threat, or affiliative lipsmacking. Direction and duration of gaze by the infant was recorded. For all categories of videos, chronic (1x or 3x per week) oxytocin treatment increased the total duration of time that the infants spent looking at the faces compared with placebo treatment. Total duration was calculated as the sum of the duration of multiple discreet fixation events. For neutral faces, the high-frequency dose increased the duration of looking. In contrast, for lipsmacks (affiliative) and open-mouth threats, both low and high frequency oxytocin increased looking duration, although the lower frequency dose increased looking duration the most. Interestingly, of the time that the infants spent looking at neutral faces, oxytocin reduced the proportion of time that the infants spent looking at the eyes. In addition to the total duration of gaze, the authors also looked at average length of each individual fixation. This showed that for neutral faces, the low dose oxytocin treatment enhanced the individual fixation length by about 25%, while the high frequency oxytocin did not increase the duration of discrete fixation for neutral faces. While there were dose by face type interactions, the main effects suggest that in rhesus macaques, chronic nebulized oxytocin given 1x or 3x per week enhances the fixation duration of distinct gaze events for neutral, affiliative, and threatening faces, with the largest effects of oxytocin seen on emotionally salient faces of both positive (lipsmacking) and negative valence (threat). Chronic oxytocin, particularly the high frequency dose, decreased looking toward the eyes of neutral faces.

Importantly, the intranasal or nebulized oxytocin in both studies were given to infant macaques without consideration of the social context. In the future, it will be important to determine if social context during the delivery of oxytocin matters for social outcomes. Also, it will be important to understand the potential effects on social behavior in the context of group living after chronic treatment with oxytocin. In sum, with the limited data available, it appears that acute treatment with oxytocin in early infancy and chronic treatment with oxytocin in older infants both appear to increase social responses in rhesus macaques.

In human infants, developmental changes in oxytocin are correlated with changes in social attention (Nishizato, Fujisawa, Kosaka, & Tomoda, 2017). As mentioned above, the measurement error in oxytocin levels may be problematic, particularly for studies in which extraction of samples was not performed. In a recent cross-sectional study in human infants and young children, unextracted salivary oxytocin levels decreased with age, as did attention to visual social stimuli. When accounting for age, oxytocin levels predicted the duration of time that an individual looked at the eyes when there was no mouth movement. Further, both oxytocin levels and visual attention to the eyes were associated with alleles of the rs53576 oxytocin receptor single nucleotide polymorphism (SNP). Individuals with the AA genotype (associated with lower general sociability in a recent meta-analysis; Li et al., 2015) had lower levels of oxytocin and lower levels of attention to eyes. Additionally, in this sample, females were more attentive to people moving, fixated longer on pointed-at objects, and were less attentive to geometric shapes than were boys. Individual differences in oxytocin (see also Nitschke, Krol, and Bartz, this volume) may be a predictor of patient populations who will respond to intranasal oxytocin intervention with improved social scores. Intranasal oxytocin delivery is in clinical trials for children with an autism spectrum disorder (ASD) diagnosis. A recent clinical trial suggests that intranasal oxytocin in children with ASD who had low starting quantities of oxytocin were more likely to respond to intranasal oxytocin treatment (Parker et al., 2017).

Neonatal rats and mice can be conditioned to associate a novel neutral odor with maternal or other unconditioned stimuli (Armstrong, DeVito, & Cleland, 2006; Bouslama, Durand, Chauviere, van den Bergh, & Gallego, 2005; Hammock et al., 2013; Honeycutt & Alberts, 2005; Moriceau, Wilson, Levine, & Sullivan, 2006; Roth et al., 2013; Roth & Sullivan, 2006). For example, pups who are co-exposed to peppermint odor with maternal cues will show orienting preferences for peppermint odor. This is thought to reflect sensitive period learning for social cues. When given before a conditioning trial, oxytocin delivered to the brain of P14 rat pups enhances preferences for an odor previously paired with the dam (Nelson & Panksepp, 1996). While oxytocin seems to increase social orienting, there is evidence in neonatal mice that AVP, acting through AVPR1A, inhibits selective social orienting as measured in an olfactory-based associative conditioning assay. In commonly used C57BL/6J mice on postnatal day 8 (Hammock et al., 2013), this orienting bias to cues previously associated with the mother was only observed in females and not in male pups, the developmental significance of which has yet to be determined. The expression of this associative learning was blocked with intracerebroventricular injections of AVP in females. In mice lacking the AVPR1A gene, learned orienting preferences were very strong and could not be blocked by AVP. These findings suggest that AVP acting through AVPR1A blocks the expression of learned odor preferences at a low dose that does not affect general motor activity. Studies in older rats show similar results. On postnatal day 17–18, AVP injections into the cisterna magna (a cerebrospinal fluid-filled subarachnoid cistern positioned beneath the cerebellum) increased the latency for rats to approach familiar nest odors and decreased the preference for familiar social cues (Sigling et al., 2009). Similarly, on postnatal day 33 (Veenema, Bredewold, & De Vries, 2012), intraseptal injections of AVP reduced the investigation preference by females for familiar individuals (it increased the investigation of novel individuals), while AVPR1A antagonist increased the investigation preference by both males and females for familiar individuals. These findings in young mice and rats suggest that AVP at the AVPR1A blocks learned orienting preferences to familiar individuals, or perhaps promotes exploration of novel stimuli, without influencing total exploration levels. It is unknown if this effect is due to a change in the perceived valence of the stimulus or perhaps due to changes in the motivation to approach or avoid particular stimuli. An additional interpretation of these results is to suggest that during the attachment phase of development, oxytocin may expand social learning to include a variety of experienced stimuli, while AVP may restrict social learning to protect the developing organism from overgeneralizing or mis-attributing social properties to non-social stimuli in the environment. This hypothesis requires further testing.

Socialization

As described above, socialization takes place after the attachment period and includes play behavior. Oxytocin and AVP modulate social play behavior in juvenile rats. Male and female rats respond differently to AVP (Veenema, Bredewold, & De Vries, 2013), in a brain-region and context-specific manner (Bredewold, Smith, Dumais, & Veenema, 2014). Research using the Brattleboro rat during the socialization period indicates that AVP-deficient rats interacting with other AVP-deficient rats showed reduced social play behavior compared to their wild-type rats interacting with wild-type littermates (Paul et al., 2016). The reduction in play behavior in the AVP-deficient dyads did not simply reflect a deficit in social behavior, but rather was accompanied by an increase in huddling time and typical levels of social investigation and allogrooming. While total lack of AVP throughout development interferes with social play in the juvenile period, the role of AVP during the juvenile period depends on sex, play context, and the brain region(s) under investigation.

After a period of normal development, male and female 5-week-old rats were cannulated and housed alone for two days during recovery and then received intracerebroventricular injections of an AVPR1A antagonist, an oxytocin receptor antagonist, or vehicle (Veenema et al., 2013). Twenty minutes later, rats were exposed to a novel same-sex intruder into their home cage. Overall, the AVPR1A antagonist seemed to enhance or even generate sex differences in social play, social investigation, non-social exploration, and nape attacks in juvenile rats (Veenema et al., 2013), suggesting a role for vasopressin in minimizing sex differences in social play (Dumais & Veenema, 2016). For example, while the AVPR1A antagonist decreased nape attacks in males, it increased nape attacks in females (Veenema et al., 2013). The oxytocin receptor antagonist did not have as much of an impact on these behaviors, in either sex (Bredewold et al., 2014; Veenema et al., 2013). Injections of AVPR1A antagonist directly into the lateral septum (Bredewold et al., 2014) of both male and female juvenile rats also showed an enhancement of sex differences. Surprisingly, the results were in the opposite direction. For example, when injected directly into the lateral septum, AVPR1A antagonist increased social play in males and decreased social play in females. Injections of AVP into the lateral septum resulted in behaviors that were not significantly different from vehicle control. It is unclear why AVPR1A antagonist injections directly into the lateral septum have different results than when AVPR1A antagonists are injected into the ventricles. The lateral septum contains high levels of AVPR1A, so perhaps direct injection of AVPR1A plays a more direct role than diffusion of the antagonist through the ventricular space.

The effects of the AVPR1A antagonist depend on sex of the study subject as well as test location (Bredewold et al., 2014). When tested with a novel animal in the familiar home cage, the AVPR1A antagonist in the lateral septum enhanced sex differences in social play. However, when the rats were tested with a novel animal in a novel cage, the AVPR1A antagonist was less effective at increasing play behavior in males and decreasing it in females. Perhaps AVPR1A signaling in the septum is part of the network for responding appropriately to social context. More experiments are needed to clarify both the role of place (novel or familiar contexts) and the role of partner (novel or familiar) in the oxytocin- and vasopressin-dependent regulation of social play.

The Developmental Uncanny Valley Hypothesis

In this section, I would like to propose the Developmental Uncanny Valley Hypothesis for oxytocin and vasopressin in the developmental emergence of social behavior. This hypothesis attempts to synthesize the available literature on the roles of oxytocin and vasopressin in social behavior in adulthood by proposing how these neuropeptides could contribute to the development of the social brain. This hypothesis was inspired by Masahiro Mori's Uncanny Valley, first proposed by Mori in 1970 (Mori, 1970, 2012) as a description of the uneasy feeling evoked when people interact with prosthetics or humanoid robots. Mori argued that people have an eerie feeling around these objects that are similar to humans but are not human enough. Mori graphed this phenomenon (Figure 28.2A) in a two-dimensional space with "human likeness" on the x-axis and affinity on the y-axis. As objects become more and more human-like on the x-axis, affinity on the y-axis also increases. Mori argues that at some point, the human likeness is close to human, but instead of more affinity, there is an "eerie" response. This dip in the otherwise positive relationship between human likeness (anthropomorphism) and affinity is Mori's Uncanny Valley (Figure 28.2).

While this description of the phenomenon of aversion to humanoid robots and prosthetics lay dormant for decades, the Uncanny Valley has recently emerged as a useful descriptor of other biases with perceptual (on the x-axis) and affective (on the y-axis) dimensions, such as xenophobia and homophobia. The Uncanny Valley may also be conceptualized as an aversive response to a norm violation. Current models of social visual perception of faces and auditory perception of voices rely heavily on norm-based coding, wherein individuals use experience

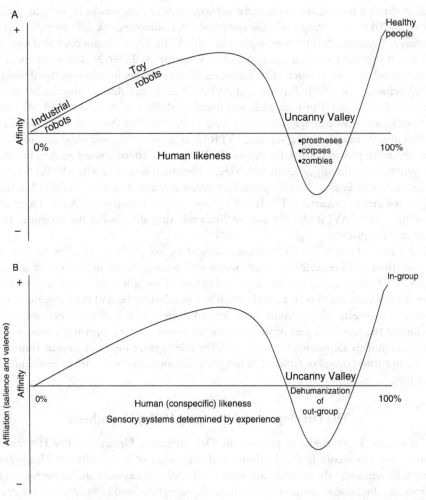

Figure 28.2 (A) Mori's (1970) original depiction of the Uncanny Valley. As human likeness increases on the x-axis, so does affinity on the y-axis, until human likeness is very similar to humans but not similar enough; then, a feeling of "eeriness" is elicited in the "Uncanny Valley". (B) In this conceptualization of the putative neural mechanisms of the Uncanny Valley, the x-axis is determined by sensory experience. Experience shapes expected visual/auditory/ chemosensory/ somatosensory perceptual "norms" for norm-based coding. Each person will, based on their experience, have a neural representation of in-group. On the y-axis, affective affiliation signals are derived from a combination of salience encoded by dopamine-based signaling related to violations of expectations and an amygdala and frontal cortical evaluation of valence. During the attachment phase of development, oxytocin may modulate the magnitude of the y-axis by contributing to the development of the amygdala and the ventral forebrain reward circuitry to enhance motivation. During the socialization phase of development, oxytocin may influence the x-axis by increasing signal:noise processing in sensory systems for social detection and result in more experience with these stimuli by increased proximity seeking to social stimuli established during the attachment period. AVP may counteract or delay this process by reducing orienting to social stimuli, resulting in less time with social stimuli, which may permit the enhancement of expertise in other domains.

with faces and voices to generate a normative expected template (Yovel & Belin, 2013). In a relatively racial-, ethnic-, and accent-homogenous environment, the generated audio and visual templates will center around one's in-group. Infrequent exposure during development to other races will generate a strong norm violation signal in adulthood. This idea is consistent with current models of perceptual narrowing (Lewkowicz & Ghazanfar, 2012) in the developmental emergence of the "other-race" effect: an individual with very little experience with other races has a harder time perceiving differences among individuals of other races, resulting in subjective comments such as "the [other race] all look alike to me, I can't tell them apart". The same experience-dependent perceptual narrowing phenomenon is thought to underlie language development and the associated difficulties with perceiving differences in closely related phonemes from other languages.

While captivating, if Mori's Uncanny Valley model of an intuitive behavioral phenomenon has relevance to neural mechanisms, then the axes must relate to brain function. Here I attempt to relate the axes of Mori's Uncanny Valley to plausible neural substrates in the adult. The x-axis, representing "human likeness", would have to be supported by neural mechanisms of sensation and perception. Visual, auditory, somatosensory, and olfactory signals all inform our neural representations of self and others. Therefore, it is perhaps easiest to conceptualize the x-axis as a sensory–perceptual axis. A structure like the fusiform face area and its enriched processing of and expertise in human faces is likely associated with this axis. In contrast, the y-axis includes positive (affiliative) or negative (fear and disgust) affective states. The y-axis could be characterized as both a salience and a valence axis. Salience would be represented by how far the measured response is from zero (absolute value) and valence would be represented by the mathematical sign. Notably, the y-axis does not include approach and avoid responses but rather only accounts for the affective response. Approach and avoid behaviors are dissociable from affective appetitive and aversive responses. The best example of this dissociation is observed in aggression behaviors where an aversive stimulus elicits an aversive affective response, but the ensuing behavior is to approach the aversive stimulus. The amygdala is arguably one of the best studied brain areas with a role in threat detection and assigning valence preceding conscious awareness (Buades-Rotger, Beyer, & Kramer, 2017). Of course, with cognition, the frontal cortex can re-assign valence as needed. If the amygdala and the frontal cortex can assign valence, there still must be a neural representation of salience – the intensity of the drive to attend to a stimulus. This may best be encoded by the activity of the dopaminergic projections from the ventral tegmental area to the nucleus accumbens (Berridge, 2007; Schultz, Dayan, & Montague, 1997; Shamay-Tsoory & Abu-Akel, 2015). Therefore, the position of y-axis response is determined by a combination of salience (absolute value), encoded by dopamine circuit activity, and a valence assignment (whether the response is appetitive (+) or aversive (-)) first by the amygdala and modified as needed by cognitive frontal circuits. The sensory–perceptual components on the x-axis interact with dopaminergic circuits as well as affective circuits. It is possible that the neural mechanisms responsible for sensory detection and perception (the x-axis) feed forward to determine salience through perceptual expertise.

The potential contributing anatomy described above is hypothesized for the underlying neural substrates of the Uncanny Valley in the adult brain. How might the Uncanny Valley develop? In general terms, another way to describe the Uncanny Valley is that it is an aversive response to perceptual norm violations. It follows then, that we are only susceptible to the phenomenon of norm violations if we know what the norms are. These norms are defined along the x-axis, with the stimuli with which we have the most experience occupying the space on the far right of the x-axis. For social stimuli, beginning in infancy, we build a lifetime of expertise in this area; there is no social stimulus expertise without experience. For example, a recent study in rhesus macaques illustrated that developmental experience with conspecific faces is required for fusiform face area expertise (Arcaro, Schade, Vincent, Ponce, & Livingstone, 2017). In contrast to monkeys reared with visual experience with other monkeys, monkeys reared by experimenters wearing welding masks spent more time looking at the hand area of pictures of monkeys than they spent looking at faces, suggesting they were relative hand experts and not face experts. In contrast, a typical monkey will spend more time looking at faces, and there is evidence that typically reared monkeys also show an Uncanny Valley response when presented with digitally fabricated unusual monkey faces (Steckenfinger & Ghazanfar, 2009). In this study, monkeys (n = 5) were shown images of typical monkey faces and digitally altered faces to create two categories of monkey faces: unrealistic and realistic but "off". All five monkeys spent less time looking at the realistic but "off" monkey faces compared to stylized but unrealistic monkey faces and actual real monkey faces. This reduction in looking preference for realistic but "off" images of monkeys is consistent with an Uncanny Valley-like response. It is tempting to predict that monkeys with no developmental face exposure would fail to show an Uncanny Valley response to faces. In contrast, they probably would show an Uncanny Valley response to atypical hands, if they had developmental expertise related to hands rather than faces, such as those monkeys in the face deprivation study (Arcaro et al., 2017). As seen by their looking behavior, hands were an atypically salient stimulus to the developmentally face deprived monkeys.

The amygdala appears not to be necessary during development for species-typical social behavior, but it is necessary for modulating some aspects of social behavior and for the appropriate expression of fear (Bauman, Lavenex, Mason, Capitanio, & Amaral, 2004a, 2004b) and conditioned reward (Baxter & Murray, 2002; Murray, 2007; Wassum & Izquierdo, 2015). Additionally, early exposure to different kinds of faces influences the later sensitivity of the amygdala to those faces (Telzer et al., 2013). If the Uncanny Valley is essentially a graphical depiction of norm violations, and neural representations of norms depend on experience, then it follows that the Uncanny Valley landscape is an experience-dependent process. Further, each individual should vary in their expected norm for how a "typical human" should look, sound, and feel. In other words, each individual has a neural template for their in-group. Attachment strength will likely influence the capacity for affiliation on the y-axis, while socialization that includes multisensory experience with conspecifics will influence the expertise on the x-axis. Social play during the socialization period is probably critical for not only refining the multisensory representation of the expected norm, but probably also for refining the capacity of frontal cortical circuits to provide top-down regulatory control of responses to salient stimuli.

How might oxytocin play a role? Oxytocin might play multiple roles during development. Oxytocin may enhance sensory detection of social stimuli through enhanced signal to noise processing, and it may also enhance orienting toward social stimuli to increase exposure to social stimuli to bias experience-dependent development. Current causal research in animals indicates that oxytocin modulates signal to noise processing in primary sensory systems, at least in adults. For example, in the auditory system, oxytocin enhances the detection of pup calls in otherwise naïve female mice (Marlin et al., 2015). This enhancement increases the probability of pup detection and retrieval – hallmark behaviors in the onset of maternal care. Oxytocin also enhances signal to noise ratios in olfactory processing of social cues (Oettl et al., 2016). Being able to detect the presence of another individual at a distance by olfaction (or vision or hearing) is a pre-requisite to social approach and further interaction. If oxytocin can play this role in enhancing signal to noise processing for primary sensory systems in adulthood, perhaps it can also play this role to bias development toward social stimuli and help to set up the x-axis of the Uncanny Valley.

In addition to potentially modulating sensory processing (the x-axis), oxytocin activity during pre-weaning development appears to increase the development of the dopamine system in the VTA and nucleus accumbens (He et al., 2017). In the Developmental Uncanny Valley model, this would increase the intensity of the y-axis. Here, I will argue that oxytocin helps us bias our expertise development toward the social world, turning up the volume on social inputs, so that social stimuli in the environment carry more weight than other stimuli. Without this built-in bias, how would an experience-dependent development stay on track? In our stimulus-rich world, this is no easy task. Oxytocin may promote the kind of sensory bias needed to attend to social stimuli during development.

Where does AVP fit in the Developmental Uncanny Valley Hypothesis? Several studies point to a role for AVP in blunting the social environment, or turning infants away from familiar social stimuli. For example, based on the results of our studies in neonatal mice (Hammock et al., 2013), developmental AVP signaling through AVPR1A seems to shift infant mice away from socially paired stimuli. Perhaps AVP helps develop a different or additional kind of expertise— to shift away from social input and instead pay more attention to the non-social environment. The solitary forager hypothesis (Reser, 2011) suggests that it could be beneficial for some individuals to orient toward non-social objects. This may also be a potential way to regulate social behavior in any individual in a context-dependent manner. While we do need to become social experts, it cannot be at the exclusion of everything else. In addition, if oxytocin helps to encode stimuli as part of the social world, this process needs some measure of context-specific regulation. Perhaps AVP helps provide a counter-measure to prevent the over-consolidation of external stimuli.

This Uncanny Valley conceptualization of the roles of oxytocin and AVP in social behavior development provides a heuristic to generate testable and falsifiable predictions. Recent evidence clearly establishes the necessity of developmental experience in the emergence of expertise required for face processing (Arcaro et al., 2017). Oxytocin may enhance the sensory and orienting bias needed to increase exposure to social stimuli to gain social experience for expertise development and AVP may reduce biased orienting to social stimuli. As an example of a falsifiable prediction of the Developmental Uncanny Valley Hypothesis, I would predict that a temporally restricted upregulation of oxytocin receptors in upper layers II/III of neocortex during a multisensory socialization period may enhance the encoding of stimuli, leading to developmental expertise and later preference in adulthood for individuals most resembling those with whom they were reared. In contrast, individuals without a developmental upregulation of oxytocin receptors in this time and place might not show preferences for or even be able to discriminate among similar individuals. This could be tested in mice with available genetic tools. The recent evidence from conspecific face deprivation in rhesus macaques is consistent with the idea that early sensory–perceptual bias may lead to enhanced attention to social stimuli, potentially leading to domain specificity in face recognition (Spunt & Adolphs, 2017). One could extend this argument by saying that an infant raised without exposure to other race faces will have relative deficits in discriminating those faces and potentially allowing them to fall into the Uncanny Valley as they come close to but fail to conform to the experience-dependent template of expected faces, thus alerting neophobic avoidance mechanisms.

Conclusions and future directions and key knowledge gaps

Oxytocin and AVP both play a role in infant attachment and socialization. The neural circuits modulated by oxytocin and AVP during these developmental epochs are not yet fully elucidated. These neuropeptides and their receptors (oxytocin receptor and AVPR1A, with more evidence needed for other AVP receptors, especially AVPR1B) are both mediators and targets of developmental experience. This system provides a foundation for later emerging social behavior. It is important to remember the difficulties of dissecting the roles of specific neural components of the experience-dependent development of social behavior. Importantly, because social behavior requires interacting partners, any treatment to one study subject that changes the behavior of the interacting partner increases the uncertainty of the direct contribution of the neural variable in question. For example, in Mongolian gerbils, AVP given to neonates on the first postnatal day later influenced parental behavior toward pups in a sex-specific manner during the neonatal attachment period and increased social contact in males only within the juvenile socialization period (Taylor, Cavanaugh, & French, 2017). The single neonatal treatment in this study could have caused a behavioral change in the infant, which altered the parental responsiveness. Then it is unknown if the later changes in social play are due to the single injection, or probably more reasonably due to an altered parent–infant relationship in the attachment period.

The Developmental Uncanny Valley Hypothesis attempts to organize and conceptualize the vast literature on the roles of oxytocin and AVP in adulthood, specifically by accounting for their hypothesized roles in development. This framework presents a heuristic to generate falsifiable predictions for the roles of these neuropeptides with primary neural targets in sensory systems, dopaminergic salience networks, and neural mechanisms of valence assignment. Further studies are needed to clarify their roles here and in approach/avoid behavioral networks which may be orthogonal to appetitive and aversive valence networks.

Affiliation and attachment require a social connection which begins with direct physical contact. Clinical trials designed to offer additional oxytocin to children and adults with ASD have thus far not focused heavily on the role of contingent experience while treating with extra oxytocin. If the oxytocin system naturally acts during times of social connection, then perhaps it is important to consider that clinically, exogenous oxytocin as medicine should also be applied in social contexts. Given the intimate nature of the caregiver–infant bond, if oxytocin really can promote social behavior, perhaps it is critical for us to consider treating the caregiver–infant (or child) dyad together as a unified whole. The overarching hypothesis that caregiver–infant interaction can cause the release of endogenous oxytocin within the infant suggests that enhanced oxytocin outside of this context might be either ineffective or perhaps even damaging to the experience-dependent development of infant social behavior. Oxytocin delivery by nebulization (Modi, Connor-Stroud, Landgraf, Young, & Parr, 2014; Parr et al., 2016) evokes an interesting scenario where both caregiver and infant might simultaneously benefit from being exposed in a nebulizing chamber where they can, without disruption, perform ethologically important behaviors such as mutual eye gaze, facial imitation, and infant-directed vocalizations. This could be piloted in non-human primates, and if effective or desirable, adapted for human use. Social behavior development requires species-appropriate social experience, and it seems misguided to consider an oxytocin intervention without also considering the environment in which it is applied.

The relationship between oxytocin and AVP effects on behavior (such as social investigation) versus oxytocin and AVP-dependent changes in sensory detection/perception and affect will need to be disentangled. These distinct components all play a role in the final observable behavior, and the relative contribution of oxytocin and AVP to each during development are not yet well characterized. The Developmental Uncanny Valley Hypothesis considers the potential roles of oxytocin and AVP in a two-dimensional space that only includes sensation/perception and affect. Therefore, a significant limitation of the Developmental Uncanny Valley Hypothesis for understanding social behavior is that it lacks a third approach/avoid axis. Based on the available data so far, the effects of AVP on social behavior may be more direct along this axis. This is critically important to keep in mind when attempting to translate observable social behavior in rodent models (which needs the missing third axis) to human behavior.

Finally, it is clear from the variety of studies presented here that research on social behavior development requires significant attention to detail. Who is the interacting partner? Is the stimulus partner familiar or a stranger? Is the environmental context familiar or new? What prior experience has the study subject already had and with whom? Oxytocin and AVP likely modulate experience-dependent social behavior development, but in social partner and context-specific ways. Sex, species, age, and individual differences in life experience will all be likely moderating factors.

References

Allin, J. T., & Banks, E. M. (1971). Effects of temperature on ultrasound production by infant albino rats. *Developmental Psychobiology, 4*(2), 149–156. doi:10.1002/dev.420040206

An, D., Chen, W., Yu, D. Q., Wang, S. W., Yu, W. Z., Xu, H., . . . Yin, S. M. (2017). Effects of social isolation, re-socialization and age on cognitive and aggressive behaviors of Kunming mice and BALB/c mice. *Animal Science Journal, 88*(5), 798–806. doi:10.1111/asj.12688

Arcaro, M. J., Schade, P. F., Vincent, J. L., Ponce, C. R., & Livingstone, M. S. (2017). Seeing faces is necessary for face-domain formation. *Nature Neuroscience, 20*, 1404–1412. doi:10.1038/nn.4635

Armstrong, C. M., DeVito, L. M., & Cleland, T. A. (2006). One-trial associative odor learning in neonatal mice. *Chemical Senses, 31*(4), 343–349. doi:10.1093/chemse/bjj038

Baarendse, P. J., Counotte, D. S., O'Donnell, P., & Vanderschuren, L. J. (2013). Early social experience is critical for the development of cognitive control and dopamine modulation of prefrontal cortex function. *Neuropsychopharmacology, 38*(8), 1485–1494. doi:10.1038/npp.2013.47

Baarendse, P. J., Limpens, J. H., & Vanderschuren, L. J. (2014). Disrupted social development enhances the motivation for cocaine in rats. *Psychopharmacology (Berl), 231*(8), 1695–1704. doi:10.1007/s00213-013-3362-8

Bauman, M. D., Lavenex, P., Mason, W. A., Capitanio, J. P., & Amaral, D. G. (2004a). The development of mother-infant interactions after neonatal amygdala lesions in rhesus monkeys. *Journal of Neuroscience, 24*(3), 711–721.

Bauman, M. D., Lavenex, P., Mason, W. A., Capitanio, J. P., & Amaral, D. G. (2004b). The development of social behavior following neonatal amygdala lesions in rhesus monkeys. *Journal of Cognitive Neuroscience, 16*(8), 1388–1411.

Baxter, M. G., & Murray, E. A. (2002). The amygdala and reward. *Nature Reviews Neuroscience, 3*(7), 563–573. doi:10.1038/nrn875

Berridge, K. C. (2007). The debate over dopamine's role in reward: The case for incentive salience. *Psychopharmacology (Berl), 191*(3), 391–431. doi:10.1007/s00213-006-0578-x

Bleickardt, C. J., Mullins, D. E., Macsweeney, C. P., Werner, B. J., Pond, A. J., Guzzi, M. F., . . . Hodgson, R. A. (2009). Characterization of the V1a antagonist, JNJ-17308616, in rodent models of anxiety-like behavior. *Psychopharmacology (Berl), 202*(4), 711–718. doi:10.1007/s00213–008–1354-x

Bouslama, M., Durand, E., Chauviere, L., van den Bergh, O., & Gallego, J. (2005). Olfactory classical conditioning in newborn mice. *Behavioural Brain Research, 161*(1), 102–106.

Branchi, I., Santucci, D., & Alleva, E. (2001). Ultrasonic vocalisation emitted by infant rodents: A tool for assessment of neurobehavioural development. *Behavioural Brain Research, 125*(1–2), 49–56.

Bredewold, R., Smith, C. J., Dumais, K. M., & Veenema, A. H. (2014). Sex-specific modulation of juvenile social play behavior by vasopressin and oxytocin depends on social context. *Frontiers in Behavioral Neuroscience, 8*, 216. doi:10.3389/fnbeh.2014.00216

Buades-Rotger, M., Beyer, F., & Kramer, U. M. (2017). Avoidant responses to interpersonal provocation are associated with increased amygdala and decreased mentalizing network activity. *eNeuro, 4*(3). doi:10.1523/ENEURO.0337-16.2017

Burghardt, G. M. (2005). *Genesis of animal play: Testing the limits.* Cambridge, MA: MIT Press.

Caldwell, H. K., & Albers, H. E. (2016). Oxytocin, vasopressin, and the motivational forces that drive social behaviors. *Current Topics in Behavioral Neurosciences, 27*, 51–103. doi:10.1007/7854_2015_390

Carter, C. S., Williams, J. R., Witt, D. M., & Insel, T. R. (1992). Oxytocin and social bonding. *Annals of the New York Academy of Sciences, 652*, 204–211.

Choe, H. K., Reed, M. D., Benavidez, N., Montgomery, D., Soares, N., Yim, Y. S., & Choi, G. B. (2015). Oxytocin mediates entrainment of sensory stimuli to social cues of opposing valence. *Neuron, 87*(1), 152–163. doi:10.1016/j.neuron.2015.06.022

Clancy, B., Darlington, R. B., & Finlay, B. L. (2001). Translating developmental time across mammalian species. *Neuroscience, 105*(1), 7–17.

Clancy, B., Kersh, B., Hyde, J., Darlington, R. B., Anand, K. J., & Finlay, B. L. (2007). Web-based method for translating neurodevelopment from laboratory species to humans. *Neuroinformatics, 5*(1), 79–94. doi:10.1385/NI:5:1:79

Cordoni, G., & Palagi, E. (2011). Ontogenetic trajectories of chimpanzee social play: Similarities with humans. *PLoS One, 6*(11), e27344. doi:10.1371/journal.pone.0027344

Denenberg, V. H., Hudgens, G. A., & Zarrow, M. X. (1964). Mice reared with rats: Modification of behavior by early experience with another species. *Science, 143*(3604), 380–381.

Dolen, G., Darvishzadeh, A., Huang, K. W., & Malenka, R. C. (2013). Social reward requires coordinated activity of nucleus accumbens oxytocin and serotonin. *Nature, 501*(7466), 179–184. doi:10.1038/nature12518

Du, P., He, Z., Cai, Z., Hao, X., Dong, N., Yuan, W., . . . Tai, F. (2017). Chronic central oxytocin infusion impairs sociability in mandarin voles. *Pharmacology, Biochemistry and Behavior, 161*, 38–46. doi:10.1016/j.pbb.2017.09.006

Dumais, K. M., & Veenema, A. H. (2016). Vasopressin and oxytocin receptor systems in the brain: Sex differences and sex-specific regulation of social behavior. *Frontiers in Neuroendocrinology, 40*, 1–23. doi:10.1016/j.yfrne.2015.04.003

Dyer, D. P., Jr., & Southwick, C. H. (1974). A possible sensitive period for juvenile socialization in mice. *Behavioral Biology, 12*(4), 551–558.

Engelmann, M., & Landgraf, R. (1994). Microdialysis administration of vasopressin into the septum improves social recognition in Brattleboro rats. *Physiology & Behavior, 55*(1), 145–149.

Feifel, D., Mexal, S., Melendez, G., Liu, P. Y., Goldenberg, J. R., & Shilling, P. D. (2009). The Brattleboro rat displays a natural deficit in social discrimination that is restored by clozapine and a neurotensin analog. *Neuropsychopharmacology, 34*(8), 2011–2018. doi:10.1038/npp.2009.15

Ferguson, J. N., Aldag, J. M., Insel, T. R., & Young, L. J. (2001). Oxytocin in the medial amygdala is essential for social recognition in the mouse. *Journal of Neuroscience, 21*(20), 8278–8285.

Ferris, C. F., Albers, H. E., Wesolowski, S. M., Goldman, B. D., & Luman, S. E. (1984). Vasopressin injected into the hypothalamus triggers a stereotypic behavior in golden hamsters. *Science, 224*(4648), 521–523.

Gunnar, M. R., & Donzella, B. (2002). Social regulation of the cortisol levels in early human development. *Psychoneuroendocrinology, 27*(1–2), 199–220.

Halldorsdottir, T., & Binder, E. B. (2017). Gene x environment interactions: From molecular mechanisms to behavior. *Annual Review of Psychology, 68*, 215–241. doi:10.1146/annurev-psych-010416-044053

Hammock, E., & Levitt, P. (2013). Oxytocin receptor ligand binding in embryonic tissue and postnatal brain development of the C57BL/6J mouse. *Frontiers in Behavioral Neuroscience, 7.* doi:10.3389/fnbeh.2013.00195

Hammock, E. A. (2015). Developmental perspectives on oxytocin and vasopressin. *Neuropsychopharmacology, 40*(1), 24–42. doi:10.1038/npp.2014.120

Hammock, E. A., Law, C. S., & Levitt, P. (2013). Vasopressin eliminates the expression of familiar odor bias in neonatal female mice through V1aR. *Hormones and Behavior, 63*(2), 352–360. doi:10.1016/j.yhbeh.2012.12.006

Hammock, E. A., & Levitt, P. (2012). Modulation of parvalbumin interneuron number by developmentally transient neocortical Vasopressin Receptor 1a (V1aR). *Neuroscience, 222C*, 20–28. doi:S0306-4522(12)00750-6 [pii] 10.1016/j.neuroscience.2012.07.025

Hammock, E. A. D., & Levitt, P. (2006). The discipline of neurobehavioral development: The emerging interface of processes that build circuits and skills. *Human Development, 49*(5), 294–309. doi:10.1159/000095581

Hatch, A. M., Wiberg, G. S., Zawidzka, Z., Cann, M., Airth, J. M., & Grice, H. C. (1965). Isolation syndrome in the rat. *Toxicology and Applied Pharmacology, 7*(5), 737–745.

He, Z., Hou, W., Hao, X., Dong, N., Du, P., Yuan, W., . . . Tai, F. (2017). Oxytocin receptor antagonist treatments alter levels of attachment to mothers and central dopamine activity in pre-weaning mandarin vole pups. *Psychoneuroendocrinology, 84*, 124–134. doi:10.1016/j.psyneuen.2017.06.020

Hodgson, R. A., Higgins, G. A., Guthrie, D. H., Lu, S. X., Pond, A. J., Mullins, D. E., . . . Varty, G. B. (2007). Comparison of the V1b antagonist, SSR149415, and the CRF1 antagonist, CP-154,526, in rodent models of anxiety and depression. *Pharmacology Biochemistry and Behavior, 86*(3), 431–440. doi:10.1016/j.pbb.2006.12.021

Hofer, M. A. (1975). Studies on how early maternal separation produces behavioral change in young rats. *Psychosomatic Medicine, 37*(3), 245–264.

Hofer, M. A. (1976). The organization of sleep and wakefulness after maternal separation in young rats. *Developmental Psychobiology, 9*(2), 189–205. doi:10.1002/dev.420090212

Hofer, M. A. (1996). Multiple regulators of ultrasonic vocalization in the infant rat. *Psychoneuroendocrinology, 21*(2), 203–217.

Hofer, M. A., & Shair, H. N. (1978). Ultrasonic vocalization during social interaction and isolation in 2-weeek-old rats. *Developmental Psychobiology, 11*(5), 495–504. doi:10.1002/dev.420110513

Hofer, M. A., Shair, H. N., & Brunelli, S. A. (2002). Ultrasonic vocalizations in rat and mouse pups. *Current Protocols in Neuroscience, 17*, 8.14.1–8.14.16. doi:10.1002/0471142301.ns0814s17

Hol, T., van den Berg, C. L., van Ree, J. M., & Spruijt, B. M. (1999). Isolation during the play period in infancy decreases adult social interactions in rats. *Behavioural Brain Research, 100*(1–2), 91–97.

Honeycutt, H., & Alberts, J. R. (2005). Housing pregnant mice (*Mus musculus*) in small groups facilitates the development of odor-based homing in offspring. *Journal of Comparative Psychology, 119*(4), 418–429. doi:2005-15842-007 [pii] 10.1037/0735-7036.119.4.418

Hung, L. W., Neuner, S., Polepalli, J. S., Beier, K. T., Wright, M., Walsh, J. J., . . . Malenka, R. C. (2017). Gating of social reward by oxytocin in the ventral tegmental area. *Science, 357*(6358), 1406–1411. doi:10.1126/science.aan4994

Iijima, M., & Chaki, S. (2005). Separation-induced ultrasonic vocalization in rat pups: Further pharmacological characterization. *Pharmacology Biochemistry and Behavior, 82*(4), 652–657. doi:10.1016/j.pbb.2005.11.005

Iijima, M., Yoshimizu, T., Shimazaki, T., Tokugawa, K., Fukumoto, K., Kurosu, S., . . . Chaki, S. (2014). Anti-depressant and anxiolytic profiles of newly synthesized arginine vasopressin V1B receptor antagonists: TASP0233278 and TASP0390325. *British Journal of Pharmacology, 171*(14), 3511–3525. doi:10.1111/bph.12699

Insel, T. R., & Winslow, J. T. (1991). Central administration of oxytocin modulates the infant rat's response to social isolation. *European Journal of Pharmacology, 203*(1), 149–152.

Johnson, Z. V., & Young, L. J. (2017). Oxytocin and vasopressin neural networks: Implications for social behavioral diversity and translational neuroscience. *Neuroscience & Biobehavioral Reviews, 76*(Pt A), 87–98. doi:10.1016/j.neubiorev.2017.01.034

Kalcher, E., Franz, C., Crailsheim, K., & Preuschoft, S. (2008). Differential onset of infantile deprivation produces distinctive long-term effects in adult ex-laboratory chimpanzees (*Pan troglodytes*). *Developmental Psychobiology, 50*(8), 777–788. doi:10.1002/dev.20330

Klengel, T., & Binder, E. B. (2015). Epigenetics of stress-related psychiatric disorders and gene x environment interactions. *Neuron, 86*(6), 1343–1357. doi:10.1016/j.neuron.2015.05.036

Kojima, S., & Alberts, J. R. (2011). Oxytocin mediates the acquisition of filial, odor-guided huddling for maternally-associated odor in preweanling rats. *Hormones and Behavior, 60*(5), 549–558. doi:10.1016/j.yhbeh.2011.08.003

Leng, G., & Ludwig, M. (2016). Intranasal oxytocin: Myths and delusions. *Biological Psychiatry, 79*(3), 243–250. doi:10.1016/j.biopsych.2015.05.003

Leng, G., & Sabatier, N. (2016). Measuring oxytocin and vasopressin: Bioassays, immunoassays and random numbers. *Journal of Neuroendocrinology, 28*(10). doi:10.1111/jne.12413

Levine, S. (2001). Primary social relationships influence the development of the hypothalamic – pituitary – adrenal axis in the rat. *Physiology & Behavior, 73*(3), 255–260.

Lewkowicz, D. J., & Ghazanfar, A. A. (2012). The development of the uncanny valley in infants. *Developmental Psychobiology, 54*(2), 124–132. doi:10.1002/dev.20583

Li, J., Zhao, Y., Li, R., Broster, L. S., Zhou, C., & Yang, S. (2015). Association of Oxytocin Receptor Gene (OXTR) rs53576 polymorphism with sociality: A meta-analysis. *PLoS One, 10*(6), e0131820. doi:10.1371/journal.pone.0131820

Lim, M. M., Wang, Z., Olazabal, D. E., Ren, X., Terwilliger, E. F., & Young, L. J. (2004). Enhanced partner preference in a promiscuous species by manipulating the expression of a single gene. *Nature, 429*(6993), 754–757.

Lin, R. E., Ambler, L., Billingslea, E. N., Suh, J., Batheja, S., Tatard-Leitman, V., . . . Siegel, S. J. (2013). Electroencephalographic and early communicative abnormalities in Brattleboro rats. *Physiological Reports, 1*(5), e00100. doi:10.1002/phy2.100

Marlin, B. J., Mitre, M., D'Amour J, A., Chao, M. V., & Froemke, R. C. (2015). Oxytocin enables maternal behaviour by balancing cortical inhibition. *Nature, 520*(7548), 499–504. doi:10.1038/nature14402

McCullough, M. E., Churchland, P. S., & Mendez, A. J. (2013). Problems with measuring peripheral oxytocin: Can the data on oxytocin and human behavior be trusted? *Neuroscience & Biobehavioral Reviews, 37*(8), 1485–1492. doi:10.1016/j.neubiorev.2013.04.018

Meng, Q., Li, N., Han, X., Shao, F., & Wang, W. (2010). Peri-adolescence isolation rearing alters social behavior and nociception in rats. *Neuroscience Letters, 480*(1), 25–29. doi:10.1016/j.neulet.2010.05.067

Miller, T. V., & Caldwell, H. K. (2015). Oxytocin during development: Possible organizational effects on behavior. *Front Endocrinol (Lausanne), 6*, 76. doi:10.3389/fendo.2015.00076

Modi, M. E., Connor-Stroud, F., Landgraf, R., Young, L. J., & Parr, L. A. (2014). Aerosolized oxytocin increases cerebrospinal fluid oxytocin in rhesus macaques. *Psychoneuroendocrinology, 45*, 49–57. doi:10.1016/j.psyneuen.2014.02.011

Mori, M. (1970). The Uncanny Valley. *Energy, 7*(4), 33–35.

Mori, M. (2012). The Uncanny Valley. *IEEE Robotics & Automation Magazine, 19*(2), 98–100. doi:10.1109/Mra.2012.2192811

Moriceau, S., Wilson, D. A., Levine, S., & Sullivan, R. M. (2006). Dual circuitry for odor-shock conditioning during infancy: Corticosterone switches between fear and attraction via amygdala. *Journal of Neuroscience, 26*(25), 6737–6748.

Murray, E. A. (2007). The amygdala, reward and emotion. *Trends in Cognitive Science, 11*(11), 489–497. doi:10.1016/j.tics.2007.08.013

Nelson, E., & Panksepp, J. (1996). Oxytocin mediates acquisition of maternally associated odor preferences in preweanling rat pups. *Behavioral Neuroscience, 110*(3), 583–592.

Nelson, E. E., & Panksepp, J. (1998). Brain substrates of infant-mother attachment: Contributions of opioids, oxytocin, and norepinephrine. *Neuroscience & Biobehavioral Reviews, 22*(3), 437–452.

Nishizato, M., Fujisawa, T. X., Kosaka, H., & Tomoda, A. (2017). Developmental changes in social attention and oxytocin levels in infants and children. *Scientific Reports, 7*(1), 2540. doi:10.1038/s41598-017-02368-x

Oettl, L. L., Ravi, N., Schneider, M., Scheller, M. F., Schneider, P., Mitre, M., . . . Kelsch, W. (2016). Oxytocin enhances social recognition by modulating cortical control of early olfactory processing. *Neuron, 90*(3), 609–621. doi:10.1016/j.neuron.2016.03.033

Oswalt, G. L., & Meier, G. W. (1975). Olfactory, thermal, and tactual influences on infantile ultrasonic vocalization in rats. *Developmental Psychobiology, 8*(2), 129–135. doi:10.1002/dev.420080205

Panksepp, J. (2003). Can anthropomorphic analyses of separation cries in other animals inform us about the emotional nature of social loss in humans? Comment on Blumberg and Sokoloff (2001). *Psychological Review, 110*(2), 376–388; discussion 389–396.

Parker, K. J., Oztan, O., Libove, R. A., Sumiyoshi, R. D., Jackson, L. P., Karhson, D. S., . . . Hardan, A. Y. (2017). Intranasal oxytocin treatment for social deficits and biomarkers of response in children with autism. *Proceedings of the National Academy of Sciences of the United States of America, 114*(30), 8119–8124. doi:10.1073/pnas.1705521114

Parr, L. A., Brooks, J. M., Jonesteller, T., Moss, S., Jordano, J. O., & Heitz, T. R. (2016). Effects of chronic oxytocin on attention to dynamic facial expressions in infant macaques. *Psychoneuroendocrinology, 74*, 149–157. doi:10.1016/j.psyneuen.2016.08.028

Paul, M. J., Peters, N. V., Holder, M. K., Kim, A. M., Whylings, J., Terranova, J. I., & de Vries, G. J. (2016). Atypical social development in vasopressin-deficient Brattleboro rats. *eNeuro, 3*(2). doi:10.1523/ENEURO.0150-15.2016

Pedersen, C. A., Ascher, J. A., Monroe, Y. L., & Prange, A. J., Jr. (1982). Oxytocin induces maternal behavior in virgin female rats. *Science, 216*(4546), 648–650.

Pedersen, C. A., & Prange, A. J., Jr. (1979). Induction of maternal behavior in virgin rats after intracerebroventricular administration of oxytocin. *Proceedings of the National Academy of Sciences of the United States of America, 76*(12), 6661–6665.

Popik, P., Vetulani, J., & van Ree, J. M. (1992). Low doses of oxytocin facilitate social recognition in rats. *Psychopharmacology (Berl), 106*(1), 71–74.

Reser, J. E. (2011). Conceptualizing the autism spectrum in terms of natural selection and behavioral ecology: The solitary forager hypothesis. *Evolutionary Psychology, 9*(2), 207–238.

Ross, H. E., Freeman, S. M., Spiegel, L. L., Ren, X., Terwilliger, E. F., & Young, L. J. (2009). Variation in oxytocin receptor density in the nucleus accumbens has differential effects on affiliative behaviors in monogamous and polygamous voles. *Journal of Neuroscience, 29*(5), 1312–1318. doi:10.1523/JNEU ROSCI.5039–08.2009

Roth, T. L., Raineki, C., Salstein, L., Perry, R., Sullivan-Wilson, T. A., Sloan, A., . . . Sullivan, R. M. (2013). Neurobiology of secure infant attachment and attachment despite adversity: A mouse model. *Genes, Brain and Behavior, 12*(7), 673–680. doi:10.1111/gbb.12067

Roth, T. L., & Sullivan, R. M. (2006). Examining the role of endogenous opioids in learned odor-stroke associations in infant rats. *Developmental Psychobiology, 48*(1), 71–78.

Scattoni, M. L., Crawley, J., & Ricceri, L. (2009). Ultrasonic vocalizations: A tool for behavioural phenotyping of mouse models of neurodevelopmental disorders. *Neuroscience & Biobehavioral Reviews, 33*(4), 508–515. doi:10.1016/j.neubiorev.2008.08.003

Scattoni, M. L., McFarlane, H. G., Zhodzishsky, V., Caldwell, H. K., Young, W. S., Ricceri, L., & Crawley, J. N. (2008). Reduced ultrasonic vocalizations in vasopressin 1b knockout mice. *Behavioural Brain Research, 187*(2), 371–378. doi:10.1016/j.bbr.2007.09.034

Schank, J. C. (2009). Early locomotor and social effects in vasopressin deficient neonatal rats. *Behavioural Brain Reserach, 197*(1), 166–177. doi:10.1016/j.bbr.2008.08.019

Schmale, H., Ivell, R., Breindl, M., Darmer, D., & Richter, D. (1984). The mutant vasopressin gene from diabetes insipidus (Brattleboro) rats is transcribed but the message is not efficiently translated. *The Embo Journal, 3*(13), 3289–3293.

Schultz, W., Dayan, P., & Montague, P. R. (1997). A neural substrate of prediction and reward. *Science, 275*(5306), 1593–1599.

Shair, H. N. (2014). Parental potentiation of vocalization as a marker for filial bonds in infant animals. *Developmental Psychobiology, 56*(8), 1689–1697. doi:10.1002/dev.21222

Shamay-Tsoory, S. G., & Abu-Akel, A. (2015). The social salience hypothesis of oxytocin. *Biological Psychiatry, 79*(3), 194–202. doi:10.1016/j.biopsych.2015.07.020

Shapiro, L. E., & Insel, T. R. (1989). Ontogeny of oxytocin receptors in rat forebrain: A quantitative study. *Synapse, 4*(3), 259–266.

Sigling, H. O., Wolterink-Donselaar, I. G., & Spruijt, B. M. (2009). Home seeking behavior in rat pups: Attachment vs. kin selection, oxytocin vs. vasopressin. *European Journal of Pharmacology, 612*(1–3), 48–53. doi:10.1016/j.ejphar.2009.03.070

Simmons, T. C., Balland, J. F., Dhauna, J., Yang, S. Y., Traina, J. L., Vazquez, J., & Bales, K. L. (2017). Early intranasal vasopressin administration impairs partner preference in adult male prairie voles (*Microtus ochrogaster*). *Front Endocrinol (Lausanne), 8*, 145. doi:10.3389/fendo.2017.00145

Simpson, E. A., Sclafani, V., Paukner, A., Hamel, A. F., Novak, M. A., Meyer, J. S., . . . Ferrari, P. F. (2014). Inhaled oxytocin increases positive social behaviors in newborn macaques. *Proceedings of the National Academy of Sciences of the United States of America, 111*(19), 6922–6927. doi:10.1073/pnas.1402471111

Smith, A. S., Williams Avram, S. K., Cymerblit-Sabba, A., Song, J., & Young, W. S. (2016). Targeted activation of the hippocampal CA2 area strongly enhances social memory. *Molecular Psychiatry, 21*(8), 1137–1144. doi:10.1038/mp.2015.189

Smith, C. J., Poehlmann, M. L., Li, S., Ratnaseelan, A. M., Bredewold, R., & Veenema, A. H. (2017). Age and sex differences in oxytocin and vasopressin V1a receptor binding densities in the rat brain: Focus on the social decision-making network. *Brain Structure and Function, 222*(2), 981–1006. doi:10.1007/s00429-016-1260-7

Snijdewint, F. G., van Leeuwen, F. W., & Boer, G. J. (1989). Ontogeny of vasopressin and oxytocin binding sites in the brain of Wistar and Brattleboro rats as demonstrated by lightmicroscopical autoradiography. *Journal of Chemical Neuroanatomy, 2*(1), 3–17.

Spunt, R. P., & Adolphs, R. (2017). A new look at domain specificity: Insights from social neuroscience. *Nature Reviews Neuroscience, 18*(9), 559–567. doi:10.1038/nrn.2017.76

Steckenfinger, S. A., & Ghazanfar, A. A. (2009). Monkey visual behavior falls into the uncanny valley. *Proceedings of the National Academy of Sciences of the United States of America, 106*(43), 18362–18366. doi:10.1073/pnas.0910063106

Sullivan, R. M., & Holman, P. J. (2010). Transitions in sensitive period attachment learning in infancy: The role of corticosterone. *Neuroscience & Biobehavioral Reviews, 34*(6), 835–844. doi:10.1016/j.neubiorev.2009.11.010

Swaab, D. F. (1995). Development of the human hypothalamus. *Neurochemical Research, 20*(5), 509–519.

Takayanagi, Y., Yoshida, M., Bielsky, I. F., Ross, H. E., Kawamata, M., Onaka, T., . . . Nishimori, K. (2005). Pervasive social deficits, but normal parturition, in oxytocin receptor-deficient mice. *Proceedings of the National Academy of Sciences of the United States of America, 102*(44), 16096–16101.

Tamborski, S., Mintz, E. M., & Caldwell, H. K. (2016). Sex differences in the embryonic development of the central oxytocin system in mice. *Journal of Neuroendocrinology.* doi:10.1111/jne.12364

Taylor, J. H., Cavanaugh, J., & French, J. A. (2017). Neonatal oxytocin and vasopressin manipulation alter social behavior during the juvenile period in Mongolian gerbils. *Developmental Psychobiology, 59*(5), 653–657. doi:10.1002/dev.21533

Telzer, E. H., Flannery, J., Shapiro, M., Humphreys, K. L., Goff, B., Gabard-Durman, L., . . . Tottenham, N. (2013). Early experience shapes amygdala sensitivity to race: An international adoption design. *Journal of Neuroscience, 33*(33), 13484–13488. doi:10.1523/JNEUROSCI.1272–13.2013

Terranova, M. L., Laviola, G., & Alleva, E. (1993). Ontogeny of amicable social behavior in the mouse: Gender differences and ongoing isolation outcomes. *Developmental Psychobiology, 26*(8), 467–481.

Trezza, V., Baarendse, P. J., & Vanderschuren, L. J. (2010). The pleasures of play: Pharmacological insights into social reward mechanisms. *Trends in Pharmacological Sciences, 31*(10), 463–469. doi:10.1016/j.tips.2010.06.008

Tribollet, E., Charpak, S., Schmidt, A., Dubois-Dauphin, M., & Dreifuss, J. J. (1989). Appearance and transient expression of oxytocin receptors in fetal, infant, and peripubertal rat brain studied by autoradiography and electrophysiology. *Journal of Neuroscience, 9*(5), 1764–1773.

Tribollet, E., Goumaz, M., Raggenbass, M., & Dreifuss, J. J. (1991). Appearance and transient expression of vasopressin and oxytocin receptors in the rat brain. *Journal of Receptor Research, 11*(1–4), 333–346.

Tribollet, E., Goumaz, M., Raggenbass, M., Dubois-Dauphin, M., & Dreifuss, J. J. (1991). Early appearance and transient expression of vasopressin receptors in the brain of rat fetus and infant. An autoradiographical and electrophysiological study. *Brain Research. Developmental Brain Research, 58*(1), 13–24.

Vaidyanathan, R., & Hammock, E. A. (2016). Oxytocin receptor dynamics in the brain across development and species. *Developmental Neurobiology, 77*(2), 143–157. doi:10.1002/dneu.22403

van Leeuwen, E. J., Mulenga, I. C., & Chidester, D. L. (2014). Early social deprivation negatively affects social skill acquisition in chimpanzees (*Pan troglodytes*). *Animal Cognition, 17*(2), 407–414. doi:10.1007/s10071-013-0672-5

Varga, J., Fodor, A., Klausz, B., & Zelena, D. (2015). Anxiogenic role of vasopressin during the early postnatal period: Maternal separation-induced ultrasound vocalization in vasopressin-deficient Brattleboro rats. *Amino Acids, 47*(11), 2409–2418. doi:10.1007/s00726-015-2034-x

Veenema, A.H. (2012). Toward understanding how early-life social experiences alter oxytocin- and vasopressin-regulated social behaviors. *Hormones and Behavior, 61*(3), 304–312. doi:10.1016/j.yhbeh.2011.12.002

Veenema, A. H., Bredewold, R., & De Vries, G. J. (2012). Vasopressin regulates social recognition in juvenile and adult rats of both sexes, but in sex- and age-specific ways. *Hormones and Behavior, 61*(1), 50–56. doi:10.1016/j.yhbeh.2011.10.002

Veenema, A. H., Bredewold, R., & De Vries, G. J. (2013). Sex-specific modulation of juvenile social play by vasopressin. *Psychoneuroendocrinology, 38*(11), 2554–2561. doi:10.1016/j.psyneuen.2013.06.002

Veenema, A. H., & Neumann, I. D. (2009). Maternal separation enhances offensive play-fighting, basal corticosterone and hypothalamic vasopressin mRNA expression in juvenile male rats. *Psychoneuroendocrinology, 34*(3), 463–467. doi:10.1016/j.psyneuen.2008.10.017

Wacker, D. W., & Ludwig, M. (2012). Vasopressin, oxytocin, and social odor recognition. *Hormones and Behavior, 61*(3), 259–265. doi:10.1016/j.yhbeh.2011.08.014

Walum, H., Waldman, I. D., & Young, L. J. (2016). Statistical and methodological considerations for the interpretation of intranasal oxytocin studies. *Biological Psychiatry, 79*(3), 251–257. doi:10.1016/j.biopsych.2015.06.016

Wassum, K. M., & Izquierdo, A. (2015). The basolateral amygdala in reward learning and addiction. *Neuroscience & Biobehavioral Reviews, 57*, 271–283. doi:10.1016/j.neubiorev.2015.08.017

Wei, L., Meaney, M. J., Duman, R. S., & Kaffman, A. (2011). Affiliative behavior requires juvenile, but not adult neurogenesis. *Journal of Neurosciences, 31*(40), 14335–14345. doi:10.1523/JNEUROSCI.1333-11.2011

Williams, J. R., Carter, C. S., & Insel, T. (1992). Partner preference development in female prairie voles is facilitated by mating or the central infusion of oxytocin. *Annals of the New York Academy of Sciences, 652*, 487–489.

Williams, J. R., Catania, K. C., & Carter, C. S. (1992). Development of partner preferences in female prairie voles (*Microtus ochrogaster*): The role of social and sexual experience. *Hormones and Behavior, 26*(3), 339–349.

Williams, J. R., Insel, T. R., Harbaugh, C. R., & Carter, C. S. (1994). Oxytocin administered centrally facilitates formation of a partner preference in female prairie voles (*Microtus ochrogaster*). *Journal of Neuroendocrinology, 6*(3), 247–250.

Winslow, J. T., Hastings, N., Carter, C. S., Harbaugh, C. R., & Insel, T. R. (1993). A role for central vasopressin in pair bonding in monogamous prairie voles. *Nature, 365*(6446), 545–548.

Winslow, J. T., Hearn, E. F., Ferguson, J., Young, L. J., Matzuk, M. M., & Insel, T. R. (2000). Infant vocalization, adult aggression, and fear behavior of an oxytocin null mutant mouse. *Hormones and Behavior, 37*(2), 145–155.

Winslow, J. T., & Insel, T. R. (1991). Infant rat separation is a sensitive test for novel anxiolytics. *Progress in Neuropsychopharmacology & Biological Psychiatry, 15*(6), 745–757.

Winslow, J. T., & Insel, T. R. (1993). Effects of central vasopressin administration to infant rats. *European Journal of Pharmacology, 233*(1), 101–107. doi:10.1016/0014-2999(93)90354-K

Workman, A. D., Charvet, C. J., Clancy, B., Darlington, R. B., & Finlay, B. L. (2013). Modeling transformations of neurodevelopmental sequences across mammalian species. *Journal of Neuroscience, 33*(17), 7368–7383. doi:10.1523/JNEUROSCI.5746-12.2013

Young, L. J. (1999). Frank A. Beach award: Oxytocin and vasopressin receptors and species-typical social behaviors. *Hormones and Behavior, 36*(3), 212–221.

Young, L. J., Wang, Z., & Insel, T. R. (1998). Neuroendocrine bases of monogamy. *Trends in Neurosciences, 21*(2), 71–75.

Young, L. J., Winslow, J. T., Nilsen, R., & Insel, T. R. (1997). Species differences in V1a receptor gene expression in monogamous and nonmonogamous voles: Behavioral consequences. *Behavioral Neuroscience, 111*(3), 599–605.

Yovel, G., & Belin, P. (2013). A unified coding strategy for processing faces and voices. *Trends in Cognitive Science, 17*(6), 263–271. doi:10.1016/j.tics.2013.04.004

Zelena, D., Domokos, A., Barna, I., Mergl, Z., Haller, J., & Makara, G. B. (2008). Control of the hypothalamo-pituitary-adrenal axis in the neonatal period: Adrenocorticotropin and corticosterone stress responses dissociate in vasopressin-deficient Brattleboro rats. *Endocrinology, 149*(5), 2576–2583. doi:10.1210/en.2007-1537

Zhang, J. B., Chen, L., Lv, Z. M., Niu, X. Y., Shao, C. C., Zhang, C., . . . Ding, Y. Q. (2016). Oxytocin is implicated in social memory deficits induced by early sensory deprivation in mice. *Molecular Brain, 9*(1), 98. doi:10.1186/s13041-016-0278-3

Zheng, J. J., Li, S. J., Zhang, X. D., Miao, W. Y., Zhang, D., Yao, H., & Yu, X. (2014). Oxytocin mediates early experience-dependent cross-modal plasticity in the sensory cortices. *Nature Neuroscience, 17*(3), 391–399. doi:10.1038/nn.3634

29

THE SOCIAL NEUROENDOCRINOLOGY AND DEVELOPMENT OF EXECUTIVE FUNCTIONS

Rosemarie E. Perry, Eric D. Finegood, Stephen H. Braren, and Clancy Blair

Introduction

Executive functions (EFs) are a constellation of effortful cognitive control abilities that support planning and goal-directed behaviors that are important for daily life and reflect some level of self-regulation (Blair, 2017; Diamond, 2013). EFs are essential to cognitive, psychological, and even social development (Blair, 2017; Diamond, 2013). Thus, EF skills influence a multitude of life outcomes, including mental and physical health, school readiness and success, job success, and overall quality of life (Diamond, 2013). While EFs are difficult to concisely define, they are commonly taxonomized into three core categories: working memory, inhibition, and cognitive flexibility (Miyake et al., 2000; Shields, Bonner, & Moons, 2015). Working memory refers to holding information in one's mind and working with it mentally. It is essential for performing mental math, understanding language, translating instructions to actions, reasoning, and updating information, among other operations (Diamond, 2013; Hofmann, Schmeichel, & Baddeley, 2012). Inhibition is the ability to volitionally control one's thoughts, emotions, and/or behavioral responses in order to selectively attend to relevant information and produce appropriate goal-directed behaviors while limiting impulsive responses (Diamond, 2013). Some aspects of inhibition include inhibitory control of attention (i.e., selective attention) (Rueda, Posner, & Rothbart, 2005), self-control (i.e., controlling one's behavior) (Hofmann, Friese, & Strack, 2009), and cognitive inhibition (i.e., resisting unwanted thoughts or memories) (Anderson & Green, 2001). Overall, working memory and inhibition support one another, as it is rare that one is needed without the other. The last core EF, cognitive flexibility, is the ability to readily switch between cognitive rules or concepts in order to adapt to changing task challenges (Diamond, 2013). For example, this includes the ability to transition between multiple trains of thought while multitasking. Although working memory, inhibition, and cognitive flexibility are related and typically operate together, factor analyses have provided strong evidence that these core EFs are functionally distinct from one another (Friedman & Miyake, 2017; Miyake et al., 2000). Furthermore, neurobiological studies involving lesioning and neuroimaging have identified distinct neurophysiological bases underlying these three core EFs (Smolker, Depue, Reineberg, Orr, & Banich, 2015; Tsuchida & Fellows, 2013).

While EFs are largely viewed and studied as cognitive processes, they are also integral to social processes, including social interactions and emotionality (Diamond, 2013). For example, poor EFs are associated with socioemotional problems such as reckless behavior, emotional outbursts, violence, and criminal activity (Broidy et al., 2003; Denson, Pederson, Friese, Hahm, & Roberts, 2011). Thus, understanding the ontogeny of EFs, including the effect of social environments on EF acquisition, is important for promoting optimal health and development. From a neurobiological perspective, research studies have focused on the role of the prefrontal cortex (PFC), with EFs being categorized as a family of "top-down" mental processes relying heavily on the involvement of the PFC via top-down regulation of lower-level brain regions and physiological processes (Blair & Ursache, 2011). The PFC is a brain area of protracted development, with development continuing through adolescence, and consequently it is particularly vulnerable to the influence of environmental input in early life (Ganzel, Kim, Gilmore, Tottenham, & Temple, 2013; Tottenham, 2015). Therefore, compromised EFs are a target mechanism by which early life stress and adversity may increase risk of later-life socioemotional and cognitive difficulties (Perry, Blair, & Sullivan, 2017). The present chapter reviews the effects of social contexts, particularly in early life, on the development of neurobiological and hormonal aspects of EFs, drawing evidence from both human and animal research. The current literature regarding the social neuroendocrinology of EFs throughout development is discussed from the perspective of identifying early life indicators of at-risk EF development, as well as developing targeted interventions for at-risk individuals.

The neuroendocrinology of executive functions

In general, research on the neurobiology underlying EF ability has identified the prefrontal cortex (PFC) as the structural and functional locus of EFs and other related higher-order cognitive processes (Fuster, 2008). For example, the PFC guides attention and is critical for working memory, impulse control, and inhibiting distracting thoughts (Arnsten, 2005). Modulation of EF ability is driven by regulation of glucocorticoid (e.g., cortisol) and catecholaminergic (e.g., norepinephrine and dopamine) activity in the PFC (Arnsten, 2009; Blair & Ursache, 2011 Lupien, Maheu, Tu, Fiocco, & Schramek, 2007; McEwen & Morrison, 2013). This is achieved via rich, reciprocal neural connections between the PFC and subcortical brain structures, which are described below.

There is considerable evidence that each core EF is supported to a large extent by subregions of the PFC (Figure 29.1; Yuan & Raz, 2014). In general, neuroimaging research using PET and fMRI has reliably indicated that working memory is predominately associated with activation in the dorsolateral PFC (dLPFC) (Smolker, 2015; Fuster, 2008; Arnsten, 2009; Yuan & Raz, 2014). Evidence from neuroimaging and lesion studies has shown that cognitive flexibility, as assessed through attention-switching tasks such as the Wisconsin Card-Sorting Task (WCST), is associated with the ventrolateral PFC (vLPFC) (Buchsbaum, Greer, Chang, & Berman, 2005; Smolker et al., 2015; Tsuchida & Fellows, 2013). Additionally, research has also implicated the ventromedial PFC (vmPFC), which includes the orbitofrontal cortex (OFC), in inhibitory control (Fuster, 2008; Suchy, 2009).

It is noteworthy that although each component EF may be more strongly associated with one brain region relative to others, EFs are not localized processes carried out only within a given brain area. Rather, the neural systems underlying EFs are highly distributed, relying on bidirectional communication between various cortical and subcortical brain regions, including not only the PFC, but also the basal ganglia, amygdala, hippocampus, and other cortices (e.g., cingulate and parietal cortex) (Fuster, 2008). Together, this allows for modulation of EFs by integrating information from various brain regions to flexibly monitor, organize, and respond to environmental demands (Fuster, 2008; Stuss, 2011). However, because various brain regions

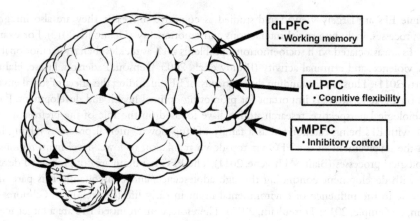

Figure 29.1 Schematic figure of principal subregions of the prefrontal cortex (PFC) that support executive functions. The dorsolateral PFC (dLPFC) has been associated primarily with working memory; the ventrolateral PFC (vLPFC) is predominately involved in cognitive flexibility; and the ventromedial PFC (vMPFC) has been implicated in inhibitory control.

support EFs, there is some theoretical disagreement and empirical inconsistency regarding the specificity of individual subregions of the PFC in their contribution to EFs. As such, a few have argued that at least some measures of EF are not necessarily specific to the PFC but are instead sensitive to frontal lobe function (Alvarez & Emory, 2006).

While it is understood that the neural networks underlying EFs are complex and widely distributed, there is a need for more detailed studies regarding the role of subcortical brain regions in EFs, as studies have primarily focused on the PFC (Diamond, 2013). Nonetheless, the limbic system – especially the amygdala and hippocampus – is intimately connected with the PFC and has been implicated in many aspects of EF, including the regulation and processing of emotions (Monk et al., 2003; Rueda et al., 2005). Furthermore, the basal ganglia, thalamus, and putamen have been implicated in sustained attention (Greene, Braet, Johnson, & Bellgrove, 2008). Other cortical regions have also been implicated in EF ability, with temporal and parietal cortices thought to be involved in inhibitory control and working memory (Collette, Hogge, Salmon, & van der Linden, 2006).

The modulation of EF ability is not solely related to structural neuroanatomy. Neurochemical substrates, in particular glucocorticoids and catecholamines, also substantially modulate PFC activity and EF ability (Arnsten & Li, 2005). Glucocorticoids (cortisol and corticosterone) and catecholamines (epinephrine, norepinephrine, and dopamine) are released in response to stress via two main pathways: the sympathetic nervous system (SNS) and the hypothalamic–pituitary–adrenal axis (HPA) (Ulrich-Lai & Herman, 2009). Broadly, the SNS is the rapid, fight-or-flight system that releases catecholamines, which increase heart rate, respiration, and vasodilation. Conversely, the HPA axis is a slower response system that secretes glucocorticoids, which regulate glucose metabolism. Neuroendocrine control of the SNS and HPA axis by an amygdala–hippocampus–PFC circuit continuously regulates circulating levels of glucocorticoids and catecholamines to facilitate resting-state (i.e., non-stressed) cognition (Ulrich-Lai & Herman, 2009). During conditions of heightened stress, levels of glucocorticoids and catecholamines rise, decreasing PFC activity and increasing amygdala activity (Ulrich-Lai & Herman, 2009). Accordingly, there is a concomitant shift from top-down, PFC-mediated executive control of EF to bottom-up, limbic regulation of EF. This switch moves cognitive resources away from more future-oriented planning tasks to more emotionally relevant stimuli and is intended to optimize an individual's response to immediate environmental challenges (Arnsten, 2009; Shields et al., 2015). However, it should be noted that relation between arousal of the stress response system and EF ability is not linear (see "Stress and the development of executive functions" below). Rather, both low and high levels of stress are associated with decreased EF abilities (Blair & Ursache, 2011).

The continual neuroendocrine regulation of basal glucocorticoid and catecholamine activity maintains optimal levels of arousal that support adaptive and flexible functioning of EFs (Arnsten, 2009; Lupien, Maheu, Tu, Fiocco, & Schramek, 2007). Animal research has demonstrated that PFC cellular activity, and thus PFC-guided behavior, is highly sensitive to small changes in the neurochemical environment (Brozoski, Brown, Rosvold, & Goldman, 1979; Granon et al., 2000), which may be the case in humans, too (Kimberg, D'Esposito, & Farah, 1997). For example, exposure to high levels of stress causes stress-evoked dopamine release in the PFC and is associated with decreased EF ability (Murphy, Arnsten, Jentsch, & Roth, 1996). This is thought to occur at least in part via regulation of dopamine activity by glucocorticoid receptors in the PFC, with increased glucocorticoid receptor binding leading to increased dopamine activity and decreased EF ability (Butts, Weinberg, Young, & Phillips, 2011). Furthermore, somewhat paradoxically, disorders of EF, such as attention-deficit/hyperactivity disorder (ADHD), are associated with decreased catecholamine inputs to the PFC (Nigg, 2006). However, the neuroendocrinology underlying EF ability is still emerging, and further research is needed to understand the potential role of additional hormones and their relation to EFs. Furthermore, as summarized here, much of the work regarding the neuroendocrinology of EFs has come from research involving adult humans and animal models. Thus, there is a need for developmental testing of the role of glucocorticoids, catecholamines, and other hormones and their association to EF ability across the lifespan.

The development of executive functions

The development of EFs does not occur linearly across the lifespan but rather in developmental bursts (Bernstein & Waber, 2007). For example, the development of EFs begins soon after birth and is particularly rapid in early childhood (Zelazo & Muller, 2002). Improvements in cognition such as working memory and attention occur during the first two years of life, allowing for engagement with the environment and providing a foundation for increased learning, social competence, and school readiness (Blair, 2002; Blair, Granger, & Peters Razza, 2005). Furthermore, it is during young adulthood, following completed myelination and synaptic pruning in the PFC, that EF skills peak (Casey, Giedd, & Thomas, 2000; Huttenlocher, 2002). The nonlinearity of EF development likely reflects differences in the brain circuitry that underlie different aspects of EF across development, including the functional emergence of brain regions and network reorganization. However, there is a need for more detailed studies exploring the association between developmental changes in EF and age-related changes in brain function (Müller & Kerns, 2015).

While neurobiological models of adult EFs thus far have been primarily modular and focused on the PFC (Stuss, 2011), there is increasing evidence that children have less neural specificity in their neural representation of EFs, with greater functional specialization occurring over time (Morton, 2010). Thus, to understand the developmental neurobiology of EFs, it is critical to consider the brain's changing organization across time (Anderson, 2001; Morton, 2010). Indeed, as mentioned above, there is mounting evidence that neurobiological operations supporting EFs are not localized in the PFC but rather are widely distributed over a network of regions (e.g., PFC, ACC, parietal cortices, basal ganglia, thalamus), with network organization changing drastically across development (Morton, 2010). In fact, fMRI studies have identified the presence of EF networks (e.g., PFC, ACC) as early as in preterm infants (Doria et al., 2010).

Furthermore, a landmark study by Jacobs and colleagues (2011) exploring EF ability in children with evidence of frontal lobe vs. extra-frontal lobe pathology found that contrary to adult lesion studies, there was little differentiation in EF skills between frontal and extra-frontal lesioned groups, providing evidence that the integrity of the whole brain is needed for adequate EFs in children (Jacobs, Harvey, & Anderson, 2011).

Increased specialization of EFs across development seems to occur not only on the neuro-biological level, but also a dimensional level. Specifically, factor analyses support a unitary EF factor structure in young children (Willoughby, Blair, Wirth, & Greenberg, 2012; Willoughby, Wirth, Blair, & Family Life Project, 2012), opposed to the three-factor EF factor structure consisting of working memory, inhibition, and cognitive flexibility commonly found in adults (Miyake et al., 2000; Shields et al., 2015). Taken together, these neurobiological and statistical findings support a "differentiation hypothesis" as it relates to the functional organization of EFs, such that development progresses from an undifferentiated state to an increasingly differentiated state, reflecting increased functional specialization of neural systems (Garrett, 1946; Johnson & Munakata, 2005). The factors that promote functional specialization as it relates to EFs, while not fully understood, are thought to result largely from the environmental/social contexts in which development is occurring (Johnson & Munakata, 2005). Indeed, the combined effect of the massive overproduction of synapses and a prolonged period of subsequent pruning in the PFC allows for optimal development of brain circuitry in a way that is adaptive to an individual's environment. Therefore, early experiences allow for multiple trajectories by which the brain circuitry underlying EF can be sculpted across development (Petanjek & Kostovic, 2012).

Social contexts and the development of EFs

Due to the protracted development of the neural systems supporting EFs, the development of EFs is vulnerable to the influences of environmental and experiential input (Ganzel et al., 2013; Tottenham, 2015). That is, EF ability is the product of integrated developmental processes at both the biological and behavioral levels that are shaped by the contexts in which development is occurring. More specifically, environmental conditions and interpersonal interactions are bio-logically embedded to ultimately shape the development of brain and behavior, including EFs (Blair & Raver, 2012). Environmental stress is particularly influential on the developing brain and EFs (see "Poverty and executive function" section below). This is especially true for young children, who depend on social support (primarily from their caregivers), for the regulation of stress. When environments become too stressful or complex and the child is unregulated, EFs shut down (Ursache, Blair, Stifter, Voegtline, & Family Life Project, 2013). Conversely, if environments are not sufficiently stimulating or become uninteresting, it becomes more likely that EFs are not called upon. Thus, the development of EFs is largely dictated by the appropriate scaffolding of a child's environment, particularly in regards to stress regulation and cognitive stimulation (Blair & Raver, 2015; Lipina et al., 2013).

Scaffolding in early life occurs primarily via interactions with adult caregivers, meaning that social contexts greatly influence the development of EFs, for better or worse (Perry et al., 2017). In early life, directive parenting (e.g., providing developmentally sensitive support in a problem-solving situation) guides the development of self-regulation and EFs (Bernier, Carlson, & Whipple, 2010; Nelson et al., 2007). Conversely, low quality care from primary caregivers is associated with decreased regulation of cortisol and catecholamines important for optimal EF development (Blair et al., 2008, 2011; Evans, Kim, Ting, Tesher, & Shannis, 2007; Watamura, Donzella, Alwin, & Gunnar, 2003). Further, longitudinal studies have identified more global family variables, such as household chaos, as also being predictive of EF (Bernier, Carlson, Deschenes, &

Matte-Gagne, 2012). While the role of social context, in particular parenting quality, on the development of EF has been strongly established, further research is needed to identify what aspects of parental scaffolding are most effective, as well as the role of parenting and/or siblings and peers in EF development in older children.

Stress and the development of executive functions

As discussed previously, rich neural connections between the PFC and subcortical brain structures enable glucocorticoids and catecholamines to modulate activity in the PFC and, as a result, EF ability (Arnsten, 2009; Lupien et al., 2007; McEwen & Morrison, 2013). Importantly, however, the relation between arousal of the stress response system and EF ability is not linear. Instead, it resembles an inverted U-shaped curve in which both low levels of physiological arousal (e.g., when fatigued) and high levels of arousal (e.g., during a high intensity stressor) are associated with diminished EF (Blair & Ursache, 2011). Conversely, moderate levels of arousal are associated with peak EF ability (Yuen et al., 2009). As glucocorticoids and catecholamines rise to moderate levels, they stimulate neural activation in areas of the PFC that underlie EFs, leading to optimal EF performance. In conditions of high stress, PFC activity is reduced while activation of brain areas important for emotional-motivational responses (e.g., amygdala) is increased (Ramos & Arnsten, 2007). For example, non-human animal research has shown that high levels of norepinephrine and dopamine in the context of high stress inhibit neuronal firing in areas of the PFC that are responsible for working memory (for review see Arnsten, 2009). The dynamic regulation of this activity is a critical aspect of optimal EF that allows for flexible adaptation to a range of environmental demands. The effects of glucocorticoid and adrenergic input on PFC functioning are particularly pronounced in the context of chronic as opposed to acute stress. For instance, research with non-human animals indicates that chronic stress causes wide-ranging structural remodeling of the PFC, including reduction in dendritic arborization of pyramidal cells in the PFC responsible for EFs (e.g., Arnsten, 2009; Liston et al., 2006; McEwen & Morrison, 2013). In humans, chronic stress exposure has also been suggested to affect the development of the PFC and concomitantly undermine EFs over time (Blair & Raver, 2012; Blair & Ursache, 2011). These developmental effects are especially pronounced in the context of poverty.

Poverty and executive function

Children in poverty are at risk of exposure to a number of poverty-related stressors, including but not limited to material deprivation, marital conflict and violence exposure, single parenthood, neighborhood disadvantage, toxin/pollution exposure, and household crowding and chaos (Evans, 2004). Consistent with the high likelihood of chronic stress exposure in these contexts, children from low income families exhibit worse EF than children from higher income families on average (e.g., Hackman, Gallop, Evans, & Farah, 2015; Noble, McCandliss, & Farah, 2007). Furthermore, cumulative poverty-related risk exposure (i.e., exposure to multitude psychosocial and physical environmental risks in these contexts) has been shown to mediate the association between poverty and early self-regulation in children (Evans & English, 2002).

Longitudinal models suggest that these relations are present early and can persist across development. In one study, for instance, Raver and colleagues (2013) found that each successive year that a child lived below the poverty line was associated with a tenth of a standard deviation (SD) reduction in EF. Consequently, by age 4, children who had spent all four years of their lives below the poverty line were estimated to score .40 of a SD lower on measures of EF compared to children who had never lived in poverty. Similarly, Evans and Schamberg (2009) showed that the proportion of childhood spent below the poverty line was negatively associated with working memory performance in adulthood. Thus, the relation between chronic financial stress of families and EF ability starts early and can persist into adulthood.

One way to explain this relation is via a stress pathway in which early life exposure to stress in the context of poverty gets "under the skin" and affects regulation of neurophysiological processes involved in the early emergence and organization of higher-order mental processes such as EF (Blair & Raver, 2012). Poverty has been associated, for instance, with individual differences in HPA axis and autonomic nervous system activity (e.g., Blair et al., 2011; Evans & English, 2002). Specifically, children in poverty evidence heightened basal levels of cortisol and norepinephrine (Chen, Cohen, & Miller, 2010; Evans & English, 2002) – physiological adaptations that are thought to be advantageous in environments characterized by chronic threat or danger (Del Giudice, Ellis, & Shirtcliff, 2011). Despite the benefits that heightened physiological activity may confer in the short term, such adaptations may come at a cost over time. Chronic over-exposure to glucocorticoids and catecholamines can be injurious to the brain and body – particularly with respect to effects on metabolic and immune processes that can have wide-ranging negative effects on physical health outcomes and neurocognitive development (McEwen, 2000; Miller & Chen, 2013). Cortisol levels, for instance, statistically mediate the association between exposure to poverty-related stress and EF ability by three years of age (Blair et al., 2011). Such relations may be present even earlier in life, given research conducted in the same sample as Blair and colleagues' (2011) suggesting that by 15 months of child age heightened cortisol levels are associated with reductions in cognitive development (Figure 29.2; Finegood et al., 2017).

Blair et al. (2011) also found evidence that the quality of children's relationships with their caregivers statistically mediates the association between poverty-related adversity exposure and both EF ability and cortisol. Specifically, higher levels of poverty were associated with lower levels of sensitive caregiving, and lower sensitive caregiving was associated with higher resting cortisol levels and lower EF ability at three years of age. These findings are consistent with neurobiological findings demonstrating the sensitivity of PFC functioning to the physiological response to stress, which is at risk of occurring at chronic levels in impoverished environments (Cerqueira, Mailliet, Almeida, Jay, & Sousa, 2007; Liston, McEwen, & Casey, 2009).

In sum, findings from developmental and neuroscience research indicate that EFs and their neuroendocrine substrates are highly susceptible to environmental input, especially early in life. Although contexts of chronic stress, such as poverty, can have substantial detrimental influence on the development of EFs, stress physiology, and the brain, there is also opportunity for intervention. That is, on the other hand, the capacity for flexible adaptation also means that an individual may be responsive to positive changes that can ameliorate some of the negative consequences of chronic stress and poverty.

Interventions for executive functions

Given the flexible functioning of EFs and the plasticity of their underlying neuroanatomy, studies have been conducted to determine whether EFs can be improved via various interventions (Blair, 2017). Overall, results of these studies have provided empirical findings that EFs tend to improve with practice. Successful interventions, as assessed by randomized controlled trials, include computerized videogame-like training, exercise, mindfulness meditation, and supplemented school curricula via the Promoting Alternative Thinking Strategies (PATHS) program or the Chicago School Readiness Project (CSRP) (Diamond, 2013; Raver et al., 2011; Riggs, Greenberg, Kusché, & Pentz, 2006). However, findings regarding the generalizability of EF intervention effects to various "real-world" scenarios are mixed, especially for

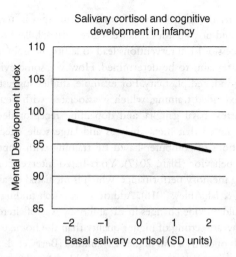

Salivary cortisol and cognitive
development in infancy

Figure 29.2   Basal salivary cortisol levels are inversely associated with cognitive development at 15 months of child age after adjusting for psychosocial and obstetric risk (n = 1,091). A one standard deviation (SD) unit increase in salivary cortisol levels is associated with a 0.11 SD unit decrease in cognitive development as measured by the Mental Development Index of the Bayley Scales of Infant Development (BSID-II). Further discussion of these results can be found in Finegood et al., 2017, Stress, 20(1), 112–121.

videogame-like/computer-based training interventions (Blair, 2017). Regardless, there are some specific elements of an intervention that reliably predict its success. Successful interventions rely on repeated practice, as well as incrementally increasing the difficulty of training to allow for gradual improvements (Diamond, 2013). An intervention's efficacy also increases as a function of how developmentally lagging an individual's EF abilities are at the start of the intervention, with the greatest gains occurring for individuals who are the most behind in terms of baseline EF abilities (Flook et al., 2010). This has huge implications regarding increasing the achievement and health of children who face social disparities as a result of being raised in disadvantaged or stressful environments. However, further research is needed to understand what dose and frequency of EF interventions lead to optimal results, as well as what factors influence the longevity of an intervention's benefits. Beyond that, there remains a great need for specific studies aimed at creating and testing age-appropriate, tailored interventions.

It has been speculated that the effects of EF interventions would be more widespread if implemented in early life. Indeed, early life interventions are of utmost importance, since EFs early in life predict lifelong achievement, health, wealth, and quality of life. Daycare programs that promote working memory, inhibition, and regulatory self-directed speech have been shown to have a positive effect on children's EF, suggesting that childcare-based interventions could provide improved results (Diamond, Barnett, Thomas, & Munro, 2007). Furthermore, parenting quality seems to be a protective factor to EF development, as it was found that sensitive parenting buffered against the impact of neurological risk (i.e., infant's corpus callosum length) on inhibition problems in preschoolers (Kok et al., 2013). Beyond parenting, other social components appear to be key aspects to successfully training EF in early life. For example, educational programs such as Tools of the Mind and Montessori promote EF development by providing opportunities for self-directed learning, but also by promoting collaboration between children. This involves structured play that encourages reflection, as well as taking on the perspective of a partner child during play. Both Tools of the Mind and Montessori have been assessed via randomized controlled trials which showed favorable outcomes in terms of EF development, academic achievement, and play abilities (Blair & Raver, 2014; Lillard & Else-Quest, 2006).

Whether or not successful EF interventions lead to lasting neurobiological and/or neuroen-docrinological changes remains to be determined. However, some evidence suggests that this may occur via training-induced plasticity. For example, studies suggest that working memory can be improved via extended training, which is associated with neurobiological changes in frontal and parietal cortex, basal ganglia, and dopamine receptor density (Klingberg, 2010). However, it should be noted that meta-analyses and large scale effectiveness trials primarily do not support associations of computer-based EF training with improvements in real world skills, such as math or behavior (Blair, 2017). Yoga-based interventions have been associated with improved working memory performance, which is mediated by an attenuated response to stress (Gothe, Keswani, & McAuley, 2016). Additional research findings suggest that caregiver-based interventions could provide changes in EF ability by way of altered HPA axis activity. For example, attending a daycare setting of higher quality than the home environment is associated with lower resting levels of cortisol and higher EF abilities (Berry et al., 2014). However, further research is needed to dissect what specific aspects of child care and parenting should be manipulated to optimize EF development. Furthermore, longitudinal data are needed to determine if early life EF interventions provide long-term benefits.

Altogether, intervention efforts to date support that EF training can favor EF development and improvement, at any age, perhaps via training-induced plasticity within the neurobiological and neuroendocrinological systems supporting EF ability. While there are a variety of promising intervention approaches, it seems that involving a social component to EF training, especially in early life, may particularly benefit the development of EFs.

Conclusion

Although it is challenging to describe EFs using a unitary definition, the cognitive processes underlying EFs are arguably the most important factors for successfully adapting to the demands of daily life. EFs such as working memory, inhibition, and cognitive flexibility are vital to many skills important for success, including reasoning, problem-solving, planning, and the general management of one's life.

Here we've provided an overview of neuroendocrinological and developmental factors that contribute to EF abilities (Figure 29.3). Although the PFC is considered the locus of EFs, the brain networks' underlying EF abilities are increasingly understood to be widely distributed and interconnected throughout the brain. Furthermore, while these networks are still poorly understood across development, they are thought to undergo massive reorganization with maturation, ultimately increasing in functional specialization. Such protracted development makes the developing circuitry underlying EFs amenable to experiential input. Thus, a variety of developmental trajectories and subsequent EF outcomes can occur as a function of life experiences, with the quality of a child's social environment significantly impacting the development of EFs. Early life experiences, especially caregiver-mediated scaffolding of a child's social interactions and cognitive stimulation, are powerful influences in the development of EF abilities, for better or worse. Indeed, exposure to stress in early life, if unregulated by caregivers, is detrimental to the development of EFs. On a neurobiological level, while moderate levels of stress lead to optimal EF performance, chronic stress exposure, such as oftentimes occurs in conditions of poverty, gets "under the skin" to disrupt regulation of neurophysiological processes involved in higher-order cognition such as EF. However, interventions aimed at improving EFs show great promise across ages, providing hope for individuals who need it the most, such as those facing the effects

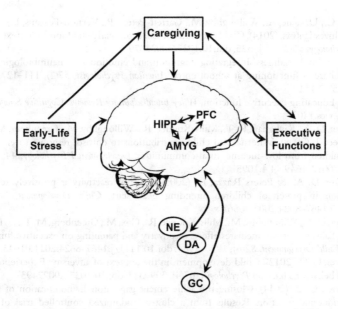

Figure 29.3   Proposed theoretical model of developmental relations between social factors, neuroendocrinology, and executive functions. Executive functions (EF) are guided by rich reciprocal connections between brain structures, namely the prefrontal cortex (PFC), hippocampus (HIPP), and amygdala (AMYG), which provide the neural regulation of hormones and neurotransmitters, such as norepinephrine (NE), dopamine (DA), and glucocorticoids (GC). Input from the social environment, such as early life stress and caregiving quality, can shape neurophysiological development, which, in turn, can influence EF.

of chronic stress exposure or low quality caregiving. While effective EF training can occur in many different forms, early life interventions targeting the improvement of social interactions with caregivers and peers may provide the most widespread benefits and should be the focus of continued research.

References

Alvarez, J. A., & Emory, E. (2006). Executive function and the frontal lobes: A meta-analytic review. *Neuropsychology Review, 16*(1), 17–42. doi:10.1007/s11065-006-9002-x

Anderson, M. C., & Green, C. (2001). Suppressing unwanted memories by executive control. *Nature, 410*(6826), 366–369. doi:10.1038/35066572

Anderson, V. (2001). Assessing executive functions in children: Biological, psychological, and developmental considerations. *Pediatric Rehabilitation, 4*(3), 119–136. doi:10.1080/713755568

Arnsten, A. F. (2009). Stress signaling pathways that impair prefrontal cortex structure and function. *Nature Reviews Neuroscience, 10*(6), 410–422. doi:10.1038/nrn2648

Arnsten, A. F., & Li, B. M. (2005). Neurobiology of executive functions: Catecholamine influences on prefrontal cortical functions. *Biological Psychiatry, 57*(11), 1377–1384. doi:10.1016/j.biopsych.2004.08.019

Bernier, A., Carlson, S. M., Deschenes, M., & Matte-Gagne, C. (2012). Social factors in the development of early executive functioning: A closer look at the caregiving environment. *Developmental Science, 15*(1), 12–24. doi:10.1111/j.1467-7687.2011.01093.x

Bernier, A., Carlson, S. M., & Whipple, N. (2010). From external regulation to self-regulation: Early parenting precursors of young children's executive functioning. *Child Development, 81*(1), 326–339. doi:10.1111/j.1467-8624.2009.01397.x

Bernstein, J. H., & Waber, D. P. (2007). Executive capacities from a developmental perspective. In *Executive function in education: From theory of practice* (pp. 39–54). New York, NY: Guilford Press.

Berry, D., Blair, C., Ursache, A., Willoughby, M., Garrett-Peters, P., Vernon-Feagans, L., . . . Family Life Project Key Investigators. (2014). Child care and cortisol across early childhood: Context matters. *Developmental Psychology, 50*(2), 514–525. doi:10.1037/a0033379

Blair, C. (2002). School readiness: Integrating cognition and emotion in a neurobiological conceptualization of children's functioning at school entry. *American Psychologist, 57*(2), 111–127. doi:10.1037/0003-066X.57.2.111

Blair, C. (2017). Educating executive function. *Wiley Interdisciplinary Reviews: Cognitive Science, 8*(1–2), 1–6. doi:10.1002/wcs.1403

Blair, C., Granger, D. A., Kivlighan, K. T., Mills-Koonce, R., Willoughby, M., Greenberg, M. T., . . . Family Life Project, I. (2008). Maternal and child contributions to cortisol response to emotional arousal in young children from low-income, rural communities. *Developmental Psychology, 44*(4), 1095–1109. doi:10.1037/0012-1649.44.4.1095

Blair, C., Granger, D. A., & Peters Razza, R. (2005). Cortisol reactivity is positively related to executive function in preschool children attending head start. *Child Development, 76*(3), 554–567. doi:10.1111/j.1467-8624.2005.00863.x

Blair, C., Granger, D. A., Willoughby, M., Mills-Koonce, R., Cox, M., Greenberg, M. T., . . . Investigators, F. L. P. (2011). Salivary cortisol mediates effects of poverty and parenting on executive functions in early childhood. *Child Development, 82*(6), 1970–1984. doi:10.1111/j.1467-8624.2011.01643.x

Blair, C., & Raver, C. C. (2012). Child development in the context of adversity: Experiential canalization of brain and behavior. *American Psychologist, 67*(4), 309–318. doi:10.1037/a0027493

Blair, C., & Raver, C. C. (2014). Closing the achievement gap through modification of neurocognitive and neuroendocrine function: Results from a cluster randomized controlled trial of an innovative approach to the education of children in Kindergarten. *PLoS One, 9*(11), e112393. doi:10.1371/journal.pone.0112393

Blair, C., & Raver, C. C. (2015). School readiness and self-regulation: A developmental psychobiological approach. *Annual Review of Psychology, 66*, 711–731. doi:10.1146/annurev-psych-010814-015221

Blair, C., & Ursache, A. (2011). A bidirectional model of executive functions and self-regulation. In *Handbook of self-regulation: Research, theory, and applications* (pp. 300–320). New York, NY: Guilford Press.

Broidy, L. M., Nagin, D. S., Tremblay, R. E., Brame, B., Dodge, K. A., & Fergusson, D. E. (2003). Developmental trajectories of childhood disruptive behaviors and adolescent delinquency: A six-site cross-national study. *Developmental Psychology, 39*(2), 222–245. Retrieved from www.ncbi.nlm.nih.gov/pmc/articles/PMC2753823/

Brozoski, T. J., Brown, R. M., Rosvold, H. E., & Goldman, P. S. (1979). Cognitive deficit caused by regional depletion of dopamine in prefrontal cortex of rhesus monkey. *Science, 205*(4409), 929–932. Retrieved from http://science.sciencemag.org/content/205/4409/929.long

Buchsbaum, B. R., Greer, S., Chang, W. L., & Berman, K. F. (2005). Meta-analysis of neuroimaging studies of the Wisconsin card-sorting task and component processes. *Human Brain Mapping, 25*(1), 35–45. doi:10.1002/hbm.20128

Butts, K. A., Weinberg, J., Young, A. H., & Phillips, A. G. (2011). Glucocorticoid receptors in the prefrontal cortex regulate stress-evoked dopamine efflux and aspects of executive function. *Proceedings of the National Academy of Sciences of the United States of America, 108*(45), 18459–18464. doi:10.1073/pnas.1111746108

Casey, B. J., Giedd, J. N., & Thomas, K. M. (2000). Structural and functional brain development and its relation to cognitive development. *Biological Psychiatry, 54*(1–3), 241–257. Retrieved from www.sciencedirect.com/science/article/pii/S0301051100000582?via%3Dihub

Cerqueira, J. J., Mailliet, F., Almeida, O. F., Jay, T. M., & Sousa, N. (2007). The prefrontal cortex as a key target of the maladaptive response to stress. *Journal of Neuroscience, 27*(11), 2781–2787. doi:10.1523/JNEUROSCI.4372–06.2007

Chen, E., Cohen, S., & Miller, G. E. (2010). How low socioeconomic status affects 2-year hormonal trajectories in children. *Psychological Science, 21*(1), 31–37. doi:10.1177/0956797609355566

Collette, F., Hogge, M., Salmon, E., & van der Linden, M. (2006). Exploration of the neural substrates of executive functioning by functional neuroimaging. *Neuroscience, 139*(1), 209–221. doi:10.1016/j.neuroscience.2005.05.035

Del Giudice, M., Ellis, B. J., & Shirtcliff, E. A. (2011). The adaptive calibration model of stress responsivity. *Neuroscience Biobehavioral Reviews, 35*(7), 1562–1592. doi:10.1016/j.neubiorev.2010.11.007

Denson, T. F., Pederson, W. C., Friese, M., Hahm, A., & Roberts, L. (2011). Understanding impulsive aggression: Angry rumination and reduced self-control capacity are mechanisms underlying the provocation-aggression relationship. *Personality and Social Psychology Bulletin, 37*(6), 850–862. doi:10.1177/0146167211401420

Diamond, A. (2013). Executive functions. *Annual Review of Psychology, 64*, 135–168. doi:10.1146/annurev-psych-113011-143750

Diamond, A., Barnett, W. S., Thomas, J., & Munro, S. (2007). Preschool program improves cognitive control. *Science, 318*(5855), 1387–1388. doi:10.1126/science.1151148

Doria, V., Beckmann, C. F., Arichi, T., Merchant, N., Groppo, M., Turkheimer, F. E., . . . Edwards, A. D. (2010). Emergence of resting state networks in the preterm human brain. *Proceedings of the National Academy of Sciences of the United States of America, 107*(46), 20015–20020. doi:10.1073/pnas.1007921107

Evans, G. W. (2004). The environment of childhood poverty. *American Psychologist, 59*(2), 77–92. doi:10.1037/0003-066X.59.2.77

Evans, G. W., & English, K. (2002). The environment of poverty: Multiple stressor exposure, psychophysiological stress, and socioemotional adjustment. *Child Development, 73*(4), 1238–1248.

Evans, G. W., Kim, P., Ting, A. H., Tesher, H. B., & Shannis, D. (2007). Cumulative risk, maternal responsiveness, and allostatic load among young adolescents. *Developmental Psychology, 43*(2), 341–351. doi:10.1037/0012-1649.43.2.341

Evans, G. W., & Schamberg, M. A. (2009). Childhood poverty, chronic stress, and adult working memory. *Proceedings of the National Academy of Sciences of the United States of America, 106*(16), 6545–6549. doi:10.1111/1467-8624.00469

Finegood, E. D., Wyman, C., O'Connor, T. G., Blair, C. B., & The Family Life Project Investigators. (2017). Salivary cortisol and cognitive development in infants from low-income communities. *Stress, 20*(1), 112–121. doi:10.1080/10253890.2017.1286325

Flook, L., Smalley, S. L., Kitil, M. J., Galla, B. M., Kaiser-Greenland, S., Locke, J., . . . Kasari, C. (2010). Effects of mindful awareness practices on executive functions in elementary school children. *Journal of Applied School Psychology, 26*, 70–95. doi:10.1080/15377900903379125

Friedman, N. P., & Miyake, A. (2017). Unity and diversity of executive functions: Individual differences as a window on cognitive structure. *Cortex, 86*, 186–204. doi:10.1016/j.cortex.2016.04.023

Fuster, J. (2008). *The prefrontal cortex.* San Diego, CA: Academic Press.

Ganzel, B. L., Kim, P., Gilmore, H., Tottenham, N., & Temple, E. (2013). Stress and the healthy adolescent brain: Evidence for the neural embedding of life events. *Development and Psychopathology, 25*(4), 879–889. doi:10.1017/S0954579413000242

Garrett, H. E. (1946). A developmental theory of intelligence. *American Psychologist, 1*(9), 372–378. Retrieved from http://psycnet.apa.org/record/1947-01421-001

Gothe, N. P., Keswani, R. K., & McAuley, E. (2016). Yoga practice improves executive function by attenuating stress levels. *Biological Psychology, 121*(Pt A), 109–116. doi:10.1016/j.biopsycho.2016.10.010

Granon, S., Passetti, F., Thomas, K. L., Dalley, J. W., Everitt, B. J., & Robbins, T. W. (2000). Enhanced and impaired attentional performance after infusion of D1 dopaminergic receptor agents into rat prefrontal cortex. *Journal of Neuroscience, 20*(3), 1208–1215. Retrieved from www.jneurosci.org/cotent/20/3/1208.long

Greene, C. M., Braet, W., Johnson, K. A., & Bellgrove, M. A. (2008). Imaging the genetics of executive function. *Biological Psychiatry, 79*(1), 30–42. doi:10.1016/j.biopsycho.2007.11.009

Hackman, D. A., Gallop, R., Evans, G. W., & Farah, M. J. (2015). Socioeconomic status and executive function: Developmental trajectories and mediation. *Developmental Science, 18*(5), 686–702. doi:10.1111/desc.12246

Hofmann, W., Friese, M., & Strack, F. (2009). Impulse and self-control from a dual-systems perspective. *Perspectives on Psychological Science, 4*(2), 162–176.

Hofmann, W., Schmeichel, B. J., & Baddeley, A. D. (2012). Executive functions and self-regulation. *Trends in Cognitive Science, 16*(3), 174–180. doi:10.1016/j.tics.2012.01.006

Huttenlocher, P. R. (2002). *Neural plasticity: The effects of environment on the development of the cerebral cortex.* Cambridge, MA: Harvard University Press.

Jacobs, R., Harvey, A. S., & Anderson, V. (2011). Are executive skills primarily mediated by the prefrontal cortex in childhood? Examination of focal brain lesions in childhood. *Cortex, 47*(7), 808–824. doi:10.1016/j.cortex.2010.06.002

Johnson, M. H., & Munakata, Y. (2005). Processes of change in brain and cognitive development. *Trends in Cognitive Science, 9*(3), 152–158. 10.1016/j.tics.2005.01.009

Kimberg, D. Y., D'Esposito, M., & Farah, M. J. (1997). Effects of bromocriptine on human subjects depend on working memory capacity. *Neuroreport, 8*(16), 3581–3585. Retrieved from https://insights.ovid.com/pubmed?pmid=9427330

Klingberg, T. (2010). Training and plasticity of working memory. *Trends in Cognitive Science*, *14*(7), 317–324. doi:10.1016/j.tics.2010.05.002

Kok, R., Lucassen, N., Bakermans-Kranenburg, M. J., van Ijzendoorn, M. H., Ghassabian, A., Roza, S. J., . . . Tiemeier, H. (2013). Parenting, corpus callosum, and executive function in preschool children. *Child Neuropsychology*, *20*(5), 583–606. doi:10.1080/09297049.2013.832741

Lillard, A., & Else-Quest, N. (2006). The early years: Evaluating Montessori education. *Science*, *313*(5795), 1893–1894. Retrieved from http://science.sciencemag.org/content/313/5795/1893.long

Lipina, S., Segretin, S., Hermida, J., Prats, L., Fracchia, C., Camelo, J. L., & Colombo, J. (2013). Linking childhood poverty and cognition: Environmental mediators of non-verbal executive control in an Argentine sample. *Developmental Science*, *16*(5), 697–707. doi:10.1111/desc.12080

Liston, C., McEwen, B. S., & Casey, B. J. (2009). Psychosocial stress reversibly disrupts prefrontal processing and attentional control. *Proceedings of the National Academy of Sciences of the United States of America*, *106*(3), 912–917. doi:10.1073/pnas.0807041106

Liston, C., Miller, M. M., Goldwater, D. S., Radley, J. J., Rocher, A. B., Hof, P. R., . . . McEwen, B. S. (2006). Stress-induced alterations in prefrontal cortical dendritic morphology predict selective impairments in perceptual attentional set-shifting. *The Journal of Neuroscience*, *26*(30), 7870–7874. doi:10.1523/JNEUROSCI.1184-06.2006

Lupien, S. J., Maheu, F., Tu, M., Fiocco, A., & Schramek, T. E. (2007). The effects of stress and stress hormones on human cognition: Implications for the field of brain and cognition. *Brain and Cognition*, *65*(3), 209–237. doi:10.1016/j.bandc.2007.02.007

McEwen, B. S. (2000). Allostasis and allostatic load: Implications for neuropsychopharmacology. *Neuropsychopharmacology*, *22*(2), 108–124. doi:10.1016/S0893-133X(99)00129-3

McEwen, B. S., & Morrison, J. H. (2013). The brain on stress: Vulnerability and plasticity of the prefrontal cortex over the lifecourse. *Neuron*, *79*(1), 16–29. doi:10.1016/j.neuron.2013.06.028

Miller, G. E., & Chen, E. (2013). The biological residue of childhood poverty. *Child Development Perspectives*, *7*(2), 67–73. doi:10.1111/cdep.12021

Miyake, A., Friedman, N. P., Emerson, M. J., Witzki, A. H., Howerter, A., & Wager, T. D. (2000). The unity and diversity of executive functions and their contributions to complex "Frontal Lobe" tasks: A latent variable analysis. *Cognitive Psychology*, *41*(1), 49–100. doi:10.1006/cogp.1999.0734

Monk, C. S., McClure, E. B., Nelson, E. E., Zarahn, E., Bilder, R. M., Leibenluft, E., . . . Pine, D. S. (2003). Adolescent immaturity in attention-related brain engagement to emotional facial expressions. *Neuroimage*, *20*(1), 420–428. doi:10.1016/S1053-8119(03)00355-0

Morton, J. B. (2010). Understanding genetic, neurophysiological, and experiential influences on the development of executive functioning: The need for developmental models. *Wiley Interdisciplinary Reviews: Cognitive Science*, *1*(5), 709–723. doi:10.1002/wcs.87

Müller, U., & Kerns, K. (2015). The development of executive function. In L. S. Liben, U. Müller, & R. M. Lerner (Eds.), *Handbook of child psychology and developmental science: Cognitive processes* (pp. 571–623). Hoboken, NJ: John Wiley & Sons Inc.

Murphy, B. L., Arnsten, A. F., Jentsch, J. D., & Roth, R. H. (1996). Dopamine and spatial working memory in rats and monkeys: Pharmacological reversal of stress-induced impairment. *Journal of Neuroscience*, *16*(23), 7768–7775. Retrieved from www.jneurosci.org/content/16/23/7768.long

Nigg, J. T. (2006). *What causes ADHD? Understanding what goes wrong and why*. New York, NY: Guilford Press.

Nelson, C. A., III, Zeanah, C. H., Fox, N. A., Marshall, P. J., Smyke, A. T., & Guthrie, D. (2007). Cognitive recovery in socially deprived young children: The Bucharest Early Intervention Project. *Science*, *318*(5858), 1937–1940. doi:10.1126/science.1143921

Noble, K. G., McCandliss, B. D., & Farah, M. J. (2007). Socioeconomic gradients predict individual differences in neurocognitive abilities. *Developmental Science*, *10*(4), 464–480. doi:10.1111/j.1467-7687.2007.00600.x

Perry, R. E., Blair, C., & Sullivan, R. M. (2017). Neurobiology of infant attachment: Attachment despite adversity and parental programming of emotionality. *Current Opinion in Psychology*, *12*(7), 673–680. doi:10.1016/j.copsyc.2017.04.022

Petanjek, Z., & Kostovic, I. (2012). Epigenetic regulation of fetal brain development and neurocognitive outcome. *Proceedings of the National Academy of Sciences of the United States of America*, *109*(28), 11062–11063. doi:10.1073/pnas.1208085109

Ramos, B. P., & Arnsten, A. F. (2007). Adrenergic pharmacology and cognition: Focus on the prefrontal cortex. *Pharmacology & Therapeutics*, *113*(3), 523–536. doi:10.1016/j.pharmthera.2006.11.006

Raver, C. C., Blair, C., Willoughby, M., & The Family Life Project Key Investigators. (2013). Poverty as a predictor of 4-year-olds' executive function: New perspectives on models of differential susceptibility. *Developmental Psychology, 49*(2), 292–304. doi:10.1037/a0028343

Raver, C. C., Jones, S. M., Li-Grining, C., Zhai, F., Bub, K., & Pressler, E. (2011). CSRP's impact on low-income preschoolers' preacademic skills: Self-regulation as a mediating mechanism. *Child Development, 82*(1), 362–378. doi:10.1111/j.1467-8624.2010.01561.x

Riggs, N. R., Greenberg, M. T., Kusché, C. A., & Pentz, M. A. (2006). The meditational role of neurocognition in the behavioral outcomes of a social-emotional prevention program in elementary school students: Effects of the PATHS curriculum. *Prevention Science, 7*(1), 91–102. doi:10.1007/s11121-005-0022-1

Rueda, M. R., Posner, M. I., & Rothbart, M. K. (2005). The development of executive attention: Contributions to the emergence of self-regulation. *Developmental Neuropsychology, 28*(2), 573–594. doi:10.1207/s15326942dn2802_2

Shields, G. S., Bonner, J. C., & Moons, W. G. (2015). Does cortisol influence core executive functions? A meta-analysis of acute cortisol administration effects on working memory, inhibition, and set-shifting. *Psychoneuroendocrinology, 58*, 91–103. doi:10.1016/j.psyneuen.2015.04.017

Smolker, H. R., Depue, B. E., Reineberg, A. E., Orr, J. M., & Banich, M. T. (2015). Individual differences in regional prefrontal gray matter morphometry and fractional anisotropy are associated with different constructs of executive function. *Brain Structure and Function, 220*(3), 1291–1306. doi:10.1007/s00429-014-0723-y

Stuss, D. T. (2011). Functions of the frontal lobes: Relation to executive functions. *Journal of the International Neuropsychological Society, 17*(5), 759–765. doi:10.1017/S1355617711000695

Suchy, Y. (2009). Executive functioning: Overview, assessment, and research issues for non-neuropsychologists. *Annals of Behavioral Medicine, 37*(2), 106–116. doi:10.1007/s12160-009-9097-4

Tottenham, N. (2015). Social scaffolding of human amygdala-mPFC circuit development. *Social Neuroscience, 10*(5), 489–499. doi:10.1080/17470919.2015.1087424

Tsuchida, A., & Fellows, L. K. (2013). Are core component processes of executive function dissociable within the frontal lobes? Evidence from humans with focal prefrontal damage. *Cortex, 49*(7), 1790–1800. doi:10.1016/j.cortex.2012.10.014

Ulrich-Lai, Y. M., & Herman, J. P. (2009). Neural regulation of endocrine and autonomic stress responses. *Nature Reviews Neuroscience, 10*(6), 397–409. doi:10.1038/nrn2647

Ursache, A., Blair, C., Stifter, C., Voegtline, K., & Family Life Project, I. (2013). Emotional reactivity and regulation in infancy interact to predict executive functioning in early childhood. *Developmental Psychology, 49*(1), 127–137. doi:10.1037/a0027728

Watamura, S. E., Donzella, B., Alwin, J., & Gunnar, M. R. (2003). Morning-to-afternoon increases in cortisol concentrations for infants and toddlers at child care: Age differences and behavioral correlates. *Child Development, 74*(4), 1006–1020. doi:10.1111/1467-8624.00583

Willoughby, M. T., Blair, C. B., Wirth, R. J., & Greenberg, M. (2012). The measurement of executive function at age 5: Psychometric properties and relationship to academic achievement. *Psychological Assessment, 24*(1), 226–239. doi:10.1037/a0025361

Willoughby, M. T., Wirth, R. J., Blair, C. B., & Family Life Project, I. (2012). Executive function in early childhood: Longitudinal measurement invariance and developmental change. *Psychological Assessment, 24*(2), 418–431. doi:10.1037/a0025779

Yuan, P., & Raz, N. (2014). Prefrontal cortex and executive functions in healthy adults: A meta-analysis of structural neuroimaging studies. *Neuroscience Biobehavioral Reviews, 42*, 180–192. doi:10.1016/j.neubiorev.2014.02.005

Yuen, E. Y., Liu, W., Karatsoereos, I. N., Feng, J., McEwen, B. S., & Yan, Z. (2009). Acute stress enhances glutamatergic transmission in prefrontal cortex and facilitates working memory. *Proceedings of the National Academy of Sciences of the United States of America, 106*(33), 14075–14079. doi:10.1073/pnas.0906791106

Zelazo, P. D., & Müller, U. (2002). Executive function in typical and atypical development. In U. Goswami (Ed.), *Handbook of childhood cognitive development* (pp. 445–469). Oxford: Blackwell.

30

SENSITIVE PERIODS OF DEVELOPMENT AND THE ORGANIZING ACTIONS OF GONADAL STEROID HORMONES ON THE ADOLESCENT BRAIN

Kalynn M. Schulz and Zoey Forrester-Fronstin

Introduction

Adolescence is the transitional period between childhood and adulthood marked by striking changes in cognitive and social behaviors. Indeed, adolescence has been characterized as a time of social "reorientation" as the importance of peer and romantic relationships increases substantially during this time (K. De Lorme, Bell, & Sisk, 2013). Another hallmark of adolescent development is the onset of pubertal secretions of gonadal steroid hormones. Puberty and adolescence are terms that are often used interchangeably but do in fact have different meanings. Puberty is the period during which an individual becomes capable of sexually reproducing. Thus, puberty is a process occurring with the larger context of adolescence. In general, pubertal onset marks the beginning of adolescence, but while sexual maturation marks the end of puberty, the end of adolescence is more difficult to define given the complexity of behaviors developing during adolescence.

While anecdotal explanations of the dramatic behavioral changes during adolescence have been ascribed to "raging hormones" for generations, rodent and human research is revealing a much more interesting, albeit complicated, interplay between pubertal timing of gonadal hormone secretions and the developing male and female adolescent brain. This chapter will present evidence from rodent models, but also emerging work in humans, that gonadal hormone secretions organize the brain and behavior during adolescence. We will distinguish between 1) organizational effects of gonadal steroid hormones occurring as a consequence of pubertal development and 2) the postnatal sensitive period(s) for steroid-dependent organization of the brain by gonadal steroid hormones. This distinction between when organizational effects normally occur and when they are possible due to the developmental parameters of brain sensitivity is important when considering how deviations in human pubertal timing increases risk for mental illness. Individuals can vary substantially in the timing of pubertal onset, and whether individuals undergo pubertal development early or late relative to their peers increases risk for mental illness (Graber, 2013). In general, late maturing boys and early maturing girls are at greatest increased risk for psychopathologies such as depression (Copeland et al., 2010; Graber, 2008; Graber, Lewinsohn, Seeley, & BrooksGunn, 1997; Negriff & Susman, 2011), disordered eating (Klump, 2013; Zehr, Culbert, Sisk, & Klump, 2007), substance abuse (Andersson & Magnusson, 1990), and disruptive behavioral disorder (Graber, Seeley, Brooks-Gunn, & Lewinsohn, 2004). Finally, we will discuss important areas of future investigation, including determining the neural mechanisms driving the opening and closing of the sensitive period(s) for steroid-dependent organization of behavior.

Organization effects vs. sensitive periods

The general theory of sensitive periods states that the organization of a system is most easily modified during periods of rapid change (Scott, Stewart, & De Ghett, 1974). Importantly, modifying factors that act during sensitive periods do not have the same impact on the system at other times during the lifespan. Modifying factors can take on any shape or form and be of exogenous or endogenous origin (e.g. sensory experience; steroid hormone exposure), depending on the developing system. As such, testing the existence of a sensitive period for a modifying factor requires systematic exposure to that factor during discrete timeframes and comparison of the impact across these timeframes.

Organizational effects refer to the impact of a modifying factor on an organism that are long-lasting or permanent. Organizational effects most often occur during sensitive periods of development; however, this is not always the case. For example, androgen treatment of adult female zebra finches, which do not normally sing, causes long-lasting increases in the volume of the brain nuclei underlying the production of song, and also induces singing behavior in these females (Gurney & Konishi, 1980). For this reason, an experimental demonstration of an organizational effect is not an automatic demonstration of a sensitive period during development, and researchers must bear this in mind when interpreting their data.

Organizational effects of gonadal steroid hormones on reproductive behavior

Phoenix, Goy, Gerall, and Young (1959) first proposed the organizational–activational hypothesis of hormone-driven sex differences in brain and behavior. The original hypothesis posited that exposure to steroid hormones during perinatal development masculinizes and defeminizes neural circuits, programming behavioral responses to hormones in adulthood (Phoenix, Goy, Gerall, & Young, 1959). In this framework, a transient rise in testosterone during prenatal or early postnatal development masculinizes and defeminizes neural circuits in males, while the absence of testosterone in females results in development of a feminine neural phenotype. Upon gonadal maturation during puberty, testicular and ovarian hormones act on previously sexually differentiated circuits to facilitate expression of sex-typical behaviors in particular social contexts.

For many years, pubertal gonadal hormone secretions were thought only to activate adult behaviors (Arnold & Breedlove, 1985). Specifically, pubertal secretions activated neural circuits that were organized by gonadal steroid hormones during the perinatal sensitive period. These scientific beliefs likely stemmed from the methods used to investigate the organizational effects of gonadal steroid hormones on behavior. For example, early studies employed neonatal castration followed by assessment of behavioral responses to steroid hormones in adulthood to determine the contribution of neonatal hormones to the process of behavioral masculinization and defeminization (Adkins-Regan, Orgeur, & Signoret, 1989; D'Occhio & Brooks, 1980; Dixon, 1993; Epple, Alveario, & Belcher, 1990; Ford, 1990; Gotz & Dorner, 1976; Larsson, 1967; Larsson,

Sodersten, Beyer, Morali, & Perez-Palacios, 1976; Shrenker, Maxson, & Ginsburg, 1985; Sodersten, 1973). However, because neonatal castration necessarily prevents exposure of the nervous system to hormone secretions during puberty, this approach confounded the contribution of neonatal hormones to the process of sexual differentiation of behavior with that of pubertal hormones. Thus, while the results of some studies employing prepubertal castration suggested that the absence of testosterone during puberty alters adult reproductive behavior (Adkins-Regan et al., 1989; Ford, 1990; Gotz & Dorner, 1976; Larsson, 1967; Sodersten, 1973), the results of other studies did not (D'Occhio & Brooks, 1980; Dixon, 1993; Epple et al., 1990; Larsson et al., 1976; Shrenker et al., 1985), and various methodological issues made it difficult to fully assess the role of pubertal hormones. For example, in some experiments, steroid-dependent activation of adult behavior in prepubertally castrated males was not always directly compared to males castrated as adults (D'Occhio & Brooks, 1980; Epple et al., 1990; Larsson et al., 1976), steroid hormones were not re-administered in adulthood prior to behavior testing (Dixon, 1993), only one measure of reproductive behavior was reported (Larsson, 1967), and sexual behavior may have been influenced by other social experiences such as aggressive encounters (Shrenker et al., 1985). Notably, the purpose of these investigations was not necessarily to assess the role of pubertal hormones in the sexual differentiation of behavior. Therefore, it is not surprising that our appreciation of pubertal hormone contributions to brain and behavioral development is relatively recent.

Two-stage model

In the decades following these important early papers, key methodological changes have allowed investigators to isolate the impact of pubertal gonadal hormone secretions on behavioral development from that of the perinatal period across several behavioral domains. These studies will be discussed in detail in the sections below. The overwhelming evidence that pubertal steroid hormones organize a wide range of adult behaviors prompted us to propose a two-stage model of behavioral development in which the perinatal period of steroid-dependent sexual differentiation is followed by a second wave of steroid-dependent neural organization during puberty and adolescence (Figure 30.1; Schulz, Molenda-Figueira, & Sisk, 2009; Schulz & Sisk, 2006; C.L. Sisk, Schulz, & Zehr, 2003; C. L. Sisk & Zehr, 2005). During the second wave, pubertal hormones first organize neural circuits in the developing adolescent brain and then facilitate the expression of adult sex-typical behaviors in specific social contexts by activating those circuits. In this model, hormone-driven organization of the adolescent brain is viewed as a refinement of the sexual differentiation that occurred during perinatal neural development. That is, perinatal brain organization determines the substrate upon which pubertal hormones act during adolescent brain development. During the adolescent phase of organization, steroid-dependent refinement of neural circuits results in long-lasting structural and functional changes that modify adult behavioral responses to hormones and socially relevant sensory stimuli, outcomes again similar to those of the perinatal phase of organization. Throughout this chapter, several terms will be used to refer to the effects of testosterone and estradiol on the developing brain. Specifically, masculinization refers to an increase in male-typical characteristics, defeminization refers to the reduction of female-typical characteristics, feminization refers to an increase in female-typical characteristics, and demasculinization refers to the reduction of male-typical characteristics.

Adolescent sensitive period?

Although organizational effects of gonadal steroid hormones on social and cognitive behavior clearly occur as a consequence of pubertal development during adolescence, whether

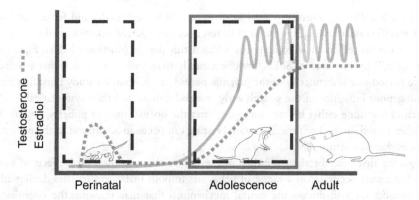

Figure 30.1 The two-stage model of postnatal brain and behavioral development. The lines depict the time course for endogenous secretions of testosterone (dotted line) in males and estradiol in females (solid line) across postnatal development. The boxes highlight the times in which endogenous gonadal steroid hormones typically organize the developing brain. Note that there are two dotted boxes and one solid box. The dotted boxes highlight that in males, transient gonadal secretions of testosterone during the perinatal period initially sexually differentiate neural circuits, and that gonadal secretions occurring during adolescence further differentiate neural circuits to bring forth adult-typical behaviors. The solid box indicates that for females, ovarian hormones acting primarily during puberty and adolescence organize neural circuits to bring forth adult-typical behaviors. Adapted from Sisk et al. (2003) and Schulz et al. (2009).

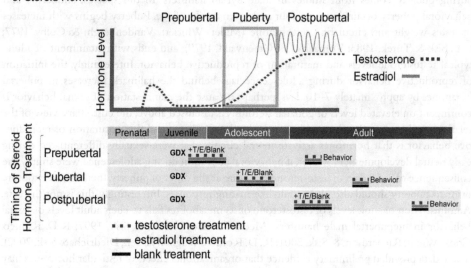

Figure 30.2 Experimental design to test sensitive period effects during adolescence. To determine whether sensitivity to the organizing actions of testosterone (males) or estradiol (females) varies across the postnatal period, all subjects are first gonadectomized prior to puberty. Steroid hormones (or blank) are then systematically administered during the timeframes of interest. In this example, before, during or after the normal time of puberty (adulthood). Following a fixed post-steroid hormone treatment interval, all subjects are behavior tested in adulthood. Depending on the behavior in question, each of the timed steroid hormone exposure (before, during, or after puberty) groups may be tested in the presence or absence of steroid hormones in adulthood.

adolescence is a discrete sensitive period for these effects in both males and females in not yet clear. A specific research design is required to test a sensitive period question, and thus far, only one study conducted in male rodents has utilized this design (discussed below, Figure 30.7; Schulz, Zehr, Salas-Ramirez, & Sisk, 2009). Specifically, to test whether adolescence is a discrete sensitive period that is distinct from the juvenile period or adulthood, a study must first remove the endogenous influence of the gonads early in development and then systematically administer steroid hormone either before, during, or after the normal time of puberty (Figure 30.2). Next, after a fixed interval of time, behavioral testing can occur in adulthood in the presence or absence of steroid hormones.

Below, we first describe the overwhelming evidence that organizational effects of gonadal steroid hormones occur across a range of behaviors in both males and females during adolescence. Second, we will discuss the neural mechanisms that may underlie the organizational effects of gonadal steroid hormones during adolescence. Third, we will review and discuss the limited data available demonstrating the parameters of a postnatal sensitive period for the effects of gonadal steroid hormones. Finally, we will discuss important future directions for this field of research.

Hormone-dependent behavioral organization during puberty and adolescence

Male reproductive behavior

Much of the empirical evidence for hormonal organization of male reproductive behavior during puberty comes from studies in male Syrian hamsters. In this species, endocrine and behavioral puberty occurs between four and seven weeks of age. Puberty begins with increases in testes weight and circulating testosterone (Miller, Whitsett, Vandenbergh, & Colby, 1977; C.L. Sisk & Turek, 1983; Vomachka & Greenwald, 1979), and ends with attainment of adult-typical testosterone levels and maturation of reproductive behavior. Interestingly, the initiation of reproductive behavior during adolescence lags behind the hallmark increases in pubertal hormones by approximately 7–10 days, perhaps because the manifestation of sexual behavior is contingent on elevated levels of gonadal steroids. As discussed above, the customary view of the relationship between the elevated hormone levels of puberty and the maturation of reproductive behavior is that hormones activate neural circuits that were sexually differentiated during early neural development. However, if behavioral activation during adolescence were simply the consequence of 7–10 days of testosterone exposure at the onset of puberty, then similar exposure prior to puberty should also elicit adult-like mating responses. Interestingly, this is not the case. Administration of adult levels of testosterone or its metabolites fails to elicit adult levels of sexual behavior in prepubertal male hamsters (Meek, Romeo, Novak, & Sisk, 1997; R.D. Romeo, Cook-Wiens, Richardson, & Sisk, 2001; R. D. Romeo, Wagner, Jansen, Diedrich, & Sisk, 2002). These data provided preliminary evidence that organizational effects of testicular hormones may be required during adolescence to permit behavioral activation by testosterone in mid- to late adolescence and adulthood.

The first tests of whether testicular hormones organize reproductive behavior during adolescence were conducted by comparing the reproductive behaviors of adult males that underwent adolescent development in the presence or absence of testicular hormones (Schulz et al., 2004). Specifically, males were gonadectomized either before puberty at 21 days of age or after puberty at 63 days of age. Six weeks following gonadectomy, when both sets of males were adults, all males were testosterone-treated to approximate adult levels of testosterone and permitted the display of testosterone-dependent sexual behavior. Behavioral testing with a receptive female occurred one week after testosterone replacement. Males gonadectomized prior to puberty displayed significantly fewer mounts, intromissions and ejaculations than males gonadectomized after puberty, suggesting that pubertal testicular secretions are necessary for complete masculinization of the developing adolescent brain. In a separate study, prepubertally gonadectomized males treated with estradiol and progesterone in adulthood displayed increased lordosis behavior relative to males gonadectomized after puberty (but were otherwise treated identically), demonstrating that testicular hormones during puberty and adolescence are also necessary for defeminization of the developing brain (Figure 30.3).

Although analogous experiments to examine the effects of prepubertal gonadectomy on adult male sexual behavior have not been performed in rats, there is nevertheless evidence that testosterone, acting during the prepubertal and early pubertal period, masculinizes and defeminizes neural circuits underlying sexual behavior. Bloch and Mills (1995) examined adult behavioral responses to either testosterone or to estradiol and progesterone in male rats that had been gonadectomized as neonates and then treated with testosterone or vehicle for a two week period of time during the juvenile/early puberty period (15–30 days of age). After testosterone priming in adulthood, rats receiving testosterone from 15–30 days of age displayed more mounts and intromissions compared with rats that received vehicle. In addition, after estradiol/progesterone priming in adulthood, rats receiving testosterone from 15–30 days of age displayed reduced lordosis and proceptive behaviors compared with rats that received vehicle. Thus, testosterone exposure during the juvenile/early pubertal period is capable of masculinizing and defeminizing sexual behavior. Although these studies in rats did not specifically investigate the role of pubertal testosterone in the expression of adult sexual behavior, they do confirm that testosterone can exert organizational influences on the prepubertal/early pubertal brain well beyond the maximally sensitive perinatal period during which initial sexual differentiation normally occurs.

A growing body of research suggests that pubertal hormones also organize sexual behavior in humans. Kinsey reported that the age at the onset of puberty appears to have long-lasting influences on the sexual behavior of human males, with earlier onset of puberty associated with higher sexual activity over the next three or four decades, and later onset of puberty associated with lower levels of sexual activity both initially and throughout the rest of adulthood (Kinsey, 1948). Although Kinsey did not discuss the concept of a sensitive period, one potential explanation of his observations is that in late-developing males, the adolescent brain is less sensitive to organizing actions of testicular hormones on sexual behavior. If so, then normal variation in the timing of puberty could cause increased behavioral organization in early bloomers versus late bloomers.

An extreme example of variation in the timing of puberty onset in human males is congenital hypogonadotropic hypogonadism (CHH), a condition in which pubertal activation of the hypothalamic–pituitary–gonadal axis fails to occur. Once diagnosed, somatic puberty is induced by hormone replacement therapy, but in most cases, hormone replacement is initiated fairly late, so that CHH males undergo adolescent development largely in the absence of testosterone. A recent study examined the effectiveness of testosterone or gonadotropin hormone replacement therapy (at least one year) in men with CHH (mean age of 37 at the time of the study) on a variety of psychosocial measures, including sexual activity (Dwyer, Quinton, Pitteloud, & Morin, 2015). In this cohort of 101 men, the mean age for diagnosis was 18, and the mean age for initiating treatment was 19, well after the normative time of pubertal onset in males. Remarkably, 26% of these men reported no history of sexual activity, which is approximately five times higher than the national average (Leigh, Temple, & Trocki, 1993). No associations between the timing of diagnosis or replacement therapy were observed in this study. However,

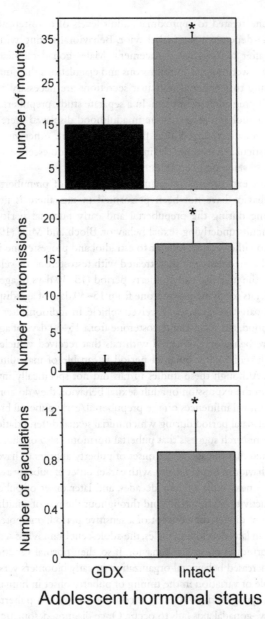

Figure 30.3 Mean number of mounts, intromissions and ejaculations displayed by sexually inexperienced
males that were gonadectomized before puberty or after puberty and tested for reproductive
behavior seven weeks later. All males were administered T for one week prior to behavior
tests. All values are expressed as means ± SEM.

Adapted from Schulz et al. (2004), *Hormones and Behavior* 45 (4) 242–249.

given that most males with CHH do not seek treatment until puberty is clearly delayed, it may
be difficult to detect effects of timing in this population. The authors conclude that existing
therapies are not effective in mitigating the well-known psychosexual problems accompanying
CHH. From the perspective of sensitive periods, we are left to speculate whether psychosexual

outcomes would indeed be improved in CHH if the timing of diagnosis and treatment occurred earlier in development.

Male agonistic behavior

Given that many social behaviors change dramatically across the adolescent period, adolescent exposure to gonadal hormones may induce organizational change in a host of male social behaviors. Indeed, organizational effects of gonadal hormones during adolescence have also been found for scent marking and territorial aggression in species as diverse as tree shrews, mice and gerbils. In tree shrews, prepubertal castration prevents testosterone from activating scent marking in adulthood (Eichmann & Holst, 1999). Similarly, mice and gerbils both display testosterone-dependent aggressive behavior in adulthood, and the ability of testosterone to activate adult aggression is substantially reduced in prepubertally castrated males (Lumia, Raskin, & Eckhert, 1977; Shrenker et al., 1985).

As with reproductive behavior, much of what is known about pubertal organization of male agonistic behaviors comes from studies of the Syrian hamster. Adult male hamsters exhibit testosterone-modulated scent marking behavior in adulthood by rubbing specialized sebaceous glands located on their dorsolateral flanks onto objects in their environment. In adult hamsters, this flank marking behavior is essential for the maintenance of dominance relationships between males, and dominant males flank mark at higher levels than submissive males (Ferris, Axelson, Shinto, & Albers, 1987; Johnston, 1970). Testosterone's ability to regulate flank marking behavior changes across adolescence, as prepubertal testosterone treatment fails to elicit flank marking behavior during social interactions with age- and weight-matched males (Schulz, Menard, Smith, Albers, & Sisk, 2006). Furthermore, males gonadectomized before puberty, but not after puberty, display reduced flank marking in response to testosterone treatment in adulthood (Figure 30.4A), suggesting that adolescent exposure to testosterone programs flank marking responses to testosterone during adult male social interactions. Flank marking behavior is regulated in part by vasopressin V1a receptors in the lateral septum, and pubertal testosterone may organize the expression of V1a, as V1a receptor binding is significantly greater in prepubertally gonadectomized males compared with males gonadectomized in adulthood (Figure 30.4B; 30.4C). It may seem counterintuitive that prepubertally gonadectomized males have more V1a binding in the lateral septum as compared to males gonadectomized in adulthood, since prepubertally gonadectomized males displayed significantly less flank-marking behavior. However, the reduced V1a binding in adult gonadectomized males may be the consequence of synaptic remodeling which normally occurs during pubertal development in both rodents and humans (Andersen, Thompson, Rutstein, Hostetter, & Teicher, 2000; Giedd et al., 1999).

During the first social encounter between two unfamiliar male hamsters in a neutral environment, an aggressive interaction initially occurs, and a dominant–subordinate relationship is typically established within a few minutes. In subsequent encounters, there is little aggression per se, but the dominant–subordinate relationship is maintained through flank marking by both males, with the dominant male flank marking more frequently than the subordinate male. This pattern of behavior, in which overt aggression is replaced by non–life-threatening flank marking, is an example of social proficiency or competence, defined as the ability of an animal to make adaptive changes in behavior as a result of social experience. Castration before puberty, but not after, disrupts this experience-dependent pattern of behavior (Figure 30.5; K. C. De Lorme & Sisk, 2013). Specifically, males gonadectomized before puberty and T-replaced in adulthood display lower levels of flank marking overall, even if they are the dominant male. Furthermore, when prepubertally gonadectomized males are re-introduced after the dominant–subordinate

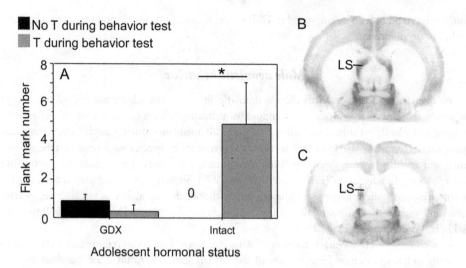

Figure 30.4   (A) Mean number of flank marks exhibited by adult males deprived of testicular hormones during adolescence (gonadectomized; GDX) and males exposed to testicular hormones during adolescence (intact; GDX in adulthood). Adult testosterone treatment significantly increased flank marking behavior during a resident/intruder test in males who were gonad-intact during adolescence (GDX in adulthood) but not males who were GDX prior to adolescence. (B&C) Photomicrographs of V1a receptor binding in the lateral septum (LS) of two testosterone-treated adult males that were either deprived of gonadal hormones during adolescence (B) or exposed to gonadal hormones during adolescence (C). Males deprived of gonadal hormones during adolescence (B) displayed significantly greater V1a receptor binding than males exposed to gonadal hormones during adolescence (C).

Adapted from Schulz et al. (2006), *Hormones and Behavior* 50 (3) 477–483.

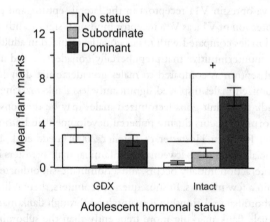

Figure 30.5   Mean number of flank marks across six trials is dependent on an interaction between pubertal testosterone, status and trial number. Status only affected the number of flank marks in males that were gonad-intact during adolescence and castrated and T-replaced in adulthood, with dominant males flank marking significantly more than no-status and subordinate intact males (+ = p < 0.05). There were no differences between no-status, subordinate or dominant males that were gonadectomized (GDX) during adolescence and T-replaced in adulthood prior to behavioral testing.

Adapted with permission from De Lorme and Sisk (2013), *Physiology & Behavior* (112–113) 1–7.

relationship was established in a prior encounter, they once again display overt aggression to re-establish the relationship, instead of maintaining the relationship via flank marking. Thus, pubertal testosterone programs the activation of flank-marking behavior, as well as flexible social communication to maintain social hierarchies (Figure 30.5).

Male anxiety-related behavior

Unlike male hamsters, male laboratory rats are not aggressive toward each other when they meet in a neutral environment. However, social interactions between males differ in familiar and unfamiliar environments: male rats spend less time interacting in a novel environment than they do in a familiar environment. The reduction in social interaction is a masculine response to a novel environment, as female rats spend similar amounts of time interacting in familiar and unfamiliar environments (Primus & Kellogg, 1990). Novel environments are considered anxiogenic to males because pretreatment with anxiolytic drugs prevents the reduction in social interaction normally induced by them (File, 1985; File & Hyde, 1978). The anxiogenic effect of a novel environment in male rats is not present until adulthood; adult males display reduced social interactions in novel environments, but prepubertal males do not (Primus & Kellogg, 1989). Although this response to novel environments is not regulated by testosterone in adulthood, depriving male rats of testosterone during adolescence prevents its development altogether, i.e., social interactions are not reduced in a novel environment in prepubertally gonadectomized rats (Primus & Kellogg, 1990). Testosterone replacement during the time of puberty in prepubertally gonadectomized rats permits the development of the masculine response (reduced social interaction) to a novel environment (Primus & Kellogg, 1990). This organizational effect of testosterone is mediated by its aromatized metabolite estradiol, as treatment with the aromatase inhibitor fadrozole during the time of puberty prevents development of the response to a novel environment (Kellogg & Lundin, 1999). More recent work has examined how the presence or absence of testosterone during puberty influences the behavior of male rats in other tests of anxiety. These studies show that compared with male rats gonadectomized in adulthood, prepubertally gonadectomized male rats spend more time in the open arms of an elevated plus maze and more time in the light section of a light–dark box, indicating in both cases that prepubertal gonadectomy results in a less anxious phenotype in adulthood (Brown, Kulbarsh, Spencer, & Duval, 2015). Together, these studies support the idea that the presence of testicular hormones during adolescence organizes anxiety-like behaviors in male rats, specifically making them more anxious after adolescence than before.

Male cognition

On average, men outperform women in tests of spatial cognition, and this sex difference in humans may be organized by pubertal hormones. Differences in spatial cognition are observed between men with prepubertal onset idiopathic hypogonadotropic hypogonadism (IHH; IHH is another term for CHH) and men with adult onset IHH (Hier & Crowley, 1982). The former group had low or undetectable levels of circulating gonadal steroids during the normal time of puberty and adolescence, whereas the latter group experienced normal levels of pubertal gonadal hormones during adolescence. Spatial cognition is impaired in men with prepubertal onset IHH, both in comparison to healthy control subjects and to men with adult onset IHH (Hier & Crowley, 1982), suggesting that the presence of testicular hormones during puberty organizes circuits underlying spatial cognition. In a separate study, women with a variation of congenital adrenal hyperplasia that leads to slightly but chronically elevated levels of adrenal androgens during childhood and early puberty performed better in a virtual Morris Water Maze (a test of spatial memory) compared with healthy subjects (Mueller et al., 2008). These data suggest that exposure to adrenal androgens during adolescence organizes (masculinizes) spatial ability in females (but see also Hines et al., 2003). Rodent work demonstrates that spatial memory is hippocampus-dependent, and synaptic plasticity in the hippocampus appears to be organized by pubertal androgens. Synaptic plasticity can be assessed by long-term depression (LTD), which is a fundamental process involved in synaptic changes underlying associative leaning. Specifically, activation of androgen receptor during puberty results in hippocampal CA1 LTD in response to a tetanizing stimulus in adulthood, whereas if androgen receptor activation is blocked during puberty, long-term potentiation occurs in response to a tetanizing stimulus in adulthood (Hebbard, King, Malsbury, & Harley, 2003). These findings in rodents provide a potential mechanism by which pubertal testosterone may organize hippocampus-dependent learning and memory in humans, including spatial cognition.

Female behavior

Feminizing and demasculinizing effects of ovarian hormones

Ovarian hormones also organize female social behaviors during adolescence, and the effects of adolescent ovarian hormones vary depending on the specific social behavior in question. Studies demonstrate that ovarian hormones during adolescence are capable of either feminizing (enhancing female-typical attributes), masculinizing (enhancing male-typical attributes), or defeminizing (suppressing female-typical attributes) adult behavior. Recently, an estrogen-deficient aromatase knockout mouse model has provided new opportunities to study the effects of estradiol during development (Bakker, Honda, Harada, & Balthazart, 2002). Although the aromatase gene knockout prevents biosynthesis of estrogen, estrogen receptors are fully functional in this model, thereby providing a unique opportunity to study the effects of exogenous estradiol administration on female behavioral development (Bakker & Baum, 2008). Female knockout mice display significantly less lordosis behavior compared to wildtype or heterozygous mice following adult ovariectomy and hormone treatment, suggesting that exposure to endogenous estrogen during adolescence feminizes reproductive responses to adult gonadal steroid hormones (Bakker et al., 2002). In a second study, estradiol was systematically administered during development prior to either the onset of normative ovarian secretions of gonadal steroid hormones (postnatal days 5–15) or the earliest timeframe for normative ovarian secretions of gonadal steroid hormones (postnatal days 15–25). Interestingly, whereas administration of estradiol between days 5–15 had no effect on lordosis behavior in wildtype or knockout animals, administration between days 15–25 significantly increased lordosis behavior in the aromatase knockout animals (Brock, Baum, & Bakker, 2011). These data provide compelling evidence for the feminization of female reproductive behavior by estradiol during early adolescent development in female mice.

Recently, the question of whether adolescent ovarian hormones impact female sexual motivation was addressed using sexual partner preference, paced mating behavior, and conditioned place preference (CPP) in prepubertally or adult ovariectomized rats. In the sexual partner preference task, sexually receptive but naïve female rats were placed in an arena with access to a sexually vigorous male and an estradiol benzoate (EB) plus progesterone (P)-treated female. During the test, behaviors of the sexually naïve female were recorded, including the time spent with the sexually vigorous male, time spent with the EB+P-treated female, and entries/exits from the compartments where the stimulus rats were kept (Meerts et al., 2017). Paced mating behavior was determined by pairing the sexually naïve female in an area with a single male and recording the timing and number of sexual behaviors (e.g. mounts, intromissions, ejaculations and lordosis). Additionally, the females were able to physically leave the presence of the male counterpart, allowing the female to "pace" the sexual experience. Conditioned place preference was induced by exposing sexually naïve females to 15 intromissions from a sexually vigorous male in one of two distinct compartments of an apparatus. Following this experience, the experimental females were placed back into the chamber, with no male counterpart, and allowed to explore the area. Place preference was determined by measuring the time spent in each chamber (Meerts et al., 2017). If sexual experience impacts conditioned place preference, the experimental females should spend more time, or prefer, the chamber that the experience took place in prior. Pubertal ovarian steroid hormones influence paced mating behaviors in female rats. Prepubertally ovariectomized rats displayed increased locomotion and withdrawal during the paced mating task relative to females ovariectomized in adulthood (Meerts et al., 2017). However, prepubertal ovariectomy did not influence partner preference or conditioned place preference (Meerts et al., 2017), suggesting that ovarian steroid hormones are not involved in all aspects of social behavior in a sexual context.

Rough and tumble play in female rats is also actively feminized by ovarian steroid hormones. Males and females display striking differences in play behavior. During adolescence, males transition from a playful defense strategy of a full supine position when contacted by a male conspecific to a partial supine position (the adult posture). In contrast, females do not show this change in play behavior across adolescence (Field & Pellis, 2008; Pellis, 2002). However, females ovariectomized neonatally or prior to puberty display the male-typical adolescent transition in play defense posture, suggesting that ovarian hormones during adolescence actively feminize and demasculinize play responses in females. Indeed, neonatal testosterone administration does not produce the male-typical play pattern (Smith, Forgie, & Pellis, 1998). Thus, play behavior in rats is a very interesting example of active feminization and demasculinization by adolescent ovarian steroid hormones. Rats also display food guarding behaviors in which sexually dimorphic postural strategies are employed to defend a food source (Field, Whishaw, Forgie, & Pellis, 2004). Both neonatal and pubertal ovariectomy shifts female defense strategies toward a more male-like pattern, whereas adult ovariectomy has no effect. Thus, these data suggest that ovarian hormones actively feminize food defense strategies during the neonatal and/or adolescent periods.

Pubertal estradiol also feminizes ingestive responses to metabolic signals in rats (Swithers, McCurley, Hamilton, & Doerflinger, 2008). Treatment with mercaptoacetate, a drug that interferes with fatty acid oxidation, increases food intake in male but not female rats. Prepubertally ovariectomized females display a male-like response to mercaptoacetate and increase their food intake in adulthood, whereas adult ovariectomized females do not increase food intake in response to mercaptoacetate. Furthermore, this effect of prepubertal ovariectomy is prevented by estradiol replacement during puberty, indicating a role for estradiol (not progesterone) in organizing (feminizing) the response to metabolic challenge (Swithers et al., 2008).

Recent evidence also suggests that maternal behavior is feminized by ovarian hormones during adolescence. Female mice ovariectomized prior to puberty spend less time with, take longer to retrieve, and retrieve fewer pups than females ovariectomized after puberty, in adulthood. However, these maternal behaviors are preserved in prepubertally ovariectomized females that receive estradiol during the time of puberty (Kercmar, Snoj, Tobet, & Majdic, 2014), again providing evidence that estradiol, in some behavioral contexts, actively feminizes the adolescent brain.

Defeminizing and masculinizing effects of ovarian hormones

In contrast to the feminizing effects of ovarian hormones during adolescence on food guarding, ingestive and maternal behaviors, ovarian hormones also cause species-specific defeminization and masculinization of mating behavior. In female Syrian hamsters, prepubertal, but not postpubertal, ovariectomy decreases lordosis latency and increases overall lordosis duration in response to adult estradiol and progesterone treatment (Figure 30.6; Schulz & Sisk, 2006), suggesting that ovarian hormone exposure during adolescence defeminizes adult lordosis behavior. In addition, estradiol treatment following prepubertal ovariectomy also defeminizes adult behavior, indicating that estradiol is the ovarian hormone driving behavioral defeminization during adolescence (Schulz & Sisk, 2006). While it may be surprising that ovarian hormones defeminize female lordosis behavior during adolescence, estrogen-receptor mediated behavioral defeminization also occurs during the perinatal period of development (Clemens & Gladue, 1978; Coniglio, Paup, & Clemens, 1973; Paup, Coniglio, & Clemens, 1972; for review see Wallen & Baum, 2002). Whether ovarian hormone-induced defeminization of lordosis behavior during adolescent development negatively impacts female reproductive success is not known. One possibility is that behavioral defeminization is a trade-off for estradiol-dependent organization of behaviors that facilitate reproductive success. For example, female hamsters are notoriously aggressive (e.g. Payne & Swanson, 1970), and socially dominant females give birth to larger litters than socially subordinate females (Huck, Lisk, & McKay, 1988). Perhaps adolescent ovarian hormones facilitate social dominance/aggression in female hamsters, as has been demonstrated for adolescent testicular hormones in male hamsters (Schulz et al., 2006; Schulz & Sisk, 2006). Thus, although defeminization of lordosis behavior by estradiol during adolescence reduces the duration of mating interactions with males, organization of other behavioral systems may ensure overall reproductive success in females.

Defeminizing and masculinizing effects of gonadal steroid hormones during adolescence have also been found in female rats. Exogenous testosterone administration in early adolescence defeminizes lordosis as well as proceptive solicitation behaviors (Bloch, Mills, & Gale, 1995). In addition, females ovariectomized after adolescence, and therefore exposed to pubertal estradiol,

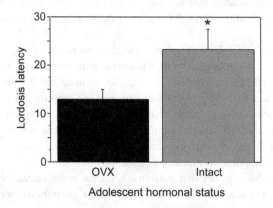

Figure 30.6 Pubertal ovarian hormones defeminize lordosis behavior. Females were ovariectomized before adolescence (OVX) or after adolescence (intact). All females were estradiol and progesterone primed in adulthood prior to behavioral testing with a stud male. Females exposed to ovarian hormones during adolescence (intact) displayed significantly longer lordosis latencies than females deprived of adolescent ovarian hormones (OVX). Asterisk indicates P < 0.05.

Adapted from Schulz and Sisk (2006), *Molecular and Cellular Endocrinology* (254–255) 120–126.

display masculinized behavioral responses to testosterone such as increased mounts of female partners and a female-oriented partner preference relative to females ovariectomized before adolescence (no exposure to pubertal estradiol). These data suggest that adolescent ovarian hormones normally partially masculinize mating behavior (de Jonge, Muntjewerff, Louwerse, & van de Poll, 1988). Interestingly, the neonatal hormonal environment may determine the extent to which adolescent ovarian hormones masculinize behavior. Adolescent ovarian hormone exposure has little effect on the reproductive behavior of neonatally androgenized female rats (de Jonge et al., 1988). Thus, neonatal androgens may render the female adolescent brain less sensitive to the organizing actions of gonadal steroid hormones during adolescence, which fits with a model of decreasing sensitivity of neural circuits to the organizing actions of steroid hormones across postnatal development (discussed further below).

Is adolescence a distinct sensitive period?

The inability of testosterone to activate adult-like reproductive and flank marking behavior in prepubertal male hamsters suggests that a second window of sensitivity to the organizing effects of gonadal hormones opens at adolescence. Alternatively, organizational effects of steroid hormones may occur prior to puberty but remain latent until requisite steroid-independent development occurs during adolescence. The experiments employing prepubertal or postpubertal gonadectomy demonstrate that organizational effects of steroid hormones are possible during adolescence, because only prepubertal gonadectomy was detrimental to behavior and these effects were long-lasting. However, the pre- and postpubertal gonadectomy experiments were not designed to determine whether adolescence is a discrete sensitive period, because they did not determine whether organizational effects of steroid hormones are possible prior to puberty, or whether cumulative life-time exposure to testosterone, regardless of when it occurs, is the key variable in expression of adult male social behaviors. Therefore, we tested the hypothesis that adolescence marks the opening of a second sensitive period for the organizing actions of testosterone on adult male reproductive behavior. This hypothesis predicts that exposure to testosterone during adolescence, but not before or after adolescence, will result in full activational responses to testosterone in adulthood.

Male hamsters were gonadectomized at 10 days of age (after the perinatal period of sexual differentiation), and then exposed to 19 days of blank- or testosterone-filled silastic capsules either before puberty (10–29d of age), during the normal time of puberty (29–48d of age) or after puberty (64–83d of age). In adulthood, four weeks following capsule removal, all gonadectomized males were implanted with testosterone-filled capsules and tested one week later with a receptive female. Both prepubertal and adolescent testosterone treatment, but not adult testosterone treatment, enhanced adult reproductive behavior, demonstrating that adolescence is not a discrete sensitive period for the organizing actions of testosterone on adult reproductive behavior (Figure 30.7). In addition, prepubertal testosterone treatment had the greatest impact on adult reproductive function, suggesting that the potential for testosterone to organize reproductive behavior decreases across postnatal development (Figure 30.7). Therefore, we propose the classical view of organizational and activational mechanisms of steroid action be revised to incorporate an extended window of decreasing postnatal sensitivity to the organization of adult social behavior by steroid hormones (Figure 30.8). If this is the case, then the two stages of hormone-dependent organization are driven by the two times that testicular hormones become elevated in males and not by the opening/closing of two discrete sensitive periods.

A recent study in humans lends support to the possibility of an extended postnatal window of decreasing sensitivity to gonadal steroid hormones. Beltz and Berenbaum (2013) hypothesized

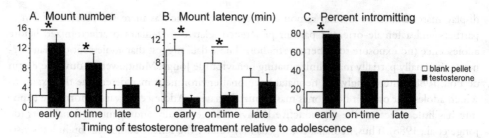

Figure 30.7 Effects of periadolescent testosterone exposure on adult reproductive behaviors. Testosterone treatments were designed to simulate early, on-time, and late pubertal development, and all behavior testing occurred in adulthood. Only pre- and mid-adolescent testosterone treatments facilitated mounting behavior in response to testosterone in adulthood. Adult intromissive behavior was only increased by pre-adolescent testosterone treatments. These data suggest that early testosterone treatments enhance behavioral responsiveness to testosterone in adulthood. Asterisk indicates a significant difference (p < 0.05) between groups.

Adapted from Schulz, Zehr, Salas-Ramirez, and Sisk (2009), *Endocrinology* 150 (9) 3690–3698.

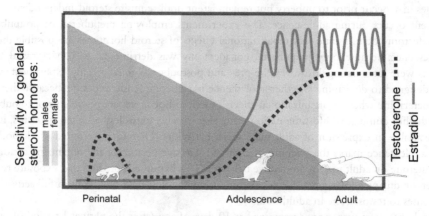

Figure 30.8 Testable working model of postnatal sensitivity to the organizing actions of gonadal steroid hormones in males and females. The triangle-shaped shading indicates that in males, current empirical evidence suggests that sensitivity to the organizing actions of gonadal steroid hormones decreases across postnatal development. The rectangular-shaped shading indicates that a more discrete period of sensitivity may occur in females. Please note that the rectangular-shaped shading is hypothetical at this point in time, given that the appropriate sensitive period test has yet to be conducted in females. Our model is testable and future studies are needed to determine the timeframe of postnatal sensitivity gonadal steroid hormones in females, and whether the model of decreasing sensitivity in males generalizes to a wider repertoire of behaviors.

that if sensitivity to organizational effects of gonadal steroid hormones decreases across adolescence, then the age at which adolescents undergo puberty should be inversely associated with the effectiveness of gonadal steroid hormones in organizing spatial (men) or verbal (women) ability. Participants reported whether they experienced specific pubertal events much earlier, somewhat earlier, the same, somewhat later, or much later than their peers to determine a pubertal timing score, and their verbal and spatial abilities were assessed. Among men, an effect of pubertal timing on three-dimensional mental rotations test scores was found, with early maturing males performing better than late maturing males (Figure 30.9). In contrast, no effects

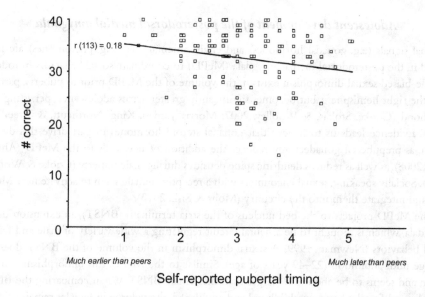

Figure 30.9   Scatterplot of pubertal timing and mental rotations scores for men. The line depicts the zero-order correlation, and open shapes depict individual data points.

Redrawn with permission from Beltz and Berenbaum (2013), *Hormones and Behavior* (63) 823–828.

of pubertal timing on verbal or spatial ability were detected in women. The authors conclude that their findings are consistent with the hypothesis of declining sensitivity to the organizing actions of testosterone throughout adolescent development. Their data further highlight the sex-specific effects of gonadal steroid hormones during human adolescent development, as is observed in rodent species.

The current working model has two key limitations (Figure 30.8). First, the model is based primarily on data generated from male rodents. It is unknown whether females similarly display a decreasing sensitivity across postnatal development to the organizing actions of gonadal steroid hormones on behavioral outcomes. Second, the model is based on male reproductive behavior. It is possible that different steroid-dependent social and cognitive behaviors have unique sensitive periods across postnatal development in males and females. As such, sensitive period experiments are needed in both males and females to determine the postnatal parameters for steroid-dependent organization of specific social and cognitive behaviors.

Neurobiological mechanisms underlying hormone-dependent organization of the adolescent brain

It is clear that pubertal gonadal hormones organize the structure and morphology of brain regions involved in behaviors organized during adolescence. However, the mechanisms of brain organization during development are still being uncovered. Thus far, the literature suggests that the timing and type of gonadal hormone exposure influences the structure of brain regions involved in adolescent maturation, which in turn mediates behavioral maturation. As a field, we are in an early but exciting phase where we can begin to correlate gonadal steroid hormone exposure and changing brain structure with the behavioral changes seen during development.

Adolescent development of the posterodorsal medial amygdala

Internal signals (e.g. gonadal hormones) and environmental cues (e.g. pheromones) are integrated in the posterodorsal medial amygdala (MePD) to coordinate social behaviors in rodents. A male-biased sexual dimorphism exists in the volume of the MePD prior to puberty, particularly the right hemisphere, but becomes significantly greater across adolescence, persisting into adulthood (Cooke, Stokas, & Woolley, 2007; Morris, Jordan, King, Northcutt, & Breedlove, 2008). Evidence leads us to believe that gonadal steroid hormones in part drive this dimorphism, as prepubertal gonadectomy reduces the addition of new cells to the MePD (Ahmed et al., 2008), as well as reduces dendritic spine densities during male puberty (Cooke & Woolley, 2009). Socially speaking, sexual encounters with a receptive female seem to activate new MePD cells and integrate them into the circuitry (Mohr & Sisk, 2013).

The MePD projects to the bed nucleus of the stria terminalis (BNST), an extension of the amygdala, which is thought to be a neural circuit regulating a wide variety of male and female social behaviors (Newman, 1999) A sexual dimorphism in the volume of the BNST does not emerge until adulthood (22–49 years of age). Similar to the MePD, this dimorphism is male-biased and seems to be about 40% larger than the female BNST. When comparing the BNST of males and females between childhood and adulthood, the volume in females remains similar across development while the BNST of males enlarges over the course of adolescent development, creating this sexual dimorphism (Chung, De Vries, & Swaab, 2002). Though we are aware of the dimorphisms seen in the BNST, it remains unclear if gonadal steroid hormones are the driving force.

Adolescent development of the cerebral cortex

Gray matter

Human neuroimaging studies demonstrate an overall decrease in gray matter volume in the cerebral cortex during adolescence. The timing of the decline, however, is sex- and cortex-specific. In both the frontal and parietal cortices, gray matter volumes increase with physical maturation, peaking around 11 years of age in females and 12.5 years of age in males, subsequently declining in volume until leveling off in the 20s, with females always having a smaller gray matter volume than males (Giedd et al., 1999). Gray matter volume of the temporal cortex peaks at approximately 16.5 years of age in both males and females, followed by a slight decline in volume (Giedd et al., 1999). The Tanner stage is an estimate of physical development in growing children (Marshall & Tanner, 1970; Marshall & Tanner, 1969). Some of the changes in gray matter volume and density can be predicted by the Tanner stage, as the age in which structural changes occur can be attributed to the changes in levels of pubertal gonadal hormones (Herting et al., 2015; Peper et al, 2011). Herting and Sowell (2017) provide a comprehensive review of both gray and white matter changes in relation to age and hormone levels. Specifically, higher levels of testosterone are predictors of decreased gray matter volume and density in males between 11 and 18 years old (Bramen et al., 2010; Paus et al., 2010; Peper et al., 2009 via Herting & Sowell, 2017). Conversely, a positive correlation between testosterone and gray matter volume exists in females aged 10–13 years old (Bramen et al., 2011 via Herting & Sowell, 2017). Rodent studies discussed below bridge the connection between changes in cortical gray matter volume with gonadal hormone levels during adolescence, which is hypothesized to contribute to social behavioral changes that occur during development.

Adolescence is accompanied by an overall decrease of cortical volume, and the extent of decline is sexually dimorphic. For example, the volume of the medial prefrontal cortex (mPFC) in adulthood is greater in male rats than in females. Koss and colleagues (2015) examined brain weight and cerebral cell numbers in adult male and female rats following prepubertal gonadectomy. Females ovariectomized prior to puberty had increased brain weight, neuron count, and glial cell count in adulthood relative to sham ovariectomized female rats. However, no differences were observed between prepubertally castrated and sham-castrated male rats (Koss et al., 2015). These results suggest a sex-specific effect of gonadal steroid hormones during puberty such that ovarian rather than testicular gonadal steroid hormones mediate changes in cortical gray matter volume.

Cortical inhibition

Piekarski and colleagues (2017) examined the influence of ovarian hormones on miniature inhibitory and excitatory post-synaptic currents (mIPSCs and mEPSCs) under an abundance of hormonal timing conditions. Specifically, mice were ovariectomized or sham ovariectomized prepubertally on day 24, and mIPSCs were measured in L2/3 pyramidal cells of the cingulate cortex. Prepubertally ovariectomized mice displayed decreased inhibitory charge transfer relative to sham females, suggesting that ovarian hormones normally increase inhibition during puberty. Importantly, this effect appears to be organizational, because postpubertal ovariectomy at day 40 did not decrease inhibitory charge transfer relative to sham ovariectomized females (Piekarski et al., 2017). Whether testicular hormones may also mediate increases in cortical inhibition is currently unknown.

White matter

Unlike the dynamic changes seen in gray matter throughout adolescence, white matter volume increases linearly across development (Paus et al., 1999; Giedd et al., 1999). Similar to gray matter, volume increases are sexually dimorphic and cortex-specific. Males have steeper increase in white matter volume, which drives the sexual dimorphism observed in adulthood, particularly in the frontal, parietal and occipital cortices (Giedd et al., 1999; Lenroot et al., 2007; Perrin et al., 2009). Quantification of white matter can be predicted by age using the Pubertal Development Scale (PDS) and hormone levels (Herting & Sowell, 2017; Herting et al., 2011; Perrin et al., 2008, 2009; Koss et al., 2015). The PDS is a self-report measure of puberty with questions related to height change, development of pubic hair, facial growth and voice change (males only), and breast development and menarche (girls only) (Petersen et al., 1988). Correlations exist between scores on PDS and white matter volume in the frontal, parietal, temporal and occipital cortices. Specifically, PDS scores accurately predicted white matter volume in 12–18-year-old males and females using magnetic transfer ratio (MTR) (Perrin et al., 2009 via Herting & Sowell, 2017). MTR, an assessment of cerebral myelination, is positively correlated with PDS scores. Lower MTR values, indicative of less overall myelination, is associated with lower PDS scores (Perrin et al., 2009 via Herting & Sowell, 2017). Hormone levels are also associated with white matter volume (Menzies et al., 2015; Herting et al., 2011, 2014; Perrin et al., 2009). Testosterone tends to predict white matter increases in boys, while estradiol predicts white matter decreases in girls (Herting et al., 2012). For example, testosterone levels predict greater cerebral white matter volumes in 12–18-year-old males and females (Perrin et al., 2008).

Rodent studies have directly examined the impact of gonadal steroid hormones on frontal white matter (Koss et al., 2015). Similar to human studies, frontal cortex white matter volume increases across adolescent development in rodents, more so in males than in females, resulting in a male-biased sexual dimorphism (Willing & Juraska, 2015). However, the hormonal determinants of the male-biased dimorphism appear to be driven by estradiol secretions in females as opposed to testosterone secretions in males. Specifically, prepubertal gonadectomy significantly increases white matter volume in females but does not affect white matter volume in males (Koss et al., 2015). Thus, under normative developmental conditions, the emergence of sex differences in white matter during adolescence in rats are due to the actions of ovarian, not testicular hormones (Juraska & Willing, 2016).

Conclusions and future directions

Adolescence is clearly a developmental period in which gonadal steroid hormones organize the brain and behavior. In males, organization of the adolescent brain builds on the sexual differentiation of neural circuits that was initiated during the perinatal period of hormone-dependent organization. In females, pubertal ovarian hormones play a central role in organizing the adolescent brain and behavior. Although 25 years of research clearly demonstrate that organizational effects of pubertal gonadal steroid hormones typically occur during adolescence, both the timeframe and degree to which the nervous system is sensitive to the organizing actions of gonadal steroid hormones across the postnatal period is less well understood. Determining these parameters in both males and females is essential given that deviations in pubertal timing is associated with psychopathologies such as depression (Copel, 2010; Graber, 2008; Graber et al., 1997; Negriff & Susman, 2011), disordered eating (Klump, 2013; Zehr et al., 2007), substance abuse (Andersson & Magnusson, 1990), and disruptive behavioral disorder (Graber et al., 2004). Scientific explanations of the relationship between pubertal timing and mental illness have primarily focused on the social and emotional consequences of off-time pubertal development relative to one's peers in boys and girls. We have proposed a biological model in which nervous system sensitivity to gonadal steroid hormones decreases across adolescent development (Schulz, Molenda-Figueira et al., 2009; Schulz & Sisk, 2016, 2017). In this framework, the developing adolescent brain is a moving target for the effects of gonadal steroid hormones, and shifts in pubertal timing may alter the course of brain development toward increased vulnerability. However, whether the model of decreasing sensitivity to the organizing actions of gonadal steroid hormones generalizes to females is not known. Indeed, given that puberty is the greatest period of organizational change by steroid hormones in females, there may exist a more discrete period of female nervous system sensitivity to gonadal steroid hormones (Figure 30.8). Our model is theoretical and testable, and experiments are needed to determine whether it extends to other social and cognitive behaviors, and females.

An exciting future direction of this research is determining the neural mechanisms governing the opening and closing of sensitive periods for steroid-dependent brain and behavioral organization. One intriguing possibility is that like other experience-dependent sensitive periods (e.g. the visual cortex), changes in GABAergic function and excitatory/inhibitory balance within neural circuits drive the opening and closing of the sensitive period (Takesian & Hensch, 2013). A recent study from Piekarski and colleagues lends support for this possibility. Reversal learning is regulated by the cingulate cortex, and decreases in reversal learning ability are normally observed after puberty in female mice (Johnson & Wilbrecht, 2011). These changes in reversal learning are concomitant with increased GABAergic signaling in the cingulate cortex. Prepubertal ovariectomy and estradiol and progesterone replacement advances both the behavioral transition to adult-like reversal learning and adult-like GABAergic signaling. Whether these changes represent the opening or closing of a sensitive period (or both) is not yet clear, but the possibilities are exciting. Understanding the factors regulating sensitive period(s) for steroid-dependent neural development holds promise for mitigating the negative consequences off-time pubertal development in humans.

References

Adkins-Regan, E., Orgeur, P., & Signoret, J. P. (1989). Sexual differentiation of reproductive behavior in pigs: Defeminizing effects of prepubertal estradiol. *Hormones and Behavior, 23*(2), 290–303.

Ahmed, E. I., Zehr, J. L., Schulz, K. M., Lorenz, B. H., DonCarlos, L. L., & Sisk, C. L. (2008). Pubertal hormones modulate the addition of new cells to sexually dimorphic brain regions. *Nature Neuroscience, 11*(9), 995–997.

Andersen, S. L., Thompson, A. T., Rutstein, M., Hostetter, J. C., & Teicher, M. H. (2000). Dopamine receptor pruning in prefrontal cortex during the periadolescent period in rats. *Synapse, 37*(2), 167–169.

Andersson, T., & Magnusson, D. (1990). Biological maturation in adolescence and the development of drinking habits and alcohol-abuse among young males – a prospective longitudinal-study. *Journal of Youth and Adolescence, 19*(1), 33–41. doi:10.1007/bf01539443

Arnold, A. P., & Breedlove, S. M. (1985). Organizational and activational effects of sex steroids on brain and behavior: A reanalysis. *Hormones and Behavior, 19*(4), 469–498.

Bakker, J., & Baum, M. J. (2008). Role for estradiol in female-typical brain and behavioral sexual differentiation. *Frontiers in Neuroendocrinology, 29*(1), 1–16. doi:10.1016/j.yfrne.2007.06.001

Bakker, J., Honda, S. I., Harada, N., & Balthazart, J. (2002). The aromatase knock-out mouse provides new evidence that estradiol is required during development in the female for the expression of sociosexual behaviors in adulthood. *Journal of Neuroscience, 22*(20), 9104–9112.

Beltz, A. M., & Berenbaum, S. A. (2013). Cognitive effects of variations in pubertal timing: Is puberty a period of brain organization for human sex-typed cognition? *Hormones and Behavior, 63*(5), 823–828. doi:10.1016/j.yhbeh.2013.04.002

Bloch, G. J., & Mills, R. (1995). Prepubertal testosterone treatment of neonatally gonadectomized male rats: Defeminization and masculinization of behavioral and endocrine function in adulthood. *Neuroscience & Biobehavioral Reviews, 19*(2), 187–200.

Bloch, G. J., Mills, R., & Gale, S. (1995). Prepubertal testosterone treatment of female rats: Defeminization of behavioral and endocrine function in adulthood. *Neuroscience & Biobehavioral Reviews, 19*(2), 177–186.

Bramen, J. E., Hranilovich, J. A., Dahl, R. E., Forbes, E. E., Chen, J., Toga, A. W., . . . Sowell, E. R. (2010). Puberty influences medial temporal lobe and cortical gray matter maturation differently in boys than girls matched for sexual maturity. *Cerebral Cortex, 21*(3), 636–646.

Brock, O., Baum, M. J., & Bakker, J. (2011). The development of female sexual behavior requires prepubertal estradiol. *Journal of Neuroscience, 31*(15), 5574–5578. doi:10.1523/jneurosci.0209-11.2011

Brown, G. R., Kulbarsh, K. D., Spencer, K. A., & Duval, C. (2015). Peri-pubertal exposure to testicular hormones organizes response to novel environments and social behaviour in adult male rats. *Hormones & Behavior, 73*, 135–141. doi:10.1016/j.yhbeh.2015.07.003

Chung, W. C., De Vries, G. J., & Swaab, D. F. (2002). Sexual differentiation of the bed nucleus of the stria terminalis in humans may extend into adulthood. *Journal of Neuroscience, 22*(3), 1027–1033.

Clemens, L. G., & Gladue, B. A. (1978). Feminine sexual behavior in rats enhanced by prenatal inhibition of androgen aromatization. *Hormones and Behavior, 11*, 190–201.

Coniglio, L. P., Paup, D. C., & Clemens, L. G. (1973). Hormonal specificity in the suppression of sexual receptivity of the female golden hamster. *Journal of Endocrinology, 57*(1), 55–61.

Cooke, B. M., Stokas, M. R., & Woolley, C. S. (2007). Morphological sex differences and laterality in the prepubertal medial amygdala. *Journal of Comparative Neurology, 501*(6), 904–915. doi:10.1002/cne.21281

Cooke, B. M., & Woolley, C. S. (2009). Effects of prepubertal gonadectomy on a male-typical behavior and excitatory synaptic transmission in the amygdala. *Developmental Neurobiology, 69*(2–3), 141–152. doi:10.1002/dneu.20688

Copeland, W., Shanahan, L., Miller, S., Costello, E. J., Angold, A., & Maughan, B. (2010). Outcomes of early pubertal timing in young women: A prospective population-based study. *American Journal of Psychiatry, 167*(10), 1218–1225. doi:10.1176/appi.ajp.2010.09081190

D'Occhio, M. J., & Brooks, D. E. (1980). Effects of androgenic and oestrogenic hormones on mating behaviour in rams castrated before and after puberty. *Journal of Endocrinology, 86*(3), 403–411.

de Jonge, F. H., Muntjewerff, J. W., Louwerse, A. L., & van de Poll, N. E. (1988). Sexual behavior and sexual orientation of the female rat after hormonal treatment during various stages of development. *Hormones and Behavior, 22*(1), 100–115.

De Lorme, K. C., Bell, M. R., & Sisk, C. L. (2013). The teenage brain: Social reorientation and the adolescent brain-the role of gonadal hormones in the male Syrian hamster. *Current Directions in Psychological Science, 22*(2), 128–133. doi:10.1177/0963721413479607

De Lorme, K. C., & Sisk, C. L. (2013). Pubertal testosterone programs context-appropriate agonistic behavior and associated neural activation patterns in male Syrian hamsters. *Physiology & Behavior, 112–113*, 1–7. doi:10.1016/j.physbeh.2013.02.003

Dixon, A. F. (1993). Sexual and aggressive behavior of adult male marmosets (*Callithrix jacchus*) castrated neonatally, prepubertally, or in adulthood. *Physiology & Behavior, 54*, 301–307.

Dwyer, A. A., Quinton, R., Pitteloud, N., & Morin, D. (2015). Psychosexual development in men with congenital hypogonadotropic hypogonadism on long-term treatment: A mixed methods study. *Sexual Medicine, 3*(1), 32–41. doi:10.1002/sm2.50

Eichmann, F., & Holst, D. V. (1999). Organization of territorial marking behavior by testosterone during puberty in male tree shrews. *Physiology & Behavior, 65*(4–5), 785–791.

Epple, G., Alveario, M. C., & Belcher, A. M. (1990). Copulatory behavior of adult tamarins (*Saguinus fuscicollis*) castrated as neonates or juveniles: Effect of testosterone treatment. *Hormones Behavior, 24*, 470–483.

Ferris, C. F., Axelson, J. F., Shinto, L. H., & Albers, H. E. (1987). Scent marking and the maintenance of dominant/subordinate status in male golden hamsters. *Physiology & Behavior, 40*(5), 661–664.

Field, E. F., & Pellis, S. M. (2008). The brain as the engine of sex differences in the organization of movement in rats. *Archives of Sexual Behavior, 37*(1), 30–42. doi:10.1007/s10508-007-9270-4

Field, E. F., Whishaw, I. Q., Forgie, M. L., & Pellis, S. M. (2004). Neonatal and pubertal, but not adult, ovarian steroids are necessary for the development of female-typical patterns of dodging to protect a food item. *Behavioral Neuroscience, 118*(6), 1293–1304.

File, S. E. (1985). Animal models for predicting clinical efficacy of anxiolytic drugs: Social behaviour. *Neuropsychobiology, 13*(1–2), 55–62.

File, S. E., & Hyde, J. R. (1978). Can social interaction be used to measure anxiety? *British Journal of Pharmacology, 62*(1), 19–24.

Ford, J. J. (1990). Differentiation of sexual behaviour in pigs. *Journal of Reproduction and Fertility Supplement, 40*, 311–321.

Giedd, J. N., Blumenthal, J., Jeffries, N. O., Castellanos, F. X., Liu, H., Zijdenbos, A., . . . Rapoport, J. L. (1999). Brain development during childhood and adolescence: A longitudinal MRI study. *Nature Neuroscience, 2*(10), 861–863.

Gotz, F., & Dorner, G. (1976). Sex hormone-dependent brain maturation and sexual behaviour in rats. *Endokrinologie, 68*(3), 275–282.

Graber, J. A. (2008). Pubertal and neuroendocrine development and risk for depression. *Adolescent Emotional Development and the Emergence of Depressive Disorders*, 74–91. doi:10.1017/cbo9780511551963.005

Graber, J. A. (2013). Pubertal timing and the development of psychopathology in adolescence and beyond. *Hormones and Behavior, 64*(2), 262–269. doi:10.1016/j.yhbeh.2013.04.003

Graber, J. A., Lewinsohn, P. M., Seeley, J. R., & BrooksGunn, J. (1997). Is psychopathology associated with the timing of pubertal development? *Journal of the American Academy of Child and Adolescent Psychiatry, 36*(12), 1768–1776.

Graber, J. A., Seeley, J. R., Brooks-Gunn, J., & Lewinsohn, P. M. (2004). Is pubertal timing associated with psychopathology in young adulthood? *Journal of the American Academy of Child and Adolescent Psychiatry, 43*(6), 718–726.

Gurney, M. E., & Konishi, M. (1980). Hormone induced sexual differentiation of brain and behavior in zebra finches. *Science, 208*, 1380–1382.

Hebbard, P. C., King, R. R., Malsbury, C. W., & Harley, C. W. (2003). Two organizational effects of pubertal testosterone in male rats: Transient social memory and a shift away from long-term potentiation following a tetanus in hippocampal CA1. *Experimental Neurology, 182*(2), 470–475.

Herting, M. M., Gautam, P., Spielberg, J. M., Dahl, R. E., & Sowell, E. R. (2015). A longitudinal study: changes in cortical thickness and surface area during pubertal maturation. *PLoS One, 10*(3), e0119774.

Herting, M. M., Gautam, P., Spielberg, J. M., Kan, E., Dahl, R. E., & Sowell, E. R. (2014). The role of testosterone and estradiol in brain volume changes across adolescence: a longitudinal structural MRI study. *Human Brain Mapping, 35*(11), 5633–5645.

Herting, M. M., Maxwell, E. C., Irvine, C., & Nagel, B. J. (2011). The impact of sex, puberty, and hormones on white matter microstructure in adolescents. *Cerebral Cortex, 22*(9), 1979–1992.

Herting, M. M., & Sowell, E. R. (2017). Puberty and structural brain development in humans. *Frontiers in Neuroendocrinology, 44*, 122–137.

Hier, D. B., & Crowley, W. F., Jr. (1982). Spatial ability in androgen-deficient men. *The New England Journal of Medicine, 306*(20), 1202–1205.

Hines, M., Fane, B. A., Pasterski, V. L., Mathews, G. A., Conway, G. S., & Brook, C. (2003). Spatial abilities following prenatal androgen abnormality: Targeting and mental rotations performance in individuals with congenital adrenal hyperplasia. *Psychoneuroendocrinology, 28*(8), 1010–1026. doi:10.1016/s0306-4530(02)00121-x

Huck, U. W., Lisk, R. D., & McKay, M. V. (1988). Social-dominance and reproductive success in pregnant and lactating golden-hamsters (*Mesocricetus-Auratus*) under seminatural conditions. *Physiology & Behavior, 44*(3), 313–319.

Johnson, C., & Wilbrecht, L. (2011). Juvenile mice show greater flexibility in multiple choice reversal learning than adults. *Developmental Cognitive Neuroscience, 1*(4), 540–551. doi:10.1016/j.dcn.2011.05.008

Johnston, R. E. (1970). *Scent marking, olfactory communication and social behavior in the golden hamster, Mesocricetus auratus* (Ph. D. Dissertation), Rockefeller, New York.

Juraska, J. M., & Willing, J. (2016). Pubertal onset as a critical transition for neural development and cognition. *Brain Research, 1654*(Pt B), 87–94. doi:10.1016/j.brainres.2016.04.012

Kellogg, C. K., & Lundin, A. (1999). Brain androgen-inducible aromatase is critical for adolescent organization of environment-specific social interaction in male rats. *Hormones and Behavior, 35*(2), 155–162.

Kercmar, J., Snoj, T., Tobet, S. A., & Majdic, G. (2014). Gonadectomy prior to puberty decreases normal parental behavior in adult mice. *Hormones and Behavior, 66*(4), 667–673. doi:10.1016/j.yhbeh.2014.09.007

Kinsey, A. C. (1948). *Sexual behavior in the human male*. Bloomington, IN: Indiana University Press.

Klump, K. L. (2013). Puberty as a critical risk period for eating disorders: A review of human and animal studies. *Hormones and Behavior, 64*(2), 399–410. doi:10.1016/j.yhbeh.2013.02.019

Koss, W. A., Lloyd, M. M., Sadowski, R. N., Wise, L. M., & Juraska, J. M. (2015). Gonadectomy before puberty increases the number of neurons and glia in the medial prefrontal cortex of female, but not male, rats. *Developmental Psychobiology, 57*(3), 305–312. doi:10.1002/dev.21290

Larsson, K. (1967). Testicular hormone and developmental changes in mating behavior of the male rat. *Journal of Comparative and Physiological Psychology, 63*(2), 223–230.

Larsson, K., Sodersten, P., Beyer, C., Morali, G., & Perez-Palacios, G. (1976). Effects of estrone, estradiol and estriol combined with dihydrotestosterone on mounting and lordosis behavior in castrated male rats. *Hormones and Behavior, 7*(4), 379–390.

Leigh, B. C., Temple, M. T., & Trocki, K. F. (1993). The sexual behavior of US adults: Results from a national survey. *American Journal of Public Health, 83*(10), 1400–1408.

Lenroot, R. K., Gogtay, N., Greenstein, D. K., Wells, E. M., Wallace, G. L., Clasen, L. S., . . . Evans, A. C. (2007). Sexual dimorphism of brain developmental trajectories during childhood and adolescence. *Neuroimage, 36*(4), 1065–1073.

Lumia, A. R., Raskin, L. A., & Eckhert, S. (1977). Effects of androgen on marking and aggressive behavior of neonatally and prepubertally bulbectomized and castrated male gerbils. *Journal of Comparative and Physiological Psychology, 91*(6), 1377–1389.

Marshall, W. A., & Tanner, J. M. (1969). Variations in pattern of pubertal changes in girls. *Archives of Disease in Childhood, 44*(235), 291.

Marshall, W. A., & Tanner, J. M. (1970). Variations in the pattern of pubertal changes in boys. *Archives of Disease in Childhood, 45*(239), 13–23.

Meek, L. R., Romeo, R. D., Novak, C. M., & Sisk, C. L. (1997). Actions of testosterone in prepubertal and postpubertal male hamsters: Dissociation of effects on reproductive behavior and brain androgen receptor immunoreactivity. *Hormones and Behavior, 31*(1), 75–88.

Meerts, S. H., Anderson, K. S., Farry-Thorn, M. E., Johnson, E. G., & Taxier, L. (2017). Prepubertal ovariectomy modulates paced mating behavior but not sexual preference or conditioned place preference for mating in female rats. *Physiology & Behavior, 171*, 142–148.

Menzies, L., Goddings, A.-L., Whitaker, K. J., Blakemore, S.-J., & Viner, R. M. (2015). The effects of puberty on white matter development in boys. *Developmental Cognitive Neuroscience, 11*, 116–128.

Miller, L. L., Whitsett, J. M., Vandenbergh, J. G., & Colby, D. R. (1977). Physical and behavioral aspects of sexual maturation in male golden hamsters. *Journal of Comparative and Physiological Psychology, 91*(2), 245–259.

Mohr, M. A., & Sisk, C. L. (2013). Pubertally born neurons and glia are functionally integrated into limbic and hypothalamic circuits of the male Syrian hamster. *Proceedings of the National Academy of Sciences of the United States America, 110*(12), 4792–4797. doi:10.1073/pnas.1219443110

Morris, J. A., Jordan, C. L., King, Z. A., Northcutt, K. V., & Breedlove, S. M. (2008). Sexual dimorphism and steroid responsiveness of the posterodorsal medial amygdala in adult mice. *Brain Research, 1190*, 115–121. doi:10.1016/j.brainres.2007.11.005

Mueller, S. C., Temple, V., Oh, E., VanRyzin, C., Williams, A., Cornwell, B., ... Merke, D. P. (2008). Early androgen exposure modulates spatial cognition in Congenital Adrenal Hyperplasia (CAH). *Psychoneuroendocrinology, 33*(7), 973–980. doi:10.1016/j.psyneuen.2008.04.005

Negriff, S., & Susman, E. J. (2011). Pubertal timing, depression, and externalizing problems: A framework, review, and examination of gender differences. *Journal of Research on Adolescence, 21*(3), 717–746. doi:10.1111/j.1532-7795.2010.00708.x

Newman, S. W. (1999). The medial extended amygdala in male reproductive behavior: A node in the mammalian social behavior network. *Annals of the New York Academy of Sciences, 877*, 242–257.

Paup, D. C., Coniglio, L. P., & Clemens, L. G. (1972). Masculinization of the female golden hamster by neonatal treatment with androgen or estrogen. *Hormones and Behavior, 3*(2), 123–131.

Paus, T., Nawaz-Khan, I., Leonard, G., Perron, M., Pike, G., Pitiot, A., ... Pausova, Z. (2010). Sexual dimorphism in the adolescent brain: role of testosterone and androgen receptor in global and local volumes of grey and white matter. *Hormones and Behavior, 57*(1), 63–75.

Paus, T., Zijdenbos, A., Worsley, K., Collins, D. L., Blumenthal, J., Giedd, J. N., ... Evans, A. C. (1999). Structural maturation of neural pathways in children and adolescents: in vivo study. *Science, 283*(5409), 1908–1911.

Payne, A. P., & Swanson, H. H. (1970). Agonistic behaviour between pairs of hamsters of same and opposite sex in a neutral observation area. *Behaviour, 36*(4), 259–&.

Pellis, S. M. (2002). Sex differences in play fighting revisited: Traditional and nontraditional mechanisms of sexual differentiation in rats. *Archives of Sex Behavior, 31*(1), 17–26.

Peper, J. S., Brouwer, R. M., Schnack, H. G., van Baal, G. C., van Leeuwen, M., van den Berg, S. M., ... Pol, H. E. H. (2009). Sex steroids and brain structure in pubertal boys and girls. *Psychoneuroendocrinology, 34*(3), 332–342.

Peper, J. S., van den Heuvel, M. P., Mandl, R. C., Pol, H. E. H., van Honk, J. (2011). Sex steroids and connectivity in the human brain: a review of neuroimaging studies. *Psychoneuroendocrinology, 36*(8), 1101–1113.

Perrin, J. S., Hervé, P.-Y., Leonard, G., Perron, M., Pike, G. B., Pitiot, A., ... Paus, T. (2008). Growth of white matter in the adolescent brain: role of testosterone and androgen receptor. *Journal of Neuroscience, 28*(38), 9519–9524.

Perrin, J. S., Leonard, G., Perron, M., Pike, G. B., Pitiot, A., Richer, L., ... Paus, T. (2009). Sex differences in the growth of white matter during adolescence. *Neuroimage, 45*(4), 1055–1066.

Petersen, A. C., Crockett, L., Richards, M., & Boxer, A. (1988). A self-report measure of pubertal status: Reliability, validity, and initial norms. *Journal of Youth and Adolescence, 17*(2), 117–133.

Phoenix, C. H., Goy, R. W., Gerall, A. A., & Young, W. C. (1959). Organizing action of prenatally administered testosterone propionate on the tissues mediating mating behavior in the female guinea pig. *Endocrinology, 65*, 369–382.

Piekarski, D. J., Johnson, C. M., Boivin, J. R., Thomas, A. W., Lin, W. C., Delevich, K., ... Wilbrecht, L. (2017). Does puberty mark a transition in sensitive periods for plasticity in the associative neocortex? *Brain Research, 1654*, 123–144.

Primus, R. J., & Kellogg, C. K. (1989). Pubertal-related changes influence the development of environment-related social interaction in the male rat. *Developmental Psychobiology, 22*(6), 633–643.

Primus, R. J., & Kellogg, C. K. (1990). Gonadal hormones during puberty organize environment-related social interaction in the male rat. *Hormones and Behavior, 24*(3), 311–323.

Romeo, R. D., Cook-Wiens, E., Richardson, H. N., & Sisk, C. L. (2001). Dihydrotestosterone activates sexual behavior in adult male hamsters but not in juveniles. *Physiology & Behavior, 73*(4), 579–584.

Romeo, R. D., Wagner, C. K., Jansen, H. T., Diedrich, S. L., & Sisk, C. L. (2002). Estradiol induces hypothalamic progesterone receptors but does not activate mating behavior in male hamsters (*Mesocricetus auratus*) before puberty. *Behavioral Neuroscience, 116*(2), 198–205.

Schulz, K. M., Menard, T. A., Smith, D. A., Albers, H. E., & Sisk, C. L. (2006). Testicular hormone exposure during adolescence organizes flank-marking behavior and vasopressin receptor binding in the lateral septum. *Hormones and Behavior, 50*(3), 477–483. doi:10.1016/j.yhbeh.2006.06.006

Schulz, K. M., Molenda-Figueira, H. A., & Sisk, C. L. (2009). Back to the future: The organizational-activational hypothesis adapted to puberty and adolescence. *Hormones and Behavior, 55*(5), 597–604. doi:10.1016/j.yhbeh.2009.03.010

Schulz, K. M., Richardson, H. N., Zehr, J. L., Osetek, A. J., Menard, T. A., & Sisk, C. L. (2004). Gonadal hormones masculinize and defeminize reproductive behaviors during puberty in the male Syrian hamster. *Hormones and Behavior, 45*(4), 242–249. doi:10.1016/j.yhbeh.2003.12.007

Schulz, K. M., & Sisk, C. L. (2006). Pubertal hormones, the adolescent brain, and the maturation of social behaviors: Lessons from the Syrian hamster. *Molecular and Cellular Endocrinology, 254–255*, 120–126. doi:10.1016/j.mce.2006.04.025

Schulz, K. M., & Sisk, C. L. (2016). The organizing actions of adolescent gonadal steroid hormones on brain and behavioral development. *Neuroscience and Biobehavioral Reviews, 70*, 148–158. doi:10.1016/j.neubiorev.2016.07.036

Schulz, K. M., & Sisk, C. L. (2017). Gonadal hormonal influences on the adolescent brain and trajectories of behavioral development. In *Hormones brain and behavior.* San Diego, CA: Academic Press.

Schulz, K. M., Zehr, J. L., Salas-Ramirez, K. Y., & Sisk, C. L. (2009). Testosterone programs adult social behavior before and during, but not after, adolescence. *Endocrinology, 150*(8), 3690–3698. doi:en.2008-1708 [pii] 10.1210/en.2008-1708

Scott, J. P., Stewart, J. M., & De Ghett, V. J. (1974). Critical periods in the organization of systems. In *Developmental psychobiology.* Hoboken, NJ: John Wiley & Sons, Inc.

Shrenker, P., Maxson, S. C., & Ginsburg, B. E. (1985). The role of postnatal testosterone in the development of sexually dimorphic behaviors in DBA/1Bg mice. *Physiology & Behavior, 35*, 757–762.

Sisk, C. L., Schulz, K. M., & Zehr, J. L. (2003). Puberty: A finishing school for male social behavior. *Annals of the New York Academy of Sciences, 1007*(Steroids and the Nervous System), 189–198.

Sisk, C. L., & Turek, F. W. (1983). Developmental time course of pubertal and photoperiodic changes in testosterone negative feedback on gonadotropin secretion in the golden hamster. *Endocrinology, 112*(4), 1208–1216.

Sisk, C. L., & Zehr, J. L. (2005). Pubertal hormones organize the adolescent brain and behavior. *Frontiers in Neuroendocrinology, 26*(3–4), 163–174.

Smith, L. K., Forgie, M. L., & Pellis, S. M. (1998). Mechanisms underlying the absence of the pubertal shift in the playful defense of female rats. *Developmental Psychobiology, 33*(2), 147–156.

Sodersten, P. (1973). Estrogen-activated sexual behavior in male rats. *Hormones and Behavior, 4*(3), 247–256.

Swithers, S. E., McCurley, M., Hamilton, E., & Doerflinger, A. (2008). Influence of ovarian hormones on development of ingestive responding to alterations in fatty acid oxidation in female rats. *Hormones and Behavior, 54*(3), 471–477. doi:10.1016/j.yhbeh.2008.05.009

Takesian, A. E., & Hensch, T. K. (2013). Balancing plasticity/stability across brain development. In M. M. Merzenich, M. Nahum, & T. M. VanVleet (Eds.), *Changing brains applying brain plasticity to advance and recover human ability* (Vol. 207, pp. 3–34). Amsterdam: Elsevier.

Vomachka, A. J., & Greenwald, G. S. (1979). The development of gonadotropin and steroid hormone patterns in male and female hamsters from birth to puberty. *Endocrinology, 105*(4), 960–966.

Wallen, K., & Baum, M. J. (2002). Masculinization and defeminization in altricial and precocial mammals: Comparative aspects of steroid hormone action. In D. W. Pfaff, A. P. Arnold, A. M. Etgen, S. E. Fahrbach, & R. T. Rubin (Eds.), *Hormones, brain and behavior* (Vol. 4, pp. 385–423). Oxford: Elsevier.

Willing, J., & Juraska, J. M. (2015). The timing of neuronal loss across adolescence in the medial prefrontal cortex of male and female rats. *Neuroscience, 301*, 268–275. doi:10.1016/j.neuroscience.2015.05.073

Zehr, J. L., Culbert, K. M., Sisk, C. L., & Klump, K. L. (2007). An association of early puberty with disordered eating and anxiety in a population of undergraduate women and men. *Hormones and Behavior, 52*(4), 427–435.

31

THE SOCIAL BIOPSYCHOLOGY OF IMPLICIT MOTIVE DEVELOPMENT

Martin G. Köllner, Kevin T. Janson, and Kira Bleck

This chapter summarizes recent evidence for organizational hormone effects (OHEs), that is, lasting organizational effects of steroid hormones on nervous system structure occurring during development (Sisk & Zehr, 2005), on the development of non-conscious motivational dispositions. We combine this evidence with earlier research on social aspects into a biopsychosocial developmental model, assuming that OHEs provide a biological basis for non-conscious motivational dispositions, which is then pruned and fine-tuned to varying degrees by later social learning experiences. We focus on human participants (for OHEs in animals please see the chapter by K. Schulz) and on non-conscious motivational dispositions. While there is evidence for influences of interactions between hormones and conscious traits on behavior (e.g., Carré et al., 2016; Slatcher, Mehta, & Josephs, 2011), this is beyond this chapter's scope, because non-conscious and conscious motivational dispositions are clearly distinct, as outlined below.

Implicit motives

Implicit motives are dispositions allowing an individual to perceive the attainment of specific types of incentives as rewarding and the confrontation with specific types of disincentives as aversive (Schultheiss, 2008; Schultheiss & Köllner, 2014). Operating outside of conscious awareness, they select, energize, and direct behavior (McClelland, 1987), partly by interacting with endocrine systems (Schultheiss, 2013).

A large body of research has focused on three implicit motives: (1) the implicit need for power (nPower) – the capacity for deriving pleasure from having impact on others while experiencing others' impact on oneself as aversive; (2) implicit need for affiliation (nAffiliation) – the capacity to derive pleasure from establishing, maintaining, and restoring positive interpersonal relationships; and (3) implicit need for achievement (nAchievement) – the capacity to derive pleasure from autonomous mastery of challenging tasks (see Schultheiss, 2008, for details). We focus on nPower, while the latter two needs are only addressed briefly.

Implicit motives differ from explicit motives (self-attributed needs and goals; McClelland, Koestner, & Weinberger, 1989), predicting different kinds of behaviors and responding to different cue types (Schultheiss, 2008; cf. meta-analysis by Spangler, 1992). While self-attributed needs predict planned behaviors like judgments and choices and respond to verbal cues, implicit motives predict spontaneous behaviors and respond to non-verbal cues (e.g., Biernat, 1989;

see Schultheiss, 2008). Moreover, implicit and explicit motives have no substantial overlap, as demonstrated by 60 years of meta-analytically combined research (Köllner & Schultheiss, 2014; Spangler, 1992), and may depend on neurobiologically distinct motivational systems (McClelland et al., 1989).

An individual's implicit motive strength is not consciously accessible and cannot be measured via questionnaires (see Schultheiss, 2008). Thus, a well-established method for motive assessment is the Picture-Story Exercise (PSE; McClelland et al., 1989), comprising four to eight pictures of persons in ambiguous social situations, such as two women working in a laboratory (see Schultheiss & Pang, 2007). These pictures are presented in random order and participants have four minutes per picture to write imaginative stories. The stories are then scored by coders who previously exceeded 85% interscorer-agreement with experts on training materials. Coders analyze the stories for imagery pertaining to specific motive domains like nPower (e.g., strong forceful actions, impressing others) following specific coding rules (e.g., Winter, 1994). Such coding rules are empirically derived by comparing stories from participants with experimentally aroused motives to stories from control participants (see Schultheiss & Köllner, in press, for an overview). These coding systems are causally valid, since resulting scores reflect experimental manipulations of the measured construct (cf. Borsboom, Mellenbergh, & van Heerden, 2004). Scores are summed within every motive domain to yield overall motive scores for each participant and are typically corrected for overall PSE story length (see Schultheiss & Pang, 2007).

Predictive validity of the implicit need for power

Implicit motives possess high predictive validity. For example, nPower is linked to various individual (e.g., proximal: behavioral expression of preference for signals of submission, Stoeckart, Strick, Bijleveld, & Aarts, 2017; distal: managerial success, McClelland & Boyatzis, 1982), biological (e.g., sympathetic activation; McClelland, 1982), and societal (e.g., engagement in wars; see Schultheiss, 2008, for an overview) criteria.

A recurrent moderator of nPower's associations with various criteria is activity inhibition (AI; McClelland & Boyatzis, 1982; Schultheiss & Brunstein, 2002; see Schultheiss, 2008). AI is measured via PSE (counting the frequency of the negation "not"; Langens, 2010) and considered a marker for greater right-hemispheric and lesser left-hemispheric engagement during stress (Schultheiss, Riebel, & Jones, 2009). High-AI individuals appear to have better access to functions associated with the right hemisphere, such as emotion-encoding and -decoding competencies (Schultheiss et al., 2009). Thus, high nPower paired with high AI, the inhibited power motive (IPM), makes individuals particularly successful in the social arena (Schultheiss & Brunstein, 2002). This may be due to their power behavior being more context-sensitive and sophisticated (Schultheiss & Köllner, in press), as can be observed for example in a proficiency in persuasive communication as indicated by factors like gesturing or speaking fluently (Schultheiss & Brunstein, 2002).

An explanation for nPower's ties to a wide range of behaviors is its affect-amplifying function (see Schultheiss & Köllner, 2014). Altering the reinforcer value of specific stimuli by enhancing affective responses to them, nPower can have scaling effects on stimulus-driven learning processes (Schultheiss & Köllner, 2014). This facilitates the acquisition of behaviors allowing an individual to exert influence on others, like persuasive communication (Schultheiss & Brunstein, 2002).

Another way for nPower to influence behavior is by interacting with endocrine systems in situational contexts that evoke dominance arousal or stress (Schultheiss, 2013; Stanton & Schultheiss, 2007, 2009). nPower is tied to activational effects of the steroid hormones testosterone (T) in men and estradiol (E2) in women (Schultheiss, 2013). Activational hormone effects are reversible hormone concentration changes promoting the display of certain behaviors (Sisk & Zehr, 2005). For example, T-increases after losing a dominance contest predict an increased inclination among men to engage in another contest, whereas T-decreases predict withdrawal from further competition (Mehta & Josephs, 2006). Although extensively researched, increases in T after winning a dominance contest and decreases in T after losing a contest cannot be found consistently in human samples (see Carré & Olmstead, 2015, for a review), with the overall effect being highly heterogeneous and the effect in lab settings being restricted to men and very weak (see Geniole, Bird, Ruddick, & Carré, 2017, for a meta-analysis). However, when nPower is considered, the expected effects are found in high-power men (Schultheiss, 2013). nPower is associated with T-changes after dominance contests in a direction depending on their outcome: High-power but not low-power men show T increases after winning and decreases in T after losing (e.g., Schultheiss, Wirth et al., 2005; Vongas & Al Hajj, 2017). These effects are assumed to be (partly) mediated by interactions of nPower with other hormonal parameters, such as epinephrine and norepinephrine release after winning (stimulating effect on testes) and cortisol release after losing a dominance contest (inhibiting effect on testes; Schultheiss, 2013; Stanton & Schultheiss, 2009; cf. Sapolsky, 1987). In women, nPower predicts E2 changes in reaction to a dominance contest in the same pattern as it predicts T changes in men: High-power but not low-power women show E2 increases after winning and decreases in E2 after losing (Stanton & Schultheiss, 2007). A recent study again found that among normally cycling women high but not low in nPower, winners had higher post-contest E2 levels than losers (Oxford, Tiedtke, Ossmann, Özbe, & Schultheiss, 2017). Thus, E2 seems to play a similar role in women as T plays in men regarding dominance behaviors and nPower (Schultheiss, 2013).

Despite nPower's broad predictive validity, not much research was devoted to its development until recently. Central among past research is a longitudinal study identifying associations of specific early child-rearing practices reported by mothers when their children were 5 years of age with specific adult implicit motive levels of these children at the age of 31 to 32 (McClelland & Pilon, 1983). For example, severity of toilet training and scheduling of feeding was associated with later nAchievement and possibly lacking maternal responsiveness for the child's crying with later nAffiliation. Most importantly, parental permissiveness for aggressive and sexual behaviors was linked to children's adult nPower. At first glance, one might assume that these parenting practices may be the roots of adult implicit motive levels. However, taking nPower as an example, this raises the question where those aggressive and sexual behaviors and their underlying inter-individual differences to which parents react to originate from in the first place. Indeed, recent findings hint at even earlier influences on motive development: OHEs (Schultheiss, 2017; Schultheiss & Zimni, 2015).

Implicit motives and organizational hormone effects

Organizational hormone effects and the marker hypothesis

OHEs differ from activational hormone effects, as the former entail lasting changes to an organism's nervous system structure and shape, especially during important developmental stages (Schultheiss, Schiepe, & Rawolle, 2012; Sisk & Zehr, 2005). Prenatal (Phoenix, Goy, Gerall, & Young, 1959) and pubertal (Sisk & Zehr, 2005) OHEs are particularly relevant for brain organization and adult behavior. In the following, we refer to prenatal and pubertal "stages", but only for ease of description: They may not be discrete events but rather part of protracted continuing development until adulthood (cf. Schulz, Molenda-Figueira, & Sisk, 2009). While the brain's sensitivity for OHEs decreases across the protracted postnatal period, increased hormone exposure during these stages renders them critical for development (see model in Schulz et al., 2009).

The brain, especially the hypothalamus, is the origin of hormonal and autonomic nervous system processes involved in motivation (see Schultheiss, 2013, for an overview). As the brain is also the target of the above-mentioned OHEs during development, it is plausible that individual differences in the functioning of the adult motivational brain are related to individual differences in earlier exposure to OHEs. But how can we retrospectively assess OHEs?

Traces of exposure to OHEs are reflected in morphological markers, as OHEs also effect bodily changes. Such correlated changes between an organism's nervous system function and body morphology, triggered by the same organizational hormones, should allow the approximation of OHEs on the developing brain and on brain-dependent motivational processes via body markers (Hönekopp, Bartholdt, Beier, & Liebert, 2007). This renders markers valuable information sources, as experimental manipulation of hormone levels in humans during development is impossible due to ethical reasons.

The ability of markers to reflect differences in OHE exposure during development is underscored by the fact that they are often sex-dimorphic, reflecting sex differences in hormone secretion during development (Ober, Loisel, & Gilad, 2008). For example, sexual dimorphisms were observed for the second-to-fourth-digit length ratio (2D:4D), with men featuring smaller ratios than women (e.g., Hönekopp et al., 2007; Zheng & Cohn, 2011). Also, the facial width-to-height ratio (fWHR), the bizygomatic width (distance between left and right zygion) divided by upper face height (distance between nasion and prosthion; e.g., Zilioli et al., 2015; cf. Weston, Friday, & Liò, 2007), is overall larger for men compared to women (see meta-analyses by Geniole, Denson, Dixson, Carré, & McCormick, 2015; Kramer, 2017, but see also Kramer's follow-up analyses within the same paper).

We argue that it may be fruitful to investigate possible connections between OHEs, reflected in morphological markers, and implicit motive development: First, hormones influence motivational development (e.g., the emergence of new motivational tendencies during puberty; Forbes & Dahl, 2010). Second, organizational hormones and social experiences may interact in shaping, for example, assertive behaviors (Schulz et al., 2009). Consequently, the above-mentioned parenting practices (McClelland & Pilon, 1983) may not constitute the actual origins of motives but instead a social learning–based modulation of a biological basis previously established by OHEs. Actually, this is very likely, as the evidence from marker studies involving 2D:4D and fWHR shows.

Prenatal hormone effects and implicit motive development: the case of 2D:4D

Evidence for 2D:4D's marker function for prenatal OHEs comes from several observations: For example, the length of the fourth digit can be experimentally increased by prenatal T and reduced by prenatal estrogen in mice (Zheng & Cohn, 2011). In addition, in humans, the sexual dimorphism in 2D:4D is already present after the first trimester of pregnancy (Malas, Dogan, Evcil, & Desdicioglu, 2006) and remains stable afterwards. Furthermore, 2D:4D is largely unrelated to adult sex hormone levels (Hönekopp et al., 2007).

There are several ways of measuring 2D:4D, including anthropometry and palm scans/photocopies (Kemper & Schwerdtfeger, 2009). Also, 2D:4D has various correlates: For example, a low 2D:4D is substantially related to athletic prowess (Hönekopp & Schuster, 2010). In the case of aggression, while the meta-analytically derived effect sizes are far too small to be considered practically meaningful, a minuscule overall association of 2D:4D with aggression and violent behavior across both genders emerged (Turanovic, Pratt, & Piquero, 2017).

2D:4D and implicit motives

A link between motives and 2D:4D was repeatedly found. Currently, two published 2D:4D samples suggest prenatal OHEs on nPower development: Schultheiss and Zimni (2015) observed an association between a more "male-typical", smaller 2D:4D, assessed with a ruler on photocopies of the hands, and PSE-nPower in the context of high AI (see Figure 31.1). This moderating effect of AI as an indicator of brain lateralization is not surprising considering the IPMs' above-mentioned relevance.

In another study featuring the PSE and hand scans, Schultheiss (2017) again found that a more "male-typical" digit ratio of the right hand was associated with simultaneously high nPower and high AI, directly replicating Schultheiss and Zimni (2015). In addition, there were sex-dimorphic relationships between digit ratio (right hand) and nPower: Women with a higher nPower, but not men, also had more female-typical higher 2D:4D.

Recently, O. C. Schultheiss (personal communication, October 19/20, 2017), corroborated this link in a large aggregation featuring more than 400 participants and including three individual studies, among them the sample of Schultheiss (2017). A sex-dimorphic relationship reflected in a Sex x nPower x AI interaction emerged for the asymmetry (left versus right) of 2D:4D, with a stronger nPower x AI effect in women. Among women, nPower correlated differently with 2D:4D-asymmetry for high-inhibition versus low-inhibition participants. In sum, OHEs seem to contribute to the development of a joint motivational syndrome involving nPower and AI, probably in a sex-dimorphic way.

Pubertal hormone effects and implicit motive development: the case of fWHR

fWHR can be considered a marker of OHEs on the pubertal brain: It is a craniofacial feature of skulls that may develop sex-dimorphically after the onset of puberty (Weston et al., 2007). While steroid hormones influence human craniofacial growth (Verdonck, Gaethofs, Carels, & de

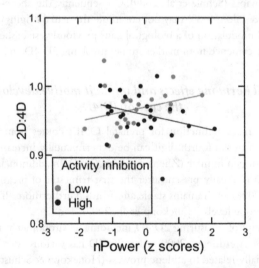

Figure 31.1 Interaction effect of nPower and activity inhibition on 2D:4D digit ratio (averaged across both hands). From: Schultheiss and Zimni (2015, Figure 2, p. 398).

Zegher, 1999), fWHR is associated with pubertal T when controlling for age (Welker, Bird, & Arnocky, 2016).

fWHR is measured for example via anthropometry or from photos (see Geniole et al., 2015, Supplementary). It has correlates like aggressive behavior in men (Carré & McCormick, 2008) or fighting ability in professional competitions (Zilioli et al., 2015). Meta-analyses revealed small associations between fWHR and male aggression (Haselhuhn, Ormiston, & Wong, 2015), as well as male threat behavior and dominance behavior across both sexes (Geniole et al., 2015). Geniole et al. (2015) concluded that fWHR may be part of an evolved intra-sexual signal system for dominance among men, but their relationship between fWHR and dominance behavior also included female participants. The latter finding is remarkable, especially as Haselhuhn et al. (2015) had a priori excluded women.

fWHR and implicit motives

fWHR's correlates suggest a possible link to nPower. Thus, we (Janson et al., 2018) tested this relationship using anthropometry and a six-picture PSE in two samples, later combining them for adequate statistical power. Controlling for BMI and age, which both influenced fWHR, we found a pattern much like the one observed by Schultheiss and Zimni (2015), however reversed, as fWHR is positively associated with dominance, not negatively like 2D:4D. The expected nPower x AI interaction on fWHR-scores emerged, with the IPM tending to predict high, and a disinhibited nPower tending to predict low, fWHR. However, when considering sex, this pattern only held for women (see Figure 31.2).

This women-specific finding seems to be at odds with fWHR's supposed status as an evolved male within-sex threat and dominance cue informative for the intra-sexual competition among men (Geniole et al., 2015). However, we offer an alternative explanation: First, the expected nPower x AI interaction was lower-order than the unexpected moderation and may be easier to replicate. Thus, the moderation by sex needs replication before it is taken seriously. Second, nPower does not deal with threat specifically but more broadly with having influence on others as a precursor of attaining dominance (cf. Schultheiss & Köllner, in press). Thus, reducing nPower to threat or aggression (in men) is inappropriate. Third, dominance behavior, a more appropriate construct when dealing with nPower in general, was associated with fWHR across both sexes meta-analytically (Geniole et al., 2015). Fourth, E2, a hormone with ties to nPower in women, may influence (facial) bone growth, too. Therefore, reducing fWHR to a marker of pubertal T only may be an oversimplification (see Janson et al., 2018, for details). We conclude that our basic nPower x AI interaction indicates that pubertal OHEs influence or refine the adult nPower in similar ways as prenatal OHEs.

The social biopsychology of implicit motive development: a tentative model

Building on these findings (for an overview of the so-far published studies, please see Table 31.1), we now discuss their implications for the bigger picture of implicit motive development (see Figure 31.3). Combined with evidence for early social influences on motives (e.g., McClelland & Pilon, 1983), they suggest a biological basis (growth-parts of Figure 31.3) which channels motive development and is later trimmed and fine-tuned by social learning experiences (Prune & Tune-parts; compare Schultheiss & Köllner, in press).

Prenatal OHEs on motive development (Growth-I) were found using 2D:4D as a marker in two published samples and showed up in a large aggregation of existing samples. This represents

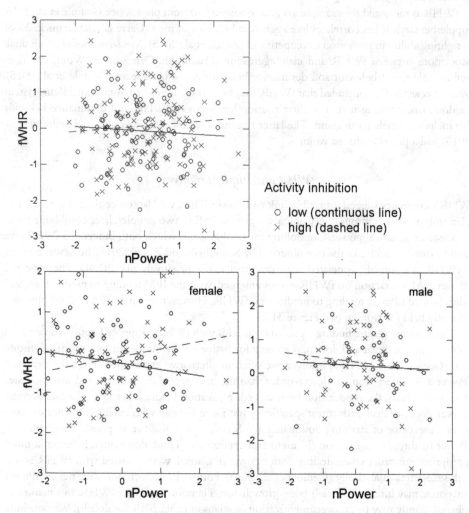

Figure 31.2 Scatter plots showing associations of fWHR and nPower in low/high AI subsamples after median split on AI variable for the overall sample (top half) and for women (bottom left) and men (bottom right), respectively. Z-scores were used for computation. AI and nPower were subjected to a square-root transformation after adding a constant of 1 and residualized for story word-count. From: Janson et al. (2018; Figure 1/3; pp. 31–32).

robust evidence, as consistently (1) nPower was associated with 2D:4D when considering (2) AI as a moderator.

How can we explain such marker–motive relationships? A possible brain basis of nPower may be found in a network of subcortical nuclei centered on the anterior hypothalamus, as the latter seems to be important for aggressive dominance in animal studies mediated by E2 and T (Schultheiss, 2013; cf. Nelson & Trainor, 2007). Though human nPower as a broad disposition should not necessarily be equated with aggressive dominance in animals, prenatal hormone

Table 31.1 Overview of the so-far published findings regarding implicit motives and organizational hormone effects

Study	N	Marker	Main association	Other associations/findings
Schultheiss & Zimni (2015)	50	2D:4D	Low 2D:4D with IPM	–
Schultheiss (2017)	144	2D:4D	Low right 2D:4D with IPM	Higher right 2D:4D with high nPower in women
Janson et al. (2018)	213	fWHR	High fWHR with IPM	Main finding moderated by sex, pattern holds for women only

Note: nPower = implicit need for power; IPM = inhibited nPower; 2D:4D = second-to-fourth-digit length ratio; fWHR = facial width-to-height ratio.

effects targeting this network may lead to lasting variations in human nPower. These variations may then for example entail inter-individual differences in the aggressive behaviors to which parental practices were found to react in the study by McClelland and Pilon (1983).

The frequent moderation of the results by AI as a marker for functional hemispheric asymmetry during stress indicates that inhibited nPower/IPM specifically is tied to prenatal OHEs. The pervasive moderation pattern may even suggest that high AI at least partly results from lateralized brain development due to early endocrine influences: Prenatal T disadvantages the left compared to the right hemisphere during development (Geschwind & Galaburda, 1987). This may explain why the left cortex is thinner in human fetuses and lateralization stronger for male ones (Kivilevitch, Achiron, & Zalel, 2010). It may also explain why male human fetuses have a larger right-hemispheric volume and why early sex steroid exposure influences brain asymmetry in rodents, with a thicker right compared to left neocortex found in males (see Toga & Thompson, 2003, for an overview). Thus, prenatal T may contribute to functional asymmetries, for example lateralization of prefrontal cortex (PFC) functions. The PFC modulates human dominance behavior, as reduced PFC-activation seems to be associated with impulsive aggression (cf. Nelson & Trainor, 2007). This may explain why AI is part of the socially effective IPM and a consistent moderator in studies involving motives and markers of OHEs. Also, this may elucidate AI's continued relevance as a moderator when examining pubertal OHEs on motives: Primate studies show dopaminergic and other circuitry changes in the PFC during adolescence, changing cortical connectivity, and almost all such adolescent brain-remodeling mechanisms can be influenced by hormones (Sisk & Zehr, 2005).

The fact that the so-far obtained findings were repeatedly sex-dimorphic (Schultheiss, 2017; O.C. Schultheiss, personal communication, October 19/20, 2017) is another noteworthy aspect of the result patterns. This brings to mind other sex-dimorphic 2D:4D-associations, for example in the BBC Internet Study (Manning & Fink, 2008) where 2D:4D was positively related to family size and reproductive success for women, but negatively for men. Also, sex-dimorphic findings in the domain of motive development are not surprising, considering what is known about activational hormone effects of the male (T) and female (E2) "dominance hormone", respectively (Schultheiss, 2013): A "male-typical" 2D:4D should represent high prenatal T-to-E2 ratio, whereas a "female-typical" 2D:4D should represent low T-to-E2 ratio (Lutchmaya, Baron-Cohen, Raggatt, Knickmeyer, & Manning, 2004; but see the partial-at-best replication by Ventura, Gomes, Pita, Neto, & Taylor, 2013).

As a side note, one study also reports some genetic influences on implicit motive strength, predominantly for nAffiliation, and on behavioral motive expression for all three motives

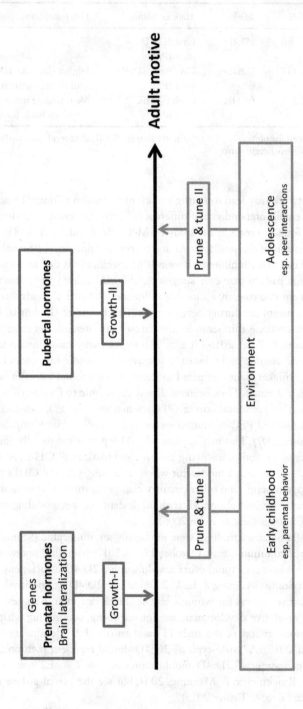

Figure 31.3 Tentative biopsychosocial model of implicit motive development. Prenatal and pubertal organizational hormone effects (Growth-I/II) provide a biological basis for an emerging implicit motive which is later "pruned and tuned" by social learning experiences in interactions with the environment during early childhood or adolescence, respectively (Prune & Tune-I/II). Until now, Prune & Tune-II has been based on grounded speculation.

(Hagemeyer & Kandler, 2014, September). Thus, we include genes in our model, but without drawing far-reaching conclusions based on a single study so far.

Regarding social learning experiences in early childhood (Prune & Tune-I), we assume a trimming and shaping of (1) a motive's strength, previously influenced by prenatal OHEs, and (2) a motive's socialization level, especially by the parents, respectively. Schultheiss and Köllner (in press) suggest that the biological basis of power motivation needs further refinement for developing socially acceptable forms, for example via contextual factors or parenting practices. This fits well with the associations of specific early parenting practices with specific adult motive levels (McClelland & Pilon, 1983).

Regarding the psychological mechanism behind this social learning, besides pruning (Schultheiss & Köllner, in press) in the sense of a necessary curtailing of the unrefined power impulses of children (and to some extent also of adolescents, see below), we believe that there is also a "tuning" aspect associated with social interactions: Interactions with the environment set the stage for Pavlovian (learning predictive cues, mediated by the amygdala) and instrumental conditioning processes (via reinforcement of successful behavior leading to incentive contact, mediated by the striatum). The effectiveness of these conditioning processes depends on the incentives reaped from those interactions via a hedonic response, which in turn depends on the strength of a given implicit motive (see Schultheiss & Köllner, 2014, for the pathways in which motives influence learning, their neuronal underpinnings, and an integrative skill-building model) to which prenatal hormones contribute in the first place.

Thus, if a child displaying behaviors like screaming or aggressive acts is unsuccessful in attracting attention or attaining influence on parental behavior or even gets punished, such outcomes will be much more aversive if the child is high in nPower and the child will try to avoid such unpleasing experiences in the future, inhibiting the behavior (pruning). Searching for alternative impact strategies, it will learn that predictive contextual cues in the appropriate situational context (for which the hippocampus mediates episodic memory that is also modulated by motive-dependent affective responses; see Schultheiss & Köllner, 2014) need to be considered and try more refined behaviors and more contextualized strategies. This way, the child will be rewarded with the desired influence on parental or peer behavior and is conditioned to use such refined behavior in future social interactions (tuning). Such shaping processes are especially likely for the IPM, to which most of the above-mentioned results regarding OHEs pertain: The results of IPM-individuals' highly refined skill building are later observable in their behavior (persuasive speech, e.g., gesturing, speaking fluently) and life outcomes in management or voluntary office holding (cf. Schultheiss & Brunstein, 2002, for an overview). Motive-dependent skill building in turn may again be influenced by hormones: Effects of nPower on implicit learning phenomena may be mediated by steroid hormones under some conditions (Schultheiss & Rohde, 2002; Schultheiss, Wirth et al., 2005), and hormones can affect all stages of learning (see Nelson & Kriegsfeld, 2017, for an overview).

As stated above, we consider early childhood factors not as the origins of motives, but as pruning and tuning of their prenatal biological basis (cf. Schultheiss & Köllner, in press). For example, regarding nPower development, parents can only be permissive towards aggressive impulses if such impulses are displayed – if not, mothers cannot accurately report their degree of permissiveness (cf. McClelland & Pilon, 1983, for problems related to linking adult traits with early child-rearing practices). In sum, the initial strength of such impulses in interaction with the degree to which parents scale back aggressiveness or channel it into more socially accepted forms of self-assertion should determine the first model-half's outcome.

Pubertal OHEs on implicit motive development (Growth-II) are suggested by our fWHR-study (Janson et al., 2018). The findings resemble those of Schultheiss and Zimni (2015) for

2D:4D, suggesting that prenatal and pubertal hormonal effects on motive development may be similar. Based on our results, a connection between pubertal OHEs and adult motive levels is very likely, but further research must corroborate this conclusion, which currently rests on a single, albeit large, two-sample study.

There is currently no research regarding adolescent social learning experiences (Prune & Tune-II). However, adolescent social pruning and fine-tuning of the outcomes of pubertal OHEs on motive development is plausible, as social experiences modulate OHEs on behavior during adolescence (Schulz et al., 2009). McClelland and Pilon (1983) state that their early childhood correlates only explain 10–30% of the variance and that later experiences during school or adulthood may contribute to specific motive levels. The role of peers during adolescence may be particularly important here, considering the heightened sensitivity to peer acceptance or rejection and an increased affective impact of peer interactions due to their rewarding nature during adolescence (see Kilford, Garrett, & Blakemore, 2016, for a review). This rewarding nature may create the incentives for similar Pavlovian and instrumental conditioning phenomena like those we assume for early childhood: Further refinement of impact strategies that were successful or socially accepted during childhood is necessary to arrive at the highly refined contextualized behavioral patterns underlying successful dominance in adult life. Peer interactions may be the testing ground for the development of such patterns. Also, if dominance is about gaining access to resources and mates (cf. Schultheiss, Pang, Torges, Wirth, & Treynor, 2005), the latter aspect should only become relevant after becoming able to sexually reproduce after the onset of puberty, demanding corresponding refinement of nPower as a precursor of attaining intra-sex dominance and thus becoming attractive to the other sex (intra-sexual selection; see Wilson, 1980, p. 159). However, these deliberations are speculative until direct evidence is available.

Our model does not deny other possible influences on adult nPower expression. For example, having younger siblings, and later having children, seems to channel nPower expression away from impulsive and towards more responsible behaviors (Winter, 1988). In addition, social environmental factors assessed at the age of 5 may be associated with later IPM specifically: For boys, primary involvement of the mother versus of the father in child-rearing seems to be associated with a disinhibited nPower, high nPower (higher than nAffiliation) combined with low AI, versus the "imperial-power-motive syndrome", high nPower (higher than nAffiliation) combined with high AI, respectively (McClelland & Pilon, 1983, p. 571). Moreover, our focus on critical developmental stages does not preclude the possibility of motive changes later in life, as brain development continues long after the end of adolescence (Pujol, Vendrell, Junqué, Martí-Vilalta, & Capdevila, 1993).

Finally, further research considering (markers of) OHEs when investigating motives and activational hormone effects is particularly promising, as the adult strength of motive-related activational hormone effects may depend on the outcomes of the two organizational stages (cf. Janson et al., 2018). Besides those mentioned above, there are many other links between motives and hormones, for example between nAffiliation and progesterone, and specific motives fluctuate across the menstrual cycle, where changes in hormone concentrations occur (Schultheiss, Dargel, & Rohde, 2003). Also, motive arousal with motive-relevant movies (e.g., the Godfather II for nPower) is associated with changing hormone levels (e.g., elevated T in high-T men; Schultheiss, Wirth, & Stanton, 2004). Checking if the strength of such motive-hormone links in adult life depends on the outcomes of brain organization during development may lead to a better understanding of the neural underpinnings of implicit motives and ultimately to an endocrinological life-span model of implicit motives (cf. Köllner & Janson, 2017)

Limitations and further research

Some general limitations regarding marker research are beyond this chapter's scope, like statistical problems with ratio scores like 2D:4D and fWHR (Cohen & Cohen, 1983) and the potential for relevant effects being obscured by other factors influencing marker scores, as has been shown in the case of BMI affecting fWHR (Lefevre et al., 2012). However, these problems are addressed to some extent in our own research findings, as Janson et al. (2018) report their fWHR-results controlling for age and BMI. Nevertheless, the relationships we obtain from less-than-optimal markers like 2D:4D measured on the body surface may attenuate and thus underestimate the relationship between nPower and OHEs: X-ray and photocopy-assessment of 2D:4D produces a correlation of only .45 (136 individuals; Manning, 2002, pp. 3 & 4) and finger fat may also affect 2D:4D measurement (Wallen, 2009).

Regarding chapter-specific limitations, there is a general lamentable dearth of research on implicit motive development over the life course and the factors that have the most impact on it. As a consequence, our model has blind spots: There is no research regarding social learning experiences in adolescence (Prune & Tune-II), for example. In addition, the model rests heavily on nPower-related findings, especially regarding prenatal and pubertal OHEs on motive development (Growth-I/II). Nevertheless, there are some cues for an association between prenatal OHEs (Growth-I) and the development of nAffiliation (Schultheiss & Zimni, 2015; r = .17, "female-typical" 2D:4D non-significantly related to nAffiliation) and findings for social learning experiences in early childhood (Prune & Tune-I) regarding nAffiliation and nAchievement (McClelland & Pilon, 1983). Consequently, we believe that the model holds for motives in general, but generalizations at this point remain speculative.

Future research

Thus, future research is essential, like testing other motives' associations with markers or our model's utility to test predictions. Such research should include additional markers potentially reflecting the influence of steroids, allowing us to map OHEs on implicit motive development onto a comprehensive marker framework.

Linear bone growth

One such possible marker is long bone length: While nPower is associated with E2 in women and T in men, estrogens and androgens are also associated with organizational influences on linear bone growth (see Juul, 2001, for an overview; cf. Cutler, 1997). Estrogens have a biphasic effect on linear bone growth in puberty. Low levels mediate the pubertal growth spurt and increase long bone growth velocity, whereas high levels stimulate epiphyseal closure and cessation of linear bone growth (Cutler, 1997; Juul, 2001). T, the main representative of androgens, is highly connected to E2, an estrogen. It can be converted into E2 by aromatization and thereby exert similar effects on bone growth as estrogens (Vanderschueren et al., 2004).

The relevance of estrogens (or T-converted-to-E2) during puberty renders long bone length a potential marker for OHEs of E2 and T (cf. Bleck, Fenkl, Jägel, & Köllner, 2016, October). We thus expected the length of long bones like ulna and fibula to be negatively associated with nPower, because high levels of E2 and T lead to shorter bones and higher nPower. As the 2D:4D findings by O. C. Schultheiss (personal communication, October 19/20, 2017) demonstrate sex-dimorphic patterns moderated by AI for the left-right-asymmetry of a bone measure, we tested our prediction with bone (ulna vs. fibula), side (left vs. right), sex, nPower, and AI as predictors while controlling for body height. The overall five-way interaction was significant in our sample including more than 100 participants, possibly indicating similar influencing variables on long bone length and 2D:4D. Among other lower-order effects, two notable patterns emerged:

First, we obtained a Bone x Sex x nPower interaction, which persisted when omitting Side and AI in a simplified model. This indicates sex-dimorphic effects on bone length. Correspondingly, Bone marginally interacted with nPower in both sexes: Women with a longer ulna and shorter fibula were higher in nPower while for men the pattern was reversed. Building on bone ratios like 2D:4D and as ulna and fibula interacted with nPower in a different way, we thus compiled an ulna-to-fibula ratio (UFR) by dividing ulna length by fibula length. UFR was highly sex-dimorphic, with higher scores for men compared to women, and predicted by a Sex x nPower interaction. As this may hint at a marker function, we will report on UFR's relationship with variables like nPower or established markers elsewhere soon.

Second, we obtained a Side x Sex x AI interaction, which marginally persisted when removing Bone and nPower from the main model. This result may be tempting regarding speculations on body (Side) and brain (AI) lateralization driven by OHEs. However, in follow-up analyses a Side x AI interaction emerged only in men and additional analyses remained inconclusive.

Nevertheless, it is an interesting pattern that nPower interacted with bone type (ulna vs. fibula) while AI interacted with body side in the above-mentioned two sex-dimorphic interactions. Sexual dimorphisms in bone length, with interactions involving AI or nPower, respectively, tentatively indicate similar influencing variables on bone length and 2D:4D (cf. O.C. Schultheiss, personal communication, October 19/20, 2017). As this was the first study concerning relationships of nPower and AI and long bone length, replication is needed before explaining our findings theoretically.

Other possible future research

While the evidence for prenatal OHEs on nPower development based on 2D:4D is sound, it should be tested if the findings extend to other possible markers of prenatal hormones like anogenital distance (AGD; Dean & Sharpe, 2013). Also, more published 2D:4D-data would clarify possible connections to nAffiliation.

Corroborating research on pubertal OHEs on motive development is needed, especially replication of our fWHR and UFR-findings. Also, other sex-dimorphic characteristics should be tested, for example facial features like cheekbone prominence or lower face/face height (Lefevre et al., 2012) or waist-to-hip ratio (Cohen-Bendahan, van de Beek, & Berenbaum, 2005).

We are currently conducting several studies to broaden the range of markers possibly associated with implicit motives. For instance, we reanalyze pictures of participants taken in two earlier studies for various facial characteristics (e.g., fWHR, cheekbone prominence) to check if pubertal changes in facial morphology can again be linked to adult motive levels. Ongoing studies include photographing participants and assessing 2D:4D via palm scans, using a newly developed software for morphometric hand and face measurements (Köllner, Schmiedl, Waßer, & Schmiedl, 2017).

However, in the long run, we should move away from only looking at less-than-optimal markers of influences on brain development and look directly at the brain itself (cf. Köllner, Janson, & Schultheiss, 2018). Do these morphological body markers, for example, co-vary with actual structural, functional, and connectivity features of the hypothalamus, which we implied as a possible brain basis of nPower? Exploring anatomical variations in hypothalamic structures as well as their functional connectivities via brain scans and doing functional magnetic resonance imaging (fMRI; Huettel, Song, & McCarthy, 2014) studies assessing their role in processing dominance-related information would be a more straightforward way of pinpointing the brain basis of human nPower.

Conclusion

In sum, there is growing evidence from marker research for OHEs on the development of adult implicit motive levels. Several 2D:4D studies consistently point to prenatal influences on nPower. Pubertal OHEs on further development and refinement of nPower are also likely, as our fWHR-study suggests. AI consistently emerged as a moderator of these results, suggesting that brain lateralization is an important factor for further theorizing. These promising results warrant further research. We consider it remarkable how much evidence for a biological basis of motives is obtained by simply looking at proxy measures like biological markers, especially given the minuscule size (Turanovic et al., 2017; meta-analysis on 2D:4D and aggression) or even absence (Kosinski, 2017, fWHR and self-reported behavioral tendencies in more than 137,000 participants) of substantial relationships obtained in conventional marker research. The consistent, repeatedly found patterns extend the success story of the PSE-based alternative approach to conceptualizing and assessing human (dominance) motivation from studies investigating activational hormone effects to OHEs. Finally, the biopsychosocial model of implicit motive development may serve as a framework to test blind spots in motive development, such as social influences during puberty.

Acknowledgments

We are grateful to Oliver C. Schultheiss for countless helpful ideas and suggestions regarding our work. We also want to thank Maryam Bonakdar, Julia Fenkl, Franziska Jägel, Lea T. Riegl, Alicia Schmidbauer, Helena and Stefan Schmiedl, and Julia Waßer for various contributions, be it hard work in conducting relevant studies or thought-stimulating exchange of ideas.

References

Biernat, M. (1989). Motives and values to achieve: Different constructs with different effects. *Journal of Personality, 57*(1), 69–95. doi:10.1111/j.1467-6494.1989.tb00761.x

Bleck, K., Fenkl, J., Jägel, F., & Köllner, M. G. (2016, October). *Zusammenhänge zwischen dem impliziten Machtmotiv, Steroidhormonen und Längen der Ulna und Fibula [Relationships between the implicit power motive, steroid hormones, and length of ulna and fibula]*. Poster presented at the 36th Colloquium on Motivational Psychology, Erlangen, Germany.

Borsboom, D., Mellenbergh, G. J., & van Heerden, J. (2004). The concept of validity. *Psychological Review, 111*(4), 1061–1071. doi:10.1037/0033-295x.111.4.1061

Carré, J. M., Geniole, S. N., Ortiz, T. L., Bird, B. M., Videto, A., & Bonin, P. L. (2016). Exogenous testosterone rapidly increases aggressive behavior in dominant and impulsive men. *Biological Psychiatry, 82*(4), 249–256. doi:10.1016/j.biopsych.2016.06.009

Carré, J. M., & McCormick, C. M. (2008). In your face: Facial metrics predict aggressive behaviour in the laboratory and in varsity and professional hockey players. *Proceedings of the Royal Society of London B, 275*, 2651–2656. doi:10.1098/rspb.2008.0873

Carré, J. M., & Olmstead, N. A. (2015). Social neuroendocrinology of human aggression: Examining the role of competition-induced testosterone dynamics. *Neuroscience, 286*, 171–186. doi:10.1016/j.neuroscience.2014.11.029

Cohen, J., & Cohen, P. (1983). *Applied multiple regression/correlation analysis for the behavioral sciences* (2nd ed.). Hillsdale, NJ: Erlbaum.

Cohen-Bendahan, C. C. C., van de Beek, C., & Berenbaum, S. A. (2005). Prenatal sex hormone effects on child and adult sex-typed behavior: Methods and findings. *Neuroscience and Biobehavioral Reviews, 29*(2), 353–384. doi:10.1016/j.neubiorev.2004.11.004

Cutler, G. B. (1997). The role of estrogen in bone growth and maturation during childhood and adolescence. *The Journal of Steroid Biochemistry and Molecular Biology, 61*(3–6), 141–144. doi:10.1016/S0960-0760(97)80005-2

Dean, A., & Sharpe, R. M. (2013). Anogenital distance or digit length ratio as measures of fetal androgen exposure: Relationship to male reproductive development and its disorders. *The Journal of Clinical Endocrinology and Metabolism, 98*(6), 2230–2238. doi:10.1210/jc.2012-4057

Forbes, E. E., & Dahl, R. E. (2010). Pubertal development and behavior: Hormonal activation of social and motivational tendencies. *Brain and Cognition, 72*(1), 66–72. doi:10.1016/j.bandc.2009.10.007

Geniole, S. N., Bird, B. M., Ruddick, E. L., & Carré, J. M. (2017). Effects of competition outcome on testosterone concentrations in humans: An updated meta-analysis. *Hormones and Behavior, 92*, 37–50. doi:10.1016/j.yhbeh.2016.10.002

Geniole, S. N., Denson, T. F., Dixson, B. J., Carré, J. M., & McCormick, C. M. (2015). Evidence from meta-analyses of the facial width-to-height ratio as an evolved cue of threat. *PLoS One, 10*(7), e0132726. doi:10.1371/journal.pone.0132726

Geschwind, N., & Galaburda, A. M. (1987). *Cerebral lateralization: Biological mechanisms, associations, and pathology.* Cambridge, MA: MIT Press.

Hagemeyer, B., & Kandler, C. (2014, September). *Einflüsse von Genen und Umwelt auf implizite Motive im hohen Alter: Eine Zwillingsstudie.* Presentation at the 34th Colloquium on Motivational Psychology, Trier, Germany.

Haselhuhn, M. P., Ormiston, M. E., & Wong, E. M. (2015). Men's facial width-to-height ratio predicts aggression: A meta-analysis. *PLoS One, 10*(4), e0122637. doi:10.1371/journal.pone.0122637

Hönekopp, J., Bartholdt, L., Beier, L., & Liebert, A. (2007). Second to fourth digit length ratio (2D:4D) and adult sex hormone levels: New data and a meta-analytic review. *Psychoneuroendocrinology, 32*, 313–321. doi:10.1016/j.psyneuen.2007.01.007

Hönekopp, J., & Schuster, M. (2010). A meta-analysis on 2D:4D and athletic prowess: Substantial relationships but neither hand out-predicts the other. *Personality and Individual Differences, 48*(1), 4–10. doi:10.1016/j.paid.2009.08.009

Huettel, S. A., Song, A. W., & McCarthy, G. (2014). *Functional magnetic resonance imaging* (3rd ed.). Sunderland, MA: Sinauer Associates Inc.

Janson, K. T., Bleck, K., Fenkl, J., Riegl, L. T., Jägel, F., & Köllner, M. G. (2018). Inhibited power motivation is associated with the facial width-to-height ratio in females. *Adaptive Human Behavior and Physiology, 4*(1), 21–41. doi:10.1007/s40750-017-0075-y

Juul, A. (2001). The effects of oestrogens on linear bone growth. *Human Reproduction Update, 7*(3), 303–313. doi:10.1111/j.1600-0463.2001.tb05758.x

Kemper, C. J., & Schwerdtfeger, A. (2009). Comparing indirect methods of digit ratio (2D:4D) measurement. *American Journal of Human Biology, 21*(2), 188–191. doi:10.1002/ajhb.20843

Kilford, E. J., Garrett, E., & Blakemore, S-J. (2016). The development of social cognition in adolescence: An integrated perspective. *Neuroscience and Biobehavioral Reviews, 70*, 106–120. doi:10.1016/j.neubiorev.2016.08.016

Kivilevitch, Z., Achiron, R., & Zalel, Y. (2010). Fetal brain asymmetry: In utero sonographic study of normal fetuses. *American Journal of Obstetrics & Gynecology, 202*, 359.e351–359.e358. doi:10.1016/j.ajog.2009.11.001

Köllner, M. G., & Janson, K. T. (2017). The sociobiological development and arousal of implicit motives: The emergence of a growth-and-prune model of motive development and the continued linkage of hormones and motives throughout the life span. *Psychoneuroendocrinology, 83S*, 70. doi:10.1016/j.psyneuen.2017.07.426

Köllner, M. G., Janson, K. T., & Schultheiss, O. C. (2018). Commentary: Sexual dimorphism of facial width-to-height ratio in human skulls and faces: A meta-analytical approach. *Frontiers in Endocrinology, 9*(227). doi:10.3389/fendo.2018.00227

Köllner, M. G., Schmiedl, H., Waßer, J., & Schmiedl, S. (2017). Face/palm measuring tool: A stand-alone software for standardized hand and face morphometry [software and manual]. *Erlangen.* Retrieved from https://github.com/swsch/FacePalm

Köllner, M. G., & Schultheiss, O. C. (2014). Meta-analytic evidence of low convergence between implicit and explicit measures of the needs for achievement, affiliation, and power. *Frontiers in Psychology, 5*(826). doi:10.3389/fpsyg.2014.00826

Kosinski, M. (2017). Facial width-to-height ratio does not predict self-reported behavioral tendencies. *Psychological Science,* 1–8. doi:10.1177/0956797617716929

Kramer, R. S. S. (2017). Sexual dimorphism of facial width-to-height ratio in human skulls and faces: A meta-analytical approach. *Evolution and Human Behavior, 38*(3), 414–420. doi:10.1016/j.evolhumbehav.2016.12.002

Langens, T. A. (2010). Activity inhibition. In O. C. Schultheiss & J. C. Brunstein (Eds.), *Implicit motives* (pp. 89–115). New York, NY: Oxford University Press.

Lefevre, C. E., Lewis, G. J., Bates, T. C., Dzhelyova, M., Coetzee, V., Deary, I. J., & Perrett, D. I. (2012). No evidence for sexual dimorphism of facial width-to-height ratio in four large adult samples. *Evolution and Human Behavior, 33*(6), 623–627. doi:10.1016/j.evolhumbehav.2012.03.002

Lutchmaya, S., Baron-Cohen, S., Raggatt, P., Knickmeyer, R., & Manning, J. T. (2004). 2nd to 4th digit ratios, fetal testosterone and estradiol. *Early Human Development, 77,* 23–28. doi:10.1016/j.earlhumdev.2003.12.002

Malas, M. A., Dogan, S., Evcil, E. H., & Desdicioglu, K. (2006). Fetal development of the hand, digits and digit ratio (2D:4D). *Early Human Development, 82*(7), 469–475. doi:10.1016/j.earlhumdev.2005.12.002

Manning, J. T. (2002). *Digit ratio: A pointer to fertility, behavior, and health.* New Brunswick, NJ: Rutgers University Press.

Manning, J. T., & Fink, B. (2008). Digit ratio (2D:4D), dominance, reproductive success, asymmetry, and sociosexuality in the BBC Internet Study. *American Journal of Human Biology, 20,* 451–461. doi:10.1002/ajhb.20767

McClelland, D. C. (1982). The need for power, sympathetic activation, and illness. *Motivation and Emotion, 6*(1), 31–41. doi:10.1007/bf00992135

McClelland, D. C. (1987). *Human motivation.* New York, NY: Cambridge University Press.

McClelland, D. C., & Boyatzis, R. E. (1982). Leadership motive pattern and long-term success in management. *Journal of Applied Psychology, 67*(6), 737–743. doi:10.1037/0021-9010.67.6.737

McClelland, D. C., Koestner, R., & Weinberger, J. (1989). How do self-attributed and implicit motives differ? *Psychological Review, 96*(4), 690–702. doi:10.1037/0033-295x.96.4.690

McClelland, D. C., & Pilon, D. A. (1983). Sources of adult motives in patterns of parent behavior in early childhood. *Journal of Personality and Social Psychology, 44*(3), 564–574. doi:10.1037/0022-3514.44.3.564

Mehta, P. H., & Josephs, R. A. (2006). Testosterone change after losing predicts the decision to compete again. *Hormones and Behavior, 50*(5), 684–692. doi:10.1016/j.yhbeh.2006.07.001

Nelson, R. J., & Kriegsfeld, L. J. (2017). *An Introduction to behavioral endocrinology* (5th ed.). Sunderland, MA: Sinauer Associates Inc.

Nelson, R. J., & Trainor, B. C. (2007). Neural mechanisms of aggression. *Nature Reviews: Neuroscience, 8,* 536–546. doi:10.1038/nrn2174

Ober, C., Loisel, D. A., & Gilad, Y. (2008). Sex-specific genetic architecture of human disease. *Nature Reviews Genetics, 9,* 911–922. doi:10.1038/nrg2415

Oxford, J. K., Tiedtke, J. M., Ossmann, A., Özbe, D., & Schultheiss, O. C. (2017). Endocrine and aggressive responses to competition are moderated by contest outcome, gender, individual versus team competition, and implicit motives. *PLoS One, 12*(7), e0181610. doi:10.1371/journal.pone.0181610

Phoenix, C. H., Goy, R. W., Gerall, A. A., & Young, W. C. (1959). Organizing action of prenatally administered testosterone propionate on the tissues mediating mating behavior in the female guinea pig. *Endocrinology, 65*(3), 369–382. doi:10.1210/endo-65-3-369

Pujol, J., Vendrell, P., Junqué, C., Martí-Vilalta, J. L., & Capdevila, A. (1993). When does human brain development end? Evidence of corpus callosum growth up to adulthood. *Annals of Neurology, 34*(1), 71–75. doi:10.1002/ana.410340113

Sapolsky, R. M. (1987). Stress, social status, and reproductive physiology in free-living baboons. In D. Crews (Ed.), *Psychobiology of reproductive behavior: An evolutionary perspective* (pp. 291–322). Englewood Cliffs, NJ: Prentice-Hall, Inc.

Schultheiss, O. C. (2008). Implicit motives. In O. P. John, R. W. Robins & L. A. Pervin (Eds.), *Handbook of personality: Theory and research* (3rd ed., pp. 603–633). New York, NY: Guilford Press.

Schultheiss, O. C. (2013). The hormonal correlates of implicit motives. *Social and Personality Psychology Compass, 7*(1), 52–65. doi:10.1111/spc3.12008

Schultheiss, O. C. (2017). Evidence for prenatal organizational effects of steroids on the motivational brain. *Psychoneuroendocrinology, 83S,* 69. doi:10.1016/j.psyneuen.2017.07.423

Schultheiss, O. C., & Brunstein, J. C. (2002). Inhibited power motivation and persuasive communication: A lens model analysis. *Journal of Personality, 70*(4), 553–582. doi:10.1111/1467-6494.05014

Schultheiss, O. C., Dargel, A., & Rohde, W. (2003). Implicit motives and gonadal steroid hormones: Effects of menstrual cycle phase, oral contraceptive use, and relationship status. *Hormones and Behavior, 43,* 293–301. doi:10.1016/S0018-506X(03)00003-5

Schultheiss, O. C., & Köllner, M. G. (2014). Implicit motives, affect, and the development of competencies: A virtuous-circle model of motive-driven learning. In R. Pekrun & L. Linnenbrink-Garcia (Eds.), *International handbook of emotions in education* (pp. 73–95). New York, NY: Taylor & Francis, Routledge.

Schultheiss, O. C., & Köllner, M. G. (in press). Implicit motives. In O. P. John & R. W. Robins (Eds.), *Handbook of personality: Theory and research* (4th ed.). New York, NY: Guilford Press.

Schultheiss, O. C., & Pang, J. S. (2007). Measuring implicit motives. In R. W. Robins, R. C. Fraley, & R. F. Krueger (Eds.), *Handbook of research methods in personality psychology* (pp. 322–344). New York, NY: Guilford Press.

Schultheiss, O. C., Pang, J. S., Torges, C. M., Wirth, M. M., & Treynor, W. (2005). Perceived facial expressions of emotion as motivational incentives: Evidence from a differential implicit learning paradigm. *Emotion, 5*(1), 41–54. doi:10.1037/1528-3542.5.1.41

Schultheiss, O. C., Riebel, K., & Jones, N. M. (2009). Activity inhibition: A predictor of lateralized brain function during stress? *Neuropsychology, 23*(3), 392–404. doi:10.1037/a0014591

Schultheiss, O. C., & Rohde, W. (2002). Implicit power motivation predicts men's testosterone changes and implicit learning in a contest situation. *Hormones and Behavior, 41*(2), 195–202. doi:10.1006/hbeh.2001.1745

Schultheiss, O. C., Schiepe, A., & Rawolle, M. (2012). Hormone assays. In H. Cooper, P. M. Camic, D. L. Long, A. T. Panter, D. Rindskopf, & K. J. Sher (Eds.), *Handbook of research methods in psychology* (Vol. 1: Foundations, planning, measures, and psychometrics, pp. 489–500). Washington, DC: American Psychological Association.

Schultheiss, O. C., Wirth, M. M., & Stanton, S. J. (2004). Effects of affiliation and power motivation arousal on salivary progesterone and testosterone. *Hormones and Behavior, 46*(5), 592–599. doi:10.1016/j.yhbeh.2004.07.005

Schultheiss, O. C., Wirth, M. M., Torges, C. M., Pang, J. S., Villacorta, M. A., & Welsh, K. M. (2005). Effects of implicit power motivation on men's and women's implicit learning and testosterone changes after social victory or defeat. *Journal of Personality and Social Psychology, 88*(1), 174–188. doi:10.1037/0022-3514.88.1.174

Schultheiss, O. C., & Zimni, M. (2015). Associations between implicit motives and salivary steroids, 2D:4D digit ratio, mental rotation performance, and verbal fluency. *Adaptive Human Behavior and Physiology, 1,* 387–407. doi:10.1007/s40750-014-0012-2

Schulz, K. M., Molenda-Figueira, H. A., & Sisk, C. L. (2009). Back to the future: The organizational-activational hypothesis adapted to puberty and adolescence. *Hormones and Behavior, 55*(5), 597–604. doi:10.1016/j.yhbeh.2009.03.010

Sisk, C. L., & Zehr, J. L. (2005). Pubertal hormones organize the adolescent brain and behavior. *Frontiers in Neuroendocrinology, 26,* 163–174. doi:10.1016/j.yfrne.2005.10.003

Slatcher, R. B., Mehta, P. H., & Josephs, R. A. (2011). Testosterone and self-reported dominance interact to influence human mating behavior. *Social Psychological and Personality Science, 2*(5), 531–539. doi:10.1177/1948550611400099

Spangler, W. D. (1992). Validity of questionnaire and TAT measures of need for achievement: Two meta-analyses. *Psychological Bulletin, 112*(1), 140–154. doi:10.1037/0033-2909.112.1.140

Stanton, S. J., & Schultheiss, O. C. (2007). Basal and dynamic relationships between implicit power motivation and estradiol in women. *Hormones and Behavior, 52*(5), 571–580. doi:10.1016/j.yhbeh.2007.07.002

Stanton, S. J., & Schultheiss, O. C. (2009). The hormonal correlates of implicit power motivation. *Journal of Research in Personality, 43*(5), 942–949. doi:10.1016/j.jrp.2009.04.001

Stoeckart, P. F., Strick, M., Bijleveld, E., & Aarts, H. (2017). The implicit power motive predicts action selection. *Psychological Research, 81,* 560–570. doi:10.1007/s00426-016-0768-z

Toga, A. W., & Thompson, P. M. (2003). Mapping brain asymmetry. *Nature Reviews Neuroscience, 4,* 37–48. doi:10.1038/nrn1009

Turanovic, J. J., Pratt, T. C., & Piquero, A. R. (2017). Exposure to fetal testosterone, aggression, and violent behavior: A meta-analysis of the 2D:4D digit ratio. *Aggression and Violent Behavior, 33,* 51–61. doi:10.1016/j.avb.2017.01.008

Vanderschueren, D., Vandenput, L., Boonen, S., Lindberg, M. K., Bouillon, R., & Ohlsson, C. (2004). Androgens and bone. *Endocrine Reviews, 25*(3), 389–425. doi:10.1210/er.2003-0003

Ventura, T., Gomes, M. C., Pita, A., Neto, M. T., & Taylor, A. (2013). Digit ratio (2D:4D) in newborns: Influences of prenatal testosterone and maternal environment. *Early Human Development, 89*(2), 107–112. doi:10.1016/j.earlhumdev.2012.08.009

Verdonck, A., Gaethofs, M., Carels, C., & de Zegher, F. (1999). Effect of low-dose testosterone treatment on craniofacial growth in boys with delayed puberty. *European Journal of Orthodontics, 21*, 137–143.

Vongas, J. G., & Al Hajj, R. (2017). The effects of competition and implicit power motive on men's testosterone, emotion recognition, and aggression. *Hormones and Behavior, 92*, 57–71. doi:10.1016/j.yhbeh.2017.04.005

Wallen, K. (2009). Does finger fat produce sex differences in second to fourth digit ratios? *Endocrinology, 150*(11), 4819–4822. doi:10.1210/en.2009-0986

Welker, K. M., Bird, B. M., & Arnocky, S. (2016). Commentary: Facial Width-to-Height Ratio (fWHR) is not associated with adolescent testosterone levels. *Frontiers in Psychology, 7*(1745). doi:10.3389/fpsyg.2016.01745

Weston, E. M., Friday, A. E., & Liò, P. (2007). Biometric evidence that sexual selection has shaped the hominin face. *PLoS One, 2*(8), e710. doi:10.1371/journal.pone.0000710

Wilson, E. O. (1980). *Sociobiology: The abridged edition.* Belknap, Cambridge, MA: Harvard University Press.

Winter, D. G. (1988). The power motive in women – and men. *Journal of Personality and Social Psychology, 54*(3), 510–519. doi:10.1037/0022-3514.54.3.510

Winter, D. G. (1994). *Manual for scoring motive imagery in running text* (4th ed.). Ann Arbor, MI: Department of Psychology, University of Michigan, Unpublished manuscript.

Zheng, Z., & Cohn, M. J. (2011). Developmental basis of sexually dimorphic digit ratios. *Proceedings of the National Academy of Sciences, 108*(39), 16289–16294. doi:10.1073/pnas.1108312108

Zilioli, S., Sell, A. N., Stirrat, M., Jagore, J., Vickerman, W., & Watson, N. V. (2015). Face of a fighter: Bizygomatic width as a cue of formidability. *Aggressive Behavior, 41*, 322–330. doi:10.1002/ab.21544

32

INTERVENTIONS, STRESS DURING DEVELOPMENT, AND PSYCHOSOCIAL ADJUSTMENT

Leslie E. Roos, Kathryn G. Beauchamp, Jessica Flannery,
Sarah Horn, and Philip A. Fisher

Over half a century of research across rodent, primate, and human studies has documented the profound effects of early life stress on biological and behavioral development (Gunnar, 2016). A complementary body of work has focused on improving outcomes for stress-exposed children through caregiver-based interventions, with several programs showing promising results for ameliorating the consequences of adverse early environments that include both maltreatment and/or caregiver psychopathology (Fisher et al., 2016). Cortisol, a primary output of the hypothalamic–pituitary–adrenal (HPA) axis, has been the focus of much of this research, as the HPA axis is responsive to both positive and negative environmental inputs and has pervasive structural and functional connections with other biological systems (e.g., immune, metabolic, central, and peripheral nervous systems; Miller, Chen, & Parker, 2011).

The examination of an environmentally sensitive system such as the HPA axis is, by nature, complex. Although stressful experiences tend to result in a short-term up-regulation of cortisol production (resulting in hypercortisolism), increasing evidence suggests that chronic exposure to severe stress might lead to downregulation of the HPA system over time (resulting in hypocortisolism). Further, children might differentially experience negative events as stressful, and the effects of adversity are believed to act along a continuum: Normative experiences (e.g., occasional separation from caregivers) have minimal effects, whereas more severe experiences (e.g., separation that is prolonged or repetitive) have negative influences on HPA function. Stressors are also often comorbid and overlapping, so research selecting children based on a given stressor (e.g., parent psychopathology) is likely to include children with varied exposure to other stressors (e.g., comorbid neglect, abuse, and community violence exposure).

We first summarize the literature regarding HPA axis measurement techniques employed in early adversity research and then discuss the theories (e.g., the allostatic load model and the adaptive calibration model) linking early life stress to alterations in HPA axis function. We then describe evidence for the impacts of environmental stress on the HPA axis and evidence for profiles of function linked to psychopathology. We next review the literature on the intervention effects on HPA axis function, followed by a section on extant methodological challenges and important future directions. Finally, we discuss the importance of understanding other key biological–regulatory systems altered by early life stress exposure (i.e., immune system, gut microbiome, and autonomic nervous system) and linked to HPA axis function. We further advocate the use of theory-driven, multisystem approaches alongside HPA axis research to delineate the effects of early adversity and interventions on development.

Developmental adversity and HPA axis measurement

Research on the HPA axis is commonly divided into basal measures (reflecting diurnal activity supporting homeostasis) and reactivity measures (reflecting responsivity to acute stress).

Basal measures

The most commonly employed assessment of basal HPA axis function is diurnal assessment. At a minimum, this involves collecting a saliva sample in-home upon waking and another just prior to bed, which provides measures of morning cortisol, evening cortisol, and the diurnal slope across the day (i.e., the difference between evening and morning levels; Adam, Klimes-Dougan, & Gunnar, 2007). Additional samples can be collected throughout the day for more data-rich measures of slopes (i.e., quadratic vs. linear). Researchers commonly report the diurnal slope, but morning or evening levels can be a useful follow-up to slope analyses to inform the relative contributions of morning or evening levels to the results of interest. In general, a blunted or flattened diurnal slope has been associated with negative physical and behavioral health (McEwen, 1998).

Measuring cortisol concentrations in hair is a relatively recent methodological approach, which reflects cumulative cortisol that becomes embedded in the hair, as a proxy for chronic stress exposure (Flom, St. John, Meyer, & Tarullo, 2017). This technique allows for the measurement of children's total exposure to cortisol because hair grows at a roughly constant speed of 1cm/month, so a small sample of hair can index a child's cumulative exposure over a period of months to years (White et al., 2017). This tool may be particularly valuable for informing questions of longitudinal HPA function and offering insight into principles of function under conditions of early adversity (Fisher, 2017).

Reactivity measures

Measuring children's reactivity to acute stress is also of interest because it reflects the ability of the HPA axis to mobilize resources in response to a stressor. Stressor paradigms involve a sample of salivary baseline cortisol, prior to, or immediately following, a stressor. This is followed by 2–5 additional samples, beginning 20 min following the onset of the stressor, which reflect reactivity and recovery, given that salivary cortisol peaks at about 20 min following acute stress. In young samples, however, this assessment can be challenging because standard adult and adolescent social stressor paradigms such as the Trier Social Stress Test (a mock job talk and mental arithmetic with high social evaluative threat), are not suitable for children (Gunnar, Talge, & Herrera, 2009). As an alternative, effective experimental manipulations of acute stressors include physical threats (e.g., immunization shots) and unresponsive caregiver paradigms (e.g., Still Face Paradigm; Haley & Stansbury, 2003; Gunnar et al., 2009) for infants and psychosocial stressors that are challenging or disappointing in early childhood (e.g., a cognitively difficult matching game performed under time pressure with negative feedback about performance; Roos et al., 2017).

Environmental stressors influence the development of HPA axis function

Programming of the HPA axis is highly influenced by early environmental inputs, which begin prenatally (Glover, O'Connor, & O'Donnell, 2010) and continue through adolescence

(Danese & McEwen, 2012). The diurnal pattern of cortisol is influenced by several factors (e.g., circadian rhythm and sleep) and begins to emerge at about 3-4 months of age, becoming more pronounced through childhood (de Weerth, Zijl, & Buitelaar, 2003). This is a period of heightened sensitivity, in which the HPA axis is susceptible to positive and negative influences that can have lasting effects on the system into adulthood (Meaney et al., 1994).

Theories of environmental influence on development and function of the HPA axis

Although alterations in HPA function (both hypocortisolism and hypercortisolism) are associated with long-term mental and physical health risk (Adam et al., 2017), two prominent theories posit that deviations might reflect evolutionarily shaped strategies for organisms encountering harsh and unpredictable environments.

Allostatic load model (ALM)

The ALM posits that activation of the body's fight-or-flight responses is critical for adaptive behavior under acute stress but incurs negative consequences (i.e., allostatic load) under conditions of chronic activation (McEwen & Seeman, 1999). The mobilization of cortisol is a key part of the body's response to stress and to the subsequent return to allostasis (i.e., ability to maintain stability through change) through interactions with metabolic, cardiovascular, and respiratory-regulatory systems (Juster, McEwen, & Lupien, 2010). The ALM proposes four profiles that can render the body more susceptible to stress-related diseases: (a) repeated hits (stressors) on the system; (b) lack of adaptation (i.e., lack of habituation to stressors); (c) prolonged stress response, in which the system fails to return to baseline; and (d) an inadequate response, or a hyporesponse, in which the system fails to respond to a stressor (McEwen & Seeman, 1999; Juster et al., 2010). The ALM model posits that these profiles of stress are associated with different cortisol responses – hypercortisol or hypocortisol production, both of which can have negative consequences – but might also protect certain bodily functions from excessive glucocorticoid exposure (i.e., hypocortisolism) or support states of hypervigilance in dangerous environments (i.e., hypercortisolism). Excess cortisol secretion can alter the development of brain regions relevant to memory, emotions, and self-regulation (i.e., hippocampus, amygdala, and prefrontal cortex; Juster et al., 2010; Lupien, McEwen, Gunnar, & Heim, 2009). However, hypoactivation of the HPA axis can result in an insufficient mobilization of resources to environmental demands (Badanes, Watamura, & Hankin, 2011). Because a well-regulated profile balances between hyper/hypoactivation and there is lack of a normalized quantification of cortisol levels across development, age-matched, healthy control samples are highly valuable for the interpretation of altered function.

Adaptive calibration model (ACM)

The ACM employs a developmental evolutionary framework to interpret the neurobiological consequences of early life stress adaptations to prepare organisms for harsh and unpredictable environments (Del Giudice, Ellis, & Shirtcliff, 2011; Ellis & Del Giudice, 2014). These adaptations are posited to shift biology and behavior towards fast life-history strategies that, over the course of evolution, maximize reproduction likelihood and species survival through processes such as early maturation, aggression, and increased vigilance to threat. However, in contemporary humans, these strategies might be challenging for children to conform to present-day contexts with constraints on behavioral expectations (e.g., school settings) and increase children's internalizing and externalizing mental health symptomatology.

Building upon the concepts of biological sensitivity to context (Boyce & Ellis, 2005) and differential susceptibility (Belsky, Bakermans-Kranenburg, & van IJzendoorn, 2007), the ACM postulates that the children most susceptible to deleterious environmental inputs are highly influenced by positive inputs. Accordingly, individuals who are most negatively affected by early life stress and exhibit biomarkers of HPA perturbation might be particularly responsive to early intervention and prevention efforts that enrich the early environment and minimize stress exposure (Laurent, Gilliam, Bruce, & Fisher, 2014). However, there has been minimal individual-difference research testing if the children who exhibit HPA perturbations are also the most responsive to intervention.

Summary of empirical studies of early adversity on HPA axis function

Infancy

Human infancy is characterized by a dependence on caregivers for food, warmth, protection, and physiological regulation (Gunnar & Donzella, 2002). During this time, caregivers can also serve as social buffers during stressful situations, resulting in lower child cortisol reactivity when caregivers are present during acutely stressful experiences (Hostinar, Sullivan, & Gunnar, 2014). Accordingly, a lack of responsive caregiving early in life is conceptualized as a chronic stressor, in which exposure to caregiver separations, stress, and depression are linked to developmental alterations in HPA axis function (N = 189; Brennan et al., 2008; N = 80; Diego et al., 2004; N = 284; Essex, Klein, Cho, & Kalin, 2002; Gunnar & Donzella, 2002).

The effects of chronic stress on the HPA axis and associated biological systems are observable in infancy (Danese & McEwen, 2012). For example, infants exposed to mothers with depression, associated with decreased maternal responsivity and sensitivity, often exhibit increased cortisol reactivity to stress (N = 189; Brennan et al., 2008) and higher basal levels of urinary cortisol (N = 80; Diego et al., 2004). In contrast, infants with secure maternal attachment and/or consistent, responsive caregiving are buffered against heightened cortisol reactivity to acute stress (Gunnar & Hostinar, 2015; Gunnar & Quevedo, 2007a).

Childhood

From toddlerhood to pre-puberty, early life stress is most commonly found to predict lower HPA axis function (i.e., blunted diurnal slope), with some notable heterogeneity. Research on post-institutionalized adoptees who had relatively similar experiences of severe environmental deprivation and caregiver neglect in infancy, followed by enriched and responsive environments post-adoption, has produced some of the most consistent results. Post-adoption children typically exhibit a blunted diurnal slope: relatively lower morning cortisol and higher evening values compared to noninstitutionalized children (n = 58 previously institutionalized; n = 47 post-institutionalized foster care; n = 50 comparison; Gunnar & Vazquez, 2001; Koss, Hostinar, Donzella, & Gunnar, 2014). Notably, the effect of institutionalized status on blunted diurnal function appears to dissipate after multiple years in adopted homes, which is theorized to reflect HPA axis recovery.

Among children exposed to maltreatment (including samples ranging from infancy to middle childhood), many studies suggest that maltreatment exposure predicts a blunted diurnal slope compared to children not exposed to maltreatment (n = 184 foster care; n = 155 comparison;

Bernard, Butzin-Dozier, Rittenhouse, & Dozier, 2010; n = 117 foster care; n = 60 comparison; Dozier et al., 2006). However, other studies have failed to find significant main effects of maltreatment status on cortisol function and have instead demonstrated that the presence of neglect is associated with more prominently blunted cortisol patterns, including lower morning cortisol (n = 55 foster care; n = 104 comparison; Bruce, Fisher, Pears, & Levine, 2009) and lower overall cortisol production assessed via hair cortisol (n = 245 maltreated; n = 292 comparison; White et al., 2017) compared to other maltreatment subtypes. This is consistent with the theory that, early in life, the absence of responsive caregiving is one of the most significant threats to survival, causing chronic activation that downregulates the HPA system.

A recent meta-analysis highlighted the importance of consistency in definitions of maltreatment with samples recruited from child protective service (CPS) agencies (believed to be exposed to relatively severe maltreatment and passing the threshold necessary for an open CPS case) tending to show lower morning cortisol (N = 3898 across 27 studies; Bernard, Frost, Bennett, & Lindhiem, 2017). Notably, this pattern was not replicated when maltreatment status was determined by self-report (believed to be both less consistent and generally less severe; Bernard et al., 2017). This meta-analysis did not find any links across studies between maltreatment status and diurnal slope measures.

Adolescence

Research indicates that alterations in HPA function associated with early life stress persist into adolescence. For example, adolescents with histories of early maltreatment have been shown to exhibit a blunted cortisol response to acute stress (n = 67 maltreated; n = 25 comparison; MacMillan et al., 2009). A longitudinal study of females with childhood sexual abuse (and those without) demonstrated that early sexual abuse predicted lower morning cortisol levels in adolescence and adulthood and provided support for the attenuation hypothesis: Cortisol levels were higher at time points closer to the abuse (i.e., hypercortisolism) and declined over time (i.e., hypocortisolism; n = 84 sexually abused; n = 89 comparison; Trickett, Noll, Susman, Shenk, & Putnam, 2010).

Animal research has indicated that the HPA axis undergoes a second period of increased environmental sensitivity during the transition into adolescence (Morley-Fletcher, Rea, Maccari, & Laviola, 2003; Romeo et al., 2006). Cross-sectional studies of previously institutionalized (PI) youths have shown that, when compared to non-adopted comparison youths, PI youths do not show a blunted slope in adolescence: Specifically, pre-pubertal PI youths display blunted cortisol profiles, whereas post-pubertal PI youth do not (n = 76 PI, n = 118; Flannery et al., 2017; n = 55 PI adopted after eight months; n = 44 PI adopted before eight months; n = 58 comparison; Quevedo, Johnson, Loman, LaFavor, & Gunnar, 2012). This putative second sensitive period in adolescence highlights the importance of considering developmental processes and longitudinal designs when examining the effects of early life stress on HPA axis function.

Although not focused on a specific developmental period, the results from a recent meta-analysis highlight the potential for the impacts of early life stress exposure (across maltreatment, parent mental illness, and family stressors) on cortisol reactivity across the lifespan (N = 4292 across 30 studies; Bunea, Szentágotai-Tătar, & Miu, 2017). This study found an overall significant and moderate effect size of early adversity exposure predicting blunted cortisol reactivity to stress, with stronger effects for samples exposed to more severe stressors (i.e., maltreatment). Interestingly, there is evidence from this meta-analysis and the aforementioned hair cortisol study (White et al., 2017) that the effects of early adversity on attenuation of HPA function (i.e., both overall cortisol production and reactivity) might be more pronounced years later or at older ages from the experiences of early adversity (Bunea et al., 2017; White et al., 2017). The suggestion that the HPA axis system takes time to downregulate following stress exposure is in line with the ALM and attenuation theories and consistent with the aforementioned longitudinal study on sexual abuse (Trickett et al., 2010).

Associations between HPA function and psychological adjustment during childhood and adolescence following early adversity

HPA axis function has been shown to relate to psychological adjustment and behavior problems in children and adolescents who have experienced early life stress. A recent meta-analysis across childhood through adulthood and including stress-exposed and non-exposed samples (N = 26,167 across 80 studies) found evidence of a blunted diurnal cortisol slope associated with both externalizing and internalizing problems (Adam et al., 2017). It has been theorized that disruptions of cortisol's circadian rhythm (i.e., a flatter slope) might affect a diverse set of central and peripheral biological systems, leading to wide-ranging negative mental health consequences (Adam et al., 2017). Another meta-analysis exclusive to children showed a small but significant association between externalizing problems and lower basal cortisol (N = 5,480 across 72 studies), as measured by total cortisol production (i.e., measured by one to five samples across the day) but not blunted cortisol reactivity (N = 2601 across 29 studies; Alink et al., 2008). Here, we review the extant literature involving developmental samples exposed to early life stress that examines associations between specific indices of HPA axis function (i.e., morning cortisol, diurnal cortisol slope, and cortisol reactivity) and internalizing and externalizing problems.

Basal HPA function and psychological adjustment

Basal homeostatic HPA axis function has been theorized to serve as a potential marker of adaptation and adjustment (or maladjustment) following early life stress (Cicchetti & Rogosch, 2001). Low arousal associated with hypoactivation of the HPA axis (i.e., lower morning cortisol levels, blunted slope, and reduced stressor reactivity) is thought to contribute to externalizing behaviors, while heightened HPA axis activation might support hypervigilance and be linked to internalizing problems.

Research on externalizing symptoms in children exposed to early life stress has shown a link between diminished basal HPA axis function, as measured by diurnal slope, and externalizing problems. Bernard, Dozier, Bick, and Gordon (2015) demonstrated an association between externalizing problems and a blunted diurnal slope (but did not report if an association was present with morning cortisol levels) in a sample of CPS children, compared to a group of control children without CPS involvement (n = 53 CPS-involved; n = 41 comparison). Notably, this pattern of blunted diurnal slope mediated the association between CPS involvement and increased externalizing problems (Bernard et al., 2015). This association has also been supported in hair cortisol research, which has shown that maltreatment exposure predicts lower cortisol levels from middle childhood to adolescence, mediating the link between maltreatment and externalizing problems (n = 245 maltreated; n = 292 comparison; White et al., 2017). However, some studies using salivary measures have failed to demonstrate an association between basal HPA function (e.g., morning levels and diurnal cortisol patterns) and externalizing symptoms in maltreated samples (n = 167 maltreated; n = 204 comparison; Cicchetti & Rogosch, 2001; n = 25 maltreated; n = 26 comparison; Puetz et al., 2016).

Although there has been relatively more research examining internalizing (vs. externalizing) problems, results in developmental samples exposed to early life stress have been more inconsistent. Some research has documented an association between lower morning cortisol and a blunted diurnal slope in maltreated children with internalizing problems (i.e., depression) compared to maltreated children without internalizing problems (n = 131 maltreated; n = 66 comparison; Hart, Gunnar, & Cicchetti, 1996). These findings are largely consistent with the aforementioned meta-analyses linking blunted diurnal cortisol patterns to internalizing problems across ages and the presence of stress exposure (Adam et al., 2017). However, other work has suggested that maltreated children with internalizing problems have higher basal cortisol (i.e., total cortisol output across the day) compared to non-maltreated controls (n = 31 maltreated; n = 51 comparison; Carrion et al., 2002; Tarullo & Gunnar, 2006). Similarly, it has been demonstrated that maltreated children living with their biological mothers who showed clinical-level internalizing problems exhibited relatively higher morning and afternoon cortisol levels (but no difference in diurnal slope) compared to maltreated children without internalizing symptoms as well as a control group of non-maltreated children with and without internalizing symptoms (Cicchetti & Rogosch, 2001).

It is theorized that the aforementioned attenuation hypothesis might explain some results here, with proximal acute stress linked to both internalizing problems and an initial hyperactivation of the HPA axis, which is followed by downregulation of the circadian rhythm and might contribute to longer term internalizing problems (Danese & McEwen, 2012). However, because the interval between the stressor and cortisol sampling has not been consistently examined across studies, it is difficult to determine if this accounts for the reported discrepancies. Further, the measurement of key covariates (e.g., child age, stressor severity, and time since stressor) vary across studies, as does the extent to which these covariates are considered to be moderators (Koss & Gunnar, 2017). Particularly for maltreated samples, the current environment is a critical variable to consider as a potential proxy for ongoing stress. Maltreatment often occurs within the context of a biological home, in which maintaining elevated HPA axis activity might be functionally relevant to maintaining vigilance. However, this might be less necessary when children are removed from the home and a sustained period of HPA axis downregulation and recovery from excessive glucocorticoid exposure would be safe.

Though few longitudinal studies offer key insights into understanding the role of stress timing and chronicity, one such investigation in a normative sample included youths exposed to parental psychopathology who were assessed for problem behaviors during childhood and early adolescence and for basal HPA function in early adolescence (N = 96; Ruttle et al., 2011). The results indicate that the childhood onset of internalizing problems is associated with lower morning cortisol levels (but not the diurnal cortisol slope) in early adolescence, suggesting that lower morning cortisol levels over time might be linked to the early onset of internalizing behavior. Such findings highlight the importance of longitudinal designs to map out the association between adjustment and HPA function.

Cortisol reactivity and psychological adjustment

The association between HPA axis function and psychological adjustment has been examined in the context of cortisol reactivity to a stressor. As with diurnal cortisol, reduced and heightened cortisol reactivity to a stressor have been linked to risk for psychopathology (Danese & McEwen, 2012; Jaffee et al., 2015). Some work has shown associations between heightened cortisol reactivity and clinical-level depression in adolescents exposed to early life stress (n = 30 maltreated; n = 25 comparison; Rao, Hammen, Ortiz, Chen, & Poland, 2008), while other research has demonstrated an association between lower total cortisol output across a stressor and heightened internalizing problems (N = 232; Keenan et al., 2013), a pattern of results consistent with allostatic load and adaptive calibration model accounts regarding short-term hyperactivity of the system linked to internalizing difficulties (Danese & McEwen, 2012; Del Giudice et al., 2011). In another community sample, children who experienced high levels of early harsh parenting and recent stressors exhibited lower cortisol reactivity to stress, a pattern associated with higher levels of internalizing and externalizing problems (N = 400; Jaffee et al., 2015). This association was not present for children who experienced recent stressors without early harsh parenting, demonstrating the potential importance of the timing and chronicity of experiences in predicting the links between HPA axis function and adaptation to stress.

The impacts of interventions on HPA axis function

Given the deleterious impacts of early life stress, as well as the importance of the timing and chronicity of adverse exposures, early intervention efforts are crucial. Interventions seeking to ameliorate negative effects of early life stress focus on improving the child's environment by decreasing levels of harshness and unpredictability and increasing responsive caregiving. Improving the child's early environment in these key ways is theorized to reduce the chronic activation of the biological stress response (e.g., HPA axis) to unpredictable and uncontrollable threats. Combined with improved scaffolding of children's stress management and prosocial behavior, this is believed to create the potential for recovery of children's neurobiological function away from developmental trajectories that include heightened risk for mental health and behavior problems (Fisher, van Ryzin, & Gunnar, 2011).

The importance of the child's early caregiving environment provides strong rationale for the development of interventions that emphasize engagement with parents and other caregivers (Shonkoff & Fisher, 2013). Several interventions have been developed to target the parent–child relationship and are shown to change children's HPA axis function, along with other socioemotional and behavioral outcomes for children exposed to early life stress (Fisher et al., 2016; Slopen, McLaughlin, & Shonkoff, 2014). These interventions illustrate the potential of intervention efforts to have longitudinal effects on stress neurobiology. Shared themes across interventions that promote social buffering include an emphasis on sensitive and responsive caregiving, behavior-management skills, didactic information on developmental milestones, motivational aspects of parental involvement, and social support (Flannery et al., 2017; Shonkoff & Fisher, 2013). Enhancement of social buffering is theorized to normalize HPA axis function, which is likely to help remediate the deleterious impacts of early life stress, such as poorer mental and physical health, academic challenges, and engagement in risky behaviors (Felitti et al., 1998; Lupien et al., 2009).

CPS and foster care interventions

CPS-involved children are among the highest risk for multiple stress and maltreatment exposures, including caregiver mental illness, substance use, incarceration, poverty, and out-of-home placements (Pears, Kim, & Fisher, 2008). Foster care involvement has been associated with dysregulated HPA axis function; however, interventions have highlighted the potential for malleability with this population (Fisher et al., 2011).

The Multidimensional Treatment Foster Care for Preschoolers (MTFC-P) program was developed for foster children aged 3–6 to promote consistent, positive parenting and placement stability using behavior-management strategies and case-management services for foster parents and children (Fisher & Chamberlain, 2000). A specific target in the development of this intervention was the reduction of stress levels for foster parents and children, with results suggesting that MTFC-P can reduce self-reported parent stress about the management of children's problem behaviors (i.e., Parent Daily Report; Chamberlain & Reid, 1987) and normalize children's cortisol patterns (i.e., so they resemble non-foster children). A randomized controlled trial (RCT) of MTFC-P showed that the children in regular foster care (RFC) receiving routine foster care services (e.g., individual psychotherapy; n = 60) showed a blunted morning-to-evening cortisol slope, while those in the MTFC-P group (n = 57) demonstrated a more typical diurnal cortisol slope comparable to a community control group (n = 60), suggesting a buffering impact of the intervention on HPA axis function (Fisher et al., 2007). Further, the foster parents in the MTFC-P group experienced reductions in self-reported parent stress, highlighting the intervention's impact on parental perceived stress and children's HPA axis function (Fisher & Stoolmiller, 2008). Comparatively, foster parents in the RFC group experienced an increase in self-reported caregiver stress levels over the course of the study. Notably, increasing levels of foster parent stress were associated with a more blunted diurnal slope for RFC children, emphasizing the likely relevance of caregiver factors in child HPA axis function (Fisher & Stoolmiller, 2008).

MTFC-P has also been demonstrated to impact cortisol reactivity in response to a naturally occurring stressor: the beginning of school. In a pilot study from a subsample of the original MTFC-P study, there was an assessment of cortisol reactivity and recovery to the beginning of the school year. Start of school year assessments are conceptualized as a normative developmental stressor leading to short-term elevations in morning cortisol and steeper diurnal slopes that typically reduce over the course of the first week (i.e., lower morning cortisol and a less steep diurnal slope), as children habituate to the new environment (Bruce, Davis, & Gunnar, 2002). Morning and evening saliva samples were collected for two consecutive days the week before the start of school, on the first day of school, and on the fifth day of school. The community control (n = 21) and MTFC-P (n = 9) children exhibited a significantly steeper cortisol slope on the first day of school compared to the week before school and no differences by the fifth day of school. In contrast, the RFC children seemed to have a delayed response to the onset of school stress, with a significantly steeper diurnal slope on the fifth day (vs. the week before) of school. This RFC diurnal slope was significantly steeper than that of the community control or MTFC-P children (Graham et al., 2012). While preliminary, this pattern of results suggests that MTFC-P children were able to habituate to the novel school environment by the fifth day of school, a pattern similar to the community control group (Graham et al., 2012).

The Attachment and Biobehavioral Catch-Up (ABC) intervention is an attachment-based intervention for infants and toddlers in foster care (Dozier et al., 2006). The ABC program involves ten weekly, in-home sessions with an intervention arm (aimed to help parents encourage regulatory capacities in children) and an active control educational intervention (aimed to develop language skills) as well as a community comparison sample (N = 164; 60 in foster care randomly assigned to ABC or active educational conditions; Dozier et al., 2006). The program utilizes an attachment perspective to improve children's regulatory capacities and create a lower stress environment. In the experimental arm, caregivers are taught to be highly responsive and effective in their interactions with children by recognizing children's needs, reducing the frequency of frightening parental behaviors, and addressing parental issues to enhance responsive engagement with their children (Bernard et al., 2015; Dozier et al., 2006). Similar to the MTFC-P program, studies indicate that the cortisol production patterns for children (ages 4–60 months) participating in the ABC intervention closely resemble those of community controls. Interestingly, however, this normative profile of function for ABC intervention and community control toddlers included lower morning and evening cortisol levels compared to the active educational control group, with no differences in slope. Additionally, there were no differences in cortisol levels between the ABC intervention and the community comparison group (Dozier et al., 2006). Because this intervention captured children's HPA function in the infant to early childhood age range, one interpretation of these results is that the HPA profile reflecting chronic stress might have been in a hypercortisolism stage before downregulation occurred.

In somewhat divergent results, another sample of children who were randomized to the ABC intervention and compared to an active educational control group demonstrated higher morning cortisol and steeper diurnal slopes (n = 49 ABC intervention; n = 51 comparison; Bernard et al., 2015). These children were followed up once they reached preschool age (3–6 years old), and the group differences in diurnal cortisol production (i.e., higher cortisol morning levels and a steeper diurnal slope for children in the ABC intervention) were maintained at follow-up (Bernard et al., 2015). Taken together, these results suggest that the ABC intervention supports children's HPA function to be consistent with either community control children's function or to reflect generally healthier profiles (i.e., steeper diurnal slope). However, the direction of effects across studies is inconsistent, and replication and further explanation are needed.

Lastly, Child–Parent Psychotherapy (CPP) is an intervention designed for toddler-aged (1–3 years) maltreated foster children. CPP is another attachment-based program that encourages sensitive interactions between caregivers and their children. Parents are encouraged to form positive representations of themselves and of their relationship with their children (Cicchetti, Rogosch, Toth, & Sturge-Apple, 2011). In a longitudinal study, CPP was compared to multiple control conditions, including a psychoeducational parenting intervention (PPI; a didactic intervention focused on parenting skills, relaxation techniques, and behaviors promoting social support; n = 56), a standard community service group (n = 35), and a non-maltreated control group (n = 52; Cicchetti et al., 2011). Mid-morning samples were collected four times over a two-year period. Results indicate that there were no baseline cortisol differences between groups; however, at the mid-intervention assessment (19 months), the maltreated children in the services-as-usual group had lower mid-morning cortisol levels that continued at a follow-up assessment seven months post-intervention. In contrast, for maltreated foster children, whose families received either intervention, cortisol patterns resembled that of the community control group beginning at the mid-intervention assessment and were maintained throughout the two-year study, again suggesting a buffering impact of parenting interventions on HPA axis function (Cicchetti et al., 2011; see Table 32.1).

Parent psychopathology intervention

Parental psychopathology might place children at elevated risk for chronic stress exposure given that psychopathology predicts less responsive and sensitive caregiving as well as family vulnerability to environmental stressors such as poverty and violence. Further, parents with psychopathology might be less effective social buffers for children when acutely stressful experiences occur because of disruptions in the attachment relationship (Adam, Gunnar, & Tanaka, 2004; De Falco et al., 2014; Flannery et al., 2017; Schechter & Willheim, 2009). Thus, parents with mental health disorders and their children represent an important demographic for intervention efforts. However, there is limited research to date examining whether interventions designed for parents exhibiting psychopathology can change HPA axis function in their children.

Caregivers at high-risk for depression often experience elevated levels of disrupted caregiving that are linked to decreased maternal responsivity and sensitivity (Brennan et al., 2008). One intervention study in this area involved a cognitive-based intervention for predominantly

Table 32.1 Effects of Interventions on HPA Axis Functioning

Intervention/ population	Aim/length/control	Study	N*	Child age (baseline)	Cortisol measure	Results
Intervention: Attachment Biobehavioral Catch-Up (ABC) Population: Foster children	Aim: Attachment perspective to improve children's regulatory capacity and create lower stress environment Length: 10 weekly, in-home sessions with parent Control: Educational intervention and community comparison	Bernard et al., 2015	100	5 months –2 years	Diurnal (morning, midday, evening) 2–3 consecutive days	The ABC Children had higher morning cortisol production and steeper diurnal slopes compared to the educational control group.
		Bernard et al., 2015	115	3–6 years	Diurnal (morning, midday, evening) 3 consecutive days	The ABC children maintained cortisol differences, with higher morning cortisol production and steeper diurnal slopes compared to the educational control group.
		Dozier et al., 2006	164	2 months –3 years	Diurnal (morning and evening) 2 consecutive days	The ABC children had similar morning and evening cortisol levels to the community control children, whereas the educational intervention children had higher morning and evening cortisol than the other groups. No differences in diurnal slope were found.
Intervention: Child–Parent Psychotherapy (CPP) Population: Foster children	Aim: Attachment-based program to encourage sensitive interactions between caregivers and children Length: About 1 year Control: Psychoeducational parenting intervention for foster children, services as usual for foster children, and community comparison	Cichetti et al., 2011	143	1–3 years	Basal Midmorning collection on four instances over 2 years	No initial differences across groups were found. At midintervention, the CPP and psychoeducational intervention children exhibited cortisol levels similar to those of the community comparison group. The services-as-usual group exhibited lower mid-morning cortisol. All results were maintained at the 2-year follow-up.

Intervention / Population	Author, year	N	Age	Cortisol measure	Results
Intervention: Cognitive–Behavioral Stress Management (CBSM) Population: Low-income pregnant women at risk for depression Aim: Create healthy environment for mothers and infants with prenatal cognitive–behavioral stress management course. Length: 12 weeks and booster sessions postpartum Control: Services as usual and community comparison	Urizar, & Muñoz, 2011	86	Infants at birth	Diurnal (morning and evening) 6 and 18 months postbirth	At 6 months, infants from standard care group had higher cortisol levels averaged across morning and evening compared to infants in intervention or community comparison groups. At 18 months postpartum, no group differences were observed.
Intervention: Multidimensional Treatment Foster Care for Preschoolers (MTFC-P) Population: Foster children Aim: Promote consistent, positive parenting and placement stability via behavior management strategies. Length: 6–9 months with 24-hour telephone support Control: Services as usual and community comparison	Fisher, Gunnar, & Burraston, 2007	117	3–6 years	Diurnal (morning and evening) 2 consecutive days	Children in intervention group exhibited a comparable diurnal slope to those in the community control group. Children in regular foster care displayed a blunted slope compared to those in the community comparison group.
	Graham et al., 2012	37	4–8 years	Diurnal (morning, midday, and evening) 2 consecutive days (1 week before start of school) and first and fifth day of school	Child in the intervention and community comparison groups had significantly steeper diurnal slope and higher morning cortisol the first day of school, compared to the week prior. Regular foster care children only had steeper diurnal slope on fifth day, compared to week prior, which was also steeper relative to intervention and community comparison groups.

* Total N is collapsed across intervention and control groups. See chapter text for participant breakdown by condition.

Spanish-speaking, low-income pregnant women at high risk of depression during the second trimester (Urizar & Muñoz, 2011). The intervention group (n = 24) underwent a 12-week, prenatal Cognitive–Behavioral Stress Management (CBSM) course that emphasized strategies for creating a healthy environment for mothers and their infants with booster sessions at 1, 3, 6, and 12 months postpartum. The study also had control standard care (n = 33) and low-risk community comparison (n = 29) groups. At six months postpartum, infants in the standard care group had higher overall cortisol levels (averaged across morning and evening levels) compared to infants in the intervention group or in the low-risk group, with no differences in diurnal slope. However, at 18 months, no group differences were observed for overall cortisol or cortisol slope between any group. These results suggest that CBSM paradigms might help to regulate biological stress in mothers and infants at certain developmental time points (Urizar & Muñoz, 2011).

Methodological considerations and future directions

There are numerous issues in the extant literature reviewed here on HPA axis activity in the context of adversity that are relevant to offering possible explanations of heterogeneous findings (e.g., positive and negative associations between internalizing and HPA axis activity) and guiding future research. Broadly, these considerations fall into two categories: (a) characteristics of early life stressors, including timing, type, and severity; and (b) methodological considerations, including measures of cortisol collection, analytic procedures, and issues of statistical power.

Regarding characteristics of early life stressors, an increasing body of evidence suggests that the time since stress occurred from the measurement of cortisol might influence results. Both cross-sectional and longitudinal work indicate that cortisol measurements close in proximity (e.g., < 6 months) to a stressor are linked to relatively higher HPA axis function, including basal measures and reactivity (White et al., 2017), and that more distal cortisol measurements from stressors are more likely to reflect downregulation of the HPA system (Trickett et al., 2010). Notably, this pattern of stress-proximal hyperactivity and stress-distal hypoactivity has been linked to psychopathology (Ruttle et al., 2011; White et al., 2017). Multiple studies have also highlighted that the type of stress experienced is relevant, with samples experiencing more severe stress (e.g., maltreatment, as determined by CPS referral) and early life neglect (vs. other types of maltreatment) more consistently exhibiting hypocortisolism profiles. It would be helpful in future work to carefully measure the timing since stressor onset (and offset, if children have been removed from stressful environments) in addition to employing more consistent measures of early life stress regarding type, severity, and duration. Some research uses coding systems such as the maltreatment classification system (Barnett, Manly, & Cicchetti, 1993), which has good replicability and consistent coding of maltreatment from CPS referrals but is less useful for community samples. Recent evidence suggests that positive caregiving experiences might buffer individuals from the detrimental effects of early adversity and could be quantified in future research (Narayan, Rivera, Bernstein, Harris, & Lieberman, in press). Finally, longitudinal research is critical for delineating the transactional relationship between early life stress, ongoing stress, and HPA axis function across development as a predictor of key outcomes such as psychopathology onset and key windows for intervention.

There are numerous methodological factors that could contribute to inconsistent findings, including the measure of HPA axis function employed (e.g., hair cortisol over time, diurnal slope, morning cortisol, and reactivity). Although certain measures might be differentially feasible based on the collection location (e.g., home, school, or laboratory), research on the standardization of techniques and best practices in at-risk samples (Valentino, De Alba, Hibel, Fondren, & McDonnel, 2017) would be valuable. As previously noted, there is a lack of established normative levels of developmental cortisol production (for either basal or reactivity) measures, in part because of differences in assay techniques across studies, which make comparisons across groups difficult. The multitude of cortisol parameters employed, combined with the variety of analytic techniques (e.g., HLM, SEM, or repeated-measures ANOVA) used to analyze them, makes drawing direct comparisons across studies or employing meta-analytic techniques more complicated.

The publication of supplementary material that includes raw values and consistency across analytic techniques could help address this issue. The potential for selective reporting is also a concern, with some studies that report diurnal slope not including the individual morning and evening parameters that go into the slope calculation. These unreported values could highlight discrepancies across studies or be useful in meta-analyses. Inconsistencies in the results reviewed could also be due to the limited sample sizes in some studies along with the minimal published research on power or effect sizes in the early life stress research. Further, there could be statistical errors in comparing the strength of associations between HPA function and psychological adjustment between groups (Nieuwenhuis, Forstmann, & Wagenmakers, 2011)

Future work investigating HPA function in children exposed to early life stress would benefit from the incorporation of open science practices, such as making datasets publicly available to encourage new analyses on existing datasets and combining datasets for meta-analytic approaches that can examine moderators, which have been suggested to influence links between adversity and HPA axis function from adult research (e.g., sex, methodological quality, and caregiver buffering; Buena et al., 2017; Flannery et al., 2017). Additionally, investigations that can incorporate larger sample sizes and replicate results across samples are important to demonstrate the consistency of findings in intervention research. Further, intervention work that can investigate the extent to which normative profiles of HPA function mediate links between intervention and mental health and behavioral outcomes would be highly valuable to demonstrate the importance of HPA function to long-term positive outcomes.

The promise of emerging multisystem approaches

The research discussed above summarizes key advances in understanding of stress neurobiology and intervention research conducted over the past 50 years. HPA axis research has been a focus of work examining the effects of early life stress on young children's biology and behavior. However, despite the importance of understanding and measuring HPA axis function, there are numerous other biological systems that might have complementary and interactive effects with the HPA axis system that are key to understanding the effects of early life stress and prevention efforts on children's well-being.

We suggest that integrating knowledge of HPA axis function with related multisystem approaches of stress-regulatory biomarkers has the potential to add to the current literature base on the biobehavioral consequences of early life stress in addition to clarifying some of the heterogeneous findings in the current cortisol-focused literature. The HPA axis is just one component of the intricate and interconnected neurobiological and physiological systems that regulate behavioral and physiological responses to stress and self-regulation, more broadly. Elucidating how the interconnected systems (e.g., autonomic nervous system) might contribute to or interact with regulation of the HPA axis could help explain inconsistent findings in the literature. For example, the coupling of activation across these systems might be a more reliable predictor of behavioral effects than measurements of one system in isolation. The emergent research on three such systems is discussed below as a key future direction to enriching our understanding of the impact of early life stress on HPA axis function and development.

Autonomic nervous system (ANS)

The ANS plays a complementary role to the HPA axis in the body's response to acute stress and other challenging and/or arousing contexts (Gunnar & Quevedo, 2007b). In particular, the sympathetic nervous system (SNS) is critically involved in the rapid engagement of the fight-or-flight response to acute stress via the release of catecholamines (e.g., epinephrine and nor-epinephrine) that drive heartrate acceleration, metabolic changes, and vigilance-related neural processes (Gunnar & Quevedo, 2007b). In contrast, the parasympathetic nervous system (PNS), with descending connections from the brainstem to the heart via the tenth-cranial vagus nerve, facilitates the rapid deceleration of heartrate and restoration of homeostatic processes and is particularly relevant for regulation of emotions and behavior (Graziano & Derefinko, 2013; Porges, 2001). Despite substantial rationale and multiple calls for the investigation of HPA and ANS function together (Bauer, Quas, & Boyce, 2002; Del Giudice et al., 2011; Obradović, 2016), there has been limited research in samples facing early life stress.

Similar to research on the HPA axis, altered function of the SNS and PNS has been linked to experiences of early adversity and psychopathology (Graziano & Derefinko, 2013; McLaughlin et al., 2015; Oosterman, De Schipper, Fisher, Dozier, & Schuengel, 2010). Anatomically, acute responsivity of the autonomic nervous system and the HPA axis are modulated by the limbic system and prefrontal cortical regions of the brain, with corticotropin-releasing hormone being critically involved in sympathetic and HPA activation (Gunnar & Quevedo, 2007b). Given the complementary functions of the ANS and the HPA axis, it has been theorized that different profiles of activation and suppression might lead to variable patterns of arousal, attention, and regulation (Del Giudice et al., 2011; Obradović, 2016).

Regarding the time course of development, the SNS matures first (by about gestational age 35 weeks), whereas the PNS continues to mature through the first year as cortical structures influencing the PNS via the brainstem develop (Porges & Furman, 2011). This time course might be relevant for understanding HPA axis function because it suggests a very early time period for ANS programming (and intervention) that might moderate the longer period of HPA axis development and plasticity (Propper & Holochwost, 2013). Although there has been limited multisystemic research to date, extant work supports such a moderating role for the ANS. In particular, more responsive PNS activity has been shown to buffer children from the links between early life stressors and altered HPA function (Blair, Berry, Mills-Koonce, Granger, & FLP Investigators, 2013). Other research findings have shown that a profile indicating a lack of coordination between SNS and HPA function is more common among maltreated children (Gordis, Granger, Susman, & Trickett, 2008). Ongoing research examining cross-system coordination and the moderating roles of the ANS might be particularly important for clarifying the effects of adversity on the HPA axis and any associated links to adjustment.

Immune system

The HPA axis and immune system are highly intertwined, as the HPA axis regulates the inflammatory arm of the immune system. During an infection, inflammatory responses serve a protective role, and sickness behaviors such as social withdrawal and loss of appetite appear temporarily, reducing once the infection has cleared (Dantzer, O'Connor, Freund, Johnson, & Kelley, 2008). Notably, these symptoms mimic those commonly observed in many stress-related psychological disorders such as depression. It has been hypothesized that chronic stress might lead to dysregulation of this adaptive behavioral response, rendering the individual more susceptible to the development of psychopathology (Pfau & Russo, 2015). Under normal conditions, cortisol is critical to downregulating immune reactions (e.g., cytokine production; Silverman, Pearce, Biron, & Miller, 2005). However, under conditions of chronic stress, excessive cortisol exposure can result in cortisol resistance of the immune system, which drives enhanced cytokine production and inflammation (Stark et al., 2001).

Clinical studies of immune mediators provide preliminary evidence that a wide range of childhood traumatic experiences are linked to altered inflammatory function (Bertone-Johnson, Whitcomb, Missmer, Karlson, & Rich-Edwards, 2012; Copeland et al., 2014; Danese & Lewis, 2016). However, few studies have examined HPA axis and immune function together in children exposed to early life stress. One recent study has examined cortisol and cytokine production and has demonstrated that, with increasing maternal stress, children's inflammatory cytokines show decreased sensitivity to cortisol production, suggesting dysregulated immune system function (Riis et al., 2016). A separate study illustrated that youths with histories of severe neglect and elevated cortisol had elevated levels of Macrophage Migration Inhibitory Factor (MIF), a cytokine closely related to HPA axis and glucocorticoid regulation (Bick et al., 2015).

Gut microbiota

Over the last decade, there has been an increasing interest in the role of gut microbiota in shaping mental and physical health outcomes, including the bidirectional relationship between the enteric nervous system (ENS) and the central nervous system (CNS; i.e., the gut–brain axis, including the HPA; Mayer, Tillisch, & Gupta, 2015). Developmentally, HPA axis development and gut microbiota colonization overlap in periods of programming. The HPA axis and gut microbiota mature postnatally and are largely shaped by environmental inputs. Early life stress leads to lasting changes in gut microbiota and has been shown in rodents to alter the early programming of the HPA axis (Sudo et al., 2004). Gut microbiota are highly responsive to environmental input prenatally, reaching adult-like stability and diversity by the age of three years (Lozupone, Stombaugh, Gordon, Jansson, & Knight, 2012), which overlaps and extends beyond the stress hyporesponsive period for the HPA axis. These systems have a dynamic relationship in which, under normal conditions, they operate to maintain symbiosis (Cryan & Dinan, 2012). However, under conditions of increased or repeated stressors, cortisol permeates the intestinal membrane and can lead to leaky gut syndrome, causing negative changes to the composition and diversity of gut microbiota (Kelly et al., 2015). Importantly, gut microbiota have a bidirectional relationship with HPA function, and disruptions along the gut–brain axis can result in changes in stress reactivity, behavior, and low-grade inflammation (Cryan & Dinan, 2012; O'Mahony et al., 2009). In fact, evidence from rodent models suggests that gut microbiota play a critical role in shaping the programming of the HPA axis, and alterations in HPA axis function associated with physical and mental health might be due to gut permeability (Kelly et al., 2015; Sudo et al., 2004).

Insights from gut microbiota research findings hold potential relevance for understanding early intervention. There is preliminary evidence in rodents that probiotics can reverse the effects on gut microbiota following early life stress and normalize HPA function (Callaghan, Cowan, & Richardson, 2016; Dinan & Cryan, 2012). Increased understanding about the interactions between HPA axis function and gut microbiota systems, as well as the bidirectional programming that occurs throughout development, could open new avenues for the development of interventions that target gut microbiota early in life.

Conclusion

The rich body of literature reviewed here demonstrates that exposure to early life stress can alter the development of HPA function as early as infancy, with effects continuing throughout development. Although altered HPA function in maltreated samples has been linked to internalizing and externalizing symptoms, it is promising that interventions for children exposed to early life stress have been shown to change stress-exposed children's cortisol function to reflect profiles found in healthy community samples. In infancy, this has included lower overall cortisol production: In childhood, this has included typically steeper diurnal slopes. Notably, these interventions tend to focus on the caregiver–child relationship as a pathway for improving not only child behaviors and psychopathology but also caregiver self-reported stress. Findings are consistent with social buffering theories about the critical nature of caregivers for providing an external source of regulation and support for children's developing stress-response systems and their ability to handle acute stress (Flannery et al., 2017).

Numerous factors might influence the discrepancies among reported findings, including heterogeneity in stressor characteristics and methodological considerations (with intervention results including notably small sample sizes). Despite these challenges, there are increasingly consistent results under certain conditions (e.g., more severe stress, neglect, and distance from stressor onset), which could provide improved guidelines for the replication and extension of effects moving forward. The inclusion of sufficiently powered studies and longitudinal designs will substantially improve the state of the evidence in the developmental adversity field and build on the preliminary HPA axis evidence to date for key principles of the ALM and ACM models, such as the attenuation hypothesis. Ultimately, continued refinement of our understanding of HPA axis function in contexts of early life stress has the potential to further basic science knowledge of this dynamic system and contribute to future intervention work that might benefit from incorporating HPA axis function as a meaningful target and/or outcome.

References

Adam, E. K., Gunnar, M. R., & Tanaka, A. (2004). Adult attachment, parent emotion, and observed parenting behavior: Mediator and moderator models. *Child Development, 75*, 110–122.

Adam, E. K., Klimes-Dougan, B., & Gunnar, M. R. (2007). Social regulation of the adrenocortical response to stress in infants, children, and adolescents. In D. Coch, G. Dawson, & K. W. Fischer (Eds.), *Human behavior, learning, and the developing brain: Atypical development* (pp. 264–304). New York, NY: Guilford Press.

Adam, E. K., Quinn, M. E., Tavernier, R., McQuillan, M. T., Dahlke, K. A., & Gilbert, K. E. (2017). Diurnal cortisol slopes and mental and physical health outcomes: A systematic review and meta-analysis. *Psychoneuroendocrinology, 83*, 25–41.

Alink, L. R., van IJzendoorn, M. H., Bakermans-Kranenburg, M. J., Mesman, J., Juffer, F., & Koot, H. M. (2008). Cortisol and externalizing behavior in children and adolescents: Mixed meta-analytic evidence for the inverse relation of basal cortisol and cortisol reactivity with externalizing behavior. *Developmental Psychobiology, 50*, 427–450.

Badanes, L. S., Watamura, S. E., & Hankin, B. L. (2011). Hypocortisolism as a potential marker of allostatic load in children: Associations with family risk and internalizing disorders. *Development and Psychopathology, 23*, 881–896.

Barnett, D., Manly, J. T., & Cicchetti, D. (1993). Defining child maltreatment: The interface between policy and research. *Child Abuse, Child Development, and Social Policy, 8*, 7–73.

Bauer, A. M., Quas, J. A., & Boyce, W. T. (2002). Associations between physiological reactivity and children's behavior: Advantages of a multisystem approach. *Journal of Developmental and Behavioral Pediatrics, 23*, 102–113.

Belsky, J., Bakermans-Kranenburg, M. J., & van IJzendoorn, M. H. (2007). For better and for worse: Differential susceptibility to environmental influences. *Current Directions in Psychological Science, 16*, 300–304.

Bernard, K., Butzin-Dozier, Z., Rittenhouse, J., & Dozier, M. (2010). Cortisol production patterns in young children living with birth parents vs children placed in foster care following involvement of child protective services. *Archives of Pediatrics and Adolescent Medicine, 164*, 438–443.

Bernard, K., Dozier, M., Bick, J., & Gordon, M. K. (2015). Intervening to enhance cortisol regulation among children at risk for neglect: Results of a randomized clinical trial. *Development and Psychopathology, 27,* 829–841.

Bernard, K., Frost, A., Bennett, C. B., & Lindhiem, O. (2017). Maltreatment and diurnal cortisol regulation: A meta-analysis. *Psychoneuroendocrinology, 78,* 57–67.

Bernard, K., Hostinar, C. E., & Dozier, M. (2015). Intervention effects on diurnal cortisol rhythms of child protective services – referred infants in early childhood: Preschool follow-up results of a randomized clinical trial. *JAMA Pediatrics, 169,* 112–119.

Bertone-Johnson, E. R., Whitcomb, B. W., Missmer, S. A., Karlson, E. W., & Rich-Edwards, J. W. (2012). Inflammation and early-life abuse in women. *American Journal of Preventive Medicine, 43,* 611–620.

Bick, J., Nguyen, V., Leng, L., Piecychna, M., Crowley, M. J., Bucala, R., . . . Grigorenko, E. L. (2015). Preliminary associations between childhood neglect, MIF, and cortisol: Potential pathways to long-term disease risk. *Developmental Psychobiology, 57,* 131–139.

Blair, C., Berry, D., Mills-Koonce, R., Granger, D., & FLP Investigators. (2013). Cumulative effects of early poverty on cortisol in young children: Moderation by autonomic nervous system activity. *Psychoneuroendocrinology, 38,* 2666–2675.

Boyce, W. T., & Ellis, B. J. (2005). Biological sensitivity to context: I. An evolutionary – developmental theory of the origins and functions of stress reactivity. *Development and Psychopathology, 17,* 271–301.

Brennan, P. A., Pargas, R., Walker, E. F., Green, P., Newport, D. J., & Stowe, Z. (2008). Maternal depression and infant cortisol: Influences of timing, comorbidity and treatment. *Journal of Child Psychology and Psychiatry, and Allied Disciplines, 49,* 1099–1107.

Bruce, J., Davis, E. P., & Gunnar, M. R. (2002). Individual differences in children's cortisol response to the beginning of a new school year. *Psychoneuroendocrinology, 27,* 635–650.

Bruce, J., Fisher, P. A., Pears, K. C., & Levine, S. (2009). Morning cortisol levels in preschool-aged foster children: Differential effects of maltreatment type. *Developmental Psychobiology, 51,* 14–23.

Bunea, I. M., Szentágotai-Tătar, A., & Miu, A. C. (2017). Early-life adversity and cortisol response to social stress: A meta-analysis. *Translational Psychiatry, 7*(12), 1274.

Callaghan, B. L., Cowan, C. S., & Richardson, R. (2016). Treating generational stress: Effect of paternal stress on development of memory and extinction in offspring is reversed by probiotic treatment. *Psychological Science, 27,* 1171–1180.

Carrion, V. G., Weems, C. F., Ray, R. D., Glaser, B., Hessl, D., & Reiss, A. L. (2002). Diurnal salivary cortisol in pediatric posttraumatic stress disorder. *Biological Psychiatry, 51*(7), 575–582.

Chamberlain, P., & Reid, J. B. (1987). Parent observation and report of child symptoms. *Behavioral Assessment, 9*(1), 97–109.

Cicchetti, D., & Rogosch, F. A. (2001). The impact of child maltreatment and psychopathology on neuroendocrine functioning. *Development and Psychopathology, 13,* 783–804.

Cicchetti, D., Rogosch, F. A., Toth, S. L., & Sturge-Apple, M. L. (2011). Normalizing the development of cortisol regulation in maltreated infants through preventive interventions. *Developmental Psychopathology, 23,* 789–800.

Copeland, W. E., Wolke, D., Lereya, S. T., Shanahan, L., Worthman, C., & Costello, E. J. (2014). Childhood bullying involvement predicts low-grade systemic inflammation into adulthood. *Proceedings of the National Academy of Sciences, 111,* 7570–7575.

Cryan, J. F., & Dinan, T. G. (2012). Mind-altering microorganisms: The impact of the gut microbiota on brain and behaviour. *Nature Reviews Neuroscience, 13,* 701–712.

Danese, A., & Lewis, S. J. (2016). Psychoneuroimmunology of early-life stress: The hidden wounds of childhood trauma? *Neuropsychopharmacology, 42,* 99–114.

Danese, A., & McEwen, B. S. (2012). Adverse childhood experiences, allostasis, allostatic load, and age-related disease. *Physiology and Behavior, 106,* 29–39.

Dantzer, R., O'Connor, J. C., Freund, G. G., Johnson, R. W., & Kelley, K. W. (2008). From inflammation to sickness and depression: When the immune system subjugates the brain. *Nature Reviews Neuroscience, 9,* 46–56.

De Falco, S., Emer, A., Martini, L., Rigo, P., Pruner, S., & Venuti, P. (2014). Predictors of mother – child interaction quality and child attachment security in at-risk families. *Frontiers in Psychology, 5,* 1–10.

Del Giudice, M., Ellis, B. J., & Shirtcliff, E. A. (2011). The adaptive calibration model of stress responsivity. *Neuroscience & Biobehavioral Reviews, 35,* 1562–1592.

de Weerth, C., Zijl, R. H., & Buitelaar, J. K. (2003). Development of cortisol circadian rhythm in infancy. *Early Human Development, 73,* 39–52.

Diego, M. A., Field, T., Hernandez-Reif, M., Cullen, C., Schanberg, S., & Kuhn, C. (2004). Prepartum, postpartum, and chronic depression effects on newborns. *Psychiatry: Interpersonal & Biological Processes*, *67*, 63–80.

Dinan, T. G., & Cryan, J. F. (2012). Regulation of the stress response by the gut microbiota: Implications for psychoneuroendocrinology. *Psychoneuroendocrinology*, *37*, 1369–1378.

Dozier, M., Manni, M., Gordon, M. K., Peloso, E., Gunnar, M. R., Stovall-McClough, K. C., . . . Levine, S. (2006). Foster children's diurnal production of cortisol: An exploratory study. *Child Maltreatment*, *11*, 189–197.

Ellis, B. J., & Del Giudice, M. (2014). Beyond allostatic load: Rethinking the role of stress in regulating human development. *Development and Psychopathology*, *26*, 1–20.

Essex, M. J., Klein, M. H., Cho, E., & Kalin, N. H. (2002). Maternal stress beginning in infancy may sensitize children to later stress exposure: Effects on cortisol and behavior. *Biological Psychiatry*, *52*, 776–784.

Felitti, V. J., Anda, R. F., Nordenberg, D., Williamson, D. F., Spitz, A. M., Edwards, V., . . . Marks, J. S. (1998). The relationship of adult health status to childhood abuse and household dysfunction. *American Journal of Preventive Medicine*, *14*, 245–258.

Fisher, P. A. (2017). Commentary: Is there a there there in hair? A reflection on child maltreatment and hair cortisol concentrations in White et al. (2017). *Journal of Child Psychology and Psychiatry*, *58*(9), 1008–1010.

Fisher, P. A., Beauchamp, K. G., Roos, L. E., Noll, L. K., Flannery, J., & Delker, B. C. (2016). The neurobiology of intervention and prevention in early adversity. *Annual Review of Clinical Psychology*, *12*, 331–357.

Fisher, P. A., & Chamberlain, P. (2000). Multidimensional treatment foster care: A program for intensive parenting, family support, and skill building. *Journal of Emotional and Behavioral Disorders*, *8*, 155–164.

Fisher, P. A., & Stoolmiller, M. (2008). Intervention effects on foster parent stress: Associations with child cortisol levels. *Developmental Psychopathology*, *20*, 1003–1021.

Fisher, P. A., Stoolmiller, M., Gunnar, M. R., & Burraston, B. O. (2007). Effects of a therapeutic intervention for foster preschoolers on diurnal cortisol activity. *Psychoneuroendocrinology*, *32*, 892–905.

Fisher, P. A., van Ryzin, M. J., & Gunnar, M. R. (2011). Mitigating HPA axis dysregulation associated with placement changes in foster care. *Psychoneuroendocrinology*, *36*, 531–539.

Flannery, J. E., Beauchamp, K. G., & Fisher, P. A. (2017). The role of social buffering on chronic disruptions in quality of care: Evidence from caregiver-based interventions in foster children. *Social Neuroscience*, *12*, 86–91.

Flannery, J. E., Gabard-Durnam, L. J., Shapiro, M., Goff, B., Caldera, C., Louie, J., . . . Tottenham, N. (2017). Diurnal cortisol after early institutional care – age matters. *Developmental Cognitive Neuroscience*, *25*, 160–166.

Flom, M., St. John, A. M., Meyer, J. S., & Tarullo, A. R. (2017). Infant hair cortisol: Associations with salivary cortisol and environmental context. *Developmental Psychobiology*, *59*, 26–38.

Glover, V., O'Connor, T. G., & O'Donnell, K. (2010). Prenatal stress and the programming of the HPA axis. *Neuroscience and Biobehavioral Reviews*, *35*, 17–22.

Gordis, E. B., Granger, D. A., Susman, E. J., & Trickett, P. K. (2008). Salivary alpha amylase – cortisol asymmetry in maltreated youth. *Hormones and Behavior*, *53*, 96–103.

Graham, A. M., Yockelson, M., Kim, H. K., Bruce, J., Pears, K. C., & Fisher, P. A. (2012). Effects of maltreatment and early intervention on diurnal cortisol slope across the start of school: A pilot study. *Child Abuse and Neglect*, *36*, 666–670.

Graziano, P., & Derefinko, K. (2013). Cardiac vagal control and children's adaptive functioning: A meta-analysis. *Biological Psychology*, *94*, 22–37.

Gunnar, M. R. (2016). Early life stress: What is the human chapter of the mammalian story? *Child Development Perspectives*, *10*, 178–183.

Gunnar, M. R., & Donzella, B. (2002). Social regulation of the cortisol levels in early human development. *Psychoneuroendocrinology*, *27*(1–2), 199–220.

Gunnar, M. R., & Hostinar, C. E. (2015). The social buffering of the hypothalamic–pituitary–adrenocortical axis in humans: Developmental and experiential determinants. *Social Neuroscience*, *10*, 479–488.

Gunnar, M. R., & Quevedo, K. M. (2007a). Early care experiences and HPA axis regulation in children: A mechanism for later trauma vulnerability. *Progress in Brain Research*, *167*, 137–149.

Gunnar, M. R., & Quevedo, K. M. (2007b). The neurobiology of stress and development. *Annual Reviews of Psychology*, *58*, 145–173.

Gunnar, M. R., Talge, N. M., & Herrera, A. (2009). Stressor paradigms in developmental studies: What does and does not work to produce mean increases in salivary cortisol. *Psychoneuroendocrinology*, *34*, 953–967.

Gunnar, M. R., & Vazquez, D. M. (2001). Low cortisol and a flattening of expected daytime rhythm: Potential indices of risk in human development. *Development and Psychopathology, 13,* 515–538.

Haley, D. W., & Stansbury, K. (2003). Infant stress and parent responsiveness: Regulation of physiology and behavior during still-face and reunion. *Child Development, 74,* 1534–1546.

Hart, J., Gunnar, M., & Cicchetti, D. (1996). Altered neuroendocrine activity in maltreated children related to symptoms of depression. *Development and Psychopathology, 8,* 201–214.

Hostinar, C. E., Sullivan, R. M., & Gunnar, M. R. (2014). Psychobiological mechanisms underlying the social buffering of the hypothalamic-pituitary-adrenocortical axis: A review of animal models and human studies across development. *Psychological Bulletin, 140,* 256–282.

Jaffee, S. R., McFarquhar, T., Stevens, S., Ouellet-Morin, I., Melhuish, E., & Belsky, J. (2015). Interactive effects of early and recent exposure to stressful contexts on cortisol reactivity in middle childhood. *Journal of Child Psychology and Psychiatry, 56,* 138–146.

Juster, R-P., McEwen, B. S., & Lupien, S. J. (2010). Allostatic load biomarkers of chronic stress and impact on health and cognition. *Neuroscience and Biobehavioral Reviews, 35,* 2–16.

Keenan, K., Hipwell, A., Babinski, D., Bortner, J., Henneberger, A., Hinze, A., . . . Sapotichne, B. (2013). Examining the developmental interface of cortisol and depression symptoms in young adolescent girls. *Psychoneuroendocrinology, 38*(10), 2291–2299.

Kelly, J. R., Kennedy, P. J., Cryan, J. F., Dinan, T. G., Clarke, G., & Hyland, N. P. (2015). Breaking down the barriers: The gut microbiome, intestinal permeability and stress-related psychiatric disorders. *Frontiers in Cellular Neuroscience, 9,* 1–20.

Koss, K. J., Hostinar, C. E., Donzella, B., & Gunnar, M. R. (2014). Social deprivation and the HPA axis in early development. *Psychoneuroendocrinology, 50,* 1–13.

Koss, K. J., & Gunnar, M. R. (2017). Annual research review: Early adversity, the hypothalamic – pituitary – adrenocortical axis, and child psychopathology. *Journal of Child Psychology and Psychiatry, 59*(4), 327–346.

Laurent, H. K., Gilliam, K. S., Bruce, J., & Fisher, P. A. (2014). HPA stability for children in foster care: Mental health implications and moderation by early intervention. *Developmental Psychobiology, 56,* 1406–1415.

Lozupone, C. A., Stombaugh, J. I., Gordon, J. I., Jansson, J. K., & Knight, R. (2012). Diversity, stability and resilience of the human gut microbiota. *Nature, 489,* 220–230.

Lupien, S. J., McEwen, B. S., Gunnar, M. R., & Heim, C. (2009). Effects of stress throughout the lifespan on the brain, behaviour and cognition. *Nature Reviews Neuroscience, 10,* 434–445.

MacMillan, H. L., Georgiades, K., Duku, E. K., Shea, A., Steiner, M., Niec, A., . . . Schmidt, L. A. (2009). Cortisol response to stress in female youths exposed to childhood maltreatment: Results of the Youth Mood Project. *Biological Psychiatry, 66,* 62–68.

Mayer, E. A., Tillisch, K., & Gupta, A. (2015). Gut/brain axis and the microbiota. *The Journal of Clinical Investigation, 125,* 926–938.

McEwen, B. S. (1998). Stress, adaptation, and disease: Allostasis and allostatic load. *Annals of the New York Academy of Sciences, 840,* 33–44.

McEwen, B. S., & Seeman, T. (1999). Protective and damaging effects of mediators of stress: Elaborating and testing the concepts of allostasis and allostatic load. *Annals of the New York Academy of Sciences, 896,* 30–47.

McLaughlin, K. A., Sheridan, M. A., Tibu, F., Fox, N. A., Zeanah, C. H., & Nelson, C. A. (2015). Causal effects of the early caregiving environment on development of stress response systems in children. *Proceedings of the National Academy of Sciences, 112*(18), 5637–5642.

Meaney, M. J., Tannenbaum, B., Francis, D., Bhatnagar, S., Shanks, N., Viau, V., . . . Plotsky, P. M. (1994). Early environmental programming hypothalamic-pituitary-adrenal responses to stress. *Seminars in Neuroscience, 6,* 247–259.

Miller, G. E., Chen, E., & Parker, K. J. (2011). Psychological stress in childhood and susceptibility to the chronic diseases of aging: Moving toward a model of behavioral and biological mechanisms. *Psychological Bulletin, 137,* 959–997.

Morley-Fletcher, S., Rea, M., Maccari, S., & Laviola, G. (2003). Environmental enrichment during adolescence reverses the effects of prenatal stress on play behaviour and HPA axis reactivity in rats. *European Journal of Neuroscience, 18,* 3367–3374.

Narayan, A. J., Rivera, L. M., Bernstein, R. E., Harris, W. W., & Lieberman, A. F. (in press). Positive childhood experiences predict less psychopathology and stress in pregnant women with childhood adversity: A pilot study of the Benevolent Childhood Experiences (BCEs) scale. *Child Abuse and Neglect.*

Nieuwenhuis, S., Forstmann, B. U., & Wagenmakers, E. J. (2011). Erroneous analyses of interactions in neuroscience: A problem of significance. *Nature Neuroscience, 14*(9), 1105.

Obradović, J. (2016). Physiological responsivity and executive functioning: Implications for adaptation and resilience in early childhood. *Child Development Perspectives, 10,* 65–70.

O'Mahony, S. M., Marchesi, J. R., Scully, P., Codling, C., Ceolho, A. M., Quigley, E. M., . . . Dinan, T. G. (2009). Early life stress alters behavior, immunity, and microbiota in rats: Implications for irritable bowel syndrome and psychiatric illnesses. *Biological Psychiatry, 65,* 263–267.

Oosterman, M., De Schipper, J. C., Fisher, P., Dozier, M., & Schuengel, C. (2010). Autonomic reactivity in relation to attachment and early adversity among foster children. *Development and Psychopathology, 22,* 109–118.

Pears, K. C., Kim, H. K., & Fisher, P. A. (2008). Psychosocial and cognitive functioning of children with specific profiles of maltreatment. *Child Abuse and Neglect, 32,* 958–971.

Pfau, M. L., & Russo, S. J. (2015). Peripheral and central mechanisms of stress resilience. *Neurobiology of Stress, 1,* 66–79.

Porges, S. W. (2001). The polyvagal theory: Phylogenetic substrates of a social nervous system. *International Journal of Psychophysiology, 42*(2), 123–146.

Porges, S. W., & Furman, S. A. (2011). The early development of the autonomic nervous system provides a neural platform for social behaviour: A polyvagal perspective. *Infant and Child Development, 20,* 106–118.

Propper, C. B., & Holochwost, S. J. (2013). The influence of proximal risk on the early development of the autonomic nervous system. *Developmental Review, 33,* 151–167.

Puetz, V. B., Zweerings, J., Dahmen, B., Ruf, C., Scharke, W., Herpertz-Dahlmann, B., & Konrad, K. (2016). Multidimensional assessment of neuroendocrine and psychopathological profiles in maltreated youth. *Journal of Neural Transmission, 123,* 1095–1106.

Quevedo, K., Johnson, A. E., Loman, M. L., LaFavor, T. L., & Gunnar, M. (2012). The confluence of adverse early experience and puberty on the cortisol awakening response. *International Journal of Behavioral Development, 36,* 19–28.

Rao, U., Hammen, C., Ortiz, L. R., Chen, L. A., & Poland, R. E. (2008). Effects of early and recent adverse experiences on adrenal response to psychosocial stress in depressed adolescents. *Biological Psychiatry, 64*(6), 521–526.

Riis, J. L., Granger, D. A., Minkovitz, C. S., Bandeen-Roche, K., DiPietro, J. A., & Johnson, S. B. (2016). Maternal distress and child neuroendocrine and immune regulation. *Social Science and Medicine, 151,* 206–214.

Romeo, R. D., Bellani, R., Karatsoreos, I. N., Chhua, N., Vernov, M., Conrad, C. D., & McEwen, B. S. (2006). Stress history and pubertal development interact to shape hypothalamic-pituitary-adrenal axis plasticity. *Endocrinology, 147,* 1664–1674.

Roos, L. E., Fisher, P. A., Shaw, D. S., Kim, H. K., Neiderhiser, J. M., Reiss, D., . . . Leve, L. D. (2016). Inherited and environmental influences on a childhood co-occurring symptom phenotype: Evidence from an adoption study. *Development and Psychopathology, 28,* 111–125.

Roos, L. E., Giuliano, R. J., Beauchamp, K. G., Gunnar, M., Amidon, B., & Fisher, P. A. (2017). Validation of autonomic and endocrine reactivity to a laboratory stressor in young children. *Psychoneuroendocrinology, 77,* 51–55.

Ruttle, P. L., Shirtcliff, E. A., Serbin, L. A., Fisher, D. B., Stack, D. M., & Schwartzman, A. E. (2011). Disentangling psychobiological mechanisms underlying internalizing and externalizing behaviors in youth: Longitudinal and concurrent associations with cortisol. *Hormones and Behavior, 59,* 123–132.

Schechter, D. S., & Willheim, E. (2009). Disturbances of attachment and parental psychopathology in early childhood. *Child and Adolescent Psychiatric Clinics of North America, 18,* 665–686.

Shonkoff, J. P., & Fisher, P. A. (2013). Rethinking evidence-based practice and two-generation programs to create the future of early childhood policy. *Development and Psychopathology, 25,* 1635–1653.

Silverman, M. N., Pearce, B. D., Biron, C. A., & Miller, A. H. (2005). Immune modulation of the Hypothalamic-Pituitary-Adrenal (HPA) axis during viral infection. *Viral Immunology, 18,* 41–78.

Slopen, N., McLaughlin, K. A., & Shonkoff, J. P. (2014). Interventions to improve cortisol regulation in children: A systematic review. *Pediatrics, 133,* 312–326.

Stark, J. L., Avitsur, R., Padgett, D. A., Campbell, K. A., Beck, F. M., & Sheridan, J. F. (2001). Social stress induces glucocorticoid resistance in macrophages. *American Journal of Physiology-Regulatory, Integrative and Comparative Physiology, 280,* R1799–R1805.

Sudo, N., Chida, Y., Aiba, Y., Sonoda, J., Oyama, N., Yu, X. N., . . . Koga, Y. (2004). Postnatal microbial colonization programs the hypothalamic – pituitary – adrenal system for stress response in mice. *The Journal of Physiology, 558*(1), 263–275.

Tarullo, A. R., & Gunnar, M. R. (2006). Child maltreatment and the developing HPA axis. *Hormones and Behavior, 50,* 632–639.

Trickett, P. K., Noll, J. G., Susman, E. J., Shenk, C. E., & Putnam, F. W. (2010). Attenuation of cortisol across development for victims of sexual abuse. *Development and Psychopathology, 22,* 165–175.

Urizar, G. G., Jr., & Muñoz, R. F. (2011). Impact of a pre-natal cognitive-behavioral stress management intervention on salivary cortisol levels in low-income mothers and their infants. *Psychoneuroendocrinology, 36,* 1480–1494.

Valentino, K., De Alba, A., Hibel, L. C., Fondren, K., & McDonnell, C. G. (2017). Adherence to diurnal cortisol sampling among mother – child dyads from maltreating and nonmaltreating families. *Child Maltreatment, 22,* 286–294.

White, L. O., Ising, M., Klitzing, K., Sierau, S., Michel, A., Klein, A. M., . . . Uhr, M. (2017). Reduced hair cortisol after maltreatment mediates externalizing symptoms in middle childhood and adolescence. *Journal of Child Psychology and Psychiatry, 58,* 998–1007.

33

DEVELOPMENTAL TRAJECTORIES OF HPA–HPG DUAL-AXES COUPLING

Implications for social neuroendocrinology

Ellen Zakreski, Andrew Richard Dismukes, Andrea Tountas,
Jenny Mai Phan, Shannin Nicole Moody,
and Elizabeth Anne Shirtcliff

Introduction

The hypothalamic–pituitary–adrenal (HPA) axis and hypothalamic–pituitary–gonadal (HPG) axis are implicated in a wide range of health, behavioral and social outcomes across development. Although often studied in isolation, there is extensive cross-talk between the HPA and HPG, and growing research suggests that their interaction may be an important determinant of health and behavior across the lifespan. While early research on HPA–HPG interactions suggested that these axes mutually inhibit one another, an emerging perspective suggests the association between HPA activity and HPG activity may be 'coupled', varying from inverse to positive depending on individual characteristics (e.g. psychopathology, sex) and contextual factors (e.g. developmental stage, competition). This chapter summarizes the physiology and function of the HPA and HPG and describe how these axes change over development and inform behavior. We then provide a historical perspective of HPA–HPG coupling and review mechanisms by which the two systems interact. We systematically review human studies that examine HPA and HPG hormones at different ages and in different contexts. For brevity, we focused on studies using cortisol as a marker of HPA activity and testosterone, dehydroepiandrosterone or dehydroepiandrosterone-sulfate as a marker of the HPG.

The HPA axis

HPA physiology

The HPA regulates a biochemical cascade (Charmandari, Tsigos, & Chrousos, 2005), beginning when corticotropin-releasing hormone (CRH) from the hypothalamus triggers release of adrenocorticotropic hormone (ACTH) from the anterior pituitary. ACTH stimulates the adrenal cortex to release glucocorticoids (cortisol in humans), which bind to glucocorticoid receptors and mineralocorticoid receptors located throughout the body and brain. In the hypothalamus and pituitary, cortisol provides negative feedback on the HPA, inhibiting further secretion of

CRH, ACTH and cortisol. The HPA influences immune function, cell growth and survival, and the control of energy supplies.

In response to acute stressors, the HPA reacts by increasing cortisol levels, inducing temporary biobehavioral changes that help the organism cope with threats or challenge (Doom & Gunnar, 2013; Stratakis & Chrousos, 1995). Chronic HPA activation due to long-term stressor exposure also induces enduring changes in the brain and other tissues through altering cell survival and morphology (Doom & Gunnar, 2013; Stratakis & Chrousos, 1995). While chronic HPA activation is typically believed to negatively impact health and development, from an evolutionary perspective, it may actually redirect development toward a phenotype that is optimal in chronically adverse conditions (Del Giudice, Ellis, & Shirtcliff, 2011; Ellis, Bianchi, Griskevicius, & Frankenhuis, 2017).

HPA and development

The HPA changes substantially across development (Shirtcliff & Ruttle, 2010). HPA activity is blunted before birth (Levine, 1994). In infancy and toddlerhood, HPA activity and reactivity is low, although the HPA may become responsive when the source of stress is a primary caregiver (Dismukes, Shirtcliff, Drury, & Theall, in press). This period, known as the stress-hyporesponsive period (SHRP), is characterized by limited cortisol reactivity to stress resulting from physiological down-regulation of the HPA (Sapolsky & Meaney, 1986; Schmidt, 2010). The SHRP occurs prior to 24 months of age and has been observed across a variety of stress paradigms (Gunnar, Brodersen, Krueger, & Rigatuso, 1996). This period potentially supports the rapid brain development that occurs in the first few years of life (Essex, Klein, Cho, & Kalin, 2002; Lupien, McEwen, Gunnar, & Heim, 2009). Like other aspects of HPA function, the SHRP is shaped by parental care. Cold, unresponsive, unpredictable or insensitive caregiving interrupts the SHRP, increasing HPA reactivity (Ainsworth, Blehar, Waters, & Wall, 2014; Gunnar, Brodersen, Nachmias, Buss, & Rigatuso, 1996). While interruption of the SHRP is frequently conceptualized as harmful, from an evolutionary perspective adverse rearing conditions, such as inconsistent caregiving and parental absence, may redirect development toward a phenotype optimized for harsh environments by advancing maturation and stress trajectories early in development (Del Giudice et al., 2011; Meaney, 2007).

HPA activity decreases from infancy to about 9 years of age (Schreiber et al., 2006). This decrease in cortisol occurs as children gradually acquire self-regulatory skills. These two events may be related such that the dyadic regulation of the HPA between a caregiver and child that emerges as the child enters the SHRP becomes internalized, as the child slowly develops self-regulatory capabilities (Adam, Klimes-Dougan, & Gunnar, 2007) – one of the hallmark developmental milestones of juvenility (Del Giudice, Angeleri, & Manera, 2009). In support, Watamura and colleagues (2004) associated lower basal cortisol with more effortful control in 3-year-olds.

Self-regulation continues to increase in adolescence, and HPA activity and reactivity also increase (Stroud et al., 2009; Sumter, Bokhorst, Miers, van Pelt, & Westenberg, 2010). Adolescent changes in HPA function could reflect increased environmental stressors relative to previous life stages due to new and challenging physical and social changes (Crone & Dahl, 2012; Gunnar & Hostinar, 2015). Social changes are important because the HPA is particularly responsive to social evaluative threat (Dickerson & Kemeny, 2004) and is more responsive among individuals with less social support. Following puberty, parents provide less social support (Dahl & Gunnar, 2009; Doom, Hostinar, van Zomeren-Dohm, & Gunnar, 2015) and youth must often navigate social situations alone. Furthermore, parents can shift from sources of social support to sources of social evaluation and/or authoritarian control in adolescence (Gecas & Schwalbe,

1986; Pettit, Laird, Dodge, Bates, & Criss, 2001) as parent–child conflict becomes normative and adolescents test parental boundaries and controls (Steinberg, 2000). While peers may provide more social support (Dahl & Gunnar, 2009; Doom, Doyle, & Gunnar, 2017; Doom et al., 2015), peer support can be unpredictable (Stanton-Salazar & Spina, 2005) and can erode quickly (Stice, Ragan, & Randall, 2004). Peer rejection and social exclusion is common in adolescence (Coie, Dodge, & Kupersmidt, 1990), and adolescents are particularly sensitive to rejection (Brown, 1990; Masten et al., 2009). Like peers, budding romantic interests and partnerships are also fragile and more likely sources of stress than support capable of buffering HPA activity (Gunnar & Hostinar, 2015).

In adulthood, individual differences predominate cortisol activity and reactivity and social support emerges as a critical factor. Low social support predicts elevated cortisol reactivity to psychosocial stress (Wirtz et al., 2006). With laboratory acute stressors, Kirschbaum, Klauer, Filipp, and Hellhammer and colleagues (1995) found that women receiving support from their romantic partners had increased cortisol responses, while men had an attenuated stress response when receiving support from their female partner. Women typically have stronger social networks than men (Kendler, Myers, & Prescott, 2005) and may respond to stress by affiliating with others as a coping mechanism (Taylor & Stanton, 2007). These findings suggest that generally men and women cope with stress differently, as indicated through cortisol levels.

At each developmental stage, there is considerable interindividual variation in HPA function. Early in life, the caregiving environment is particularly influential, establishing set points for activity and reactivity of the HPA (Anand, Coskun, Thrivikraman, Nemeroff, & Plotsky, 1999; Del Giudice et al., 2011; Tarullo, Bruce, & Gunnar, 2007). Individual differences in HPA function may depend on self-regulatory skills that develop across childhood (Adam et al., 2007; Gunnar & Donzella, 2002; Hostinar & Gunnar, 2013). By adolescence, however, self-regulation resources may be overwhelmed by social evaluation, conflict and rejection from parents, peers and romantic relationships, in addition to reduced social support. Taken together, social dynamics inform HPA activity, and those social dynamics are different across the lifespan according to the particular challenges and milestones of each developmental stage.

HPA and human behavior

Altered HPA activity at baseline and under stress is implicated in a wide range of stress-related pathologies across development (Doom & Gunnar, 2013; McEwen & Stellar, 1993), including depression (Pariante & Lightman, 2008), anxiety (Kallen et al., 2008), and aggression (Böhnke, Bertsch, Kruk, & Naumann, 2010; Lopez-Duran, Olson, Hajal, Felt, & Vazquez, 2008), as well as internalizing and externalizing problems overall (Ruttle et al., 2011). The Adaptive Calibration Model (ACM; Del Giudice et al., 2011) provides a useful model for understanding which behavioral outcomes should be shaped by the HPA axis. The ACM describes how salient social contexts such as uncontrollability/unpredictability, parental care, social threat or opportunity and novel environmental experiences shift the HPA to adapt and calibrate to these contexts, filtering out unimportant information and amplifying salient signals of the quality of the social ecology. This, in turn, helps shape the individual's development, regulating their behavior and ultimately increasing individual differences in behavioral traits such as competition and risk-taking, pair bonding and caregiving as well as more physiological development including growth and learning, maturation and fertility. Several of these behavioral outcomes can be framed as mental health problems, yet, from the perspective of the ACM, even undesirable behavioral outcomes and physiological adaptations may nonetheless serve a purpose that helps direct growth and development toward the best option for that individual in their context. In sum, alterations to the HPA provide a key link between adverse early conditions and the development of psychopathology, as predicted by the ACM.

The HPG axis

HPG physiology

The hypothalamus releases gonadotropin releasing hormone (GnRH), which triggers release of luteinizing hormone (LH) and follicle-stimulating hormone (FSH) from the anterior pituitary. LH and FSH trigger the gonads and adrenal cortex to release sex steroids into the bloodstream. Sex steroids include androgens (testosterone, dihydrotestosterone, DHEA, DHEAS), progestins (e.g. progesterone) and estrogens (e.g. estradiol). These hormones respectively bind to androgen receptors, progesterone receptors, and estrogen receptors. Sex steroid receptors exist throughout the body and brain. In the hypothalamus and pituitary, sex steroids provide positive and negative feedback on the HPG.

HPG and development

HPG activity spikes during prenatal development and again at birth. Perinatal sex steroids establish primary sexual characteristics and organize the brain, facilitating the expression of sex-typical behaviors later in life (Hines, 2010). For instance, children with high prenatal exposure to testosterone show increased preference for toys and games typically preferred by boys such as rough and tumble play while low prenatal testosterone levels is associated with more female typical play (e.g. playing with dolls) (Hines, 2010).

During childhood, the HPG is relatively inactive (Styne & Grumbach, 2011). Suppression of reproduction, and thus the HPG, early in life is likely adaptive since immature organisms lack sufficient resources to produce or rear offspring (Hill & Kaplan, 1999). According to Ellis (2004), HPG inactivity during childhood allows for skeletal and brain development which would otherwise be impeded by high sex hormone levels.

Adrenarche (adrenal puberty), which occurs roughly around age 6–8, marks a gradual increase in the production of adrenal androgens such as DHEA and DHEAS (Havelock, Auchus, & Rainey, 2004), an early hallmark of puberty. Del Giudice et al. (2009) theorize that the surge in DHEA acts as a premature sex hormone, and others have theorized that adrenarche may initiate several classic puberty-related changes such as sexual attraction or interest (McClintock & Herdt, 1996). In support, one study in juvenile boys found that physical competition increased DHEA rather than testosterone (McHale, Zava, Hales, & Gray, 2015).

After adrenarche, children enter puberty when surges in testosterone, estrogen and progesterone facilitate the further development of secondary sexual characteristics that will provide signals of sexual maturity. The HPG becomes more active; GnRH secretion becomes pulsatile, and testosterone and estrogen levels rise in both boys and girls (Shirtcliff, 2009). The adrenal glands continue to produce increasing levels of DHEA through this period, which are directly responsible for several hallmark signs of puberty (e.g. body odor, acne, pubic hair; Auchus & Rainey, 2004). Testosterone exposure during adolescence and into young adulthood also affects numerous brain regions implicated in reward sensitivity, emotion-regulation and social perception, and temporarily augments neural plasticity (Sisk & Zehr, 2005). Studies on youth associate adverse rearing conditions with faster puberty in boys and girls (Belsky, Steinberg, Houts, Halpern-Felsher, & NICHD Early Child Care Research Network, 2010; Ellis, Shirtcliff, Boyce, Deardorff, & Essex, 2011). Thus, the HPG, like the HPA, may be programmed by the early caregiving environment.

In middle adulthood, HPG activity gradually decreases and testosterone levels decline. This is observed in DHEA as well, which undergoes a gradual decline in the later decades of life (Kroboth, Salek, Pittenger, Faban, & Frye, 1999). The decrease in testosterone may help redirect resources away from mating toward parenting (McGlothlin, Jawor, & Ketterson, 2007). Consistent with this idea, for both men and women, parents have lower testosterone than non-parents (Gray, Kahlenberg, Barrett, Lipson, & Ellison, 2002; Kuzawa, Gettler, Huang, & McDade, 2010), and parents with lower testosterone levels invest more in caring for their offspring (Alvergne, Faurie, & Raymond, 2009; O'Neal, Reichard, Pavilis, & Ketterson, 2008).

The HPG and human behavior

The HPG is best known for facilitating sex and reproduction. Testosterone promotes development of primary and secondary male sexual characteristics (Wilson, George, & Griffin, 1981) and spermatogenesis (Short, 1975). Estrogen promotes development of primary and secondary female sexual characteristics (Wilson et al., 1981) and ovulation (Docke & Dorner, 1965). Progesterone promotes breast development (Javed & Lteif, 2013), and prepares the uterus and other organs for pregnancy (Spencer & Bazer, 2002). According to Archer (2006), testosterone promotes the development and expression of social behaviors and motivations conducive to sex and mating, particularly for males, as well as aggression (Book, Starzyk, & Quinsey, 2001), dominance and status seeking (Rowe, Maughan, Worthman, Costello, & Angold, 2004), although findings are inconsistent. While testosterone is often called a "male" sex hormone, it is relevant across reproductive behaviors in both sexes. For instance, in women, exogenous testosterone promotes sexual arousal (Cappelletti & Wallen, 2016) and is correlated with aggression (Harris, Rushton, Hampson, & Jackson, 1996) and dominance (Grant & France, 2001). Men and women with higher testosterone also have more sexual partners (van Anders, Hamilton, & Watson, 2007).

DHEA is sometimes called the 'anti-aging hormone' because of its protective effects on memory, neuronal growth and neuronal activity (Havelock et al., 2004). DHEA binds to a range of receptors, including estrogen receptors (Maninger, Wolkowitz, Reus, Epel, & Mellon, 2009), and serves as a prohormone for estrogen and testosterone. DHEA can broadly influence physiology through its conversion to other sex steroids and metabolites, indicating the potential for a diverse pattern of peripheral downstream effects. DHEA has been associated with externalizing disorders such as disruptive behavior disorder (Brown et al., 2008; van Goozen et al., 2000) as well as internalizing disorders such as anxiety (Boudarene, Legros, & Timsit-Berthier, 2002) and depression (Shirtcliff, Zahn-Waxler, Klimes-Dougan, & Slattery, 2007; Wolkowitz et al., 1995), marking this as a particularly important emerging biomarker in the study of social neuroendocrinology. It is worth noting that many of the behaviors that are implicated as an outcome of the HPG are also correlates of the HPA.

Coupling and other forms of HPG–HPG axis interplay

The HPA and HPG develop in parallel, with low activity early in life and higher activity in adolescence. While these axes are typically regarded as separate, both affect social behaviors and both are shaped by environmental forces (e.g. parental care, early life adversity). Across development, the HPA and HPG communicate centrally and peripherally. End-products of the HPA (e.g. cortisol) and the HPG (e.g. testosterone, DHEA) are measured to probe HPA–HPG regulatory interplay under various contexts and across development. This cross-axis coordination extends across basal (waking), diurnal (hormone trajectory across a day) and reactive (acute increases in hormone levels) time frames as well as early, extreme and concurrent stress exposure and across a range of behavioral outcomes (Shirtcliff et al., 2015).

This chapter focuses on HPA–HPG coupling, which is in its simplest form a bivariate correlation between HPA and HPG markers within individuals. Positive coupling is when HPA hormones and HPG hormones move in the same direction within an individual. Inverse coupling occurs when hormones move in opposite directions. Decoupling is a non-significant correlation. Most frequently, coupling has been assessed within individuals over time using techniques such as hierarchical linear modeling (e.g. Black, Lerner, Shirtcliff, & Klein, 2018; Dismukes, Johnson, Vitacco, Iturri, & Shirtcliff, 2015; Dismukes, Shirtcliff et al., 2015; Marceau et al., 2013; Phan et al., 2017). Insights into coupling can be unmasked through cross-sectional analyses (across individuals). For instance, Casto, Rivell, and Edwards (2017) compare basal cortisol and basal testosterone across individuals. Nonetheless, correlation across individuals is an imperfect proxy of within-individual processes (Kraemer, Yesavage, Taylor, & Kupfer, 2000). Alternatively, some researchers use area under the curve (AUC) to summarize the change or total output of each hormone over time for each subject, then they compare this value between subjects. For instance, Han and colleagues (2015) correlated DHEA AUC with cortisol AUC. This approach has utility, yet does not provide information on whether HPA and HPG hormone levels are correlated at the same time. It must be noted that the HPA–HPG axis interaction is a distinct facet of HPA–HPG interplay which captures whether one axis moderates the effects of another axis on a trait or state. As Mehta and Prasad (2015) review (and as discussed elsewhere in this handbook), several traits depend on HPA–HPG interactions.

Marceau and colleagues (2014) have provided a framework for fully decomposing coupling in longitudinal hormone data involving a four-step analytic approach. First, data are probed for basic within-individual associations between hormones. Second, time as a covariate is added so that deviations of one hormone from its slope can be associated with deviations of another hormone. The 'slope' could be reactivity scores, diurnal declines or longitudinal trajectories. Third, residual scores of a hormone from its slope are extracted for each collection point and modeled in the prediction of another hormone, e.g. the residual score of testosterone at each time point predicting cortisol, allowing for an interrogation of the way that deviations of one hormone from its diurnal slope or trajectory are associated with deviations of another hormone from its slope. Lastly, estimates of the slope term of time predicting a hormone are saved and entered as a between-individual predictor of another hormone, e.g. the DHEA slope can be entered as a between-individual predictor of intercept and time predicting cortisol. To our knowledge, this strategy represents the most robust and full decomposition method for analyzing coupling in longitudinal hormone data.

The classic view on coupling

An overview of classical coupling

Inverse HPA-HPG coupling seems consistent with the classsic view that the HPA and HPG inhibit each other. Animal and human research dating back to Hans Selye (1939) has informed the way scientists think about processes modulating HPA–HPG outputs under stressful contexts. The classic fight-or-flight response of an organism under threat suggests the HPA inhibits reproductive functioning. In the presence of imminent threat (i.e. a bear chasing), survival mode prioritizes physiologic functioning over reproduction, and the HPA takes the lead over the HPG, which is more concerned with sex, sexual development and reproduction. Much of the stress literature emphasizes chronic or prolonged stress that results in elevated levels of cortisol, CRH or ACTH (Plotsky & Sawchenko, 1987) and lower levels of testosterone, estrogen, progesterone and HPG intermediaries (Breen et al., 2004; Whirledge & Cidlowski, 2010). Recently, literature within acute stress contexts has provided meaningful insight into the complexity of HPA–HPG coupling, demonstrating these axes' adaptive functioning. We expand below on studies focusing on acute stress contexts (laboratory stress) as well as prolonged stress (early life adversity) displaying inhibitory effects of the HPA on the HPG (glucocorticoids suppressing gonadal functioning and reproduction).

HPA activity inhibits HPG activity

Glucocorticoids have a negative feedback mechanism designed to regulate metabolic, immuno-logic and other physiologic functions (e.g. autonomic physiological responses). HPG hormones can have a negative feedback (progesterone and testosterone) or a positive feedback (estrogen) regulatory function. Glucocorticoids can exhibit inhibitory effects on HPG hormones through HPG intermediaries, such as LH (Breen et al., 2004; Saketos, Sharma, & Santoro, 1993; Viau, 2002), GnRH and FSH (Rivier & Rivest, 1991; Tilbrook, Turner, & Clarke, 2000). Chronic suppression of LH leads to infertility problems in both men and women and has been found to cause Kallmann's syndrome, a condition of hypogonadotropic hypogonadism (in men), and amenorrhea (in women). Down-regulation of HPA on HPG also involves CRH suppressing GnRH levels in hypophyseal portal blood, and ACTH suppressing LH, evidenced by admin-istration studies in animals (Phogat, Smith, & Dobson, 1997; Phogat, Smith, & Dobson, 1999a, 1999b). Chronic or prolonged stress in humans and extended exposure to stressors or administration of exogenous glucocorticoids in animals is thought to exacerbate inhibitory effects. It is thought that the HPA may inhibit the HPG under stress so that energy spent on reproductive functions can be used for survival. More recently, researchers have suggested that the HPA may protect the HPG from the effects of chronic stress (Maeda & Tsukamura, 2006; Matsuwaki, Kayasuga, Yamanouchi, & Nishihara, 2006; Matsuwaki, Suzuki, Yamanouchi, & Nishihara, 2004; Matsuwaki, Watanabe, Suzuki, Yamanouchi, & Nishihara, 2003), which offers further insight into the complexity of these two axes.

HPG activity inhibits HPA axis activity

The inhibitory effects of the HPG on the HPA involves testosterone at the level of the medial preoptic area (MPOA) of the hypothalamus and at the pituitary (Viau, 2002; Viau & Meaney, 1996), and is evident in both males and females. In men, exogenous testosterone has been found to suppress cortisol responsivity to CRH stimulation (Rubinow et al., 2005). Increases in tes-tosterone likely slow down cortisol release by enhancing HPA negative feedback (Viau, 2002), which can be viewed as stress regulation. Indeed, Stephens, Mathon, McCaul and Wand (2016) found that high basal testosterone attenuated cortisol responsivity to psychosocial stress. Con-trary to the notion that the HPG inhibits the HPA, Knight et al. (2017) found that exogenous testosterone actually enhanced rather than suppressed cortisol responsivity to a psychosocial stressor.

Coupling: a modern perspective

Whether inverse HPA–HPG coupling is empirically supported is not our primary question. Rather, the ubiquity of inhibition is under scrutiny by emerging data (reviewed below), which suggests that acute and chronic stress can upregulate (rather than suppress) the HPG in some contexts.

Drawing from life history theory, Wingfield and Sapolsky (2003) suggest inverse coupling and positive coupling may be adaptive but in different contexts. Inverse coupling may be adaptive for organisms with high future reproductive potential when they encounter threat or challenge. HPA activation suppresses inflammation and focuses energy on survival. HPA activation during stress liberates energy, sensitizes the individual to social feedback and facilitates self-regulation by acting as an anxiolytic (Putman, Antypa, Crysovergi, & van der Does, 2010) and preventing overactivation of the adrenocortical and autonomic stress responses (Sapolsky, Romero, & Munck, 2000). HPG inhibition postpones reproduction until conditions become more auspicious.

Postponing reproduction is likely maladaptive for organisms with limited chances to reproduce, such as organisms living in harsh conditions (Wingfield & Sapolsky, 2003). Organisms can maintain reproductive capacity even under stressful conditions by down-regulating HPA activity, freeing the HPG from inhibition. The majority of studies in humans associate chronic stress with blunted basal and reactive cortisol levels (Miller, Chen, & Zhou, 2007), in addition to increased reproductive effort (Chisholm, Quinlivan, Petersen, & Coall, 2005; Gettler, McDade, Bragg, Feranil, & Kuzawa, 2015; Kogan et al., 2015). Longitudinal studies have also observed low cortisol and accelerated puberty in maltreated children, indirectly implicating HPG modulation (Ellis et al., 2011; Negriff, Saxbe, & Trickett, 2015; Saxbe, Negriff, Susman, & Trickett, 2015).

Down-regulating HPA activity may help maintain the HPG; however, it also limits the organism's capacity to cope with stressors and desensitizes the individual to social feedback. Positive coupling may therefore come on-line in challenging situations where organisms require both the HPA and HPG; adolescents, for example, may require co-activation of the HPA and HPG. Increased HPG activity stimulates development of secondary sexual characteristics (Shirtcliff, Dahl, & Pollak, 2009) and prepares adolescents for reproduction by enhancing other characteristics that help individuals compete for and attract mates (Ballonoff Suleiman, Johnson, Shirtcliff, & Galván, 2015). High HPA reactivity helps adolescents cope with unpredictability/uncontrollability and social evaluative threat in a context of limited and variable social support. As Somerville (2013) reviews, high HPA reactivity may sensitize adolescents to social evaluation, which could help them learn adult roles and responsibilities.

Whether an organism exhibits positive or inverse coupling could therefore depend on contextual factors affecting the relative importance of functions dependent on the HPA (e.g. sensitivity to social feedback) versus functions dependent on the HPG (e.g. reproduction). In addition to normative developmental challenges (e.g. adolescence), other contexts may also favor positive coupling, such as early life adversity. According to Del Giudice and colleagues (2011), early life adversity (e.g. low maternal care) signals low future reproductive potential. Given Wingfield and Sapolsky's (2003) claim that inverse coupling is maladaptive for organisms with low future reproductive potential, one might expect positive coupling or decoupling among survivors of early life adversity. This could partly explain why high cortisol predicted low sexual functioning in women with low childhood adversity, but for women who experienced childhood sexual abuse, cortisol and sexual functioning were unrelated (Meston & Lorenz, 2013).

Potential mechanisms of positive HPA–HPG coupling

With this functional perspective of coupling in mind, we can speculate upon permissive mechanisms for how positive coupling is instantiated in the body, although much of the extant literature on mechanisms underlying HPA–HPG interplay was designed to explain HPA–HPG inhibition (reviewed above). Epigenetic modulation, a bridge between environmental context and the genetic code (Geng, Gao, & Yang, 2013) varies according to developmental stage (Hochberg et al., 2011), and it is possible that developmental stages such as infancy and the pubertal transition, characterized by epigenetic flexibility and plasticity, allow for more HPA–HPG communication than other developmental stages. In support, new research is finding that pubertal onset is epigenetically controlled (Aylwin, Toro, Shirtcliff, & Lomniczi, in press).

Upstream neural activation of both axes may be parallel, regulated by similar brain regions. The HPA and HPG are modulated by prefrontal and orbitofrontal cortical activation and connectivity as well as the amygdala (Derntl et al., 2009; Radke et al., 2015; Jankord & Herman, 2008). If an individual appraises a context as a challenge or social evaluative threat, both axes may be centrally activated, culminating in reactivity of the end-products of the HPA and HPG over the course of minutes, long before one axis is able to inhibit the other.

Inhibition occurs within and between the HPA and HPG. For instance, CRH and cortisol are positively coupled, since CRH promotes cortisol release, but at later times, e.g. during negative feedback when cortisol inhibits CRH, cortisol and CRH are inversely coupled. GnRH and testosterone function in a parallel fashion as CRH and cortisol. Another possible explanation for coupling between axes may be that cortisol could enhance HPG functioning by shutting itself off and that testosterone could enhance HPA activity by shutting itself off. While speculatory, this mechanistic principle is worth investigating to explain variance associated in HPA–HPG cross-talk. Previously, we also illustrated the role of DHEA as an end-product of both axes, as well as intra-cellular conversion between HPA and HPG hormones as a hint toward the plausibility of positive coupling (Shirtcliff et al., 2015). This is not an exhaustive list of potential mechanisms, but rather aims to suggest that positive coupling is physiologically plausible through meaningful social neuroendocrinological pathways.

Evidence from 2015

A special issue of *Developmental Psychobiology* (Shirtcliff et al., 2015) highlighted the role of positive coupling in a series of studies across diverse contexts (Bobadilla, Asberg, Johnson, & Shirtcliff, 2015; Dismukes, Johnson, et al., 2015; Dismukes, Shirtcliff, Hanson, & Pollak, 2015; Han, Miller, Cole, Zahn-Waxler, & Hastings, 2015; Marceau et al., 2014; Ruttle et al., 2015). These papers suggest that coupling is a robust phenomenon with implications for mental health in adolescents and longitudinal predictive utility (Han et al., 2015; Ruttle et al., 2015). HPA–HPG interplay as a function of early stress exposure was clearly supported in Dismukes, Shirtcliff, et al. (2015). Ruttle and colleagues (2015) found tight coupling (strong correlation between HPA and HPG) within early adolescence followed by an early switch to an adult-like pattern within those with early life adversity. Simmons and colleagues (2015) found positive coupling within male adolescents exposed to high levels of maternal aggression but did not find the same pattern within females or traumatized youth. Dismukes, Johnson, and colleagues (2015) also found more positive coupling in adolescents exposed to early life adversity. A consistent picture emerged for HPA–HPG coupling with more proximal stressors, such that coupling was stronger within those exposed to greater stress defined by a difficult laboratory-day (Dismukes, Shirtcliff et al., 2015), during acute laboratory stressors (Marceau et al., 2014) or as combat experiences in adulthood within military veterans (Bobadilla et al., 2015).

In sum, this special issue provided mounting evidence for the phenomenon of context-dependent HPA–HPG coupling and served as an early call to systematically begin to consider when and for whom positive coupling occurs.

A review of the literature since 2015

To determine any updates to the HPA–HPG coupling literature presented in the Special issue in 2015, we conducted a review of published peer-reviewed journal articles.

Systematic literature search

We performed a systematic review of the literature using the database PubMed in March 2018 with the following sets of search and Boolean terms: cortisol OR HPA OR "hypothalamic-pituitary-adrenal" AND testosterone OR DHEA OR dehydroepiandrosterone OR HPG OR "hypothalamic-pituitary-gonadal" AND interaction OR joint OR jointly OR ratio OR coupling OR dual OR coupled. The terms interaction and ratio were included since these studies typically report correlations between HPA and HPG hormones. In addition, we applied the parameters that the studies must include humans, be published since January 1, 2013, and have the full text made available. We chose commonly used terms in our field to capture our variables of interest. We chose the cut-off date of January 1, 2013 for our search as these may not have been integrated into the special issue of Developmental Psychobiology highlighting HPA–HPG coupling. This resulted in a total of 502 results. We also conducted forward searching, which utilizes studies cited by other articles from our search results, as well as a search in Google Scholar using "dual hormone" and "hormonal coupling" as these terms repeatedly surfaced on the relevant articles located through PubMed, contributing ten more articles.

INCLUSION/EXCLUSION CRITERIA

There were several inclusion criteria articles had to meet: 1) report an association between cortisol and either DHEA or testosterone assessed at the same time; 2) age of the sample reported; 3) inclusion of an effect size or sufficient information to determine if there was a significant relationship about coupling; 4) include human participants; 5) have undergone peer-review; and 6) be written in English. Reviews or meta-analyses were excluded. We analyzed but ultimately excluded associations between HPA and HPG markers at different times, such as associations between basal cortisol and testosterone reactivity, since this review focuses specifically on hormone coupling. Figure 33.1 illustrates our inclusion and exclusion process, which culminated in systematic review of N = 41 papers. Table 33.1 summarizes articles that found a significant positive association between HPA and HPG markers. Table 33.2 summarizes articles that found a statistically non-significant association (i.e. p > 0.05). Table 33.3 shows studies that found group differences in either the strength or direction of coupling. Initially, we also sought to summarize articles that found significant inverse coupling, following the classic view of HPA–HPG axis inhibition, but we were unable to locate articles which showed, on average, inverse HPA–HPG axis correlations.

Emerging themes since 2015   Of the 41 relevant original peer-reviewed research papers identified through our systematic review, 26 studies reported an overall positive association between cortisol and either DHEA or testosterone, suggesting that positive HPA–HPG coupling has largely replicated as a robust phenomenon (Black et al., 2018; Ruttle et al., 2015). New themes in the coupling literature have emerged. This emerging research suggests that HPA and HPG markers tend to correlate positively both between and within individuals (e.g. Harden et al., 2016) across multiple developmental stages (Harden et al., 2016; Turan et al., 2015); that positive coupling as a phenomenon is observed across multiple contexts (Phan et al., 2017; Casto et al., 2017;

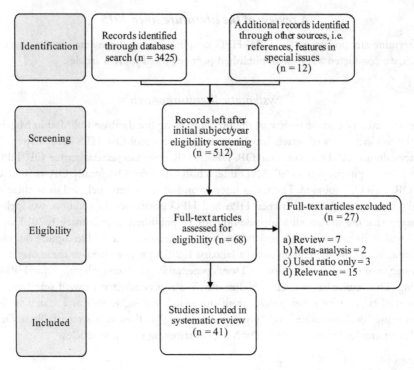

Figure 33.1   PRISMA (Preferred Reporting Items of Systematic Reviews and Meta-Analyses) flowchart for PubMed database search.

Panizzon et al., 2018); that coupling appears for both genders (e.g. Casto et al., 2017; Taylor et al., 2017) but nevertheless sex differences may be an important consideration (Black et al., 2018; Barel, Shahrabani, & Tzischinsky, 2017; Zilioli, Ponzi, Henry, & Maestripieri, 2015); that the population under study persists as a key predictor of coupling (Bobadilla et al., 2015; Dismukes, Johnson, et al., 2015); and that coupling plays a role in the etiology of psychopathological traits (Black et al., 2018; Jin et al., 2016; Turan et al., 2015).

The notion that positive coupling is specific to a particular developmental stage is challenged. Shirtcliff et al. (2015) propose that coupling is positive in adolescence but becomes inverse in adulthood. Many of the studies reviewed here report positive coupling in early adulthood (e.g. Casto et al., 2017; Phan et al., 2017) and mid–late adulthood (Panizzon et al., 2018; Sherman, Lerner, Josephs, Renshon, & Gross, 2016; Wilcox, Granger, Szanton, & Clark, 2014). Harden et al. (2016) found positive coupling from age 11–88 years. Nonetheless, other studies show developmental changes such that coupling becomes more positive as children enter adolescence and then less positive as adolescents approach adulthood (Black et al., 2018; Marceau et al., 2014; Ruttle et al., 2015). Both adolescence and adulthood may be permissive developmental stages for positive coupling, but adolescence may be characterized by circumstances that cultivate positive coupling.

Table 33.1 illustrates that both males and females demonstrate positive coupling. Nonetheless, given sex differences in HPA and HPG functioning, it is unsurprising that in several studies, coupling differed between males and females. Interestingly, the nature of this difference appears to depend on developmental stage. Among the studies reporting sex differences in coupling, girls showed stronger coupling than boys (Marceau et al., 2013; Simmons et al., 2015), while

Table 33.1 Studies showing overall significant[1] positive HPA–HPG coupling

Authors, year	Sex	N	Task	Life stage	Measure(s)
Edwards & Casto, 2013[1]	F	88	Athletic competition	Adult	Basal/Reactive
Marceau et al., 2013	M/F	213	Psychosocial stress	Adolescent	Reactive/Diurnal
Grasso et al., 2014	M	25		Adult	Basal
Johnson et al., 2014	M	50		Adolescent	Diurnal
Marceau et al., 2014	M/F	213	Psychosocial stress	Adolescent	Basal/Reactive
Wilcox, Granger, Szanton, & Clark, 2014	M/F	460		Adult	Diurnal
Dismukes, Johnson et al., 2015[2]	M	50		Adolescent	Diurnal
Dismukes, Shirtcliff et al., 2015	M/F	118	Low-level stressor; MRI stressor	Adolescent	Reactive/Diurnal
Edwards & Casto, 2015	F	97	Athletic competition	Adult	Basal/Reactive
Ota, Yatsuya, Mase, & Ono, 2015	F	115		Adult	Diurnal
Mehta & Prasad, 2015	M/F	280		Adult	Basal
Turan, Tackett, Lechtreck, & Browning, 2015	M/F	138	Psychosocial stress	Adult	Reactive
Zilioli et al., 2015	M/F	469		Adult	Basal
Harden et al., 2016	M/F	292		Adolescent; Adult	Diurnal
Jin et al., 2016	M/F	38		Adult	Basal
Laurent, Pierce, Goetz, & Granger, 2016	M/F	54	Psychosocial stress	Adult	Reactive
Sherman et al., 2016	M	78		Adult	Baseline
Shields, Lam, Trainor, & Yonelinas, 2016	M/F	129	Psychosocial stress	Adult	Reactive
Sollberger, Bernauer, & Ehlert, 2016	M	147		Adult	Basal
Casto et al., 2017	F	25	Athletic competition	Adult	Basal/Reactive
Phan et al., 2017	M/F	63	Psychosocial stress	Adult	Reactive
Taylor et al., 2017	M	57		Adult	Diurnal
Wu, Eisenegger, Zilioli, Watson, & Clark, 2017	M	166		Adult	Basal
Black, Lerner, Shirtcliff, & Klein, 2018	M/F	405		Adrenarche	Diurnal
Nofsinger, Patterson, & Shank, 2018	M/F	39		Adult	Basal
Panizzon et al., 2018	M	741		Adult	Diurnal

Notes:
1 Significant means the p-value of the association between HPA and HPG markers was < 0.05.
2 Sample of incarcerated adolescent boys.

Table 33.2 Studies showing overall non-significant[1] HPA–HPG coupling

Author, year	Sex	N	Task	Life stage	Measure
Bobadilla, Asberg, Johnson, & Shirtcliff, 2015[2]	M	45	Frustration task	Adult	Reactive
Han et al., 2015	M/F	51	Anger task; anxiety task	Adolescent	Reactive
Barel, Shahrabani, & Tzischinsky, 2017	M/F	77		Adult	Basal
Chatzittofis et al., 2013[3]	M/F	47	Lumbar puncture	Adult	Basal
Denson, Mehta, & Ho Tan, 2013	F	53		Adult	Basal
Kupchak et al., 2014[4]	M	12	Athletic competition	Adult	Reactive
Mehta, DesJardins, van Vugt, & Josephs, 2017[2]	M/F	98	Hawk–Dove game	Adult	Basal/Reactive
Pauly, Lay, Nater, Scott, & Hoppmann, 2017	M	185		Adult	Diurnal
Pfattheicher, 2017[5]	M	153		Adult	Basal

Notes:
1 Non-significant means the p-value of the association was > 0.05.
2 Basal testosterone and cortisol were positively correlated at the trend level ($p < 0.10$).
3 Sample of suicide attempters and healthy participants.
4 Correlation was calculated from subject's raw data.
5 Raw cortisol and testosterone were significantly positively correlated but non-significantly positively correlated after log-transformation.

Table 33.3 Studies showing group differences in HPA–HPG coupling

Author, year	Sex	N	Task	Life stage	Measure(s)
Aguilar, Jiménez, & Alvero-Cruz, 2013	M	7	Athletic competition	Adult	Basal/Reactive
Johnson et al., 2014	M	50		Adolescent	Diurnal
Schneiderman, Kanat-Maymon, Zagoory-Sharon, & Feldman, 2014	M/F	160		Adult	Basal
Wilcox, Granger, Szanton, & Clark, 2014	M/F	460		Adult	Diurnal
Bobadilla et al., 2015	M	45	Frustration task	Adult	Reactive
Dismukes, Johnson et al., 2015	M	50		Adolescent	Diurnal
Dismukes, Shirtcliff et al., 2015	M/F	118	Low-level stressor; MRI stressor	Adolescent	Reactive/ Diurnal
do Vale et al., 2015	F	21		Adult	Basal
Simmons et al., 2015	M/F	76		Adolescent	Basal
Ruttle, Shirtcliff, Armstrong, Klein, & Essex, 2015	M/F	346		Adolescent	Diurnal
Turan et al., 2015	M/F	138	Psychosocial stress	Adult	Reactive
Zilioli et al., 2015	M/F	469		Adult	Basal
Jin et al., 2016	M/F	38		Adult	Basal
Barel et al., 2017	M/F	77		Adult	Basal
Mehta et al., 2017	M/F	98	Hawk–Dove game	Adult	Basal/Reactive
Black et al., 2018	M/F	405		Adrenarche	Diurnal

women showed weaker coupling than men (Barel et al., 2017; Zilioli et al., 2015; Schneiderman, Kanat-Maymon, Zagoory-Sharon, & Feldman, 2014). Sex differences may also depend on task and method. Mehta et al. (2017) observed stronger (not weaker) correlation between cortisol and testosterone reactivity in women compared to men, while studies reporting weaker coupling in women compared HPA and HPG hormone levels at baseline only.

Nine studies reported a non-significant association between HPA–HPG markers. Potentially this could occur if coupling varies between participants in a sample (e.g. Bobadilla et al., 2015). Coupling appears to vary according to individual and contextual factors which may in turn interact with age and sex. Adversity is associated with tighter, more positive coupling (Bobadilla et al., 2015; Dismukes, Johnson, et al., 2015). Interestingly, the effect of adversity on coupling differs between boys and girls, underscoring the importance of sex when considering HPA–HPG coupling. Both Simmons et al. (2015) and Black et al. (2018) associated adversity with more positive coupling in boys yet less positive coupling in girls.

Many behaviors (e.g. depression, aggression) involve both the HPA and HPG, which is not surprising given extant theories (reviewed above), which frame a suite of behaviors as being calibrated by these biomarkers to help the individual adapt to their social context (Del Giudice et al., 2011). Several studies associate coupling with psychopathology and behavior. In adolescence, Johnson et al. (2014) observed tighter, more positive coupling in children with psychopathic traits. In adults, DHEAS–cortisol coupling was more positive in depressed patients than in healthy controls (Jin et al., 2016). Turan and colleagues (2015) associated positive testosterone-cortisol coupling with negative affect in boys and girls. In men, more positive testosterone-cortisol coupling predicted anxiety (women were not tested). These data suggest that coupling may be relevant to several psychopathologies across development. While certain clinical populations may exhibit more positive coupling than healthy controls, it is nonetheless important to note the presence of positive coupling is not an indicator of pathology. Many studies reviewed here observed positive coupling in healthy adults (e.g. Phan et al., 2017; Ota et al., 2015; Sollberger et al., 2016).

Limitations and future directions

Methodological limitations

We excluded unpublished studies and dissertations because peer-review is an important quality check. Including only published studies, however, may create a file-drawer problem and potentially bias our review. Many studies measure HPG and HPA hormones simultaneously, yet few actually report the relationship between these hormones, further indicating a potential file-drawer problem. We suspect this indicates the infancy of the field rather than publication bias because the file-drawer problem usually pertains to findings that run counter to established theoretical concepts. The notion of positive coupling itself runs counter to the classical view of dual-axis inhibition, so it is more likely that positive coupling findings have been scrapped for the file-drawer in prior decades rather than systematically dominate the field. Surprisingly, despite this obstacle, we were unable to find studies reporting a significant inverse association that met our inclusion criteria, while we found 26 studies reporting significant positive coupling.

Another limitation is an overall lack of standardization in methods. Different classifications for baseline (i.e. days, minutes or hours before task, etc.) and reactivity measures complicate our ability to draw firm conclusions between studies. Method did not clearly delineate studies finding significant positive coupling from studies that did not; methodological variation complicates identification of moderating factors. It is notable, however, that since 2015 consistencies in positive coupling has emerged despite substantial variation across studies, across methods and within studies that have not yet been specifically designed to reveal positive coupling.

Another limiting factor may be that many of the studies we reviewed assessed salivary hormones, presenting the possibility that coupling is an artifact of hormone measurement; Marceau et al.'s (2013) study utilizing blood was consistent with salivary findings of coupling. Another potential artifact may arise from tools used to assess hormone concentrations, such as liquid chromatography tandem mass spectrometry (LC-MS/MS) or enzyme immunoassays (EIAs). Since most studies utilize EIA, there is a possibility that positive coupling may result from cross-reactivity. However, Welker et al. (2016) reported that the correlation between cortisol and testosterone was equivalent across EIA and LC/MS-MS.

It will be important, moving forward, to work toward enhancing methodological cohesion necessary to make specific predictions and design studies to uncover when, why and how positive coupling occurs and to disentangle the unavoidable and inherent complications that come with studying dual-axis communication. To accomplish this, we now consider important future directions for the field to both minimize these limitations and advance the field of social neuroendocrinology.

Future direction: longitudinal studies of coupling across development

Much of what we know about HPA–HPG coupling across development comes from cross-sectional studies at different age ranges. Although cross-sectional research provides insights on positive coupling throughout the lifespan, taking a longitudinal approach may be key to understanding how dual-axis coupling changes across the lifespan (Ruttle et al., 2015). Longitudinal studies of hormone coupling across development will improve our understanding of coupling and ecological antecedents and behavioral correlates.

Coupling during adolescence and adulthood has been investigated, but there is a dearth of research covering coupling in infancy, early childhood and middle childhood. It would be fruitful to study coupling early in development, particularly since social neuroendocrinological developmental events occur, such as the SHRP and adrenarche (Byrne et al., 2017; Del Giudice et al., 2009).

Future direction: gender and the inclusion of additional sex steroids

There is a known limitation about gender such that most hormone research is conducted in males (Carré & Olmstead, 2015; Casto & Prasad, 2017; Geniole et al., 2017). The situation has improved over the last decade, yet gender continues to be a thorny issue because females are under-represented in extant literature, but also their hormonal release is often cyclical, and levels of testosterone in females are present in biofluids at a minute fraction relative to males (Davison & Davis, 2003). Additionally, many females take hormonal contraceptives, and effects of exogenous hormones on cross-axes communication is poorly understood. Casto and Edwards (2016) found that females taking hormonal contraceptives generally displayed lower levels of testosterone at baseline in the context of competition but similar testosterone reactivity; however, cortisol levels increased during the period of competition.

Measurement issues are not only present for females as some HPG end-products (e.g. estradiol) are also virtually unstudied in males. This could partly be due to the fact that estrogen is too low in male saliva for current assays to detect reliably (Shirtcliff et al., 2000), and plasma may be necessary to reliably measure these hormones. Nonetheless, estrogen and progesterone are important components of the HPG. For example, Barel and colleagues (2017) found that the relationship between risk-taking and estrogen was stronger than the relationship between testosterone and risk-taking in both men and women, providing useful hints toward HPA–HPG coupling. As studies on dual-axis communication gain momentum, it will be important to expand the repertoire of sex steroids beyond cortisol, testosterone and DHEA and fully embrace the complexities of hormone challenges in both genders.

Future direction: coupling across longer time periods

So far, coupling has been examined primarily by measuring hormones in saliva and plasma. This provides insight into coupling over short periods of time but does not provide information on coupling over longer periods of time (i.e. months). To capture long-term coupling, researchers can use cumulative hormone measurements instead of brief 'snap shots'. By measuring hormones in hair, hormone levels can be captured over months. Recently, hair testosterone and DHEA assays have been developed (Gao et al., 2013; Wang, Moody, & Shirtcliff, 2016) and hair cortisol assays established (Short et al., 2016), suggesting it may be feasible to further explore basal HPA–HPG cross-talk across longer time periods. This technique may be especially important for studies aimed at understanding how coupling unfolds across developmental stages.

Future direction: advancing mechanistic insights into positive coupling

The studies reviewed in this chapter rely on cortisol, testosterone and DHEA as markers of the HPA and HPG. These biomarkers reflect the totality of changes that have led to their coupling, but they do not provide detail on how that coupling occurred. Above, we speculate on upstream mechanism of positive coupling that remain to be explicated. It would be helpful for future work to probe these axes at each level through other biomarkers (e.g. ACTH, LH, FSH), to consider other axes or systems that display parallel developmental trajectories (e.g. estradiol, progesterone) or are theorized to also have life history relevance (e.g. oxytocin). Endocrine measures can be integrated into neuroimaging investigations (Eatough, Shirtcliff, Hanson, & Pollak, 2009), so studies can also be designed to understand central activation of social- and emotion-related neurocircuitry that leads to positive dual-axis activation.

Future direction: clinical and behavioral implications

Research devoted to understanding HPA–HPG coupling is not merely academic exploits. If positive coupling happens, it likely happens for a reason, and this functional view hints toward important behavioral and clinical implications. Emerging research is elucidating how a variety of health-related behaviors, such as callous–unemotional traits (Johnson, Vitacco, & Shirtcliff, 2017) and externalizing behaviors (Susman, Peckins, Bowes, & Dorn, 2017; Tackett et al., 2017) depend on both the HPA and HPG functioning. As researchers begin to explore behavioral and health correlates of coupling, it will be important to consider context and individual factors (e.g. sex) when planning experiments and comparing results between studies. Taken one step further, since there is a functional developmental role for positive coupling – potentially predominating the findings in adolescents more than adults – the clinical and behavioral implications of positive coupling may be particularly important for adolescents for whom many forms of psychopathology emerge.

Conclusion

We described how the HPA and HPG change over development and the social forces that drive these changes. Using a developmental lens, we expanded how the HPA adapts to changes in social evaluation and social support across the lifespan, while the HPG changes to prepare the individual for reproduction. We described how and why these axes change over development, and then reviewed evidence for dual-axis communication between the HPA–HPG axes. In 2015, a special issue of *Developmental Psychobiology* originally postulated a conservative view that positive coupling was a paradox constrained by certain contextual forces, ecological niches or developmental challenges that required the organism to override the established classical view of dual-axis inhibition. Since 2015, a surprisingly large number of studies have emerged, which pertain to the HPA–HPG coupling as well as a 2017 special issue in *Hormones and Behavior* that pertains to HPA–HPG interactions. Collectively, this research provides tangible support for the idea that these axes work together to shape development and, specifically, provides support to the hunch about positive coupling may have conceptual grounding. Nonetheless, concerned with our own positive biases, we utilized this handbook chapter to systematically review studies that examine HPA and HPG interactions and generally confirmed the hypothesis that positive coupling occurs across a range of contexts, in both genders and at multiple developmental stages under baseline and stressful conditions. The next step for the field is, at minimum, to cease accepting the classical view of HPA–HPG axis inhibition at face value and to simply report the bivariate associations between hormones even if counterintuitive, as has been done in prior work (Mehta & Josephs, 2010). In addition, it would behoove the field to advance from questioning this emerging phenomenon toward forming a priori hypotheses for when, why and for whom we expect positive coupling. To accomplish this goal requires a functional view about these hormonal biomarkers and how they may help individuals adapt to their circumstances.

References

Adam, E. K., Klimes-Dougan, B., & Gunnar, M. (2007). Social regulation of the adrenocortical response to stress in infants, children and adolescents. In D. Coch, G. Dawson, & K. W. Fischer (Eds.), *Human behavior and the developing brain: Atypical·development* (pp. 264–304). New York, NY: Guilford Press.

Aguilar, R., Jiménez, M., & Alvero-Cruz, J. R. R. (2013). Testosterone, cortisol and anxiety in elite field hockey players. *Physiology & Behavior, 119*, 38–42.

Ainsworth, M., Blehar, M. C., Waters, E., & Wall, S. (2014). *Patterns of attachment: A psychological study of the strange situation*. London, England: Psychology Press.

Alvergne, A., Faurie, C., & Raymond, M. (2009). Variation in testosterone levels and male reproductive effort: Insight from a polygynous human population. *Hormones and Behavior, 56*(5), 491–497.

Anand, K. J., Coskun, V., Thrivikraman, K. V., Nemeroff, C. B., & Plotsky, P. M. (1999). Long-term behavioral effects of repetitive pain in neonatal rat pups. *Physiology & Behavior, 66*(4), 627–637.

Archer, J. (2006). Testosterone and human aggression: An evaluation of the challenge hypothesis. *Neuroscience and Biobehavioral Reviews, 30*(3), 319–345.

Auchus, R. J., & Rainey, W. E. (2004). Adrenarche – physiology, biochemistry and human disease. *Clinical Endocrinology, 60*(3), 288–296.

Aylwin, C. F., Toro, C. A., Shirtcliff, E. A., & Lomniczi, A. (in press). Emerging genetic and epigenetic mechanisms underlying pubertal maturation in adolescence. *Journal of Research in Adolescence*.

Ballonoff Suleiman, A., Johnson, M., Shirtcliff, E. A., & Galván, A. (2015). School-based sex education and neuroscience: What we know about sex, romance, marriage, and adolescent brain development. *The Journal of School Health, 85*(8), 567–574.

Barel, E., Shahrabani, S., & Tzischinsky, O. (2017). Sex hormone/cortisol ratios differentially modulate risk-taking in men and women. *Evolutionary Psychology: An International Journal of Evolutionary Approaches to Psychology and Behavior, 15*(1), 147470491769733.

Belsky, J., Steinberg, L., Houts, R. M., Halpern-Felsher, B. L., & NICHD Early Child Care Research Network. (2010). The development of reproductive strategy in females: Early maternal harshness – > earlier menarche – > increased sexual risk taking. *Developmental Psychology, 46*(1), 120–128.

Black, S. R., Lerner, M. D., Shirtcliff, E. A., & Klein, D. N. (2018). Patterns of neuroendocrine coupling in 9-year-old children: Effects of sex, body-mass index, and life stress. *Biological Psychology, 132*, 252–259.

Bobadilla, L., Asberg, K., Johnson, M., & Shirtcliff, E. A. (2015). Experiences in the military may impact dual-axis neuroendocrine processes in veterans. *Developmental Psychobiology, 57*(6), 719–730.

Böhnke, R., Bertsch, K., Kruk, M. R., & Naumann, E. (2010). The relationship between basal and acute HPA axis activity and aggressive behavior in adults. *Journal of Neural Transmission, 117*(5), 629–637.

Book, A. S., Starzyk, K. B., & Quinsey, V. L. (2001). The relationship between testosterone and aggression: A meta-analysis. *Aggression and Violent Behavior, 6*(6), 579–599.

Boudarene, M., Legros, J. J., & Timsit-Berthier, M. (2002). Study of the stress response: Role of anxiety, cortisol and DHEAs. *L'Encephale*. Retrieved from http://europepmc.org/abstract/med/11972140

Breen, K. M., Stackpole, C. A., Clarke, I. J., Pytiak, A. V., Tilbrook, A. J., Wagenmaker, E. R., . . . Karsch, F. J. (2004). Does the type II glucocorticoid receptor mediate cortisol-induced suppression in pituitary responsiveness to gonadotropin-releasing hormone? *Endocrinology, 145*(6), 2739–2746.

Brown, B. B. (1990). Peer groups and peer cultures. In S. S. Feldman & G. R. Elliott (Eds.), *At the threshold: The developing adolescent* (pp. 171–196). Cambridge, MA: Harvard University Press.

Brown, G. L., McGarvey, E. L., Shirtcliff, E. A., Keller, A., Granger, D. A., & Flavin, K. (2008). Salivary cortisol, dehydroepiandrosterone, and testosterone interrelationships in healthy young males: A pilot study with implications for studies of aggressive behavior. *Psychiatry Research, 159*(1–2), 67–76.

Byrne, M. L., Whittle, S., Vijayakumar, N., Dennison, M., Simmons, J. G., & Allen, N. B. (2017). A systematic review of adrenarche as a sensitive period in neurobiological development and mental health. *Developmental Cognitive Neuroscience, 25*, 12–28.

Cappelletti, M., & Wallen, K. (2016). Increasing women's sexual desire: The comparative effectiveness of estrogens and androgens. *Hormones and Behavior, 78*, 178–193.

Carré, J. M., & Olmstead, N. A. (2015). Social neuroendocrinology of human aggression: Examining the role of competition-induced testosterone dynamics. *Neuroscience, 286*, 171–186.

Casto, K. V., & Edwards, D. A. (2016). Testosterone and reconciliation among women: After-competition testosterone predicts prosocial attitudes towards opponents. *Adaptive Human Behavior and Physiology, 2*(3), 220–233.

Casto, K. V., & Prasad, S. (2017). Recommendations for the study of women in hormones and competition research. *Hormones and Behavior, 92*, 190–194.

Casto, K. V., Rivell, A., & Edwards, D. A. (2017). Competition-related testosterone, cortisol, and perceived personal success in recreational women athletes. *Hormones and Behavior, 92*, 29–36.

Charmandari, E., Tsigos, C., & Chrousos, G. (2005). Endocrinology of the stress response. *Annual Review of Physiology, 67*, 259–284.

Chatzittofis, A., Nordström, P., Hellström, C., Arver, S., Åsberg, M., & Jokinen, J. (2013). CSF 5-HIAA, cortisol and DHEAS levels in suicide attempters. *European Neuropsychopharmacology: The Journal of the European College of Neuropsychopharmacology, 23*(10), 1280–1287.

Chisholm, J. S., Quinlivan, J. A., Petersen, R. W., & Coall, D. A. (2005). Early stress predicts age at menarche and first birth, adult attachment, and expected lifespan. *Human Nature, 16*(3), 233–265.

Coie, J. D., Dodge, K. A., & Kupersmidt, J. B. (1990). Peer rejection in childhood. In S. R. Asher & J. D. Coie (Eds.), *Studies in social and emotional development* (pp. 17–59). New York, NY: Cambridge University Press.

Crone, E. A., & Dahl, R. E. (2012). Understanding adolescence as a period of social – affective engagement and goal flexibility. *Nature Reviews. Neuroscience, 13*(9), 636–650.

Dahl, R. E., & Gunnar, M. R. (2009). Heightened stress responsiveness and emotional reactivity during pubertal maturation: Implications for psychopathology. *Development and Psychopathology, 21*(1), 1–6.

Davison, S. L., & Davis, S. R. (2003). Androgens in women. *The Journal of Steroid Biochemistry and Molecular Biology, 85*(2–5), 363–366.

Del Giudice, M., Angeleri, R., & Manera, V. (2009). The juvenile transition: A developmental switch point in human life history. *Developmental Review, 29*(1), 1–31.

Del Giudice, M., Ellis, B. J., & Shirtcliff, E. A. (2011). The adaptive calibration model of stress responsivity. *Neuroscience and Biobehavioral Reviews, 35*(7), 1562–1592.

Denson, T. F., Mehta, P. H., & Ho Tan, D. (2013). Endogenous testosterone and cortisol jointly influence reactive aggression in women. *Psychoneuroendocrinology, 38*(3), 416–424.

Derntl, B., Windischberger, C., Robinson, S., Kryspin-Exner, I., Gur, R. C., Moser, E., & Habel, U. (2009). Amygdala activity to fear and anger in healthy young males is associated with testosterone. *Psychoneuroendocrinology, 34*(5), 687–693.

Dickerson, S. S., & Kemeny, M. E. (2004). Acute stressors and cortisol responses: A theoretical integration and synthesis of laboratory research. *Psychological Bulletin, 130*(3), 355–391.

Dismukes, A. R., Johnson, M. M., Vitacco, M. J., Iturri, F., & Shirtcliff, E. A. (2015). Coupling of the HPA and HPG axes in the context of early life adversity in incarcerated male adolescents. *Developmental Psychobiology, 57*(6), 705–718.

Dismukes, A. R., Shirtcliff, E. A., Drury, S. S., & Theall, K. T. (in press). The development of the cortisol response to dyadic stressors in black and white infants. *Development and Psychopathology*.

Dismukes, A. R., Shirtcliff, E. A., Hanson, J. L., & Pollak, S. D. (2015). Context influences the interplay of endocrine axes across the day. *Developmental Psychobiology, 57*(6), 731–741.

Docke, F., & Dorner, G. (1965). The mechanism of the induction of ovulation by oestrogens. *The Journal of Endocrinology, 33*(3), 491–499.

Doom, J. R., Doyle, C. M., & Gunnar, M. R. (2017). Social stress buffering by friends in childhood and adolescence: Effects on HPA and oxytocin activity. *Social Neuroscience, 12*(1), 8–21.

Doom, J. R., & Gunnar, M. R. (2013). Stress physiology and developmental psychopathology: Past, present, and future. *Development and Psychopathology, 25*(4 Pt 2), 1359–1373.

Doom, J. R., Hostinar, C. E., VanZomeren-Dohm, A. A., & Gunnar, M. R. (2015). The roles of puberty and age in explaining the diminished effectiveness of parental buffering of HPA reactivity and recovery in adolescence. *Psychoneuroendocrinology, 59*, 102–111.

do Vale, S., Selinger, L., Martins, J. M., Bicho, M., do Carmo, I., & Escera, C. (2015). Dehydroepiandrosterone (DHEA) and Dehydroepiandrosterone-Sulfate (DHEAS) and emotional processing – a behavioral and electrophysiological approach. *Hormones and Behavior, 73*, 94–103.

Eatough, E. M., Shirtcliff, E. A., Hanson, J. L., & Pollak, S. D. (2009). Hormonal reactivity to MRI scanning in adolescents. *Psychoneuroendocrinology, 34*(8), 1242–1246.

Edwards, D. A., & Casto, K. V. (2013). Women's intercollegiate athletic competition: Cortisol, testosterone, and the dual-hormone hypothesis as it relates to status among teammates. *Hormones and Behavior, 64*(1), 153–160.

Edwards, D. A., & Casto, K. V. (2015). Baseline cortisol moderates testosterone reactivity to women's intercollegiate athletic competition. *Physiology & Behavior, 142*, 48–51.

Ellis, B. J. (2004). Timing of pubertal maturation in girls: An integrated life history approach. *Psychological Bulletin, 130*(6), 920–958.

Ellis, B. J., Bianchi, J., Griskevicius, V., & Frankenhuis, W. E. (2017). Beyond risk and protective factors: An adaptation-based approach to resilience. *Perspectives on Psychological Science: A Journal of the Association for Psychological Science, 12*(4), 561–587.

Ellis, B. J., Shirtcliff, E. A., Boyce, T. W., Deardorff, J., & Essex, M. J. (2011). Quality of early family relationships and the timing and tempo of puberty: Effects depend on biological sensitivity to context. *Development and Psychopathology, 23*(1), 85–99.

Essex, M. J., Klein, M. H., Cho, E., & Kalin, N. H. (2002). Maternal stress beginning in infancy may sensitize children to later stress exposure: Effects on cortisol and behavior. *Biological Psychiatry, 52*(8), 776–784.

Gao, W., Stalder, T., Foley, P., Rauh, M., Deng, H., & Kirschbaum, C. (2013). Quantitative analysis of steroid hormones in human hair using a column-switching LC-APCI-MS/MS assay. *Journal of Chromatography. B, Analytical Technologies in the Biomedical and Life Sciences, 928*, 1–8.

Gecas, V., & Schwalbe, M. L. (1986). Parental behavior and adolescent self-esteem. *Journal of Marriage and the Family, 48*(1), 37.

Geng, Y., Gao, L., & Yang, J. (2013). Epigenetic flexibility underlying phenotypic plasticity. In *Progress in botany* (pp. 153–163). Berlin, Heidelberg: Springer.

Geniole, S. N., Bird, B. M., Ruddick, E. L., & Carré, J. M. (2017). Effects of competition outcome on testosterone concentrations in humans: An updated meta-analysis. *Hormones and Behavior, 92*, 37–50.

Gettler, L. T., McDade, T. W., Bragg, J. M., Feranil, A. B., & Kuzawa, C. W. (2015). Developmental energetics, sibling death, and parental instability as predictors of maturational tempo and life history scheduling in males from Cebu, Philippines. *American Journal of Physical Anthropology, 57*(S13), S1–S26.

Grant, V. J., & France, J. T. (2001). Dominance and testosterone in women. *Biological Psychology, 58*, 41–47.

Grasso, D., Lanteri, P., Di Bernardo, C., Mauri, C., Porcelli, S., Colombini, A., . . . Lombardi, G. (2014). Salivary steroid hormone response to whole-body cryotherapy in elite rugby players. *Journal of Biological Regulators & Homeostatic Agents, 28*, 291–300.

Gray, P. B., Kahlenberg, S. M., Barrett, E. S., Lipson, S. F., & Ellison, P. T. (2002). Marriage and fatherhood are associated with lower testosterone in males. *Evolution and Human Behavior: Official Journal of the Human Behavior and Evolution Society*, *23*(3), 193–201.

Gunnar, M. R., Brodersen, L., Krueger, K., & Rigatuso, J. (1996). Dampening of adrenocortical responses during infancy: Normative changes and individual differences. *Child Development*, *67*(3), 877.

Gunnar, M. R., Brodersen, L., Nachmias, M., Buss, K., & Rigatuso, J. (1996). Stress reactivity and attachment security. *Developmental Psychobiology*, *29*(3), 191–204.

Gunnar, M. R., & Donzella, B. (2002). Social regulation of the cortisol levels in early human development. *Psychoneuroendocrinology*, *27*(1–2), 199–220.

Gunnar, M. R., & Hostinar, C. E. (2015). The social buffering of the hypothalamic–pituitary–adrenocortical axis in humans: Developmental and experiential determinants. *Social Neuroscience*, *10*(5), 479–488.

Han, G., Miller, J. G., Cole, P. M., Zahn-Waxler, C., & Hastings, P. D. (2015). Adolescents' internalizing and externalizing problems predict their affect-specific HPA and HPG axes reactivity. *Developmental Psychobiology*, *57*(6), 769–785.

Harris, J. A., Rushton, J. P., Hampson, E., & Jackson, D. N. (1996). Salivary testosterone and self-report aggressive and pro-social personality characteristics in men and women. *Aggressive Behavior*, *22*, 321–331.

Harden, K. P., Wrzus, C., Luong, G., Grotzinger, A., Bajbouj, M., Rauers, A., . . . Riediger, M. (2016). Diurnal coupling between testosterone and cortisol from adolescence to older adulthood. *Psychoneuroendocrinology*, *73*, 79–90.

Havelock, J. C., Auchus, R. J., & Rainey, W. E. (2004). The rise in adrenal androgen biosynthesis: Adrenarche. *Seminars in Reproductive Medicine*, *22*(4), 337–347.

Hill, K., & Kaplan, H. (1999). Life history traits in humans: Theory and empirical studies. *Annual Review of Anthropology*, *28*, 397–430.

Hines, M. (2010). Sex-related variation in human behavior and the brain. *Trends in Cognitive Sciences*, *14*(10), 448–456.

Hochberg, Z., Feil, R., Constancia, M., Fraga, M., Junien, C., Carel, J-C., . . . Albertsson-Wikland, K. (2011). Child health, developmental plasticity, and epigenetic programming. *Endocrine Reviews*, *32*(2), 159–224.

Hostinar, C. E., & Gunnar, M. R. (2013). Future directions in the study of social relationships as regulators of the HPA axis across development. *Journal of Clinical Child and Adolescent Psychology: The Official Journal for the Society of Clinical Child and Adolescent Psychology, American Psychological Association, Division 53*, *42*(4), 564–575.

Jankord, R., & Herman, J. P. (2008). Limbic regulation of hypothalamo-pituitary-adrenocortical function during acute and chronic stress. *Annals of the New York Academy of Sciences*, *1148*, 64–73.

Javed, A., & Lteif, A. (2013). Development of the human breast. *Seminars in Plastic Surgery*, *27*(1), 5–12.

Jin, R. O., Mason, S., Mellon, S. H., Epel, E. S., Reus, V. I., Mahan, L., . . . Wolkowitz, O. M. (2016). Cortisol/DHEA ratio and hippocampal volume: A pilot study in major depression and healthy controls. *Psychoneuroendocrinology*, *72*, 139–146.

Johnson, M. M., Dismukes, A. R., Vitacco, M. J., Breiman, C., Fleury, D., & Shirtcliff, E. A. (2014). Psychopathy's influence on the coupling between hypothalamic – pituitary – adrenal and -gonadal axes among incarcerated adolescents. *Developmental Psychobiology*, *56*(3), 448–458.

Johnson, M. M., Vitacco, M. J., & Shirtcliff, E. A. (2017). Callous-unemotional traits and early life stress predict treatment effects on stress and sex hormone functioning in incarcerated male adolescents. *Stress*, 1–9.

Kallen, V. L., Tulen, J. H. M., Utens, E. M. W. J., Treffers, P. D. A., De Jong, F. H., & Ferdinand, R. F. (2008). Associations between HPA axis functioning and level of anxiety in children and adolescents with an anxiety disorder. *Depression and Anxiety*, *25*(2), 131–141.

Kendler, K. S., Myers, J., & Prescott, C. A. (2005). Sex differences in the relationship between social support and risk for major depression: A longitudinal study of opposite-sex twin pairs. *The American Journal of Psychiatry*, *162*(2), 250–256.

Kirschbaum, C., Klauer, T., Filipp, S. H., & Hellhammer, D. H. (1995). Sex-specific effects of social support on cortisol and subjective responses to acute psychological stress. *Psychosomatic Medicine*, *57*(1), 23–31.

Knight, E. L., Christian, C. B., Morales, P. J., Harbaugh, W. T., Mayr, U., & Mehta, P. H. (2017). Exogenous testosterone enhances cortisol and affective responses to social evaluative stress in dominant men. *Psychoneuroendocrinology*, *85*, 151–157.

Kogan, S. M., Cho, J., Simons, L. G., Allen, K. A., Beach, S. R. H., Simons, R. L., & Gibbons, F. X. (2015). Pubertal timing and sexual risk behaviors among rural African American male youth: Testing a model based on life history theory. *Archives of Sexual Behavior*, *44*(3), 609–618.

Kraemer, H. C., Yesavage, J. A., Taylor, J. L., & Kupfer, D. (2000). How can we learn about developmental processes from cross-sectional studies, or can we? *American Journal of Psychiatry, 152*(2), 163–171.

Kroboth, P. D., Salek, F. S., Pittenger, A. L., Faban, T. J., & Frye, R. F. (1999). DHEA and DHEA-S: A review. *Journal of Clinical Pharmacology, 39,* 327–348.

Kupchak, B. R., Kraemer, W. J., Hoffman, M. D., Phinney, S. D., & Volek, J. S. (2014). The impact of an ultramarathon on hormonal and biochemical parameters in men. *Wilderness & Environmental Medicine, 25*(3), 278–288.

Kuzawa, C. W., Gettler, L. T., Huang, Y-Y., & McDade, T. W. (2010). Mothers have lower testosterone than non-mothers: Evidence from the Philippines. *Hormones and Behavior, 57*(4–5), 441–447.

Laurent, H. K., Lucas, T., Pierce, J., Goetz, S., & Granger, D. A. (2016). Coordination of cortisol response to social evaluative threat with autonomic and inflammatory responses is moderated by stress appraisals and affect. *Biological Psychology, 118,* 17–24.

Levine, S. (1994). The ontogeny of the hypothalamic-pituitary-adrenal axis. The influence of maternal factors. *Annals of the New York Academy of Sciences, 746,* 275–288; discussion 289–293.

Lopez-Duran, N. L., Olson, S. L., Hajal, N. J., Felt, B. T., & Vazquez, D. M. (2008). Hypothalamic pituitary adrenal axis functioning in reactive and proactive aggression in children. *Journal of Abnormal Child Psychology, 37*(2), 169–182.

Lupien, S. J., McEwen, B. S., Gunnar, M. R., & Heim, C. (2009). Effects of stress throughout the lifespan on the brain, behaviour and cognition. *Nature Reviews. Neuroscience, 10*(6), 434–445.

Maeda, K-I., & Tsukamura, H. (2006). The impact of stress on reproduction: Are glucocorticoids inhibitory or protective to gonadotropin secretion? *Endocrinology, 147*(3), 1085–1086.

Maninger, N., Wolkowitz, O. M., Reus, V. I., Epel, E. S., & Mellon, S. H. (2009). Neurobiological and neuropsychiatric effects of Dehydroepiandrosterone (DHEA) and DHEA sulfate (DHEAS). *Frontiers in Neuroendocrinology, 30*(1), 65–91.

Marceau, K., Ruttle, P. L., Shirtcliff, E. A., Hastings, P. D., Klimes-Dougan, B., & Zahn-Waxler, C. (2013). Within-person coupling of changes in cortisol, testosterone, and DHEA across the day in adolescents. *Developmental Psychobiology, 57*(6), 654–669.

Marceau, K., Shirtcliff, E. A., Hastings, P. D., Klimes-Dougan, B., Zahn-Waxler, C., Dorn, L. D., & Susman, E. J. (2014). Within-adolescent coupled changes in cortisol with DHEA and testosterone in response to three stressors during adolescence. *Psychoneuroendocrinology, 41,* 33–45.

Masten, C. L., Eisenberger, N. I., Borofsky, L. A., Pfeifer, J. H., McNealy, K., Mazziotta, J. C., & Dapretto, M. (2009). Neural correlates of social exclusion during adolescence: Understanding the distress of peer rejection. *Social Cognitive and Affective Neuroscience, 4*(2), 143–157.

Matsuwaki, T., Kayasuga, Y., Yamanouchi, K., & Nishihara, M. (2006). Maintenance of gonadotropin secretion by glucocorticoids under stress conditions through the inhibition of prostaglandin synthesis in the brain. *Endocrinology, 147*(3), 1087–1093.

Matsuwaki, T., Suzuki, M., Yamanouchi, K., & Nishihara, M. (2004). Glucocorticoid counteracts the suppressive effect of tumor necrosis factor-alpha on the surge of luteinizing hormone secretion in rats. *The Journal of Endocrinology, 181*(3), 509–513.

Matsuwaki, T., Watanabe, E., Suzuki, M., Yamanouchi, K., & Nishihara, M. (2003). Glucocorticoid maintains pulsatile secretion of luteinizing hormone under infectious stress condition. *Endocrinology, 144*(8), 3477–3482.

McClintock, M. K., & Herdt, G. (1996). Rethinking puberty. *Current Directions in Psychological Science, 5*(6), 178–183.

McEwen, B. S., & Stellar, E. (1993). Stress and the individual: Mechanisms leading to disease. *Archives of Internal Medicine, 153*(18), 2093–2101.

McGlothlin, J. W., Jawor, J. M., & Ketterson, E. D. (2007). Natural variation in a testosterone-mediated trade-off between mating effort and parental effort. *The American Naturalist, 170*(6), 864–875.

McHale, T. S., Zava, D. T., Hales, D., & Gray, P. B. (2015). Physical competition increases Dehydroepiandrosterone (DHEA) and androstenedione rather than testosterone among Juvenile boy soccer players. *Adaptive Human Behavior and Physiology, 2*(1), 44–56.

Meaney, M. J. (2007). Environmental programming of phenotypic diversity in female reproductive strategies. *Advances in Genetics, 59,* 173–215.

Mehta, P. H., & Josephs, R. A. (2010). Testosterone and cortisol jointly regulate dominance: Evidence for a dual-hormone hypothesis. *Hormones and Behavior, 58*(5), 898–906.

Mehta, P. H., Lawless DesJardins, N. M., van Vugt, M., & Josephs, R. A. (2017). Hormonal underpinnings of status conflict: Testosterone and cortisol are related to decisions and satisfaction in the hawk-dove game. *Hormones and Behavior, 92,* 141–154.

Mehta, P. H., & Prasad, S. (2015). The dual-hormone hypothesis: A brief review and future research agenda. *Current Opinion in Behavioral Sciences, 3*, 163–168.

Meston, C. M., & Lorenz, T. A. (2013). Physiological stress responses predict sexual functioning and satisfaction differently in women who have and have not been sexually abused in childhood. *Psychological Trauma: Theory, Research, Practice and Policy, 5*(4), 350–358.

Miller, G. E., Chen, E., & Zhou, E. S. (2007). If it goes up, must it come down? Chronic stress and the hypothalamic-pituitary-adrenocortical axis in humans. *Psychological Bulletin, 133*(1), 25–45.

Negriff, S., Saxbe, D. E., & Trickett, P. K. (2015). Childhood maltreatment, pubertal development, HPA axis functioning, and psychosocial outcomes: An integrative biopsychosocial model. *Developmental Psychobiology, 57*(8), 984–993.

Nofsinger, J., Patterson, F., & Shank, C. (2018). Decision-making, financial risk aversion, and behavioral biases: The role of testosterone and stress. *Economics & Human Biology, 29*, 1–16.

O'Neal, D., Reichard, D., Pavilis, K., & Ketterson, E. (2008). Experimentally-elevated testosterone, female parental care, and reproductive success in a songbird, the Dark-eyed Junco (*Junco hyemalis*). *Hormones and Behavior, 54*(4), 571–578.

Ota, A., Yatsuya, H., Mase, J., & Ono, Y. (2015). Psychological job strain, social support at work and daytime secretion of Dehydroepiandrosterone (DHEA) in healthy female employees: Cross-sectional analyses. *Scientific Reports, 5*, 15844.

Panizzon, M. S., Hauger, R. L., Xian, H., Jacobson, K., Lyons, M. J., Franz, C. E., & Kremen, W. S. (2018). Interactive effects of testosterone and cortisol on hippocampal volume and episodic memory in middle-aged men. *Psychoneuroendocrinology, 91*, 115–122.

Pariante, C. M., & Lightman, S. L. (2008). The HPA axis in major depression: Classical theories and new developments. *Trends in Neurosciences, 31*(9), 464–468.

Pauly, T., Lay, J. C., Nater, U. M., Scott, S. B., & Hoppmann, C. A. (2017). How we experience being alone: Age differences in affective and biological correlates of momentary solitude. *Gerontology, 63*(1), 55–66.

Pettit, G. S., Laird, R. D., Dodge, K. A., Bates, J. E., & Criss, M. M. (2001). Antecedents and behavior-problem outcomes of parental monitoring and psychological control in early adolescence. *Child Development, 72*(2), 583–598.

Pfattheicher, S. (2017). Illuminating the dual-hormone hypothesis: About chronic dominance and the interaction of cortisol and testosterone. *Aggressive Behavior, 43*(1), 85–92.

Phan, J. M., Schneider, E., Peres, J., Miocevic, O., Meyer, V., & Shirtcliff, E. A. (2017). Social evaluative threat with verbal performance feedback alters neuroendocrine response to stress. *Hormones and Behavior, 96*, 104–115.

Phogat, J. B., Smith, R. F., & Dobson, H. (1997). The influence of stress on neuroendocrine control of the hypothalamic-pituitary-ovarian axis. *Veterinary Bulletin (United Kingdom), 67*. Retrieved from http://agris.fao.org/agris-search/search.do?recordID=GB9717961

Phogat, J. B., Smith, R. F., & Dobson, H. (1999a). Effect of adrenocorticotrophic hormone (ACTH1-24) on ovine pituitary gland responsiveness to exogenous pulsatile GnRH and oestradiol-induced LH release in vivo. *Animal Reproduction Science, 55*(3), 193–203.

Phogat, J. B., Smith, R. F., & Dobson, H. (1999b). Effect of transport on pituitary responsiveness to exogenous pulsatile GnRH and oestradiol-induced LH release in intact ewes. *Journal of Reproduction and Fertility, 116*(1), 9–18.

Plotsky, P. M., & Sawchenko, P. E. (1987). Hypophysial-portal plasma levels, median eminence content, and immunohistochemical staining of corticotropin-releasing factor, arginine vasopressin, and oxytocin after pharmacological adrenalectomy. *Endocrinology, 120*(4), 1361–1369.

Putman, P., Antypa, N., Crysovergi, P., & van der Does, W. A. J. (2010). Exogenous cortisol acutely influences motivated decision making in healthy young men. *Psychopharmacology, 208*(2), 257–263.

Radke, S., Volman, I., Mehta, P., van Son, V., Enter, D., Sanfey, A., . . . Roelofs, K. (2015). Testosterone biases the amygdala toward social threat approach. *Science Advances, 1*(5), e1400074.

Rivier, C., & Rivest, S. (1991). Effect of stress on the activity of the hypothalamic-pituitary-gonadal axis: Peripheral and central mechanisms. *Biology of Reproduction, 45*(4), 523–532.

Rowe, R., Maughan, B., Worthman, C. M., Costello, E. J., & Angold, A. (2004). Testosterone, antisocial behavior, and social dominance in boys: Pubertal development and biosocial interaction. *Biological Psychiatry, 55*(5), 546–552.

Rubinow, D. R., Roca, C. A., Schmidt, P. J., Danaceau, M. A., Putnam, K., Cizza, G., & Chrousos, G. (2005). Testosterone suppression of CRH-stimulated cortisol in men. *Neuropsychoendocrinology, 30*(10) 1906–1923.

Ruttle, P. L., Shirtcliff, E. A., Armstrong, J. M., Klein, M. H., & Essex, M. J. (2015). Neuroendocrine coupling across adolescence and the longitudinal influence of early life stress. *Developmental Psychobiology*, *57*(6), 688–704.

Ruttle, P. L., Shirtcliff, E. A., Serbin, L. A., Fisher, D. B-D., Stack, D. M., & Schwartzman, A. E. (2011). Disentangling psychobiological mechanisms underlying internalizing and externalizing behaviors in youth: Longitudinal and concurrent associations with cortisol. *Hormones and Behavior*, *59*(1), 123–132.

Saketos, M., Sharma, N., & Santoro, N. F. (1993). Suppression of the hypothalamic-pituitary-ovarian axis in normal women by glucocorticoids. *Biology of Reproduction*, *49*(6), 1270–1276.

Sapolsky, R. M., & Meaney, M. J. (1986). Maturation of the adrenocortical stress response: Neuroendocrine control mechanisms and the stress hyporesponsive period. *Brain Research Reviews*, *11*(1), 65–76.

Sapolsky, R. M., Romero, L. M., & Munck, A. U. (2000). How do glucocorticoids influence stress responses? Integrating permissive, suppressive, stimulatory, and preparative actions. *Endocrine Reviews*, *21*(1), 55–89.

Saxbe, D. E., Negriff, S., Susman, E. J., & Trickett, P. K. (2015). Attenuated hypothalamic-pituitary-adrenal axis functioning predicts accelerated pubertal development in girls 1 year later. *Development and Psychopathology*, *27*(3), 819–828.

Schmidt, M. V. (2010). Molecular mechanisms of early life stress – lessons from mouse models. *Neuroscience and Biobehavioral Reviews*, *34*(6), 845–852.

Schneiderman, I., Kanat-Maymon, Y., Zagoory-Sharon, O., & Feldman, R. (2014). Mutual influences between partners' hormones shape conflict dialog and relationship duration at the initiation of romantic love. *Social Neuroscience*, *9*(4), 337–351.

Schreiber, J., Shirtcliff, E., Hulle, C., Lemerychalfant, K., Klein, M., Kalin, N., . . . Goldsmith, H. (2006). Environmental influences on family similarity in afternoon cortisol levels: Twin and parent – offspring designs. *Psychoneuroendocrinology*, *31*(9), 1131–1137.

Selye, H. (1939). The effect of adaptation to various damaging agents on the female sex organs in the rat. *Endocrinology*, *25*(4), 615–624.

Sherman, G. D., Lerner, J. S., Jospehs, R. A, Renshon, J., & Gross, J. J. (2016). The interaction of testosterone and cortisol is associated with attained status in male executives. *Journal of Personality and Social Psychology*, *110*(6), 921–929.

Shields, G. S., Lam, J. C., Trainor, B. C., & Yonelinas, A. P. (2016). Exposure to acute stress enhances decision-making competence: Evidence for the role of DHEA. *Psychoneuroendocrinology*, *67*, 51–60.

Shirtcliff, E. A. (2009). Biologic underpinnings of adolescent development. In R. A. Crosby & J. S. R. DiClemente (Eds.), *Adolescent health: Understanding and preventing risk behaviors and adverse health outcomes* (pp. 95–114). New York, NY: John Wiley & Sons, Inc.

Shirtcliff, E. A., Dahl, R. E., & Pollak, S. D. (2009). Pubertal development: Correspondence between hormonal and physical development. *Child Development*, *80*(2), 327–337.

Shirtcliff, E. A., Dismukes, A. R., Marceau, K., Ruttle, P. L., Simmons, J. G., & Han, G. (2015). A dual-axis approach to understanding neuroendocrine development. *Developmental Psychobiology*, *57*(6), 643–653.

Shirtcliff, E. A., Granger, D. A., Schwartz, E. B., Curran, M. J., Booth, A., & Overman, W. H. (2000). Assessing estradiol in biobehavioral studies using saliva and blood spots: Simple radioimmunoassay protocols, reliability, and comparative validity. *Hormones and Behavior*, *38*(2), 137–147.

Shirtcliff, E. A., & Ruttle, P. (2010). Immunological and neuroendocrine dysregulation following early deprivation and stress. In K. Heinz Brisch (Ed.), *Attachment and early disorders of development*. Munich: Klett-Cotta & Stuttgart.

Shirtcliff, E. A., Zahn-Waxler, C., Klimes-Dougan, B., & Slattery, M. (2007). Salivary dehydroepiandrosterone responsiveness to social challenge in adolescents with internalizing problems. *Journal of Child Psychology and Psychiatry, and Allied Disciplines*, *48*(6), 580–591.

Short, R. V. (1975). Hormonal control of spermatogenesis. *Nature*, *254*(5496), 103–103.

Short, S. J., Stalder, T., Marceau, K., Entringer, S., Moog, N. K., Shirtcliff, E. A., . . . Buss, C. (2016). Correspondence between hair cortisol concentrations and 30-day integrated daily salivary and weekly urinary cortisol measures. *Psychoneuroendocrinology*, *71*, 12–18.

Simmons, J. G., Byrne, M. L., Schwartz, O. S., Whittle, S. L., Sheeber, L., Kaess, M., . . . Allen, N. B. (2015). Hormonal coupling in adolescence and the moderating influence of prior trauma and aversive maternal parenting. *Developmental Psychobiology*, *57*(6), 670–687.

Sisk, C. L., & Zehr, J. L. (2005). Pubertal hormones organize the adolescent brain and behavior. *Frontiers in Neuroendocrinology*, *26*(3–4), 163–174.

Sollberger, S., Bernauer, T., & Ehlert, U. (2016). Salivary testosterone and cortisol are jointly related to pro-environmental behavior in men. *Social Neuroscience*, *11*(5), 553–566.

Somerville, L. H. (2013). Special issue on the teenage brain: Sensitivity to social evaluation. *Current Directions in Psychological Science, 22*(2), 121–127.

Spencer, T. E., & Bazer, F. W. (2002). Biology of progesterone action during pregnancy recognition and maintenance of pregnancy. *Frontiers in Bioscience: A Journal and Virtual Library, 7,* d1879–98.

Stanton-Salazar, R. D., & Spina, S. U. (2005). Adolescent peer networks as a context for social and emotional support. *Youth & Society, 36*(4), 379–417.

Steinberg, L. (2000). The family at adolescence: Transition and transformation. *Journal of Adolescent Health Care: Official Publication of the Society for Adolescent Medicine, 27*(3), 170–178.

Stephens, M. A. C., Mathon, P. B., McCaul, M. E., & Wand, G. S. (2016). Hypothalamic-pituitary-adrenal axis response to acute psychosocial stress: Effects of biological stress and circulating sex hormones. *Psychoneuroendocrinology, 66,* 47–55.

Stice, E., Ragan, J., & Randall, P. (2004). Prospective relations between social support and depression: Differential direction of effects for parent and peer support? *Journal of Abnormal Psychology, 113*(1), 155–159.

Stratakis, C. A., & Chrousos, G. P. (1995). Neuroendocrinology and pathophysiology of the stress system. *Annals of the New York Academy of Sciences, 771,* 1–18.

Stroud, L. R., Foster, E., Papandonatos, G. D., Handwerger, K., Granger, D. A., Kivlighan, K. T., & Niaura, R. (2009). Stress response and the adolescent transition: Performance versus peer rejection stressors. *Development and Psychopathology, 21*(1), 47–68.

Styne, D. M., & Grumbach, M. M. (2011). Puberty, ontogeny, neuroendocrinology, physiology, and disorders. In S. Melmed, K. S. Polonsky, P. R. Larsen, & H. M. Kronenberg (Eds.), *Williams textbook of endocrinology* (12th ed., pp. 1074–1218). Philadelphia, PA: Elsevier.

Sumter, S. R., Bokhorst, C. L., Miers, A. C., van Pelt, J., & Westenberg, P. M. (2010). Age and puberty differences in stress responses during a public speaking task: Do adolescents grow more sensitive to social evaluation? *Psychoneuroendocrinology, 35*(10), 1510–1516.

Susman, E. J., Peckins, M. K., Bowes, J. L., & Dorn, L. D. (2017). Longitudinal synergies between cortisol reactivity and diurnal testosterone and antisocial behavior in young adolescents. *Development and Psychopathology, 29*(4), 1353–1369.

Tackett, J. L., Reardon, K. W., Herzhoff, K., Page-Gould, E., Harden, K. P., & Josephs, R. A. (2015). Estradiol and cortisol interactions in youth externalizing psychopathology. *Psychoneuroendocrinology, 55,* 146–153.

Tarullo, A. R., Bruce, J., & Gunnar, M. R. (2007). False belief and emotion understanding in post-institutionalized children. *Social Development, 16*(1), 57–78.

Taylor, M. K., Hernández, L. M., Kviatkovsky, S. A., Schoenherr, M. R., Stone, M. S., & Sargent, P. (2017). The "yin and yang" of the adrenal and gonadal systems in elite military men. *Stress, 20*(3), 258–264.

Taylor, S. E., & Stanton, A. L. (2007). Coping resources, coping processes, and mental health. *Annual Review of Clinical Psychology, 3,* 377–401.

Tilbrook, A. J., Turner, A. I., & Clarke, I. J. (2000). Effects of stress on reproduction in non-rodent mammals: The role of glucocorticoids and sex differences. *Reviews of Reproduction, 5*(2), 105–113.

Turan, B., Tackett, J. L., Lechtreck, M. T., & Browning, W. R. (2015). Coordination of the cortisol and testosterone responses: A dual axis approach to understanding the response to social status threats. *Psychoneuroendocrinology, 62,* 59–68.

van Anders, S. M., Hamilton, L. D., & Watson, N. V. (2007). Multiple partners are associated with higher testosterone in North American men and women. *Hormones and Behavior, 51*(3), 454–459.

van Goozen, S. H., van den Ban, E., Matthys, W., Cohen-Kettenis, P. T., Thijssen, J. H., & van Engeland, H. (2000). Increased adrenal androgen functioning in children with oppositional defiant disorder: A comparison with psychiatric and normal controls. *Journal of the American Academy of Child and Adolescent Psychiatry, 39*(11), 1446–1451.

Viau, V. (2002). Functional cross-talk between the hypothalamic-pituitary-gonadal and -adrenal axes. *Journal of Neuroendocrinology, 14*(6), 506–513.

Viau, V., & Meaney, M. J. (1996). The inhibitory effect of testosterone on hypothalamic-pituitary-adrenal responses to stress is mediated by the medial preoptic area. *The Journal of Neuroscience: The Official Journal of the Society for Neuroscience, 16*(5), 1866–1876.

Wang, W., Moody, S. N., & Shirtcliff, E. A. (2016). Noninvasive hair assay for sex hormones: Preliminary protocol validation. *Psychoneuroendocrinology, 71,* 45.

Watamura, S. E., Donzella, B., Kertes, D. A., & Gunnar, M. R. (2004). Developmental changes in baseline cortisol activity in early childhood: Relations with napping and effortful control. *Developmental Psychobiology, 45*(3), 125–133.

Welker, K. M., Lassetter, B., Brandes, C. M., Prasad, S., Koop, D. R., & Mehta, P. H. (2016). A comparison of salivary testosterone measurement using immunoassay and tandem mass spectrometry. *Psychoneuroendocrinology, 71*, 180–188.

Whirledge, S., & Cidlowski, J. A. (2010). Glucocorticoids, stress, and fertility. *Minerva Endocrinologica, 35*(2), 109–125.

Wilcox, R. R., Granger, D. A., Szanton, S., & Clark, F. (2014). Diurnal patterns and associations among salivary cortisol, DHEA and alpha-amylase in older adults. *Physiology & Behavior, 129*, 11–16.

Wilson, J. D., George, F. W., & Griffin, J. E. (1981). The hormonal control of sexual development. *Science, 211*(4488), 1278–1284.

Wingfield, J. C., & Sapolsky, R. M. (2003). Reproduction and Resistance to Stress: When and How. *Journal of Neuroendocrinology, 15*(8), 711–724.

Wirtz, P. H., von Känel, R., Mohiyeddini, C., Emini, L., Ruedisueli, K., Groessbauer, S., & Ehlert, U. (2006). Low social support and poor emotional regulation are associated with increased stress hormone reactivity to mental stress in systemic hypertension. *The Journal of Clinical Endocrinology and Metabolism, 91*(10), 3857–3865.

Wolkowitz, O. M., Reus, V. I., Roberts, E., Manfredi, F., Chan, T., Ormiston, S., ... Weingartner, H. (1995). Antidepressant and cognition-enhancing effects of DHEA in major depression. *Annals of the New York Academy of Sciences, 774*, 337–339.

Wu, Y., Eisenegger, C., Zilioli, S., Watson, N. V., & Clark, L. (2017). Comparison of clear and narrow outcomes on testosterone levels in social competition. *Hormones and Behavior, 92*, 51–56.

Zilioli, S., Ponzi, D., Henry, A., & Maestripieri, D. (2015). Testosterone, Cortisol and Empathy: Evidence for the Dual-Hormone Hypothesis. *Adaptive Human Behavior and Physiology, 1*(4), 421–433.

SECTION 7

Mental and physical health

34

NEUROENDOCRINOLOGICAL ASPECTS OF SOCIAL ANXIETY AND AGGRESSION-RELATED DISORDERS

Dorien Enter, Moniek H. M. Hutschemaekers, and Karin Roelofs

Steroid hormones, like cortisol and testosterone, play an important role in the regulation of social motivational behavior. Whereas testosterone facilitates threat approach, presumably by facilitating dopaminergic projections from the amygdala to the striatum (de Souza Silva, Mattern, Topic, Buddenberg, & Huston, 2009; Hermans et al., 2010; Radke et al., 2015), cortisol increases threat avoidance, particularly in highly socially anxious individuals (van Peer et al., 2007; van Peer, Spinhoven, Dijk, & Roelofs, 2009). Interestingly, social motivational disorders, such as social anxiety and aggression-related disorders, show an imbalance in these steroid hormones: social anxiety has been associated with increased cortisol stress-responses and decreased testosterone levels (Gerra et al., 2000; Giltay et al., 2012; Roelofs, Minelli, Mars, van Peer, & Toni, 2009), while aggressive psychopathologies have been linked to increased testosterone levels (Glenn, Raine, Schug, Gao, & Granger, 2011; Montoya, Terburg, Bos, & van Honk, 2012; Volman et al., 2016). In this chapter, we discuss the role of these steroid hormones and the neuropeptide oxytocin in social psychopathologies, especially social anxiety and psychopathy. First, we will give a description of the neuroendocrine aspects of social motivational behavior, including social approach and avoidance behaviors. Then we will focus on the neuroendocrine aspects of social anxiety and aggression-related disorders. Finally, motivational and psychiatric findings will be integrated, followed by a research agenda, aiming to provide starting points for clinical applications.

Social motivational action

The term motivation reflects a broad concept related to anything that may prompt the person to act in a certain way, or to develop an inclination for specific behavior. In this chapter though, we will focus largely on social motivational actions that can be roughly divided into social approach and social avoidance (Davidson, Ekman, Saron, Senulis, & Friesen, 1990; Gray, 1994). These action tendencies involve a basic response to stimulus valence. They are mediated by primary motivational systems of the brain -whereby reward potentiates behavioral activation, while punishment promotes behavioral inhibition or avoidance - and are thought to underlie every complex emotional responding (Carver & White, 1994; Gray & MacNaughton, 2000). Successful social functioning depends on adaptive regulation of these social approach and avoidance responses.

Both automatic defensive action tendencies and more instrumental (or goal-directed) mechanisms shape an individual's behavior. When an individual encounters a social stimulus (e.g., an angry facial expression directed at him/her), he/she will engage in an automatic defensive freeze and flight-or-fight response, a quick and automatic sequence of defensive responses stages (Bradley, Codispoti, Cuthbert, & Lang, 2001). During threat exposure in particular, an initial freezing response is activated during which the individual ceases all ongoing activity and perception is enhanced to quickly assess the situation in order to optimize subsequent fight-or-flight responses (Blanchard, Griebel, Pobbe, & Blanchard, 2011; Lojowska, Gladwin, Hermans, & Roelofs, 2015; Roelofs, Hagenaars, & Stins, 2010). This is an automatic process, and the evaluation directly results in a behavioral disposition towards the stimulus: aversive stimuli generally elicit the tendency to move away from the stimulus and appetitive stimuli will elicit a tendency to move towards the stimulus (Lang, Bradley, & Cuthbert, 1997). Such automatic tendencies can also influence more complex, instrumental approach–avoidance decision making (Geurts, Huys, den Ouden, & Cools, 2013; Guitart-Masip, Duzel, Dolan, & Dayan, 2014). For instance, Ly and colleagues (2014) tested such influence in 45 healthy human individuals using an experimental set-up in which automatic freezing reactions towards negatively (versus positively) valenced stimuli were disentangled from instrumental approach–avoidance decisions (guided by monetary rewards and punishments). Critically, the transfer of valence (and related automatic reactions) to the instrumental approach–avoidance actions were systematically tested. The valence of angry (versus happy) faces was indeed found to transfer to instrumental decision making, in such a way that it induced an instrumental avoidance bias. The extent of freezing elicited by the angry faces was significantly correlated to the instrumental avoidance bias.

Both automatic freeze–fight–flight tendencies and more instrumental approach and avoidance biases have been suggested to play a prominent role in the maintenance and perhaps even cause of psychopathology (Blanchard et al., 2011; Rudaz, Ledermann, Margraf, Becker, & Craske, 2017; Turk, Lerner, Heimberg, & Rapee, 2001; Wong & Moulds, 2011). Aggression, for instance, has been conceptualized as a defensive response system in which automatic *fight*-responses are triggered too easily and in which instrumental threat–*approach* tendencies become well-learned and rewarded (Blair, 2013; Blanchard et al., 2011; Ly et al., 2016). On the contrary, persistent avoidance in anxiety disorders has been thought of as a defensive response system in which automatic *flight*–responses are easily triggered and in which instrumental threat–*avoidance* tendencies become rewarded and well-learned (Blanchard et al., 2011).

Rolls (2000) emphasized the importance of facial expressions as input for these systems, as they convey social information. When applied in social approach–avoidance tasks (AATs), healthy people show a general tendency to move away from angry expressions and to approach happy faces (Bradley et al., 2001; Chen & Bargh, 1999; Heuer, Rinck, & Becker, 2007; Roelofs, Minelli et al., 2009; Volman, Toni, Verhagen, & Roelofs, 2011). Social AATs using emotional faces have therefore been used to objectively measure the motor responses that are brought about by the automatic and instrumentally driven tendency to approach or avoid a certain stimulus (Chen & Bargh, 1999; Heuer et al., 2007; Roelofs, Elzinga, & Rotteveel, 2005; Rotteveel & Phaf, 2004). A commonly used type is a manual reaction time task which requires participants to approach and to avoid socially appetitive and aversive visually presented stimuli (happy and angry faces, respectively) by pulling (approach) or pushing away (avoidance) a joystick (see Figure 34.2E). In zooming versions of the AAT, pulling or pushing the joystick increases or decreases the size of the picture respectively, giving the impression of moving towards or moving away from the participant (Heuer et al., 2007). Affect–behavior congruence (i.e., approaching happy or avoiding angry faces) leads to quicker responses than when automatic tendencies need to be overridden, as is the case with affect–behavior incongruence (i.e., approaching angry or avoiding happy faces). Highly socially anxious individuals have been shown to avoid socially threatening (i.e., angry) faces, compared to low anxious controls (Heuer et al., 2007; Roelofs, Putman et al., 2010), while psychopathic offenders show diminished avoidance tendencies of angry faces, compared to controls (von Borries et al., 2012).

Neurobiology underlying social motivational behavior

Approach and avoidance-related behaviors are mediated by complex interacting neural networks, which can be categorized in the so-called emotional network, reward network, and cognitive control network (Cremers & Roelofs, 2016), which will be broadly described hereafter. The amygdala plays a central role in the emotional network; its subnuclei process salient information from the environment, such as emotional facial expressions, and trigger behavioral responses in response to these environmental stimuli. The basolateral amygdala (BLA) receives input from the thalamus and sensory cortices (such as fusiform gyrus, involved in face processing), whereas the central amygdala (CeA) orchestrates autonomic responses by projections to the periaqueductal gray (PAG) initiating freeze, to brainstem nuclei for release of neurotransmitters, and the hypothalamus for release of oxytocin, corticotropin releasing hormone (CRH), and gonadotropin releasing hormone (GnRH). This eventually leads to enhanced cortisol and testosterone levels, respectively. The amygdala is also connected to the reward network, which comprises the ventral tegmental area (VTA), striatum (including the nucleus accumbens (NAcc)), and medial prefrontal cortex (mPFC) (Haber & Knutson, 2010). Striatal dopamine transmission is essential for the adaptive regulation of social behavior as it is involved in reward learning (i.e., obtaining social reward but also avoiding punishment; see Delgado, Jou, LeDoux, & Phelps, 2009), behavioral activation, and motivational behavior (Cools, 2008; Yacubian & Büchel, 2009). The anterior prefrontal cortex plays a crucial role in the cognitive control network as it is involved in the regulation of emotion (Damásio, 1994; Rolls, 1999). It also has a role in social motivational behavior as it inhibits the amygdala, making it possible to control and override automatic behavioral approach and avoidance tendencies (Roelofs, Minelli, Mars, van Peer, & Toni, 2009; Volman et al., 2011). Furthermore, it modulates mesolimbic striatal activity (Grace, Floresco, Goto, & Lodge, 2007; Wager, Davidson, Hughes, Lindquist, & Ochsner, 2008). Naturally, this description is a highly simplified one, and many other brain regions partake in these networks (Cremers & Roelofs, 2016).

Hormonal regulation of social motivational behavior

Testosterone

The hypothalamus–pituitary–gonadal (HPG) axis with its end product testosterone plays a key role in the neuroendocrine regulation of social motivational behavior in both sexes. Testosterone levels follow a pulsatile, seasonal, and diurnal cycle in which levels are highest upon waking and typically decline by 50% during the day (Dabbs, 1990). Gonadotropin-releasing hormone (GnRH) is secreted from the hypothalamus, which stimulates the production of luteinizing hormone (LH) and follicle-stimulating hormone (FSH) in the pituitary gland, which in turn triggers production of testosterone and estradiol in the gonads (i.e., testes and ovaries). The secreted estradiol and testosterone in turn inhibit the hypothalamus and pituitary, thus forming a negative feedback loop. In addition, small amounts of testosterone are produced in the adrenal cortex and synthesized in the brain from cholesterol and other steroid precursors. Testosterone is able to cross the blood–brain barrier, and besides having (epigenetic) organizational effects on brain structures during pre- and early postnatal development, testosterone also influences emotion, motivation, and behavior later in life (i.e., activational effects; Lombardo et al., 2012; McHenry, Carrier, Hull, & Kabbaj, 2014). Actions of testosterone are brought about directly via androgen receptors but also via metabolites such as estradiol, dihydrotestosterone, and 3α-diol, which binds to the γ-aminobutyric acid (GABA-A) receptor (Balthazart & Ball, 2006; Wood, 2008). The effects can either be slow and long-lasting (i.e., hours–days) via a genomic pathway featuring intracellular steroid receptors, or rapid (i.e., seconds–minutes) via membrane-bound (steroid) receptors, which exert non-genomic actions in the cell. Importantly, testosterone acts through a steroid-responsive network which includes the amygdala, hypothalamus, hippocampus, and PAG, among other limbic areas (Wood, 1996), and hence influences the flight–fight response.

Naturally, testosterone interacts with other neurotransmitters and peptides, such as serotonin (probably via estradiol), vasopressin, oxytocin, and dopamine. With regard to the latter, testosterone enhances dopamine transmission in the mesolimbic system, which in turn can lead to increased reward sensitivity and augmented motivational behavior by promoting dopaminergic projections form the amygdala to the striatum (de Souza Silva, Mattern, Topic, Buddenberg, & Huston, 2009; Hermans et al., 2010; Welker, Gruber, & Mehta, 2015).

Baseline hormone levels are in general predictive of psychological traits and behavior (Welker et al., 2015), whereas social events are typically associated with a temporary surge or decline in hormone levels (Casto & Edwards, 2016; Maner, Miller, Schmidt, & Eckel, 2008; Sapolsky, 1991). The social challenge hypothesis states that testosterone levels rise in preparation to a challenging encounter in which social status might be threatened, thereby initiating approach motivation and simultaneously reducing fear (Archer, 2006; Mazur & Booth, 1998; Wingfield, Hegner, Dufty Jr., & Ball, 1990). Several studies featuring single-dose testosterone administration, which leads to a transient increase in testosterone levels, to healthy female participants confirmed the causal relationship between testosterone and its effects on the social motivational system. The findings show that testosterone administration reduces fear and sensitivity to threat and punishment, enhances reward sensitivity, and promotes social approach motivation aimed at achieving social status (i.e., social reward; see for a review Bos, Panksepp, Bluthe, & van Honk, 2012; Enter, Spinhoven, & Roelofs, 2014). These actions have been suggested to be brought about by anxiolytic effects (GABA, androgen receptors; McHenry et al., 2014) and upregulation of the dopaminergic system (de Souza Silva et al., 2009), in addition to biasing the amygdala towards threat approach (Radke et al., 2015) and reducing prefrontal control over the amygdala (Schutter & van Honk, 2004; van Wingen, Mattern, Verkes, Buitelaar, & Fernández, 2010; Volman et al., 2011). Although associated with aggression (Montoya et al., 2012), the effects of testosterone on social motivational behavior depend on social context and individual differences and thus do not entail aggressive behavior per se, but could also lead to prosocial behavior when this is more appropriate to ensure an increase in social status (Boksem et al., 2013; Carré et al., 2016; Eisenegger, Haushofer, & Fehr, 2011; Mehta & Josephs, 2010; Stanton & Schultheiss, 2009; van Honk, Terburg, & Bos, 2011; sample sizes in these studies ranged from $n = 54$ to $n = 121$).

Cortisol

For decades cortisol has been a popular biomarker to index acute and chronic social and psychological stress (Hellhammer, Wüst, & Kudielka, 2009). Individual differences in the diurnal pattern are associated with psychopathology (Adam et al., 2017); however, most research has focused on stress-induced cortisol surges. Like testosterone, this hormone follows a pulsatile and diurnal pattern, in which levels are high in the morning, surging within 30–40 minutes after waking, followed by a steep drop for a few hours and a steady decline until the lowest point at bedtime. Cortisol is the end product of the hypothalamus–pituitary–adrenal (HPA) axis. The hypothalamus secretes corticotropin-releasing hormone (CRH), which stimulates the anterior pituitary to release adrenocorticotropic hormone (ACH); this travels via the bloodstream to the adrenal cortex where it stimulates the production of cortisol. Cortisol in turn inhibits the pituitary and the hypothalamus, forming a negative feedback loop, and is able to exert both rapid non-genomic and slow genomic effects in the brain (Joëls, Pu, Wiegert, Oitzl, & Krugers, 2006). Cortisol binds to glucocorticoid and mineralocorticoid receptors in brain areas important in regulating the fight–flight response, such as frontal areas, amygdala, and hippocampus (Lupien, Maheu, Tu, Fiocco, & Schramek, 2007). It has an important role in regulating homeostatic systems, affecting arousal, metabolic processes, and the immune system (Sapolsky, Romero, & Munck, 2000). During the initial phase of the stress response, epinephrine from the adrenal medulla triggers norepinephrine release in the basolateral amygdala, among other regions, which induces an increase in vigilance by prioritizing sensory processing and activation of the amygdala (Osborne, Pearson-Leary, & McNay, 2015). Subsequent cortisol release regulates the stress response by downregulating amygdala responsivity and decreasing anxiety-driven selective attention to threat (Henckens, Wingen, Joëls, & Fernández, 2010, $n = 72$; Putman & Roelofs, 2011; van Peer et al., 2009, $n = 21$, small effect sizes), besides affecting activity in areas involved in the planning and execution of motor responses (Montoya, Bos, Terburg, Rosenberger, & van Honk, 2014, $n = 20$). Animal research has shown that higher cortisol levels are associated with social avoidance behavior (Sapolsky, 1990). Studies featuring stress-induced cortisol surges and cortisol administration in healthy humans extend these findings by showing that elevated levels of cortisol are associated with increased avoidance of social threat on the AAT (Roelofs et al., 2005, $n = 22$, small to medium effect sizes; van Peer et al., 2007, $n = 40$, large effect sizes).

The HPG axis works in antagonism with the hypothalamus–pituitary–adrenal (HPA) axis, in such a way that the end product of the latter (i.e., cortisol, released in response to stress) disrupts production and inhibits actions of testosterone, which in turn inhibits the stress-induced activation of the HPA axis at the hypothalamus (Viau, 2002). Both neuroendocrine axes are important in the regulation of social–motivational behavior and show a complex interaction: basically, higher basal cortisol levels, and low testosterone, are associated with social subordination stress and avoidance behavior, whereas higher basal testosterone and low cortisol facilitate social dominance and approach behavior (Bedgood, Boggiano, & Turan, 2014; Mehta & Josephs, 2010; Mehta, Lawless DesJardins, van Vugt, & Josephs, 2017; Sapolsky, 1990, 1991; van Honk et al., 1999).

Oxytocin

Originally considered as having a key role in labor and lactation, in the past decade the neuropeptide oxytocin has gained more and more interest as a modulator of social cognition and behavior. Oxytocin has a very similar structure to vasopressin, and both neuropeptides are synthesized in the supraoptic and paraventricular nuclei of the hypothalamus (Johnson & Young, 2017). From there they are released, via the anterior pituitary, in the bloodstream. In addition, there are projections to the amygdala, lateral septum, nucleus accumbens, hippocampus, and ventral tegmental area (Ross & Young, 2009), which are areas involved in the fight–flight response. Oxytocin inhibits the output of the central amygdala to the PAG, whereas vasopressin excites this pathway (Huber, Veinante, & Stoop, 2005). There are indications that oxytocin attenuates the cortisol stress response (Cardoso, Kingdon, & Ellenbogen, 2014), and it is thought to have anxiolytic effects (Heinrichs & Domes, 2008). In addition, oxytocin enhances the salience of social information by increasing attention towards social cues and also increases the reward value of social stimuli (see for a review Crespi, 2016). During the control of social approach–avoidance behavior, oxytocin decreases amygdala responses during threat approach as a result of its anxiolytic properties (Radke et al., 2017, n = 57, medium effect sizes). Also, oxytocin administration promotes threat approach in low socially anxious men (Radke, Roelofs, & de Bruijn, 2013, n = 24, medium to large effect sizes). It has been proposed that oxytocin and testosterone have opposite effects on social cognition and behavior: where testosterone facilitates a dominance-related approach strategy which serves individual status defense, oxytocin promotes social exploration and in-group protection (Bos, Panksepp, Bluthe, & van Honk, 2012; Reimers & Diekhof, 2015). It is important to note that the effects of oxytocin depend on social context and individual differences and can have both positive and negative social effects. Shamay-Tsoory and Abu-Akel (2016) argue that oxytocin increases the salience of safety signals in a positive and supportive context, but on the other hand triggers orienting responses to threat and enhances anxiety in an unpredictable and threatening situation. It is likely that interactions between phasic dopaminergic signaling and oxytocin in the ventral tegmental area, nucleus accumbens, and amygdala modulate the effects of context and individual differences. Interactions of oxytocin and serotonin in the nucleus accumbens have been shown to be important in social interaction (Dölen, Darvishzadeh, Huang, & Malenka, 2013).

Before discussing the potential role of these hormones and peptides in social psychopathologies, we will introduce two types of pathologies that show marked alterations in social motivational processing: social anxiety and psychopathy.

Social psychopathology

Social anxiety disorder

Social anxiety disorder (SAD) is one of the most common mental health disorders (e.g., Bandelow & Michaelis, 2015). SAD is characterized by an intense fear of social situations in which the individual may be scrutinized by others (American Psychiatric Association, 2013). The affected individual fears that he/she will behave, or show anxiety symptoms, in a way that will be negatively evaluated and will lead to rejection by others. Social situations, such as social interactions, are therefore avoided or endured with intense fear or anxiety. Avoidance behavior plays a crucial role in the persistence of the disorder and hinders extinction of fear in social situations as it reduces the opportunity for accommodation to and reevaluation of the situation (Clark & Wells, 1995). In addition, when engaging in social interaction, someone with SAD typically tends to avoid eye contact (Stein & Stein, 2008). As eye contact is important in social communication, this characteristic hinders social interactions and influences how others respond to the person with SAD, reinforcing the social fear–avoidance cycle. Furthermore, there is evidence that SAD persists because of biased processing of social information, favoring disorder-relevant information, which leads to interpretation of the situation as more negative than it was in reality (Heeren, Lange, Philippot, & Wong, 2014; Stein & Stein, 2008). With a lifetime prevalence rate of 7–12%, SAD is the most common anxiety disorder and among the most common psychiatric disorders (Kessler et al., 2005). Onset occurs in childhood or early adolescence, and SAD affects more women than men. The disorder typically leads to significant distress and, when left untreated, tends to follow a chronic, unremitting course leading to substantial impairments in vocational and social functioning. Treatment of SAD consist of pharmacotherapy and/

or psychotherapy, mainly cognitive behavioral therapy aiming at acquiring the behavioral and cognitive skills to function effectively. Exposure therapy is part of the latter and aims at fear extinction by repeated or prolonged exposure to feared social situations, leading to a reduction of anxiety and avoidance behavior. Notwithstanding the efficacy of current evidence-based psychological and pharmacological treatments in SAD, nonresponse rates in large clinical trials have been up to 50% (Hofmann & Bögels, 2006; Stein & Stein, 2008), leaving considerable room for improvement.

Neuroendocrinology of social anxiety disorder

Social anxiety disorder (SAD) is associated with deviations in the neuroendocrine brain circuits underlying social motivational behavior. Unfortunately, evidence is inconsistent, and may be due to relatively small sample sizes (averaging 12 patients per group) and differences in methods and analyses. Nevertheless, several meta-analytic studies have consistently shown a hyperactive amygdala in response to social threat, probably reflecting enhanced processing of and attention to threat (Brühl, Delsignore, Komossa, & Weidt, 2014; Cremers & Roelofs, 2016; Fouche, van Der Wee, Roelofs, & Stein, 2013). In addition, prefrontal structures are also more active than in healthy controls; however, prefrontal–amygdala connectivity seems to be reduced (Brühl et al., 2014; Cremers & Roelofs, 2016; Fouche et al., 2013), indicating an inability to regulate subcortical regions. Interestingly, pharmaco- and psychotherapy seem to "normalize" deviating activation patterns in SAD (Fouche et al., 2013; Freitas-Ferrari et al., 2010). Studies also show alterations in striatal functioning in SAD, but findings are mixed (Freitas-Ferrari et al., 2010). A recent fMRI study in patients with SAD ($n = 20$), compared to healthy controls ($n = 20$) reported reduced striatal activity in anticipation of social reward and relative increased striatal activity for avoiding social punishment (Cremers, Veer, Spinhoven, Rombouts, & Roelofs, 2014). These findings suggest that patients with SAD show a reduced motivation to obtain social reward and relative increased motivation to avoid social punishment compared to healthy controls. In addition, patients with SAD showed a reduced pattern of fronto-striatal connectivity during reward and punishment anticipation, relative to healthy controls.

Patients with SAD ($n = 18$) show an increased cortisol response to social stress, compared to healthy participants (n = 22) and patients with Post-Traumatic Stress Disorder (PTSD; $n = 17$; small to medium effect sizes), and this response was associated with social avoidance behavior (large effect sizes) (Roelofs, van Peer et al., 2009). Studies combining cortisol administration with electroencephalography (EEG) in patients with SAD confirmed a causal relationship between cortisol and increased early processing of emotional faces during social avoidance (Van Peer, Spinhoven, & Roelofs, 2009, $n = 21$, large effect size), and modulation of early threat processing depending on motivational context and symptom severity (van Peer, Spinhoven, & Roelofs, 2010, $n = 18$). In addition, both higher baseline levels of cortisol and exogenous cortisol are associated with EEG wave activity patterns related to anxiety and behavioral inhibition (Schutter & van Honk, 2005, $n = 28$; van Peer, Roelofs, & Spinhoven, 2008, $n = 40$), whereas testosterone has an opposite effect (Schutter & van Honk, 2004, $n = 16$).

Studies on testosterone in SAD are scarce, and although previous results on the relation between SAD and baseline testosterone levels show no differences (Gerra et al., 2000, $n = 40$; Maner et al., 2008, $n = 64$), recent findings from a large cohort study show reduced testosterone levels in women with SAD compared to women without a lifetime history of anxiety or depressive disorders. (Giltay et al., 2012, $n = 2102$, small–medium effect size). Interestingly, testosterone administration to women with SAD promotes social threat approach on the AAT (Enter et al.,

2014, *n* = 24, medium effect size) and socially dominant gaze behavior. For example, patients with SAD have been shown to display reduced fixations on the eye-regions of angry (versus neutral) faces (Enter, Terburg, Harrewijn, Spinhoven, & Roelofs, 2016, SAD *n* = 18, HC *n* = 19; Horley, Williams, Gonsalvez, & Gordon, 2004, SAD *n* = 22, HC *n* = 22). Administration of 0.5 mg testosterone in 18 patients with SAD resulted in normalization of the gaze pattern, increasing the number of first fixations to the eye-region of angry faces (see Figure 34.1). These results suggest that testosterone is able to promote social dominant behavior by its anxiolytic and reward-promoting properties, presumably by influencing early automatic mechanisms (van Peer, Enter, van Steenbergen, Spinhoven, & Roelofs, 2017, SAD *n* = 19, HC *n* = 19).

Quite a few studies have focused on the role of oxytocin in SAD, but the results should be interpreted with caution, as statistical power tends to be low (Walum, Waldman, & Young, 2016). There is no evidence of altered baseline levels in SAD compared to healthy controls, although higher levels of oxytocin were associated with more severe social anxiety symptomatology and less satisfaction in social relationships in one study (*n* = 46) (Hoge, Pollack, Kaufman, Zak, & Simon, 2008). Oxytocin administration studies in SAD (18 SAD patients versus 18 healthy controls) have shown that this neuropeptide is able to dampen heightened amygdala and prefrontal responses (Labuschagne et al., 2010, 2011) and to normalize amygdala–frontal connectivity during resting state (Dodhia et al., 2014, *n* = 36). Interestingly, oxytocin administration promotes other-oriented reward motivation, but only in patients with generalized SAD who have less severe social interaction anxiety (Fang, Treadway, & Hofmann, 2017, *n* = 52).

In sum, individuals with SAD show alterations in the regulation of social motivational behavior characterized by persistent social avoidance, reduced testosterone levels, increased cortisol responses, enhanced threat sensitivity, and probably reduced reward processing, a pattern that is associated with socially submissive behavior. Results on the role of oxytocin in SAD are inconclusive and need to be elucidated in future research.

Psychopathy

Psychopathy is a multidimensional personality condition which overlaps partly with anti-social personality disorder, sharing an anti-social lifestyle, but distinguished by affective–interpersonal impairments (Brazil, van Dongen, Maes, Mars, & Baskin-Sommers, 2016). The full clinical manifestation affects less than 1% of the general population, and approximately 15–25% of the prison population. Characterization in the literature is inconsistent, but psychopathy has often been defined based on the Hare Psychopathy Checklist, which describes psychopathy along two distinct dimensions: Factor 1 (comprising lack of guilt and empathy, shallow affect, and pathological lying), and Factor 2 (including impulsivity, anti-social behavior, and sensation-seeking) (Hare & Neumann, 2008). Alternatively, a distinction between primary and secondary psychopathy has been made, with similar symptoms but a difference in anxiety levels (Anderson & Kiehl, 2012; Brazil et al., 2016; van Honk & Schutter, 2006). Whereas primary psychopathy is characterized by low anxiety, secondary psychopathy is defined by higher anxiety levels. Both show pronounced problems in emotional processing (e.g., reduced guilt, empathy, etc.), increased goal-directed behavior, instrumental aggression (i.e., goal-oriented self-serving aggression), and an increase in impulsive behavior and uncontrolled aggression after emotional provocation.

Psychological and behavioral interventions give mixed results in effectiveness, depending on different types of anti-social individuals (Brazil et al., 2016). In general, psychopathic individuals are not responsive to treatment due to the specific characteristics of the disorder and a lack of motivation to seek treatment.

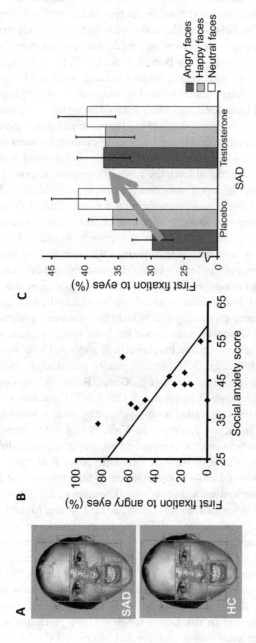

Figure 34.1 Adapted from Enter, Terburg, Harrewijn, Spinhoven, and Roelofs (2016). Panel A provides an illustration of a gaze path measured using eye-tracking while a patient with social anxiety disorder (SAD) and a healthy control participant (HC) were viewing an angry facial expression. Panel B: A correlation between percentage first fixations on angry eyes and LSAS social anxiety scores (Liebowitz, 1987) in the placebo condition indicated that SAD participants with stronger anxiety symptomatology showed increased gaze avoidance of angry eye contact ($r = -.561, p = .046$). Panel C: Testosterone administration, compared to placebo, alleviated gaze avoidance of angry eye contact by increasing the percentage first fixations towards angry eyes.

Neuroendocrinology of psychopathy

Research on the neuroendocrinological underpinnings of psychopathy suffers from small sample sizes, especially for individuals scoring high on the psychopathy checklist, and also from lack of one clear definition of the different subtypes of psychopathy (Brazil et al., 2016; Koenigs, Baskin-Sommers, Zeier, & Newman, 2011). One of the few studies with psychopathic offenders (n = 17) featuring the AAT indicates that this maladaptive behavior already stems from early automatic mechanisms by showing reduced avoidance tendencies towards angry faces compared to healthy control participants (n = 15) (von Borries et al., 2012). In addition, this effect was related to higher levels of instrumental aggression and reduced feelings of discomfort when observing another's negative experiences. Neuroimaging studies of psychopathic offenders show structural deviations in several brain areas, including reduced amygdala and prefrontal volume, increased striatal volume, and an abnormal shape of the hippocampus (Koenigs et al., 2011). In addition, psychopathy is associated with impaired amygdala–prefrontal connections in a relatively small sample (n = 22) and a larger sample (n = 147; Hoppenbrouwers et al., 2013; Wolf et al., 2015, respectively). On a functional level, the amygdala seems to respond less to aversive stimuli, fearful faces, and pictures of moral violations (Anderson & Kiehl, 2012; Decety, Chen, Harenski, & Kiehl, 2015, n = 155), in addition to atypical activity of the aPFC during various tasks. Interestingly, striatal activity is enhanced, suggesting an increase in reward sensitivity (van Honk & Schutter, 2006). During the control of social approach–avoidance behavior, psychopathic offenders (n = 15) show reduced anterior prefrontal cortex activity and less anterior prefrontal cortex–amygdala connectivity (versus 19 healthy controls), and this was modulated by endogenous testosterone levels (Volman et al., 2016). These findings suggest that higher testosterone levels are associated with less prefrontal control over amygdala-driven actions.

Because of its social dominance-promoting effects, including dampening of punishment sensitivity and increasing reward sensitivity, testosterone has been in the picture with regard to the biological underpinnings of psychopathy. Psychopathy is associated with social dominance (Lobbestael, Arntz, Voncken, & Potegal, 2018). Studies yielded mixed results in trying to relate endogenous testosterone to psychopathy scores (e.g., Glenn, Raine, Schug, Gao, & Granger, 2011, n = 178; Welker, Lozoya, Campbell, Neumann, & Carré, 2014), and rather found relationships with typical personality traits associated with psychopathy, such as impulsivity and antisocial aspects (Stålenheim, Eriksson, von Knorring, & Wide, 1998, n = 61). Importantly, several studies showed that the relation between testosterone and psychopathy was modulated by cortisol (Glenn et al., 2011; Loomans, Tulen, de Rijke, & van Marle, 2016; Welker et al., 2014, sample sizes were respectively 178, 166, and 237). A combination of high testosterone levels and low cortisol levels tends to be associated with psychopathy (Loomans et al., 2016), which predisposes individuals to aggressive behavior (Montoya et al., 2012; Terburg, Morgan, & van Honk, 2009). However, Welker et al. (2014) showed a different pattern of results in which the positive relationship between testosterone and psychopathy only emerged when cortisol was high. High testosterone levels in utero, during adolescence, and in response to stress might predispose to psychopathy, in combination with individual and environmental risk factors (Yildirim & Derksen, 2012). Testosterone likely dampens oxytocinergic effects on social empathy (see Yildirim & Derksen, 2012 for a review). Both lower oxytocin levels and certain variations in oxytocin receptor polymorphisms are related to risk factors for developing psychopathy (e.g., callous–unemotional traits and conduct problems) in children and adolescents (Dadds et al., 2014; Levy et al., 2015). Taken together, the pattern that emerges is that psychopathy is associated with structural and functional brain deviations. Alterations in social approach–avoidance behavior, such as decreased social threat avoidance, are likely associated with reduced prefrontal control

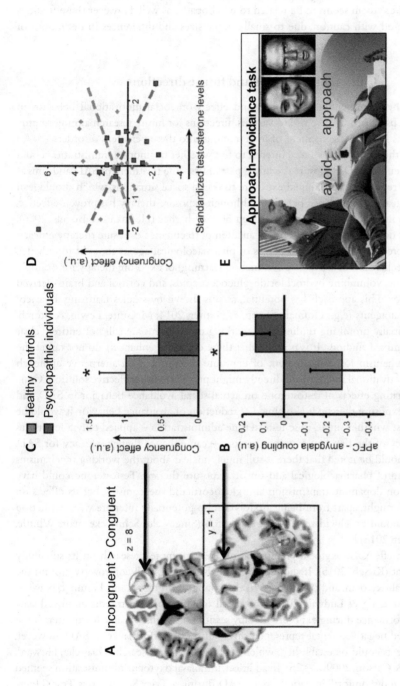

Figure 34.2 Adapted from Volman et al., 2016. Panels A and B: Psychopathic individuals (violent offenders with high psychopathic traits) show reduced pattern of negative coupling between the anterior prefrontal cortex (aPFC) and the amygdala when they have to control their emotional actions on the approach–avoidance task (AAT, see panel E), compared to healthy matched controls. Panel C: Psychopathic individuals (compared to controls) show reduced local activity in the aPFC when they exert approach-avoidance control, and this effect is modulated by their testosterone levels (Panel D). Panel E: fMRI-adapted AAT– people make affect-congruent reactions by pulling a joystick towards their body when detecting a happy face or by pushing the joystick away from their body in response to an angry face. In contrast, affect-incongruent responses involved the opposite reactions to the emotional faces, which requires AA control and is typically associated with increased reaction times and increased aPFC activity (Volman et al., 2011, 2013).

over limbic structures. Testosterone plays a role in modulation of prefrontal–amygdala connectivity, and is associated with psychopathic tendencies, a relationship that seems to be modulated by cortisol. Lower oxytocin seems to be related to psychopathy as well. However these findings should be considered with caution, due to small sample sizes and differences in definitions of psychopathy.

Clinical implications and future directions

The above-described neuroendocrine aspects and effects on social motivational behavior in social anxiety and psychopathy give rise to various directions for future research aiming to provide starting points for the enhancement of interventions into these persistent disorders.

It would be of theoretical and clinical interest to test whether hormone administration could benefit the treatment of SAD. Exposure therapy is part of first-line treatment of SAD and aims at fear extinction by repeated or prolonged exposure to feared social situations, which should lead to a reduction in fear and avoidance behavior. Although exposure therapy has proven effective, nonresponse rates in large clinical trials have been 50% or higher (Hofmann & Bögels, 2006), and many patients do not achieve remission. In an attempt to enhance exposure therapy efficacy, research has explored the augmentation effects of pharmacological agents thought to enhance the underlying mechanisms of action (e.g., extinction learning) of exposure therapy, for example using D-cycloserine, yohimbine hydrochloride, glucocorticoids, and cortisol and brain-derived neurotrophic factor. This approach has potential, as was shown by studies featuring a variety of pharmacological agents (e.g., Hofmann, Fang, & Gutner, 2014; McGuire, Lewin, & Storch, 2014). Despite initially promising findings, the working mechanisms are still not entirely clear and studies yield mixed findings. It is possible that these cognitive enhancers do not target the most optimal mechanism for enhancement of exposure therapy, and an alternative approach targeting social motivational mechanisms directly might provide a more effective solution. Considering the alleviating effects of testosterone on actual social avoidance behavior in SAD, and considering that exposure therapy is also aimed at reduction of avoidance behavior, it would be of relevance to test whether single-dose testosterone administration – applied only a few times to enhance efficacy of the first few exposure sessions – can enhance therapy efficacy for SAD. Nevertheless, it should be noted that there is still much unclear about the working mechanisms of testosterone and of pharmacological add-ons in exposure therapy. Testosterone could have beneficial effects on dopamine transmission and glucocorticoid mechanisms, but its effects on the GABA system might, apart from being anxiolytic, also potentially interfere with extinction learning, which should be elucidated in future research (Singewald, Schmuckermair, Whittle, Holmes, & Ressler, 2015).

The anxiolytic effects of oxytocin administration have prompted research on its suitability for SAD treatment (Kirsch, 2015). It should be noted that there is still controversy around the effects of intranasal oxytocin, and that there is likely a publication bias (Lane, Luminet, Nave, & Mikolajczak, 2016; Leng & Ludwig, 2016). Intranasal oxytocin administration improved self-evaluation of performance during exposure therapy sessions, and thus was able to counteract the typical exaggerated negative mental representations after social performance in SAD; however, no long-term effects could be established, which warrants further research (Guastella, Howard, Dadds, Mitchell, & Carson, 2009, $n = 25$). In addition, intranasal oxytocin administration seemed to reduce "physical discomfort" in patients with SAD during a Trier Social Stress Test (Heinrichs et al., 2006). The ability of oxytocin to make social interactions more rewarding might be beneficial for certain subtypes of SAD patients who lack the motivation to engage in social interaction (van Honk, Bos, Terburg, Heany, & Stein, 2015).

Finally, an initial study with cortisol administration to promote extinction learning during exposure sessions in 40 patients with SAD led to reduced heart rate and self-reported anxiety during the sessions (Soravia et al., 2006). However, long-term effects of cortisol on persistent avoidance tendencies in SAD have not been investigated.

Another interesting approach would be to explore whether the automatic avoidance tendencies in SAD and psychopathy could be diminished by approach–avoidance training on the AAT. Research on this topic across various disciplines has shown positive results (e.g., Wiers, Eberl, Rinck, Becker, & Lindemeyer, 2011; for review see Woud & Becker, 2014). Two studies featuring socially anxious participants showed that, after being required to approach positive social stimuli on the AAT (e.g., smiling faces), they subsequently showed more approach behavior during social interactions, elicited more positive reactions by their interaction partners (Taylor & Amir, 2012, *n* = 47, large effect sizes), and reported better mood and less anxiety after a social challenge (Rinck et al., 2013, *n* = 40, medium to large effect sizes). A study featuring approach–avoidance training in alcoholism (20 alcohol dependents versus 17 healthy controls) showed that amygdala activity reduced in response to alcohol-related stimuli (Wiers et al., 2014). This finding suggests that the affective evaluation of the stimulus was altered by the training; however, the mechanisms behind approach–avoidance training are not clear to date. It is also possible that the training increases prefrontal control over amygdala-driven approach–avoidance responses. Single-dose testosterone administration in SAD might aid the training process by biasing the brain towards social approach, although this effect is likely specific for social threat faces.

All these studies would be helped by increased clarity on the neuroendocrine mechanisms underlying deviations in social motivational behavior in SAD. Research featuring neuroimaging techniques should shed more light on this matter. Future studies could combine social approach and avoidance tasks with fMRI, endogenous hormone/neuropeptide measurements (e.g., Volman, et al., 2011), and/or testosterone/oxytocin administration to find out how these neuroendocrine agents modulate social approach/avoidance behavior in SAD. In addition, it would be interesting to try to probe the functioning of the emotion-network (e.g., fear reduction by GABA-ergic mechanisms) and the reward network (dopaminergic mechanisms) in SAD, by using single photon emission computed tomography (SPECT) or positron emission tomography (PET) scanning (e.g., van der Wee et al., 2008; Schneier, Kent, Star, & Hirsch, 2009), in combination with testosterone administration. It would be particularly interesting to add genotyping for androgen and dopaminergic receptor genes. Furthermore, future research featuring EEG or magnetoencephalography (MEG) should further elucidate the temporal dynamics of these processes in both healthy individuals and those with SAD.

The same line of reasoning holds for aggression-related disorders, such as psychopathy, for which identification of biological underpinnings of subtypes and adaptive treatment is still in its infancy (e.g., Brazil et al., 2016). More research is needed to obtain starting points for studying the effects of hormone manipulations on the management of social aggression. Pioneering evidence in autism spectrum disorders, where aggression plays an important role as well, suggests that oxytocin has the potential to enhance motivation and attention to social cues in patients with autism spectrum disorder (Yamasue, 2016). A recent review and meta analyses concluded that studies on autism did show significant effect sizes (combined effect size of d = 57, e.g., medium effect); however, oxytocin seemed less effective in other psychopathologies (Bakermans-Kranenburg & van IJzendoorn, 2013; Guastella & Hickie, 2016). On the other hand, no significant meta-analytic effect of oxytocin on the social domain in autism was found by Ooi and colleagues (2017). More sophisticated and targeted clinical trials are required, due to a limited number of studies and small sample sizes. Whether similar interventions may be effective for aggression-related disorders, such as psychopathy, remains to be determined. It is conceivable that the social salience enhancing effects of oxytocin could make matters worse in psychopathy.

Finally, increasing evidence suggests that the effects of testosterone, cortisol, and oxytocin on social motivational behavior are modulated by individual differences and social context. For example, the effects of testosterone and oxytocin on social motivational behavior in healthy individuals were modulated by social anxiety scores (Enter et al., 2014; Radke et al., 2013). Future research should address these influences in order to optimize indications for potential hormonal interventions.

Conclusion

Steroid hormones, like cortisol and testosterone, and neuropeptides such as oxytocin, play a role in the regulation of social motivational behavior. Both social anxiety and aggression-related disorders show an imbalance in these steroid hormones. Given the important interaction between steroid hormones and the main motivational systems in healthy individuals as well as individuals with social psychopathologies, future studies should explore the potential role of hormones in enhancing therapy efficacy.

References

Adam, E. K., Quinn, M. E., Tavernier, R., McQuillan, M. T., Dahlke, K. A., & Gilbert, K. E. (2017). Diurnal cortisol slopes and mental and physical health outcomes: A systematic review and meta-analysis. *Psychoneuroendocrinology*, *83*, 25–41. https://doi.org/10.1016/j.psyneuen.2017.05.018

American Psychiatric Association. (2013). Social anxiety disorder (social phobia). In *Diagnostic and statistical manual of mental disorders: DSM-V* (pp. 202–208). Washington, DC: American Psychiatric Association.

Anderson, N. E., & Kiehl, K. A. (2012). The psychopath magnetized: Insights from brain imaging. *Trends in Cognitive Sciences*, *16*(1), 52–60. https://doi.org/10.1016/j.tics.2011.11.008

Archer, J. (2006). Testosterone and human aggression: An evaluation of the challenge hypothesis. *Neuroscience & Biobehavioral Reviews*, *30*(3), 319–345. https://doi.org/10.1016/j.neubiorev.2004.12.007

Bakermans-Kranenburg, M. J., & van IJzendoorn, M. H. (2013). Sniffing around oxytocin: Review and meta-analyses of trials in healthy and clinical groups with implications for pharmacotherapy. *Translational Psychiatry*, *3*(5), e258. https://doi.org/10.1038/tp.2013.34

Balthazart, J., & Ball, G. F. (2006). Is brain estradiol a hormone or a neurotransmitter? *Trends in Neurosciences*, *29*(5), 241–249. https://doi.org/10.1016/j.tins.2006.03.004

Bandelow, B., & Michaelis, S. (2015). Epidemiology of anxiety disorders in the 21st century. *Dialogues in Clinical Neuroscience*, *17*(3), 327–335.

Bedgood, D., Boggiano, M. M., & Turan, B. (2014). Testosterone and social evaluative stress: The moderating role of basal cortisol. *Psychoneuroendocrinology*, *47*, 107–115. https://doi.org/10.1016/j.psyneuen.2014.05.007

Blair, R. J. J. (2013). The neurobiology of psychopathic traits in youths. *Nature Reviews. Neuroscience*, *14*(11), 786–799. https://doi.org/10.1038/nrn3577

Blanchard, D. C., Griebel, G., Pobbe, R., & Blanchard, R. J. (2011). Risk assessment as an evolved threat detection and analysis process. *Neuroscience and Biobehavioral Reviews*, *35*(4), 991–998. https://doi.org/10.1016/j.neubiorev.2010.10.016

Boksem, M. A. S., Mehta, P. H., van den Bergh, B., van Son, V., Trautmann, S. T., Roelofs, K., . . . Sanfey, A. G. (2013). Testosterone inhibits trust but promotes reciprocity. *Psychological Science*, *24*(11), 2306–2314. https://doi.org/10.1177/0956797613495063

Bos, P. A., Panksepp, J., Bluthe, R.-M., & van Honk, J. (2012). Acute effects of steroid hormones and neuropeptides on human social-emotional behavior: A review of single administration studies. *Frontiers in Neuroendocrinology*, *33*(1), 17–35. http://dx.doi.org/10.1016/j.yfrne.2011.01.002

Bradley, M. M., Codispoti, M., Cuthbert, B. N., & Lang, P. J. (2001). Emotion and motivation I: Defensive and appetitive reactions in picture processing. *Emotion*, *1*(3), 276–298. https://doi.org/10.1037/1528-3542.1.3.276

Brazil, I. A., van Dongen, J. D. M., Maes, J. H. R., Mars, R. B., & Baskin-Sommers, A. R. (2016). Classification and treatment of antisocial individuals: From behavior to biocognition. *Neuroscience and Biobehavioral Reviews*. https://doi.org/10.1016/j.neubiorev.2016.10.010

Brühl, A. B., Delsignore, A., Komossa, K., & Weidt, S. (2014). Neuroimaging in social anxiety disorder – a meta-analytic review resulting in a new neurofunctional model. *Neuroscience & Biobehavioral Reviews*, *47*, 260–280. https://doi.org/10.1016/j.neubiorev.2014.08.003

Cardoso, C., Kingdon, D., & Ellenbogen, M. A. (2014). A meta-analytic review of the impact of intranasal oxytocin administration on cortisol concentrations during laboratory tasks: Moderation by method and mental health. *Psychoneuroendocrinology*, *49*, 161–170. https://doi.org/10.1016/j.psyneuen.2014.07.014

Carré, J. M., Geniole, S. N., Ortiz, T. L., Bird, B. M., Videto, A., & Bonin, P. L. (2016). Exogenous testosterone rapidly increases aggressive behavior in dominant and impulsive men. *Biological Psychiatry*, *0*(0). https://doi.org/10.1016/j.biopsych.2016.06.009

Carver, C. S., & White, T. L. (1994). Behavioral inhibition, behavioral activation, and affective responses to impending reward and punishment: The BIS/BAS scales. *Journal of Personality and Social Psychology*, *67*(2), 319–333. https://doi.org/10.1037/0022-3514.67.2.319

Casto, K. V., & Edwards, D. A. (2016). Testosterone, cortisol, and human competition. *Hormones and Behavior*, *82*, 21–37. https://doi.org/10.1016/j.yhbeh.2016.04.004

Chen, M., & Bargh, J. A. (1999). Consequences of automatic evaluation: Immediate behavioral predispositions to approach or avoid the stimulus. *Personality and Social Psychology Bulletin*, *25*(2), 215–224. https://doi.org/10.1177/0146167299025002007

Clark, D. M., & Wells, A. (1995). A cognitive model of social phobia. In *Social phobia: Diagnosis, assessment and treatment* (pp. 69–93). New York, NY: Guilford Press.

Cools, R. (2008). Role of dopamine in the motivational and cognitive control of behavior. *The Neuroscientist*, *14*(4), 381–395. https://doi.org/10.1177/1073858408317009

Cremers, H. R., & Roelofs, K. (2016). Social anxiety disorder: A critical overview of neurocognitive research. *Wiley Interdisciplinary Reviews. Cognitive Science*, *7*, 218–232. https://doi.org/10.1002/wcs.1390

Cremers, H. R., Veer, I. M., Spinhoven, P., Rombouts, S. A. R. B., & Roelofs, K. (2014). Neural sensitivity to social reward and punishment anticipation in social anxiety disorder. *Frontiers in Behavioral Neuroscience*, *8*, 439. https://doi.org/10.3389/fnbeh.2014.00439

Crespi, B. J. (2016). Oxytocin, testosterone, and human social cognition. *Biological Reviews of the Cambridge Philosophical Society*, *91*(2), 390–408. https://doi.org/10.1111/brv.12175

Dabbs, J. M. (1990). Salivary testosterone measurements: Reliability across hours, days, and weeks. *Physiology & Behavior*, *48*(1), 83–86.

Dadds, M. R., Moul, C., Cauchi, A., Dobson-Stone, C., Hawes, D. J., Brennan, J., . . . Ebstein, R. E. (2014). Polymorphisms in the oxytocin receptor gene are associated with the development of psychopathy. *Development and Psychopathology*, *26*(1), 21–31. https://doi.org/10.1017/S0954579413000485

Damásio, A. R. (1994). *Descartes' error: Emotion, reason, and the human brain*. New York, NY: Quill.

Davidson, R. J., Ekman, P., Saron, C. D., Senulis, J. A., & Friesen, W. V. (1990). Approach-withdrawal and cerebral asymmetry: Emotional expression and brain physiology: I. *Journal of Personality and Social Psychology*, *58*(2), 330–341. https://doi.org/10.1037/0022-3514.58.2.330

Decety, J., Chen, C., Harenski, C. L., & Kiehl, K. A. (2015). Socioemotional processing of morally-laden behavior and their consequences on others in forensic psychopaths. *Human Brain Mapping*, *36*(6), 2015–2026. https://doi.org/10.1002/hbm.22752

Delgado, M. R., Jou, R. L., LeDoux, J. E., & Phelps, E. A. (2009). Avoiding negative outcomes: Tracking the mechanisms of avoidance learning in humans during fear conditioning. *Frontiers in Behavioral Neuroscience*, *3*. https://doi.org/10.3389/neuro.08.033.2009

de Souza Silva, M. A., Mattern, C., Topic, B., Buddenberg, T. E., & Huston, J. P. (2009). Dopaminergic and serotonergic activity in neostriatum and nucleus accumbens enhanced by intranasal administration of testosterone. *European Neuropsychopharmacology*, *19*(1), 53–63. https://doi.org/10.1016/j.euroneuro.2008.08.003

Dodhia, S., Hosanagar, A., Fitzgerald, D. A., Labuschagne, I., Wood, A. G., Nathan, P. J., & Phan, K. L. (2014). Modulation of resting-state amygdala-frontal functional connectivity by oxytocin in generalized social anxiety disorder. *Neuropsychopharmacology: Official Publication of the American College of Neuropsychopharmacology*, *39*(9), 2061–2069. https://doi.org/10.1038/npp.2014.53

Dölen, G., Darvishzadeh, A., Huang, K. W., & Malenka, R. C. (2013). Social reward requires coordinated activity of nucleus accumbens oxytocin and serotonin. *Nature*, *501*(7466), 179–184. https://doi.org/10.1038/nature12518

Eisenegger, C., Haushofer, J., & Fehr, E. (2011). The role of testosterone in social interaction. *Trends in Cognitive Sciences, 15*(6), 263–271. https://doi.org/10.1016/j.tics.2011.04.008

Enter, D., Spinhoven, P., & Roelofs, K. (2014). Alleviating social avoidance: Effects of single dose testosterone administration on approach-avoidance action. *Hormones and Behavior, 65*(4), 351–354. https://doi.org/10.1016/j.yhbeh.2014.02.001

Enter, D., Terburg, D., Harrewijn, A., Spinhoven, P., & Roelofs, K. (2016). Single dose testosterone administration alleviates gaze avoidance in women with social anxiety disorder. *Psychoneuroendocrinology, 63*, 26–33. https://doi.org/10.1016/j.psyneuen.2015.09.008

Fang, A., Treadway, M. T., & Hofmann, S. G. (2017). Working hard for oneself or others: Effects of oxytocin on reward motivation in social anxiety disorder. *Biological Psychology, 127*, 157–162. https://doi.org/10.1016/j.biopsycho.2017.05.015

Fouche, J-P., van Der Wee, N. J. A., Roelofs, K., & Stein, D. J. (2013). Recent advances in the brain imaging of social anxiety disorder. *Human Psychopharmacology: Clinical and Experimental, 28*(1), 102–105. https://doi.org/10.1002/hup.2281

Freitas-Ferrari, M. C., Hallak, J. E. C., Trzesniak, C., Filho, A. S., Machado-de-Sousa, J. P., Chagas, M. H. N., . . . Crippa, J. A. S. (2010). Neuroimaging in social anxiety disorder: A systematic review of the literature. *Progress in Neuro-Psychopharmacology and Biological Psychiatry, 34*(4), 565–580. https://doi.org/10.1016/j.pnpbp.2010.02.028

Gerra, G., Zaimovic, A., Zambelli, U., Timpano, M., Reali, N., Bernasconi, S., & Brambilla, F. (2000). Neuroendocrine responses to psychological stress in adolescents with anxiety disorder. *Neuropsychobiology, 42*(2), 82–92. https://doi.org/10.1159/000026677

Geurts, D. E. M., Huys, Q. J. M., den Ouden, H. E. M., & Cools, R. (2013). Aversive Pavlovian control of instrumental behavior in humans. *Journal of Cognitive Neuroscience, 25*(9), 1428–1441. https://doi.org/10.1162/jocn_a_00425

Giltay, E. J., Enter, D., Zitman, F. G., Penninx, B. W. J. H., van Pelt, J., Spinhoven, P., & Roelofs, K. (2012). Salivary testosterone: Associations with depression, anxiety disorders, and antidepressant use in a large cohort study. *Journal of Psychosomatic Research, 72*(3), 205–213. https://doi.org/10.1016/j.jpsychores.2011.11.014

Glenn, A. L., Raine, A., Schug, R. A., Gao, Y., & Granger, D. A. (2011). Increased testosterone-to-cortisol ratio in psychopathy. *Journal of Abnormal Psychology, 120*(2), 389–399. https://doi.org/10.1037/a0021407

Grace, A. A., Floresco, S. B., Goto, Y., & Lodge, D. J. (2007). Regulation of firing of dopaminergic neurons and control of goal-directed behaviors. *Trends in Neurosciences, 30*(5), 220–227. https://doi.org/10.1016/j.tins.2007.03.003

Gray, J. A., & MacNaughton, N. (2000). *The neuropsychology of anxiety: An enquiry into the functions of the septo-hippocampal system* (2nd ed.). Oxford, New York, NY: Oxford University Press.

Gray, J. R. (1994). Personality dimensions and emotion systems. In P. Ekman & R. J. Davidson (Eds.), *The nature of emotion* (pp. 329–331). New York, NY: Oxford University Press.

Guastella, A. J., & Hickie, I. B. (2016). Oxytocin treatment, circuitry, and autism: A critical review of the literature placing oxytocin into the autism context. *Biological Psychiatry, 79*(3), 234–242. https://doi.org/10.1016/j.biopsych.2015.06.028

Guastella, A. J., Howard, A. L., Dadds, M. R., Mitchell, P., & Carson, D. S. (2009). A randomized controlled trial of intranasal oxytocin as an adjunct to exposure therapy for social anxiety disorder. *Psychoneuroendocrinology, 34*(6), 917–923. https://doi.org/10.1016/j.psyneuen.2009.01.005

Guitart-Masip, M., Duzel, E., Dolan, R., & Dayan, P. (2014). Action versus valence in decision making. *Trends in Cognitive Sciences, 18*(4), 194–202. https://doi.org/10.1016/j.tics.2014.01.003

Haber, S. N., & Knutson, B. (2010). The reward circuit: Linking primate anatomy and human imaging. *Neuropsychopharmacology: Official Publication of the American College of Neuropsychopharmacology, 35*(1), 4–26. https://doi.org/10.1038/npp.2009.129

Hare, R. D., & Neumann, C. S. (2008). Psychopathy as a clinical and empirical construct. *Annual Review of Clinical Psychology, 4*(1), 217–246. https://doi.org/10.1146/annurev.clinpsy.3.022806.091452

Heeren, A., Lange, W-G., Philippot, P., & Wong, Q. J. J. (2014). Biased cognitions and social anxiety: Building a global framework for integrating cognitive, behavioral, and neural processes. *Frontiers in Human Neuroscience, 8*. https://doi.org/10.3389/fnhum.2014.00538

Heinrichs, M., & Domes, G. (2008). Neuropeptides and social behaviour: Effects of oxytocin and vasopressin in humans. *Progress in Brain Research, 170*, 337–350. https://doi.org/10.1016/S0079-6123(08)00428-7

Heinrichs, M., Soravia, L. M., Neumann, I. D., Stangier, U., de Quervain, D. J. F., & Ehlert, U. (2006). Effects of oxytocin on social phobia. *Neuropsychopharmacology, 31*, S10.

Hellhammer, D. H., Wüst, S., & Kudielka, B. M. (2009). Salivary cortisol as a biomarker in stress research. *Psychoneuroendocrinology, 34*(2), 163–171. https://doi.org/10.1016/j.psyneuen.2008.10.026

Henckens, M. J. A. G., Wingen, G. A. van, Joëls, M., & Fernández, G. (2010). Time-dependent effects of corticosteroids on human amygdala processing. *Journal of Neuroscience, 30*(38), 12725–12732. https://doi.org/10.1523/JNEUROSCI.3112-10.2010

Hermans, E. J., Bos, P. A., Ossewaarde, L., Ramsey, N. F., Fernández, G., & van Honk, J. (2010). Effects of exogenous testosterone on the ventral striatal BOLD response during reward anticipation in healthy women. *NeuroImage, 52*(1), 277–283. https://doi.org/10.1016/j.neuroimage.2010.04.019

Heuer, K., Rinck, M., & Becker, E. S. (2007). Avoidance of emotional facial expressions in social anxiety: The approach-avoidance task. *Behaviour Research and Therapy, 45*(12), 2990–3001. https://doi.org/10.1016/j.brat.2007.08.010

Hofmann, S. G., & Bögels, S. M. (2006). Recent advances in the treatment of social phobia. *Journal of Cognitive Psychotherapy, 20*, 3–5.

Hofmann, S. G., Fang, A., & Gutner, C. A. (2014). Cognitive enhancers for the treatment of anxiety disorders. *Restorative Neurology and Neuroscience, 32*(1), 183–195. https://doi.org/10.3233/RNN-139002

Hoge, E. A., Pollack, M. H., Kaufman, R. E., Zak, P. J., & Simon, N. M. (2008). Oxytocin levels in social anxiety disorder. *CNS Neuroscience & Therapeutics, 14*(3), 165–170. https://doi.org/10.1111/j.1755-5949.2008.00051.x

Hoppenbrouwers, S. S., Nazeri, A., de Jesus, D. R., Stirpe, T., Felsky, D., Schutter, D. J. L. G., ... Voineskos, A. N. (2013). White matter deficits in psychopathic offenders and correlation with factor structure. *PLoS One, 8*(8). https://doi.org/10.1371/journal.pone.0072375

Horley, K., Williams, L. M., Gonsalvez, C., & Gordon, E. (2004). Face to face: Visual scanpath evidence for abnormal processing of facial expressions in social phobia. *Psychiatry Research, 127*(1), 43–53. https://doi.org/10.1016/j.psychres.2004.02.016

Huber, D., Veinante, P., & Stoop, R. (2005). Vasopressin and oxytocin excite distinct neuronal populations in the central amygdala. *Science (New York, N.Y.), 308*(5719), 245–248. https://doi.org/10.1126/science.1105636

Joëls, M., Pu, Z., Wiegert, O., Oitzl, M. S., & Krugers, H. J. (2006). Learning under stress: How does it work? *Trends in Cognitive Sciences, 10*(4), 152–158. https://doi.org/10.1016/j.tics.2006.02.002

Johnson, Z. V., & Young, L. J. (2017). Oxytocin and vasopressin neural networks: Implications for social behavioral diversity and translational neuroscience. *Neuroscience and Biobehavioral Reviews, 76*(Pt A), 87–98. https://doi.org/10.1016/j.neubiorev.2017.01.034

Kessler, R. C., Berglund, P., Demler, O., Jin, R., Merikangas, K. R., & Walters, E. E. (2005). Lifetime prevalence and age-of-onset distributions of DSM-IV disorders in the National Comorbidity Survey Replication. *Archives of General Psychiatry, 62*(6), 593–602. https://doi.org/10.1001/archpsyc.62.6.593

Kirsch, P. (2015). Oxytocin in the socioemotional brain: Implications for psychiatric disorders. *Dialogues in Clinical Neuroscience, 17*(4), 463–476.

Koenigs, M., Baskin-Sommers, A., Zeier, J., & Newman, J. P. (2011). Investigating the neural correlates of psychopathy: A critical review. *Molecular Psychiatry, 16*(8), 792–799. https://doi.org/10.1038/mp.2010.124

Labuschagne, I., Phan, K. L., Wood, A., Angstadt, M., Chua, P., Heinrichs, M., ... Nathan, P. J. (2010). Oxytocin attenuates amygdala reactivity to fear in generalized social anxiety disorder. *Neuropsychopharmacology: Official Publication of the American College of Neuropsychopharmacology, 35*(12), 2403–2413. https://doi.org/10.1038/npp.2010.123

Labuschagne, I., Phan, K. L., Wood, A., Angstadt, M., Chua, P., Heinrichs, M., ... Nathan, P. J. (2011). Medial frontal hyperactivity to sad faces in generalized social anxiety disorder and modulation by oxytocin. *The International Journal of Neuropsychopharmacology*, 1–14. https://doi.org/10.1017/S1461145711001489

Lane, A., Luminet, O., Nave, G., & Mikolajczak, M. (2016). Is there a publication bias in behavioural intranasal oxytocin research on humans? Opening the file drawer of one laboratory. *Journal of Neuroendocrinology, 28*(4). https://doi.org/10.1111/jne.12384

Lang, P. J., Bradley, M. M., & Cuthbert, B. N. (1997). Motivated attention: Affect, activation, and action. In P. J. Lang, R. F. Simons, & M. F. Balaban (Eds.), *Attention and orienting: Sensory and motivational processes* (pp. 97–135). Hillsdale, NJ: Erlbaum.

Leng, G., & Ludwig, M. (2016). Intranasal oxytocin: Myths and delusions. *Biological Psychiatry, 79*(3), 243–250. https://doi.org/10.1016/j.biopsych.2015.05.003

Levy, T., Bloch, Y., Bar-Maisels, M., Gat-Yablonski, G., Djalovski, A., Borodkin, K., & Apter, A. (2015). Salivary oxytocin in adolescents with conduct problems and callous-unemotional traits. *European Child & Adolescent Psychiatry, 24*(12), 1543–1551. https://doi.org/10.1007/s00787-015-0765-6

Lobbestael, J., Arntz, A., Voncken, M., & Potegal, M. (2018). Responses to dominance challenge are a function of psychopathy level: A multimethod study. *Personality Disorders, 9*, 305–314. https://doi.org/10.1037/per0000252

Lojowska, M., Gladwin, T. E., Hermans, E. J., & Roelofs, K. (2015). Freezing promotes perception of coarse visual features. *Journal of Experimental Psychology: General, 144*(6), 1080–1088. https://doi.org/10.1037/xge0000117

Lombardo, M. V., Ashwin, E., Auyeung, B., Chakrabarti, B., Lai, M-C., Taylor, K., . . . Baron-Cohen, S. (2012). Fetal programming effects of testosterone on the reward system and behavioral approach tendencies in humans. *Biological Psychiatry, 72*(10), 839–847. https://doi.org/10.1016/j.biopsych.2012.05.027

Loomans, M. M., Tulen, J. H. M., de Rijke, Y. B., & van Marle, H. J. C. (2016). A hormonal approach to anti-social behaviour. *Criminal Behaviour and Mental Health: CBMH, 26*(5), 380–394. https://doi.org/10.1002/cbm.1968

Lupien, S. J., Maheu, F., Tu, M., Fiocco, A., & Schramek, T. E. (2007). The effects of stress and stress hormones on human cognition: Implications for the field of brain and cognition. *Brain and Cognition, 65*(3), 209–237. https://doi.org/10.1016/j.bandc.2007.02.007

Ly, V., Huys, Q. J. M., Stins, J. F., Roelofs, K., & Cools, R. (2014). Individual differences in bodily freezing predict emotional biases in decision making. *Frontiers in Behavioral Neuroscience, 8*. https://doi.org/10.3389/fnbeh.2014.00237

Ly, V., von Borries, A. K. L., Brazil, I. A., Bulten, B. H., Cools, R., & Roelofs, K. (2016). Reduced transfer of affective value to instrumental behavior in violent offenders. *Journal of Abnormal Psychology, 125*(5), 657–663. https://doi.org/10.1037/abn0000166

Maner, J. K., Miller, S. L., Schmidt, N. B., & Eckel, L. A. (2008). Submitting to defeat – social anxiety, dominance threat, and decrements in testosterone. *Psychological Science, 19*(8), 764–768. https://doi.org/10.1111/j.1467-9280.2008.02154.x

Mazur, A., & Booth, A. (1998). Testosterone and dominance in men. *Behavioral and Brain Sciences, 21*(3), 353–363.

McGuire, J. F., Lewin, A. B., & Storch, E. A. (2014). Enhancing exposure therapy for anxiety disorders, obsessive-compulsive disorder and post-traumatic stress disorder. *Expert Review of Neurotherapeutics, 14*(8), 893–910. https://doi.org/10.1586/14737175.2014.934677

McHenry, J., Carrier, N., Hull, E., & Kabbaj, M. (2014). Sex differences in anxiety and depression: Role of testosterone. *Frontiers in Neuroendocrinology, 35*(1), 42–57. https://doi.org/10.1016/j.yfrne.2013.09.001

Mehta, P. H., & Josephs, R. A. (2010). Testosterone and cortisol jointly regulate dominance: Evidence for a dual-hormone hypothesis. *Hormones and Behavior, 58*(5), 898–906. https://doi.org/10.1016/j.yhbeh.2010.08.020

Mehta, P. H., Lawless DesJardins, N. M., van Vugt, M., & Josephs, R. A. (2017). Hormonal underpinnings of status conflict: Testosterone and cortisol are related to decisions and satisfaction in the hawk-dove game. *Hormones and Behavior, 92*, 141–154. https://doi.org/10.1016/j.yhbeh.2017.03.009

Montoya, E. R., Bos, P. A., Terburg, D., Rosenberger, L. A., & van Honk, J. (2014). Cortisol administration induces global down-regulation of the brain's reward circuitry. *Psychoneuroendocrinology, 47*, 31–42. https://doi.org/10.1016/j.psyneuen.2014.04.022

Montoya, E. R., Terburg, D., Bos, P. A., & van Honk, J. (2012). Testosterone, cortisol, and serotonin as key regulators of social aggression: A review and theoretical perspective. *Motivation and Emotion, 36*(1), 65–73. https://doi.org/10.1007/s11031-011-9264-3

Ooi, Y. P., Weng, S-J., Kossowsky, J., Gerger, H., & Sung, M. (2017). Oxytocin and autism spectrum disorders: A systematic review and meta-analysis of randomized controlled trials. *Pharmacopsychiatry, 50*(1), 5–13. https://doi.org/10.1055/s-0042-109400

Osborne, D. M., Pearson-Leary, J., & McNay, E. C. (2015). The neuroenergetics of stress hormones in the hippocampus and implications for memory. *Frontiers in Neuroscience, 9*. https://doi.org/10.3389/fnins.2015.00164

Putman, P., & Roelofs, K. (2011). Effects of single cortisol administrations on human affect reviewed: Coping with stress through adaptive regulation of automatic cognitive processing. *Psychoneuroendocrinology, 36*(4), 439–448. https://doi.org/10.1016/j.psyneuen.2010.12.001

Radke, S., Roelofs, K., & de Bruijn, E. R. A. (2013). Acting on anger: Social anxiety modulates approach-avoidance tendencies after oxytocin administration. *Psychological Science, 24*(8), 1573–1578. https://doi.org/10.1177/0956797612472682

Radke, S., Volman, I., Kokal, I., Roelofs, K., de Bruijn, E. R. A., & Toni, I. (2017). Oxytocin reduces amygdala responses during threat approach. *Psychoneuroendocrinology*, *79*, 160–166. https://doi.org/10.1016/j.psyneuen.2017.02.028

Radke, S., Volman, I., Mehta, P., Son, V. van, Enter, D., Sanfey, A., . . . Roelofs, K. (2015). Testosterone biases the amygdala toward social threat approach. *Science Advances*, *1*(5), e1400074. https://doi.org/10.1126/sciadv.1400074

Reimers, L., & Diekhof, E. K. (2015). Testosterone is associated with cooperation during intergroup competition by enhancing parochial altruism. *Frontiers in Neuroscience*, *9*, 183. https://doi.org/10.3389/fnins.2015.00183

Rinck, M., Telli, S., Kampmann, I. L., Woud, M. L., Kersholt, M., te Velthuis, S., . . . Becker, E. S. (2013). Training approach-avoidance of smiling faces affects emotional vulnerability in socially anxious individuals. *Frontiers in Human Neuroscience*, *7*. https://doi.org/10.3389/fnhum.2013.00481

Roelofs, K., Elzinga, B. M., & Rotteveel, M. (2005). The effects of stress-induced cortisol responses on approach – avoidance behavior. *Psychoneuroendocrinology*, *30*(7), 665–677. https://doi.org/10.1016/j.psyneuen.2005.02.008

Roelofs, K., Hagenaars, M. A., & Stins, J. (2010). Facing freeze: Social threat induces bodily freeze in humans. *Psychological Science*, *21*(11), 1575–1581. https://doi.org/10.1177/0956797610384746

Roelofs, K., Minelli, A., Mars, R. B., van Peer, J., & Toni, I. (2009). On the neural control of social emotional behavior. *Social Cognitive and Affective Neuroscience*, *4*(1), 50–58. https://doi.org/10.1093/scan/nsn036

Roelofs, K., Putman, P., Schouten, S., Lange, W-G., Volman, I., & Rinck, M. (2010). Gaze direction differentially affects avoidance tendencies to happy and angry faces in socially anxious individuals. *Behaviour Research and Therapy*, *48*(4), 290–294. https://doi.org/10.1016/j.brat.2009.11.008

Roelofs, K., van Peer, J., Berretty, E., de Jong, P., Spinhoven, P., & Elzinga, B. M. (2009). Hypothalamus-pituitary-adrenal axis hyperresponsiveness is associated with increased social avoidance behavior in social phobia. *Biological Psychiatry*, *65*(4), 336–343. https://doi.org/10.1016/j.biopsych.2008.08.022

Rolls, E. T. (1999). *The brain and emotion*. Oxford: Oxford University Press.

Rolls, E. T. (2000). On the brain and emotion. *Behavioral and Brain Sciences*, *23*(2), 219–228. https://doi.org/10.1017/S0140525X00512424

Ross, H. E., & Young, L. J. (2009). Oxytocin and the neural mechanisms regulating social cognition and affiliative behavior. *Frontiers in Neuroendocrinology*, *30*(4), 534–547. https://doi.org/10.1016/j.yfrne.2009.05.004

Rotteveel, M., & Phaf, R. H. (2004). Automatic affective evaluation does not automatically predispose for arm flexion and extension. *Emotion*, *4*(2), 156–172. https://doi.org/10.1037/1528-3542.4.2.156

Rudaz, M., Ledermann, T., Margraf, J., Becker, E. S., & Craske, M. G. (2017). The moderating role of avoidance behavior on anxiety over time: Is there a difference between social anxiety disorder and specific phobia? *PLoS One*, *12*(7). https://doi.org/10.1371/journal.pone.0180298

Sapolsky, R. M. (1990). A. E. Bennett Award paper. Adrenocortical function, social rank, and personality among wild baboons. *Biological Psychiatry*, *28*(10), 862–878.

Sapolsky, R. M. (1991). Testicular function, social rank and personality among wild baboons. *Psychoneuroendocrinology*, *16*(4), 281–293.

Sapolsky, R. M., Romero, L. M., & Munck, A. U. (2000). How do glucocorticoids influence stress responses? Integrating permissive, suppressive, stimulatory, and preparative actions. *Endocrine Reviews*, *21*(1), 55–89. https://doi.org/10.1210/edrv.21.1.0389

Schneier, F. R., Kent, J. M., Star, A., & Hirsch, J. (2009). Neural circuitry of submissive behavior in social anxiety disorder: A preliminary study of response to direct eye gaze. *Psychiatry Research*, *173*(3), 248–250. https://doi.org/10.1016/j.pscychresns.2008.06.004

Schutter, D. J. L. G., & van Honk, J. (2004). Decoupling of midfrontal delta-beta oscillations after testosterone administration. *International Journal of Psychophysiology: Official Journal of the International Organization of Psychophysiology*, *53*(1), 71–73. https://doi.org/10.1016/j.ijpsycho.2003.12.012

Schutter, D. J. L. G., & van Honk, J. (2005). Salivary cortisol levels and the coupling of midfrontal delta-beta oscillations. *International Journal of Psychophysiology: Official Journal of the International Organization of Psychophysiology*, *55*(1), 127–129. https://doi.org/10.1016/j.ijpsycho.2004.07.003

Shamay-Tsoory, S. G., & Abu-Akel, A. (2016). The social salience hypothesis of oxytocin. *Biological Psychiatry*, *79*(3), 194–202. https://doi.org/10.1016/j.biopsych.2015.07.020

Singewald, N., Schmuckermair, C., Whittle, N., Holmes, A., & Ressler, K. J. (2015). Pharmacology of cognitive enhancers for exposure-based therapy of fear, anxiety and trauma-related disorders. *Pharmacology & Therapeutics*, *149*, 150–190. https://doi.org/10.1016/j.pharmthera.2014.12.004

Soravia, L. M., Heinrichs, M., Aerni, A., Maroni, C., Schelling, G., Ehlert, U., . . . de Quervain, D. J.-F. (2006). Glucocorticoids reduce phobic fear in humans. *Proceedings of the National Academy of Sciences, 103*(14), 5585–5590. https://doi.org/10.1073/pnas.0509184103

Stålenheim, E. G., Eriksson, E., von Knorring, L., & Wide, L. (1998). Testosterone as a biological marker in psychopathy and alcoholism. *Psychiatry Research, 77*(2), 79–88.

Stanton, S. J., & Schultheiss, O. C. (2009). The hormonal correlates of implicit power motivation. *Journal of Research in Personality, 43*(5), 942–949. https://doi.org/10.1016/j.jrp.2009.04.001

Stein, M. B., & Stein, D. J. (2008). Social anxiety disorder. *Lancet, 371*(9618), 1115–1125. https://doi.org/10.1016/S0140-6736(08)60488-2

Taylor, C. T., & Amir, N. (2012). Modifying automatic approach action tendencies in individuals with elevated social anxiety symptoms. *Behaviour Research and Therapy, 50*(9), 529–536. https://doi.org/10.1016/j.brat.2012.05.004

Terburg, D., Morgan, B., & van Honk, J. (2009). The testosterone-cortisol ratio: A hormonal marker for proneness to social aggression. *International Journal of Law and Psychiatry, 32*(4), 216–223. https://doi.org/10.1016/j.ijlp.2009.04.008

Turk, C. L., Lerner, J., Heimberg, R. G., & Rapee, R. M. (2001). An integrated cognitive – behavioral model of social anxiety. In S. G. Hofmann & P. M. DiBartolo (Eds.), *From social anxiety to social phobia: Multiple perspectives* (pp. 281–303). Needham Heights, MA: Allyn and Bacon.

van der Wee, N. J., van Veen, J. F., Stevens, H., van Vliet, I. M., Rijk, P. P., & Westenberg, H. G. (2008). Increased serotonin and dopamine transporter binding in psychotropic medication – naïve patients with generalized social anxiety disorder shown by 123I-β-(4-Iodophenyl)-Tropane SPECT. *Journal of Nuclear Medicine, 49*(5), 757–763. https://doi.org/10.2967/jnumed.107.045518

van Honk, J., Bos, P. A., Terburg, D., Heany, S., & Stein, D. J. (2015). Neuroendocrine models of social anxiety disorder. *Dialogues in Clinical Neuroscience, 17*(3), 287–293.

van Honk, J., & Schutter, D. J. L. G. (2006). Unmasking feigned sanity: A neurobiological model of emotion processing in primary psychopathy. *Cognitive Neuropsychiatry, 11*(3), 285–306. https://doi.org/10.1080/13546800500233728

van Honk, J., Terburg, D., & Bos, P. A. (2011). Further notes on testosterone as a social hormone. *Trends in Cognitive Sciences, 15*(7), 291–292. https://doi.org/10.1016/j.tics.2011.05.003

van Honk, J., Tuiten, A., Verbaten, R., van den Hout, M., Koppeschaar, H., Thijssen, J., & de Haan, E. (1999). Correlations among salivary testosterone, mood, and selective attention to threat in humans. *Hormones and Behavior, 36*(1), 17–24. https://doi.org/10.1006/hbeh.1999.1521

van Peer, J. M., Enter, D., van Steenbergen, H., Spinhoven, P., & Roelofs, K. (2017). Exogenous testosterone affects early threat processing in socially anxious and healthy women. *Biological Psychology, 129*, 82–89. https://doi.org/10.1016/j.biopsycho.2017.08.003

van Peer, J. M., Roelofs, K., Rotteveel, M., van Dijk, J. G., Spinhoven, P., & Ridderinkhof, K. R. (2007). The effects of cortisol administration on approach – avoidance behavior: An event-related potential study. *Biological Psychology, 76*(3), 135–146. https://doi.org/10.1016/j.biopsycho.2007.07.003

van Peer, J. M., Roelofs, K., & Spinhoven, P. (2008). Cortisol administration enhances the coupling of midfrontal delta and beta oscillations. *International Journal of Psychophysiology, 67*(2), 144–150. https://doi.org/10.1016/j.ijpsycho.2007.11.001

van Peer, J. M., Spinhoven, P., Dijk, J. G. van, & Roelofs, K. (2009). Cortisol-induced enhancement of emotional face processing in social phobia depends on symptom severity and motivational context. *Biological Psychology, 81*(2), 123–130. https://doi.org/10.1016/j.biopsycho.2009.03.006

van Peer, J. M., Spinhoven, P., & Roelofs, K. (2010). Psychophysiological evidence for cortisol-induced reduction in early bias for implicit social threat in social phobia. *Psychoneuroendocrinology, 35*(1), 21–32. https://doi.org/10.1016/j.psyneuen.2009.09.012

van Wingen, G., Mattern, C., Verkes, R. J., Buitelaar, J., & Fernández, G. (2010). Testosterone reduces amygdala – orbitofrontal cortex coupling. *Psychoneuroendocrinology, 35*(1), 105–113. https://doi.org/10.1016/j.psyneuen.2009.09.007

Viau, V. (2002). Functional cross-talk between the hypothalamic-pituitary-gonadal and -adrenal axes. *Journal of Neuroendocrinology, 14*(6), 506–513. https://doi.org/10.1046/j.1365-2826.2002.00798.x

Volman, I., Roelofs, K., Koch, S., Verhagen, L., & Toni, I. (2011). Anterior prefrontal cortex inhibition impairs control over social emotional actions. *Current Biology, 21*(20), 1766–1770. https://doi.org/10.1016/j.cub.2011.08.050

Volman, I., Toni, I., Verhagen, L., & Roelofs, K. (2011). Endogenous testosterone modulates prefrontal-amygdala connectivity during social emotional behavior. *Cerebral Cortex, 21*(10), 2282–2290. https://doi.org/10.1093/cercor/bhr001

Volman, I., Verhagen, L., den Ouden, H. E. M., Fernandez, G., Rijpkema, M., Franke, B., . . . Roelofs, K. (2013). Reduced serotonin transporter availability decreases prefrontal control of the amygdala. *Journal of Neuroscience, 33*(21), 8974–8979. https://doi.org/10.1523/JNEUROSCI.5518-12.2013

Volman, I., von Borries, A. K. L., Bulten, B. H., Verkes, R. J., Toni, I., & Roelofs, K. (2016). Testosterone modulates altered prefrontal control of emotional actions in psychopathic offenders (1,2,3). *ENeuro, 3*(1). https://doi.org/10.1523/ENEURO.0107-15.2016

von Borries, A. K. L., Volman, I., de Bruijn, E. R. A., Bulten, B. H., Verkes, R. J., & Roelofs, K. (2012). Psychopaths lack the automatic avoidance of social threat: Relation to instrumental aggression. *Psychiatry Research, 200*(2–3), 761–766. https://doi.org/10.1016/j.psychres.2012.06.026

Wager, T. D., Davidson, M. L., Hughes, B. L., Lindquist, M. A., & Ochsner, K. N. (2008). Prefrontal-subcortical pathways mediating successful emotion regulation. *Neuron, 59*(6), 1037–1050. https://doi.org/10.1016/j.neuron.2008.09.006

Walum, H., Waldman, I. D., & Young, L. J. (2016). Statistical and methodological considerations for the interpretation of intranasal oxytocin studies. *Biological Psychiatry, 79*(3), 251–257. https://doi.org/10.1016/j.biopsych.2015.06.016

Welker, K. M., Gruber, J., & Mehta, P. H. (2015). A positive affective neuroendocrinology approach to reward and behavioral dysregulation. *Frontiers in Psychiatry, 6*, 93. https://doi.org/10.3389/fpsyt.2015.00093

Welker, K. M., Lozoya, E., Campbell, J. A., Neumann, C. S., & Carré, J. M. (2014). Testosterone, cortisol, and psychopathic traits in men and women. *Physiology & Behavior, 129*, 230–236. https://doi.org/10.1016/j.physbeh.2014.02.057

Wiers, C. E., Stelzel, C., Park, S. Q., Gawron, C. K., Ludwig, V. U., Gutwinski, S., . . . Bermpohl, F. (2014). Neural correlates of alcohol-approach bias in alcohol addiction: The spirit is willing but the flesh is weak for spirits. *Neuropsychopharmacology, 39*(3), 688–697. https://doi.org/10.1038/npp.2013.252

Wingfield, J. C., Hegner, R. E., Dufty, A. M., Jr., & Ball, G. F. (1990). The "challenge hypothesis": Theoretical implications for patterns of testosterone secretion, mating systems, and breeding strategies. *The American Naturalist, 136*, 829–846.

Wolf, R. C., Pujara, M. S., Motzkin, J. C., Newman, J. P., Kiehl, K. A., Decety, J., . . . Koenigs, M. (2015). Interpersonal traits of psychopathy linked to reduced integrity of the uncinate fasciculus. *Human Brain Mapping, 36*(10), 4202–4209. https://doi.org/10.1002/hbm.22911

Wong, Q. J. J., & Moulds, M. L. (2011). The relationship between the maladaptive self-beliefs characteristic of social anxiety and avoidance. *Journal of Behavior Therapy and Experimental Psychiatry, 42*(2), 171–178. https://doi.org/10.1016/j.jbtep.2010.11.004

Wood, R. I. (1996). Functions of the steroid-responsive neural network in the control of male hamster sexual behavior. *Trends in Endocrinology and Metabolism: TEM, 7*(9), 338–344.

Wood, R. I. (2008). Anabolic-androgenic steroid dependence? Insights from animals and humans. *Frontiers in Neuroendocrinology, 29*(4), 490–506. https://doi.org/10.1016/j.yfrne.2007.12.002

Woud, M. L., & Becker, E. S. (2014). Editorial for the special issue on cognitive bias modification techniques: An introduction to a time traveller's tale. *Cognitive Therapy and Research, 38*(2), 83–88. https://doi.org/10.1007/s10608-014-9605-0

Yacubian, J., & Büchel, C. (2009). The genetic basis of individual differences in reward processing and the link to addictive behavior and social cognition. *Neuroscience, 164*(1), 55–71. https://doi.org/10.1016/j.neuroscience.2009.05.015

Yamasue, H. (2016). Promising evidence and remaining issues regarding the clinical application of oxytocin in autism spectrum disorders. *Psychiatry and Clinical Neurosciences, 70*(2), 89–99. https://doi.org/10.1111/pcn.12364

Yildirim, B. O., & Derksen, J. J. L. (2012). A review on the relationship between testosterone and the interpersonal/affective facet of psychopathy. *Psychiatry Research, 197*(3), 181–198. https://doi.org/10.1016/j.psychres.2011.08.016

35

THE SOCIAL NEUROENDOCRINOLOGY OF TRAUMA AND POST-TRAUMATIC STRESS DISORDER

Amy Lehrner and Rachel Yehuda

Introduction

The emergent field of social neuroendocrinology, with its emphasis on understanding hormones, brain, and behavior within their social contexts, provides a unique analytic framework for understanding the effects of psychological trauma. Post-trauma mental health disorders are unlike other psychiatric disorders in that they, by definition, develop in response to a life-threatening experience. While trauma exposure does not always result in post-traumatic stress disorder (PTSD), it is a diagnostically necessary precipitant. The necessary environmental precipitant of PTSD and the other stressor-related disorders (acute stress disorder, adjustment disorders, reactive attachment disorder, disinhibited social engagement disorder (American Psychiatric Association, 2013)) invites examination of the interplay between social and biological processes.

This chapter provides a brief overview of the literature on the neuroendocrinology of trauma and PTSD with an emphasis on the relevance of social context for risk, resilience, disorder, and recovery. The influence of trauma-related neuroendocrinology on social behavior, such as sex and violence, will be explored and lacunae in the literature will be highlighted.

Psychological trauma and PTSD

Although the concept of trauma is widely used in everyday language and popular culture, the Diagnostic and Statistical Manual of Mental Disorders (DSM; American Psychiatric Association, 2013) – the dominant diagnostic nosological framework in the United States – defines specific kinds of traumatic events that may lead to a diagnosis of PTSD. This definition privileges experiences of threat to life or bodily integrity, which will be critical to understanding hormonal and behavioral sequelae. Although this definition has been criticized as not fully encompassing the totality of experiences that many people find highly distressing and potentially life changing (Hoge et al., 2016), the current DSM definition of trauma is exposure to "actual or threatened death, serious injury or sexual violation" (American Psychiatric Association, 2013).

When PTSD was first codified in the DSM, it was conceptualized as the normative, expected response to an extremely rare event. Through the Western eyes of those involved in formulating and describing the diagnosis, the experience of a monumental trauma was seen as unusual. Prolonged symptoms following such an event were the expected response. In this sense, the social context was seen to have a deterministic influence on subsequent functioning. However, following the formalization of the disorder, epidemiological research was undertaken to gather data on the incidence and prevalence of trauma and PTSD. Such research revealed that trauma exposure is a relatively common, if potentially hidden, experience, and that it is the subsequent development of PTSD that is the rare outcome. Recent survey data documented that the vast majority (89.7%) of U.S. adults have experienced at least one DSM-5 Criterion A trauma, with 53.1% reporting interpersonal victimization and 29.7% reporting sexual assault (Kilpatrick et al., 2013). Epidemiological research using representative samples suggests that among adults in the U.S., lifetime prevalence rates of PTSD are approximately 9.4%. Women are more than twice as likely to have had PTSD than men (12.8% versus 5.7%, respectively).

Although diagnostic criteria for PTSD have changed over time as the DSM has been revised, diagnostic criteria for core symptoms have not changed. In its current iteration, the diagnosis of PTSD requires the following symptoms following a Criterion A trauma: 1) persistent re-experiencing of the event, such as intrusive thoughts, nightmares, flashbacks, and physical or emotional reactivity after a reminder (one symptom required); 2) avoidance of trauma-related thoughts or feelings, or trauma-related reminders (such as people, places, or activities); 3) pervasive and distorted negative thoughts or feelings, such as negative thoughts about oneself, others, or the world, self-blame, negative emotional states, inability to recall important aspects of the trauma (i.e., traumatic amnesia), loss of interest in activities, feeling estranged or isolated, and difficulty experiencing positive emotions (two symptoms required); and 4) trauma-related arousal and reactivity, such as irritability or aggression, hypervigilance, heightened startle reaction, difficulty concentrating or sleeping, and risky behavior (two symptoms required). A notable change in DSM-5 from the previous version is the removal of the diagnostic criterion requiring an acute emotional response (fear, horror, or helplessness) to the trauma. To warrant a diagnosis of PTSD, these symptoms must begin or worsen following the trauma; they must last for more than a month; they must not be due to medication, substance use, or other illness; and they must cause significant distress or functional impairment (e.g., social, occupational, self-care). Of note, the revised diagnostic criteria of PTSD have been criticized as lacking in precision (Hoge et al., 2016), and in fact there are now more than half a million possible symptom combinations that would meet the diagnostic criteria of PTSD (Galatzer-Levy & Bryant, 2013), contributing to significant phenotypic heterogeneity. These changes make clear that it is not only the mental disorder that is socially embedded, but also the construct definition itself. Changes in diagnostic criteria and conceptualizations of the nature of the phenomenon are decided and contested within a social context.

Social neuroendocrinology of PTSD

Hypothalamic–pituitary–adrenal (HPA) axis response to trauma

Survival is one of our most profound and instinctual imperatives. Humans, like other animals, mount a "fight–flight–freeze" response to acute life threat in order to maximize the chance of survival. This response is rapidly implemented hormonally, neuronally, and behaviorally before higher-order cognitive functions go online for conscious decision making. The threat response prepares the organism to fight, escape, or survive. The sympathetic nervous system (SNS) and hypothalamic–pituitary–adrenal (HPA) axis are central to the acute threat response (Sapolsky, 2002). Upon perception of a threat by the amygdala, the SNS is activated, rapidly releasing catecholamines such as norepinephrine and epinephrine. Heart rate accelerates, blood pressure increases, and pupils dilate. In preparation to fight or flee, blood flows to large muscles in the extremities, oxygen intake increases, digestion slows, the immune system shuts down, and attention becomes acutely focused through loss of peripheral vision.

Concurrently, the release of cortisol initiates a glucocorticoid signaling cascade through the HPA axis and across multiple biological systems. Under conditions of threat, the paraventricular nucleus of the hypothalamus rapidly synthesizes and secretes corticotropin releasing hormone (CRH) and arginine vasopressin (AVP). These peptides stimulate the anterior pituitary to secrete adrenocorticotropic hormone (ACTH), which in turn stimulates the adrenal cortex to produce cortisol. Cortisol, the main stress hormone in humans, has many effects on the body. Rapid, stress-related release of cortisol (in conjunction with catecholamines) ensures an adequate burst of energy through increased blood sugar, blood pressure, and suppressed immune system. In the brain, cortisol primarily binds with high affinity mineral glucocorticoid receptors. However, under stressful conditions it also binds to low affinity glucocorticoid receptors as the mineral glucocorticoid receptors become saturated. This glucocorticoid binding initiates a negative feedback loop at the hypothalamus and pituitary that downregulates the HPA axis, slowing further release of CRH, AVP, ACTH, and cortisol. Ultimately, this process leads to homeostasis as the hormonal milieu returns to baseline following resolution of the threat (McEwen, 1998). The stress response has been very well described as a reaction occurring in all organisms exposed to threat (Chrousos & Gold, 1992; De Kloet, Joëls, & Holsboer, 2005). The question one can raise is the extent to which these rather normal responses occurring at the time of challenge are relevant to the biobehavioral response that ensues.

Adaptivity depends on context

The organism's immediate physiological and behavioral response to threat depends in part on the context – the assessed likelihood of surviving a fight, opportunity to flee, degree of immobility, etc. As with many aspects of human behavior, the flexibility of this response is adaptive, allowing for social–contextual information to inform and interact with the neuroendocrine system. The individual's social information processing skills (which influence the interpretation of potentially ambiguous stimuli), life history (e.g., past experiences of threat, coping style), personality, and hormonal milieu interact with the perception of control over the situation and other situational factors to shape a behavioral response that leverages these factors for maximum efficacy. After surviving a traumatic threat, the ability to store and retrieve threat memories, with acute sensitivity to contextual cues rendered salient by the trauma, is evolutionarily adaptive. In individuals with PTSD, however, the healthy and adaptive response to trauma goes into overdrive. The trauma feels ever-present, emerging in nightmares and intrusive images, triggering panic at reminders and requiring constant hypervigilance against a perpetual sense of threat and dread. The context has changed, but the memory does not recede, even years after the trauma. In some ways, PTSD represents a mismatch between the social context and the individual's psychological, behavioral, and biological state.

HPA axis in PTSD

Because people with PTSD present themselves as persons who are still in some way responding to a threat (e.g., hypervigilance, heightened startle, intrusive images, insomnia), initial theorizing about PTSD started from the assumption that the pathophysiology of the disorder would mirror an exaggerated stress response. Starting from healthy HPA axis functioning, such an assumption predicted chronically heightened cortisol, reflecting an activated threat response. However, initial studies found relatively low basal cortisol levels, heightened HPA axis negative feedback inhibition as evidenced by an exaggerated suppression of cortisol following dexamethasone administration, and heightened peripheral and central catecholamines in individuals with PTSD (Bremner, Vermetten, & Kelley, 2007; Yehuda et al., 1990). These seemingly paradoxical findings have led to a central hypothesis in the literature: that PTSD represents a failure of the organism to contain the threat response and return to homeostasis (Yehuda, 2002). Adequate levels of cortisol are required for negative feedback and down-regulation of the SNS system. Without such a glucocorticoid cascade, the result may be a prolonged and potentially intensified SNS response. The extended and elevated levels of catecholamines have been hypothesized to contribute to arousal and hypervigilance symptoms and reinforcement of avoidance behaviors (Yehuda, 2002). While glucocorticoid alterations in PTSD have been widely reported, findings have been mixed, and it has been difficult to establish whether low cortisol and attenuated glucocorticoid receptor sensitivity is a consequence of trauma exposure, a biomarker of PTSD, or a pre-existing risk factor reflecting individual differences in biology or adverse early experiences (Lehrner, Daskalakis, & Yehuda, 2016; Morris, Compas, & Garber, 2012). Differences in sampling and biological methods, the presence of comorbid disorders or histories of previous trauma, the influence of diurnal and circadian rhythms, and underpowered studies likely contribute to mixed findings and complicate interpretation. However, the inability to link PTSD with high levels of cortisol – which should be the case in those who are under chronic or extreme stress – was an observation worthy of follow up because it represented a clue that PTSD may not simply represent the standard biological response to a stressor.

In addition to low basal levels of cortisol, potential mechanisms that may influence the disrupted HPA axis recovery observed in PTSD, and confer increased risk or resilience, include heightened glucocorticoid receptor sensitivity and genetic and epigenetic factors. Higher glucocorticoid receptor sensitivity or density could account for lower levels of basal or acute peri-traumatic cortisol through rapid uptake of cortisol such that there is inadequate circulating cortisol to trigger the negative feedback loop at the hypothalamus and pituitary. The low-dose dexamethasone suppression test (DST) is widely used to test glucocorticoid receptor sensitivity in response to a glucocorticoid challenge. Individuals with PTSD demonstrate an exaggerated response to the DST indicative of glucocorticoid receptor hypersensitivity (Yehuda, Halligan, Golier, Grossman, & Bierer, 2004; Yehuda, Southwick et al., 1993). In vitro assays of glucocorticoid sensitivity in lymphocytes also indicate higher glucocorticoid sensitivity in PTSD (Yehuda, Golier, Yang, & Tischler, 2004). Animal models corroborate these findings. Brain and blood glucocorticoid receptor signaling is associated with differences in the behavioral response to predator scent stress in a rat model of PTSD; specifically, the glucocorticoid signaling pathway is associated with an extreme behavioral response to a stressor, considered a "PTSD-like" vulnerability (Daskalakis, Cohen, Cai, Buxbaum, & Yehuda, 2014). Individuals with PTSD have a greater number of glucocorticoid receptors than those with any other psychiatric disorder (Yehuda, Boisoneau, Mason, & Giller, 1993), and combat veterans with PTSD have shown a higher density of glucocorticoid receptors than those without PTSD (Yehuda, Lowy, Southwick, Shaffer, & Giller, 1991). Genetic and epigenetic factors that may contribute to disrupted HPA axis functioning in PTSD are beyond the scope of this chapter; recent reviews include Mehta and Binder (2012) and Yehuda, Koenen, Galea, and Flory (2011).

Social neuroendocrinology of risk and resilience factors

The foregoing describes a flexible and adaptive repertoire of survival processes and behaviors that can be mobilized in the face of threat, and alterations in neuroendocrinology that may reflect the pathophysiology of PTSD. However, it is clear that neither the experience of trauma nor the biological response to it are adequate to predict who will recover and who will remain trapped in their memories. A social neuroendocrinology approach highlights the multifactorial nature of PTSD, as myriad aspects of the social and hormonal milieu prior to, during, and following a traumatic experience interact to influence risk of disorder or resilience.

Pre-traumatic risk factors

Whereas there are some individuals who experience a single discrete trauma in the context of a life lived in relative safety (e.g., an accident or natural disaster), epidemiological data makes clear that for many others, the trauma understood to be the immediate precipitant of PTSD follows a lifetime of trauma exposure, which may include child abuse, family violence, community violence, and sexual assault. Research that takes a developmental approach, including early life adversity, has identified interactions of biological risk factors with environmental insults that sensitize the individual to later trauma and subsequent psychopathology (Daskalakis, Bagot, Parker, Vinkers, & de Kloet, 2013). Pre-traumatic risk factors include experiential, psychological, and biological factors from *in utero* to adulthood. Across meta-analyses, childhood abuse or trauma has consistently been found to confer risk for subsequent PTSD (Brewin, Andrews, & Valentine, 2000; Ozer, Best, Lipsey, & Weiss, 2003). Prior psychological problems, which may indicate poor adaptation to early stressors or biological vulnerability, and family history of psychopathology also increase risk for PTSD, and all of these social factors may be mediated by neuroendocrinology.

The HPA axis is a dynamic system that can recalibrate in response to environmental and biological demands, and there may be developmental windows of plasticity during which there is increased vulnerability to stress or trauma, or during which resilient pathways or mechanisms are strengthened. The HPA axis and related brain regions begin to develop prenatally, and stress-induced adaptation in its development may begin *in utero* (Welberg & Seckl, 2001). For example, a study of women who were directly exposed to the World Trade Center attack on 9/11/01 during pregnancy found lower cortisol levels in mothers who developed PTSD and in their one-year-old babies (Yehuda et al., 2005). Furthermore, there was a trimester effect such that lower cortisol levels were observed in babies of mothers exposed during the third trimester, highlighting the relevance of developmental windows on HPA axis development. There are *in utero* protections against the effect of maternal stress hormones on the developing HPA axis, particularly placental 11B-hydroxysteroid dehydrogenase type 2 (11B-HSD2), which minimizes corticosteroid exposure to the fetus. However, repeated maternal stress exposure reduces 11B-HSD2 and allows fetal corticosteroid exposure, which may influence fetal HPA axis development. Animal models show that postnatal prolonged or chronic separation induced stress sensitizes components of the HPA axis (van Bodegom, Homberg, & Henckens, 2017). Epigenetic modifications may also mediate the effects of maternal stress on offspring; a recent meta-analysis of 977 participants identified a positive correlation between methylation levels at CpG site 36 at the 1F promoter region of the NR3C1 gene, which is the glucocorticoid receptor gene, and prenatal stress (Palma-Gudiel, Cordova-Palomera, Eixarch, Deuschle, & Fananas, 2015). Such sensitization may confer adaptive advantage to offspring born into social environments of high threat or challenge but may also confer vulnerability to psychiatric disorder.

There is an extensive clinical and pre-clinical literature on the impact of early life stress on the neuroendocrinology of the developing organism (Murgatroyd et al., 2009; Tarullo & Gunnar, 2006). In animals, early life stress exposure associated specifically with early social deprivation has been linked with HPA axis hypoactivity similar to that observed in PTSD, whereas stress related to prenatal influences, maternal separation, or fragmented maternal care have been linked with HPA axis hyperreactivity consistent with that observed in major depression (van Bodegom et al., 2017). Early social deprivation isolates pups from both mother and litter mates and houses them in a novel environment, considered an extreme and acute (although possibly recurrent) stressor. In humans, severely stressed children have also demonstrated low basal cortisol (van Bodegom et al., 2017). A recent meta-analysis of 4,292 individuals ranging from children to adults identified an association between early life adversity and blunted cortisol response to social stress (g = −0.39), an association that was strongest in adults, and among those reporting childhood maltreatment compared with other adversities (Bunea, Szentágotai-Tătar, & Miu, 2017). These patterns of association highlight the long-term impact maltreatment may have on the developing HPA axis, with reduced cortisol reactivity to stress apparent in adulthood, long after the abuse. Research on the effects of early life stress in humans has led to the hypothesis that hypocortisolism can result from chronic traumatization involving sustained HPA axis stress reactivity (Fries, Hesse, Hellhammer, & Hellhammer, 2005; Trickett, Noll, Susman, Shenk, & Putnam, 2010). Developmental timing of the stressor and type of trauma likely influence the nature of HPA axis dysregulation. This literature points to the exquisite sensitivity during programming of the HPA axis to social and environmental variations, even prenatal and neonatal stressors, and the long lasting adaptations that can occur after sustained periods of threat.

Later trauma exposure in adolescence or adulthood also increases vulnerability to PTSD following a subsequent trauma (Breslau, Chilcoat, Kessler, & Davis, 1999), and a more sensitized HPA axis characterized by low cortisol levels and enhanced glucocorticoid sensitivity may partially mediate this risk (Yehuda, McFarlane, & Shalev, 1998). For example, among adult female rape victims assessed in a hospital emergency department in the aftermath of the assault, those with a history of prior assault had lower cortisol levels and were more likely to develop PTSD after the rape (Resnick, Yehuda, Pitman, & Foy, 1995). A comprehensive developmental approach recognizes the dynamic interaction of the stress response system and the social environment across the entire lifespan. Later enrichment following early adversity may reverse or otherwise buffer early developmental programming (Morley-Fletcher, Rea, Maccari, & Laviola, 2003), or conversely, chronic social stressors such as racism and poverty may potentiate such programming (Jackson, Knight, & Rafferty, 2010), possibly through epigenetic mechanisms.

Genetic, epigenetic, and molecular factors that regulate the HPA axis have all been implicated in pre-trauma risk for PTSD (Mehta & Binder, 2012; Yehuda & Bierer, 2009). For example, the FKBP5 gene, a co-chaperone to the glucocorticoid receptor (GR) gene with a role in the regulation of the HPA axis, has been found to interact with childhood trauma in several cohorts (Binder et al., 2008; K. C. Koenen & Uddin, 2010; Roy, Gorodetsky, Yuan, Goldman, & Enoch, 2010). In a widely cited study, Binder and colleagues (2008) identified four FKBP5 polymorphisms that interacted with severity of child abuse to predict adult PTSD (Binder et al., 2008). A specific genotype of a known GR polymorphism (BclI GG) has been associated with low basal cortisol and higher PTSD symptom severity among Vietnam era veterans with PTSD (Bachmann et al., 2005). A prospective study of 448 male soldiers assessed prior to combat zone deployment found that variations in the GR pathway predicted postdeployment development of PTSD. Significant predictors were: high numbers of GR, low FKBP5 mRNA expression, and high GILZ (a GR target gene) mRNA expression (Van Zuiden et al., 2012). Furthermore, there was an interaction of a GR haplotype with childhood trauma on GR number. This literature increasingly shows the importance of environmental stimuli in potentiating individual differences in genetic, molecular, and neuroendocrine factors along the glucocorticoid signaling pathway.

The influence of pre-traumatic risk factors, from prenatal to early life stress to trauma in adulthood, reflects the importance of context in rendering an adaptation either health- or disease-promoting. Hypervigilance to threat may be adaptive in a dangerous environment but maladaptive in conditions of relative safety. Thus, early life stress can confer advantage or disadvantage for later environmental challenges, as reflected in the match/mismatch hypothesis (Santarelli et al., 2014). Pre-trauma risk factors are also likely mediated by other, more proximal factors, such as the severity of the trauma, the presence of injury, the person's response to the trauma, and the degree of social support received.

Peri-traumatic risk factors

Trauma severity and chronicity have been shown to increase risk of PTSD, as does the perception of life threat, intensity of peri-traumatic emotional response, and experience of peri-traumatic dissociation (Ozer et al., 2003). A series of biologic studies of trauma survivors in the acute aftermath of trauma, specifically in the emergency department, have identified peri-traumatic cortisol reactivity as a predictor of the development of PTSD, although negative findings have also been published (Bonne et al., 2003; Shalev et al., 2008). Similar to the study of rape survivors described above, victims of motor vehicle accidents admitted to hospital who subsequently developed PTSD demonstrated lower serum and urinary acute cortisol levels compared to those who did not develop the disorder (Delahanty, Raimonde, & Spoonster, 2000; McFarlane, Atchison, & Yehuda, 1997). Importantly, these biological risk factors were observed prior the development of disorder and were stronger predictors than post-traumatic emotional or behavioral symptoms assessed concurrently with the biological collections. Experimental work provides additional support for the hypothesis that the failure to mount an adequate glucocorticoid response to threat may contribute to risk for PTSD. Urban police officers who demonstrated a blunted cortisol response to an experimental stressor were more likely to follow a trajectory of chronic, increasing distress over four years of active duty than those who showed an acute rise in cortisol, which was associated with resilience and recovery trajectories (Galatzer-Levy et al., 2014).

Peri-traumatic dissociation, a risk factor for PTSD, is considered an analog of immobilization/freezing in animals and may have unique neuroendocrine and brain function correlates. For example, there is preliminary evidence for an association of two of the same FKBP5 polymorphisms studied by Binder et al. (2004) with peri-traumatic dissociation in children with acute medical injuries assessed following admission to hospital (Koenen et al., 2005). In a prospective study of police recruits, a greater salivary cortisol awakening response prior to law enforcement critical incident exposure was associated with peri-traumatic dissociation over a three-year period but not with development of PTSD symptoms (Inslicht et al., 2011).

Post-traumatic risk factors

One of the most robust findings in the risk literature is the influence of perceived post-traumatic social support and additional post-traumatic life stress on the development of PTSD symptoms and diagnosis. For example, a meta-analysis analyzing 14 putative risk factors, including childhood abuse, previous trauma, and psychiatric history, drawn from 77 articles, found that lack of social support demonstrated the single greatest effect size (weighted average r = .40, range of effect size = −0.02–00.54; effect size for other risk factors range = 0.05–00.32) (Brewin et al.,

2000). These effects were unchanged based on gender, retrospective vs. prospective design, or whether the trauma occurred in childhood. A second widely cited meta-analysis also identified social support as a significant predictor (weighted $r = |.28|$), the effects of which were stronger when time since trauma was greater than three years (Ozer et al., 2003). Charuvastra and Cloitre (2008) propose a "social ecology of PTSD," emphasizing the centrality of social factors such as support, social cognition, and attachment in the development of PTSD. They note the potential relevance and distinctive nature of both positive and negative social responses. Positive social support after trauma has been shown to promote resilience across a wide variety of populations, for example among Vietnam veterans, prisoners of war, civilians exposed to civil war, children exposed to physical and sexual abuse, rape survivors, and multiply traumatized women (Charuvastra & Cloitre, 2008).

Research attempting to identify the neurobiological signatures or mechanisms through which these risk factors operate is limited. Social support is associated with myriad physiological and neuroendocrine indicators of stress and disease, such as blood pressure, heart rate, and atherosclerosis, and may influence risk and resilience through effects on the HPA axis, the noradrenergic system, and oxytocin (Ozbay et al., 2007). The role of social support and oxytocin are reviewed in more detail below.

Social implications of trauma-related neuroendocrinology

The interplay between hormones, brain, behavior, and the social context in PTSD are particularly crucial for important social behaviors such as intimacy and sexual function, and violence and aggression.

Intimacy, attachment, and sexual function

Problems with sexual function are not explicitly specified as a symptom of PTSD, but difficulty with intimacy and attachment are directly implied. The current diagnostic criteria for PTSD include "feelings of detachment or estrangement from others" and "persistent inability to experience positive emotions (e.g., inability to experience happiness, satisfaction, or loving feelings)" (American Psychiatric Association, 2013). PTSD has been associated with relationship difficulties, including marital separation, divorce, and domestic violence (Marshall, Panuzio, & Taft, 2005; Schnurr, Lunney, Bovin, & Marx, 2009). Feelings of numbness and detachment are antithetical to strong romantic attachment and physical closeness. Additional PTSD symptoms such as hypervigilance, irritability, and avoidance of trauma-related triggers (which may include feelings of vulnerability) further challenge the maintenance or establishment of intimate relationships.

Feelings of detachment and anhedonia have been conceptualized as resulting from dysfunction in the reward system in the brain, compromising the individual's ability to benefit from social support and reducing approach behavior. Inadequate social support is a robust predictor of PTSD following trauma, and impairment in the ability to appreciate and respond to social reward may contribute to a negative cycle of withdrawal, isolation, and rejection that exacerbates PTSD and irreparably damages social relationships. Neuropeptides such as oxytocin and vasopressin have been associated with prosocial, affiliative behavior, and a small body of research has investigated whether these hormones are dysregulated in PTSD and associated with attachment failures and social deficits (Olff, Langeland, Witteveen, & Denys, 2010). For example, male police officers with PTSD demonstrated lower salivary oxytocin than trauma-exposed controls (Frijling et al., 2015). Oxytocin is also known to have anxiolytic effects (Heinrichs, Baumgartner,

Kirschbaum, & Ehlert, 2003), promoting a sense of safety and facilitating a downregulation of the threat response system once the threat is over. The oxytocin system thus engages in cross-talk with the HPA axis, possibly through a reduction in stress-induced cortisol (Cardoso, Ellenbogen, Orlando, Bacon, & Joober, 2013). It is not clear how this relationship works in the context of a hypoactive glucocorticoid response in PTSD, and there have been problems with replication (see Schultheiss & Mehta's chapter in this volume). The hormone progesterone, which has been linked to motivation for affiliation and social contact (Wirth, 2011), may also mediate the effects of social support (Brown et al., 2009), but this has not yet been studied in PTSD.

Research has investigated the potential for oxytocin to improve top-down fear regulation, and to increase feelings of safety, trust, and motivation for social connection, which could potentiate the therapeutic alliance, an important predictor of treatment response. Oxytocin has been suggested as a potential therapeutic agent for PTSD, either alone or in conjunction with psychotherapy, and is currently being investigated, but to date there have been few trials (Olff et al., 2010). Intranasal oxytocin increased baseline skin conductance but did not affect PTSD symptoms in response to personal combat imagery among male Vietnam veterans (Pitman, Orr, & Lasko, 1993), and reduced anxiety, irritability, intensity of thoughts about the trauma, and severity of PTSD symptoms while also improving mood and self-reported desire for social interaction (Yatzkar & Klein, 2010). A within-subject, double-blind, randomized placebo controlled study of 35 female PTSD patients found that intranasal oxytocin led to a reduction in PTSD symptoms, in particular avoidance, following trauma-script provocation (Sack et al., 2017). Importantly, there is increasing evidence that the effects of oxytocin administration vary by important individual differences, including sex, developmental history, and psychiatric status, and by contextual factors (Bartz, Zaki, Bolger, & Ochsner, 2011; Olff et al., 2013). If oxytocin renders the individual more sensitive to social cues, the resulting emotional and behavioral responses will be highly influenced by the perceptual lens of the individual. In other words, oxytocin's effects will not be uniform but will be highly dependent on the social environment and the individual's interpretation of that environment.

The question of whether PTSD-related neuroendocrinology specifically contributes to problems in sexual functioning is an area of growing interest. Initial research on trauma-related problems with sexual function understandably focused on behavioral sequelae of sexual trauma. However, a growing body of research documents problems with sexual function even among those exposed to non-sexual traumas, such as accidents, assaults, and combat (Yehuda, Lehrner, & Rosenbaum, 2015). Furthermore, sexual dysfunction appears to be associated not with trauma exposure *per se*, but with the development of PTSD in its aftermath. Rates of sexual dysfunction in PTSD have been estimated as high as 85% (Cosgrove et al., 2002), and PTSD has been shown to significantly increase the odds of a sexual dysfunction (Breyer et al., 2014; Letourneau, Resnick, Kilpatrick, Saunders, & Best, 1996). It has been hypothesized that sexual function in PTSD may be compromised not only by symptoms such as numbness, avoidance, anhedonia, and irritability, but also by the underlying neurobiology of PTSD (Lehrner, Flory et al., 2016; Yehuda et al., 2015).

The neuroendocrinology of PTSD parallels that of sexual arousal and behavior in many ways. Whether physiological arousal is one of pleasure or fear has everything to do with the context. Impaired glucocorticoid signaling in PTSD may prolong the SNS response with elevations in catecholamines, as described above. This prolonged and intense physiological arousal is paired with a sense of threat and fear. Sexual desire and arousal includes increased heart rate, blood pressure, breathing rate, and muscle tension, followed by rapidly increasing norepinephrine during sexual activity. However, there is a curvilinear relationship of hormones to sexual function. Moderate levels of norepinephrine support optimal sexual behavior but if too elevated, norepinephrine becomes sexually inhibitory. Similarly, moderate levels of cortisol are likely consistent with sexual arousal, but if too high or low they may be inhibiting. Downregulation of the amygdala, medial temporal lobe and ventromedial prefrontal cortex during sexual arousal and orgasm allow physiological arousal to occur in a context in which the brain feels safe. However, an overactive limbic system in PTSD, in which the amygdala is hypersensitive to threat and inhibitory processes are compromised, may override the sexual context. If physiological arousal has been conditioned to imply danger, and physical and emotional vulnerability are felt to increase risk of harm, the inability to downregulate the threat response is likely to have a chilling effect on sexual functioning.

There is some initial evidence in support of this hypothesis. A case report documented the treatment of a 25-year-old man with PTSD who presented to the emergency department with spontaneous ejaculation concurrent with an increase in PTSD symptom severity (Öznur, Akarsu, Karaahmetoğlu, & Doruk, 2014). Organic causes were ruled out and treatment with an SSRI resulted in decreased frequency of ejaculations and PTSD symptoms. The authors hypothesized that the increase in PTSD symptoms activated the adrenergic system to the point that the patient was having spontaneous ejaculation in the absence of any sexual stimuli. Conversely, there are anecdotal reports of intrusive trauma-related imagery apparently triggered by heightened arousal during sexual activity. Preliminary data also showed an association of neuroendocrine indicators, known to be related to PTSD, with sexual problems in male veterans with PTSD (Lehrner et al., 2016). Lower levels of basal plasma DHEA and cortisol, and an attenuated cortisol decline following a low dose dexamethasone suppression test (which assesses HPA axis glucocorticoid sensitivity), were associated with loss of interest in sex in the prior seven days. Heightened catecholamines were associated with problems during sex and intrusive symptoms. In a separate sample of treatment-seeking veterans with PTSD, urinary norepinephrine was associated with difficulty achieving orgasm. There is almost no literature on the treatment of sexual problems in PTSD, but one small, prospective, naturalistic study found that adjunctive sex therapy in combination with PTSD psychotherapy resulted in improvements across all domains of sexual functioning and in PTSD symptoms (Chudakov et al., 2008).

Violence and aggression

Violence and aggression, and the subjective experience of anger and irritability, are symptoms of PTSD and a common complaint in patients seeking treatment. It is surprising, therefore, that despite a literature on the neuroendocrinology of aggression, there is little work investigating potential relationships of biological dysregulations in PTSD with violence and aggression. This is particularly surprising given the close relationship of the HPA axis with hypothalamic–pituitary–gonadal (HPG) axis (Viau, 2002). The HPG axis produces testosterone, which in addition to its function as a sex hormone is involved in the stress response and has effects on mood, cognition, and behavior (including aggression). Cortisol inhibits the HPG axis, suppressing testosterone, and this may contribute to impaired sexual functioning under stress. Conversely, testosterone inhibits HPA axis activity, suppressing ACTH and glucocorticoids and confers direct anxiolytic effects. Testosterone effects are also potentiated by vasopressin and estradiol. In addition, low cortisol has been associated with aggression in experimental and clinical samples (McBurnett, Lahey, Rathouz, & Loeber, 2000; Oxford, Tiedtke, Ossmann, Özbe, & Schultheiss, 2017), although results are mixed (Scerbo & Kolko, 1994; van Bokhoven et al., 2005).

Research findings on testosterone in PTSD have been inconsistent. Low testosterone has been identified in men with PTSD (Mulchahey, 2001) and after extreme military training (Gomez-Merino, 2005). In animal models of PTSD, multiple types of stressors lead to lower testosterone (Andersen, Bignotto, Machado, & Tufik, 2004). But no difference in testosterone was observed in men with combat-related PTSD compared with controls (Karlovic; Mulchahey 2001; Spivak, Maayan, Mester, & Weizman, 2003) and elevated levels have been observed in PTSD inpatients (Mason, Giller, Kosten, & Wahby, 1990). Male rats exposed to predator scent stress that developed a disturbed behavioral phenotype (akin to PTSD) evidenced lower levels of plasma testosterone (Cohen, Kozlovsky, Alona, Matar, & Joseph, 2012) and a reduction in brain expression of androgen and estrogen receptors (Fenchel et al., 2015). Treatment with testosterone or a testosterone receptor antagonist led to higher rates of a resilience phenotype.

When comorbid psychiatric conditions were considered, combat veterans with PTSD alone showed significantly higher levels of testosterone compared with controls and those with comorbid major depressive disorder or alcohol abuse (Karlovic et al., 2012). Testosterone has also been associated with avoidance symptoms (Spivak, 2003). In a prospective longitudinal military study following male soldiers for two years starting prior to combat deployment, plasma testosterone moderately increased following a four-month deployment (Reijnen, Geuze, & Vermetten, 2015). Testosterone levels were not associated with PTSD symptoms postdeployment, but low pre-deployment testosterone predicted the development of PTSD at one and two years postdeployment. There were no interactions of testosterone with cortisol at pre-deployment.

Given evidence for a mutually influential relationship between the HPA and HPG axes, a dual-systems approach to research on stress-related disorders has been promoted (Viau, 2002). For example, gonadectomized rats show elevations in HPA axis hormones ACTH and corticosterone, which are reduced by administration of testosterone (Handa et al., 1994). There is a body of literature investigating the interaction of HPA and HPG axis activity on behavior and psychopathology. Mehta and Josephs (2010) have proposed a dual-hormone hypothesis that dominance behaviors are jointly regulated by testosterone and cortisol in men and women. In healthy subjects, they observed that the combination of high testosterone and low cortisol was associated with dominance, and that those with high cortisol demonstrated a null or reversed relationship between testosterone and dominance behavior. There is some evidence, however, that this relationship may vary under conditions of threat or provocation, in which a combination of high testosterone and cortisol may contribute to aggressive behavior (Denson, Mehta, & Tan, 2013).

Of potential relevance to PTSD, aggression has been associated with the combination of high testosterone and low cortisol in delinquent male adolescents (Popma et al., 2007). Furthermore, in a prospective study of military service members, salivary cortisol and testosterone reactivity to a pre-deployment CO_2 challenge had interactive effects on the development of PTSD symptoms following warzone trauma exposure (Josephs, Cobb, Lancaster, Lee, & Telch, 2017). A combination of baseline hyporeactivity of both cortisol and testosterone predicted emergence of PTSD symptoms following combat exposure. However, baseline high cortisol reactivity in conjunction with testosterone hyporeactivity conferred resilience to combat trauma. These results were moderated by differences in overall stress exposure between soldiers, whereas within person deviations in the average number of monthly stressors was not significant. The authors suggest that this pattern supports a dose-response model of the relationship of stress hormones and development of psychopathology, such that chronic elevations have more deleterious effects. These findings also highlight the importance of contextual factors, such as chronicity versus variation in trauma exposure, on neuroendocrine mediated elevations in PTSD symptoms. While these relationships remain to be further explored in PTSD, a small, uncontrolled pilot study of treatment-resistant combat PTSD (n = 10) found increased sex drive, improved partner relations, and overall reductions in PTSD symptoms over six months of treatment with an experimental soy formulation that increased testosterone, cortisol, and other steroids such as estradiol (Gocan, Bachg, Schindler, & Rohr, 2012).

Fenchel et al. (2015) propose that testosterone has time-dependent effects on anxiety behaviors due to its influence on glucocorticoids. In an animal model of PTSD, they observed lower levels of corticosterone in rats treated with testosterone immediately following stress exposure. However, treatment with a testosterone receptor antagonist, but not testosterone, 60 minutes after exposure was associated with a resilience phenotype. Delayed treatment with testosterone seven days post-exposure reduced extreme responding to the stressor. The authors hypothesize that high levels of corticosterone interfere with memory consolidation following trauma, whereas low levels promote consolidation. Testosterone may thus differentially affect risk for PTSD through its effects on glucocorticoids depending on timing of administration. In the acute aftermath of trauma, memory consolidation is reinforced through lowered glucocorticoid levels (increasing risk), but in the post-trauma period after memory consolidation and onset of behavioral symptoms testosterone's influence on the HPA axis may attenuate anxiety behaviors. This hypothesis is supported by animal research showing that high doses of corticosterone immediately following stress exposure prevented a PTSD-like phenotype, whereas a low dose increased rates of this phenotype (Cohen, Matar, Buskila, Kaplan, & Zohar, 2008).

Despite this body of work on the potential cross-talk between HPA and HPG axes, the association of the HPG axis and aggression, and the significant problem of anger and aggression in PTSD, there is little research on neuroendocrine mediation of PTSD-related aggression. For irritability and aggression to be considered symptoms of PTSD, they must begin or worsen following the trauma or represent a significant change from pre-trauma baseline. It is possible that PTSD-related aggression involves specific hormonal and neural networks that differ from those engaged in individuals with a history of aggression. As described above, the experience of childhood trauma and abuse is known to affect HPA axis development and to increase risk for a variety of deleterious social and behavioral outcomes, including antisocial behavior, substance abuse, and aggression. It is not known whether such developmental influences contribute to PTSD-related aggression. It is also not known whether the presence of violent and aggressive behavior represents a subgroup of patients with PTSD with specific neuroendocrine signatures.

The feeling of anger and irritability is different from the behavioral expression of aggression and violence, and the mechanisms underlying the ability to effectively contain such emotions and avoid aggressive behavior are likely different than those mediating the subjective experience of anger. Furthermore, PTSD-related aggression and violence are likely moderated by many additional factors, including sex, personality, and other hormonal, genetic, and physiological systems (Liening & Josephs, 2010). Overall, despite evidence for the potential relevance of both the HPA and HPG axes on anger, irritability, and aggression in PTSD, there has been very limited research into potential neuroendocrine mediators of these clinical symptoms in this population, and this poses an opportunity for translational research with important clinical relevance.

Social neuroendocrinology of resilience and recovery

Many factors across social, behavioral, and neuroendocrine levels that are implicated in risk and disease may of course also be considered through the inverse lens of resilience. A well-functioning HPA axis, an absence of early childhood trauma, the presence of social support, healthy bonding, and attachment are all factors that may influence resilience to, and recovery from, PTSD following trauma. A number of hormones, neurotransmitters, and neuropeptides are implicated in stress response and may influence resilience and coping. In terms of HPA axis function, the ability of the organism to mount a rapid acute response to threat and then to efficiently return to homeostasis in its aftermath has been associated with resilience. The presence of higher levels of the stress hormone dehydroepiandrosterone (DHEA), which has antiglucocorticoid and GABA-ergic effects (Morgan et al., 2004; Yehuda, Brand, Golier, & Yang, 2006), and progesterone (see Walf & Frye's chapter, this volume), have also been associated with resilience.

Beyond the HPA axis, noradrenergic, serotonergic, and dopaminergic systems are all implicated in stress response or fear extinction, but their role in promoting or inhibiting resilience is not yet well known. Neuropeptide Y (NPY), which has anxiolytic and cognition enhancing effects, has been more studied in PTSD, and higher levels have been associated with peak performance during extreme military training and with resilience to PTSD after combat exposure (Feder, Nestler, & Charney, 2009; Morgan et al., 2000; Yehuda, Brand, & Yang, 2006). These findings are supported by animal research showing that administration of NPY impairs fear conditioning and enhances its extinction (Gutman, Yang, Ressler, & Davis, 2008), and minimizes anxious-like behavioral responses to restraint (Sajdyk et al., 2008).

As emphasized by Feder et al. (2009), resilience should not be conceptualized only as the absence of disorder, but also as an active process whereby "more adaptive functioning of fear, reward, emotion regulation or social-behaviour circuits … underlie a resilient individual's capacity to face fears, experience positive emotions, search for positive ways to reframe stressful events and derive benefit from supportive friendships." Research on the mechanisms that mediate resilience, and possible psychotherapeutic or pharmacologic interventions to promote or support it, is still in its early stages, but promises much for our understanding of how individuals face, survive, and at times even thrive following trauma.

Conclusion

Social neuroendocrinology is a reasonable framework through which to understand the interactions of the social environment with hormones, psychology, and behavior in PTSD. The threat reaction system, primarily regulated by the HPA axis, is universal and adaptive. A prolonged and disabling failure of the natural process of recovery and homeostasis in the context of safety is the hallmark of PTSD and suggests a dysregulation in this system. PTSD represents a mismatch between social environment and neuroendocrinology; cognitions and behaviors become "symptoms" when they no longer promote life-preserving behaviors but instead become fixed, disabling, and distressing. The HPA axis is dynamic and flexible, responding and recalibrating to environmental inputs throughout the lifespan, from prenatal to adulthood. When the HPA axis becomes dysregulated, it may impair flexibility and adaptivity to changing social stimuli, contributing to rigid cognitions and behavior and fueling the development of PTSD.

The interactions of social environmental inputs with neuroendocrinology are relevant across the continuum from risk or resilience to disorder to recovery. This review has highlighted two areas in which social neuroendocrinology may be particularly relevant to PTSD-related behavior: sex and intimacy, and violence. Sex and attachment are partly mediated by neuroendocrine mechanisms, such as catecholamines and oxytocin, and it is possible that problems in sexual function and intimacy are not only psychologically but also biologically initiated and maintained. Although anger and aggressive behavior are explicit symptoms of PTSD with possible HPA and HPG axis correlates, this review identified gaps in the literature regarding the neuroendocrinology of this phenotype. Further investigation and clarification of the relationship of these neuroendocrine pathways with problems with sex and aggression in PTSD has the potential to empower patients and inform development of new treatments. It remains challenging to describe any feedback loop, particularly one influenced by higher-order emotional and cognitive factors such as attributions for the trauma, the meaning made of the experience, and the perceptions and interactions with social support systems in the aftermath of survival. Despite these challenges, future research taking a social neuroendocrinology approach to PTSD will benefit from incorporating multiple levels of analysis, from the molecular to the phenomenological, carefully evaluating contextual factors, and emphasizing system functioning through experimental provocation and longitudinal analysis. It is clear that PTSD is not a static state but a constellation of symptoms that vary over time and contexts, and further understanding of relevant neuroendocrinology must address the dynamic interplay of the social environment on PTSD-related cognitions, emotions, and behaviors.

References

American Psychiatric Association. (2013). *Diagnostic and statistical manual of mental disorders* (5th ed.). Washington, DC: American Psychiatric Association.

Andersen, M. L., Bignotto, M., Machado, R. B., & Tufik, S. (2004). Different stress modalities result in distinct steroid hormone responses by male rats. *Brazilian Journal of Medical and Biological Research, 37*(6), 791–797.

Bachmann, A. W., Sedgley, T. L., Jackson, R. V., Gibson, J. N., Young, R. M., & Torpy, D. J. (2005). Glucocorticoid receptor polymorphisms and post-traumatic stress disorder. *Psychoneuroendocrinology, 30*(3), 297–306.

Bartz, J. A., Zaki, J., Bolger, N., & Ochsner, K. N. (2011). Social effects of oxytocin in humans: Context and person matter. *Trends in Cognitive Sciences, 15*(7), 301–309.

Binder, E. B., Bradley, R. G., Liu, W., Epstein, M. P., Deveau, T. C., Mercer, K. B., . . . Nemeroff, C. B. (2008). Association of FKBP5 polymorphisms and childhood abuse with risk of posttraumatic stress disorder symptoms in adults. *JAMA, 299*(11), 1291–1305.

Bonne, O., Brandes, D., Segman, R., Pitman, R. K., Yehuda, R., & Shalev, A. Y. (2003). Prospective evaluation of plasma cortisol in recent trauma survivors with posttraumatic stress disorder. *Psychiatry Research, 119*(1), 171–175.

Bremner, D., Vermetten, E., & Kelley, M. E. (2007). Cortisol, dehydroepiandrosterone, and estradiol measured over 24 hours in women with childhood sexual abuse-related posttraumatic stress disorder. *Journal of Nervous and Mental Disease, 195*(11), 919–927. doi:10.1097/NMD.0b013e3181594ca0

Breslau, N., Chilcoat, H. D., Kessler, R. C., & Davis, G. C. (1999). Previous exposure to trauma and PTSD effects of subsequent trauma: Results from the Detroit Area Survey of Trauma. *American Journal of Psychiatry, 156*(6), 902–907.

Brewin, C. R., Andrews, B., & Valentine, J. D. (2000). *Meta-analysis of risk factors for posttraumatic stress disorder in trauma-exposed adults.* Washington, DC: American Psychological Association.

Breyer, B. N., Cohen, B. E., Bertenthal, D., Rosen, R. C., Neylan, T. C., & Seal, K. H. (2014). Sexual dysfunction in male Iraq and Afghanistan war veterans: Association with posttraumatic stress disorder and other combat-related mental health disorders: A population-based cohort study. *The Journal of Sexual Medicine, 11*(1), 75–83.

Brown, S. L., Fredrickson, B. L., Wirth, M. M., Poulin, M. J., Meier, E. A., Heaphy, E. D., . . . Schultheiss, O. C. (2009). Social closeness increases salivary progesterone in humans. *Hormones and Behavior, 56*(1), 108–111.

Bunea, I. M., Szentágotai-Tătar, A., & Miu, A. C. (2017). Early-life adversity and cortisol response to social stress: A meta-analysis. *Translational Psychiatry, 7*(12), 1274.

Cardoso, C., Ellenbogen, M. A., Orlando, M. A., Bacon, S. L., & Joober, R. (2013). Intranasal oxytocin attenuates the cortisol response to physical stress: A dose – response study. *Psychoneuroendocrinology, 38*(3), 399–407.

Charuvastra, A., & Cloitre, M. (2008). Social bonds and posttraumatic stress disorder. *Annual Reviews of Psychology, 59*, 301–328.

Chrousos, G. P., & Gold, P. W. (1992). The concepts of stress and stress system disorders: Overview of physical and behavioral homeostasis. *JAMA, 267*(9), 1244–1252.

Cohen, H., Kozlovsky, N., Alona, C., Matar, M. A., & Joseph, Z. (2012). Animal model for PTSD: From clinical concept to translational research. *Neuropharmacology, 62*(2), 715–724.

Cohen, H., Matar, M. A., Buskila, D., Kaplan, Z., & Zohar, J. (2008). Early post-stressor intervention with high-dose corticosterone attenuates posttraumatic stress response in an animal model of posttraumatic stress disorder. *Biological Psychiatry*, 64(8), 708–717.

Cosgrove, D. J., Gordon, Z., Bernie, J. E., Hami, S., Montoya, D., Stein, M. B., & Monga, M. (2002). Sexual dysfunction in combat veterans with post-traumatic stress disorder. *Urology*, 60(5), 881–884.

Daskalakis, N. P., Bagot, R. C., Parker, K. J., Vinkers, C. H., & de Kloet, E. R. (2013). The three-hit concept of vulnerability and resilience: Toward understanding adaptation to early-life adversity outcome. *Psychoneuroendocrinology*, 38(9), 1858–1873.

Daskalakis, N. P., Cohen, H., Cai, G., Buxbaum, J. D., & Yehuda, R. (2014). Expression profiling associates blood and brain glucocorticoid receptor signaling with trauma-related individual differences in both sexes. *Proceedings of the National Academy of Sciences*, 111(37), 13529–13534.

De Kloet, E. R., Joëls, M., & Holsboer, F. (2005). Stress and the brain: From adaptation to disease. *Nature Reviews. Neuroscience*, 6(6), 463.

Delahanty, D. L., Raimonde, A. J., & Spoonster, E. (2000). Initial posttraumatic urinary cortisol levels predict subsequent PTSD symptoms in motor vehicle accident victims. *Biological Psychiatry*, 48(9), 940–947.

Denson, T. F., Mehta, P. H., & Tan, D. H. (2013). Endogenous testosterone and cortisol jointly influence reactive aggression in women. *Psychoneuroendocrinology*, 38(3), 416–424.

Feder, A., Nestler, E. J., & Charney, D. S. (2009). Psychobiology and molecular genetics of resilience. *Nature Reviews. Neuroscience*, 10(6), 446.

Fenchel, D., Levkovitz, Y., Vainer, E., Kaplan, Z., Zohar, J., & Cohen, H. (2015). Beyond the HPA-axis: The role of the gonadal steroid hormone receptors in modulating stress-related responses in an animal model of PTSD. *European Neuropsychopharmacology*, 25(6), 944–957. doi:10.1016/j.euroneuro.2015.02.004

Fries, E., Hesse, J., Hellhammer, J., & Hellhammer, D. H. (2005). A new view on hypocortisolism. *Psychoneuroendocrinology*, 30(10), 1010–1016.

Frijling, J. L., van Zuiden, M., Nawijn, L., Koch, S. B., Neumann, I. D., Veltman, D. J., & Olff, M. (2015). Salivary oxytocin and vasopressin levels in police officers with and without post-traumatic stress disorder. *Journal of Neuroendocrinology*, 27(10), 743–751. doi:10.1111/jne.12300

Galatzer-Levy, I. R., & Bryant, R. A. (2013). 636,120 ways to have posttraumatic stress disorder. *Perspectives on Psychological Science*, 8(6), 651–662.

Galatzer-Levy, I. R., Steenkamp, M. M., Brown, A. D., Qian, M., Inslicht, S., Henn-Haase, C., ... Marmar, C. R. (2014). Cortisol response to an experimental stress paradigm prospectively predicts long-term distress and resilience trajectories in response to active police service. *Journal of Psychiatric Research*, 56, 36–42.

Gocan, A. G., Bachg, D., Schindler, A. E., & Rohr, U. D. (2012). Balancing steroidal hormone cascade in treatment-resistant veteran soldiers with PTSD using a fermented soy product (FSWW08): A pilot study. *Hormone Molecular Biology and Clinical Investigation*, 10(3), 301–314.

Gutman, A. R., Yang, Y., Ressler, K. J., & Davis, M. (2008). The role of neuropeptide Y in the expression and extinction of fear-potentiated startle. *Journal of Neuroscience*, 28(48), 12682–12690.

Handa, R. J., Nunley, K. M., Lorens, S. A., Louie, J. P., McGivern, R. F., & Bollnow, M. R. (1994). Androgen regulation of adrenocorticotropin and corticosterone secretion in the male rat following novelty and foot shock stressors. *Physiology & Behavior*, 55(1), 117–124.

Heinrichs, M., Baumgartner, T., Kirschbaum, C., & Ehlert, U. (2003). Social support and oxytocin interact to suppress cortisol and subjective responses to psychosocial stress. *Biological Psychiatry*, 54(12), 1389–1398.

Hoge, C. W., Yehuda, R., Castro, C. A., McFarlane, A. C., Vermetten, E., Jetly, R., ... Rauch, S. A. (2016). Unintended consequences of changing the definition of posttraumatic stress disorder in DSM-5: Critique and call for action. *JAMA Psychiatry*, 73(7), 750–752.

Inslicht, S. S., Otte, C., McCaslin, S. E., Apfel, B. A., Henn-Haase, C., Metzler, T., ... Marmar, C. R. (2011). Cortisol awakening response prospectively predicts peritraumatic and acute stress reactions in police officers. *Biological Psychiatry*, 70(11), 1055–1062.

Jackson, J. S., Knight, K. M., & Rafferty, J. A. (2010). Race and unhealthy behaviors: Chronic stress, the HPA axis, and physical and mental health disparities over the life course. *American Journal of Public Health*, 100(5), 933–939.

Josephs, R. A., Cobb, A. R., Lancaster, C. L., Lee, H-J., & Telch, M. J. (2017). Dual-hormone stress reactivity predicts downstream war-zone stress-evoked PTSD. *Psychoneuroendocrinology*, 78, 76–84.

Karlovic, D., Serretti, A., Marcinko, D., Martinac, M., Silic, A., & Katinic, K. (2012). Serum testosterone concentration in combat-related chronic posttraumatic stress disorder. *Neuropsychobiology*, 65(2), 90–95. doi:10.1159/000329556

Kilpatrick, D. G., Resnick, H. S., Milanak, M. E., Miller, M. W., Keyes, K. M., & Friedman, M. J. (2013). National estimates of exposure to traumatic events and PTSD prevalence using DSM-IV and DSM-5 criteria. *Journal of Traumatic Stress, 26*(5), 537–547.

Koenen, K., Saxe, G., Purcell, S., Smoller, J., Bartholomew, D., Miller, A., . . . Moulton, S. (2005). Polymorphisms in FKBP5 are associated with peritraumatic dissociation in medically injured children. *Molecular Psychiatry, 10*(12), 1058–1058.

Koenen, K. C., & Uddin, M. (2010). FKBP5 polymorphisms modify the effects of childhood trauma. *Neuropsychopharmacology, 35*(8), 1623.

Lehrner, A., Daskalakis, N., & Yehuda, R. (2016). Cortisol and the hypothalamic – pituitary – adrenal axis in PTSD. *Posttraumatic Stress Disorder: From Neurobiology to Treatment*, 265.

Lehrner, A., Flory, J. D., Bierer, L. M., Makotkine, I., Marmar, C. R., & Yehuda, R. (2016). Sexual dysfunction and neuroendocrine correlates of posttraumatic stress disorder in combat veterans: Preliminary findings. *Psychoneuroendocrinology, 63*, 271–275.

Letourneau, E. J., Resnick, H. S., Kilpatrick, D. G., Saunders, B. E., & Best, C. L. (1996). Comorbidity of sexual problems and posttraumatic stress disorder in female crime victims. *Behavior Therapy, 27*(3), 321–336.

Liening, S. H., & Josephs, R. A. (2010). It is not just about testosterone: Physiological mediators and moderators of testosterone's behavioral effects. *Social and Personality Psychology Compass, 4*(11), 982–994.

Marshall, A. D., Panuzio, J., & Taft, C. T. (2005). Intimate partner violence among military veterans and active duty servicemen. *Clinical Psychology Review, 25*(7), 862–876.

Mason, J. W., Giller, E. L., Kosten, T. R., & Wahby, V. S. (1990). Serum testosterone levels in post-traumatic stress disorder inpatients. *Journal of Traumatic Stress, 3*(3), 449–457.

McBurnett, K., Lahey, B. B., Rathouz, P. J., & Loeber, R. (2000). Low salivary cortisol and persistent aggression in boys referred for disruptive behavior. *Archives of General Psychiatry, 57*(1), 38–43.

McEwen, B. S. (1998). Stress, adaptation, and disease: Allostasis and allostatic load. *Annals of the New York Academy of Sciences, 840*(1), 33–44.

McFarlane, A. C., Atchison, M., & Yehuda, R. (1997). The acute stress response following motor vehicle accidents and its relation to PTSD. *Annals of the New York Academy of Sciences, 821*(1), 437–441.

Mehta, D., & Binder, E. B. (2012). Gene× environment vulnerability factors for PTSD: The HPA-axis. *Neuropharmacology, 62*(2), 654–662.

Mehta, P. H., & Josephs, R. A. (2010). Testosterone and cortisol jointly regulate dominance: Evidence for a dual-hormone hypothesis. *Hormones and Behavior, 58*(5), 898–906.

Morgan, C. A., Southwick, S., Hazlett, G., Rasmusson, A., Hoyt, G., Zimolo, Z., & Charney, D. (2004). Relationships among plasma dehydroepiandrosterone sulfate and cortisol levels, symptoms of dissociation, and objective performance in humans exposed to acute stress. *Archives of General Psychiatry, 61*(8), 819–825.

Morgan, C. A., Wang, S., Southwick, S. M., Rasmusson, A., Hazlett, G., Hauger, R. L., & Charney, D. S. (2000). Plasma neuropeptide-Y concentrations in humans exposed to military survival training. *Biological Psychiatry, 47*(10), 902–909.

Morley-Fletcher, S., Rea, M., Maccari, S., & Laviola, G. (2003). Environmental enrichment during adolescence reverses the effects of prenatal stress on play behaviour and HPA axis reactivity in rats. *European Journal of Neuroscience, 18*(12), 3367–3374.

Morris, M. C., Compas, B. E., & Garber, J. (2012). Relations among posttraumatic stress disorder, comorbid major depression, and HPA function: A systematic review and meta-analysis. *Clinical Psychology Review, 32*(4), 301–315.

Murgatroyd, C., Patchev, A. V., Wu, Y., Micale, V., Bockmühl, Y., Fischer, D., . . . Spengler, D. (2009). Dynamic DNA methylation programs persistent adverse effects of early-life stress. *Nature Neuroscience, 12*(12), 1559–1566.

Olff, M., Frijling, J. L., Kubzansky, L. D., Bradley, B., Ellenbogen, M. A., Cardoso, C., . . . van Zuiden, M. (2013). The role of oxytocin in social bonding, stress regulation and mental health: An update on the moderating effects of context and interindividual differences. *Psychoneuroendocrinology, 38*(9), 1883–1894.

Olff, M., Langeland, W., Witteveen, A., & Denys, D. (2010). A psychobiological rationale for oxytocin in the treatment of posttraumatic stress disorder. *CNS Spectrums, 15*(8), 522–530.

Oxford, J. K., Tiedtke, J. M., Ossmann, A., Özbe, D., & Schultheiss, O. C. (2017). Endocrine and aggressive responses to competition are moderated by contest outcome, gender, individual versus team competition, and implicit motives. *PLoS One, 12*(7), e0181610.

Ozbay, F., Johnson, D. C., Dimoulas, E., Morgan III, C., Charney, D., & Southwick, S. (2007). Social support and resilience to stress: From neurobiology to clinical practice. *Psychiatry (Edgmont), 4*(5), 35.

Ozer, E. J., Best, S. R., Lipsey, T. L., & Weiss, D. S. (2003). Predictors of posttraumatic stress disorder and symptoms in adults: A meta-analysis. *Psychological Bulletin, 129*(1), 52.

Öznur, T., Akarsu, S., Karaahmetoğlu, B., & Doruk, A. (2014). A rare symptom in posttraumatic stress disorder: Spontaneous ejaculation. *The American Journal of Case Reports, 15,* 69.

Palma-Gudiel, H., Cordova-Palomera, A., Eixarch, E., Deuschle, M., & Fananas, L. (2015). Maternal psychosocial stress during pregnancy alters the epigenetic signature of the glucocorticoid receptor gene promoter in their offspring: A meta-analysis. *Epigenetics, 10*(10), 893–902.

Pitman, R. K., Orr, S. P., & Lasko, N. B. (1993). Effects of intranasal vasopressin and oxytocin on physiologic responding during personal combat imagery in Vietnam veterans with posttraumatic stress disorder. *Psychiatry Research, 48*(2), 107–117.

Popma, A., Vermeiren, R., Geluk, C. A., Rinne, T., van den Brink, W., Knol, D. L., . . . Doreleijers, T. A. (2007). Cortisol moderates the relationship between testosterone and aggression in delinquent male adolescents. *Biological Psychiatry, 61*(3), 405–411.

Reijnen, A., Geuze, E., & Vermetten, E. (2015). The effect of deployment to a combat zone on testosterone levels and the association with the development of posttraumatic stress symptoms: A longitudinal prospective Dutch military cohort study. *Psychoneuroendocrinology, 51,* 525–533.

Resnick, H. S., Yehuda, R., Pitman, R. K., & Foy, D. W. (1995). Effect of previous trauma on acute plasma cortisol level following rape. *The American Journal of Psychiatry, 152*(11), 1675.

Roy, A., Gorodetsky, E., Yuan, Q., Goldman, D., & Enoch, M-A. (2010). Interaction of FKBP5, a stress-related gene, with childhood trauma increases the risk for attempting suicide. *Neuropsychopharmacology, 35*(8), 1674–1683.

Sack, M., Spieler, D., Wizelman, L., Epple, G., Stich, J., Zaba, M., & Schmidt, U. (2017). Intranasal oxytocin reduces provoked symptoms in female patients with posttraumatic stress disorder despite exerting sympathomimetic and positive chronotropic effects in a randomized controlled trial. *BMC Medicine, 15*(1), 40.

Sajdyk, T. J., Johnson, P. L., Leitermann, R. J., Fitz, S. D., Dietrich, A., Morin, M., . . . Shekhar, A. (2008). Neuropeptide Y in the amygdala induces long-term resilience to stress-induced reductions in social responses but not hypothalamic – adrenal – pituitary axis activity or hyperthermia. *Journal of Neuroscience, 28*(4), 893–903.

Santarelli, S., Lesuis, S. L., Wang, X-D., Wagner, K. V., Hartmann, J., Labermaier, C., . . . Schmidt, M. V. (2014). Evidence supporting the match/mismatch hypothesis of psychiatric disorders. *European Neuropsychopharmacology, 24*(6), 907–918.

Sapolsky, R. M. (2002). Endocrinology of the stress-response.

Scerbo, A. S., & Kolko, D. J. (1994). Salivary testosterone and cortisol in disruptive children: Relationship to aggressive, hyperactive, and internalizing behaviors. *Journal of the American Academy of Child & Adolescent Psychiatry, 33*(8), 1174–1184.

Schnurr, P. P., Lunney, C. A., Bovin, M. J., & Marx, B. P. (2009). Posttraumatic stress disorder and quality of life: Extension of findings to veterans of the wars in Iraq and Afghanistan. *Clinical Psychology Review, 29*(8), 727–735.

Shalev, A. Y., Videlock, E. J., Peleg, T., Segman, R., Pitman, R. K., & Yehuda, R. (2008). Stress hormones and post-traumatic stress disorder in civilian trauma victims: A longitudinal study. Part I: HPA axis responses. *International Journal of Neuropsychopharmacology, 11*(3), 365–372.

Spivak, B., Maayan, R., Mester, R., & Weizman, A. (2003). Plasma testosterone levels in patients with combat-related posttraumatic stress disorder. *Neuropsychobiology, 47*(2), 57–60.

Tarullo, A. R., & Gunnar, M. R. (2006). Child maltreatment and the developing HPA axis. *Hormones and Behavior, 50*(4), 632–639.

Trickett, P. K., Noll, J. G., Susman, E. J., Shenk, C. E., & Putnam, F. W. (2010). Attenuation of cortisol across development for victims of sexual abuse. *Development and Psychopathology, 22*(1), 165–175.

van Bodegom, M., Homberg, J. R., & Henckens, M. J. (2017). Modulation of the hypothalamic-pituitary-adrenal axis by early life stress exposure. *Frontiers in Cellular Neuroscience, 11.*

Van Bokhoven, I., van Goozen, S., van Engeland, H., Schaal, B., Arseneault, L., Seguin, J., . . . Tremblay, R. (2005). Salivary cortisol and aggression in a population-based longitudinal study of adolescent males. *Journal of Neural Transmission, 112*(8), 1083–1096.

Van Zuiden, M., Geuze, E., Willemen, H. L., Vermetten, E., Maas, M., Amarouchi, K., . . . Heijnen, C. J. (2012). Glucocorticoid receptor pathway components predict posttraumatic stress disorder symptom development: A prospective study. *Biological Psychiatry, 71*(4), 309–316.

Viau, V. (2002). Functional cross-talk between the hypothalamic-pituitary-gonadal and-adrenal axes. *Journal of Neuroendocrinology*, *14*(6), 506–513.

Welberg, L. A., & Seckl, J. R. (2001). Prenatal stress, glucocorticoids and the programming of the brain. *Journal of Neuroendocrinology*, *13*(2), 113–128.

Wirth, M. M. (2011). Beyond the HPA axis: Progesterone-derived neuroactive steroids in human stress and emotion. *Frontiers in Endocrinology*, *2*.

Yatzkar, U., & Klein, E. (2010). P.3.026 intranasal oxytocin in patients with post traumatic stress disorder: A single dose, pilot double blind crossover study. *European Neuropsychopharmacology*, *20*, S84.

Yehuda, R. (2002). Post-traumatic stress disorder. *The New England Journal of Medicine*, *346*(2), 108–114. doi:10.1056/NEJMra012941

Yehuda, R., & Bierer, L. M. (2009). The relevance of epigenetics to PTSD: Implications for the DSM-V. *Journal of Traumatic Stress*, *22*(5), 427–434.

Yehuda, R., Boisoneau, D., Mason, J. W., & Giller, E. L. (1993). Glucocorticoid receptor number and cortisol excretion in mood, anxiety, and psychotic disorders. *Biological Psychiatry*, *34*(1), 18–25.

Yehuda, R., Brand, S., Golier, J., & Yang, R. K. (2006). Clinical correlates of DHEA associated with post-traumatic stress disorder. *Acta Psychiatrica Scandinavica*, *114*(3), 187–193.

Yehuda, R., Brand, S., & Yang, R-K. (2006). Plasma neuropeptide Y concentrations in combat exposed veterans: Relationship to trauma exposure, recovery from PTSD, and coping. *Biological Psychiatry*, *59*(7), 660–663.

Yehuda, R., Engel, S. M., Brand, S. R., Seckl, J., Marcus, S. M., & Berkowitz, G. S. (2005). Transgenerational effects of posttraumatic stress disorder in babies of mothers exposed to the World Trade Center attacks during pregnancy. *The Journal of Clinical Endocrinology & Metabolism*, *90*(7), 4115–4118.

Yehuda, R., Golier, J. A., Yang, R-K., & Tischler, L. (2004). Enhanced sensitivity to glucocorticoids in peripheral mononuclear leukocytes in posttraumatic stress disorder. *Biol Psychiatry*, *55*(11), 1110–1116.

Yehuda, R., Halligan, S. L., Golier, J. A., Grossman, R., & Bierer, L. M. (2004). Effects of trauma exposure on the cortisol response to dexamethasone administration in PTSD and major depressive disorder. *Psychoneuroendocrinology*, *29*(3), 389–404.

Yehuda, R., Koenen, K. C., Galea, S., & Flory, J. D. (2011). The role of genes in defining a molecular biology of PTSD. *Disease Markers*, *30*(2–3), 67–76.

Yehuda, R., Lehrner, A., & Rosenbaum, T. Y. (2015). PTSD and sexual dysfunction in men and women. *The Journal of Sexual Medicine*, *12*(5), 1107–1119.

Yehuda, R., Lowy, M. T., Southwick, S. M., Shaffer, D., & Giller, E. L. (1991). Lymphocyte glucocorticoid receptor number in posttraumatic stress disorder. *The American Journal of Psychiatry*, *144*(4), 499–504.

Yehuda, R., McFarlane, A., & Shalev, A. (1998). Predicting the development of posttraumatic stress disorder from the acute response to a traumatic event. *Biological Psychiatry*, *44*(12), 1305–1313.

Yehuda, R., Southwick, S. M., Krystal, J. H., Bremner, D., Charney, D. S., & Mason, J. W. (1993). Enhanced suppression of cortisol following dexamethasone administration in posttraumatic stress disorder. *American Journal of Psychiatry*, *150*, 83–86.

Yehuda, R., Southwick, S. M., Nussbaum, G., Wahby, V., Giller, E. L., Jr., & Mason, J. W. (1990). Low urinary cortisol excretion in patients with posttraumatic stress disorder. *Journal of Nervous and Mental Disease*, *178*(6), 366–369.

36

ATTACHMENT AND DEPRESSION

Is oxytocin the shared link?

Allison M. Perkeybile and C. Sue Carter

Oxytocin as a social peptide

Oxytocin is a nine-amino-acid peptide primarily produced in the magnocellular division of the paraventricular hypothalamic nucleus (PVN) and in the supraoptic hypothalamic nucleus (SON). From those sites, oxytocin is transported to the neurohypophyseal system and is then secreted into the periphery from the posterior pituitary. The release of oxytocin from this pathway targets the smooth muscle of the uterus to produce contractions during labor and the myoepithelial cells of the mammary glands to cause milk letdown during lactation. Central oxytocin projections arise primarily from parvocellular cells in the PVN. This central release occurs not just from axon terminals but also via release from dendrites and cell bodies (see Landgraf & Neumann, 2004 and Grinevich, Knobloch-Bollmann, Eliava, Busnelli, & Chini, 2016 for reviews). The central targets for oxytocin include limbic structures involved in mood, emotion, memory, and social behavior regulation such as the amygdala, hippocampus, and lateral septum (Buijs, 1978; Buijs, Swaab, Dogterom, & Vanleeuwen, 1978; Grinevich et al., 2016; Stoop, Hegoburu, & van den Burg, 2015), allowing for potentially rapid modulation of emotion regulation by oxytocin.

The production and release pathways of oxytocin are shared with the closely related nonapeptide arginine vasopressin. The two neuropeptides are similar in molecular structure and hypothesized to have both evolved from vasotocin (Goodson & Kingsbury, 2013). There is an extensive literature on the role these neuropeptides play in a variety of social behaviors across species, including social affiliation and group formation, aggression, parental care, mother–infant attachment, and social attachments (for review see Caldwell, 2017; Dumais & Veenema, 2016; Feldman, Monakhov, Pratt, & Ebstein, 2016; French, Taylor, Mustoe, & Cavanaugh, 2016; Numan & Young 2016). This chapter will focus on maternal–infant attachment and social attachments.

Defining attachment and the role of oxytocin in regulating its different forms

The concept of emotional attachment is a hypothetical construct. We infer attachment relationships from physiological and behavioral measures (Carter & Keverne, 2017). The objective criteria most often used to define an attachment relationship include (1) proximity by choice, (2) distress upon separation, (3) reduced distress upon reunion, and (4) social stress buffering

(Mason & Mendoza, 1998). An attached individual is likely to seek out and maintain spatial proximity to the individual (or object) of their attachment, typically showing preference for their attachment figure over other individuals. When involuntarily separated from the attachment figure, the attached individual will typically display signs of distress, such as increases in vocalizations or locomotor behavior; this distress is ameliorated by reunion with the attachment figure. The attachment figure will also provide some measure of physiological stress buffering for the attached individual in the presence of a threatening stimulus.

Oxytocin has repeatedly been implicated in attachment formation in human populations (Bernaerts et al., 2017; Carter, 2017; Feldman, 2012, 2017; Hurlemann & Scheele, 2016; Swain et al., 2014). There is also evidence in several animal models that oxytocin is critical for maternal, filial, and adult pair attachments.

Maternal attachment

Oxytocin is active in the periphery during labor and birth, helping to contract the uterus to expel the fetus, and is responsible for milk letdown during lactation post-birth. At the same time, oxytocin is also active centrally to facilitate selective attachment to the infant in many species. An excellent model for oxytocin involvement in maternal attachment is that of sheep. Upon birth of the lamb, ewes rapidly develop a specific recognition of and attachment to their lamb and will actively reject attempts to suckle made by unrelated lambs within just a few hours after birth. This recognition and attachment is regulated in part by oxytocin. In late pregnancy, ewes experience a drastic rise in sex steroids, in particular estradiol (Kendrick & Keverne, 1991; Keverne, Levy, Poindron, & Lindsay, 1983). This estradiol surge is thought to prime the animal for engaging in maternal behavior by increasing mRNA expression of both the oxytocin peptide (Broad, Kendrick, Sirinathsinghji, & Keverne, 1993) and its receptor (Broad et al., 1999) in brain regions responsible for controlling maternal behavior (including bed nucleus of the stria terminalis (BNST), lateral septum, and medial preoptic area). Oxytocin is released in response to the vaginal–cervical stimulation that occurs at birth (Kendrick, Keverne, Hinton, & Goode, 1991). A female must experience the rise in both estradiol and oxytocin to stimulate the onset of maternal behavior and subsequent attachment to her infant.

Ewes do show variation in both maternal behavior and oxytocin sensitivity based on parity. Experiments demonstrate that maternal behavior can be induced in inexperienced females following an intracerebroventricular (ICV) infusion of oxytocin (Kendrick, Keverne, & Baldwin, 1987). Estradiol priming in combination with vaginocervical stimulation increases positive maternal behaviors while reducing aggression towards or withdrawal from the lamb in multiparous but not nulliparous ewes (Kendrick & Keverne, 1991). This outcome is likely due to a rise in hypothalamic oxytocin release or sensitivity following estradiol administration and vaginocervical stimulation (Kendrick, Fabrenys, Blache, Goode, & Broad, 1993). There is also a greater increase in oxytocin in the olfactory bulbs, a region that is vital in this species for recognition of a specific lamb and, hence, attachment to offspring, in multiparous compared to primiparous ewes (Levy, Kendrick, Goode, Guevaraguzman, & Keverne, 1995), suggesting that a prior birth experience may increase a ewe's sensitivity to oxytocin stimulation and perhaps allow her to form an attachment to her lamb more quickly.

Filial attachment

Just as mothers of some species develop attachments to their infants, so too do infants form attachments to their parent(s), typically to their mother in non-human mammals. These filial attachments do not always occur simultaneously with a maternal attachment to the infant; several species display filial attachments without a concurrent selective maternal or, more broadly, parental attachment (for example, guinea pigs (Hennessy & Ritchey, 1987; Pettijohn, 1979) and titi monkeys (Hoffman, Mendoza, Hennessy, & Mason, 1995; Mendoza & Mason, 1986b)). Similar to maternal attachment, there is evidence in lambs that filial attachments may be regulated in part by oxytocin. Lambs begin to develop a selective attachment to the ewe within hours after birth. Some of the first contact these lambs have with the ewe involves suckling. If access to suckling just after birth is blocked without preventing non-nutritive contact with the ewe, the development of this selective preference for the ewe is delayed (Nowak et al., 1997). Blocking oxytocin in the lamb with an antagonist in this same time frame will also delay filial attachment formation (Nowak, Keller, & Levy, 2011), suggesting a link between nursing, oxytocin, and attachment in very early life. Indeed, there is a rise in plasma oxytocin just following suckling in lambs (Nowak et al., 2011), leading to the hypotheses that nursing promotes the development of selective filial attachment in lambs in part by inducing a rise in central oxytocin levels, similar to what has been described in ewes (see "Maternal attachment" above). How the peripheral rise in oxytocin is related to central oxytocin levels remains unclear. Plasma oxytocin may act via indirect mechanisms, including vagal pathways, to influence central activity.

Adult pair bonds

Attachment formation between adults is relatively rare in mammalian species, with only approximately 5% of species displaying a selective attachment to another individual within the context of monogamy (Kleiman, 1977). Best studied of these are prairie voles (*Microtus ochrogaster*), small rodents which form selective bonds with an opposite sex partner that are oxytocin-dependent. Comparisons between monogamous and nonmonogamous vole species have shown that the monogamous nature of the prairie vole is regulated not solely by species differences in the oxytocin peptide (Wang, Zhou, Hulihan, & Insel, 1996) but by differences in oxytocin receptor distribution, which is upregulated in the prairie vole in the BNST, nucleus accumbens, and prefrontal cortex (Insel & Shapiro, 1992). These three regions are heavily involved in the regulation of various kinds of social behaviors and social reward. Of these regions, the nucleus accumbens appears to be particularly important for bond formation. Release of oxytocin in the nucleus accumbens is increased with mating (Ross et al., 2009), and this peptide release is important for the development of an attachment to the partner (Williams, Insel, Harbaugh, & Carter, 1994a), as is extended cohabitation (DeVries & Carter, 1999).

Early studies of the role of oxytocin in pair bonding focused almost exclusively on females. We now know that oxytocin works in both sexes to influence pair bonding, although not always in the same fashion. ICV infusion of oxytocin facilitates the rapid development of a partner preference in both males and females, while administering an oxytocin antagonist in the same manner blocks the bond formation, even in the presence of endogenous oxytocin release (mating) and exogenous oxytocin exposure (ICV) (Cho, DeVries, Williams, & Carter, 1999; Williams, Insel, Harbaugh, & Carter, 1994b). Site-specific oxytocin manipulations have shown sex-specific effects. In females, oxytocin delivered directly to the nucleus accumbens promotes pair bond formation even in the absence of mating (Liu & Wang, 2003), while blocking oxytocin in the prelimbic cortex, a region involved in goal-directed and attentional behavior, blocks pair bond formation even in the presence of mating (Young, Lim, Gingrich, & Insel, 2001). Blocking oxytocin action in the lateral septum of males has the same effect of disrupting pair bonding (Liu, Curtis, & Wang, 2001).

Often active in conjunction with oxytocin, vasopressin is also critical to pair bond formation in the prairie vole. Similar to oxytocin, ICV administration of vasopressin promotes pair bonding and blockade of the vasopressin receptor V1a prevents bonding in both males and females (Cho et al., 1999; Donaldson, Spiegel, & Young, 2010; Winslow, Hastings, Carter, Harbaugh, & Insel, 1993; Young, Nilsen, Waymire, MacGregor, & Insel, 1999). Two regions appear to be especially important with regard to vasopressin regulation of pair bonding in males. V1a receptors are very dense in the ventral pallidum (a component of the limbic system, regulating reward and motivation behaviors) of the monogamous prairie vole but not the polygamous meadow vole. This high density of V1a receptors in part regulates bonding behavior; increasing V1a receptors in the ventral pallidum of male meadow voles using a viral vector V1a gene transfer from prairie voles resulted in the display of a preference for an opposite sex partner (Lim et al., 2004). Mating increases ventral pallidum neural activity through V1a receptors in male prairie voles (Lim & Young, 2004), providing further evidence that V1a receptors in this region modulate bond formation. Upregulating V1a receptors in this area promotes pair bonding in the absence of mating (Pitkow et al., 2001), while blocking V1a receptors in the ventral pallidum disrupts bond formation (Lim & Young, 2004), even in the presence of mating (Barrett et al., 2013).

The lateral septum is similarly involved in attachment formation in males. There is an increase in vasopressin release in the lateral septum in males following mating or cohabitation with a female partner (Bamshad, Novak, & Devries, 1994). Infusion of vasopressin into this region promotes pair bonding without mating, while blocking V1a receptors in the lateral septum prevents bond formation even with mating (Liu et al., 2001), indicating the vasopressin release in the lateral septum associated with mating is critical for attachment formation to occur.

The consequences of attachment

Stable social attachments provide a number of health benefits to the attached individual, including beneficial effects on immune, cardiovascular, and endocrine systems, the promotion of better mental health, and the reduction of morbidity and mortality rates (see reviews by Cacioppo et al., 2007; House, Landis, & Umberson, 1988; Uchino, Cacioppo, & Kiecolt-Glaser, 1996). In contrast to the benefits stable attachments confer to individuals, disruption of these attachments is associated with a number of detrimental physiological and behavioral outcomes, including psychopathology and substance abuse (Buisman-Pijlman et al., 2014; MacDonald, Berlow, & Thomas, 2013; Toepfer et al., 2017). These effects are also found in a variety of animal models, including mimicking behaviors observed in major depressive disorder. Several of these responses highlight the four criteria for attachment relationships outlined above and are found in maternal, filial, and adult pair attachments.

Maternal attachment disruption

In the examples used previously, ewes form a strong and selective attachment to their lamb within hours of giving birth. Subsequently, separating ewes from their lamb results in increased high-pitched bleating (distress vocalizations), increased line crossings (a measure of locomotion behaviors) in an open field arena, and increased nosing of the enclosure walls. This response is unique to infant separation in ewes, as being separated from familiar conspecifics does not produce this reaction in new mothers (Poindron, Caba, Arrati, Krehbiel, & Beyer, 1994). A similar response is seen in macaques; separation from their infant leads to mothers engaging in a high amount of vocalizing and showing increased aggression toward caretakers in both rhesus macaques (*Macaca mulatta*) (B. Seay, Hansen, & Harlow, 1962) and pigtail macaques (*Macaca nemestrina*), species that also display very high levels of maternal behavior when they are reunited with their infant (Jensen & Tolman, 1962). In squirrel monkeys (*Saimiri sciureus*), separation from the infant, even short-term, is also accompanied by a rise in plasma cortisol, even in the presence of a familiar adult conspecific (Coe, Mendoza, Smotherman, & Levine, 1978; Mendoza, Coe, Smotherman, Kaplan, & Levine, 1980), providing evidence for a hypothalamic–pituitary–adrenal (HPA) response to disrupted maternal attachment as well as a behavioral response.

Filial attachment disruption

In 1946, René Spitz described a series of behavioral responses in children following separation from their mother in the first year of life, what he described as anaclitic depression. Upon initial separation, infants often cried and showed apprehension and agitation, but as the separation persisted, the children began to withdraw and reject attempted interactions. They showed a loss of appetite, decreased reactions and slowed movements, and often adopted a hunched posture (Spitz, 1946). If the infant was subsequently reunited with their mother, their behaviors recovered quickly and typically completely. These same behavioral responses were later characterized in older children, 2–3 years old, and were termed "protest" (the initial active phase of crying and agitation) and "despair" (the later withdrawal phase following prolonged separation) (J. Robertson & Bowlby, 1952). A child's attachment style likely influences the coping strategy they adopt in response to disruption within the caregiver/child relationship. The attachment style of children to their caregiver can be classified using Ainsworth's Strange Situation paradigm (Ainsworth, 1985). A brief period of separation from the caregiver in this test leads to increases in plasma cortisol in children who exhibit insecure–avoidant and disorganized, compared to secure, attachments (Spangler & Grossmann, 1993).

Additional work on these "protest" and "despair" stages of the separation response have linked these phases with two of the primary process regulators of emotion, PANIC/GRIEF and SEEKING functions (Panksepp & Watt, 2011; Watt & Panksepp, 2009). As separation from the attachment figure occurs, the initial "protest" phase is characterized by increases in both the PANIC/GRIEF and SEEKING systems. The behavioral response during this phase, namely increases in vocalizing behaviors, is accompanied by decreases in both the opioid and oxytocinergic systems, and increases in HPA functioning and glutamatergic drive in neurocircuitry that controls the PANIC/GRIEF system. If reunion with the attachment figure does not occur, the resulting "despair" phase includes a PANIC/GRIEF system that remains overactive, while the SEEKING system begins to shut down. The authors theorize that a depression phenotype arises at this point as a protective mechanism to block the effects of prolonged elevation of the PANIC/GRIEF system (Panksepp & Watt, 2011; Watt & Panksepp, 2009).

Since these descriptions of separation response in human infants, this response to disruption of filial attachments has been modeled in both primates and rodents. Over the course of a six-week separation, rhesus macaque infants initially vocalize and move around their enclosure at high rates, but then shift to the "despair" stage, including decreased movement and withdrawal. Similar to humans, reunion with the mother ameliorated the distress behaviors and infants returned to their pre-separation state (B. Seay et al., 1962). The same response is found in pigtail macaques, although there is some evidence that being the infant of the mother at the top of the social dominance hierarchy may be protective against the "despair" stage (Kaufman & Rosenblum, 1967). As is the case in maternal attachment disruption, there is also an HPA response to filial attachment disruption. In titi monkeys (*Callicebus cupreus*), a biparental new world monkey species in which infants form an attachment to their father but not their mother (Mendoza &

Mason, 1986b), separation from the father causes a rise in plasma cortisol over the course of an hour (Hoffman et al., 1995). This response is not seen when separated from the mother, providing further evidence of their selective paternal filial attachment.

This two-phase response to separation seen in humans and non-human primates has also been characterized in the guinea pig (*Cavia porcellus*). When separated from their mother, infant guinea pigs will emit high rates of distress vocalizations, especially if they are isolated in a novel environment (Hennessy & Ritchey, 1987; Pettijohn, 1979). During this initial "protest" phase there is a rise in adrenocorticotropic hormone and plasma cortisol (Hennessy & Ritchey, 1987; Hennessy, Tamborski, Schiml, & Lucot, 1989), although this elevation in cortisol is only seen when the infant is separated in a novel enclosure; if the mother is simply removed from the home cage, the infant does not show this HPA response (Hennessy & Moorman, 1989). Guinea pig pups will transition to the "despair" stage after approximately one hour of separation in a novel environment, much faster than primates do, showing behaviors such as a crouched posture, closed eyes, and piloerection of the fur (Hennessy, Long, Nigh, Williams, & Nolan, 1995). With this shift toward a passive response phase, vocalizations decrease, but HPA activity continues to remain elevated (Hennessy & Moorman, 1989).

Pair bond disruption

The consequences of disruptions to adult pair bonds are perhaps more challenging to study in animal models than are maternal and filial attachments given the infrequent occurrence rate of social monogamy in mammalian species. A comparison of the monogamous titi monkey and the polygamous squirrel monkey shows titi monkeys display a greater increase in distress vocalizations and a larger increase in heart rate when separated from their bonded pair mate than do squirrel monkeys separated from a familiar conspecific (Cubicciotti & Mason, 1975). When the pair bond is disrupted, titi monkeys also show greater amounts of agitation and distress and have higher plasma cortisol levels (Fragaszy & Mason, 1978; Mendoza & Mason, 1986a). As is seen in filial attachments, the presence of an unfamiliar companion in place of the pair mate is not sufficient to reduce this emotional response, although reunion with the pair mate does eliminate it (Cubicciotti & Mason, 1975).

In the prairie vole, loss of the pair mate increases depressive behaviors in a forced swim chamber in both male and female partners (Bosch et al., 2016; McNeal et al., 2014; Sun, Smith, Lei, Liu, & Wang, 2014). These depressive behaviors may be moderated in part by oxytocin. With extended separation from the pair mate, oxytocin-immunoreactive cells are increased in both the PVN and SON (Sun et al., 2014). Oxytocin neurons originating in these hypothalamic nuclei project to the nucleus accumbens, where they facilitate social bonding (Ross et al., 2009). Oxytocin receptors within the nucleus accumbens shell are decreased in males in the days following partner loss. These males also demonstrate an increase in passive stress-coping behavior (floating) in a forced swim chamber, perhaps mimicking the "despair" phase of separation. The effects of this bond disruption on circulating oxytocin peptide levels is unknown. Infusing oxytocin directly into the nucleus accumbens shell in these males decreases the passive coping seen following bond disruption, while blocking oxytocin receptors in the region increases passive coping in males in intact pair bonds, mimicking the behaviors seen following bond disruption (Bosch et al., 2016). Oxytocin activity in this region, then, appears to be an important link between depressive behaviors and disruption of the pair bond – oxytocin activity in the nucleus accumbens facilitates bond formation and is decreased upon bond disruption, at which point depressive or "despair" behaviors increase. Stimulating nucleus accumbens oxytocin following bond disruption may then allow for a new bond to form, in part by overcoming the depressive behaviors.

The effects of oxytocin on the autonomic nervous system and social engagement

The autonomic nervous system is an important neural substrate for the behavioral effects of oxytocin, including its effects on the development of attachments and responses to the absence of an attachment figure. The actions of oxytocin on the autonomic nervous system may help to explain the dynamic capacity for care-giving and attachment behaviors. Conversely, deficiencies in the oxytocin system, either in the peptide or receptor, contribute to the tendency of separated or abandoned infants to show agitation and eventually despair and depression (Panksepp & Watt, 2011; Watt & Panksepp, 2009). However, the effects of oxytocin on the autonomic nervous system are complex, reflecting the evolution of that system, the adaptive role of oxytocin on different components of the autonomic nervous system, and the dynamic behavioral responses necessary for attachments to be expressed.

The autonomic nervous system consists of sympathetic and parasympathetic components. Embedded within the parasympathetic nervous system are two systems: an ancient unmyelinated branch with cells of origin in the brainstem region known as the dorsal vagal complex, and a more evolutionarily modern myelinated brain, with cells of origin in the ventral vagal complex. All components of the autonomic nervous system can be affected by the presence or absence of oxytocin, although these effects are most obvious in the presence of a challenge or stressor (Yee et al., 2016).

Oxytocin can support both active and passive social engagement and parenting, perhaps depending on whether oxytocin is experienced acutely or chronically. Acute release of or exposure to oxytocin is permissive for active social behaviors and may affect the sympathetic nervous system. In a safe environment, the chronic actions of oxytocin may reduce sympathetic activation and allow an increase in parasympathetic/vagal functions necessary for quiet social interactions. "Immobility without fear" characterizes parenting and pair bonding and appears to be facilitated by oxytocin (Kenkel et al., 2013; Porges, 1998). "Immobility with fear," shown in the face of threat or abandonment, is a component of despair and depression; this more primitive response may occur in the absence of oxytocin. Shut-down reactions or despair, including immobility, such as those seen in separated infants or abandoned partners, are common reactions to the absence of significant others.

Studies in isolated prairie voles have revealed that oxytocin has protective actions on the myelinated, newer branch of the vagus (Grippo, Trahanas, Zimmerman, Porges, & Carter, 2009). The myelinated vagus protects the heart, assuring adequate oxygenation of the neocortex, which in turn is necessary for social interactions and cognition (Porges, 1998). Oxytocin also may directly co-opt the unmyelinated vagus, acting in an inhibitory capacity to protecting mammals from the more primitive "reptile-like" freezing pattern (Porges, 2011).

Oxytocin works in conjunction with vasopressin, allowing a dynamic role in the regulation of the autonomic nervous system (Grippo et al., 2009; Yee et al., 2016). Oxytocin and vasopressin receptors are also found in brainstem regions that regulate social behaviors. Both peptides modulate the sympathetic system, but it is probably oxytocin that normally restrains the over-reactivity of the cardiovascular and HPA systems. In the face of extreme or chronic stress, oxytocin has direct actions on the parasympathetic component of the autonomic nervous system, permitting and promoting some of the health benefits of social engagement. This role of oxytocin in promoting engagement may be in part occurring via interactions with progesterone and its product allopregnanolone, both of which are released in response to a stressor to downregulate HPA activity. Interestingly, progesterone and allopregnanolone also appear to promote social engagement in response to a stressor in a fashion similar to that of oxytocin

(Wirth, 2011). We suspect that in the absence of a partner, reduced oxytocin, and possibly pro-gesterone/allopregnanolone, may leave an individual vulnerable initially to over-reactivity. This perhaps reflects the actions of vasopressin, while in the absence of oxytocin; over time these systems (oxytocin, vasopressin, progesterone, allopregnanolone) may all downregulate at the level of the peptide, the receptor, or both, with the response in this case being that of a "shut-down" response, including a depression phenotype and lack of social engagement. This response is adaptive in conserving energy but is not optimal for supporting social behaviors (Porges, 2011).

Oxytocin's role in psychopathologies

Studies in animal models of the various types of attachment relationships, including rodents, large mammals, and non-human primates, all indicate that involuntary separation from the attach-ment figure has negative consequences for the attached individual. These behavioral responses are remarkably similar across species and strongly resemble behaviors characteristic of human depression. Given that these attachment relationships are also regulated in part by oxytocin, it seems likely that there is a link between oxytocin system functioning and depressive disorders (Panksepp & Watt, 2011; Watt & Panksepp, 2009). Indeed, there is growing evidence in humans and in a number of rodent models that this is the case.

Major depression

Major depressive disorder negatively impacts functioning and quality of life each year in an estimated 16.1 million adults aged 18 or older in the United States (as reported by the National Institute of Mental Health). Diagnostic criteria listed in the Diagnostic and Statistical Manual – V include: a depressed mood; loss of interest in activities; changes in weight or appetite; dis-rupted sleep patterns; disrupted motor movement; fatigue; feelings of worthlessness; inability to concentrate; and recurrent thoughts of suicide or death, per the American Psychiatric Associa-tion (2013). Individuals must demonstrate at least five of these symptoms within a two-week period to warrant a diagnosis of major depressive disorder.

Evidence in clinical populations that oxytocin dysfunction is related to major depressive disorder symptomology is inconsistent. Measures of circulating oxytocin peptide, for example, have often shown opposing outcomes. There are several reports that individuals with increased depressive symptoms show increased circulating plasma oxytocin (Holt-Lunstad, Birming-ham, & Light, 2011; Parker et al., 2010; J. S. Seay et al., 2014). Similar results have also been found postmortem; people with major depressive disorder had a greater number of oxytocin-immunoreactive cells in the PVN compared to controls (Purba, Hoogendijk, Hofman, & Swaab, 1996). Conversely, several studies show a decrease in peripheral oxytocin with increased depressive symptoms (Frasch, Zetzsche, Steiger, & Jirikowski, 1995; Ozsoy, Esel, & Kula, 2009; Scantamburlo et al., 2007; J. S. Seay et al., 2014). There are also reports of increased variability in plasma oxytocin levels in people with depressive symptoms compared to controls (Cyranowski et al., 2008; vanLonden et al., 1997). Interestingly, there were no differences in central oxytocin levels as measured in cerebrospinal fluid between males with and without major depressive dis-order (Sasayama et al., 2012), raising the question of what the functional relationship is between central and peripheral oxytocin.

The variability seen in outcomes of these studies is somewhat striking, with several possible explanations. Study design varies, including factors such as the sex of participants or the time of day samples were collected. This may also include issues of adequate statistical power within samples, making a lack of replication of findings perhaps misleading. There is also currently a debate on the validity of assays measuring peripheral oxytocin levels (see, for example, Leng & Sabatier, 2016; McCullough, Churchland, & Mendez, 2013; Szeto et al., 2011). It is important to note that oxytocin and vasopressin contain disulfide bonds that allow these peptides to quickly bind to other molecules, making measurement and comparison across different methods difficult (Brandtzaeg et al., 2016; Martin & Carter, 2013). Issues such as these are likely to contribute to the variability found in study outcomes.

In addition to methodological points, individual differences in the subjects, such as genetics and early life experiences, may in turn lead to variability in these neuropeptides as well as in vulnerability to depression. Another possibility of potential relevance and perhaps one that is highly likely to play a role is that multiple mechanisms are involved in major depressive disorder, allowing different physiological profiles to present in different individuals. The list of diagnostic criteria for depression has several symptoms, not all of which need to be present for a diagnosis. Each of these symptoms is likely regulated by different mechanisms. Different individuals, then, can experience varying sets of symptoms with potentially different underlying causes, yet each have the same diagnosis. Thus, it is not surprising that physiological outcomes are not always consistent across this clinical diagnosis.

Animal models of depression and the effects of oxytocin

Data from human samples suggest that the relationship between depressive disorders and oxytocin levels may be diverse, suggesting an equally diverse etiology. This presents a particular problem when trying to develop a useful animal model of oxytocin and depression. Many neuropsychiatric disorders, in particular depressive disorders, do not demonstrate a single set of identifiable changes in neural circuitry or signaling. This diverse etiology makes it challenging to model the full extent of a particular human psychiatric condition in a single animal model. Instead, scientists have aimed to examine specific components of depression, focusing on specific models.

One of the first demonstrations of a connection between oxytocin and depressive behaviors came in mice, where ICV administration of oxytocin decreased immobility in a forced swim test (Meisenberg, 1981). The effects of oxytocin mimicked the effects of antidepressant administration on this same behavior. The results of that study suggested that oxytocin may act like an antidepressant to block passive coping or shutting down in the face of intense stressors. In the forced swim model, physical immobility or a failure to try to escape has been described as a "despair" behavior, similar to the despair phase of separation; Porsolt, Anton, Blavet, & Jalfre, 1978). One frequently studied rat model of depression is "learned helplessness" (a condition where, after repeated exposure to an inescapable stressor, a subject adopts a helpless approach and stops trying to escape); in this model, treatment with ICV oxytocin was also associated with fewer learned helplessness behaviors (Meisenberg, 1982). Peripheral oxytocin administration appears to have similar consequences. Intraperitoneal injections of oxytocin in mice decrease forced swim immobility (Arletti & Bertolini, 1987), although this may not always be the case (see Slattery & Neumann, 2010). In rats, peripheral oxytocin also decreases forced swim immobility (Nowakowska, Kus, Bobkiewicz-Kozlowska, & Hertmanowska, 2002) and decreases learned helplessness behaviors in a foot shock test, where rats treated with oxytocin escaped the foot shock faster (Arletti & Bertolini, 1987). The mechanism of action for this peripherally administered oxytocin remains unclear. Although oxytocin does not readily cross the blood–brain barrier, as mentioned previously it may impact central signaling through peripheral sites of action such as vagal pathways.

More recent studies have provided additional support for the idea that oxytocin can act similarly to antidepressants to block depressive behaviors. The oxytocin agonist carbetocin, as well as a tricyclic antidepressant, both decrease immobility and increase active coping behaviors such as swimming escape attempts in a forced swim test, regardless of whether they are administered peripherally or centrally. These effects of carbetocin are blocked by concurrent administration of atosiban, an oxytocin receptor antagonist, indicating that the depressive behavioral responses seen in these models are likely due to oxytocin receptor activity in the brain (Broadbear, Kabel, Tracy, & Mak, 2014).

Depressive symptoms are more common in females

One of the hallmarks of major depressive disorder is the strong sex bias in prevalence, with women two to four times more likely to receive this diagnosis (Piccinelli & Wilkinson, 2000). Despite this known sex disparity, most basic research modeling depression has not specifically studied females (Beery & Zucker, 2011) but rather may combine males and females or present data exclusively on male subjects. Two promising animal models of depressive-like behaviors in females include social defeat in the California mouse and chronic social isolation in the prairie vole.

Social defeat has been used as a stressor in a variety of species. The paradigm involves placing the focal animal into the home cage of an unfamiliar resident, where the focal animal will very likely be attacked by the resident. Repeated daily exposure to this aggression will reliably produce depressive-like behaviors in the focal animal (see Solomon, 2017, for review). This paradigm is most useful in males in many species because females simply do not engage in high enough levels of aggression. One exception to this is the California mouse (*Peromyscus californicus*), a monogamous species in which both males and females defend their territory and females will reliably display aggression toward an intruder (Davis & Marler, 2003). Following repeated social defeat, female California mice will avoid social interaction with a novel conspecific, even several weeks following the defeat (Koolhaas et al., 1999; Steinman et al., 2016; Trainor et al., 2011). The response to these defeats is regulated in part by the oxytocin system. Following extended social defeat, females have increased oxytocin/c-fos co-localization in both the rostral PVN and the medioventral BNST in a social context. This increase is also seen in non-social situations in only the medioventral BNST. The elevated oxytocin/c-fos activity is related to an increased preference for an empty chamber in a test of social approach (Steinman et al., 2016). Together these data provide strong evidence that the decrease in social interaction seen in females following chronic social defeat, a behavior that is believed to be similar to social withdrawal seen in depression in humans, is related to an increase in oxytocin release. In this case, and perhaps especially in females, the release of endogenous oxytocin may reflect a "stress-coping" mechanism.

Social behavior is critically intertwined with stress management. Oxytocin pathways are protective against a number of adverse events, including over-reactivity to stressors. Social bonds can form in response to extreme stressors, especially when survival depends on the presence of another individual. Under comparatively intense stress, oxytocin is released, leading to the formation of social bonds (Carter, 1998). In rodents and other social mammals, chronic social isolation is associated with increases in measures of depression, anxiety, and physiological arousal, including changes in basal heart rate and reductions in ventral vagal parasympathetic activity in the prairie vole (Grippo et al., 2009).

Work in the prairie vole has highlighted the role attachment and social affiliation may play in avoiding depressive-like behaviors. As discussed previously, this species is typically found living in a social group, and social isolation is a potent stressor. This appears to be the case especially for females. Chronic isolation housing of at least four weeks in duration results in an increase in a number of depressive-like and anxiety-like behaviors, including increased immobility in a forced swim test, increased anhedonia (lack of a preference for a rewarding stimulus, which is seen as an indicator of a depressive-like mood; Willner, Muscat, & Papp, 1992), decreased exploration in an open field arena and an elevated plus maze, and increased aggression toward novel infants (Grippo, Cushing, & Carter, 2007; Grippo, Gerena et al., 2007; Grippo et al., 2009; Grippo, Wu, Hassan, & Carter, 2008; Lieberwirth, Liu, Jia, & Wang, 2012).

Isolation or other forms of chronic stress also may reduce gene expression for the oxytocin receptor (Pournajafi-Nazarloo et al., 2013), possibly creating insensitivity to the beneficial effects of oxytocin. Concurrently, in female prairie voles isolation is accompanied by an increase in blood levels of oxytocin (Grippo et al., 2009). The autonomic components of voles' responses to chronic isolation are prevented or reversed by chronic treatment with exogenous oxytocin, further implicating oxytocin in social support. Thus, in the prairie vole model, isolation-associated elevations in endogenous oxytocin are not sufficient to fully protect against the autonomic and behavioral consequences of living alone. Whether comparable changes occur in humans remains to be determined, but the presence of a companion, especially an attachment figure, via functional increases in oxytocin or its receptor, could potentially reverse some effects of chronic stress. Thus, the presence of a safe partner or other conditions that favor activation of oxytocin-regulated processes may enhance resilience in the face of stressful experiences.

Several of the animal models discussed above present apparently conflicting findings with regard to oxytocin system activity, social bonds, and depressive-like behaviors. Oxytocin transmission is elevated and in fact necessary during the formation of social bonds (Carter, 1998; Cho et al., 1999; Ross et al., 2009). Yet it is also elevated in models of depressive behaviors, which inherently include a lack of social bond formation, including social defeat (Steinman et al., 2016) and chronic social isolation (Grippo et al., 2009). The reasons for these contradictions are not immediately clear. Oxytocin likely serves dual purposes in this regard. It may be that, while it is necessary for displays of pro-social behaviors, increased oxytocin activity in the absence of these pro-social interactions may serve as a protection mechanism for some, but not all, consequences of exposure to stressful conditions. Additional work to understand the role of the oxytocin system in these conflicting scenarios is warranted and may serve to provide a better understanding of potential links between oxytocin and depressive disorders.

Postpartum depression

Instances of depression that may be particularly related to altered oxytocin system functioning are those occurring in the postpartum period in mothers. As discussed previously, the peripartum period is a time when women experience dynamic changes in the oxytocin system. Given oxytocin's known role in the peripartum and postpartum period in mothers, as well as the connection between oxytocin dysfunction and major depressive disorders, researchers have begun to examine the relationship between the oxytocin network and postpartum depression (PPD). Major depressive disorder and PPD symptoms manifest themselves almost identically, so much so that PPD and major depressive disorder have the same diagnostic criteria in the Diagnostic and Statistical Manual – V (American Psychiatric Association, 2013) with the added stipulation that PPD occurs "with peripartum onset," meaning the onset of depressive episodes occurring any time from pregnancy through the first four weeks postpartum. In practicality, though, the diagnosis of PPD is often applied to the onset of symptoms occurring within 12 months of parturition (O'Hara & McCabe, 2013). This range in diagnostic timeline likely is related to the variation in reported prevalence rates, which have been reported as occurring in up to 19% of new mothers (O'Hara & McCabe, 2013).

While definitive causes of PPD are unknown, two classes of risk factors have been identified: genetic/biological factors and environmental/social factors. Research strongly suggests that variation in the oxytocin system may be a biological risk factor for PPD. Decreased levels of plasma oxytocin both prenatally and postnatally have repeatedly been associated with increased PPD symptomology (Cox et al., 2015; Garfield et al., 2015; Skrundz, Bolten, Nast, Hellhammer, & Meinlschmidt, 2011; Stuebe, Grewen, & Meltzer-Brody, 2013). Specific polymorphisms within both the oxytocin peptide gene, OXT (Jonas et al., 2013), and the oxytocin receptor gene, OXTR (Apter-Levy, Feldman, Vakart, Ebstein, & Feldman, 2013; Mileva-Seitz et al., 2013), both appear to confer vulnerability to developing PPD. In addition, epigenetic modification of OXTR via DNA methylation at a specific CpG site in the promoter region, which theoretically should decrease OXTR transcription and lead to a downstream reduction in oxytocin receptors, also increases the risk of PPD in a genotype-specific manner (Bell et al., 2015). Taken together, these data indicate that disruption to the oxytocin system at a number of different points may act to increase a woman's vulnerability to developing PPD.

A key environmental risk factor for developing PPD is perceived psychosocial stress throughout pregnancy and in the postpartum period. Women who report experiencing higher levels of psychosocial stress are more likely to experience symptoms of PPD (Beck, 2001; E. Robertson, Grace, Wallington, & Stewart, 2004; Yim, Stapleton, Guardino, Hahn-Holbrook, & Schetter, 2015). This relationship may be mediated by oxytocin levels, as women with higher reported levels of psychosocial stress in early pregnancy and postpartum had lower depressive symptoms if they had higher levels of circulating oxytocin (Zelkowitz et al., 2014). At least some of the individual variation in PPD may be due to early life experiences and attachment, which in turn can be moderated by the sensitivity of the oxytocin receptor and the capacity to release oxytocin. Oxytocin, then, may be protective against the development of PPD symptoms, possibly in part by reducing susceptibility to social or environmental stressors.

This idea that oxytocin may be protective against PPD has been explored with regard to breastfeeding in the postpartum period, a behavior that facilitates the release of maternal (and infant) oxytocin. Breastfeeding has been hypothesized to be protective against risk for PPD by increasing levels of oxytocin. Evidence for this protective effect, however, is mixed. Women who had negative breastfeeding experiences in the early postpartum period, including painful or difficult feedings, had greater rates of PPD symptoms (Watkins, Meltzer-Brody, Zolnoun, & Stuebe, 2011). Other studies have found that increased breastfeeding duration was associated with decreased PPD risk (Figueiredo, Dias, Brandao, Canario, & Nunes-Costa, 2013) or have found no clear association between breastfeeding and PPD (Dias & Figueiredo, 2015). Several others have concluded there is no association between breastfeeding and PPD after accounting for other PPD risk factors (Ahn & Corwin, 2015; Davey, Tough, Adair, & Benzies, 2011; McKee, Zayas, & Jankowski, 2004; Pope, Mazmanian, Bedard, & Sharma, 2016), suggesting that breastfeeding may not serve to lower PPD risk through elevating oxytocin levels.

Conclusion

Here we review the role oxytocin plays in the formation and maintenance of maternal, filial, and adult attachment relationships and how involuntary breaking of these attachments results in behavioral responses, seen across many species that resemble at least some of the behavioral symptoms of major depressive disorder. It is clear that attachment formation is regulated in part by the oxytocin system and that disruption of these attachments is associated with depressive-like behaviors. The link between these disrupted bonds and "despair" may well be a dysfunction in oxytocin activity (see Figure 36.1). For example, disrupting an attachment relationship may

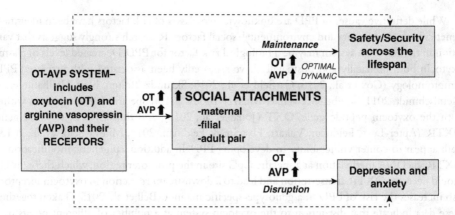

Figure 36.1 Hypothetical protective and adaptive effects of social attachments via oxytocin and vasopressin and their receptors. Oxytocin and especially vasopressin will differ between males and females, and by context.

disrupt or downregulate oxytocin, possibly allowing an over-expression of vasopressin or other stress hormones in the attached individual; such changes in turn could manifest as depressive-like or shutting down behavioral traits. Animal models of depressive-like behaviors appear to support this hypothesis. Behaviors such as immobility, anhedonia, and social withdrawal are all related to altered oxytocin functioning following social stressors that model depression. While findings in humans are still mixed due to methodological variations and statistical power issues, these models suggest that, at least for some symptoms and some individuals, the oxytocin system, including the functions of the related peptide vasopressin, could offer a viable target for understanding the etiology of major depressive disorders. If correct, knowledge of the role of oxytocin, as well as vasopressin, in attachment behaviors may help in the development of hormonally informed treatment strategies for these and related forms of psychopathology.

References

Ahn, S., & Corwin, E. J. (2015). The association between breastfeeding, the stress response, inflammation, and postpartum depression during the postpartum period: Prospective cohort study. *International Journal of Nursing Studies, 52*(10), 1582–1590. doi:10.1016/j.ijnurstu.2015.05.017

Ainsworth, M. D. S. (1985). Patterns of infant-mother attachments – antecedents and effects on development. *Bulletin of the New York Academy of Medicine, 61*(9), 771–791.

American Psychiatric Association. (2013). *Diagnostic and statistical manual of mental disorders* (5th ed.). Arlington, VA: American Psychiatric Association.

Apter-Levy, Y., Feldman, M., Vakart, A., Ebstein, R. P., & Feldman, R. (2013). Impact of maternal depression across the first 6 years of life on the child's mental health, social engagement, and empathy: The moderating role of oxytocin. *American Journal of Psychiatry, 170*(10), 1161–1168. doi:10.1176/appi.ajp.2013.12121597

Arletti, R., & Bertolini, A. (1987). Oxytocin acts as an antidepressant in 2 animal models of depression. *Life Sciences, 41*(14), 1725–1730. doi:10.1016/0024-3205(87)90600-x

Bamshad, M., Novak, M. A., & Devries, G. J. (1994). Cohabitation alters vasopressin innervation and paternal behavior in prairie voles (*Microtus ochrogaster*). *Physiology & Behavior, 56*(4), 751–758. doi:10.1016/0031-9384(94)90238-0

Barrett, C. E., Keebaugh, A. C., Ahern, T. H., Bass, C. E., Terwilliger, E. F., & Young, L. J. (2013). Variation in vasopressin receptor (Avpr1 a) expression creates diversity in behaviors related to monogamy in prairie voles. *Hormones and Behavior, 63*(3), 518–526. doi:10.1016/j.yhbeh.2013.01.005

Beck, C. T. (2001). Predictors of postpartum depression – an update. *Nursing Research, 50*(5), 275–285. doi:10.1097/00006199-200109000-00004

Beery, A. K., & Zucker, I. (2011). Sex bias in neuroscience and biomedical research. *Neuroscience and Biobehavioral Reviews, 35*(3), 565–572. doi:10.1016/j.neubiorev.2010.07.002

Bell, A. F., Carter, C. S., Steer, C. D., Golding, J., Davis, J. M., Steffen, A. D., . . . Connelly, J. J. (2015). Interaction between oxytocin and receptor DNA methylation and genotype is associated with risk of postpartum depression in women without depression in pregnancy. *Frontiers in Genetics, 6*, 243-Article No.: 243. doi:10.3389/fgene.2015.00243

Bernaerts, S., Prinsen, J., Berra, E., Bosmans, G., Steyaert, J., & Alaerts, K. (2017). Long-term oxytocin administration enhances the experience of attachment. *Psychoneuroendocrinology, 78*, 1–9. doi:10.1016/j.psyneuen.2017.01.010

Bosch, O. J., Dabrowska, J., Modi, M. E., Johnson, Z. V., Keebaugh, A. C., Barrett, C. E., . . . Young, L. J. (2016). Oxytocin in the nucleus accumbens shell reverses CRFR2-evoked passive stress-coping after partner loss in monogamous male prairie voles. *Psychoneuroendocrinology, 64*, 66–78. doi:10.1016/j.psyneuen.2015.11.011

Brandtzaeg, O. K., Johnsen, E., Roberg-Larsen, H., Seip, K. F., MacLean, E. L., Gesquiere, L. R., . . . Wilson, S. R. (2016). Proteomics tools reveal startlingly high amounts of oxytocin in plasma and serum. *Scientific Reports, 6*. doi:10.1038/srep31693

Broad, K. D., Kendrick, K. M., Sirinathsinghji, D. J. S., & Keverne, E. B. (1993). Changes in oxytocin immunoreactivity and messenger-RNA expression in the sheep brain during pregnancy, parturition and lactation and in response to estrogen and progesterone. *Journal of Neuroendocrinology, 5*(4), 435–444. doi:10.1111/j.1365-2826.1993.tb00505.x

Broad, K. D., Levy, F., Evans, G., Kimura, T., Keverne, E. B., & Kendrick, K. M. (1999). Previous maternal experience potentiates the effect of parturition on oxytocin receptor mRNA expression in the paraventricular nucleus. *European Journal of Neuroscience, 11*(10), 3725–3737. doi:10.1046/j.1460-9568.1999.00782.x

Broadbear, J. H., Kabel, D., Tracy, L., & Mak, P. (2014). Oxytocinergic regulation of endogenous as well as drug-induced mood. *Pharmacology Biochemistry and Behavior, 119*, 61–71. doi:10.1016/j.pbb.2013.07.002

Buijs, R. M. (1978). Intrahypothalamic and extrahypothalamic vasopressin and oxytocin pathways in rat – pathways to limbic system, medulla oblongata and spinal cord. *Cell and Tissue Research, 192*(3), 423–435.

Buijs, R. M., Swaab, D. F., Dogterom, J., & Vanleeuwen, F. W. (1978). Intrahypothalamic and extrahypothalamic vasopressin and oxytocin pathways in rat. *Cell and Tissue Research, 186*(3), 423–433.

Buisman-Pijlman, F. T. A., Sumracki, N. M., Gordon, J. J., Hull, P. R., Carter, C. S., & Tops, M. (2014). Individual differences underlying susceptibility to addiction: Role for the endogenous oxytocin system. *Pharmacology Biochemistry and Behavior, 119*, 22–38. doi:10.1016/j.pbb.2013.09.005

Cacioppo, J. T., Amaral, D. G., Blanchard, J. J., Cameron, J. L., Carter, C. S., Crews, D., . . . Quinn, K. J. (2007). Social neuroscience progress and implications for mental health. *Perspectives on Psychological Science, 2*(2), 99–123. doi:10.1111/j.1745-6916.2007.00032.x

Caldwell, H. K. (2017). Oxytocin and vasopressin: Powerful regulators of social behavior. *Neuroscientist, 23*(5), 517–528. doi:10.1177/1073858417708284

Carter, C. S. (1998). Neuroendocrine perspectives on social attachment and love. *Psychoneuroendocrinology, 23*(8), 779–818.

Carter, C. S. (2017). The role of oxytocin and vasopressin in attachment. *Psychodynamic Psychiatry, 45*(4), 499–518.

Carter, C. S., & Keverne, E. B. (2017). The neurobiology of social affiliation and pair bonding. In D. W. Pfaff & M. Joels (Eds.), *Hormones, brain, and behavior* (3rd ed., pp. 117–143). Oxford: Academic Press.

Cho, M. M., DeVries, A. C., Williams, J. R., & Carter, C. S. (1999). The effects of oxytocin and vasopressin on partner preferences in male and female prairie voles (*Microtus ochrogaster*). *Behavioral Neuroscience, 113*(5), 1071–1079. doi:10.1037/0735-7044.113.5.1071

Coe, C. L., Mendoza, S. P., Smotherman, W. P., & Levine, S. (1978). Mother-infant attachment in squirrel monkey – adrenal response to separation. *Behavioral Biology, 22*(2), 256–263. doi:10.1016/s0091-6773(78)92305-2

Cox, E. Q., Stuebe, A., Pearson, B., Grewen, K., Rubinow, D., & Meltzer-Brody, S. (2015). Oxytocin and HPA stress axis reactivity in postpartum women. *Psychoneuroendocrinology, 55*, 164–172. doi:10.1016/j.psyneuen.2015.02.009

Cubicciotti, D. D., & Mason, W. A. (1975). Comparative studies of social behavior in *Callicebus* and *Saimiri*: Male-female emotional attachments. *Behavioral Biology, 16*, 185–197.

Cyranowski, J. M., Hofkens, T. L., Frank, E., Seltman, H., Cai, H-M., & Amico, J. A. (2008). Evidence of dysregulated peripheral oxytocin release among depressed women. *Psychosomatic Medicine, 70*(9), 967–975. doi:10.1097/PSY.0b013e318188ade4

Davey, H. L., Tough, S. C., Adair, C. E., & Benzies, K. M. (2011). Risk factors for sub-clinical and major postpartum depression among a community cohort of Canadian women. *Maternal and Child Health Journal, 15*(7), 866–875. doi:10.1007/s10995-008-0314-8

Davis, E. S., & Marler, C. A. (2003). The progesterone challenge: Steroid hormone changes following a simulated territorial intrusion in female Peromyscus californicus. *Hormones and Behavior, 44*(3), 185–198. doi:10.1016/s0018-506x(03)00128-4

DeVries, A. C., & Carter, C. S. (1999). Sex differences in temporal parameters of partner preference in prairie voles (*Microtus ochrogaster*). *Canadian Journal of Zoology-Revue Canadienne De Zoologie, 77*(6), 885–889. doi:10.1139/cjz-77-6-885

Dias, C. C., & Figueiredo, B. (2015). Breastfeeding and depression: A systematic review of the literature. *Journal of Affective Disorders, 171*, 142–154. doi:10.1016/j.jad.2014.09.022

Donaldson, Z. R., Spiegel, L., & Young, L. J. (2010). Central vasopressin V1a receptor activation is independently necessary for both partner preference formation and expression in socially monogamous male prairie voles. *Behavioral Neuroscience, 124*(1), 159–163. doi:10.1037/a0018094

Dumais, K. M., & Veenema, A. H. (2016). Vasopressin and oxytocin receptor systems in the brain: Sex differences and sex-specific regulation of social behavior. *Frontiers in Neuroendocrinology, 40*, 1–23. doi:10.1016/j.yfrne.2015.04.003

Feldman, R. (2012). Oxytocin and social affiliation in humans. *Hormones and Behavior, 61*(3), 380–391. doi:10.1016/j.yhbeh.2012.01.008

Feldman, R. (2017). The neurobiology of human attachments. *Trends in Cognitive Sciences, 21*(2), 80–99. doi:10.1016/j.tics.2016.11.007

Feldman, R., Monakhov, M., Pratt, M., & Ebstein, R. P. (2016). Oxytocin pathway genes: Evolutionary ancient system impacting on human affiliation, sociality, and psychopathology. *Biological Psychiatry, 79*(3), 174–184. doi:10.1016/j.biopsych.2015.08.008

Figueiredo, B., Dias, C. C., Brandao, S., Canario, C., & Nunes-Costa, R. (2013). Breastfeeding and postpartum depression: State of the art review. *Jornal De Pediatria, 89*(4), 332–338. doi:10.1016/j.jped.2012.12.002

Fragaszy, D. M., & Mason, W. A. (1978). Response to novelty in *Saimiri* and *Callicebus* influence of social context. *Primates, 19*(2), 311–332. doi:10.1007/bf02382800

Frasch, A., Zetzsche, T., Steiger, A., & Jirikowski, G. F. (1995). Reduction of plasma oxytocin levels in patients suffering from major depression. In R. Ivell & J. A. Russell (Eds.), *Oxytocin: Cellular and molecular approaches in medicine and research* (Vol. 395, pp. 257–258). London and New York: Plenum Press.

French, J. A., Taylor, J. H., Mustoe, A. C., & Cavanaugh, J. (2016). Neuropeptide diversity and the regulation of social behavior in New World primates. *Frontiers in Neuroendocrinology, 42*, 18–39. doi:10.1016/j.yfrne.2016.03.004

Garfield, L., Giurgescu, C., Carter, C. S., Holditch-Davis, D., McFarlin, B. L., Schwertz, D., . . . White-Traut, R. (2015). Depressive symptoms in the second trimester relate to low oxytocin levels in African-American women: A pilot study. *Archives of Women's Mental Health, 18*(1), 123–129. doi:10.1007/s00737-014-0437-4

Goodson, J. L., & Kingsbury, M. A. (2013). What's in a name? Considerations of homologies and nomenclature for vertebrate social behavior networks. *Hormones and Behavior, 64*(1), 103–112. doi:10.1016/j.yhbeh.2013.05.006

Grinevich, V., Knobloch-Bollmann, H. S., Eliava, M., Busnelli, M., & Chini, B. (2016). Assembling the puzzle: Pathways of oxytocin signaling in the brain. *Biological Psychiatry, 79*(3), 155–164. doi:10.1016/j.biopsych.2015.04.013

Grippo, A. J., Cushing, B. S., & Carter, C. S. (2007). Depression-like behavior and stressor-induced neuroendocrine activation in female prairie voles exposed to chronic social isolation. *Psychosomatic Medicine, 69*(2), 149–157. doi:10.1097/PSY.0b013e31802f054b

Grippo, A. J., Gerena, D., Huang, J., Kumar, N., Shah, M., Ughreja, R., & Carter, C. S. (2007). Social isolation induces behavioral and neuroendocrine disturbances relevant to depression in female and male prairie voles. *Psychoneuroendocrinology, 32*(8–10), 966–980. doi:10.1016/j.psyneuen.2007.07.004

Grippo, A. J., Trahanas, D. M., Zimmerman, R. R., 2nd, Porges, S. W., & Carter, C. S. (2009). Oxytocin protects against negative behavioral and autonomic consequences of long-term social isolation. *Psychoneuroendocrinology, 34*(10), 1542–1553. doi:10.1016/j.psyneuen.2009.05.017

Grippo, A. J., Wu, K. D., Hassan, I., & Carter, C. S. (2008). Social isolation in prairie voles induces behaviors relevant to negative affect: Toward the development of a rodent model focused on co-occurring depression and anxiety. *Depress Anxiety, 25*(6), E17–26. doi:10.1002/da.20375

Hennessy, M. B., Long, S. J., Nigh, C. K., Williams, M. T., & Nolan, D. J. (1995). Effects of peripherally administered Corticotropin-Releasing Factor (CRF) and a CRF antagonist: Does peripheral CRF activity mediate behavior of guinea pig pups during isolation? *Behavioral Neuroscience, 109*(6), 1137–1145. doi:10.1037//0735-7044.109.6.1137

Hennessy, M. B., & Moorman, L. (1989). Factors influencing cortisol and behavioral responses to maternal separation in guinea pigs. *Behavioral Neuroscience, 103*(2), 378–385.

Hennessy, M. B., & Ritchey, R. L. (1987). Hormonal and behavioral attachment responses in infant guinea pigs. *Developmental Psychobiology, 20*(6), 613–625. doi:10.1002/dev.420200607

Hennessy, M. B., Tamborski, A., Schiml, P., & Lucot, J. (1989). The influence of maternal separation on plasma concentrations of ACTH, epinephrine, and norepinephrine in guinea pig pups. *Physiology & Behavior, 45*(6), 1147–1152. doi:10.1016/0031-9384(89)90101-7

Hoffman, K. A., Mendoza, S. P., Hennessy, M. B., & Mason, W. A. (1995). Responses of infant titi monkeys, *Callicebus moloch*, to removal of one or both parents – evidence for paternal attachment. *Developmental Psychobiology, 28*(7), 399–407. doi:10.1002/dev.420280705

Holt-Lunstad, J., Birmingham, W., & Light, K. C. (2011). The influence of depressive symptomatology and perceived stress on plasma and salivary oxytocin before, during and after a support enhancement intervention. *Psychoneuroendocrinology, 36*(8), 1249–1256. doi:10.1016/j.psyneuen.2011.03.007

House, J. S., Landis, K. R., & Umberson, D. (1988). Social relationships and health. *Science, 241*(4865), 540–545. doi:10.1126/science.3399889

Hurlemann, R., & Scheele, D. (2016). Dissecting the role of oxytocin in the formation and loss of social relationships. *Biological Psychiatry, 79*(3), 185–193. doi:10.1016/j.biopsych.2015.05.013

Insel, T. R., & Shapiro, L. E. (1992). Oxytocin receptor distribution reflects social-organization in monogamous and polygamous voles. *Proceedings of the National Academy of Sciences of the United States of America, 89*(13), 5981–5985. doi:10.1073/pnas.89.13.5981

Jensen, G. D., & Tolman, C. W. (1962). Mother-infant relationship in monkey, *Macaca nemestring* – effect of brief separation and mother-infant specificity. *Journal of Comparative and Physiological Psychology, 55*(1), 131–&. doi:10.1037/h0048498

Jonas, W., Mileva-Seitz, V., Girard, A. W., Bisceglia, R., Kennedy, J. L., Sokolowski, M., . . . Team, M. R. (2013). Genetic variation in oxytocin rs2740210 and early adversity associated with postpartum depression and breastfeeding duration. *Genes Brain and Behavior, 12*(7), 681–694. doi:10.1111/gbb.12069

Kaufman, I. C., & Rosenblum, L. A. (1967). Reaction to separation in infant monkeys – anaclitic depression and conservation withdrawal. *Psychosomatic Medicine, 29*(6), 648–+.

Kendrick, K. M., Fabrenys, C., Blache, D., Goode, J. A., & Broad, K. D. (1993). The role of oxytocin release in the mediobasal hypothalamus of the sheep in relation to female sexual receptivity. *Journal of Neuroendocrinology, 5*(1), 13–21. doi:10.1111/j.1365-2826.1993.tb00359.x

Kendrick, K. M., & Keverne, E. B. (1991). Importance of progesterone and estrogen priming for the induction of maternal behavior by vaginocervical stimulation in sheep – effects of maternal experience. *Physiology & Behavior, 49*(4), 745–750. doi:10.1016/0031-9384(91)90313-d

Kendrick, K. M., Keverne, E. B., & Baldwin, B. A. (1987). Intracerebroventricular oxytocin stimulates maternal behaviour in the sheep. *Neuroendocrinology, 46*(1), 56–61.

Kendrick, K. M., Keverne, E. B., Hinton, M. R., & Goode, J. A. (1991). Cerebrospinal-fluid and plasma concentrations of oxytocin and vasopressin during parturition and vaginocervical stimulation in the sheep. *Brain Research Bulletin, 26*(5), 803–807. doi:10.1016/0361-9230(91)90178-m

Kenkel, W. M., Paredes, J., Lewis, G. F., Yee, J. R., Pournajafi-Nazarloo, H., Grippo, A. J., . . . Carter, C. S. (2013). Autonomic substrates of the response to pups in male prairie voles. *PLoS One, 8*(8), e69965. doi:10.1371/journal.pone.0069965

Keverne, E. B., Levy, F., Poindron, P., & Lindsay, D. R. (1983). Vaginal stimulation – an important determinant of maternal bonding in sheep. *Science, 219*(4580), 81–83. doi:10.1126/science.6849123

Kleiman, D. G. (1977). Monogamy in mammals. *Quarterly Review of Biology, 52*(1), 39–69. doi:10.1086/409721

Koolhaas, J. M., Korte, S. M., De Boer, S. F., van Der Vegt, B. J., van Reenen, C. G., Hopster, H., . . . Blokhuis, H. J. (1999). Coping styles in animals: Current status in behavior and stress physiology. *Neuroscience and Biobehavioral Reviews, 23*(7), 925–935. doi:10.1016/s0149-7634(99)00026-3

Landgraf, R., & Neumann, I. D. (2004). Vasopressin and oxytocin release within the brain: A dynamic concept of multiple and variable modes of neuropeptide communication. *Frontiers in Neuroendocrinology*, *25*(3–4), 150–176. doi:10.1016/j.yfrne.2004.05.001

Leng, G., & Sabatier, N. (2016). Measuring oxytocin and vasopressin: Bioassays, immunoassays and random numbers. *Journal of Neuroendocrinology*, *28*(10). doi:10.1111/jne.12413

Levy, F., Kendrick, K. M., Goode, J. A., Guevaraguzman, R., & Keverne, E. B. (1995). Oxytocin and vasopressin release in the olfactory bulb of parturient ewes – changes with maternal experience and effects on acetylcholine, gamma-aminobutyric-acid, glutamate and noradrenaline release. *Brain Research*, *669*(2), 197–206. doi:10.1016/0006-8993(94)01236-b

Lieberwirth, C., Liu, Y., Jia, X., & Wang, Z. (2012). Social isolation impairs adult neurogenesis in the limbic system and alters behaviors in female prairie voles. *Hormones and Behavior*, *62*(4), 357–366. doi:10.1016/j.yhbeh.2012.03.005

Lim, M. M., Wang, Z. X., Olazabal, D. E., Ren, X. H., Terwilliger, E. F., & Young, L. J. (2004). Enhanced partner preference in a promiscuous species by manipulating the expression of a single gene. *Nature*, *429*(6993), 754–757. doi:10.1038/nature02539

Lim, M. M., & Young, L. J. (2004). Vasopressin-dependent neural circuits underlying pair bond formation in the monogamous prairie vole. *Neuroscience*, *125*(1), 35–45. doi:10.1016/j.neuroscience.2003.12.008

Liu, Y., Curtis, J. T., & Wang, Z. X. (2001). Vasopressin in the lateral septum regulates pair bond formation in male prairie voles (*Microtus ochrogaster*). *Behavioral Neuroscience*, *115*(4), 910–919. doi:10.1037//0735-7044.115.4.910

Liu, Y., & Wang, Z. X. (2003). Nucleus accumbens oxytocin and dopamine interact to regulate pair bond formation in female prairie voles. *Neuroscience*, *121*(3), 537–544. doi:10.1016/s0306-4522(03)00555-4

MacDonald, K., Berlow, R., & Thomas, M. L. (2013). Attachment, affective temperament, and personality disorders: A study of their relationships in psychiatric outpatients. *Journal of Affective Disorders*, *151*(3), 932–941. doi:10.1016/j.jad.2013.07.040

Martin, W., & Carter, C. S. (2013). *Oxytocin and vasopressin are sequestered in plasma*. Paper presented at the World Congress of Neurohypophyseal Hormones, Bristol, UK.

Mason, W. A., & Mendoza, S. P. (1998). Generic aspects of primate attachments: Parents, offspring and mates. *Psychoneuroendocrinology*, *23*(8), 765–778.

McCullough, M. E., Churchland, P. S., & Mendez, A. J. (2013). Problems with measuring peripheral oxytocin: Can the data on oxytocin and human behavior be trusted? *Neuroscience and Biobehavioral Reviews*, *37*(8), 1485–1492. doi:10.1016/j.neubiorev.2013.04.018

McKee, M. D., Zayas, L. H., & Jankowski, K. R. B. (2004). Breastfeeding intention and practice in an urban minority population: Relationship to maternal depressive symptoms and mother infant closeness. *Journal of Reproductive and Infant Psychology*, *22*(3), 167–181. doi:10.1080/02646830410001723751

McNeal, N., Scotti, M. A., Wardwell, J., Chandler, D. L., Bates, S. L., Larocca, M., . . . Grippo, A. J. (2014). Disruption of social bonds induces behavioral and physiological dysregulation in male and female prairie voles. *Autonomic Neuroscience*, *180*, 9–16. doi:10.1016/j.autneu.2013.10.001

Meisenberg, G. (1981). Short-term behavioral effects of posterior pituitary peptides in mice. *Peptides*, *2*(1), 1–8. doi:10.1016/s0196-9781(81)80003-4

Meisenberg, G. (1982). Short-term behavioral effects of neurohypophyseal hormones – pharmacological characteristics. *Neuropharmacology*, *21*(4), 309–316. doi:10.1016/0028-3908(82)90093-4

Mendoza, S. P., Coe, C. L., Smotherman, W. P., Kaplan, J., & Levine, S. (1980). Functional consequences of attachment: A comparison of two species. In R. W. Bell & W. P. Smotherman (Eds.), *Maternal influences and early behavior* (pp. 235–252). New York, NY: Spectrum Publications.

Mendoza, S. P., & Mason, W. A. (1986a). Contrasting responses to intruders and to involuntary separation by monogamous and polygynous new world monkeys. *Physiology & Behavior*, *38*(6), 795–801. doi:10.1016/0031-9384(86)90045-4

Mendoza, S. P., & Mason, W. A. (1986b). Parental division of labor and differentiation of attachments in a monogamous primate (*Callicebus moloch*). *Animal Behaviour*, *34*, 1336–1347. doi:10.1016/s0003-3472(86)80205-6

Mileva-Seitz, V., Steiner, M., Atkinson, L., Meaney, M. J., Levitan, R., Kennedy, J. L., . . . Fleming, A. S. (2013). Interaction between oxytocin genotypes and early experience predicts quality of mothering and postpartum mood. *PLoS One*, *8*(4). doi:e61443 10.1371/journal.pone.0061443

Nowak, R., Keller, M., & Levy, F. (2011). Mother-young relationships in sheep: A model for a multidisciplinary approach of the study of attachment in mammals. *Journal of Neuroendocrinology*, *23*(11), 1042–1053. doi:10.1111/j.1365-2826.2011.02205.x

Nowak, R., Murphy, T. M., Lindsay, D. R., Alster, P., Andersson, R., & UvnasMoberg, K. (1997). Development of a preferential relationship with the mother by the newborn lamb: Importance of the sucking activity. *Physiology & Behavior, 62*(4), 681–688. doi:10.1016/s0031-9384(97)00079-6

Nowakowska, E., Kus, K., Bobkiewicz-Kozlowska, T., & Hertmanowska, H. (2002). Role of neuropeptides in antidepressant and memory improving effects of venlafaxine. *Polish Journal of Pharmacology, 54*(6), 605–613.

Numan, M., & Young, L. J. (2016). Neural mechanisms of mother–infant bonding and pair bonding: Similarities, differences, and broader implications. *Hormones and Behavior, 77*, 98–112. doi:10.1016/j.yhbeh.2015.05.015

O'Hara, M. W., & McCabe, J. E. (2013). Postpartum depression: Current status and future directions. In S. Nolen-Hoeksema (Ed.), *Annual review of clinical psychology* (Vol. 9, pp. 379–407). Palo Alto, CA: Annual Reviews.

Ozsoy, S., Esel, E., & Kula, M. (2009). Serum oxytocin levels in patients with depression and the effects of gender and antidepressant treatment. *Psychiatry Research, 169*(3), 249–252. doi:10.1016/j.psychres.2008.06.034

Panksepp, J., & Watt, D. (2011). Why does depression hurt? ancestral primary-process separation-distress (panic/grief) and diminished brain reward (seeking) processes in the genesis of depressive affect. *Psychiatry-Interpersonal and Biological Processes, 74*(1), 5–13.

Parker, K. J., Kenna, H. A., Zeitzer, J. M., Keller, J., Blasey, C. M., Amico, J. A., & Schatzberg, A. F. (2010). Preliminary evidence that plasma oxytocin levels are elevated in major depression. *Psychiatry Research, 178*(2), 359–362. doi:10.1016/j.psychres.2009.09.017

Pettijohn, T. F. (1979). Attachment and separation distress in the infant guinea pig. *Developmental Psychobiology, 12*(1), 73–81. doi:10.1002/dev.420120109

Piccinelli, M., & Wilkinson, G. (2000). Gender differences in depression – critical review. *British Journal of Psychiatry, 177*, 486–492. doi:10.1192/bjp.177.6.486

Pitkow, L. J., Sharer, C. A., Ren, X. L., Insel, T. R., Terwilliger, E. F., & Young, L. J. (2001). Facilitation of affiliation and pair-bond formation by vasopressin receptor gene transfer into the ventral forebrain of a monogamous vole. *Journal of Neuroscience, 21*(18), 7392–7396.

Poindron, P., Caba, M., Arrati, P. G., Krehbiel, D., & Beyer, C. (1994). Responses of maternal and nonmaternal ewes to social and mother-young separation. *Behavioural Processes, 31*(1), 97–110. doi:10.1016/0376-6357(94)90039-6

Pope, C. J., Mazmanian, D., Bedard, M., & Sharma, V. (2016). Breastfeeding and postpartum depression: Assessing the influence of breastfeeding intention and other risk factors. *Journal of Affective Disorders, 200*, 45–50. doi:10.1016/j.jad.2016.04.014

Porges, S. W. (1998). Love: An emergent property of the mammalian autonomic nervous system. *Psychoneuroendocrinology, 23*(8), 837–861.

Porges, S. W. (2011). *The polyvagal theory: Neurophysiological foundations of emotions, attachment, communication, and self-regulation* (1st ed.). New York, NY: W. W. Norton & Company.

Porsolt, R. D., Anton, G., Blavet, N., & Jalfre, M. (1978). Behavioral despair in rats – new model sensitive to antidepressant treatments. *European Journal of Pharmacology, 47*(4), 379–391. doi:10.1016/0014-2999(78)90118-8

Pournajafi-Nazarloo, H., Kenkel, W., Mohsenpour, S. R., Sanzenbacher, L., Saadat, H., Partoo, L., ... Carter, C. S. (2013). Exposure to chronic isolation modulates receptors mRNAs for oxytocin and vasopressin in the hypothalamus and heart. *Peptides, 43*, 20–26. doi:10.1016/j.peptides.2013.02.007

Purba, J. S., Hoogendijk, W. J. G., Hofman, M. A., & Swaab, D. F. (1996). Increased number of vasopressin- and oxytocin-expressing neurons in the paraventricular nucleus of the hypothalamus in depression. *Archives of General Psychiatry, 53*(2), 137–143.

Robertson, E., Grace, S., Wallington, T., & Stewart, D. E. (2004). Antenatal risk factors for postpartum depression: A synthesis of recent literature. *General Hospital Psychiatry, 26*(4), 289–295. doi:10.1016/j.genhosppsych.2004.02.006

Robertson, J., & Bowlby, J. (1952). Responses of young children to separation from their mothers. *Courrier Centre Internaternational Enfance, 2*, 131.

Ross, H. E., Cole, C. D., Smith, Y., Neumann, I. D., Landgraf, R., Murphy, A. Z., & Young, L. J. (2009). Characterization of the oxytocin system regulating affiliative behavior in female prairie voles. *Neuroscience, 162*(4), 892–903. doi:10.1016/j.neuroscience.2009.05.055

Sasayama, D., Hattori, K., Teraishi, T., Hori, H., Ota, M., Yoshida, S., ... Kunugi, H. (2012). Negative correlation between cerebrospinal fluid oxytocin levels and negative symptoms of male patients with schizophrenia. *Schizophrenia Research, 139*(1–3), 201–206. doi:10.1016/j.schres.2012.06.016

Scantamburlo, G., Hansenne, M., Fuchs, S., Pitchot, W., Marechal, P., Pequeux, C., ... Legros, J. J. (2007). Plasma oxytocin levels and anxiety in patients with major depression. *Psychoneuroendocrinology, 32*(4), 407–410. doi:10.1016/j.psyneuen.2007.01.009

Seay, B., Hansen, E., & Harlow, H. F. (1962). Mother-infant separation in monkeys. *Journal of Child Psychology and Psychiatry and Allied Disciplines, 3*(3–4), 123–132. doi:10.1111/j.1469-7610.1962.tb02047.x

Seay, J. S., Lattie, E., Schneiderman, N., Antoni, M. H., Fekete, E. M., Mendez, A. J., ... Fletcher, M. A. (2014). Linear and quadratic associations of plasma oxytocin with depressive symptoms in ethnic minority women living with HIV. *Journal of Applied Biobehavioral Research, 19*(1), 70–78. doi:10.1111/jabr.12016

Skrundz, M., Bolten, M., Nast, I., Hellhammer, D. H., & Meinlschmidt, G. (2011). Plasma oxytocin concentration during pregnancy is associated with development of postpartum depression. *Neuropsychopharmacology, 36*(9), 1886–1893. doi:10.1038/npp.2011.74

Slattery, D. A., & Neumann, I. D. (2010). Chronic ICV oxytocin attenuates the pathological high anxiety state of selectively bred Wistar rats. *Neuropharmacology, 58*(1), 56–61. doi:10.1016/j.neuropharm.2009.06.038

Solomon, M. B. (2017). Evaluating social defeat as a model for psychopathology in adult female rodents. *Journal of Neuroscience Research, 95*(1–2), 763–776. doi:10.1002/jnr.23971

Spangler, G., & Grossmann, K. E. (1993). Biobehavioral organization in securely and insecurely attached infants. *Child Development, 64*(5), 1439–1450. doi:10.1111/j.1467-8624.1993.tb02962.x

Spitz, R. A. (1946). An inquiry into the genesis of psychiatric conditions in early childhood, II. *Psychoanalytic Study of the Child, 2*, 313–342.

Steinman, M. Q., Duque-Wilckens, N., Greenberg, G. D., Hao, R., Campi, K. L., Laredo, S. A., ... Trainor, B. C. (2016). Sex-specific effects of stress on oxytocin neurons correspond with responses to intranasal oxytocin. *Biological Psychiatry, 80*(5), 406–414. doi:10.1016/j.biopsych.2015.10.007

Stoop, R., Hegoburu, C., & van den Burg, E. (2015). New opportunities in vasopressin and oxytocin research: A perspective from the amygdala. *Annual review of neuroscience, 38*(1), 369–388).

Stuebe, A. M., Grewen, K., & Meltzer-Brody, S. (2013). Association between maternal mood and oxytocin response to breastfeeding. *Journal of Women's Health, 22*(4), 352–361. doi:10.1089/jwh.2012.3768

Sun, P., Smith, A. S., Lei, K., Liu, Y., & Wang, Z. (2014). Breaking bonds in male prairie voles: Long-term effects on emotional and social behavior, physiology, and neurochemistry. *Behavioural Brain Research, 265*, 22–31.

Swain, J. E., Kim, P., Spicer, J., Ho, S. S., Dayton, C. J., Elmadih, A., & Abel, K. M. (2014). Approaching the biology of human parental attachment: Brain imaging, oxytocin and coordinated assessments of mothers and fathers. *Brain Research, 1580*, 78–101. doi:10.1016/j.brainres.2014.03.007

Szeto, A., McCabe, P. M., Nation, D. A., Tabak, B. A., Rossetti, M. A., McCullough, M. E., ... Mendez, A. J. (2011). Evaluation of enzyme immunoassay and radioimmunoassay methods for the measurement of plasma oxytocin. *Psychosomatic Medicine, 73*(5), 393–400. doi:10.1097/PSY.0b013e31821df0c2

Toepfer, P., Heim, C., Entringer, S., Binder, E., Wadhwa, P., & Buss, C. (2017). Oxytocin pathways in the intergenerational transmission of maternal early life stress. *Neuroscience and Biobehavioral Reviews, 73*, 293–308. doi:10.1016/j.neubiorev.2016.12.026

Trainor, B. C., Pride, M. C., Landeros, R. V., Knoblauch, N. W., Takahashi, E. Y., Silva, A. L., & Crean, K. K. (2011). Sex differences in social interaction behavior following social defeat stress in the monogamous California mouse (*Peromyscus californicus*). *PLoS One, 6*(2). doi:10.1371/journal.pone.0017405

Uchino, B. N., Cacioppo, J. T., & Kiecolt-Glaser, J. K. (1996). The relationship between social support and physiological processes: A review with emphasis on underlying mechanisms and implications for health. *Psychological Bulletin, 119*(3), 488–531. doi:10.1037/0033-2909.119.3.488

vanLonden, L., Goekoop, J. G., vanKempen, G. M. J., FrankhuijzenSierevogel, A. C., Wiegant, V. M., vanderVelde, E. A., & DeWied, D. (1997). Plasma levels of arginine vasopressin elevated in patients with major depression. *Neuropsychopharmacology, 17*(4), 284–292. doi:10.1016/s0893-133x(97)00054-7

Wang, Z. X., Zhou, L., Hulihan, T. J., & Insel, T. R. (1996). Immunoreactivity of central vasopressin and oxytocin pathways in microtine rodents: A quantitative comparative study. *Journal of Comparative Neurology, 366*(4), 726–737.

Watkins, S., Meltzer-Brody, S., Zolnoun, D., & Stuebe, A. (2011). Early breastfeeding experiences and postpartum depression. *Obstetrics and Gynecology, 118*(2), 214–221. doi:10.1097/AOG.0b013e3182260a2d

Watt, D. F., & Panksepp, J. (2009). Depression: An evolutionarily conserved mechanism to terminate separation-distress? A review of aminergic, peptidergic, and neural network perspectives. *Neuropsychoanalysis, 11*, 5–104.

Williams, J. R., Insel, T. R., Harbaugh, C. R., & Carter, C. S. (1994a). Oxytocin administered centrally facilitates formation of a partner preference in female prairie voles (*Microtus ochrogaster*). *Journal of Neuroendocrinology, 6*(3), 247–250.

Williams, J. R., Insel, T. R., Harbaugh, C. R., & Carter, C. S. (1994b). Oxytocin administered centrally facilitates formation of a partner preference in female prairie votes (*Microtus ochrogaster*). *Journal of Neuroendocrinology, 6*(3), 247–250. doi:10.1111/j.1365-2826.1994.tb00579.x

Willner, P., Muscat, R., & Papp, M. (1992). Chronic mild stress-induced anhedonia – a realistic animal model of depression. *Neuroscience and Biobehavioral Reviews, 16*(4), 525–534. doi:10.1016/s0149-7634(05)80194-0

Winslow, J. T., Hastings, N., Carter, C. S., Harbaugh, C. R., & Insel, T. R. (1993). A role for central vasopressin in pair bonding in monogamous prairie voles. *Nature, 365*(6446), 545–548. doi:10.1038/365545a0

Wirth, M. M. (2011). Beyond the HPA axis: Progesterone-derived neuroactive steroids in human stress and emotion. *Front Endocrinol (Lausanne), 2*, 19.

Yee, J. R., Kenkel, W. M., Frijling, J. L., Dodhia, S., Onishi, K. G., Tovar, S., . . . Carter, C. S. (2016). Oxytocin promotes functional coupling between paraventricular nucleus and both sympathetic and parasympathetic cardioregulatory nuclei. *Hormones and Behavior, 80*, 82–91. doi:10.1016/j.yhbeh.2016.01.010

Yim, I. S., Stapleton, L. R. T., Guardino, C. M., Hahn-Holbrook, J., & Schetter, C. D. (2015). Biological and psychosocial predictors of postpartum depression: Systematic review and call for integration. In T. D. Cannon & T. Widiger (Eds.), *Annual review of clinical psychology* (Vol. 11, pp. 99–137). Palo Alto, CA: Annual Reviews.

Young, L. J., Lim, M. M., Gingrich, B., & Insel, T. R. (2001). Cellular mechanisms of social attachment. *Hormones and Behavior, 40*(2), 133–138. doi:10.1006/hbeh.2001.1691

Young, L. J., Nilsen, R., Waymire, K. G., MacGregor, G. R., & Insel, T. R. (1999). Increased affiliative response to vasopressin in mice expressing the V-1a receptor from a monogamous vole. *Nature, 400*(6746), 766–768.

Zelkowitz, P., Gold, I., Feeley, N., Hayton, B., Carter, C. S., Tulandi, T., . . . Levin, P. (2014). Psychosocial stress moderates the relationships between oxytocin, perinatal depression, and maternal behavior. *Hormones and Behavior, 66*(2), 351–360. doi:10.1016/j.yhbeh.2014.06.014

37

SEXUAL DIMORPHISM IN DRUG ADDICTION

An influence of sex hormones

Linda I. Perrotti, Brandon D. Butler, and Saurabh S. Kokane

Addiction is a debilitating neuropsychiatric disorder characterized by a loss of control over drug-seeking behavior and high levels of drug intake that is followed by repeated cycles of abstinence and relapse to drug-seeking and use (Reid, Lingford-Hughes, Cancela, & Kalivas, 2012). Although both men and women become addicted to drugs of abuse, women transition to addiction faster and experience greater difficulties remaining abstinent (J. B. Becker & Koob, 2016). Evidence identifying important differences in the patterns of drug use and abuse between men and women suggests that a person's sex influences the course and treatment of substance use disorder. Among populations of men and women vulnerable to addiction, addiction-vulnerable women progress from casual use of the drug to actual dependence on the drug more rapidly. They also experience higher levels of craving and relapse during periods of abstinence, take larger amounts of the drug during relapse, and are less likely to seek treatment for their addiction than men (Bobzean, DeNobrega, & Perrotti, 2014; Brady & Randall, 1999; Ignjatova & Raleva, 2009; T. R. Kosten, Rounsaville, & Kleber, 1985). During attempts to abstain from drug use, women experience more unpleasant physical symptoms than men do and report more intense feelings of "drug craving" (Back et al., 2009; J. B. Becker & Koob, 2016; Fox, Sofuoglu, Morgan, Tuit, & Sinha, 2013; Hogle & Curtin, 2006; Hudson & Stamp, 2011; T. A. Kosten, Gawin, Kosten, & Rounsaville, 1993). Moreover, the effects of drug withdrawal on mood and anxiety and general stress responsivity are greater in women than men. Lastly, a more severe drug addiction syndrome has been seen in women who enter drug abuse treatment programs as compared to men (Back, Lawson, Singleton, & Brady, 2011; Yates, Booth, Reed, Brown, & Masterson, 1993). Women who successfully manage to surmount the barriers to treatment (Greenfield et al., 2007) have similar treatment outcomes for substance use disorders compared to men. However, these women remain more susceptible to sporadic relapse related to negative affect (Greenfield et al., 2007), which may be related to the more intense negative affect experienced by them during abstinence/withdrawal from the drug (Hudson & Stamp, 2011; Sinha, Garcia, Paliwal, Kreek, & Rounsaville, 2006).

The mesolimbic reward system

The mesolimbic reward system is necessary for organisms to engage in behaviors that are reinforcing and to motivate actions that produce rewarding feelings of pleasure. Accordingly, this system plays a critical role in modulating information flow through the limbic system to regulate and/or promote behaviors related to survival and perpetuation of the species (i.e., feeding, drinking, mating, paternal behaviors, and social interactions) (Gardner, 2011; Hone-Blanchet & Fecteau, 2014). In drug addiction, there is a chronic enhanced activation of this system by drugs of abuse which results in long-term functional changes of this system. This, in turn, alters the motivational process arising from this system in a way such that the drive to obtain and use drugs supersedes the drive to obtain natural rewards.

The mesolimbic pathway is composed of neural circuits that originate from cell bodies in the ventral tegmental area of the midbrain and project onto target cells in the nucleus accumbens, dorsal striatum, the frontal cortex (Gardner, 2011; Koob, 1992), and other regions of the forebrain (Figure 37.1). Activation of cells in the ventral tegmental area results in the release of the neurotransmitter dopamine onto the dopamine receptors in the nucleus accumbens. This neurotransmission is one of the major components in a series of events that mediates the positive subjective emotional effects of reward in response to a stimulus (eating, drinking, sexual behavioral, etc.) (Gardner, 2011; Nestler, 2005). As such, drugs of abuse and their associated stimuli act to modulate this pathway to influence reward associated with consumption of the drug and drug-seeking behavior (Di Chiara & Imperato, 1988; Owesson-White et al., 2009; Phillips, Setzu, Vugler, & Hitchcott, 2003; Pierce & Kumaresan, 2006).

Typically, dopaminergic neurotransmission within the mesolimbic pathway plays an important role in mediating neural activity through the limbic system to modulate reward-motivated behaviors (Gardner, 2011). However, drugs of abuse hijack this pathway by inducing an overly enhanced activation of mesolimbic dopamine neurotransmission and increased extracellular dopamine, which leads to long-term morphological and functional changes in this pathway (Hedges, Staffend, & Meisel, 2010). An example of one such drug-induced morphological change is increased dendritic branching in medium spiny neurons in the nucleus accumbens

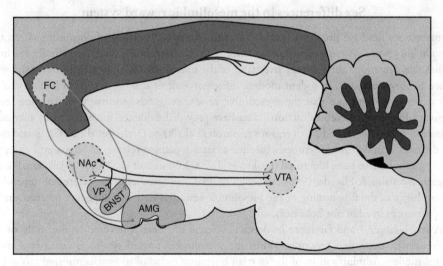

Figure 37.1 Mesolimbic reward circuits. The mesolimbic pathway originates with dopaminergic cell bodies in the ventral tegmental area (VTA). Dopamine (black) cell bodies in the VTA are tonically inhibited by GABA neurons in the VTA. Dopamine cells send projections primarily to the nucleus accumbens (NAc), but there are also projections to the bed nucleus of stria terminalis (BNST), and frontal cortex (FC). Both the VTA and NAc are modulated by rich innervation from GABAergic (dark grey) and glutamatergic systems (light grey).

upon administration of psychostimulant drugs, e.g., cocaine and amphetamine (Robinson & Kolb, 1997, 1999b). Inversely, other drugs, like morphine and its derivatives, have been shown to induce a decrease in the dendritic branching complexity in the same type of neurons in the nucleus accumbens (Robinson & Kolb, 1999a). Long-term exposure to such drugs of abuse can lead to persistent neuroadaptations in the mesolimbic neurocircuitry that lead to the development of hypersensitivity to drug-associated stimuli, such as environmental cues that are associated with drug consumption (Di Chiara et al., 1999; Everitt & Wolf, 2002; Nestler, 2002a, 2002b). Such persistent neuroadaptations can render affected individuals neurologically vulnerable to relapse even after prolonged abstinence from drug use.

Generally speaking, the nucleus accumbens plays an important role in processing rewarding stimuli and regulating the appropriate behavioral responses to those stimuli (Belin & Everitt, 2008), while the dorsal striatum is involved in shifting these behavioral responses to more habitual, automatic, compulsive behaviors (Willuhn, Burgeno, Everitt, & Phillips, 2012). Progression to more addictive patterns of drug-taking behaviors (movement from casual/pleasurable use to avid and compulsive use) is thought to reflect an increase in neural activity in the dorsal striatum and reduced activity in the nucleus accumbens (Everitt & Robbins, 2005; Porrino, Smith, Nader, & Beveridge, 2007; Willuhn et al., 2012). Incentive-sensitization theory explains that the initial feelings of pleasure associated with the drug are referred to as drug "liking" and may be transient; but the "wanting" or craving for a drug eventually becomes the stronger drive for use (Berridge & Robinson, 2016). Accordingly, neural activation (by opioid transmitters) of portions of the nucleus accumbens is important for the initial pleasure or "liking" reaction, while a shift to increases in dopamine activity in other regions of the nucleus accumbens and portions of the dorsal striatum is critical for the development of craving or "wanting" (Berridge, 1996; Berridge & Kringelbach, 2015). This shift in the balance of neurotransmission may reflect some of the neuroadaptations that occur early in the addiction process (George & Koob, 2017).

Sex differences in the mesolimbic reward system

Numerous studies have provided evidence that the functional activity of dopamine within the mesolimbic reward system varies in accordance with the hormonal milieu (specifically, sex hormones that determine the reproductive state) of the individual. While the majority of this evidence has been obtained in rodent models, sufficient – albeit scant – data from human studies also exists to demonstrate that the mesolimbic reward system is sensitive to fluctuating levels of gonadal hormones. Neurofunctional data have provided evidence for hormonally mediated activation of reward-related brain regions (Adinoff et al., 2006; Dreher et al., 2007). In addition, sex differences in dopamine synthesis, baseline striatal dopamine release, and dopamine receptor binding affinity have been identified (Laakso et al., 2002; Munro et al., 2006; Pohjalainen, Rinne, Nagren, Syvalahti, & Hietala, 1998). Although limited, these studies demonstrate sex-dependent dimorphisms in the functioning of the mesolimbic reward system and suggest a mechanism for sex differences in addictive behaviors.

A much larger – and far more in-depth – volume of research devoted to the study of sex differences in dopamine function within the mesolimbic reward system is conducted using animal models. Administration of the ovarian hormone estradiol to ovariectomized rats affects both pre-and postsynaptic components of dopamine neurotransmission. In terms of presynaptic changes, acute injections of estradiol increase dopamine release and turnover and also increase dopamine uptake in the striatum (J. B. Becker & Beer, 1986; J. B. Becker & Ramirez, 1981; Di Paolo, 1994). In terms of postsynaptic changes, estradiol acutely increases dopamine receptor density and dopamine binding in the striatum (Di Paolo, 1994; Di Paolo, Rouillard, & Bedard,

1985; Levesque & Di Paolo, 1989; Shieh & Yang, 2008). Evidence from studies using intact rodents add to the above studies and clearly demonstrate sex differences in baseline dopamine activity and stimulated dopamine activity in the striatum (J. B. Becker, 1999; Jill B. Becker & Hu, 2008; J. B. Becker, Perry, & Westenbroek, 2012). More specifically, female rats exhibit greater basal concentrations of dopamine and stimulated dopamine concentrations in the striatum compared to those of males (Castner, Xiao, & Becker, 1993; Walker, Rooney, Wightman, & Kuhn, 2000). Microdialysis studies in rodents support these findings as they demonstrate that in the nucleus accumbens, basal levels of dopamine and its metabolite-3,4-Dihydroxyphenylacetic acid (DOPAC) are modulated by different levels of sex hormones corresponding to different stages of the estrous cycle (Shimizu & Bray, 1993). The ratio of levels of striatal DOPAC/dopamine (a measure of neurotransmitter turnover) are highest during the proestrus stage of the estrous cycle as compared to the other stages of the cycle, suggesting a greater magnitude of dopamine turnover when circulating levels of estrogen are high (Xiao & Becker, 1994). The fact that estrogen plays a modulatory role in the mesolimbic reward system implies the presence of estrogen receptors in the neurons of that same system. In fact, it has long been known that the mesolimbic reward system contains a high density of estrogen alpha- and beta-type receptors (Creutz & Kritzer, 2002, 2004). Specifically, the activation of estrogen receptor type–alpha seems to play a crucial role in the regulation of estrogen on dopamine receptors by increasing their expression and binding in the striatum (Di Paolo, 1994; Lammers et al., 1999; Landry, Levesque, & Di Paolo, 2002; Le Saux, Morissette, & Di Paolo, 2006; Levesque & Di Paolo, 1989; Morissette et al., 2008; Zhou, Cunningham, & Thomas, 2002). The ventral tegmental area, the region that sends out dopaminergic neural projections in the mesolimbic pathway, also exhibits neuroanatomical differences based on sex and fluctuating levels of ovarian hormones (Gillies & McArthur, 2010; Johnson et al., 2010; Morissette et al., 2008). Female rodents have a significantly greater proportion of dopamine neurons in the ventral tegmental area compared to their male counterparts (Kritzer & Creutz, 2008). Estrogen affects the activity of dopamine neurons within the ventral tegmental area, including the firing rate, spontaneous activity, release of dopamine, and overall responsiveness of these cells to dopamine (J. B. Becker, 1999; J. B. Becker & Rudick, 1999; Calipari et al., 2017; Dazzi et al., 2007; McEwen & Alves, 1999; Vandegrift, You, Satta, Brodie, & Lasek, 2017; Zhang, Yang, Yang, Jin, & Zhen, 2008). Dopaminergic neurons of the ventral tegmental area express estrogen receptors (Creutz & Kritzer, 2002; Milner et al., 2010; Shughrue, Lane, & Merchenthaler, 1997), and intra-ventral tegmental area injections of estradiol have been shown to influence an animal's response for a sucrose reward (Richard, Lopez-Ferreras, Anderberg, Olandersson, & Skibicka, 2017).

Taken together, these data lend support to the hypothesis that in females, changes in the activation of dopaminergic neurotransmission within the mesolimbic reward system correspond with the fluctuations in ovarian hormone levels during the reproductive cycle. Moreover, these studies implicate the hormonal modulation of dopamine neurotransmission in the mesolimbic pathway as a critical mediator of the susceptibility to addiction.

Sex differences in dysregulation of the reward system

Accumulating evidence indicates that fluctuations in ovarian sex hormones over the course of the menstrual cycle modulate the mesolimbic reward system and influence reward behavior. The data have consistently shown that women experience greater positive subjective effects of psychostimulant drugs (cocaine and amphetamine) during the follicular phase of the menstrual cycle compared to the luteal phase of the cycle (Evans, Haney, & Foltin, 2002; Justice & de Wit, 1999, 2000a; White, Justice, & de Wit, 2002). However, the rationale to interpret these findings – and used to approach further study – has been split. One view is that high levels of estrogen during the late follicular phase augment the effects of psychostimulants. The other perspective posits that the presence of progesterone during the luteal phase attenuate the positive effects of psychostimulants.

Clinical investigations into the role of estrogen in enhancing the effects of psychostimulants did not reveal a convincing relationship between increased levels of estrogen and the positive subjective effects of the drugs. One such study compared the effects of amphetamine given during the early and late portions of the follicular phase (characterized by low and moderate levels of estrogen, respectively) and reported no differences on the effects of amphetamine between the early and late portions (Justice & De Wit, 2000a). In another study, women were pretreated with estradiol (via transdermal patch) and amphetamine was administered during the follicular or mid-luteal phases; no effect of estradiol treatment was observed (Justice & de Wit, 2000b). Further clinical studies exploring effects of progesterone demonstrated that elevations in levels of progesterone attenuated the effects of psychostimulant drugs. (Carroll & Anker, 2010; Evans, 2007; Evans & Foltin, 2010). Women cocaine users administered with cocaine in the luteal phase of their menstrual cycle had attenuated positive subjective effects of the drug (diminished feelings of "high") compared to women in the follicular phase of the menstrual cycle and to men (Evans et al., 2002; Sofuoglu, Dudish-Poulsen, Nelson, Pentel, & Hatsukami, 1999; Sofuoglu, Babb, & Hatsukami, 2002). This suggests that high circulating levels of progesterone in the luteal phase attenuated the subjective effects of cocaine. Accordingly, progesterone pretreatment given to women during the early follicular phase of their menstrual cycle diminished some of the subjective effects of cocaine (specifically, the ratings of "feel the effect of the last dose" were diminished) but had no effect on cocaine self-administration behavior (Sofuoglu, Mitchell, & Kosten, 2004). Later studies showed that in women, administration of progesterone during the follicular phase of the menstrual cycle attenuated the "Good Drug Effect" cluster scores after repeated doses of smoked cocaine (Evans, 2007; Evans & Foltin, 2006). Taken together, these clinical studies indicate that progesterone decreases the subjective effects of cocaine in women.

To overcome limitations of study design in clinical settings and also to gain a more complete and unequivocal understanding of the modulation of drug addiction by gonadal hormones, it is necessary to use preclinical animal models. As such, most of the research on how gonadal hormones influence drug addiction has been conducted in rats and mice. As clinical evidence of sex differences in drug-taking behaviors (patterns of use and drug addiction) between men and women accumulated (Griffin, Weiss, Mirin, & Lange, 1989; T. A. Kosten et al., 1993; Mendelson et al., 1999), preclinical researchers began to investigate sex differences in drug self-administration behavior in rodent populations. The drug self-administration paradigm is an operant conditioning procedure used in preclinical research wherein an operant response (generally, a lever press or nose poke) is reinforced by the effects of a drug. It comprises of acquisition (initiation of drug intake and drug-seeking behavior), escalation (loss of control over drug intake and drug-seeking), extinction (abstinence from drug consumption), and reinstatement (relapse to drug use) phases which replicate the different stages of drug addiction in humans.

The operant behavior of intact female rats is more robust than that of males during the acquisition phase of self-administration, escalation of drug intake, and reinstatement of extinguished drug-seeking behavior (Lynch & Carroll, 1999, 2000; Roth & Carroll, 2004). Moreover, female rats acquire intravenous self-administration of cocaine and heroin more quickly and at lower doses than males (Davis, Clinton, Akil, & Becker, 2008; Lynch & Carroll, 1999). Phase of the estrous cycle has been shown to influence an animal's motivation to self-administer cocaine (Roberts, Loh, & Vickers, 1989); for example, cocaine self-administration is highest during proestrus and estrus (when estrogen levels are high, similar to the follicular phase in humans) and lowest during diestrus (when progesterone levels are high) (Feltenstein, Henderson, & See, 2011). The notion that different levels of circulating ovarian hormones are important for differences in the reinforcing properties of drugs are further supported by self-administration paradigms using ovariectomized hormone-treated rodents. These have consistently demonstrated a role for estrogen in enhancing the responsivity to cocaine. More specifically, ovariectomy decreased the rate of acquisition of cocaine self-administration and reinstatement of cocaine-seeking behavior; thereafter, estradiol administration to these ovariectomized animals restored cocaine self-administration rates to levels comparable with intact female rodents (Frye, 2007; Larson, Roth, Anker, & Carroll, 2005; Lynch, Roth, Mickelberg, & Carroll, 2001; Hu & Becker, 2003; Hu, Crombag, Robinson, & Becker, 2004). This effect was specific for female rodents since there was no effect of castration or testosterone/estradiol administration on the cocaine self-administration behavior of male rodents (Jackson, Robinson, & Becker, 2006). In this way, the effects of estrogen on cocaine self-administration are sexually dimorphic. Studies of self-administration also provide support for the hypothesis that progesterone dampens the reinforcing effects of drugs of abuse. For example, progesterone administration reduced the acquisition (Jackson et al., 2006) and escalation (Larson, Anker, Gliddon, Fons, & Carroll, 2007) of cocaine self-administration. These findings have been extended to the progesterone metabolite allopregnanolone, which has also been shown to have an attenuating effect on acquisition of cocaine-self administration. Furthermore, allopregnanolone inhibited escalation of cocaine self-administration and proved more effective than progesterone at blocking cocaine-primed reinstatement of self-administration suggesting an important role for progesterone in limiting the initiation of drug-seeking behavior and preventing escalation of drug use and relapse (Anker & Carroll, 2010a).

Cue reactivity and exposure to cues are important factors in continued drug use and relapse to former patterns of drug use (Enmark et al., 1997; O'Brien, Childress, McLellan, & Ehrman, 1990). The conditioned place preference paradigm is used to determine the conditioned rewarding effects of drugs in rodents because the contextual (environmental) cues used within the paradigm acquire secondary appetitive properties when paired with a rewarding stimulus (i.e., drug of abuse) (Bardo & Bevins, 2000; Tzschentke, 2007). Female rats acquire conditioned place preference to lower doses of cocaine compared to males (Russo, Jenab et al., 2003; Zakharova, Wade, & Izenwasser, 2009). In addition, reinstatement of extinguished cocaine-induced conditioned place preference is more pronounced in female rats (Bobzean, Dennis, Addison, & Perrotti, 2010). The magnitude of conditioned place preference is influenced by circulating levels of ovarian hormones. Ovariectomy attenuated conditioned place preference for cocaine, whereas chronic combined estradiol and progesterone treatment potentiated conditioned place preference (Russo, Festa et al., 2003). Interestingly, progesterone treatment alone inhibited cocaine conditioned place preference, which again adds additional support to the hypothesis that progesterone blunts the rewarding effects of drugs of abuse, specifically in females (Russo et al., 2008).

As previously mentioned, estrogen exhibits modulatory effects on the actions of drugs of abuse within the mesolimbic reward system. Interactions between estrogen and cocaine have also been demonstrated in that estrogen enhances the sensitivity of the dopaminergic neurons of the ventral tegmental area to cocaine as well as cocaine-induced dopamine release in the striatum (Peris, Decambre, Coleman-Hardee, & Simpkins, 1991; Zhang et al., 2008). Moreover, the cocaine-induced inhibitory effect on dopaminergic neurotransmission of the ventral tegmental area is stronger in female rats during the proestrus (higher estrogen and progesterone) phase of the cycle compared to those in the estrus (moderate estrogen and low progesterone) phase (Zhang et al., 2008). Additionally, ovariectomized females did not exhibit this cocaine-induced inhibitory effect on the dopaminergic neurotransmission of the ventral tegmental area and this was rescued by estradiol administration (Zhang et al., 2008). A more recent study demonstrated a positive association between calcium transmission within ventral tegmental area cell bodies in estrus-stage female mice compared to diestrus-stage female and to male mice during the time they were learning to associate an environment with cocaine administration (Calipari et al., 2017).

Overall, the current literature demonstrates that fluctuating levels of ovarian hormones over the menstrual/estrous cycle of the female influence the effects of drugs of abuse on neuronal dopamine systems and the resultant behavior. More specifically, the animal data show that estrogen influences dopamine activity within the mesolimbic reward system such that, in females, drug-directed behaviors that are normally rewarding and reinforcing become enhanced when circulating levels of estrogen are high. Data from human and emerging data from rodent studies demonstrate that high levels of progesterone attenuate rewarding effects of psychostimulant drugs of abuse.

Brain stress systems

Drug addiction typically progresses through three stages; (1) compulsion to seek and take the drug, (2) loss of control in limiting intake, and (3) emergence of a negative emotional state when access to drug is prevented. Studies of the early phases of drug-seeking and taking have identified important anatomical circuits in the mesolimbic reward system (discussed in previous section) as playing a critical role in mediating these behaviors. As addiction progresses, neuroadaptations take place within this mesolimbic reward system (proponent reward) to accommodate overactivity of reward processing associated with addiction. These modifications to these proponent reward (pro-reward) systems result in a decrease in reward function and, over time, result in the development of tolerance. Meanwhile, the excessive engagement of the reward circuit leads to neuroadaptations within a different circuit (brain stress circuit). These neuroadaptations of the brain stress circuit lead to its activation, which works to oppose the proponent activities of the reward systems. In this way, the opponent brain reward processes work to inhibit brain reward and progressively increase in strength over time. This phenomenon has been suggested to lead to the excessive consumption of the drug and eventual loss of control of drug intake (George & Koob, 2017). The negative emotional state accompanies abstinence from an abused drug and dominates the motivational state of the user. Thus, during abstinence, the principal motivation for drug use is relief from the internal negative emotional state (withdrawal), which is aversive and may include symptoms of dysphoria, anxiety, irritability, and sleep disturbances. At this point, the motivation to use the drug is no longer driven by a desire to obtain a euphoric mood state (positive reinforcement); the user is instead motivated to alleviate the aversive feelings associated with withdrawal (negative reinforcement). This negative reinforcement mechanism represents a shift in motivation that is characteristic of individuals who are persistent long-term drug users (Koob & Le Moal, 2001, 2008a, 2008b).

Opponent process theory (Solomon & Corbit, 1974) postulates that every emotional process has an affective balance (pleasant or unpleasant). These affective processes are thought to be modulated by neural mechanisms to reduce the intensity of these states. Conceptually, the a-process includes a positive mood state (i.e., the net hedonic effects of drugs) and the b-processes includes negative mood state or processes to counteract the a-processes (i.e., withdrawal). Changes in the a-processes occur within the mesolimbic reward system while the changes in the b-processes occur within brain stress systems. The changes in the a-processes gradually compromise those processes which, in effect, reduce the positive reinforcement properties of drugs of abuse. With the diminishing reward, these changes render the user more likely to consume increasing amounts of a drug in order to re-experience the positive rewards and to counteract the diminishing function of the a-processes. The changes in the b-process also become sensitized with repeated drug exposure and compel drug use to avoid the aversive symptoms associated with withdrawal (negative reinforcement) (Edwards & Koob, 2010; George, Le Moal, & Koob, 2012).

Both the hypothalamic–pituitary–adrenal (HPA) axis and central brain stress systems (extended amygdala) are regulated by corticotrophin releasing factor (CRF). Hypothalamic–pituitary–adrenal axis activation is triggered by stressful stimuli or stressful events. Neurons in the paraventricular nucleus of the hypothalamus secrete CRF into the anterior pituitary gland in order to promote the synthesis and secretion of adrenocorticotrophic hormone into general circulation (Figure 37.2). In turn, adrenocorticotrophic hormone stimulates the adrenal glands to secrete glucocorticoids (i.e., cortisol in humans and corticosterone in rodents) that are essential for a stress response. This response is fine-tuned via negative feedback from circulating glucocorticoids that act on glucocorticoid receptors in the paraventricular nucleus of the hypothalamus and the hippocampus. However, the paraventricular nucleus of the hypothalamus is not only source of corticotrophin releasing factor; it is widely distributed throughout the

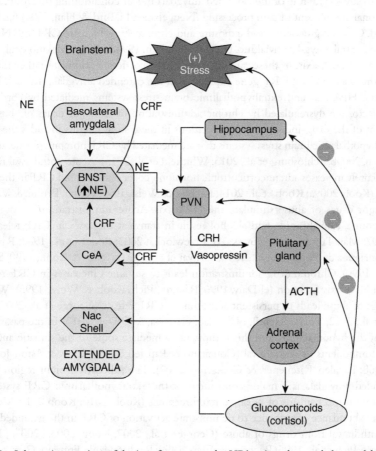

Figure 37.2 Schematic overview of the interface among the HPA axis and extended amygdala.

The extended amygdala is comprised of the central amygdala (CeA), bed nucleus of stria terminalis (BNST), and the nucleus accumbens shell (NAc Shell). This circuit receives corticotropin releasing factor (CRF) from the paraventricular nucleus of the hypothalamus (PVH) and norepinephrine (NE) from pontine nuclei in the brainstem.

nervous system (Merchenthaler, 1984). Of primary interest to this discussion are the central nucleus of the amygdala and the bed nucleus of stria terminalis which comprise the extended amygdala (Heimer & Alheid, 1991). Glucocorticoid receptors are located outside of the HPA axis in regions such as the neocortex, extended amygdala, and hippocampus axis and also serve to control autonomic and behavioral responses to stress. Glucocorticoids can bind to available associated receptors (glucocorticoid and mineralocorticoid receptors) and have the ability to influence neural excitability and synaptic and neuronal plasticity (McEwen, 2001; Roozendaal, McEwen, & Chattarji, 2009). In this way, stress-induced glucocorticoid secretion can stimulate CRF expression in the central brain systems. The distribution of CRF in extrahypothalamic circuits of the brain functions to establish and integrate a complex system to regulate multiple aspects of the stress response (de Kloet, Jolës, & Holsboer, 2005; Bale & Vale, 2004; Smith et al., 1998; Korosi & Baram, 2008; Inda, Armando, Dos Santos Claro, & Solberstein, 2017). The extended amygdala (Heimer & Alheid, 1991) is a macrostructure composed of several basal forebrain structures: the bed nucleus of stria terminalis, central medial amygdala, and a transition zone in the medial shell subregion of the nucleus accumbens (i.e., posterior shell) (Heimer & Alheid, 1991). Within the extended amygdala, CRF acts to regulate behavioral and autonomic responses to stress. The role of the extended amygdala in fear conditioning (LeDoux, 2000) and the emotional component of pain processing (Neugebauer, Li, Bird, & Han, 2004) has been well established. Chronic glucocorticoid exposure and chronic stress increase CRF mRNA expression in the central amygdala (Makino, Gold, & Schulkin, 1994a, 1994b; Makino et al., 1999). In contrast to the HPA axis, in these circuits, excess glucocorticoids stimulate rather than inhibit CRF synthesis and induce CRF gene expression in the extended amygdala (Kovacs, 2013).

Both the HPA axis and extrahypothalimic brain stress systems mediated by corticotrophin releasing factor are dysregulated by chronic administration of all major drugs of abuse. A core component of the drug-induced neuroadaptations in these stress circuits includes the HPA axis and extrahypothalamic brain stress systems that are mediated by CRF, norepinephrine, and dynorphin (Koob, 2009b; Schlosburg et al., 2013; Whitfield et al., 2015). Acute withdrawal from drugs of abuse acutely increases adrenocorticotropic hormone, corticosterone, and CRF in the extended amygdala (Koob, 2009a; Koob et al., 2014; Richter & Weiss, 1999; Rivier, Bruhn, & Vale, 1984).

All major drugs of abuse stimulate the HPA axis. Acute administration of cocaine, morphine, nicotine, cannabinoids, and alcohol result in transient increases in CRF release (Gardi et al., 1997; Maj, Turchan, Smialowska, & Przewlocka, 2003; Puder et al., 1982; Rivier et al., 1984; Rodriguez de Fonseca et al., 1996; Sarnyai et al., 1993) (Ignar & Kuhn, 1990; Spencer & McEwen, 1990). Chronic drug administration leads to sustained increases in CRF release and associated HPA axis function (el Daly, 1996; Richter, Pich, Koob, & Weiss, 1995). Withdrawal from drugs of abuse leads to persistent activation of CRF release (George et al., 2007; Lowery-Gionta et al., 2012; Torres, Gentil, Natividad, Carcoba, & O'Dell, 2013) in the paraventricular nucleus of the hypothalamus, and this is thought to mediate some of the somatic and negative affective components of withdrawal (Contarino & Papaleo, 2005; Harris & Aston-Jones, 2007; Koob, 2008; Papaleo, Kitchener, & Contarino, 2007). The subcortical brain region known as the extended amygdala is a major constituent of the extrahypothalamic CRF system that is associated with mechanisms of negative reinforcement (Koob, 2010; Koob & Le Moal, 2005). There is an abundance of evidence to demonstrate activation of CRF in the extended amygdala during withdrawal from drugs of abuse (George et al., 2007; Koob, 2003a, 2009b; Maj et al., 2003; Merlo Pich et al., 1995; Richter & Weiss, 1999; Rodriguez de Fonseca, Carrera, Navarro, Koob, & Weiss, 1997; Zorrilla et al., 2012; Koob et al., 2014). Anxiety and aversion to novel or aversive stimuli are common phenotypes observed during acute withdrawal from all major drugs of abuse and, as such, can be used as measures to determine the presence and severity of the addiction syndrome. Moreover, these phenotypes are often indicative of extended amygdala activation (external stress-induced or pharmacologically induced) when observed outside the context of drug withdrawal. CRF receptor antagonists reverse anxiety and aversive responses during acute withdrawal and protracted abstinence (Koob, 2008; Koob et al., 2013; Rassnick, Heinrichs, Britton, & Koob, 1993). In addition, CRF receptor antagonists block withdrawal-induced anxiety and aversion affective states (Basso, Spina, Rivier, Vale, & Koob, 1999; Over-street & Griebel, 2004; Overstreet, Keeney, & Hogg, 2004).

In contrast to the HPA response during withdrawal, extended amygdala brain stress systems become sensitized. Studies have demonstrated evidence that the negative reinforcement-driven motivational effects of drug withdrawal are dependent on CRF signaling in the extended amygdala (Delfs, Zhu, Druhan, & Aston-Jones, 2000; Heinrichs, Menzaghi, Schulteis, Koob, & Stinus, 1995; Schulteis, Markou, Gold, Stinus, & Koob, 1994). For example, it has been shown in male animals that CRF efferent signaling from the central amygdala to the bed nucleus of the stria terminalis is critical in facilitating stress-induced reinstatement of drug-seeking behavior (Erb, Salmaso, Rodaros, & Stewart, 2001). Moreover, CRF receptors within the bed nucleus of the stria terminalis are also implicated in stress-induced reinstatement of drug-seeking (Buffalari & See, 2011; Mantsch, Baker, Funk, Le, & Shaham, 2016; Sartor & Aston-Jones, 2012; Wang, Fang, Liu, & Lu, 2006) as inactivation of the bed nucleus of stria terminalis reduces stress- and cue-induced reinstatement to drug-seeking behavior. Other studies provide pharmacological evidence to support the hypothesis for the role of bed nucleus of the stria terminalis in drug reinstatement. Local injections of CRF within the bed nucleus of the stria terminalis lead to reinstatement, while infusions of CRF (and adrenergic) receptor antagonists attenuated stress-induced reinstatement (Erb & Stewart, 1999; Wang et al., 2006). Taken together, these studies provide evidence that the bed nucleus of the stria terminalis plays an essential role in the modulation of the stress response and in the long-term actions of drugs of abuse (Aston-Jones, Delfs, Druhan, & Zhu, 1999; Delfs et al., 2000; Epping-Jordan, Markou, & Koob, 1998; Georges & Aston-Jones, 2001; Koob, 2003b).

Gonadal hormone regulation of brain stress systems

Sex differences in stress reactivity in HPA axis activation are extensively reported. To date, clinical studies have revealed conflicting findings regarding sex differences in neuroendocrine response to stress, likely because none of the longitudinal studies have been sufficiently powered to detect sex differences (Bangasser & Valentino, 2012). In contrast, reliable sex differences in HPA axis activity are found in rodents (Bangasser & Valentino, 2014). Female rats have higher basal and stress-induced corticosterone levels than male rats (Viau, Bingham, Davis, Lee, & Wong, 2005; Weinstock, Razin, Schorer-Apelbaum, Men, & McCarty, 1998). In addition, females exhibit a higher stress-induced activation of the HPA axis, in particular greater secretion of ACTH, a higher production rate of corticosterone, and a faster onset and higher circulating levels of corticosterone (Armario, Gavalda, & Marti, 1995; Haleem, Kennett, & Curzon, 1988; Handa, Burgess, Kerr, & O'Keefe, 1994; Heinsbroek, van Haaren, Feenstra, Endert, & van de Poll, 1991; Jones, Brush, & Neame, 1972; Kant et al., 1983; Kitay, 1961, 1963; Le Mevel, Abitbol, Beraud, & Maniey, 1979; Rivier, 1999; Yoshimura et al., 2003; Young, 1996). In adult animals, these sex differences are attributed to fluctuations in levels of ovarian hormones throughout the menstrual/estrous cycle of the female (Oyola & Handa, 2017).

One way ovarian hormones influence HPA axis functioning is by modulating the sensitivity to negative feedback (Young, 1995). For example, during the proestrus phase of the estrous cycle, when circulating estrogen and progesterone levels are at their highest, females rats tend to exhibit higher secretion of ACTH and increased subsequent production of corticosterone compared to the diestrus phase, when such hormones are circulating at their lowest levels (Viau & Meaney, 1991). Moreover, estrogen replacement to ovariectomized females prolongs stress-induced corticosterone release and impairs dexamethasone suppression (Burgess & Handa, 1992; Viau & Meaney, 1991; Young, 1996). Similarly, women exhibit less sensitivity to dexamethasone-induced feedback during the luteal phase than during the early follicular phase of the menstrual cycle, suggesting that the circulating levels of both estrogen and progesterone modulate the degree of sensitivity to glucocorticoid-induced negative feedback (Altemus et al., 1997; Burgess & Handa, 1992; Ferrini, Lima, & De Nicola, 1995; Patchev, Hayashi, Orikasa, & Almeida, 1995; Rousseau, Baxter, & Tomkins, 1972).

Females can manifest an increased vulnerability to stress due to sexually dimorphic structural and molecular characteristics of the CRF activation in brain stress systems (Bangasser et al., 2010; Bangasser & Valentino, 2012; Salvatore et al., 2018). Unfortunately, most of the subjects in studies examining the extended amygdala system and its involvement in drug addiction behavior have been male. As such, our knowledge on the interactions between the extended amygdala system and drugs of abuse in females is limited at this point. The few studies that do focus on females implicate the CRF systems in both the HPA axis and the extended amygdala in enhancing the responses to drugs of abuse. Some of these studies provide evidence of female rats exhibiting enhanced CRF responses during acute withdrawal (Bradshaw, Miller, Ling, Malsnee, & Ruda, 2000; Garcia-Carmona, Baroja-Mazo, Milanes, & Laorden, 2015; Silva & Madeira, 2012; Torres et al., 2013) when compared to males. In addition, females also show greater yohimbine-induced (a pharmacological stress) reinstatement of cocaine-seeking behavior (Anker & Carroll, 2010b; Feltenstein et al., 2011).

As addiction progresses (dependence and withdrawal develop), mesolimbic reward systems are compromised and extended amygdala CRF stress (anti-reward) systems of the extended amygdala are recruited (Koob, 2015). The extended amygdala is proposed to be the site where homeostatic dysregulation becomes adapted to meet a new set of demands. Opponent process theory of motivation suggests that the strong motivational effects of brain reward systems are opposed by brain stress systems (Koob & Le Moal, 2001). Following chronic drug use, the opponent processes that normally limit reward function become dysregulated and a new drug-modified set point must be established (Koob & Le Moal, 2001). This altered set point is referred to as allostasis, which represents a chronic deviation of the reward set point to return to a normal homeostatic range (Koob & Le Moal, 2001; Koob & Volkow, 2010). The affective processes that are thought to be modulated by these changes include the a-processes (i.e., the net hedonic effects of drugs) and the b-processes (i.e., the processes to counteract the a-processes). It has been recently proposed that because females exhibit stronger positive effects (i.e., a-process) to drugs of abuse, those effects will in turn recruit stress systems (b-process) to a greater degree than is observed in males (O'Dell & Torres, 2014). Clinical, preclinical, and epidemiological studies demonstrate that females display an enhanced recruitment of opponent process systems during long-term nicotine use, which leads to a greater stress response during nicotine withdrawal as compared to males (O'Dell & Torres, 2014) (J. B. Becker et al., 2012).

Addiction has been presented as an attempt to self-medicate stress and mood or anxiety disorders in some individuals (Back, Payne et al., 2011; Brady & Randall, 1999; Conway, Compton, Stinson, & Grant, 2006), thus emphasizing the basic need to influence negative reinforcement processes (relief from stress and aversive mood states). It is consistently reported that drug-dependent women are more likely to suffer from negative emotional states and have higher rates of major depression and anxiety than men (Back, Lawson et al., 2011; Green, Grimes Serrano, Licari, Budman, & Butler, 2009; Griffin et al., 1989; Maremmani et al., 2007; Teesson et al.,

2005). Moreover, these negative emotional states are more likely to trigger craving and relapse in women than in men (Fox & Sinha, 2009; McKay, Rutherford, Cacciola, Kabasakalian-McKay, & Alterman, 1996). In addition, women report being motivated to use prescription opioid drugs by negative reinforcement processes more often than men (cope with interpersonal stress; cope with negative affect) (Back, Payne et al., 2011). Under negative reinforcement, the principal motivation for drug use is self-medication and relief from internal distress states, which may be aversive states (i.e., depressive or anxiety disorders) that preceded drug use or may be the result of drug withdrawal (which includes symptoms of dysphoria, anxiety, irritability, and sleep disturbances). Indeed, there is evidence for a higher degree of comorbidity between psychiatric and mood disorders and drug abuse disorders in women as compared to men (Zilberman, Tavares, Blume, & el-Guebaly, 2003). This distinction in reinforcement mechanisms/motivations (positive vs negative) of drug-seeking behavior is greatly dependent on (1) aforementioned neuroadaptations that occur in the mesolimbic and brain stress systems as a result of chronic drug use; and/or (2) preexisting vulnerabilities in brain stress pathways which give way to increased risk to stress, depression, anxiety, and/or other aversive mood states causing women to be more vulnerable than men to the negative reinforcing effects of drugs of abuse.

In all, the studies reviewed above indicate that the neural circuits and neurochemical factors underlying the CRF systems in both the HPA axis and the extended amygdala likely represent the biological substrates that mediate the acute drug withdrawal syndrome and the negative effects of compulsive drug use on reward processing systems (Koob, Sanna, & Bloom, 1998). The neuroadaptations that occur in these systems may represent the transition from the cognitive regulatory control of drug use to compulsive drug use, and these alterations are sex-specific. These alterations recruit opponent processes during long-term drug use which then diminish the positive reinforcement properties of the drugs and increase the stress response during drug withdrawal, i.e., negative reinforcement compelling drug-seeking behavior (Koob & Le Moal, 2005). However, negative affective states (i.e., anxiety or depression) often precede drug-taking behaviors, especially in women (Zilberman, Tavares, & el-Guebaly, 2003; Zilberman, Tavares, Blume, et al., 2003). Clinical and animal model studies indicate that stress can induce drug craving and increase the probability of relapsing back into drug use (Sinha, 2001). Additionally, the studies reviewed above support the notion that addiction is not simply a phenomenon in which long-term drug abuse leads to a tolerance of the positive reward effects, but also one in which increased internal distress is due to sensitization of the arousal/CRF circuits in the HPA axis and extended amygdala (i.e., stress/anti-reward pathway and opponent process) which require increased amounts of the drug to attenuate this internal distress. However, more study is needed to properly model this in women and female animal models to account for the fluctuations of ovarian hormones.

Summary

Sex differences in response to drugs of abuse are the result of molecular neuroadaptations that develop over the course of addiction. Ovarian hormones can sensitize a specific set of target neurons to the effects of other hormones, which may be released under the influence of a particular drug of abuse. Such interactions may explain sex differences in behaviors motivated by drug reward.

References

Adinoff, B., Williams, M. J., Best, S. E., Harris, T. S., Chandler, P., & Devous, M. D., Sr. (2006). Sex differences in medial and lateral orbitofrontal cortex hypoperfusion in cocaine-dependent men and women. *Gender Medicine, 3*(3), 206–222. doi:S1550-8579(06)80209-3 [pii]

Altemus, M., Redwine, L., Leong, Y. M., Yoshikawa, T., Yehuda, R., Detera-Wadleigh, S., & Murphy, D. L. (1997). Reduced sensitivity to glucocorticoid feedback and reduced glucocorticoid receptor mRNA expression in the luteal phase of the menstrual cycle. *Neuropsychopharmacology, 17*(2), 100–109. doi:S0893-133X(97)00039-0 [pii] 10.1016/S0893-133X(97)00039-0

Anker, J. J., & Carroll, M. E. (2010a). The role of progestins in the behavioral effects of cocaine and other drugs of abuse: Human and animal research. *Neuroscience & Biobehavioral Review, 35*(2), 315–333. doi:10.1016/j.neubiorev.2010.04.003

Anker, J. J., & Carroll, M. E. (2010b). Sex differences in the effects of allopregnanolone on yohimbine-induced reinstatement of cocaine seeking in rats. *Drug and Alcohol Dependence, 107*(2–3), 264–267. doi:10.1016/j.drugalcdep.2009.11.002

Anker, J. J., & Carroll, M. E. (2010c). Sex differences in the effects of allopregnanolone on yohimbine-induced reinstatement of cocaine seeking in rats. *Drug and Alcohol Dependence, 107*(2–3), 264–267. doi:S0376-8716(09)00409-8 [pii] 10.1016/j.drugalcdep.2009.11.002

Armario, A., Gavalda, A., & Marti, J. (1995). Comparison of the behavioural and endocrine response to forced swimming stress in five inbred strains of rats. *Psychoneuroendocrinology, 20*(8), 879–890. doi:0306453095000186 [pii]

Aston-Jones, G., Delfs, J. M., Druhan, J., & Zhu, Y. (1999). The bed nucleus of the stria terminalis. A target site for noradrenergic actions in opiate withdrawal. *Annals of the New York Academy of Science, 877*, 486–498.

Back, S. E., Lawson, K. M., Singleton, L. M., & Brady, K. T. (2011). Characteristics and correlates of men and women with prescription opioid dependence. *Addictive Behaviors, 36*(8), 829–834. doi:S0306-4603(11)00109-2 [pii] 10.1016/j.addbeh.2011.03.013

Back, S. E., Payne, R. A., Waldrop, A. E., Smith, A., Reeves, S., & Brady, K. T. (2009). Prescription opioid aberrant behaviors: A pilot study of sex differences. *The Clinical Journal of Pain, 25*(6), 477–484. doi:10.1097/AJP.0b013e31819c2c2f 00002508-200907000-00004 [pii]

Back, S. E., Payne, R. L., Wahlquist, A. H., Carter, R. E., Stroud, Z., Haynes, L., . . . Ling, W. (2011). Comparative profiles of men and women with opioid dependence: Results from a national multisite effectiveness trial. *The American Journal of Drug and Alcohol Abuse, 37*(5), 313–323. doi:10.3109/00952 990.2011.596982

Bale, T. L., & Vale, W. W. (2004). CRF and CRF receptors: role in stress responsivity and other behaviors. *Annual Review of Pharmacology and Toxicology, 44*, 525–557.

Bangasser, D. A., Curtis, A., Reyes, B. A., Bethea, T. T., Parastatidis, I., Ischiropoulos, H., . . . Valentino, R. J. (2010). Sex differences in corticotropin-releasing factor receptor signaling and trafficking: Potential role in female vulnerability to stress-related psychopathology. *Molecular Psychiatry, 15*(9), 877, 896–904. doi:10.1038/mp.2010.66

Bangasser, D. A., & Valentino, R. J. (2012). Sex differences in molecular and cellular substrates of stress. *Cellular and Molecular Neurobiology, 32*(5), 709–723. doi:10.1007/s10571-012-9824-4

Bangasser, D. A., & Valentino, R. J. (2014). Sex differences in stress-related psychiatric disorders: Neurobiological perspectives. *Frontiers in Neuroendocrinology, 35*(3), 303–319. doi:10.1016/j.yfrne.2014.03.008

Bardo, M. T., & Bevins, R. A. (2000). Conditioned place preference: What does it add to our preclinical understanding of drug reward? *Psychopharmacology (Berl), 153*(1), 31–43.

Basso, A. M., Spina, M., Rivier, J., Vale, W., & Koob, G. F. (1999). Corticotropin-releasing factor antagonist attenuates the "anxiogenic-like" effect in the defensive burying paradigm but not in the elevated plus-maze following chronic cocaine in rats. *Psychopharmacology (Berl), 145*(1), 21–30.

Becker, J. B. (1999). Gender differences in dopaminergic function in striatum and nucleus accumbens. *Pharmacology, Biochemistry, and Behavior, 64*(4), 803–812. doi:S0091-3057(99)00168-9 [pii]

Becker, J. B., & Beer, M. E. (1986). The influence of estrogen on nigrostriatal dopamine activity: Behavioral and neurochemical evidence for both pre- and postsynaptic components. *Behavioural Brain Research, 19*(1), 27–33. doi:0166-4328(86)90044-6 [pii]

Becker, J. B., & Hu, M. (2008). Sex differences in drug abuse. *Frontiers in Neuroendocrinology, 29*(1), 36–47.

Becker, J. B., & Koob, G. F. (2016). Sex differences in animal models: Focus on addiction. *Pharmacological Reviews, 68*(2), 242–263. doi:10.1124/pr.115.011163

Becker, J. B., Perry, A. N., & Westenbroek, C. (2012). Sex differences in the neural mechanisms mediating addiction: A new synthesis and hypothesis. *Biology of Sex Differences, 3*(1), 14. doi:10.1186/2042-6410-3-14

Becker, J. B., & Ramirez, V. D. (1981). Experimental studies on the development of sex differences in the release of dopamine from striatal tissue fragments in vitro. *Neuroendocrinology, 32*(3), 168–173.

Becker, J. B., & Rudick, C. N. (1999). Rapid effects of estrogen or progesterone on the amphetamine-induced increase in striatal dopamine are enhanced by estrogen priming: A microdialysis study. *Pharmacology Biochemistry and Behavior, 64*(1), 53–57. doi:S0091-3057(99)00091-X [pii]

Belin, D., & Everitt, B. J. (2008). Cocaine seeking habits depend upon dopamine-dependent serial connectivity linking the ventral with the dorsal striatum. *Neuron, 57*(3), 432–441. doi:10.1016/j.neuron.2007.12.019

Berridge, K. C. (1996). Food reward: Brain substrates of wanting and liking. *Neuroscience & Biobehavioral Reviews, 20*(1), 1–25.

Berridge, K. C., & Kringelbach, M. L. (2015). Pleasure systems in the brain. *Neuron, 86*(3), 646–664. doi:10.1016/j.neuron.2015.02.018

Berridge, K. C., & Robinson, T. E. (2016). Liking, wanting, and the incentive-sensitization theory of addiction. *American Psychology, 71*(8), 670–679. doi:10.1037/amp0000059

Bobzean, S. A., Dennis, T. S., Addison, B. D., & Perrotti, L. I. (2010). Influence of sex on reinstatement of cocaine-conditioned place preference. *Brain Research Bulletin, 83*(6), 331–336. doi:S0361-9230(10)00208-X [pii] 10.1016/j.brainresbull.2010.09.003

Bobzean, S. A., DeNobrega, A. K., & Perrotti, L. I. (2014). Sex differences in the neurobiology of drug addiction. *Experimental Neurology, 259*, 64–74. doi:10.1016/j.expneurol.2014.01.022

Bradshaw, H., Miller, J., Ling, Q., Malsnee, K., & Ruda, M. A. (2000). Sex differences and phases of the estrous cycle alter the response of spinal cord dynorphin neurons to peripheral inflammation and hyperalgesia. *Pain, 85*(1–2), 93–99.

Brady, K. T., & Randall, C. L. (1999). Gender differences in substance use disorders. *Psychiatric Clinics of North America, 22*(2), 241–252.

Buffalari, D. M., & See, R. E. (2011). Inactivation of the bed nucleus of the stria terminalis in an animal model of relapse: Effects on conditioned cue-induced reinstatement and its enhancement by yohimbine. *Psychopharmacology (Berl), 213*(1), 19–27. doi:10.1007/s00213-010-2008-3

Burgess, L. H., & Handa, R. J. (1992). Chronic estrogen-induced alterations in adrenocorticotropin and corticosterone secretion, and glucocorticoid receptor-mediated functions in female rats. *Endocrinology, 131*(3), 1261–1269.

Calipari, E. S., Juarez, B., Morel, C., Walker, D. M., Cahill, M. E., Ribeiro, E., . . . Nestler, E. J. (2017). Dopaminergic dynamics underlying sex-specific cocaine reward. *Nature Communications, 8*, 13877. doi:10.1038/ncomms13877

Carroll, M. E., & Anker, J. J. (2010). Sex differences and ovarian hormones in animal models of drug dependence. *Hormones and Behavior, 58*(1), 44–56. doi:10.1016/j.yhbeh.2009.10.001

Castner, S. A., Xiao, L., & Becker, J. B. (1993). Sex differences in striatal dopamine: In vivo microdialysis and behavioral studies. *Brain Research, 610*(1), 127–134.

Contarino, A., & Papaleo, F. (2005). The corticotropin-releasing factor receptor-1 pathway mediates the negative affective states of opiate withdrawal. *Proceedings of the National Academy of Sciences of United States of America, 102*(51), 18649–18654. doi:10.1073/pnas.0506999102

Conway, K. P., Compton, W., Stinson, F. S., & Grant, B. F. (2006). Lifetime comorbidity of DSM-IV mood and anxiety disorders and specific drug use disorders: Results from the national epidemiologic survey on alcohol and related conditions. *The Journal of Clinical Psychiatry, 67*(2), 247–257.

Creutz, L. M., & Kritzer, M. F. (2002). Estrogen receptor-beta immunoreactivity in the midbrain of adult rats: Regional, subregional, and cellular localization in the A10, A9, and A8 dopamine cell groups. *Journal of Comparative Neurology, 446*(3), 288–300. doi:10.1002/cne.10207 [pii]

Creutz, L. M., & Kritzer, M. F. (2004). Mesostriatal and mesolimbic projections of midbrain neurons immunoreactive for estrogen receptor beta or androgen receptors in rats. *Journal of Comparative Neurology, 476*(4), 348–362. doi:10.1002/cne.20229

Davis, B. A., Clinton, S. M., Akil, H., & Becker, J. B. (2008). The effects of novelty-seeking phenotypes and sex differences on acquisition of cocaine self-administration in selectively bred High-Responder and Low-Responder rats. *Pharmacology Biochemistry and Behavior, 90*(3), 331–338. doi:S0091-3057(08)00093-2 [pii] 10.1016/j.pbb.2008.03.008

Dazzi, L., Seu, E., Cherchi, G., Barbieri, P. P., Matzeu, A., & Biggio, G. (2007). Estrous cycle-dependent changes in basal and ethanol-induced activity of cortical dopaminergic neurons in the rat. *Neuropsychopharmacology, 32*(4), 892–901. doi:10.1038/sj.npp.1301150

de Kloet, E. R., Joëls, M., & Holsboer, F. (2005). Stress and the brain: From adaptation to disease. *Nature Reviews Neuroscience, 6*(6), 463–475. doi:10.1038/nrn1683

Delfs, J. M., Zhu, Y., Druhan, J. P., & Aston-Jones, G. (2000). Noradrenaline in the ventral forebrain is critical for opiate withdrawal-induced aversion. *Nature*, *403*(6768), 430–434. doi:10.1038/35000212

Di Chiara, G., & Imperato, A. (1988). Drugs abused by humans preferentially increase synaptic dopamine concentrations in the mesolimbic system of freely moving rats. *Proceedings of the National Academy of Sciences of the United States of America*, *85*(14), 5274–5278.

Di Chiara, G., Tanda, G., Bassareo, V., Pontieri, F., Acquas, E., Fenu, S., . . . Carboni, E. (1999). Drug addiction as a disorder of associative learning. Role of nucleus accumbens shell/extended amygdala dopamine. *Annals of the New York Academy of Sciences*, *877*, 461–485.

Di Paolo, T. (1994). Modulation of brain dopamine transmission by sex steroids. *Reviews in the Neurosciences*, *5*(1), 27–41.

Di Paolo, T., Rouillard, C., & Bedard, P. (1985). 17 beta-Estradiol at a physiological dose acutely increases dopamine turnover in rat brain. *European Journal of Pharmacology*, *117*(2), 197–203. doi:0014-2999(85)90604-1 [pii]

Dreher, J. C., Schmidt, P. J., Kohn, P., Furman, D., Rubinow, D., & Berman, K. F. (2007). Menstrual cycle phase modulates reward-related neural function in women. *Proceedings of the National Academy of Sciences of the United States of America*, *104*(7), 2465–2470. doi:0605569104 [pii] 10.1073/pnas.0605569104

Edwards, S., & Koob, G. F. (2010). Neurobiology of dysregulated motivational systems in drug addiction. *Future Neurology*, *5*(3), 393–401. doi:10.2217/fnl.10.14

el Daly, E. S. (1996). Influence of acute and chronic morphine or stadol on the secretion of adrenocorticotrophin and its hypothalamic releasing hormone in the rat. *Life Sciences*, *59*(22), 1881–1890.

Enmark, E., Pelto-Huikko, M., Grandien, K., Lagercrantz, S., Lagercrantz, J., Fried, G., . . . Gustafsson, J. A. (1997). Human estrogen receptor beta-gene structure, chromosomal localization, and expression pattern. *Journal of Clinical Endocrinology & Metabolism*, *82*(12), 4258–4265.

Epping-Jordan, M. P., Markou, A., & Koob, G. F. (1998). The dopamine D-1 receptor antagonist SCH 23390 injected into the dorsolateral bed nucleus of the stria terminalis decreased cocaine reinforcement in the rat. *Brain Research*, *784*(1–2), 105–115.

Erb, S., Salmaso, N., Rodaros, D., & Stewart, J. (2001). A role for the CRF-containing pathway from central nucleus of the amygdala to bed nucleus of the stria terminalis in the stress-induced reinstatement of cocaine seeking in rats. *Psychopharmacology (Berl)*, *158*(4), 360–365. doi:10.1007/s002130000642

Erb, S., & Stewart, J. (1999). A role for the bed nucleus of the stria terminalis, but not the amygdala, in the effects of corticotropin-releasing factor on stress-induced reinstatement of cocaine seeking. *Journal of Neuroscience*, *19*(20), RC35.

Evans, S. M. (2007). The role of estradiol and progesterone in modulating the subjective effects of stimulants in humans. *Experimental and Clinical Psychopharmacology*, *15*(5), 418–426. doi:2007-14661-002 [pii] 10.1037/1064-1297.15.5.418

Evans, S. M., & Foltin, R. W. (2006). Exogenous progesterone attenuates the subjective effects of smoked cocaine in women, but not in men. *Neuropsychopharmacology*, *31*(3), 659–674. doi:1300887 [pii] 10.1038/sj.npp.1300887

Evans, S. M., & Foltin, R. W. (2010). Does the response to cocaine differ as a function of sex or hormonal status in human and non-human primates? *Hormones and Behavior*, *58*(1), 13–21. doi:10.1016/j.yhbeh.2009.08.010

Evans, S. M., Haney, M., & Foltin, R. W. (2002). The effects of smoked cocaine during the follicular and luteal phases of the menstrual cycle in women. *Psychopharmacology (Berl)*, *159*(4), 397–406. doi:10.1007/s00213-001-0944-7

Everitt, B. J., & Robbins, T. W. (2005). Neural systems of reinforcement for drug addiction: From actions to habits to compulsion. *Nature Neuroscience*, *8*(11), 1481–1489. doi:nn1579 [pii] 10.1038/nn1579

Everitt, B. J., & Wolf, M. E. (2002). Psychomotor stimulant addiction: A neural systems perspective. *Journal of Neuroscience*, *22*(9), 3312–3320. doi:20026356 22/9/3312 [pii]

Feltenstein, M. W., Henderson, A. R., & See, R. E. (2011). Enhancement of cue-induced reinstatement of cocaine-seeking in rats by yohimbine: Sex differences and the role of the estrous cycle. *Psychopharmacology (Berl)*, *216*(1), 53–62. doi:10.1007/s00213-011-2187-6

Ferrini, M., Lima, A., & De Nicola, A. F. (1995). Estradiol abolishes autologous down regulation of glucocorticoid receptors in brain. *Life Sciences*, *57*(26), 2403–2412. doi:0024320595022363 [pii]

Fox, H. C., & Sinha, R. (2009). Sex differences in drug-related stress-system changes: Implications for treatment in substance-abusing women. *Harvard Review of Psychiatry*, *17*(2), 103–119. doi:10.1080/1067 3220902899680

Fox, H. C., Sofuoglu, M., Morgan, P. T., Tuit, K. L., & Sinha, R. (2013). The effects of exogenous progesterone on drug craving and stress arousal in cocaine dependence: Impact of gender and cue type. *Psychoneuroendocrinology, 38*(9), 1532–1544. doi:10.1016/j.psyneuen.2012.12.022

Frye, C. A. (2007). Progestins influence motivation, reward, conditioning, stress, and/or response to drugs of abuse. *Pharmacology Biochemistry and Behavior, 86*(2), 209–219. doi:S0091-3057(06)00253-X [pii] 10.1016/j.pbb.2006.07.033

Garcia-Carmona, J. A., Baroja-Mazo, A., Milanes, M. V., & Laorden, M. L. (2015). Sex differences between CRF1 receptor deficient mice following naloxone-precipitated morphine withdrawal in a conditioned place aversion paradigm: Implication of HPA axis. *PLoS One, 10*(4), e0121125. doi:10.1371/journal. pone.0121125

Gardi, J., Biro, E., Sarnyai, Z., Vecsernyes, M., Julesz, J., & Telegdy, G. (1997). Time-dependent alterations in corticotropin-releasing factor-like immunoreactivity in different brain regions after acute cocaine administration to rats. *Neuropeptides, 31*(1), 15–18.

Gardner, E. L. (2011). Addiction and brain reward and antireward pathways. *Advances in Psychosomatic Medicine, 30*, 22–60. doi:10.1159/000324065

George, O., Ghozland, S., Azar, M. R., Cottone, P., Zorrilla, E. P., Parsons, L. H., . . . Koob, G. F. (2007). CRF-CRF1 system activation mediates withdrawal-induced increases in nicotine self-administration in nicotine-dependent rats. *Proceedings of the National Academy of Sciences of the United States of America, 104*(43), 17198–17203. doi:10.1073/pnas.0707585104

George, O., & Koob, G. F. (2017). Individual differences in the neuropsychopathology of addiction. *Dialogues in Clinical Neuroscience, 19*(3), 217–229.

George, O., Le Moal, M., & Koob, G. F. (2012). Allostasis and addiction: Role of the dopamine and corticotropin-releasing factor systems. *Physiology & Behavior, 106*(1), 58–64. doi:10.1016/j.physbeh.2011.11.004

Georges, F., & Aston-Jones, G. (2001). Potent regulation of midbrain dopamine neurons by the bed nucleus of the stria terminalis. *Journal of Neuroscience, 21*(16), RC160.

Gillies, G. E., & McArthur, S. (2010). Independent influences of sex steroids of systemic and central origin in a rat model of Parkinson's disease: A contribution to sex-specific neuroprotection by estrogens. *Hormones and Behavior, 57*(1), 23–34. doi:10.1016/j.yhbeh.2009.06.002

Green, T. C., Grimes Serrano, J. M., Licari, A., Budman, S. H., & Butler, S. F. (2009). Women who abuse prescription opioids: Findings from the Addiction Severity Index-Multimedia Version Connect prescription opioid database. *Drug and Alcohol Dependence, 103*(1–2), 65–73. doi:S0376-8716(09)00094-5 [pii] 10.1016/j.drugalcdep.2009.03.014

Greenfield, S. F., Brooks, A. J., Gordon, S. M., Green, C. A., Kropp, F., McHugh, R. K., . . . Miele, G. M. (2007). Substance abuse treatment entry, retention, and outcome in women: A review of the literature. *Drug and Alcohol Dependence, 86*(1), 1–21. doi:S0376-8716(06)00177-3 [pii] 10.1016/j.drugalcdep.2006.05.012

Griffin, M. L., Weiss, R. D., Mirin, S. M., & Lange, U. (1989). A comparison of male and female cocaine abusers. *Archives of General Psychiatry, 46*(2), 122–126.

Haleem, D. J., Kennett, G., & Curzon, G. (1988). Adaptation of female rats to stress: Shift to male pattern by inhibition of corticosterone synthesis. *Brain Research, 458*(2), 339–347. doi:0006-8993(88)90476-3 [pii]

Handa, R. J., Burgess, L. H., Kerr, J. E., & O'Keefe, J. A. (1994). Gonadal steroid hormone receptors and sex differences in the hypothalamo-pituitary-adrenal axis. *Hormones and Behavior, 28*(4), 464–476. doi:S0018-506X(84)71044-0 [pii] 10.1006/hbeh.1994.1044

Harris, G. C., & Aston-Jones, G. (2007). Activation in extended amygdala corresponds to altered hedonic processing during protracted morphine withdrawal. *Behavioural Brain Research, 176*(2), 251–258. doi:10.1016/j.bbr.2006.10.012

Hedges, V. L., Staffend, N. A., & Meisel, R. L. (2010). Neural mechanisms of reproduction in females as a predisposing factor for drug addiction. *Frontiers in Neuroendocrinology, 31*(2), 217–231. doi:10.1016/j. yfrne.2010.02.003

Heimer, L., & Alheid, G. F. (1991). Piecing together the puzzle of basal forebrain anatomy. *Advances in Experimental Medicine and Biology, 295*, 1–42.

Heinrichs, S. C., Menzaghi, F., Schulteis, G., Koob, G. F., & Stinus, L. (1995). Suppression of corticotropin-releasing factor in the amygdala attenuates aversive consequences of morphine withdrawal. *Behavioural Pharmacology, 6*(1), 74–80.

Heinsbroek, R. P., van Haaren, F., Feenstra, M. G., Endert, E., & van de Poll, N. E. (1991). Sex- and time-dependent changes in neurochemical and hormonal variables induced by predictable and unpredictable footshock. *Physiology & Behavior, 49*(6), 1251–1256.

Hogle, J. M., & Curtin, J. J. (2006). Sex differences in negative affective response during nicotine withdrawal. *Psychophysiology, 43*(4), 344–356. doi:10.1111/j.1469-8986.2006.00406.x

Hone-Blanchet, A., & Fecteau, S. (2014). Overlap of food addiction and substance use disorders definitions: Analysis of animal and human studies. *Neuropharmacology, 85,* 81–90. doi:10.1016/j.neuropharm.2014.05.019

Hu, M., Crombag, H. S., Robinson, T. E., & Becker, J. B. (2004). Biological basis of sex differences in the propensity to self-administer cocaine. *Neuropsychopharmacology, 29*(1), 81–85. doi:10.1038/sj.npp.1300301

Hu, M., & Becker, J. B. (2003). Effects of sex and estrogen on behavioral sensitization to cocaine in rats. *Journal of Neuroscience, 23*(2), 693–699.

Hudson, A., & Stamp, J. A. (2011). Ovarian hormones and propensity to drug relapse: A review. *Neuroscience & Biobehavioral Review, 35*(3), 427–436. doi:10.1016/j.neubiorev.2010.05.001

Ignar, D. M., & Kuhn, C. M. (1990). Effects of specific mu and kappa opiate tolerance and abstinence on hypothalamo-pituitary-adrenal axis secretion in the rat. *Journal of Pharmacology and Experimental Therapeutics, 255*(3), 1287–1295.

Ignjatova, L., & Raleva, M. (2009). Gender difference in the treatment outcome of patients served in the mixed-gender program. *Bratislava Lekarske Listy, 110*(5), 285–289.

Inda, C., Armando, N. G., Dos Santos Claro, P. A., & Solberstein, S. (2017). Endocrinology and the brain: Corticotropin-releasing hormone signaling. *Endocrine Connections, 6*(6), R99–R120. doi:10.1530EC-17-0111

Jackson, L. R., Robinson, T. E., & Becker, J. B. (2006). Sex differences and hormonal influences on acquisition of cocaine self-administration in rats. *Neuropsychopharmacology, 31*(1), 129–138. doi:1300778 [pii] 10.1038/sj.npp.1300778

Johnson, M. L., Ho, C. C., Day, A. E., Walker, Q. D., Francis, R., & Kuhn, C. M. (2010). Oestrogen receptors enhance dopamine neurone survival in rat midbrain. *Journal of Neuroendocrinology, 22*(4), 226–237. doi:10.1111/j.1365-2826.2010.01964.x

Jones, M. T., Brush, F. R., & Neame, R. L. (1972). Characteristics of fast feedback control of corticotrophin release by corticosteroids. *Journal of Endocrinology, 55*(3), 489–497.

Justice, A. J., & de Wit, H. (1999). Acute effects of d-amphetamine during the follicular and luteal phases of the menstrual cycle in women. *Psychopharmacology (Berl), 145*(1), 67–75.

Justice, A. J., & de Wit, H. (2000a). Acute effects of d-amphetamine during the early and late follicular phases of the menstrual cycle in women. *Pharmacology Biochemistry and Behavior, 66*(3), 509–515.

Justice, A. J., & de Wit, H. (2000b). Acute effects of estradiol pretreatment on the response to d-amphetamine in women. *Neuroendocrinology, 71*(1), 51–59. doi:10.1159/000054520

Kant, G. J., Lenox, R. H., Bunnell, B. N., Mougey, E. H., Pennington, L. L., & Meyerhoff, J. L. (1983). Comparison of stress response in male and female rats: Pituitary cyclic AMP and plasma prolactin, growth hormone and corticosterone. *Psychoneuroendocrinology, 8*(4), 421–428.

Kitay, J. I. (1961). Sex differences in adrenal cortical secretion in the rat. *Endocrinology, 68,* 818–824.

Kitay, J. I. (1963). Pituitary-adrenal function in the rat after gonadectomy and gonadal hormone replacement. *Endocrinology, 73,* 253–260.

Koob, G. F. (1992). Neural mechanisms of drug reinforcement. *Annals of the New York Academy of Sciences, 654,* 171–191.

Koob, G. F. (2003a). Alcoholism: Allostasis and Beyond. *Alcoholism: Clinical and Experimental Research, 27*(2), 232–243. doi:10.1097/01.ALC.0000057122.36127.C2

Koob, G. F. (2003b). Neuroadaptive mechanisms of addiction: Studies on the extended amygdala. *European Neuropsychopharmacology, 13*(6), 442–452.

Koob, G. F. (2008). A role for brain stress systems in addiction. *Neuron, 59*(1), 11–34. doi:10.1016/j.neuron.2008.06.012

Koob, G. F. (2009a). Brain stress systems in the amygdala and addiction. *Brain Research, 1293,* 61–75. doi:10.1016/j.brainres.2009.03.038

Koob, G. F. (2009b). Neurobiological substrates for the dark side of compulsivity in addiction. *Neuropharmacology, 56*(Suppl. 1), 18–31. doi:S0028-3908(08)00328-6 [pii] 10.1016/j.neuropharm.2008.07.043

Koob, G. F. (2010). The role of CRF and CRF-related peptides in the dark side of addiction. *Brain Research, 1314,* 3–14. doi:S0006-8993(09)02400-7 [pii] 10.1016/j.brainres.2009.11.008

Koob, G. F. (2015). The dark side of emotion: The addiction perspective. *European Journal of Pharmacology, 753,* 73–87. doi:10.1016/j.ejphar.2014.11.044

Koob, G. F., Buck, C. L., Cohen, A., Edwards, S., Park, P. E., Schlosburg, J. E., … George, O. (2014). Addiction as a stress surfeit disorder. *Neuropharmacology, 76*(Pt B), 370–382. doi:10.1016/j.neuropharm.2013.05.024

Koob, G. F., & Le Moal, M. (2001). Drug addiction, dysregulation of reward, and allostasis. *Neuropsychopharmacology, 24*(2), 97–129. doi:10.1016/S0893-133X(00)00195-0

Koob, G. F., & Le Moal, M. (2005). Plasticity of reward neurocircuitry and the "dark side" of drug addiction. *Nature Neuroscience, 8*(11), 1442–1444. doi:10.1038/nn1105–1442

Koob, G. F., & Le Moal, M. (2008a). Addiction and the brain antireward system. *Annual Review of Psychology, 59*, 29–53. doi:10.1146/annurev.psych.59.103006.093548

Koob, G. F., & Le Moal, M. (2008b). Review: Neurobiological mechanisms for opponent motivational processes in addiction. *Philosophical Transactions of the Royal Society of London. Series B, Biological Sciences, 363*(1507), 3113–3123. doi:C54412M472226253 [pii] 10.1098/rstb.2008.0094

Koob, G. F., Sanna, P. P., & Bloom, F. E. (1998). Neuroscience of addiction. *Neuron, 21*(3), 467–476.

Koob, G. F., & Volkow, N. D. (2010). Neurocircuitry of addiction. *Neuropsychopharmacology, 35*(1), 217–238. doi:10.1038/npp.2009.110

Korosi, A., & Baram, T. Z. (2008). The central corticortripin releasing factor system during development and adulthood. *European Journal of Pharmacology, 583*(2–3), 204–214. doi10.1016/j.ejphar.2007.11.006

Kosten, T. A., Gawin, F. H., Kosten, T. R., & Rounsaville, B. J. (1993). Gender differences in cocaine use and treatment response. *Journal of Substance Abuse Treatment, 10*(1), 63–66.

Kosten, T. R., Rounsaville, B. J., & Kleber, H. D. (1985). Ethnic and gender differences among opiate addicts. *International Journal of the Addictions, 20*(8), 1143–1162.

Kovacs, K. J. (2013). CRH: The link between hormonal-, metabolic- and behavioral responses to stress. *Journal of Chemical Neuroanatomy, 54*, 25–33. doi:10.1016/j.jchemneu.2013.05.003

Kritzer, M. F., & Creutz, L. M. (2008). Region and sex differences in constituent dopamine neurons and immunoreactivity for intracellular estrogen and androgen receptors in mesocortical projections in rats. *Journal of Neuroscience, 28*(38), 9525–9535. doi:10.1523/JNEUROSCI.2637-08.2008

Laakso, A., Vilkman, H., Bergman, J., Haaparanta, M., Solin, O., Syvalahti, E., . . . Hietala, J. (2002). Sex differences in striatal presynaptic dopamine synthesis capacity in healthy subjects. *Biological Psychiatry, 52*(7), 759–763.

Lammers, C. H., D'Souza, U. M., Qin, Z. H., Lee, S. H., Yajima, S., & Mouradian, M. M. (1999). Regulation of striatal dopamine receptors by corticosterone: An in vivo and in vitro study. *Brain Research. Molecular Brain Research, 69*(2), 281–285. doi:S0169328X99001059 [pii]

Landry, M., Levesque, D., & Di Paolo, T. (2002). Estrogenic properties of raloxifene, but not tamoxifen, on D2 and D3 dopamine receptors in the rat forebrain. *Neuroendocrinology, 76*(4), 214–222. doi:nen76214 [pii]

Larson, E. B., Anker, J. J., Gliddon, L. A., Fons, K. S., & Carroll, M. E. (2007). Effects of estrogen and progesterone on the escalation of cocaine self-administration in female rats during extended access. *Experimental and Clinical Psychopharmacology, 15*(5), 461–471. doi:2007-14661-006 [pii] 10.1037/1064-1297.15.5.461

Larson, E. B., Roth, M. E., Anker, J. J., & Carroll, M. E. (2005). Effect of short- vs. long-term estrogen on reinstatement of cocaine-seeking behavior in female rats. *Pharmacology Biochemistry and Behavior, 82*(1), 98–108. doi:S0091-3057(05)00249-2 [pii] 10.1016/j.pbb.2005.07.015

LeDoux, J. E. (2000). Emotion circuits in the brain. *Annual Review of Neuroscience, 23*, 155–184. doi:10.1146/annurev.neuro.23.1.155

Le Mevel, J. C., Abitbol, S., Beraud, G., & Maniey, J. (1979). Temporal changes in plasma adrenocorticotropin concentration after repeated neurotropic stress in male and female rats. *Endocrinology, 105*(3), 812–817.

Le Saux, M., Morissette, M., & Di Paolo, T. (2006). ERbeta mediates the estradiol increase of D2 receptors in rat striatum and nucleus accumbens. *Neuropharmacology, 50*(4), 451–457. doi:S0028-3908(05)00365-5 [pii] 10.1016/j.neuropharm.2005.10.004

Levesque, D., & Di Paolo, T. (1989). Chronic estradiol treatment increases ovariectomized rat striatal D-1 dopamine receptors. *Life Sciences, 45*(19), 1813–1820.

Lowery-Gionta, E. G., Navarro, M., Li, C., Pleil, K. E., Rinker, J. A., Cox, B. R., . . . Thiele, T. E. (2012). Corticotropin releasing factor signaling in the central amygdala is recruited during binge-like ethanol consumption in C57BL/6J mice. *Journal of Neuroscience, 32*(10), 3405–3413. doi:10.1523/JNEUROSCI.6256-11.2012

Lynch, W. J., & Carroll, M. E. (1999). Sex differences in the acquisition of intravenously self-administered cocaine and heroin in rats. *Psychopharmacology (Berl), 144*(1), 77–82.

Lynch, W. J., & Carroll, M. E. (2000). Reinstatement of cocaine self-administration in rats: Sex differences. *Psychopharmacology (Berl), 148*(2), 196–200. doi:01480196.213 [pii]

Lynch, W. J., Roth, M. E., Mickelberg, J. L., & Carroll, M. E. (2001). Role of estrogen in the acquisition of intravenously self-administered cocaine in female rats. *Pharmacology Biochemistry and Behavior, 68*(4), 641–646. doi:S0091-3057(01)00455-5 [pii]

Maj, M., Turchan, J., Smialowska, M., & Przewlocka, B. (2003). Morphine and cocaine influence on CRF biosynthesis in the rat central nucleus of amygdala. *Neuropeptides, 37*(2), 105–110.

Makino, S., Gold, P. W., & Schulkin, J. (1994a). Corticosterone effects on corticotropin-releasing hormone mRNA in the central nucleus of the amygdala and the parvocellular region of the paraventricular nucleus of the hypothalamus. *Brain Research, 640*(1–2), 105–112.

Makino, S., Gold, P. W., & Schulkin, J. (1994b). Effects of corticosterone on CRH mRNA and content in the bed nucleus of the stria terminalis; comparison with the effects in the central nucleus of the amygdala and the paraventricular nucleus of the hypothalamus. *Brain Research, 657*(1–2), 141–149.

Makino, S., Shibasaki, T., Yamauchi, N., Nishioka, T., Mimoto, T., Wakabayashi, I., . . . Hashimoto, K. (1999). Psychological stress increased corticotropin-releasing hormone mRNA and content in the central nucleus of the amygdala but not in the hypothalamic paraventricular nucleus in the rat. *Brain Research, 850*(1–2), 136–143.

Mantsch, J. R., Baker, D. A., Funk, D., Le, A. D., & Shaham, Y. (2016). Stress-induced reinstatement of drug seeking: 20 years of progress. *Neuropsychopharmacology, 41*(1), 335–356. doi:10.1038/npp.2015.142

Maremmani, I., Pacini, M., Pani, P. P., Perugi, G., Deltito, J., & Akiskal, H. (2007). The mental status of 1090 heroin addicts at entry into treatment: Should depression be considered a "dual diagnosis"? *Annals of General Psychiatry, 6*, 31. doi:1744-859X-6-31 [pii] 10.1186/1744-859X-6-31

McEwen, B. S. (2001). From molecules to mind. Stress, individual differences, and the social environment. *Annals of the New York Academy of Sciences, 935*, 42–49.

McEwen, B. S., & Alves, S. E. (1999). Estrogen actions in the central nervous system. *Endocrine Reviews, 20*(3), 279–307.

McKay, J. R., Rutherford, M. J., Cacciola, J. S., Kabasakalian-McKay, R., & Alterman, A. I. (1996). Gender differences in the relapse experiences of cocaine patients. *Journal of Nervous and Mental Disease, 184*(10), 616–622.

Mendelson, J. H., Mello, N. K., Sholar, M. B., Siegel, A. J., Kaufman, M. J., Levin, J. M., . . . Cohen, B. M. (1999). Cocaine pharmacokinetics in men and in women during the follicular and luteal phases of the menstrual cycle. *Neuropsychopharmacology, 21*(2), 294–303. doi:10.1016/S0893-133X(99)00020-2

Merchenthaler, I. (1984). Corticotropin Releasing Factor (CRF)-like immunoreactivity in the rat central nervous system: Extrahypothalamic distribution. *Peptides, 5*(Suppl. 1), 53–69.

Merlo Pich, E., Lorang, M., Yeganeh, M., Rodriguez de Fonseca, F., Raber, J., Koob, G. F., & Weiss, F. (1995). Increase of extracellular corticotropin-releasing factor-like immunoreactivity levels in the amygdala of awake rats during restraint stress and ethanol withdrawal as measured by microdialysis. *Journal of Neuroscience, 15*(8), 5439–5447.

Milner, T. A., Thompson, L. I., Wang, G., Kievits, J. A., Martin, E., Zhou, P., . . . Waters, E. M. (2010). Distribution of estrogen receptor beta containing cells in the brains of bacterial artificial chromosome transgenic mice. *Brain Research, 1351*, 74–96. doi:10.1016/j.brainres.2010.06.038

Morissette, M., Le Saux, M., D'Astous, M., Jourdain, S., Al Sweidi, S., Morin, N., . . . Di Paolo, T. (2008). Contribution of estrogen receptors alpha and beta to the effects of estradiol in the brain. *Journal of Steroid Biochemistry and Molecular Biology, 108*(3–5), 327–338. doi:S0960-0760(07)00262-2 [pii] 10.1016/j.jsbmb.2007.09.011

Munro, C. A., McCaul, M. E., Wong, D. F., Oswald, L. M., Zhou, Y., Brasic, J., . . . Wand, G. S. (2006). Sex differences in striatal dopamine release in healthy adults. *Biological Psychiatry, 59*(10), 966–974. doi:10.1016/j.biopsych.2006.01.008

Nestler, E. J. (2002a). Common molecular and cellular substrates of addiction and memory. *Neurobiology of Learning and Memory, 78*(3), 637–647. doi:S1074742702940840 [pii]

Nestler, E. J. (2002b). From neurobiology to treatment: Progress against addiction. *Nature Neuroscience, 5*(Suppl.), 1076–1079. doi:10.1038/nn945 nn945 [pii]

Nestler, E. J. (2005). Is there a common molecular pathway for addiction? *Nat Neuroscience, 8*(11), 1445–1449. doi:10.1038/nn1578

Neugebauer, V., Li, W., Bird, G. C., & Han, J. S. (2004). The amygdala and persistent pain. *Neuroscientist, 10*(3), 221–234. doi:10.1177/1073858403261077

O'Brien, C. P., Childress, A. R., McLellan, T., & Ehrman, R. (1990). Integrating systemic cue exposure with standard treatment in recovering drug dependent patients. *Addictive Behaviors, 15*(4), 355–365.

O'Dell, L. E., & Torres, O. V. (2014). A mechanistic hypothesis of the factors that enhance vulnerability to nicotine use in females. *Neuropharmacology, 76*(Pt B), 566–580. doi:10.1016/j.neuropharm.2013.04.055

Overstreet, D. H., & Griebel, G. (2004). Antidepressant-like effects of CRF1 receptor antagonist SSR125543 in an animal model of depression. *European Journal of Pharmacology, 497*(1), 49–53. doi:10.1016/j.ejphar.2004.06.035

Overstreet, D. H., Keeney, A., & Hogg, S. (2004). Antidepressant effects of citalopram and CRF receptor antagonist CP-154,526 in a rat model of depression. *European Journal of Pharmacology, 492*(2–3), 195–201. doi:10.1016/j.ejphar.2004.04.010

Owesson-White, C. A., Ariansen, J., Stuber, G. D., Cleaveland, N. A., Cheer, J. F., Wightman, R. M., & Carelli, R. M. (2009). Neural encoding of cocaine-seeking behavior is coincident with phasic dopamine release in the accumbens core and shell. *European Journal of Neuroscience, 30*(6), 1117–1127. doi:10.1111/j.1460-9568.2009.06916.x

Oyola, M. G., & Handa, R. J. (2017). Hypothalamic-pituitary-adrenal and hypothalamic-pituitary-gonadal axes: Sex differences in regulation of stress responsivity. *Stress, 20*(5), 476–494. doi:10.1080/10253890.2017.1369523

Papaleo, F., Kitchener, P., & Contarino, A. (2007). Disruption of the CRF/CRF1 receptor stress system exacerbates the somatic signs of opiate withdrawal. *Neuron, 53*(4), 577–589. doi:10.1016/j.neuron.2007.01.022

Patchev, V. K., Hayashi, S., Orikasa, C., & Almeida, O. F. (1995). Implications of estrogen-dependent brain organization for gender differences in hypothalamo-pituitary-adrenal regulation. *FASEB Journal, 9*(5), 419–423.

Peris, J., Decambre, N., Coleman-Hardee, M. L., & Simpkins, J. W. (1991). Estradiol enhances behavioral sensitization to cocaine and amphetamine-stimulated striatal [3H]dopamine release. *Brain Research, 566*(1–2), 255–264. doi:0006-8993(91)91706-7 [pii]

Phillips, G. D., Setzu, E., Vugler, A., & Hitchcott, P. K. (2003). Immunohistochemical assessment of mesotelencephalic dopamine activity during the acquisition and expression of Pavlovian versus instrumental behaviours. *Neuroscience, 117*(3), 755–767.

Pierce, R. C., & Kumaresan, V. (2006). The mesolimbic dopamine system: The final common pathway for the reinforcing effect of drugs of abuse? *Neuroscience & Biobehavioral Reviews, 30*(2), 215–238. doi:S0149-7634(05)00069-2 [pii] 10.1016/j.neubiorev.2005.04.016

Pohjalainen, T., Rinne, J. O., Nagren, K., Syvalahti, E., & Hietala, J. (1998). Sex differences in the striatal dopamine D2 receptor binding characteristics in vivo. *American Journal of Psychiatry, 155*(6), 768–773. doi:10.1176/ajp.155.6.768

Porrino, L. J., Smith, H. R., Nader, M. A., & Beveridge, T. J. (2007). The effects of cocaine: A shifting target over the course of addiction. *Progress in Neuropsychopharmacology & Biological Psychiatry, 31*(8), 1593–1600. doi:10.1016/j.pnpbp.2007.08.040

Puder, M., Weidenfeld, J., Chowers, I., Nir, I., Conforti, N., & Siegel, R. A. (1982). Corticotrophin and corticosterone secretion following delta 1-Tetrahydrocannabinol, in intact and in hypothalamic deafferentated male rats. *Experimental Brain Research, 46*(1), 85–88.

Rassnick, S., Heinrichs, S. C., Britton, K. T., & Koob, G. F. (1993). Microinjection of a corticotropin-releasing factor antagonist into the central nucleus of the amygdala reverses anxiogenic-like effects of ethanol withdrawal. *Brain Research, 605*(1), 25–32.

Reid, A. G., Lingford-Hughes, A. R., Cancela, L. M., & Kalivas, P. W. (2012). Substance abuse disorders. *Handbook of Clinical Neurology, 106*, 419–431. doi:10.1016/B978-0-444-52002-9.00024-3

Richard, J. E., Lopez-Ferreras, L., Anderberg, R. H., Olandersson, K., & Skibicka, K. P. (2017). Estradiol is a critical regulator of food-reward behavior. *Psychoneuroendocrinology, 78*, 193–202. doi:10.1016/j.psyneuen.2017.01.014

Richter, R. M., Pich, E. M., Koob, G. F., & Weiss, F. (1995). Sensitization of cocaine-stimulated increase in extracellular levels of corticotropin-releasing factor from the rat amygdala after repeated administration as determined by intracranial microdialysis. *Neuroscience Letters, 187*(3), 169–172.

Richter, R. M., & Weiss, F. (1999). In vivo CRF release in rat amygdala is increased during cocaine withdrawal in self-administering rats. *Synapse, 32*(4), 254–261. doi:10.1002/(SICI)1098-2396(19990615)32:4<254::AID-SYN2>3.0.CO;2-H

Rivier, C. (1999). Gender, sex steroids, corticotropin-releasing factor, nitric oxide, and the HPA response to stress. *Pharmacology Biochemistry and Behavior, 64*(4), 739–751.

Rivier, C., Bruhn, T., & Vale, W. (1984). Effect of ethanol on the hypothalamic-pituitary-adrenal axis in the rat: Role of Corticotropin-Releasing Factor (CRF). *Journal of Pharmacology and Experimental Therapeutics, 229*(1), 127–131.

Roberts, D. C., Loh, E. A., & Vickers, G. (1989). Self-administration of cocaine on a progressive ratio schedule in rats: Dose-response relationship and effect of haloperidol pretreatment. *Psychopharmacology (Berl), 97*(4), 535–538.

Robinson, T. E., & Kolb, B. (1997). Persistent structural modifications in nucleus accumbens and prefrontal cortex neurons produced by previous experience with amphetamine. *Journal of Neuroscience, 17*(21), 8491–8497.

Robinson, T. E., & Kolb, B. (1999a). Alterations in the morphology of dendrites and dendritic spines in the nucleus accumbens and prefrontal cortex following repeated treatment with amphetamine or cocaine. *European Journal of Neuroscience, 11*(5), 1598–1604.

Robinson, T. E., & Kolb, B. (1999b). Morphine alters the structure of neurons in the nucleus accumbens and neocortex of rats. *Synapse, 33*(2), 160–162. doi:10.1002/(SICI)1098-2396(199908)33:2<160:: AID-SYN6>3.0.CO;2-S

Rodriguez de Fonseca, F., Carrera, M. R., Navarro, M., Koob, G. F., & Weiss, F. (1997). Activation of corticotropin-releasing factor in the limbic system during cannabinoid withdrawal. *Science, 276*(5321), 2050–2054.

Rodriguez de Fonseca, F., Rubio, P., Menzaghi, F., Merlo-Pich, E., Rivier, J., Koob, G. F., & Navarro, M. (1996). Corticotropin-Releasing Factor (CRF) antagonist [D-Phe12,Nle21,38,C alpha MeLeu37]CRF attenuates the acute actions of the highly potent cannabinoid receptor agonist HU-210 on defensive-withdrawal behavior in rats. *Journal of Pharmacology and Experimental Therapeutics, 276*(1), 56–64.

Roozendaal, B., McEwen, B. S., & Chattarji, S. (2009). Stress, memory and the amygdala. *Nature Reviews Neuroscience, 10*(6), 423–433. doi:10.1038/nrn2651

Roth, M. E., & Carroll, M. E. (2004). Sex differences in the escalation of intravenous cocaine intake following long- or short-access to cocaine self-administration. *Pharmacology Biochemistry and Behavior, 78*(2), 199–207. doi:10.1016/j.pbb.2004.03.018 S0091305704001029 [pii]

Rousseau, G. G., Baxter, J. D., & Tomkins, G. M. (1972). Glucocorticoid receptors: Relations between steroid binding and biological effects. *Journal of Molecular Biology, 67*(1), 99–115. doi:0022-2836(72)903 89-0 [pii]

Russo, S. J., Festa, E. D., Fabian, S. J., Gazi, F. M., Kraish, M., Jenab, S., & Quinones-Jenab, V. (2003). Gonadal hormones differentially modulate cocaine-induced conditioned place preference in male and female rats. *Neuroscience, 120*(2), 523–533. doi:S0306452203003178 [pii]

Russo, S. J., Jenab, S., Fabian, S. J., Festa, E. D., Kemen, L. M., & Quinones-Jenab, V. (2003). Sex differences in the conditioned rewarding effects of cocaine. *Brain Research, 970*(1–2), 214–220. doi:S00068 99303023461 [pii]

Russo, S. J., Sun, W. L., Minerly, A. C., Weierstall, K., Nazarian, A., Festa, E. D., . . . Quinones-Jenab, V. (2008). Progesterone attenuates cocaine-induced conditioned place preference in female rats. *Brain Research, 1189*, 229–235. doi:10.1016/j.brainres.2007.10.057

Salvatore, M., Wiersielis, K. R., Luz, S., Waxler, D. E., Bhatnagar, S., & Bangasser, D. A. (2018). Sex differences in circuits activated by corticotropin releasing factor in rats. *Hormones and Behavior, 97*, 145–153. doi:10.1016/j.yhbeh.2017.10.004

Sarnyai, Z., Biro, E., Gardi, J., Vecsernyes, M., Julesz, J., & Telegdy, G. (1993). Alterations of corticotropin-releasing factor-like immunoreactivity in different brain regions after acute cocaine administration in rats. *Brain Research, 616*(1–2), 315–319.

Sartor, G. C., & Aston-Jones, G. S. (2012). A septal-hypothalamic pathway drives orexin neurons, which is necessary for conditioned cocaine preference. *Journal of Neuroscience, 32*(13), 4623–4631. doi:10.1523/ JNEUROSCI.4561-11.2012

Schlosburg, J. E., Whitfield, T. W., Jr., Park, P. E., Crawford, E. F., George, O., Vendruscolo, L. F., & Koob, G. F. (2013). Long-term antagonism of kappa opioid receptors prevents escalation of and increased motivation for heroin intake. *Journal of Neuroscience, 33*(49), 19384–19392. doi:10.1523/ JNEUROSCI.1979-13.2013

Schulteis, G., Markou, A., Gold, L. H., Stinus, L., & Koob, G. F. (1994). Relative sensitivity to naloxone of multiple indices of opiate withdrawal: A quantitative dose-response analysis. *Journal of Pharmacology and Experimental Therapeutics, 271*(3), 1391–1398.

Shieh, K. R., & Yang, S. C. (2008). Effects of estradiol on the stimulation of dopamine turnover in mesolimbic and nigrostriatal systems by cocaine- and amphetamine-regulated transcript peptide in female rats. *Neuroscience, 154*(4), 1589–1597. doi:S0306-4522(08)00162-0 [pii] 10.1016/j.neuroscience.2008.01.086

Shimizu, H., & Bray, G. A. (1993). Effects of castration, estrogen replacement and estrus cycle on monoamine metabolism in the nucleus accumbens, measured by microdialysis. *Brain Research, 621*(2), 200–206.

Shughrue, P. J., Lane, M. V., & Merchenthaler, I. (1997). Comparative distribution of estrogen receptor-alpha and -beta mRNA in the rat central nervous system. *Journal of Comparative Neurology, 388*(4), 507–525.

Silva, S. M., & Madeira, M. D. (2012). Effects of chronic alcohol consumption and withdrawal on the response of the male and female hypothalamic-pituitary-adrenal axis to acute immune stress. *Brain Research, 1444*, 27–37. doi:10.1016/j.brainres.2012.01.013

Sinha, R. (2001). How does stress increase risk of drug abuse and relapse? *Psychopharmacology (Berl)*, *158*(4), 343–359. doi:10.1007/s002130100917

Sinha, R., Garcia, M., Paliwal, P., Kreek, M. J., & Rounsaville, B. J. (2006). Stress-induced cocaine craving and hypothalamic-pituitary-adrenal responses are predictive of cocaine relapse outcomes. *Archives of General Psychiatry*, *63*(3), 324–331. doi:10.1001/archpsyc.63.3.324

Smith, G. W., Aubry, J. M., Dellu, F., Contarino, A., Bilezikjian, L. M., Gold, L. H., . . . Lee, K. F. (1998). Corticotropin releasing factor receptor 1-deficient mice display decreased anxiety impared stress response, and abberant neuroendocrine development. *Neuron, 20*(6), 1093–1102.

Sofuoglu, M., Dudish-Poulsen, S., Nelson, D., Pentel, P. R., & Hatsukami, D. K. (1999). Sex and menstrual cycle differences in the subjective effects from smoked cocaine in humans. *Experimental and Clinical Psychopharmacology*, 7(3), 274–283.

Sofuoglu, M., Babb, D. A., & Hatsukami, D. K. (2002). Effects of progesterone treatment on smoked cocaine response in women. *Pharmacology Biochemistry and Behavior*, *72*(1–2), 431–435. doi:10.1016/S0091-3057(02)00716-5

Sofuoglu, M., Mitchell, E., & Kosten, T. R. (2004). Effects of progesterone treatment on cocaine responses in male and female cocaine users. *Pharmacology Biochemistry and Behavior*, *78*(4), 699–705. doi:10.1016/j.pbb.2004.05.004 S0091305704001443 [pii]

Solomon, R. L., & Corbit, J. D. (1974). An opponent-process theory of motivation. I. Temporal dynamics of affect. *Psychological Review*, *81*(2), 119–145.

Spencer, R. L., & McEwen, B. S. (1990). Adaptation of the hypothalamic-pituitary-adrenal axis to chronic ethanol stress. *Neuroendocrinology*, *52*(5), 481–489. doi:10.1159/000125632

Teesson, M., Havard, A., Fairbairn, S., Ross, J., Lynskey, M., & Darke, S. (2005). Depression among entrants to treatment for heroin dependence in the Australian Treatment Outcome Study (ATOS): Prevalence, correlates and treatment seeking. *Drug and Alcohol Dependence*, *78*(3), 309–315. doi:S0376-8716(04)00350-3 [pii] 10.1016/j.drugalcdep.2004.12.001

Torres, O. V., Gentil, L. G., Natividad, L. A., Carcoba, L. M., & O'Dell, L. E. (2013). Behavioral, biochemical, and molecular indices of stress are enhanced in female versus male rats experiencing nicotine withdrawal. *Frontiers in Psychiatry*, *4*, 38. doi:10.3389/fpsyt.2013.00038

Tzschentke, T. M. (2007). Measuring reward with the Conditioned Place Preference (CPP) paradigm: Update of the last decade. *Addiction Biology*, *12*(3–4), 227–462. doi:ADB070 [pii] 10.1111/j.1369-1600.2007.00070.x

Vandegrift, B. J., You, C., Satta, R., Brodie, M. S., & Lasek, A. W. (2017). Estradiol increases the sensitivity of ventral tegmental area dopamine neurons to dopamine and ethanol. *PLoS One*, *12*(11), e0187698. doi:10.1371/journal.pone.0187698

Viau, V., Bingham, B., Davis, J., Lee, P., & Wong, M. (2005). Gender and puberty interact on the stress-induced activation of parvocellular neurosecretory neurons and corticotropin-releasing hormone messenger ribonucleic acid expression in the rat. *Endocrinology*, *146*(1), 137–146. doi:10.1210/en.2004-0846

Viau, V., & Meaney, M. J. (1991). Variations in the hypothalamic-pituitary-adrenal response to stress during the estrous cycle in the rat. *Endocrinology*, *129*(5), 2503–2511.

Walker, Q. D., Rooney, M. B., Wightman, R. M., & Kuhn, C. M. (2000). Dopamine release and uptake are greater in female than male rat striatum as measured by fast cyclic voltammetry. *Neuroscience*, *95*(4), 1061–1070.

Wang, J., Fang, Q., Liu, Z., & Lu, L. (2006). Region-specific effects of brain corticotropin-releasing factor receptor type 1 blockade on footshock-stress- or drug-priming-induced reinstatement of morphine conditioned place preference in rats. *Psychopharmacology (Berl)*, *185*(1), 19–28. doi:10.1007/s00213-005-0262-6

Weinstock, M., Razin, M., Schorer-Apelbaum, D., Men, D., & McCarty, R. (1998). Gender differences in sympathoadrenal activity in rats at rest and in response to footshock stress. *International Journal of Developmental Neuroscience*, *16*(3–4), 289–295.

White, T. L., Justice, A. J., & de Wit, H. (2002). Differential subjective effects of D-amphetamine by gender, hormone levels and menstrual cycle phase. *Pharmacology Biochemistry and Behavior*, *73*(4), 729–741.

Whitfield, T. W., Jr., Schlosburg, J. E., Wee, S., Gould, A., George, O., Grant, Y., . . . Koob, G. F. (2015). kappa Opioid receptors in the nucleus accumbens shell mediate escalation of methamphetamine intake. *Journal of Neuroscience*, *35*(10), 4296–4305. doi:10.1523/JNEUROSCI.1978-13.2015

Willuhn, I., Burgeno, L. M., Everitt, B. J., & Phillips, P. E. (2012). Hierarchical recruitment of phasic dopamine signaling in the striatum during the progression of cocaine use. *Proceedings of the National Academy of Sciences of the United States of America*, *109*(50), 20703–20708. doi:10.1073/pnas.1213460109

Xiao, L., & Becker, J. B. (1994). Quantitative microdialysis determination of extracellular striatal dopamine concentration in male and female rats: Effects of estrous cycle and gonadectomy. *Neuroscience Letters*, *180*(2), 155–158.

Yates, W. R., Booth, B. M., Reed, D. A., Brown, K., & Masterson, B. J. (1993). Descriptive and predictive validity of a high-risk alcoholism relapse model. *Journal of Studies on Alcohol and Drugs*, *54*(6), 645–651.

Yoshimura, S., Sakamoto, S., Kudo, H., Sassa, S., Kumai, A., & Okamoto, R. (2003). Sex-differences in adrenocortical responsiveness during development in rats. *Steroids*, *68*(5), 439–445. doi:S0039128X03000 45X [pii]

Young, E. A. (1995). The role of gonadal steroids in hypothalamic-pituitary-adrenal axis regulation. *Critical Reviews in Neurobiology*, *9*(4), 371–381.

Young, E. A. (1996). Sex differences in response to exogenous corticosterone: A rat model of hypercortisolemia. *Molecular Psychiatry*, *1*(4), 313–319.

Zakharova, E., Wade, D., & Izenwasser, S. (2009). Sensitivity to cocaine conditioned reward depends on sex and age. *Pharmacology Biochemistry and Behavior*, *92*(1), 131–134. doi:S0091-3057(08)00365-1 [pii] 10.1016/j.pbb.2008.11.002

Zhang, D., Yang, S., Yang, C., Jin, G., & Zhen, X. (2008). Estrogen regulates responses of dopamine neurons in the ventral tegmental area to cocaine. *Psychopharmacology (Berl)*, *199*(4), 625–635. doi:10.1007/s00213-008-1188-6

Zhou, W., Cunningham, K. A., & Thomas, M. L. (2002). Estrogen regulation of gene expression in the brain: A possible mechanism altering the response to psychostimulants in female rats. *Brain Research. Molecular Brain Research*, *100*(1–2), 75–83. doi:S0169328X02001341 [pii]

Zilberman, M., Tavares, H., & el-Guebaly, N. (2003). Gender similarities and differences: The prevalence and course of alcohol- and other substance-related disorders. *Journal of Addictive Disease*, *22*(4), 61–74.

Zilberman, M. L., Tavares, H., Blume, S. B., & el-Guebaly, N. (2003). Substance use disorders: Sex differences and psychiatric comorbidities. *Canadian Journal of Psychiatry*, *48*(1), 5–13.

Zorrilla, E. P., Wee, S., Zhao, Y., Specio, S., Boutrel, B., Koob, G. F., & Weiss, F. (2012). Extended access cocaine self-administration differentially activates dorsal raphe and amygdala corticotropin-releasing factor systems in rats. *Addiction Biology*, *17*(2), 300–308. doi:10.1111/j.1369-1600.2011.00329.x

38

NEUROENDOCRINE–IMMUNE INTERACTIONS IN HEALTH AND DISEASE

Nicolas Rohleder

Introduction

Neuroendocrine systems interact with each other and with the immune system, and thereby maintain our inner homeostasis. Several neuroendocrine systems also interact with behavior, but most important for human health are interactions of the stress systems with the immune system, and the modulation of each of these systems, as well as their interactions, by social and psychological factors. Stress system regulation of different aspects of immune activity is the most important area to study, because stress systems are the ones most consistently affected by mental states, and are also the most likely to contribute to diseases related to different mental states, including chronic stress exposure, trauma, and affective disorders.

Interaction of neuroendocrine and immune system

In this section, I will first describe how the immune system is controlled by the central nervous system through the communication pathways provided by the neuroendocrine system, followed by a description of how the immune system can affect the central nervous system.

How neuroendocrine signals regulate immune function

As already alluded to, the most important neuroendocrine pathways regulating the immune system in the context of mental states and health are stress pathways. The main stress pathways are the Autonomic Nervous System (ANS), consisting of the Sympathetic and the Parasympathetic Nervous System (SNS and PNS) as well as the hypothalamus–pituitary–adrenal (HPA) axis.

Both systems originate deep in the central nervous system and communicate a number of different states to the periphery of the body, not all of which are necessarily related to mental states. For example, both ANS and the HPA axis play important roles in energy metabolism and other housekeeping functions of the body that are unrelated to mental states and immune function (e.g. Chrousos, Charmandari, & Kino, 2004; Joseph-Bravo, Jaimes-Hoy, & Charli, 2015). However, interpretation of situations as dangerous or threatening will increase SNS activity while decreasing PNS activity to promote the so-called fight-or-flight response (Cannon, 1932), which includes, among many important functions, activation of several components of the immune system (e.g. Naliboff et al., 1991). Similarly, the HPA axis will be activated in response to threat perceptions, albeit with a different temporal pattern, i.e. a delay in activation as well as deactivation, and in response to a different set of stimuli (Dickerson & Kemeny, 2004; Kirschbaum, Pirke, & Hellhammer, 1993). HPA axis activation will also, among many other effects, affect the immune system (McEwen & Stellar, 1993). While SNS activation (and PNS deactivation) only requires a low threshold of activity and can also be achieved through arousal and focused attention (Goldstein & Kopin, 2008; Messina et al., 2016), the HPA axis has a much higher activation threshold and only responds if a situation is perceived as threatening and, at the same time, uncontrollable and important for survival or social standing (Dickerson & Kemeny, 2004). It is believed that the concerted activation and subsequent deactivation of SNS and the HPA axis characterizes a healthy organism and permits unharmed survival of threatening life challenges (Sapolsky, Romero, & Munck, 2000).

While activation and deactivation of such acute stress responses is thought to be a require-ment for survival and under normal circumstances does not endanger the organism's health, a different picture emerges when a human being is under long-term or chronic stress, going through the aftermath of traumatization, or suffering from an affective disorder. Such adverse mental states are associated with altered basal activity of the neuroendocrine system. In fact, both stress-responsive systems show typical patterns of alterations in humans affected by long-term adverse mental states. The neuroendocrine systems discussed so far are characterized not only by their ability to respond to acute stress, but also through showing basal activity, with pronounced circadian activity linked to the individual's activity, i.e. sleep–wake cycle (Van Cauter, 1995). While the HPA axis shows a diurnal rhythm characterized by a sharp increase of activity, as pri-marily seen in cortisol concentrations upon waking up, and subsequent decline throughout the day, the SNS shows the opposite pattern, with generally higher activity in the second half of the day (Miller et al., 2016; Rohleder, Nater, Wolf, Ehlert, & Kirschbaum, 2004).

Adverse mental states such as chronic stress are associated with typical alterations in the basal activity of these systems. The SNS shows increased activity with higher plasma concentrations of epinephrine and norepinephrine, and higher SNS-driven target systems such as higher heart rate and blood pressure, or lower heart rate variability in, for example, depression and posttrau-matic stress disorder (PTSD; Grippo & Johnson, 2009; Southwick et al., 1997). It also shows similar alterations in states of chronic stress (Hänsel, Hong, Cámara, & von Känel, 2010). Altera-tions of the HPA axis are more complex and have only recently been understood and described by a comprehensive model. In short, early studies were equivocal with findings of hyper- as well as hypocortisolism associated with chronic stress and affective disorders. In a meta-analysis summarizing a large number of studies, Miller, Chen, and Zhou (2007) reported that timing and type of stressor matter: Generally, chronic stress or affective states are more likely to be associated with hypercortisolism in the earlier stages of an ongoing stressful state or, in the case of a trauma, in participants with a recent trauma. In contrast, long-term chronic stress or a longer period of time since experiencing a traumatic event are associated with hypocortisolism (Miller, Chen, & Zhou, 2007).

When studying how neuroendocrine systems affect the immune system, a number of factors have to be taken into account, including timing: Short-term, acute changes in neuroendocrine systems have to be distinguished from long-term, chronic alterations in neuroendocrine systems. Furthermore, each of these systems uses different signaling molecules to communicate with the immune system, and different sub-components of the immune system are differentially responsive to neuroendocrine signals. These factors, as well as the interaction between different neuroendocrine signals, have to be considered in any analysis of neuroendocrine effects on the immune system.

It is important to understand in this context that the immune system is in fact an organ comprised of many different components with different tasks within the organism. One of the most important distinctions has to be made between innate and adaptive immunity. Innate immunity refers to defense mechanisms that are present from birth and have been shaped by phylogenetic learning. These are able to immediately conquer invading pathogens, and one important component of this part of the immune system is the inflammatory response cascade. Inflammatory processes are central in immediate host defense and in wound healing (Chaplin, 2003). Adaptive immunity refers to defense mechanisms that are shaped by learning experiences in interaction with pathogens an individual organism is exposed to during its development. These mechanisms target a specific pathogen and therefore take several days to activate. Adaptive immunity includes cellular mechanisms, which mainly target viruses, and humoral immunity, which mainly targets single or multicellular pathogens like bacteria or parasites (Alam & Gorska, 2003).

Innate and adaptive immunity are differentially affected by neuroendocrine signaling. Innate immunity, and in particular inflammatory mechanisms, is typically stimulated by norepinephrine secreted by the SNS through well-described receptors on inflammatory immune cells like monocytes and macrophages (Padro & Sanders, 2014). Inflammatory mechanisms are also affected by the PNS, mainly through acetylcholine signaling taking place in lymph nodes (Pavlov, Wang, Czura, Friedman, & Tracey, 2003). While this anti-inflammatory effect of the PNS is still not well understood, the well-established main anti-inflammatory neuroendocrine pathway is the HPA axis. Cortisol, the main signaling molecule of the HPA axis in humans, has strong anti-inflammatory effects by binding to glucocorticoid receptors (GR) on immune cells relevant for the inflammatory response (Sapolsky et al., 2000). Through these pathways, acute exposure to threatening situations has been shown to at first activate inflammatory defense mechanisms, presumably to prepare the organism for potential injury requiring defense against invading pathogens, as well as wound healing (Bierhaus et al., 2003). Delayed increases of cortisol are then thought to downregulate inflammatory mechanisms once a stress situation is resolved (Wolf, Rohleder, Bierhaus, Nawroth, & Kirschbaum, 2009). These mechanisms are of particular importance in the context of long-term adverse mental states, in which a disinhibition of inflammatory processes occurs, which has many negative health effects (see below).

Stress system effects on adaptive immunity are more complex, which is related to the differential responsiveness of the different cellular as well as humoral components of the adaptive immune system to different stress mediators. Receptors for norepinephrine are expressed differently on cells responsible for antibody production versus cells responsible for targeting viruses, for example (Nance & Sanders, 2007). Cortisol has stronger effects on the cellular component of the adaptive immune system, while antibody production by humoral immunity is largely unaffected. This leads to a relatively stronger suppression of cellular immunity, targeting viruses, when cortisol concentrations are high and higher susceptibility to viral diseases such as the common cold and influenza (Wilder & Elenkov, 1999). Due to lesser effects of cortisol on humoral immunity, defense against bacteria and parasites is not compromised in a similar fashion by adverse mental states.

How immune system signals affect the central nervous system

Research on immune system effects on the central nervous system (CNS) has long been hampered by the assumption that the brain would be shielded from immune cells, as well as messenger molecules of the immune system, by the blood–brain barrier. In fact, neither immune cells nor cytokines, the messenger molecules of the immune system, are small enough to cross the blood–brain barrier.

However, a number of immune effects on the CNS have been observed and known for a long time. Most prominent are the effects of acute infections with fever on brain and behavior, such as nausea, fatigue, loss of interest in social and physical activities, and declines in cognitive function such as memory and attention. In animal models, these changes have been described with the term sickness behavior and are clear evidence that in fact the immune system can exert powerful effects on the CNS (Dantzer, O'Connor, Freund, Johnson, & Kelley, 2008). The first human evidence that these effects also play a role in the absence of acute infection and fever came from patients that were treated with specific messenger molecules of the immune system, so-called cytokines, to boost immune system function to fight cancer or hepatitis. Those patients showed symptoms of severe clinical depression (Denicoff et al., 1987; Renault et al., 1987).

In animal models, injection of these and other immune system mediators reliably induces sickness behavior, and the responsible mechanisms have become well understood (Dantzer et al., 2008): While the brain is indeed protected from many substances circulating in the blood, including immune cells and their messengers, there are pathways that allow the brain to sense immune activity in the periphery that circumvent the blood–brain barrier. One of these pathways makes use of nerves such as the vagus, which in the periphery have receptors for cytokines, and their afferent projections reach brain regions relevant for mood and pain regulation (e.g. amygdala and periaqueductal gray (PAG), among many others) (Bluthé, Michaud, Kelley, & Dantzer, 1996; Watkins & Maier, 2005). These vagal afferents also reach the paraventricular nucleus of the hypothalamus, through which peripheral inflammation can influence the HPA axis (Fleshner et al., 1995). This stimulating effect of cytokines on the HPA axis is a key component of the neuroendocrine–immune feedback loop, as part of which the immune system communicates with the CNS (Besedovsky, del Rey, Sorkin, & Dinarello, 1986). Another pathway operates through immune cells residing in blood vessels surrounding the brain's ventricles that will, in response to immune mediators circulating in the blood, produce local inflammatory signals that can be released into the brain (Quan, Whiteside, Kim, & Herkenham, 1997). In addition, research has identified active cytokine transporters that can move cytokines through the blood–brain barrier (Banks, Ortiz, Plotkin, & Kastin, 1991). Furthermore, cytokine receptors have been discovered on cells of the CNS vasculature that, upon stimulation, induce prostaglandin secretion into the brain (Konsman, Vigues, Mackerlova, Bristow, & Blomqvist, 2004). As this research shows, the brain – despite its blood–brain barrier – is not shielded from the immune system and is able to perceive, and respond to, immune system activation.

Neuroendocrine–immune interactions in the healthy organism

What do we need these mechanisms for? It has been suggested that the ability of the brain to control the immune system could be important for priming the immune system in preparation for anticipated infections. When the brain senses a threat to the integrity of the organism, the inflammatory system readies its arsenal of effector cells and mechanisms, allowing for faster response to wounds and infections. The HPA axis helps to downregulate this arsenal and return the system to a homeostatic state. With regard to immune-to-brain pathways, it is striking to observe that the sickness response leads to changes in physiology and behavior that put the immune system in a much better position to fight infections. Increased body temperature during fever helps the immune system fight pathogens. Decreased appetite and social motivation, as well as fatigue, force the organism into a resting state that also helps the immune system by shunting the organism's available energy and nutrients to it. It has therefore been suggested that the immune system, through its messenger molecules, can shape our behavior to allow it to work more efficiently. In the healthy organism, the immune system and HPA axis form a neuroendocrine feedback loop that appears to be important for physical as well as psychological health (Dantzer et al., 2008; del Rey & Besedovsky, 2000; Sternberg, Chrousos, Wilder, & Gold, 1992). How dysregulations of this feedback loop can lead to physical and mental disease will be described in the next section.

Role of alterations of neuroendocrine–immune interactions for health

The importance of the neuroendocrine feedback loop becomes apparent when looking at consequences of disruptions of this feedback system, which will be discussed here.

Neuroendocrine–immune interactions in physical disease

Physiological consequences of a disrupted neuroendocrine–immune feedback loop were first observed in animal models. In a series of studies using animal models of autoimmune inflammatory diseases, Sternberg et al. (1989) found strong support for the essential role of the HPA axis for the maintenance of health. While investigating the pathophysiology of rheumatoid arthritis using a rat model of this disease, they observed that one rat strain would die within a few days after induction, while other strains recovered. It was subsequently discovered that rats that did not survive were unable to mount an HPA axis response upon disease induction. Follow-up studies pinpointed their susceptibility to the disease to lack of HPA axis activation, and specifically to glucocorticoid effects, on the rat's immune system (Sternberg, Hill et al., 1989; Sternberg, Young et al., 1989). A similar importance of the HPA axis was found for a rat model of multiple sclerosis (del Rey, Klusman, & Besedovsky, 1998).

Similarly well-controlled experimental studies are not possible in humans, but HPA axis dysregulations have been studied in a variety of human autoimmune and inflammatory diseases. There are some reports of similar deficiencies in HPA axis responses in humans. Buske-Kirschbaum et al., for example, reported lower stress-induced cortisol increases in patients with atopic dermatitis (Buske-Kirschbaum, Geiben, Hollig, Morschhauser, & Hellhammer, 2002) and children with asthma (Buske-Kirschbaum et al., 2003). Lower HPA axis responses were also found in patients with rheumatoid arthritis (Dekkers et al., 2001) and fibromyalgia (Crofford et al., 1994). However, there are also many reports in which lower HPA axis reactivity was not found and in which basal HPA axis activity was even higher in patients compared to controls (e.g. Michelson et al., 1994; Heesen et al., 2002).

More recent evidence suggests that the disruption of the neuroendocrine–immune feedback loop occur not at the level of HPA axis regulation but at the level of the immune cell. In particular in the case of multiple sclerosis, there is now evidence showing that patients' immune cells are less able to respond to the anti-inflammatory effects of cortisol, both at baseline (Gold et al., 2005) and in response to acute stress (Kern, Rohleder, Eisenhofer, Lange, & Ziemssen, 2014). In this latter study, we were also able to show that timing matters. Longer disease duration appears to be associated with stronger HPA axis changes. Although we have no definitive data yet from experimental and longitudinal studies on the flow of causal effects between the stress system and the immune system, these findings may suggest that HPA axis changes are more likely a consequence rather than a cause of susceptibility to autoimmune diseases.

Neuroendocrine–immune interactions in mental disease

Even more so than in physiological disease, alterations in neuroendocrine–immune interactions play a role in mental disease. In particular, depression and PTSD are associated with pronounced changes in neuroendocrine activity, albeit with strikingly different patterns (Rohleder, Wolf, & Wolf, 2010; Yehuda, Teicher, Trestman, Levengood, & Siever, 1996; see also Lehrner & Yehuda, this volume). Both disorders come with very distinct alterations in HPA axis activity that range from the CNS level to the level of target tissue responsiveness to HPA axis hormones. Both diseases also show characteristic changes in ANS activity.

Depression is characterized by increased corticotropin-releasing hormone (CRH) levels in the hypothalamus; reduced negative feedback sensitivity, meaning that more cortisol is needed to exert negative feedback to suppress HPA axis activity; and higher responses to injections of CRH (Ising et al., 2005; Nemeroff, 1996). These central changes are often related to a state of hypercortisolism, i.e. increased plasma concentrations of cortisol (e.g. Deuschle et al., 1997), although more recent summaries conclude that a disturbed circadian rhythm in the shape of a reduced circadian dynamic of cortisol release is a more consistent finding than hypercortisolism (e.g. Miller et al., 2007). SNS activity in depression is frequently found to be increased, as evidenced, for example, through increased plasma norepinephrine concentrations (e.g. Miller, Cohen, & Herbert, 1999). PTSD shows similar overactivity of CRH in the hypothalamus (Baker et al., 1999), but other, more downstream indicators of HPA axis activity differ markedly from depression. Typical for PTSD is an increased HPA axis feedback sensitivity and lower plasma and salivary cortisol concentrations, indicating a state of hypocortisolism (N. Rohleder & Karl, 2006; Wessa, Rohleder, Kirschbaum, & Flor, 2006; R. Yehuda, 2001). Similarly to depression, though, the SNS is overactive in PTSD, as evidenced for example by increased central (Geracioti et al., 2001) and peripheral norepinephrine (Mason, Giller, Kosten, Ostroff, & Podd, 1986) concentrations.

While these two representatives of mental disorders are different with regard to their HPA axis dysregulations, both are characterized by similar immune alterations, notably increased inflammation (depression: Alesci et al., 2005; Maes et al., 1995; Miller, Stetler, Carney, Freedland, & Banks, 2002; PTSD: Maes et al., 1999; Spitzer et al., 2010; Spivak et al., 1997). The fact that neuroendocrine alterations are so different, but immune changes are so similar in depression and PTSD, points to differences in neuroendocrine–immune interactions in both disorders.

This difference can be attributed to differences in inflammatory cells' sensitivity to glucocorticoid signaling. In depression, inflammatory activity is increased despite high concentrations of circulating cortisol. While increased inflammation could be the result of higher SNS activity and higher immune stimulating effects of norepinephrine, cortisol's anti-inflammatory effects should normally downregulate inflammation. However, depressed patients' immune cells have been shown to be less responsive to inhibition by cortisol (e.g. Lowy, Reder, Antel, & Meltzer, 1984; Pariante, 2004). In PTSD, inflammatory activity is increased as well, which is in line with the assumption that higher SNS signaling and lower cortisol availability should be predictive of inflammatory disinhibition. However, glucocorticoid responsiveness of immune cells is frequently found to be upregulated (Rohleder, Joksimovic, Wolf, & Kirschbaum, 2004; Yehuda, Golier, Yang, & Tischler, 2004), which could be interpreted as a counter-regulatory mechanism that nevertheless does not quite compensate for the overall low cortisol levels characteristic of PTSD and, hence, higher inflammatory activity (Rohleder et al., 2010).

Immune-to-brain signaling is of particular relevance for depression. Since the early findings of cytokine therapies leading to full-blown major depression in some patients, researchers have proposed a more central role of the neuroendocrine–immune feedback loop, and its disruption, in the pathogenesis of depression (e.g. Dantzer et al., 2008; Maes, 1995; Raison, Capuron, & Miller, 2006). The magnitude of the relative contribution of inflammation to major depression is still a matter of debate, but the immune-to-brain signaling pathways described above, in particular the fact that peripheral cytokines target regions such as the amygdala, anterior cingulate cortex (ACC), and serotonergic and dopaminergic systems, show how strong the immune system's impact on the brain is.

Effects of social interactions on the neuroendocrine–immune interplay

Social interactions exert a powerful influence on the neuroendocrine system and, through these systems, also on the immune system. As introduced above, both acute and chronic stress are associated with marked changes in activity and reactivity of the neuroendocrine system, and also with changes in immune system function.

Everyday and acute social stress and the neuroendocrine–immune interplay

Through the pathways already described, the brain communicates the presence of a threat to the body's periphery, including the immune system. Many of the findings already described were gained from controlled laboratory studies using standardized laboratory stress tests. The aim of this section is to discuss the relevance of these changes in real life situations.

In addition to situations that are reasonably similar to laboratory stress tests, there are daily hassles which might be perceived as less stressful but which can accumulate to amount to similar or even stronger changes (Almeida, 2005). Furthermore, it will be important to understand individual differences in how stressful these hassles are experienced and how strongly they activate the neuroendocrine and the immune system. Recent research has shown that daily hassles, and in particular an individual's responses to such stressors, can have long-term effects on the organism. Piazza et al., for example, found that stronger self-reported emotional responses to daily hassles were predictive of higher rates of health conditions such as cardiovascular or digestive issues, but also pain and cancer ten years later (Piazza, Charles, Sliwinski, Mogle, & Almeida, 2013). Similar findings emerged for the likelihood to self-report an affective disorder after ten years (Charles, Piazza, Mogle, Sliwinski, & Almeida, 2013). In terms of mechanisms, cross-sectional analyses found that those individuals with higher emotional reactivity to daily stressors showed signs of ANS alterations, with lower parasympathetic activity (Sin, Sloan, McKinley, & Almeida, 2016), changes in HPA axis activity characterized by higher cortisol levels during days with more daily stressors (Stawski, Cichy, Piazza, & Almeida, 2013), and higher inflammation (Sin, Graham-Engeland, Ong, & Almeida, 2015). Taken together, these findings show that everyday stressors can affect the neuroendocrine–immune interplay. They also suggest that these effects on the neuroendocrine–immune interplay are relevant for an individual's health, as higher emotional reactivity predicts long-term declines in health.

Chronic social stress and the neuroendocrine–immune interplay

Chronic life stress, together with mental disorders, is one of the strongest forces interrupting the neuroendocrine–immune interplay. Above, we discussed associations of chronic stress with HPA axis activity and reported that the most appropriate summary of HPA axis changes in chronic stress is that hypercortisolism is present in early stages of chronic stress, while with prolonged exposure, the system reverts to an under-active state characterized by hypocortisolism and flat diurnal profiles (Miller et al., 2007). At the level of the SNS, a recent systematic review (Allen et al., 2017) reported rather inconsistent findings for differences between people living with and taking care of a family member with a chronic debilitating illness, typically referred to as caregivers, with chronic stress, as compared with non-caregivers. The authors summarize that the cardiovascular system shows signs of an overactive SNS in this population. This is reflected in, for example, findings of higher heart rate and blood pressure in chronically stressed caregivers, compared to controls. But the authors discuss that findings are inconclusive and in need of replication. With regard to neuroendocrine measures of SNS activity, findings in caregivers were similarly mixed, with only half of the studies finding higher epinephrine and norepinephrine concentrations (Allen et al., 2017). These inconsistent findings might in part be explained by the difficulty of obtaining blood samples for neuroendocrine measurements in chronically stressed individuals, which might be due to the low number of available studies. An alternative, less-invasive measure, salivary alpha-amylase (sAA), has been suggested more recently, and first results using this parameter provide some indication of SNS alterations in chronic stress. We found, for example, that sAA daily rhythms, which are typically pronounced, with a drop in the morning and high afternoon concentrations, flatten out over a one-year period of participants caring for a family member with brain cancer (Nicolas Rohleder, Marin, Ma, & Miller, 2009). We also found altered sAA diurnal rhythms in refugees with PTSD (Thoma, Joksimovic, Kirschbaum, Wolf, & Rohleder, 2012). Liu et al. reported that stress caused by caring for a family member was associated with higher afternoon sAA concentrations (Liu et al., 2017). While these findings are still emerging, they point to pattern changes in diurnal SNS activity, with a relative loss of circadian rhythmicity.

Clear evidence exists for the relationship of chronic life stress with increased activity of the inflammatory system. Higher blood concentrations of markers of systemic low-grade inflammation such as interleukin-6 (IL-6) and C-reactive Protein (CRP) have been found in populations of individuals with experiences of childhood adversity (Danese et al., 2011), work stress (Melamed, Shirom, Toker, Berliner, & Shapira, 2006), caregiving stress (Rohleder et al., 2009), and also with related social states such as loneliness (McDade, Hawkley, & Cacioppo, 2006) and low socioeconomic status (Friedman & Herd, 2010). Several systematic reviews have provided summaries and analyses of the literature and uniformly conclude that there is a continuous relationship between chronically experienced adverse psychosocial factors and systemic low-grade inflammation (e.g. Hänsel et al., 2010; Rohleder, 2014; Wirtz & von Känel, 2017).

The neuroendocrine–immune interplay is critical for understanding the underlying causes of increased activity of the inflammatory system in these chronic stress conditions. While findings of lower HPA axis activity in chronic stress would be consistent with dysregulated inflammation, there are many reports in the literature of increased inflammation in the absence of hypocortisolism (e.g. Rohleder et al., 2009). Furthermore, evidence for SNS alterations, as summarized above, is inconsistent and does not support the simple notion of SNS overactivity in chronic stress, which could also be a factor stimulating inflammation. It has therefore been proposed that one of the key factors for development of an overactive inflammatory system is an alteration in neuroendocrine–immune communication, in particular an inability of inflammatory cells to respond to the suppressing effects of cortisol (e.g. Miller, Cohen, & Ritchey, 2002; Raison & Miller, 2003; Rohleder, 2012). In fact, reduced glucocorticoid sensitivity has been found in many conditions of chronic stress, such as in our own caregiver study (Rohleder et al., 2009), in chronic fatigue states (Strahler, Skoluda, Rohleder, & Nater, 2016), and in adults who experienced childhood adversity (Miller et al., 2009; for a summary, see Rohleder, 2012). Furthermore, chronic stress has also been found to be associated with changes in the ability of the inflammatory immune cells to respond to SNS system signals (Mausbach et al., 2008). Taken together, altered neuroendocrine–immune interplay plays a crucial role in the development of systemic low-grade inflammation in chronically adverse psychosocial states.

Conclusions and outlook

Alterations of the complicated interplay between the neuroendocrine and the immune system play an important role in the development of disease. Such alterations can be caused by conditions of psychosocial stress and adversity, as well as by affective disorders such as depression and PTSD. Alterations, however, can also originate in the periphery in response to immune system activation by chronic infections or by immune system disorders such as autoimmune and inflammatory diseases. Functional bi-directional communication between the immune system and the brain and by extension the neuroendocrine system is important for the maintenance of health. In particular, inflammatory system over-activation without infectious causes has been identified as a predictor of severe and life-shortening diseases such as cardiovascular diseases, type 2 diabetes, cancers, and conditions of older age, such as osteoporosis and frailty. In the quest to understand the pathways between psychosocial factors and these diseases, neuroendocrine systems alone have proven insufficient as predictors of disease, but their interactions with the immune system have been shown to lead to inflammation. While a specific form of disruption of neuroendocrine–immune signaling, i.e. ability of immune cells to respond to suppressive glucocorticoid signals, has emerged as a likely culprit, other forms of disruption, such as those between the ANS and the immune system, as well as immune-to-brain signaling, are less well-understood. Future work will therefore need to focus on disentangling those relationships, which will likely improve our ability to diagnose, and potentially treat, psychosocial effects on health and longevity.

References

Alam, R., & Gorska, M. (2003). 3. Lymphocytes. *The Journal of Allergy and Clinical Immunology, 111*(2 Suppl.), S476–85.

Alesci, S., Martinez, P. E., Kelkar, S., Ilias, I., Ronsaville, D. S., Listwak, S. J., . . . Gold, P. W. (2005). Major depression is associated with significant diurnal elevations in plasma interleukin-6 levels, a shift of its circadian rhythm, and loss of physiological complexity in its secretion: Clinical implications. *The Journal of Clinical Endocrinology and Metabolism, 90*(5), 2522–2530.

Allen, A. P., Curran, E. A., Duggan, Á., Cryan, J. F., Chorcoráin, A. N., Dinan, T. G., . . . Clarke, G. (2017). A systematic review of the psychobiological burden of informal caregiving for patients with dementia: Focus on cognitive and biological markers of chronic stress. *Neuroscience and Biobehavioral Reviews, 73*, 123–164.

Almeida, D. M. (2005). Resilience and vulnerability to daily stressors assessed via diary methods. *Current Directions in Psychological Science, 14*(2), 64–68.

Baker, D. G., West, S. A., Nicholson, W. E., Ekhator, N. N., Kasckow, J. W., Hill, K. K., . . . Geracioti, T. D., Jr. (1999). Serial CSF corticotropin-releasing hormone levels and adrenocortical activity in combat veterans with posttraumatic stress disorder. *The American Journal of Psychiatry, 156*(4), 585–588.

Banks, W. A., Ortiz, L., Plotkin, S. R., & Kastin, A. J. (1991). Human interleukin (IL) 1 alpha, murine IL-1 alpha and murine IL-1 beta are transported from blood to brain in the mouse by a shared saturable mechanism. *The Journal of Pharmacology and Experimental Therapeutics, 259*(3), 988–996.

Besedovsky, H., del Rey, A., Sorkin, E., & Dinarello, C. A. (1986). Immunoregulatory feedback between interleukin-1 and glucocorticoid hormones. *Science, 233*(4764), 652–654.

Bierhaus, A., Wolf, J., Andrassy, M., Rohleder, N., Humpert, P. M., Petrov, D., . . . Nawroth, P. P. (2003). A mechanism converting psychosocial stress into mononuclear cell activation. *Proceedings of the National Academy of Sciences of the United States of America, 100*(4), 1920–1925.

Bluthé, R. M., Michaud, B., Kelley, K. W., & Dantzer, R. (1996). Vagotomy attenuates behavioural effects of interleukin-1 injected peripherally but not centrally. *Neuroreport, 7*(9), 1485–1488.

Buske-Kirschbaum, A., Geiben, A., Hollig, H., Morschhauser, E., & Hellhammer, D. (2002). Altered responsiveness of the hypothalamus-pituitary-adrenal axis and the sympathetic adrenomedullary system to stress in patients with atopic dermatitis. *The Journal of Clinical Endocrinology and Metabolism, 87*(9), 4245–4251.

Buske-Kirschbaum, A., von Auer, K., Krieger, S., Weis, S., Rauh, W., & Hellhammer, D. (2003). Blunted cortisol responses to psychosocial stress in asthmatic children: A general feature of atopic disease? *Psychosomatic Medicine, 65*(5), 806–810.

Cannon, W. B. (1932). *The wisdom of the body.* New York, NY: W. W. Norton & Company.

Chaplin, D. D. (2003). 1. Overview of the immune response. *The Journal of Allergy and Clinical Immunology, 111*(2 Suppl.), S442–59.

Charles, S. T., Piazza, J. R., Mogle, J., Sliwinski, M. J., & Almeida, D. M. (2013). The wear and tear of daily stressors on mental health. *Psychological Science, 24*(5), 733–741.

Chrousos, G. P., Charmandari, E., & Kino, T. (2004). Glucocorticoid action networks – an introduction to systems biology. *The Journal of Clinical Endocrinology and Metabolism, 89*(2), 563–564.

Crofford, L. J., Pillemer, S. R., Kalogeras, K. T., Cash, J. M., Michelson, D., Kling, M. A., . . . Wilder, R. L. (1994). Hypothalamic-pituitary-adrenal axis perturbations in patients with fibromyalgia. *Arthritis and Rheumatism, 37*(11), 1583–1592.

Danese, A., Caspi, A., Williams, B., Ambler, A., Sugden, K., Mika, J., . . . Arseneault, L. (2011). Biological embedding of stress through inflammation processes in childhood. *Molecular Psychiatry, 16*(3), 244–246.

Dantzer, R., O'Connor, J. C., Freund, G. G., Johnson, R. W., & Kelley, K. W. (2008). From inflammation to sickness and depression: When the immune system subjugates the brain. *Nature Reviews. Neuroscience, 9*(1), 46–56.

Dekkers, J. C., Geenen, R., Godaert, G. L., Glaudemans, K. A., Lafeber, F. P., van Doornen, L. J., & Bijlsma, J. W. (2001). Experimentally challenged reactivity of the hypothalamic pituitary adrenal axis in patients with recently diagnosed rheumatoid arthritis. *The Journal of Rheumatology, 28*(7), 1496–1504.

del Rey, A., & Besedovsky, H. O. (2000). The cytokine-HPA axis circuit contributes to prevent or moderate autoimmune processes. *Zeitschrift Fur Rheumatologie, 59*(Suppl. 2), II/31–5.

del Rey, A., Klusman, I., & Besedovsky, H. O. (1998). Cytokines mediate protective stimulation of glucocorticoid output during autoimmunity: Involvement of IL-1. *The American Journal of Physiology, 275*(4 Pt 2), R1146–51.

Denicoff, K. D., Rubinow, D. R., Papa, M. Z., Simpson, C., Seipp, C. A., Lotze, M. T., . . . Rosenberg, S. A. (1987). The neuropsychiatric effects of treatment with interleukin-2 and lymphokine-activated killer cells. *Annals of Internal Medicine, 107*(3), 293–300.

Deuschle, M., Schweiger, U., Weber, B., Gotthardt, U., Körner, A., Schmider, J., . . . Heuser, I. (1997). Diurnal activity and pulsatility of the hypothalamus-pituitary-adrenal system in male depressed patients and healthy controls. *The Journal of Clinical Endocrinology and Metabolism, 82*(1), 234–238.

Dickerson, S. S., & Kemeny, M. E. (2004). Acute stressors and cortisol responses: A theoretical integration and synthesis of laboratory research. *Psychological Bulletin, 130*(3), 355–391.

Fleshner, M., Goehler, L. E., Hermann, J., Relton, J. K., Maier, S. F., & Watkins, L. R. (1995). Interleukin-1 beta induced corticosterone elevation and hypothalamic NE depletion is vagally mediated. *Brain Research Bulletin, 37*(6), 605–610.

Friedman, E. M., & Herd, P. (2010). Income, education, and inflammation: Differential associations in a national probability sample (The MIDUS study). *Psychosomatic Medicine, 72*(3), 290–300.

Geracioti, T. D., Jr, Baker, D. G., Ekhator, N. N., West, S. A., Hill, K. K., Bruce, A. B., . . . Kasckow, J. W. (2001). CSF norepinephrine concentrations in posttraumatic stress disorder. *The American Journal of Psychiatry, 158*(8), 1227–1230.

Gold, S. M., Mohr, D. C., Huitinga, I., Flachenecker, P., Sternberg, E. M., & Heesen, C. (2005). The role of stress-response systems for the pathogenesis and progression of MS. *Trends in Immunology.* Retrieved from www.ncbi.nlm.nih.gov/entrez/query.fcgi?cmd=Retrieve&db=PubMed&dopt=Citation&list_uids=16214415

Goldstein, D. S., & Kopin, I. J. (2008). Adrenomedullary, adrenocortical, and sympathoneural responses to stressors: A meta-analysis. *Endocrine Regulations, 42*(4), 111–119.

Grippo, A. J., & Johnson, A. K. (2009). Stress, depression and cardiovascular dysregulation: A review of neurobiological mechanisms and the integration of research from preclinical disease models. *Stress, 12*(1), 1–21.

Hänsel, A., Hong, S., Cámara, R. J. A., & von Känel, R. (2010). Inflammation as a psychophysiological biomarker in chronic psychosocial stress. *Neuroscience and Biobehavioral Reviews, 35*(1), 115–121.

Heesen, C., Schulz, H., Schmidt, M., Gold, S., Tessmer, W., & Schulz, K-H. (2002). Endocrine and cytokine responses to acute psychological stress in multiple sclerosis. *Brain, Behavior, and Immunity, 16*(3), 282–287.

Ising, M., Künzel, H. E., Binder, E. B., Nickel, T., Modell, S., & Holsboer, F. (2005). The combined dexamethasone/CRH test as a potential surrogate marker in depression. *Progress in Neuro-Psychopharmacology & Biological Psychiatry, 29*(6), 1085–1093.

Joseph-Bravo, P., Jaimes-Hoy, L., & Charli, J-L. (2015). Regulation of TRH neurons and energy homeostasis-related signals under stress. *The Journal of Endocrinology, 224*(3), R139–59.

Kern, S., Rohleder, N., Eisenhofer, G., Lange, J., & Ziemssen, T. (2014). Time matters – acute stress response and glucocorticoid sensitivity in early multiple sclerosis. *Brain, Behavior, and Immunity, 41*, 82–89.

Kirschbaum, C., Pirke, K.-M., & Hellhammer, D. H. (1993). The "Trier Social Stress Test" - a tool for investigating psychobiological stress responses in a laboratory setting. *Neuropsychobiology, 28*, 76–81.

Konsman, J. P., Vigues, S., Mackerlova, L., Bristow, A., & Blomqvist, A. (2004). Rat brain vascular distribution of interleukin-1 type-1 receptor immunoreactivity: Relationship to patterns of inducible cyclooxygenase expression by peripheral inflammatory stimuli. *The Journal of Comparative Neurology, 472*(1), 113–129.

Liu, Y., Granger, D. A., Kim, K., Klein, L. C., Almeida, D. M., & Zarit, S. H. (2017). Diurnal salivary alpha-amylase dynamics among dementia family caregivers. *Health Psychology: Official Journal of the Division of Health Psychology, American Psychological Association, 36*(2), 160–168.

Lowy, M. T., Reder, A. T., Antel, J. P., & Meltzer, H. Y. (1984). Glucocorticoid resistance in depression: The dexamethasone suppression test and lymphocyte sensitivity to dexamethasone. *The American Journal of Psychiatry, 141*(11), 1365–1370.

Maes, M. (1995). Evidence for an immune response in major depression: A review and hypothesis. *Progress in Neuro-Psychopharmacology & Biological Psychiatry, 19*(1), 11–38.

Maes, M., Lin, A. H., Delmeire, L., van Gastel, A., Kenis, G., De Jongh, R., & Bosmans, E. (1999). Elevated serum interleukin-6 (IL-6) and IL-6 receptor concentrations in posttraumatic stress disorder following accidental man-made traumatic events. *Biological Psychiatry, 45*(7), 833–839.

Maes, M., Vandoolaeghe, E., Ranjan, R., Bosmans, E., Bergmans, R., & Desnyder, R. (1995). Increased serum interleukin-1-receptor-antagonist concentrations in major depression. *Journal of Affective Disorders, 36*(1–2), 29–36.

Mason, J. W., Giller, E. L., Kosten, T. R., Ostroff, R. B., & Podd, L. (1986). Urinary free-cortisol levels in posttraumatic stress disorder patients. *The Journal of Nervous and Mental Disease, 174*(3), 145–149.

Mausbach, B. T., Aschbacher, K., Mills, P. J., Roepke, S. K., von Känel, R., Patterson, T. L., . . . Grant, I. (2008). A 5-year longitudinal study of the relationships between stress, coping, and immune cell beta(2)-adrenergic receptor sensitivity. *Psychiatry Research, 160*(3), 247–255.

McDade, T. W., Hawkley, L. C., & Cacioppo, J. T. (2006). Psychosocial and behavioral predictors of inflammation in middle-aged and older adults: The Chicago health, aging, and social relations study. *Psychosomatic Medicine, 68*(3), 376–381.

McEwen, B. S., & Stellar, E. (1993). Stress and the individual. Mechanisms leading to disease. *Archives of Internal Medicine, 153*(18), 2093–2101.

Melamed, S., Shirom, A., Toker, S., Berliner, S., & Shapira, I. (2006). Burnout and risk of cardiovascular disease: Evidence, possible causal paths, and promising research directions. *Psychological Bulletin, 132*(3), 327–353.

Messina, G., Chieffi, S., Viggiano, A., Tafuri, D., Cibelli, G., Valenzano, A., . . . Monda, M. (2016). Parachute jumping induces more sympathetic activation than cortisol secretion in first-time parachutists. *Asian Journal of Sports Medicine, 7*(1), e26841.

Michelson, D., Stone, L., Galliven, E., Magiakou, M. A., Chrousos, G. P., Sternberg, E. M., & Gold, P. W. (1994). Multiple sclerosis is associated with alterations in hypothalamic-pituitary-adrenal axis function. *The Journal of Clinical Endocrinology and Metabolism, 79*(3), 848–853.

Miller, G. E., Chen, E., Fok, A. K., Walker, H., Lim, A., Nicholls, E. F., . . . Kobor, M. S. (2009). Low early-life social class leaves a biological residue manifested by decreased glucocorticoid and increased proinflammatory signaling. *Proceedings of the National Academy of Sciences of the United States of America, 106*(34), 14716–14721.

Miller, G. E., Chen, E., & Zhou, E. S. (2007). If it goes up, must it come down? Chronic stress and the hypothalamic-pituitary-adrenocortical axis in humans. *Psychological Bulletin, 133*(1), 25–45.

Miller, G. E., Cohen, S., & Herbert, T. B. (1999). Pathways linking major depression and immunity in ambulatory female patients. *Psychosomatic Medicine, 61*(6), 850–860.

Miller, G. E., Cohen, S., & Ritchey, A. K. (2002). Chronic psychological stress and the regulation of pro-inflammatory cytokines: A glucocorticoid-resistance model. *Health Psychology: Official Journal of the Division of Health Psychology, American Psychological Association, 21*(6), 531–541.

Miller, G. E., Stetler, C. A., Carney, R. M., Freedland, K. E., & Banks, W. A. (2002). Clinical depression and inflammatory risk markers for coronary heart disease. *The American Journal of Cardiology, 90*(12), 1279–1283.

Miller, R., Stalder, T., Jarczok, M., Almeida, D. M., Badrick, E., Bartels, M., . . . Kirschbaum, C. (2016). The CIRCORT database: Reference ranges and seasonal changes in diurnal salivary cortisol derived from a meta-dataset comprised of 15 field studies. *Psychoneuroendocrinology, 73*, 16–23.

Naliboff, B. D., Benton, D., Solomon, G. F., Morley, J. E., Fahey, J. L., Bloom, E. T., . . . Gilmore, S. L. (1991). Immunological changes in young and old adults during brief laboratory stress. *Psychosomatic Medicine, 53*(2), 121–132.

Nance, D. M., & Sanders, V. M. (2007). Autonomic innervation and regulation of the immune system (1987–2007). *Brain, Behavior, and Immunity, 21*(6), 736–745.

Nemeroff, C. B. (1996). The Corticotropin-Releasing Factor (CRF) hypothesis of depression: New findings and new directions. *Molecular Psychiatry, 1*(4), 336–342.

Padro, C. J., & Sanders, V. M. (2014). Neuroendocrine regulation of inflammation. *Seminars in Immunology, 26*(5), 357–368.

Pariante, C. M. (2004). Glucocorticoid receptor function in vitro in patients with major depression. *Stress, 7*(4), 209–219.

Pavlov, V. A., Wang, H., Czura, C. J., Friedman, S. G., & Tracey, K. J. (2003). The cholinergic anti-inflammatory pathway: A missing link in neuroimmunomodulation. *Molecular Medicine, 9*(5–8), 125–134.

Piazza, J. R., Charles, S. T., Sliwinski, M. J., Mogle, J., & Almeida, D. M. (2013). Affective reactivity to daily stressors and long-term risk of reporting a chronic physical health condition. *Annals of Behavioral Medicine: A Publication of the Society of Behavioral Medicine, 45*(1), 110–120.

Quan, N., Whiteside, M., Kim, L., & Herkenham, M. (1997). Induction of inhibitory factor kappaBalpha mRNA in the central nervous system after peripheral lipopolysaccharide administration: An in situ hybridization histochemistry study in the rat. *Proceedings of the National Academy of Sciences of the United States of America, 94*(20), 10985–10990.

Raison, C. L., Capuron, L., & Miller, A. H. (2006). Cytokines sing the blues: Inflammation and the pathogenesis of depression. *Trends in Immunology, 27*(1), 24–31.

Raison, C. L., & Miller, A. H. (2003). When not enough is too much: The role of insufficient glucocorticoid signaling in the pathophysiology of stress-related disorders. *The American Journal of Psychiatry, 160*(9), 1554–1565.

Renault, P. F., Hoofnagle, J. H., Park, Y., Mullen, K. D., Peters, M., Jones, D. B., . . . Jones, E. A. (1987). Psychiatric complications of long-term interferon alfa therapy. *Archives of Internal Medicine, 147*(9), 1577–1580.

Rohleder, N. (2012). Acute and chronic stress induced changes in sensitivity of peripheral inflammatory pathways to the signals of multiple stress systems – 2011 Curt Richter Award Winner. *Psychoneuroendocrinology, 37*(3), 307–316.

Rohleder, N. (2014). Stimulation of systemic low-grade inflammation by psychosocial stress. *Psychosomatic Medicine, 76*(3), 181–189.

Rohleder, N., Joksimovic, L., Wolf, J. M., & Kirschbaum, C. (2004). Hypocortisolism and increased glucocorticoid sensitivity of pro-Inflammatory cytokine production in Bosnian war refugees with post-traumatic stress disorder. *Biological Psychiatry, 55*(7), 745–751.

Rohleder, N., & Karl, A. (2006). Role of endocrine and inflammatory alterations in comorbid somatic diseases of post-traumatic stress disorder. *Minerva Endocrinologica, 31*(4), 273–288.

Rohleder, N., Marin, T. J., Ma, R., & Miller, G. E. (2009). Biologic cost of caring for a cancer patient: Dysregulation of pro- and anti-inflammatory signaling pathways. *Journal of Clinical Oncology: Official Journal of the American Society of Clinical Oncology, 27*(18), 2909–2915.

Rohleder, N., Nater, U. M., Wolf, J. M., Ehlert, U., & Kirschbaum, C. (2004). Psychosocial stress-induced activation of salivary alpha-amylase: An indicator of sympathetic activity? *Annals of the New York Academy of Sciences, 1032*, 258–263.

Rohleder, N., Wolf, J. M., & Wolf, O. T. (2010). Glucocorticoid sensitivity of cognitive and inflammatory processes in depression and posttraumatic stress disorder. *Neuroscience and Biobehavioral Reviews, 35*(1), 104–114.

Sapolsky, R. M., Romero, L. M., & Munck, A. U. (2000). How do glucocorticoids influence stress responses? Integrating permissive, suppressive, stimulatory, and preparative actions. *Endocrine Reviews, 21*(1), 55–89.

Sin, N. L., Graham-Engeland, J. E., Ong, A. D., & Almeida, D. M. (2015). Affective reactivity to daily stressors is associated with elevated inflammation. *Health Psychology: Official Journal of the Division of Health Psychology, American Psychological Association, 34*(12), 1154–1165.

Sin, N. L., Sloan, R. P., McKinley, P. S., & Almeida, D. M. (2016). Linking daily stress processes and laboratory-based heart rate variability in a national sample of midlife and older adults. *Psychosomatic Medicine, 78*(5), 573–582.

Southwick, S. M., Morgan, C. A., III, Bremner, A. D., Grillon, C. G., Krystal, J. H., Nagy, L. M., & Charney, D. S. (1997). Noradrenergic alterations in posttraumatic stress disorder. *Annals of the New York Academy of Sciences, 821*, 125–141.

Spitzer, C., Barnow, S., Völzke, H., Wallaschofski, H., John, U., Freyberger, H. J., . . . Grabe, H. J. (2010). Association of posttraumatic stress disorder with low-grade elevation of C-reactive protein: Evidence from the general population. *Journal of Psychiatric Research, 44*(1), 15–21.

Spivak, B., Shohat, B., Mester, R., Avraham, S., Gil-Ad, I., Bleich, A., . . . Weizman, A. (1997). Elevated levels of serum interleukin-1 beta in combat-related posttraumatic stress disorder. *Biological Psychiatry, 42*(5), 345–348.

Stawski, R. S., Cichy, K. E., Piazza, J. R., & Almeida, D. M. (2013). Associations among daily stressors and salivary cortisol: Findings from the national study of daily experiences. *Psychoneuroendocrinology, 38*(11), 2654–2665.

Sternberg, E. M., Chrousos, G. P., Wilder, R. L., & Gold, P. W. (1992). The stress response and the regulation of inflammatory disease. *Annals of Internal Medicine, 117*(10), 854–866.

Sternberg, E. M., Hill, J. M., Chrousos, G. P., Kamilaris, T., Listwak, S. J., Gold, P. W., & Wilder, R. L. (1989). Inflammatory mediator-induced hypothalamic-pituitary-adrenal axis activation is defective in streptococcal cell wall arthritis-susceptible Lewis rats. *Proceedings of the National Academy of Sciences of the United States of America, 86*(7), 2374–2378.

Sternberg, E. M., Young, W. S., III, Bernardini, R., Calogero, A. E., Chrousos, G. P., Gold, P. W., & Wilder, R. L. (1989). A central nervous system defect in biosynthesis of corticotropin-releasing hormone is associated with susceptibility to streptococcal cell wall-induced arthritis in Lewis rats. *Proceedings of the National Academy of Sciences of the United States of America, 86*(12), 4771–4775.

Strahler, J., Skoluda, N., Rohleder, N., & Nater, U. M. (2016). Dysregulated stress signal sensitivity and inflammatory disinhibition as a pathophysiological mechanism of stress-related chronic fatigue. *Neuroscience and Biobehavioral Reviews, 68*, 298–318. https://doi.org/10.1016/j.neubiorev.2016.05.008

Thoma, M. V., Joksimovic, L., Kirschbaum, C., Wolf, J. M., & Rohleder, N. (2012). Altered salivary alpha-amylase awakening response in Bosnian War refugees with posttraumatic stress disorder. *Psychoneuroendocrinology, 37*(6), 810–817.

Van Cauter, E. (1995). Endocrine rhythms. In K. L. Becker (Ed.), *Principles and practice of endocrinology and metabolism* (pp. 41–50). Philadelphia, PA: J.B. Lippincott Company.

Watkins, L. R., & Maier, S. F. (2005). Immune regulation of central nervous system functions: From sickness responses to pathological pain. *Journal of Internal Medicine, 257*(2), 139–155.

Wessa, M., Rohleder, N., Kirschbaum, C., & Flor, H. (2006). Altered cortisol awakening response in posttraumatic stress disorder. *Psychoneuroendocrinology, 31*(2), 209–215.

Wilder, R. L., & Elenkov, I. J. (1999). Hormonal regulation of tumor necrosis factor-alpha, interleukin-12 and interleukin-10 production by activated macrophages. A disease-modifying mechanism in rheumatoid arthritis and systemic lupus erythematosus? *Annals of the New York Academy of Sciences, 876*, 14–31.

Wirtz, P. H., & von Känel, R. (2017). Psychological stress, inflammation, and coronary heart disease. *Current Cardiology Reports, 19*(11), 111.

Wolf, J. M., Rohleder, N., Bierhaus, A., Nawroth, P. P., & Kirschbaum, C. (2009). Determinants of the NF-kappaB response to acute psychosocial stress in humans. *Brain, Behavior, and Immunity, 23*(6), 742–749.

Yehuda, R. (2001). Biology of posttraumatic stress disorder. *The Journal of Clinical Psychiatry, 62*(Suppl. 17), 41–46.

Yehuda, R., Golier, J. A., Yang, R-K., & Tischler, L. (2004). Enhanced sensitivity to glucocorticoids in peripheral mononuclear leukocytes in posttraumatic stress disorder. *Biological Psychiatry, 55*(11), 1110–1116.

Yehuda, R., Teicher, M. H., Trestman, R. L., Levengood, R. A., & Siever, L. J. (1996). Cortisol regulation in posttraumatic stress disorder and major depression: A chronobiological analysis. *Biological Psychiatry, 40*(2), 79–88.

39

THE SOCIAL NEUROENDOCRINOLOGY OF ATHLETIC COMPETITION

David A. Edwards and Kathleen V. Casto

At the 2017 International Association of Athletics Federations (IAAF) World Championships for track and field, USA runners Emma Coburn and Courtney Frerich were not predicted to win a medal in their event, the 3,000-meter steeplechase – a grueling race of speed, endurance, strength, and toughness where athletes must leap over four barriers per lap, one with a slanted pit of water on the other side of it. As the runners approached the water jump for the first time in the 15-person final for the event, Beatrice Chepkoech, a Kenyan runner and early leader, perhaps nudged from behind, ran wide of the jump and had to double back after the entire field had cleared the barrier. Amazingly, with a burst of speed, she quickly recovered lost ground to join the lead pack of six runners which included the two Americans. The pack surged ahead at a blistering pace. In the final lap Emma took the water jump cleanly and, perhaps feeding off the excitement of a championship final and the unexpected possibility of victory, sprinted ahead with Courtney on her heels to take the first and second positions as they turned into the final stretch, holding their places through the finish to secure the gold and silver medals with personal best times, bettering the American and World Championship records for this event. Beatrice Chepkoech finished fourth, a remarkable achievement considering that because of her miss on the first water jump she had to run at least 30 meters farther than all the other racers.

At moments like this we see athletes at their very best. And it's not just about physical talent – to win against others at the highest level one must surpass opponents in strategy, tenacity, courage, and determination. In a sport setting, the desire for status achieved by winning, more concealed in other circumstances, is fierce, palpable, and authentically on display. Competition is part of the human condition and, for some, the desire to compete (and win) is a foundational part of their psychological character. In this chapter, we describe our research having to do with the hormonal response to competition and close with a bit of discussion about the implications of this work for sport performance and mental and physical health.

Levels of cortisol and testosterone increase in association with athletic competition

In the early 1980s, two studies – one with tennis players (Mazur & Lamb, 1980) and the other with wrestlers (Elias, 1981) – showed that athletic competition was associated with an increase in blood levels of testosterone and cortisol in men. The development of accurate assays for salivary concentrations of testosterone and cortisol facilitated study of the hormonal correlates of human athletic and non-athletic competition; for the most part, these studies were conducted with men (for review, Casto & Edwards, 2016a).

In the fall of 1999, one of us (DE) began what would turn out to be the first of many studies designed to determine how athletic competition concurrently affects levels of testosterone and cortisol in women. For the Emory University women's soccer team (N= 15), saliva was collected for each of two home games played two weeks apart near the end of the fall season (details of saliva collection, storage, and hormone assays for all the Emory University studies can be found elsewhere, e.g., Edwards, Wetzel, & Wyner, 2006; Edwards & Kurlander, 2010; Casto & Edwards, 2016b). The first game was a 1–2 loss and the second was a 5–0 victory. For each match, participants gave saliva samples before a one-hour warm-up and then immediately after the end of the match. For women who played (winning game, n = 15; losing game, n = 11, Figure 39.1), after-match levels of testosterone and cortisol were significantly higher than before-match levels for both the winning and losing games (for cortisol, Cohen's d = 1.09 and 2.11 for winning and losing games, respectively; for testosterone, d = .90 and 1.02). Importantly, actual participation in the competition appears to make an essential contribution to this effect – levels of testosterone and cortisol did not increase for members of the team who watched the competition from the sidelines. This was true in all our subsequent studies of women athletes, and we will comment on this a bit later in the chapter.

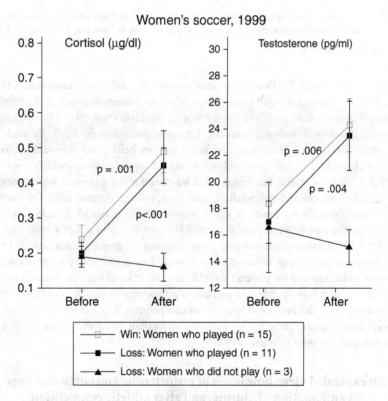

Figure 39.1 Mean before- and after-game salivary hormone levels for women soccer players. Error bars = 1 SEM.

Redrawn from Edwards et al., 2006.

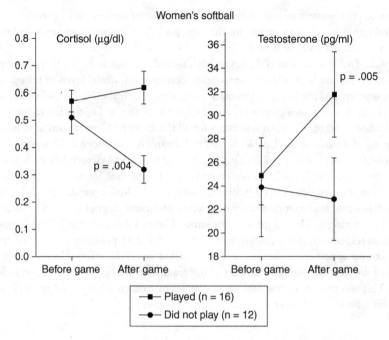

Figure 39.2   Mean before- and after-game saliva levels of cortisol and testosterone plotted for games in which women played and for games in which women did not play. Error bars = 1 SEM.

Redrawn from Edwards et al., 2007.

Subsequent studies with the Emory women's varsity volleyball teams corroborated the "competition effect" for testosterone and cortisol seen in soccer players (Edwards et al., 2006). Looking for this effect in another sport, the Emory women's softball team (N = 16) was followed for almost their entire season, running from late February through early April (Edwards, Waters, Weiss, & Jarvis, 2007). Team members gave saliva samples before and after each of five games (three wins and two losses). Testosterone levels increased for the games in which women played (Figure 39.2; Cohen's *d* = .83) but remained at baseline for the games in which they did not play. In contrast to soccer and volleyball competitions, average cortisol levels for softball players increased only slightly for games in which women played (Cohen's *d* = .16), an effect that seemingly resists the significant decline in cortisol level for games in which women did not play (Cohen's *d* = 1.03). To determine whether game outcome (victory or defeat) affected hormone levels, we compared after-game testosterone and cortisol values for every possible combination of game-won and game-lost for players who played in each. In all but one instance, before- and after-game hormone values for winning and losing games were so similar as to suggest that game outcome did not affect the hormonal response to competition. The exception: mean after-game cortisol level for one losing game was significantly lower than mean after-game cortisol level for another game that was won (Cohen's *d* = .98).

An expanded view: how levels of testosterone and cortisol change in anticipation of, during, and after athletic competition

In virtually all sports, participants "warm up" prior to competing. A typical warm-up consists of sport-specific stretching and exercise/practice intended to decrease the potential for physical injury and physically and mentally prepare for the contest to come. A meta-analysis of 32 relevant studies generally supports the idea that warm-up improves physical performance (Fradkin, Zazryn, & Smoliga, 2010). In studies involving women volleyball and tennis players (Edwards & Kurlander, 2010), considering those who would go on to play in the competition (volleyball, n = 10; tennis, n = 6), warm-up was associated with a substantial increase in testosterone (for the volleyball players, Cohen's $d = 1.02$; for the tennis players, $d = 1.32$), with testosterone either continuing to increase (for the volleyball players, $d = .99$.) or remain at after warm-up levels (for the tennis players) during the period of actual competition. On average, cortisol levels were little changed as women warmed up in preparation for intercollegiate competition.

A study with the members of the 2013 Emory women's soccer team (N = 25) expanded on earlier studies in as much as we obtained saliva samples at the time of consent to provide neutral-day baseline values for testosterone and cortisol. Then, for each of two intercollegiate matches, participants gave a saliva sample 10–15 minutes before the start of an hour-long warm-up, another sample immediately after warm-up (a few minutes before the start of the match), a third sample immediately after match completion, and a final sample 30 minutes later. Figure 39.3 (adapted from Casto & Edwards, 2016a) gives a picture of how levels of testosterone and cortisol change from neutral-day baseline to the start of game-day warm-up, then during warm-up and competition, and finally during the first 30 minutes after the end of competition. By the start of

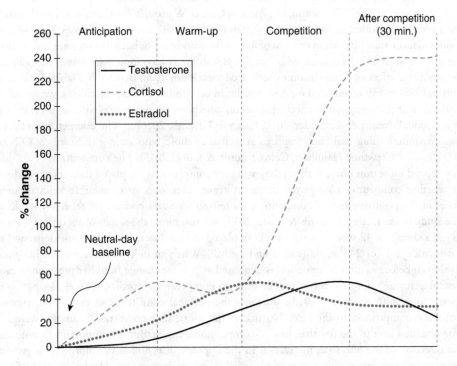

Figure 39.3   The average percent change in T and C from neutral day baseline to before warm-up (Anticipation), from before to after warm-up (Warm-up), from before to after competition (Competition), and within the 30 minutes after competition in varsity women soccer players. Lines represent best-fit curves for changing hormone levels measured at four different points relative to neutral-day baseline.

Redrawn from Casto & Edwards, 2016a.

warm-up on game-day, salivary cortisol levels had increased by more than 50 percent relative to neutral-day baseline (η^2 = .22 and .37, for the first and second games, respectively) – an effect noted by others for both women and men (Alix-Sy, Le Scanff, & Filaire, 2008; Bateup, Booth, Shirtcliff, & Granger, 2002; Filaire, Ferrand, & Verger, 2009; Salvador, Suay, González-Bono, & Serrano, 2003). In keeping with our earlier studies, on average, cortisol levels were relatively unchanged during the warm-up (η^2 = .04 and .14) but increased dramatically (131 percent and 142 percent) during the period of competition (η^2 = .51 and .54) and remained elevated for at least 30 minutes after match completion (η^2 = .01 and .14). Before warm-up, game-day testosterone levels were little different from those for neutral-day baseline. Consonant with earlier research with volleyball and tennis players (Edwards & Kurlander, 2010) and cross-country runners (Casto, Elliot, & Edwards, 2014), testosterone levels increased during warm-up (η^2 = .68 and .77) and continued to increase during the period of competition (η^2 = .24 and .51), then (unlike cortisol) decreased to near-baseline levels during the 30-minute period after the end of competition (η^2 = .67 and .88). This is the only published study of ours in which saliva samples were also assayed for estradiol. Average estradiol level increased leading up to the day of competition and increased further during warm-up by almost 20 percent relative to before-warm up levels (η^2 = .34 and .76), and remained at nearly these levels for the full duration of the contest and for at least 30 minutes after its end.

The competition effect – an increase in testosterone and cortisol associated with athletic competition – has been, by now, well-documented in women athletes in a variety of sports (e.g., Bateup et al., 2002; Hamilton, van Anders, Cox, & Watson, 2009; Casto & Edwards, 2016a for a review). Provided women actually play in the competition, we see increases in these hormones in more than 80 percent of the women we have studied. For both testosterone and cortisol, the effect is seen only in women who actually play in the competition – we found no evidence for a positive effect of competition experienced vicariously (e.g., Bernhardt, Dabbs, Fielden, & Lutter, 1998) in any of our studies. Additionally, in our studies of women athletes, we found no evidence that the competition effect depends on whether a competition is won or lost (Edwards et al., 2006; Edwards & Kurlander, 2010; Casto & Edwards, 2016b).[1] The competition effect is seen in women using oral contraceptives as well as in those who are not (Edwards & O'Neal, 2009, but see Crewther, Hamilton, Casto, Kilduff, & Cook, 2015). The competition effect does not depend on season nor is it affected by whether competitions are played indoors or outdoors or whether competitions are played in the morning, afternoon, or evening. Individual differences in the positive effect of competition on testosterone and cortisol are relatively stable. In one study of the matter (Edwards & Casto, 2013), we combined the results of six different teams to get a sample of 42 women, each of whom played in two different competitions separated by a day (volleyball) or 2–3 weeks (soccer and softball). When an individual's change in hormone level from before to after competition is expressed as percent change from her pre-competition baseline, change values are correlated for the two competitions (cortisol, $r(40)$ = .44, p = .004; testosterone, $r(40)$ = .38, p = .013), affirming the personal consistency of endocrine response from one competition to the next. No matter the sport, after-competition samples were *ipso facto* obtained later in the day than before-competition samples. But it is important to note that the direction of the effect (an increase) is in the opposite direction as the morning-to-evening decrease in levels that occurs as part of a normal circadian rhythm (e.g., Harden et al., 2016).

Relationships between changing levels of testosterone and cortisol

In our individual studies, baseline (before warm-up) levels of testosterone and cortisol in women athletes are sometimes positively correlated (e.g., Edwards et al., 2006; Edwards & Casto,

2013). Levels of both these hormones increase during competition (Figure 39.3), and when competition-related changes in levels are calculated as percent change from baseline, increases in testosterone and cortisol from before warm-up to after the end of competition are positively correlated (Edwards & Casto, 2013). But testosterone levels also typically increase during warm-up, while levels of cortisol do not (Edwards & Kurlander, 2010, and see Figure 39.3). Combining studies in which we have hormone values for warm-up and competition, a total of 57 participants, percent change in testosterone and cortisol are significantly positively correlated across both the warm-up and competition periods (Figure 39.4).

These results seem consonant with recent reports of within-person associations (coupling) between salivary cortisol and testosterone levels in adolescent and adult men and women (Harden et al., 2016; Marceau et al., 2013) and coordinated reactivity of these two hormones in response to social status threats in men, boys, and girls (Turan, Tackett, Lechtreck, & Browning, 2015). In women, androgens are produced by the ovaries and adrenal glands. The correspondence between changes in cortisol and testosterone during warm-up and competition could reflect a common source for the two hormones – the adrenal cortex, since cortisol is produced exclusively by this gland. Or, perhaps testosterone and cortisol reactivity to competition are similar because the adrenal glands and gonads are responding similarly to physical and/or psychological elements of competition. The proximate physiological mechanisms by which athletic competition increases salivary cortisol and testosterone cannot be determined from any of the studies reported here. A recent review (Casto & Edwards, 2016a) provides discussion on matters of source and mechanisms.

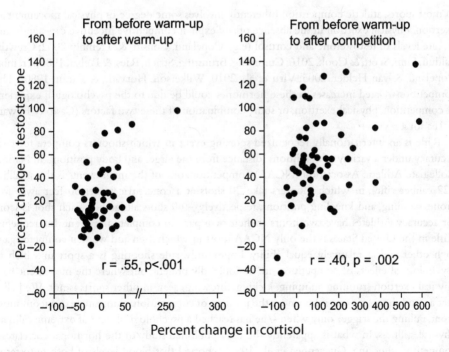

Figure 39.4 Correlations between the changes in cortisol and testosterone expressed as percent of before-warm-up baseline. The figure on the left shows the percent by which hormone levels changed during warm-up. The figure on the right shows the percent by which hormone levels changed from before warm-up to immediately after the end of competition.

Hormone levels for most of the studies with Emory athletes were assayed using kits from Salimetrics (Carlsbad, CA) in which cross-reactivity for testosterone and cortisol is essentially zero (Salimetrics.com). That said, we cannot discount the possibility that correlations between testosterone and cortisol levels are an artifact of less-than-perfect assay specificity. Future studies using more specific methods such a mass spectrometry will surely clarify this issue (e.g., Welker et al., 2016).

While the average change in cortisol during warm-up is close to zero, when considered at the level of the individual athlete, there is considerable variability in the direction and magnitude of change in cortisol relative to baseline. During warm-up, some individuals show an increase in cortisol while others show a decrease, making the group average essentially zero. Considering only the average change, one would conclude that cortisol levels are not affected by warm-up. But looking at the data for individuals (Figure 39.4), cortisol levels do appear to be affected by warm-up, but differently depending on the individual. In some athletes cortisol increases; in others it decreases or does not change much at all. During warm-up, 26 of the 57 athletes showed a decrease in cortisol level but showed an increase in testosterone level for the same period – for these individuals, levels of cortisol and testosterone are changing in opposite directions during warm-up. From before to after competition, 9 of the 57 athletes showed a decrease in cortisol level but showed an increase in testosterone over this same period. For these participants, cortisol and testosterone appear to be uncoupled. The extent which individual differences in changing levels of cortisol and testosterone are reflected in psychological reactions to competition remains to be explored.

Hormonal correlates of intercollegiate rifle shooting

In most sports, athletic competition inherently involves some degree of physical movement and exertion. Physical exertion in the absence of any explicit competitive incentive can significantly elevate levels of testosterone and cortisol (e.g., Copeland, Consitt, & Trembly, 2002; Crewther, Kilduff, Finn, Scott, & Cook, 2016; Cumming, Brunsting, Strich, Ries, & Rebar, 1986; Tremblay, Copeland, & van Helder, 2005; Viru et al., 2010; Wilkerson, Horvath, & Gutin, 1980). Thus, competition-related increases in these hormones could be due to the psychological experience of competition, physical exertion, or some combination of these two factors (Casto & Edwards, 2016a for a review).

Rifle is an internationally recognized sporting event in which shooters compete for target accuracy under a variety of conditions (distance from the target and body position). In National Collegiate Athletic Association (NCAA) competition, one of the main events is the smallbore (.22 caliber rifle), in which shooters take 20 shots at a concentric target 50 feet away from prone, standing, and kneeling positions, respectively – 60 shots altogether. Each shot is scored for accuracy. Athletes have two hours at their own pace to complete the event. Intercollegiate Rifle in the United States is the only NCAA sport in which men and women compete against each other and at relatively equal ability. Importantly, rifle shooting is a sport in which the psychological effects of competition are undoubtedly present, but where the movement-based physical exertion (running, jumping, kicking, throwing) seen in other sports is not. We believe that a good shooter is one who, under the pressure of competition, eliminates extraneous movement, pulling the trigger only when s/he has reached a psychological state of extreme calm and physical stillness. In what is apparently the only published study of the hormonal correlates of competitive shooting, Guezennec et al. (1992) reported that blood levels of both testosterone and cortisol increased over the course of the shooting event for men competing in a modern pentathlon.

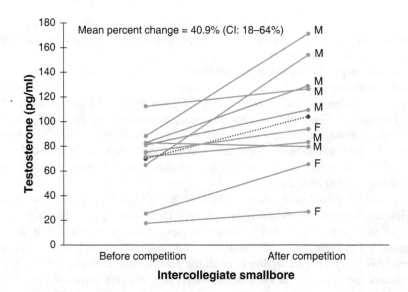

Figure 39.5   Testosterone levels before and after an intercollegiate smallbore rifle competition for male (M) and female (F) shooters. Each solid line represents single individual; the dotted line represents the mean testosterone levels averaged across all participants (three women and seven men). These data are from an unpublished 2016 study by Kathleen Casto and David Edwards.

To test hormone reactivity to rifle competition, we collected saliva samples from a mixed-sex group of ten trained shooters from the United States Military Academy 10–15 minutes before and immediately following an intercollegiate competition held in the early afternoon at the team's home facility. Figure 39.5 shows levels of salivary testosterone for the shooters for samples obtained before and after the competition.

For all but one of the shooters, testosterone levels increased over the course of competition by amounts typical for sports that require far more vigorous levels of physical exertion. Unlike other sports that we have studied (excepting softball), cortisol levels appeared relatively unaffected by the shooting competition, increasing across the competition in some athletes and decreasing for others.

Baseline levels of testosterone and cortisol relate to status among teammates

For many of the teams that we worked with, consenting participants completed a 15-item Player Rating Scale (PRS) on which they used a 5-point scale ranging from "fair" (1 point) to "excellent" (5 points) to rate each of their teammates on a variety of different athletic and/or leadership abilities. The use of this questionnaire was premised on the idea that an individual's testosterone level might be related to her status with teammates (e.g., Cashdan, 1995). Typical items: "She inspires her teammates to play at their highest level"; "She works effectively with her teammates to help create a sense of team unity"; and "She plays and competes with a passion for the game." The fifteenth item asked participants to "provide an overall rating of the individual's abilities as a team leader." (A complete list of all the items in the PRS can be found in Casto & Edwards, 2013). We used the average score of an individual's combined teammate ratings as a measure of her status among teammates. For each woman, these ratings are based on hours together with her teammates in practice and competition during the course of at least one and sometimes more than one competitive season.

Mehta and Josephs' (2010) report of a dual-hormone effect on dominance i.e., testosterone is positively related to dominance, but only in individuals with low cortisol levels, prompted a retrospective consideration of data collected with women athletes (Edwards & Casto, 2013 for details). Participants – 74 in all – were the consenting members of the Emory University 1999 women's soccer team, the 2002, 2005, and 2008 women's volleyball teams, the 2004 softball team, and the 2009 tennis team. Consonant with the "dual hormone hypothesis" (Mehta & Josephs, 2010), testosterone was positively related to status, but only when cortisol levels were low ($R^2 change$ = .09) (Figure 39.6).

As we wrote in considering this result (Edwards & Casto, 2013, p. 159), in women's sports teams, leaders assert themselves in a variety of ways. To promote an individual's status among teammates, those actions have to be shown in a manner that is neither overtly dominating nor aggressive. For individuals with low levels of cortisol, perhaps the higher an athlete's testosterone level, the greater her ability to reach the delicate balance between being gentle and being overbearing in matters of authority in interactions with teammates. Why this relationship should be compromised in women with the highest levels of cortisol is not known, but it does add complexity to consideration of the endocrine correlates of dominance motivation and status.

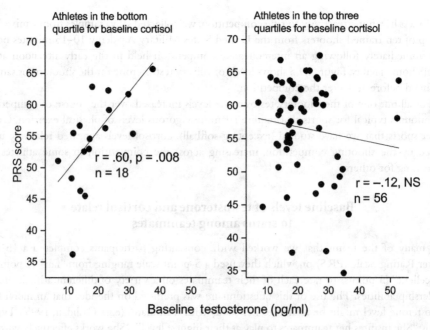

Figure 39.6 The relationship between an athlete's baseline (before-competition) level of salivary testosterone and her score on the Player Rating Scale (PRS), a measure of her status with teammates. The figure on the left shows this relationship for athletes in the bottom quartile with respect to baseline level of cortisol. The figure on the right shows the absence of this relationship for athletes in the top three quartiles with respect to baseline level of cortisol.

Redrawn from Edwards and Casto (2013).

Functional considerations

Sport performance

Transient elevations in testosterone or cortisol are perhaps beneficial for achieving status in competition (Bos, Hermans, Montoya, Ramsey, & van Honk, 2010; Carré, McCormick, & Hariri, 2011; Eisenegger, Naef, Snozzi, Heinrichs, & Fehr, 2010, Eisenegger, Haushofer, & Fehr, 2011; Hermans, Putman, & van Honk, 2006; Mehta et al., 2015; Radke et al., 2015). In men competing in laboratory competitions, testosterone increases during competition appear to predispose losers (Mehta & Josephs, 2006) and aggressive individuals (Carré & McCormick, 2008) to compete again against the same opponent, and for decisive winners to compete against a different opponent (Mehta, Snyder, Knight, & Lassetter, 2015). In a recent study with women soccer players (Casto & Edwards, 2016c), the higher an athlete's testosterone remained during the 30 minutes after the end competition, the greater her willingness to reconcile with her opponent – a prosocial strategy for status maintenance.

Testosterone change during or after competition could also affect social bonding among teammates in a way that positively affects future performances (Kraus, Huang, & Keltner, 2010). Testosterone levels and, to a lesser degree, testosterone change associated with competition have been positively related to after-competition appraisal of one's own performance (Casto, Rivell, & Edwards, 2017; Trumble et al., 2012) and confidence (Eisenegger, Kumsta, Naef, Gromoll, & Heinrichs, 2017), perhaps to the benefit of subsequent competitive performance.

Only a few studies have directly tested the relationship between transient changes in testosterone levels and sport performance. Cook and Crewther (2012a) experimentally increased salivary testosterone levels in male rugby players by having them watch video clips of successful skill execution combined with coach feedback 15 minutes before they played a rugby match. Larger individual testosterone responses were linked with better game performance as retrospectively assessed by coaches. In another study (Cook & Crewther, 2012b), highly trained male athletes were shown a variety of videos over six different sessions and relative increases in testosterone and cortisol were noted for each session for every participant. Shortly after watching each video, athletes completed a workout that included measurement of their performance on squat exercises, a test of strength where performance reflects a combination of physical strength and the will to achieve a higher maximum in the presence of others. Positive within-individual correlations between testosterone increases (and to a lesser extent, cortisol increases) and subsequent squat performance were noted, suggesting a causal link between transient hormonal changes and the physical performance that followed shortly thereafter.

Power imagery

Informed by research on the relationship between testosterone and cortisol and feelings of dominance or power (Schultheiss & Rohde, 2002; Schultheiss, Campbell, & McClelland, 1999; Schultheiss et al., 2005; Stanton & Schultheiss, 2009; Wirth, Welsh, & Schultheiss, 2006) and research on the effectiveness of mental imagery in sports (Holmes & Collins, 2001; Williams, Cooley, Newell, Weibull, & Cumming, 2013), we developed a novel cognitive intervention intended to induce a transient increase in endogenous testosterone level that could potentially improve sports performance. Power imagery is imagining oneself in a position of dominance or power (Winter, 1973, 1992). For two separate sports, field hockey and rifle, one of us (KC) wrote sport-specific scripts that described a competition experience in which the athletes performed well, masterly executed their skill, and were in complete control over the outcome (key words like powerful, dominate, control, master, and greatness were used throughout the scripts). The scenarios were scripted with the intention of provoking feelings of confidence, excitement, and joy, and vivid mental images of success. We collected saliva samples immediately before and after a ten-minute power imagery session (athletes sat quietly in a room with their eyes closed while the experimenter read the script). We began with separate sessions for 20 female United States Olympic Team field hockey players and a mixed-sex group of 12 West Point Military Academy rifle shooters. Nineteen of the 32 participants showed an increase in testosterone relative to before-session baseline (mean increase = 52 percent); the remaining 13 participants showed a decrease in testosterone (mean decrease = 18 percent). While these results should be considered preliminary, it seems clear that for some individuals a guided power imagery session can produce a substantial increase in salivary testosterone levels. This research continues; understanding the variables that determine individual differences in testosterone reactivity to power imaging sessions is one of the essential goals of this research. To the extent that increases in testosterone levels benefit athletic effort, power imagery shortly before a competition could be used with the intention of improving performance in competition. Good coaches are motivators, and it is altogether possible (but as yet unstudied) that the motivating effects of an effective pre-game "pep talk" accrue, in part, from the hormonal responses of their athletes to that talk.

Small sample field studies: statistical considerations

Nearly all of the individual studies discussed in this chapter were conducted with relatively small samples of participants. Pooling the results for six different teams in four different sports (see Edwards & Casto, 2013) gave us a sample size of 54 and 52 women athletes competing in a first or second competition, respectively. For the vast majority of athletes, cortisol and testosterone increased from before warm-up to immediately after the end of competition (for the first and second competitions, respectively: Cohen's d for cortisol = .80 and .60; Cohen's d for testosterone = .91 and .63). For any one study, small sample size limits confidence in the replicability of the study's results. That athletic competition increases salivary testosterone and cortisol levels in so many sports and in so many different studies attests to the robust nature of the competition effect for these hormones.

Small sample size is an almost unavoidable complication for studies of athletic teams and other "special" populations. But these populations afford the opportunity to study the hormonal effects of competition in ecologically valid and personally meaningful settings not easily achieved in large-sample laboratory studies. Indeed, the special nature of these populations is what makes them an invaluable resource as we work towards an understanding of the social neuroendocrinology of competition.

Physical and mental health

Sex-steroid modulated reward mechanisms

Research on hormones and competition has relevance in matters of physical and mental health. The psychoactive effects of testosterone (and other androgens) include feelings of pleasure (Bless, McGinnis, Mitchell, Hartwell, & Mitchell, 1997; Frye, Rhodes, Rosellini, & Svare, 2002; Hermans et al., 2010; Packard, Cornell, & Gerianne, 1997), and testosterone positively affects reinforcement learning in humans and rodents (e.g., Hermans et al., 2010; Op de Macks et al., 2011; Spritzer et al., 2011; Wood, 2004). Further, synthetic testosterone has been used in the treatment of depression and anxiety disorders (Pope, Cohane, Kanayama, Siegel, & Hudson, 2003). It is perhaps no coincidence that physical activity and sport participation have also been shown to reduce clinical symptoms of depression and anxiety (Ströhle, 2009). Although participation in sports can increase social engagement and physical health, the physiological and neural mechanisms by which exercise and sport affect depression symptomology is not well understood (but see Heyman et al., 2012; Laske et al., 2010). Studies of the role of testosterone in this process are surely warranted. Neuroendocrine dysfunction has also been linked to fibromyalgia syndrome (FMS) and chronic fatigue syndrome (CFS), two similar disorders marked by severe deficits in motivation, among other symptoms (Demitrack, 1997; Neeck & Crofford, 2000; Crofford et al., 2004). Testosterone has been explored as a treatment therapy for FMS and CFS (White & Robinson, 2015; White et al., 2015). Athletic competition could perhaps be effectively used to treat these conditions in place of (or in combination with) synthetic steroids, adding to the several other exercise-related behavioral interventions (e.g., graded exercise therapy) currently employed (for more about these interventions: Chambers, Bagnall, Hempel, & Forbes, 2006; Edmonds, McGuire, & Price, 2004; Moss-Morris, Sharon, Tobin, & Baldi, 2005).

Oral contraceptives and other hormone-based forms of contraception typically lower testosterone levels in women (e.g., Zimmerman, Eijkemans, Coelingh Bennink, Blankenstein, & Fauser, 2013). Given the relationship between androgens, motivation, and reward, lower testosterone levels in hormonal contraceptive users are perhaps cause for concern. Although the health and sport performance effects of hormonal contraceptives have been explored (e.g., Frankovich & Lebrun, 2000), there has been less attention to how these drugs impact subtle aspects of motivation and behavior in competitive settings (Buser, 2012; Pearson & Schipper, 2013; Schultheiss, Dargel, & Rohde, 2003). Success in sport as well as in day-to-day goal-achievement involves numerous competitive interactions and status contests with others. Thus, research in this area would have implications for the general health and well-being of women, the retention of women in competitive sport, and the ability of women to achieve career success and positions of leadership.

Resilience to stress

In the physiological toughness model, Dienstbier (1989) describes how the combination of habitual exposure to a stressor, with adequate recovery, and a positive psychological state (e.g., sense of control; positive cognitive appraisal) result in adaptive changes in the neuroendocrine response to subsequent stress. Specifically, individuals who have been "toughened" show higher catecholamine and lower cortisol responses to stress and correspondingly lower emotional reactivity, and better stress tolerance and immune function. Exercise and sport, particularly in competitive settings, can toughen an individual, and the psychological experience of winning and losing could be beneficial for developing psychological and physiological resilience to stress (Dienstbier, 1989). The psychological and social benefits of sport participation are well-documented (e.g., Eime, Young, Harvey, Charity, & Payne, 2013) as are the positive effects exercise on brain health (e.g., Cotman, Berchtold, & Christie, 2007; Duman, Schlesinger, Russell, & Duman, 2008). The extent to which hormones are involved in this process remains to be determined.

Concluding remarks

It is by now clear that participating in an athletic competition increases salivary (and presumably blood) levels of testosterone and cortisol, regardless of competition outcome and even in sports that require almost no movement. While the most proximate physiological causes of these increases remain to be established (see Casto & Edwards, 2016a), competition-related increases in testosterone and cortisol will elevate the concentration of these hormones at target tissues in the brain and body and could have important effects on psychological states relevant to status-motivation, competitive behavior, sport performance, and physical and mental health. The potential benefits of athletic competition and power imagery as health and performance enhancing interventions are surely worth exploring.

We believe there are three factors that help promote hormone increases during athletic and perhaps non-athletic competition as well. First, participants must be psychologically engaged in the competition. While not discounting the possible role of physical exertion in the competition effect for athletes, actually playing in the competition makes an important contribution to the effect, and we assume that play is a surrogate index of psychological engagement. Second, related to this, the outcome of the competition has to matter to the participant. Third, the participant must feel some agency with respect to outcome, i.e., have a sense that his/his performance can affect the outcome of the competition. Laboratory studies of hormones and competition can be useful. But it is, we believe, difficult to completely satisfy these conditions in laboratory studies where the outcome may be of little personal consequence for participants. It is perhaps for this reason that increases in testosterone in non-sport related competitions have been so inconsistently demonstrated (see Casto & Edwards, 2016a for a review).

The reliably robust increases in testosterone and cortisol that are provoked by athletic competition can be exploited to study the psychological effects of these hormones in a naturalistic competitive context. Competitive athletic encounters often involve both inter- and intra-group status negotiations. But analogous negotiations occur in a variety of everyday social circumstances. The study of competitive and cooperative interactions, within and between groups, in athletic and other naturalistic settings offers the opportunity for a better understanding of how hormones affect and are affected by social behavior as well as their potential for improving mental and physical health.

Note

1 If the psychological experiences of winning or losing are to affect hormone levels, the influences are most likely to be evident in instances where there is a delay of some minutes between the end of competition and the collection of saliva (e.g., Jiménez, Aguilar, & Alvero-Cruz, 2012; Casto & Edwards, 2016a for more discussion).

References

Alix-Sy, D., Le Scanff, C., & Filaire, E. (2008). Psychophysiological responses in the pre-competition period in elite soccer players. *Journal of Sports Science and Medicine, 7*, 446–454.

Bateup, H. S., Booth, A., Shirtcliff, E. A., & Granger, D. A. (2002). Testosterone, cortisol, and women's competition. *Evolution and Human Behavior, 23*, 181–192.

Bernhardt, P. C., Dabbs, J. M., Jr., Fielden, J. A., & Lutter, C. D. (1998). Testosterone changes during vicarious experiences of winning and losing among fans at sporting events. *Physiology and Behavior, 65*, 59–62.

Bless, E. P., McGinnis, K. A., Mitchell, A. L., Hartwell, A., & Mitchell, J. B. (1997). The effects of gonadal steroids on brain stimulation reward in female rats. *Behavioural Brain Research, 82*, 235–244.

Bos, P. A., Hermans, E. J., Montoya, E. R., Ramsey, N. F., & van Honk, J. (2010). Testosterone administration modulates neural responses to crying infants in young females. *Psychoneuroendocrinology, 35*, 114–121.

Buser, T. (2012). The impact of the menstrual cycle and hormonal contraceptives on competitiveness. *Journal of Economic Behavior & Organization, 83*, 1–10.

Carré, J. M., & McCormick, C. M. (2008). Aggressive behavior and change in salivary testosterone concentrations predict willingness to engage in a competitive task. *Hormones and Behavior, 54*, 403–409.

Carré, J. M., McCormick, C. M., & Hariri, A. R. (2011). The social neuroendocrinology of human aggression. *Psychoneuroendocrinology, 36*, 935–944.

Cashdan, E. (1995). Hormones, sex, and status in women. *Hormones and Behavior, 29*, 354–366.

Casto, K. V., & Edwards, D. A. (2016a). Testosterone, cortisol, and human competition. *Hormones and Behavior, 82*, 21–37.

Casto, K. V., & Edwards, D. A. (2016b). Before, during, and after: How phases of competition differentially affect testosterone, cortisol, and estradiol levels in women athletes. *Adaptive Human Behavior and Physiology, 2*, 11–25.

Casto, K. V., & Edwards, D. A. (2016c). Testosterone and reconciliation among women: After-competition testosterone predicts prosocial attitudes towards opponents. *Adaptive Human Behavior and Physiology, 2*, 220–233.

Casto, K. V., Elliott, C. M., & Edwards, D. A. (2014). Intercollegiate cross country competition: Effects of warm-up and racing on salivary levels of cortisol and testosterone. *International Journal of Exercise Science, 7*, 318–328.

Casto, K. V., Rivell, A., Edwards, D. A. (2017). Competition-related testosterone, cortisol, and perceived personal success in recreational women athletes. *Hormones and Behavior, 92*, 29–36.

Chambers, D., Bagnall, A. M., Hempel, S., & Forbes, C. (2006). Interventions for the treatment, management and rehabilitation of patients with chronic fatigue syndrome/myalgic encephalomyelitis: An updated systematic review. *Journal of the Royal Society of Medicine, 99*, 506–520.

Cook, C. J., & Crewther, B. T. (2012a). Changes in salivary testosterone concentrations and subsequent voluntary squat performance following the presentation of short video clips. *Hormones and Behavior, 61*, 17–22.

Cook, C. J., & Crewther, B. T. (2012b). The effects of different pre-game motivational interventions on athlete free hormonal state and subsequent performance in professional rugby union matches. *Physiology & Behavior, 106*, 683–688.

Copeland, J. L., Consitt, L. A., & Tremblay, M. S. (2002). Hormonal responses to endurance and resistance exercise in females aged 19–69 years. *The Journals of Gerontology: Series A, 57*, B158–B165.

Cotman, C. W., Berchtold, N. C., & Christie, L. A. (2007). Exercise builds brain health: Key roles of growth factor cascades and inflammation. *Trends in Neurosciences, 30*, 464–472.

Crewther, B. T., Hamilton, D., Casto, K., Kilduff, L. P., & Cook, C. J. (2015). Effects of oral contraceptive use on the salivary testosterone and cortisol responses to training sessions and competitions in elite women athletes. *Physiology and Behavior, 147*, 84–90. Crewther, B. T., Kilduff, L. P., Finn, C., Scott, P., & Cook, C. J. (2016). Salivary testosterone responses to a physical and psychological stimulus and subsequent effects on physical performance in healthy adults. *Hormones, 15*, 248–255.

Crofford, L. J., Young, E. A., Engleberg, N. C., Korszun, A., Brucksch, C. B., McClure, L. A., . . . Demitrack, M. A. (2004). Basal circadian and pulsatile ACTH and cortisol secretion in patients with fibromyalgia and/or chronic fatigue syndrome. *Brain, Behavior, and Immunity, 18*, 314–325.

Cumming, D. C., Brunsting, L. A., Strich, G., Ries, A. L., & Rebar, R. W. (1986). Reproductive hormone increases in response to acute exercise in men. *Medicine and Science in Sports and Exercise, 18*, 369–373.

Demitrack, M. A. (1997). Neuroendocrine correlates of chronic fatigue syndrome: A brief review. *Journal of Psychiatric Research, 31*(1), 69–82.

Dienstbier, R. A. (1989). Arousal and physiological toughness: Implications for mental and physical health. *Psychological Review, 96*, 84–100.

Duman, C. H., Schlesinger, L., Russell, D. S., & Duman, R. S. (2008). Voluntary exercise produces antidepressant and anxiolytic behavioral effects in mice. *Brain Research, 1199*, 148–158.

Edmonds, M., McGuire, H., & Price, J. (2004). Exercise therapy for chronic fatigue syndrome. *Cochrane Database of Systematic Reviews*, CD003.

Edwards, D. A., & Casto, K. V. (2013). Women's intercollegiate athletic competition: Cortisol, testosterone, and the dual-hormone hypothesis as it relates to status among teammates. *Hormones and Behavior, 64*, 153–160.

Edwards, D. A., & Kurlander, L. S. (2010). Women's intercollegiate volleyball and tennis: Effects of warm-up, competition, and practice on saliva levels of cortisol and testosterone. *Hormones and Behavior, 58*, 606–613.

Edwards, D. A., & O'Neal, J. L. (2009). Oral contraceptives decrease saliva testosterone but do not affect the rise in testosterone associated with athletic competition. *Hormones and Behavior, 56*, 195–198.

Edwards, D. A., Waters, J., Weiss, A., & Jarvis, A. (2007). Intercollegiate athletics: Competition increases saliva testosterone in women soccer, volleyball, and softball players. In L. I. Ardis (Ed.), *Testosterone research trends* (pp. 195–209). Hauppage, NY: Nova Science Publishers, Inc.

Edwards, D. A., Wetzel, K., & Wyner, D. R. (2006). Intercollegiate soccer: Saliva cortisol and testosterone are elevated during competition, and testosterone is related to status and social connectedness with teammates. *Physiology and Behavior, 87*, 135–143.

Eime, R. M., Young, J. A., Harvey, J. T., Charity, M. J., & Payne, W. R. (2013). A systematic review of the psychological and social benefits of participation in sport for children and adolescents: Informing development of a conceptual model of health through sport. *International Journal of Behavioral Nutrition and Physical Activity, 10*, 98. doi:10.1186/1479-5868-10-98

Eisenegger, C., Haushofer, J., & Fehr, E. (2011). The role of testosterone in social interaction. *Trends in Cognitive Sciences, 15*, 263–271.

Eisenegger, C., Kumsta, R., Naef, M., Gromoll, J., & Heinrichs, M. (2017). Testosterone and androgen receptor gene polymorphism are associated with confidence and competitiveness in men. *Hormones and Behavior, 92*, 93–102.

Eisenegger, C., Naef, M., Snozzi, R., Heinrichs, M., & Fehr, E. (2010). Prejudice and truth about the effect of testosterone on human bargaining behaviour. *Nature, 463*, 356–359.

Elias, M. (1981). Serum cortisol, testosterone, and testosterone-binding globulin responses to competitive fighting in human males. *Aggressive Behavior, 7*, 215–224.

Fradkin, A. J., Zazryn, T. R., & Smoliga, J. M. (2010). Effects of warming-up on physical performance: A systematic review with meta-analysis. *Journal of Strength and Conditioning Research, 24*, 140–148.

Frankovich, R. J., & Lebrun, C. M. (2000). Menstrual cycle, contraception, and performance. *Clinics in Sports Medicine, 19*, 251–271.

Filaire, E., Alix, D., Ferrand, C., & Verger, M. (2009). Psychophysiological stress in tennis players during the first single match of a tournament. *Psychoneuroendocrinology, 34*, 150–157.

Frye, C. A., Rhodes, M. E., Rosellini, R., & Svare, B. (2002). The nucleus accumbens as a site of action for rewarding properties of testosterone and its 5α-reduced metabolites. *Pharmacology Biochemistry and Behavior, 74*, 119–127.

Guezennec, G. Y., Oliver, C., Lienhard, F., Seyfried, D., Huet, F., & Pesce, G. (1992). Hormonal and metabolic response to a pistol-shooting competition. *Science & Sports, 7*, 27–32.

Hamilton, L. D., van Anders, S. M., Cox, D. N., & Watson, N. V. (2009). The effect of competition on salivary testosterone in elite female athletes. *International Journal of Sports Physiology and Performance, 4*, 538–542.

Harden, K. P., Wrzus, C., Luong, G., Grotzinger, A., Bajbouj, M., Rauers, A., Wagner, G. G., & Riediger, M. (2016). Diurnal coupling between testosterone and cortisol from adolescence to older adulthood. *Psychoneuroendocrinology, 73*, 79–90.

Hermans, E. J., Bos, P. A., Ossewaarde, L., Ramsey, N. F., Fernández, G., & van Honk, J. (2010). Effects of exogenous testosterone on the ventral striatal BOLD response during reward anticipation in healthy women. *Neuroimage, 52*, 277–283.

Hermans, E. J., Putman, P., & van Honk, J. (2006). Testosterone administration reduces empathic behavior: A facial mimicry study. *Psychoneuroendocrinology, 31*, 859–866.

Heyman, E., Gamelin, F. X., Goekint, M., Piscitelli, F., Roelands, B., Leclair, E., & Meeusen, R. (2012). Intense exercise increases circulating endocannabinoid and BDNF levels in humans – possible implications for reward and depression. *Psychoneuroendocrinology, 37*, 844–851.

Holmes, P. S., & Collins, D. J. (2001). The PETTLEP approach to motor imagery: A functional equivalence model for sport psychologists. *Journal of Applied Sport Psychology, 13*, 60–83.

Jiménez, M., Aguilar, R., & Alvero-Cruz, J. R. (2012). Effects of victory and defeat on testosterone and cortisol response to competition: Evidence for same response patterns in men and women. *Psychoneuroendocrinology, 37*, 1577–1581.

Kraus, M. W., Huang, C., & Keltner, D. (2010). Tactile communication, cooperation, and performance: An ethological study of the NBA. *Emotion, 10*, 745–749.

Laske, C., Banschbach, S., Stransky, E., Bosch, S., Straten, G., Machann, J., . . . Eschweiler, G. W. (2010). Exercise-induced normalization of decreased BDNF serum concentration in elderly women with remitted major depression. *International Journal of Neuropsychopharmacology, 13*, 595–602.

Marceau, K., Ruttle, P. L., Shirtcliff, E. A., Hastings, P. D., Klimes-Dougan, B., Zahn-Waxler, C. (2013). Within-person coupling of changes in cortisol, testosterone, and DHEA across the day in adolescents. *Developmental Psychobiology, 57*, 654–669.

Mazur, A., & Lamb, T. A. (1980). Testosterone, status, and mood in human males. *Hormones and Behavior, 14*, 236–246.

Mehta, P. H., & Josephs, R. A. (2006). Testosterone change after losing predicts the decision to compete again. *Hormones and Behavior, 50*, 684–692.

Mehta, P. H., & Josephs, R. A. (2010). Testosterone and cortisol jointly regulate dominance: Evidence for a dual-hormone hypothesis. *Hormones and Behavior, 58,* 898–906.

Mehta, P. H., Snyder, N. A., Knight, E. L., & Lassetter, B. (2015). Close versus decisive victory moderates the effect of testosterone change on competitive decisions and task enjoyment. *Adaptive Human Behavior and Physiology, 1,* 291–311.

Mehta, P. H., van Son, V., Welker, K. M., Prasad, S., Sanfey, A. G., Smidts, A., & Roelofs, K. (2015). Exogenous testosterone in women enhances and inhibits competitive decision-making depending on victory – defeat experience and trait dominance. *Psychoneuroendocrinology, 60,* 224–236.

Moss-Morris, R., Sharon, C., Tobin, R., & Baldi, J. C. (2005). A randomized controlled graded exercise trial for chronic fatigue syndrome: Outcomes and mechanisms of change. *Journal of Health Psychology, 10,* 245–259.

Neeck, G., & Crofford, L. J. (2000). Neuroendocrine perturbations in fibromyalgia and chronic fatigue syndrome. *Rheumatic Disease Clinics of North America, 26,* 989–1002.

Op de Macks, Z. A., Moor, B. G., Overgaauw, S., Güroğlu, B., Dahl, R. E., & Crone, E. A. (2011). Testosterone levels correspond with increased ventral striatum activation in response to monetary rewards in adolescents. *Developmental Cognitive Neuroscience, 1,* 506–516.

Pearson, M., & Schipper, B. C. (2013). Menstrual cycle and competitive bidding. *Games and Economic Behavior, 78,* 1–20.

Packard, M. G., Cornell, A. H., & Alexander, G. M. (1997). Rewarding affective properties of intra-nucleus accumbens injections of testosterone. *Behavioral Neuroscience, 111,* 219–224.

Pope, H. G., Cohane, G. H., Kanayama, G., Siegel, A. J., & Hudson, J. I. (2003). Testosterone gel supplementation for men with refractory depression: A randomized, placebo-controlled trial. *American Journal of Psychiatry, 160,* 105–111.

Radke, S., Volman, I., Mehta, P., van Son, V., Enter, D., Sanfey, A., Toni, I., de Bruijn, E. R. A., & Roelofs, K. (2015). Testosterone biases the amygdala toward social threat approach. *Science Advances, 1,* e1400074.

Salvador, A., Suay, F., González-Bono, E., & Serrano, M. A. (2003). Anticipatory cortisol, testosterone and psychological responses to judo competition in young men. *Psychoneuroendocrinology, 28,* 364–375.

Schultheiss, O. C., Campbell, K. L., & McClelland, D. C. (1999). Implicit power motivation moderates men's testosterone responses to imagined and real dominance success. *Hormones and Behavior, 36,* 234–241.

Schultheiss, O. C., Dargel, A., & Rohde, W. (2003). Implicit motives and gonadal steroid hormones: Effects of menstrual cycle phase, oral contraceptive use, and relationship status. *Hormones and Behavior, 43,* 293–301.

Schultheiss, O. C., & Rohde, W. (2002). Implicit power motivation predicts men's testosterone changes in implicit learning in a contest situation. *Hormones and Behavior, 41,* 195–202.

Schultheiss, O. C., Wirth, M. M., Torges, C. M., Pang, J. S., Villacorta, M. A., & Welsh, K. M. (2005). Effects of implicit power motivation on men's and women's implicit learning and testosterone changes after social victory or defeat. *Journal of Personality and Social Psychology, 88,* 174–188.

Spritzer, M. D., Daviau, E. D., Coneeny, M. K., Engelman, S. M., Prince, W. T., & Rodriguez-Wisdom, K. N. (2011). Effects of testosterone on spatial learning and memory in adult male rats. *Hormones and Behavior, 59,* 484–496.

Stanton, S. J., & Schultheiss, O. C. (2009). The hormonal correlates of implicit power motivation. *Journal of Research in Personality, 43,* 942–949.

Ströhle, A. (2009). Physical activity, exercise, depression and anxiety disorders. *Journal of Neural Transmission, 116,* 777.

Tremblay, M. S., Copeland, J. L., & van Helder, W. (2005). Influence of exercise duration on post-exercise steroid hormone responses in trained males. *European Journal of Applied Physiology, 94,* 505–513.

Trumble, B. C., Cummings, D., von Rueden, C., O'Connor, K. A., Smith, E. A., Gurven, M., & Kaplan, H. (2012). Physical competition increases testosterone among Amazonian forager-horticulturalists: A test of the "challenge" hypothesis. *Proceedings of the Royal Society. B, 279,* 2907–2912.

Turan, B., Tackett, J. L., Lechtreck, M. T., & Browning, W. R. (2015). Coordination of the cortisol and testosterone responses: A dual axis approach to understanding the response to social status threats. *Psychoneuroendocrinology, 62,* 59–68.

Viru, M., Hackney, A., Karelson, K., Janson, T., Kuus, M., & Viru, A. (2010). Competition effects on physiological responses to exercise: Performance, cardiorespiratory and hormonal factors. *Acta Physiologica Hungarica, 97,* 22–30.

Welker, K. M., Lassetter, B., Brandes, C. M., Prasad, S., Koop, D. R., & Mehta, P. H. (2016). A comparison of salivary testosterone measurement using immunoassays and tandem mass spectrometry. *Psychoneuroendocrinology, 71,* 180–188.

White, H. D., & Robinson, T. D. (2015). A novel use for testosterone to treat central sensitization of chronic pain in fibromyalgia patients. *International Immunopharmacology*, *27*, 244–248.

White, H. D., Brown, L. A., Gyurik, R. J., Manganiello, P. D., Robinson, T. D., Hallock, L. S., . . . Yeo, K. T. J. (2015). Treatment of pain in fibromyalgia patients with testosterone gel: Pharmacokinetics and clinical response. *International Immunopharmacology*, *27*, 249–256.

Wilkerson, J. E., Horvath, S. M., & Gutin, B. (1980). Plasma testosterone during treadmill exercise. *Journal of Applied Physiology*, *49*, 249–253.

Williams, S. E., Cooley, S. J., Newell, E., Weibull, F., & Cumming, J. (2013). Seeing the difference: Developing effective imagery scripts for athletes. *Journal of Sport Psychology in Action*, *4*, 109–121.

Winter, D. G. (1973). *The power motive*. New York, NY: Free Press.

Winter, D. G. (1992). Power motivation revisited. In C. P. Smith (Ed.), *Motivation and personality: Handbook of thematic content analysis* (pp. 301–310). New York, NY: Cambridge University Press.

Wirth, M. M., Welsh, K. M., & Schultheiss, O. C. (2006). Salivary cortisol changes in humans after winning or losing a dominance contest depend on implicit power motivation. *Hormones and Behavior*, *49*, 346–352.

Wood, R. I. (2004). Reinforcing aspects of androgens. *Physiology and Behavior*, *83*, 279–289.

Zimmerman, Y., Eijkemans, M. J. C., Coelingh Bennink, H. J. T., Blankenstein, M. A., & Fauser, B. C. J. M. (2013). The effect of combined oral contraception on testosterone levels in healthy women: A systematic review and meta-analysis. *Human Reproduction Update*, *20*, 76–105.

INDEX

17β-estradiol see estradiol
2D:4D see digit ratio
3β-hydroxysteroid dehydrogenase/Δ5−4 isomerase (3β-HSD) 71, 173–177
5α-reductase 173–177; deficiency 265, 273; inhibitor 172

accessory olfactory bulb 484
acetylcholine 719
ACTH *see* adrenocorticotropic hormone
activational hormone effects 74, 163–192, 265, 371–372, 376, 380–384, 436, 557, 569–570, 575, 578, 581, 638
activity inhibition 569–581
adaptation 114, 152–153, 300, 309–312, 318, 326, 424–437, 441, 454–455, 465, 535–536, 588, 591, 593, 610, 660–662
Adaptive Calibration Model (ACM) 586, 588–589, 593
adaptive immunity 719
addiction 420, 437, 694–705
adolescence 1, 10, 107–108, 127, 360, 479–496, 544–563, 575–579, 587, 590–615, 618, 622, 640, 644, 661
adoptive parenting 299, 305, 308
adrenarche 611, 619–620, 622
adrenocorticotropic hormone (ACTH) 9, 152, 319, 442, 455–456, 461, 465–466, 489, 511, 608–609, 614, 623, 639, 658, 665–666, 679, 701–704
adversity 212, 215–216, 305, 310, 312, 461, 531, 536, 586–591, 598–602, 612, 614–616, 621, 661, 724–725
affiliation 1–2, 17, 51, 81, 107, 147, 156, 166, 178, 193–200, 205–210, 214, 216, 224–225, 282, 318, 321, 485, 487–488, 491, 504, 514–515, 518–522, 568, 570, 575, 578–580, 610, 658,

663–664, 674, 683, 696; implicit motive 568–586; social affiliation 147–224
age 1, 34, 107, 211, 284–285, 287, 289, 292, 323, 338, 344–348, 376–377, 380, 394, 459–461, 481, 490–491, 511, 535–537, 549, 557–558, 560–561, 570, 573, 578–579, 595–596, 601, 609, 611, 617–618, 621–622; adolescence 479–503, 544–567; and social behaviour 504–529; and stress 586–607
aggression 1–3, 13, 16, 54, 65, 67–76, 82–93, 99–103, 107, 113, 119–129, 133–141, 163, 177, 206, 212–215, 225–232, 286–287, 291–293, 309, 317, 326–327, 338, 392, 435, 447, 464, 484, 487, 493, 504–505, 509, 551–556, 571, 573, 581, 588, 610, 616, 621, 635–648, 657, 665–666, 674–675, 683
aggressive punishment 119–122, 127
agonistic behavior 166, 551
allocation trade-offs 151, 334
allomaternal care 299, 305, 308
alloparenting 305, 312, 327
allopregnanolone 164–165, 168, 171–182, 405, 426, 432, 680–681, 699
allostasis 455, 588, 704
allostatic load model 586, 588
alpha amylase 11, 32, 179, 724
ambulatory assessment (AA) 454, 459
amniotic fluid 259, 260–264, 269
amphetamine 696–698
amygdala 19, 135, 139–140, 166, 197–198, 213–214, 229–230, 302–312, 359, 373, 382, 405–415, 431–435, 442, 445, 518–519, 531, 535, 539, 577, 588, 616, 635, 637–647, 658, 665, 674, 720, 723; central 138, 230, 637, 639, 701–703; medial 68, 88, 139, 303, 434–435, 484–488, 495, 560
androgen receptor (AR) 71–71, 75, 86, 125, 265, 273, 372, 380–381, 432, 554, 638

747